Best Wishes

Forty Years of Stock Car Racing

The
Superspeedway
Boom
1959 - 1964

Second of a Four Volume Series

By Greg Fielden

The Galfield Press
P.O. Box 15009
Surfside Beach, S.C. 29587
(803) 238-2404

"Forty Years of Stock Car Racing"
Volume II, The Superspeedway Boom, 1959-1964"

ISBN   0-9621580-1-1

First Printing, September 1988
Second Printing, August 1989
Third Printing, February 1991
Fourth Printing, March 1992
Fifth Printing, November 1993

Published by The Galfield Press
Manufactured in the United States of America

Other Books by The Galfield Press
"Forty Years of Stock Car Racing"
Vol. I, The Beginning 1949-1958
Vol. III, Big Bucks & Boycotts 1965-1971
Vol. IV, The Modern Era 1972-1989
High Speed At Low Tide
Rumblin' Ragtops
Tim Flock - Race Driver

Cover Photo: The first lap of the inaugural Daytona 500 on
February 22, 1959 at the Daytona International Speedway

about the author . . . . . **Greg Fielden**

Mr. Fielden, a native of Charlotte, NC, has devoted his life to the sport of Stock Car racing beginning with his first race as a 5 year-old spectator at the Lakeside Speedway in Denver, Colorado. By the time he was a teen in the Washington, DC area, he was totally addicted, studying various motorsports publications and collecting historical data as far back as 1906.

Greg Fielden

He has written for several daily newspapers and authored articles and columns in various auto racing trade papers.

Fielden is also Statistician and Historian for several auto racing telecasts on network and cable television.

The Publisher

To my readers:

This is the second edition of "Forty Years of Stock Car Racing", our series of four books on the history of NASCAR Winston Cup Grand National stock car racing. Our effort is to provide the fans and participants (past and present) with a chronicle of the history of the sport.

I would like to thank all the individuals who have contributed to the success of the first volume, "The Beginning, 1949-1958", which was released in February 1988. It is gratifying to know that so many people have a sincere interest in the history of the most exciting sport in America.

In Volume I, we documented the first 381 Strictly Stock and Grand National events staged under NASCAR sanction. It was an exhaustive project, but one that was extremely rewarding. It required 336 pages to trace those early years.

In this the second volume, entitled "The Superspeedway Boom", 309 Grand National races have been documented. Volume II is devoted to the era in which new superspeedways were built in many sections of the country with as many as 62 races in a single year.

Our third volume traces the happenings from 1965 through 1971, an era when the automotive factories pumped millions of dollars into the sport and NASCAR racing approached major league status. Entitled "Big Bucks and Boycotts", Volume III contains each and every race in a time span when Chrysler Corporation walked out (1965), Ford Motor Company boycotted (1966) and when the drivers staged their infamous strike at Talladega (1969).

Completing the series is Volume IV, "The Modern Era"", covering 477 races from 1972 through 1989, the series' 40th anniversary. This is the premier volume of the series, totalling 688 pages with an 8 page section of color photographs.

I hope you will continue to enjoy the books as much as I have enjoyed preparing them for you.

Greg Fielden
715 - 5th Avenue South
Surfside Beach, S.C. 29575

Credits

The author wishes to extend a special thanks to P.J. Hollebrand for his invaluable
assistance in compiling data for this publication

Elizabeth Baker	Larry Fielden	Tony Martin
Larry Balewski	Patricia Fielden	John Mauk
Fred Bince	Tim & Frances Flock	Jeanie & Morris Metcalfe
Russell Branham	Gene Granger	Graham Niven
Allan E Brown	Sam Gulino	Don O'Reilly
Richard Cole	Jerry Haislip	Doris Roberts
Irma Combs	Bill Hennecy	Dave Rodman
Phil Combs	Bob Hoffman	Marti Rompf
Bob Costanzo	Jim Hunter	Hank Schoolfield
Paul Dalton	Larry Jendras, Jr.	Mary Stacy
Dorothy Davis	Kenny Kane	Mitzi Teague
Larry Eanes	Bob Kelly	Paul Vinson
Chris Economaki	Bill Kiser	Chip Williams
Ernie Elkins	Bob Latford	Fletcher Williams
	Houston Lawing	

Dedication

*This series of books is dedicated to
those individuals who paid the ultimate price
in NASCAR Winston Cup Grand National Stock Car Racing
The sport they loved*

Larry Mann
Frank Arford
Lou Figaro
John McVitty
Clint McHugh
Cotton Priddy
Bobby Myers
Gwyn Staley
Joe Weatherly
Fireball Roberts
Jimmy Pardue
Billy Wade
Buren Skeen
Harold Kite
Billy Foster
Talmadge Prince
Friday Hassler
Larry Smith
Tiny Lund
Ricky Knotts
Terry Schoonover
Bruce Jacobi
Grant Adcox
J.D. McDuffie

Forty Years of Stock Car Racing
Volume II
The Superspeedway Boom   1959 - 1964

Preface

In the first ten years of NASCAR Grand National (Winston Cup) stock car racing, only 22 of the 381 events were staged on "superspeedways" -- and three of those were in the Convertible Division, which do not appear in the Winston Cup Grand National records or statistics. A superspeedway race has been classified as a long distance event presented on an oval track of a mile or more in length. These **superspeedway** events were run on tracks designed for **super speeds**, hence the title.

Over the next six years, some 47 superspeedway events were conducted. With Bill France's new Daytona International Speedway leading the way, big fancy ovals began to spring up on both the East and West coasts.

One of the genuine superspeedways which has been all but forgotten or ignored over the years was a 1.4-mile high-banked paved oval in Hanford, California. Marchbanks Speedway hosted two NASCAR Grand National races. Although it lasted only a short period of time, Marchbanks Speedway's contribution to the sport and NASCAR should not be forgotten.

Fireball Roberts made history in the 250-mile superspeedway race at Marchbanks on March 12, 1961. Driving a Pontiac owned by J.D. Braswell and tuned by Lyle Stelter, Roberts led every lap. To this day, it is the only superspeedway race in which a driver led from flag-to-flag.

In the 1959 season, the first year in this second edition of *Forty Years of Stock Car Racing,* NASCAR was winding up its Convertible Division, which was originally an offspring of NASCAR's merger in 1956 with the Society of Autosports and Fellowship Education (SAFE). It lasted only four years.

The Convertible Division was a carbon copy of the headlining Grand National Circuit -- only without the tops on the cars. Convertibles were frequently driven in Grand National races; the drivers and car owners used "zipper tops" -- easily attached roofs -- to comply with Grand National standards.

Richard Petty, in his first full year driving NASCAR stocks in 1959, competed in many Convertible races. He also drove in 21 events which offered points toward the Grand National championship.

Today's records indicate that young Petty drove in 22 Grand National events in 1959. An extra race has been erroneously added -- the 100-mile Convertible race held at Daytona in preparation for the inaugural Daytona 500.

The first Daytona 500 was a Sweepstakes race -- open to both Grand National hardtops and Convertibles. Richard Petty entered a 1957 Oldsmobile Convertible.

He finished third in the 100-mile qualifying race for the Convertible cars. No points were awarded to the Grand National standings -- all points for all drivers went toward the Convertible championship. Over the years, somehow Petty's participation in this race has been credited to his Grand National (Winston Cup) records. By finishing third, he earned $400. In today's records the third place finish does not count. Neither does the $400 he earned on that day. Only the start has been added to his record, a misleading statistic to be sure.

Petty's participation in the Daytona 500 two days later in the same car does count on his Winston Cup Grand National record. As pointed out in Volume I of *Forty Years of Stock Car Racing*, in 1969 sanctioning NASCAR decided to count all driver records and finishing positions for those men who drove Convertible cars in the Sweepstakes races. Following NASCAR's lead, this practice has remained consistent -- and will remain so -- throughout all four volumes of *Forty Years of Stock Car Racing*. Documenting records in a consistent manner has been at or near the top of our objectives in compiling these books.

The superspeedway boom, 1959 - 1964, was one of the most progressive eras of the sport. This was a heavy transitional period -- a changing of the guard. Very few of the stars from the 1950's made it past the early 1960's. For example, only ten drivers in the top 50 point standings in 1958 were listed in the top 50 by 1964. New faces were arriving -- along with the big speedy ovals -- and many old familiar faces were fading away.

Table of Contents

The 1959 Season
The Daytona International Speedway Opens

Volume two of a four volume series . . . . . The Superspeedway Boom 1959 - 1964

1959

In February of 1954, NASCAR announced during SpeedWeeks that the famous old Beach and Road course activities would move to the new Daytona Beach Motor Speedway in 1955. Rapid development along the shoreline south of Daytona Beach most certainly had numbered the days of the 4.1-mile beachfront facility.

NASCAR President Bill France, an individual with decisive foresightedness, dreamed of building the ultimate - a huge, high-banked paved track that had no equal anywhere in the world. A number of factors -- politics, rejected proposals, tight money markets, referendum delays and balks by the Civil Aeronautics Board -- prevented France from meeting his target date of February 1955. Seemingly endless postponements pushed the grand opening of the "World's Most Modern Racing Facility" up to February of 1959.

By mid-1958, the newly named Daytona International Speedway had cleared all the obstacles. France's massive project, once tagged "Pipe Dream Speedway" by the *Indianapolis Star,* was only several weeks away from becoming a reality.

During the final stages of construction, nearly all the car owners, drivers and accessory representatives stopped by the project. Many were impressed. Others were awe-struck. Some admitted to having a tinge of fear. Everyone had something to say about the two-and-a-half mile D-shaped oval:

John Holman, Car Owner: *"This track is a tribute to Bill France for his interest in racing. It's a dream of a track for race drivers."*

Marvin Panch, Driver: *"I had decided to quit racing.*

But not now. Not until I test this track."

Buck Baker, Driver: *"It's the darndest thing you ever saw. It's the Hollywood of racing. For the man who really wants to race, this is it."*

Dave Evans, Goodyear Racing Director: *"This is the greatest track I've ever seen, and it should be as safe as it is fast."*

Hans Turner, Italian Journalist: *"This Daytona track has revolutionized the entire racing business."*

Fireball Roberts, Driver: *"This is the track where you can step on the accelerator and let it roll. You can flatfoot it all the way."*

Jimmy Thompson, Driver: *"There have been other tracks that separated the men from the boys. This is the track that will separate the brave from the weak after the boys are gone."*

Aerial view of the site of Daytona International Speedway. Preliminary grading has begun just above Highway 92. Daytona Kennel Club is visible at right

Sometime later, national champion Lee Petty said, *"I'll tell you what, there wasn't a man there who wasn't scared to death of the place. We never had raced on a track like that before. Darlington was big, but it wasn't banked like Daytona. What it amounted to*

Early Stages of earth moving required for the high banks of Daytona

was that we were all rookies going 30 to 40 miles per hour faster than we had ever gone before. There were some scared cats out there."

Entry blanks for the first annual "500 Mile International Sweepstakes" race were mailed from NASCAR headquarters on January 6, 1959. Posted awards were $67,760 including a $5,000 bonus for the winner if he was driving a '59 model car. France felt it was important for a flock of brand new American cars to adorn the wind-whipped banks of his new speedway in the grand opening. He dangled the crisp five-grand as an extra incentive.

Curiously, Jaguar automobiles were eligible to compete in the first Daytona 500. France offered a $500 bonus to the highest "3.4 five-passenger Jaguar to finish in addition to other prize money earned." No one showed up with a Jag.

But plenty of other 1959 models did appear. Lee Petty purchased a new 1959 Oldsmobile "for about $2,500 cash from Newton-Chappell Motors in Reidsville, NC". Holman-Moody's T-Bird Power Products Division built eight new Thunderbirds with a $5,500 price tag. Each T-Bird was identically prepared and equipped with roll bars, safety belts, shoulder harness, asbestos floor mat, reinforced suspension, heavy-duty spindles, 22 gallon gas tank, tachometer and a Holman-Moody prepared **legal** engine.

NASCAR issued a new set of standards for drivers who were entered in the inaugural Daytona 500. "It will be necessary for drivers and relief drivers to prove their ability on the Speedway by driving at least 25 miles at speeds of 100 mph or more under observation of NASCAR officials," read a statement mailed to each NASCAR member. The sanctioning body also declared that a physical examination for drivers competing at Daytona would be mandatory. The Daytona medical staff, headed by Dr. A. A. Monaco, would conduct the physical. Price of the examination was $14.

On February 1, 1959, race cars got on the Daytona International Speedway for the first time. Among those participating in the shakedown runs were Curtis Turner, who wheeled his Doc White-owned T-Bird at 143.1 mph; Fireball Roberts, who drove his Fish Carburetor Ford Modified at 145.7 mph; and Bill France, who steered the '59 Pontiac Catalina pace car around the track at 114 mph.

Following that Sunday afternoon of practice, the track was closed so that work on the guard rail could be completed.

The official open house for Daytona was on Sunday, February 7, 1959. Some 6,500 spectators showed up for the opening round of qualifying. Thirteen cars were ready for qualifying, but six had failed inspection. Only seven cars made qualifying runs, which disappointed the crowd. Fireball Roberts pierced the timing lights at 140.581 mph to gain the pole position for the 100-mile Grand National qualifying race. Tim Flock's T-Bird followed at 138.121, Joe Weatherly drove a Chevrolet at 137.741, Jack Smith

The Daytona 31 degree high banked turns get a coat of asphalt

ran 136.425 in a Chevy and Bobby Johns took a two year old Chevy around at 126.528.

A pair of Convertibles took their turns in the race against the clock. Marvin Panch tooled Glen Wood's Ford at 128.810 mph and Gene White posted a 120.048 in a '57 Chevrolet.

The next morning Chapman Root, of Terre Haute, Indiana, unveiled a new Sumar Special Indianapolis car in the garage area. With native Daytonan Marshall Teague handling the controls, the duo was set to make an assault on the world record of 177.038 mph established by Tony Bettenhausen at Monza, Italy on June 28, 1958. Root had built a unique specimen - an Indy car with a hand-crafted aerodynamic canopy attached over the cockpit and fenders covering the wheels. He and Teague felt confident the world record would be theirs in a matter of days.

Teague toured the high banks of Daytona at 171.82 mph in his opening run. "I was just playing around," he said. "We won't get serious until later in the week." Car owner Root remarked that "we are not geared right for this speedway."

France had booked a United States Auto Club Indy Car race for April 4th, and he openly invited the Indy cars to engage in practice sessions at his new plant. Initially, USAC officials turned thumbs down on the invitation and denied permission to any of their drivers to participate in the NASCAR-oriented gala festival.

However, France applied a little pressure to the USAC offices in Indianapolis, and USAC President Thomas Binford relented. He agreed to a two-hour practice session on specified days - from 10 am to noon. "The drivers will be covered by USAC insurance," declared Binford. "We will have prescribed familiarization runs on this new course for the drivers who are entered in the April race."

Joining Teague was Jim Rathmann in the D-A Lubricant Special. High winds hampered Rathmann, and his fast lap was 170.06 mph.

On Wednesday, February 11, Teague went onto the Speedway shortly after 10 am. On his first warm-up lap, the dark blue Sumar was clocked at 128.42 mph. Teague upped the pace on the next time around to over 140 mph. On his third lap he was timed at 160.25 mph. As Teague entered the first turn of his fourth lap, the car lifted slightly and slid down the track. As the car hit the safety apron, it flipped. The car overturned five times and traveled some 1,500 feet from the first roll-over until it stopped. Teague, still strapped into his seat, was thrown out and landed 150 feet ahead of

where the car stopped. He was dead on arrival at the hospital.

Moments before the fateful run, Teague had said,

An aerial view of the new Daytona International Speedway on race day

"We're trying to get the gears and the weight adjustment and everything set up for this speedway. This is the finest speedway in the world. It's deceptive, though. When you're going 165 mph you feel like you're coasting at 135. I feel safer on this speedway than I do on U.S. 92."

NASCAR qualifying continued through four sessions. Tom Pistone was fastest in the second round with a speed of 141.376 mph in his T-Bird. Lee Petty's Olds topped the third round with a 141.709 effort, and Cotton Owens' Pontiac turned in the quickest time of SpeedWeeks with a 143.198 mph lap in the final session.

The 100-mile Convertible qualifying race on Friday, February 20, was the first competitive event staged at Daytona International Speedway. Four cars in the field of 21 broke away from the pack -- but they were unable to break away from each other. Glen Wood, Shorty Rollins, Richard Petty and Marvin Panch swapped the lead five times in the final nine laps. Wood led the charge into the final lap, but slipped to fourth at the finish line as a freight train motored past him. Rollins nipped Panch at the strip by a bumper bolt. Petty was third.

Rollins nearly missed the race. "I blew my good engine during practice yesterday (Thursday)," said the 1958 Rookie of the Year. "This engine is a junk one that we installed last night. We were still working on it right up to race time."

Rollins expressed surprise that his 'junk engine'

Fireball Roberts and Joe Weatherly in Firecracker 250 victory lane.
Weatherly hooked up in Roberts' draft and discovered he could run 5 mph faster

was able to keep up and actually win the race. "How in the world could that happen?" he queried.

Thirty-eight hard top sedans lined up for the Grand National qualifier. Bob Welborn, manning a Chevrolet, led all but seven laps, but could not pull away from Fritz Wilson, who had bought one of the Holman-Moody T-Birds. Welborn edged Wilson by a half car length at the finish.

"There I was breaking the wind for him and I couldn't seem to shake him," Welborn said in victory lane. "I let him go around me twice to shake him. But when I would regain the lead, he would latch on to me again."

Welborn, who had qualified at 140.121 mph, averaged 143.198 mph for the 100 miles. Drivers, including Welborn, were wondering what was going on. How could all of these cars running together suddenly be going decidedly faster than when they had qualified?

On Saturday, the day before the Daytona 500, a 200-mile Modified-Sportsman race was staged for the NASCAR "Weekend Warriors". Edwin "Banjo" Matthews lapped the field and won $2,400 for his efforts. Junior Johnson finished in fourth place, worth $500, but he became the first driver to be disqualified at Daytona International Speedway when NASCAR officials discovered his fuel tank was much larger than the maximum 20 gallons allowed.

Jack Smith, who had qualified at 136.425 mph,

won the 25-mile Grand National consolation event at an average speed of 141.288 mph. The remainder of the 59-car Daytona 500 field was determined in the consolation event.

Race day dawned warm and sunny. Johnny Bruner, Sr. waved the green flag from the apron of the tri-oval area -- unquestionably the bravest act of SpeedWeeks -- and the 59 cars roared off. Three, four, five abreast they went -- in a neat and noisy formation.

Bob Welborn and Tom Pistone traded the lead in the opening laps. Fireball Roberts, who started 46th, stormed around the clumps of traffic in a bold charge to the front. Tim Flock and Jack Smith, who started 42nd and 41st respectively, latched onto Fireball's bumper and the speedy trio quickly scampered to the front. By the 23rd lap, Roberts' big Pontiac was on the point. And a funny thing happened, he was able to pull away from the field without having any rival tag along for a "free ride". Roberts was stretching his lead until fuel pump problems intervened after 56 laps.

Jack Smith's Chevrolet led most of the laps after Roberts' departure, heading the field for 47 laps of a 61 lap stretch. However, recurring tire troubles knocked the Sandy Springs, GA veteran four laps off the pace in the caution-free event. Curtis Turner and Tim Flock, front runners in the Lincoln powered T-Birds, encountered blistered tires and dropped well off the pace.

As the field became depleted, Johnny Beauchamp and Lee Petty were left in the lead lap by themselves. In the last 125 miles, they traded the lead a dozen times. All eyes were on Beauchamp's T-Bird and Petty's Oldsmobile as the final laps wound down. It was clearly evident that the race would be a down-to-the-wire affair between Petty -- a two-time NASCAR

Johnny Bruner, Sr. gives green flag to the Daytona 500 field -- from the inside of the track

Grand National champ -- and Beauchamp -- a newcomer out of the International Motor Contest Association ranks.

The two drivers raced furiously with each other lap after lap. Soon, they caught up with Joe Weatherly, who was running two laps down. The three cars toured the high banks with reckless abandon.

Petty led by a single car length as Johnny Bruner waved the white flag. The cluster of cars -- Petty, Beauchamp and Weatherly -- raced around the track and the impossible happened. The three cars danced across the finish line side-by-side-by-side.

The crowd of 41,921 were on their collective feet, cheering wildly. The finish was so close that no one seemed to know who had won the thing. Lots of shrugged shoulders in the grandstands.

France and Bruner, standing together in the flag-stand, called Beauchamp the winner in unison. When the announcement was made over the public address system, howls of protests and jeers rose from the area near the finish line.

Bernard Kahn, *Daytona Beach News Journal* Sports Editor, polled 12 accredited newsmen who saw the two cars cross the finish line together -- and all of them claimed that Petty had won. Confusion reigned supreme.

Unofficial winner Johnny Beauchamp with Scottie McCormick

"To me and John, it looked like Beauchamp by about two feet," declared France. "There has never been a photo camera used in auto racing before, but I'm going to see if such a device would be practical right away."

"I never want to call another one this close," said Bruner. "I want an electronic eye or camera, if I have to buy it myself."

Petty drove his Oldsmobile to victory lane, but found NASCAR and Speedway officials calling for Beauchamp. "A man who finished two feet ahead of another is supposed to be the winner," said Petty. "I just hope that the man who got to that finish line collects the first prize money. I am confident I won."

Beauchamp defended the original decision and said, "I won."

Roy Burdick of Omaha who owned the T-Bird Beauchamp drove, declared his man won "beyond the

shadow of a doubt. We would have won by a decisive margin if it hadn't been for that rough riding by Weatherly," said Burdick.

Weatherly, although two laps down and coming up to complete his 198th lap, refused to give an inch and actually outran the principles who were vying for victory. "As they hit the finish line, I was about a hood length ahead of Petty," said Weatherly. "And Petty was about the same distance ahead of Beauchamp. If Petty didn't win this race, he never won a race. I don't know what the argument is all about. Petty won easily."

By virtue of beating Petty and Beauchamp to the finish line, Weatherly was able to complete another lap. He got credit for fifth place, completing 199 laps.

Upon hearing all the protests, France declared the finish "unofficial". He solicited all available still photographs and said he would wait until conclusive evidence supported either Petty or Beauchamp. He also solicited film footage of the finish, but that may take days, he was told.

At trackside, Peter DePaolo, a former Indy 500 winner who had watched the finish, said, "It's one of those fantastic finishes that couldn't happen -- but it did. Hollywood would have rejected a race script like this as too unbelievable."

At least seven still photographs were examined by France and other NASCAR officials. Each one indicated that Petty was slightly ahead as they came to the finish line, but none caught the cars at the moment they crossed the line. Finally on Wednesday, three days after the race had ended, newsreel film shot by *Hearst Metrotone News of the Week* in New York arrived in Daytona Beach. The film proved conclusively that Lee Petty had won the Daytona 500.

At 6 pm Wednesday February 25, 61 hours after the checkered flag fell, Petty was officially declared the winner. "The newsreel substantiated that the cars of Petty and Beauchamp did not change positions from the time those other still photographs were taken just before the finish," said France. "Petty is the winner."

The final laps of the Daytona 500 were a wide open scramble for first place. Neither Petty nor Beauchamp employed any scheming. Rather than **outsmarting** the other, they were concerned with **outrunning** the other. Both Petty and Beauchamp felt little bits of trickery with the wind currents while they were scrapping closely for the $19,000 top prize. They were far too busy with the task at hand to explore the wonderous art of "drafting".

Most of the front runners knew the winds were doing something. Speeds would suddenly escalate when the cars were running in nose-to-tail formation. But it took a little scar-faced squirt from Norfolk, VA to **utilize** the effects of "drafting" at Daytona on NAS-CAR's return visit on July 4.

Joe Weatherly was entered in a Convertible T-Bird owned by Doc White, an Orlando dentist, in the inaugural Firecracker 250 -- a Sweepstakes event open to both Grand National and Convertible cars.

Weatherly qualified his ragtop T-Bird at a two lap average speed of 139.664 mph, which earned him the 12th starting position. Pole sitter was Fireball Roberts, who drove his hard top Pontiac at a speed of 144.997 mph. Second fastest qualifier was Bob Burdick's Convertible T-Bird, which was timed at 140.911 mph. Young Burdick had replaced Johnny Beauchamp in the saddle of the car owned by his dad, Roy.

Weatherly knew his only chance was to try to follow the fleet Fireball. At the drop of the green flag, Weatherly

USAC Indy cars zoom through Daytona's fourth turn.

whisked past several slower cars that had lined up in front of him (Weatherly had qualified on the second day), and caught Roberts' rear bumper by the backstretch.

Weatherly, described by some members of the media as an individual who spoke in shorthand, explained his Firecracker 250 game plan: "I stuck the nose of my 'Bird under the rear of 'Ball's Big Indian and he took me for a ride." Translated, Li'l Joe said he drove his Thunderbird close behind the rear of Fireball Roberts' big Pontiac and hooked up in a delightful draft.

A statistical account of the 250-miler on Independence Day proved Weatherly was perhaps the first to *utilize* the full effects of the draft. Although he qualified at 139-plus, his car was clocked at an average speed of 144.000 mph for the first 25 miles. After 50 miles, he had averaged 143.769 mph. After 100 miles, his speed was logged at 142.857 mph. After the first round of pit stops, Roberts shook the pesky Weatherly.

Roberts won the Firecracker at an average speed of

140.581 mph. Weatherly wound up second, 57 seconds behind Roberts. Weatherly's time for the 250 miles was 139.340, only a fraction off his qualifying speed.

Both NASCAR events at Daytona International Speedway, the Daytona 500 and the Firecracker 250, were run without any wrecks. Such was not the case when the USAC Indy Cars came to the world's fastest speedway on April 4.

George Amick, who had finished second in the 1958 Indianapolis 500 in his rookie year, topped qualifying for the 100-mile Indy Car race with a 176.887 mph lap. Jim Rathmann completed the 100 miles in 35 minutes, 14.4 seconds for a world record average speed of 170.261 mph.

At the precise moment Rathmann sailed under the checkered flag, Amick, battling for third place, lost control of his car, and it darted into the outside retaining wall at an estimated 190 mph. The front end of the car was sheared off, eight sturdy fence posts were reduced to splinters, and Amick slid 900 feet upside down on the backstretch. George Amick died instantly.

Rathmann won a 50-mile Indy Car race later that same afternoon. It was shortened from the scheduled 100 mile distance due to "driver fatigue, high winds, electrifying speeds", and the uncertainty of the stability of Indy Cars on a track like Daytona.

USAC Competition Director Henry Banks, said the upcoming 300-mile event slated for July 4 at the 2.5-mile Daytona tri-oval would be cancelled. "The Daytona track is still way ahead of the equipment we now have available," he remarked. "We have a little research to do as far as Daytona is concerned. We have to find out just what our problems are. We knew we would reach high speeds at Daytona, but we had not foreseen the problems."

Banks said the high speeds -- over 175 mph -- were nearing "air speed, and the USAC Speedway cars have a tendency to lift off the ground. We need further testing before we ever come back to Daytona."

The Indy Car race was replaced with the Firecracker 250. The Indy Cars never came back to Daytona. During their short tenure at Bill France's new creation, they resoundly established Daytona as the fastest track in the world. It wasn't until 1971 that Indy Cars would break George Amick's Daytona record at Indianapolis.

Race No. 1

Welborn Takes Fayetteville in Sweep

FAYETTEVILLE, NC (Nov 9, 1958) -- Bob Welborn took the lead in the 43rd lap and led the rest of the way to capture the 1959 Grand National season opener at Champion Speedway. It was the seventh career win for Welborn in NASCAR's premier series.

Glen Wood finished in second place with Buck Baker third. Roy Tyner finished fourth and Junior Johnson fifth.

Welborn earned the pole with quick time in qualifications, won a 25 lap heat race and led all but 33 laps in the 150 lap feature at the .333-mile paved oval. Rex White passed Welborn in the 10th lap and was leading when overheating problems forced him off the pace. White limped home 10th in the field of 25.

Welborn averaged 56.001 mph in the 53 minute event.

Grand National Race No. 1
150 Laps at Champion Speedway
Fayetteville, NC
50 Miles on .333-mile Paved Track
November 9, 1958

Fin	St	No.	Driver	Team / Car	Laps	Money	Status
1	1	46	Bob Welborn	Julian Petty '57 Chevy	150	$600	Running
2	4	21	Glen Wood	Wood Brothers '58 Ford	150	475	Running
3	5	86	Buck Baker	Baker '58 Chevrolet	150	350	Running
4	3	49	Roy Tyner	Tyner '57 Chevrolet	149	250	Running
5	12	11	Junior Johnson	Paul Spaulding '57 Ford	148	215	Running
6	9	6	Tommy Irwin	'57 Ford	148	190	Running
7	14	36	Tiny Lund	'58 Ford	147	170	Running
8	11	77	Joe Lee Johnson	S T Campbell '57 Chevy	147	170	Running
9	6	42	Lee Petty	Petty Eng '57 Olds	146	180	Running
10	2	40	Rex White	'58 Chevrolet	146	190	Running
11	10	14	George Dunn	Manley Britt '57 Mercury	145	130	Running
12	7	8	Jimmy Thompson	'57 Chevrolet	145	150	Running
13	13	24	Richard Petty	Petty Eng '57 Olds	140	100	Running
14	21	96	Bobby Keck	Keck '57 Chevrolet	139	120	Running
15	19	711	Bill Poor	Poor '56 Chevrolet	139	90	Running
16	18	32	Brownie King	Jess Potter '57 Chevrolet	139	90	Running
17	16	74	L D Austin	Austin '56 Chevrolet	138	75	Running
18	20	94	Clarence DeZalia	DeZalia '56 Ford	136	60	Running
19	22	66	Jimmy Pardue	A M Crawford '57 Plym	131	50	Running
20	17	78	Shep Langdon	Langdon '56 Ford	129	65	Running
21	12	2	Jimmie Lewallen	'57 Ford	102	35	Vapor Lk
22	24	81	Harvey Hege	'57 Ford	41	25	Steering
23	23	63	R L Combs	'56 Ford	25	25	Distrib
24	15	17	Fred Harb	Harb '57 Mercury	21	25	Engine
25	25	18	Charley Griffith	Red Bank '57 Pontiac	0	---	Engine

Time of Race: 53 minutes, 31 seconds
Average Speed: 56.001 mph
Pole Winner: Bob Welborn - 61.985 mph
Lap Leaders: Bob Welborn 1-9, Rex White 10-42, Welborn 43-150
Cautions:
Margin of Victory:
Attendance:

Grand National Race No. 2
40 Laps at Daytona International Speedway
Daytona Beach, FL
100 Miles on 2.5-mile Paved Track
February 20, 1959

Fin	St	No.	Driver	Team / Car	Laps	Money	Status
1	7	49	Bob Welborn	Welborn '59 Chevrolet	40	$800	Running
2	15	64	Fritz Wilson	Museum of Speed '59 T-Bird	40	525	Running
3	6	59	Tom Pistone	Rupert Safety Belt '59 T-Bird	40	350	Running
4	3	48	Joe Weatherly	E C Wilson '59 Chevrolet	40	250	Running
5	18	37	Eduardo Dibos	Peru '59 T-Bird	39	225	Running
6	23	6	Cotton Owens	W H Watson '58 Pontiac	39	200	Running
7	17	88	Tiny Lund	Buck Baker '59 Chevrolet	39	165	Running
8	14	42	Lee Petty	Petty Eng '59 Olds	39	150	Running
9	9	18	Charley Griffith	Red Bank '57 Pontiac	38	140	Running
10	24	4	Rex White	Idlewild Homes '59 Chevrolet	38	130	Running
11	8	73	Johnny Beauchamp	Roy Burdick '59 T-Bird	38	125	Running
12	28	81	Bernie Hentges	'59 DeSoto	38	110	Running
13	27	29	Dick Freeman	'59 Chevrolet	38	100	Running
14	38	71	Dick Joslin	'57 Dodge	38	85	Running
15	5	72	Bobby Johns	Shorty Johns '57 Chevrolet	38	70	Running
16	12	1	Speedy Thompson	Steve Pierce '57 Chevrolet	38	60	Running
17	21	11	Junior Johnson	Paul Spaulding '57 Ford	37	50	Running
18	30	38	Raul Cilloniz	Cilloniz '58 Ford	37	50	Running
19	20	53	Ken Johnson	'57 Ford	37	50	Running
20	26	7	Jim Reed	Reed '59 Chevrolet	35	50	Running
21	22	69	Harold Smith	'59 Studebaker	35	50	Running
22	33	19	Herman Beam	Beam '57 Chevrolet	35	50	Running
23	13	86	Carl Tyler	Tyler '57 Ford	34	50	Running
24	2	15	Tim Flock	Beau Morgan '59 T-Bird	30	50	Push Rod
25	29	9	Roy Tyner	Tyner '57 Chevrolet	29	---	Coil
26	10	58	Roscoe Thompson	'57 Chevrolet	28	---	Engine
27	4	47	Jack Smith	Bud Moore Garage '59 Chevy	20	---	Crash
28	16	87	Buck Baker	Baker '59 Chevrolet	20	---	Crash
29	37	41	Curtis Turner	Delta Auto Sales '59 T-Bird	17	---	Trans
30	11	10	Elmo Langley	'57 Ford	17	---	Heating
31	19	95	Bob Duell	Julian Buesink '59 Ford	17	---	Heat
32	32	16	Jim McGuirk	'59 Pontiac	15	---	Distrib
33	1	3	Fireball Roberts	Jim Stephens '59 Pontiac	14	---	Distrib
34	25	24	Bob Potter	'59 Chevrolet	13	---	Tires
35	36	83	Bob Pronger	'58 Ford	13	---	Gasket
36	31	80	Bobby Rose	Sam Arena '57 Chevrolet	11	---	Steering
37	34	66	Dick Foley	'59 Chevrolet	9	---	Engine
38	35	74	L D Austin	Austin '57 Chevrolet	1	---	Steering

Time of Race: 41 minutes, 54 seconds
Average Speed: 143.198 mph
Pole Winner: Fireball Roberts - 140.581 mph
Fastest Qualifier: Cotton Owens - 143.198 mph
Lap Leaders: Joe Weatherly 1, Bob Welborn 2-6, Curtis Turner 7, Welborn 8-12, Turner 13, Welborn 14-23, Fritz Wilson 24-26, Welborn 27, Wilson 28, Welborn 29-40
Cautions: None
Margin of Victory: 1/2 Car Length
Attendance: 17,000

Race No. 2

Welborn Nips Fritz Wilson In Daytona 100-miler

DAYTONA BEACH, FL (Feb 20) -- Bob Welborn scampered to the front and held off a pesky Fritz Wilson to win the Grand National qualifying race at Daytona International Speedway. Welborn's feat earned him the coveted pole position for the inaugural Daytona 500.

The 30 year-old Summerfield, NC Chevrolet driver led for 33 of the 40 laps around the 2.5-mile super-speedway, but had to use all his savvy to hold off Wilson's Thunderbird by three feet at the finish line. Just behind the leaders, Tom Pistone squeaked past Joe Weatherly to gain third place. Eduardo Dibos came in fifth.

Welborn started seventh on the grid but had the lead by the second lap. He was in front for all but seven laps, four of those led by Wilson. "That T-Bird should have averaged 10 miles per hour better than our car," remarked Welborn afterwards. "It has a 430 cubic inch engine compared to our 348. But the way those T-Birds are designed, they're built like a box."

Buck Baker blew a tire in the first turn midway through the race and spun into Jack Smith. Baker spun into the grass as Smith limped to the pit area. Both were sidelined, but the incident did not bring out the caution flag.

Welborn, who qualified at 140.121 mph, averaged 143.198 mph for the full 100 miles. Ironically, Welborn's race speed matched Cotton Owens' quick time trial during SpeedWeeks.

Shorty Rollins won a 100-mile qualifier for Convertibles just before the Grand National event. Rollins passed Glen Wood in the final lap as the crowd of 17,000 watched in near disbelief.

Race No. 3

Petty and Beauchamp in Dead Heat Finish in Daytona 500

DAYTONA BEACH, FL (Feb 22) -- Daytona International Speedway's inaugural 500 mile race produced a finish that will be talked about for generations

Pure gasoline attendants fuel up Rex White's Chevy

Grand National Race No. 3
200 Laps at Daytona Int'l Speedway
Daytona Beach, FL
500 Miles on 2.5-mile Paved Track
February 22, 1959

Fin	St	No.	Driver	Team / Car	Laps	Money	Status
1	15	42	Lee Petty	Petty Eng '59 Olds GN	200	`$19,050	Running
2	21	73	Johnny Beauchamp	Roy Burdick '59 T-Bird GN	200	7,650	Running
3	17	18	Charley Griffith	Red Bank '57 Pontiac GN	199	4,600	Running
4	11	6	Cotton Owens	W H Watson '58 Pontiac GN	199	2,525	Running
5	7	48	Joe Weatherly	E C Wilson '59 Chevrolet GN	199	1,875	Running
6	39	7	Jim Reed	Reed '59 Chevrolet GN	196	1,075	Running
7	41	47	Jack Smith	Bud Moore '59 Chevrolet GN	196	2,625	Running
8	5	59	Tom Pistone	Rupert Sfty Blt '59 T-Bird GN	195	1,825	Running
9	42	15	Tim Flock	Beau Morgan '59 T-Bird GN	193	800	Running
10	31	1	Speedy Thompson	Steve Pierce '57 Chevy GN	193	600	Running
11	59	8	Johnny Allen	'57 Chevrolet GN	192	400	Running
12	35	38	Raul Cilloniz	Cilloniz '59 T-Bird GN	192	500	Running
13	43	41	Curtis Turner	Delta Auto '59 T-Bird GN	189	425	Running
14	33	11	Junior Johnson	Paul Spaulding '57 Ford GN	189	250	Running
15	25	29	Dick Freeman	'59 Chevrolet GN	188	250	Running
16	16	77	Joe Lee Johnson	Honest Charley '57 Chevy C	187	975	Running
17	4	98	Marvin Panch	Tom Vernon '58 Ford C	185	775	Running
18	10	25	Gene White	White '57 Chevrolet C	185	600	Running
19	57	9	Roy Tyner	Tyner '57 Chevrolet GN	184	200	Running
20	18	2	Jimmy Thompson	Bruce Thompson '57 Chevy C	182	500	Running
21	49	19	Herman Beam	Beam '57 Chevrolet GN	182	165	Running
22	22	92	Wilbur Rakestraw	B J Jones '57 Ford C	181	250	Running
23	53	16	Jim McGuirk	'59 Pontiac GN	181	150	Running
24	12	76	Larry Frank	Carolina Plating '57 Chevy C	178	250	Running
25	48	10	Elmo Langley	Ratus Walters '57 Ford GN	175	175	Running
26	19	4	Rex White	Idlewild Homes '50 Chevy GN	174	100	Engine
27	30	55	Ben Benz	H. Friedland '57 Chevy GN	169	200	Running
28	27	71	Dick Joslin	'57 Dodge GN	167	100	Piston
29	24	14	Ken Rush	Manley Britt '57 Mercury C	163	200	Engine
30	55	80	Bobby Rose	Sam Arena '57 Chevrolet GN	162	100	Running
31	50	69	Harold Smith	'59 Studebaker GN	159	110	Running
32	44	66	Dick Foley	'59 Chevrolet GN	157	150	Running
33	28	32	Brownie King	Jess Potter '58 Chevrolet C	152	150	Engine
34	8	21	Glen Wood	Wood Brothers '58 Ford C	149	100	Clutch
35	47	83	Bob Pronger	'58 Ford GN	143	125	Running
36	26	39	Billy Carden	Davis Brothers '57 Mercury C	140	100	Running
37	23	81	Bernie Hentges	'59 DeSoto GN	138	100	Engine
38	2	99	Shorty Rollins	Shorty's '58 Ford C	115	100	Engine
39	22	82	Joe Eubanks	Don Every '58 Ford C	95	100	Trans
40	13	88	Tiny Lund	Buck Baker '59 Chevrolet GN	92	100	Timing
41	1	49	Bob Welborn	Welborn '59 Chevrolet GN	75	325	Engine
42	54	87	Buck Baker	Buck Baker '59 Chevrolet GN	75	100	Timing
43	37	53	Ken Johnson	'57 Ford GN	67	100	Push Rod
44	58	74	L D Austin	Austin '57 Chevrolet GN	65	100	Generator
45	46	3	Fireball Roberts	Jim Stephens '59 Pontiac GN	56	650	Fuel Pmp
46	40	45	Paul Bass	'58 Edsel C	52	100	Engine
47	29	72	Bobby Johns	Shorty Johns '57 Chevy GN	46	100	Heating
48	9	37	Eduardo Dibos	"Peru" '59 T-Bird GN	44	100	Susp
49	36	50	Gober Sosebee	Cherokee Gar '57 Chevy C	44	100	Trans
50	20	89	Bob Said	'58 Chevrolet C	42	100	Trans
51	51	95	Bob Duell	Julian Buesink '59 Ford GN	38	100	Distrib
52	32	36	Pete Kelly	'57 Chevrolet C	34	100	Engine
53	45	24	Bob Potter	'59 Chevrolet GN	33	150	Timing
54	52	86	Carl Tyler	Tyler '57 Ford GN	29	100	Heating
55	34	33	George Green	City Motors '57 Chevrolet C	21	100	Cooling
56	3	64	Fritz Wilson	Museum of Spd '59 T-Bird GN	15	100	Piston
57	6	43	Richard Petty	Petty Eng '57 Olds C	8	100	Engine
58	38	79	Larry Odo	'57 Ford C	3	100	Engine
59	56	75	Ken Marriott	'58 Ford C	1	100	Engine

Time of Race: 3 hours, 41 minutes, 22 seconds   Average Speed: 135.521 mph
Pole Winner: Bob Welborn - 140.121 mph
Fastest Qualifier: Cotton Owens - 143.198 mph
Lap Leaders: Bob Welborn 1, Tom Pistone 2-3, Welborn 4-7, Pistone 8, Welborn 9-10, Joe Weatherly 11-13, Pistone 14-16, Weatherly 17-18, Welborn 19-20, Pistone 21, Weatherly 22, Fireball Roberts 23-43, Johnny Beauchamp 44-49, Pistone 50-57, Jack Smith 58-65, Pistone 66, Smith 67, Pistone 68-86, Smith 87-102, Beauchamp 107-116, Smith 117-148, Beachamp 149, Lee Petty 150-154, Beauchamp 155-161, Petty 162-182, Beauchamp 183-184, Petty 185-187, Beauchamp 188, Petty 189, Beauchamp 190-191, Petty 192-195, Beauchamp 196, Petty 197-200.
Cautions: None   Margin of Victory: 2 feet   Attendance: 41,921

as Lee Petty's Oldsmobile and Johnny Beauchamp's T-Bird crossed the finish line in a dead heat. The two cars were clocked at 135.521 mph.

The dash to the finish line was so unexpectedly dramatic that it took NASCAR officials some 61 hours to determine a clear-cut winner. Beauchamp was initially instructed to go to victory lane and he went through all the ceremonies. Supporters from the Petty camp and most of the newsmen who were in a position to see the finish, claimed the Oldsmobile of the two-time Grand National champ was in front. As the uproar continued, Bill France, President of NASCAR and the new speedway, declared the finish "unofficial" and results would be pending on photographic and film evidence of the thrilling climax. The finish was even more incredible considering there was not a single caution flag.

Daytona's famous finish

As evidence arrived daily at NASCAR headquarters, the decision started to swing in Petty's favor. Seven photographs by seven different photographers seemed to indicate Petty was ahead as Johnny Bruner waved the checkered flag. Film footage sent by *Hearst Metrotone News of the Week* in New York removed all doubt on Wednesday when examined by France. Petty was ahead by about two feet as the cars crossed the line.

Charley Griffith, driving the same Pontiac that Cotton Owens drove to victory in 1957 on the sands of

Daytona Beach, came in third. Owens was fourth and Joe Weatherly fifth. Weatherly crossed the finish line a fender in front of the Petty-Beauchamp tango, almost two laps behind.

The lead swapped hands 33 times among seven different drivers. Besides Petty and Beauchamp, Bob Welborn, Tom Pistone, Weatherly, Fireball Roberts and Jack Smith shared the lead in the $67,760 event.

Smith's Pontiac seemed to have the upper hand in the middle stages, but the Sandy Springs, GA driver had problems "chunking" tires. He made several pit stops under the green flag and lost four laps. He wound up in seventh place in the field of 59 cars.

Fireball Roberts started 46th, but had the lead by the 23rd lap. He had shaken loose from the rest of the contenders and was leading by a comfortable margin when fuel pump failure sidelined his Pontiac. Welborn blew an engine in his Chevrolet after 75 laps.

Joe Lee Johnson's Convertible Chevrolet was the highest finisher in the ragtop division. The Chattanooga, TN pilot ran 187 of the 200 laps, good enough for 16th place.

Richard Petty drove an Oldsmobile Convertible but blew the engine after just eight laps.

Fritz Wilson departed with engine problems after 15 laps, and Shorty Rollins lost his engine on lap 115.

Johnny Beauchamp in victory lane after first Daytona 500. Four days later he was relegated to second place

Race No. 4

Welborn Runs Dry; Turner Wins Wild Hillsboro in Final Lap

HILLSBORO, NC (Mar 1) -- Bob Welborn's Chevrolet ran out of gas while leading in the final lap. Curtis Turner seized the opportunity and won the 99-mile Grand National race at Orange Speedway. It was the first win for Turner since April 18, 1958, when he won at Charlotte.

Tom Pistone trailed Turner by just three car lengths at the finish of the 110 lap ding-dong duel on the famous .9-mile oval. Welborn got credit for third place, one lap behind. Lee Petty came in fourth and Buck Baker was fifth.

Welborn had snatched the lead from Pistone with four laps to go. Turner followed Welborn past Pistone and was challenging in the final lap when Welborn jerked his car to the inside of the track - his fuel tank dry.

Grand National Race No. 4
110 Laps at Orange Speedway
Hillsboro, NC
99 miles on .9-mile Dirt Track
March 1, 1959

Fin	St	No.	Driver	Team / Car	Laps	Money	Status
1	1	41	Curtis Turner	Delta Auto Sales '59 T-Bird	110	$800	Running
2	2	59	Tom Pistone	Rupert Saf Belt '59 T-Bird	110	525	Running
3	5	49	Bob Welborn	Welborn '59 Chevrolet	109	350	Fuel
4	3	42	Lee Petty	Petty Eng '57 Olds	109	250	Running
5	7	88	Buck Baker	Baker '59 Chevrolet	109	225	Running
6	8	21	Glen Wood	Wood Bros '58 Ford	106	200	Running
7	16	33	Brownie King	Jess Potter '58 Chevrolet	105	165	Running
8	15	82	Joe Eubanks	Don Every '58 Ford	104	150	Running
9	4	6	Cotton Owens	W H Watson '58 Pontiac	104	140	Running
10	20	27	Jimmy Pardue	'58 Plymouth	99	130	Running
11	14	9	Roy Tyner	Tyner '57 Chevrolet	99	125	Running
12	19	81	Harvey Hege	Hege '57 Ford	98	110	Running
13	9	1	Speedy Thompson	Steve Pierce '57 Chevrolet	96	100	Fuel
14	12	89	Tiny Lund	Buck Baker '58 Chevrolet	96	85	Running
15	22	96	Bobby Keck	Keck '57 Chevrolet	95	70	Running
16	11	76	Larry Frank	Carolina Plating '58 Chevy	94	60	Crash
17	13	10	Elmo Langley	'57 Ford	93	50	Running
18	21	74	L D Austin	Austin '57 Chevrolet	90	50	Running
19	6	11	Junior Johnson	Paul Spaulding '57 Ford	66	50	Coil
20	10	26	Tommy Irwin	'58 Ford	24	50	Crash
21	17	7	Jimmie Lewallen	'58 Ford	21	50	Engine
22	18	80	Bobby Rose	Sam Arena '57 Che;vrolet	9	50	Rear End

Time of Race: 1 hour, 12 minutes, 47 seconds
Average Speed: 81.612 mph
Pole Winner: Curtis Turner - 87.544 mph
Lap Leaders: Curtis Turner 1, Tom Pistone 2, Turner 3-13, Pistone 14-50, Turner 51-103, Pistone 104-106, Bob Welborn 107-109, Turner 110
Cautions: 2
Margin of Victory: 3 car lengths
Attendance: 7,500

Grand National Race No. 5
200 Laps at New Concord Speedway
Concord, NC
100 Miles on Half-mile Dirt Track
March 8, 1959

Fin	St	No.	Driver	Team / Car	Laps	Money	Status
1	4	41	Curtis Turner	Delta Auto Sales '59 T-Bird	200	$800	Running
2	3	6	Cotton Owens	W H Watson '58 Pontiac	199	525	Running
3	6	42	Lee Petty	Petty Engineering '57 Olds	198	350	Running
4	10	11	Junior Johnson	Paul Spaulding '57 Ford	196	250	Running
5	7	1	Speedy Thompson	Steve Pierce '57 Chevrolet	196	225	Running
6	13	26	Tommy Irwin	'57 Ford	195	200	Running
7	8	44	Chester Barron	Barron '57 Chevrolet	192	165	Running
8	9	10	Elmo Langley	Ratus Walters '57 Ford	191	150	Running
9	17	19	Herman Beam	Beam '57 Chevrolet	179	140	Running
10	18	74	L D Austin	Austin '57 Chevrolet	168	130	Running
11	14	96	Bobby Keck	Keck '57 Chevrolet	156	125	Running
12	16	80	Neil Castles	Castles '57 Chevrolet	155	110	Running
13	12	8	Johnny Allen	'57 Chevrolet	151	100	Fuel Line
14	11	4	Rex White	White '59 Chevrolet	109	85	Rock Arm
15	15	81	Harvey Hege	Hege '57 Ford	101	70	Engine
16	2	59	Tom Pistone	Rupert Saf Belt '59 T-Bird	62	60	Crash
17	5	49	Bob Welborn	Welborn '59 Chevrolet	19	50	Fire
18	1	88	Buck Baker	Baker '59 Chevrolet	15	50	Valve
19	19	0	Bunk Moore	'57 Chevrolet	2	50	Crash

Time of Race: 1 hour, 41 minutes, 17 seconds
Average Speed: 59.239 mph
Pole Winner: Buck Baker - 66.420 mph
Lap Leaders: Buck Baker 1-13, Tom Pistone 14-15, Curtis Turner 16-200
Cautions: 2
Margin of Victory: 1 lap plus 4 seconds
Attendance: 11,500

Turner swerved his T-Bird past Welborn and held off Pistone in the stretch duel.

The Roanoke, VA lumberman gave car owner Dr. Bradford White of Orlando his first Grand National victory.

The crowd of 7,500 watched the lead change hands seven times in one of the finest races witnessed at this tight-turned facility. Turner led on four occasions, Pistone led three times and Welborn once.

Empty fuel tank cost Bob Welborn Hillsboro victory

Two caution flags slowed Turner's winning speed to 81.612 mph. Tommy Irwin sailed off into the woods in the 24th lap when his throttle hung open. He was unhurt. With 13 laps to go, Larry Frank rocketed off the first turn. His leg was bruised when his Chevy struck a tree.

Race No. 5

Turner Tames Field In Concord 100

CONCORD, NC (Mar 8) -- Curtis Turner outlasted and outran a 19-car field and won the 100 miler at Concord Speedway. A crowd of 11,500 turned out in 57 degree weather in what was termed the largest crowd for a sporting event in Cabarrus County.

Turner shoved his Thunderbird around Tom Pistone in the 16th lap and led the rest of the way. Cotton Owen's Pontiac was second, Lee Petty came in third and Junior Johnson was fourth. Fifth place went to Speedy Thompson.

Pole sitter Buck Baker led the first 13 laps in his Chevrolet. But a heavy smoke screen sidelined the former champion out of Charlotte.

Pistone led for two laps before Turner set sail. Pistone was holding down second place in the 62nd lap when a wheel bearing broke on his T-Bird, causing it to turn over in the second turn. Tiger Tom was not injured in the mishap.

Petty's third place finish enabled him to hold a 328 point lead over Owens in the Grand National point standings.

Race No. 6

Beauchamp Champ in Lakewood's 100 Miler

ATLANTA, GA (Mar 22) -- Johnny Beauchamp of Harlan, IA, who lost the Daytona 500 by a couple of feet, won the 100-miler at Lakewood Speedway by a mile. It was the first career win for the Thunderbird chauffeur.

Buck Baker finished in second place over a lap behind. Beauchamp led all the way, lapping Baker's Chevrolet in the 87th lap on the one-mile dirt track.

Tom Pistone finished third, Speedy Thompson was fourth and Joe Eubanks fifth.

The expected rematch between Beauchamp and Petty with all its emotional overtones failed to materialize. Petty started seventh and had moved into fourth place when an axle broke on his Oldsmobile after 39 laps. Petty got credit for 17th place in the field of 21.

Johnny Beauchamp

Beauchamp started on the pole as the crowd of 15,000 watched him build his lead with every turn of the wheel. He averaged 75.172 mph in giving Thunderbirds their third straight Grand National triumph.

Grand National Race No. 6
100 Laps at Lakewood Speedway
Atlanta, GA
100 Miles on 1-mile Dirt Track
March 22, 1959

Fin	St	No.	Driver	Team / Car	Laps	Money	Status
1	2	73	Johnny Beauchamp	Roy Burdick '59 T-Bird	100	$800	Running
2	1	87	Buck Baker	Baker '59 Chevrolet	99	525	Running
3	15	59	Tom Pistone	Rupert Safety Belt '59 T-Bird	97	350	Running
4	6	1	Speedy Thompson	Steve Pierce '57 Chevrolet	96	250	Running
5	14	82	Joe Eubanks	Don Every '58 Ford	95	225	Running
6	17	99	Shorty Rollins	Rollins '58 Ford	94	200	Running
7	21	39	Billy Carden	Davis Bros '57 Mercury	93	165	Running
8	4	22	Fireball Roberts	Jim Stephens '59 Chevrolet	85	150	Rear End
9	8	5	Tiny Lund	'57 Chevrolet	83	140	Trans
10	5	49	Bob Welborn	Welborn '59 Chevrolet	82	130	Rear End
11	16	16	Jim McGuirk	Happy Steigel '59 Pontiac	81	125	Running
12	13	35	Sam Massey	'57 Ford	73	110	Running
13	11	58	Roscoe Thompson	'57 Chevrolet	68	100	Crash
14	9	6	Cotton Owens	W H Watson '58 Pontiac	54	85	Engine
15	12	68	J C Hendrix	'57 Plymouth	52	70	Crash
16	18	44	Chester Barron	Barron '57 Chevrolet	45	60	Clutch
17	7	42	Lee Petty	Petty Engineering '57 Olds	39	50	L R Axle
18	19	8	Johnny Allen	'57 Chevrolet	23	50	Heating
19	20	36	Pete Kelly	'57 Chevrolet	10	50	Hd Gasket
20	10	18	Charley Griffith	Red Bank '57 Pontiac	2	50	Axle
21	3	47	Jack Smith	Bud Moore '59 Chevrolet	1	50	Engine

Time of Race: 1 hour, 19 minutes, 49 seconds
Average Speed: 75.172 mph
Pole Winner: Buck Baker - 77.888 mph
Lap Leaders: Johnny Beauchamp 1-100
Cautions:
Margin of Victory: 1 lap
Attendance: 15,000

Race No. 7

Johnson Wins at Wilson As Grandstand Burns

WILSON, NC (Mar 29) -- The action at Wilson Speedway was not confined to the race track as an Easter Day crowd of 8,800 saw a spectacular 'double feature'.

Junior Johnson passed Curtis Turner in the 177th lap and drove his Ford to a 3.0 second victory in the 200-lap Grand National event at the half mile dirt track. But the close finish was anti-climactic as the main grandstand caught fire.

The incident occurred at 1:45 pm - before the race had started. The spectators who were watching prac-

Grand National Race No. 7
200 Laps at Wilson Speedway
Wilson, NC
100 Miles on Half-mile Dirt Track
March 29, 1959

Fin	St	No.	Driver	Team / Car	Laps	Money	Status
1	22	11	Junior Johnson	Paul Spaulding '57 Ford	200	$800	Running
2	5	41	Curtis Turner	Delta Auto Sales '59 T-Bird	200	525	Running
3	21	43	Richard Petty	Petty Engineering '57 Olds	198	350	Running
4	10	42	Lee Petty	Petty Engineering '57 Olds	196	250	Running
5	8	59	Tom Pistone	Rupert Safety Belt '59 T-Bird	196	225	Running
6	15	9	Roy Tyner	Tyner '57 Chevrolet	194	200	Running
7	17	82	Joe Eubanks	Don Every '58 Ford	190	165	Running
8	11	33	Brownie King	Jess Potter '57 Chevrolet	189	150	Running
9	2	40	Joe Weatherly	'57 Chevrolet	188	140	Engine
10	19	64	Shep Langdon	Langdon '58 Ford	186	130	Running
11	3	6	Cotton Owens	W H Watson '58 Pontiac	186	125	Running
12	14	74	L D Austin	Austin '57 Chevrolet	182	110	Running
13	24	81	Harvey Hege	Hege '57 Ford	181	100	Running
14	18	96	Bobby Keck	Keck '57 Chevrolet	177	85	Running
15	4	88	Buck Baker	Baker '59 Chevrolet	175	70	Rear End
16	20	0	Bunk Moore	'57 Chevrolet	164	60	Steering
17	9	5	Tiny Lund	'57 Chevrolet	137	50	Running
18	6	10	Elmo Langley	Ratus Walters '58 Ford	110	50	Engine
19	13	99	Shorty Rollins	Shorty's '58 Ford	95	50	Fuel Line
20	12	49	Bob Welborn	Welborn '59 Chevrolet	81	50	Heating
21	7	1	Speedy Thompson	Steve Pierce '57 Chevrolet	78	50	Ball Joint
22	16	3	Marvin Panch	Don Angel '58 Ford	37	50	Engine
23	23	16	Jim McGuirk	Happy Steigel '59 Pontiac	37	---	Rear End
24	1	14	Ken Rush	Manley Britt '57 Mercury	33	---	Clutch

Time of Race: 1 hour, 59 minutes, 17 seconds
Average Speed: 50.300 mph
Poel Winner: Drew for Position
Lap Leaders: Joe Weatherly 1-4, Bob Welborn 5-10, Curtis Turner 11-176, Junior Johnson 177-200
Cautions:
Margin of Victory: 3 seconds
Attendance: 8,800

Grand National Race No. 8
200 Laps at Bowman Gray Stadium
Winston-Salem, NC
50 Miles on Quarter-mile Paved Track
March 30, 1959

Fin	St	No.	Driver	Team / Car	Laps	Money	Status
1	20	7	Jim Reed	Reed '57 Ford	200	$550	Running
2	3	43	Lee Petty	Petty Engineering '57 Olds	200	480	Running
3	1	4	Rex White	White '59 Chevrolet	200	350	Running
4	16	49	Bob Welborn	Welborn '59 Chevrolet	198	270	Running
5	7	89	Buck Baker	Baker '59 Chevrolet	197	230	Running
6	11	78	Jimmie Lewallen	'58 Ford	196	190	Running
7	5	97	Barney Shore	'57 Chevrolet	196	170	Running
8	10	11	Glen Wood	Paul Spaulding '57 Ford	195	165	Running
9	12	42	Richard Petty	Petty Engineering '57 Olds	195	150	Running
10	13	82	Cotton Owens	Don Every '58 Ford	193	160	Running
11	9	99	Shorty Rollins	Shorty's '58 Ford	192	180	Running
12	22	33	Brownie King	Jess Potter '57 Chevrolet	192	120	Running
13	21	3	Speedy Thompson	Don Angel '58 Ford	190	100	Running
14	19	27	Jimmy Pardue	'58 Plymouth	186	100	Running
15	4	44	Ken Rush	Chester Barron '57 Chevrolet	182	90	Running
16	24	74	L D Austin	Austin '57 Chevrolet	178	75	Running
17	14	8	Whitey Norman	'57 Chevrolet	175	105	Running
18	18	15	Max Berrier	'58 Plymouth	173	60	Rear End
19	8	14	Pee Wee Jones	Manley Britt '57 Mercury	150	50	Engine
20	6	17	Fred Harb	Harb '57 Mercury	126	75	Trans
21	15	96	Bobby Keck	Keck '57 Chevrolet	89	25	Engine
22	2	41	Curtis Turner	Delta Auto Sales '59 T-Bird	81	75	Wheel
23	23	81	Harvey Hege	Hege '57 Ford	25	25	Battery
24	17	45	Bobby Waddell	'57 Pontiac	11	40	Rear End

Time of Race: 1 hour, 8 minutes, 52 seconds
Average Speed: 43.562 mph
Pole Winner: Rex White - 46.296 mph
Lap Leaders: - - - - - - - - - - - - - - Jim Reed   -200
Cautions:
Margin of Victory:
Attendance:

tice were led to safety by public address announcer Sammy Bland, who directed them to the backstretch bleachers. The old wooden structure was ablaze within minutes and burned to the ground.

The fire cost Promoter Paul Sawyer and Race Director Joe Weatherly several thousand dollars as state police detoured cars around the track to make room for firefighting equipment.

Turner finished a close second to Johnson. Richard Petty enjoyed his first top five finish by taking third. Lee Petty was fourth and Tom Pistone fifth.

No time trials were held due to the fire. Race Director Weatherly led the first four laps, but yielded to Bob Welborn, who led for six laps. Turner passed Welborn on lap 11 and led until the late stages when Johson's Ford went to the front.

Johnson averaged 50.300 mph for his 12th career Grand National victory.

Race No. 8

Reed's Charge Impressive at Bowman-Gray

WINSTON-SALEM, NC (Mar 30) -- Jim Reed, starting 20th on the grid, charged his Ford to victory in the 50-mile Grand National event at the Bowman-Gray Stadium.

Reed missed qualifications and was forced to start near the rear of the 24 car field. Despite the obvious disadvantage on the flat quarter mile track, Reed knifed his way through his rivals quickly. He took the lead late in the race and beat Lee Petty to the finish line.

Rex White, who started on the pole, wound up third. Bob Welborn was fourth and Buck Baker fifth.

Jimmie Lewallen finished in sixth place, his first top 10 finish since the 1956 season.

Petty's runner-up effort enabled him to extend his point lead to 376 points over Cotton Owens, who finished 10th.

Curtis Turner started second, but the right front wheel locked up on his T-Bird in the 81st lap, putting him out of action.

Reed averaged 43.562 mph for his fifth career Grand National triumph.

Race No. 9

Jack Smith Beats Upstart Ned Jarrett at Columbia

COLUMBIA, SC (Apr 4) -- Jack Smith drove his Chevrolet to a narrow victory over upstart rookie Ned Jarrett to win the 100 miler at Columbia Speedway.

Smith, wheeling a Chevy wrenched by Bud Moore, started on the pole. After Bob Welborn fell out on lap 28, Smith only had to contend with Jarrett, a Sportsman hot shot from Conover, NC.

Jarrett got a ride in a Ford owned by Paul Spaulding

Buck Baker gives son, Buddy, some pointers at Columbia. It was Buddy's first Grand National start

as regular driver Junior Johnson was unable to make the race. Jarrett started eighth and handled himself like a veteran on the half-mile dirt track.

Third place went to point leader Lee Petty. Tiny Lund was fourth and Cotton Owens fifth.

Buddy Baker, son of two-time champ Buck Baker, made his first Grand National start in a Chevrolet owned by his dad. Young Baker wound up 14th in the field of 21 after his Chevrolet broke a shock absorber.

Smith became the seventh different winner in the nine 1959 Grand National Races run to date. He averaged 57.343 mph.

Grand National Race No. 9
200 Laps at Columbia Speedway
Columbia, SC
100 Miles on Half-mile Dirt Track
April 4, 1959

Fin	St	No.	Driver	Team / Car	Laps	Money	Status
1	1	47	Jack Smith	Bud Moore '59 Chevrolet	200	$900	Running
2	8	11	Ned Jarrett	Paul Spaulding '57 Ford	200	525	Running
3	5	42	Lee Petty	Petty Engineering '57 Olds	191	350	Running
4	6	5	Tiny Lund	'57 Chevrolet	190	250	Running
5	11	6	Cotton Owens	W H Watson '58 Pontiac	186	225	Running
6	15	33	George Green	Jess Potter '57 Chevrolet	181	200	Running
7	16	81	Harvey Hege	Hege '57 Ford	180	165	Running
8	14	64	Shep Langdon	Langdon '58 Ford	177	150	Running
9	13	68	J C Hendrix	'57 Plymouth	175	140	Running
10	19	74	L D Austin	Austin '57 Chevrolet	174	130	Running
11	17	19	Herman Beam	Beam '57 Chevrolet	147	125	Running
12	9	25	Gene White	White '57 Chevrolet	98	110	Heating
13	4	2	Speedy Thompson	Bruce Thompson '57 Chevy	94	100	Rear End
14	18	89	Buddy Baker	Buck Baker '58 Chevrolet	53	85	Shocks
15	3	59	Curtis Turner	Rupert Safety Belt '59 T-Bird	46	70	Ball Jnt
16	10	0	Bunk Moore	'57 Chevrolet	41	60	Engine
17	12	15	Max Berrier	'58 Plymouth	41	50	A Frame
18	2	49	Bob Welborn	Welborn '59 Chevrolet	18	50	Piston
19	7	88	Buck Baker	Buck Baker '59 Chevrolet	13	50	Rear End
20	20	27	Jimmy Pardue	'58 Plymouth	2	50	R R hub
21	21	99	Shorty Rollins	Shorty's '58 Ford	0	50	Crash

Time of Race: 1 hour, 44 minutes, 38 seconds
Average Speed: 57.343 mph
Pole Winner: Jack Smith - 60.73 mph
Lap Leaders: - - - - - - - - - - - - - - Jack Smith   -200
Cautions:
Margin of Victory:
Attendance:

Race No. 10

Petty Wins 2nd of Year At North Wilkesboro

N. WILKESBORO, NC (Apr 5) -- Lee Petty swept into the lead in the 108th lap and went on to win the 100-mile Grand National contest at North Wilkesboro Speedway. It was the second win of the year for the Oldsmobile driver and the 39th of his illustrious career.

Jack Smith followed in second place with Cotton Owens third. Tiny Lund came in fourth and Fred Harb fifth.

Speedy Thompson led the first 88 laps from the pole position. His Chevrolet was padding his advantage until a right front wheel bearing burned out, knocking him out of action. Curtis Turner picked up first place and led until mechanical problems kayoed his T-Bird after 107 laps. Petty took the lead at that point and led the final 53 laps.

After Turner pitted, he dismounted and stomped off. When his Doc White team repaired the trouble enough to get back into the race, Turner was nowhere to be found. Tom Pistone was summoned to take the helm. The little Chicago driver took the car to 11th place in the final rundown, falling out with a bent push rod late in the race.

Petty averaged 71.985 mph before 10,000 spectators. Four minor spin outs were responsible for four short cautions for a total of nine laps.

Grand National Race No. 10
160 Laps at N. Wilkesboro Speedway
North Wilkesboro, NC
100 Miles on .625-mile Paved Track
April 5, 1959

Fin	St	No.	Driver	Team / Car	Laps	Money	Status
1	4	43	Lee Petty	Petty Engineering '57 Olds	160	$800	Running
2	8	47	Jack Smith	Bud Moore '59 Chevrolet	160	525	Running
3	7	6	Cotton Owens	W H Watson '58 Pontiac	159	350	Running
4	9	5	Tiny Lund	'57 Chevrolet	159	250	Running
5	10	17	Fred Harb	Harb '57 Mercury	154	225	Running
6	17	19	Herman Beam	Beam '57 Chevrolet	147	200	Running
7	20	74	L D Austin	Austin '57 Chevrolet	147	165	Running
8	18	33	George Green	Jess Potter '57 Chevrolet	145	150	Running
9	3	99	Shorty Rollins	Shorty's '58 Ford	143	140	Running
10	15	81	Harvey Hege	Hege '57 Ford	142	130	Running
11	6	59	Curtis Turner*	Rupert Safety Belt '59 T-Bird	141	125	Bent Rod
12	12	45	Bobby Waddell	'57 Pontiac	136	110	Heating
13	19	3	Don Angel	Angel '58 Ford	131	100	R F Lugs
14	14	27	Jimmy Pardue	'58 Plymouth	124	85	R R Axle
15	23	44	G C Spencer	Chester Barron '57 Chevrolet	122	70	Running
16	13	40	Paul Walton	'57 Chevrolet	112	60	Piston
17	1	1	Speedy Thompson	Steve Pierce '57 Chevrolet	88	50	Bearing
18	22	64	Shep Langdon	Langdon '58 Ford	87	50	Engine
19	21	8	Whitey Norman	'57 Chevrolet	60	50	Fuel Line
20	2	21	Glen Wood	Wood Bros '58 Ford	35	50	Engine
21	16	88	Buck Baker	Baker '59 Chevrolet	23	50	Rear End
22	5	11	Junior Johnson	Paul Spaulding '57 Ford	19	50	Bearing
23	11	2	Jimmy Thompson	Bruce Thompson '57 Chevy	11	50	Engine

Time of Race: 1 hour, 23 minutes, 21 seconds
Average Speed: 71.985 mph
Pole Winner: Speedy Thompson - 85.746 mph
Lap Leaders: Speedy Thompson 1-88, Curtis Turner 89-107, Lee Petty 108-160
Cautions: 4 for 9 laps
Margin of Victory:
Attendance: 10,000

Grand National Race No. 11
200 Miles at Reading Speedway
Reading, PA
100 Miles on Half-mile Dirt Track
April 26, 1959

Fin	St	No.	Driver	Team / Car	Laps	Money	Status
1	11	11	Junior Johnson	Paul Spaulding '57 Ford	200	$800	Running
2	1	1	Speedy Thompson	Steve Pierce '57 Chevrolet	196	525	Running
3	59	59	Tom Pistone	Rupert Safety Belt '59 T-Bird	196	350	Running
4	36	36	Tommy Irwin	Irwin '59 T-Bird	192	250	Running
5	90	90	Buzz Woodward	'57 Ford	191	225	Running
6	42	42	Lee Petty	Petty Engineering '57 Olds	189	200	Axle
7	79	79	Tiny Benson	'57 Chevrolet	187	165	Running
8	70	70	Jim Parsley	'57 Chevrolet	177	150	Running
9	50	50	Ben Benz	Harry Friedland '57 Chevy	166	150	Running
10	99	99	Shorty Rollins	Shorty's '58 Ford	161	130	Engine
11	52	52	John Seely	'57 Chevrolet	160	125	Running
12	88	88	Reds Kagle	'57 Chevrolet	158	110	Fuel Line
13	33	33	Al White	White '58 Ford	148	100	Running
14	6	6	Cotton Owens	W H Watson '58 Pontiac	128	85	Heating
15	53	53	Kenny Johnson	'57 Ford	121	70	H Gasket
16	200	200	Ray Fanning	'57 Chevrolet	117	60	Heating
17	100	100	Jim Findley	'57 Chevrolet	116	50	Hose
18	31	31	Gus Wilson	'57 Chevrolet	100	50	Front End
19	4	4	Rex White	'59 Chevrolet	97	50	Push Rod
20	72A	72A	Bobby Johns	Shorty Johns '57 Chevrolet	96	50	Ignition
21	73	73	Johnny Beauchamp	Roy Burdick '57 Ford	92	50	Brakes
22	10	10	Elmo Langley	Ratus Walters '57 Ford	76	50	Heating
23	3	3	Don Angel	Angel '58 Ford	36	---	Fumes
24	7	7	Jim Reed	Reed '57 Ford	22	---	Engine
25	791	791	Dave Marburger	'57 Ford	22	---	Crash

Time of Race: 1 hour, 53 minutes, 11 seconds
Average Speed: 53.011 mph
Pole Winner: No Time Trials
Lap Leaders: Lee Petty 1-188, Junior Johnson 189-200
Cautions: 1 for 12 laps
Margin of Victory: 4 laps plus
Attendance: 2,500

Race No. 11

Johnson Outlasts Petty To Win Reading 100

READING, PA (Apr 26) -- Junior Johnson dogged Lee Petty for most of the race, finally made the decisive pass and went on to win the 100 miler at Reading Speedway by four laps.

Speedy Thompson wound up second, Tom Pistone was third, Tommy Irwin fourth and Buzz Woodward fifth.

Petty led the first 188 laps in his Oldsmobile. With 13 laps to go, he pitted for fuel, but when he returned to the track, he broke an axle. He was forced to retire and received sixth place money based on his 189 laps complete. Johnson took the lead and coasted to the finish.

A slim crowd of 2,500 was on hand in wet weather. The qualifying was washed out.

Dave Marburger rolled his Ford in the 22nd lap. The caution came out for 12 laps while the wreckage was cleared. Johnson averaged 53.011 mph for his second win of the year.

Grand National Race No. 12
250 laps at Hickory Speedway
Hickory, NC
100 Miles on .4-mile Dirt Track
May 2, 1959

Fin	St	No.	Driver	Team / Car	Laps	Money	Status
1	1	11	Junior Johnson	Paul Spaulding '57 Ford	250	$800	Running
2	7	41	Joe Weatherly	Delta Auto Sales '59 T-Bird	248	525	Running
3	2	42	Lee Petty	Petty Engineering '57 Olds	247	350	Running
4	3	40	Ken Rush	'57 Chevrolet	246	250	Running
5	11	6	Cotton Owens	W H Watson '58 Pontiac	246	225	Running
6	17	1	Speedy Thompson	Steve Pierce '57 Chevrolet	237	200	Oil Press
7	9	64	Shep Langdon	Langdon '58 Ford	237	165	Running
8	16	74	L D Austin	Austin '57 Chevrolet	221	150	Running
9	8	38	Ned Jarrett	'57 Chevrolet	220	140	Running
10	20	19	Herman Beam	Beam '57 Chevrolet	214	130	Running
11	15	81	Harvey Hege	Hege '57 Ford	209	125	Running
12	12	22	Harlan Richardson	'58 Ford	193	110	Engine
13	6	7	Jim Reed	Reed '57 Ford ST	182	100	R R Axle
14	4	34	G C Spencer	'57 Chevrolet	179	85	Trans
15	18	87	Buck Baker	Baker '59 Chevrolet	167	70	Oil Press
16	14	96	Bobby Keck	Keck '57 Chevrolet	133	60	Fan
17	19	39	Buck Brigance	'57 Chevrolet	125	50	Batt Cable
18	10	45	Bobby Waddell	'57 Pontiac	81	50	Piston
19	13	27	Jimmy Pardue	'58 Plymouth	73	50	R F Hub
20	21	0	Bunk Moore	'57 Chevrolet	28	50	Engine
21	5	5	Rex White	'57 Chevrolet ST	27	50	Trans

Time of Race: 1 hour, 36 minutes, 31 seconds
Average Speed: 62.165 mph
Pole Winner: Junior Johnson - 68.900 mph
Lap Leaders: Junior Johnson 1-25, Speedy Thompson 26-50, Joe Weatherly 51-100,
 Buck Baker 101-124, Thompson 125-237, Johnson 238-250
Cautions: 4
Margin of Victory: 2 and a half laps
Attendance: 5,000

Race No. 12

Johnson Flips Ford; Then Wins at Hickory

HICKORY, NC (May 2) -- Junior Johnson rolled his Ford in a practice session but came back to win the Hickory 250 at Hickory Speedway. It was the third win of the year for the Ronda, NC mountain man.

Johnson slipped into first place 13 laps from the finish when engine problems sent leader Speedy Thompson to the pits. As Thompson's Chevrolet limped down pit road, Johnson sailed to a two-lap victory over Joe Weatherly's T-Bird. Third place went to Lee Petty, Ken Rush was fourth and Cotton Owens fifth.

Johnson spun out in a practice run, flipping his Paul Spaulding Ford. The car landed on its wheels and Johnson drove back to the pit area. "It just skinned it up a little," remarked Johnson.

The 27 year old leadfoot started on the pole and led the first 25 laps, giving way to Thompson in lap 26. Thompson then engaged in a tight battle with Joe Weatherly and Buck Baker. All led the race before Thompson got the lead from Baker in lap 125.

The Monroe, NC driver, looking for his first win of the year, led for 113 straight laps before the oil pressure dropped in his Chevy with 13 laps to go.

Johnson averaged 62.165 mph as four cautions broke the action.

Race No. 13

Petty Beats Beauchamp by 5 Laps in Virginia 500

MARTINSVILLE, VA (May 3) -- Old Hoss Lee Petty motored into the lead on lap 309 and trotted to an easy victory in the Virginia 500 at Martinsville Speedway. It was the 40th career Grand National win for the 45 year-old Randleman, NC Oldsmobile driver.

Petty finished five laps ahead of a Chevrolet driven by Johnny Beauchamp and relief driver Larry Frank. The tag-team of Junior Johnson and Ned Jarrett captured third place. Tom Pistone was fourth and Roy Tyner fifth.

Johnson was holding better than a lap lead when he pitted on lap 308, giving the lead to Petty for good. A long stay in the pits dropped him to third place. On lap 347, Johnson pitted again and passed out. Jarrett took the wheel and drove the car home third. Johnson later said exhaust fumes had overcome him.

Petty bagged $3,630 for his third win of the 1959 campaign. He stretched his point lead to 608 points over Cotton Owens, who finished 10th.

Pole sitter Bobby Johns led the first 72 laps. Glen Wood, who started 19th but hustled to the front quickly, passed Johns and led for 13 laps. Petty and

Johnson swapped the lead three times the rest of the way.

Petty averaged 59.512 mph before a crowd of 14,000. Three cautions for minor incidents plus a 30 minute red flag for rain showers interrupted the hot pace.

Race No. 14

Tiger Tom Tops Trenton 150

TRENTON, NJ (May 17) -- Tiger Tom Pistone of Chicago, passed Jim Reed in the 106th lap and led the rest of the way to nail down his first Grand National win at Trenton Speedway.

Pistone, the 5'3" little dynamo, drove his Rupert Safety Belt T-Bird across the finish line 11.8 seconds in front of Cotton Owens to bag the $1,450 top prize in the 150-mile event on the one-mile paved track. Third place went to point leader Lee Petty. Reed fell to fourth in the closing laps, and Tommy Irwin was fifth. Pedro Rodriguez, noted Mexican

Bob Burdick won pole in first Grant National Start at Trenton

Grand National Race No. 13
500 Laps at Martinsville Speedway
Martinsville, Virginia
"Virginia 500"
250 Miles on Half-mile Paved Track
May 3, 1959

Fin	St	No.	Driver	Team / Car	Laps	Money	Status
1	24	42	Lee Petty	Petty Engineering '57 Olds	500	$3,630	Running
2	20	76	* J. Beauchamp	Carolina Plating '57 Chevy	495	1,625	Running
3	32	11	** Junior Johnson	Paul Spaulding '57 Ford	495	1,205	Running
4	10	59	Tom Pistone	Rupert Safety Belts '59 T-Bird	491	775	Running
5	18	9	Roy Tyner	Tyner '57 Chevrolet	491	600	Running
6	34	49	Bob Welborn	Welborn '57 Chevrolet	490	500	Running
7	25	43	Richard Petty	Petty Engineering '57 Olds	490	375	Running
8	31	41	Joe Weatherly	Delta Auto Sales '59 T-Bird	489	375	Running
9	17	99	Shorty Rollins	Shorty's '58 Ford	486	300	Running
10	3	6	Cotton Owens	W H Watson '58 Pointiac	484	300	Running
11	19	21	Glen Wood	Wood Bros '58 Ford	482	230	Running
12	11	40	Dave White	'58 Chevrolet	479	150	Running
13	16	5	Tiny Lund	'57 Chevrolet	478	135	Running
14	39	29	Dick Freeman	'59 Chevrolet	469	125	Vapor Lk
15	9	4	Rex White	White '59 Chevrolet	468	125	Running
16	4	44	Ken Rush	Chester Barron '57 Chevrolet	468	110	Running
17	12	34	G C Spencer	'57 Chevrolet	467	110	Running
18	6	32	Brownie King	Jess Potter '58 Chevrolet	466	100	Running
19	14	1	Speedy Thompson	Steve Pierce '57 Chevrolet	464	100	Bearing
20	7	19	Herman Beam	Beam '57 Chevrolet	462	100	Running
21	33	17	Fred Harb	Harb '57 Mercury	461	100	Running
22	35	3	Bunk Moore	'58 Ford	460	100	Running
23	5	64	Shep Langdon	Langdon '58 Ford	453	90	Running
24	8	74	L D Austin	Austin '57 Chevrolet	453	90	Running
25	28	48	Fireball Roberts	E C Wilson '59 Chevrolet	385	85	Rear End
26	40	78	Jim Paschal	'58 Ford	371	80	Engine
27	21	81	Harvey Hege	Hege '57 Ford	339	75	Crash
28	22	114	Fritz Wilson	Wilson '59 T-Bird	333	75	Fuel Pmp
29	1	72	Bobby Johns	Shorty Johns '57 Chevrolet	297	75	Rear End
30	2	77	Joe Lee Johnson	Honest Charley '57 Chevy	297	125	H Gasket
31	37	79	Jerry Draper	'57 Chevrolet	278	50	Engine
32	15	36	Tommy Irwin	Irwin '59 T-Bird	275	50	Engine
33	30	88	Reds Kagle	'57 Chevrolet	222	50	Engine
34	27	96	Bobby Keck	Keck '57 Chevrolet	208	50	Engine
35	13	33	George Green	Jess Potter'57 Chevrolet	143	50	Engine
36	26	7	Barney Shore	'57 Chevrolet	76	---	Oil Press
37	36	7	Jim Reed	Reed '59 Chevrolet	47	---	Vapor Lk
38	38	55	Ben Benz	Harry Friedland '57 Chevrolet	40	---	Brakes
39	23	87	Buck Baker	Baker '59 Chevrolet	31	---	Trans
49	29	46	Whitey Norman	'57 Chevrolet	23	---	R R Axle

Time of Race: 4 hours, 12 minutes, 3 seconds
Average Speed: 59.512 mph
Pole Winner: Bobby Johns - 66.03 mph
* Relieved by Larry Frank
** Relieved by Ned Jarrett
Lap Leaders: Bobby Johns 1-72, Glen Wood 73-85, Lee Petty 86-230,
  Junior Johnson 231-308, Lee Petty 309-500
Cautions: 3
Margin of Victory: 5 laps plus
Attendance: 14,000

Grand National Race No. 14
150 Laps at Trenton Speedway
Trenton, NJ
150 Miles on 1.0-mile Paved Track
May 17, 1959

Fin	St	No.	Driver	Team / Car	Laps	Money	Status
1	3	59	Tom Pistone	Rupert Safety Belt '59 T-Bird	150	$1,450	Running
2	2	6	Cotton Owens	W H Watson '58 Pontiac	150	750	Running
3	8	42	Lee Petty	Petty Eng '59 Plymouth	149	575	Running
4	5	7	Jim Reed	Reed '59 Chevrolet	148	375	Running
5	4	36	Tommy Irwin	Irwin '59 T-Bird	147	350	Running
6	10	10	Pedro Rodriguez	Ratus Walters '57 Ford	144	300	Running
7	13	55	Ben Benz	Harvey Friedland '57 Chevy	139	250	Running
8	14	27	Dominick Persicketti	'57 Ford	137	225	Running
9	17	61	Ernie Gesell	'57 Ford	115	200	Running
10	16	79	Tiny Benson	'56 Chevrolet	111	185	Running
11	6	11	Junior Johnson	Paul Spaulding '57 Ford	103	175	Running
12	11	43	Richard Petty	Petty Engineering '57 Olds	95	165	Crash
13	9	16	Charlie Cregar	Happy Steigel '59 Pontiac	95	150	Rear End
14	18	74	L D Austin	Austin '57 Chevrolet	87	130	Carb
15	1	73	Bob Burdick	Roy Burdick '59 T-Bird	64	100	Fire
16	7	88	Reds Kagle	'57 Chevrolet	53	90	Oil Leak
17	15	33	Al White	White '58 Ford	52	75	U Joint
18	12	110	Elmo Langley	Ratus Walters '57 Ford	25	75	Clutch

Time of Race: 1 hour, 43 minutes, 2 seconds
Fastest Speed: 87.350 mph
Pole Winner: Bob Burdick - 88.95 mph
Lap Leaders: Cotton Owens 1-95, Tom Pistone 96-102, Jim Reed 103-105,
  Pistone 106-150
Cautions:
Margin of Victory: 11.8 seconds
Attendance:

road racer, finished sixth in his first Grand National start.

Bob Burdick, the 22 year-old newcomer out of Omaha, won the pole position in his very first Grand National start. The crew-cut kid, who replaced Johnny Beauchamp in his dad Roy's powerful T-Bird, qualified quickest at 88.95 mph, but never led. He departed after 64 laps when a rear wheel caught on fire. Burdick got credit for 15th place in the 18-car field.

Tom Pistone won his first Grand National race at Trenton

Owens led the first 95 laps with Pistone in hot pursuit. When Owens went to the pits, Pistone took the lead for seven laps. Pistone then pitted on lap 102, getting 102 miles out of a full tank of fuel in his heavy Thunderbird. Reed fell heir to the lead at this point. But three laps later Tiger Tom again grabbed first place for good.

In the only crash of the day, Richard Petty's Oldsmobile thumped the wall on lap 97, putting him out of the race.

Pistone, who won in his 14th career start, averaged 87.350 mph in a caution-free race.

Grand National Race No. 15
200 Laps at Charlotte Fairgrounds
Charlotte, NC
100 Miles on Half-mile Dirt Track
May 22, 1959

Fin	St	No.	Driver	Team / Car	Laps	Money	Status
1	4	42	Lee Petty	Petty Engineering '57 Olds	200	$800	Running
2	3	5	Tiny Lund	'57 Chevrolet	200	525	Running
3	9	82	Cotton Owens	Don Every '58 Ford	200	350	Running
4	7	2	Speedy Thompson	Bruce Thompson '57 Chevy	200	250	Running
5	6	87	Buck Baker	Baker '59 Chevrolet	199	225	Running
6	18	1	Richard Riley	'57 Chevrolet	198	200	Running
7	10	79	Jerry Draper	'57 Chevrolet	197	165	Running
8	1	49	Bob Welborn	Welborn '57 Chevrolet	196	150	Running
9	16	17	Fred Harb	Harb '58 Ford	194	140	Running
10	13	47	Jack Smith	Bud Moore Gar '59 Chevrolet	193	130	Running
11	8	38	Ned Jarrett	Jarrett '57 Chevrolet	189	125	Running
12	22	34	G C Spencer	'57 Chevrolet	171	110	Rear End
13	23	74	L D Austin	Austin '57 Chevrolet	163	100	Running
14	19	62	Buck Brigance	'57 Chevrolet	159	85	Running
15	21	19	Herman Beam	Beam '57 Chevrolet	146	70	Running
16	2	41	Joe Weatherly	Delta Auto Sales '59 T-Bird	142	60	Rear End
17	20	9	Roy Tyner	Tyner '57 Chevrolet	129	50	Engine
18	14	11	Junior Johnson	Paul Spaulding '57 Ford	122	50	RR Axle
19	11	43	Richard Petty	Petty Engineering '57 Olds	108	50	Engine
20	15	21	Larry Frank	Wood Bros '58 Ford	90	50	Axle
21	25	96	Bobby Keck	Keck '57 Chevrolet	82	50	Engine
22	17	64	Shep Langdon	Langdon '58 Ford	55	50	RR Axle
23	12	45	Bobby Waddell	'57 Pontiac	47	---	Piston
24	5	99	Fritz Wilson	Shorty Rollins '58 Ford	17	---	Radiator
25	24	80	Cliff Timberman	'57 Chevrolet	2	---	Engine

Time of Race: 1 hour, 48 minutes, 30 seconds
Average Speed: 55.300 mph
Pole Winner: Bob Welborn - 57.95 mph
Lap Leaders: Bob Welborn 1-7, Joe Weatherly 8-22, Buck Baker 23-80,
    Weatherly 81-142, Lee Petty 143-200
Cautions: 3 for 12 laps
Margin of Victory: 20 yards
Attendance: 4,200

Race No. 15

Petty Fastest in 100-miler At Charlotte

CHARLOTTE, NC (May 22) -- Lee Petty gunned his Oldsmobile past Joe Weatherly in the 143rd lap and sped to victory in the 100-miler at the Charlotte Fairgrounds.

Tiny Lund finished in second place, just 20 yards behind Petty at the checkered flag. Cotton Owens was third, Speedy Thompson fourth and Buck Baker fifth.

A crowd of 4,200 watched the lead change hands four times among four drivers. Bob Welborn led the first seven laps, but fell off the pace and wound up eighth, four laps behind.

Weatherly led twice for a total of 77 laps in his Thunderbird. The Norfolk, VA driver was heading the field when rear end failure put him out, paving the way

for Petty.

Fritz Wilson, who ran so strong at Daytona, returned to action, driving Shorty Rollins' Ford. Wilson went only 17 laps before he was sidelined with a split radiator.

Petty averaged 55.300 mph after three caution flags for 12 laps slowed the race.

Race No. 16

Rex White Outduels Johnson And Irwin at Nashville

NASHVILLE, TN (May 24) -- Rex White ended an 11 month famine with an impressive drive at Fairgrounds Speedway in Nashville. The Silver Spring, MD Chevrolet driver grabbed the lead with five laps to

Grand National Race No. 16
200 Laps at Fairgrounds Speedway
Nashville, TN
100 Miles on Half-mile Paved Track
May 24, 1959

Fin	St	No.	Driver	Team / Car	Laps	Money	Status
1	1	4	Rex White	White, 59 Chevrolet	200	$900	Running
2	7	11	Junior Johnson	Paul Spaulding '57 Ford	200	525	Running
3	3	36	Tommy Irwin	Irwin '59 Thunderbird	199	350	Running
4	5	87	Buck Baker	Baker '59 Chevrolet	198	250	Running
5	4	77	Joe Lee Johnson	Honest Charley '57 Chevrolet	198	225	Running
6	2	42	Lee Petty	Petty Eng '59 Plymouth	196	200	Running
7	8	18	Charley Griffith	Red Bank '57 Pontiac	193	165	Running
8	6	6	Cotton Owens	W H Watson '58 Pontiac	193	150	Running
9	9	73	Bob Burdick	Roy Burdick '59 Thunderbird	192	140	Running
10	11	19	Herman Beam	Beam '57 Chevrolet	179	130	Running
11	10	34	G C Spencer	'57 Chevrolet	171	125	Running
12	12	13	Tommy Thompson	'59 Chevrolet	160	110	Running

Time of Race: 1 hour, 24 minutes, 30 seconds
Average Speed: 71.006 mph
Pole Winner: Rex White - 70.89 mph
Lap Leaders: Lee Petty 1-37, Tommy Irwin 38-148, Rex White 149-183
    Junior Johnson 184-195, White 196-200
Cautions: None
Margin of Victory:
Attendance: 9,634

Pole sitter Rex White #4 and Lee Petty take the green flag at Nashville. White won the 100-miler

go and edged Junior Johnson in the 100-miler on the half-mile paved track.

Tommy Irwin finished in third place, Buck Baker was fourth and Joe Lee Johnson fifth.

Twelve cars started the race and all 12 finished. It was the first time in Grand National history that every car that started the race was running at the finish.

Lee Petty led the first 37 laps in his Oldsmobile. Rookie Tommy Irwin shoved his T-Bird into the lead on lap 38 and led for 111 laps. He relinquished the lead to White when he pitted.

White, who was trying to go the full 200 laps on the half-mile paved track without a pit stop, had to come down pit road on lap 183. His crew added a couple of gallons and he was on his way. Johnson also gambled on going the distance, but his engine sputtered on lap 195. White roared into the lead when Johnson pitted and held on for the victory. It was his third Grand National win and his first since June 29, 1958.

The winner averaged 71.006 mph before an audience of 9,634. The event was uninterrupted by caution flags.

Grand National Race No. 17
500 Laps at Ascot Stadium
Los Angeles, CA
200 Miles on .4-mile Dirt Track
May 30, 1959

Fin	St	No.	Driver	Team / Car	Laps	Money	Status
1	4	97	Parnelli Jones	Vel Miletich '59 Ford ST	487	$1,805	Running
2	11	44	Lloyd Dane	Vada Dane '57 Ford ST	487	900	Running
3	12	12	Marvin Porter	Porter '57 Ford ST	485	700	Running
4	6	34	Bob Ross	'57 Chevrolet ST	482	600	Running
5	27	11	Bob Keefe	'58 Plymouth ST	459	500	Running
6	21	10	Lucky Long	'57 Chevrolet ST	457	400	Running
7	17	8	Dave James	'57 Chevrolet ST	454	350	Running
8	29	5	John Potter	'58 Ford ST	453	300	Running
9	5	55	Mel Larson	'57 Mercury ST	451	250	Running
10	15	3	Eddie Pagan	'59 Thunderbird ST	439	375	Running
11	3	9	Bob Price	'57 Chevrolet ST	419	225	Running
12	30	26	Jim Lamport	'56 Ford C	414	150	Running
13	14	37	Bob Hogie	'57 Pontiac ST	409	140	Heating
14	10	61	Dick Santee	'57 Ford ST	407	130	Running
15	19	18	Bob Tyrrell	'57 Chevrolet ST	406	120	Heating
16	31	22	Harlan Richardson	'57 Ford GN	393	110	Running
17	23	23	Bob Perry	'59 Plymouth ST	359	250	Rear End
18	24	21	Ronny Myers	'56 Ford C	369	100	Heating
19	9	1	Scotty Cain	'59 Ford ST	367	200	Piston
20	16	84	Don Taylor	'57 Chevrolet ST	360	100	Heating
21	13	43	Bill Jarick	'58 Mercury ST	346	75	Running
22	32	87	Arley Scranton	'57 Pontiac ST	339	75	Running
23	26	2	Ron Hornaday	'57 Chevrolet ST	325	75	Radiator
24	18	91	Jim Cook	'59 Plymouth ST	270	175	Plugs
25	22	14	Tom Edmonds	'56 Mercury C	239	75	A Frame
26	28	40	Dick Carter	'58 Mercury ST	230	75	Running
27	8	0	Danny Letner	'57 Pontiac ST	224	100	Camshaft
28	2	98	Eddie Gray	Vel Miletich '57 Ford ST	217	170	Heating
29	1	7	Jim Reed	Reed '59 Chevrolet ST	134	134	Engine
30	33	4	Dick Getty	'59 Chevrolet ST	132	175	Sway Bar
31	20	47	George Norton	'57 Chevrolet ST	73	50	Bearing
32	25	31	Kirby Miller	'59 Chevrolet ST	47	150	Drive Shft
33	7	20	Gene Peltier	'57 Chevrolet ST	36	50	Piston

* Race Shortened to 487 laps by rain
Time of Race: 3 hours, 49 minutes, 15.5 seconds
Average Speed: 50.982 mph
Pole Winner: Jim Reed - 53.59 mph
Lap Leaders: - - - - - - - - - - - - - Parnelli Jones   -487
Cautions:
Margin of Victory:
Attendance:

Race No. 17

Parnelli Jones First in Ascot Stadium Sweepstakes Race

LOS ANGELES, CA (May 30) -- Parnelli Jones drove his Ford to victory in a rain-shortened 195-miler at Ascot Stadium. The scheduled 200-mile Sweepstakes race was the third career win for the Torrance, CA speedster.

Lloyd Dane finished in second place with Marvin Porter third. Fourth place went to Bob Ross, and Bob Keefe was fifth.

The Sweepstakes event pitted Short Track division cars, Convertibles and Grand Nationals together. Twenty-nine of the cars in the 33 car field were Short Track cars. There were three Convertibles and one lone Grand National.

Harlan Richardson drove the lone Grand National and wound up 16th, 94 laps behind winner Jones. Richardson, however, received 500 points in the Grand National point race since he was the only Grand National entrant. Jones was awarded 500 Short Track points for winning the race.

Jones collected $1,805 for his Vel Miletich owned team. He averaged 50.982 mph on the .4-mile dirt track.

Grand National Race No. 19
200 Laps at Greenville-Pickens Speedway
Greenville, SC
100 Miles on Half-mile Dirt Track
June 13, 1959

Fin	St	No.	Driver	Team / Car	Laps	Money	Status
1	11	11	Junior Johnson	Paul Spaulding '57 Ford	200	$800	Running
2	7	9	Roy Tyner	Tyner '57 Chevrolet	198	525	Running
3	4	42	Lee Petty	Petty Engineering '57 Olds	198	350	Running
4	12	5	Tiny Lund	'57 Chevrolet	196	250	Running
5	3	36	Tommy Irwin	Irwin '59 Thunderbird	193	225	Running
6	6	88	Buck Baker	Baker '59 Chevrolet	192	200	Running
7	20	34	G C Spencer	'57 Chevrolet	192	165	Running
8	15	2	Richard Riley	Bruce Thompson '57 Chevy	191	150	Running
9	22	74	L D Austin	Austin '57 Chevrolet	185	140	Running
10	17	30	Doug Cox	'58 Ford	181	130	LR Spring
11	21	64	Shep Langdon	Langdon '58 Ford	181	125	Running
12	18	28	Fred Harb	Harvey Hege '57 Mercury	179	110	Running
13	24	19	Herman Beam	Beam '57 Chevrolet	178	100	Running
14	23	51	Fred Boles	'58 Plymouth	165	85	Running
15	5	1	Speedy Thompson	Steve Pierce '57 Chevrolet	164	70	Bearing
16	2	6	Cotton Owens	W H Watson '58 Pontiac	130	60	Bearing
17	19	89	Buddy Baker	Buck Baker '58 Chevrolet	125	50	Running
18	8	49	Bob Welborn	Welborn '57 Chevrolet	120	50	Running
19	25	79	Jerry Draper	'57 Chevrolet	108	50	Spindle
20	1	47	Jack Smith	Bud Moore Gar '59 Chevrolet	107	50	Wtr Pmp
21	16	32	Browne King	Jess Potter '58 Chevrolet	105	50	LR Axle
22	14	38	Ned Jarrett	Jarrett '57 Chevrolet	101	50	LR Axle
23	13	62	Bunk Moore	'57 Chevrolet	32	---	Rear End
24	9	99	Fritz Wilson	Shorty Rollins '58 Ford	27	---	Crash
25	10	82	Joe Eubanks	Don Every '58 Ford	16	---	Engine

Time of Race: 1 hour, 56 minutes, 33 seconds
Average Speed: 51.480 mph
Pole Winner: Jack Smith - 65.838 mph
Lap Leaders:- - - - - - - - - - - - - Junior Johnson   -200
Cautions:
Margin of Victory: 2 laps plus
Attendance:

Grand National Race No. 18
200 Laps at Hub City Speedway
Spartanburg, SC
100 Miles on Half-mile Dirt Track
June 5, 1959

Fin	St	No.	Driver	Team / Car	Laps	Money	Status
1	9	47	Jack Smith	Bud Moore '59 Chevrolet	200	$1,000	Running
2	5	82	Joe Eubanks	Don Every '58 Ford	199	525	Running
3	8	11	Junior Johnson	Paul Spaulding '57 Ford	198	350	Running
4	15	34	G C Spencer	'57 Chevrolet	197	250	Running
5	6	9	Roy Tyner	Tyner '57 Chevrolet	195	225	Running
6	20	79	Jerry Draper	'57 Chevrolet	190	200	Running
7	16	74	L D Austin	Austin '57 Chevrolet	183	165	Running
8	13	30	Doug Cox	'58 Ford	180	150	Running
9	18	19	Herman Beam	Beam '57 Chevrolet	180	140	Running
10	3	99	Fritz Wilson	Shorty Rollins '58 Ford	170	130	Running
11	10	88	Buck Baker	Baker '59 Chevrolet	170	125	Running
12	7	42	Lee Petty	Petty Engineering '57 Olds	131	110	RR Axle
13	11	2	Richard Riley	Bruce Thompson '57 Chevy	120	100	Engine
14	4	1	Speedy Thompson	Steve Pierce '57 Chevrolet	101	85	Rear End
15	1	6	Cotton Owens	W H Watson '58 Pontiac	86	70	Fan Belt
16	14	0	Bunk Moore	'57 Chevrolet	77	60	Engine
17	17	27	Jimmy Pardue	'58 Plymouth	42	50	Engine
18	2	5	Tiny Lund	'57 Chevrolet	36	50	Crash
19	12	89	Shorty Rollins	Buck Baker '58 Chevrolet	15	50	Bearing
20	19	49	Bob Welborn	Welborn '57 Chevrolet	4	50	Bearing

Time of Race: 1 hour, 48 minutes, 01 second
Average Speed: 55.547 mph
Pole Winner: Cotton Owens - 63.180 mph
Lap Leaders:- - - - - - - - - - - - - Jack Smith   -200
Cautions:
Margin of Victory: 1 lap plus
Attendance:

Race No. 18

Jack Smith Takes Hub City Speedway Hundred

SPARTANBURG, SC (June 5) -- Jack Smith, 36-year old veteran out of Sandy Springs, GA, wheeled his Chevrolet to the first win of the year in the 100-miler at Hub City Speedway.

Smith's Chevy, tuned by mechanic Bud Moore, finished a lap ahead of runner-up Joe Eubanks. Junior Johnson came in third with G.C. Spencer fourth and Roy Tyner fifth.

Cotton Owens started on the pole, but his Pontiac lasted just 86 laps before a fan belt broke, putting him out. Owens' misfortune put him 636 points behind Lee Petty in the Grand National point standings. Petty went 131 laps before being sidelined by a broken axle.

Smith averaged 55.547 mph for his ninth career Grand National win.

Race No. 19

Easy Pickin' for Johnson at Greenville-Pickens

GREENVILLE, SC (June 13) -- Junior Johnson lapped the field twice and ran away with the 100-miler

For the first time in NASCAR history, a father-son team had finished 1-2 in a Grand National race. Son Richard Petty had beaten his dad Lee in the 150 lapper at Lakewood Speedway. Lee protested the scoring of the race -- and was later declared official winner.

at Greenville-Pickens Speedway. It was the fourth win of the year for the Ford driver and the 15th of his career.

Finishing second was Roy Tyner of Red Springs, NC, who turned in his finest effort of his three year career. Lee Petty wound up third and boosted his point lead to 900 points over Cotton Owens, who wound up 16th after wheel bearing problems.

Tiny Lund finished fourth and Tommy Irwin came in fifth.

Pole sitter Jack Smith went out on lap 107 with a broken water pump. Wheel bearing difficulties knocked out Speedy Thompson after 164 laps, Ned Jarrett departed with a broken axle and Fritz Wilson crashed his Ford.

Johnson averaged 51.480 mph in the 100 mile grind on the half-mile dirt track.

Race No. 20

Pettys In Atlanta Tiff; Dad First in Sweepstakes 150

ATLANTA, GA (June 14) -- Richard Petty drove his Convertible Oldsmobile under the checkered flag first, but dad Lee Petty wound up pocketing first place money in the 150-mile Sweepstakes race at Lakewood Speedway.

Richard, the 21 year-old sensation out of Randleman, NC, appeared to have won his first big league NASCAR event when he was flagged first in the 150-lapper on the dusty Lakewood oval. However, the runner-up protested and asked that the score cards be checked out. The runner-up was Richard's dad, Lee.

After an hour, Lee was declared the winner, and he nailed down the $2,200 first prize. Richard got $1,400 for second place. Buck Baker finished third and Curtis Turner was fourth. The first four cars all completed the prescribed 150 lap distance. Fifth place went to Tom Pistone who was two laps down.

Lee Petty started 37th in the 40 car field. Time trials were not held due to an early morning rain. Richard drew 27th place. The Pettys charged through the pack as wrecks slimmed down the field. Accidents took out Bob Burdick, Ken Rush, Johnny Allen, Mike Price, Gene White and Harlan Richardson. No serious injuries were reported in any of the incidents.

Lee Petty won the race at an average speed of 58.499 mph for his 42nd career victory.

Grand National Race No. 20
150 Laps at Lakewood Speedway
Atlanta, GA
150 Miles on 1-mile Dirt Track
June 14, 1959

Fin	St	No.	Driver	Team / Car	Laps	Money	Status
1	37	42	Lee Petty	Petty Eng '59 Plymouth GN	150	$2,200	Running
2	27	43	Richard Petty	Petty Eng '57 Olds C	150	1,400	Running
3	5	87	Buck Baker	Baker '59 Chevrolet GN	150	1,025	Running
4	30	22	Curtis Turner	Ogden Ridgeway '59 Chev C	150	950	Running
5	25	59	Tom Pistone	Rupert Safety '59 T-Bird GN	148	625	Running
6	13	88	Fireball Roberts	Buck Baker '59 Chevrolet GN	148	525	Running
7	7	47	Jack Smith	Bud Moore '59 Chevrolet GN	146	450	Running
8	22	99X	Wilbur Rakestraw	R J Jones '57 Mercury C	145	475	Running
9	39	36	Tommy Irwin	Irwin '59 T-Bird GN	142	300	Running
10	34	92	George Alsobrook	D J Jones '57 Ford C	142	325	Running
11	26	5	Tiny Lund	'57 Chevrolet C	142	275	Running
12	10	79	Roy Tyner	'57 Chevrolet C	141	250	Running
13	1	68	J C Hendrix	'57 Plymouth GN	134	150	Running
14	32	21	Johnny Beauchamp	Wood Bros '58 Ford C	132	190	Running
15	33	41	Joe Weatherly	Delta Auto Sales '59 T-Bird C	132	225	Running
16	12	27	Billy Carden	'57 Chevrolet C	131	110	Running
17	38	19	Herman Beam	Beam '57 Chevrolet GN	126	100	Running
18	2	76	Larry Frank	Carolina Plating '57 Chevy C	119	100	Trans
19	16	77	Joe Lee Johnson	Honest Charley '57 Chevy C	119	100	Battery
20	36	13	Tommy Thompson	'59 Chevrolet GN	117	100	Running
21	3	11	Junior Johnson	Paul Spaulding '57 Ford GN	115	75	Rear End
22	14	34	G C Spencer	'57 Chevrolet C	111	75	Running
23	28	32	Brownie King	Jess Potter '58 Chevrolet C	108	75	Running
24	17	2	Richard Riley	Bruce Thompson '57 Chevy C	101	75	Running
25	19	6	Cotton Owens	W H Watson '58 Pontiac GN	91	75	RR Axle
26	9	1	Speedy Thompson	Steve Pierce '57 Chevy GN	91	50	Clutch
27	35	74	L D Austin	Austin '57 Chevrolet GN	85	50	Engine
28	21	122	Harlan Richardson	'57 Ford GN	81	50	Crash
29	6	25	Gene White	White '57 Chevrolet C	73	50	Crash
30	23	71	Mike Price	'57 Chevrolet GN	72	50	Crash
31	18	38	Ned Jarrett	Jarrett '57 Chevrolet C	64	50	Drv Shft
32	29	9	Johnny Allen	Roy Tyner '57 Chevrolet C	57	50	Crash
33	40	99	Fritz Wilson	Shorty Rollins '58 Ford GN	49	50	Radiator
34	31	20	Benny Rakestraw	'57 Mercury C	35	50	Battery
35	8	44	Chester Barron	Barron '59 Chevrolet C	34	50	Steering
36	15	83	Bunk Moore	'58 Ford GN	24	---	Radiator
37	24	49	Bob Welborn	Welborn '59 Chevrolet C	15	---	Engine
38	20	4	Ken Rush	'57 Chevrolet C	13	---	Crash
39	11	18	Charley Griffith	Red Bank '57 Pontiac GN	6	---	Engine
40	4	73	Bob Burdick	Roy Burdick '59 T-Bird C	3	---	Crash

Time of Race: 2 hours, 33 minutes, 51 seconds
Average Speed: 58.499 mph
Pole Winner: No Time Trials
Lap Leaders: - - - - - - - - - - - - - - - Lee Petty   -150
Cautions:
Margin of Victory:
Attendance:

Race No. 21

Weatherly Hurt as Petty Wins at Columbia

COLUMBIA, SC (June 18) -- Lee Petty's late surge netted him a victory in the 100-mile Grand National event at Columbia Speedway. Joe Weatherly injured his back when his T-Bird crashed into G.C. Spencer and Richard Riley early in the race.

Tommy Irwin nabbed second place honors and

Buck Baker was third despite blowing his engine in the final lap. Benny Rakestraw was fourth and Weatherly's car, driven by relief driver Jimmy Thompson took fifth spot.

Weatherly started second and led the first 43 laps. As he and Junior Johnson sped into the first turn, they piled into Spencer and Riley, who had spun out. Weatherly wrenched his back when rear-ended by Johnson and had to give up the seat to Thompson. Johnson, Spencer and Riley were out for the day.

Bob Burdick won the pole for the second time of the season and finished sixth. It was only Burdick's fourth career Grand National start.

Bob Welborn and Doug Cox wrecked in the first lap and finished at the rear of the 20 car field.

Buddy Baker finished seventh, the first time the Charlotte youngster had cracked the top 10 in a Grand National event.

Petty passed Buck Baker in the 194th lap and beat Irwin to the finish line by five car lengths to win the $900 top prize.

Grand National Race No. 21
200 Laps at Columbia Speedway
Columbia, SC
100 Miles on Half-mile Dirt Track
June 18, 1959

Fin	St	No.	Driver	Team / Car	Laps	Money	Status
1	3	42	Lee Petty	Petty Eng '59 Plymouth	200	$900	Running
2	10	36	Tommy Irwin	Irwin '59 T-Bird	200	525	Running
3	4	87	Buck Baker	Baker '59 Chevrolet	200	350	Running
4	11	20	Benny Rakestraw	'57 Mercury	196	250	Running
5	2	41	* Joe Weatherly	Delta Auto Sales '59 T-Bird	196	225	Running
6	1	73	Bob Burdick	Roy Burdick '59 T-Bird	194	200	Running
7	12	89	Buddy Baker	Buck Baker '58 Chevrolet	193	165	Running
8	18	74	L D Austin	Austin '57 Chevrolet	188	150	Running
9	19	19	Herman Beam	Beam '57 Chevrolet	188	140	Running
10	16	28	Harvey Hege	'57 Mercury	169	130	Running
11	20	64	Shep Langdon	Langdon '58 Ford	167	125	Running
12	5	9	Roy Tyner	Tyner '59 Chevrolet	165	110	Trans
13	9	4	Ken Rush	'57 Chevrolet	146	100	RF Hub
14	17	0	Curtis Crider	'57 Chevrolet	119	85	Engine
15	7	6	Cotton Owens	W H Watson '58 Pontiac	108	70	Heating
16	8	11	Junior Johnson	Paul Spaulding '57 Ford	43	60	Crash
17	15	34	G C Spencer	'57 Chevrolet	42	50	Crash
18	6	1	Richard Riley	Steve Pierce '57 Chevrolet	42	50	Crash
19	13	49	Bob Welborn	Welborn '57 Chevrolet	1	50	Crash
20	14	30	Doug Cox	'58 Ford	1	50	Crash

* Relieved by Jimmy Thompson
Time of Race: 1 hour, 42 minutes, 10 seconds
Average Speed: 58.726 mph
Pole Winner: Bob Burdick - 64.865 mph
Lap Leaders: Joe Weatherly 1-43, Buck Baker 44-126, Tommy Irwin 127-189, Baker 190-193, Petty 194-200
Cautions:
Margin of Victory: 5 car lengths
Attendance:

Race No. 22

Johnson Jaunts to Victory at Wilson

WILSON, NC (June 20) -- Junior Johnson scored his fifth win of the 1959 season in the 100-mile Grand National event at Wilson Speedway.

The Ronda, NC Ford driver started 18th in the field of 25, but muscled his way around the half-mile dirt oval and edged Tom Pistone's T-Bird at the finish line. Glen Wood came in third, four laps behind. Lee Petty and Buck Baker rounded out the top five.

Johnson drew the 18th starting position from a hat shortly before the race. No time trials were held. Rookie Ned Jarrett started on the pole, but engine problems knocked him out after 80 laps.

Joe Weatherly, back from an injury two nights earlier, was among the leading contenders, but a right front hub broke on his T-Bird after just 52 laps. He wound up 23rd in the final order.

Johnson averaged a record 58.065 mph in gaining his 16th career big league victory.

Grand National Race No. 22
200 Laps at Wilson Speedway
Wilson, NC
100 Miles on Half-mile Dirt Track
June 20, 1959

Fin	St	No.	Driver	Team / Car	Laps	Money	Status
1	18	11	Junior Johnson	Paul Spaulding '57 Ford	200	$800	Running
2	8	59	Tom Pistone	Rupert Safety Belt '59 T-Bird	200	525	Running
3	19	21	Glen Wood	Wood Bros '58 Ford	196	350	Running
4	10	42	Lee Petty	Petty Engineering '57 Olds	194	250	Running
5	16	87	Buck Baker	Baker '59 Chevrolet	194	225	Running
6	2	5	Tiny Lund	'57 Chevrolet	193	200	Running
7	7	89	Buddy Baker	Buck Baker '58 Chevrolet	188	165	Running
8	20	74	L D Austin	Austin '57 Chevrolet	187	150	Running
9	11	28	Fred Harb	Harvey Hege '57 Mercury	186	140	Running
10	9	9	Roy Tyner	Tyner '57 Chevrolet	186	130	Running
11	17	6	Cotton Owens	W H Watson '58 Pontiac	186	125	Running
12	15	4	Joe Halton	'57 Chevrolet	181	110	Running
13	24	19	Herman Beam	Beam '57 Chevrolet	171	100	Running
14	5	34	G C Spencer	'57 Chevrolet	162	85	Running
15	6	22	Harlan Richardson	'57 Ford	160	70	Running
16	4	96	Bobby Keck	Keck '57 Chevrolet	142	60	Rear End
17	25	0	Richard Riley	'57 Chevrolet	137	50	Running
18	23	64	Shep Langdon	Langdon '58 Ford	108	50	Engine
19	21	82	Joe Eubanks	Don Every '58 Ford	106	50	Engine
20	1	38	Ned Jarrett	Jarrett '57 Chevrolet	80	50	Engine
21	22	36	Tommy Irwin	Irwin '59 T-Bird	80	50	Heating
22	14	62	Buck Brigance	'57 Chevrolet	67	50	Oil Pan
23	12	41	Joe Weatherly	Delta Auto Sales '59 T-Bird	52	---	RF Hub
24	3	12	Speedy Thompson	'57 Chevrolet	42	---	Brakes
25	13	20	Benny Rakestraw	'57 Mercury	6	---	Rkr Arm

Time of Race: 1 hour, 43 minutes, 20 seconds
Average Speed: 58.065 mph
Pole Winner: No Time Trials
Laps Leaders:- - - - - - - - - - - - - - - Junior Johnson   - 200
Cautions:
Margin of Victory:
Attendance:

Race No. 23

Pistone's Late Charge Nets Richmond Victory

RICHMOND, VA (June 21) -- Tiger Tom Pistone, the little Italian Thunderbird chauffeur, made a late race surge into first place and won the 100 mile Grand National race at the Atlantic Rural Fairgrounds in Richmond, VA.

Tiger Tom Pistone and car owner Carl Rupert

It was Pistone's second victory in his first full season on NASCAR's premier tour.

Glen Wood finished a close second and Buck Baker was third. Bob Welborn came in fourth and Cotton Owens was fifth.

Point leader Lee Petty fell victim to engine trouble and wound up 18th in the field of 22. Despite his misfortune at Richmond, he still held a 956 point lead over Owens in the driver standings.

Freshman driver Tommy Irwin had been running in the top five most of the race, but late engine problems put him out after 186 laps had been completed. He managed to finish sixth in the final order.

Joe Weatherly qualified second, but wrecked his T-Bird in the 81st lap. Junior Johnson crashed his Ford after 22 laps.

Pistone averaged 56.881 mph for the 100 miles.

Race No. 24

White Nips Rush in Bowman-Gray Bumper Tag

WINSTON-SALEM, NC (June 27) -- Rex White led all the way to win the 50-mile Grand National race at Bowman-Gray Stadium, but he had to repel a stiff challenge from Ken Rush to pocket the $675 first prize.

White got the jump on pole sitter Lee Petty in the first lap and was never headed. Petty hugged White's bumper for 43 laps until he was forced to make an unscheduled pit stop when the distributor cap jarred loose. Petty leaped out of his Plymouth, made the repairs himself and rejoined the race 14 laps behind.

White led by a comfortable margin through the midway point. But Rush, the 1957 NASCAR Rookie of the Year, caught a second wind with 34 laps remaining. The High Point, NC Ford driver tagged the rear of White's Chevrolet repeatedly in the final 10 miles, but White held his ground.

Rush finished second with Bob Welborn, Junior Johnson and Jim Reed filling out the top five. Petty wound up in 10th place, 14 laps behind. Young Richard Petty qualified third, but was the first car out of the race when transmission failure knocked his Olds out after 14 laps.

White averaged 41.228 mph in the 200 laps contest on the quarter-mile paved track.

Grand National Race No. 24
200 Laps at Bowman-Gray Stadium
Winston-Salem, NC
50 Miles on Quarter-mile Paved Track
June 27, 1959

Fin	St	No.	Driver	Team / Car	Laps	Money	Status
1	2	4	Rex White	White '59 Chevrolet	200	$675	Running
2	6	14	Ken Rush	Manley Britt '57 Ford	200	480	Running
3	4	49	Bob Welborn	Welborn '57 Chevrolet	199	375	Running
4	10	11	Junior Johnson	Paul Spaulding '57 Ford	198	270	Running
5	7	7	Jim Reed	Reed '59 Chevrolet	196	235	Running
6	11	5	Tiny Lund	'57 Chevrolet	193	205	Running
7	14	97	Barney Shore	'57 Chevrolet	192	185	Running
8	19	34	G C Spencer	'57 Chevrolet	190	150	Running
9	20	89	Buck Baker	Baker '58 Chevrolet	189	150	Engine
10	1	42	Lee Petty	Petty Eng '59 Plymouth	186	170	Running
11	15	82	Cotton Owens	Don Every '58 Ford	186	155	Running
12	13	28	Shorty York	Harvey Hege '57 Mercury	185	120	Running
13	12	40	Dave White	'58 Chevrolet	184	100	Running
14	22	63	R L Combs	'57 Ford	184	100	Running
15	17	96	Bobby Keck	Keck '57 Chevrolet	184	75	Running
16	24	74	L D Austin	Austin '57 Chevrolet	178	75	Running
17	18	64	Shep Langdon	Langdon '58 Ford	173	75	Oil Pres
18	23	32	George Green	Jess Potter '57 Chevrolet	171	60	A Frame
19	5	21	Glen Wood	Wood Bros '58 Ford	165	65	Engine
20	16	41	Joe Halton	'57 Chevrolet	164	50	A Frame
21	8	9	Roy Tyner	Tyner '57 Chevrolet	153	25	Crnkshft
22	21	79	Jerry Draper	'57 Chevrolet	87	25	Fuel Filt
23	9	17	Fred Harb	Harb '57 Ford	33	15	Heating
24	3	43	Richard Petty	Petty Engineering '57 Olds	14	50	Trans

Time of Race: 1 hour, 12 minutes, 46 seconds
Average Speed: 41.228 mph
Pole Winner: Lee Petty - 47.071 mph
Lap Leaders: Rex White 1-200
Cautions:
Margin of Victory: 1 car length
Attendance:

Grand National Race No. 23
200 Laps at Atlantic Rural Fairgrounds
Richmond, VA
100 Miles on Half-mile Dirt Track
June 21, 1959

Fin	St	No.	Driver	Team / Car	Laps	Money	Status
1	12	59	Tom Pistone	Rupert Safety Belt '59 T-Bird	200	$900	Running
2	3	21	Glen Wood	Wood Bros '58 Ford	200	525	Running
3	1	87	Buck Baker	Baker '59 Chevrolet	200	350	Running
4	5	79	Bob Welborn	'57 Chevrolet	199	250	Running
5	11	6	Cotton Owens	W H Watson '58 Pontiac	191	225	Running
6	8	36	Tommy Irwin	Irwin '59 T-Bird	186	200	Engine
7	17	19	Herman Beam	Beam '57 chevrolet	186	165	Running
8	13	32	George Green	Jess Potter '58 Chevrolet	171	150	Running
9	16	51	Aubrey Boles	'58 Plymouth	165	140	Running
10	4	2	Speedy Thompson	Bruce Thompson '57 Chevy	159	130	Running
11	7	5	Tiny Lund	'57 Chevrolet	159	125	Running
12	18	0	Richard Riley	'57 Chevrolet	152	110	Running
13	20	33	Ken Hundley	Jess Potter '57 Chevrolet	141	100	Running
14	15	74	L D Austin	Austin '57 Chevrolet	139	85	Running
15	14	62	Buck Brigance	'57 Chevrolet	122	70	Running
16	2	41	Joe Weatherly	Delta Auto Sales '59 T-Bird	81	60	Crash
17	9	22	Harlan Richardson	'57 Ford	79	50	Engine
18	6	42	Lee Petty	Petty Eng '59 Plymouth	77	50	Engine
19	19	89	Buddy Baker	Buck Baker '58 Chevrolet	33	50	Heating
20	10	11	Junior Johnson	Paul Spaulding '57 Ford	22	50	Crash
21	21	82	Joe Eubanks	Don Every '58 Ford	1	50	Engine
22	22	9	Roy Tyner	Tyner '57 Chevrolet	1	50	Engine

Time of Race: 1 hour, 45 minutes, 29 seconds
Average Speed: 56.881 mph
Pole Winner: Buck Baker - 66.42 mph
Lap Leaders: - - - - - - - - - - - - - - - Tom Pistone   -200
Cautions:
Margin of Victory:
Attendance:

Jim Reed chats with Rex White. White won at
Winston-Salem with Reed finishing 5th

Race No. 25

Weaverville Hundred Falls to Rex White

WEAVERVILLE, NC (June 28) -- Rex White pushed his gold and white Chevrolet to a narrow triumph over Lee Petty's Plymouth to win the 100-miler at Asheville-Weaverville Speedway. It was White's second win in a row and the third of the season for the diminutive Silver Spring, MD speedster.

Junior Johnson grabbed third place, four laps behind the leaders. Roy Tyner took fourth place and Herman "The Turtle" Beam was fifth.

Glen Wood started on the pole, but his Ford had to make several pit stops. The Stuart, VA short track specialist eventually finished 13th in the field of 20.

Petty extended his point lead to 988 points over Cotton Owens, who finished sixth.

White averaged 72.934 mph for his fifth career Grand National win.

Grand National Race No. 25
200 Laps at Asheville-Weaverville Speedway
Weaverville, NC
100 Miles on Half-mile Paved Track
June 28, 1959

Fin	St	No.	Driver	Team / Car	Laps	Money	Status
1	4	4	Rex White	White '59 Chevrolet	200	$900	Running
2	3	42	Lee Petty	Petty Eng '59 Plymouth	200	525	Running
3	8	11	Junior Johnson	Paul Spaulding '57 Ford	196	350	Running
4	16	9	Roy Tyner	Tyner '57 Chevrolet	194	250	Running
5	10	19	Herman Beam	Beam '57 Chevrolet	190	225	Running
6	5	82	Cotton Owens	Don Every '58 Ford	190	200	Running
7	12	89	Buddy Baker	Buck Baker '58 Chevrolet	189	165	Running
8	13	32	Jerry Draper	'57 Chevrolet	189	150	Running
9	15	32	George Green	Jess Potter '58 Chevrolet	187	140	Running
10	17	40	Dave White	'58 Chevrolet	185	130	Running
11	2	49	Bob Welborn	Welborn '57 Chevrolet	174	125	Running
12	18	74	L D Austin	Austin '57 Chevrolet	173	110	Running
13	1	16	Glen Wood	Wood Bros '58 Ford	172	100	Running
14	6	2	Speedy Thompson	Bruce Thompson '57 Chevy	156	85	Engine
15	20	31	Brownie King	Jess Potter '57 Chevrolet	97	70	Engine
16	9	5	Tiny Lund	'57 Chevrolet	79	60	LR Axle
17	11	62	Buck Brigance	'57 Chevrolet	35	50	Fuel Pmp
18	14	45	Bobby Waddell	'57 Pontiac	32	50	Heating
19	7	34	G C Spencer	'57 Chevrolet	18	50	Fan Belt
20	19	64	Shep Langdon	Langdon '58 Ford	1	50	Bearing

Time of Race: 1 hour, 22 minutes, 16 seconds
Average Speed: 72.934 mph
Pole Winner: Glen Wood - 76.82 mph
Lap Leaders: - - - - - - - - - - - - - - - Rex White   -200
Cautions:
Margin of Victory:
Attendance:

Grand National Race No. 26
100 Laps at Daytona International Speedway
Daytona Beach, FL
"Firecracker 250"
250 Miles on 2.5-mile Paved Track
July 4, 1959

Fin	St	No.	Driver	Team / Car	Laps	Money	Status
1	1	3	Fireball Roberts	Jim Stephens '59 Pontiac GN	100	$7,050	Running
2	12	12	Joe Weatherly	Bob Bennett Mtr '59 T-Bird C	100	4,625	Running
3	11	22	Johnny Allen	Smith Radiator '59 Chevrolet	99	1,925	Running
4	5	47	Jack Smith	Bud Moore Gar '59 Chevrolet	99	1,175	Running
5	3	37	Eduardo Dibos	"Peru" '59 Thunderbird	98	725	Running
6	2	73	Bob Burdick	Roy Burdick '59 T-Bird C	97	1,850	Running
7	13	59	Tom Pistone	Rupert Safety Belt '59 T-Bird	96	720	Running
8	21	6	Cotton Owens	W H Watson '59 T-Bird	95	500	Running
9	14	36	Tommy Irwin	Irwin '59 T-Bird C	95	1,100	Running
10	7	7	Jim Reed	Reed '59 Chevrolet	95	400	Running
11	17	41	Speedy Thompson	Delta Auto Sales '59 T-Bird	94	375	Running
12	6	44	Gene White	'59 Chevrolet C	92	700	Running
13	18	20	Bennie Rakestraw	'57 Mercury C	92	500	Running
14	16	92	George Alsobrooke	B J Jones '57 Ford C	92	450	Running
15	29	13	Tommy Thompson	'59 Chevrolet	90	300	Running
16	34	83	Shorty Rollins	'58 Ford	90	300	Running
17	22	76	* Larry Frank	Carolina Plating '57 Chevy C	89	350	Disqual
18	37	19	Herman Beam	Beam '57 Chevrolet	89	200	Running
19	20	77	Joe Lee Johnson	Honest Charley '57 Chevy C	88	325	Running
20	24	14	Ken Rush	Manley Britt '58 Ford C	88	300	Running
21	31	71	Dick Joslin	'57 dodge	87	150	Oil Leak
22	10	99	Wilbur Rakestraw	Talmadge Cochrane '57 Mer	87	300	Running
23	23	4	Rex White	Idlewild Homes '59 Chevy	86	135	Running
24	33	86	Larry Flynn	'57 Ford	85	125	Running
25	32	89	Roy Ryner	Tyner '58 Chevrolet	84	125	Running
26	4	43	Richard Petty	Petty Eng '59 Plymouth C	78	200	Fuel Pmp
27	27	49	Bob Welborn	Welborn '59 Chevrolet	77	210	Running
28	26	32	Geroge Green	Jess Potter '58 Chevrolet C	73	150	Fan
29	15	16	Charlie Cregar	Happy Steigel '59 pontiac	70	110	Engine
30	9	60	John Paschall	'58 Ford	67	100	Running
31	35	66	Dick Foley	'59 Chevrolet	60	100	Timing
32	36	97	Jim Austin	'59 Ford	33	100	Wtr Pmp
33	19	42	Lee Petty	Petty Eng '59 Plymouth	27	200	Fuel Pmp
34	30	34	G C Spencer	'57 Chevrolet C	16	135	Engine
35	25	87	Buck Baker	Baker '59 Chevrolet	12	100	Bent Rod
36	8	10	Elmo Langley	Ratus Walters '59 Buick C	11	125	Engine
37	28	82	Joe Eubanks	Don Every '58 Pontiac C	2	125	Bearing

Time of Race: 2 hour, 46 minutes, 42 seconds
Averaage Speed: 140.581 mph
Pole Winner: Fireball Roberts - 144.997 mph
Lap Leaders: Fireball Roberts 1-2, Joe Weatherly 3, Jack Smith 4, Roberts 5-41, Pistone 42-48, Roberts 49-77, Weatherly 78-84, Roberts 85-100
Cautions: None
Margin of Victory: 57 Seconds
Attendance: 12,017
* Larry Frank disqualified for violation of pit rule

Race No. 26

Fireball's Pontiac Pounces on Field in Firecracker 250

DAYTONA BEACH, FL (July 4) -- Fireball Roberts led all but 16 laps and won the inaugural Firecracker 250 at Daytona International Speedway in a breeze. It was the Fireball's 21st victory on NASCAR's Grand National circuit.

Jack Smith #47, Eduardo Dibos #37 and Joe Weatherly #12 speed through
Daytona's Tri-oval in Firecracker 250

Roberts drove his black and gold Stephens Pontiac into the lead for the final time in the 85th lap and beat runner-up Joe Weatherly to the finish line by 57 seconds. He collected $7,050 for his efforts. Johnny Allen finished third, with Jack Smith fourth and Eduardo Dibos fifth. Weatherly was the only top five finisher driving a convertible in the $25,525 Sweepstakes event.

Roberts made two pit stops en route to the victory, but it wasn't until late in the event that he was able to shake the pesky Weatherly, who had "drafted" Roberts' swift Pontiac for most of the race.

Tom Pistone had mapped out a strategy beforehand to make only one pit stop. He was leading Roberts by nearly a full lap on the 48th circuit when his T-Bird ran out of gas. His Carl Rupert-owned car coasted to a halt on the backstretch and he lost four laps in the process. "I was trying to make it to half-way (lap 50), but missed it by two laps," said Pistone, who eventually finished seventh.

Fireball Roberts leads Eduardo Dibos
at Daytona

Roberts averaged 140.581 mph in the caution free event. Ironically, the speed matched Roberts' qualifying speed for the Daytona 500 in February.

Larry Frank was disqualified on lap 89 when he overshot his pit area and was refueled outside his designated space. He got credit for 17th place, based on the 89 laps he completed.

Fireball Roberts

Race No. 27

Reed Pockets 50-miler At Heidelberg

PITTSBURGH, PA (July 21) -- Jim Reed of Peekskill, NY passed Rex White in the 155th lap and led the rest of the way to win the 50-mile race at Heidelberg Raceway. It was the second win of the year for the Chevrolet driver.

White finished in second place with Lee Petty third. Marvin Potter came in fourth and Cotton Owens was fifth.

Dick Bailey stunned the veterans in qualifying by winning the pole in his Plymouth. Bailey led

Jim Reed

Grand National Race No. 27
200 Laps at Heidelberg Raceway
Pittsburgh, PA
50 Miles on Quarter-mile Dirt Track
July 21, 1959

Fin	St	No.	Driver	Team / Car	Laps	Money	Status
1	6	7	Jim Reed	Reed '59 Chevrolet	200	$900	Running
2	2	4	Rex White	White '59 Chevrolet	200	525	Running
3	3	42	Lee Petty	Petty Eng '59 Plymouth	197	350	Running
4	4	12	Marvin Porter	Porter '57 Ford	195	250	Running
5	5	6	Cotton Owens	W H Watson '59 Pontiac	193	225	Running
6	10	89	Don Dahle	'57 Chevrolet	192	200	Running
7	16	1	Bill Brown	'56 Chevrolet	183	165	Running
8	9	53	Ken Johnson	'57 Ford	183	150	Running
9	21	69	Don Strain	'56 Ford	181	140	Running
10	18	83	Lennie Page	'57 Ford	180	130	Running
11	12	33	Al White	White '58 Ford	180	125	Running
12	15	97	Jim Austin	'59 Ford	180	110	Running
13	11	25	August Sand	'57 Ford	133	100	Engine
14	4	V2	Russ Gemberling	'56 Dodge	127	85	RF Wheel
15	14	88	Bill Woolkin	'57 Plymouth	109	70	RF Wheel
;16	22	96	L Lyndstrum	'57 Ford	99	60	Rear End
17	7	10	Elmo Langley	Ratus Walters '57 Ford	99	50	RR Axle
18	13	93	Ted Chamberlain	Chamberlain '57 Chevrolet	68	50	Heating
19	1	2	Dick Bailey	'59 Plymouth	54	50	Heating
20	17	17	Russ Whitman	'57 Ford	27	50	Oil Pres
21	20	26	Scott Sandman	'58 Edsel	20	50	Spindle
22	19	75	Jim Brickstaff	'56 Ford	12	50	LR Axle

Time of Race: 1 hour, 6 minutes, 40 seconds
Average Speed: 45.000 mph
Pole Winner: Dick Bailey - 47.97 mph
Lap Leaders: Dick Bailey 1-3, Russ Gemberling 4-6, Rex White 7-154, Jim Reed 155-200
Cautions: 1 for 4 laps
Margin of Victory:
Attendance: 6,000

Grand National Race No. 28
200 Laps at Charlotte Fairgrounds
Charlotte, NC
100 Miles on Half-mile Dirt Track
July 26, 1959

Fin	St	No.	Driver	Team / Car	Laps	Money	Status
1	5	47	Jack Smith	Bud Moore Gar '59 Chevy	200	$900	Running
2	33	49	Bob Welborn	Welborn '57 Chevrolet	200	525	Running
3	1	87	Buck Baker	Baker '59 Chevrolet	200	350	Running
4	7	6	Cotton Owens	W H Watson '58 Pontiac	200	250	Running
5	28	76	Larry Frank	Carolina Plating '57 Chevy	200	225	Running
6	3	72	Ralph Moody	John Dodd '59 Ford	197	200	Running
7	25	9	Roy Tyner	Tyner '57 Chevrolet	196	165	Running
8	17	88	Buddy Baker	Buck Baker '59 Chevrolet	194	150	Running
9	2	21	Glen Wood	Wood Bros '58 Ford	193	140	Vapor Lk
10	4	42	Lee Petty	Petty Eng '59 Plymouth	193	230	RF Wheel
11	8	5	Tiny Lund	'57 Chevrolet	191	125	Running
12	11	43	Richard Petty	Petty Eng '57 Olds	189	110	Spindle
13	19	32	George Green	Jess Potter '58 Chevrolet	185	100	Running
14	23	62	Buck Brigance	'57 Chevrolet	182	85	Running
15	21	97	Jim Austin	'59 Ford	182	70	Running
16	32	19	Herman Beam	Beam '57 Chevrolet	182	60	Running
17	24	28	Neil Castles	Harvey Hege '57 Mercury	179	50	Running
18	27	0	Richard Riley	'57 Chevrolet	177	50	Running
19	20	96	Bobby Keck	Keck '57 Chevrolet	174	50	Running
20	6	30	Doug Cox	'58 Ford	170	50	Distrib
21	34	74	L D Austin	Austin '57 Chevrolet	166	50	Running
22	12	82	Elmo Henderson	'58 Ford	160	50	Heating
23	30	14	Gene White	Manley Britt '58 Ford	155	---	Crash
24	10	2	Speedy Thompson	Bruce Thompson '57 Chevy	138	---	Engine
25	26	89	Banjo Matthews	Buck Baker '58 Chevrolet	137	---	Trans
26	9	41	Joe Weatherly	Delta Auto Sales '59 T-Bird	129	---	Crash
27	13	34	G C Spencer	'57 Chevrolet	114	---	Rear End
28	22	15	Aubrey Boles	'58 Plymouth	114	---	Heating
29	35	711	Bill Poor	Poor '57 Chevrolet	64	---	Fuel Pmp
30	16	36	Tommy Irwin	Irwin '59 T-Bird	55	---	Heating
31	14	45	Bobby Waddell	'57 Pontiac	41	---	Gas Line
32	29	4	Joe Halton	'57 Chevrolet	35	---	Spindle
33	15	63	R L Combs	'57 Ford	28	---	Rear End
34	31	17	Fred Harb	Harb '57 Ford	16	---	Radiator
35	18	11	Junior Johnson	Paul Spaulding '57 Ford	7	---	Engine

Time of Race: 2 hours, 1 minute, 5 seconds
Average Speed: 49.553 mph
Pole Winner: Buck Baker - 63.07 mph
Lap Leaders: - - - - - - - - - - - - - - Jack Smith   -200
Cautions: 9 for 22 laps
Margin of Victory:
Attendance: 6,000

the first three laps before Russ Gemberling took the lead. Gemberling lost a left front wheel on lap 127, putting him out of action.

Reed averaged 45.000 mph as one caution slowed the field for four laps. A crowd of 6,000 was on hand for the Tuesday evening presentation.

Race No. 28

Smith Tops 35-car Field at Charlotte Fairgrounds

CHARLOTTE, NC (July 26) -- Jack Smith held his Chevrolet in front for most of the way and finished first in the caution-filled 100-miler at the Charlotte Fairgrounds. It was the third win of the season for the Sandy Springs, GA veteran.

Bob Welborn, who started in 33rd position, came through the field to finish second. Pole sitter Buck Baker wound up third, Cotton Owens was fourth and Larry Frank fifth. The first five finishers completed the 200 laps on the half-mile dirt track as nine caution flags kept the field tightly bunched.

Point leader Lee Petty broke a right front wheel in the 193rd lap, knocking him down to 10th in the final order. The Randleman, NC Plymouth jockey had his point lead sliced to 388 points over Owens.

Joe Weatherly and Gene White crashed their cars in separate incidents. Neither driver was injured.

Other top threats Junior Johnson, Tommy Irwin, Richard Petty and Banjo Matthews failed to finish.

Old Pro Ralph Moody donned a helmet and drove John Dodd's Ford to a sixth place finish.

Smith averaged only 49.553 mph as 22 laps were run under the caution flag.

Race No. 29

Jarrett Notches First Grand National Win at Myrtle Beach

MYRTLE BEACH, SC (Aug 1) -- Ned Jarrett, NASCAR Sportsman titlist in 1957 and 1958, had been seeking a first class Grand National ride for several months. When no car owner would let the Conover, NC hotshot drive his car, Jarrett was forced to improvise.

He purchased a '57 Ford from Paul Spaulding, post-dating a check. "I didn't have any money in the bank, but I figured I could go out and win a couple of races and have enough money to cover the $2,000 check," Jarrett later said.

At Myrtle Beach Rambi Raceway he started in 9th place and worked his way up to the front, finishing a lap ahead of runner-up Jim Paschal. The win covered $800 of his $2,000 check. Tommy Irwin placed third, Glen Wood fourth and Joe Weatherly fifth.

Paschal was in a position to challenge Jarrett for top honors, but a right front wheel bearing burned out on his Chevrolet in the final lap.

Cotton Owens and Larry Flynn crashed on the rough half-mile dirt track.

Pole sitter Bob Welborn left after just five laps when he sputtered to the pits. His crew discovered that some water had gotten into his fuel tank.

Jarrett averaged 52.941 mph.

Grand National Race No. 29
200 Laps at Rambi Raceway
Myrtle Beach, SC
100 Miles on Half-mile Dirt Track
August 1, 1959

Fin	St	No.	Driver	Team / Car	Laps	Money	Status
1	9	11	Ned Jarrett	Jarrett '57 Ford	200	$800	Running
2	8	48	Jim Paschal	'57 Chevrolet	199	525	Bearing
3	7	36	Tommy Irwin	Irwin '57 Ford	199	350	Running
4	6	21	Glen Wood	Wood Bros '58 Ford	198	250	Running
5	3	41	Joe Weatherly	Delta Auto Sales '59 T-Bird	197	225	Running
6	2	42	Lee Petty	Petty Eng '59 Plymouth	197	300	Running
7	5	72	John Dodd, Sr	Dodd '59 Ford	196	165	Running
8	11	9	Roy Tyner	Tyner '57 Chevrolet	194	150	Running
9	4	14	Earl Moss	Manley Britt '57 Ford	194	140	Running
10	13	22	Harlan Richardson	'58 Ford	192	130	Axle
11	23	89	Buddy Baker	Buck Baker '58 Chevrolet	187	125	Running
12	14	34	G C Spencer	'57 Chevrolet	186	110	Running
13	21	28	Neil Castles	Harvey Hege '57 Mercury	184	100	Running
14	22	97	Jim Austin	'59 Ford	178	85	Running
15	17	62	Buck Brigance	'57 Chevrolet	178	70	Running
16	19	96	Bobby Keck	Keck '57 Chevrolet	177	60	Running
17	25	74	L D Austin	Austin '57 Ford	175	50	Running
18	18	711	Bill Poor	Poor '57 Chevrolet	173	50	Running
19	26	82	Cotton Owens	Don Every '58 Ford	171	50	Crash
20	15	88	Buck Baker	Baker '59 Chevrolet	158	50	Engine
21	24	0	Curtis Crider	'57 Chevrolet	125	50	Oil Pres
22	27	2	Speedy Thompson	Bruce Thompson '57 Chevy	124	50	Crash
23	16	197	Barney Shore	'57 Chevrolet	52	---	Trans
24	20	86	Larry Flynn	'57 Ford	42	---	Crash
25	12	17	Fred Harb	Harb '57 Ford	38	---	Axle
26	1	49	Bob Welborn	Welborn '59 Chevrolet	5	---	Fuel Tnk
27	10	43	Richard Petty	Petty Engieering '57 Olds	4	---	Ball Jnt

Time of Race: 1 hour, 54 minutes, 20 seconds
Average Speed: 52.941 mph
Pole Winner: Bob Welborn - 66.47 mph
Lap Leaders: - - - - - - - - - - - - - - Ned Jarrett   -200
Cautions:
Margin of Victory: I lap plus
Attendance:

Race No. 30

Jarrett Wins 2nd in Row, Makes Good on Check

CHARLOTTE, NC (Aug 2) -- Ned Jarrett, with Junior Johnson and Joe Weatherly providing crucial relief driving assignments, won the 100-miler at Charlotte Fairgrounds. The $800 first place money enabled Jarrett to pocket $1,600 in weekend events. "I was able to come up with the other $400 to make my $2,000 check to Paul Spaulding good on Monday morning," said Jarrett. The former Sportsman champ had purchased the Ford from Spaulding with a post-dated check and only pennies in his bank account.

Jarrett started 10th in the field of 29, but had to get

Grand National Race No. 30
200 Laps at Charlotte Fairgrounds
Charlotte, NC
100 Miles on Half-mile Dirt Track
August 2, 1959

Fin	St	No.	Driver	Team / Car	Laps	Money	Status
1	10	11	* Ned Jarrett	Jarrett '57 Ford	200	$800	Running
2	5	48	Jim Paschal	'57 Chevrolet	199	525	Running
3	1	49	Bob Welborn	Welborn '59 Chevrolet	199	350	Running
4	8	36	Tommy Irwin	Irwin '57 Ford	193	250	Running
5	12	76	Larry Frank	Carolina Plating '57 Chevy	190	225	Running
6	19	22	Harlan Richardson	'58 Ford	190	300	Running
7	17	4	Joe Halton	'57 Chevrolet	188	165	Running
8	26	19	Herman Beam	Beam '57 Chevrolet	179	150	Running
9	4	82	Joe Eubanks	Don Every '58 Ford	176	140	Heating
10	27	74	L D Austin	Austin '57 Chevrolet	175	130	Running
11	25	2	Richard Riley	Bruce Thompson '57 Chevy	166	125	Running
12	16	45	Bobby Waddell	'57 Pontiac	164	110	Running
13	3	87	Buck Baker	Baker '59 Chevrolet	162	100	Engine
14	9	17	Fred Harb	Harb '57 Ford	161	85	Battery
15	29	5	Tiny Lund	'57 Chevrolet	159	70	Running
16	22	62	Buck Brigance	'57 Chevrolet	149	60	Battery
17	20	63	R L Combs	'57 Ford	143	50	Running
18	2	42	Lee Petty	Petty Eng '59 Plymouth	131	50	Engine
19	28	96	Bobby Keck	Keck '57 Chevrolet	121	50	Running
20	13	43	Richard Petty	Petty Engineering '57 Olds	114	50	Crash
21	15	89	Buddy Baker	Buck Baker '58 Chevrolet	112	50	Axle
22	23	711	Bill Poor	Poor '57 Chevrolet	108	50	Running
23	24	32	George Green	Jess Potter '58 Chevrolet	98	---	Running
24	14	14	Earl Moss	Manley Britt '57 Ford	85	---	Trans
25	11	21	Junior Johnson	Wood Bros '58 Ford	76	---	Engine
26	21	86	Larry Flynn	'57 Ford	68	---	Spindle
27	6	72	John Dodd, Sr	Dodd '59 Ford	20	---	Engine
28	18	34	G C Spencer	'57 Chevrolet	15	---	Engine
29	7	6	Cotton Owens	W H Watson '58 Pontiac	1	---	Engine

* Joe Weatherly and Junior Johnson relieved Jarrett
Time of Race: 1 hour, 53 minutes, 39 seconds
Average Speed: 52.794 mph
Pole Winner: Bob Welborn - 62.54 mph
Lap Leaders: - - - - - - - - - - - - - Ned Jarrett   -200
Cautions:
Margin of Victory: 1 lap plus
Attendance: 5,300

Race No. 31

Joe Lee Johnson Wins First In Nashville Sweeps Event

NASHVILLE, TN (Aug 9) -- Joe Lee Johnson led a 1-2-3 sweep for Convertible cars in the 150 mile Sweepstakes race at the Nashville Fairgrounds. It was Johnson's first big league victory.

Larry Frank finished second, three laps behind. Elmo Langley enjoyed his best finish by taking third. Lee Petty and Tommy Irwin were fourth and fifth, both in Grand National hardtops.

Rex White started on the pole and led for over half of the 300 lap event on the half-mile paved track. Rear gearing failure foiled White's bid. He got paid for 24th

Grand National Race No. 31
300 Laps at Fairgrounds Speedway
Nashville, TN
150 Miles on Half-mile Paved Track
August 9, 1959

Fin	St	No.	Driver	Team / Car	Laps	Money	Status
1	2	77	Joe Lee Johnson	Honest Charley '57 Chevy C	300	$2,912	Running
2	4	76	Larry Frank	Carolina Plating '57 Chevy C	297	1,453	Running
3	12	10	Elmo Langley	Ratus Walters '59 Buick C	297	1,125	Running
4	3	42	Lee Petty	Petty Eng '59 Plymouth GN	297	900	Running
5	10	36	Tommy Irwin	'59 T-Bird C	295	750	Running
6	16	9	Cotton Owens	Roy Tyner '57 Chevrolet GN	290	450	Running
7	22	41	Joe Weatherly	Delta Auto Sales '59 T-Bird C	289	500	Running
8	14	25	Gene White	White '57 Chevrolet C	286	350	Running
9	11	12	Bob Reuther	Marvin Porter '58 Ford GN	284	250	Running
10	5	16	Bud Crothers	'57 Chevrolet C	283	225	Running
11	7	87	Buck Baker	Baker '59 Chevrolet GN	281	250	Running
12	20	34	G C Spencer	'57 Chevrolet C	278	175	Axle
13	26	192	George Alsobrook	B J Jones '57 Ford C	277	150	Running
14	30	32	George Green	Jess Potter '57 Chevrolet C	273	140	Running
15	17	19	Herman Beam	Beam '57 Chevrolet GN	262	125	Running
16	25	74	L D Austin	Austin '57 Chevrolet GN	251	110	Running
17	19	92	Gerald Duke	Duke '59 T-Bird	249	125	Running
18	6	49	Bob Welborn	Welborn '59 Chevrolet C	234	200	Axle
19	13	22	Harlan Richardson	'58 Ford GN	224	100	Running
20	9	189	Herb Lewis	'58 Chevrolet GN	221	100	Ball Jnt
21	29	20	Benny Rakestraw	'57 Mercury C	213	75	Running
22	21	97	Jim Austin	'59 Ford GN	211	75	Rear End
23	15	110	Jim Mairs	'57 Ford GN	202	75	Engine
24	1	4	Rex White	White '59 Chevrolet	176	510	Rear End
25	24	31	Brownie King	Jess Potter '57 Chevrolet C	84	75	Fan Blt
26	23	13	Andy Hampton	'59 Chevrolet GN	76	50	Bearing
27	27	59	Tom Pistone	Rupert Saf Blt '59 T-Bird GN	51	50	Engine
28	18	44	Tiny Lund	'59 Chevrolet C	30	50	Heating
29	8	43	Richard Petty	Petty Eng '59 Plymouth C	12	50	Engine
30	28	89	Buddy Baker	Buck Baker '58 Chevrolet C	10	50	Engine

Time of Race: 2 hours, 22 minutes, 05 seconds
Average Speed: 63.343 mph
Pole Winner: Rex White - 74.044 mph
Lap Leaders: Rex White 1 - , - - - - - - - - - - - - - Joe Lee Johnson   -200
Cautions:
Margin of Victory: 3 laps plus
Attendance:

out of the car early. His hands had been cut by steering wheel tape in a race at Myrtle Beach the night before. Joe Weatherly, just spectatoring at Charlotte, helped Jarrett out for about 50 laps. During a caution period, Junior Johnson, who had departed with a blown engine on lap 76, hopped into Jarrett's Ford and carried it to victory lane. Johnson had driven the former Spaulding Ford for two years.

Jim Paschal scored his second straight runner-up finish. Bob Welborn was third, Tommy Irwin fourth and Larry Frank fifth.

Richard Petty started 13th in an Oldsmobile and crashed after 114 laps. Lee Petty started second but fell out after 131 laps with a blown engine. His point lead was 476 points over Cotton Owens, who went only one lap before the engine blew in his Pontiac.

The Jarrett-Weatherly-Johnson combo averaged 52.794 mph before a crowd of 5,300.

place in the field of 30, but picked up an extra $435 in lap prizes.

Second generation drivers Richard Petty and Buddy Baker both blew engines in their cars early and were awarded next-to-last and last place.

Local driver Bob Reuther filled in for Marvin Porter and finished ninth. Reuther holds the all-time qualifying record on the sands of Daytona with a 150.250 mph mark in a Modified '38 Plymouth. He set his record in 1957.

Johnson averaged 63.343 mph and won $2,912 for his Honest Charley Speed Shop team.

Ned Jarrett #11 and Herman Beam #19 crash at Weaverville. Also involved was Richard Petty's Plymouth Convertible

Race No. 32

Welborn's Convertible Chevy Wins Western North Carolina 500

WEAVERVILLE, NC (Aug 16) -- Bob Welborn, three time NASCAR Convertible champion, outran the field by three laps to win the Western North Carolina 500 Sweepstakes event at the Asheville-Weaverville Speedway. It was his ninth career win on NASCAR's premier tour.

The Summerfield, NC Chevrolet driver won $3,200 and beat runner-up Lee Petty by three laps. Jack Smith finished third, Joe Lee Johnson was fourth and Rex White fifth.

Twenty cars in the starting field of 41 were around at the finish. Richard Petty was eliminated in a four car scramble on lap 286. Petty's was the only car unable to continue.

Glen Wood was the fastest Convertible qualifier, but a drive shaft snapped in his Ford and wound up 28th. Herman Beam, Roy Tyner and Dave White exited with broken axles. Neil Castles went out with a broken spindle and Banjo Matthews departed with worn out shock absorbers as the half-mile paved track broke up before the half-way point.

Petty's second place finish enabled him to pad his point lead to 580 points over Cotton Owens, who wound up seventh.

Welborn averaged 71.833 mph for his first win since Daytona's SpeedWeeks in February.

Race No. 33

White Wins Winston-Salem Sweepstakes Event

WINSTON-SALEM, NC (Aug 21) -- Rex White hopped in his Short Track Division Chevrolet and scampered to an easy victory in the 200-lap Sweepstakes race at Bowman Gray Stadium. It was the fourth win of the year for the 130-pounder from Silver Spring, Md.

Glen Wood finished second, 10 sec-

Pace lap for Asheville-Weaverville Western North Carolina 500. Rex White and Glen Wood are on the front row

Grand National Race No. 32
500 Laps at Asheville-Weaverville Speedway
Weaverville, NC
"Western North Carolina 500"
250 Miles on Half-mile Paved Track
August 16, 1959

Fin	St	No.	Driver	Team / Car	Laps	Money	Status
1	4	49	Bob Welborn	Welborn '59 Chevrolet C	500	$3,200	Running
2	9	42	Lee Petty	Petty Eng '59 Plymouth GN	497	2,025	Running
3	5	47	Jack Smith	Bud Moore '59 Chevrolet GN	493	1,325	Running
4	6	77	Joe Lee Johnson	Honest Charley '57 Chevy C	489	975	Running
5	1	4	Rex White	White '59 Chevrolet GN	489	800	Running
6	12	76	Larry Frank	Carolina Plating '57 Chevy C	486	700	Running
7	19	6	Cotton Owens	W H Watson '59 T-Bird GN	484	625	Running
8	11	88	Buck Baker	Baker '59 Chevrolet GN	484	575	Running
9	27	12	Marvin Porter	Porter '58 Ford GN	480	455	Running
10	3	72	Bobby Johns	Shorty Johns '57 Chevy GN	470	425	Running
11	37	95	Bob Duell	Julian Buesink '59 Ford GN	466	400	Running
12	31	34	G C Spencer	'57 Chevrolet GN	463	375	Fuel
13	29	64	Shep Langdon	Langdon '58 Ford GN	457	325	Running
14	13	5	Tiny Lund	'57 Chevrolet GN	455	275	Running
15	38	74	L D Austin	Austin '57 Chevrolet GN	454	250	Running
16	26	32	George Green	Jess Potter '57 Chevrolet C	453	250	Running
17	21	11	Ned Jarrett	Jarrett '57 Ford GN	452	250	Running
18	36	27	Dominick Persicketti	'57 Ford GN	444	225	Running
19	28	192	George Alsobrook	B J Jones '57 Ford C	425	225	Running
20	30	20	Benny Rakestraw	'57 Mercury C	420	220	Fuel
21	23	19	Herman Beam	Beam '57 Chevrolet GN	410	210	LR Axle
22	18	9	Roy Tyner	Tyner '57 Chevrolet C	407	200	RR Axle
23	8	10	Elmo Langley	Ratus Walters '59 Buick C	379	175	Rear End
24	25	22	Harlan Richardson	'58 Ford GN	342	150	Running
25	41	46	Whitey Norman	'57 Chevrolet GN	339	140	Running
26	22	43	Richard Petty	Petty Engineering '59 Plym C	281	100	Crash
27	24	16	Bud Crothers	'57 Chevrolet C	266	100	Oil Pres
28	2	21	Glen Wood	Wood Bros '58 Ford C	254	100	Drv Shft
29	17	40	Dave White	'58 Chevrolet GN	216	100	LR Axle
30	35	13	Earl Balmer	'59 Chevrolet GN	202	100	Engine
31	7	36	Tommy Irwin	Irwin '59 T-Bird GN	187	---	Engine
32	20	25	Gene White	White '57 Chevrolet C	158	---	Engine
33	34	86	Neil Castles	Castles '56 Ford C	144	---	Spindle
34	39	59	Tom Pistone	Rupert Belt '59 T-Bird GN	142	---	Engine
35	10	93	Banjo Matthews	T-Bird Pwr Prod '59 T-Bird C	123	---	Shocks
36	16	17	Fred Harb	Harb '57 Ford C	83	---	Engine
37	15	92	Speedy Thompson	Gerald Duke '59 T-Bird GN	75	---	RF Hub
38	33	23	Bill Scott	'57 Chevrolet GN	65	---	Heating
39	40	18	Freddy Fryar	Red Bank '57 Pontiac GN	53	---	Pistons
40	14	41	Joe Weatherly	Delta Auto Sales '59 T-Bird C	44	---	Engine
41	32	31	Brownie King	Jess Potter '57 Chevrolet 'GN	44	---	Fan Belt

Time of Race: 3 hours, 28 minutes, 49 seconds
Average Speed: 71.833 mph
Pole Winner: Rex White - 77.687 mph
Lap Leaders: - - - - - - - - - - - - - - Bob Welborn   -500
Cautions:
Margin of Victory: 3 Laps plus
Attendance:

Track cars together. White was one of four drivers who entered the race under the Short Track Division.

Twenty cars in the 24 car field finished the race. Jim Paschal was the only notable who failed to finish, falling out on lap 170 with gearing failure.

White averaged 44.085 mph as two cautions flags broke the brisk pace.

Grand National Race No. 33
200 Laps at Bowman Gray Stadium
Winston-Salem, NC
50 Miles on Quarter-mile Paved Track
August 21, 1959

Fin	St	No.	Driver	Team / Car	Laps	Money	Status
1	1	4	Rex White	White '59 Chevrolet ST	200	$1,125	Running
2	2	16	Glen Wood	Wood Bros '58 Ford C	200	690	Running
3	3	42	Lee Petty	Petty Eng '59 Plymouth GN	198	595	Running
4	16	49	Bob Welborn	Welborn '59 Chevrolet C	197	425	Running
5	5	7	Jim Reed	Reed '57 Ford ST	196	290	Running
6	12	14	Ken Rush	Manley Britt '57 Ford C	196	240	Running
7	4	21	Joe Weatherly	Wood Bros '58 Ford C	196	200	Running
8	8	9	Roy Tyner	Tyner '57 Chevrolet C	193	190	Running
9	19	5	Tom Pistone	'57 Chevrolet GN	192	175	Running
10	10	17	Fred Harb	Harb '57 Ford C	191	160	Running
11	17	34	G C Spencer	'57 Chevrolet GN	189	150	Running
12	7	40	Dave White	'58 Chevrolet ST	189	180	Running
13	18	40X	Ermon Rush	'57 Chevrolet C	188	140	Running
14	20	32	George Green	Jess Potter '57 Chevrolet C	186	145	Running
15	21	96	Bobby Keck	Keck '57 Chevrolet GN	182	100	Running
16	24	63	R L Combs	'57 Ford C	182	110	Running
17	13	12	Marvin Porter	Porter '57 Ford C	179	125	Running
18	22	31	Brownie King	Jess Potter '57 Chevrolet C	176	115	Running
19	23	4	Joe Halton	'57 Chevrolet C	173	115	Running
20	15	74	L D Austin	Austin '57 Chevrolet GN	172	125	Running
21	6	48	Jim Paschal	'57 Chevrolet C	170	140	Rear End
22	14	97	Barney Shore	'57 Chevrolet C	50	70	Bearing
23	11	46	Whitey Norman	'57 Chevrolet GN	43	75	Points
24	9	64	Shep Langdon	Langdon '58 Ford GN	26	80	Rear End

Time of Race: 1 hour, 8 minutes, 3 seconds
Average Speed: 44.085 mph
Pole Winner: Rex White - 47.443 mph
Lap Leaders: Rex White 1-200
Cautions: 2
Margin of Victory: 10 seconds
Attendance: 11,500

onds behind winner White. Lee Petty was third, Bob Welborn fourth and Jim Reed fifth.

White got the jump at the green flag and was never headed in the 50-mile sprint on the flat quarter-mile paved track. Petty challenged early, but had drifted two laps off the pace when the checkered flag fell.

A crowd of 11,500, termed the largest in Bowman Gray history, was on hand for the Sweepstakes event which pitted Grand Nationals, Convertibles and Short

Race No. 34

Buck Baker
Grand at Greenville

GREENVILLE, SC (Aug 22) -- Venerable Charlotte veteran Buck Baker ended an 11-month slump and roared to his first win of the year in the 100-mile Grand National event at Greenville-Pickens Speedway.

Baker's Chevrolet nosed out Cotton Owens and Ned Jarrett to capture the $800 first prize. Jack Smith borrowed a T-Bird from Gerald Duke and finished fourth. Fifth place went to Jim Paschal.

Lee Petty won the pole and was leading when he wrecked with L D Austin in the 20th lap. Austin was running four laps behind at the time. Petty was left with an 18th place finish in the field of 19 but still held a 808 point lead over Owens in the Grand National standings.

Baker's 40th career Grand National triumph came at an average speed of 58.055 mph.

ond since switching from Oldsmobile to Plymouth.

Tiny Lund finished in second place and Fred Harb was third. Roy Tyner came in fourth with Glen Wood fifth.

Only 13 cars started and only six were running at the finish of the 200 lapper on the half-mile dirt track. Only five cars got points, including Petty, who upped his lead to 1,010 points over Cotton Owens, who did not enter. Eight of the 13 cars were Convertibles with zipper tops. No rear windows were in these automobiles and therefore the drivers were not awarded any championship points.

No time trials were held. Ned Jarrett drew the pole position in a blind draw for the second time in the '59 season. Jarrett went out on lap 152 with a blown engine, but still got credit for eighth place.

Petty averaged 48.264 mph for his 44th career win.

Grand National Race No. 34
200 Laps at Greenville-Pickens Speedway
Greenville, SC
100 Miles on Half-mile Dirt Track
August 22, 1959

Fin	St	No.	Driver	Team / Car	Laps	Money	Status
1	4	88	Buck Baker	Baker '59 Chevrolet	200	$800	Running
2	3	6	Cotton Owens	W H Watson '58 Pontiac	200	525	Running
3	7	11	Ned Jarrett	Jarrett '57 Ford	200	375	Running
4	15	92	Jack Smith	Gerald Duke '59 T-Bird	196	275	Running
5	5	48	Jim Paschal	'57 Chevrolet	190	250	Running
6	19	36	Tommy Irwin	'57 Ford	187	215	Running
7	13	25	Gene White	White '57 Chevrolet	186	175	Running
8	14	12	Marvin Porter	Porter '57 Ford	176	150	Running
9	9	82	Joe Eubanks`	Don Every '58 Ford	171	140	Running
10	16	45	Curtis Crider	'57 Pontiac	163	130	Running
11	11	9	Roy Tyner	Tyner '57 Chevrolet	163	125	Running
12	6	5	Tiny Lund	'57 Chevrolet	125	110	RF Tire
13	17	19	Herman Beam	Beam '57 Chevrolet	122	100	Running
14	18	15	Aubrey Boles	Aubrey Boles '58 Plymouth	112	85	Running
15	10	34	G C Spencer	'57 Chevrolet	75	70	Running
16	2	49	Bob Welborn	Welborn '59 Chevrolet	65	60	Shocks
17	8	64	Shep Langdon	Langdon '58 Ford	55	50	Fuel Pmp
18	1	42	Lee Petty	Petty Eng '59 Plymouth	20	150	Crash
19	12	74	L D Austin	Austin '57 Chevrolet	16	50	Crash

Time of Race: 1 hour, 43 minutes, 21 seconds
Average Speed: 58.055 mph
Pole Winner: Lee Petty - 63.313 mph
Lap Leaders: Lee Petty 1-20, ---------- Buck Baker - 200
Cautions:
Margin of Victory:
Attendance:

Grand National Race No. 35
200 Laps at Columbia Speedway
Columbia, SC
100 Miles on Half-mile Dirt Track
August 29, 1959

Fin	St	No.	Driver	Team / Car	Laps	Money	Status
1	9	42	Lee Petty	Petty Eng '59 Plymouth	200	$900	Running
2	3	5	Tiny Lund	'57 Chevrolet	199	525	Running
3	12	17	Fred Harb	Harb '57 Ford	197	375	Running
4	4	9	Roy Tyner	Tyner '57 Chevrolet	194	275	Running
5	10	21	Glen Wood	Wood Bros '58 Ford	193	250	Running
6	2	32	George Green	Jess Potter '57 Chevrolet	192	215	Running
7	8	34	G C Spencer	'57 Chevrolet	165	175	Clutch
8	1	38	Ned Jarrett	Jarrett '57 Ford	152	150	Engine
9	5	82	Joe Eubanks	Don Every '58 Ford	98	140	Engine
10	6	12	L D Austin	'57 Ford	78	130	Engine
11	11	36	Tommy Irwin	Irwin '57 Ford	69	125	Steering
12	7	45	Curtis Crider	'57 Pontiac	46	110	Oil Pres
13	13	96	Bobby Keck	Keck '57 Chevrolet	29	100	Engine

Time of Race: 2 hours 4 minutes, 19 seconds
Average Speed: 48.264 mph
Pole Position: No Time Trials
Lap Leaders: - - - - - - - - - - - - - - - Lee Petty - 200
Cautions:
Margin of Victory: 1 lap plus
Attendance:

Race No. 35

Petty Wins at Columbia; Only 6 Cars Finish

COLUMBIA, SC (Aug 29) -- Lee Petty drove his Plymouth to victory in the 100 mile Grand National race at Columbia Speedway. It was the seventh win of the season for the Randleman, NC champ, and his sec-

Race No. 36

Jim Reed Outlasts Field To Snare Southern 500

DARLINGTON, SC (Sept 7) -- Jim Reed kept a steady pace and outlasted his rivals to win the 10th annual Southern 500 at Darlington Raceway. The storied event was the first time Reed, a short track ace, had ever led a lap at superspeedway competition.

Finishing second was Bob Burdick's T-Bird, driven by Joe Weatherly at the end. Bobby Johns came in third with Richard Petty fourth and Tommy Irwin fifth.

only 54 laps before retiring behind the wall with no oil pressure. The swash-buckling Norfolk veteran then relieved rookie Bob Burdick and brought the car home second. Car owner Roy Burdick elected to take his son

Fireball Roberts #3 leads Elmo Langley #10 and Richard Petty in opening lap of Southern 500

Joe Caspolich, Joe Weatherly and Shep Langdon talk things over before Southern 500. Weatherly's T-Bird was sponsored by Coca-Cola

Reed, who kept his Chevrolet in the lead for a total of 152 laps, said he charted a course and stuck to it. "I raced the car against the track and tried to stay clear of the traffic jams," said the 33 year-old former truck driver. "I planned a steady pace. If the pace I was running wasn't fast enough, I wouldn't have won. Everything went according to plan."

Richard Petty, 22 year-old Plymouth driver was poised to give Reed a run for the money. He led for seven laps early in the race then turned the wheel over to veteran Marvin Panch. Panch had caught Reed late in the going but lost a wheel. "If that wheel would have stayed on, we'd have won the race," claimed Panch.

Even Reed was not sure he could have beaten the Petty-Panch team. "I might have been able to stay with him for a while, but not too long," commented Reed.

Pole sitter Fireball Roberts went through several sets of tires en route to a seventh place finish. Second fastest qualifier Elmo Langley drove only 41 laps before blowing the engine in his Buick. Speedy Thompson led the first few laps, but went out with suspension problems late in the going.

Joe Weatherly drove his T-Bird

Movie star Rory Calhoun makes pit stop during the Southern 500. Scenes were being shot for the Hollywood production "Thunder in Carolina". Alan Hale is the crew chief

Action in rookie Richard Petty's pit during the Southern 500

Grand National Race No. 36
364 Laps at Darlington Raceway
Darlington, SC
"Southern 500"
500 Miles on 1.375-mile Paved Track
September 7, 1959

Fin	St	No.	Driver	Team / Car	Laps	Money	Status
1	14	7	Jim Reed	Reed '57 Chevrolet	364	$17,250	Running
2	5	73	* Bob Burdick	Roy Burdick '59 T-Bird	362	7,760	Running
3	22	72	Bobby Johns	Shorty Johns '57 Chevrolet	362	4,760	Running
4	6	43	** Richard Petty	Petty Eng '59 Plymouth	361	2,830	Running
5	16	36	Tommy Irwin	Irwin '59 T-Bird	358	2,010	Running
6	23	88	Jim Paschal	Buck Baker '59 Chevrolet	356	1,460	Running
7	1	3	Fireball Roberts	Jim Stephens '59 Pontiac	354	2,330	Running
8	20	76	Larry Frank	Carolina Plating '57 Chevy	350	1,025	Running
9	15	87	Buck Baker	Baker '59 Chevrolet	347	875	Running
10	18	41	Jimmy Thompson	Delia Auto Sales '59 T-Bird	346	805	Running
11	28	64	Shep Langdon	Langdon '58 Ford	345	600	Running
12	25	27	Bill Champion	'57 Ford	343	500	Running
13	12	2	Joe Caspolich	City of Florence '59 Olds	342	470	Running
14	3	22	Speedy Thompson	Ogden-Ridgeway '59 Chevy	333	565	Spring
15	29	16	Charlie Cregar	Happy Steigel '59 Pontiac	331	300	Running
16	34	19	Herman Beam	Beam '57 Chevrolet	328	250	Running
17	4	4	Rex White	White 59 Chevrolet	326	310	Drv Shft
18	39	66	L D Austin	Austin '57 Ford	326	225	Running
19	19	6	Cotton Owens	Thunder Chicken '59 T-Bird	320	600	Running
20	9	42	Lee Petty	Petty Eng '59 Plymouth	319	300	Running
21	32	56	Bud Crothers	'57 Chevrolet	318	150	Running
22	47	35	Al White	Salad Bowl Rest '58 Ford	286	150	Running
23	31	34	G C Spencer	'57 Chevrolet	272	150	Battery
24	30	13	Earl Balmer	'59 Chevrolet	234	150	Piston
25	27	26	Dick Blackwell	'57 Ford	225	150	Crash
26	24	20	Tiny Lund	A M Crawford '58 Ford	221	150	Clutch
27	33	30	Cale Yarborough	'58 Ford	219	150	Tires
28	10	47	Jack Smith	Bud Moore '59 Chevy	218	150	Axle
29	21	98	Marvin Panch	Tom Vernon '59 Ford	194	150	Cam Shft
30	50	55	Johnny Patterson	'57 Chevrolet	180	150	Axle
31	7	93	Banjo Matthews	T-Bird Power Prod '59 T-Bird	178	1,915	Crash
32	46	32	George Green	Jess Potter '58 Chevrolet	175	150	Engine
33	35	9	Roy Tyner	Tyner '57 Chevrolet	166	150	Timing
34	38	5	Bob Duell	Julian Buesink '59 Ford	151	150	Pistons
35	11	49	Bob Welborn	Welborn '59 Chevrolet	130	200	Crash
36	17	59	Tom Pistone	Rupert Safety Blt '59 T-Bird	119	325	Engine
37	41	91	Neil Castles	'57 Ford	92	150	Running
38	13	92	Possum Jones	Gerald Duke '59 T-Bird	74	295	Brakes
39	43	83	Lennie Page	'57 Ford	71	150	Engine
40	40	95	Buddy Baker	Julian Buesink '59 Ford	64	150	Engine
41	42	23	Bob Perry	'59 Plymouth	63	150	Engine
42	49	44	Joe Lee Johnson	Chester Barron '59 Chevrolet	58	150	Trans
43	8	12	Joe Weatherly	Coca-Cola '59 T-Bird	54	210	Oil Pres
44	36	71	Dick Joslin	'57 Dodge	46	150	Hd Gasket
45	2	10	Elmo Langley	Ratus Walters '59 Buick	41	180	Engine
46	26	61	Joe Eubanks	W H Watson '58 Pontiac	26	190	Pistons
47	48	15	Marvin Porter	Porter '57 Ford	19	150	Hd Gasket
48	45	82	Elmo Henderson	'58 Ford	16	150	Engine
49	44	86	Larry Flynn	'58 Ford	11	150	Rear End
50	37	14	Carl Burris	'57 Ford	2	150	Engine

Time of Race: 4 hours, 28 minutes, 30 seconds
Average Speed: 111.836 mph
Pole Winner: Fireball Roberts - 123.734 mph
Lap Leaders: Speedy Thompson 1-2, Fireball Roberts 3-44, Banjo Matthews 45-61, Cotton Owens 62-85, Bobby Johns 86-92, Richard Petty 93-99, Matthews 100-137, Johns 138-187, Jim Reed 188-238, Bob Burdick 239-263, Reed 264-364
Cautions: 2 for 12 laps
Margin of Victory: 2 laps plus
Attendance: 78,000
* Relieved by Joe Weatherly
** Relieved by Marvin Panch

out of the car in favor of the more experienced Weatherly. "Weatherly can take the knocks a little better," said Burdick. "Where Bob was having trouble, Joe was breezing through." Ironically, Burdick had claimed Weatherly was "rough riding" in the February 22nd

Daytona 500, which he said cost then driver Johnny Beauchamp the race.

Buddy Baker's Ford was equipped with a two-way radio so he could talk to car owner Julian Buesink. Baker retired after 64 laps with engine problems.

Reed averaged 111.836 mph for his third win of the year. A standing room crowd of 78,000 was on hand to view the action.

Grand National Race No. 37
250 Laps at Hickory Speedway
Hickory, NC
100 Miles on .4-mile Dirt Track
September 11, 1959

Fin	St	No.	Driver	Team / Car	Laps	Money	Status
1	13	42	Lee Petty	Petty Eng '59 Plymouth	250	$900	Running
2	3	88	Buck Baker	Baker '59 Chevrolet	249	525	Running
3	10	4	Rex White	White '59 Chevrolet ST	248	375	Running
4	2	21	Junior Johnson	Wood Brothers '58 Ford	248	275	Running
5	4	31	Brownie King	Jess Potter '57 Chevrolet	243	250	Running
6	9	17	Fred Harb	Harb '57 Ford	238	215	Running
7	12	62	Buck Brigance	'57 Chevrolet	238	175	Running
8	14	19	Herman Beam	Beam '57 Chevrolet	233	150	Running
9	7	23	Fuzz Clifton	'57 Chevrolet	214	140	Running
10	5	55	L D Austin	'57 Chevrolet	183	130	Running
11	1	63	R L Combs	'57 Ford	177	125	Running
12	8	12	Marvin Porter	Porter '58 Ford ST	162	110	Running
13	11	47	Jack Smith	Bud Moore '59 Chevrolet	148	100	A Frame
14	6	34	G C Spencer	'57 Chevrolet	74	185	Crank Sh

Time of Race: 1 hour, 34 minutes, 40 seconds
Average Speed: 63.380 mph
Pole Position: No Time Trials - Drew for positions
Lap Leaders: - - - - - - - - - - - - - - - Lee Petty - 250
Cautions:
Margin of Victory: 1 lap plus
Attendance:

Race No. 37

Bad Luck Foils Smith; Petty Wins at Hickory

HICKORY, NC (Sept 11) -- Lee Petty took the lead when suspension troubles sidetracked Jack Smith and won the 100 mile race at Hickory Speedway. It was Petty's eighth win of the 1959 season.

Jack Smith had gotten around early leader Junior Johnson and was setting the pace when a lower A Frame broke on his Chevrolet. Petty's Plymouth took charge and beat runner-up Buck Baker by more than one lap. Rex White finished third, Johnson was fourth and Brownie King fifth.

Since no time trials were held, Petty had to come

from 13th starting spot in the slim 14-car field. R.L. Combs won the pole position in a blind draw, with Johnson starting second. Johnson, driving the Wood Brothers Ford, led in the early going before dropping off the pace.

Rex White and Marvin Porter, two drivers vying for NASCAR's Short Track Division title, requested that their points count toward the Short Track standings. The sanctioning body obliged.

Petty averaged 63.380 mph for his 45th career Grand National win.

Owens' victory left him 1,120 points behind Petty in the Grand National standings.

Glen Wood and Jack Smith, second and third fastest qualifiers, fell out of the race. Wood's Ford blew a tire and hit the fence after 152 laps; Smith's Chevrolet popped its engine on lap 11.

Owens averaged 60.382 mph for his third career Grand National victory.

Grand National Race No. 38
200 Laps at Atlantic Rural Fairgrounds
Richmond, VA
100 Miles on Half-mile Dirt Track
September 13, 1959

Fin	St	No.	Driver	Team / Car	Laps	Money	Status
1	1	6	Cotton Owens	Thunder-Chicken '59 T-Bird	200	$800	Running
2	15	42	Lee Petty	Petty Eng '59 Plymouth	200	625	Running
3	4	59	Tom Pistone	Rupert Safety Blt '59 T-Bird	198	375	Running
4	9	88	Reds Kagle	'57 Chevrolet	194	275	Running
5	5	90	Runt Harris	Junie Donlavey '57 Chevy	193	250	Running
6	7	64	Shep Langdon	Langdon '58 Ford	191	215	Running
7	13	19	Herman Beam	Beam '57 Chevrolet	189	175	Running
8	6	31	Brownie King	Jess Potter '57 Chevrolet	187	150	Pistons
9	10	23	Bill Scott	'57 Chevrolet	179	140	Running
10	16	55	L D Austin	'57 Chevrolet	172	130	Running
11	14	35	Al White	Salad Bowl Rest '58 Ford	160	125	Running
12	2	21	Glen Wood	Wood Brothers '58 Ford	152	110	Crash
13	12	32	George Green	Jess Potter '57 Chevrolet	146	100	Engine
14	11	34	G C Spencer	'57 Chevrolet	76	85	Engine
15	8	38	Ned Jarrett	Jarrett '57 Ford	50	70	Wheel
16	3	47	Jack Smith	Bud Moore '59 Chevrolet	11	60	Engine

Time of Race: 1 hour, 39 minutes, 22 seconds
Average Speed: 60.382 mph
Pole Winner: Cotton Owens - 62.674 mph
Lap Leaders: - - - - - - - - - - - - - - Cotton Owens   - 200
Cautions:
Margin of Victory:
Attendance:

Grand National Race No. 39
100 Laps at Sacramento Fairgrounds
Sacramento, CA
100 Miles on 1-mile Dirt Track
September 13, 1959

Fin	St	No.	Driver	Team / Car	Laps	Money	Status
1	19	1	Eddie Gray	Vel Miletich '59 Ford	100	$700	Running
2	13	3	Scotty Cain	'59 T-Bird	100	500	Running
3	20	16	Danny Weinberg	'58 Mercury	100	425	Running
4	2	34	Bob Ross	'57 Chevrolet	100	335	Running
5	3	10	Lucky Long	'57 Chevrolet	97	300	Running
6	25	5	Johnny Potter	'58 Ford	96	250	Running
7	24	44	Lloyd Dane	'59 Ford	91	200	Running
8	10	0	Jim Cook	'57 Pontiac	87	150	Engine
9	18	23	Bob Perry	'59 Plymouth	87	100	Running
10	12	55	Mel Larson	'57 Mercury	78	100	Heating
11	23	97	Parnelli Jones	Vel Miletich '59 Ford	73	100	Heating
12	16	84	Don Taylor	'57 Chevrolet	70	100	Running
13	17	25	Chuck Webb	'58 Ford	63	100	Heating
14	6	11	Owen Loggins	'58 Plymouth Fury	57	100	Hose
15	11	17	Jack Austin	'58 Ford	54	75	Crash
16	9	91	Jim Blomgren	'59 Plymouth	49	50	Engine
17	21	22	Jack D McCoy	'58 Chevrolet	42	50	Heating
18	7	32	Harlan Richardson	'57 Ford	39	50	Engine
19	26	40	Dick Carter	'58 Mercury	39	50	Running
20	24	8	Dave James	'57 Chevrolet	35	50	Engine
21	14	37X	Charles Sanchez	'57 Ford	35	25	Engine
22	4	87	Arley Scranton	'57 Pontiac	22	25	Crash
23	8	37	Bob Hogle	'57 Pontiac	20	25	Crash
24	1	43	Bill Jarick	'58 Mercury	14	25	Engine
25	5	9	Bob Price	'59 Chevrolet	8	---	Engine
26	15	4	Dick Getty	'59 Chevrolet	6	---	Engine

Time of Race: 1 hour, 49 minutes, 35 seconds
Average Speed: 54.753 mph
Pole Winner: No Time Trials, Drew for Position
Lap Leaders: - - - - - - - - - - - - - - Eddie Gray   - 100
Cautions:
Margin of Victory:
Attendance:

Race No. 38

Owens Gets First '59 Win at Richmond

RICHMOND, VA (Sept 13) -- Cotton Owens drove his Thunder-Chicken Thunderbird to his first triumph of the season in the 100 miler at the Atlantic Rural Fairgrounds.

Owens started on the pole and held off Lee Petty to take the $800 first prize. Tom Pistone was third, Reds Kagle fourth and Runt Harris fifth. Harris was tooling a Chevrolet tuned by Junie Donlavey.

Race No. 39

Eddie Gray Victorious In Sacramento 100

SACRAMENTO, CA (Sept 13) -- Eddie Gray of Gardena, CA drove his Ford to victory in the 100-mile Grand National event at the Sacramento Fairgrounds.

It was Gray's first win of the season.

Scotty Cain finished second with Danny Weinberg third. Fourth place went to Bob Ross and Lucky Long was fifth.

Only 10 cars in the starting field of 26 finished. Three drivers, Arlie Scranton, Bob Hogle and Jack Austin, flipped their cars. None of the drivers were injured.

Gray started 19th on the grid as poor track conditions prevented qualifying from taking place. Gray shoved his Vel Miletich Ford through the field and took the lead in the second half of the event.

Gray averaged 54.753 mph for his second career victory.

Race No. 40

Johnson Delights Crowd But is Disqualified -- Petty Wins

HILLSBORO, NC (Sept 20) -- Lee Petty was declared the winner of the 99-mile Grand National event at the Orange Speedway for his ninth win of the year.

Cotton Owens finished a lap behind in second place; Richard Petty was third. Larry Frank got paid for fourth place and Roy Tyner fifth.

Junior Johnson dazzled the crowd with his relentless charge. The Ronda, NC Ford driver arrived at the track late and started 22nd in the 22 car field. He ran on the ragged edge and had moved up to seventh place by the **fourth** lap. He was third by the 22nd lap but was caught up in a crash on the 28th lap. George Green spun, and Johnson collected the Chevrolet.

Johnson continued in the race to finish third in the poorly handling car. After the race, NASCAR officials discovered an illegal differential and dropped Johnson to the rear of the field with no pay.

Richard Petty was running second when the rear axle broke in his Plymouth, knocking him out of the race. He still completed enough laps to get third place money.

Petty averaged 77.868 mph for his 46th career Grand National win.

Grand National Race No. 40
110 Laps at Orange Speedway
Hillsboro, NC
99 Miles on .9-mile Dirt Track
September 20, 1959

Fin	St	No.	Driver	Team / Car	Laps	Money	Status
1	7	42	Lee Petty	Petty Eng '59 Plymouth	110	$900	Running
2	4	6	Cotton Owens	Thunder-Chicken '59 T-Bird	109	525	Running
3	2	43	Richard Petty	Petty Eng '59 Plymouth	100	375	Axle
4	13	76	Larry Frank	Carolina Plating '57 Chevy	100	250	Running
5	16	9	Roy Tyner	Tyner '57 Chevrolet	100	250	Running
6	18	19	Herman Beam	Beam '57 Chevrolet	99	250	Running
7	14	63	R L Combs	'57 Ford	98	175	Running
8	15	34	G C Spencer	'57 Chevrolet	95	150	Engine
9	19	23	Bill Scott	'57 Chevrolet	93	140	Heating
10	6	59	Tom Pistone	Rupert Safety Belt '59 T-Bird	89	130	Spindle
11	11	64	Shep Langdon	Langdon '58 Ford	85	125	Running
12	5	88	Buck Baker	Baker '59 Chevrolet	82	110	Sway Bar
13	9	17	Fred Harb	Harb '57 Ford	69	100	Engine
14	10	32	George Greene	Jess Potter '57 Chevrolet	68	85	Running
15	17	62	Buck Brigance	'57 Chevrolet	65	70	Running
16	1	47	Jack Smith	Bud Moore '59 Chevrolet	48	60	Axle
17	8	15	Rex White	Beau Morgan '58 Ford	43	50	Axle Hub
18	3	61	Speedy Thompson	W H Watson '58 Pontiac	29	50	A Frame
19	12	38	Ned Jarrett	Jarrett '57 Ford	18	50	Axle
20	20	96	Bobby Keck	Keck '57 Chevrolet	12	50	Hd Gasket
21	21	27	E J Trivette	'57 Plymouth	2	50	Trans
22	22	11	Junior Johnson	Paul Spaulding '59 Dodge	108	---	Disqual

Time of Race: 1 hour, 16 minutes, 17 seconds
Average Speed: 77.868 mph
Pole Winner: Jack Smith - 85.533 mph
Lap Leaders: Jack Smith 1-50, Tom Pistone 51-89, Lee Petty 90-100
Cautions:
Margin of Victory: 1 lap plus
Attendance:

Race No. 41

Petty Clinches Championship; White Wins Martinsville

MARTINSVILLE, VA (Sept 27) -- Rex White led the final 195 laps and won the Virginia Sweepstakes 500 at Martinsville Speedway. It was the fifth win of the season for the compact Chevrolet driver.

Glen Wood, who started on the pole and led for 85 laps, finished second in his Ford convertible. Jim Reed was third, Tommy Irwin was fourth and Speedy Thompson fifth.

Seven cautions broke the pace, but there were no driver injuries.

The only serious incident occurred midway in the race when Richard Petty ran over his crew chief, Red Myler. On a routine pit stop, Myler had gone underneath the Petty Plymouth. None of the other crew members were aware that Myler was making adjustments to the car and signaled for 22 year-old Richard to pull out of the pits. The rear wheel ran over Myler's chest. Myler was released from Martinsville General

Tom Pistone spins his T-Bird at Martinsville

Hospital after treatments for burns of the chest and bruises. X-rays revealed no broken bones. Petty went on to finish 15th.

Lee Petty drove his Plymouth to a 10th place finish, clinching his third Grand National championship. His point lead stood at 1,380 points with three events left on the 1959 slate.

White started 14th and first took the lead on lap 165. He led for just seven laps before making a pit stop. He passed Larry Frank on lap 306 and led the rest of the way. Frank finished sixth.

White averaged 60.500 mph before 13,500 spectators. It was White's seventh win of his career.

Race No. 42

Petty Paces Field at Asheville-Weaverville

WEAVERVILLE, NC (Oct 11) -- Lee Petty racked up his 10th win of the year with a victory in the 100-mile event at Asheville-Weaverville Speedway.

Glen Wood finished in second place with Jack Smith, Rex White and Richard Petty rounding out the top five.

Tommy Irwin, rookie T-Bird driver, won the pole but went only 96 laps before his engine expired. He wound up 28th in the field of 29.

Tiny Lund crashed his Ford in the 119th lap, but he

Grand National Race No. 41
500 Laps at Martinsville Speedway
Martinsville, VA
"Virginia Sweepstakes 500"
250 Miles on Half-mile Paved Track
September 27, 1959

Fin	St	No.	Driver	Team / Car	Laps	Money	Status
1	14	4	Rex White	White '59 Chevrolet GN	500	$3,250	Running
2	1	16	Glen Wood	Wood Bros '58 Ford C	500	1,975	Running
3	24	7	Jim Reed	Reed '59 Chevrolet GN	497	1,425	Running
4	2	36	Tommy Irwin	Irwin '59 T-Bird GN	497	1,175	Running
5	16	22	Speedy Thompson	Ogden-Ridgeway '59 Ch GN	497	900	Running
6	7	76	Larry Frank	Carolina Plating '57 Chev C	496	750	Running
7	4	59	Tom Pistone	Rupert Saf Blt '59 T-Bird GN	492	675	Running
8	5	77	Joe Lee Johnson	Honest Charley '58 Chev C	490	600	Running
9	15	9	Roy Tyner	Tyner '57 Chevrolet C	490	500	Running
10	6	42	Lee Petty	Petty Eng '59 Plymouth GN	488	575	Running
11	26	75	John Dodd, Sr	Dodd '59 Ford GN	488	375	Running
12	39	38	Ned Jarrett	Jarrett '57 Ford GN	484	275	Running
13	27	41	Ken Rush	'57 Chevrolet C	476	250	Running
14	32	87	Buck Baker	Baker '59 Chevrolet GN	476	225	Running
15	3	43	Richard Petty	Petty Eng '59 Plymouth C	470	275	Running
16	19	32	George Green	Jess Potter '58 Chevrolet C	469	200	Running
17	37	15	L D Austin	Beau Morgan '57 Ford GN	469	180	Running
18	36	18	Jerry Smith	Red Bank '57 Pontiac GN	466	165	Running
19	12	20	Tiny Lund	A M Crawford '58 Ford GN	451	155	Running
20	4	5	Bunk Moore	'57 Chevrolet GN	451	150	Running
21	42	19	Herman Beam	Beam '57 Chevrolet GN	447	130	Running
22	21	14	Bill Taylor	Manley Britt '58 Ford C	439	125	Engine
23	17	31	Brownie King	Jess Potter '57 Chevrolet C	434	110	Engine
24	8	72	Bobby Johns	Shorty Johns '57 Chevy GN	431	100	Running
25	28	64	Shep Langdon	Langdon '58 Ford GN	425	85	Running
26	29	45	Aubrey Boles	Aubrey Boles '57 Plym C	405	75	Running
27	23	63	R L Combs	'57 Ford C	404	75	Running
28	9	2	Jimmy Thompson	Bruce Thompson '57 Chevy C	318	75	Running
29	22	47	Jack Smith	Bud Moore '59 Chevrolet GN	305	75	Rear End
30	30	88	Fireball Roberts	Buck Baker '59 Chevrolet GN	303	75	Rear End
31	25	86	Erwin Carpenter	Neil Castles '56 Ford C	299	75	Crash
32	31	27	E J Trivette	'58 Plymouth C	293	75	Radiator
33	10	6	Cotton Owens	Thunder-Chick '59 T-Bird C	279	75	Rear End
34	34	34	G C Spencer	'57 Chevrolet GN	263	75	Trans
35	35	46	Whitey Norman	'57 Chevrolet GN	259	75	Axle
36	41	62	Buck Brigance	'57 Chevrolet GN	229	75	Rear End
37	13	25	Gene White	White '57 Chevrolet C	224	75	Engine
38	18	98	Marvin Panch	Tom Vernon '59 Ford GN	224	75	Fuel Pmp
39	20	93	Banjo Matthews	Power Prod '59 T-Bird GN	216	75	Rear End
40	11	10	Elmo Langley	Ratus Walters '59 Buick GN	180	75	Clutch
41	33	40	Joe Halton	'57 Chevrolet C	157	25	Engine
42	43	55	Ben Benz	'57 Chevrolet GN	151	25	Clutch
43	44	33	Bill Scott	'57 Chevrolet GN	151	25	Clutch
44	47	17	Fred Harb	Harb '57 Ford C	76	25	Engine
45	46	58	Johnny Beauchamp	'57 Chevrolet GN	50	25	Steering
46	48	49	Bob Welborn	Welborn '57 Chevrolet C	37	25	Engine
47	38	78	Jimmie Lewallen	'57 Ford GN	2	25	Crash

Time of Race: 4 hours 7 minutes, 56 seconds
Average Speed: 60.500 mph
Pole Winner: Glen Wood - 69.471 mph
Lap Leaders: Glen Wood 1-85, Lee Petty 86-164, Rex White 165-171, L Petty 172-179, Jim Reed 180-266, Larry Frank 267-305, White 306-500
Cautions: 7
Margin of Victory:
Attendance: 13,500

was not hurt.

Twenty-nine cars started the 200 lapper on the half-mile paved track and 21 were running at the finish.

Petty's 47th career victory came at an average speed of 76.433 mph after Irwin earned the pole at 78.568 mph.

Grand National Race No. 42
200 Laps at Asheville-Weaverville Speedway
Weaverville, NC
100 Miles on Half-mile Paved Track
October 11, 1959

Fin	St	No.	Driver	Team / Car	Laps	Money	Status
1	4	42	Lee Petty	Petty Eng '59 Plymouth	200	$900	Running
2	2	16	Glen Wood	Wood Bros '58 Ford	200	525	Running
3	6	47	Jack Smith	Bud Moore '59 Chevrolet	199	375	Running
4	9	4	Rex White	White '59 Chevrolet	199	275	Running
5	8	43	Richard Petty	Petty Eng '59 Plymouth	198	250	Running
6	3	76	Larry Frank	Carolina Plating '57 Chevy	197	215	Running
7	14	77	Joe Lee Johnson	Honest Charley '57 Chevy	197	175	Running
8	19	38	Ned Jarrett	Jarrett '57 Ford	195	150	Running
9	11	11	Junior Johnson	Paul Spaulding '59 Dodge	194	140	Running
10	15	9	Roy Tyner	Tyner '57 Chevrolet	193	130	Running
11	7	6	Cotton Owens	Thunder Chicken '59 T-Bird	192	125	Running
12	13	88	Buck Baker	Baker '59 Chevrolet	192	110	Running
13	18	15	Speedy Thompson	Beau Morgan '57 Ford	187	100	Running
14	16	17	Fred Harb	Harb '57 Ford	184	85	Running
15	26	12	Benny Rakestraw	'57 Mercury	182	70	Running
16	28	64	L D Austin	Shep Langdon '58 Ford	180	60	Running
17	23	78	Jimmie Lewallen	'57 Ford	179	50	Running
18	25	18	Jerry Smith	Red Bank '57 Pontiac	178	50	Running
19	20	19	Herman Beam	Beam '57 Chevrolet	177	50	Running
20	24	26	Dick Blackwell	'57 Ford	175	50	Running
21	5	72	Bobby Johns	Shorty Johns '57 Chevrolet	171	50	Engine
22	29	62	Buck Brigance	'57 Chevrolet	169	50	Rear End
23	22	66	Bill Morton	'58 Ford	164	---	Engine
24	21	31	Brownie King	Jess Potter '57 Chevrolet	138	---	Running
25	27	13	Chuck Tombs	'59 Chevrolet	134	---	RF Hub
26	17	32	Rayman Utsman	Jess Potter '57 Chevrolet	124	---	Spindle
27	10	20	Tiny Lund	A M Crawford '58 Ford	119	---	Crash
28	1	36	Tommy Irwin	Irwin '59 T-Bird	96	---	Engine
29	12	49	Bob Welborn	Welborn '59 Chevrolet	81	---	Sway Bar

Time of Race: 1 hour, 18 minutes, 30 seconds
Average Speed: 76.433 mph
Pole Winner: Tommy Irwin - 78.568 mph
Lap Leaders: - - - - - - - - - - - - - - Lee Petty   - 200
Cautions:
Margin of Victory:
Attendance:

Race No. 43

Petty Wins at Wilkesboro -- Matches Herb Thomas' 48 Victories

N. WILKESBORO, NC (October 18) -- Lee Petty led all the way and won the 100-miler at North Wilkesboro Speedway. It was the 11th win of the season for the old man from Randleman, NC, and it tied him with Herb Thomas for the most Grand National victories. Both men have 48 big league triumphs.

Rex White was running directly behind Petty most of the way, but he had to slacken his pace when a tire blistered. He still held onto second place, just ahead of

Richard Petty, who grabbed third. Tom Pistone finished fourth with Junior Johnson fifth.

There were three caution flags during the running of the 160-lap race; all of them for minor spins. The most serious altercation came in qualifying when Bob Welborn tagged the wall coming off the fourth turn. The car flipped over three times and scattered pit row occupants in all directions. Welborn was only shaken but his Chevrolet was a total wipeout.

An audience of 5,500 watched Petty win at an average speed of 74.829 mph.

Lee Petty -- win number 48

Grand National Race No. 43
160 Laps at N. Wilkesboro Speedway
North Wilkesboro, NC
100 Miles on .625-mile Paved Track
October 18, 1959

Fin	St	No.	Driver	Team / Car	Laps	Money	Status
1	2	42	Lee Petty	Petty Eng '59 Plymouth	160	$900	Running
2	6	4	Rex White	White '59 Chevrolet	160	525	Running
3	5	43	Richard Petty	Petty Eng '59 Plymouth	160	375	Running
4	8	49	Tom Pistone	Rupert Safety Belt '59 T-Bird	159	275	Running
5	18	11	Junior Johnson	Paul Spaulding '59 Dodge	159	250	Running
6	3	76	Larry Frank	Carolina Plating '57 Chevy	159	215	Running
7	1	16	Glen Wood	Wood Bros '58 Ford	158	175	Running
8	11	87	Buck Baker	Baker '59 Chevrolet	154	150	Running
9	15	64	Shep Langdon	Langdon '58 Ford	154	140	Running
10	16	31	Brownie King	Jess Potter '57 Chevrolet	154	130	Running
11	7	47	Jack Smith	Bud Moore '59 Chevrolet	154	125	Running
12	20	94	Bill Taylor	'57 Ford	153	110	Running
13	19	56	Bill Morton	'58 Ford	152	100	Running
14	21	19	Herman Beam	Beam '57 Chevrolet	147	85	Running
15	13	15	Speedy Thompson	Beau Morgan '57 Ford	147	70	Running
16	25	34	G C Spencer	'59 Chevrolet	147	60	Running
17	17	26	Dick Blackwell	'57 Ford	144	50	Running
18	23	27	E J Trivette	'57 Plymouth	136	50	Running
19	26	96	Bobby Keck	Keck '57 Chevrolet	136	50	Running
20	22	32	Layman Utsman	Jess Potter '58 Chevrolet	111	50	Rear End
21	24	33	Bill Scott	'57 Chevrolet	97	50	Bearing
22	9	9	Roy Tyner	Tyner '57 Chevrolet	80	50	Engine
23	4	36	Tommy Irwin	Irwin '59 T-Bird	77	---	Oil Pres
24	12	46	Barney Shore	'57 Chevrolet	62	---	Oil Pres
25	10	38	Ned Jarrett	Jarrett '57 Ford	55	---	Clutch
26	14	78	Jimmie Lewallen	'57 Ford	9	---	Piston

Time of Race: 1 hour, 20 minutes, 11 seconds
Average Speed: 74.829 mph
Pole Winner: Glen Wood - 86.806 mph
Lap Leaders: Lee Petty 1-160
Cautions: 3
Margin of Victory:
Attendance: 5,500

Race No. 44

Smith Wins Finale At Concord; Chooses New Automobile as Prize

CONCORD, NC (Oct 25) -- Jack Smith passed Cotton Owens in the 90th lap and led the rest of the way to win the Lee Kirby Memorial at the New Concord Speedway. It was the final race of the 1959 Grand National season.

Smith was offered his choice for winning by pro-

Jack Smith and wife Betty are all smiles after winning a new car

moter Bruton Smith -- a new 1960 Ford or first place money of $1,500. Smith chose the new automobile and was presented the keys by Janice Kirby, daughter of the late sportscaster Lee Kirby, for whom the race was named.

Lee Petty finished second and was crowned Grand National champion for the third time. Petty wound up with 11,792 points, 1,830 more than runner-up Cotton Owens.

Third place in the 150-mile race on the half-mile dirt track went to Buck Baker. Buddy Baker finished fourth in a sterling performance. Fifth place went to Glen Wood.

Owens led the first 89 laps. Smith nosed his Chevrolet into the lead on lap 90 and was never headed.

Owens went 111 laps before a broken water hose sidelined his T-Bird.

Smith had to come from 18th starting spot. No time trials were held and drivers drew for starting psoition. Curtis Turner, making a return from back surgery, started 22nd and had moved to fifth place when transmission troubles knocked his Ford out of the race.

Smith averaged 54.005 mph as two cautions slowed the field. A crowd of 7,500 was on hand.

Grand National Race No. 44
300 Laps at New Concord Speedway
Concord, NC
"Lee Kirby Memorial"
150 Miles on Half-mile Dirt Track
October 25, 1959

Fin	St	No.	Driver	Team / Car	Laps	Money	Status
1	18	47	Jack Smith	Bud Moore '59 Chevrolet	300	$1,500	Running
2	9	42	Lee Petty	Petty Eng '59 Plymouth	299	1,000	Running
3	3	87	Buck Baker	Baker '59 Chevrolet	293	700	Running
4	8	88	Buddy Baker	Buck Baker '59 Chevrolet	291	500	Running
5	23	98	Glen Wood	Tom Vernon '59 Ford	288	400	Running
6	14	64	Shep Langdon	Langdon '58 Ford	284	300	Running
7	11	43	Richard Petty	Petty Eng '59 Plymouth	283	275	Running
8	7	2	Speedy Thompson	Bruce Thompson '57 Chevy	282	225	Running
9	12	59	Tom Pistone	Rupert Safety Belt '59 T-Bird	279	200	Trans
10	31	74	L D Austin	Austin '58 Chevrolet	279	150	Running
11	15	20	Tiny Lund	A M Crawford '58 Ford	268	125	Running
12	24	9	Roy Tyner	Tyner '57 Chevrolet	266	125	Running
13	34	19	Herman Beam	Beam '57 Chevrolet	260	125	Running
14	5	15	Rex White	Beau Morgan '57 Ford	258	125	Running
15	30	76	Larry Frank	Carolina Plating '57 Chev	255	100	Engine
16	19	96	Bobby Keck	Keck '57 Chevrolet	248	90	Running
17	28	11	Junior Johnson	Paul Spaulding '59 Dodge	244	75	Heating
18	17	63	R L Combs	'57 Ford	237	75	Spindle
19	25	94	Bill Taylor	'57 Ford	235	75	Engine
20	21	31	Brownie King	Jess Potter '57 Chevrolet	234	75	Axle
21	32	33	Bill Scott	'57 Chevrolet	220	75	Running
22	16	4	Ken Rush	Rex White '57 Chevrolet	177	75	Heating
23	33	77	Joe Lee Johnson	Honest Charley '57 Chevy	173	75	Hd Gasket
24	22	75	Curtis Turner	'59 Ford	159	75	Trans
25	29	32	Bill Morton	Jess Potter '58 Chevrolet	149	---	Engine
26	20	36	Tommy Irwin	Irwin '59 T-Bird	121	---	Spindle
27	10	62	Buck Brigance	'57 Chevrolet	117	---	Rear End
28	2	6	Cotton Owens	Thunder Chicken '59 T-Bird	111	---	Hose
29	6	27	E J Trivette	'57 Plymouth	103	---	Clutch
30	13	34	G C Spencer	'59 Chevrolet	102	---	Spindle
31	1	17	Fred Harb	Harb '57 Ford	82	---	Radiator
32	4	56	Bill Morton	'58 Ford	82	---	Radiator
33	26	5	Bunk Moore	'57 Chevrolet	71	---	Gen
34	27	38	Ned Jarrett	Jarrett '57 Ford	69	---	Engine

Time of Race: 2 hours, 16 minutes, 39 seconds
Average Speed: 54.005 mph
Pole Winner: No Time Trials. Drew for position
Lap Leaders: Cotton Owens 1-89, Jack Smith 90-200
Cautions: 2
Margin of Victory: 1 lap plus 2 car lengths
Attendance: 7,500

1959 NASCAR Season
Final Point Standings - Grand National Division

Rank	Driver	Points	Starts	Wins	Top 5	Top 10	Winnings
1	Lee Petty	11,792	42	11	27	35	$49,219.15
2	Cotton Owens	9,962	36	1	13	22	14,639.35
3	Speedy Thompson	7,684	29	0	5	9	6,815.63
4	Herman Beam	7,396	30	0	1	12	6,379.48
5	Buck Baker	7,170	35	1	14	19	11,060.04
6	Tom Pistone	7,050	22	2	12	18	12,724.43
7	L D Austin	6,519	38	0	0	12	4,670.35
8	Jack Smith	6,150	21	4	9	12	13,289.38
9	Jim Reed	5,744	13	3	6	8	23,533.58
10	Rex White	5,526	23	5	11	13	12,359.85
11	Junior Johnson	4,864	27	5	14	15	9,674.67
12	Shep Langdon	4,768	21	0	0	6	3,525.21
13	G C Spencer	4,260	28	0	1	5	3,700.21
14	Tommy Irwin	3,876	24	0	10	17	9,189.21
15	Richard Petty	3,694	21	0	6	9	8,110.21
16	Fireball Roberts	3,676	8	1	1	4	10,660.14
17	Bob Welborn	3,588	28	2	9	12	6,490.14
18	Joe Weatherly	3,404	17	0	6	10	9,815.14
19	Bobby Johns	2,732	8	0	1	2	5,950.14
20	Tiny Lund	2,634	27	0	5	10	4,940.14
21	Bob Burdick	2,392	6	0	1	3	10,050.00
22	Larry Frank	2,256	15	0	4	9	5,993.00
23	Bobby Keck	2,186	18	0	0	0	1,270.00
24	Curtis Turner	2,088	10	2	4	4	3,845.00
25	Jim Paschal	1,792	6	0	3	4	2,980.00
26	Buddy Baker	1,692	12	0	1	5	1,705.00
27	Shorty Rollins	1,600	10	0	0	4	1,500.00
28	Elmo Langley	1,568	13	0	1	2	2,286.00
29	Jimmy Thompson	1,528	5	0	0	1	1,580.00
30	Brownie King	1,480	18	0	1	5	1,875.00
31	Tim Flock	1,464	2	0	0	1	850.00
32	Joe Eubanks	1,432	13	0	2	7	2,000.00
33	Roy Tyner	1,416	28	0	7	14	5,425.00
34	Charlie Cregar	1,408	3	0	0	0	550.00
35	Dick Freeman	1,352	3	0	0	0	475.00
36	Raul Cilloniz	1,272	2	0	0	0	550.00
37	Ned Jarrett	1,248	17	2	4	7	3,860.00
38	Dave White	1,228	5	0	0	1	660.00
39	Dick Joslin	1,224	4	0	0	0	485.00
40	Tommy Thompson	1,168	3	0	0	0	510.00
41	Harvey Hege	1,152	10	0	0	3	955.00
42	Eduardo Dibos	1,128	3	0	2	2	1,050.00
43	Bill Champion	1,120	1	0	0	0	500.00
44	Joe Caspolich	1,040	1	0	0	0	470.00
45	Jim Austin	1,016	5	0	0	0	440.00
46	Marvin Porter	984	7	0	2	4	1,940.00
47	Jim McGuirk	928	4	0	0	0	325.00
48	Harlan Richardson	924	10	0	0	2	1,120.00
49	Al White	872	5	0	0	0	575.00
50	Richard Riley	760	10	0	0	2	910.00

The 1960 Season
Three New Superspeedways
and Live Television

Volume two of a four volume series . . . . . The Superspeedway Boom 1959 - 1964

1960

NASCAR Grand National stock car racing was born and bred on the short dirt tracks of the Southeast. There was always a certain flair with watching big American-made passenger cars locked in a four-wheel drift through the corners of a dirt track.

From 1949 - 1958, 381 Grand National events had been presented, 293 of them on dirt tracks of a mile or less in length. There had been three superspeedways in operation during the early years of NASCAR, but somewhat shockingly, two of them had gone out of business by 1959.

Construction work begins at Charlotte Motor Speedway

Raleigh Speedway, a one-mile banked paved oval, joined NASCAR in 1953 and ran its last lap in 1958. Memphis-Arkansas Speedway, a giant 1.5-mile steeply banked dirt track, lasted from 1954 to 1957. Only Darlington had prospered during the decade of the 50's.

There were a number of hardcore traditionalists who whispered that NASCAR would follow Raleigh and West Memphis into a fatal passage if too much emphasis was put on the *"super fast tracks"*. The dirt tracks were the backbone of the sport, the traditionalists argued, and stock car racing would wilt and collapse without the spinal cord intact.

NASCAR President Bill France did not subscribe to that theory. He felt the dirt tracks had their place in Grand National racing in the 60's, but the superspeedways underscored progress. And Big Bill was certainly an advocate of progress.

"Upgrading the facilities was one of the most important phases of NASCAR stock car racing," France stressed. "The big tracks simply accelerated that movement. The spectators could watch the races in comfort, and it was entertainment the whole family could enjoy."

In 1960, three new superspeedways were built. B.L. Marchbanks, an extravagant California sportsman, supervised the construction of a 1.4-mile banked paved track in Hanford, CA. He promptly named the facility after himself. Marchbanks Speedway scheduled its first race on June 12, 1960, and press releases boldly stated that the 250-miler was "the biggest race ever held West of the Mississippi River."

Marvin Porter, a journeyman driver out of Lakewood, CA, won the first California 250 at 88.032 mph. He collected $2,000 from the $17,425 total purse.

Most of the 33 cars in the starting

Charlotte Motor Speedway was just a pile of dirt and rocks in the spring of 1960

field were made up of Pacific Coast Late Model regulars -- a forerunner to today's Winston West Series. "They weren't paying enough money to get all of us Easterners out there," explained defending Grand National champion Lee Petty. "All of us who were running for the points got together and decided it would be best for our pocketbooks not to go all the way out to California and back. Not for no $2,000. Each of us knew that if

Lee and Richard Petty were disqualified from the Charlotte's first World 600

one guy made the trip, we'd all have to go to get them points. And we'd all lose money if we did that.

"Next thing I knew, Rex White had slipped out the back door and gone to California," continued Petty. "He got lots of points too. That helped him win the championship that year."

White finished eighth in the California 250 and earned 456 points. He leaped to within 390 points of leaders Richard and Lee Petty in the point standings and was never out of contention after that.

Only 7,000 fans turned out for the Marchbanks Speedway inaugural. Temperatures which hit 104 degrees were a major factor in the slim turnout. Sixteen cars dropped out of the race, but no race officials bothered to find out why. There was a major communications breakdown.

One week later, Charlotte Motor Speedway opened its doors with the first annual World 600. Track President Curtis Turner and General Manager Bruton Smith both wanted the event at Charlotte's 1.5-mile tri-oval to host the "world's longest and most grueling late model stock car race". They had considered a 501 mile

race with the checkered flag being thrown on the backstretch of the 334th lap. However, they opted to tack on another 99 miles and call it the World 600.

The race, originally slated for May 29, was advanced three weeks so construction crews could finish the project. Light poles were erected so crews could work in two 12 hour shifts around the clock.

Pavement was completed the morning of the first round of qualifying. It had not had time to settle and huge holes were ripped into the turns. "You could have half-hidden a big Chevrolet Impala in some of those holes," quipped Buck Baker.

Patch work on the pavement was done daily, and the drivers prepared for the worst. "Most of the cars looked like army tanks," recalled Lee Petty. "We knew the track wouldn't hold up for 600 miles with 60 cars on the track. Heck, it wasn't holding up for four laps while one car qualified. We put big screens over the grill and windshield to keep flying rocks and chunks of asphalt out of the radiators. Hopefully, it would keep flying objects out of the driver's compartment. We even put tire flaps over the rear tires on our Plymouths to keep all the debris from flying up into the guy following us."

In the driver's meeting, NASCAR Executive Manager Pat Purcell told the drivers to keep off the infield area which separated pit road from the homestretch. There had not been time to plant any grass in that area, and NASCAR officials were fearful of a blinding dust storm if any cars cut across the infield to enter the pit area.

Early in the race, Junior Johnson lost control of his Pontiac coming off the fourth turn. His car skidded into the dusty infield area and plowed into the Victory

Construction crews had to patch up holes in Charlotte Motor Speedway after it broke up during the World 600 qualifying

Lane structure which had been placed on the edge of pit road. He tore out 30 feet of chain-link fence and came to rest on pit road. He stopped in the pits while his pit crew made quick repairs. Johnson continued in the race, completing 287 laps, good enough for 30th place in the field of 60 cars.

"Not long after that, I spun out in the same area," said Lee Petty. "Charlotte's home stretch was unique and it fooled a lot of us drivers. I managed to miss the Victory Lane. Junior had already wiped that out. I think I had my eyes closed most of the time. With all the dust swirling around, I couldn't see, so I closed my eyes. When I finally opened them, I had stopped right in my pit area. That was a stroke of luck I thought. My boys checked everything over and I was on my way. Finished fifth."

But Johnson and Petty received a severe reprimand from NASCAR several days later. "It was three, four, maybe five days later when NASCAR told me that I had been disqualified from the 600 for making an improper entrance to the pits," said Petty. "They disqualified a whole bunch of us. Really, what was I supposed to do, having spun out like that?"

Along with Petty and Johnson, Richard Petty, Paul Lewis, Lennie Page and Bob Welborn were all disqualified from the World 600 and placed at the bottom of the order. No points. No money.

Jim Foster, Sports Editor of the *Spartanburg Herald*, who would join NASCAR as an assistant to the President in 1967, defended NASCAR's decision. "Actually, if the drivers were warned that they would be disqualified if they entered the pits by any route other than pit road, then the Pettys should have been disqualified," said Foster. "Stock car racing has been criticized for a long time for its lack of rules and its laxity in enforcing the rules it does have. Racing rules are made for safety reasons. Let's hope that NASCAR will continue to be as strict in enforcement of its rules as it was at Charlotte."

Jack Smith made all of his pit stops according to the rules. He had built up a seemingly insurmountable five lap lead with less than 50 laps to go. Smith was just cruising around at a conservative pace when a chunk of pavement gouged the fuel tank of his Pontiac.

Car owner Bud Moore and mechanic Pop Eargle slid under the car and attempted to stop the gasoline from gushing out. They tried stuffing rags and steel wool into the opening, but it was no use.

"Anybody got any Octagon soap?" yelled Moore.

A spectator came up with a bar of Camay, but it was too small and too hard. "A cake of the larger, softer Octogon soap might have plugged the hole," muttered a dejected Moore.

Smith departed on lap 352 of the 400 lapper and got credit for 12th place. Joe Lee Johnson, of Chattanooga, TN, was deposited in the lead and led the final 48 laps to win $27,150 of the $106,250 purse. A crowd of 35,462 spent over five and a half hours in the grandstands watching a slice of

history.

Six weeks after the 600, Atlanta International Raceway held its inaugural meet -- the Dixie 300. The mile and a half oval, with wide sweeping turns accounting for a full mile, had scheduled its opening for November of 1959. But construction delays and a short cash flow jeopardized the facility for over eight months.

Finishing touches were put on the Atlanta track the week of the race -- a la Charlotte Motor Speedway. Tents were used to shelter the garage area, there wasn't a blade of grass on the site and concrete was poured into the grandstands during race week. Despite the rush, some 25,000 fans turned out to watch the 300-miler on July 31, 1960.

During the race, starter Ernie Moore was struck down by a piece of flying metal while he was in the flagstand. A lengthy caution came out while an ambulance drove onto the track. Moore was transported to a hospital where he later recovered.

Assistant starter Roby Combs handled the flagging duties the rest of the race, waving the checkered flag over Fireball Roberts at the end of 200 laps. It was the first superspeedway win for Roberts in over a year.

Although the three new superspeedways had encountered an assortment of problems getting off the ground and spectator turnout was less than expected, they did draw national attention to NASCAR stock car racing. With the superspeedway boom working its way up through the gears, the Grand National circuit became a focal point for television cameras.

CBS-Television announced that it would take a bold step -- one that no other network had dared to try. On Sunday, January 31, 1960, the program "*CBS Sports Spectacular*" would televise -- live -- Grand National Pole Position races and a pair of Compact Car events at the Big D.

CBS had sent 50 technicians from New York to Daytona to cover the action. The two-hour program was devoted entirely to the stock car races at Daytona. Bud Palmer was assigned to handle the anchorman duties. Although relatively unrehearsed in auto racing, Palmer described the action that was put on the monitor. Cotton Owens nipped Jack Smith in a stirring finish to win the first 25-lap Pole Position race, thereby earning the

CBS announcer Bud Palmer prepares for first live network telecast at Daytona

inside front row starting position for the second annual Daytona 500. Smith nosed out Bobby Johns to take the second twin 10-miler as everyone but Owens was eligible to enter the second race.

The first ever Compact Car race was staged over the 3.81-mile road course. Marvin Panch prevailed in the 10-lapper driving a Plymouth Valiant. Panch also won the 50-miler staged on the "speedway course", beating Roy Schecter by several car lengths. The two contests were open to small American cars and an assortment of foreign entries including Volvos and Simcas.

Some of the cars in the 37-car crash in Daytona's Modified-Sportsman race

According to reports, some 17,000,000 viewers watched the races on the tube. CBS elected not to tackle the task of a long distance event. They felt it was more suitable to a television audience to show a series of short races. Each of the Grand National Pole Position races were 10 minutes in length, and the two Compact Car races were 24 and 25 minutes long.

It was only 12 days later that NBC jumped on the racing bandwagon. On Friday, February 12, 1960, a four lap Autolite Challenge race -- a special 10-mile event open by invitation -- was televised on NBC's *Today* show. NBC's presentation was on a tape-delayed basis. Johnny Beauchamp squeaked past Ned Jarrett and won the race by mere inches. The race was completed in less than five minutes.

History was made at Daytona International Speedway on Saturday, February 13, 1960 -- history of the dubious kind. Track officials permitted 73 cars to start the 250-mile Modified-Sportsman race, and the most incredible multi-car crash took place less than 90 seconds after the green flag.

Coming out of the fourth turn to complete the second lap, 37 cars -- that's right, 37 -- crashed. A dozen cars flipped. Twenty-four were knocked out of the race. Forty-four cars were said to have survived the melee.

It all started when Dick Foley's Chevrolet lurched sideways. Foley was able to bring his car under control on the apron of the track. In fact, he continued and eventually finished 10th. But mayhem tore loose directly behind Foley. Some of the drivers eliminated in the crash included Larry Frank, Speedy Thompson, Ralph Earnhardt, Wendell Scott, Joe Lee Johnson, Hooker Hood, Sonny Palmer and Johnny Roberts.

"That number 66 car (Foley) bobbled in the turn and everything happened all at once," explained Larry Frank. "My car flipped once, became airborne and sailed completely over the 21 car (Earl Moss)."

"It was the worst accident I've ever seen," said Speedy Thompson. "It's just a miracle that no one got hurt any worse than they did."

Eight drivers went to the hospital. Four were released: Dick Freeman, Carl Tyler, Stan Kross and Francis Allen. Four drivers were admitted to Halifax Hospital and kept at least overnight: Jack McLaughlin (neck injury), Bill Wark (fractured leg), Billy Rafter (injured lower leg, left elbow and shoulder) and Will Cagle (neck injury).

Five ambulances rushed to the crash site and reporters on the scene said it was a record for speedy treatment of injured drivers. "Thank goodness there was no fire," said driver Stan Kross.

It took wrecker crews only 39 minutes to clean up the wreckage. Marion "Bubba" Farr of Augusta, GA, won the wreck-marred race at 116.612 mph. The 38 year-old lunch room oper-

The 37-car crash in the Daytona Modified-Sportsman race left many cars crumpled badly

ator was driving a '56 Ford Modified powered by a 430 cubic inch 1958 Lincoln engine with six carburetors. Carl Burris finished second in a Sportsman Ford.

The Daytona 500 on February 14 was a wreck-marred event. High winds, gusting up to 30 mph, played havoc with the beefed up NASCAR stock cars. Tommy Herbert, young Miami driver, suffered a badly broken arm and a severe eye injury when his T-Bird flew apart after crashing on the backstretch. In all, 32 laps were run under the caution flag.

So many cars were banged up that NASCAR of-

Rex White drove this Chevrolet to the 1960 NASCAR Grand National Championship

ficials cancelled a pair of Grand National events in South Florida scheduled for the following week. One hundred-milers at Palmetto Speedway in Miami and Hollywood Speedway in Hallandale were taken off the slate because, NASCAR said, too many cars had been damaged in the 500.

However, Kelly Kellum, promoter at Hollywood Speedway, was irked that only two drivers -- Rex White and Jim Reed -- had sent in entries for his race. "I can't pay $4,200 for a match race between Reed and White," huffed Kellum.

On May 11, Erwin G. "Cannonball" Baker, NAS-CAR's Commissioner since its inception in 1948, died of a heart attack in Indianapolis. He was 78 at the time. 'Bake' had made his final public appearance four days earlier at Darlington in pre-race ceremonies for the Rebel 300.

Baker became famous for his high speed antics, including 143 cross-country runs against time -- on motorcycles and in automobiles. In 1914, a New York newspaper tagged him with the name "Cannonball" after he arrived in the City following a transcontinental record run. He had estimated that he had driven 5,500,000 miles by motorcycle and car, collecting a few scars and many trophies along the way. He considered his greatest feat a drive from New York to Chicago in a Franklin automobile in 1928, beating the time of the 20th Century Limited train.

Baker also won the very first event at the Indianapolis Motor Speedway -- a motorcycle event in 1909. In 1933, he drove from New York to Los Angeles, covering the 3,224 miles in 53.5 hours, an accomplishment which would stand for decades. On that trip, he slept only 30 minutes.

A successor to the Commissioner's post was not named until November, when NASCAR President Bill France gave the nod to Harley J. Earl, former Vice-President of General Motors.

On the competitive side of the ledger, nine superspeedway races were staged, producing nine different winners. Six of the victors had never won on a high-banked oval before. Score one for parity.

Rex White won the Grand National driving championship by 3,936 points over runner-up Richard Petty. White won six of the 44 races -- no other driver won as many -- and bagged a record $57,524.85 including point money.

Race No. 1

Smith Laps Field in Caution-Filled Charlotte Race

CHARLOTTE, NC (Nov 8, 1959) -- Jack Smith, the 'Red Fox' out of Sandy Springs, GA, outdueled Bob Welborn and dodged a rash of caution flags to win the 100-mile 1960 Grand National season opener at the Charlotte Fairgrounds.

Smith, driving his Bud Moore Garage Chevrolet, finished a lap and a half ahead of Welborn to post his 12th career win on NASCAR's premier stock car racing tour. Buck Baker came in third after losing four laps in the pits to repair damage received in a tangle with Richard Petty. Baker and Petty swapped sheet metal in the 109th lap.

Fourth place went to Roy Tyner and Speedy Thompson was fifth.

California driver Scotty Cain escaped serious injury when his T-Bird burst into flames on the backstretch in the 124th lap. Although 10 minutes were required to extinguish the blaze, Cain suffered only minor burns.

A crowd of 6,000 watched the lead change hands six times among four drivers. Smith grabbed first place in the 134th lap and led the rest of the way.

Marvin Panch led twice for 24 laps, but the Oakland, CA native crashed his Ford after 66 laps. He wound up 22nd in the 28 car field.

Smith averaged 52.409 mph as eight caution flags broke the action.

Grand National Race No. 1
200 Laps at Charlotte Fairgrounds
Charlotte, NC
100 Miles on Half-mile Dirt Track
November 8, 1959

Fin	St	No.	Driver	Team / Car	Laps	Money	Status
1	3	47	Jack Smith	Bud Moore Gar '59 Chevrolet	200	$800	Running
2	8	22	Bob Welborn	Ogden-Ridgeway '59 Chevy	199	525	Running
3	1	87	Buck Baker	Baker '59 Chevrolet	198	375	Running
4	14	9	Roy Tyner	Tyner '57 Chevrolet	196	275	Running
5	19	2	Speedy Thompson	Bruce Thompson '57 Chevy	193	250	Running
6	18	31	Brownie King	Jess Potter '57 Chevrolet	189	215	Running
7	10	42	Lee Petty	Petty Eng '59 Plymouth	188	175	Running
8	23	62	Buck Brigance	'57 Chevrolet	187	150	Running
9	7	20	Tiny Lund	'58 Ford	187	140	Running
10	4	59	Tom Pistone	Rupert Safety Blt '59 T-Bird	183	130	Engine
11	20	34	G C Spencer	'57 Chevrolet	177	125	Running
12	13	43	Richard Petty	Petty Eng '59 Plymouth	174	110	Axle
13	15	77	Joe Lee Johnson	Honest Charley '59 Chevrolet	172	100	Rear End
14	27	15	Rex White	'57 Ford	172	85	Running
15	24	32	Richard Riley	Jess Potter '57 Chevrolet	172	70	Running
16	17	64	Shep Langdon	Langdon '58 Ford	168	60	Engine
17	11	45	Bobby Waddell	'57 Pontiac	168	50	Running
18	21	3	Scotty Cain	'59 T-Bird	99	50	Eng Fire
19	28	49	Jim Paschal	'57 Chevrolet	98	50	Heating
20	25	46	Barney Shore	'57 Chevrolet	93	50	Crash
21	6	36	Tommy Irwin	Irwin '59 T-Bird	84	50	Rear End
22	2	98	Marvin Panch	Tom Vernon '59 Ford	66	50	Crash
23	16	5	Bunk Moore	'57 Chevrolet	66	---	Engine
24	26	68	Bud Parnell	'58 Plymouth	57	---	Axle
25	22	17	Fred Harb	Harb '57 Ford	56	---	Crash
26	9	38	Ned Jarrett	Jarrett '57 Ford	50	---	Rear End
27	12	88	Buddy Baker	Buck Baker '59 Chevrolet	34	---	Fuel Tank
28	5	11	Junior Johnson	Paul Spaulding '59 Dodge	11	---	Heating

Time of Race: 1 hour, 54 minutes, 29 seconds
Average Speed: 52.409 mph
Pole Winner: Buck Baker - 64.103 mph
Lap Leaders: Marvin Panch 1-9, Buck Baker 10-17, Panch 18-30, Baker 31-57,
   Bob Welborn 58-133, Jack Smith 134-200
Cautions: 8
Margin of Victory: 1.5 laps
Attendance: 6,000

Grand National Race No. 2
200 Laps at Columbia Speedway
Columbia, SC
100 Miles on Half-mile Dirt Track
November 26, 1959

Fin	St	No.	Driver	Team / Car	Laps	Money	Status
1	3	38	Ned Jarrett	Jarrett '57 Ford	200	$800	Running
2	7	47	Jack Smith	Bud Moore Gar '59 Chevy	200	525	Running
3	2	77	Joe Lee Johnson	Honest Charley '59 Chevrolet	200	375	Running
4	5	42	Lee Petty	Petty Eng '59 Plymouth	200	275	Running
5	13	72	Bobby Johns	Shorty Johns '57 Chevrolet	195	250	Running
6	6	43	Richard Petty	Petty Eng '59 Plymouth	190	215	Running
7	22	64	Shep Langdon	Langdon '58 Ford	189	175	Running
8	9	74	L D Austin	Austin '58 Chevrolet	183	150	Running
9	16	58	Pappy Crane	'59 Chevrolet	181	140	Running
10	12	32	Richard Riley	Jess Potter '57 Chevrolet	179	130	Running
11	18	19	Herman Beam	Beam '57 Chevrolet	166	125	Running
12	20	9	Roy Tyner	Tyner '57 Chevrolet	158	110	Crash
13	17	68	Bill Parnell	'58 Plymouth	158	100	Running
14	21	2	Bunk Moore	Bruce Thompson '57 Chevy	147	85	Running
15	4	34	G C Spencer	'59 Chevrolet	134	70	Diff
16	15	62	Buck Brigance	'57 Chevrolet	110	60	Engine
17	14	36	Tommy Irwin	Irwin '57 Chevrolet	108	50	Crash
18	10	7	Hubert Johnson	'57 Chevrolet	105	50	Crash
19	1	11	Junior Johnson	Paul Spaulding '59 Dodge	87	50	Carb
20	11	59	Tom Pistone	Rupert Safety Blt '59 T-Bird	85	50	Springs
21	19	5	Tiny Lund	'57 Chevrolet	54	50	Gener
22	8	22	Bob Welborn	Ogden-Ridgeway '59 Chevy	0	50	Crash

Time of Race: 1 hour, 48 minutes, 57 seconds
Average Speed: 55.071 mph
Pole Winner: Junior Johnson - 65.217 mph
Lap Leaders: - - - - - - - - - - - - - - - Ned Jarrett   -200
Cautions:
Margin of Victory:
Attendance:

Race No. 2

Jarrett Triumphs in Columbia 100

COLUMBIA, SC (Nov 26, 1959) -- Ned Jarrett of Conover, NC drove his Ford to a close victory over Jack Smith and won the 100-miler at Columbia Speedway. It was Jarrett's third career win.

The first four cars finished all 200 laps on the half-mile dirt track. Joe Lee Johnson, 1959 Convertible champ, wound up third with Lee Petty fourth. Fifth place finisher Bobby Johns was five laps in arrears.

Johnson, of Chattanooga, TN, was the 1959 Convertible titlist in its last year of existence. NASCAR officials expressed hope that the Grand National circuit would attract more entries.

Junior Johnson started on the pole in his Dodge, but carburetor trouble knocked him out after 87 laps. It was the first time a Dodge automobile had been on the pole in a Grand National event since 1956.

Wrecks took out a number of contenders. Bob Welborn, driving the Ogden-Ridgeway Chevrolet, crashed in the first lap. Tommy Irwin and Roy Tyner were kayoed with wrecks as was rookie Hubert Johnson.

Jarrett averaged 55.071 mph after starting third in his Ford.

Race No. 3

Roberts Wins Daytona Qualifier; Irwin Lands in Lake

DAYTONA BEACH, FL (Feb 12) -- Fireball Roberts pushed his John Hines Pontiac into the lead in the opening lap and led all the way to win the 100-mile Grand National qualifying race at Daytona International Speedway. It was the 22nd career victory for the hometown throttle stomper.

Cotton Owens wound up second, only one second behind Roberts. Third place went to former USAC champion Fred Lorenzen, who announced his intentions of coming South for the 1960 stock car racing season. Joe Weatherly picked up fourth place money and Junior Johnson finished fifth.

A wild first lap collision sent sophomore driver Tommy Irwin's T-Bird nose first into Lake Lloyd.

Herman Beam forgot to put on his helmet before racing at Daytona

Gene White, Dave Hirshfield and Irwin locked horns coming off the second turn in the first lap. Irwin shot through the infield, catapulted over the dirt embankment and was nearly completely submerged in the lake. He swam to safety.

Roberts averaged 137.614 mph as five laps were run under the caution flag.

Grand National Race No. 3
40 Laps at Daytona International Speedway
Daytona Beach, FL
100 Miles on 2.5-mile Paved Track
February 12, 1960

Fin	St	No.	Driver	Team / Car	Laps	Money	Status
1	2	22	Fireball Roberts	John Hines '60 Pontiac	40	$1,000	Running
2	1	6	Cotton Owens	Owens '60 Pontiac	40	600	Running
3	16	28	Fred Lorenzen	Lorenzen '60 Ford	40	400	Running
4	15	12	Joe Weatherly	Holman Moody '60 Ford	40	300	Running
5	13	27	Junior Johnson	John Masoni '59 Chevy	40	275	Running
6	24	69	Johnny Allen	Hanley Dawson '60 Chevrolet	40	250	Running
7	3	52	Bob Burdick	Roy Burdick Gar '60 Ford	40	200	Running
8	17	85	Emanuel Zervakis	Monroe Shook '60 Chevrolet	39	175	Running
9	23	94	Speedy Thompson	Banjo Matthews '59 T-Bird	39	150	Running
10	43	43	Richard Petty	Petty Eng '60 Plymouth	39	140	Running
11	12	39	Herb Tillman	Ralph Stark '60 Chevrolet	39	135	Running
12	31	66	Dick Foley	Foley '59 Chevrolet	39	125	Running
13	14	61	Joe Caspolich	Doc White '59 T-Bird	39	115	Running
14	29	34	G C Spencer	'59 Chevrolet	39	100	Running
15	6	87	Buck Baker	Baker '60 Chevrolet	39	85	Running
16	19	63	Whitey Gerkin	Frank Skinner '59 Pontiac	38	75	Running
17	20	67	David Pearson	Pearson '59 Chevrolet	38	50	Running
18	22	35	Mel Larson	Sun City '60 Pontiac	38	50	Running
19	25	1	Brownie King	Faircloth '60 Chevrolet	38	50	Running
20	36	88	Red Farmer	'60 Ford	38	50	Running
21	10	60	Jim Whitman	Dick Stanley '60 Dodge	38	50	Running
22	21	8	Dick Dixon	Ray Boynton '60 Chevrolet	37	50	Running
23	37	78	Roy Tyner	E C Wilson '60 Chevrolet	37	50	Running
24	34	50	Dick Freeman	Freeman '60 Ford	36	50	Running
25	8	33	Reb Wickersham	Wickersham '60 Olds	35	---	Running
26	27	98	Marvin Panch	Air Port Automotive '60 Ford	34	---	Hood
27	4	77	Joe Lee Johnson	Billie Ridgeway '60 Ford	33	100	Tire
28	30	2	Dave Hirshfield	Lloyd Chick '69 Buick	29	---	Crash
29	26	45	Tiny Lund	Bill Gazaway '69 Olds	21	---	
30	18	76	Larry Frank	Thor '59 Chevrolet	13	---	Drv shft
31	28	44	Bill Lutz	Bob Chapman '60 Ford	13	---	
32	7	13	Harold Smith	Damon Leonard '60 Plymouth	11	---	
33	11	24	Arnold Gardner	Harry Huhn '60 Ford	10	---	
34	35	18	Fritz Wilson	Wilson '60 Ford	9	---	Engine
35	9	79	Harold McCann	Robert Ranney '59 T-Bird	8	---	
36	32	41	Gene White	'60 Ford	0	---	Crash
37	33	36	Tommy Irwin	Irwin '59 T-Bird	0	---	Crash

Time of Race: 45 minutes, 32 seconds
Average Speed: 137.614 mph
Pole Winner: Cotton Owens - 149.892 mph
Fastest Qualifier: Fireball Roberts - 151.556 mph
Lap Leaders: Fireball Roberts 1-40
Cautions: 2 for 5 laps
Margin of Victory: 1 second
Attendance: 12,500

Race No. 4

Smith Sizzles in Daytona 100

DAYTONA BEACH, FL (Feb 12) -- Jack Smith set a sizzling record of 146.520 mph in winning the second 100-mile qualifying race at Daytona International Speedway. It was the second win of the season for the Pontiac driver.

Bobby Johns wound up second, 2.0 seconds behind Smith. Third place went to Jim Reed, Rex White was fourth and Bob Welborn fifth.

Smith set the 100-mile race record despite a pair of

Lee Petty leads Ned Jarrett on Daytona's high banks

short caution periods when two cars spun out. John Rostek spun out on lap six which brought out the yellow flag for only one lap. Johnny Dodd, Jr. crashed into the wall on lap 15 forcing another single lap caution.

Herman Beam of Johnson City, TN had the dubious distinction of being the first driver to be black-flagged from a race at Daytona. The "Turtle" *forgot* to put on his safety helmet and had run eight laps before NASCAR officials noticed he had left the head gear in the pits.

Twenty-nine cars in the starting field of 40 finished the race before a crowd of 12,500 fans.

Curtis Turner and Johnny Beauchamp, both driving Holman-Moody Fords, crashed in separate incidents which did not bring out the yellow flag. Neither driver was injured

Smith led the entire 40 laps from the pole. It was the 13th win of his career.

Grand National Race No. 4
40 Laps at Daytona International Speedway
Daytona Beach, FL
100 Miles on 2.5-mile Paved Track
February 12, 1960

Fin	St	No.	Driver	Team / Car	Laps	Money	Status
1	1	47	Jack Smith	Boomershine '60 Pontiac	40	$1,000	Running
2	2	3	Bobby Johns	Jim Stephens '59 Pontiac	40	600	Running
3	17	7	Jim Reed	Reed '60 Chevrolet	40	400	Running
4	16	4	Rex White	Piedmont/Friendly '60 Chevy	40	300	Running
5	22	49	Bob Welborn	Welborn '60 Chevrolet	40	275	Running
6	12	48	Darrell Dake	Weldon Wagner '60 Chevy	40	250	Running
7	3	42	Lee Petty	Petty Eng '60 Plymouth	40	200	Running
8	30	71	Gene Marmor	'59 Pontiac	39	175	Running
9	6	73	Bud Burdick	Roy Burdick '59 T-Bird	39	150	Running
10	7	29	Bob Potter	Potter '60 Chevrolet	39	140	Running
11	15	93	Banjo Matthews	Sunbeam Systems '59 T-Bird	39	135	Running
12	27	70	Elmo Henderson	W H Watson '58 Pontiac	39	125	Running
13	35	15	Johnny Sudderth	Beau Morgan '60 Ford	39	115	Running
14	14	64	Shep Langdon	Bobby Langdon '60 Ford	39	100	Running
15	8	16	Dick Joslin	Happy Stiegel '59 Pontiac	39	85	Running
16	21	52	Salvatore Tovella	Frank Filizer '60 Ford	38	75	Running
17	5	56	Ken Johnson	Charles French '60 Chevrolet	38	50	Running
18	9	30	Bob Kosiske	Joe Kosiske '59 T-Bird	38	50	Running
19	19	54	Jim Pardue	Lowe's '59 Dodge	38	50	Running
20	13	51	Burrhead Nantz	Roy McDonald '59 Olds	38	50	Running
21	29	95	Bob Duell	Julian Buesink '60 Ford	38	50	Running
22	33	97	Parnelli Jones	Vel Miletich '60 Ford	38	50	Running
23	34	32	George Green	Jess Potter '58 Chevrolet	37	50	Running
24	36	25	Tommy Herbert	Don Angel '59 T-Bird	37	50	Running
25	28	99	Wilbur Rakestraw	Talmadge Cochrane '60 Ford	37	---	Running
26	4	59	Tom Pistone	Thor '60 Chevrolet	36	---	Pulley
27	24	74	L D Austin	Austin '58 Chevrolet	36	---	Running
28	37	14	Paul Parks	Parks '60 Ford	36	---	Running
29	38	38	Eddie Gray	Charles Chapman '60 Ford	36	---	Running
30	26	9	Carl Burris	A J Blackwelder '60 Ford	35	---	Running
31	20	26	Curtis Turner	Holman-Moody '60 Ford	26	---	Crash
32	11	10	Elmo Langley	Ratus Walters '59 Buick	26	---	Heating
33	25	31	Johnny Beauchamp	Holman-Moody '60 Ford	19	---	Crash
34	32	90	Runt Harris	Junie Donlavey '60 Ford	15	---	
35	18	11	Ned Jarrett	Jarrett '60 Ford	14	---	Crash
36	34	75	John Dodd Jr	Dodd '60 Ford	14	---	Crash
37	39	19	Herman Beam	Beam '60 Ford	8	---	Flagged
38	23	92	Charley Griffith	Robert Davis '59 T-Bird	8	---	
39	10	96	John Rostek	Rostek '60 Ford	5	---	Crash
40	40	86	Johnny Dollar	M DeMatthews '60 Chevrolet	5	---	Engine

Time of Race: 40 minutes, 57 seconds
Average Speed: 146.520 mph
Pole Winner: Jack Smith - 148.157
Lap Leaders: Jack Smith 1-40
Cautions: 2 for 2 laps
Margin of Victory: 2 seconds
Attendance: 12,500

Tommy Irwin's T-Bird wound up in Lake Lloyd during Daytona's 100 miler

Grand National Race No. 5
200 Laps at Daytona International Speedway
Daytona Beach, FL
"Daytona 500"
500 Miles on 2.5-mile Paved Track
February 14, 1960

Fin	St	No.	Driver	Team / Car	Laps	Money	Status
1	9	27	Junior Johnson	John Masoni '59 Chevy	200	$19,600	Running
2	4	3	Bobby Johns	Jim Stephens '59 Pontiac	200	8,600	Running
3	19	43	Richard Petty	Petty Eng '60 Plymouth	200	6,450	Running
4	14	42	Lee Petty	Petty Eng '60 Plymouth	200	3,650	Running
5	11	69	Johnny Allen	Hanley Dawson '60 Chevrolet	199	3,300	Running
6	54	11	Ned Jarrett	Jarrett '60 Ford	199	2,075	Running
7	53	26	Curtis Turner	Holman-Moody '60 Ford	199	1,650	Running
8	5	28	Fred Lorenzen	Lorenzen '60 Ford	198	1,150	Running
9	8	4	Rex White	Piedmont/Friendly '60 Chevy	198	925	Running
10	15	85	Emanuel Zervakis	Monroe Shook '60 Chevrolet	197	800	Running
11	18	73	Bud Burdick	Roy Burdick Gar '59 T-Bird	197	600	Running
12	52	59	Tom Pistone	Thor '60 Chevrolet	196	500	Crash
13	10	49	Bob Welborn	Welborn '60 Chevrolet	195	400	Running
14	6	7	Jim Reed	Reed '60 Chevrolet	195	350	Running
15	20	29	Bob Potter	Potter '60 Chevrolet	195	350	Running
16	12	48	Darrell Dake	Weldon Wagner '60 Chevy	195	325	Running
17	31	63	Whitey Gerkin	Frank Skinner '59 Pontiac	195	325	Running
18	29	87	Buck Baker	Baker '60 Chevrolet	194	300	Running
19	22	93	Banjo Matthews	Sunbeam Systems '59 T-Bird	193	375	Running
20	28	64	Shep Langdon	Bobby Langdon '60 Ford	192	300	Running
21	38	54	Jimmy Pardue	Lowe's '59 Dodge	192	200	Running
22	60	76	Larry Frank	Thor '59 Chevrolet	191	200	Running
23	2	47	Jack Smith	Boomershine '60 Pontiac	191	900	Running
24	50	99	Wilbur Rakestraw	Talmadge Cochrane '60 Ford	189	200	Running
25	25	61	Joe Caspolich	Doc White '50 T-Bird	188	200	Running
26	61	41	Gene White	'60 Ford	187	200	Running
27	34	56	Ken Johnson	Charles French '60 Ford	186	200	Running
28	33	67	David Pearson	Pearson '59 Chevrolet	185	200	Running
29	16	71	Gene Marmor	'59 Pontiac	184	200	Running
30	37	1	Brownie King	Faircloth '60 Chevrolet	183	200	Running
31	27	34	G C Spencer	'59 Chevrolet	183	200	Running
32	62	19	Herman Beam	Beam '60 Ford	175	200	Running
33	49	33	Reb Wickersham	Wickersham '60 Olds	175	700	Running
34	63	74	L D Austin	Austin '58 Chevrolet	175	100	Running
35	30	16	Dick Joslin	Happy Stiegel '59 Pontiac	171	200	Running
36	35	35	Mel Larson	Sun City '60 Pontiac	166	275	Running
37	65	14	Paul Parks	Parks '60 Ford	164	200	Running
38	56	24	Arnold Gardner	Harry Huhn '60 Ford	160	300	Running
39	21	39	Herb Tillman	Ralph Stark '60 Chevrolet	155	200	Running
40	1	6	Cotton Owens	Owens '60 Pontiac	149	200	Trans
41	7	12	Joe Weatherly	Holman-Moody '60 Ford	146	300	Crnk Sh
42	43	8	Dick Dixon	Ray Boynton '60 Chevrolet	144	200	
43	45	78	Roy Tyner	E C Wilson '60 Chevrolet	143	200	Crash
44	36	30	Bob Kosiske	Joe Kosiske '59 T-Bird	125	200	
45	48	25	Tommy Herbert	Don Angel '60 Ford	118	200	Crash
46	51	98	Marvin Panch	Air Port Auto '60 Ford	117	300	Oil Leak
47	41	60	Jim Whitman	Dick Stanley '60 Dodge	116	700	Engine
48	26	15	Johnny Sudderth	Beau Morgan '60 Ford	110	200	Engine
49	59	13	Harold Smith	Damon Leonard '60 Plymouth	94	200	Engine
50	67	58	Pappy Crane	Monty Walden '59 Chevrolet	89	200	Crash
51	64	45	Tiny Lund	Bill Gazaway '60 Olds	83	100	Steering
52	55	10	Elmo Langley	Ratus Walters '59 Buick	77	275	Crnk Sh
53	58	44	Bill Lutz	Bob Chapman '60 Ford	75	250	Engine
54	44	97	Parnelli Jones	Vel Miletich '60 Ford	73	200	Engine
55	46	32	George Green	Jess Potter '58 Chevrolet	67	200	Fire
56	39	88	Red Farmer	'60 Ford	65	200	
57	3	22	Fireball Roberts	John Hines '60 Pontiac	51	400	Engine
58	42	95	Bob Duell	Julian Buesink '60 Ford	50	200	Engine
59	24	70	Elmo Henderson	W H Watson '58 Pontiac	31	200	
60	13	53	Bob Burdick	Roy Burdick Gar '60 Ford	31	275	
61	23	66	Richard Foley	Foley '59 Chevrolet	30	200	
62	17	94	Speedy Thompson	Banjo Matthews '60 Ford	28	200	Engine
63	66	2	Dave Hirschfield	Lloyd Chick '60 Buick	21	100	Axle
64	57	77	Joe Lee Johnson	Billie Ridgeway '60 Ford	18	200	Engine
65	68	92	Charley Griffith	Robert Davis '60 Ford	14	100	
66	40	51	Burrhead Nantz	Roy McDonald '59 Olds	11	200	Clutch
67	32	52	Sal Tovella	Frank Kilizer '60 Ford	5	200	Engine
68	47	50	Richard Freeman	Freeman '60 Ford	5	200	

Race No. 5

Johns Spins; Johnson Wins Daytona 500

DAYTONA BEACH, FL (Feb 14) -- Robert "Junior" Johnson, the well-fed mountain kid from Ronda, NC, took advantage of Bobby Johns' freak mishap and swept to first place honors in the second annual Daytona 500-mile International Sweepstakes.

Johnson and his Daytona Kennel Club Chevrolet motored past the spinning Johns in the 192nd lap and cruised to a 23 second victory.

Johns recovered from his spin off the second turn, which did not bring out the caution flag, and managed to salvage second place. Richard Petty came in third, just ahead of his dad, Lee Petty. Johnny Allen finished fifth, one lap back.

Johns had taken the lead for the first time on the brisk, sunny afternoon in the 172nd lap and appeared to be on his way to victory when an unusual incident took place. As the Miami Pontiac driver was nursing a seven second lead, a wind pocket sucked the rear window out of Johns' car and he looped in the second turn. Johns skidded to within a matter of inches of Lake Lloyd, and Johnson raced into the lead.

Johnson averaged 124.740 mph in the wreck-

Eventual Daytona 500 winner Junior Johnson #27 ducks under rookie David Pearson #67

Time of Race: 4 hours, 30 seconds
Average Speed: 124.740 mph
Pole Winner: Cotton Owens - 149.892 mph
Fastest Qualifier: Fireball Roberts - 151.556 mph
Lap Leaders: Fireball Roberts 1-19, Jack Smith 20-28, Junior Johnson 29-36, Smith 37-41, Johnson 42-46, Lee Petty 47-54, Tom Pistone 55-80, Rex White 81-89, Johnson 90-134, Richard Petty 135-163, L Petty 164-169, Bobby Johns 170-191, Johnson 192-200
Cautions: ? for 32 laps
Margin of Victory: 23 seconds
Attendance: 38,775

Five wide on the short chute in Daytona International Speedway's Daytona 500

marred 500 miler and collected $19,600 for his first place efforts. Two drivers were injured in the event, and 32 laps were run under the yellow flag. Tommy Herbert of Miami crashed his T-Bird into the back stretch guard rail in the 118th lap and flipped, utterly destroying the car. The engine was ripped from the chassis and flew down the pavement as the front end assembly shot nearly 75 feet in the air. Pappy Crane spun to avoid Herbert and the debris flipped his Chevrolet. Herbert suffered a mangled right arm and a severe eye injury. Crane was unhurt.

Ray Fox and Junior Johnson in Daytona victory lane

Tom Pistone, who led for 26 laps, lost control of his Chevrolet in the 198th lap and rapped the wall in the fourth turn. Pistone suffered a concussion, a broken collar bone and internal injuries.

George Green's Chevrolet caught fire in the tri-oval when his fuel tank burst. The sergeant, based out of Frankfurt, Germany, calmly drove his fiery car to the safety apron and leaped out.

Johnson's car owner, John Masoni of Cleveland, gave all the net earnings to charity, claiming that "we're in this racing game for fun, not profit."

There were so many torn up race cars that NASCAR officials were forced to cancel the next two scheduled Grand National events for fear of car shortages. The 100-milers at Palmetto Speedway in Miami and Hollywood Speedway in Hallandale were taken off the 1960 slate.

Johnny Allen #69 passes Jimmy Pardue #54 en route to 5th place in Daytona 500

Race No. 6

Richard Petty Grabs First GN Win at Charlotte

CHARLOTTE, NC (Feb 28) -- Richard Petty, 22 year-old second generation driver, grabbed his first Grand National win with a big assist from his papa Lee in the 100-miler at the Charlotte Fairgrounds.

Petty pushed his Plymouth around Rex White with 18 laps to go and won by six car lengths. Lee Petty, driving in relief of Doug Yates, popped White's Chevrolet as he challenged young Richard on lap 187. White nearly spun out as Richard hustled to the checkered flag.

Yates got credit for finishing third, point leader Junior Johnson was fourth in the Wood Brothers Ford and Joe Eubanks came in fifth.

Young Petty started seventh on the grid and kept the leaders in sight for the entire 200 laps on the half-mile dirt oval.

Attrition took out many of the top qualifiers. Pole sitter Lee Petty went out after 38 laps with fouled spark plugs. Second fastest qualifier Buck Baker lost an en-

Safety workers try to free Johnny Beauchamp's Ford from muddy infield at Charlotte Fairgrounds

gine in his Chevrolet. Johnny Beauchamp, who started third, wound up in a muddy ditch when he crashed his Holman-Moody Ford in the 83rd lap. Joe Lee Johnson and Tom Pistone were kayoed by mechanical problems.

Only seven cars in the starting field of 21 finished the event on the rough and choppy half-mile dirt surface.

Petty won $800 for his 53.404 mph victory, witnessed by a crowd of 7,849. Afterwards Petty said he planned his strategy. "I saw Rex hit a big bump as we

came out of the first turn," said Richard from victory lane. "That was my chance to get under him at the bend of the turn."

Lee admitted to questioning that, "I didn't hurt his (Richard's) chances", when he nearly took White out of the race in the late stages.

The pace lap at Charlotte Fairgrounds. Richard Petty won his first Grand National race in the final NASCAR event at the half-mile dirt oval

Grand National Race No. 6
200 Laps at Charlotte Fairgrounds Charlotte, NC
100 Miles on Half-mile Dirt Track
February 28, 1960

Fin	St	No.	Driver	Team / Car	Laps	Money	Status
1	7	43	Richard Petty	Petty Eng '59 Plymouth	200	$800	Running
2	6	4	Rex White	Piedmont/ Friendly '59 Chevy	200	525	Running
3	10	23	Doug Yates *	Yates '59 Plymouth	199	375	Running
4	8	21	Junior Johnson	Wood Brothers '59 Ford	198	275	Running
5	13	82	Joe Eubanks	'59 Chevrolet	193	250	Running
6	11	78	Roy Tyner	E C Wilson '59 Chevrolet	192	215	Running
7	15	54	Jimmy Pardue	Lowe's '59 Dodge	178	175	Axle
8	14	92	Gerald Duke	Robert Davis '59 T-Bird	167	150	Rear End
9	5	59	Tom Pistone	Thor '59 Chevrolet	144	140	Distrib
10	18	19	Herman Beam	Beam '60 Ford	141	130	Running
11	12	11	Ned Jarrett	Courtesy Ford '60 Ford	138	125	Rear End
12	17	32	George Green	Jess Potter '58 Chevrolet	133	110	Rear End
13	2	87	Buck Baker	Baker '60 Chevrolet	118	100	Engine
14	20	30	Cale Yarborough	'58 Ford	114	85	Rear End
15	9	67	David Pearson	Pearson '59 Chevrolet	84	70	Rear End
16	3	31	Johnny Beauchamp	Holman-Moody '60 Ford	83	60	Crash
17	4	77	Joe Lee Johnson	Billie Ridgeway '60 Ford	74	50	H Gasket
18	21	14	Paul Parks	Parks '60 Ford	73	50	Heating
20	19	68	Bill Parnell	R L Baird '58 Plymouth	66	50	Rear End
20	1	42	Lee Petty	Petty Eng '60 Plymouth	38	150	Plugs
21	16	64	Bunkie Blackburn	A M Crawford '58 Ford	8	50	A Frame

* Relieved by Lee Petty
Time of Race: 1 hour, 52 minutes, 21 seconds
Average Speed: 53.404 mph
Pole Winner: Lee Petty - 62.11 mph
Lap Leaders: - - - - - - - Rex White -182, Richard Petty 183-200
Cautions:
Margin of Victory: 6 car lengths
Attendance: 7,849

Grand National Race No. 7
160 Laps at N. Wilkesboro Speedway
North Wilkesboro, NC
100 Miles on .625-mile Paved Track
March 27, 1960

Fin	St	No.	Driver	Team / Car	Laps	Money	Status
1	8	42	Lee Petty	Petty Eng '60 Plymouth	160	$900	Running
2	6	4	Rex White	Piedmont/Friendly '59 Chevy	160	525	Running
3	2	21	Glen Wood	Wood Brothers '59 Ford	160	375	Running
4	3	11	Ned Jarrett	Courtesy '60 Ford	160	275	Running
5	1	27	Junior Johnson	John Masoni '59 Chevy	160	250	Running
6	11	23	Doug Yates	Yates '59 Plymouth	160	215	Running
7	21	78	Roy Tyner	E C Wilson '59 Chevrolet	159	175	Running
8	15	54	Jimmy Pardue	Lowe's '59 Dodge	158	150	Running
9	18	1	Buddy Baker	Faircloth '59 Chevrolet	158	140	Running
10	7	31	Joe Weatherly	Holman-Moody '60 Ford	157	130	Running
11	13	74	L D Austin	Austin '58 Chevrolet	155	125	Running
12	20	32	Paul Lewis	Jess Potter '58 Chevrolet	149	110	Running
13	14	64	Bunkie Blackburn	A M Crawford '58 Ford	149	100	Running
14	5	87	Buck Baker	Baker '60 Chevrolet	144	85	Engine
15	22	35	E J Trivette	'58 Plymouth	142	70	Running
16	12	50	Cotton Owens	Richard Freeman '60 Ford	137	60	Rear End
17	9	94	Banjo Matthews	Matthews '59 Ford	127	50	Crash
18	4	43	Richard Petty	Petty Eng '59 Plymouth	125	50	Engine
19	17	67	David Pearson	Pearson '59 Chevrolet	18	50	Crash
20	16	51	Burrhead Nantz	Roy McDonald '59 Olds	17	50	Handling
21	19	80	Neil Castles	Castles '58 Ford	14	50	Engine
22	10	77	Joe Lee Johnson	Billie Ridgeway '60 Ford	9	50	Oil Press

Time of Race: 1 hour, 30 minutes, 26 seconds
Average Speed: 66.347 mph
Pole Winner: Junior Johnson - 83.86 mph
Lap Leaders: Glen Wood 1, Junior Johnson 2-146, Lee Petty 147-160
Cautions: 6
Margin of Victory:
Attendance: 9,200

Race No. 7

Lee Petty Beats Junior Johnson in Wilkesboro Slugfest

N WILKESBORO, NC (Mar 27) -- After five cancellations in the last six races, the Grand National tour finally got back into action with the touring pros engaging in a mechanical slugfest at North Wilkesboro Speedway.

Lee Petty spun Junior Johnson from the lead with 14 laps to go and won the 100-miler at the .625-mile paved oval. The 45 year-old Randleman, NC pilot faced his toughest challenge immediately after the finish of the 160 lapper when Johnson supporters pelted the three-time champion with rocks, bottles and items

that fit all descriptions.

Most of the 9,200 spectators who attended the race in the Carolina mountains, only a stone's throw from the Johnson garage, were incensed when Petty shoved leader Johnson into the guard rail in the closing stages. The winner grabbed the microphone and pleaded his case with the huge throng, only to be pelted again with miscellaneous debris amid a roar of jeers.

Rex White finished second and later remarked, "Something's got to be done. The Old Man (Lee Petty) is getting rougher and rougher. If this sort of thing keeps up, there is going to be a lot of equipment torn up and some drivers badly hurt."

Glen Wood finished third, Ned Jarrett was fourth and Johnson fifth. Johnson led for 145 laps.

Veteran Banjo Matthews and rookie David Pearson were taken out by wrecks.

Six caution flags held Petty's winning speed to 66.347 mph.

The victory was Petty's 49th of his career, making him the Grand National all-time leader, passing the retired Herb Thomas.

Grand National Race No. 8
100 Laps at Arizona State Fairgrounds
Phoenix, AZ
"Copper Cup Championship"
100 Miles on 1 Mile Dirt Track
April 3, 1960

Fin	St	No.	Driver	Team / Car	Laps	Money	Status
1		19	John Rostek	Rostek '58 Ford	100	$800	Running
2	1	35	Mel Larson	Sun City '60 Pontiac	100	525	Running
3		4	Scotty Cain	'59 T-Bird	97	375	Running
4		48	Fritz Wilson	'58 Ford	95	275	Running
5		44	Lloyd Dane	'59 Ford	95	250	Running
6		97	Parnelli Jones	Vel Miletich '60 Ford	93	215	Running
7		91	Bruce Worrell	'59 Plymouth	91	175	Running
8		5	Jim Blomgren	'58 Ford	88	150	Tie Rod
9		26	Clyde Mitchell	'58 Ford	88	140	Running
10		6	Eddie Gray	'58 Ford	87	130	Crash
11		16	Danny Weinberg	'60 Ford	84	125	Fuel
12		2	Ron Hornaday	'60 Ford	75	110	Running
13		7	Don Noel	'59 Ford	66	100	Running
14		3	Dick Getty	'58 Mercury	57	85	Brakes
15		9	Bob Price	'59 Chevrolet	46	70	Fuel
16		55	Lyle Stelter	Stelter '58 Mercury	44	60	Fuel Pmp
17		23	Bob Perry	'59 Plymouth	33	50	A Frame
18	2	98	Marvin Porter	Porter '59 Ford	11	50	Oil Line
19		38	Bob Ross	'60 Ford	1	50	Drv Shft

Time of Race: 1 hour, 23 minutes, 27 seconds
Average Speed: 71.899 mph
Pole Winner: Mel Larson - 78.930 mph
Lap Leaders: Marvin Porter 1-11, Parnelli Jones 12-36, Mel Larson 37-42,
    John Rostek 43-100
Cautions:
Margin of Victory:
Attendance:

Race No. 8

John Rostek Drives Ford to Win at Phoenix

PHOENIX, AZ (Apr 3) -- John Rostek of Ft. Collins, CO surged past Mel Larson in the 43rd lap and went on to win the Copper Cup Championship 100-mile race at the Arizona State Fairgrounds. It was the first Grand National win of Rostek's career and it came in only his second start.

Larson started on the pole in his Sun City Pontiac, led for six laps and eventually finished second.

Scotty Cain finished third, Fritz Wilson was fourth and Lloyd Dane fifth.

Marvin Porter of Lakewood, California led the first 11 laps. He was leading when his Ford fell victim to a broken oil line. Parnelli Jones took the lead at that point and led until Larson retook the lead in the 37th lap.

Rostek muscled his way past Larson just short of the half-way point and led the rest of the way. He averaged 71.899 mph on the one-mile dirt oval.

Race No. 9

Rex White Nabs Columbia Flag

COLUMBIA, SC (Apr 5) -- Rex White of Silver Spring, MD snared his first win of the season in the 100-miler at Columbia Speedway to become the eighth different winner in the first nine races of the 1960 season.

White pushed his Chevrolet to a full lap win over runner-up Buck Baker. Doug Yates finished in third place, Lee Petty

Rex White

was fourth and Joe Lee Johnson fifth.

David Pearson, rookie driver out of Spartanburg, SC, continued to have his problems during his freshman year on the big league stock car racing circuit. Pearson started sixth, but crashed his Chevrolet in the 147th lap. Tommy Irwin filled in for the injured Tom Pistone in the Thor Chevrolet and finished seventh.

Joe Weatherly replaced Johnny Beauchamp in one of the Holman-Moody Fords, but crashed on lap 127 after qualifying second.

White averaged 50.697 mph for his eighth win.

Grand National Race No. 9
200 Laps at Columbia Speedway
Columbia, SC
100 Miles on Half-mile Dirt Track
April 5, 1960

Fin	St	No.	Driver	Team / Car	Laps	Money	Status
1	3	4	Rex White	Piedmont/Friendly '60 Chevy	200	$800	Running
2	11	87	Buck Baker	Baker '60 Chevrolet	199	525	Running
3	1	23	Doug Yates	Yates '59 Plymouth	199	375	Running
4	5	42	Lee Petty	Petty Eng '60 Plymouth	199	375	Running
5	8	78	Joe Lee Johnson	E C Wilson '59 Chevrolet	197	350	Running
6	7	43	Richard Petty	Petty Eng '59 Plymouth	196	215	Running
7	13	59	Tommy Irwin	Thor '60 Chevrolet	196	175	Running
8	4	27	Junior Johnson	John Masoni '59 Chevy	195	150	Running
9	14	48	G C Spencer	Weldon Wagner '59 Chevy	191	140	Running
10	12	64	Bunkie Blackburn	A M Crawford '58 Ford	189	130	Running
11	9	11	Ned Jarrett	Courtesy Ford '60 Ford	177	125	Axle
12	18	74	L D Austin	Austin '58 Chevrolet	172	110	Running
13	20	19	Herman Beam	Beam '60 Ford	159	100	Running
14	10	80	Neil Castles	Castles '58 Ford	149	85	Rear End
15	6	67	David Pearson	Pearson '59 Chevrolet	140	70	Crash
16	16	83	Curtis Crider	Crider '58 Ford	133	60	Heating
17	19	1	Buddy Baker	Faircloth '60 Chevrolet	129	50	Rkr Arm
18	2	31	Joe Weatherly	Holman-Moody '60 Ford	127	50	Crash
19	17	39	Bobby Johns	Ralph Stark '60 Chevrolet	57	50	Tires
20	21	82	Joe Eubanks	'59 Chevrolet	22	50	Crash
21	15	9	Roy Tyner	Tyner '59 Chevrolet	17	50	Carb

Time of Race: 1 hour, 58 minutes, 21 seconds
Average Speed: 50.697 mph
Pole Winner: Doug Yates - 66.03 mph
Lap Leaders: - - - - - - - - - - - - - - - Rex White   -200
Cautions:
Margin of Victory:
Attendance:

Race No. 10

Richard Petty Tops at Martinsville; Takes Point Lead

MARTINSVILLE, VA (Apr 10) -- Richard Petty breezed into the lead when Bobby Johns spun from first place and coasted to victory in the Virginia 500 at Martinsville Speedway. It was the second win of the season for the Randleman Rocket.

With his $3,340 triumph, Petty grabbed first place in the Grand National point standings, 50 points up on Junior Johnson who finished eighth.

Petty's Plymouth crossed the finish line a quarter lap ahead of runner-up Jimmy Massey's Ford. Glen Wood, Rex White and Bob Welborn rounded out the first five finishers.

Wood paced the opening 152 laps from his pole position. Following one of the day's eight caution periods, Wood pitted. White, Massey, Fred Lorenzen, Johns and Petty swapped the lead eight times before Petty assumed command for good.

Johns had led for 49 laps before spinning out for the second time in a major event. The Miami driver lost the Daytona 500 when he spun out with nine laps left. Johns eventually wound up 14th in the field of 37, falling out in the final stages with rear gearing failure.

Petty averaged 63.943 mph before a crowd of 12,500.

Grand National Race No. 10
500 Laps at Martinsville Speedway
Martinsville, VA
"Virginia 500"
250 Miles on Half-mile Paved Track
April 10, 1960

Fin	St	No.	Driver	Team / Car	Laps	Money	Status
1	4	43	Richard Petty	Petty Eng '60 Plymouth	500	$3,340	Running
2	2	21	Jimmy Massey	Wood Bros '58 Ford	500	1,535	Running
3	1	24	Glen Wood	Wood Bros '58 Ford	499	1,155	Running
4	7	4	Rex White	Piedmont/Friendly '60 Chevy	499	835	Running
5	23	49	Bob Welborn	Welborn '60 Chevrolet	495	650	Running
6	3	42	Lee Petty	Petty Eng '60 Plymouth	495	650	Running
7	12	69	Johnny Allen	Hanley Dawson '60 Chevy	495	425	Running
8	11	27	Junior Johnson	Daytona Kennel '59 Chevy	492	375	Running
9	6	85	Emanuel Zervakis	Monroe Shook '60 Chevy	491	300	Running
10	14	11	Ned Jarrett	Courtesy Ford '60 Ford	488	300	Running
11	28	71	Gene Marmor	'59 Pontiac	485	200	Running
12	8	29	Bob Potter	Potter '60 Chevrolet	474	150	Running
13	30	48	G C Spencer	Weldon Wagner '58 Chevy	471	135	Running
14	10	41	Bobby Johns	'59 Chevrolet	470	195	Rear End
15	32	55	Ernie Gahan	Gahan '59 Chevrolet	468	125	Rear End
16	5	31	Joe Weatherly	Holman-Moody '60 Ford	466	110	Rear End
17	25	39	Herb Tillman	Ralph Stark '60 Chevrolet	458	110	Running
18	9	28	Fred Lorenzen	Lorenzen '60 Ford	454	190	Engine
19	17	54	Jimmy Pardue	Lowe's '59 Dodge	448	100	Running
20	35	64	Bunkie Blackburn	A M Crawford '58 Ford	429	100	Running
21	33	32	Paul Lewis	Jess Potter '58 Chevrolet	400	100	Running
22	16	7	Jim Reed	Reed '60 Chevrolet	354	100	Engine
23	37	1	Buddy Baker	Faircloth '60 Chevrolet	335	90	Engine
24	29	99	Wilbur Rakestraw	Talmadge Cochrane '60 Ford	284	90	Crash
25	27	19	John Rostek	Rostek '58 Ford	284	85	RF Hub
26	24	87	Buck Baker	Baker '60 Chevrolet	230	80	Engine
27	13	10	Elmo Langley	Ratus Walters '59 Buick	229	75	Axle
28	34	24	Arnie Gardner	Harry Huba '60 Ford	187	75	Oil Pres
29	19	77	Joe Lee Johnson	Billie Ridgeway '60 Ford	155	175	Rear End
30	21	17	Fred Harb	Harb '58 Ford	155	75	Piston
31	26	70	Elmo Henderson	W H Watson '58 Pontiac	130	50	Axle
32	20	59	Tom Pistone	Thor '60 Chevrolet	102	50	RR seal
33	36	15	Aubrey Boles	'58 Plymouth	97	50	Engine
34	31	52	Pat Moore	'59 Ford	72	50	Engine
35	15	23	Doug Yates	Yates '59 Plymouth	70	50	Crash
36	18	95	Bob Duell	Julian Buesink '60 Ford	69	---	Crash
37	22	78	Tommy Irwin	E C Wilson '60 Chevrolet	59	---	Crash

Time of Race: 3 hours, 54 minutes, 35 seconds
Average Speed: 63.943 mph
Pole Winner: Glen Wood - 69.15 mph
Lap Leaders: Glen Wood 1-152, Rex White 153-184, Jimmy Massey 185-209, Fred Lorenzen 210-302, Wood 303-315, Richard Petty 316-333, Bobby Johns 334-382, Massey 383, R Petty 384-500
Cautions: 8
Margin of Victory: 1/4 lap
Attendance: 12,500

Grand National Race No 11
250 Laps at Hickory Speedway
Hickory, NC
100 Miles on .4-mile Dirt Track
April 15, 1960

Fin	St	No.	Driver	Team / Car	Laps	Money	Status
1	2	12	Joe Weatherly	Holman-Moody '60 Ford	250	$800	Running
2	5	11	Ned Jarrett	Courtesy Ford '60 Ford	250	525	Running
3	3	43	Richard Petty	Petty Eng '60 Plymouth	249	375	Running
4	12	49	Bob Welborn	Welborn '60 Chevrolet	247	275	Running
5	15	59	Tom Pistone	Thor '60 Chevrolet	246	250	Running
6	11	78	Joe Lee Johnson	E C Wilson '60 Chevrolet	246	315	Running
7	16	17	Fred Harb	Harb '58 Ford	240	175	Running
8	13	36	Tommy Irwin	Irwin '59 T-Bird	238	150	Running
9	14	80	Neil Castles	Castles '58 Ford	235	140	Running
10	18	79	James Norton	'58 Mercury	235	130	Running
11	8	42	Lee Petty	Petty Eng '60 Plymouth	233	225	Running
12	4	87	Buck Baker	Baker '60 Chevrolet	226	110	Running
13	20	19	Herman Beam	Beam '60 Ford	202	100	Running
14	1	4	Rex White	Piedmont/Friendly '59 Chevy	187	85	Rear End
15	17	64	Bunkie Blackburn	A M Crawford '58 Ford	183	70	Running
16	21	32	Paul Lewis	Jess Potter '58 Chevrolet	166	60	Rear End
17	23	1	Buddy Baker	Faircloth '58 Ford	95	50	Rear End
18	19	35	E J Trivette	'58 Plymouth	88	50	Ball Jnt
19	7	23	Doug Yates	Yates '59 Plymouth	85	50	Engine
20	9	48	G C Spencer	Weldon Wagner '58 Chevy	63	50	Engine
21	22	9	Roy Tyner	Tyner '58 Mercury	59	50	Drv Shft
22	6	54	Jimmy Pardue	Lowe's '59 Dodge	15	50	Generato
23	10	27	Junior Johnson	Daytona Kennel '59 Chevy	10	---	Axle

Time of Race: 1 hour, 30 minutes, 26 seconds
Average Speed: 66.347 mph
Pole Winner: Rex White - 71.08 mph
Lap Leaders: ------------------ Ned Jarrett -172, Joe Weatherly 173-250
Cautions:
Margin of Victory: 3 car lengths
Attendance: 7,460

Race No. 11

Weatherly Runs Down Jarrett; Captures Hickory 100

HICKORY, NC (Apr 16) -- Joe Weatherly of Norfolk wheeled his Holman-Moody Ford to a close win in the 100-miler at Hickory Speedway. It was the first Grand National for Weatherly since August 10, 1958, when he won a Sweepstakes event at Nashville, TN.

The 5'8" former motorcycle racer took the lead from Ned Jarrett with 28 laps to go and nipped his Ford rival by three car lengths to nail down the $800 first prize. Third place went to Richard Petty with Bob Welborn fourth and Tom Pistone fifth.

A crowd of 7,460 watched Weatherly win at an average speed of 66.347 mph for the 250 laps on the .4-mile dirt track.

Junior Johnson broke a left rear axle in the 10th lap and finished last in the 23 car field. Pole sitter Rex White left after 187 laps with rear gearing failure and wound up 14th.

Pole sitter Rex White left the race after 187 laps with rear gearing failure.

Weatherly took home the first place winnings of $1,275.

Zervakis' Monroe Shook-owned Chevrolet was closely inspected by NASCAR officials following the 200 lap contest on the half-mile dirt track. The fuel tank was found to be oversized, and Zervakis was promptly disqualified and placed at the rear of the 19 car field.

Lee Petty got credit for finishing second, one lap behind Weatherly's Ford. Tom Pistone pocketed third place money with Rex White fourth and Buck Baker fifth. Zervakis had earned the pole position, and was allowed to keep that honor in the NASCAR official record despite his disqualification from the race.

Point leader Richard Petty wound up seventh in his Plymouth, eight laps behind.

Weatherly averaged 55.113 mph for his third career Grand National triumph.

Grand National Race No. 12
200 Laps at Wilson Speedway
Wilson, NC
100 Miles on Half-mile Dirt Track
April 17, 1960

Fin	St	No.	Driver	Team / Car	Laps	Money	Status
1	5	12	Joe Weatherly	Holman-Moody '60 Ford	200	$1,275	Running
2	6	42	Lee Petty	Petty Eng '60 Plymouth	199	750	Running
3	11	59	Tom Pistone	Thor '60 Chevrolet	199	525	Running
4	4	4	Rex White	Piedmont/Friendly '50 Chevy	198	275	Running
5	2	87	Buck Baker	Baker '60 Chevrolet	198	250	Running
6	16	78	Joe Lee Johnson	E C Wilson '60 Chevrolet	195	215	Running
7	13	43	Richard Petty	Petty Eng '59 Plymouth	192	175	Running
8	10	49	Bob Welborn	Welborn '60 Chevrolet	189	150	Running
9	15	80	Neil Castles	Castles '58 Ford	185	140	Running
10	8	27	Junior Johnson	John Masoni '59 Chevy	177	130	Running
11	7	64	Bunkie Blackburn	A M Crawford '58 Ford	177	125	Running
12	14	84	Al Tasnady	'58 Ford	172	110	Running
13	3	11	Ned Jarrett	Courtesy '60 Ford	162	100	Rear End
14	17	1	Buddy Baker	Faircloth '60 Chevrolet	128	85	Running
15	12	32	Paul Lewis	Jess Potter '58 Chevrolet	119	70	Running
16	9	74	L D Austin	Austin '58 Chevrolet	18	60	Engine
17	18	9	Roy Tyner	Tyner '58 Mercury	15	50	Trans
18	19	51	Bob Roberts	Roy McDonald '59 Olds	10	50	Flagged
19	1	85	Emanuel Zervakis	Monroe Shook '60 Chevrolet	200	---	Disqual

Time of Race: 1 hour, 48 minutes, 52 seconds
Average Speed: 55.113 mph
Pole Winner: Emanuel Zervakis - 60.50 mph
Lap Leaders: - - - - - - - - - - - - - - - Joe Weatherly　-200
Cautions:
Margin of Victory:
Attendance:

Race No. 12

Weatherly Declared Winner at Wilson; Zervakis Disqualified

WILSON, NC (Apr 17) -- Emanuel Zervakis, the "Golden Greek" out of Richmond, crossed the finish line first in the 100-miler at Wilson Speedway, but Joe

Race No. 13

Glen Wood All The Way At Winston-Salem

WINSTON-SALEM, NC (Apr 18) -- Glen Wood of Stuart, VA, one of the outstanding Modified drivers, grabbed his first Grand National victory in the 50-miler at Bowman-Gray Stadium.

Wood started on the pole and held his Ford in front for the entire 200 laps on the flat quarter mile oval.

Rex White finished second in his Chevrolet and Jimmy Massey was third in another Wood Brothers

Jimmy Pardue leads Ned Jarrett and company at Winston-Salem

Ford. Richard Petty came in fourth with Ned Jarrett fifth.

Wood's first Grand National triumph came on his 44th start, and he became the 10th different winner in the 13 Grand National events staged thus far into the 1960 season.

Junior Johnson borrowed a Chevrolet, but qualified last and finished last in the 15 car field. The engine blew after just two laps.

Richard Petty's point lead increased to 194 points over his dad, Lee, who wound up 12th after engine problems sidelined his Plymouth.

Wood averaged 43.082 mph in giving Ford its third straight Grand National win.

Grand National Race No. 13
200 Laps at Bowman Gray Stadium
Winston-Salem, NC
50 Miles on Quarter-mile Paved Track
April 18, 1960

Fin	St	No.	Driver	Team / Car	Laps	Money	Status
1	1	16	Glen Wood	Wood Brothers '58 Ford	200	$600	Running
2	3	4	Rex White	Piedmont/Friendly '60 Chevy	200	475	Running
3	2	21	Jimmy Massey	Wood Brothers '59 Ford	199	400	Running
4	4	43	Richard Petty	Petty Eng '60 Plymouth	199	305	Running
5	5	11	Ned Jarrett	Courtesy Ford '60 Ford	196	245	Running
6	9	59	Tom Pistone	Thor '59 Chevrolet	195	220	Running
7	6	17	Fred Harb	Harb '58 Ford	193	205	Running
8	7	54	Jimmy Pardue	Lowe's '59 Dodge	190	160	Running
9	14	49	Bob Welborn	Welborn '60 Chevrolet	180	165	Running
10	12	64	Bunkie Blackburn	A M Crawford '58 Ford	169	140	Running
11	10	32	Paul Lewis	Jess Potter '58 Chevrolet	114	145	Spindle
12	8	42	Lee Petty	Petty Eng '60 Plymouth	113	250	Engine
13	13	80	Neil Castles	Castles '58 Ford	96	125	Running
14	11	71	Jimmie Lewallen	'58 Ford	61	115	Radiator
15	15	14	Junior Johnson	'59 Chevrolet	2	75	Engine

Time of Race: 1 hour, 09 minutes, 38 seconds
Average Speed: 43.082 mph
Pole Winner: Glen Wood - 47.24 mph
Lap Leaders: Glen Wood 1-200
Cautions:
Margin of Victory:
Attendance:

Race No. 14

Jarrett Jaunts to Victory at Greenville

GREENVILLE, SC (Apr 23) -- Ned Jarrett gunned his Ford around Lee Petty in the 140th lap and went on to post his second victory of the season in the 100-miler at Greenville-Pickens Speedway.

Lee and Richard Petty, the formidable father-son Plymouth team, took second and third in the 200 lap

Grand National Race No. 14
200 Laps at Greenville-Pickens
Speedway
Greenville, SC
100 Miles on Half-mile Dirt Track
April 23, 1960

Fin	St	No.	Driver	Team / Car	Laps	Money	Status
1	5	11	Ned Jarrett	Courtesy '60 Ford	200	$800	Running
2	2	42	Lee Petty	Petty Eng '60 Plymouth	200	625	Running
3	3	43	Richard Petty	Petty Eng '60 Plymouth	199	375	Running
4	14	36	Tommy Irwin	Irwin '59 T-Bird	194	275	Running
5	9	49	Bob Welborn	Welborn '60 Chevrolet	192	250	Running
6	18	92	Gerald Duke	Robert Davis '59 T-Bird	188	215	Running
7	20	80	Neil Castles	Castles '58 Ford	173	175	Running
8	4	67	David Pearson	Pearson '59 Chevrolet	153	150	Engine
9	8	4	Rex White	Piedmont/Friendly '59 Chevy	136	140	Rear End
10	21	68	Bill Parnell	R L Baird '58 Plymouth	126	130	RF Hub
11	6	70	Elmo Henderson	W H Watson '58 Pontiac	120	125	Rear End
12	10	50	Junior Johnson	Thor '59 Chevrolet	113	110	Fuel Pmp
13	12	17	Fred Harb	Harb '58 Ford	96	100	Engine
14	17	64	Bunkie Blackburn	A M Crawford '58 Ford	93	85	Engine
15	13	26	Joe Weatherly	Holman-Moody '60 Ford	88	70	H Gasket
16	1	26	Curtis Turner	Holman-Moody '60 Ford	85	60	Heating
17	7	87	Buck Baker	Baker '60 Chevrolet	75	50	Running
18	19	79	James Norton	'58 Mercury	56	50	Steering
19	15	54	Jimmy Pardue	Lowe's '59 Dodge	51	50	Steering
20	16	32	Paul Lewis	Jess Potter '58 Chevrolet	38	50	Tie Rod
21	11	48	G C Spencer	Weldon Wagner '58 Chevy	34	50	A Frame
22	22	9	Roy Tyner	Tyner '58 Mercury	12	50	Engine

Time of Race: 1 hour, 36 minutes, 15 seconds
Average Speed: 62.337 mph
Pole Winner: Curtis Turner - 64.72 mph
Lap Leaders: Curtis Turner 1-85, Lee Petty 86-139, Ned Jarrett 140-200
Cautions: None
Margin of Victory: 5 seconds
Attendance: 8,000

event. Tommy Irwin came in fourth and Bob Welborn fifth.

Curtis Turner, making only his third start in the 1960 season, won the pole and led the first 85 laps. His Holman-Moody Ford was comfortably out front when steam whined from his overheated radiator. Turner was out for the day.

Lee Petty picked up first place on lap 86 and held it for 54 laps until Jarrett grabbed the lead for good.

Tommy Irwin came from 14th to 4th at Greenville in his T-Bird

Twenty-two cars started the race but only eight were running at the finish, including Buck Baker's Chevrolet, which was 125 laps behind.

Jarrett averged 62.337 mph for his fourth career win. A crowd of 8,000 watched the caution-free event.

Race No. 15

Petty Claims 50th Career Win In Disputed Weaverville Race

WEAVERVILLE, NC (Apr 24) -- Lee Petty of Randleman, NC drove his Plymouth to victory in the abbreviated 100 miler at the Asheville-Weaverville Speedway. The event was halted for over an hour due to track deterioration and finally curtailed after 167 laps when driving conditions became too hazardous to continue.

A crowd of 5,000 showed up on the pleasant spring afternoon and saw Jack Smith lead the first 35 laps after starting third.

The track started digging up after 25 laps. Smith ran over a hole in the third turn that ruptured the oil pan on his

Pontiac. Local star Banjo Matthews took the lead when Smith departed. Matthews held his big T-Bird in front for nine laps when Bob Welborn surged into the lead. Welborn's Chevrolet was leading when the red flag came out on lap 62 to allow safety workers to sweep the crushed asphalt back into the holes to make driving safer.

Petty got around Welborn on lap 63 and was in

Lee Petty leads field down backstretch at Weaverville

front when NASCAR officials flagged the field to a halt.

Joe Lee Johnson finished second but filed a protest. His E.C. Wilson Chevrolet team was convinced their car had finished first. A check of the score cards revealed Petty to be the winner.

Third place went to Ned Jarrett with Welborn fourth and G.C. Spencer fifth.

Junior Johnson started a Wood Brothers Ford on the pole, but went only 49 laps before bending a tie rod on a hole in the track. Glen Wood, in another Wood Brothers Ford, punctured his oil pan after 39 laps on the rough track.

Matthews was knocked out of the race when he tangled with Richard Petty, Larry Frank and Rex White.

Lee Petty's 50th win came at an average speed of 63.368 mph.

Grand National Race No. 15
200 Laps at Asheville-Weaverville Speedway
Weaverville, NC
100 Miles on Half-mile Paved Track
April 24, 1960

Fin	St	No.	Driver	Team / Car	Laps	Money	Status
1	8	42	Lee Petty	Pettty Eng '60 Plymouth	167	$900	Running
2	18	78	Joe Lee Johnson	E C Wilson '60 Chevrolet	166	625	Running
3	6	11	Ned Jarrett	Courtesy'60 Ford	164	375	Running
4	11	49	Bob Welborn	Welborn '60 Chevrolet	158	275	Running
5	12	48	G C Spencer	Weldon Wagner '58 Chevy	157	250	Running
6	16	32	Paul Lewis	Jess Potter '58 Chevrolet	153	215	Running
7	4	4	Rex White	Piedmont/Friendly '60 Chevy	145	175	Running
8	14	87	Buck Baker	Baker '60 Chevrolet	139	150	Running
9	7	43	Richard Petty	Petty Eng '60 Plymouth	127	140	Running
10	9	59	Larry Frank	Thor '59 Chevrolet	118	130	Fuel Pmp
11	10	17	Fred Harb	Harb '58 Ford	118	125	Running
12	15	79	James Norton	'58 Mercury	111	110	Crash
13	5	94	Banjo Matthews	Matthews '59 T-Bird	81	100	Crash
14	13	54	Jimmy Pardue	Lowe's '59 Dodge	73	85	Engine
15	1	21	Junior Johnson	Wood Bros '59 Ford	49	70	Tie Rod
16	2	16	Glen Wood	Wood Bros '58 Ford	39	60	Oil Pan
17	3	47	Jack Smith	Boomershine '60 Pontiac	35	50	Oil Pan
18	19	80	Neil Castles	Castles '58 Ford	13	50	A Frame
19	17	9	Roy Tyer	Tyner '58 Mercury	5	50	Engine
20	20	64	Bunkie Blackburn	A M Crawford '58 Ford	1	50	H Gasket

* Race was shortened to 167 laps due to track deterioration
Time of Race: 1 hour, 17 minutes, 50 seconds
Average Speed: 63.368 mph
Pole Winner: Junior Johnson - 78.09 mph
Lap Leaders: Jack Smith 1-35, Banjo Matthews 36-44, Bob Welborn 45-62, Lee Petty 63-167
Cautions:
Margin of Victory: 1 1/2 Laps
Attendance: 5,000

Race No. 16

Weatherly Wins Two-part Rebel 300 at Darlington

DARLINGTON, SC (May 14) -- Joe Weatherly outlasted Fireball Roberts both on and off the track and emerged victorious in the fourth annual Rebel 300 Convertible Grand National race at Darlington Raceway

Johnny Allen sails over the wall at Darlington ....

.... and chops down the scoring stand

The 300 miler on the 1.375-mile oval was scheduled to be run on May 7, but the yellow flag came out as rain began to fall on lap 58. The race was called after 74 laps had been completed to be resumed a week later on May 14th with Fireball Roberts in the lead. The cars were not to be refueled or serviced during the idle week. Unlike most of the leaders, Weatherly had pitted during the rain, while under the yellow flag and was ready to go full bore the following week. However, NASCAR officials opted to restart the race the following Saturday under the caution flag rather than under the green. Weatherly objected to NASCAR's ruling, because he lost the advantage a full tank of fuel gave him. Roberts, of course, supported the sanctioning body's position.

Track president Bob Colvin intervened and made a compromise. He said the Raceway was forced to abide by NASCAR's ruling, but added that he would be behind the wheel of the pace car. "Those first five laps will be the fastest caution laps ever run," declared Colvin.

During the week between runnings, Weatherly stayed in the Darlington area and went on a promotional tear, going on television and radio programs, bid-

Johnny Allen's convertible Chevrolet was destroyed after flight over the guard rail in Rebel 300

ding for a green flag restart. Public support was evident when the following Saturday rolled around and 37,000 race fans showed up for the completion of the race. Thousands of these fans were waving small green flags. Only 25,000 fans had been on hand on May 7.

On May 14 Colvin hopped aboard the pace car and clicked off a few laps in excess of 100 mph. Roberts made his pit stop and rejoined the field, still on the lead lap. He worked his way back to the front and recaptured the lead on lap 167. But seven laps later the A-frame broke in his Pontiac forcing him to the sidelines. Weatherly took the lead on lap 174 and led the rest of the way. The Norfolk, VA Ford driver collected $9,250 for his 102.640 mph drive.

Richard Petty finished second in the lightly regarded Petty Engineering Plymouth. Rex White was a lap behind in third place, with Lee Petty fourth. Buck Baker came from 31st starting spot to finish a strong fifth.

Johnny Allen survived a horrendous crash in the 148th lap when a tire blew on his Chevrolet, and he soared over the guard rail. The airborne car plowed into the scoring stand, knocking part of it down. Some 48 occupants were trapped on one teetering corner of the structure.

Allen received a scratch on his nose.

Bunkie Blackburn and Carl Burris were eliminated in a 47th lap wreck.

Grand National Race No. 16
219 Laps at Darlington Raceway
Darlington, SC
"Rebel 300"
300 Miles on 1.375-mile Paved Track
May 14, 1960

Fin	St	No.	Driver	Team / Car	Laps	Money	Status
1	2	12	Joe Weatherly	Holman-Moody '60 Ford	219	$9,250	Running
2	7	43	Richard Petty	Petty Eng '60 Plymouth	219	4,875	Running
3	3	4	Rex White	Piedmont/Friendly '60 Chevy	218	2,900	Running
4	11	42	Lee Petty	Petty Eng '60 Plymouth	218	1,940	Running
5	31	87	Buck Baker	Thor '60 Chevrolet	216	1,500	Running
6	10	93	Bobby Johns	Sunbeam Systems '59 T-bird	215	1,160	Running
7	23	49	Bob Welborn	Welborn '60 Chevrolet	214	925	Running
8	14	85	Emanuel Zervakis	Monroe Shook '60 Ford	214	825	Running
9	5	15	Tim Flock	Beau Morgan '60 Ford	213	700	Running
10	15	77	Marvin Panch	Billie Ridgeway '60 Ford	213	600	Running
11	28	39	Herb Tillman	Ralph Stark '60 Chevrolet	213	500	Running
12	21	45	Joe Caspolich	Bill Gazaway '60 Olds	213	400	Running
13	4	5	Cotton Owens	Owens '60 Pontiac	213	350	Running
14	19	78	Joe Lee Johnson	E C Wilson '60 Chevrolet	210	400	Running
15	25	48	G C Spencer	Weldon Wagner '58 Chevy	208	250	Running
16	9	11	Ned Jarrett	Courtesy '60 Ford	206	225	Running
17	26	1	Buddy Baker	Faircloth '60 Chevrolet	202	200	Running
18	16	76	Larry Frank	Thor '59 Chevrolet	201	200	Oil Pres
19	8	26	Curtis Turner	Holman-Moody '60 Ford	194	200	Bearing
20	1	22	Fireball Roberts	John Hines '60 Pontiac	173	250	A Frame
21	13	61	Jimmy Thompson	Doc White '59 T-Bird	158	200	Push Rd
22	6	69	Johnny Allen	Hanley Dawson '60 Chevrolet	148	265	Crash
23	12	59	Tom Pistone	Thor '60- Chevrolet	119	265	Piston
24	17	26	Junior Johnson	John Masoni '60 Chevy	95	220	Steering
25	20	64	Bunkie Blackburn	A M Crawford '60 Ford	47	200	Crash
26	22	9	Carl Burris	A J Blackwelder '60 Ford	46	200	Crash
27	24	94	Banjo Matthews	Matthews '59 T-Bird	11	200	Engine
28	30	90	Runt Harris	Junie Donlavey '60 Chevy	9	200	Steering
29	18	23	Doug Yates	Yates '59 Plymouth	3	200	H Gasket
30	27	86	Johnny Dollar	Mat DeMatthews '58 Ford	3	200	Crash
31	32	83	Curtis Crider	Crider '58 Ford	2	100	Rear End
32	29	80	Neil Castles	Castles '58 Ford	2	200	Engine

Time of Race: 2 hours, 56 minutes 01 seconds
Average Speed: 102.640 mph
Pole Winner: Fireball Roberts - 127.750 mph
Lap Leaders: Fireball Roberts 1-8, Joe Weatherly 9-11, Roberts 12-74, Lee Petty 75-91
    Weatherly 92-149, Cotton Owens 150-166, Roberts 167-173, Weatherly 174-219
Cautions: 4
Margin of Victory:
Attendance: 25,000 (May 7); 37,000 (May 14)

Race No. 17

Jarrett-Massey Team Wins Spartanburg 100

SPARTANBURG, SC (May 28) -- Ned Jarrett, with relief help from Jimmy Massey, won the 100-mile Grand National race at Hub City Speedway. It was the fifth time in NASCAR history that a relief driver had carried a car to victory lane.

Lee Petty came in second and Cotton Owens was third. Tommy Irwin finished fourth as rookie David Pearson took fifth place.

Jarrett, starting 16th on the grid, had to signal for relief midway through the race. Massey, not an entrant, was summoned from the pits to handle Jarrett's Ford the rest of the way.

Buddy Baker and Larry Frank were involved in a crash in the 57th lap. Neither could continue in the race. Frank was driving the Thor Chevrolet previously driven by Tom Pistone.

Richard Petty finished 11th and held a 158 point lead over his dad, Lee, in the Grand National point standings.

Jarrett and Massey averaged 51.843 mph on the half-mile dirt track.

Grand National Race No. 17
200 Laps at Hub City Speedway
Spartanburg, SC
100 Miles on Half-mile Dirt Track
May 28, 1960

Fin	St	No.	Driver	Team / Car	Laps	Money	Status
1	16	11	* Ned Jarrett	Courtesy '60 Ford	200	$800	Running
2	9	42	Lee Petty	Petty Eng '60 Plymouth	200	625	Running
3	3	5	Cotton Owens	Owens '60 Pontiac	199	375	Running
4	5	36	Tommy Irwin	Irwin '59 T-Bird	198	275	Running
5	10	67	David Pearson	Pearson '59 Chevrolet	198	250	Running
6	14	48	G C Spencer	Welson Wagner '58 Che;vy	192	215	Running
7	20	92	Gerald Duke	Robert Davis '59 T-Bird	191	175	Running
8	6	23	Doug Yates	Yates '59 Plymouth	190	150	Axle
9	2	87	Buck Baker	Thor '60 Chevrolet	190	140	Running
10	17	24	Bunkie Blackburn	A M Crawford '58 Ford	189	130	Running
11	11	43	Richard Petty	Petty Eng '60 Plymouth	186	125	Crash
12	4	4	Rex White	Piedmont-Friendly '60 Chevy	183	110	Running
13	22	19	Herman Beam	Beam '60 Ford	175	100	Running
14	19	83	Curtis Crider	Crider '58 Ford	173	85	Running
15	13	78	Joe Lee Johnson	E C Wilson '60 Chevrolet	168	170	Rear End
16	21	1	Paul Lewis	Faircloth '60 Chevrolet	167	60	Crash
17	18	17	Fred Harb	Harb '60 Ford	156	50	Running
18	1	47	Jack Smith	Boomershine '60 Pontiac	79	50	Frame
19	8	59	Larry Frank	Thor '59 Chevrolet	57	50	Crash
20	15	32	Buccy Baker	Jess Potter '58 Chevrolet	54	50	Crash
21	12	77	Curtis Turner	Billie Ridgeway '60 Ford	10	50	Rear End
22	7	93	Bobby Johns	Sunbeam Systems '59 T-Bird	5	50	Radiator

* Relieved by Jimmy Massey
Time of Race: 1 hour, 55 minutes 44 seconds
Average Speed: 51.843 mph
Pole Winner: Jack Smith - 64.22 mph
Lap Leaders: -------------- Ned Jarrett   -200
Cautions:
Margin of Victory:
Attendance:

Race No. 18

Petty Punches Plymouth; Pockets Hillsboro 99

HILLSBORO NC (May 29) -- Lee Petty led the entire distance and came home the winner in the 99-mile Grand National event at Orange Speedway. It was the third win of the season for the 46 year-old Plymouth driver.

Richard and Lee Petty earned the front row starting positions -- the first time the father and son team had done so. Papa Lee was never challenged and wound up two laps in front of Ned Jarrett, who finished second in his Ford. Jack Smith, Tommy Irwin and Buck Baker rounded out the top five. Richard Petty finished sixth, three laps back.

Curtis Turner and Junior Johnson, a pair of dust-slinging throttle stompers, ran side by side for almost six laps early in the race before Johnson spun out. Tur-

ner clobbered Johnson's Chevrolet, but both were able to continue. Johnson went on to finish ninth. Turner was later taken out when the drive shaft broke on his Wood Brothers' Ford and he sailed over the bank and into a clump of trees.

David Pearson qualified fourth but departed late in the race when an axle broke on his Chevrolet.

Petty's average speed was 83.583 mph for his 51st career victory.

Grand National Race No. 18
110 Laps at Orange Speedway
Hillsboro, NC
99 Miles on .9-mile Dirt Track
May 29, 1960

Fin	St	No.	Driver	Team / Car	Laps	Money	Status
1	2	42	Lee Petty	Petty Eng '60 Plymouth	110	$900	Running
2	8	11	Ned Jarrett	Courtesy '60 Ford	108	525	Running
3	5	47	Jack Smith	Boomershine '60 Pontiac	108	375	Running
4	14	36	Tommy Irwin	Irwin '59 T-Bird	107	275	Running
5	23	87	Buck Baker	Thor '60 Chevrolet	107	250	Running
6	1	43	Richard Petty	Petty Eng '60 Plymouth	107	215	Running
7	3	85	Emanuel Zervakis	Monroe Shook '60 Chevrolet	105	175	Rear End
8	10	82	Joe Eubanks	'59 Chevrolet	105	150	Running
9	9	27	Junior Johnson	John Masoni '60 Chevy	104	140	Running
10	16	92	Gerald Duke	Robert Davis '59 T-Bird	104	130	Running
11	6	4	Rex White	Piedmont/Friendly '60 Chevy	103	125	Running
12	11	5	Cotton Owens	Owens '60 Pontiac	103	110	Running
13	17	74	L D Austin	Austin '58 Chevrolet	103	100	Running
14	4	67	David Pearson	Pearson '59 Chevrolet	97	85	Axle
15	19	19	Herman Beam	Beam '60 Ford	96	70	Running
16	22	24	Spook Crawford	Crawford '58 Ford	91	60	Axle
17	12	21	Curtis Turner	Wood Bros '59 Ford	78	50	Crash
18	18	48	G C Spencer	Weldon Wagner '58 Chevy	69	50	Rear End
19	7	12	Joe Weatherly	Holman-Moody '60 Ford	55	50	Heating
20	21	51	Roy Tyner	Roy McDonald '59 Olds	44	50	Trans
21	20	17	Fred Harb	Harb '58 Ford	39	50	Brakes
22	13	64	Bunkie Blackburn	A M Crawford '60 Ford	18	50	Conn Rd
23	15	23	Doug Yates	Yates '59 Plymouth	16	---	Brakes

Time of Race: 1 hour, 12 minutes, 44 seconds
Average Speed: 83.583 mph
Pole Winner: Richard Petty - 88.19 mph
Lap Leaders: Lee Petty 1-110
Cautions: 1 for 6 laps
Margin of Victory:
Attendance:

Grand National Race No. 19
200 Laps at Atlantic Rural Fairgrounds
Richmond, VA
100 Miles on Half-mile Dirt Track
June 5, 1960

Fin	St	No.	Driver	Team / Car	Laps	Money	Status
1	10	42	Lee Petty	Petty Eng '60 Plymouth	200	$900	Running
2	3	4	Rex White	Piedmont/Friendly '59 Chevy	200	525	Running
3	1	11	Ned Jarrett	Courtesy '60 Ford	199	375	Running
4	5	23	Doug Yates	Yates '59 Plymouth	198	275	Running
5	8	21	Glen Wood	Wood Bros '59 Ford	197	250	Running
6	11	43	Richard Petty	Petty Eng '60 Plymouth	196	215	Running
7	12	54	Nace Mattingly	'58 Ford	189	175	Running
8	19	87	Buck Baker	Thor '60 Chevrolet	189	150	Running
9	16	74	L D Austin	Austin '58 Chevrolet	183	140	Running
10	13	19	Herman Beam	Beam '60 Ford	182	130	Running
11	15	80	Neil Castles	Castles '58 Ford	180	125	Running
12	17	9	Jim Austin	Roy Tyner '60 Ford	175	110	Running
13	18	51	Roy Tyner	Roy McDonald '59 Olds	155	100	Running
14	6	27	Junior Johnson	John Masoni '59 Chevy	138	85	Spindle
15	14	12	Joe Weatherly	'60 Valiant	90	70	Engine
16	7	78	Joe Lee Johnson	E C Wilson '60 Chevrolet	73	160	Sw Bar
17	2	5	Cotton Owens	Owens '60 Pontiac	69	50	Air Filter
18	9	85	Emanuel Zervakis	Monroe Shook '60 Chevy	42	50	A Frame
19	4	75	John Dodd Jr	Dodd '60 Ford	37	50	Engine

Time of Race: 1 hour, 36 minutes, 23 seconds
Average Speed: 62.251 mph
Pole Winner: Ned Jarrett - 64.56 mph
Lap Leaders: Cotton Owens 1-11, Ned Jarrett 12-76, Junior Johnson 77-128, Rex White 129-131, Doug Yates 132-170, White 171-182, Lee Petty 183-200
Cautions: 1 for 6 laps
Margin of Victory: 1 second
Attendance: 6,100

Race No. 19

Lee Petty Edges Rex White at Richmond

RICHMOND, VA (June 5) -- Lee Petty rallied from a tire blowout and roared back to take first place in the 100-miler at the Atlantic Rural Fairgrounds. It was Petty's fourth win of the season.

Petty was running in third place when a tire blew on

his Plymouth on lap 125. He stopped his car on the track, bringing out the caution flag. The Old Master was able to get a new tire on without losing a lap.

Petty charged back and passed rival Rex White for good with 18 laps to go. White finished in second place 1.0 second behind. Ned Jarrett was third, a lap back. Doug Yates wound up fourth with Glen Wood fifth.

Joe Weatherly drove a compact Plymouth Valiant and wound up 15th in the field of 19 starters. The little car ran for 90 laps before the engine blew.

Lee Petty

The lead changed hands seven times among six drivers in the hotly contested event. Independent Yates passed White in the 132nd lap and paced the field for 39 laps. Yates' bid for his first Grand National win was foiled when he had to make a late pit stop.

One caution flag for six laps held Petty's average speed to 62.251 mph.

Race No. 20

Marvin Porter Bags California 250 at Marchbanks

HANFORD, CA (June 12) -- Marvin Porter of Lakewood, CA pushed his Ford into the lead 50 laps from the finish and won the California 250 at the new 1.4-mile banked Marchbanks Speedway. It was Porter's second Grand National win.

The 179 lap affair was an endurance contest as 104 degree temperatures played havoc with the drivers and the machinery. Some 17 cars fell out of the race, but no track officials or NASCAR officials bothered to find out why. It was believed that many quit due to driver fatigue.

Joe Weatherly started 32nd in the 33 car field and managed to finish second. His Vel Miletich Ford was 46 seconds behind Porter's independent Ford at the finish. Third place went to John Rostek, fourth to Fritz Wilson and fifth to Don Noel.

Weatherly filed a protest afterwards, claiming a pit

road official wrongfully held him up a lap while he was exiting the pit area. NASCAR upheld Porter's first superspeedway victory.

Lloyd Dane had taken the lead from Mel Larson in the 41st lap and was leading when he drove his Chevrolet into the pit area. No word was given as to why Dane pulled out of the race.

Only 7,000 spectators turned out for the heat-seared show, far below expectations. Rex White, who finished eighth, had lavishing praise for the new superspeedway. "This is an outstanding track, and I'll let everyone know back East when I return home."

Porter covered the 250 miles at an 88.032 mph clip.

Grand National Race No. 20
179 Laps at Marchbanks Speedway
Hanford, CA
"California 250"
250 Miles on 1.4-mile Paved Track
June 12, 1960

Fin	St	No.	Driver	Team / Car	Laps	Money	Status
1	8	98	Marvin Porter	Porter '59 Ford	179	$2,000	Running
2	32	97	Joe Weatherly	Vel Miletich '60 Ford	179	1,250	Running
3	2	19	John Rostek	Rostek '60 Ford	175	750	Running
4	5	48	Fritz Wilson	'58 Ford	173	600	Running
5	15	7	Don Noel	'59 Ford	172	575	Running
6	11	18	Dick Smith	'57 Mercury	170	550	Running
7	7	22N	Art Watts	'60 Ford	168	525	Running
8	9	41	Rex White	'59 Ford	162	500	Running
9	12	35	Mel Larson	Sun City '60 Pontiac	161	475	DNF
10	25	99	Al Self	'58 Chevrolet	157	450	Running
11	6	6	Eddie Gray	'58 Ford	155	425	Running
12	13	38	Charlie Chapman	Chapman '60 Ford	152	400	Running
13	19	91	Bruce Worrell	'59 Plymouth	152	375	Running
14	23	28	Ed Andrews	'60 Olds	150	350	Running
15	10	23	Bob Perry	'59 Plymouth	145	325	DNF
16	30	3	Dick Getty	'57 Mercury	141	300	DNF
17	18	9	Bob Price	'59 Chevrolet	139	275	Running
18	26	17	Bill Cook	'58 Ford	137	200	Running
19	3	44	Lloyd Dane	'60 Chevrolet	129	200	DNF
20	31	11	Owen Loggins	'60 Plymouth	126	100	Running
21	14	0	Jim Cook	'60 Dodge	117	100	DNF
22	21	2	Ron Hornaday	'60 Ford	112	100	DNF
23	27	5	Jim Blomgren	'60 Ford	109	100	DNF
24	20	55	Lyle Stelter	'57 Mercury	86	100	DNF
25	22	25	Johnny Potter	'58 Ford	79	100	DNF
26	4	4	Scotty Cain	'59 T-Bird	55	100	DNF
27	1	86	Frank Secrist	'60 Ford	45	100	DNF
28	28	16	Danny Weinberg	'60 Ford	37	100	DNF
29	33	20	Bob Ross	'59 Chevrolet	30	100	DNF
30	29	28N	Kuzie Kuzmanich	'60 Pontiac	22	100	DNF
31	16	68	Johnny Mello	'60 Ford	22	---	DNF
32	24	77	Brownie Brown	'59 Ford	12	---	DNF
33	17	69	Bob Hogle	'58 Pontiac	3	---	DNF

Time of Race: 2 hours, 50 minutes, 48 seconds
Average Speed: 88.032 mph
Pole Winner: Frank Secrist - 93.04 mph
Lap Leaders: Frank Secrist 1-8, Scotty Cain 9-27, Mel Larson 28-40, Lloyd Dane 41-129, Marvin Porter 130-179
Cautions:
Margin of Victory: 46 seconds
Attendance: 7,000

Race No. 21

Down by 5 Laps, Joe Lee Johnson Takes First World 600

CHARLOTTE, NC (June 19) -- Joe Lee Johnson, journeyman driver out of Chattanooga, TN, cashed in on the biggest prize of his career with a victory in the inaugural World 600 at Charlotte Motor Speedway.

It was the second Grand National victory for the 29 year old Chevrolet pilot.

Johnson steered his Paul McDuffie prepared mount around the large chuck holes on the track surface and cruised into the lead 48 laps from the finish. Jack Smith, driving a Pontiac had taken the lead from Tiger Tom Pistone on lap 160 and had led for 193 laps. The Sandy Springs, GA veteran had built up a five lap lead over Johnson when a chunk of asphalt tore open a hole in his fuel tank.

Joe Lee Johnson won first World 600

Johnson went uncontested the final 72 miles and finished four laps ahead of Johnny Beauchamp's Chevrolet, driven in relief by Johnny Allen. The three

Lee Petty's Plymouth was equipped with protective grille and windshield screens

car Petty Engineering team took third through fifth with Bobby Johns, Richard and Lee Petty at the wheels.

A few days after the race, Richard and Lee Petty, along with four other drivers, were disqualified for making improper entrances to the pits. The disqualification was termed "fatal" to Richard's title hopes as he fell to fourth in the standings after what would have been an 870 point lead.

Papa Lee, when informed of NASCAR's decision, muttered, "I might as well go back to chopping wood for a living." Others disqualified were Junior Johnson, Bob Welborn, Lennie Page and Paul Lewis.

Lee Petty leads World 600 field out of 4th turn

Smith, starting from the middle of the front row, had moved to a commanding lead by the half-way point. His Bud Moore led pit crew tried stuffing rags into the opening in the gas tank, but it was no use. The entire 22-gallon capacity had leaked out by the time he drove around the track.

Rookie David Pearson had moved up to second behind Johnson in a sparkling drive, but distributor problems knocked him down to 10th at the finish.

Gerald Duke was moved up to fourth with the rash of disqualifications, and Buck Baker took fifth place.

Johnson won $27,150 and leaped to sixth place in the point standings. Sixth place finisher Rex White moved into the point lead by a margin of 1,110 points over Johns.

Track officials announced the crowd at 78,000, but actually 35,462 were on hand. The 400-lapper on the new mile-and-a-half tri-oval was originally scheduled for May 20, but it was necessary to advance the date three weeks so the speedway could be completed. Actual paving was continued during the qualifying trials, and most of the cars were armed with protective screens and tire flaps.

Johnson averaged 107.735 mph after 45 laps were run under the caution flag. Johnny Wolford's Ford was demolished in a sixth lap crack-up with Cotton Owens and Johnny Allen.

Grand National Race No. 21
400 Laps at Charlotte Motor Speedway
Charlotte, NC
"World 600"
600 Miles on 1.5-mile Paved Track
June 19, 1960

Fin	St	No.	Driver	Team / Car	Laps	Money	Status
1	20	89	Joe Lee Johnson	Paul McDuffie '60 Chevrolet	400	$27,150	Running
2	38	73	Johnny Beauchamp *	'60 Chevrolet	396	9,110	Running
3	6	46	Bobby Johns	Petty Eng '60 Plymouth	394	6,975	Running
4	44	92	Gerald Duke	Robert Davis '59 T-Bird	388	3,675	Running
5	14	87	Buck Baker	Thor '60 Chevrolet	386	3,075	Running
6	7	4	Rex White	Piedmont/Friendly '60 Chevy	378	2,250	Running
7	31	94	Banjo Matthews	Matthews '60 Ford	377	2,350	Running
8	40	63	Tiny Lund	'59 Pontiac	375	1,350	Running
9	39	81	Shorty Rollins	Rolins '60 Ford	374	1,100	Running
10	19	67	David Pearson	Pearson '59 Chevrolet	367	1,150	Running
11	58	78	Charley Griffith	E C Wilson '60 Chevrolet	365	750	Engine
12	2	47	Jack Smith	Boomershine '60 Pontiac	352	3,680	Fuel Tnk
13	49	55	Ernie Gahan	Gahan '59 Chevrolet	350	500	Running
14	59		Herman Beam	Beam '60 Ford	344	400	Running
15	51	38	Jim Cook	Charles Chapman '60 Ford	343	400	Running
16	55	35	Jimmy Pardue	'59 Plymouth	343	400	Running
17	32	77	Marvin Panch	Billie Ridgeway '60 Ford	341	400	A Frame
18	42	21	Jimmy Massey	'59 Chevrolet	333	400	Trans
19	48	20	Buddy Baker	A M Crawford '58 Ford	332	400	Running
20	28	91	Larry Frank	'60 Ford	320	400	Engine
21	37	48	G C Spencer	Weldon Wagner '58 Chevy	316	300	Engine
22	24	45	Joe Caspolich	Bill Gazaway '60 Olds	313	1025	Engine
23	26	64	Bunkie Blackburn	A M Crawford '60 Ford	311	300	H Gasket
24	23	61	Jimmy Thompson	Doc White '59 T-Bird	310	300	Spindle
25	10	90	Speedy Thompson	Junie Donlavey '60 Ford	287	550	Valve
26	50	33	Reb Wickersham	Wickersham '60 Olds	260	200	Running
27	41	24	Arnie Gardner	Harry Hahn '60 Ford	257	200	Running
28	13	7	Jim Reed	Reed '60 Chevrolet	246	500	Crash
29	54	17	Shorty York	Fred Harb '58 Ford	243	200	Fuel Pmp
30	5	11	Ned Jarrett	Courtesy '60 Ford	233	350	Crash
31	9	59	Tom Pistone	Thor '60 Chevrolet	221	840	Brakes
32	22	70	Elmo Henderson	W H Watson '58 Pontiac	212	275	Running
33	16	85	Emanuel Zervakis	Monroe Shook '60 Chevy	209	225	Axle
34	33	15	Johnny Sudderth	Beau Morgan '60 Ford	202	200	Rear End
35	1	22	Fireball Roberts	John Hines '60 Pontiac	191	2090	Crash
36	21	23	Doug Yates	Yates '59 Plymouth	176	350	Crash
37	46	51	Roy Tyner	Roy McDonald '59 Olds	176	200	Axle
38	47	50	George Tet	Richard Freeman '60 Ford	171	200	H Gasket
39	3	26	Curtis Turner	Holman-Moody '60 Ford	154	660	H Gasket
40	27	39	Herb Tillman	Ralph Starke '60 Chevrolet	138	200	Crash
41	18	28	Fred Lorenzen	Lorenzen '60 Ford	118	500	H Gasket
42	52	32	Richard Riley	Jess Potter '58 Chevrolet	115	200	Fuel Pmp
43	15	12	Joe Weatherly	Holman-Moody '60 Ford	85	250	Crash
44	36	99	Wilbur Rakestraw	Talmadge Cochrane'60 Ford	57	200	H Gasket
45	30	82	Joe Eubanks	'59 Chevrolet	46	200	Spindle
46	35	2	Possum Jones	'60 Chevrolet	39	200	A Frame
47	53	74	L D Austin	Austin '58 Chevrolet	33	200	Exhaust
48	43	86	Ed Marksteller	Mat DeMatthews '58 Ford	27	200	Crash
49	25	71	Gene Marmor	'59 Pontiac	24	200	Valve
50	57	9	Jim Austin	Roy Tyner '60 Ford	24	200	Oil Press
51	4	6	Cotton Owens	Owens '60 Pontiac	6	500	Crash
52	17	69	Johnny Allen	Hanley Dawson '60 Chevrolet	6	700	Crash
53	45	95	Bob Duell	Julian Buesink '59 Ford	6	200	Timing
54	56	88	Johnny Wolford	'60 Ford	5	200	Crash
55	11	43	Richard Petty	Petty Eng '60 Plymouth	---	---	Disqual
56	8	42	Lee Petty	Petty Eng '60 Plym	---	---	Disqual
57	12	49	Bob Welborn	Welborn '60 Ford	---	---	Disqual
58	34	1	Paul Lewis	Faircloth '60 Chevrolet	---	---	Disqual
59	29	27	Junior Johnson	John Masoni '60 Chevy	---	---	Disqual
60	60	83	Lennie Page	'59 T-Bird	---	---	Disqual

* Relieved by Johnny Allen
Time of Race: 5 hours, 34 minutes, 6 seconds
Average Speed: 107.735 mph
Pole Winner: Fireball Roberts - 133.904 mph
Lap Leaders: Fireball Roberts 1-65, Tom Pistone 66-73, Junior Johnson 74-78,
    Curtis Turner 79-94, Jack Smith 95-96, Roberts 97-140, Smith 141-143,
    Roberts 144-148, Turner 149-153, Pistone 154-159, Smith 160-352,
    Joe Lee Johnson 353-400
Cautions: 8 for 45 laps   Margin of Victory: 4 Laps plus   Attendance: 35,462

Rade No. 22

Wood's Ford Wins International 200 as Corvettes, MG's Fizzle

WINSTON SALEM, NC (June 26) -- Glen Wood, the 'Old Woodchopper' from Stuart, Virginia, turned in a flawless performance and won the International Sweepstakes 200 at Bowman-Gray Stadium. It was the second Grand National win for Wood at this quarter-mile facility, leading from wire to wire both times. The win netted the winner $1,125.

Lee Petty finished second, a half-lap back, Rex White was third, Richard Petty fourth and Ned Jarrett fifth.

Joe Weatherly finished sixth in a Plymouth Valiant. Jack Hart's 14th place effort in a '57 Triumph was the best the tiny sports cars could do.

Charles Kolb, an SCCA amateur participant, elected to withdraw moments before the start of the race to retain his amateur status. Kolb had won his 25 lap heat race after starting last.

Wood averaged 45.872 mph. Bob Welborn was seated in the other Wood Brothers entry but a right front wheel bearing knocked him out after 127 laps.

Grand National Race No. 22
200 Laps at Bowman-Gray Stadium
Winston-Salem, NC
50 Miles on Quarter-mile Paved Track
June 26, 1960

Fin	St	No.	Driver	Team / Car	Laps	Money	Status
1	3	16	Glen Wood	Wood Bros '58 Ford	200	$1,125	Running
2	1	42	Lee Petty	Petty Eng '60 Plymouth	200	595	Running
3	5	4	Rex White	Piedmont/Friendly '59 Chevy	198	415	Running
4	2	43	Richard Petty	Petty Eng '60 Plymouth	197	250	Running
5	6	11	Ned Jarrett	Courtesy '60 Ford	195	255	Running
6	7	12	Joe Weatherly	'60 Valiant	193	265	Running
7	9	36	Tommy Irwin	Irwin '59 T-Bird	192	215	Running
8	8	74	Buck Baker	L D Austin '58 Chevrolet	189	175	Running
9	11	17	Fred Harb	Harb '58 Ford	187	170	Running
10	13	54	Jimmy Pardue	Lowe's '59 Dodge	186	175	Running
11	10	9	Roy Tyner	Tyner '60 Ford	185	175	Running
12	12	1	Paul Lewis	Faircloth '58 Chevrolet	176	155	Running
13	4	21	Bob Welborn	Wood Bros '59 Ford	127	125	Bearing
14	15	79	Jack Hart	'57 Triumph	76	145	Running
15	18	25	Bill Massey	'59 MG	71	130	Axle
16	16	17X	Bill Whitley	'54 Corvette	6	145	Heating
17	14	78	Jimmie Lewallen	'57 Ford	2	100	Engine
18	17	3	Smokey Cook	'52 MG	1	140	Steering

Time of Race: 1 hour, 05 minutes, 24 seconds
Average Speed: 45.872 mph
Pole Winner: Lee Petty - 47.85 mph
Lap Leaders: Glen Wood 1-200
Cautions:
Margin of Victory: 1/2 lap
Attendance: 10,500

Grand National Race No. 23
100 Laps at Daytona International Speedway
Daytona Beach, FL
"Firecracker 250"
250 Miles on 2.5-mile Paved Track
July 4, 1960

Fin	St	No.	Driver	Team / Car	Laps	Money	Status
1	1	47	Jack Smith	Boomershine '60 Pontiac	100	$11,500	Running
2	4	6	Cotton Owens	Owens '60 Pontiac	100	5,100	Running
3	11	28	Fred Lorenzen	Lorenzen '60 Ford	99	2,600	Running
4	12	42	Lee Petty	Petty Eng '60 Plymouth	99	1,525	Running
5	15	64	Bunkie Blackburn	A M Crawford '60 Ford	98	1,150	Running
6	8	4	Rex White	Piedmont/Friendly '60 Chevy	98	1,050	Running
7	13	11	Ned Jarrett	Courtesy '60 Ford	97	800	Running
8	9	94	Banjo Matthews	Matthews '60 Chevrolet	97	775	Running
9	21	92	Gerald Duke	Robert Davis '59 T-Bird	97	650	Running
10	16	21	Jimmy Massey	'59 Chevrolet	96	575	Running
11	6	43	Richard Petty	Petty Eng '60 Plymouth	96	600	Running
12	14	99	Wilbur Rakestraw	Talmadge Cochrane '60 Ford	96	375	Running
13	22	49	Jim Paschal	Bob Welborn '60 Chevrolet	95	320	Running
14	18	77	Marvin Panch	Billie Ridgeway '60 Ford	95	300	Running
15	17	27	Junior Johnson	John Masoni '60 Chevy	94	270	Running
16	26	81	Shorty Rolins	Rollins '60 Ford	93	270	Running
17	24	16	Dick Joslin	Happy Stiegel '59 Pontiac	92	250	Running
18	27	67	David Pearson	Pearson '59 Chevrolet	91	250	Running
19	35	17	Jimmy Pardue	'60 Dodge	89	225	Running
20	32	19	Herman Beam	Beam '60 Ford	89	250	Running
21	31	60	Jim Whitman	Dick Stanley '60 Dodge	88	250	Running
22	36	8	Joe Caspolich	'60 Chevrolet	85	225	Running
23	29	33	Reb Wickersham	Wickersham '60 Olds	80	250	Running
24	37	83	Curtis Crider	Crider '58 Ford	80	200	Running
25	10	59	Tom Pistone	Thor '60 Chevrolet	66	300	Engine
26	7	12	Joe Weatherly	Holman-Moody '60 Ford	65	300	Engine
27	5	69	Johnny Allen	Hanley Dawson '60 Chevrolet	61	300	Valve
28	20	87	Buck Baker	Thor '60 Chevrolet	58	150	Engine
29	23	1	Paul Lewis	Faircloth '60 Chevrolet	55	150	Running
30	3	3	Bobby Johns	Jim Stephens '59 Pontiac	52	500	Axle
31	2	22	Fireball Roberts	John Hines '60 Pontiac	40	750	Oil Filter
32	19	10	Elmo Langley	Ratus Walters '59 Buick	26	150	Crank Sh
33	30	89	Joe Lee Johnson	Paul McDuffie '60 Chevrolet	25	250	Rods
34	28	18	Tim Flock	'60 Plymouth	22	150	Engine
35	34	51	Roy Tyner	Ray McDonald '59 Olds	14	125	Axle
36	25	2	Possum Jones	'60 Chevrolet	8	150	Rkr Arm
37	33	86	Ed Markstellar	'58 Ford	7	125	Heating

Time of Race: 1 hour, 42 minutes, 09 seconds
Average Speed: 146.842 mph
Pole Winner: Jack Smith - 152.129 mph
Lap Leaders: Jack Smith 1-4, Fireball Roberts 5-7, Smith 8, Roberts 9-10, Smith 11-12, Roberts 13-15, Smith 16-38, Cotton Owens 39-44, Smith 45-77, Owens 78-96, Smith 97-100
Cautions: None
Margin of Victory: 30 feet
Attendance: 15,919

Race No. 23

Smith's Pontiac, Equipped With 2-way Radio; Wins Firecracker 250

DAYTONA BEACH, FL (July 4) -- Jack Smith ran down Cotton Owens in a nerve-jabbing stretch dash and won the second annual Firecracker 250 be-fore 15,919 spectators at Daytona International Speedway. It was Smith's third win of the year.

Smith's Boomershine Pontiac zipped past Owens four laps from the finish and edged his cross-town rival by 30 feet to win $11,500. Fred Lorenzen was third, Lee Petty fourth, and Bunkie Blackburn fifth.

Smith won the pole at 152.129 mph and eclipsed the race record with an astonishing 146.842 mph mark.

It was a Pontiac parade throughout the 100-lap speed-happy contest. The lead changed hands 10 times among three drivers with Smith leading for a total of 67 laps.

Fireball Roberts and Bobby Johns, driving team cars wrenched by Smokey Yunick, failed to finish after offering strong challenges. Roberts went out on lap 40 with a bad oil filter, and Johns broke an axle after 52 laps.

After Roberts and Johns went out, Smith and Owens settled the outcome between themselves. Owens held a 9-second lead after 85 laps when Smith, equipped with a 2-way radio, started his charge. With 10 laps remaining, he was six seconds back. Smith caught Owens on lap 95 and made the pass two laps later.

Smith said he didn't communicate with crew chief Bud Moore during his stretch run. "I didn't interrupt his concentration," said Moore. "He knew what he had to do."

Grand National Race No. 24
200 Laps at Heidelberg Stadium
Pittsburgh, PA
100 Miles on Half-mile Dirt Track
July 10, 1960

Fin	St	No.	Driver	Team / Car	Laps	Money	Status
1	1	42	Lee Petty	Petty Eng '60 Plymouth	188	$900	Running
2	4	43	Richard Petty	Petty Eng '60 Plymouth	185	525	Running
3	3	4	Rex White	Piedmont/Friendly '59 Chevy	184	375	Running
4	9	1	Nook Walters	'59 Chevrolet	179	275	Running
5	17	74	L D Austin	Austin '58 Chevrolet	174	250	Running
6	16	3	Al White	'58 Ford	173	215	Running
7	12	8	Lennie Page	'59 T-Bird	173	175	Running
8	14	20	Spook Crawford	Crawford '58 Ford	172	150	Running
9	13	54	Jimmy Pardue	Lowes '59 Dodge	172	140	Running
10	6	80	Neil Castles	Castles '58 Ford	170	130	Running
11	11	19	Herman Beam	Beam '60 Ford	169	125	Running
12	8	95	Bob Duell	Julian Buesink '60 Ford	167	110	Running
13	5	64	Bunkie Blackburn	A M Crawford '60 Ford	152	100	Running
14	15	87	Lee Parris	'60 Chevrolet	129	100	Rear End
15	10	83	Curtis Crider	Crider '58 Ford	124	100	Running
16	2	11	Ned Jarrett	Courtesy '60 Ford	38	100	Engine
17	7	56	Ken Johnson	Charles French '60 Ford	17	100	Piston

* Race shortened to 188 laps due to rain
Time of Race: 1 hour, 23 minutes, 37 seconds
Average Speed: 67.450 mph
Pole Winner: Lee Petty - 71.97 mph
Lap Leaders: Ned Jarrett 1-19, Lee Petty 20-188
Cautions:
Margin of Victory:
Attendance: 6,800

Race No. 24

Petty and Petty 1-2 In Heidelberg 200

PITTSBURGH, PA (July 10) -- Lee Petty grabbed his fifth win of the season with a victory in the rain-shortened Heidelberg 200 at Heidelberg Stadium. The event was flagged to a halt 12 laps from the finish when a thunderstorm hit the half-mile dirt track.

Richard Petty came in second, three laps behind, providing the crowd with the second father-son finish in NASCAR Grand National racing. Point leader Rex White took third and increased his point lead to a commanding 2,342 points over Bobby Johns, the part-timer who concentrates only on major events. Nook Walters came in fourth and L. D. Austin was fifth.

Ned Jarrett led the first 19 laps in his Ford. Petty made the pass and was never threatened. Jarrett was running second when his engine blew on lap 38.

A crowd of 6,800 watched the twin Petty Plymouths take the top two spots.

Papa Lee averaged 67.450 mph for his 53rd big league triumph.

Grand National Race No. 25
100 Laps at Montgomery Air Base
Montgomery, NY
"Empire State 200"
200 Miles on 2-mile Paved Track
July 17, 1960

Fin	St	No.	Driver	Team / Car	Laps	Money	Status
1	3	4	Rex White	Piedmont/Friendly '60 Chevy	100	$2,970	Running
2	2	43	Richard Petty	Petty Eng '60 Plymouth	99	1,600	Running
3	7	42	Lee Petty	Petty Eng '60 Plymouth	97	1,200	Running
4	6	11	Ned Jarrett	Courtesy '60 Ford	96	725	Running
5	4	87	Buck Baker	Thor '60 Chevrolet	96	625	Running
6	15	8	Lennie Page	'59 T-Bird	94	550	Running
7	1	1	John Rostek	Rostek '60 Ford	94	425	Running
8	8	95	Bob Duell	Julian Buesink '60 Ford	92	375	Running
9	11	19	Herman Beam	Beam '60 Ford	90	300	Running
10	12	74	L D Austin	Austin '58 Chevrolet	87	300	Engine
11	19	54	Jimmy Pardue	Lowe's '59 Dodge	87	200	Running
12	13	20	Buddy Baker	A M Crawford '58 Ford	87	150	Running
13	5	7	Jim Reed	Reed '60 Chevrolet	86	165	Engine
14	16	83	Curtis Crider	Crider '58 Ford	84	125	Running
15	9	80	Neil Castles	Castles '58 Ford	80	125	Running
16	10	56	Ken Johnson	'60 Ford	76	110	Running
17	14	0	Eddie Riker	'58 Ford	61	110	Engine
18	11	64	Bunkie Blackburn	A M Crawford '60 Ford	39	100	Drive Sh
19	18	60	Jim Whitman	Dick Stanley '60 Dodge	5	100	Engine

Time of Race: 2 hours, 15 minutes, 24 seconds
Average Speed: 88.626 mph
Pole Winner: John Rostek - 91.650 mph
Lap Leaders: Buck Baker 1-2, Rex White 3-6, John Rostek 7-13, White 14-48
   Jim Reed 49-76, White 77-100
Cautions: 1
Margin of Victory:
Attendance: 5,000

Race No. 25

Point Leader White Captures 200-miler at Montgomery Air Base

MONTGOMERY, NY (July 17) -- Rex White of Silver Spring, MD, took the lead from Jim Reed in the 77th lap and went on to win the Empire State 200 at the Montgomery Air Force Base. It was the second win of

Rex White won Montgomery, NY race on airport runways

the season for the title-bound Chevrolet driver.

Richard Petty finished second, Lee Petty was third and Ned Jarrett fourth. Fifth place went to Buck Baker.

Jarrett was foiled by three pit stops to replace worn tires.

Reed was closing in on leader White with 14 laps to go, but engine problems put his Chevrolet out of the race.

The two-mile layout on the runways of the Air Force Base was in a triangular shape with no right turns required. The flat, tight turns were a severe test for tires. Most of the drivers cut across the dirt in a wide series of fishtails in order to save their tires. One caution was waved to allow track workers to drag hay bales from the long straightaways after cars had carried them from the turns.

The lead changed hands six times on the hot, sultry afternoon. John Rostek started on the pole and led for seven laps in the early going. But Rostek drifted to a seventh place finish, six laps off the pace.

A crowd of 5,000 watched White average 88.626 mph for the 100-lapper.

Race No. 26

Baker Gets First '60 Win At Myrtle Beach

MYRTLE BEACH, SC (July 23) -- Buck Baker of Charlotte took his first win of the year with a triumph in the 100-miler at Rambi Raceway. It was the 41st career victory for the 41 year-old veteran.

Baker started 11th in the 17 car field and edged Lee Petty to take the $800 top prize. Baker became the 13th different winner in the 1960 Grand National season.

Third place went to Rex White. Junior Johnson was fourth with Richard Petty fifth.

White held a 2,660 point lead over Lee Petty in the point standings. Had Petty not been disqualified from a fifth place finish in Charlotte's World 600, he would have had a 1,000 point lead.

Fred Harb crashed his Ford in the 55th lap for the only accident of the race.

Baker averaged 60.985 mph and maintained fifth place in the point standings.

Grand National Race No. 26
200 Laps at Rambi Raceway
Myrtle Beach, SC
100 Miles on Half-Mile Dirt Track
July 23, 1960

Fin	St	No.	Driver	Team Car	Laps	Money	Status
1	11	87	Buck Baker	Baker '60 Chevrolet	200	$800	Running
2	5	42	Lee Petty	Petty Eng '60 Plymouth	200	625	Running
3	4	4	Rex White	Piedmont/Friendly '60 Chevy	198	375	Running
4	2	27	Junior Johnson	John Masoni '60 Chevy	197	275	Running
5	8	43	Richard Petty	Petty Eng '60 Plymouth	197	250	Running
6	1	11	Ned Jarrett	Jarrett '60 Ford	197	215	Running
7	14	23	Doug Yates	Yates '59 Plymouth	196	175	Running
8	3	36	Tommy Irwin	Irwin '59 T-Bird	196	150	Tire
9	7	9	Roy Tyner	Tyner '60 Ford	189	140	Running
10	9	99	Wilbur Rakestraw	Talmadge Cochrane '60 Ford	185	130	Running
11	10	67	David Pearson	Pearson '59 Chevrolet	184	125	Running
12	16	20	Bunkie Blackburn	A M Crawford '58 Ford	181	110	Running
13	17	83	Curtis Crider	Crider '58 Ford	133	100	Running
14	12	54	Jimmy Pardue	Lowe's '59 Dodg	99	85	Rear End
15	13	80	Neil Castles	Castles '58 Ford	83	70	Trans
16	6	61	Jimmy Thompson	Doc White '59 T-Bird	75	60	Rear End
17	15	17	Fred Harb	Harb '58 Ford	55	50	Crash

Time of Race: 1 hour, 38 minutes, 23 seconds
Average Speed: 60.985 mph
Pole Winner: Ned Jarrett - 64.61 mph
Lap Leaders - - - - - - - - - - - - - - - Buck Baker   -200
Cautions:
Margin of Victory:
Attendance:

Grand National Race No. 27
200 Laps at Atlanta International Raceway
Hampton, GA
"Dixie 300"
300 Miles on 1.5-mile Paved Track
July 31, 1960

Fin	St	No.	Driver	Team / Car	Laps	Money	Status
1	1	22	Fireball Roberts	John Hines '60 Pontiac	200	$10,130	Running
2	5	6	Cotton Owens	Owens '60 Pontiac	200	5,215	Running
3	2	47	Jack Smith	Boomershine '60 Pontiac	200	3,090	Running
4	3	3	Bobby Johns	Stephens '60 Pontiac	199	1,865	Running
5	4	28	Fred Lorenzen	Lorenzen '60 Ford	199	1,565	Running
6	9	44	Jim Paschal	Petty Eng '60 Plymouth	198	1,185	Running
7	13	18	Roz Howard	'59 Chevrolet	197	1,050	Running
8	14	42	Lee Petty	Petty Eng '60 Plymouth	197	1,050	Running
9	7	69	Johnny Allen	Hanley Dawson '60 Chevrolet	193	900	Running
10	16	85	Emanuel Zervakis	Monroe Shook '58 Chevrolet	193	800	Running
11	18	99	Wilbur Rakestraw	Talmadge Cochrane '60 Ford	193	700	Running
12	23	90	Speedy Thompson	Junie Donlavey '59 Ford	192	650	Crash
13	29	2	Possum Jones	'60 Chevrolet	192	600	Running
14	24	23	Doug Yates	Yates '59 Plymouth	192	550	Running
15	15	11	Ned Jarrett	Jarrett '60 Ford	191	575	Running
16	36	39	Herb Tillman	'59 Chevrolet	191	450	Running
17	26	77	Marvin Panch	Billie Ridgeway '60 Ford	191	450	Running
18	11	59	Tom Pistone	Thor '60 Chevrolet	188	505	Running
19	34	82	Joe Eubanks	'59 Chevrolet	188	450	Running
20	12	43	Richard Petty	Petty Eng '60 Plymouth	186	475	Running
21	30	61	Jimmy Thompson	Doc White '59 T-Bird	185	350	Running
22	31	15	Curtis Turner	Beau Morgan '59 Ford	185	350	Running
23	22	4	Rex White	Piedmont/Friendly '60 Chevy	185	350	Running
24	44	55	Herb Shannon	'59 T-Bird	184	350	Running
25	8	94	Banjo Matthews	Matthews '60 Ford	182	400	Running
26	43	33	Reb Wickersham	Wickersham '59 Olds	181	300	Running
27	39	19	Herman Beam	Beam '60 Ford	181	300	Running
28	28	79	Johnny Miller	'59 Ford	181	300	Running
29	38	74	L D Austin	Austin '58 Chevrolet	180	300	Running
30	40	45	Tiny Lund	'59 Olds	178	300	Running
31	21	87	Buck Baker	Baker '60 Chevrolet	177	250	Running
32	35	67	David Pearson	Pearson '59 Chevrolet	168	250	Running
33	32	73	Johnny Beauchamp	'60 Chevrolet	155	250	Engine
34	17	81	Shorty Rollins	'59 Ford	154	250	Engine
35	6	12	Joe Weatherly	Holman-Moody '60 Ford	148	545	Engine
36	27	21	Jimmy Massey	'60 Chevrolet	128	250	Valve
37	19	64	Bunkie Blackburn	A M Crawford '60 Ford	123	250	Rods
38	45	86	Curtis Crider	Crider '58 Ford	122	250	Engine
39	41	9	Roy Tyner	Tyner '60 Olds	86	250	Engine
40	33	78	Charley Griffith	E C Wilson '59 Chevrolet	80	250	Engine
41	25	92	Gerald Duke	Robert Davis '59 T-Bird	65	200	Distrib
42	10	89	Joe Lee Johnson	Paul McDuffie '60 Chevrolet	45	350	Rkr Arm
43	20	27	Junior Johnson	John Masoni '60 Chevy	38	200	Engine
44	37	16	Jim Reed	Reed '60 Pontiac	35	200	Axle
45	42	54	Jimmy Pardue	Lowe's '59 dodge	19	200	Fan

Time of Race: :2 hours, 39 minutes, 47 seconds
Averqage Speed: 112.652 mph
Pole Winner: Fireball Roberts - 133.870 mph
Lap Leaders: Fireball Roberts 1, Jack Smith 2-4, Bobby Johns 5, Joe Weatherly 6-14,
    Cotton Owens 15-17, Weatherly 18-33, Roberts 34-47, Weatherly 48, Roberts 49,
    Tom Pistone 50-52, Weatherly 53-70, Owens 71-188, Roberts 189-200
Cautions:
Margin of Victory: Under Caution
Attendance: 25,000

Race No. 27

Fireball Overcomes 'Trance'; Takes Dixie 300

HAMPTON, GA (July 31) -- Fireball Roberts

overcame a mid-race 'trance' and shot past Cotton Owens 12 laps from the finish to win the inaugural Dixie 300 at the new Atlanta International Raceway.

The final two laps were run under the caution flag

Smokey Yunick finely tunes his Pontiac as driver Fireball Roberts looks on

when Speedy Thompson crashed while running ninth. Thompson suffered three broken ribs in the mishap.

The finish was protested by Bud Moore, chief mechanic of the third place car driven by Jack Smith. Moore and Smith felt they had finished second behind Owens. NASCAR upheld Roberts' victory which was achieved at a speed of 112.652 mph.

Roberts said he felt a tire going flat in the 137th lap and rolled down pit road. Later, he claimed he was in a 'trance', explaining why he motored right past his pits and proceeded to return to the track. "I felt sort of goofy," admitted Roberts. "I thought a tire was about ready to blow. I was hot, tired and exhausted, and I was sort of in a trance. But after that, I was okay."

Owens was not sure where he finished, but Smith felt sure the crafty Spartanburg veteran had won. "Fireball made a stop on green and Cotton and I made one under yellow," said Smith. "I thought Owens had won."

Smith did make one of his pit stops under the yellow flag, but it took one minute and 40 seconds to service the car.

Bobby Johns finished in fourth place with Fred Lorenzen fifth.

A small crowd of 25,000 was on hand to watch the grand opening of the mile-and-a-half oval. Construction and financial problems delayed the first race almost eight months.

Point leader Rex White finished 23rd and Lee Petty wound up eighth. Petty closed to within 1,626 points of White in the point race.

Race No. 28

Jarrett Wins at Birmingham; Pettys Finish 2nd, 3rd & 8th

BIRMINGHAM, AL (Aug 3) -- Ned Jarrett wheeled his Ford to victory in the 100-miler at Dixie Speedway for his fourth win of the year. The Conover, NC driver wound up two full laps ahead of runner-up Richard Petty.

Lee Petty finished third, Joe Lee Johnson fourth and Johnny Beauchamp fifth.

Rex White finished ninth in a two year-old Chevrolet normally driven by L. D. Austin and emerged with a 1,570 point lead.

Maurice Petty made his first Grand National start and finished eighth in a Petty Engineering Plymouth.

Only 16 cars started the race and 11 were running at the finish.

Jarrett averaged 54.463 mph on the quarter-mile paved track and led all the way.

No caution flags were waved in the 50-mile event.

Grand National Race No. 28
200 Laps at Dixie Speedway
Birmingham, AL
50 Miles on Quarter-mile Paved Track
August 3, 1960

Fin	St	No.	Driver	Team / Car	Laps	Money	Status
1	1	11	Ned Jarrett	Courtesy '60 Ford	200	$770	Running
2	2	43	Richard Petty	Petty Eng '60 Plymouth	198	535	Running
3	3	42	Lee Petty	Petty Eng '60 Plymouth	196	485	Running
4	9	89	Joe Lee Johnson	Paul McDuffie '60 Chevy	195	365	Running
5	4	73	Johnny Beauchamp	'60 Chevrolet	192	245	Running
6	8	48	G C Spencer	Weldon Wagner '58 Chevy	192	210	Running
7	6	87	Buck Baker	Thor '60 Chevrolet	189	195	Running
8	5	44	Maurice Petty	Petty Eng '60 Plymouth	183	150	Running
9	7	74	Rex White	L D Austin '58 Chevrolet	182	140	Heating
10	15	17	Jimmy Pardue	'60 Dodge	178	130	Running
11	14	83	Curtis Crider	Crider '58 Ford	178	125	Running
12	13	20	Spook Crawford	Crawford '58 Ford	176	110	Running
13	10	79	James Norton	'58 Mercury	125	100	Trans
14	12	80	Neil Castles	Castles '58 Ford	98	85	Wheel
15	11	61	Jimmy Thompson	Doc White '59 T-Bird	81	80	Axle
16	16	64	L D Austin	A M Crawford '60 Ford	2	60	Engine

Time of Race: 55 minutes, 05 seconds
Average Speed: 54.463 mph
Pole Winner: Ned Jarrett - 55.866 mph
Lap Leaders: Ned Jarrett 1-200
Cautions: None
Margin of Victory: 2 laps
Attendance:

Race No. 29

Beauchamp Champ in Nashville's Rain-shortened 200-miler

NASHVILLE, TN (Aug. 7) -- Johnny Beauchamp, the "Flying Iowan", won the rain-shortened 200-miler at the Nashville Fairgrounds Speedway. It was the first win of the year for the former IMCA stock car champion and the second of his NASCAR career.

Paul Lewis spins into fence at Nashville

Grand National Race No. 29
400 Laps at Fairgrounds Speedway
Nashville, TN
200 Miles on Half-mile Paved Track
August 7, 1960

Fin	St	No.	Driver	Team / Car	Laps	Money	Status
1	2	73	Johnny Beauchamp	'60 Chevrolet	333	$3,666	Running
2	1	4	Rex White	Piedmont/Friendly '60 Chevy	333	2,390	Running
3	10	87	Buck Baker	Thor '60 Chevrolet	331	1,225	Running
4	5	42	Lee Petty	Petty Eng '60 Plymouth	330	825	Running
5	3	89	Joe Lee Johnson	Paul McDuffie '60 Chevrolet	330	718	Running
6	9	43	Richard Petty	Petty Eng '60 Plymouth	329	500	Running
7	8	44	Jim Paschal	Petty Eng '60 Plymouth	327	425	Running
8	22	23	Doug Yates	Yates '59 Plymouth	327	375	Running
9	7	18	Roz Howard	'60 Chevrolet	325	300	Running
10	12	48	G C Spencer	Weldon Wagner '58 Chevy	321	225	Running
11	6	59	Tom Pistone	Thor '60 Chevrolet	313	200	Running
12	13	19	Herman Beam	Beam '60 Ford	301	175	Running
13	18	79	James Norton	'58 Mercury	287	150	Running
14	14	64	Bob Reuther	A M Crawford '60 Ford	285	140	Rear End
15	17	83	Curtis Crider	Crider '58 Ford	273	125	Running
16	23	1	Paul Lewis	Faircloth '60 Chevrolet	250	110	Running
17	20	34	Chuck Tomes	'59 Chevrolet	205	100	Running
18	16	80	Neil Castles	Castles '58 Ford	107	100	Conn Rd
19	11	99	Wilbur Rakestraw	Talmadge Cochrane '60 Ford	77	100	Crash
20	4	11	Jed Jarrett	Courtesy '60 Ford	73	100	A Frame
21	15	17	Jimmy Pardue	'60 Dodge	62	75	Hub
22	21	9	Roy Tyner	Tyner '59 Olds	7	75	Trans
23	19	74	L D Austin	Austin '58 Chevrolet	1	75	Crank Sh

* Race Shortened to 333 laps (166 miles) due to rain
Time of Race: 2 hours, 55 minutes, 22 seconds
Average Speed: 56.966 mph
Pole Winner: Rex White - 74.81 mph
Lap Leaders:
Cautions:
Margin of Victory:
Attendance:

The race was halted after 333 laps of the scheduled 400-lapper because of rain. Beauchamp collected the winner's prize of $3,666.

Rex White finished in second place and Buck Baker was third, giving Chevrolet a 1-2-3 sweep. Lee Petty finished fourth with Joe Lee Johnson fifth.

The only crash occurred when Wilbur Rakestraw blew a tire on his Ford and smashed into the guard rail. He was not hurt.

Ned Jarrett started his Ford in the second row and ran with the leaders in the early laps. He was forced to the sidelines when an A Frame snapped after 73 laps. Jarrett was credited with a 20th place finish in the field of 23.

Beauchamp's victory came at an average speed of 56.966 mph. White upped his point lead to 1,610 over Lee Petty.

Jack Smith and Rex White on front row for start of Western North Carolina 500

Race No. 30

Pistone Blows; White Wins Western N.C. 500

WEAVERVILLE, NC (Aug 14) -- Rex White forged into the lead on lap 389 and pulled away from the field to win the Western North Carolina 500 at Asheville-Weaverville Speedway. It was White's third win of the year and the 10th of his career.

Lewis "Possum" Jones finished second, four laps back. Emanuel Zervakis was third, eight laps off the pace. Bobby Johns drove Cotton Owens' Pontiac to fourth place, a whopping 21 laps behind. Jack Smith was fifth.

A crowd of 12,500 race fans packed the grandstands in this hillside community and watched six drivers trade the lead eight times.

Johns started seventh but leaped to the front by the

fifth lap. He led for 166 laps before making his first pit stop. Tom Pistone put his Thor Chevrolet up front on two occasions for a total of 140 laps, and was heading the field when a blown engine ended his bid.

White took the lead when Pistone went to the pits and was never challenged.

Thirty-four cars started the 500 lapper on the half-mile paved track, but only 10 finished. Tenth place finisher Paul Lewis was 81 laps behind when the checkered flag fell.

Richard Petty, Fred Harb, Chuck Tomes and Joe Lee Johnson were taken out by wrecks.

White averaged 65.024 mph on what had been billed as the "fastest half-mile track in the nation".

Grand National Race No. 30
500 Laps at Asheville-Weaverville Speedway
Weaverville, NC
"Western North Carolina 500"
250 Miles on Half-mile Dirt Track
August 14, 1960

Fin	St	No.	Driver	Team / Car	Laps	Money	Status
1	2	4	Rex White	Piedmont/Friendly '60 Chevy	500	$3,650	Running
2	18	2	Possum Jones	'60 Chevrolet	496	2,225	Running
3	15	85	Emanuel Zervakis	Monroe Shook '60 Chevy	492	1,525	Running
4	7	5	Bobby Johns	Cotton Owens '60 Pontiac	479	975	Running
5	1	47	Jack Smith	Boomershine '60 Pontiac	479	800	Running
6	4	16	Glen Wood	Wood Bros '59 Ford	479	700	Running
7	24	74	L D Austin	Austin '58 Chevrolet	473	625	Running
8	14	42	Lee Petty	Petty Eng '60 Plymouth	464	675	Running
9	27	83	Curtis Crider	Crider '58 Ford	433	455	Running
10	26	1	Paul Lewis	Faircloth '60 Chevrolet	419	425	Running
11	10	99	Wilbur Rakestraw	Talmadge Cochrane '60 Ford	413	400	Wheel
12	6	59	Tom Pistone	Thor '60 Chevrolet	388	375	Engine
13	13	11	Ned Jarrett	Courtesy '60 Ford	377	325	Engine
14	11	21	Fred Harb	Wood Bros '58 Ford	370	275	Crash
15	16	43	Richard Petty	Petty Eng '60 Plymouth	359	250	Crash
16	20	19	Herman Beam	Beam '60 Ford	349	250	H Gasket
17	21	48	G C Spencer	'58 Chevrolet	330	250	Axle
18	32	80	Neil Castles	Castles '58 Ford	316	225	Trans
19	9	89	Joe Lee Johnson	Paul McDuffie '60 Chevrolet	314	325	Crash
20	3	73	Johnny Beauchamp	'60 Chevrolet	303	220	Sway Bar
21	17	92	Gerald Duke	Robert Davis '59 T-Bird	289	210	Rear End
22	5	44	Jim Paschal	Petty Eng '60 Plymouth	272	200	Rear End
23	12	23	Doug Yates	Yates '59 Plymouth	240	175	Trans
24	33	7	Jimmy Pardue	'60 Dodge	202	150	Clutch
25	23	18	Roz Howard	'60 Chevrolet	154	140	U Bolts
26	8	94	Banjo Matthews	Matthews '60 Ford	116	100	Seals
27	22	87	Buck Baker	Thor '60 Chevrolet	108	100	Shocks
28	19	64	Buddy Baker	A M Crawford '60 Ford	76	100	A Frame
29	28	17	Harvey Hege	Fred Harb '58 Ford	62	100	Steering
30	29	27	Junior Johnson	John Masoni '60 Chevy	58	100	Heating
31	25	34	Chuck Tomes	'59 Chevrolet	22	---	Crash
32	34	9	Roy Tyner	Tyner '60 Ford	21	---	Axle
33	30	77	Marvin Panch	Billie Ridgeway '60 Ford	11	---	Rear End
34	31	35	E J Trivette	'59 Dodge	6	---	Coil

Time of Race: 3 hours, 50 minutes, 41 seconds
Average Speed: 65.024 mph
Pole Winner: Jack Smith - 77.85 mph
Lap Leaders: Jack Smith 1-4, Bobby Johns 5-170, Jim Paschal 171-181, Johns 182-183, Rex White 184-199, Tom Pistone 200-310, Richard Petty 311-359, Pistone 360-388, White 389-500
Cautions:
Margin of Victory: 4 laps
Attendance: 12,500

Grand National Race No. 31
200 Laps at Hub City Speedway
Spartanburg, SC
100 Miles on Half-mile Dirt Track
August 16, 1960

Fin	St	No.	Driver	Team / Car	Laps	Money	Status
1	1	5	Cotton Owens	Owens '60 Pontiac	200	$800	Running
2	6	42	Lee Petty	Petty Eng '60 Plymouth	200	625	Running
3	11	27	Junior Johnson	John Masoni '60 Chevy	198	375	Running
4	5	11	Ned Jarrett	Courtesy '60 Ford	198	275	Running
5	9	4	Rex White	Piedmont/Friendly '60 Chevy	198	250	Running
6	7	36	Tommy Irwin	Irwin '59 T-Bird	197	215	Running
7	2	92	Gerald Duke	Robert Davis '59 T-Bird	196	175	Running
8	18	74	L D Austin	Austin '58 Chevrolet	181	150	Running
9	3	87	Buck Baker	Baker '60 Chevrolet	180	140	Running
10	20	54	Jimmy Pardue	Lowe's '59 Dodge	178	130	Running
11	15	19	Herman Beam	Beam '60 Ford	172	125	Running
12	16	83	Curtis Crider	Crider '58 Ford	148	110	Running
13	4	43	Richard Petty	Petty Eng '60 Plymouth	147	100	Batt Pst
14	8	2	Possum Jones	'60 Chevrolet	143	85	A Frame
15	12	64	Buddy Baker	A M Crawford '60 Ford	81	70	Rear End
16	14	82	Joe Eubanks	'59 Chevrolet	79	60	Wheel
17	19	80	Neil Castles	Castles '58 Ford	67	50	Ball Jnt
18	10	67	David Pearson	Pearson '59 Chevrolet	59	50	Rear End
19	13	48	G C Spencer	Weldon Wagner '58 Chevy	43	50	Ball Jnt
20	17	23	Doug Yates	Yates '59 Plymouth	6	50	Heating
21	21	93	Bobby Johns	Sunbeam Systems '59 T-Bird	2	50	Heating

Time of Race: 1 hour, 40 minutes, 32 seconds
Average Speed: 59.681 mph
Pole Winner: Cotton Owens - 63.25 mph
Lap Leader: - - - - - - - - - - - - - - Cotton Owens   -200
Cautions:
Margin of Victory: 20 yards
Attendance: 6,000

Race No. 31

Cotton Owens Wins on Neighborhood Track

SPARTANBURG, SC (Aug. 16) -- Cotton Owens, the hometown boy, grabbed first place in the 100 mile Grand National event at Hub City Speedway. The 36 year-old Pontiac chauffeur became the 15th different driver to post a win during the 1960 season.

Cotton Owens is congratulated after Spartanburg win

A crowd of 6,000 watched Owens cross under the checkered flag 20 yards ahead of runner-up Lee Petty. Junior Johnson was third, Ned Jarrett fourth and Rex White fifth.

Three young drivers, striving to make a name for themselves on the big league stock car racing circuit, encountered problems. Richard Petty, flashy newcomer out of Randleman, NC, fell out after 147 laps with a broken battery post. Buddy Baker departed after 81 laps with rear gearing failure. And David Pearson fell out on lap 59 with rear end failure.

Owens won the pole at 63.25 mph and took the 100-miler at a speed of 59.681 mph. It was the fourth win of his career.

Grand National Race No. 32
300 Laps at Columbia Speedway
Columbia, SC
150 Miles on Half-mile Dirt Track
August 18, 1960

Fin	St	No.	Driver	Team / Car	Laps	Money	Status
1	7	4	Rex White	Piedmont/Friendly '60 Chevy	300	$1,000	Running
2	9	43	Richard Petty	Petty Eng '60 Plymouth	300	600	Running
3	6	87	Buck Baker	Baker '60 Chevrolet	293	450	Running
4	21	11	Ned Jarrett	Courtesy '60 Ford	293	350	Running
5	1	36	Tommy Irwin	Irwin '59 T-Bird	293	325	Running
6	17	2	Possum Jones	'60 Chevrolet	285	300	Running
7	10	42	Lee Petty	Petty Eng '60 Plymouth	278	350	Rear End
8	15	74	L D Austin	Austin '58 Chevrolet	273	225	Running
9	14	19	Herman Beam	Beam '60 Ford	273	215	Running
10	19	83	Curtis Crider	Crider '58 Ford	255	205	Running
11	20	35	E J Trivette	'59 Plymouth	239	200	Running
12	11	64	Bunkie Blackburn	A M Crawford '60 Ford	209	160	Rear End
13	25	82	Joe Eubanks	'58 Ford	189	150	Running
14	24	1	Paul Lewis	Faircloth '60 Chevrolet	188	140	Running
15	8	5	Cotton Owens	Owens '60 Pontiac	187	120	Rear End
16	23	17	Fred Harb	Harb '58 Ford	184	110	Spindle
17	22	80	Neil Castles	Castles '58 Ford	181	100	Running
18	3	23	Doug Yates	Yates '59 Plymouth	150	100	Engine
19	4	67	David Pearson	Pearson '59 Chevrolet	134	100	Rear End
20	12	93	Bobby Johns	Sunbeam Systems '59 T-Bird	128	100	A Frame
21	18	54	Jimmy Pardue	Lowe's '59 Dodge	102	100	Crash
22	16	99	Wilbur Rakestraw	Talmadge Cochrane '60 Ford	91	100	Rear End
23	5	92	Gerald Duke	Robert Davis '59 T-Bird	80	50	Fuel Pmp
24	13	27	Junior Johnson	John Masoni '60 Chevy	54	50	Steering
25	26	61	Joe Weatherly	Doc White '59 T-Bird	49	50	Rear End
26	2	48	G C Spencer	Weldon Wagner '58 Chevy	42	---	Rear End

Time of Race: 2 hours, 45 minutes, 51 seconds
Average Speed: 54.265 mph
Pole Winner: Tommy Irwin - 60.36 mph
Lap Leaders: - - - - - - - - - - - - - - - Rex White   -300
Cautions:
Margin of Victory:
Attendance:

Race No. 32

Independents Fade; White Grabs Columbia Victory

COLUMBIA, SC (Aug. 18) -- Rex White continued his drive to the 1960 NASCAR Grand National championship with a victory in the 150-miler at Columbia Speedway. It was the fourth win of the year for the 31 year-old Chevrolet driver.

Richard Petty, finishing second, was the only driver other than White to complete the 300 laps on the half-mile dirt track. Buck Baker took third with Ned Jarrett fourth and pole sitter Tommy Irwin fifth.

Lee Petty had been running in third place, but rear end failure in the closing stages put him down to seventh in the final rundown.

Second fastest qualifier G. C. Spencer encountered tough luck and finished last in the 26 car field.

White won the 150-miler at an average speed of 54.265 mph after Irwin won the pole at 60.36 mph. The first five qualifiers were a major surprise as relative newcomers Doug Yates, David Pearson and Gerald Duke lined up behind the front row of Irwin and Spencer to take the green flag.

Race No. 33

Johnson Cops South Boston As Jarrett Blows

SOUTH BOSTON, VA (Aug. 20) -- Junior Johnson ended a six-month famine and won the 37.5 -mile race at the South Boston Speedway for his first victory since winning the Daytona 500 in February. It was the 18th career win for the Ronda Road Runner.

Johnson and Ned Jarrett swapped the lead 12 times before the Chevrolet driver took the lead for good on lap 109. Jarrett was holding down a narrow lead when the engine blew in his Ford, giving the race to Johnson.

Possum Jones finished second, a lap behind the fleet Johnson. Rex White came in third with Buck Baker fourth and Fred Harb fifth.

Lee Petty, feeling his Plymouth was not as strong as his son Richard's, swapped cars at the last moment. Richard finished sixth in Lee's #42 and Lee was seventh in Richard's #43.

Johnson averaged 50.732 mph.

Wood led the entire 200 laps on the quarter-mile paved oval. The Ford driver has led a remarkable 600 consecutive laps at this facility in Grand National competition.

Lee Petty dogged Wood in the early stages, but could not keep up. He wound up second, a lap off the pace. Junior Johnson came in third with Rex White fourth and Buck Baker fifth.

Sixteen cars in the field of 17 were running at the finish. The only dropout was G. C. Spencer in his Chevrolet. It was the third consecutive race in which Spencer has finished dead last, a dubious honor which may never be broken.

Wood won $770 for his 44.389 mph victory.

Grand National Race No. 33
150 Laps at South Boston Speedway
South Boston, VA
37.5 Miles on Quarter-mile Dirt Track
August 20, 1960

Fin	St	No.	Driver	Team / Car	Laps	Money	Status
1	2	27	Junior Johnson	Daytona Kennel '59 Chevy	150	$810	Running
2	14	2	Possum Jones	'60 Chevrolet	149	545	Running
3	4	4	Rex White	Piedmont/Friendly '59 Chevy	148	410	Running
4	15	87	Buck Baker	Baker '60 Chevrolet	147	290	Running
5	9	17	Fred Harb	Harb '58 Ford	146	260	Running
6	3	42	Richard Petty	Petty Eng '60 Plymouth	144	235	Running
7	10	43	Lee Petty	Petty Eng '60 Plymouth	144	275	Running
8	6	80	Neil Castles	Castles '58 Ford	144	150	Running
9	11	74	L D Austin	Austin '58 Chevrolet	142	140	Running
10	7	35	Jimmy Pardue	'59 Dodge	135	130	Running
11	13	19	Herman Beam	Beam '60 Ford	131	125	Running
12	12	83	Curtis Crider	Crider '59 Ford	130	110	Running
13	5	93	Bobby Johns	Sunbeam Systems '59 T-Bird	125	115	Running
14	1	11	Ned Jarrett	Courtesy '60 Ford	108	120	Engine
15	8	48	G C Spencer	Weldon Wagner '58 Chevy	22	70	Rear End

Time of Race: 44 minutes, 21 seconds
Average Speed: 50.732 mph
Pole Winner: Ned Jarrett - 51.903 mph
Lap Leaders: 12 lead changes, --- Jarrett ...-108, Johnson 109-150
Cautions:
Margin of Victory:
Attendance:

Grand National Race No. 34
200 Laps at Bowman-Gray Stadium
Winston-Salem, NC
50 Miles on Quarter-mile Paved Track
August 23, 1960

Fin	St	No.	Driver	Taam / Car	Laps	Money	Status
1	1	16	Glen Wood	Wood Bros '58 Ford	200	$770	Running
2	2	42	Lee Petty	Petty Eng '60 Plymouth	199	635	Running
3	5	27	Junior Johnson	Junior Johnson '59 Chevy	199	365	Running
4	4	4	Rex White	Piedmont/Friendly '59 Chevy	199	260	Running
5	6	87	Buck Baker	Baker '60 Chevrolet	198	245	Running
6	9	21	Fred Harb	Harb '59 Ford	198	200	Running
7	11	12	Joe Weatherly	'60 Valiant	195	180	Running
8	7	93	Bobby Johns	Sunbeam Systems '59 T-Bird	194	165	Running
9	3	43	Richard Petty	Petty Eng '60 Plymouth	194	175	Running
10	8	11	Ned Jarrett	Courtesy '60 Ford	193	140	Running
11	13	17	Shorty York	'58 Ford	191	125	Running
12	12	74	L D Austin	Austin '58 Chevrolet	186	110	Running
13	17	54	Jimmy Pardue	Lowe's '59 Dodge	177	100	Running
14	14	1	Paul Lewis	Faircloth '58 Chevrolet	176	85	Running
15	15	83	Curtis Crider	Crider '58 Ford	174	70	Running
16	16	35	E J Trivette	'59 Plymouth	173	60	Running
17	10	48	G C Spencer	Weldon Wagner '58 Chevy	62	50	Sway Bar

Time of Race: 1 hour, 7 minutes, 35 seconds
Average Speed: 44.389 mph
Pole Winner: Glen Wood - 46.97 mph
Lap Leaders: Glen Wood 1-200
Cautions: 1 for 3 laps
Margin of Victory: 1 lap plus
Attendance:

Race No. 34

Glen Wood 3-for-3 At Winston-Salem

WINSTON-SALEM, NC (Aug. 23) -- Glen Wood proved he was the "Master of the Madhouse" with his third win of the season in the 50-mile Grand National race at Bowman-Gray Stadium.

Race No. 35

Three Die as Buck Baker Wins Southern 500

DARLINGTON, SC (Sept. 5) -- Buck Baker, an old pro long overdue, rode a flat tire to victory in the 11th annual Southern 500 at Darlington Raceway. The event was filled with tragedy, caution flags and confusion.

One accident left two mechanics and a race official dead, while in a separate incident another mechanic was badly injured.

The dead were mechanics Paul McDuffie and

Bobby Johns' Pontiac lies upside down after tragic crash that killed three at Darlington

Charles Sweatlund, both of Atlanta, and NASCAR official Joe Taylor of Paterson, NJ. They were fatally injured when the Pontiac of Bobby Johns slammed into the unprotected pit area after brushing Roy Tyner's Oldsmobile. McDuffie, Sweatlund and Taylor were cut down by flying chunks of concrete in the backstretch

Elmo Langley crashed into the pits in Southern 500

accident.

Seriously injured in the same accident were Ralph Byers, Roger Vermillion, Jr. and John Blalock, all pit attendants on Joe Lee Johnson's Chevrolet. McDuffie, car owner and crew chief for Johnson, withdrew from the race moments after the crash.

Ankrum "Spook" Crawford of Fayetteville, NC was seriously injured when Elmo Langley's T-Bird crashed into the pits in the front chute in an earlier wreck. Debris from the crash struck Crawford.

Grand National Race No. 35
364 Laps at Darlington Raceway
Darlington, SC
"Southern 500"
500 Miles on 1.375-mile Paved Track
September 5, 1960

Fin	St	No.	Driver	Team / Car	Laps	Money	Status
1	2	47	Buck Baker	Boomershine '60 Pontiac	364	$19,900	Running
2	7	4	Rex White	Piedmont/Friendly '60 Chevy	364	9,780	Running
3	3	44	Jim Paschal	Petty Eng '60 Plymouth	362	5,595	Running
4	16	85	Emanuel Zervakis	Monroe Shook '60 Chevrolet	362	3,125	Running
5	20	11	Ned Jarrett	Courtesy '60 Ford	362	2,000	Running
6	8	43	Richard Petty	Petty Eng '60 Plymouth	361	2,575	Running
7	17	94	Banjo Matthews	Matthews '60 Ford	361	1,255	Running
8	21	73	Johnny Beauchamp	'60 Chevrolet	358	1,025	Running
9	1	22	Fireball Roberts	John Hines '60 Pontiac	353	2,175	Axle
10	34	23	Doug Yates	Yates '59 Plymouth	353	775	Running
11	24	77	Marvin Panch	Billie Ridgeway '60 Ford	351	700	Running
12	26	70	Elmo Henderson	W H Watson '58 Pontiac	338	600	Running
13	39	38	Clem Proctor	Charles Chapman '60 Ford	338	500	Running
14	36	1	Paul Lewis	Faircloth '60 Chevrolet	335	450	Engine
15	29	81	Shorty Rollins	Rollins '60 Ford	331	500	Running
16	35	60	Jim Whitman	Dick Stanley '60 Dodge	320	350	Engine
17	41	74	L D Austin	Austin '58 Chevrolet	310	300	Running
18	37	19	Herman Beam	Beam '60 Ford	305	250	Running
19	32	45	Tiny Lund	Bill Gazaway '59 Olds	304	250	Crash
20	43	83	Curtis Crider	Crider '58 Ford	304	250	Crash
21	4	12	Joe Weatherly	Holman-Moody '60 Ford	303	200	Crash
22	44	20	G C Spencer	A M Crawford '58 Ford	301	200	Running
23	25	61	Jimmy Thompson	Doc White '59 T-Bird	278	200	Axle
24	6	6	Cotton Owens	Owens '60 Pontiac	277	510	Axle
25	45	10	T C Hunt	'60 Plymouth	260	200	Crash
26	30	99	Wilbur Rakestraw	Talmadge Cochrane '60 Ford	217	200	Axle
27	22	67	David Pearson	Pearson '59 Chevrolet	214	200	Axle
28	14	28	Fred Lorenzen	Rupert Safety Belt '60 Ford	188	250	Engine
29	42	16	Steve McGrath	Happy Stiegel '59 Pontiac	188	200	Engine
30	9	42	Lee Petty	Petty Eng '60 Plymouth	188	470	Crash
31	33	39	Herb Tillman	Ralph Stark '60 Chevrolet	180	200	Rear End
32	38	33	Reb Wickersham	Wickersham '60 Olds	163	200	Axle
33	46	54	Jimmy Pardue	Lowe's '59 Dodge	143	200	Oil Pres
34	23	87	Buddy Baker	Buck Baker '60 Chevrolet	136	200	Fuel Pmp
35	47	96	Gene White	'60 Chevrolet	134	200	Engine
36	28	7	Jim Reed	Reed '60 Chevrolet	130	200	A Frame
37	13	69	Johnny Allen	Hanley Dawson '60 Chevy	125	220	Engine
38	12	59	Tom Pistone	Thor '60 Chevrolet	115	230	Engine
39	19	90	Speedy Thompson	Junie Donlavey '60 Ford	110	250	Engine
40	5	5	Bobby Johns	Cotton Owens '60 Pontiac	95	210	Crash
41	11	89	Joe Lee Johnson	Paul McDuffie '60 Chevrolet	95	550	Withdrew
42	40	9	Roy Tyner	Tyner '59 Olds	86	200	Crash
43	15	2	Possum Jones	'60 Chevrolet	76	200	C Pulley
44	31	79	Johnny Miller	'60 Ford	26	200	Crash
45	18	92	Elmo Langley	Robert Davis '59 T-Bird	25	220	Crash
46	27	64	Bunkie Blackburn	A M Crawford '60 Ford	24	200	Crash
47	10	27	Junior Johnson	John Masoni '60 Chevy	17	200	Engine
48	48	35	E J Trivette	'59 Plymouth	1	200	Handling

Time of Race: 4 hours, 43 minutes, 34 seconds
Average Speed: 105.901 mph
Pole Winner: Fireball Roberts - 125.459 mph
Fastest Qualifier: Cotton Owens - 126.146 mph
Lap Leaders: Buck Baker 1-6, Fireball Roberts 7-26, Baker 27-42   Roberts 43-75
    Owens 76-84, Richard Petty 85, Bobby Johns 86-89, Rex White 90-93, Baker 94-155,
    R Petty 156-170, Lee Petty 171-183, Baker 184-224, R Petty 225-314, Baker 315-364
Cautions: 5 for 61 laps
Margin of Victory: 25 seconds
Attendance: 80,000

Baker, Fireball Roberts and young Richard Petty treated the standing room only crowd of 80,000 to a terrific duel. Petty pushed his lightly regarded Plymouth to the limit and hounded the powerful Pontiac favorite.

Baker, who put Bud Moore's Pontiac into the lead

on five occasions for 175 laps, was cruising toward the checkered flag when the day's fifth and final caution came out for Tiny Lund's solo crack-up with 20 laps to go. Roberts and Petty closed in on the rear of Baker, poised for an electrifying shoot-out.

Roberts was sniffing Baker's exhaust when the engine in his Smokey Yunick-prepared Pontiac belched fatal smoke with 11 laps remaining. Petty popped a tire

Ned Jarrett took his gas can onto the track at Darlington

Grand National Race No. 36
250 Laps at Hickory Speedway
Hickory, NC
"Buddy Shuman Memorial"
100 Miles on .4-mile Dirt Track
September 9, 1960

Fin	St	No.	Driver	Team / Car	Laps	Money	Status
1	2	27	Junior Johnson	John Masoni '60 Chevy	250	$800	Running
2	5	2	Possum Jones	'60 Chevrolet	249	525	Running
3	7	4	Rex White	Piedmont/Friendly '59 Chevy	246	375	Running
4	9	67	David Pearson	Pearson '59 Chevrolet	246	275	Running
5	3	11	Ned Jarrett	Courtesy '60 Ford	241	250	Running
6	10	54	Jimmy Pardue	Lowe's '59 Dodge	237	215	Running
7	11	17	Fred Harb	Harb '58 Ford	235	175	Running
8	6	42	Lee Petty	Petty Eng '60 Plymouth	234	250	Running
9	13	19	Herman Beam	Beam '60 Ford	228	140	Running
10	14	1	Paul Lewis	Faircloth '60 Chevrolet	224	130	Running
11	4	48	G C Spencer	Weldon Wagner '58 Chevy	202	125	Running
12	8	43	Richard Petty	Petty Eng '60 Plymouth	201	110	Engine
13	12	83	Curtis Crider	Crider '58 Ford	198	100	Running
14	15	35	E J Trivette	'59 Plymouth	173	85	Running
15	1	87	Buck Baker	Baker '60 Chevrolet	68	70	Fuel Pmp

Time of Race: 1 hour, 25 minutes, 43 seconds
Average Speed: 69.998 mph
Pole Winner: Buck Baker - 71.18 mph
Lap Leaders: - - - - - - - - - - - - - - Junior Johnson   -250
Cautions:
Margin of Victory:
Attendance:

with three laps left, taking him out of the victory hunt.

Baker was left alone in the lead lap. However the Charlotte veteran blew a tire and spun crazily with a lap and a half to go. Rex White, who suddenly found himself in second place, received two white flags and finally the checkered flag as Baker limped on the apron of the track for the final two miles.

Confusion broke loose immediately after the race. Chief Scorer Joe Epton examined the score cards and determined that Baker had completed the 500 miles first.

Baker, in winning his first superspeedway race in six years, did not officially lay claim to the $19,900 first prize until nearly 7:00 p.m.

White got credit for second and all but assured himself of the 1960 Grand National Championship. Third place went to Jim Paschal, fourth to Emanuel Zervakis and fifth to Ned Jarrett. Richard Petty wound up sixth.

A crowd of 80,000 was on hand in mid-90 degree weather. The temperature of the track surface soared to 145 degrees, the hottest Southern 500 ever.

Best seat in the house

Race No. 36

Johnson Beats Jones in Buddy Shuman Memorial

HICKORY, NC (Sept 9) -- Junior Johnson nabbed his third win of the season in the Buddy Shuman Memorial 100-miler at Hickory Speedway. It was the 19th career triumph for the Chevrolet driver.

Possum Jones finished second for the third time in the 1960 season. Rex White came in third, David Pearson was fourth and Ned Jarrett fifth.

Buck Baker, fresh from his Southern 500 victory, started on the pole with a speed of 71.18 mph. However a faulty fuel pump sidelined his Chevrolet after 68 laps and he wound up last in the 15 car field.

Only one other starter failed to finish. Richard Petty dropped out with a blown engine after 201 of the 250 laps.

Johnson averaged 69.998 mph in his Daytona Kennel Club Chevrolet.

Race No. 37

Jim Cook's Dodge Tops at Sacramento

SACRAMENTO, CA (Sept 11) -- Jim Cook drove his Dodge to victory in the 100-miler at the Sacramento Fairgrounds for his first Grand National triumph. The win came in Cook's 23rd start, and he became the 16th different driver in the 1960 season.

Scotty Cain finished second in a T-Bird, Lloyd Dane was third and Ron Hornaday fourth. Fifth place went to Danny Weinberg, who fell out with five laps remaining when the engine in his Ford overheated.

Fritz Wilson, a top contender in the inaugural Daytona races in 1959, was kayoed in a seventh lap crash. Eddie Gray and Marshall Sargent were put out after an opening lap accident. There were no injuries.

Al Pombo started 12th and finished 16th in a Ford. It was Pombo's first Grand National start since August 19, 1956 at San Mateo, CA. In that race, Pombo spun

Grand National Race No. 37
100 Laps at Sacramento Fairgrounds
Sacramento, CA
100 Miles on 1-Mile Dirt Track
September 11, 1960

Fin	St	No.	Driver	Team / Car	Laps	Money	Status
1	1	0	Jim Cook	'60 Dodge	100	$1,100	Running
2	3	4	Scotty Cain	'59 T-Bird	100	700	Running
3	6	44	Lloyd Dane	'59 Ford	99	500	Running
4	2	2	Ron Hornaday	'60 Ford	96	400	Running
5	7	16	Danny Weinberg	'60 Ford	95	300	Heating
6	11	28N	Kuzie Kuzmanich	'60 Pontiac	93	250	Running
7	4	18	Dick Smith	'58 Mercury	92	200	Running
8	20	5	Jim Blomgren	'60 Ford	91	150	Running
9	9	91	Bruce Worrell	'59 Plymouth	90	100	Running
10	15	23	Bob Perry	'59 Plymouth	78	100	Running
11	16	43	Bob Ross	'58 Mercury	74	100	Running
12	18	5	Bob Price	'59 Chevrolet	73	100	Running
13	23	99	Al Self	'58 Chevrolet	70	100	Heating
14	21	20	Jack Norton	'59 Chevrolet	65	100	RR Axle
15	8	86	Frank Secrist	'60 Ford	60	75	Heating
16	12	3	Al Pombo	'58 Ford	52	50	Running
17	17	25	Johnny Potter	'58 Ford	47	50	Rear End
18	22	69	Clyde Mitchell	'58 Pontiac	47	50	RF Wheel
19	10	97	Marvin Porter	Vel Miletich '59 Ford	33	50	H Gasket
20	14	48	Fritz Wilson	'58 Ford	7	50	Crash
21	5	7	Don Noel	'59 Ford	2	50	Clutch
22	13	11	Marshall Sargent	'60 Plymouth	1	25	Crash
23	19	6	Eddie Gray	'58 Ford	1	25	Crash

Time of Race: 1 hour, 24 minutes, 57 seconds
Average Speed: 70.629 mph
Pole Winner: Jim Cook - 78.45 mph
Lap Leaders: - - - - - - - - - - - - - - - Jim Cook　　-100
Cautions:
Margin of Victory:
Attendance:

Grand National Race No. 38
200 Laps at Gamecock Speedway
Sumter, SC
50 Miles on Quarter-mile Dirt Track
September 15, 1960

Fin	St	No.	Driver	Team / Car	Laps	Money	Status
1	2	11	Ned Jarrett	Courtesy '60 Ford	200	$770	Running
2	1	67	David Pearson	Pearson '59 Chevrolet	200	535	Running
3	8	27	Junior Johnson	John Masoni '60 Chevy	199	385	Running
4	13	48	G C Spencer	Weldon Wagner '58 Chevy	195	270	Running
5	10	42	Lee Petty	Petty Eng '60 Plymouth	195	325	Running
6	6	4	Rex White	Piedmont / Friendly '59 Chevy	194	200	Running
7	4	43	Richard Petty	Petty Eng '60 Plymouth	194	190	Running
8	12	54	Jimmy Pardue	Lowe's '59 Dodge	191	165	Running
9	5	74	L D Austin	Austin '58 Chevrolet	187	140	Running
10	11	87	Buck Baker	Thor '60 Chevrolet	183	130	Running
11	9	9	Curtis Crider	'59 Olds	110	125	Axle
12	7	17	Fred Harb	Harb '58 Ford	107	125	Engine
13	3	23	Doug Yates	Yates '59 Plymouth	34	110	RF Hub

Time of Race: 1 hour, 12 minutes, 48 seconds
Average Speed: 41.208 mph
Pole Winner: David Pearson - 45.07 mph
Lap Leaders: - - - - - - - - - - - - - - Ned Jarrett　　-200
Cautions:
Margin of Victory:
Attendance:

off the course and watched a police officer get run over. The officer had trotted across the track to check on the condition of Pombo.

Cook averaged 70.629 mph after starting on the pole at 78.45 mph.

Race No. 38

Jarrett Gobbles Up Field In Gamecock Victory

SUMTER, SC (Sept. 15) -- Ned Jarrett held off rookie David Pearson in a stretch duel and won the 50-mile Grand National event at Gamecock Speedway. It was the fifth win of the year for the two-time NASCAR Sportsman champion.

Pearson started on the pole in his Chevrolet and gave Jarrett a run for his money throughout the 200 lapper on the quarter-mile dirt track.

Only 13 cars were on hand, testimony of the car-killing Southern 500 ten days earlier. Curtis Crider, Fred Harb and third fastest qualifier Doug Yates were the only drivers not around at the finish.

Junior Johnson finished third with G C Spencer fourth. Fifth place went to Lee Petty. Rex White came in sixth and held a 3,660 point lead over Richard Petty, who finished seventh.

Jarrett averaged 41.208 mph for his seventh career Grand National win.

Grand National Race No. 39
110 Laps at Orange Speedway
Hillsboro, NC
99 Miles on .9-mile Dirt Track
September 18, 1960

Fin	St	No.	Driver	Team / Car	Laps	Money	Status
1	1	43	Richard Petty	Petty Eng '60 Plymouth	110	$800	Running
2	4	11	Ned Jarrett	Courtesy '60 Ford	109	525	Running
3	6	4	Rex White	Piedmont /Friendly '59 Chevy	106	375	Running
4	16	19	Herman Beam	Beam '60 Ford	103	275	Running
5	13	54	Jimmy Pardue	Lowe's '59 Dodge	103	250	Running
6	8	36	Tommy Irwin	Irwin '59 T-Bird	102	215	Wheel
7	14	74	L D Austin	Austin '58 Chevrolet	102	175	Running
8	11	87	Buck Baker	Thor '60 Chevrolet	101	150	Running
9	17	9	Roy Tyner	Tyner '59 Olds	101	140	Running
10	15	1	Paul Lewis	Faircloth '60 Chevrolet	99	130	Running
11	7	42	Lee Petty	Petty Eng '60 Plymouth	87	225	Rear End
12	12	17	Fred Harb	Harb '58 Ford	85	110	Rear End
13	2	27	Junior Johnson	John Masoni '59 Chevy	75	110	Crash
14	10	61	Elmo Langley	Doc White '59 T-Bird	70	85	Rear End
15	9	67	David Pearson	Pearson '59 Chevrolet	55	70	Axle
16	3	23	Doug Yates	Yates '59 Plymouth	50	60	Axle
17	18	35	Curtis Crider	'59 Plymouth	45	50	Rear End
18	5	76	Larry Frank	'59 T-Bird	8	50	Heating

Time of Race: 1 hour, 14 minutes, 06 seconds
Average Speed: 80.161 mph
Polle Winner: Richard Petty - 85.285 mph
Lap Leaders: Richard Petty 1-110
Cautions: 1 for 3 laps
Margin of Victory: 1 lap plus
Attendance:

Race No. 39

Richard Roars to Victory in Orange Speedway 99

HILLSBORO, NC (Sept 18) -- Richard Petty scored his third win of the season in impressive style by taking the 99-mile Grand National race at Orange Speedway.

The 23 year-old hotshot started on the pole and led all 110 laps on the gently banked .9-mile dirt oval. His blue Plymouth was a full lap ahead of runner-

Richard Petty in uniform -- a sleeveless button-up shirt

up Ned Jarrett's Ford. Rex White was third, and Herman Beam registered a mild surprise by taking fourth place. Jimmy Pardue was fifth.

Junior Johnson started second and pressured Petty for 75 laps. As Johnson went sliding into the first turn in the 75th lap, the rear end broke loose on his Chevrolet. Johnson spun over the banking and landed in the woods. He was through for the day.

Lee Petty moved up to second with Johnson's departure, but he broke an axle with 13 laps remaining. He got credit for 11th place in the final rundown.

Tommy Irwin was running third with just five laps to go when the lug nuts broke on his right front wheel. Irwin's T-Bird screeched to a halt in a turn, and narrowly missed being T-boned by other cars. He dropped to sixth in the final order.

One caution flag interrupted Petty's hot pace. He averaged 80.161 mph.

Race No. 40

White Nips Weatherly In Old Dominion 500

MARTINSVILLE, VA (Sept 25) -- Little Rex White passed Joe Weatherly with nine laps to go and prevailed in a stirring duel to win the Old Dominion Sweepstakes 500 at Martinsville Speedway. It was the fifth win of the year for the 5'4", 145 pounder.

Herman Beam spins at Martinsville

Weatherly finished second, one car length behind White as the crowd of 15,000 were on their feet for the finish. Junior Johnson came in third, Jim Paschal was

Lee and Richard Petty crashed together at Martinsville

fourth and Buck Baker fifth.

Richard and Lee Petty virtually lost all hopes of winning the championship when they crashed together on lap 290. Bobby Johns' T-Bird was also involved.

Glen Wood started on the pole for the 10th time in his career. The Stuart, VA driver challenged early but fell out after 232 laps with a leaking rear grease seal. He got credit for 25th in the field of 31.

Jimmy Massey started third in a Wood Brothers Ford, but retired on lap 136 with brake failure.

Rookie David Pearson wound up seventh in one of his best Grand National efforts to date.

White's 12th career win came at an average speed of 60.439 mph.

Grand National Race No. 40
500 Laps at Martinsville Speedway
Martinsville, VA
"Old Dominion 500"
250 Miles on Half-mile Paved Track
September 25, 1960

Fin	St	No.	Driver	Team / Car	Laps	Money	Status
1	2	4	Rex White	Piedmont/Friendly '60 Chevy	500	$3,110	Running
2	4	12	Joe Weatherly	Holman-Moody '60 Ford	500	1,790	Running
3	15	27	Junior Johnson	John Masoni '59 Chevy	499	975	Running
4	16	44	Jim Paschal	Petty Eng '60 Plymouth	497	625	Running
5	18	87	Buck Baker	Thor '60 Chevrolet	494	575	Running
6	9	81	Larry Frank	Shorty Rollins '60 Ford	493	525	Running
7	10	67	David Pearson	Pearson '59 Chevrolet	493	400	Running
8	8	85	Emanuel Zervakis	Monroe Shook '60 Chevy	492	325	Running
9	13	73	Johnny Beauchamp	'60 Chevrolet	489	275	Running
10	20	59	Tom Pistone	Thor '60 Chevrolet	489	250	Running
11	23	3	Al White	'58 Ford	470	235	Running
12	11	28	Fred Lorenzen	Lorenzen '60 Ford	468	150	Running
13	26	19	Herman Beam	Beam '60 Ford	467	150	Running
14	25	54	Jimmy Pardue	Lowe's '59 Dodge	462	140	Running
15	30	74	L D Austin	Austin '58 Chevrolet	455	100	Running
16	28	48	G C Spencer	Weldon Wagner '58 Chevy	438	100	Running
17	27	8	Lennie Page	'59 T-Bird	419	125	Gr Seal
18	24	79	Jimmy Thompson	Robert Ranney '60 Ford	397	125	Heating
19	21	61	Elmo Langley	Doc White '59 T-Bird	393	200	Rear End
20	22	90	Runt Harris	Junie Donlavey '60 Ford	367	150	Brakes
21	6	23	Doug Yates	Yates '59 Plymouth	354	100	U Joint
22	17	43	Richard Petty	Petty Eng '60 Plymouth	290	75	Crash
23	7	42	Lee Petty	Petty Eng '60 Plymouth	285	200	Crash
24	5	93	Bobby Johns	Sunbeam Systems '59 T-Bird	246	125	Crash
25	1	21	Glen Wood	Wood Bros '60 Ford	232	225	Gr Seal
26	12	17	Fred Harb	Harb '58 Ford	143	75	Engine
27	3	16	Jimmy Massey	Wood Bros '58 Ford	136	150	Brakes
28	14	11	Ned Jarrett	Courtesy '60 Ford	103	75	Engine
29	19	2	Possum Jones	'60 Chevrolet	98	75	Handling
30	31	1	Paul Lewis	Faircloth '60 Chevrolet	43	75	Engine
31	29	83	Curtis Crider	Crider '58 Ford	1	50	Con Rod

Time of Race: 4 hours, 08 minutes, 11 seconds
Average Speed: 60.439 mph
Pole Winner: Glen Wood - 68.44 mph
Lap Leaders: ---- Joe Weatherly -491, Rex White 492-500
Cautions:
Margin of Victory: 1 Car length
Attendance: 15,000

Race No. 41

White Outdrives Johnson
To Win Wilkes 200

NORTH WILKESBORO, NC (Oct 2) -- Rex White breezed into the lead when Cotton Owens crashed with 79 laps to go and hustled to his sixth win of the year in the Wilkes 200 at North Wilkesboro Speedway.

White fended off Junior Johnson in the late stages to win the $2,200 first prize. Possum Jones came in third, Joe Weatherly was fourth and Buck Baker fifth.

Owens started 11th on the grid but quickly established his dominance. The Spartanburg Pontiac driver was pulling away when a ball joint broke, sending him into the wall.

Winner White admitted, "I kind of fell into this one. Owens' Pontiac was the fastest thing I have ever seen on a five-eighths mile track."

Jim Paschal was pressing White for the lead when he blew a tire on his Petty Engineering Plymouth and clobbered the wall. The mishap occurred with just 11 laps left. The High Point, NC driver got credit for 10th place in the field of 24.

Lee Petty wrecked for the third time in the last six races. A right front tire blew on his Plymouth in the 129th lap and he struck the retaining wall.

Five caution flags held White's average speed to 77.444 mph after he had won the pole at 93.399 mph.

Grand National Race No. 41
320 Laps at North Wilkesboro
Speedway
North Wilkesboro, NC
"Wilkes 200"
200 Miles on .625-mile Paved Track
October 2, 1960

Fin	St	No.	Driver	Team / Car	Laps	Money	Status
1	1	4	Rex White	Piedmont/Friendly '60 Chevy	320	$2,200	Running
2	10	27	Junior Johnson	John Masoni '60 Chevy	320	1,225	Running
3	6	2	Possum Jones	'60 Chevrolet	320	800	Running
4	5	16	Joe Weatherly	Wood Bros '58 Ford	318	525	Running
5	4	87	Buck Baker	Thor '60 Chevrolet	314	375	Running
6	2	43	Richard Petty	Petty Eng '60 Plymouth	314	315	Running
7	7	11	Ned Jarrett	Courtesy '60 Ford	313	275	Running
8	18	67	David Pearson	Pearson '59 Chevrolet	313	250	Running
9	12	59	Tom Pistone	Thor '60 Chevrolet	311	230	Running
10	3	44	Jim Paschal	Petty Eng '60 Plymouth	309	220	Crash
11	14	17	Fred Harb	Harb '59 Ford	309	200	Running
12	16	54	Jimmy Pardue	Lowe's '59 Dodge	305	150	Running
13	21	7	Buddy Baker	Bake.'58 Ford	302	110	Running
14	19	19	Herman Beam	Beam '60 Ford	298	100	Running
15	23	83	Curtis Crider	Crider '58 Frod	297	100	Running
16	20	74	L D Austin	Austin '60 Chevrolet	293	100	Running
17	17	48	G C Spencer	Weldon Wagner '58 Chevy	280	75	Running
18	11	6	Cotton Owens	Owens '60 Pontiac	241	75	Crash
19	9	23	Doug Yates	Yates '59 Plymouth	233	75	Crash
20	8	42	Lee Petty	Petty Eng '60 Plymouth	129	175	Crash
21	22	35	E J Trivette	'59 Plymouth	109	75	Fuel Pmp
22	13	76	Larry Frank	'59 T-Bird	85	75	Rear End
23	15	61	Elmo Langley	Doc White '59 T-Bird	13	50	Rear End
24	24	1	Paul Lewis	Faircloth '60 Chevrolet	9	50	Engine

Time of Race: 2 hours, 34 minutes, 57 seconds
Average Speed: 77.444 mph
Pole Winner: Rex White - 93.399 mph
Lap Leaders: ---- Owens - 241, White 242-320
Cautions: 5
Margin of Victory: Half lap
Attendance:

Race No. 42

Forgotten Speedy Thompson Wins Charlotte 400 in Wood Brothers Ford

CHARLOTTE, NC (Oct 16) -- Speedy Thompson outlasted a parade of blowouts and crack-ups to win the inaugural National 400 at Charlotte Motor Speedway. It was the 19th career win for the all-but-forgotten Monroe, NC veteran.

Thompson got the assignment in the Wood Brothers Ford and led the final 35 laps. His big opportunity came on lap 233 when leader Fireball Roberts blew a tire and rapped the retaining wall. Thompson outdistanced Richard Petty by one lap and 12 seconds to win $12,710 before an audience of 29,166.

The race was marred by a spectacular collision be-

Grand National Race No. 42
267 Laps at Charlotte Motor Speedway
Charlotte, NC
"National 400"
400 Miles on 1.5-mile Paved Track
October 16, 1960

Fin	St	No.	Driver	Team / Car	Laps	Money	Status
1	3	21	Speedy Thompson	Wood Bros '60 Ford	267	$12,710	Running
2	21	43	Richard Petty	Petty Eng '60 Plymouth	266	5,550	Running
3	11	11	Ned Jarrett	Courtesy '60 Ford	266	3,275	Running
4	6	5	Bobby Johns	Cotton Owens '60 Pontiac	265	2,880	Running
5	14	27	Junior Johnson	John Masoni '60 Pontiac	265	1,855	Running
6	4	4	Rex White	Piedmont/Friendly '60 Chevy	265	2,050	Running
7	9	85	Emanuel Zervakis	Monroe Shook '60 Chevy	263	1,100	Running
8	7	44	Jim Paschal	Petty Eng '60 Plymouth	261	920	Running
9	30	59	Tom Pistone	Lynn Holloway '59 Pontiac	260	700	Running
10	17	94	Banjo Matthews	Matthews '60 Ford	259	725	Running
11	31	15	Roscoe Thompson	Beau Morgan '60 Ford	258	500	Running
12	12	73	Johnny Beauchamp	'60 Chevrolet	256	400	Running
13	34	23	Doug Yates	Yates '59 Plymouth	254	350	Running
14	23	49	Bob Welborn	Welborn '60 Ford	250	350	Running
15	16	2	Possum Jones	'60 Chevrolet	248	350	Running
16	41	48	G C Spencer	Weldon Wagner '58 Chevy	245	350	Running
17	37	61	Elmo Langley	Doc White '59 T-Bird	244	300	Running
18	10	87	Buck Baker	Baker '60 Chevrolet	243	530	Running
19	49	—	Wes Morgan	'60 Chevrolet	239	300	Running
20	43	19	Herman Beam	Beam '60 Ford	238	300	Running
21	29	67	David Pearson	Pearson '59 Chevrolet	236	225	Running
22	22	78	Friday Hassler	E C Wilson '60 Chevrolet	235	225	Running
23	1	22	Fireball Roberts	John Hines '60 Pontiac	232	2,435	Crash
24	40	74	L D Austin	Austin '58 Chevrolet	229	225	Running
25	39	33	Reb Wickersham	Wickersham '60 Olds	225	925	Running
26	18	69	Johnny Allen	Hanley Dawson '60 Chevy	220	200	Tire
27	47	—	Bunk Moore	'60 Ford	203	200	Running
28	38	34	Charlie Glotzbach	'59 Chevrolet	192	200	A Frame
29	24	81	Larry Frank	Shorty Rollins '60 Ford	191	310	A Frame
30	46	17	Bob Barron	'60 Dodge	186	900	Coil
31	28	55	Jerry Roedell	'59 T-Bird	168	200	Oil Pres
32	8	26	Curtis Turner	Holman-Moody '60 Ford	159	200	Engine
33	26	76	Jimmy Thompson	'59 T-Bird	157	325	Engine
34	50	83	Richard Riley	Curtis Crider '58 Ford	143	200	Rear End
35	15	89	Joe Lee Johnson	Johnson '60 Chevrolet	133	395	Wiring
36	19	42	Lee Petty	Petty Eng '60 Plymouth	119	300	Brakes
37	44	64	Curtis Crider	A M Crawford '60 Ford	108	200	Engine
38	36	1	Paul Lewis	Faircloth '60 Chevrolet	99	200	Radiator
39	20	35	Don O'Dell	Sun City '60 Pontiac	90	200	Crash
40	13	7	Jim Reed	Reed '60 Chevrolet	89	325	Crash
41	42	3	Lennie Page	'59 T-Bird	88	200	Crash
42	35	54	Jimmy Pardue	Lowe's '59 Dodge	79	200	Radiator
43	45	31	E J Trivette	'59 Plymouth	69	200	Heating
44	2	47	Jack Smith	Boomershine '60 Pontiac	60	375	Crash
45	5	12	Joe Weatherly	Holman-Moody '60 Ford	22	250	Crash
46	25	10	T C Hunt	'60 Plymouth	20	200	Piston
47	48	9	Roy Tyner	Tyner '59 Olds	19	200	Crash
48	27	77	Marvin Panch	Billie Ridgeway '60 Ford	17	200	Fuel Pmp
49	32	39	Herb Tillman	Ralph Stark '60 Chevrolet	15	200	Bearing
50	33	28	Fred Lorenzen	Lorenzen '60 Ford	4	200	Vibration

Time of Race: 3 hours, 32 minutes, 50 seconds
Average Speed: 112.905 mph
Pole Winner: Fireball Roberts - 133.465 mph
Lap Leaders: Fireball Roberts 1-33, Jack Smith 34-35, Roberts 36-64,
   Jimmy Thompson 65-73, Roberts 74-141, Ned Jarrett 142-154, Larry Frank 155-165,
   Roberts 166-232, Thompson 233-267
Cautions: 7 for 34 laps
Margin of Victory: I lap plus 12 seconds
Attendance: 29,166

tween Lennie Page and Don O'Dell in the 93rd lap. Page's T-Bird hit the wall and bounced into the path of O'Dell, who hit him squarely. O'Dell was only shaken, but Page was knocked unconscious with a brain concussion, several broken ribs and a deep neck puncture. Quick acting by Chris Economaki, taking photos for National Speed Sport News, saved Page's life. Economaki took off his shirt, wrapped Page's neck

Lennie Page crashes hard in National 400 at Charlotte

tightly and administered treatment until an ambulance arrived. The Buffalo, NY driver was reported in serious condition at Presbyterian Hospital in Charlotte.

Rex White wrapped up the championship by taking sixth place. In the weeks leading up to the race, speedway officials threatened to turn down White's entry blank after he put a "rap" on the track surface.

The problems stemmed from a practice session a week before the race. Tom Pistone and White were engaged in shake-down sessions, and Pistone's car was wiped out in a crash. White discontinued further tests and blamed the track for the accident.

Ned Jarrett finished in third place with Bobby Johns fourth and Junior Johnson fifth.

Thompson averaged 112.905 mph for his third superspeedway victory.

Race No. 43

Thompson Speedy in Richmond 100

RICHMOND, VA (Oct 23) -- Silent for over a year, Speedy Thompson romped to his second straight

Grand National Race No. 43
200 Laps at Atlantic Rural Fairgrounds
Richmond, VA
100 Miles on Half-mile Dirt Track
October 23, 1960

Fin	St	No.	Driver	Team / Car	Laps	Money	Status
1	3	21	Speedy Thompson	Wood Bros '60 Ford	200	$800	Running
2	8	27	Junior Johnson	John Masoni '59 Chevy	200	525	Running
3	1	11	Ned Jarrett	Courtesy '60 Ford	200	375	Running
4	5	43	Richard Petty	Petty Eng '60 Plymouth	197	275	Running
5	11	17	Fred Harb	Harb '59 Ford	197	250	Running
6	6	87	Buck Baker	Thor '60 Chevrolet	196	215	Running
7	10	36	Tommy Irwin	Irwin '59 T-Bird	195	175	Running
8	12	4	Rex White	Piedmont/Friendly '59 Chevy	194	150	Running
9	13	42	Maurice Petty	Petty Eng '60 Plymouth	192	140	Running
10	9	10	Bill Morgan	Ratus Walters '59 Buick	183	130	Engine
11	19	74	L D Austin	Austin '58 Chevrolet	179	125	Running
12	14	5	Nace Mattingly	'58 Ford	172	110	Running
13	18	83	Curtis Crider	Crider '58 Ford	171	100	Running
14	16	61	Elmo Langley	Doc White '59 T-Bird	107	85	RR Axle
15	4	23	Doug Yates	Yates '59 Plymouth	90	70	Piston
16	2	16	Joe Weatherly	Wood Bros '58 Ford	76	60	Fuel Pmp
17	7	54	Jimmy Pardue	Lowe's '59 Dodge	54	50	Tie Rod
18	17	14	Wes Morgan	'60 Chevrolet	38	50	RF Hub
19	15	7	Buddy Baker	'58 Ford	0	50	Crash

Time of Race: 1 hour, 34 minutes, 08 seconds
Average Speed: 63.739 mph
Pole Winner: Ned Jarrett - 64.41 mph
Lap Leaders: Ned Jarrett 1-19, Speedy Thompson 20-111, Junior Johnson 112-119, Thompson 120-200
Cautions:
Margin of Victory: 1/4 lap
Attendance: 7,500

victory in the 100-miler at the Atlantic Rural Fairgrounds

Thompson, who led for 173 of the 200 laps on the half-mile dirt oval, pushed his Wood Brothers Ford past Junior Johnson in the 120th lap and kept it to the finish. Johnson came in second, Ned Jarrett was third and Richard Petty fourth. Fifth place went to Fred Harb.

Defending champion Lee Petty elected not to start the race, giving his son, Maurice, a crack at the wheel. Maurice, who

Speedy Thompson

had gained a reputation as a mechanic and race car preparer, finished ninth, one spot behind the new Grand National champion, Rex White.

A crowd of 7,500 watched Thompson take his 20th career win at an average speed of 63.739 mph.

Grand National Race No. 44
334 Laps at Atlanta International Raceway
Hampton, GA
"Atlanta 500"
500 Miles on 1.5 -mile Paved Track
October 30, 1960

Fin	St	No.	Driver	Team / Car	Laps	Money	Status
1	5	5	Bobby Johns	Cotton Owens '60 Pontiac	334	$15,975	Running
2	37	69	Johnny Allen	Hanley Dawson '60 Chevrolet	333	7,475	Running
3	13	44	Jim Paschal	Petty Eng '60 Plymouth	333	4,425	Running
4	19	21	Speedy Thompson	Wood Bros '60 Ford	330	2,475	Running
5	8	4	Rex White	Piedmont/Friendly '60 Chevy	330	1,850	Running
6	25	42	Lee Petty	Petty Eng '60 Plymouth	329	1,450	Running
7	12	43	Richard Petty	Petty Eng '60 Plymouth	327	1,075	Running
8	6	12	Joe Weatherly	Holman-Moody '60 Ford	323	1,300	Running
9	14	49	Bob Welborn	Welborn '60 Chevrolet	323	825	Running
10	4	28	Fred Lorenzen	Lorenzen '60 Ford	318	1,000	Running
11	38	39	Herb Tillman	Ralph Stark '60 Chevrolet	316	700	Running
12	20	1	Paul Lewis	Faircloth '60 Chevrolet	311	625	Running
13	39	74	L D Austin	Austin '58 Chevrolet	310	500	Running
14	40	64	Curtis Crider	A M Crawford '60 Ford	309	450	Running
15	33	81	Larry Frank	Shorty Rollins '60 Ford	307	500	Running
16	41	19	Herman Beam	Beam '60 Ford	306	350	Running
17	21	55	Jimmy Thompson	'59 T-Bird	303	300	Running
18	27	2	Tommy Irwin	'60 Chevrolet	300	260	Running
19	35	92	Gerald Duke	Robert Davis '59 T-Bird	297	300	Running
20	24	87	Buck Baker	Thor '60 Chevrolet	294	250	Running
21	34	61	Possum Jones	Doc White '59 T-Brid	291	275	Running
22	30	23	Doug Yates	Yates '59 Plymouth	255	200	Fuel Pmp
23	28	59	Tom Pistone	'59 Pontiac	224	200	Gas Tank
24	3	27	Junior Johnson	John Masoni '60 Pontiac	212	450	Axle
25	17	67	David Pearson	Pearson '59 Chevrolet	212	225	Crash
26	2	47	Jack Smith	Boomershine '60 Pontiac	154	445	Engine
27	23	15	Roscoe Thompson	Beau Morgan '60 Ford	144	210	Crash
28	29	89	Charley Griffith	'60 Chevrolet	132	200	A Frame
29	16	73	Johnny Beauchamp	'60 Chevrolet	85	240	Crash
30	9	85	Emanuel Zervakis	Monroe Shook '60 Chevy	83	250	Con Rod
31	32	34	Charlie Glotzbach	'59 Chevrolet	74	200	Axle
32	22	10	T C Hunt	'60 Plymouth	73	200	A Frame
33	18	82	LeeRoy Yarbrough	'59 Chevrolet	60	225	Crash
34	1	22	Fireball Roberts	John Hines '60 Pontiac	58	665	Axle
35	36	17	Jimmy Pardue	'60 Dodge	58	225	Engine
36	10	90	Tiny Lund	Junie Donlavey '60 Ford	52	250	Engine
37	7	94	Banjo Matthews	Matthews '60 Ford	51	275	Crash
38	15	77	Marvin Panch	Billie Ridgeway '60 Ford	46	225	Brakes
39	25	01	Bob Eichlor	'60 Ford	39	200	Crash
40	43	16	Elmo Langley	Happy Steigel '59 Pontiac	24	200	Engine
41	45	99	Wilbur Rakestraw	Talmadge Cochrane '60 Ford	23	200	Engine
42	31	78	Friday Hassler	E C Wilson '60 Chevrolet	16	200	Engine
43	11	11	Ned Jarrett	Courtesy '60 Ford	5	225	Engine
44	42	79	Paul Norris	'60 Ford	1	200	Engine
45	44	45	Bill Gazaway	Gazaway '60 Olds	1	200	Rear End

Time of Race: 4 hours, 36 minutes, 44 seconds
Average Speed: 108.408 mph
Pole Winner: Fireball Roberts - 134.596 mph
Lap Leaders: Fireball Roberts 1-41, Jack Smith 42-72, Joe Weatherly 73-87,
   Bobby Johns 88-92, Smith 93-121, Johns 122-130, Smith 131-154, Johns 155-334
Cautions:
Margin of Victory:
Attendance: 30,000

Junior Johnson, Joe Weatherly, Johnny Beauchamp and T C Hunt zoom through Atlanta turn

Bobby Johns pits in Atlanta 500

Bobby Johns #5 leads Joe Weatherly #12 in Atlanta 500

Race No. 44

Johns Finally Breaks Through; Wins Atlanta 500

HAMPTON, GA (Oct 30) -- Bobby Johns of

Miami ended a year of frustration with a victory in the first Atlanta 500 at Atlanta International Raceway.

Johns held his Cotton Owens Pontiac steady

through a nagging rain shower that forced officials to run 51 of the last 64 laps under the caution flag.

Johnny Allen, still looking for his first Grand National win, finished second in a Chevrolet. Jim Paschal, Speedy Thompson and Rex White rounded out the top five.

Tire failures were the by-word on the heavily overcast afternoon. Blown tires leading to wrecks took out Banjo Matthews, Johnny Beauchamp, Roscoe Thompson, David Pearson and a newcomer named LeeRoy Yarbrough.

For Johns, the drive was more rewarding than the $15,975 pay-off. The 27 year-old driver had lost major events at Daytona and Martinsville when he spun in the closing stages. He was also involved in the tragic collision at Darlington. The Atlanta 500 triumph was the first for Johns on the Grand National circuit.

Fireball Roberts won the pole at 134.596 mph, but a broken axle put the Daytona Beach charger out after 58 laps. Jack Smith led three times for 84 laps, but his Pontiac went out on lap 154 with a blown engine. Smith was leading at the time.

Johns averaged 108.408 mph despite the rain.

White won the lucrative Grand National Championship by 3,936 points over Richard Petty.

1960 NASCAR Season
Final Point Standings - Grand National Division

Rank	Driver	Points	Starts	Wins	Top 5	Top 10	Winnings
1	Rex White	21,164	40	6	25	35	$57,524.85
2	Richard Petty	17,228	40	3	16	30	41,872.95
3	Bobby Johns	14,964	19	1	8	9	46,114.92
4	Buck Baker	14,674	37	2	15	24	38,398.31
5	Ned Jarrett	14,660	40	5	20	26	25,437.38
6	Lee Petty	14,510	39	5	21	30	31,282.19
7	Junior Johnson	9,932	34	3	14	18	38,989.16
8	Emanuel Zervakis	9,720	12	0	1	10	12,123.97
9	Jim Paschal	8,968	10	0	3	7	15,095.94
10	Banjo Matthews	8,458	12	0	0	4	15,616.99
11	Johnny Beauchamp	8,306	11	1	3	5	17,373.78
12	Herman Beam	7,776	26	0	1	6	5,915.94
13	Joe Lee Johnson	7,352	22	1	6	8	34,518.94
14	Jack Smith	6,944	13	3	7	7	24,720.94
15	Fred Lorenzen	6,764	10	0	3	5	9,135.94
16	Bob Welborn	6,732	15	0	6	10	6,193.96
17	Jimmy Pardue	6,682	32	0	1	11	5,609.96
18	Tom Pistone	6,572	20	0	2	8	6,713.96
19	Johnny Allen	6,506	10	0	2	5	14,788.96
20	Joe Weatherly	6,380	24	3	7	11	20,123.96
21	Doug Yates	6,374	24	0	3	18	5,205.00
22	L D Austin	6,180	27	0	1	10	4,785.00
23	David Pearson	5,956	22	0	3	7	5,030.00
24	Gerald Duke	5,950	11	0	1	7	5,930.00
25	Speedy Thompson	5,658	9	2	4	5	18,035.00
26	Marvin Panch	5,268	11	0	0	1	3,225.00
27	Paul Lewis	5,212	22	0	0	4	3,535.00
28	Curtis Crider	4,720	24	0	0	2	3,645.00
29	Fireball Roberts	4,700	8	2	2	3	19,895.00
30	Shorty Rollins	4,374	4	0	0	1	2,120.00
31	Possum Jones	4,270	13	0	4	5	6,330.00
32	Tiny Lund	4,124	8	0	0	2	2,440.00
33	G C Spencer	3,986	26	0	2	6	3,910.00
34	Larry Frank	3,634	11	0	0	2	2,440.00
35	Herb Tillman	3,504	9	0	0	0	2,605.00
36	Curtis Turner	3,300	9	0	0	1	3,220.00
37	Bunkie Blackburn	3,252	18	0	1	4	3,400.00
38	Buddy Baker	3,070	15	0	0	1	1,745.00
39	Cotton Owens	3,050	14	1	5	5	14,065.00
40	Charley Griffith	2,684	5	0	0	0	1,300.00
41	Wilbur Rakestraw	2,676	12	0	0	1	2,695.00
42	Jimmy Massey	2,662	6	0	2	3	3,310.00
43	Jimmy Thompson	2,472	9	0	0	0	1,940.00
44	Jim Reed	2,340	8	0	1	1	2,240.00
45	Jim Cook	2,178	3	1	1	1	1,600.00
46	Ernie Gahan	2,080	2	0	0	0	625.00
47	Elmo Henderson	2,072	7	0	0	0	1,425.00
48	Bob Burdick	1,970	3	0	0	1	850.00
49	Roz Howard	1,810	3	0	0	2	1,490.00
50	Bob Potter	1,800	3	0	0	1	640.00

The 1961 Season
The Ultimate Challenge --
NASCAR vs Teamsters

Volume two of a four volume series . . . . . The Superspeedway Boom 1959 - 1964

1961

In twelve short years the NASCAR Grand National Circuit had become a big healthy boy. From 1949-1961, Bill France's homespun stock car racing game had, for the most part, busted out of its backwoods image. Gone -- or declining in numbers -- were the weekend racers who spent Monday through Friday hauling 'bathtub brewed' joy-juice from one hamlet to another. Gone were the days when race promoters high-tailed through dimly lit gates halfway through the feature -- their pockets crammed with the cash that was supposed to go to the poor slobs out on the track who were risking life and limb while bustin' heads and fenders.

No more driving the family automobile to the track, taping up the headlights, strapping the doors shut and going racing with all the other individuals of the same mold. In the early years, stock car racers were said to be a direct reflection of the failure of the educational system.

Grand National racing and sanctioning NASCAR had gained a fair measure of respectability by 1961. The drivers had become semi-conscious of their public image. Some actually began talking with members of the media. Others began to wear driver's uniforms. Many would rather be photographed with a soda in their hands rather than a brown-bagged bottle of Jack Daniels.

New speedways -- many of them huge ovals with enormous seating capacities -- were being built around the country. The superspeedway races attracted a larger audience and drew more national attention. Bill France himself started the new "superspeedway boom" by building the ultimate -- the Daytona International Speedway. In 1960, three more big ovals joined the circuit -- Marchbanks Speedway in Hanford, CA; Atlanta International Raceway in Hampton, GA; and the Charlotte Motor Speedway in North Carolina's Queen City.

Bill France threatened to plow up his Daytona International Speedway and plant corn in the infield if the Union effort was successful

All three new speedways that spawned in 1960 had to overcome varying degrees of problems in order to become a reality. Charlotte Motor Speedway had to overcome nearly impossible odds, and ramifications of those problems carried on to the summer of 1961 which produced the biggest challenge Bill France and NASCAR ever had to face -- a vicious battle with the Teamsters Union.

On July 29, 1959, ground breaking ceremonies were held on a tract of land on US 29 just inside the Cabarras County line north of Charlotte. From that day on, things went downhill. Projected costs of about $1,000,000 were greatly underestimated. "I had the financing all worked out," said Curtis Turner, first president of Charlotte Motor Speedway. "Everything was okay until we hit rock. The core-drill report said it was boulders. So, in the contract for moving dirt, I also got the boulders moved for 18 cents a yard. But instead of hitting boulders we hit a half-million yards of solid granite. That cost a dollar a yard to move, plus the dynamite. (It) cost $70,000 worth of dynamite just getting through the first turn. The whole thing cost a half-million dollars more than it should have."

It was a miracle that the speedway was ever completed. Turner and Vice-President Bruton Smith solicited money lenders -- and even in their darkest hours, they managed to come up with enough funds to survive another day.

The combatants - Bill France, President of NASCAR, and...

Before the first World 600 was staged on June 19, 1960, there were $500,000 in debts outstanding. At the eleventh hour, Turner came up with enough money to place an escrow account to cover the $106,000 purse. It is assumed that Turner pulled one of his famous -- or infamous -- transactions in order to cover the purse.

A crowd of 35,462 showed up for the first World 600. Ticket sales were enough to cover the immediate loans for the racing purse, but a long line of creditors lined up outside the office demanding to be paid.

It was reported that shortly after the first World 600, Turner approached the Teamsters Union for an $800,000 loan to bail the speedway out. William R. Rabin, an accountant and lawyer, was hired to set up the books of Charlotte Motor Speedway. More importantly, Mr. Rabin was a confidante of big monied people including Teamster boss Jimmy Hoffa. Rabin was instrumental in persuading each creditor to give the Speedway management more time to solve its financial problems. He also acted as liaison between Turner and the Teamsters in their original discussions. In return for the $800,000 loan, Turner was asked to unionize the drivers as part of the deal. Turner did a little 'feeling around' in the driver ranks, but later abandoned the idea of the union.

Within 12 months, Charlotte Motor Speedway was slowly -- but steadily -- working its way out from under the pile of debts. But not nearly fast enough to appease the creditors and strike a harmonic note among

stockholders. Turner was ousted as president in early June of 1961, and Bruton Smith resigned as vice-president. Smith was kept on temporarily as "promotion director".

The board of directors held a pre-meeting to which Turner was not invited, a practice not strictly legal under North Carolina law. He was dismissed in a "stormy" meeting the following day. Allan Nance was electedpresident and C.D. "Duke" Ellington was elected vice-president and appointed general manager. Turner did not contest the fact that he had not been invited to a board of director's meeting.

He chose an alternate method, which he hoped would get the speedway that he had built back in his hands. He went back to the Teamsters and this time, he agreed to round up the NASCAR stock car drivers. The Teamsters were prepared to spend heavily, if necessary, in their efforts to unionize professional athletes from all levels of the sporting industry.

During the week of August 7, Turner and other racing people were in Chicago to talk with leading Teamster officials - Nick Torzeski, who was directly involved with the organizing of professional athletes and Harold Gibbons, administrative aide to Hoffa.

Quietly, and without fanfare, several leading race drivers from the NASCAR and USAC ranks, met and formed the Federation of Professional Athletes. The

Curtis Turner, Race Driver turned Entrepreneur

purpose, they said, was to form a union of all professional drivers cutting across NASCAR, USAC, IMCA and other boundaries. Targeted benefits for members were, "(1) better purses, (2) pension plans, (3) more adequate insurance coverage, (4) a scholarship fund for children of deceased members, and (5) upgraded facilities for drivers at the speedways -- including shower areas and lounge facilities."

Reported at the meeting were Fireball Roberts and Tim Flock of NASCAR and Paul Goldsmith of USAC. Don Branson of USAC had been invited but did not attend. Unconfirmed reports named

1956 Indianapolis 500 winner, Pat Flaherty, and 1952 AAA champion Chuck Stevenson among those most interested in the FPA, which was the name given by the Teamsters to the drivers' union.

John Marcum, President of the Midwest Association of Race Cars, predecessor of ARCA, was offered the job of vice-president of FPA. After several days of personal deliberation, Marcum turned down the offer.

Turner told Nick Torzeski and Hal Gibbons that he would lead the efforts to organize the stock car drivers. In return, Turner would get $850,000 -- plenty of cash to bail Charlotte Motor Speedway out of its impending bankruptcy.

*Tim Flock
Union Supporter*

Turner set up his home base in the Nissen Building in Winston-Salem, NC. He released a statement on August 8, 1961: "A majority of the drivers on the Grand National Circuit have signed applications and paid initiation dues of $10 for membership in the Federation of Professional Athletes."

The proverbial mess hit the fan when Big Bill France heard that one.

"No known Teamster member can compete in a NASCAR race," France fired back. "And I'll use a pistol to enforce it."

The Grand Nationals were scheduled to run a 37.5-miler at Winston-Salem's Bowman-Gray Stadium on August 9. Bill France hustled up to Winston-Salem and met with the drivers in a vacant building not far from the track. He made his pitch.

"Gentlemen, before I have this union stuffed down my throat, I will plow up my two-and-a-half-mile track

*Fireball Roberts - early supporter,
then withdrew*

at Daytona Beach and plant corn in the infield." To prove his point, France, acting as President of NASCAR, promptly suspended Turner, Flock and Roberts, who had participated in union work. The suspensions were for "conduct detrimental to auto racing" and essentially, they were "for life".

France also declared "Auto racing is one of the few sports which has never had a scandal. We'll fight this union to the hilt."

Turner counteracted with a prepared written statement which was distributed to most of the drivers, all of the signed members and many of the daily newspapers and racing tabloids. Turner's written statement, in its entirety:

"I would like to explain some of the needs for the Federation of Professional Athletes.

First of all, this is not the Teamsters Union. The FPA is a union of its own, affiliated with the Brotherhood of Teamsters, Chauffeurs, Warehousemen and Helpers of America. The entire staff is made up of people from racing, elected and governed by you, the members. Our affiliation with the Teamsters Union means we gain the support of an organization of 1,700,000 members, their experience, finances and other forms of aid.

PRIZE MONEY: As racing grows, the promoters are requiring drivers to be present for two and in some cases three weeks in advance of a race. This means $15 per man per day, or for two weeks, $210. Five to a crew means over $1,000 per crew. Assuming 50 cars in the race: $50,000. At Daytona you wear out one set of tires in practice. There's another $11,000. Then you need a minimum of six tires to start the race. That's another $16,500. Damage to cars at Daytona will average $50,000. Your entry fee is $25 or another $1,250. This makes a total of $112,250 - (actual cash money put up by the owners and drivers) - not to mention pit passes, driver's physicals, car registration, etc. This is only figured on 50 cars and the figure is low. So the drivers are spending approximately twice as much as they can win (if they come in first) while the promoter is charging admission for your practice and time trials, plus the race.

We feel the drivers should get 40% of the time trial money.

Stop false advertising of purse, such as prize money for Continental Lincoln, Imperial Chrysler, Cadillacs, etc. Eliminate double totals of accessory awards as you cannot win both Champion and Autolite awards, and the same goes for Firestone and Goodyear. However, both are included in the advertised purse. This is just a small part of what we intend to do for you.

PENSIONS:
Pensions are almost unheard of in professional sports, and yet they are one of the greatest needs. Professional athletes are old before their time by virtue of the pressing pace their profession demands. Because of this great need for security when the athlete reaches the age considered "old" for his profession, a liberal pension program ranks high on the objectives list of the Federation of Professional Ath-

*Rex White - joined union -
then withdrew*

letes.

DEATH BENEFITS: Death benefits have been discussed by sports associations for as many years as
there have been professional sports.Yet, no real answer
has been found for this problem. Associations at their
best have no collective
strength, unity of purpose or
enough money to get the job
done. The insurance program
currently offered professional
athletes is totally inadequate
and serves no other purpose
than a burial. Families of fatally injured athletes are often
hard put to meet this expense,
much less being able to keep
their home and pay due bills.
Very often families have to be
split up because of a fatal accident. It is for these reasons
and a host of other needs
equally important that Death
Benefits are another major
goal earmarked for you and your family by the Federation of Professional Athletes.

Ed Otto - a calm voice in a
storm

HEALTH AND WELFARE: Health and Welfare
benefits go hand-in-hand with Death Benefits inasmuch
as they greatly affect the family budget in time of illness
or accident. The Federation of Professional Athletes
has placed these benefits high on the collective bargaining agenda. The Health and Welfare program
includes a negotiated schedule of hospital and
medical benefits for professional athletes
which will lessen the financial burden on Federation members when accident or illness
strike them or their dependents.

SCHOLARSHIP FUND: A scholarship
fund for children of deceased members will
also become a part of the objectives of the
Federation. This program is a mainstay in the
Federation's plans to bring social benefits to
Federation members as well as improved eco-
nomic conditions.

COMPLAINT PROCEDURES: Complaint
Procedures have been absent too long in asso-
ciations dealing with professional sports.
Strong and meaningful complaint provisions
will be clearly spelled out by the Federation of
Professional Athletes in all contracts.

SAFETY: Adequate safety conditions are
another problem which has been neglected in
many professional sports because of the lack
of unity and central strength. Since many
sports always contain the element of danger,
safety conditions and safer and more adequate
equipment will be given special attention by
the Federation.

Because we want to give you this help, Bill France
says, "I'll use my pistol, I've done it before and I'll do
it again."

Last week he stated he would plow up all his tracks
before he would let a union come in. I believe he would
have to check with his creditors and stockholders before doing this.

You have our permission to sign any papers that he
may dictate to you to sign. They are of no value and
you are still members of the FPA and in good standing.

We want to help you, and we will. Ten years ago
NASCAR was paying $4,000 for a 100-mile Grand
National. You could build a race car for $3,000. To-
day, they are still paying $4,000 while it costs $6,000
(to build) a race car and NASCAR membership has increased from $5 per year to $20.

France states the drivers don't realize the money in-
vested in these tracks. I know, because I built the best
one in the nation and paid the largest purse, and I also
realized a field of race cars represents over a half million dollars while damage to the tracks is a small percentage of damages to the race cars.

Bill France knows we are right. He's already begun
to make you more promises.

Drivers all over America are continuing to sign up in
the Federation of Professional Atheletes. We are rolling.

If you are not already a member, sign the attached
membershp application and mail it to Curtis Turner,
231 Nissen Building, Winston-Salem, North Carolina.

Yours truly,
Curtis Turner

One item not included
in the prepared statement
by Turner was the inten-
tion of the Federation of
Professional Atheltes to
include pari-mutuel bet-
ting on auto races. Tur-
ner stated that the pari-
mutuel betting had been
given a 14 month tempo-
rary approval in a south-
ern state -- he declined to
say which one -- and
that betting would start
"in a matter of weeks",
as soon as the proper
equipment could be in-
stalled at the track site.
He further stated that approval for pari-mutuel
betting in a midwestern
state was expected in the
near future.

Bill France, no ama-

Pat Purcell, NASCAR Executive Manager - led
the Grand National Advisory Board,
the management solution to the Union which
gave drivers a platform where they could be heard

teur at power plays, issued a prepared statement of his own:

"A recent newspaper story suggsts that I might be some rootin', tootin', hootin', shootin' cuss, waving a pistol and itching to shoot up anyone who might disagree with me.

Honest, I'm nothing like that. But I am an American who believes our constitution and our laws - and that bearing of arms to repel invasion is a part of our great American Heritage.

For 14 years I have had the honor and responsibility of heading, as President, the building of a house called NASCAR -- the National Association for Stock Car Auto Racing, Inc. -- at Daytona Beach, Florida.

In the center of that house, I have collected a staff of fine people devoted to the expansion and improvement of the great sport of auto racing by building public respect and interest in the sport, and by guiding and helping the people who take part in that sport.

In one wing of that NASCAR house, we have gathered a large group of business people who are something more than just business people when it comes to the sport of automobile racing. They are the promoters -- the people who promote and build the sport by tremendous investments of lands, monies, work, sweat and thought, to build and run modern, safe race tracks and plants for the presentation of auto races. They put up the purses and the many other very substantial costs of preparing and presenting race meets -- and when the whims of weather and other uncontrollable circumstances permit, and the public responds to their expensive advertising and publicity selling each race meet, they are able to pay their bills, get some return on their investments and with luck -- some profit. Too often, weather, other circumstances, and lack of public response produce sad losses instead of hoped-for profits. It is a terrible risky business that relatively few people undertake; those who do take those risks generally do it for the love of the sport more than for the dubious profits. One of our big jobs in NASCAR is to help the promoters do a good job of building, maintaining and operating their tracks for good, safe racing, with fair purses and proper regard for the safety and well being of our contestants, and with the maximum comfort, safety and gratification of our racing fans. The growth of our sport bespeaks some success in our efforts.

In the other wing of our NASCAR house we have our contestants -- the greatest group of people engaged in building, maintaining and driving the greatest groups of racing autos ever collected under one banner -- NASCAR!

Our big job for our driver, owner and mechanic members of NASCAR consists of setting-up, modifying and keeping up-to-date, and enforcing fair and effective rules, regulations and specifications governing classes of auto racing with maximum safety, and fair, balanced competition for fair, guaranteed purses.

Further NASCAR pioneered in developing and providing the Benefit Plan that has always given its members the "best break" in the sport in the event of injury at the race track; NASCAR's administration of its Benefit Plan has saved countless lives and limbs for its membership, and has eased many of the pains of race track casualties.

NASCAR's rule books and specification sheets are read and interpreted identically for all contestants by trained officials who are qualified for their assignments. Outstanding members of the sport and of the automobile industry have contributed generously and effectively over the years to the building of these rules and their proper application. Appeals and grievance procedures under the directing of outstanding national commissioners, have been fairly and effectively applied over the years.

Point funds have been set up and administered to afford proper honor and recognition as well as payments to our contestants.

Cooperation and recognition of the automotive industries in support of our sport has been built up by NASCAR.

And when bigger and better ideas and plans for the benefit and betterment of our sport and the folks in it are developed -- NASCAR will continue to be up front and working sincerely and effectively for them, with years of experience and achievement to build from.

For 14 years, we in NASCAR have been working and striving for the growth and improvement of the great sport of auto racing and the great number of nice folks who have graced our rolls as members -- promoters, drivers, car owners and mechanics -- trying, and usually succeeding, in balancing their various needs for their respective progress in the sport. We honestly feel that ours is a record of solid achievement and progress for our members and for our sport.

And when out of a clear blue sky, in a period of continuing growth and progress in the sport, I am suddenly confronted with the fact that a few of the boys who have grown to stature and respect in the sport as NASCAR members, and with the help and support of NASCAR over many years which have been good and profitable for them, engage in activity which is disruptive -- and actually poisonous to the sport -- I hope it's not too hard to understand why I might be a bit mad.

I'm not quite sure, yet, if it's just plain foolishness, stupidity or avarice that makes these boys get associated with movements which can only hurt and degrade our sport and injure the people and organization that helped them grow.

But I do know that organized gambling would be bad for our sport -- and would spill innocent blood on our race track -- I'll fight it to the end! And with the help of all decent auto racing people and their fans, we will lick it.

And I know and believe that trade unions have a good place in the American way of life. However, the kind those boys are working with can't do anything but hurt racing, and all the nice folks who have been building our great sport.

Bill France, NASCAR President

On Friday, August 11, 1961, Fireball Roberts resigned from the union. "I drove slowly from Charlotte this morning and took the long way by Lake Lure and I thought this thing over from all angles," he said. "I'm withdrawing my support from the union and am resigning from the Federation of Professional Athletes. It's as simple as that.

"I don't know for sure what the motives of the other FPA officers were," Roberts added, "but I assume they were the same as mine. My motives were clear. I simply wanted to better the positions of race drivers, car owners, myself and racing in general. I can see now that by affiliating the FPA with the Teamsters, we could possibly accomplish more harm than good for racing. The Teamsters people have implied that to force this issue there might be injunctions and litigations which might disrupt all racing in the South. If that happened, there might be a lot of individuals who would be hurt very badly. Personally, I could live five years without getting behind another wheel, but there are several on the racing circuit who aren't that fortunate. I feel if I do anything to hurt the least man in racing, I will be doing a disservice to my fellow drivers who have been my friends for 15 years. And I will have no part of that." Roberts was reinstated by NASCAR later that same afternoon.

The verbal sparring between Curtis Turner and Bill France continued. "I understand that Bill France has been talking about pistols and threatening my life and Fireball Roberts' life," said Turner. "I guess Fireball decided he didn't want to get shot, but I think he is still with us."

Turner brought up the subject of expenses and purses again. "It costs more to go race today," he said. "Traveling expenses are greater, you have to pay the mechanics more. Motel fees are going up every year. Everything has gone up but the purses."

"Ten years ago, Darlington was paying $25,000 for its Southern 500." France shot back, "Today, the purse is nearly $100,000."

"There are 72,000 men in the racing business in the United States," said Turner. "There are 432 tracks which hold non-sanctioned events. Bill France looks pretty small to all the racing activity and all the people in the United States.

"The majority of the drivers aren't as dumb as France thinks they are," Turner continued. "They've heard empty promises for 15 years. All that has resulted is the drivers getting leaner and the promoters getting fatter."

France served a volley of his own. "If the drivers unionize, any support from the factories will be withdrawn. And the car owners, if they hire mechanics, then they will have to pay him time-and-a-half on Saturday and double-time on Sunday. They don't know what they're getting into."

Through all the heated argument and accusations, it was the cool hand of Ed Otto, NASCAR Vice President of Maplewood, NJ, who spoke in a different nature -- without emotion.

"In my many years in motor sports promotions and other businesses, I have had occasion to deal with many of the unions in connection with my employment of help, with my fair share of bickering as to wages and hours and other details involved with the dealings of an employer with employees through their recognized and respected unions," said Otto.

"I understand and respect our unions and have enjoyed a good relationship with them, and I surely appreciate the fact that their steps toward improving the status, income and living standards of the people of our country have been one of the major factors in enabling so many Americans to afford attendance at and enjoy the thrills and excitement of the great sport to which I have devoted the major part of my lifetime efforts and from which I have been able to earn a decent livelihood for myself and my family. I am sure I am a friend of labor, not an enemy.

"I am surprised at the vagaries of memory among the contestants, promoters, and sanctioning bodies," continued Otto. "In our sport in the past 10 or 12 years there have been many instances which conclusively indicate that the relationships of the people involved in automobile racing do not constitute a proper basis for unionization. It can only hurt the sport and it cannot help any union that attempts involvement in the sport on behalf of the contestants in the sport.

"Let me briefly remind racing personnel, promoters and sanctioning bodies in automobile racing of past events that should guide their thinking in connection with proposals toward unionization of contestants. And I hope proponents of the idea and the union people who are considering reacting toward the idea, note these remarks and consider them fairly, honestly and sincerely, as I offer them.

"In the late '40s, the unfortunate deaths of two Midget auto racers at Freeport Stadium in Long Island, resulted in workmen's compensation actions against the promoter -- very substantial judgements resulted from the compensation board ruling that the drivers were "employees". Because of the unavailability of compensation insurance required by law for the benefits of "employees", every auto and motorcycle track in the state of New York was in a position to be shut down and abolished, and the precedent would probably have followed in other states. I was able to obtain the cooperation of other responsible promoters in helping the

Freeport Stadium promoters to appeal the case to the courts. In 1951, the Appellate Division reversed the board action, ruling that auto racers are not "employees", but contestants and independent contractors. The impossible insurance became unnecesary and the race tracks remained in business. The New York decision has since been followed in many other states."

"Automobile racing has enjoyed the devotion of too many dedicated people, some of whom have expanded their very lives, in becoming the great sport that it is. And having no scandals during all these years it has grown to such great heights of popularity and dignity. Current reports of attempts to organize gambling on auto races coincide so closely with union activity, that many responsible persons in the sport are led to suspect that a union is being improperly "used". Gambling interests have too long been trying to get into auto racing, and their steps toward such contamination of our sport have been many and devious, and completely unsuccessful.

"I ask my friends and colleagues in racing, all contestants, promoters, sanctioning bodies and auto racing fans, to help keep auto racing free of the dangers and contaminating influences that gambling would bring to our beloved sport. From the court decisions on the subjects, from all practical consideration, and from the very nature of the many fine people that build and drive racing automobiles, I am sure that our personnel are true, honest and vigorous contestants, not "employees".

"Unions know their job is the representation of "employees" in the bargaining with "employers". For lack of full honest disclosure of facts and circumstances, they, like any of us, can sometimes be misled.

"I hope that all persons interested in auto racing await the full development and disclosure of the facts, the complete and true facts, and help bring them out in appropriate action. And I hope enough of my good friends in the unions can help me to help the sport and the standing of their unions in connection with the problems presented," concluded Otto.

One of the first steps NASCAR took during the dispute was to form a Grand National Advisory Board. The panel would be made up of two drivers, two NASCAR executives, two car owners and two promoters. Ned Jarrett and Rex White would represent the drivers, Ed Otto and Pat Purcell would sit in for NASCAR, Rex Lovette and Lee Petty would represent the car owners and promoters Clay Earles and Enoch Staley would be present for all the meetings.

"The Advisory Board, aided by two NASCAR officials, will evaluate the current rule book, race entry regulations, prize money payoffs and make a comprehensive study of pension plan possibilities -- and the

The Winner - and still Champion

overall promotion of racing for the benefit of all concerned," said NASCAR Executive Manager Pat Purcell.

"The success of the Advisory Board depends upon the efforts of the members, the cooperation of all concerned in getting their ideas across. I do not think anyone will be foolish to think the Advisory Board can accomplish in a few weeks more than NASCAR has built up in more than 12 years of operation," Purcell hastened to add. "But intelligent changes can be made and will be made. The purpose of the Advisory Board is to work for the overall betterment of everyone active in any phase of the sport. It is a big job and will take some solid thinking and doing."

The first meeting was slated for September 16 in Atlanta.

Rex White, defending Grand National champion, resigned from the Federation of Professional Athletes. "I joined this union and I've been thinking about it ever since," he said. "Drivers have legitimate beefs and the drivers want a fair deal and more money. Let's let this board France has appointed decide what's good for racing. I'll admit the union offer of a retirement plan sold me, but from now on, I'll think a week before I sign anything else."

Ned Jarrett, current point leader, turned in his resignation too. "I signed the union paper, but I didn't consider everything," said Jarrett. "A lot of us drivers have beefs but this was going about it in the wrong way."

With virtually all of the NASCAR drivers back in Bill France's fold, Turner and Flock -- the only two who held their positions in the union effort -- were unforgiven by France's sanctioning body. The "life" suspension were upheld.

Turner and Flock filed a number of lawsuits. One was to be reinstated in NASCAR under the Florida right to work law. And the biggie -- a $300,000 suit for actual and punitive damages along with a request for a temporary injunction.

Circuit Judge Robert E. Wingfield dismissed the temporary injunction on January 13, 1962. "While the testimony was being given," said Flock, "the judge was up in his chair reading comic books. We didn't have a chance."

Only days later, Turner was advised by his attorneys to drop the entire suit. The clincher was that the Teamsters union could not have made a loan to a company that they were attempting to organize. Turner and Flock were left out on a limb -- way out. France held his guns and kicked Turner and Flock out of NASCAR.

Big Bill France and NASCAR had prevailed in the ultimate challenge -- the battle with the Teamsters Union.

The Grand National Advisory Board accomplished some things too. A more equitable purse distribution crept into the Grand National ranks, and death and dismemberment benefits were increased.

In the summer of 1961, Curtis Turner and Tim Flock fought the NASCAR law -- and the law won.

Race No. 1

Weatherly Drives Wood Bros. Ford To Victory at Charlotte

CHARLOTTE, NC (Nov 6, 1960) -- Joe Weatherly of Norfolk, VA emerged victorious in a brutal 100 miler at the Charlotte Fairgrounds. It was the opening event of the 1961 NASCAR Grand National season and it marked the fifth career triumph for the stubby ex-motorcycle champ.

Weatherly, driving the Wood Brothers' Ford, overcame flying glass, Rex White and Lee Petty to earn the $800 top prize. The condition of the half-mile dirt track was less than ideal and the turns were described as "washboards", which contributed to eleven of the twenty starters being knocked from the race.

Weatherly grabbed the lead from White in the 161st lap and led the rest of the way. White held on to finish second despite breaking a shock absorber on his Chevrolet. Lee Petty came in third with Buck Baker fourth and David Pearson fifth.

The huge pot holes in the track surface broke A-frames and motor mounts on some of the cars and cracked windshields in others. The track was littered with pieces of glass in the late stages. Weatherly said his own windshield was pitted by flying debris and that he had to drive with his head out of the window in order to see.

Junior Johnson, the crowd-pleaser out of Ronda, NC, snapped two rear axles while attempting to qualify his Pontiac. A fan from the infield who owned a new Pontiac offered to loan Johnson the rear axle from his own street car. Johnson accepted.

Johnson started in 20th position and resembled a wild bull rider at the drop of the green flag. After seven laps, Johnson was in eighth place. By the 21st lap of the 200 lap event, Johnson was running in third place. He moved past Petty to take second in the 34th lap and moved in on leader White. As he took the high groove to pass White on lap 35, the borrowed rear axle broke and he was out of the race.

Weatherly did not receive any points because his car was not equipped with a rear window. A crowd of 4,000 was on hand to watch the 37 year-old veteran average 59.435 mph.

Race No. 2

Lee Petty's 54th Win Comes at Jacksonville

JACKSONVILLE, FL (Nov 20, 1960) -- Lee

Grand National Race No. 1
200 Laps at Charlotte Fairgrounds
Charlotte, NC
100 Miles on Half-mile Dirt Track
November 6, 1960

Fin	St	No.	Driver	Team / Car	Laps	Money	Status
1	11	16	Joe Weatherly	Wood Bros '58 Ford	200	$800	Running
2	2	4	Rex White	Piedmont/Friendly '59 Chevy	200	525	Running
3	1	42	Lee Petty	Petty Eng '60 Plymouth	196	375	Running
4	10	87	Buck Baker	Thor '60 Chevrolet	194	275	Running
5	5	67	David Pearson	Pearson '59 Chevrolet	190	250	Running
6	14	19	Herman Beam	Beam '60 Ford	183	215	Running
7	16	1	Paul Lewis	Faircloth '60 Chevrolet	183	175	Running
8	18	74	L D Austin	Austin '58 Chevrolet	174	150	Running
9	19	83	Bob Barron	'59 Ford	157	140	Running
10	8	23	Doug Yates	Yates '59 Plymouth	152	130	Rear End
11	6	43	Richard Petty	Petty Eng '60 Plymouth	142	125	A Frame
12	3	61	Elmo Langley	Doc White '59 T-Bird	133	110	Rear End
13	17	35	Jimmy Pardue	'60 Dodge	112	100	A Frame
14	13	17	Fred Harb	Harb '59 Ford	110	85	Oil Pres
15	4	36	Tommy Irwin	Irwin '59 T-Bird	97	70	Mtr Mnt
16	7	11	Ned Jarrett	Courtesy '60 Ford	60	60	Heating
17	15	7	Buddy Baker	'59 Ford	59	50	Dr Shaft
18	20	27	Junior Johnson	Holly Farms '60 Pontiac	35	50	RR Axle
19	9	64	Curtis Crider	Crider '60 Ford	35	50	Rear End
20	12	59	Tom Pistone	'59 Pontiac	17	50	Cr Shaft

Time of Race: 1 hour, 40 minutes, 57 seconds
Average Speed: 59.435 mph
Pole Winner: Lee Petty - 63.581 mph
Lap Leaders: Lee Petty 1-17, Rex White 18-49, L Petty 50-140, White 141-160, Weatherly 161-200.
Cautions: 4
Margin of Victory:
Attendance: 4,000

Petty grabbed first place and the lead in the point standings with a triumph in the 100-mile Grand National race at Speedway Park. It was the 54th victory for the 46 year-old Plymouth driver.

Tommy Irwin finished second after leading for 166 laps. Rex White came in third with Richard Petty fourth and Doug Yates fifth.

Petty drove his blue Plymouth around Irwin in the 183rd lap and led the rest of the way on the oil-based half-mile dirt track. Irwin had to pit his Chevrolet late in the race, which dropped him a lap off the pace.

Buck Baker led the first 15 laps, but he blew a head gasket in his Chevrolet on lap 137. Bob Welborn led briefly in the early stages but drifted to a ninth place finish.

Junior Johnson won the pole but departed after four laps when his Pontiac encountered distributor problems.

By winning this event, Petty, starting 13th, posted a victory in 13 consecutive Grand National seasons, a feat unmatched by any other driver.

A crowd of 5,000 was on hand to watch Petty average 64.400 mph.

Grand National Race No. 2
200 Laps at Speedway Park
Jacksonville, FL
100 Miles on Half-mile Dirt Track
November 20, 1960

Fin	St	No.	Driver	Team / Car	Laps	Money	Status
1	13	42	Lee Petty	Petty Eng '60 Plymouth	200	$800	Running
2	3	2	Tommy Irwin	Irwin '60 Chevrolet	199	525	Running
3	6	4	Rex White	Piedmont/Friendly '59 Chevy	198	475	Running
4	8	43	Richard Petty	Petty Eng '60 Plymouth	197	275	Running
5	16	23	Doug Yates	Yates '59 Plymouth	194	250	Running
6	15	19	Herman Beam	Beam '60 Ford	191	215	Running
7	14	16	Elmo Langley	Doc White '59 Pontiac	190	175	Running
8	21	74	L D Austin	Austin '58 Chevrolet	180	150	Running
9	5	49	Bob Welborn	Welborn '60 Chevrolet	176	140	Running
10	20	1	Paul Lewis	Faircloth '60 Chevrolet	163	130	RR Tire
11	2	87	Buck Baker	Thor '60 Chevrolet	137	125	H Gasket
12	22	7	Bob Barron	'60 Dodge	127	110	Running
13	18	35	Jimmy Pardue	'59 Plymouth	126	100	Running
14	17	33	Reb Wickersham	Wickersham '60 Olds	125	85	Running
15	12	64	Curtis Crider	Crider '60 Ford	120	70	Running
16	4	67	David Pearson	Pearson '59 Chevrolet	102	60	Running
17	7	55	Jimmy Thompson	'59 T-Bird	92	50	Engine
18	19	83	David Ezell	'58 Ford	87	50	Wheel
19	10	11	Ned Jarrett	Courtesy '60 Ford	67	50	H Gasket
20	11	92	Gerald Duke	'59 T-Bird	39	50	Heating
21	9	17	Fred Harb	Harb '59 Ford	35	50	Heating
22	1	27	Junior Johnson	Holly Farms '60 Pontiac	4	50	Distrib

Time of Race: 1 hour, 33 minutes, 10 seconds
Average Speed: 64.400 mph
Pole Winner: Junior Johnson 68.623 mph
Lap Leaders: Buck Baker 1-15, Bob Welborn 16, Tommy Irwin 17-182,
   Lee Petty 183-200
Cautions:
Margin of Victory: 1 lap plus
Attendance: 5,000

Dave Mader #00 and Marshall Sargent crash in opening 100-miler

Junior Johnson's Pontiac, one of many wiped out in qualifiers

Race No. 3

Roberts Avoids Wrecks;
Wins Daytona Qualifier

DAYTONA BEACH, FL (Feb 24) -- Fireball Roberts squeaked past a thundering last lap collision and roared home first in the crash torn 100-mile qualifying race at Daytona International Speedway.

The event was flagged to a halt after 39 of the scheduled 40 laps had been completed. Five drivers went to the hospital as 13 cars were wiped out in an endless series of mishaps. Junior Johnson was running side-by-side with eventual winner Roberts when his Pontiac ran over some debris. Johnson's car nicked Richard Petty's Plymouth, sending Petty airborne over the wall. Johnson turned into the wall head on, smashing the engine up into the driver's compartment. Petty suffered abrasions of both eyes and a cut hand. Johnson suffered a lacerated chin and possible jaw injuries.

Earlier, Pete Boland suffered multiple lacerations of both hands when his Ford whacked the wall in the 32nd lap. Wes Morgan was taken to the hospital with

Richard Petty's Plymouth - over the wall

spinal injuries after flipping several times when tangling with Dave Mader. Mader was treated for neck injuries.

A crowd of 17,500 was left limp after watching the destruction.

Jim Paschal finished second and Jack Smith was third, giving the big Pontiacs a 1-2-3 sweep. Buck Baker's Chrysler was fourth and Ned Jarrett fifth in a Chevrolet.

Roberts averaged 129.711 mph for the 97.5-mile event.

Grand National Race No. 3
40 Laps at Daytona International Speedway
Daytona Beach, FL
100 Miles on 2.5-mile Paved Track
February 24, 1961

Fin	St	No.	Driver	Team / Car	Laps	Money	Status
1	1	22	Fireball Roberts	Smokey Yunick '61 Pontiac	39	$1,000	Running
2	2	3	Jim Paschal	Daytona Kennel '61 Pontiac	39	600	Running
3	13	47	Jack Smith	Smith '61 Pontiac	39	400	Running
4	11	87	Buck Baker	Baker '61 Chrysler	39	300	Running
5	19	11	Ned Jarrett	B G Holloway '61 Chevrolet	39	275	Running
6	4	72	Bobby Johns	Shorty Johns '61 Ford	39	250	Running
7	8	29	Nelson Stacy	Holt-Stacy '61 Ford	39	200	Runing
8	6	53	Bob Burdick	McKenzie '61 Pontiac	39	175	Running
9	7	31	Paul Goldsmith	Ray Nichels '61 Pontiac	39	150	Running
10	3	27	Junior Johnson	Holly Farms '61 Pontiac	38	140	Crash
11	23	2	Tommy Irwin	Tom Daniels '60 Chevrolet	38	135	Running
12	18	10	T C Hunt	Fred Wheat '60 Dodge	38	125	Running
13	10	24	Roscoe Thompson	James Turner '60 Pontiac	37	115	Crash
14	5	49	Bob Welborn	Welborn '61 Pontiac	37	100	Crash
15	9	83	Bob Pronger	Jack Meeks '61 Ford	37	85	Crash
16	14	43	Richard Petty	Petty Eng '61 Plymouth	37	75	Crash
17	16	56	Jim Hendrickson	Charles French '60 Chevrolet	37	75	Crash
18	26	62	Curtis Crider	Crider '60 Ford	37	75	Running
19	20	19	Herman Beam	Beam '60 Ford	37	50	Running
20	15	76	Larry Frank	Dick Wright '60 Ford	37	50	Running
21	12	4	Rex White	White-Clements '61 Chevy	36	50	Running
22	24	30	Friday Hassler	Fred Clark '60 Chevrolet	36	50	Crnk Sh
23	30	55	Ernie Gahan	John Koszeln '59 Che;vrolet	36	50	Running
24	29	60	George Tet	Tetsno Fuchigami '60 Ford	36	50	Running
25	32	64	Paul Parks	'60 Ford	35	---	Running
26	27	88	Harlan Richardson	Jim White '61 Ford	34	---	Running
27	25	63	Pete Boland	Boland '60 Ford	32	---	Crash
28	34	41	Charlie Chapman	Chapman '60 Ford	32	---	Running
29	33	39	Marshall Sargent	'59 Pontiac	21	---	
30	17	37	Joe Kelly	Don House '61 Ford	12	---	
31	31	38	Ed Marksteller	Mat DeMatthews '61 Ford	8	---	
32	28	57	Wes Morgan	J I Divers '60 Chevrolet	7	---	Crash
33	22	18	Darell Dake	Weldon Wagner '61 Chevy	7	---	
34	21	00	Dave Mader	Mader '61 Chevrolet	6	---	Crash

** Race shortened to 39 laps due to crash
Time of Race: 45 minutes, 06 seconds
Average Speed: 129.711 mph
Pole Winner: Fireball Roberts - 133.037 mph
Lap Leaders: - - - - - - - - - - - - - - Fireball Roberts   -39
Cautions: 5 for 10 laps
Margin of Victory: 1 car length (under caution)
Attendance: 17,500

Grand National Race No. 4
40 Laps at Daytona International Speedway
Daytona Beach, FL
100 Miles on 2.5-mile Paved Track
February 24, 1961

Fin	St	No.	Driver	Team / Car	Laps	Money	Status
1	1	8	Joe Weatherly	Bud Moore '61 Pontiac	40	$1,000	Running
2	5	20	Marvin Panch	Smokey Yunick '60 Pontiac	40	600	Running
3	3	6	Cotton Owens	Owens '61 Pontiac	40	400	Running
4	4	94	Banjo Matthews	Warrior Motel '61 Ford	39	300	Crash
5	12	32	Darel Dieringer	Ray Nichels '61 Pontiac	39	275	Running
6	20	89	Joe Lee Johnson	Johnson '61 Chevroelt	39	250	Running
7	16	85	Emanuel Zervakis	Toots Transfer '61 Chevrolet	39	200	Running
8	22	7	Jim Reed	Reed '61 Chevrolet	39	175	Running
9	6	59	Tom Pistone	Lynn Holloway '61 Pontiac	38	150	Running
10	9	75	Don O'Dell	J D Braswell '61 Pontiac	38	140	Running
11	10	65	Charlie Glotzbach	Melvin Black '61 Pontiac	38	135	Running
12	25	54	Jimmy Pardue	Pardue '60 Chevrolet	38	125	Running
13	13	91	Robert Roeber	R G Henschel '60 Pontiac	38	115	Running
14	21	86	Buddy Baker	Buck Baker '61 Chrysler	38	100	Running
15	15	42	Lee Petty	Petty Eng '61 Pontiac	37	85	Crash
16	24	73	Johnny Beauchamp	Dale Swanson '61 Chevrolet	37	75	Crash
17	8	66	David Pearson	Tony Lavati '61 Pontiac	37	75	Running
18	28	52	Tom Dill	Julian Buesink '61 Ford	37	75	Running
19	26	68	Ed Livingston	Curtis Crider '60 Ford	37	50	Running
20	29	40	Bobby Allison	Ralph Stark '60 Chevrolet	37	50	Running
21	27	16	Elmo Langley	Happy Steigel '509 Pontiac	36	50	Running
22	30	33	Reb Wickersham	Wickersham '60 Olds	36	50	Running
23	33	50	Ken Johnson	'60 Ford	33	50	Running
24	31	15	Red Hollingsworth	Hollingsworth '60 Chevrolet	33	50	Running
25	18	23	Sal Tovella	Bob Rose '61 Ford	27	---	Running
26	2	21	Curtis Turner	Courtesy '61 Ford	21	---	
27	23	1	Paul Lewis	Jess Potter '61 Chevrolet	14	---	
28	11	80	Tubby Gonzales	Gonzales '61 Ford	9	---	
29	19	99	Wilbur Rakestraw	B J Jones '61 Ford	8	---	
30	14	69	Johnny Allen	B G Holloway '61 Chevrolet	6	---	
31	32	36	Frank Secrist	Warner Bros '60 Ford	4	---	
32	7	78	Brian Naylor	Fred Lovette '60 Pontiac	1	---	
33	17	77	Buzz McCann	McCann's Auto '61 Ford	1	---	

Time of Race: 39 minutes, 19 seconds
Average Speed: 152.671 mph
Pole Winner: Joe Weatherly - 154.122 mph
Lap Leaders: Weatherly 1, Banjo Matthews 2-3, Curtis Turner 4-7, Matthews 8-10, Turner 11-21, Matthews 22-33, Weatherly 34, Matthews 35-39, Weatherly 40
Cautions:
Margin of Victory: 3 car lengths
Attendance: 17,500

Race No. 4

Weatherly Nips Matthews in Final Lap; Lee Petty Gravely Injured

DAYTONA BEACH, FL (Feb 24) -- Joe Weatherly nosed past a spinning Banjo Matthews 400 yards from the finish line and came home a winner in the second twin 100-mile qualifying race at Daytona International Speedway.

Lee Petty and Johnny Beauchamp, principles in the stunning inaugural Daytona 500 finish in 1959, were

Beauchamp's Chevrolet - a pile of junk after Daytona wreck

involved in a bone-snapping, horrifying crash in the last lap. Petty's Plymouth and Beauchamp's Chevrolet locked bumpers in the third turn and both machines

Rescue workers prepare stretcher for injured Lee Petty

hurtled the guard rail while traveling at 150 mph. Petty was gravely injured. Speedway Medical Director A. A. Monaco said Petty suffered a punctured lung, multiple fractures of the left chest, a fractured left thigh, a broken collar bone and multiple internal injuries. Beauchamp suffered head injuries. Spectator A. B. Kelly of Nashville, TN received a severely lacerated right hand while trying to administer to Petty moments after the crash. Petty's car rolled over on Kelly's hand.

Matthews, who had led entering the final lap, lost control of his Ford in the fourth turn. His car bounced off Weatherly's Pontiac and slapped the wall. He was not injured and accepted blame for the accident afterwards.

Marvin Panch finished second, three car lengths behind Weatherly, who averaged a record 152.671 mph. Cotton Owens wound up third. Matthews got credit for fourth place and Darel Dieringer was fifth.

Modified hot shot Bobby Allison of Miami entered his first Grand National race and finished 20th in a Chevrolet.

Grand National Race No. 5
200 Laps at Daytona International Speedway
Daytona Beach, FL
"Daytona 500"
500 Miles on 2.5-mile Paved Track
February 26, 1961

Fin	St	No.	Driver	Team / Car	Laps	Money	Status
1	4	20	Marvin Panch	Smokey Yunick '60 Pontiac	200	$21,050	Running
2	2	8	Joe Weatherly	Bud Moore '61 Pontiac	200	9,150	Running
3	17	31	Paul Goldsmith	Ray Nichels '61 Pontiac	200	5,900	Running
4	45	80	Fred Lorenzen	Tubby Gonzales '61 Ford	198	3,825	Running
5	6	6	Cotton Owens	Owens '61 Pontiac	198	2,975	Running
6	5	47	Jack Smith	Smith '61 Pontiac	197	2,075	Running
7	9	11	Ned Jarrett	B G Holloway '61 Chevrolet	196	1,550	Running
8	47	69	Johnny Allen	B G Holloway '61 Chevrolet	196	1,050	Running
9	7	87	Buck Baker	Baker '61 Chrysler	196	850	Running
10	18	59	Tom Pistone	Lynn Holloway '61 Pontiac	196	750	Running
11	29	49	Bob Welborn	Welborn '61 Pontiac	194	600	Running
12	41	4	Rex White	White '61 Chevrolet	194	500	Running
13	16	7	Jim Reed	Reed '61 Chevrolet	194	400	Running
14	46	23	Sal Tovella	Bob Rose '61 Ford	191	350	Running
15	22	65	Charlie Glotzbach	Melvin Black '61 Pontiac	191	350	Running
16	10	32	Darel Dieringer	Ray Nichels '61 Pontiac	191	325	Running
17	32	52	Tom Dill	Julian Buesink '61 Ford	190	325	Running
18	14	85	Emanuel Zervakis	Toots Transfer '61 Chevrolet	189	300	Running
19	49	37	Joe Kelly	Don House '61 Ford	188	300	Running
20	1	22	Fireball Roberts	Smokey Yunick '61 Pontiac	187	4,750	Engine
21	30	66	David Pearson	Tony Lavati '61 Pontiac	186	200	Running
22	37	30	Friday Hassler	Fred Clark '60 Chevrolet	186	200	Running
23	57	41	Elmo Henderson	Charlie Chapman '60 Ford	184	200	Running
24	31	83	Tim Flock	Jack Meeks '61 Ford	184	200	Running
25	38	16	Elmo Langley	Happy Steigel '59 Pontiac	184	200	Running
26	50	88	Harlan Richardson	Jim White '61 Ford	184	200	Running
27	8	94	Banjo Matthews	Warrior Motel '61 Ford	181	250	Crash
28	26	91	Bob Roeber	R G Wenschel '60 Pontiac	170	200	Running
29	34	68	Ed Livingstonn	Curtis Crider '60 Ford	177	200	Running
30	24	54	Jimmy Pardue	Pardue '60 Chevrolet	176	200	Engine
31	36	40	Bobby Allison	Ralph Stark '60 Chevrolet	175	200	Running
32	53	64	Paul Parks	'60 Ford	173	200	Running
33	27	24	Roscoe Thompson	James Turner '60 Pontiac	169	200	Timing Ch
34	39	19	Herman Beam	Beam '60 Ford	167	200	Running
35	40	33	Reb Wickersham	Wickersham '60 Olds	158	200	Engine
36	15	53	Bob Burdick	McKenzie '61 Pontiac	157	200	Engine
37	12	89	Joe Lee Johnson	Johnson '61 Chevrolet	153	200	Engine
38	25	76	Larry Frank	Dick Wright '60 Ford	152	200	Fuel Pmp
39	48	1	Paul Lewis	Jess Potter '61 Chevrolet	149	200	Running
40	28	86	Buddy Baker	Buck Baker '61 Chrysler	145	200	Running
41	54	39	Marshall Sargent	'59 Pontiac	115	200	Trans
42	58	36	Brian Naylor	Warner Bros '60 Ford	85	200	Engine
43	56	38	Ed Markstellar	Mat DeMatthews '61 Ford	81	200	Oil Leak
44	13	29	Nelson Stacy	Holt-Stacy '61 Ford	79	200	Engine
45	19	2	Tommy Irwin	Tom Daniels '60 Chevrolet	67	200	Engine
46	35	18	Darrell Dake	Weldon Wagner '61 Chevy	47	200	Fuel Pmp
47	43	27	Junior Johnson	Holly Farms '60 Pontiac	44	300	Engine
48	51	15	Red Hollingsworth	Hollingsworth '60 Chevrolet	35	200	Rock Arm
49	3	3	Jim Paschal	Daytona Kennel '61 Pontiac	30	200	Seal
50	11	72	Bobby Johns	Shorty Johns '61 Ford	26	200	Heating
51	55	60	George Tet	Tetsno Fuchigami '60 Ford	24	200	Valve
52	21	10	T C Hunt	Fred Wheat '60 Dodge	23	200	Engine
53	23	62	Curtis Crider	Crider '60 Ford	12	200	Oil Pres
54	20	75	Don O'Dell	J D Braswell '61 Pontiac	10	200	Bearing
55	33	21	Curtis Turner	Courtesy '61 Ford	6	200	Engine
56	44	99	Wilbur Rakestraw	B J Jones '61 Ford	5	200	Engine
57	52	55	Ernie Gahan	John Koszeln '59 Chevrolet	3	200	Wtr Pmp
58	42	50	Ken Johnson	'60 Ford	3	200	H Gasket

Time of Race: 3 hours, 20 minutes, 32 seconds
Average Speed: 149.601 mph
Pole Winner: Fireball Roberts - 155.709 mph
Lap Leaders: Fireball Roberts 1-12, Banjo Matthews 13-15, Nelson Stacy 16-17,
    Roberts 18-30, Stacy 31-33, Junior Johnson 34-37, Stacy 38-39, Johnson 40-42,
    Roberts 43-187, Marvin Panch 188-200
Cautions: None
Margin of Victory: 16 seconds
Attendance: 51,287

Race Number 5

Panch Takes Daytona 500 as Roberts Breaks Near End

DAYTONA BEACH, FL (Feb 26) -- Marvin Panch inherited the lead with 13 laps remaining and raced home first in the third annual Daytona 500 before a sell out audience of 51,287.

Panch was running nearly a lap behind teammate Fireball Roberts in the waning stages of the caution-free event, but found himself in the catbird seat for the $21,050 top prize when Roberts' Pontiac limped to the pits trailing smoke.

Roberts had dominated the affair in his Smokey Yunick prepared Pontiac, leading all but 17 laps. Panch, wheeling a year-old Pontiac from the Yunick stable, led the final 13 laps and finished 16 seconds ahead of runner-up Joe Weatherly. Paul Goldsmith came in third

Bobby Allison #40 and Rex White #4 in the Daytona 500

with Fred Lorenzen fourth and Cotton Owens fifth.

Roberts' 187 laps completed left him with a 20th place finish. The hometown star did manage to pocket $4,450 in lap money. It was the third straight year that Roberts was foiled by sour luck while leading the Daytona 500.

Panch averaged 149.601 mph for the 200 trips around Daytona's 2.5-mile track, shattering the previous record of 135.521 mph by over 12 mph.

Edwin "Banjo" Matthews was running in second place five laps before Roberts departed. However bad luck again bit the Asheville, NC Ford driver as he blew his engine with 19 laps to go. Buddy Baker, son of Buck Baker, had the dubious distinction of running all

afternoon, but finishing no better than 40th for his efforts.

Panch took the lead in the point standings with a 110 point margin over Weatherly.

Lorenzen, former USAC stock car champion, came to Daytona without a ride, but was itching to test his skills against the NASCAR stars. He managed to talk Tubby Gonzales into letting him drive his Ford and he responded brilliantly with a fourth place effort.

Grand National Race No. 6
200 Laps at Piedmont Interstate Fairgrounds
Spartanburg, SC
100 Miles on Half-mile Dirt Track
March 4, 1961

Fin	St	No.	Driver	Team / Car	Laps	Money	Status
1	4	5	Cotton Owens	Owens '60 Pontiac	200	$800	Running
2	3	43	Richard Petty	Petty Eng '60 Plymouth	199	525	Running
3	6	67	David Pearson	Pearson '60 Chevrolet	197	375	Running
4	15	54	Jimmy Pardue	Pardue '59 Chevrolet	195	275	Running
5	12	23	Doug Yates	Yates '59 Plymouth	193	250	Running
6	10	55	Ernie Gahan	John Koszeln '59 Chevrolet	192	215	Crash
7	5	4	Rex White	White '60 Chevrolet	188	275	Running
8	11	19	Herman Beam	Beam '60 Ford	187	150	Running
9	14	97	Harry Leake	'59 Chevrolet	183	140	Running
10	2	27	Junior Johnson	Holly Farms '60 Pontiac	182	130	Fuel Line
11	7	62	Curtis Crider	Crider '60 Ford	180	125	Running
12	17	7	E J Trivette	'59 Plymouth	173	110	Running
13	13	2	Tommy Irwin	Tom Daniels '60 Chevrolet	162	100	Sway Bar
14	16	68	Ed Livingston	Curtis Crider '60 Ford	133	85	Wheel
15	18	65	Charlie Glotzbach	Melvin Black '59 Chevrolet	92	70	Carb Fire
16	1	11	Ned Jarrett	B G Holloway '60 Ford	54	60	Oil Pres
17	9	87	Wendell Scott	'60 Chevrolet	52	50	Oil Pres
18	8	17	Fred Harb	Harb '59 Ford	29	50	Heating

Time of Race: 1 hour, 41 minutes, 26 seconds
Average Speed: 59.152 mph
Pole Winner: Ned Jarrett - 63.92 mph
Lap Leaders: Junior Johnson 1-102, Cotton Owens 103-109, Johnson 110-182, Owens 183-200
Cautions: 3
Margin of victory: 1 lap plus
Attendance: 6,000

Race No. 6

Hometowner Owens Laps Field at Spartanburg

SPARTANBURG, SC (Mar 4) -- Cotton Owens survived billowing dust and outlasted Junior Johnson to win the 100-mile Grand National race at the Piedmont Interstate Fairgrounds. It was Owens' fifth career win on the major league stock car tour, curiously one in each of the last five years.

Richard Petty finished second, a lap behind. David Pearson was third with Jimmy Pardue fourth and Doug Yates fifth.

Johnson took the lead from pole sitter Ned Jarrett at the outset and led most of the way. With 18 laps remaining, a broken fuel line put him out of the race, opening the door for the blond-thatched Owens.

Dust was a terrible problem for the 18 competitors, but more than that, it left the estimated attendance of 6,000 looking like wooden Indians.

Young Petty, driving in his first race since his dad had a life threatening crash at Daytona, was the sentimental favorite of the crowd. The 23 year-old Plymouth driver made a strong bid for victory, but he was foiled by an unscheduled pit stop and a spin with 30 laps to go.

Owens averaged 59.152 mph in his white Pontiac.

Grand National Race No. 7
200 Laps at Asheville-Weaverville Speedway
Weaverville, NC
100 Miles on Half-mile Dirt Track
March 5, 1961

Fin	St	No.	Driver	Team / Car	Laps	Money	Status
1	1	4	Rex White	White '61 Chevrolet	200	$900	Running
2	4	5	Cotton Owens	Owens '60 Pontiac	200	525	Running
3	9	11	Ned Jarrett	B G Holloway '60 Ford	200	375	Running
4	10	43	Richard Petty	Petty Eng '60 Plymouth	196	275	Running
5	5	85	Emanuel Zervakis	Monroe Shook '61 Chevrolet	194	250	Running
6	8	54	Jimmy Pardue	Pardue '59 Chevrolet	194	215	Running
7	12	23	Doug Yates	Yates '59 Plymouth	191	175	Running
8	13	1	Paul Lewis	Jess Potter '61 Chevrolet	190	150	Running
9	11	19	Herman Beam	Beam '60 Ford	186	140	Running
10	15	7	E J Trivette	'59 Plymouth	135	130	RR Axle
11	2	27	Junior Johnson	Holly Farms '60 Pontiac	91	125	Rear End
12	6	89	Joe Lee Johnson	Johnson '61 Chevrolet	87	110	Crnk Sh
13	3	42	Jim Paschal	Petty Eng '60 Plymouth	25	100	Steering
14	7	2	Tommy Irwin	Tom Daniels '60 Chevrolet	25	85	Engine
15	14	68	Curtis Crider	Crider '60 Ford	3	70	Crash

Time of Race: 1 hour, 22 minutes, 46 seconds
Average Speed: 72.492 mph
Pole Winner: Rex White - 79.295 mph
Lap Leaders: Rex White 1-200
Cautions: 2
Margin of Victory: 6 seconds
Attendance: 8,500

Race No. 7
White Edges Owens in Weaverville 100

WEAVERVILLE, NC (Mar 5) -- Perky Rex White of Silver Spring, MD drove his gold and white Chevrolet to a flag-to-flag triumph in the 100-miler at

Asheville-Weaverville Speedway.

The 5'4" White became the sixth different winner on the Grand National trail in the first seven races. He fought back the challenges of Junior Johnson in the early going, then repelled a late effort by Cotton Owens to bag his 14th career win.

A crowd of 8,500 watched White cross the finish line six seconds in front of Owens to snare the $900 top prize. Ned Jarrett came in third in the lead lap while fourth place finisher Richard Petty was four laps back. Emanuel Zervakis came in fifth.

Johnson pressured White through most of the first half of the race, but was knocked out by rear gearing failure. He got credit for 11th place in the 15 car field.

Owens moved into second place in the point standings with his runner-up effort. Point leader Marvin Panch was not entered, but still held a 98 point lead. White moved into ninth place, 774 points behind Panch.

White averaged 72.492 mph for the 100 miles and also established an all time qualifying record of 79.295 mph for a half-mile track.

Race No. 8

Roberts Leads All The Way in Inaugural Marchbanks 250

HANFORD, CA (Mar 12) -- Fireball Roberts of Daytona Beach drove the J.D. Braswell Pontiac to an overwhelming victory in the 250-mile Grand National race at the new Marchbanks Speedway. It was the ninth superspeedway victory in the last six years for the 32 year-old veteran. He led all 178 laps on the 1.4-mile banked paved oval. It was the first time a driver has ever led the entire distance on a superspeedway.

Finishing a distant second was Eddie Gray in a Ford. Danny Letner was third and Tubby Gonzales finished fourth. Fifth place went to Eddie Pagan.

Roberts had one close encounter en route to the $2,000 pay-off. Danny Weinberg, running in second place on lap 113, passed Roberts on the low side. However his angle into the first turn was too sharp and he crashed into the wall. Roberts looped his car to miss the Weinberg Ford.

Only one driver in the top 10 point standings entered the race. Rex White managed a sixth place finish, vaulting him from ninth to fourth in the point tally.

Roberts' 25th career win came at an average speed of 95.621 mph.

Grand National Race No. 8
178 Laps at Marchbanks Speedway
Hanford, CA
250 Miles on 1.4-mile Paved Track
March 12, 1961

Fin	St	No.	Driver	Team / Car	Laps	Money	Status
1	2	75	Fireball Roberts	J D Braswell '61 Pontiac	178	$2,000	Running
2	3	98	Eddie Gray	Gray '61 Ford	176	1,250	Running
3	33	76	Danny Letner	Guy Kimball '61 Ford	175	750	Running
4	28	80	Tubby Gonzales	'61 Ford	168	600	Running
5	7	45	Eddie Pagan	Bill Clinton '61 Ford	168	575	Running
6	14	47	Rex White	'60 Chevrolet	167	550	Running
7	18	0	Jim Cook	Floyd Johnson '60 Dodge	166	525	Running
8	6	4	Scotty Cain	'60 T-Bird	165	500	Running
9	5	44	Lloyd Dane	Dane '61 Chevrolet	165	450	Running
10	36	84	Bob Perry	'60 Ford	159	425	Running
11	23	77	Dick Santee	'59 Ford	159	400	Running
12	10	7	Don Noel	Chuck Parkko '61 Ford	157	400	Oil Pres
13	25	91	Dick Cook	'60 Plymouth	157	350	Running
14	4	36	Frank Secrist	'60 Ford	146	350	Running
15	34	00	Dick Getty	'59 Chevrolet	135	300	Running
16	27	20	Jack Norton	William Peach '59 Chevrolet	134	300	Running
17	22	61N	Dick Brown	'59 Chevrolet	133	250	Running
18	19	15	Marvin Heinis	'60 Ford	130	200	Engine
19	31	38	Mike Saathoff	'59 Edsel	129	200	Running
20	13	26N	Carl Joiner	'61 Chevrolet	125	100	Running
21	29	11	Dick Carter	'60 Plymouth	119	100	Engine
22	17	14	Ed Negre	'59 Ford	116	100	Engine
23	16	16	Danny Weinberg	Guy Kimball '61 Ford	113	100	Crash
24	21	10	Jim Blomgren	Bob Smith '60 Ford	107	100	Rear End
25	11	46	Marvin Porter	'60 Olds	95	100	Lugs
26	8	22N	Art Watts	'60 Ford	85	100	Engine
27	12	5	Bruce Worrell	Bob Smith '60 Ford	66	100	Rear End
28	15	94	Banjo Matthews	'61 Ford	66	100	Brakes
29	32	88	Harlan Richardson	'61 Ford	44	100	Engine
30	20	41	Charles Chapman	'60 Ford	35	100	Fuel Pmp
31	9	2	Ron Hornaday	'60 Ford	34	---	Engine
32	30	23	Tom Guffy	'59 Plymouth	29	---	Handling
33	35	12	Chuck Webb	'59 Ford	23	---	Rear End
34	1	51	Bob Ross	'60 Ford	13	---	Crash
35	26	25	Al Brand	'60 Ford	11	---	Piston
36	24	17	Brownie Brown	'59 Ford	6	---	Engine

Time of Race: 2 hours, 36 minutes, 22 seconds
Average Speed: 95.621 mph
Pole Winner: Bob Ross - 98.370 mph
Lap Leaders: Fireball Roberts 1-178
Cautions:
Margin of Victory: 2 laps plus
Attendance:

The 24 year-old Burdick, who has shown promise but lacks the funds from his family operated team, outlasted a 46 car field while motoring around the 1.5-mile oval on used tires, a borrowed rear end and service by a rag-tag rookie pit crew.

Rex White finished second and was on Burdick's bumper when the race ended under the caution flag. Ralph Earnhardt came in third. Fourth place went to Nelson Stacy and Ned Jarrett was fifth. White was originally flagged in fourth place, but a recheck of the score cards revealed he was in the lead lap rather than a lap down.

Marvin Panch, driving the Daytona Kennel Club Pontiac, appeared to be on his way to another big win. The native Californian was holding down a comfortable lead when he broke an axle with 42 laps left. Panch's Ray Fox led pit crew replaced the axle in five laps, and he came back to finish sixth.

Fred Lorenzen, driving the Holman-Moody Ford, was leading in the 106th lap when he slugged the retaining wall while trying to avoid the spinning cars of Wilbur Rakestraw, Johnny Allen, Herman Beam and Bobby Allison. He was unhurt.

Joe Lee Johnson was treated and released from the infield hospital for a banged up knee when his Chevrolet collided with T. C. Hunt's Dodge.

Fireball Roberts, Banjo Matthews and Curtis Turner all led in the early stages, but all failed to finish. Only 13 of the starting 46 cars were running at the end.

A crowd of 43,000 filled every available seat to watch the Grand National pilots wrestle for top honors on the sunny afternoon. Burdick won $15,775 and averaged 124.172 mph. Panch had posted the top qualifying effort of 135.755 mph.

White assumed command of the point race, leaping from fourth to first in one race. Panch was second, 66 points behind the new leader.

Race No. 9

Bob Burdick Stuns Favorites in Atlanta 500

HAMPTON, GA (Mar 26) -- Bob Burdick of Omaha, NE, drove his Pontiac into the lead in the 292nd lap and led the rest of the way to score a popular upset victory in the second annual Atlanta 500 at Atlanta International Raceway.

Bob Burdick upset the favorites in Atlanta 500

Grand National Race No. 9
334 Laps at Atlanta International Raceway
Hampton, GA
"Atlanta 500"
500 Miles on 1.5-mile Paved Track
March 26, 1961

Fin	St	No.	Driver	Team / Car	Laps	Money	Status
1	7	53	Bob Burdick	Roy Burdick Gar '61 Pontiac	334	$15,775	Running
2	4	4	Rex White	White-Clements '61 Chevrolet	334	8,850	Running
3	13	6	Ralph Earnhardt	Cotton Owens '61 Pontiac	334	4,850	Running
4	17	29	Nelson Stacy	Holt-Stacy '61 Ford	333	2,475	Running
5	18	11	Ned Jarrett	B G Holloway '61 Chevrolet	332	1,775	Running
6	1	3	Marvin Panch	Daytona Kennel '61 Pontiac	329	3,035	Running
7	24	66	Red Kagle	Cafe Burgundy '60 Ford	326	1,125	Running
8	14	59	Tom Pistone	Lynn Holloway '61 Pontiac	325	1,100	Running
9	19	85	Emanuel Zervakis	Monroe Shook '61 Chevrolet	322	825	Running
10	21	2	Tommy Irwin	Tom Daniels '60 Chevrolet	315	775	Fuel
11	12	54	Jimmy Pardue	Pardue '60 Chevrolet	312	700	Running
12	15	7	Jim Reed	Reed '61 Chevrolet	309	675	Rear End
13	6	49	Bob Welborn	Welborn '61 Pontiac	308	550	Running
14	39	62	Curtis Crider	Crider '60 Ford	293	450	Running
15	40	86	Buck Baker	Baker '61 Chrysler	290	400	Running
16	10	94	Banjo Matthews	Matthews '61 Ford	267	755	H Gasket
17	36	16	Elmo Langley	Happy Steigel '59 Pontiac	233	300	Lugs
18	43	39	Marshall Sargent	'59 pontiac	233	250	Rear End
19	33	78	Darel Dieringer	Billie Ridgeway '60 Ford	231	250	Crash
20	9	21	Curtis Turner	Wood Bros '61 Ford	216	565	H Gasket
21	11	47	Jack Smith	Smith '61 Pontiac	212	225	Engine
22	5	8	Joe Weatherly	Bud Moore '61 Pontiac	179	275	Lugs
23	34	56	Jim Hendrickson	'60 Chevrolet	171	200	Fuel Pmp
24	22	43	Richard Petty	Petty Eng '60 Plymouth	155	200	Engine
25	37	68	Ed Livingston	Curtis Crider '60 Ford	151	200	Bearings
26	16	23	Sal Tovella	Bob Rose '61 Ford	144	250	Engine
27	23	27	Junior Johnson	Holly Farms '61 Pontiac	126	300	Crash
28	25	89	Joe Lee Johnson	Johnson '61 Chevrolet	124	250	Crash
29	27	72	Bobby Johns	Shorty Johns '61 Ford	124	250	Crash
30	20	10	T C Hunt	Fred Wheat '61 Dodge	124	225	Crash
31	46	14	Freddy Fryar	'61 Chevrolet	116	200	Engine
32	38	9	Roy Tyner	'61 Chevrolet	109	200	Pulley
33	3	28	Fred Lorenzen	Holman-Moody '61 Ford	106	1,320	Crash
34	42	99	Wilbur Rakestraw	B J Jones '61 Ford	100	200	Crash
35	32	96	Johnny Allen	J L Cheatham '60 Chevrolet	96	200	Crash
36	35	19	Herman Beam	Beam '70 Ford	94	200	Crash
37	31	40	Bobby Allison	Ralph Stark '60 Chevrolet	94	200	Crash
38	8	76	Larry Frank	Dick Wright '60 Ford	90	225	Engine
39	41	15	Tim Flock	Beau Morgan '61 Ford	82	200	Steering
40	30	26	David Pearson	Pearson '61 Pontiac	80	200	Engine
41	29	30	Friday Hassler	Fred Clark '60 Chevrolet	53	200	Drv Shft
42	2	22	Fireball Roberts	Smokey Yunick '61 Pontiac	29	860	Engine
43	28	65	Charlie Glotzbach	Melvin Black '61 Pontiac	23	200	Engine
44	26	88	Harlan Richardson	Jim White '61 Ford	22	225	Engine
45	44	64	Johnny Sudderth	'60 Ford	22	200	Rear End
46	45	1	Paul Lewis	Jess Potter '61 Chevrolet	1	200	Engine

Time of Race: 4 hours, 02 minutes, 05 seconds
Average Speed: 124.172 mph

Pole Winner: Marvin Panch - 135.755 mph
Lap Leaders: Marvin Panch 1-4, Fireball Roberts 5-29, Panch 30-33, Fred Lorenzen 34-106,
  Panch 107-.......... Matthews-..........Panch 257-291, Burdick 292-334
Total Laps Led: Panch 116, Lorenzen 73, Turner 11, Roberts 25, Matthews 66,
  Burdick 43
Cautions: 2
Margin of Victory: 1 car length (Under Caution)

Race No. 10
"Golden Greek" Great
At Greenville

GREENVILLE, SC (Apr 1) -- Emanuel Zervakis,

the 'Golden Greek', passed a spinning Rex White in the 176th lap and breezed to victory in the 100-mile Grand National race at Greenville-Pickens Speedway. It was Zervakis' first Grand National win, although he was flagged the victor at Wilson, NC on April 17, 1960, only to have his car disqualified.

White was holding down first place with David Pearson and Zervakis in tow. White and Pearson tangled as they ran through a hole in the third turn and both spun out. Zervakis found an opening and shot his Chevrolet into the lead for good. Zervakis gave car owner Monroe Shook his first big time NASCAR victory.

Richard Petty finished in second place as a crowd of 5,000 watched the action packed affair. White recovered from his spin to take third, G.C. Spencer was fourth and Buck Baker fifth. Pearson got straightened out after his loop, but ran out of gas with 19 laps left. He got credit for 10th place in the final order.

Junior Johnson started on the pole and led the first 69 laps. A broken fuel pump put his Rex Lovette-owned Pontiac out at that point.

Zervakis became the eighth different winner in the 10 Grand National events staged in the 1961 season.

Grand National Race No. 10
200 Laps at Greenville-Pickens Speedway
Greenville, SC
100 Miles on Half-mile Dirt Track
April 1, 1961

Fin	St	No.	Driver	Team / Car	Laps	Money	Status
1	2	85	Emanuel Zervakis	Monroe Shook '60 Chevrolet	200	$800	Running
2	5	43	Richard Petty	Petty Eng '60 Plymouth	200	525	Running
3	4	4	Rex White	White-Clements '60 Chevrolet	199	475	Running
4	10	48	G C Spencer	'60 Chevrolet	199	275	Running
5	7	86	Buck Baker	Baker '61 Chrysler	196	250	Running
6	11	54	Jimmy Pardue	Pardue '59 Chevrolet	195	215	Running
7	13	7	Fred Harb	Harb '59 Ford	186	175	Running
8	17	35	George Green	'59 Plymouth	186	150	Running
9	15	0	Bobby Waddell	'59 Dodge	182	140	Running
10	8	67	David Pearson	Pearson '60 Chevrolet	181	130	Fuel
11	18	62	Curtis Crider	Crider '60 Ford	177	125	Running
12	21	30	Doug Cox	'59 T-Bird	150	110	Running
13	19	19	Herman Beam	Beam '60 Ford	149	100	Axle
14	9	11	Ned Jarrett	B G Holloway '60 Ford	100	85	Heating
15	14	9	Roy Tyner	Tyner '60 Ford	99	70	Trans
16	1	27	Junior Johnson	Holly Farms '60 Pontiac	69	60	Fuel Pmp
17	12	2	Tommy Irwin	Tom Daniels '59 T-Bird	68	50	Steering
18	20	71	Bob Barron	'60 Dodge	54	50	Clutch
19	3	47	Jack Smith	Smith '61 Pontiac	49	50	Engine
20	16	1	Paul Lewis	Jess Potter '61 Chevrolet	33	50	Crash
21	6	23	Doug Yates	Yates '59 Plymouth	8	50	Drv Shft

Time of Race: 1 hour, 54 minutes, 58 seconds
Average Speed: 52.189 mph
Pole Winner: Junior Johnson - 62.09 mph
Lap Leaders: Junior Johnson 1-69, Rex White 70-175, Emanuel Zervakis 176-200
Cautions: 4 for 20 laps
Margin of Victory:
Attendance: 5,000

Grand National Race No. 11
110 Laps at Orange Speedway
Hillsboro, NC
99 Miles on .9-mile Dirt Track
April 2, 1961

Fin	St	No.	Driver	Team / Car	Laps	Money	Status
1	3	6	Cotton Owens	Owens '60 Pontiac	110	$800	Running
2	4	42	Richard Petty	Petty Eng '60 Plymouth	110	525	Running
3	6	86	Buck Baker	Baker '61 Chrysler	110	375	Running
4	2	27	Junior Johnson	Holly Farms '60 Pontiac	109	275	Running
5	11	4	Rex White	White-Clements '60 Chevrolet	109	350	Running
6	8	54	Jimmy Pardue	Pardue '59 Chevrolet	108	215	Running
7	9	2	Tommy Irwin	Tom Daniels '59 T-Bird	108	175	Running
8	5	23	Doug Yates	Yates '59 Plymouth	107	150	Engine
9	10	48	G C Spencer	'60 Chjevrolet	106	140	Running
10	20	9	Roy Tyner	Tyner '60 Ford	102	140	Running
11	17	97	Harry Leake	'60 Chevrolet	102	125	Running
12	15	19	Herman Beam	Beam '60 Ford	99	110	Running
13	18	34	Wendell Scott	Scott '60 Chevrolet	98	100	Running
14	7	85	Emanuel Zervakis	Monroe Shook '60 Chevrolet	90	85	Running
15	12	43	Maurice Petty	Petty Eng '60 Plymouth	83	70	A Frame
16	13	17	Fred Harb	Harb '59 Ford	79	60	Running
17	19	35	George Green	'59 Plymouth	75	50	Axle
18	16	0	Bobby Waddell	'59 Dodge	39	50	Engine
19	1	11	Ned Jarrett	B G Holloway '61 Chevrolet	9	50	LR Hub
20	14	62	Curtis Crider	Crider '60 Ford	7	50	Radiator

Time of Race: 1 hour, 10 minutes, 08 seconds
Average Speed: 84.695 mph
Pole Winner: Ned Jarrett - 91.836 mph
Lap Leaders: Ned Jarrett 1-9, Cotton Owens 10-11, Junior Johnson 12-92,
  Owens 93-110
Cautions:
Margin of Victory:
Attendance: 4,900

Race No. 11

Checkered Flag Surprises Owens at Hillsboro

HILLSBORO, NC (Apr 2) -- Cotton Owens was a surprised victor as he rode home first in the 99-mile Grand National race at Orange Speedway. It was the fifth career win for the Spartanburg Pontiac driver.

Owens was running more than a lap behind in the late stages of the race when leader Junior Johnson was forced to make a lengthy pit stop to repair a faulty distributor. Owens, unaware of Johnson's misfortune, drove into the lead in the 93rd lap and led the rest of the way in the 110 lapper on Hillsboro's .9-mile dirt oval.

Owens was startled in the victory lane ceremonies. Richard Petty came in second and Buck Baker was third. Johnson came back to finish fourth, one lap off the pace. Rex White was fifth.

Ned Jarrett established a new qualifying record at

the famed dirt facility, pushing his Chevrolet around at a clip of 91.836 mph. Jarrett led the first nine laps before the left rear hub broke on his car. Owens drove into the lead for two laps before Johnson broke into a big lead.

A crowd of 4,900 were on hand despite a cold, biting 20 mph wind. The race had originally been schedule for March 19th, but rain forced postponement.

Owens won the race with an average speed of 84.695 mph.

Grand National Race No. 12
150 Laps at Bowman-Gray Stadium
Winston-Salem, NC
37.5 Miles on Quarter-mile Paved Track
April 3, 1961

Fin	St	No.	Driver	Team / Car	Laps	Money	Status
1	2	4	Rex White	White - Clements '60 Chevy	150	$700	Running
2	1	21	Glen Wood	Wood Bros '61 Ford	150	500	Running
3	6	43	Richard Petty	Petty Eng '60 Plymouth	147	375	Running
4	4	17	Fred Harb	Harb '59 Ford	147	305	Running
5	7	11	Ned Jarrett	B G Holloway '61 Chevrolet	147	245	Running
6	10	54	Jimmy Pardue	Pardue '59 Chevrolet	145	215	Running
7	8	23	Doug Yates	Yates '59 Plymouth	145	200	Running
8	5	27	Junior Johnson	Holly Farms '60 Pontiac	145	185	Running
9	9	2	Tommy Irwin	Tom Daniels '59 T-Bird	144	165	Running
10	16	48	G C Spencer	'60 Chevrolet	143	155	Running
11	12	34	Wendell Scott	Scott '60 Chevrolet	141	130	Running
12	13	19	Herman Beam	Beam '60 Ford	140	120	Running
13	3	85	Emanuel Zervakis	Monroe Shook '60 Chevrolet	136	140	Running
14	15	42	Maurice Petty	Petty Eng '60 Plymouth	135	115	Running
15	11	62	Curtis Crider	Crider '60 Ford	132	75	Running
16	18	86	Buck Baker	Baker '61 Chrysler	129	75	Axle
17	17	35	E J Trivette	'59 Plymouth	129	75	Running
18	14	97	Harry Leake	'60 Chevrolet	3	60	Engine

Time of Race: 49 minutes, 27 seconds
Average Speed: 45.500 mph
Pole Winner: Glen Wood - 48.70 mph
Lap Leaders: - - - - - - - - - - - - - - - Rex White   -150
Cautions:
Margin of Victory:
Attendance:

Race No. 12

Rex White Outmuscles Glen Wood for Bowman-Gray Win

WINSTON-SALEM, NC (Apr 3) -- Rex White took his second win of the year in the Easter Monday 37.5-mile Grand National race at Bowman-Gray Stadium. The victory enabled the Silver Spring, MD Chevrolet driver to open up a 782 point lead over Ned Jarrett in the 1961 point battle.

Pole sitter Glen Wood finished a close second. Richard Petty was third, three laps behind on the quarter-mile paved oval. Fred Harb, a part-timer who prefers the short tracks to the superspeedways, wound up in fourth place. Jarrett came in fifth.

A field of 18 took the green flag and 16 were running at the finish. Buck Baker and Harry Leake were the only drivers unable to make the distance.

Emanuel Zervakis qualified a strong third but fell to 13th in the final rundown, 14 laps off the pace. Maurice Petty struggled to finish 14th in a Petty Engineering Plymouth.

White averaged 45.500 mph for his 15th career Grand National victory.

Grand National Race No. 13
500 Laps at Martinsville Speedway
Martinsville, VA
"Virginia 500"
250 Miles on Half-mile Paved Track
April 9, 1961

Fin	St	No.	Driver	Team / Car	Laps	Money	Status
1	2	28	Fred Lorenzen	Holman-Moody '61 Ford	149	$1,150	Running
2	1	4	Rex White	White-Clements '61 Ford	149	1,275	Running
3	3	21	Glen Wood	Wood Bros '61 Ford	147	500	Running
4	16	85	Emanuel Zervakis	Monroe Shook '61 Chevrolet	147	325	Running
5	5	11	Ned Jarrett	B G Holloway '61 Chevrolet	147	450	Running
6	6	27	Junior Johnson	Holly Farms '61 Pontiac	146	315	Running
7	23	69	Johnny Allen	B G Holloway '61 Chevrolet	146	245	Running
8	9	43	Richard Petty	Petty Eng '61 Plymouth	146	175	Running
9	8	15	Tim Flock	Beau Morgan '61 Ford	146	215	Running
10	22	2	Tommy Irwin	Tom Daniels '60 Chevrolet	146	215	Running
11	7	72	Bobby Johns	Shorty Johns '61 Ford	145	150	Running
12	13	86	Buck Baker	Baker '61 Chrysler	144	160	Running
13	21	6	Cotton Owens	Owens '60 Pontiac	143	300	Running
14	12	87	Buddy Baker	Buck Baker '61 Chrysler	142	120	Running
15	25	48	G C Spencer	'60 Chevrolet	141	95	Running
16	15	55	Ernie Gahan	John Koszeln '59 Chevrolet	141	60	Running
17	10	54	Jimmy Pardue	Pardue '60 Chevrolet	140	110	Running
18	11	23	Doug Yates	Yates '59 Plymouth	139	85	Running
19	17	19	Herman Beam	Beam '60 Ford	136	50	Running
20	20	35	George Green	'59 Plymouth	136	50	Running
21	27	97	Harry Leake	'60 Chevrolet	134	50	Running
22	4	66	Reds Kagle	Cafe Burgandy '60 Ford	117	150	Fuel Tank
23	24	17	Fred Harb	Harb '59 Ford	113	75	Running
24	14	34	Wendell Scott	Scott '60 Chevrolet	109	50	Running
25	18	62	Curtis Crider	Crider '60 Ford	102	50	Running
26	19	9	Roy Tyner	Tyner '60 Ford	77	50	Brakes
27	26	71	Bob Barron	'60 Dodge	21	75	Engine

** Rain forced a halt after 149 laps had been completed
Time of Race: 1 hour, 05 minutes, 23 seconds
Average Speed: 68.366 mph
Pole Winner: Rex White - 70.28 mph
Lap Leaders: Rex White 1-118, Fred Lorenzen 119-149
Cautions: 2
Margin of Victory: 1 car length, Under Caution
Attendance:

Race No. 13

Lorenzen Gets First Win in Virginia 500 Minus 351

MARTINSVILLE, VA (Apr 9) -- Fred Lorenzen of Elmhurst, IL, was declared the official winner of the rain-abbreviated Virginia 500 at Martinsville Speedway as sanctioning NASCAR made an unusual ruling. Although only 29.8% of the race had been completed -- far short of the required 50% -- NASCAR officials declared the event as a full race.

A pelting rain forced a halt to the scheduled 500 lapper after 149 laps had been completed. NASCAR President Bill France, on hand for the race, said the full 500 lapper would be rescheduled for April 30 and the 149 laps completed before the rain fell would count as a 100-mile official race with drivers keeping their qualifying and lap leading bonus awards plus their position earnings. For the first time in NASCAR Grand National history, a runner-up took home more money than the race winner. Lorenzen got $1,150 for winning and White carted home $1,275 for position and bonus money.

Rex White was running second to Lorenzen when the race was red flagged. Glen Wood got credit for third place. Emanuel Zervakis was fourth and Ned Jarrett fifth.

White led the first 118 laps. Lorenzen, recently assigned to drive the Holman-Moody Ford after a superlative effort at Daytona in a lightly regarded car, slipped under White on lap 119 and led to the finish of the 74.5-mile race.

Race No. 14

White Bags Gwyn Staley Memorial At N. Wilkesboro

NORTH WILKESBORO, NC (Apr 16) -- Rex White ran down Curtis Turner with 104 laps to go and scored a two lap victory in the inaugural Gwyn Staley Memorial 400 at North Wilkesboro Speedway.

White bagged $2,455 and padded his point lead to 1,190 in the 400 lap event over the .625-mile paved track. A standing room only crowd of 12,500 was on hand to watch White average 83.248 mph. The event attracted considerable interest in the news media as several reporters sat cramped in a make-do press box.

Tommy Irwin scampered home second and Richard Petty was third. Fireball Roberts crossed the line in fourth place with Johnny Allen fifth.

Allen blew a tire and crashed his Chevrolet in the final five laps and did not finish.

Three different drivers, all major stars, fell out of the race while leading the pack. Pole winner Junior Johnson led the first 62 laps. His transmission broke at that point, leaving new star Fred Lorenzen in first place. Lorenzen led until the 123rd lap when a rocker arm broke on his Ford, allowing White to assume command. Curtis Turner caught White on lap 241 and took over the lead, but the Virginia lumberman's rear end burned out, knocking him from the lead. White then led the rest of the way for a two-lap victory.

Grand National Race No. 14
400 Laps at North Wilkesboro Speedway
North Wilkesboro, NC
250 Miles on .625-mile Paved Track
April 16, 1961

Fin	St	No.	Driver	Team / Car	Laps	Money	Status
1	2	4	Rex White	White-Clements '61 Chevrolet	400	$2,455	Running
2	6	2	Tommy Irwin	Tom Daniels '60 Chevrolet	398	1,175	Running
3	3	43	Richard Petty	Petty Eng '61 Plymouth	396	900	Running
4	19	22	Fireball Roberts	Smokey Yunick '60 Pontiac	390	575	Running
5	7	69	Johnny Allen	B G Holloway '61 Chevrolet	387	575	Crash
6	13	85	Emanuel Zervakis	Monroe Shook '61 Chevrolet	385	475	Running
7	10	87	Buddy Baker	Buck Baker '61 Chrysler	369	375	Trans
8	14	17	Fred Harb	Harb '59 Ford	366	325	Running
9	16	19	Herman Beam	Beam '60 Ford	346	325	Runing
10	21	33	Reb Wickersham	Wickersham '60 Olds	333	250	Running
11	18	71	Bob Barron	'60 Dodge	329	250	Running
12	24	62	Curtis Crider	Crider '60 Ford	319	175	Running
13	12	35	George Green	'59 Plymouth	310	175	Running
14	4	21	Curtis Turner	Wood Bros '61 Ford	296	250	Rear End
15	23	34	Wendell Scott	Scott '60 Chevrolet	276	100	Running
16	20	9	Roy Tyner	Tyner '60 Ford	252	100	Clutch
17	8	54	Jimmy Pardue	Pardue '59 Chevrolet	230	125	Rear End
18	15	48	G C Spencer	'60 Chevrolet	168	125	Rear End
19	5	28	Fred Lorenzen	Holman-Moody '61 Ford	123	210	Rock Arm
20	17	0	Bobby Waddell	'59 Dodge	109	125	Rear End
21	25	1	Paul Lewis	Jess Potter '61 Chevrolet	100	75	Rock Arm
22	1	27	Junior Johnson	Holly Farms '61 Pontiac	62	285	Trans
23	22	23	Doug Yates	Yates '59 Plymouth	30	75	Rear End
24	9	11	Ned Jarrett	B G Holloway '61 Chevrolet	29	100	Pistons
25	11	86	Buck Baker	Baker '61 Chrysler	27	100	Rear End

Time of Race: 3 hours, 11 seconds
Average Speed: 83.248 mph
Pole Winner: Junior Johnson - 95.66 mph
Lap Leaders: Junior Johnson 1-62, Fred Lorenzen 63-123, Rex White 124-240, Curtis Turner 241-296, White 297-400
Cautions: 6 for 33 laps
Margin of Victory: 2 laps plus
Attendance: 12,500

Grand National Race No. 15
200 Laps at Columbia Speedway
Columbia, SC
100 Miles on Half-mile Dirt Track
April 20, 1961

Fin	St	No.	Driver	Team / Car	Laps	Money	Status
1	2	6	Cotton Owens	Owens '60 Pontiac	200	$950	Running
2	1	11	Ned Jarrett	B G Holloway '61 Chevrolet	199	625	Running
3	3	85	Emanuel Zervakis	Monroe Shook '60 Chevrolet	199	425	Running
4	12	48	G C Spencer	'60 Chevrolet	197	275	Running
5	9	4	Rex White	White-Clements '60 Chevrolet	197	350	Running
6	7	43	Richard Petty	Petty Eng '60 Plymouth	193	215	Running
7	6	17	Fred Harb	Harb '59 Ford	192	175	Running
8	11	62	Curtis Crider	Crider '60 Ford	191	150	Running
9	15	97	Harry Leake	'60 Chevrolet	182	140	Running
10	13	19	Herman Beam	Beam '60 Ford	171	130	Running
11	16	34	Wendell Scott	Scott '60 Chevrolet	167	125	Crash
12	10	23	Doug Yates	Yates '59 Plymouth	167	110	Fuel Pmp
13	17	71	Bob Barron	'60 Dodge	165	100	Running
14	5	67	David Pearson	Pearson '60 Chevrolet	149	85	A Frame
15	19	93	Lee Reitzel	Reitzel '60 Ford	122	70	Running
16	4	86	Buck Baker	Baker '61 Chrysler	103	60	Axle
17	21	30	Doug Cox	'59 T-Bird	100	50	Axle
18	22	33	Bryant Wallace	Reb Wickersham '60 Olds	72	50	Brakes
19	14	35	George Green	'59 Plymouth	67	50	Crash
20	8	2	Tommy Irwin	Tom Daniels '59 T-Bird	23	50	Rear End
21	18	47	Jack Smith	Smith '61 Pontiac	12	50	Head
22	20	54	Jimmy Pardue	Pardue '59 Chevrolet	5	50	Push Rod

Time of Race: 1 hour, 55 minutes, 31 seconds
Average Speed: 51.940 mph
Pole Winner: Ned Jarrett - 64.38 mph
Lap Leaders: Ned Jarrett 1-196, Cotton Owens 197-200
Cautions:
Margin of Victory: 1 lap plus
Attendance:

Race No. 15

Owens' Third Win of Year Comes at Columbia

COLUMBIA, SC (Apr 20) -- Cotton Owens snared his third win of the season by taking the 100-miler at Columbia Speedway. It was the eighth win in 15 races for the Pontiac nameplate.

Ned Jarrett, who started on the pole, finished second, a lap behind. Emanuel Zervakis, competing in his first full year on the Grand National tour, wound up third. G.C. Spencer came in fourth and Rex White fifth. Jarrett led the first 196 laps and was a shoo-in for victory, but his Chevrolet ran out of gas with two miles remaining. "From now on whenever I come into the pits at any race, someone's going to be there pouring gas into the tank if it runs over every time," declared Jarrett.

Jarrett shaved 48 points off of White's point lead,

reducing his deficit to 1,242 points. Marvin Panch, who has started only three races, still ranked third in the point standings by virtue of his Febraury win at Daytona.

Accidents took out a pair of independent drivers. George Green crashed his Plymouth after 67 laps and Wendell Scott, black driver out of Danville, VA, crashed on lap 167.

Owens averaged 51.940 mph for his seventh career victory.

Grand National Race No. 16
250 Laps at Hickory Speedway
Hickory, NC
100 Miles on .4-mile Dirt Track
April 22, 1961

Fin	St	No.	Driver	Team / Car	Laps	Money	Status
1	1	27	Junior Johnson	Holly Farms '61 Pontiac	250	$950	Running
2	8	86	Buck Baker	Baker '62 Chrysler	250	625	Running
3	7	4	Rex White	White-Clements '60 Chevrolet	245	525	Running
4	23	48	G C Spencer	'60 Chevrolet	245	275	Running
5	14	54	Jimmy Pardue	Pardue '59 Chevrolet	242	250	Running
6	11	61	Elmo Langley	Doc White '59 T-Bird	241	215	Running
7	10	1	Paul Lewis	Jess Potter '61 Chevrolet	239	175	Running
8	6	69	Johnny Allen	B G Holloway '60 Chevrolet	236	150	Running
9	15	0	Bobby Waddell	'59 Dodge	235	140	Running
10	2	21	Curtis Turner	Holly Farms '60 Pontiac	233	130	Running
11	17	97	Harry Leake	'60 Chevrolet	232	125	Running
12	9	19	Herman Beam	Beam '60 Ford	229	110	Running
13	22	47	Jack Smith	Smith '61 Pontiac	228	100	Running
14	20	71	Bob Barron	'60 Dodge	215	85	Running
15	21	35	George Green	'59 Plymouth	210	70	Running
16	13	23	Doug Yates	Yates '59 Plymouth	195	60	Rans
17	3	85	Emanuel Zervakis	Monroe Shook '60 Chevrolet	190	50	Crash
18	19	93	Lee Reitzel	Reitzel '60 Ford	178	50	A Frame
19	5	11	Ned Jarrett	B G Holloway '61 Chevrolet	138	50	A Frame
20	4	43	Richard Petty	Petty Eng '60 Plymouth	100	50	Radiator
21	16	62	Curtis Crider	Crider '60 Ford	47	50	Rear End
22	12	17	Fred Harb	Harb '59 Ford	20	50	A Frame
23	18	33	Bryant Wallace	Reb Wickersham '60 Olds	9	50	Handling

Time of Race: 1 hour, 30 minutes, 1 second
Average Speed: 66.654 mph
Pole Winner: Junior Johnson - 74.074 mph
Lap Leaders: Curtis Turner 1-3, Junior Johnson 4-70, Richard Petty 71-98, Johnson 99-250
Cautions: 4 for 19 laps
Margin of Victory: 3/4 lap
Attendance: 10,000

Race No. 16

Johnson's Pontiac Holds Together; Wins at Hickory

HICKORY, NC (Apr 22) -- Junior Johnson had entered 12 races in 1961 prior to the 100-miler at Hickory Speedway, finishing only three. But everything under the hood of his Rex Lovette-owned, Holly Farms

sponsored Pontiac held together and the Ronda, NC charger registered his first win of the year.

Johnson drove past Richard Petty in the 99th lap and led the rest of the way in the 250 lapper on the .4-mile dirt track. Petty was hampered by a hole in his radiator, which forced him to the sidelines two laps after giving the lead to Johnson.

Buck Baker wound up second in his Chrysler. Rex White, G.C. Spencer and Jimmy Pardue rounded out the top five.

Curtis Turner, driving a Pontiac out of the Lovette stable, led the opening three laps but faded to a 10th place finish.

Emanuel Zervakis flipped his Chevrolet four times on the front stretch after brushing Rex White on lap 190. Zervakis, running sixth at the time of the mishap, was unhurt.

A crowd of 10,000 was on hand to see Johnson average 66.654 mph for his 20th career Grand National triumph.

Grand National Race No. 17
200 Laps at Atlantic Rural Fairgrounds
Richmond, VA
100 Miles on Half-mile Dirt Track
April 23, 1961

Fin	St	No.	Driver	Team / Car	Laps	Money	Status
1	1	43	Richard Petty	Petty Eng '60 Plymouth	200	$950	Running
2	4	6	Cotton Owens	Owens '60 Pontiac	199	625	Running
3	7	86	Buck Baker	Baker '61 Chrysler	193	425	Running
4	2	11	Ned Jarrett	B G Holloway '61 Chevrolet	186	275	Running
5	8	61	Elmo Langley	Doc White '59 T-Bird	186	250	Running
6	6	48	G C Spencer	'60 Chevrolet	176	215	Running
7	11	19	Herman Beam	Beam '60 Ford	168	175	Engine
8	12	71	Bob Barron	'60 Dodge	159	150	A Frame
9	10	35	George Green	'59 Plymouth	146	140	Engine
10	5	4	Rex White	White-Clements '60 Chevrolet	134	230	Fuel Pmp
11	3	69	Johnny Allen	B G Holloway '60 Chevrolet	128	125	A Frame
12	9	54	Jimmy Pardue	Pardue '59 Chevrolet	123	110	A Frame

Time of Race: 1 hour, 36 minutes, 4 seconds
Average Speed: 62.456 mph
Pole Winner: Richard Petty - 66.667 mph
Lap Leaders: Ned Jarrett 1-18, Richard Petty 19-200
Cautions:
Margin of Victory: I lap plus
Attendance: 7,000

Race No. 17

Only 6 Finish as Richard Petty Wins at Richmond

RICHMOND, VA (Apr 23) -- Richard Petty stormed past Ned Jarrett in the 19th lap and drove his Plymouth to an easy victory in the 100-mile Grand National race at the Atlantic Rural Fairgrounds. It was the first win for the 23 year-old Randleman, NC Plymouth driver since his father Lee was felled by critical injuries at Daytona.

Petty's fourth career win netted him $950 and moved him into 10th place in the point standings.

A crowd of 7,000 turned out to see only a dozen cars start the 200 lapper. Ned Jarrett led the first 18 laps before Petty took the lead for good. Cotton Owens finished second with Buck Baker, Jarrett and Elmo Langley following in that order. Only six cars finished the race.

Point leader Rex White fell out after 134 laps and wound up 10th. He still maintained a 1,386 point lead over Jarrett in his bid to repeat as NASCAR Grand National champion. Petty averaged 62.456 mph for his hour and a half ride.

Tim Flock #15 in one of his final appearances. He finished 7th in Virginia 500

Grand National Race No. 18
500 Laps at Martinsville Speedway
Martinsville, VA
"Virginia 500 Sweepstakes"
250 Miles on Half-mile Paved Track
April 30, 1961

Fin	St	No.	Driver	Team / Car	Laps	Money	Status
1	17	27	Junior Johnson	Holly Farms '61 Pontiac GN	500	$2,315	Running
2	5	85	Emanuel Zervakis	Monroe Shook '61 Chevy C	496	1,200	Running
3	26	75	Fireball Roberts	Smokey Yunick '61 Pont GN	496	825	Running
4	21	2	Tommy Irwin	Tom Daniels '60 Chevy GN	491	625	Running
5	24	86	Buck Baker	Baker '61 Chrysler C	491	550	Running
6	4	11	Ned Jarrett	B G Holloway '61 Chevy C	484	500	Running
7	7	15	Tim Flock	Beau Morgan '61 Ford GN	479	375	Running
8	22	97	Harry Leake	'60 Chevrolet GN	475	325	Running
9	1	4	Rex White	White-Clements '61 Chevy C	474	580	Running
10	6	29	Nelson Stacy	Holt-Stacy '61 Ford C	465	300	Rear End
11	2	28	Fred Lorenzen	Holman Moody '61 Ford	465	705	Running
12	10	19	Herman Beam	Beam '60 Ford GN	463	275	Running
13	18	48	G C Spencer	'60 Chevrolet GN	450	285	Running
14	9	23	Doug Yates	Yates '59 Plymouth GN	442	225	Running
15	15	34	Wendell Scott	Scott '60 Chevrolet GN	432	175	Running
16	28	69	Johnny Allen	B G Holloway '60 Chevy GN	431	150	Engine
17	29	74	L D Austin	Austin '61 Chevrolet GN	417	150	Running
18	27	9	Roy Tyner	Tyner '60 Ford C	416	150	Running
19	19	72	Bobby Johns	Shorty Johns '61 Ford C	414	175	Running
20	23	93	Lee Reitzel	Reitzel '60 Ford GN	403	150	Running
21	14	72	Bob Barron	'60 Dodge GN	312	150	Running
22	16	21	Glen Wood	Wood Bros '61 Ford GN	266	225	Rear End
23	3	43	Richard Petty	Petty Eng '61 Plymouth C	243	200	Distribut
24	30	62	Curtis Crider	Crider '60 Ford GN	236	125	Con Rod
25	11	54	Jimmy Pardue	Pardue '59 Chevrolet GN	211	150	Axle
26	20	1	Paul Lewis	Jess Potter '61 Chevrolet GN	209	150	Oil Pres
27	12	30	Bob Welborn	Fred Clark '60 Chevrolet GN	112	150	Piston
28	13	33	Reb Wickersham	Wickersham '60 Olds GN	48	150	Handling
29	8	17	Fred Harb	Harb '59 Ford GN	35	150	Handling
30	25	8	Allen Franklin	'60 Rambler GN	5	125	Handling

Time of Race: 3 hours, 46 minutes, 19 seconds
Average Speed: 66.278 mph
Pole Winner: Rex White - 71.32 mph
Lap Leaders: Rex White 1-31, Fred Lorenzen 32-365, Junior Johnson 366-500
Cautions: 1 for 6 laps
Margin of Victory: 4 laps plus
Attendance: 16,000

Race No. 18

Johnson Victorious in Virginia 500 Sweepstakes

MARTINSVILLE, VA (Apr 30) -- Junior Johnson, seemingly well out of contention in the middle stages, came to life with Fred Lorenzen's mechanical failure and walked off with top honors in Martinsville Speedway's Virginia 500 Sweepstakes race.

Johnson was four laps behind Lorenzen's fleet Holman-Moody Ford when engine problems put the Elmhurst, IL driver into the pits for a lengthy stay. His pit crew got him running again 37 laps later. Returning to the fray, Lorenzen blitzed the half-mile track with abandon, making up two of the lost laps. He managed to finish 11th.

Emanuel Zervakis finished second to Johnson in a Convertible. Fireball Roberts was third, Tommy Irwin fourth and Buck Baker fifth. Track officials encouraged the use of Convertible cars in the 250 miler, and eight of them showed up.

Johnson was left with a two lap lead when Lorenzen retreated to the pits. His pit crew repeatedly gave him the "E-Z" sign on the pit board, but Johnson refused to slack up. He continued to drive at break-neck speeds, which raised the ire of car owner Rex Lovette.

On Johnson's final pit stop, Lovette threatened Johnson with a sledge hammer, ordering his driver to ease off the throttle with the race well in hand. Johnson obliged somewhat reluctantly. He eventually won by a four-lap margin.

Johnson's 21st career Grand National win came at an average speed of 66.278 mph. Rex White finished ninth and had a 1,326 point lead over Ned Jarrett, who finished sixth.

Curtis Turner leads Fred Lorenzen in dramatic final laps of Rebel 300

Race No. 19
Lorenzen Beats Turner In Wild Darlington Shoot-out

DARLINGTON, SC (May 6) - Fair-haired Fred Lorenzen and old Pro Curtis Turner literally fought each other with fists of steel in Darlington Raceway's fifth annual Rebel 300 in a death-defying slugfest which decided perhaps the most exciting stock car race of all time.

Lorenzen emerged the winner in a vicious, fender-slamming duel between two angry and determined men

Grand National Race No. 19
219 Laps at Darlington Raceway
Darlington, SC
"Rebel 300"
300 Miles on 1.375-mile Paved Track
May 6, 1961

Fin	St	No.	Driver	Team / Car	Laps	Money	Status
1	1	28	Fred Lorenzen	Holman-Moody '61 Ford	219	$8,420	Running
2	8	21	Curtis Turner	Wood Bros '61 Ford	219	4,600	Running
3	9	69	Johnny Allen	B G Holloway '61 Chevrolet	218	3,200	Running
4	10	53	Bob Burdick	Roy Burdick Gar '61 Pontiac	218	2,400	Running
5	2	22	Fireball Roberts	Bud Moore '61 Pontiac	218	1,665	Running
6	17	3	Marvin Panch	Daytona Kennel '61 Pontiadc	217	1,050	Running
7	6	6	Ralph Earnhardt	Cotton Owens '61 Pontiac	216	925	Running
8	3	94	Banjo Matthews	Matthews '61 Ford	215	865	Running
9	5	72	Bobby Johns	Shorty Johns '61 Pontiac	215	700	Running
10	11	11	Ned Jarrett	B G Holloway '61 Chevrolet	215	650	Running
11	7	29	Nelson Stacy	Holt-Stacy '61 Ford	212	500	Running
12	18	47	Larry Frank	Jack Smith '61 Pontiac	212	400	Running
13	14	85	Emanuel Zervakis	Monroe Shook '61 Chevrolet	211	370	Running
14	22	54	Jimmy Pardue	Pardue '60 Chevrolet	209	300	Running
15	4	8	Joe Weatherly	Bud Moore '61 Pontiac	206	250	Running
16	26	00	Dave Mader	Mader '61 Chevrolet	205	275	Running
17	20	48	G C Spencer	'60 Chevrolet	200	200	Running
18	21	2	Tommy Irwin	Tom Daniels '60 Chevrolet	200	200	Running
19	25	82	Larry Flynn	'59 Chevrolet	195	200	Running
20	13	87	Buck Baker	Baker '61 Chrysler	192	565	Running
21	28	68	Ed Livingston	Curtis Crider '60 Ford	187	200	Running
22	32	62	Curtis Crider	Crider '61 Mercury	181	500	Running
23	29	38	Ed Marsteller	'61 Ford	177	200	Running
24	12	4	Rex White	White-Clements '61 Chevy	173	340	Crash
25	15	86	Buddy Baker	Buck Baker '61 Chrysler	115	200	Crash
26	24	55	Jimmy Thompson	'59 T-Bird	62	200	Crash
27	23	52	Tom Dill	Julian Buesink '61 Ford	46	230	Crash
28	19	1	Paul Lewis	Jess Potter '61 Chevrolet	38	200	Oil Pres
29	30	71	Bobby Waddell	'60 Dodge	22	220	Oil Pres
30	16	15	Tim Flock	Beau Morgan '61 Ford	16	200	Handling
31	27	61	Elmo Langley	Doc White '50 T-Bird	14	200	Handling
32	31	43	Richard Petty	Petty Eng '61 Plymouth	11	200	Engine

Time of Race: 2 hours, 31 minutes, 10 seconds
Average Speed: 119.520 mph
Pole Winner: Fred Lorenzen - 128.965 mph
Lap Leaders: Fred Lorenzen 1-5, Fireball Roberts 6-9, Lorenzen 10-71,
  Joe Weatherly 72-74, Ralph Earnhardt 75, Curtis Turner 76-77, Johnny Allen 78-79,
  Banjo Matthews 80, Roberts 81-142, Turner 143-146, Weatherly 147-149,
  Bob Burdick 150, Earnhardt 151-155, Allen 156, Roberts 157-198, Turner 199-217,
  Lorenzen 218-219
Cautions: 1
Margin of Victory: 6 car lengths
Attendance: 32,000

Car owner Cotton Owens and driver Ralph Earnhardt. The Pontiac team finished 7th in Rebel 300

who threw caution and common sense out the window.

Turner had taken the lead on lap 199 when tire trouble held Fireball Roberts in check. Turner then engaged in a thundering battle with upstart Lorenzen that had the crowd of 32,000 on their collective feet. "He bumped me 50 times and I bumped him 50 times in the last 20 laps," said Lorenzen.

Lorenzen repeatedly tried to muscle his way past Turner on the high side of the one groove race track. Turner would drift high and block Lorenzen's move, often forcing him into the guard rail. With two laps to go, Lorenzen faked a high pass then scooted under

Turner's Wood Brothers' Ford. The two slapped considerable sheet metal in the first and second turns before Lorenzen skated to a six car length lead, which he held until the finish.

"If I could have caught him before he got the checkered flag," steamed Turner, "I guarantee you he never would have finished the race."

Johnny Allen finished third, a lap behind the leaders. Bob Burdick was fourth as Roberts fell to fifth. Lorenzen won $8,420 for his 119.520 mph victory.

Point leader Rex White was eliminated in a two car crash in the 173rd lap. His point lead was cut to 262 points as Ned Jarrett finished 10th.

The lead changed hands 16 times among eight drivers on the overcast afternoon.

Grand National Race No. 20
67 Laps at Charlotte Motor Speedway
Charlotte, NC
100 Miles on 1.5-mile Paved Track
May 21, 1961

Fin	St	No.	Driver	Team / Car	Laps	Money	Status
1	7	43	Richard Petty	Petty Eng '61 Plymouth	67	$800	Running
2	3	6	Ralph Earnhardt	Cotton Owens '61 Pontiac	67	525	Running
3	5	47	Bob Welborn	Jack Smith '61 Pontiac	67	375	Running
4	4	72	Bobby Johns	Shorty Johns '61 Ford	67	275	Running
5	1	28	Fred Lorenzen	Holman-Moody '61 Ford	67	250	Running
6	18	75	Fireball Roberts	Smokey Yunick '61 Pontiac	66	215	Running
7	2	94	Banjo Matthews	Matthews '61 Ford	66	175	Running
8	6	11	Ned Jarrett	B G Holloway '61 Chevrolet	66	150	Running
9	8	69	Johnny Allen	B G Holloway '61 Chevrolet	66	140	Running
10	10	48	G C Spencer	'60 Chevrolet	65	130	Running
11	12	82	Joe Eubanks	'61 Ford	64	125	Running
12	9	54	Jimmy Pardue	Pardue '60 Chevrolet	64	110	Running
13	16	97	E J Trivette	'60 Chevrolet	56	100	Running
14	11	4	Rex White	White-Clements '61 Chevrolet	41	185	Running
15	13	85	Emanuel Zervakis	Monroe Shook '61 Chevrolet	28	70	Engine
16	14	62	Curtis Crider	Crider '61 Mercury	18	60	Trans
17	17	35	Bobby Waddell	'59 Plymouth	3	50	Rear End
18	15	27	Bobby Isaac	Holly Farms '61 Pontiac	2	50	Coil
19	19	9	Roy Tyner	Tyner '60 Ford	1	50	Handling

Time of Race: 45 minutes, 09 seconds
Average Speed: 133.554 mph
Pole Winner: Fred Lorenzen - 137.48 mph
Lap Leaders: Fred Lorenzen 1-34, Ralph Earnhardt 35-43, Richard Petty 44-67
Cautions: None
Margin of victory: 8 seconds
Attendance: 10,000

Race No. 20

Petty Trims Earnhardt in Charlotte 100-mile Qualifier

CHARLOTTE, NC (May 21) -- Richard Petty gunned his Plymouth to victory in the opening 100-mile qualifying race for the upcoming World 600, showing that his previously underpowered 'Mayflower' car is ready to be competitive on the big speedways.

Petty edged Ralph Earnhardt by 8.0 seconds to take the $800 first prize at Charlotte Motor Speedway's first attempt to stage qualifying races. Bob Welborn came in third with Bobby Johns fourth and Fred Lorenzen fifth.

A crowd of 10,000 turned out to watch the two qualifiers, an attempt by Speedway management to get out of the financial ointment they have been in for more than a year.

Petty took the lead from Earnhardt in the 44th lap of the 67 lap contest and stretched his advantage slowly until Roby Combs' checkered flag fell. The triumph earned Petty the coveted pole position for the World 600 as only the front row of starting positions were up for grabs.

Bobby Isaac drove Junior Johnson's Pontiac in the first 100-miler, finishing 18th after his coil burned out. It was the first Grand National start for the Catawba, NC Modified driver.

Petty averaged 133.554 mph for his second win of the 1961 season.

Race No. 21

Turner Crashes; Weatherly Takes Second Charlotte Qualifier

CHARLOTTE, NC (May 21) -- Joe Weatherly scrubbed past Junior Johnson with three laps to go and won the second half of Charlotte Motor Speedway's twin bill 100-mile qualifying races.

Johnson wound up second, just six car lengths behind Weatherly's Bud Moore Pontiac. Third place went to Jack Smith with Nelson Stacy fourth and Marvin Porter fifth.

Curtis Turner, President of the Charlotte Motor Speedway, jumped out to an early lead and was running away when a tire blew on his Ford, sending it into the wall. He was done for the day, setting the stage for the Weatherly-Johnson duel. Turner was unhurt in the mishap, but his Wood Brothers Ford tore out six sturdy fence posts.

Speedy Thompson and Tommy Irwin crashed in the second lap, but neither driver was hurt.

The caution flag came out twice for a total of 14 laps, reducing Weatherly's average speed to 115.591 mph.

Johnson was the fastest qualifier at 136.951 mph in the Ray Fox prepared Pontiac.

Grand National Race No. 21
67 Laps at Charlotte Motor Speedway
Charlotte, NC
100 Miles on 1.5-mile Paved Track
May 21, 1961

Fin	St	No.	Driver	Team / Car	Laps	Money	Status
1	3	8	Joe Weatherly	Bud Moore '61 Pontiac	67	$800	Running
2	1	3	Junior Johnson	Daytona Kennel '61 Pontiac	67	525	Running
3	9	46	Jack Smith	Smith '61 Pontiac	66	375	Running
4	8	29	Nelson Stacy	Holt-Stacy '61 Ford	66	275	Running
5	11	44	Marvin Porter	'60 Plymouth	66	250	Running
6	6	15	Tim Flock	Beau Morgan '61 Ford	65	215	Running
7	13	12	Buck Fulp	'61 Ford	65	175	Running
8	12	19	Herman Beam	Beam '60 Ford	60	150	Running
9	14	93	Lee Reitzel	Reitzel '60 Ford	59	140	Running
10	17	74	L D Austin	Austin '61 Chevrolet	57	130	Running
11	2	21	Curtis Turner	Wood Bros '61 Ford	52	125	Crash
12	4	87	Buck Baker	Baker '61 Chrysler	39	110	Cut Tire
13	15	71	Bob Barron	'60 Dodge	18	100	Rear End
14	10	89	Joe Lee Johnson	Adcox-Kirby '61 Chevrolet	17	85	Clutch
15	19	86	Buddy Baker	Buck Baker '61 Chrysler	12	70	Clutch
16	16	18	Cotton Owens	'61 Pontiac	11	60	Trans
17	5	16	Speedy Thompson	Beau Morgan '61 Ford	2	50	Crash
18	7	2	Tommy Irwin	Tom Daniels '60 Chevrolet	1	50	Crash
19	18	31	Gene Stokes	Stokes '61 Studebaker	1	50	Fuel Pmp

Time of Race: 52 minutes, 16 seconds
Average Speed: 115.591 mph
Pole Winner: Junior Johnson - 136.951 mph
Lap Leaders: Curtis Turner 1-52, Junior Johnson 53-64, Joe Weatherly 65-67
Cautions: 2 for 14 laps
Margin of Victory: 6 car lengths
Attendance: 10,000

Grand National Race No. 22
39 Laps at Riverside International
Raceway
Riverside, CA
100 Miles on 2.58-Mile Road Course
May 21, 1961

Fin	St	No.	Driver	Team / Car	Laps	Money	Status
1	2	44	Lloyd Dane	Dane '61 Chevrolet	39	$825	Running
2	7	7	Don Noel	Chuck Parkko '61 Ford	39	505	Running
3	8	18	Dick Smith	'60 Ford	38	350	Running
4	4	0	Jim Cook	Floyd Johnson '60 Dodge	38	290	Running
5	9	84	Bob Perry	'59 Ford	38	250	Running
6	5	76	Danny Weinberg	Guy Kimball '61 Ford	38	215	Running
7	12	10	Jim Blomgren	Bob Smith '60 Ford	38	160	Running
8	3	45	Eddie Pagan	Bill Clinton '61 Ford	38	160	Running
9	10	5	Bruce Worrell	Bob Smith '60 Ford	37	140	Running
10	20	20	Jack Norton	Jim Peach '59 Chevrolet	37	130	Running
11	6	4	Scotty Cain	'60 T-Bird	37	130	Running
12	13	41	Charlie Chapman	Chapman '60 Ford	36	100	Running
13	16	91	Dick Cook	'59 Plymouth	36	90	Running
14	15	27	Gus Newman	'59 Chevrolet	35	80	Running
15	18	3	Dick Miller	'58 Ford	33	70	Running
16	1	98	Eddie Gray	Gray '61 Ford	33	85	Running
17	17	25	Al Brand	'60 Ford	32	55	Running
18	14	11	Cliff Hill	'60 Plymouth	31	50	Running
19	27	9	Bob Price	'59 Chevrolet	23	50	Running
20	11	2	Ron Hornaday	'60 Ford	13	50	Engine
21	26	00	Dick Getty	'59 Chevrolet	5	50	Fuel Pmp
22	23	35	Mike Mitchell	'58 Ford	5	50	Heating
23	21	21	Arley Scranton	'58 Ford	3	---	Heating
24	25	75	Clem Proctor	'61 Corvair	3	---	Flagged
25	24	88	Joe Clark	'61 Chevrolet	3	---	Flagged
26	22	17	Marvin Heinis	'61 Chevrolet	2	---	Flagged
27	19	15	Bill Clifton	'60 Ford	1	---	Radiator

Time of Race: 1 hour, 13 minutes, 10 seconds
Average Speed: 82.512 mph
Pole Winner: Eddie Gray - 85.21 mph
Lap Leaders: - - - - - - - - - - - - - - Lloyd Dane   -39
Cautions: None
Margin of Victory:
Attendance:

Race No. 22

Dane's Chevrolet Tops Field in Riverside 100

RIVERSIDE, CA (May 21) -- Lloyd Dane drove his Chevrolet to victory in the 100-mile Grand National race at Riverside International Raceway to become the 12th different winner of the 1961 NASCAR season. It was Dane's fourth Grand National win since 1957.

Don Noel, the only other driver to complete the prescribed 39 lap distance on the 2.58-mile road course, wound up second. Dick Smith was third, Jim Cook fourth and Bob Perry fifth.

Eddie Gray won the pole, but his Ford fell off the pace and wound up 6th in the field of 27, six laps off the pace.

Clem Proctor entered a new compact Chevrolet Corvair, but was flagged off the course after three laps for not maintaining race speeds.

The 100-miler was the 10th road race in NASCAR Grand National history, and it was the second staged in the California desert.

Dane averaged 82.512 mph as the race was uninterrupted by accidents.

Race No. 23

Eddie Gray Grabs Win at Ascot Speedway

LOS ANGELES, CA (May 27) -- Eddie Gray, driving a Ford owned and prepared by himself, lapped the field in the 100-mile event at Ascot Speedway. It was the third career win for the Gardena, CA speedster.

Don Noel finished in second place, and pole sitter Danny Weinberg was third. Jim Blomgren wound up fourth with Ron Hornaday fifth.

Ford automobiles swept the first nine spots in the 200 lap event on the half-mile dirt track.

Weinberg won the pole in Guy Kimball's Ford, but

ell four laps off the pace. Gray was in command most of the way.

Gray, author of one of the scariest crashes in NAS-CAR history in the 1958 Southern 500, averaged 68.833 mph.

Grand National Race No.23
200 Laps at Ascot Speedway
Los Angeles, CA
100 Miles on Half-mile Dirt Track
May 27, 1961

Fin	St	No.	Driver	Team / Car	Laps	Money	Status
1	2	98	Eddie Gray	Gray '61 Ford	200	$850	Running
2	7	7	Don Noel	Chuck Parkko '61 Ford	199	500	Running
3	1	76	Danny Weinberg	Guy Kimball '61 Ford	196	370	Running
4	4	10	Jim Blomgren	Bob Smith '60 Ford	196	305	Running
5	9	2	Ron Hornaday	'60 Ford	196	250	Running
6	8	5	Bruce Worrell	Bob Smith '60 Ford	194	200	Running
7	15	14	Ed Negre	'59 Ford	192	160	Running
8	11	45	Eddie Pagan	Bill Clinton '61 Ford	192	150	Running
9	12	84	Bob Perry	'59 Ford	191	140	Running
10	16	9	Bob Price	'59 Chevrolet	181	130	Running
11	20	15	Bill Clinfton	'60 Ford	166	120	Running
12	18	25	Al Brand	'60 Ford	162	100	Running
13	5	44	Lloyd Dane	'61 Chevrolet	161	90	Running
14	21	46	Bill Ferrier	'59 Ford	132	80	Clutch
15	17	3	Dick Miller	'58 Ford	101	70	Engine
16	19	20	Jack Norton	William Peach '59 Chevrolet	93	60	RF Hub
17	14	00	Dick Getty	'59 Chevrolet	81	50	Running
18	13	91	Dick Cook	'60 Plymouth	80	50	Trans
19	10	18	Dick Smith	'60 Ford	67	50	Piston
20	3	0	Jim Cook	Floyd Johnson '60 Dodge	39	60	Piston
21	6	4	Scotty Cain	'60 T-Bird	14	50	Piston
22	22	27	Gus Newman	'59 Chevrolet	5	50	Bearing

Time of Race: 1 hour, 27 minutes, 10 seconds
Average Speed: 68.833 mph
Pole Winner: Danny Weinberg - 71.94 mph
Lap Leaders: - - - - - - - - - - - - - - Eddie Gray   -200
Cautions:
Margin of Victory: 1 lap plus
Attendance:

Race No. 24

David Pearson Captures World 600 on Three Wheels

CHARLOTTE, NC (May 28) -- David Pearson led the final 129 laps and crossed the finish line in a shower of sparks as he drove a Pontiac to victory in a stunning upset in the World 600 at Charlotte Motor Speedway. It was Pearson's first Grand National win, and he became the 14th different winner in the first half of the 1961 season.

The wreck-marred endurance contest, in which 57 laps were run under the caution flag, sent Richard "Reds" Kagle to Cabarrus Memorial Hospital in serious condition after doctors amputated his left leg above the

Grand National Race No. 24
400 Laps at Charlotte Motor Speedway
Charlotte, NC
"World 600"
600 Miles on 1.5-mile Paved Track
May 28, 1961

Fin	St	No.	Driver	Team / Car	Laps	Money	Status
1	3	3	David Pearson	Daytona Kennel '61 Pontiac	400	$24,280	Running
2	10	22	Fireball Roberts	Smokey Yunick '61 Pontiac	398	9,320	Running
3	8	4	Rex White	White-Clements '61 Chevrolet	397	7,070	Running
4	11	11	Ned Jarrett	B G Holloway '61 Chevrolet	397	4,475	Running
5	25	14	Jim Paschal	'61 Pontiac	394	3,150	Running
6	39	30	Tiny Lund	Fred Clark '60 Chevrolet	392	2,450	Running
7	19	46	Jack Smith	Smith '61 Pontiac	392	1,710	Running
8	14	47	Bob Welborn	Jack Smith '61 Pontiac	392	1,350	Running
9	23	27	Junior Johnson	Holly Farms '61 Pontiac	390	1,100	Running
10	2	8	Joe Weatherly	Bud Moore '61 Pontiac	389	1,040	Running
11	6	6	Ralph Earnhardt	Cotton Owens '61 Pontiac	386	1,570	Running
12	30	1	Paul Lewis	Jess Potter '61 Chevrolet	386	650	Running
13	33	82	Joe Eubanks	'61 Ford	384	1,350	Running
14	37	10	T C Hunt	Fred Wheat '61 Dodge	376	1,200	Running
15	17	85	Emanuel Zervakis	Monroe Shook '61 Chevrolet	375	400	Running
16	54	93	Lee Reitzel	Reitzel '60 Ford	371	400	Running
17	44	61	Elmo Langley	Doc White '59 T-Bird	371	400	Running
18	43	96	Friday Hassler	'60 Chevrolet	368	400	Running
19	12	72	Bobby Johns	Shorty Johns'61 Ford	367	445	Running
20	7	18	Tommy Irwin	'61 Pontiac	361	500	Drv Shft
21	38	5	Bobby Waddell	'59 Chevrolet	361	300	Running
22	41	38	Ed Marksteller	'61 Ford	350	300	Running
23	48	23	Doug Yates	Yates '61 Plymouth	358	1,100	Running
24	42	19	Herman Beam	Beam '60 Ford	357	250	Running
25	49	57	Wes Morgan	'61 Chevrolet	347	250	Running
26	32	86	Buddy Baker	Buck Baker '61 Chrysler	342	1,000	Rear End
27	13	53	Bob Burdick	Roy Burdick Gar '61 Pontiac	338	200	Crash
28	18	94	Banjo Matthews	Matthews '61 Ford	336	250	Engine
29	36	80	Tubby Gonzales	Gonzales '61 Ford	336	200	Rear End
30	1	43	Richard Petty	Petty Eng '61 Plymouth	332	670	Engine
31	26	48	G C Spencer	'60 Ford	325	200	Running
32	55	71	Bob Barron	'60 Dodge	291	200	Flagged
33	21	69	Johnny Allen	B G Holloway '61 Chevrolet	283	200	Rear End
34	29	2	Reds Kagle	Cafe Burgandy '61 Ford	277	220	Crash
35	5	28	Fred Lorenzen	Holman-Moody '61 Ford	274	275	A Frame
36	50	9	Roy Tyner	Tyner '60 Ford	266	200	Crash
37	24	15	Tim Flock	Beau Morgan '61 Ford	255	200	Engine
38	45	68	Ed Livingston	Curtis Crider '60 Ford	254	200	Engine
39	35	54	Jimmy Pardue	Pardue '60 Chevrolet	221	200	Bel Hsng
40	46	62	Curtis Crider	Crider '61 Mercury	203	1,000	Crank Sh
41	9	16	Speedy Thompson	Beau Morgan '61 Ford	186	225	Cam Sh
42	15	87	Buck Baker	Baker '61 Chrysler	147	200	Heating
43	4	20	Marvin Panch	Smokey Yunick '60 Pontiac	140	230	Crash
44	20	21	Curtis Turner	Wood Bros '61 Ford	139	220	Crash
45	31	44	Marvin Porter	'60 Plymouth	136	200	Engine
46	22	29	Nelson Stacy	Holt-Stacy '671 Ford	128	200	Bearing
47	34	66	Jimmy Thompson	Cafe Burgandy '60 Ford	113	200	Axle
48	53	31	Gene Stokes	Stokes '61 Studebaker	95	200	Oil Pres
49	27	7	Jim Reed	Reed '61 Chevrolet	93	250	Valve Spg
50	16	24	Roscoe Thompson	James Turner '60 Pontiac	70	200	Clutch
51	47	40	Bobby Allison	Ralph Stark '60 Chevrolet	53	200	Axle
52	28	89	Joe Lee Johnson	Adcox-Kirby '61 Chevrolet	40	230	Crash
53	40	75	Larry Frank	'61 Pontiac	10	225	Timing
54	51	51	Doug Cox	'59 T-Bird	6	200	Engine
55	52	35	E J Trivette	'59 Plymouth	3	200	Axle

Time of Race: 5 hours, 22 minutes, 29 seconds
Average Speed: 111.633 mph
Pole Winner: Richard Petty - 131.611 mph
Fastest Qualifier: David Pearson - 138.381 mph
Lap Leaders: Joe Weatherly 1, David Pearson 2, Weatherly 3-15, Ralph Earnhardt 16-33,
  Jack Smith 34-36, Earnhardt 37-48, Pearson 49-52, Earnhardt 53-69, Pearson 70-80,
  Ned Jarrett 81-110, Earnhardt 111-138, Pearson 139-177, Richard Petty 178-200,
  Fireball Roberts 201-206, Pearson 207-247, Petty 248-271, Pearson 272-400
Cautions: 7 for 57 laps
Margin of Victory: 2 laps plus
Attendance: 46,538

knee. The Greenbelt, MD driver had been running in third place when a tire popped on his Ford, sending it into the guard rail. The steel rail was overlapped at the posts in reverse, and when Kagle's car struck the bolt-

Reds Kagle's Ford tore through Charlotte's guard rail. He lost a leg in the mishap

ed part, the rail sliced through the car. The engine was cut in half, the steering column was destroyed and Kagle's leg was badly cut. In addition to his other injuries, Kagle suffered a fractured right ankle.

Fireball Roberts finished in second place, two laps behind Pearson. The winner blew a tire with two laps to go, but he stayed on the track and finished the race in a shower of sparks.

Third place went to Rex White, Ned Jarrett was fourth and Jim Paschal fifth.

Pearson was piloting Ray Fox's Pontiac -- a car which did not have a driver earlier in the week. Pearson, the 1960 Rookie of the Year, had just about given up hope of finding a

David Pearson enjoys first trip to victory lane with Nancy Ann Harrison and June Wilkinson

home on the Grand National circuit. He was forced to park his own Chevrolet due to under financing.

The lead changed hands 17 times among seven different drivers. Pearson averaged 111.633 mph and won $24,280 before a crowd of 46,538.

Tim Flock drove Beau Morgan's Ford to a 37th place finish in the field of 55. It would be the final Grand National effort for the Atlanta driver, winner of two championships.

Race No. 25

Paschal Ends Three Year Drought; Wins at Spartanburg

SPARTANBURG, SC (June 2) -- Jim Paschal of High Point, NC drove his Pontiac to a two-lap victory in the 100-mile race at the Piedmont Interstate Fairgrounds, ending a winless skid dating back to 1958. The last Grand National win for Paschal came on July 12, 1958, when he won at Asheville, NC.

Paschal became the 15th different winner of the 1961 season.

Jim Paschal

Cotton Owens finished in second place and Maurice Petty was third. It was Petty's best finish of his young career. Herman Beam, the "Turtle" out of Johnson City, TN, wound up fourth, 12 laps behind. Ned Jarrett came in fifth.

Owens was leading the event with only 20 laps to go when a wheel on his Pontiac broke, sending him to the pits.

Point leader Rex White finished 10th and saw his point lead shaved to 246 over Jarrett.

Joe Weatherly and Richard Petty were eliminated in a 70th lap crash. Neither driver was hurt.

Paschal averaged 55.495 mph for his eighth career Grand National victory.

Grand National Race No. 25
200 Laps at Piedmont Interstate
Fairgrounds
Spartanburg, SC
100 Miles on Half-mile Dirt Track
June 2, 1961

Fin	St	No.	Driver	Team / Car	Laps	Money	Status
1	11	14	Jim Paschal	'61 Pontiac	200	$800	Running
2	2	6	Cotton Owens	Owens '60 Pontiac	198	525	Running
3	19	42	Maurice Petty	Petty Eng '60 Plymouth	197	375	Running
4	21	19	Herman Beam	Beam '60 Ford	188	275	Running
5	5	11	Ned Jarrett	B G Holloway '61 Chevrolet	187	250	Running
6	12	54	Jimmy Pardue	Pardue '59 Chevrolet	187	215	Running
7	18	17	Fred Harb	Harb '59 Ford	177	175	Engine
8	13	48	G C Spencer	'60 Chevrolet	130	150	Running
9	4	47	Jack Smith	Smith '61 Pontiac	125	140	Running
10	7	4	Rex White	White-Clements '60 Chevrolet	108	230	Rear Sus
11	3	86	Buck Baker	Baker '61 Chrysler	104	125	Rear End
12	14	55	Elmo Henderson	'59 T-Bird	84	110	Crash
13	9	51	Doug Cox	'59 T-Bird	84	100	Engine
14	1	8	Joe Weatherly	Bud Moore '61 Pontiac	70	85	Crash
15	8	43	Richard Petty	Petty Eng '60 Plymouth	70	70	Crash
16	16	99	Wilbur Rakestraw	B J Jones '61 Ford	62	60	A Frame
17	17	67	David Pearson	Pearson '60 Chevrolet	37	50	Heating
18	15	62	Curtis Crider	Crider '60 Ford	24	50	Heating
19	6	27	Junior Johnson	Holly Farms '61 Pontiac	13	50	A Frame
20	20	71	Bob Barron	'60 Dodge	5	50	Heating
21	10	93	Darel Dieringer	L L Reitzel '60 Ford	1	50	Spindle

Time of Race: 4 hours, 48 minutes, 07 seconds
Average Speed: 55.495 mph
Pole Winner: Joe Weatherly - 61.25 mph
Lap Leaders: ------- Cotton Owens -180, Jim Paschal 181-200
Cautions:
Margin of Victory: 2 laps plus
Attendance:

Grand National Race No. 26
200 Laps at Alabama State Fairgrounds
Birmingham, AL
100 Miles on Half-mile Dirt Track
June 4, 1961

Fin	St	No.	Driver	Team / Car	Laps	Money	Status
1	4	11	Ned Jarrett	B G Holloway '61 Chevrolet	200	$800	Running
2	6	14	Jim Paschal	'61 Pontiac	198	525	Running
3	2	46	Jack Smith	Smith '61 Pontiac	198	375	Running
4	5	4	Rex White	White-Clements '60 Chevrolet	197	375	Running
5	10	39	Tommy Wells	'60 Chevrolet	192	250	Running
6	9	19	Herman Beam	Beam '60 Ford	190	215	Running
7	7	99	Wilbur Rakestraw	B J Jones '61 Ford	185	175	Running
8	13	71	Bob Barron	'60 Dodge	168	150	Running
9	11	48	G C Spencer	'60 Chevrolet	110	140	Rear End
10	1	69	Johnny Allen	B G Holloway '61 Chevrolet	91	130	A Frame
11	3	86	Buck Baker	Baker '61 Chrysler	44	125	RF Hub
12	12	89	Bob Welborn	Adcox-Kirby '61 Chevrolet	7	110	Con Rod
13	8	54	Jimmy Pardue	Pardue '59 Chevrolet	3	100	Crash

Time of Race: 1 hour, 38 minutes, 15 seconds
Average Speed: 61.068 mph
Pole Winner: Johnny Allen - 65.91 mph
Lap Leaders: - - - - - - - - - - - - - Ned Jarrett   -200
Cautions:
Margin of Victory: 2 laps plus
Attendance:

Race No. 26

Ned Jarrett Breaks Through for First '61 Win at Birmingham

Birmingham, AL (June 4) -- Gentleman Ned Jarrett of Conover, NC grabbed his first win of the year and inched closer to the Grand National point lead with a victory in the 100-mile race at the Alabama State Fairgrounds.

Jarrett, wheeling the Bee Gee Holloway Chevrolet, wound up two laps ahead of runner-up Jim Paschal. Jack Smith was third with Rex White fourth. Tommy Wells, making his first Grand National start since 1951, finished in fifth place.

Chevrolets from the Holloway shops took top honors in both the race and qualifying. Johnny Allen started on the pole but left the race after 91 laps with a broken A-Frame.

Jarrett's eighth career victory moved him to within 198 points of leader White.

Ned Jarrett

The only accident occurred in the third lap when Jimmy Pardue's Chevrolet hit the wall.

Jarrett averaged a speed of 61.068 mph for the 100 miles on the half-mile dirt track.

Race No. 27

Jack Smith is Tenth Different Winner in Last Ten Races

GREENVILLE, SC (June 8) -- Jack Smith became the 10th different winner in the last 10 Grand National races by driving his Pontiac to victory in the 100-miler at Greenville-Pickens Speedway. It was the first win for the 37 year-old veteran since he won the 1960 Firecracker 250 at Daytona.

Smith started seventh and chased leader Ned Jarrett for the first 170 laps. After catching his friendly rival, Smith made the decisive pass and led the rest of the way.

Jarrett finished in second place with Emanual Zervakis third. Joe Weatherly took fourth spot and Jim Paschal fifth.

Rex White finished eighth, 10 laps behind and had his point lead sliced to 102 points over Jarrett.

Junior Johnson started second but departed early when the fan belt came off his Pontiac. Buck Baker, Paul Lewis and Doug Cox crashed, but nobody was hurt.

In other developments, Curtis Turner and Bruton Smith resigned from Charlotte Motor Speedway after a stormy Board of Directors meeting. President Turner and Vice-president Smith were replaced by Allan Nance and Duke Ellington.

Grand National Race No. 27
200 Laps at Greenville-Pickens
Speedway
Greenville, SC
100 Miles on Half-mile Dirt Track
June 8, 1961

Fin	St	No.	Driver	Team / Car	Laps	Money	Status
1	7	47	Jack Smith	Smith '61 Pontiac	200	$800	Running
2	1	11	Ned Jarrett	B G Holloway '61 Chevrolet	199	525	Running
3	4	85	Emanuel Zervakis	Monroe Shook '61 Chevrolet	198	375	Running
4	10	8	Joe Weatherly	Bud Moore '61 Pontiac	198	275	Running
5	3	14	Jim Paschal	'61 Pontiac	196	250	Running
6	11	7	Elmo Henderson	'60 Pontiac	193	215	Running
7	23	42	Maurice Petty	Petty Eng '60 Plymouth	191	175	Running
8	6	4	Rex White	White-Clements '61 Chevrolet	190	150	Running
9	9	48	G C Spencer	'60 Chevrolet	186	140	Running
10	15	54	Jimmy Pardue	Pardue '59 Chevrolet	183	130	Running
11	26	19	Herman Beam	Beam '60 Ford	181	125	Running
12	22	62	Curtis Crider	Crider '60 Ford	177	110	Running
13	17	71	Bob Barron	'60 Dodge	172	100	Running
14	24	35	E J Trivette	'59 Plymouth	171	85	Running
15	18	93	Lee Reitzel	Reitzel '60 Ford	164	70	Running
16	8	43	Richard Petty	Petty Eng '60 Plymouth	130	60	A Frame
17	5	67	David Pearson	Pearson '60 Chevrolet	123	50	Steering
18	14	89	Bob Welborn	Adcox-Kirby '61 Chevrolet	110	50	Rear End
19	19	58	Bunk Moore	'60 Ford	91	50	Piston
20	12	17	Fred Harb	Harb '59 Ford	85	50	Rear End
21	13	51	Doug Cox	'59 T-Bird	27	50	Crash
22	16	86	Buck Baker	Baker '61 Chrysler	23	50	Crash
23	21	1	Paul Lewis	Jess Potter '61 Chevrolet	23	---	Crash
24	25	55	Bob Gossett	'59 T-Bird	19	---	Oil Pres
25	2	27	Junior Johnson	Holly Farms '61 Pontiac	13	---	Fan Belt
26	20	99	George Alsobrook	B J Jones '61 Ford	8	---	Heating

Time of Race: 1 hour, 42 minutes, 40 seconds
Average Speed: 58.441 mph
Pole Winner: Ned Jarrett - 65.48 mph
Lap Leaders: Jarrett 1-170, Smith 171-200
Cautions:
Margin of Victory: 1 lap plus
Attendance:

Grand National Race No. 28
200 Laps at Bowman-Gray Stadium
Winston-Salem, NC
"Myers Brothers Memorial"
50 Miles on Quarter-mile Paved Track
June 10, 1961

Fin	St	No.	Driver	Team / Car	Laps	Money	Status
1	4	4	Rex White	White-Clements '60 Chevrolet	200	$900	Running
2	3	7	Jim Reed	Reed '61 Chevrolet	200	525	Running
3	1	27	Junior Johnson	Holly Farms '60 Pontiac	199	375	Running
4	8	85	Emanuel Zervakis	Monroe Shook '60 Chevrolet	198	275	Running
5	6	43	Richard Petty	Petty Eng '60 Plymouth	198	250	Running
6	7	11	Ned Jarrett	B G Holloway '61 Chevrolet	196	215	Running
7	22	86	Buck Baker	Baker '61 Chrysler	195	175	Running
8	20	48	G C Spencer	'60 Chevrolet	193	150	Running
9	18	54	Jimmy Pardue	Pardue '59 Chevrolet	192	140	Running
10	13	23	Doug Yates	Yates '59 Plymouth	188	130	Running
11	5	14	Jim Paschal	'61 Pontiac	186	125	RR Tire
12	11	68	Pete Boland	Curtis Crider '60 Ford	185	110	Running
13	10	42	Maurice Petty	Petty Eng '60 Plymouth	184	100	Running
14	15	19	Herman Beam	Beam '60 Ford	183	85	Running
15	14	62	Curtis Crider	Crider '60 Ford	181	70	Running
16	19	71	Bob Barron	'60 Dodge	174	60	Running
17	21	8	Larry Thomas	'60 Chevrolet	150	50	RR Tire
18	2	21	Glen Wood	Wood Bros '61 Ford	124	50	Brakes
19	12	97	Harry Leake	'59 Chevrolet	87	50	W Hose
20	16	17	Fred Harb	Harb '59 Ford	83	50	Door
21	9	34	Wendell Scott	Scott '60 Chevrolet	78	50	Brakes
22	17	93	Lee Reitzel	Reitzel '60 Ford	36	50	Brakes

Time of Race: 1 hour, 10 minutes, 14 seconds
Average Speed: 42.714 mph
Pole Winner: Junior Johnson - 47.72 mph
Lap Leaders: - - - - - - - - - - - - - - - Rex White   -200
Cautions 1 for 5 laps
Margin of Victory: 1/2 lap
Attendance: 12,500

Race No. 28

White Outruns Reed to Win Myers Brothers Memorial

WINSTON-SALEM, NC (June 10) -- Rex White bagged his fourth triumph of the year in the Myers Brothers Memorial at Bowman-Gray Stadium. The 200 lapper on the quarter-mile tight oval was named in honor of Billy and Bobby Myers, late stock car racing pioneers from the Winston-Salem area. The diminutive Silver Spring, MD driver tacked on to the incredible string as he became the 11th different winner of the last 11 Grand National events.

A crowd of 12,500 who braved threatening skies watched White finish a half-lap ahead of runner-up Jim Reed to win the $900 first prize. Junior Johnson started on the pole and finished third, Emanual Zervakis was fourth and Richard Petty fifth. Ned Jarrett was sixth and fell 182 points behind White in the point race.

Maurice Petty, second generation driver, had plenty of difficulty in the race, spinning out and finishing 16 laps off the pace. He wound up 13th in the field of 22.

One caution flag for a total of five laps slowed White's average speed to 42.714 mph. It was his 17th career Grand National victory.

complained to NASCAR officials that Zervakis had made an improper pit stop. NASCAR studied White's protest, but said that no conclusive evidence was found to support White's claim. Zervakis got credit for his second win of the year.

Ned Jarrett finished third in the 500 lap contest on the quarter-mile paved track. Buck Baker took fourth place, 24 laps behind. Jim Reed pocketed fifth place money.

White started on the pole and led the first 125 laps. Zervakis took the lead on lap 126 and held it until passed by Ned Jarrett on lap 249. Jarrett led for 14 laps before Zervakis overtook him and regained the lead for good.

Only one caution flag broke the brisk pace as Zervakis averaged 53.827 mph. Budd Olsen was disqualified in the 168th lap for an unexplained reason.

Grand National Race No. 29
500 Laps at Norwood Arena
Norwood, MA
"Yankee 500"
125 Miles on Quarter-mile Asphalt
June 17, 1961

Fin	St	No.	Driver	Team / Car	Laps	Money	Status
1	3	85	Emanuel Zervakis	Monroe Shook '60 Chevrolet	500	$2,250	Running
2	1	4	Rex White	White-Clements '60 Chevrolet	500	1,000	Running
3	9	11	Ned Jarrett	B G Holloway '61 Chevrolet	491	800	Running
4	5	86	Buck Baker	Baker '61 Chrysler	476	700	Running
5	4	7	Jim Reed	Reed '61 Chevrolet	473	600	Running
6	2	14	Jim Paschal	'61 Pontiac	467	500	Running
7	11	90	Buzz Woodward	'59 Ford	456	400	Running
8	14	27	Dom Persecketti	'59 Ford	450	300	Running
9	13	38	Sam Packard	'61 Ford	444	275	Running
10	8	34	Wendell Scott	Scott '60 Chevrolet	426	250	Running
11	7	55	Ernie Gahan	John Koszeln '59 Chevrolet	335	225	Running
12	17	60	Ed Flemke	'61 Dodge Dart	231	175	Axle
13	12	56	Budd Olsen	'60 Chevrolet	168	175	Disqual
14	15	64	Harold Wilcox	'59 Olds	112	150	W Bearing
15	10	24	Bob Devine	'61 Chevrolet	92	150	Rock Arm
16	16	54	Jimmy Pardue	Pardue '61 Chevrolet	2	150	Piston
17	6	66	Hoss Kagle	Cafe Burgandy '60 Ford	2	125	Engine
18	18	57	Jim Mairs	'61 Chevrolet	2	125	Con Rd

Time of Race: 2 hours, 19 minutes, 20 seconds
Average Speed: 53.827 mph
Pole Winner: Rex White - 55.87 mph
Lap Leaders: Rex White 1-125, Emanuel Zervakis 126-248, Ned Jarrett 249-262,
   Zervakis 263-500
Cautions: 1
Margin of Victory: 1/4 lap
Attendance:

Race No. 29

Zervakis Zaps Rivals in Yankee 500 Win

NORWOOD, MA (June 17) -- Emanuel Zervakis of Richmond, VA took the lead in the 263rd lap and led the remaining distance to win the Yankee 500 at the Norwood Arena. Rex White filed a protest, but NASCAR officials upheld Zervakis' victory.

Zervakis became the 12th different winner in the last 12 Grand National races. White, who finished second,

Grand National Race No. 30
150 Laps at Hartsville Speedway
Hartsville, SC
50 Miles on .333-mile Dirt Track
June 23, 1961

Fin	St	No.	Driver	Team / Car	Laps	Money	Status
1	3	86	Buck Baker	Baker '61 Chrysler	150	$760	Running
2	9	47	Jack Smith	Smith '61 Pontiac	150	520	Running
3	6	4	Rex White	White-Clements '60 Chevrolet	149	460	Running
4	7	67	David Pearson	Pearson '60 Chevrolet	148	265	Running
5	4	27	Junior Johnson	Holly Farms '60 Pontiac	148	260	Running
6	2	11	Ned Jarrett	B G Holloway '61 Chevrolet	147	220	Running
7	13	54	Jimmy Pardue	Pardue '50 Chevrolet	144	215	Running
8	16	97	Harry Leake	'60 Chevorlet	138	150	Running
9	12	34	Wendell Scott	Scott '60 Chevrolet	137	140	Running
10	14	93	Lee Reitzel	Reitzel '60 Ford	131	130	Running
11	17	19	Herman Beam	Beam '60 Ford	131	125	Running
12	11	62	Homer Galloway	Curtis Crider '60 Ford	127	110	Running
13	8	68	Curtis Crider	Crider '60 Ford	124	100	Running
14	15	71	Bob Barron	'60 Dodge	120	85	Running
15	18	77	Joe Jones	'60 Ford	118	70	RR Axle
16	1	85	Emanuel Zervakis	Monroe Shook '60 Chevrolet	101	60	Crash
17	10	43	Richard Petty	Petty Eng '61 Plymouth	69	65	Engine
18	5	17	Fred Harb	Harb '59 Ford	68	50	RR Axle

Time of Race: 1 hour, 05 minutes, 01 second
Average Speed: 46.234 mph
Pole Winner: Emanuel Zervakis - 54.97 mph
Lap Leaders: - - - - - - - - - - - - - - Buck Baker   -150
Cautions:
Margin of Victory:
Attendance:

Race No. 30

Baker's Chrysler First at Hartsville Speedway

HARTSVILLE, SC (June 23) -- Buck Baker drove his Chrysler to victory in the 50-mile Grand National

Race at Hartsville Speedway. The 42 year-old Charlotte veteran became the 13th different driver to win as many Grand National Races -- a NASCAR record.

Baker, in giving Chrysler its first Grand National win since the 1956 season finale, beat Jack Smith by about a half lap. Point leader Rex White was third, David Pearson was fourth and Junior Johnson fifth.

Emanuel Zervakis put the Monroe Shook Chevrolet on the pole, but the Richmond, VA native fell out on lap 101 when steering failure put him into the wall.

Baker averaged 46.234 mph for his 43rd career Grand National victory and his first since winning the 1960 Southern 500 at Darlington.

Richard Petty was taken out by engine failure in the 69th lap.

Grand National Race No. 31
150 Laps at Starkey Speedway
Roanoke, VA
37.5 Miles on Quarter-mile Paved Track
June 24, 1961

Fin	St	No.	Driver	Team / Car	Laps	Money	Status
1	2	27	Junior Johnson	Holly Farms '60 Pontiac	150	$900	Running
2	1	4	Rex White	White-Clements '60 Chevrolet	149	725	Running
3	3	14	Jim Paschal	'61 Pontiac	149	475	Running
4	4	43	Richard Petty	Petty Eng '61 Plymouth	147	295	Running
5	18	85	Emanuel Zervakis	Monroe Shook '60 Chevrolet	146	250	Running
6	20	23	Doug Yates	Yates '59 Plymouth	144	200	Running
7	9	48	G C Spencer	'60 Chevrolet	144	175	Running
8	13	34	Wendell Scott	Scott '60 Chevrolet	140	170	Running
9	10	86	Buck Baker	Baker '61 Chrysler	140	175	Running
10	14	57	Wes Morgan	'61 Chevrolet	139	155	Running
11	5	11	Ned Jarrett	B G Holloway '61 Chevrolet	136	155	Running
12	17	71	Bob Barron	'60 Dodge	134	120	Running
13	12	19	Herman Beam	Beam '60 Ford	134	110	Running
14	11	8	Larry Thomas	'60 Chevrolet	133	115	Running
15	15	62	Curtis Crider	Crider '60 Ford	132	80	Running
16	19	93	Lee Reitzel	Reitzel '60 Ford	130	50	Running
17	16	77	Joe Jones	'60 Ford	119	25	Running
18	8	97	Harry Leake	'60 Chevrolet	113	35	RR Axle
19	6	68	Charles Williamson	Curtis Crider '60 Ford	107	30	Tires
20	7	54	Jimmy Pardue	Pardue '59 Chevrolet	27	45	Radiator

Time of Race: 45 minutes, 05 seconds
Average Speed: 49.907 mph
Pole Winner: Rex White - 53.70 mph
Lap Leaders: - - - - - - - - - - - - - - - Junior Johnson   -150
Cautions:
Margin of Victory: 1 lap plus
Attendance:

Race No. 31
Junior's Pontiac Speedy at Starkey Speedway

ROANOKE, VA (June 24) -- Junior Johnson, outracing the traveling troup of Grand National drivers in the 37.5-mile race at Starkey Speedway, ended the string of different winners in as many races at 13.

Rex White came in second, a lap behind. Jim Paschal took third place money with Richard Petty fourth and Emanuel Zervakis fifth.

Johnson, the 30 year-old Ronda, NC Pontiac driver, registered his 22nd career victory and his third of the 1961 season.

White extended his point lead to 396 over Ned Jarrett, who struggled to an 11th place finish. Twenty cars started the 150 lapper on the quarter-mile paved track, and 17 were around at the finish.

Only three cars failed to finish. Rookie Charles Williamson departed on lap 107 when he blew a tire. Williamson had qualified a lightly regarded Curtis Crider Ford sixth fastest, but went out because his pit crew did not have enough rubber. Harry Leake departed on lap 113 with rear axle trouble. And Jimmy Pardue made only 27 laps with a red hot radiator.

Johnson averaged 49.907 mph in the 500th NASCAR Grand National race.

Race No. 32

Pearson Outduels Lorenzen in Daytona's Firecracker 250

DAYTONA BEACH, FL (July 4) -- Li'l David Pearson, loading his sling with brains, speed and a gambling spirit, outran the Goliaths of stock car racing in the third annual Firecracker 250 at Daytona International Speedway. It was Pearson's second superspeedway win of the year and his second start in what is considered first rate machinery.

Pearson shoved the nose of his Ray Fox Pontiac around Fred Lorenzen two laps from the finish and took the first place payoff of $8,450 by two car lengths. Lorenzen was second in his Holman-Moody Ford and Jack Smith was a lap back in third. Marvin Panch finished fourth as Fireball Roberts fell to fifth in the last 20 laps.

Roberts had led 58 of the first 80 laps, but went into a spin in the fourth turn when a tire blew on his Smokey Yunick Pontiac. Lorenzen dove to the apron to avoid a collision and took the lead in the process. The Elmhurst, IL newcomer held the lead until Pearson ran him down in the stretch duel.

Pearson's average speed was 154.294 mph. Roberts had won the pole at 157.150 mph.

Ned Jarrett took the lead in the tight point race despite finishing back in 12th place. Rex White, leader entering the second half of the season, fell out after 63 laps with engine failure and finished 23rd. Jarrett's lead stood at 200 points after the 100 lap race on the 2.5-mile high banked tri-oval.

Joe Weatherly turned in one of the most dedicated efforts in racing history. The gear shift in his Bud Moore Pontiac would not stay in place. He coped with the situation by wrapping his right leg around the gear shift lever to keep it in place and drove with his left foot. The Norfolk, VA veteran managed to finish sixth in the 30 car field.

Richard Petty was a notable absentee. The Randleman, NC hot-shot opted to drive a NASCAR Eastern Late Model race in Pennsylvania.

Race No. 33

Lorenzen Avoids Early Crash, Drives Ford to Victory in Festival 250

HAMPTON, GA (July 9) -- Fred Lorenzen avoided a wholesale opening lap crash and outlasted the field in the hastily promoted "Festival 250" at Atlanta International Raceway. The event was tossed into the 1961 Grand National schedule only a week earlier when the United States Auto Club pulled its drivers out of an Indy race at the last moment.

USAC President Henry Banks notified Raceway President Nelson Weaver that he was canceling the USAC Indy Car race when his findings determined the track was unsafe. Banks stated the open wheelers' lives would have been "seriously jeopardized" had they gone through with the race. Weaver, expresssing his anger with USAC, told the press that USAC had no business withdrawing the sanction of a race 36 hours before they were supposed to check in.

Lorenzen led 52 laps of the 167 lap event and won $7,085 for his third win of the season. Bob Welborn finished second in a Pontiac owned by Jack Smith. Richard Petty, Emanuel Zervakis and Smith completed the top five.

Big track star David Pearson started second, but spun in the first lap, taking a dozen cars with him. Although the cars involved suffered much sheet metal damage, only three cars were eliminated in the melee. None of the drivers were hurt, although Robert Higgenbottom, driver of the wrecker, was shaken up when his vehicle flipped while trying to retrieve the crashed race cars.

Grand National Race No. 32
100 Laps at Daytona International Speedway
Daytona Beach, FL
"Firecracker 250"
250 Miles on 2.5-mile Paved Track
July 4, 1961

Fin	St	No.	Driver	Team / Car	Laps	Money	Status
1	2	3	David Pearson	Daytona Kennel '61 Pontiac	100	$8,450	Running
2	7	28	Fred Lorenzen	Holman-Moody '61 Ford	100	4,275	Running
3	10	46	Jack Smith	Smith '61 Pontiac	99	2,700	Running
4	6	20	Marvin Panch	Smokey Yunick '60 Pontiac	99	1,525	Running
5	1	22	Fireball Roberts	Smokey Yunick '61 Pontiac	98	1,525	Running
6	3	8	Joe Weatherly	Bud Moore '61 Pontiac	98	1,250	Running
7	13	29	Nelson Stacy	Holt-Stacy '61 Ford	98	800	Running
8	11	24	Roscoe Thompson	James Turner '60 Pontiac	97	825	Running
9	14	76	Larry Frank	Dick Wright '61 Ford	97	675	Running
10	8	6	Ralph Earnhardt	Cotton Owens '61 Pontiac	96	700	Running
11	12	15	Jim Bennett	Beau Morgan '61 Ford	96	500	Running
12	17	11	Ned Jarrett	B G Holloway '61 Chevrolet	96	350	Running
13	19	69	Johnny Allen	B G Holloway '61 Chevrolet	96	320	Running
14	21	89	Herb Tillman	Adcox-Kirby '61 Chevrolet	95	300	Running
15	5	72	Bobby Johns	Shorty Johns '61 Ford	94	420	H Gasket
16	15	82	Marvin Porter	'61 Ford	94	295	Running
17	9	27	Junior Johnson	Holly Farms '61 Pontiac	93	300	Running
18	16	5	Woodie Wilson	'61 Pontiac	92	275	Running
19	27	54	Jimmy Pardue	Pardue '60 Chevrolet	92	250	Running
20	28	75	Tiny Lund	J D Braswell '61 Pontiac	91	250	Running
21	23	19	Herman Beam	Beam '60 Ford	91	250	Running
22	4	94	Banjo Matthews	Matthews '61 Ford	82	600	Engine
23	26	4	Rex White	White-Clements '61 Chevrolet	63	350	Con Rod
24	25	62	Curtis Crider	Crider '61 Mercury	52	250	Flagged
25	30	33	Reb Wickersham	Wickersham '60 Olds	49	250	Flagged
26	18	99	George Alsobrook	B J Jones '61 Ford	27	150	Con Rod
27	20	86	Buddy Baker	Buck Baker '61 Chrysler	15	150	Engine
28	22	38	Roy Tyner	DeMatthews '61 Ford	8	150	Engine
29	24	85	Emanuel Zervakis	Monroe Shook '61 Ford	4	150	Cam Sh
30	29	87	Buck Baker	Baker '61 Chrysler	2	150	Trans

Time of Race: 1 hour, 37 minutes, 13 seconds
Average Speed: 154.294 mph
Pole Winner: Fireball Roberts - 157.150 mph
Lap Leaders: Fireball Roberts 1-5, Joe Weatherly 6-7, Roberts 8-12, Weatherly 13-16, Roberts 17-42, David Pearson 43-45, Banjo Matthews 46-48, Bobby Johns 49-51, Roberts 52-58, Pearson 59-64, Roberts 65-80, Fred Lorenzen 81-98, Pearson 99-100
Cautions: None
Margin of Victory: 2 car lengths
Attendance: 18,370

David Pearson's Pontiac on the hook after Festival 250 crash

Joe Weatherly, Junior Johnson and Nelson Stacy all led the race, but none finished. Fireball Roberts led the field for 51 laps but had to make an extended pit stop to correct mechanical problems. The Daytona Beach Pontiac driver wound up 12th in the field of 42.

A disappointing crowd of 18,000 watched Lorenzen win the race at an average speed of 118.067 mph.

Rex White, who wound up 10th, took over the point lead from 14th place finisher Ned Jarrett. The exciting point race stood in favor of White by a mere 40 points.

Grand National Race No. 33
167 Laps at Atlanta International Raceway
Hampton, GA
"Festival 250"
250 Miles on 1.5-Mile Paved Track
July 9, 1961

Fin	St	No.	Driver	Team / Car	Laps	Money	Status
1	5	28	Fred Lorenzen	Holman-Moody '61 Ford	167	$7,085	Running
2	7	47	Bob Welborn	Jack Smith '61 Pontiac	166	3,580	Running
3	39	43	Richard Petty	Petty Eng '61 Plymouth	164	2,275	Running
4	21	85	Emanuel Zervakis	Monroe Shook '61 Chevrolet	163	1,475	Running
5	12	46	Jack Smith	Smith '61 Pontiac	161	1,310	Running
6	19	87	Buck Baker	Baker '61 Chrysler	160	1,150	Running
7	23	96	Friday Hassler	J L Cheatham '60 Chevrolet	159	1,025	Running
8	20	86	Buddy Baker	Buck Baker '61 Chrysler	159	925	Running
9	30	48	G C Spencer	'60 Chevrolet	158	850	Running
10	11	4	Rex White	White-Clements '61 Chevrolet	157	900	Running
11	8	6	Ralph Earnhardt	Cotton Owens '61 Pontiac	157	750	Running
12	1	22	Fireball Roberts'	Smokey Yunick '61 Pontiac	155	1,025	Running
13	18	82	Marvin Porter	'61 Ford	154	625	Running
14	16	11	Ned Jarrett	B. G Holloway '61 Chevrolet	153	550	Engine
15	15	5	Woody Wilson	'61 Pontiac	153	550	Running
16	26	1	Paul Lewis	Jess Potter '61 Chevrolet	152	450	Running
17	33	74	L D Austin	Austin '61 Chevrolet	152	450	Running
18	24	19	Herman Beam	Beam '60 Ford	151	450	Running
19	38	38	Roy Tyner	Tyner '61 Ford	150	450	Running
20	35	93	Lee Reitzel	Reitzel '60 Ford	149	450	Running
21	29	99	George Alsobrook	B J Jones '61 Ford	148	300	Rock Arm
22	28	30	Gene White	Fred Clark '60 Chevrolet	147	300	Running
23	41	77	Hank Tillman	'60 Ford	146	300	Running
24	34	62	Curtis Crider	Crider '61 Mercury	145	300	Running
25	36	39	Tommy Wells	'60 Chevrolet	143	300	Running
26	40	69	Johnny Allen	B G Holloway '61 Chevrolet	140	300	Engine
27	31	2	Frank Graham	'60 Ford	140	300	Running
28	3	8	Joe Weatherly	Bud Moore '61 Pontiac	133	490	Engine
29	37	71	Bob Barron	'60 Dodge	123	300	Rear end
30	42	75	Tiny Lund	J D Braswell '61 Pontiac	115	300	Fuel Pmp
31	9	27	Junior Johnson	Holly Farms '61 Pontiac	109	5	Timing
32	32	64	Eddie Pagan	'60 Ford	89	---	Rear End
33	6	94	Banjo Matthews	Matthews '61 Ford	82	---	Axle
34	17	15	Jim Bennett	Beau Morgan '61 Ford	74	---	H Gasket
35	13	72	Bobby Johns	Shorty Johns '61 Ford	66	---	Engine
36	22	23	Doug Yates	Yates '61 Plymouth	48	---	Engine
37	4	29	Nelson Stacy	Holt-Stacy '61 Ford	36	60	Engine
38	25	54	Jimmy Pardue	Pardue '60 Chevrolet	28	---	Piston
39	27	10	T C Hunt	Fred Wheat '61 Dodge	20	---	Con Rod
40	2	3	David Pearson	Daytona Kennel '61 Pontiac	3	75	Crash
41	10	24	Roscoe Thompson	James Turner '60 Pontiac	1	---	Crash
42	14	89	Herb Tillman	Adcox-Kirby '61 Chevrolet	1	---	Crash

Time of Race: 2 hours, 07 minutes, 18 seconds
Average Speed: 118.067 mph
Pole Winner: Fireball Roberts - 136.088 mph
Lap Leaders: Fred Lorenzen, 52 laps; Fireball Roberts, 51 laps; Joe Weatherly, 28 laps;
  Bob Welborn, 26 laps; Nelson Stacy, 7 laps; Jack Smith, 2 laps; Junior Johnson, 1 lap
Cautions: 1 for 12 laps
Margin of Victory: 1 lap plus
Attendance: 18,000

Grand National Race No. 34
200 Laps at Columbia Speedway
Columbia, SC
100 Miles on Half-mile Dirt Track
July 20, 1961

Fin	St	No.	Driver	Team / Car	Laps	Money	Status
1	1	6	Cotton Owens	Owens '60 Pontiac	200	$950	Running
2	7	14	Jim Paschal	Joe Lee Johnson '61 Chevy	200	625	Running
3	3	11	Ned Jarrett	B G Holloway '61 Chevrolet	200	425	Running
4	14	27	Junior Johnson	Holly Farms '60 Pontiac	198	275	Running
5	2	8	Joe Weatherly	Bud Moore '61 Pontiac	198	250	Running
6	5	85	Emanuel Zervakis	Monroe Shook '61 Chevrolet	197	215	Running
7	8	43	Richard Petty	Petty Eng '60 Plymouth	194	175	Running
8	11	48	G C Spencer	'60 Chevrolet	191	150	Running
9	16	74	L D Austin	Austin '61 Chevrolet	188	140	Running
10	13	19	Herman Beam	Beam '61 Ford	186	130	Running
11	15	71	Bob Barron	'60 Dodge	181	125	Running
12	19	18	Larry Thomas	'60 Chevrolet	180	110	Running
13	9	63	Tiny Lund	Pete Boland '60 Ford	175	100	Running
14	4	4	Rex White	White-Clements '60 Chevrolet	173	185	Running
15	12	86	Buck Baker	Baker '61 Chrysler	163	70	Engine
16	21	77	Jimmy Pardue	Pardue '60 Ford	119	60	Drv Shft
17	18	67	David Pearson	Pearson '60 Chevrolet	109	50	Crash
18	6	47	Jack Smith	Smith '60 Pontiac	95	50	Oil Leak
19	10	23	Doug Yates	Yates '59 Plymouth	81	50	Engine
20	17	9	Bunkie Blackburn	'60 Ford	64	50	Air Intake
21	20	62	Curtis Crider	Crider '61 Mercury	19	50	Sway Bar

Time of Race: 1 hour, 36 minutes, 28 seconds
Average Speed: 62.198 mph
Pole Winner: Cotton Owens - 67.65 mph
Lap Leaders: Joe Weatherly 1-50, Jim Paschal 51-192, Cotton Owens 193-200
Cautions:
Margin of Victory: 3 car lengths
Attendance:

Race No. 34

Owens Beats Paschal at Columbia with Late Race Pass

COLUMBIA, SC (July 20) -- Cotton Owens wheeled his white Pontiac around Jim Paschal with eight laps remaining and took first place in the 100-mile Grand National race at Columbia Speedway. It was the fourth win of the year for the 37 year-old Spartanburg, SC veteran.

Paschal finished second in Joe Lee Johnson's Chevrolet. He was only three car lengths behind when the checkered flag fell. Ned Jarrett finished third and re-took the lead in the point standings. Junior Johnson came in fourth with Joe Weatherly fifth.

Rex White, leader in the point standings entering the 200 lap event on the half-mile dirt track, experienced problems and struggled to a 14th place finish. He was 136 points behind Jarrett after the 34th race of the 1961 season.

Weatherly led the opening 50 laps before being passed by Paschal. The High Point, NC driver led until Owens passed him four miles from the finish.

Sophomore sensation David Pearson blew a tire on his Chevrolet and popped the wall in the 109th lap. It was the day's only accident.

Owens covered the 100 miles at an average speed of 62.198 mph. It was his eighth career victory on NASCAR's premier stock car racing tour.

Jim Paschal finished second, the only other driver to complete the 200 laps on the half-mile dirt track. Ned Jarrett came in third, George Green was fourth and Emanuel Zervakis fifth.

Jarrett extended his lead to 258 points as Rex White broke a left rear hub, knocking him down to a 10th place finish.

Fireball Roberts made a rare short track appearance in the town where he frequently competed in Modified events in the '50s. The 32 year-old Daytona Beach driver got an assignment in a Rex Lovette-owned Pontiac. However, Roberts fell out early on lap 27 with a blown engine. Junior Johnson departed on lap 16 with a broken ball joint.

Weatherly averaged 57.655 mph for the 200 laps.

Grand National Race No. 35
200 Laps at Rambi Raceway
Myrtle Beach, SC
100 Miles on Half-mile Dirt Track
July 22, 1961

Fin	St	No.	Driver	Team / Car	Laps	Money	Status
1	1	8	Joe Weatherly	Bud Moore '61 Pontiac	200	$950	Running
2	6	14	Jim Paschal	Joe Lee Johnson '61 Pontiac	200	625	Running
3	5	11	Ned Jarrett	B G Holloway '61 Chevrolet	199	425	Running
4	19	77	George Green		188	275	Running
5	13	85	Emanuel Zervakis	Monroe Shook '61 Chevrolet	185	250	Running
6	18	19	Herman Beam	Beam '60 Ford	184	215	Running
7	20	74	L D Austin	Austin '61 Chevrolet	184	175	Running
8	21	18	Larry Thomas	Wade Younts '60 Chevrolet	178	150	Running
9	17	71	Bob Barron	'60 Dodge	149	140	Running
10	9	4	Rex White	White-Clements '61 Chevrolet	145	230	LR Hub
11	22	54	Jimmy Pardue	Pardue '60 Chevrolet	145	125	Running
12	10	23	Doug Yates	Yates '61 Plymouth	126	110	RR Lugs
13	3	86	Buck Baker	Baker '61 Chrysler	111	100	Rear End
14	14	93	Lee Reitzel	Reitzel '60 Ford	104	185	Running
15	11	63	Tiny Lund	Pete Boland '60 Ford	104	70	Running
16	8	48	G C Spencer	'60 Chevrolet	52	60	Engine
17	4	43	Richard Petty	Petty Eng '61 Plymouth	43	50	Con Rd
18	15	42	Maurice Petty	Petty Eng '60 Plymouth	40	50	Clutch
19	16	62	Curtis Crider	Crider '60 Ford	36	50	Heating
20	7	47	Jack Smith	Smith '61 Pontiac	30	50	Oil Leak
21	12	127	Fireball Roberts	Holly Farms '61 Pointiac	27	50	Engine
22	2	27	Junior Johnson	Holly Farms '60 Pontiac	16	50	Ball Joint

Time of Race: 1 hour, 44 minutes, 04 seconds
Average Speed: 57.655 mph
Pole Winner: Joe Weatherly - 66.69 mph
Lap Leaders: - - - - - - - - - - - - - - - Joe Weatherly   -200
Cautions:
Margin of Victory:
Attendance

Race No. 35

Weatherly Grabs Third of Year at Rambi Raceway

MYRTLE BEACH, SC (July 22) -- Joe Weatherly drove his Bud Moore Pontiac to his third win of the year in the 100-miler at Rambi Raceway. It was the eighth win of his career for the 39 year-old Norfolk, VA speedster.

Race No. 36

Johnny Allen Gets Win for Jack Smith in Volunteer 500

BRISTOL, TN (July 29) -- Veteran Jack Smith captured the first annual Volunteer 500 at the new Bristol International Speedway with a crucial assist from Johnny Allen. It was Smith's 16th career victory.

Allen drove Smith's Pontiac for 209 laps and kept it in front all the way. Smith said heat was coming up through the floorboard and burned his right foot. Allen was available for the pinch-hitting role when his Chevrolet broke an axle and fell out after 106 laps.

Fireball Roberts finished second, two laps and 22 seconds behind the winning Smith-Allen combo. Ned Jarrett was

Johnny Allen relief drove Jack Smith's Pontiac to victory at Bristol

third, Richard Petty fourth and Buddy Baker fifth.

Eight caution flags held Smith's average speed to 68.373 mph. Fred Lorenzen had won the pole at

79.225 mph, but 'Fearless Freddy' failed to lead a single lap. Differential problems put Lorenzen out after 175 laps.

Ken Rush crashed hard into the retaining wall after 332 laps. His Ford had run over a wheel that had come off Bob Welborn's Pontiac. Rush was treated for knee injuries and released from the hospital.

Junior Johnson, surviving a wreck with Joe Weatherly and Tiny Lund, drove for about 200 laps with no driver's door on his Pontiac. He wound up 22nd after differential problems kayoed him out of the race.

When Allen took over for Smith, he had a three lap lead. By continuing to charge hard, the cushion rose to six laps before he backed off and took an insurance pit stop in the late stages.

Jarrett extended his point lead to 918 over Rex White, who blew his engine and wound up 25th in the field of 42.

The race had three brothers competing. Sherman, Dub and Layman Utsman became the first triple brother act in Grand National racing since the famous Flock gang.

Grand National Race No. 37
500 Laps at Fairgrounds Speedway
Nashville, TN
"Nashville 500"
250 Miles on Half-mile Paved Track
August 6, 1961

Fin	St	No.	Driver	Team / Car	Laps	Money	Status
1	10	44	Jim Paschal	J H Petty '61 Pontiac	403	$2,523	Running
2	4	11	Ned Jarrett	B G Holloway '61 Chevrolet	403	1,275	Running
3	3	14	Johnny Allen	Joe Lee Johnson '61 Chevy	401	975	Running
4	5	86	Buck Baker	Baker '61 Chrysler	401	675	Running
5	8	85	Emanuel Zervakis	Monroe Shook '61 Chevrolet	397	575	Running
6	12	99	George Alsobrook	B J Jones '61 Ford	397	450	Running
7	9	54	Jimmy Pardue	Pardue '60 Chevrolet	397	400	Running
8	14	48	G C Spencer	'60 Chevrolet	386	350	Axle
9	15	1	Paul Lewis	Jess Potter '61 Chevrolet	383	300	Running
10	18	74	L D Austin	Austin '61 Chevrolet	381	225	Running
11	17	19	Herman Beam	Beam '60 Ford	374	200	Running
12	22	71	Bob Barron	'60 Dodge	367	175	Running
13	20	61	Crash Bond	'60 Ford	367	150	Running
14	2	43	Richard Petty	Petty Eng '61 Plymouth	366	1,226	Engine
15	6	46	Jack Smith	Smith '61 Pontiac	363	125	Crash
16	21	62	Curtis Crider	Crider '61 Mercury	356	110	Running
17	24	41	Charles Chapman	Chapman '60 Ford	344	100	Running
18	16	39	Tommy Wells	'60 Chevrolet	199	100	Oil Leak
19	7	27	Junior Johnson	Holly Farms '60 Pontiac	134	100	Studs
20	23	5	Bob Presnell	'59 Chevrolet	104	100	Steering
21	19	96	Dave Mader	J L Cheatham '61 Chevrolet	50	75	W Bearing
22	11	87	Buddy Baker	Buck Baker '61 Chrysler	34	75	Rear End
23	1	4	Rex White	White-Clements '61 Chevrolet	15	175	Crash
24	13	23	Doug Yates	Yates '61 Plymouth	1	75	Trans

** Race shortened to 403 laps due to rain
Time of Race: 3 hours, 34 minutes, 09 seconds
Average Speed: 56.455 mph
Pole Winner: Rex White - 76.69 mph
Lap Leaders: Richard Petty 1-362, Jim Paschal 363-403
Cautions: 3 for 172 laps
Margin of Victory: 1 car length, under caution
Attendance: 12,081

Grand National Race No. 36
500 Laps at Bristol International Speedway
"Volunteer 500"
250 Miles on Half-mile paved track
July 30, 1961

Fin	St	No.	Driver	Team / Car	Laps	Money	Status
1	12	46	* Jack Smith	Smith '61 Pontiac	500	$3,025	Running
2	16	22	Fireball Roberts	Smokey Yunick '61 Pontiac	498	1,325	Running
3	8	11	Ned Jarrett	B G Holloway '61 Chevrolet	495	1,125	Running
4	4	43	Richard Petty	Petty Eng '61 Plymouth	493	800	Running
5	21	87	Buddy Baker	Buck Baker '61 Chrysler	492	750	Running
6	11	8	Joe Weatherly	Bud Moore '61 Pontiac	491	725	Running
7	13	85	Emanuel Zervakis	Monroe Shook '61 Chevrolet	490	575	Running
8	19	44	Jim Paschal	J H Petty '61 Pontiac	485	525	Running
9	20	26	Sherman Utsman	'61 Ford	481	450	Running
10	7	75	Tiny Lund	J D Braswell '61 Pontiac	476	400	Running
11	18	1	Paul Lewis	Jess Potter '61 Chevrolet	474	350	Running
12	30	74	L D Austin	Austin '61 Chevrolet	465	275	Running
13	25	19	Herman Beam	Beam '60 Ford	460	250	Running
14	36	36	Larry Thomas	Wade Younts '60 Chevrolet	434	225	Running
15	41	62	Curtis Crider	Crider '60 Ford	425	150	Running
16	23	14	Herb Tillman	Joe Lee Johnson '61 Chevy	422	150	Spun Out
17	35	71	Bob Barron	'60 Dodge	422	150	Running
18	10	47	Bob Welborn	Jack Smith '61 Pontiac	416	150	Studs
19	26	23	Doug Yates	Yates '61 Plymouth	414	150	Running
20	40	33	Reb Wickersham	Wickersham '60 Olds	377	150	Running
21	22	54	Jimmy Pardue	Pardue '60 Chevrolet	348	125	Running
22	2	27	Junior Johnson	Holly Farms '61 Pontiac	340	405	Rear End
23	42	12	Ken Rush	'59 Ford	332	125	Crash
24	31	34	Wendell Scott	Scott '60 Chevrolet	319	125	Rear End
25	6	4	Rex White	White-Clements '61 Chevrolet	285	280	Engine
26	39	64	Bill Morton	'60 Chevrolet	245	125	Rock Arm
27	28	71	George Green	'60 Ford	236	125	Con Rod
28	32	82	Marvin Porter	'61 Ford	235	125	Axle
29	33	38	Dub Utsman	'61 Ford	200	125	Rock Arm
30	3	3	David Pearson	Daytona Kennel '61 Pontiac	198	125	Engine
31	37	39	Tommy Wells	'60 Chevrolet	193	100	Engine
32	15	29	Nelson Stacy	Holt-Stacy '61 Ford	182	125	Crash
33	1	28	Fred Lorenzen	Holman-Moody '61 Ford	175	250	Rear End
34	29	48	G C Spencer	'60 Chevrolet	125	100	Engine
35	17	76	Larry Frank	Dick Wright '61 Ford	107	125	Clutch
36	34	69	Johnny Allen	B G Holloway '61 Chevrolet	106	100	On Fire
37	5	86	Buck Baker	Baker '61 Chrysler	78	150	Valve
38	27	99	George Alsobrook	B J Jones '61 Ford	59	100	Axle
39	9	2	Tommy Irwin	Tom Daniels '60 Chevrolet	48	125	Heating
40	14	6	Cotton Owens	Owens '60 Pontiac	46	125	H GAsket
41	24	17	Fred Harb	Harb '61 Ford	35	100	Handling
42	38	25	Layman Utsman	'60 Dodge	35	100	Handling

* Johnny Allen, driving relief from lap 292, finished Jack Smith's Pontiac first, but Smith gets credit for victory
Time of Race: 3 hours, 39 minutes, 23 seconds
Average Speed: 68.373 mph
Pole Winner: Fred Lorenzen - 79.225 mph
Lap Leaders: Junior Johnson 1-124, Bob Welborn 125-150, Jack Smith 151-160, Richard Petty 161-179, Johnson 180-225, Rex White 226-267, Smith 268-500
Cautions: 8
Margin of Victory: 2 laps and 22 seconds
Attendance: 25,000

Race No. 37

Paschal's Petty Pontiac Picks Music City Prize

NASHVILLE, TN (Aug 6) -- Steady Jim Paschal drove his J.H. Petty-owned Pontiac into the lead in the 363rd lap and held on to win a soggy Nashville 500 at

Fairgrounds Raceway. The scheduled 250 miler was called off after 403 laps due to rain.

Ned Jarrett came in second and cemented his strong hold on the point lead. Johnny Allen was third, Buck Baker fourth and Emanuel Zervakis fifth.

Richard Petty started second and led the first 362 laps. At that point the engine in his Plymouth soured, and he was on the sidelines four laps later.

Paschal took the lead and stayed in front for 41 laps when the race was red flagged. The event was the second for J.H. "Julian" Petty, who just recently got back into Grand National racing as a car owner.

Rex White started on the pole and was running second to Petty when the right front tire blew, sending his Chevrolet up and over the guard rail and into a giant billboard. He was not hurt, but fell 1,338 points behind Jarrett in the chase for the national driving title.

Junior Johnson provided the fireworks for the sell-out audience of 12,081 as he charged from seventh place to challenge Petty in the early going. He spun once but charged back into contention until a broken wheel put him out after 134 laps.

A staggering total of 172 laps were run under the caution flag, most of them weather related. At one point the race was run for 130 straight laps under the yellow flag.

Grand National Race No. 38
150 Laps at Bowman-Gray Stadium
Winston-Salem, NC
37.5 Miles on Quarter-mile Paved Track
August 9, 1961

Fin	St	No.	Driver	Team / Car	Laps	Money	Status
1	3	4	Rex White	White-Clements '60 Chevy	150	$665	Running
2	2	21	Glen Wood	Wood Bros '61 Ford	150	500	Running
3	4	11	Ned Jarrett	B G Holloway '61 Chevrolet	150	370	Running
4	8	85	Emanuel Zervakis	Monroe Shook '60 Chevrolet	149	305	Running
5	6	43	Richard Petty	Petty Eng '61 Plymouth	149	225	Running
6	11	48	G C Spencer	'60 Chevrolet	147	215	Running
7	9	34	Wendell Scott	Scott '60 Chevrolet	145	180	Running
8	12	57	Jim Mairs	'61 Chevrolet	145	190	Running
9	13	97	Harry Leake	'60 Chevrolet	145	175	Running
10	18	36	Larry Thomas	Wade Younts '60 Chevrolet	143	165	Running
11	14	71	Bob Barron	'60 Dodge	140	145	Running
12	16	5	Jimmy Pardue	'59 Chevrolet	139	120	Running
13	17	32	Robert Berrier	'54 MG	137	110	Running
14	20	62	Curtis Crider	Crider '60 Ford	136	115	Running
15	22	77	Doc Lee	'60 Austin Healey	135	75	Running
16	5	23	Doug Yates	Yates '61 Plymouth	105	95	Crash
17	19	12	T R Miller	'59 Ford	96	75	RF Tire
18	21	71S	Jack Hart	'58 Austin Healey	52	60	Heating
19	1	27	Junior Johnson	Holly Farms '60 Pontiac	44	100	Crash
20	10	17X	Bill Whitley	'54 Corvette	39	50	Crash
21	15	44	Maurice Petty	Petty Eng '60 Valiant	32	25	Clutch
22	7	17	Fred Harb	Harb '61 Ford	23	25	Engine
23	23	75	Paul Lions	'60 Sprite	4	---	Flagged

Time of Race: 53 minutes
Average Speed: 42.452 mph
Pole Winner: Junior Johnson - 48.05 mph
Lap Leaders: Glen Wood 1-138, Rex White 139-150
Cautions:
Margin of Victory: 2 car lengths
Attendance:

Race No. 38

White Prevails in Close Winston-Salem Finish

WINSTON-SALEM, NC (Aug 9) -- Rex White dipped under Glen Wood eight laps from the finish and scored his fifth win of the season in the 37.5-mile Grand National race at Bowman-Gray Stadium.

Wood came in second, two car lengths behind White's Chevrolet. Ned Jarrett finished third to protect his point lead and Emanuel Zervakis was fourth. Fifth place went to Richard Petty.

Wood passed pole sitter Junior Johnson in the first turn and led the first 138 laps. The Stuart, VA Ford driver held his Ford in the lead until White made his bid in the final three miles.

The event had international flavor as small sports cars were permitted to compete. Bill Whitley drove a seven year old Corvette but crashed in the 39th lap. Robert Berrier, manning a '54 MG, was the highest finisher in the smaller cars, coming home in 13th place. Paul Lions, driving a 1960 Sprite was flagged off the track for not running up to race speed.

The biggest news was made in Winston-Salem with the announcement that Curtis Turner, Tim Flock and Fireball Roberts were leading an attempt to organize the NASCAR drivers into the Teamsters Union. NASCAR President Bill France boldly stated that he would use his pistol if any union member tried to enter a Grand National event.

Roberts later resigned from the union while Turner and Flock held their position. France said Roberts would be accepted back into the good graces of the sanctioning body while Turner and Flock would be barred "for life".

Race No. 39

Fans Hold Drivers Hostage in Shortened Weaverville Event

WEAVERVILLE, NC (Aug 13) -- A disintegrating track halved the Western North Carolina 500 and triggered a riot in which all participating drivers and pit crews were held hostage for nearly four hours at the Asheville-Weaverville Speedway.

Junior Johnson was declared the winner after the 500-lapper on the half-mile paved oval was halted after

A mob of about 4,000 mill around the Asheville-Weaverville Speedway after shortened Western North Carolina 500

258 laps due to impossible track conditions. Joe Weatherly was flagged in second place with Rex White third, Ned Jarrett fourth and Emanuel Zervakis fifth.

Over 10,000 spectators turned out to see both the race and the expected clash between the Teamsters Union and NASCAR officials. The union, headed by drivers Curtis Turner and Tim Flock, did not make an appearance although they had said they would be present.

During a red flag period on lap 208 for a crash involving Dick Behling, driving in relief of Bunk Moore, NASCAR Executive Manager Pat Purcell told the drivers that after another 50 laps the race would be halted for good. "I hope you can make it," Purcell told the drivers and car owners. With the additional 50 laps in the books, the race would go over half-way, therefore constituting a completed Grand National event.

Drivers prepared for the final 50 lap dash as safety crews swept loose pavement into the holes in the track.

As the teams gamely tried racing in the final 50 laps, all NASCAR personnel removed their black and white uniforms and left the facility. When the race was red flagged, some 4,000 spectators remained on the grounds and a few of them started to riot.

A pick-up truck was dragged across the access road leading to the infield, essentially locking the racing teams inside. Some of the fans requested their money back. "I paid five bucks to see a 500 lap race," one of them shouted. "Somebody owes me some laps or some money."

One infield occupant, acting as an impromptu mediator, approached the leaders of the mob. He was bodily thrown into a lake. Another person was heaved over a tall fence. Buncombe County sheriff deputies were called to the scene, but they were unable to get the mob to disperse. The State Highway Patrol was summoned, but their efforts also failed.

As darkness approached, Pop Eargle, a six-foot-six 285 pound crewman for the Bud Moore team, went to the gate to discuss the matter with one leader of the group. Eargle was jabbed in the stomach with a 2x4

piece of lumber. Incensed, Eargle grabbed the big piece of wood and whacked the mobster in the head. Shortly after that happened, the drivers and crew members were allowed to leave.

In the end, four spectators were treated in nearby hospitals for injuries and several arrests were made.

Johnson led all the way and finished three laps ahead of Weatherly. He averaged 65.704 mph for his 23rd career victory.

Race No. 40

Johnson Leads Every Lap To Win Southside Event

RICHMOND, VA Aug 18) -- Junior Johnson kept his Pontiac on the point for the entire distance and won the 37.5-mile Grand National race at Southside Speedway. It was the fifth win of the eyar for the 30 year-old Ronda Road Runner.

The dispute with the Teamsters Union, operating as the Federation of Professional Athletes, appeared to simmer down following the opening fusillades at Weaverville five days previous to the Southside event.

Johnson led all 150 laps on the quarter-mile paved oval, the second race in a row he has led all the way. Ned Jarrett wound up second a lap behind. Emanuel Zervakis finished third, Rex White was fourth and Jimmy Pardue fifth.

Johnson won $600 for his 51.605 mph victory as a crowd of 3,500 looked on.

Jarrett upped his Grand National point lead to 1,300 over second place White.

Nineteen cars started the event and 14 were running at the finish. One caution flag came out for eight laps in the 43 minutes race.

Race No. 41

Junior Johnson Snares Third in Row at South Boston

SOUTH BOSTON, VA (Aug 27) -- Junior Johnson became the first 1961 driver to win three races in a row by taking the 50-mile feature at South Boston Speedway. The rotund Pontiac driver was the first man

Grand National Race No. 39
500 Laps at Asheville-Weaverville Speedway
Weaverville, NC
"Western North Carolina 500"
250 Miles on Half-mile Paved Track
August 13, 1961

Fin	St	No.	Driver	Team / Car	Laps	Money	Status
1	2	27	Junior Johnson	Holly Farms '60 Pontiac	258	$2,000	Running
2	5	8	Joe Weatherly	Bud Moore '61 Pontiac	255	1,400	Running
3	11	4	Rex White	White-Clements '61 Chevy	254	1,100	Running
4	9	11	Ned Jarrett	B G Holloway '61 Chevrolet	254	850	Running
5	7	85	Emanuel Zervakis	Monroe Shook '61 Chevrolet	254	750	Running
6	1	44	Jim Paschal	J H Petty '61 Pontiac	254	650	Running
7	13	2	Tommy Irwin	Tom Daniels '60 Chevrolet	253	600	Running
8	33	14	Johnny Allen	Joe Lee Johnson '61 Chevy	253	550	Running
9	4	47	Jack Smith	Smith '61 Pontiac	252	455	Running
10	21	29	Nelson Stacy	Holt-Stacy '61 Ford	252	425	Running
11	8	43	Richard Petty	Petty Eng '61 Plymouth	249	400	Running
12	15	99	George Alsobrook	B J Jones '61 Ford	234	375	Crash
13	17	19	Herman Beam	Beam '60 Ford	233	325	Running
14	18	82	Marvin Porter	'61 Ford	231	275	Running
15	27	41	Charles Chapman	Chapman '60 Ford	228	250	Running
16	16	87	Buddy Baker	Buck Baker '61 Chrysler	227	250	Running
17	21	74	L D Austin	Austin '61 Chevrolet	227	250	Running
18	26	97	Harry Leake	'59 Chevrolet	227	225	Running
19	20	54	Jimmy Pardue	Pardue '60 Chevrolet	225	225	Running
20	31	1	Paul Lewis	Jess Potter '61 Chevrolet	218	220	Running
21	25	33	Reb Wickersham	Wickersham '60 Olds	217	210	Running
22	28	62	Curtis Crider	Crider '60 Ford	214	200	Running
23	34	25	John V Hamby	'60 Dodge	208	175	Running
24	35	34	Wendell Scott	Scott '60 Chevrolet	204	150	Running
25	32	5	Bob Presnell	'59 Chevrolet	200	140	Running
26	22	64	Bill Morton	'60 Chevrolet	198	100	Running
27	19	48	G C Spencer	'60 Chevrolet	196	100	Fuel Pmp
28	6	86	Buck Baker	Baker '61 Chrysler	185	100	Running
29	36	58	* Bunk Moore	'60 Ford	182	100	Crash
30	29	148	Bill McDonald	'61 Chevrolet	180	100	Too Slow
31	37	59	Fireball Roberts	Lynn Holloway '61 Pontiac	144	---	Axle
32	23	36	Larry Thomas	Wade Younts '50 Chevrolet	136	---	Running
33	3	17	Fred Harb	Harb '61 Ford	135	---	Running
34	10	94	Banjo Matthews	Matthews '61 Ford	102	---	Crash
35	38	164	Earl Wilcox	'59 Olds	81	---	Too Slow
36	30	23	Doug Yates	Yates '61 Plymouth	75	---	Oil Filter
37	24	71	Bob Barron	'60 Dodge	67	---	RF Hub
38	14	96	Dave Mader	J L Cheatham '61 Chevrolet	64	---	RF Wheel

* Relieved by Dick Behling

** Race Shortened from 500 laps to 258 laps due to track deterioration

Time of Race: 1 hour, 57 minutes 48 seconds
Average Speed: 65.704 mph
Pole Winner: Jim Paschal - 80.43 mph
Lap Leaders: Junior Johnson 1-258
Cautions:
Margin of Victory: 3 laps plus
Attendance: 10,000

Grand National Race No. 40
150 Laps at Southside Speedway
Richmond, VA
37.5 Miles on Quarter-mile Paved Track
August 18, 1961

Fin	St	No.	Driver	Team / Car	Laps	Money	Status
1	1	27	Junior Johnson	Holly Farms '60 Pontiac	150	$600	Running
2	5	11	Ned Jarrett	B G Holloway '61 Chevrolet	149	475	Running
3	3	85	Emanuel Zervakis	Monroe Shook '61 Chevrolet	149	380	Running
4	2	4	Rex White	White-Clements '60 Chevrolet	148	425	Running
5	6	54	Jimmy Pardue	Pardue '60 Chevrolet	148	225	Running
6	9	23	Doug Yates	Yates '60 Plymouth	147	215	Running
7	7	57	Jim Mairs	'61 Chevrolet	146	195	Running
8	19	61	Elmo Langley	Doc White '59 T-Bird	143	160	Running
9	4	43	Richard Petty	Petty Eng '61 Plymouth	143	180	Running
10	15	12	Fred Harb	Harb '59 Ford	141	140	Running
11	12	74	L D Austin	Austin '61 Chevrolet	139	145	Running
12	8	5	Curtis Crider	Crider '59 Chevrolet	136	120	Running
13	13	112	Ronnie Fones	'59 Chevrolet	135	110	Running
14	16	36	Larry Thomas	Wade Younts '60 Chevrolet	132	125	Running
15	11	86	Buck Baker	Baker '61 Chrysler	117	95	Engine
16	10	34	Wendell Scott	Scott '60 Chevrolet	90	95	Fuel Tnk
17	14	71	Bob Barron	'60 Dodge	84	90	Running
18	17	41	Charles Chapman	Chapman '60 Ford	27	60	Heating
19	18	62	Bob Presnell	Curtis Crider '60 Ford	1	50	Trans

Time of Race: 43 minutes, 36 seconds
Average Speed: 51.605 mph
Pole Winner: Junior Johnson - 58.86 mph
Lap Leaders: Junior Johnson 1-150
Cautions: 1 for 8 laps
Margin of Victory: 1 lap plus
Attendance: 3,500

Grand National Race No. 41
200 Laps at South Boston Speedway
South Boston, VA
50 Miles on Quarter-mile Paved Track
August 27, 1961

Fin	St	No.	Driver	Team / Car	Laps	Money	Status
1	3	27	Junior Johnson	Holly Farms '60 Pontiac	200	$800	Running
2	2	7	Jim Reed	Reed '61 Chevrolet	199	525	Running
3	8	11	Ned Jarrett	B G Holloway '61 Chevrolet	197	375	Running
4	17	85	Emanuel Zervakis	Monroe Shook '60 Chevrolet	196	275	Running
5	5	4	Rex White	White-Clements '60 Chevrolet	195	350	Running
6	9	54	Jimmy Pardue	Pardue '60 Chevrolet	192	215	Running
7	15	36	Larry Thomas	Wade Younts '60 Chevrolet	189	175	Running
8	11	97	Harry Leake	'60 Chevrolet	189	150	Running
9	14	71	Bob Barron	'60 Dodge	184	140	Running
10	20	5	Bob Presnell	'59 Chevrolet	184	130	Running
11	12	57	Bill Morgan	'61 Chevrolet	182	125	Running
12	4	61	Elmo Langley	Doc White '60 T-Bird	181	110	Running
13	21	12	Harvey Hege	'59 Ford	166	100	Running
14	10	23	Doug Yates	Yates '59 Plymouth	158	85	Crash
15	18	17	Fred Harb	Harb '61 Ford	117	70	Engine
16	6	34	Wendell Scott	Scott '60 Chevrolet	114	60	Crash
17	1	6	Cotton Owens	Owens '60 Pontiac	75	50	Trans
18	13	77	Joe Jones	'60 Ford	71	50	Engine
19	16	48	G C Spencer	'60 Chevrolet	62	50	Rear End
20	7	43	Richard Petty	Petty Eng '60 Plymouth	32	50	Engine
21	19	25	John V Hamby	'60 Dodge	22	50	Handling

Time of Race: 1 hour, 02 minutes, 03 seconds
Average Speed: 48.348 mph
Pole Winner: Cotton Owens - 52.63 mph
Lap Leaders: Jim Reed 1-32, Junior Johnson 33-200
Cautions:
Margin of Victory: 1 lap plus
Attendance:

to pull a 'hat trick' since he won three in a row in 1958.

Jim Reed led the first 32 laps and eventually finished second. Ned Jarrett was third with Emanuel Zervakis fourth. Fifth place went to Rex White.

Doug Yates and rookie Wendell Scott were taken out by crashes in the quarter-mile paved track. Pole sitter Cotton Owens departed on lap 75 with transmission failure and Richard Petty went to the sidelines on lap 32 with a blown engine.

Johnson averaged 48.348 mph for his 25th career Grand National victory.

Race No. 42

Nelson Stacy Bags Southern 500 in Final Laps

DARLINGTON, SC (Sept 4) -- Nelson Stacy, the little 'Bull Fighter' out of Cincinnati, ran down Marvin

Grand National Race No. 42
364 Laps at Darlington Raceway
Darlington, SC
"Southern 500"
500 Miles on 1.375-mile Paved Track
September 4, 1961

Fin	St	No.	Driver	Team / Car	Laps	Money	Status
1	3	29	Nelson Stacy	Holt-Stacy '61 Ford	364	$18,430	Running
2	1	22	* Fireball Roberts	Smokey Yunick '61 Pontiac	364	10,670	Running
3	9	3	David Pearson	Daytona Kennel '61 Pontiac	363	5,060	Running
4	7	44	Jim Paschal	Neill '61 Pontiac	359	2,625	Running
5	20	85	Emanuel Zervakis	Monroe Shook '61 Chevrolet	359	2,450	Running
6	33	11	Ned Jarrett	B G Holloway '61 Chevrolet	354	1,500	Running
7	26	14	Johnny Allen	Joe Lee Johnson '61 Chevy	348	1,195	Running
8	18	24	Roscoe Thompson	James Turner '60 Pontiac	347	1,195	Running
9	6	6	Ralph Earnhardt	Cotton Owens '61 Pontiac	346	875	Engine
10	36	47	Rex White	Jack Smith '61 Pontiac	345	925	Running
11	12	72	Bobby Johns	Shorty Johns '61 Ford	344	750	Running
12	16	66	Bill Morgan	Cafe Burgandy '61 Ford	342	700	Running
13	32	30	Elmo Langley	Fred Clark '60 Chevrolet	341	500	Running
14	14	27	Junior Johnson	Holly Farms '61 Pontiac	337	450	Running
15	24	59	Tiny Lund	Lynn Holloway '61 Pontiac	323	650	Crash
16	40	74	L D Austin	Austin '61 Chevrolet	321	350	Running
17	35	54	Jimmy Pardue	Pardue '60 Chevrolet	316	300	Running
18	39	62	Curtis Crider	Crider '61 Mercury	312	750	Running
19	23	19	Herman Beam	Beam '60 Ford	312	250	Running
20	17	46	Larry Frank	Jack Smith '61 Pontiac	273	480	Spindle
21	25	90	Dave Mader	'61 Chevrolet	262	280	Timing
22	4	8	Joe Weatherly	Bud Moore '61 Pontiac	229	370	RF Hub
23	31	7	Jim Reed	Reed '61 Chevrolet	228	200	Brakes
24	15	86	Buddy Baker	Buck Baker '61 Chrysler	221	700	Bearings
25	34	10	T C Hunt	Fred Wheat '61 Dodge	206	700	Rear End
26	5	43	Richard Petty	Petty Eng '61 Plymouth	201	1,110	Engine
27	11	87	Buck Baker	Baker '61 Chrysler	190	220	Con Rod
28	21	2	Tommy Irwin	Tom Daniels '61 Chevrolet	164	200	Rock Arm
29	2	28	Fred Lorenzen	Holman-Moody '61 Ford	158	950	Throttle
30	19	52	Cale Yarborough	Julian Buesink '61 Ford	135	200	Engine
31	8	42	Marvin Panch	Petty Eng '61 Plymouth	94	200	Carb
32	28	82	Marvin Porter	'61 Ford	85	200	Crash
33	29	1	Paul Lewis	Jess Potter '61 Chevrolet	81	200	Crash
34	30	5	Woody Wilson	Leroy Faucett '61 Pontiac	79	200	Crash
35	38	68	E Livingston	Curtis Crider '61 Ford	79	200	H Gasket
36	10	94	Banjo Matthews	Matthews '61 Ford	65	430	Engine
37	22	32	Joe Caspolich	'61 Ford	50	200	Rear End
38	27	80	Darel Dieringer	Tubby Gonzales '61 Ford	45	300	Rear End
39	13	9	Bunkie Blackburn	'61 Ford	34	200	H Gasket
40	37	96	Friday Hassler	J L Cheatham '60 Chevrolet	22	200	Brakes
41	43	99	George Alsobrook	B J Jones '61 Ford	2	200	Handling
42	41	75	Red Hollingsworth	J D Braswell '60 Chevrolet	2	200	Handling
43	42	93	Lee Reitzel	Reitzel '60 Ford	2	200	Handling

* Relieved by Marvin Panch

Time of Race: 4 hours, 54 minutes, 45 seconds
Average Speed: 117.787 mph
Pole Winner: Fireball Roberts - 128.680 mph
Lap Leaders: Fireball Roberts 1-15, Fred Lorenzen 16-63, Roberts 64-79,
   Richard Petty 80-82, David Pearson 83-86, Lorenzen 87-90, Joe Weatherly 91-103,
   Roberts 104-112, Nelson Stacy 113-123, Roberts 124-131, Petty 132-169,
   Stacy 170-182, Roberts 183-225, Stacy 226-240, Roberts 241-258, Pearson 259-260,
   Roberts 261-276, Stacy 277-302, Roberts 303-357, Stacy 358-364
Cautions: 6 for 21 laps
Margin of Victory: 2.64 seconds
Attendance: 80,000

Panch with seven laps remaining and sped to an upset victory in the storied Southern 500 at Darlington Raceway. Stacy, a former Midwest Auto Racing Club champion, became the 19th different winner of the year on the Grand National circuit.

Panch was driving in relief of Fireball Roberts, who was forced to get out of his high powered Smokey Yunick Pontiac with 87 laps left due to neck cramps. Stacy reached the finish line 2.64 seconds in front of the Roberts-Panch car.

Third place went to David Pearson; Jim Paschal was fourth with Emanuel Zervakis fifth. Stacy made five pit stops during the afternoon, averaging 46.2 seconds each.

Ned Jarrett finished sixth and saw his point lead rise to 1,812 over Rex White. Jarrett, leading White throughout the past several

Nelson Stacy won the storied Southern 500 in his first try

months in the point race, filed a protest claiming White's car was illegal. Norris Friel, NASCAR technical inspector, supported Jarrett's protest, finding the engine of White's Chevrolet to be lowered and moved back about one inch. White, scrambling for a ride, bor-

Nelson Stacy gets checkered flag in Southern 500

rowed a Pontiac from Jack Smith to run the race.

A crowd of 30,000 watched Stacy re-write the record books with his 117.787 mph triumph. It was a popular victory for Stacy, who was driving The Holt-Stacy Ford prepared by the famed Holman-Moody team. It was the former MARC champion's first win in 13 Grand National starts.

Marvin Porter, Paul Lewis and Woody Wilson were involved in a fourth turn crash on lap 86. Porter was taken to a Florence hospital for treatment of a concussion and leg bruises.

The lead changed hands 19 times among six different drivers as 6 caution flags slowed the race for a total of 21 laps.

Nelson Stacy and Marvin Panch race side-by-side in final laps of the Darlington Classic

Race No. 43

White Wins Buddy Shuman Memorial Before 10,500

HICKORY, NC (Sept 8) -- Rex White surged into the lead with 11 laps left and went on to win the Buddy Shuman Memorial at Hickory Speedway. It was the sixth win of the season for the 5'4", 32 year-old Chevrolet chauffeur.

An overflow crowd of 10,500 saw White outlast challengers Ned Jarrett, Junior Johnson, Buck Baker and Jack Smith in a tense 100-mile struggle around the .4-mile dirt oval. Jarrett had the lead and was apparently headed for victory when the rear axle snapped on his Chevrolet with 11 laps remaining.

Johnson grabbed the lead at the start and led the first 58 laps in a masterful display of side-tracking. However, he crashed while trying to lap fourth place runner Jarrett. Johnson poked the nose of his Pontiac between Jarrett and Cotton Owens, but found the opening too

Grand National Race No. 43
250 Laps at Hickory Speedway
Hickory, NC
"Buddy Shuman Memorial"
100 Miles on .4-mile Dirt Track
September 8, 1961

Fin	St	No.	Driver	Team / Car	Laps	Money	Status
1	1	4	Rex White	White-Clements '61 Chevrolet	250	$900	Running
2	13	47	Jack Smith	Smith '61 Pontiac	249	525	Running
3	5	86	Buck Baker	Baker '61 Chrysler	249	375	Running
4	8	6	Cotton Owens	Owens '60 Pontiac	248	275	Running
5	11	85	Emaneul Zervakis	Monroe Shook '60 Chevrolet	246	250	Running
6	12	48	G C Spencer	'60 Chevrolet	242	215	Running
7	9	17	Fred Harb	Harb '61 Ford	240	175	Running
8	7	11	Ned Jarrett	B G Holloway '61 Chevrolet	239	150	LR Axle
9	18	74	L D Austin	Austin '61 Chevrolet	233	140	Running
10	15	93	Lee Reitzel	Reitzel '60 Ford	225	130	Running
11	16	3	Mark Hurley	'59 T-Bird	224	125	Running
12	19	5	Paul Lewis	'59 Chevrolet	222	110	Running
13	14	19	Herman Beam	Beam '60 Ford	221	100	Running
14	4	54	Jimmy Pardue	Pardue '60 Chevrolet	194	85	LR Axle
15	3	7	* Joe Weatherly	'60 Pontiac	189	70	Ball Jnt
16	20	71	Bob Barron	'60 Dodge	162	60	Rear End
17	6	42	Richard Petty	Petty Eng '61 Plymouth	102	60	Rear End
18	17	36	Larry Thomas	Wade Younts '60 Chevrolet	89	50	Rear End
19	10	23	Doug Yates	Yates '59 Plymouth	61	50	Clutch
20	2	27	Junior Johnson	Holly Farms '61 Pontiac	58	50	Crash

* Relieved by Junior Johnson

Time of Race: 1 hour, 28 minutes, 51 seconds
Average Speed: 67.529 mph
Pole Winner: Rex White - 72.29 mph
Lap Leaders: Junior Johnson 1-58, Rex White 59-60, Ned Jarrett 61-189, White 190-208, Jarrett 209-239, White 240-250
Cautions: 2
Margin of Victory: 1 lap plus
Attendance: 10,500

narrow. He wound up last in the 20 car field.

Johnson then hopped into Joe Weatherly's Pontiac during a caution period.He drove that car until lap 189 when the ball joint broke, putting him out for the day.

White and Jarrett swapped the lead five times after Johnson fell out.

White averaged 67.529 mph for his 19th career Grand National victory.

Weatherly. Rex White came in third, Ned Jarrett wa: fourth and Jim Paschal fifth.

White stayed alive in the battle for the national driving title. He trails Jarrett by 1,302 points with two su- perspeedway races left on the 1961 slate, both with a combined total of 4,100 points to win.

Johnson won the pole and was in contention all day. Weatherly, starting seventh, came on strong in the late stages and outdrove his rival on the half-mile dirt track. He averaged 61.677 mph.

Cotton Owens and Richard Petty, both of whom qualified in the top 10, failed to finish. Owens dropped out after 171 laps with rear gearing failure, and Petty blew the engine in his Plymouth after 157 laps.

Grand National Race No. 44
250 Laps at Atlantic Rural Fairgrounds
Richmond, VA
125 Miles on Half-mile Dirt Track
September 10, 1961

Fin	St	No.	Driver	Team / Car	Laps	Money	Status
1	7	8	Joe Weatherly	Bud Moore '61 Pontiac	250	$1,350	Running
2	1	27	Junior Johnson	Holly Farms '60 Pontiac	250	850	Running
3	5	4	Rex White	White-Clements '61 Chevrolet	249	750	Running
4	2	11	Ned Jarrett	B G Holloway '61 Chevrolet	249	450	Running
5	12	44	Jim Paschal	J H Petty '61 Pontiac	248	300	Running
6	4	85	Emanuel Zervakis	Monroe Shook '60 Chevrolet	246	250	Running
7	3	66	Bill Morgan	Cafe Burgandy '60 Ford	239	225	Running
8	19	61	Elmo Langley	Doc White '59 T-Bird	224	200	Running
9	9	19	Herman Beam	Beam '60 Ford	223	175	Running
10	17	48	G C Spencer	'60 Chevrolet	219	150	Running
11	11	23	Doug Yates	Yates '61 Plymouth	217	150	Running
12	23	17	Fred Harb	Harb '61 Ford	215	125	Running
13	14	119	Al Disney	'59 Buick	214	125	Running
14	10	34	Wendell Scott	Scott '60 Chevrolet	201	110	Running
15	13	86	Buck Baker	Baker '61 Chrysler	189	110	Running
16	20	36	Larry Thomas	Wade Younts '60 Chevrolet	176	100	Rear End
17	6	6	Cotton Owens	Owens '60 Pontiac	171	90	Rear End
18	8	42	Richard Petty	Petty Eng '61 Plymouth	157	80	Engine
19	18	74	L D Austin	Austin '61 Chevrolet	155	75	Spindle
20	21	57	Harvey Henderson	'61 Chevrolet	153	75	Brakes
21	15	90	Johnny Roberts	Junie Donlavey '60 Ford	113	75	H Gasket
22	22	112	Ronnie Fones	'59 Chevrolet	82	75	Rear End
23	24	5	Jimmy Pardue	'59 Chevrolet	70	75	Spindle
24	25	71	Bob Barron	'60 Dodge	63	75	Rear End
25	16	62	Curtis Crider	Crider '61 Mercury	7	75	Heating

Time of Race: 2 hours, 01 minute, 36 seconds
Average Speed: 61.677 mph
Pole Winner: Junior Johnson - 65.01 mph
Lap Leaders: - - - - - - - - - - - - - - Joe Weatherly   -250
Cautions:
Margin of Victory: 2 car lengths
Attendance:

Race No. 44

Weatherly Defeats Johnson in Richmond Barn-Burner

RICHMOND, VA (Sept 10) -- Joe Weatherly edged Junior Johnson in a close finish in the 125-miler at the Atlantic Rural Fairgrounds. It was the fourth win of the season for the 5'7" Norfolk, VA Pontiac driver.

Johnson finished second, two car lengths behind

Grand National Race No. 45
100 Laps at Sacramento Fairgrounds
Sacramento, CA
100 Miles on 1-mile Dirt Track
September 10, 1961

Fin	St	No.	Driver	Team / Car	Laps	Money	Status
1		98	Eddie Gray	Gray '61 Ford	100	$1,300	Running
2		6	Bob Ross	'61 Olds	99	800	Running
3		76	Danny Weinberg	Guy Kimball '61 Ford	99	500	Running
4		36	Frank Secrist	'60 Ford	99	400	Running
5		7	Don Noel	Chuck Parkko '61 Ford	98	300	Running
6		41	Clem Proctor	'60 Ford	97	250	Running
7		4	Chuck Webb	'59 Ford	97	200	Running
8		28	Kuzie Kuzmanich	'61 Pontiac	97	150	Running
9		26N	Carl Jaemar	'61 Chevrolet	95	100	Running
10		45	Eddie Pagan	Bill Clinton '61 Ford	94	100	Running
11		5	Bruce Worrel	Bob Smith '60 Ford	94	100	Running
12		11	Jim Stewart	'60 Plymouth	93	100	Running
13		00	Dick Getty	'59 Chevrolet	89	100	Running
14		20	Jack Norton	William Peach '59 Chevrolet	88	100	Running
15		18	Dick Smith	'60 Ford	86	75	Running
16		46	Bill Ferrier	'59 Ford	82	50	Running
17		94	Ed Brown	'61 Ford	74	50	Crash
18		85	Keith Wilkinson	'61 Ford	74	50	Running
19		91	Oren Prosser	'61 Plymouth	73	50	Running
20		0	Jim Cook	Floyd Johnson '60 Dodge	71	50	Running
21		23	Bill Foster	'60 Ford	61	25	Engine
22		10	Jim Blomgren	Bob Smith '61 Ford	60	25	Trans
23		43	Joe Clark	'60 Ford	53	25	Heating
24		2	Ron Hornaday	'60 Ford	40	25	Running
25		84	Bob Perry	'59 Ford	36	25	Bearing
26		44	Lloyd Dane	'61 Chevrolet	31	25	Sway Bar
27		21	Jerry Plotts	'59 Ford	30	25	Crash
28	1	98N	Bill Amick	'60 Pontiac	25	25	Rear End
29		8	Clyde Palmer	'59 Dodge	16	25	Fuel Pmp
30		15	Bill Clifton	'60 Ford	16	25	Crash
31		61N	Dick Baron	'59 Chevrolet	5	25	Axle
32		12N	Scotty Cain	'60 T-Bird	2	25	Crank Sh

Time of Race: Not recorded
Average Speed: Not Recorded
Pole Winner: Bill Amick - 79.26 mph
Lap Leaders: Bill Amick 1-25, Eddie Gray 26-100
Cautions:
Margin of Victory: 1 lap plus
Attendance:

Race No. 45

Amick's Comeback Foiled; Gray Wins at Sacramento

SACRAMENTO, CA (Sept 10) -- Eddie Gray of Gardena, CA took the lead in the 26th lap and led the rest of the way to win the 100-miler at the Sacramento Fairgrounds. It was the second win of the season for the Ford driver.

Bob Ross wound up second, a lap behind. Danny Weinberg finished third, Frank Secrist fourth and Don Noel fifth.

Bill Amick of Portland made his return to the Grand National circuit. Driving in his first big NASCAR race since 1957, Amick won the pole and led the first 25 laps. However, bad luck haunted his Ford in the form of differential problems, and he wound up 28th in the field of 32.

Gray took the lead when Amick pulled into the pits and led the rest of the way.

Bill Clifton, Jerry Plotts and Ed Brown were all eliminated in separate crashes.

No official time was kept by the NASCAR scorers.

Race No. 46

Pearson Leads Only Last Lap to Win Dixie 400

HAMPTON, GA (Sept 17) -- Confusion and pandemonium held sway in Atlanta as David Pearson of Spartanburg, SC took his third superspeedway win of the year in the disputed Dixie 400 at Atlanta International Raceway.

It seemed no one was willing to accept victory as the final laps around the 1.5-mile speedway featured four lap changes and a protest as to who was the real winner.

Banjo Matthews, hard charging driver out of Asheville, NC, had a 15.3 second lead with five laps to go. The 29 year-old Ford jockey seemed poised to gain his first Grand National victory. But as he moved toward the shadow of the checkered flag, smoke erupted from beneath his red car, and he dejectedly pulled behind pit wall for good.

Fireball Roberts breezed into the lead. It had been a long day for the Fireball, with the clutch slipping badly in his Pontiac. As the Daytona Beach veteran cruised

Grand National Race No. 46
267 Laps at Atlanta International Raceway
Hampton, GA
"Dixie 400"
400 Miles on 1.5-mile Paved Track
September 17, 1961

Fin	St	No.	Driver	Team / Car	Laps	Money	Status
1	5	3	David Pearson	Daytona Kennel '61 Pontiac	267	$9,330	Running
2	9	27	* Junior Johnson	Holly Farms '61 Pontiac	267	4,795	Running
3	1	22	Fireball Roberts	Smokey Yunick '61 Pontiac	267	3,165	Running
4	13	47	Jack Smith	Smith '61 Pontiac	264	2,250	Running
5	26	43	Richard Petty	Petty Eng '61 Plymouth	264	1,625	Running
6	24	14	Johnny Allen	Joe Lee Johnson '61 Chevy	264	1,325	Running
7	17	11	Ned Jarrett	B G Holloway '61 Chevrolet	264	1,225	Running
8	23	46	Bob Welborn	Jack Smith '61 Pontiac	264	1,100	Running
9	22	51	Woody Wilson	Leroy Faucett '61 Pontiac	262	1,000	Running
10	11	6	Marvin Panch	Cotton Owens '61 Pontiac	262	875	Running
11	7	94	Banjo Matthews	Matthews '61 Ford	262	1,485	Engine
12	8	72	Bobby Johns	Shorty Johns '61 Ford	261	705	Running
13	14	44	Jim Paschal	J H Petty '61 Pontiac	260	650	Running
14	15	85	Emanuel Zervakis	Monroe Shook '61 Chevrolet	259	575	Running
15	30	30	Tiny Lund	Fred Clark '60 Chevrolet	259	550	Running
16	3	8	Joe Weatherly	Bud Moore '61 Pontiac	256	520	Running
17	21	59	Ken Rush	Lynn Holloway '61 Pontiac	255	450	Running
18	10	4	Rex White	White-Clements '61 Chevrolet	254	550	Running
19	2	29	Nelson Stacy	Holt-Stacy '61 Ford	243	845	Engine
20	6	24	Darel Dieringer	James Turner '60 Pontiac	238	575	Crash
21	35	74	L D Austin	Austin '61 Chevrolet	238	350	Running
22	37	19	Herman Beam	Beam '60 Ford	235	350	Running
23	25	68	Ed Livingston	Curtis Crider '61 Ford	234	350	Running
24	36	93	Lee Reitzel	Reitzel '60 Ford	226	350	Running
25	16	87	Buck Baker	Baker '61 Chrysler	209	375	Engine
26	20	32	Bill Morgan	'61 Ford	203	325	Piston
27	32	78	J C Hendrix	Billie Ridgeway '60 Ford	202	300	Con Rod
28	33	96	Elmo Langley	J L Cheatham '60 Chevrolet	180	300	Engine
29	12	9	Bunkie Blackburn	'61 Ford	174	375	Engine
30	28	10	T C Hunt	Fred Wheat '61 Dodge	153	300	Engine
31	34	48	G C Spencer	'60 Chevrolet	124	250	Engine
32	38	71	Bob Barron	'60 Chevrolet	104	250	Engine
33	39	23	Doug Yates	Yates '61 Plymouth	65	250	Oil Pres
34	31	99	George Alsobrook	R J Jones '61 Ford	63	250	Piston
35	29	5	Ralph Earnhardt	Leroy Faucett '60 Pontiac	62	250	Trans
36	4	28	Fred Lorenzen	Holman-Moody '61 Ford	52	315	Crash
37	19	90	Dave Mader	'61 Chevrolet	51	250	Crash
38	17	80	Tubby Gonzales	Gonzales '61 Ford	47	250	Engine
39	18	86	Herb Tillman	Buck Baker '61 Chrysler	46	275	Oil Pres
40	42	15	Jesse James Taylor	Beau Morgan '61 Ford	10	250	Engine
41	41	62	Curtis Crider	Crider '61 Mercury	3	200	Bearing
42	40	2	Tommy Irwin	Tom Daniels '61 Chevrolet	---	200	Piston

* Relieved by Bunkie Blackburn

Time of Race: 3 hours, 11 minutes, 39 seconds
Average Speed: 125.384 mph
Pole Winner: Fireball Roberts - 136.294 mph
Fastest Qualifier: David Pearson - 136.778 mph
Lap Leaders: Fireball Roberts 1-37, Nelson Stacy 38-52, Banjo Matthews 53-200, Stacy 201-243, Matthews 244-262, Roberts 263-265, Johnson 266, David Pearson 267
Cautions:
Margin of Victory: 5 seconds
Attendance: 30,000

for the checkered flag, his fuel tank ran dry. With only two laps left in the race, he headed down pit road to take on gas.

Pandemonium cut loose in the Holly Farms pits. Bunkie Blackburn, driving in relief of Junior Johnson, swept into first place as the white flag was given to the field. On the backstretch, Blackburn slowed, taking the third turn in the low groove. The Fayetteville, NC driver shook the tail of his Pontiac in order to get every speck of fuel in his carburetor. He was out of gas, running slowly.

Blackburn took the winner's flag from starter Ernie Moore, going about 50 mph.

David Pearson, who had passed Blackburn in the fourth turn of the final lap, immediately filed a protest. For an hour, NASCAR officials studied the score cards and discovered that Pearson was right. The sophomore sensation had indeed reached the finish line first.

Johnson got credit for finishing second with Blackburn in relief. Roberts came in third, Jack Smith was fourth and Richard Petty fifth.

Pearson, who wound up 5.0 seconds in front of the Johnson-Blackburn team, averaged 125.384 mph before 30,000 spectators.

David Pearson, winner at Atlanta

When the final decision was made, it was found that Pearson led only the last lap of the 267 lap event. Curiously, the Johnson car also led only one lap -- the white flag lap.

Fred Lorenzen was taken out by a spectacular crash. The engine blew in his Ford on lap 52, and he went sliding backwards into the retaining wall. The blond bomber crawled out of his car unhurt.

Darel Dieringer qualified a strong sixth in a lightly regarded Pontiac owned by James Turner, but he hit the fence after blowing a tire on lap 238. Rookie Dave Mader tagged the wall on lap 51.

Point Leader Ned Jarrett wound up seventh and held a 2,182 point lead over Rex White, who limped to an 18th place finish.

Race No. 47

Weatherly Holds Off White to Win Old Dominion 500

MARTINSVILLE, VA (Sept 24) -- Joe Weatherly withstood a tenacious challenge from Rex White and emerged victorious in the Old Dominion 500 at Martinsville Speedway. It was the sixth win of the season for the squatty Pontiac driver.

Weatherly pushed his Bud Moore Pontiac into the lead on lap 418 and held off White in the stretch duel. White reeled Weatherly in during the late stages, but his engine began sputtering with seven laps to go, knocking him off the pace.

Weatherly was home free, it appeared, until he ran out of gas in the final lap. The Norfolk, VA veteran crossed the finish line with no power. White was nearly three-quarters of a lap back in second place.

Junior Johnson finished third, Fireball Roberts was fourth and Ken Rush fifth.

A crowd of 18,000 filled the seats to watch Weatherly win at an average speed of 62.586 mph. All 16,000 seats were sold out before the race and another 2,000 were admitted for standing room only.

Pole sitter Fred Lorenzen led the first 57 laps, but

Grand National Race No. 47
500 Laps at Martinsville Speedway
Martinsville, VA
"Old Dominion 500"
250 Miles on Half-mile Paved Track
September 24, 1961

Fin	St	No.	Driver	Team / Car	Laps	Money	Status
1	4	8	Joe Weatherly	Bud Moore '61 Pontiac	500	$3,595	Running
2	2	4	Rex White	White-Clements '61 Pontiac	500	2,000	Running
3	9	27	Junior Johnson	Holly Farms '61 Pontiac	499	1,570	Running
4	8	6	Fireball Roberts	Cotton Owens '61 Pontiac	496	850	Running
5	16	59	Ken Rush	Lynn Holloway '61 POntiac	494	750	Running
6	11	54	Jimmy Pardue	Pardue '60 Chevrolet	494	650	Running
7	12	85	Emanuel Zervakis	Monroe Shook '61 Chevrolet	492	550	Running
8	15	42	Art Malone	Petty Eng '61 Plymouth	484	500	Running
9	24	36	Larry Thomas	'60 Chevrolet	476	425	Running
10	17	64	Bill Morton	'60 Chevrolet	473	365	Running
11	21	48	G C Spencer	'60 Chevrolet	469	425	Running
12	18	19	Herman Beam	Beam '60 Ford	464	275	Running
13	6	11	Ned Jarrett	B G Holloway '61 Chevrolet	407	285	Engine
14	5	17	Fred Harb	Harb '61 Ford	407	275	Running
15	19	23	Doug Yates	Yates '61 Plymouth	395	150	Trans
16	26	25	John V Hamby	Hamby '61 Dodge	395	175	Running
17	7	43	Richard Petty	Petty Eng '61 Plymouth	319	175	Engine
18	1	28	Fred Lorenzen	Holman-Moody '61 Ford	300	350	Rear End
19	14	44	Jim Paschal	J H Petty '61 Pontiac	284	150	Rear End
20	3	21	Glen Wood	Wood Bros '61 Ford	264	225	Rear End
21	13	86	Buck Baker	Baker '61 Chrysler	214	100	Rock Arm
22	22	74	L D Austin	Austin '61 Chevrolet	179	150	Engine
23	28	71	Bob Barron	'60 Dodge	120	100	Handling
24	25	12	Wayne Lambeth	'59 Ford	117	125	Fuel Leak
25	23	62	Curtis Crider	Crider '61 Mercury	17	135	Heating
26	27	5	Bob Presnell	'59 Chevrolet	5	100	Engine
27	10	2	Tommy Irwin	Tom Daniels '61 Chevrolet	2	125	Rock Arm
28	20	34	Wendell Scott	Scott '60 Chevrolet	1	100	Crash
29	29	77	Joe Jones	'60 Ford	0	125	Engine

Time of Race: 3 hours, 59 minutes, 40 seconds
Average Speed: 62.586 mph
Pole Winner: Fred Lorenzen - 70.73 mph
Lap Leaders: Fred Lorenzen 1-57, Junior Johnson 58-112, Joe Weatherly 113-127,
   Fireball Roberts 128-129, Ned Jarrett 130-137, Johnson 138-299, Weatherly 300-317,
   Johnson 318-359, Rex White 360-417, Weatherly 418-500
Cautions: 7
Margin of Victory: 3/4 Lap
Attendance: 18,000

Ned Jarrett #11 leads Richard Petty #43 through turn at Martinsville

Grand National Race No. 48
320 Laps at North Wilkesboro Speedway
North Wilkesboro, NC
"Wilkes 200"
200 Miles on .625-mile Paved Track
October 1, 1961

Fin	St	No.	Driver	Team / Car	Laps	Money	Status
1	3	4	Rex White	White-Clements '61 Chevrolet	320	$ 3,105	Running
2	6	18	Fireball Roberts	Bud Moore '61 Pontiac	319	1,125	Running
3	13	42	Richard Petty	Petty Eng '61 Plymouth	316	850	Running
4	1	27	Junior Johnson	Holly Farms '61 Pontiac	315	1,265	Running
5	10	11	Ned Jarrett	B G Holloway '61 Chevrolet	315	575	Running
6	14	85	Emanuel Zervakis	Monroe Shook '61 Chevrolet	312	450	Running
7	24	54	Jimmy Pardue	Pardue '59 Chevrolet	312	400	Running
8	5	8	Joe Weatherly	Bud Moore '61 Pontiac	311	355	Running
9	18	64	Bill Morton	'60 Chevroelt	300	300	Running
10	20	23	Doug Yates	Yates '61 Plymouth	299	225	Running
11	8	2	Tommy Irwin	Tom Daniels '61 Chevrolet	296	200	Crash
12	19	36	Larry Thomas	'60 Chevrolet	294	175	Running
13	21	34	Wendell Scott	Scott '60 Chevrolet	293	150	Running
14	22	62	Curtis Crider	Crider '61 Mercury	293	140	Running
15	17	19	Herman Beam	Beam '60 Ford	291	125	Running
16	26	20	Paul Lewis	'60 Chevrolet	262	110	Running
17	27	74	L D Austin	Austin '61 Chevrolet	253	100	Heating
18	12	17	Fred Harb	Harb '61 Ford	241	100	Engine
19	23	71	Bob Barron	'60 Dodge	218	100	Running
20	2	21	Banjo Matthews	Wood Bros '61 Ford	202	100	Rear End
21	4	44	Jim Paschal	J H Petty '61 Pontiac	200	75	Drive Sh
22	15	14	Johnny Allen	Joe Lee Johnson '61 Chevy	198	75	Crash
23	16	48	G C Spencer	'60 Chevrolet	194	75	Crash
24	7	46	Jack Smith	Smith '61 Pontiac	190	75	Piston
25	11	6	Cotton Owens	Owens '61 Pontiac	189	75	Oil Pres
26	28	25	John Handy	'61 Dodge	120	50	Trans
27	9	86	Buck Baker	Baker '61 Chrysler	28	50	Engine
28	29	97	Harry Leake	'60 Chevrolet	26	50	Engine
29	25	59	Ken Rush	Lynn Holloway '61 Pontiac	8	50	Engine
30	30	12	Joe Jones	'59 Ford	2	50	Handling

Time of Race: 2 hours, 21 minutes, 43 seconds
Average Speed: 84.675 mph
Pole Winner: Junior Johnson - 94.54 mph
Lap Leaders: Junior Johnson 1-79, Joe Weatherly 80, Johnson 81-119, White 120-320
Cautions: 4 for 23 laps
Margin of Victory: 1 lap plus
Attendance: 9,000

eventually went out with rear end trouble. Seven caution flags slowed the action, the most serious happening in the second lap when Bob Barron broadsided Wendell Scott. Scott was knocked out of the race and Barron limped another 120 laps before calling it quits.

Six drivers traded the lead nine times. Ned Jarrett, starting in sixth place, went out on lap 407 with engine problems. His point lead was cut to 1,852 over White.

Ned Jarrett pits on the grass at Martinsville

Race No. 48

White Whitewashes Field In Wilkes 200

NORTH WILKESBORO, NC (Oct 1) -- Rex White zipped past Junior Johnson in the 120th lap and outdistanced his rivals to win the Wilkes 200 at North Wilkesboro Speedway. It was the 20th career win for the 145 pound Chevrolet driver.

Fireball Roberts hopped in a back-up Bud Moore Pontiac and finished second, a lap behind. Richard Petty came in third, Johnson was fourth and Ned Jarrett fifth.

Johnson scorched the .625-mile paved oval in the

early going, leading the first 79 laps. Joe Weatherly grabbed the lead in the 80th lap, but Johnson snatched it right back. Johnson kept his Holly Farms Pontiac out front until White passed him with 201 laps remaining.

Hard luck Tommy Irwin was running in the top 10 when his Chevrolet blew an engine and crashed into the fence. Johnny Allen and G.C. Spencer were kayoed from the race by a crack-up on lap 201.

White made the entire 320 laps on one pit stop and averaged 84.675 mph.

Race No. 49

Weatherly Edges Petty in National 400 Thriller

CHARLOTTE, NC (Oct 15) -- Joe Weatherly outsprinted Richard Petty and Bob Welborn in a three-car showdown to win the second annual National 400 at Charlotte Motor Speedway. Weatherly's triumph silenced critics who said the classy veteran was 'featherfooting' his car in recent outings. Among those critics was car owner Bud Moore.

National 400 winner Joe Weatherly and Miss Pontiac Linda Vaughn in victory lane

Moore entered two cars in the 400-miler, the second being manned by Bob Welborn. Weatherly passed Welborn with five laps to go and held off Petty's late challenge to win by a car length and a half.

Cotton Owens came in fourth and Rex White was fifth. Ned Jarret slipped to 18th in the final rundown and watched his point lead drop to 1,062 over White.

Fireball Roberts survived a grisly crash when his Pontiac

Fireball Roberts' Pontiac took a severe lick from Bill Morgan's Ford in Charlotte Motor Speedway's National 400

Grand National Race No. 49
267 Laps at Charlotte Motor Speedway
Charlotte, NC
"National 400"
400 Miles on 1.5-mile Paved Track
October 15, 1961

Fin	St	No.	Driver	Team / Car	Laps	Money	Status
1	6	8	Joe Weatherly	Bud Moore '61 Pontiac	267	$9,510	Running
2	22	43	Richard Petty	Petty Eng '61 Plymouth	267	4,870	Running
3	14	18	Bob Welborn	Bud Moore '61 Pontiac	267	3,275	Running
4	21	6	Cotton Owens	Owens '61 Pontiac	266	2,275	Running
5	13	4	Rex White	White-Clements '61 Chevrolet	264	1,800	Running
6	29	42	Darel Dieringer	Petty Eng '61 Plymouth	263	1,375	Running
7	24	85	Emanuel Zervakis	Monroe Shook '61 Chevrolet	261	1,250	Running
8	25	14	Joe Lee Johnson	Johnson '61 Chevrolet	258	1,125	Running
9	12	27	Junior Johnson	Holly Farms '61 Pontiac	256	1,535	Wheel
10	30	30	J C Hendrix	Fred Clark '60 Chevrolet	254	875	Running
11	10	21	Speedy Thompson	Wood Bros '61 Ford	252	825	Engine
12	40	15	Johnny Allen	Beau Morgan '61 Ford	249	650	Running
13	34	74	L D Austin	Austin '61 Chevrolet	243	600	Running
14	26	5	Woody Wilson	Leroy Faucett '61 Pontiac	242	600	Running
15	36	96	Tiny Lund	J L Cheatham '60 Chevrolet	234	550	Running
16	32	19	Herman Beam	Beam '60 Ford	233	450	Running
17	19	87	Buck Baker	Baker '61 Chrysler	232	525	Running
18	15	11	Ned Jarrett	B G Holloway '61 Chevrolet	223	550	Engine
19	31	54	Jimmy Pardue	Pardue '59 Chevrolet	221	450	Running
20	33	77	Joe Jones	'60 Ford	220	450	Running
21	1	3	David Pearson	Daytona Kennel '61 Pontiac	217	470	Fuel Pmp
22	42	34	Wendell Scott	Scott '60 Chevrolet	191	350	Running
23	43	1	George Green	Jess Potter '61 Chevrolet	175	350	Running
24	18	32	Elmo Langley	'61 Ford	169	360	Engine
25	35	23	Doug Yates	Yates '61 Plymouth	140	350	Drive Shft
26	5	20	Marvin Panch	Smokey Yunick '60 Pontiac	136	600	Crash
27	23	82	Elmo Henderson	'61 Ford	122	310	Running
28	28	68	Ed Livingston	Curtis Crider '60 Ford	121	310	Running
29	2	22	Fireball Roberts	Smokey Yunick '61 Pontiac	113	1,110	Crash
30	20	66	Bill Morgan	Cafe Burgandy '61 Ford	111	300	Crash
31	4	28	Fred Lorenzen	Holman-Moody '61 Ford	104	275	H Gasket
32	8	72	Bobby Johns	Shorty Johns '61 Ford	55	250	Crash
33	3	94	Banjo Matthews	Matthews '61 Ford	54	300	Engine
34	27	86	Herb Tillman	Buck Baker '61 Chrysler	45	275	Rear End
35	11	9	Bunkie Blackburn	'61 Ford	42	325	Crash
36	41	80	Tubby Gonzales	Gonzales '61 Ford	38	250	Engine
37	7	47	Jack Smith	Smith '61 Pontiac	34	550	Fuel Pmp
38	38	83	Sal Tovella	'61 Ford	31	250	Distributo
39	39	93	Lee Reitzel	Reitzel '60 Ford	31	250	H Gasket
40	37	62	Curtis Crider	Crider '61 Mercury	27	250	Engine
41	9	29	Nelson Stacy	Holt-Stacy '61 Ford	27	400	Heating
42	16	2	Tommy Irwin	Tom Daniels '61 Chevrolet	20	350	Rod
43	17	59	Ken Rush	Lynn Holloway '61 Pontiac	16	275	Rock Arm

Time of Race: 3 hours, 20 minutes, 20 seconds
Average Speed: 119.950 mph
Pole Winner: David Pearson - 138.577 mph
Lap Leaders: David Pearson 1-3, Fireball Roberts 4-73, Pearson 74, Junior Johnson 75-76, Roberts 77-113, Johnson 114-139, Bob Welborn 140-179, Johnson 180,196, Welborn 197, Johnson 198-199, Welborn 200-203, Johnson 204-256, Welborn 257-262, Joe Weatherly 263-267
Cautions: 3 for 18 laps
Margin of Victory: 1 1/2 car lengths

ost power and was creamed by Bill Morgan. White paint from the front of Morgan's Ford was clearly visible on Roberts' bucket seat. No one was seriously injured although Roberts later said, "I picked glass from my neck and back for two weeks." Morgan was treated for a broken rib and facial cuts.

Weatherly was practically counted out of the race when rookie Woody Wilson spun, taking Little Joe for a harrowing 200 yard slide through the first turn. Weatherly spent the rest of the afternoon catching up and did not lead in the race except for the final five laps.

Three caution flags for 18 laps failed to keep Weatherly from setting a race record of 119.950 mph. A crowd of 35,821 was on hand in pleasant autumn weather.

Race No. 50

Weatherly Overcomes Five Lap Deficit; Wins Southeastern 500

BRISTOL, TN (Oct 22) -- Sour luck foiled Junior Johnson as he was knocked out while holding a five lap lead in the Bristol International Speedway's Southeastern 500. Johnson's misfortune became Joe Weatherly's good fortune. The heavy-footed Pontiac driver sneaked home first for his 12th career win.

Rex White finished second, 7.0 seconds behind Weatherly in the 500 lap event on the half-mile paved tri-oval. Nelson Stacy wound up third with Jim Paschal

Jim Paschal spins down front chute in Southeastern 500. He recovered and finished 4th

Grand National Race No. 50
500 Laps at Bristol International Speedway
Bristol, TN
"Southeastern 500"
250 Miles on Half-mile Paved Track
October 22, 1961

Fin	St	No.	Driver	Team / Car	Laps	Money	Status
1	2	8	Joe Weatherly	Bud Moore '61 Pontiac	500	$3,680	Running
2	8	4	Rex White	White-Clements '61 Chevrolet	500	2,365	Running
3	18	29	Nelson Stacy	Holt-Stacy '61 Ford	500	1,525	Running
4	17	44	Jim Paschal	J H Petty '61 Pontiac	498	1,125	Running
5	5	85	Emanuel Zervakis	Monroe Shook '61 Chevrolet	495	950	Running
6	16	11	Ned Jarrett	B G Holloway '61 Chevrolet	491	825	Running
7	13	54	Jimmy Pardue	Pardue '60 Chevrolet	482	725	Running
8	12	59	Ken Rush	Lynn Holloway '61 Pontiac	481	675	Running
9	23	64	Bill Morton	'60 Chevrolet	481	600	Running
10	3	18	Bob Welborn	Bud Moore '61 Pontiac	480	585	Running
11	20	86	Buck Baker	Baker '61 Chrysler	480	450	Running
12	14	48	G C Spencer	'60 Chevrolet	478	400	Running
13	30	74	L D Austin	Austin '61 Chevrolet	474	325	Running
14	9	19	Herman Beam	Beam '60 Ford	471	325	Running
15	36	62	Curtis Crider	Crider '61 Mercury	460	290	Running
16	33	34	Wendell Scott	Scott '60 Chevrolet	459	280	Running
17	1	47	Bobby Johns	Jack Smith '61 Pontiac	457	440	Running
18	28	16	Brownie King	'59 T-Bird	442	250	Running
19	31	69	Bill Latham	'60 Chevrolet	440	250	Running
20	21	17	Fred Harb	Harb '61 Ford	439	250	Engine
21	24	46	Jack Smith	Smith '61 Pontiac	421	240	Wheel
22	26	30	Tiny Lund	Fred Clark '60 Chevrolet	414	225	Rear End
23	11	43	Richard Petty	Petty Eng '61 Plymouth	394	245	Rear End
24	7	27	Junior Johnson	Holly Farms '61 Pontiac	394	495	Rear End
25	15	14	Joe Lee Johnson	'61 Chevrolet	370	225	Engine
26	4	22	Fireball Roberts	Holly Farms '60 Pontiac	323	310	Fuel Pmp
27	19	32	Bill Morgan	'61 Ford	237	225	Rear End
28	38	1	George Green	Jess Potter '60 Chevrolet	197	200	Engine
29	25	96	Johnny Allen	J L Cheatham '60 Chevrolet	169	200	Rear End
30	10	9	Bunkie Blackburn	'61 Ford	164	225	Engine
31	20	20	Paul Lewis	'61 Chevrolet	149	200	Crash
32	36	36	Larry Thomas	Wade Younts '60 Chevrolet	120	200	Crank Sh
33	25	25	Gene Blackburn	'60 Dodge	117	100	Axle
34	39	39	Friday Hassler	'60 Chevrolet	115	100	Rear End
35	77	77	Joe Jones	'60 Ford	111	100	Rear End
36	23	23	Doug Yates	Yates '61 Plymouth	35	100	Fan Belt
37	2	2	Tommy Irwin	Tom Daniels '61 Chevrolet	19	125	Crash
38	88	88	Allen Franklin	'59 Nash	3	100	Too Slow

Time of Race: 3 hours, 27 minutes, 02 seconds
Average Speed: 72.452 mph
Pole Winner: Bobby Johns - 80.645 mph
Lap Leaders: Bobby Johns 1-30, Junior Johnson 31-212, Johns 213-231, Fireball Roberts 232-282, Johnson 283-394, Rex White 395-418, Joe Weatherly 419-500
Cautions: 3
Margin of Victory: 7 car lengths
Attendance: 17,000

fourth and Emanual Zervakis fifth.

Johnson and Fireball Roberts, both driving Pontiacs owned by Rex Lovette, were the dominant factors, leading for 334 laps collectively. But Roberts parked his car with fuel pump failure on lap 323 and Johnson suffered a heartbreaker 70 laps later. He was coasting with a five-lap cushion when his Pontiac slowed on lap 394. Differential problems put him behind the wall for good. White took over the lead on lap 395

Jim Paschal was running second to Johnson midway in the race but hit a spinning Tiny Lund and had to go to the pits for minor surgical work. White took first place on lap 395 and led until Weatherly passed him on lap 419. Paschal was over a half lap ahead of White and Weatherly when he got tangled up with Lund only a few laps before Johnson fell out.

Weatherly averaged 72.452 mph for his $3,680 triumph. Bobby Johns had won the pole at 80.645 mph and led the first 30 laps. The Miami driver wound up 17th, 43 laps behind.

Ned Jarrett finished sixth and held a 894 point lead over White, thus clinching the Grand National championship. Only two races remained with a total first place point value of 800 points.

100-miler at Greenville-Pickens Speedway.

Weatherly recovered to finish second, a lap behind Johnson. Rex White was third with Richard Petty fourth and Curtis Crider fifth.

Buck Baker earned the pole in his No. 86 Chrysler and led the first 98 laps. Johnson passed Baker on lap 99 and led through lap 116 when Weatherly grabbed the lead. Little Joe was comfortably ahead when the tire let go on his Pontiac, sending him to the pits.

Baker's bid for victory ended on lap 98 when he lost his clutch.

Junior Johnson

Johnson averaged 63.346 mph for his seventh win of the season.

Point leader Ned Jarrett wound up sixth.

Grand National Race No. 51
200 Laps at Greenville-Pickens Speedway
Greenville, SC
100 Miles on Half-mile Dirt Track
October 28, 1961

Fin	St	No.	Driver	Team / Car	Laps	Money	Status
1	3	27	Junior Johnson	Holly Farms '61 Pontiac	200	$950	Running
2	2	8	Joe Weatherly	Bud Moore '61 Pontiac	199	625	Running
3	10	4	Rex White	White-Clements '61 Chevrolet	198	425	Running
4	9	42	Richard Petty	Petty Eng '61 Plymouth	195	275	Running
5	16	62	Curtis Crider	Crider '61 Mercury	192	250	Running
6	6	11	Ned Jarrett	B G Holloway '61 Chevrolet	191	215	Running
7	15	43	Maurice Petty	Petty Eng '61 Plymouth	190	175	Running
8	2	34	Wendell Scott	Scott '60 Chevrolet	190	150	Running
9	11	14	Joe Lee Johnson	Johnson '61 Chevrolet	188	140	Running
10	8	44	Jim Paschal	J H Petty '61 Pontiac	183	130	Rear End
11	13	19	Herman Beam	Beam '60 Ford	181	125	Running
12	14	93	Lee Reitzel	Reitzel '60 Ford	181	110	Running
13	18	17	Fred Harb	Harb '61 Ford	171	100	Running
14	7	46	Jack Smith	Smith '61 Pontiac	169	85	Crash
15	17	77	Joe Jones	'60 Ford	159	70	Running
16	5	22	Fireball Roberts	Holly Farms '60 Pontiac	116	60	Rear End
17	1	86	Buck Baker	Baker '61 Chrysler	98	50	Clutch
18	4	54	Jimmy Pardue	Pardue '59 Chevrolet	51	50	Distributor

Time of Race: 1 hour, 34 minutes, 43 seconds
Average Speed: 63.346 mph
Pole Winner: Buck Baker -66.667 mph
Lap Leaders: Buck Baker 1-98, Junior Johnson 99-116, Joe Weatherly 117-192, Johnson 193-200
Cautions:
Margin of victory: 1 lap plus
Attendance:

Race No. 51

Johnson Wins Greenville After Weatherly Blows Tire

GREENVILLE, SC (Oct 28) -- Junior Johnson slipped into first place when leader Joe Weatherly blew a tire with eight laps remaining and went on to win the

Grand National Race No. 52
165 Laps at Orange Speedway
Hillsboro, NC
148.5 Miles on .9-mile Dirt Track
October 29, 1961

Fin	St	No.	Driver	Team / Car	Laps	Money	Status
1	1	8	Joe Weatherly	Bud Moore '61 Pontiac	165	$1,150	Running
2	2	4	Rex White	White-Clements '61 Chevrolet	164	850	Running
3	6	11	Ned Jarrett	B G Holloway '61 Chevrolet	163	475	Running
4	10	42	Maurice Petty	Petty Eng '61 Plymouth	155	375	Running
5	4	22	Fireball Roberts	Holly Farms '61 Pontiac	154	325	Engine
6	16	17	Fred Harb	Harb '61 Ford	150	275	Running
7	13	19	Herman Beam	Beam '60 Ford	147	225	Running
8	20	74	L D Austin	Austin '61 Chevrolet	142	200	Running
9	15	97	Harry Leake	'60 Chevrolet	139	200	Running
10	5	43	Richard Petty	Petty Eng '61 Plymouth	133	200	Trans
11	11	62	Curtis Crider	Crider '61 Mercury	121	175	Running
12	3	27	Junior Johnson	Holly Farms '60 Pontiac	117	125	Clutch
13	20	68	Ed Livingston	Curtis Crider '61 Ford	104	150	Heating
14	7	85	Tommy Irwin	Monroe Shook '61 Chevrolet	103	150	Brakes
15	17	34	Wendell Scott	Scott '60 Chevrolet	101	150	Engine
16	19	77	Joe Jones	'60 Ford	95	125	Engine
17	9	86	Buck Baker	Baker '61 Chrysler	80	125	Distributor
18	18	93	Lee Reitzel	Reitzel '60 Ford	54	125	Heating
19	14	23	Doug Yates	Yates '60 Plymouth	38	125	Seals
20	8	44	Jim Paschal	J H Petty '61 Pontiac	6	100	Rear End

Time of Race: 1 hour, 44 minutes, 31 seconds
Average Speed: 85.249 mph
Pole Winner: Joe Weatherly - 95.154 mph
Lap Leaders: Joe Weatherly 1-100, Junior Johnson 101, Weatherly 102-165
Cautions:
Margin of Victory: 1 lap plus
Attendance:

Race No. 52

Weatherly Grabs Season-ending 148.5-miler at Hillsboro

HILLSBORO, NC (Oct 29) -- Joe Weatherly polished off the exhaustive 1961 NASCAR campaign with an overwhelming victory in the season-ending 148.5-mile race at Orange Speedway. It was Weatherly's ninth win of the year.

Rex White finished second, a lap behind and Ned Jarrett was third. Maurice Petty came in fourth with Fireball Roberts fifth.

Weatherly led all but one lap in the 165 lap event on the .9-mile banked dirt oval. Junior Johnson led one lap during a caution flag. Johnson retired on lap 117 with clutch failure. Roberts, running mate with Johnson, blew his engine on lap 154 but still drove enough laps to get fifth place in the final order.

Jarrett was officially crowned Grand National champion of 1961, winning by 830 points over White. He won only once but managed 34 top 10 finishes.

Only nine of the twenty cars starting the race were running at the finish of the event which was erroneously billed as a 150-miler.

Ned Jarrett, 1961 NASCAR Grand National Champion

1961 NASCAR Season
Final Point Standings - Grand National Division

Rank	Driver	Points	Starts	Wins	Top 5	Top 10	Winnings
1	Ned Jarrett	27,272	46	1	23	34	$41,055.90
2	Rex White	26,442	47	7	29	38	56,394.60
3	Emanuel Zervakis	22,312	38	2	19	28	27,280.65
4	Joe Weatherly	17,894	25	9	14	18	47,078.36
5	Fireball Roberts	17,600	21	2	13	14	50,266.09
6	Junior Johnson	17,178	40	7	16	22	28,540.44
7	Jack Smith	15,186	24	2	10	14	21,409.81
8	Richard Petty	14,984	41	2	18	23	25,238.52
9	Jim Paschal	13,922	23	2	12	16	18,099.91
10	Buck Baker	13,746	42	1	11	15	13,696.91
11	Jimmy Pardue	13,408	44	0	3	16	10,561.91
12	Johnny Allen	13,114	22	0	3	11	13,126.91
13	David Pearson	13,088	19	3	7	8	51,910.21
14	Bob Welborn	12,570	14	0	3	7	13,486.91
15	Herman Beam	11,382	41	0	1	14	9,391.91
16	Nelson Stacy	10,436	15	1	4	8	27,607.94
17	Ralph Earnhardt	10,182	8	0	2	5	11,472.94
18	Marvin Panch	9,392	9	1	3	6	30,477.94
19	Fred Lorenzen	9,316	15	3	6	6	30,394.94
20	G C Spencer	9,128	31	0	3	18	7,362.94
21	Curtis Crider	8,414	41	0	1	2	7,420.00
22	Cotton Owens	8,032	17	4	11	11	11,560.00
23	Tiny Lund	7,740	10	0	0	2	5,545.00
24	Bobby Johns	7,590	14	0	1	3	5,010.00
25	L D Austin	7,306	20	0	0	8	4,530.00
26	Tommy Irwin	7,300	26	0	3	8	7,170.00
27	Doug Yates	5,878	7	0	0	2	1,090.00
28	Paul Lewis	5,712	21	0	0	5	4,095.00
29	Bob Barron	5,412	30	0	0	5	3,725.00
30	Elmo Langley	5,376	15	0	1	5	3,530.00
31	Banjo Matthews	4,924	14	0	1	3	5,560.00
32	Wendell Scott	4,726	23	0	0	5	3,240.00
33	Jim Reed	4,705	8	0	3	3	3,350.00
34	Fred Harb	4,526	27	0	1	8	3,460.00
35	Darel Dieringer	4,416	7	0	1	2	3,150.00
36	Bob Burdick	4,382	5	1	2	3	18,750.00
37	Lee L Reitzel	4,380	17	0	0	3	2,910.00
38	Tom Pistone	3,766	4	0	0	3	2,050.00
39	Buddy Baker	3,668	14	0	1	3	4,965.00
40	Roscoe Thompson	3,602	6	0	0	2	2,535.00
41	Woodie Wilson	3,580	5	0	0	1	2,625.00
42	Larry Frank	3,162	8	0	0	1	2,380.00
43	Larry Thomas	3,140	13	0	0	4	2,015.00
44	Harry Leake	3,092	15	0	0	7	2,000.00
45	Paul Goldsmith	2,930	2	0	1	2	6,050.00
46	Joe Lee Johnson	2,700	9	0	0	3	2,615.00
47	Bill Morgan	2,430	6	0	0	1	1,900.00
48	T C Hunt	2,430	7	0	0	0	2,750.00
49	Marvin Porter	2,326	8	0	1	1	2,070.00
50	Joe Eubanks	2,320	2	0	0	0	1,475.00

The 1962 Season
Auto Industry Back in Racing - Ford Leads the Way

Volume two of a four volume series . . . . . The Superspeedway Boom 1959 - 1964

1962

In June of 1957, the Automobile Manufacturers Association recommended unanimously that all of its members "disassociate itself" entirely from stock car racing. The resolution was adopted by the big motor companies after Congressional pressure based on a contention that promotion of speed and horsepower would be detrimental to the safety of the general motoring public of America.

It specified that the "AMA members would take no part or assist in any way automobile races or other competitive events in which speed or horsepower were emphasized. It also recommended that members of the automotive industry not advertise or publicize actual or comparative capabilities of passenger cars for speed, or specific engine size, torque, horsepower or ability to accelerate or perform, in any context that suggests speed."

But the factories had cars to sell, and stock car racing would sell them. It seemed that the agreement would be violated to some extent by one or all of the manufacturers.

By 1959 -- after one year in which the automobile industry's aid to racing, if any, was not particularly evident -- it returned.

That was the year the Daytona International Speedway opened its gates, ushering in a new and fruitful era of stock car racing. NASCAR Grand National racing was all set to surge to a higher level. Media attention jumped tremendously. Spectator interest soared dramatically.

Spectators of auto racing events also happened to buy new automobiles. And therein lay the motives.

All along, the AMA considered auto racing a prohibited substance. It didn't require a whole lot of ingenuity for the racing factories to side-step that issue. They merely supplied the hardware and provided the necessary funding on an "under the table" basis. In the Detroit area, this practice was done by "consulting engineers".

And presto! The newest and latest cars had a habit of showing up at the race tracks. Big shiny engines appeared in the garage area of some of the better stock car racers, with nobody having any idea how they got there.

The practice had increased to the point that the AMA ban on racing was being widely ignored, although no one would admit it.

Fireball Roberts won everything in sight at Daytona in 1962 -- despite General Motors insistence they were "not involved" in racing

On Monday, June 11, 1962, the Ford Motor Company broke with the automobile industry's policy against participation in racing.

In a letter to the Automobile Manufacturers Association, Henry Ford II, the company's board chairman and newly elected president of the AMA, said that his firm thought the 1957 resolution opposing such participation "no longer had either purpose or effect."

"Accordingly," Ford said, "we are withdrawing from it."

Ford II, whose company acquired a $2 million racing operation as part of its $28 million purchase of the Autolite Company, said, "For a while other member companies endorsed the soundness of the principles stated in the resolution. As time passed, however, some car divisions, including our own, interpreted the resolution more and more freely, with the result that increasing emphasis was placed on speed and racing.

"As a result," he continued, "Ford Motor Company feels that the resolution has no purpose. We have notified the Board of Directors of the Automobile Manufacturers Association that we feel we can better establish our own standards of conduct with respect to the matter in which the performance of our vehicles is to be promoted and advertised."

First reaction from the other automobile companies left the immediate outlook somewhat confused, but the

want to see our cars win races," he said, adding that the industry believes that racing "definitely sells cars."

Within a few weeks, Chrysler announced that it would develop "high performance" parts for stock car racing, but General Motors remained mute.

Ford Motor Company absorbed the initial credit for starting the trend toward "open factory participation" on the NASCAR Grand National circuit.

Bill France made an announcement of his own -- and he clamped down on possible intentions on the part of the factories to produce "out of sight" engines in special limited edition highway vehicles just to get them inside the fences at the race tracks. The engine displacement limit was set at 428 inches, although Ford reportedly had a 483 cubic inch power plant under development. "The ruling was discussed with Ford several months before Ford announced its withdrawal of the AMA," said France. "Ford and other Detroit manufacturers have been most cooperative and interested in helping us establish a realistic engine limit."

Reaction among non-Ford drivers, as expected, was mixed. "Sounds to me like an alibi for Ford's poor showing on the tracks this year," said Rex White. "Ford hadn't won a major race until Darlington's Rebel

In the early part of 1962 Grand National season, the Pontiacs were way out front. Near the end of the season the situation had changed

united stand in support of the resolution obviously was broken.

A Chrysler Corporation spokesman said the expressed withdrawal by Ford made it "inoperative" so far as Chrysler was concerned.

General Motors said that it was "continuing to endorse the soundness of the principles of the resolution."

Ford noted that racing accomplishments in recent seasons have sharply boosted Pontiac sales. "We also

300 in May. Fords won the World 600 and the Atlanta 500, but everybody in racing knows it was pure luck rather than performance."

Junior Johnson, a Pontiac chauffeur in 1961, was irked on one occasion when he set fast time in qualifying and a Ford team requested an engine teardown. It happened at Martinsville when Johnson appeared to have won the pole in a record qualifying lap. "Those Ford drivers will do anything to win," steamed Johnson. "They can't beat the Pontiacs on the track, so they try to get at us some other way. I wouldn't mind letting NASCAR inspectors tear my engine down, but why should I be the guinea pig just to satisfy the curiosity of the Ford guys?

"The Ford drivers haven't done anything but run their mouths," Johnson added. "If their cars were as fast as their mouths, they wouldn't have lost a race this season."

At Martinsville, Johnson's qualification attempt was disqualified. When he made necessary changes in the engine, he qualified 20th.

In the second half of the year, Ford won only three out of 25 Grand National races. It took 17 races from the July 4 Firecracker 250 before they won their first race. However, one of those wins was in the storied Southern 500 when Larry Frank scored a disputed victory over Junior Johnson's Pontiac. Although the results weren't dramatic the ground work was laid for the 1963 season.

The youngest car owner on record emerged in 1962 within the Ford camp. The owner was a 19 year-old out of Asheville, NC -- and the owner just happened to be a woman. Mamie Reynolds, daughter of U.S. Senator Robert R. Reynolds, purchased a new 1962 Ford and made her debut in the Southern 500 at Darlington. Darel Dieringer was assigned to drive the car. After qualifying 15th, Dieringer was caught up in a multi-car pile-up in the 184th lap. The new car was crunched and caught on fire. It was destroyed.

Undaunted, Miss Reynolds ordered another new Ford from Holman-Moody and Fred Lorenzen drove it twice within a few days -- finishing as high as third at Richmond, VA. In his next start, on September 13th at Augusta, GA, Lorenzen passed Ned Jarrett with 19 laps to go and won the 100 miler. Mamie Reynolds entered the elusive ranks of a winning car owner in only her fourth start, although technically, the car was a Holman-Moody machine.

Along the weekly dirt track trail an attractive brunette, Wanda Tallent, of Hickory, NC became one of

the best known race drivers in the Carolinas. Her activity was, however, confined to "Powder Puff" derbies, special novice events for women drivers only. Tallent won 18 out of 20 races in her first five seasons at Hickory Speedway. Even with that enviable record, she

Fred Lorenzen #28, driver of the Holman-Moody Ford, benefitted from Ford Motor Co's plunge into stock car racing

didn't feel she had accomplished all that much. "Ah, I drive faster on the highway than I do in those Powder Puff races," she once said. "The other women don't like to drive fast or take chances. I usually lap 'em at least once."

Hickory Speedway promoter, Grafton Burgess, decided to spice up the Powder Puff Derby one Saturday night. Unknown to any of the lady contestants, one of the track's hot-shot Sportsman drivers -- Bennett Clontz -- was dressed in female attire, with appropriate padding, and entered the race. The plot was that, in victory lane, he was to be exposed and disqualified.

"I found out about that, but I wasn't supposed to have," said Wanda. "They put that boy at the rear of the field. So I went back there with

Fireball Roberts and David Pearson set the pace for World 600 field

him, pretendin' not to know who he was. I didn't want him sayin' he came from last to beat me.

"That was the hardest race I ever had," she continued. "I was just determined he wasn't gonna pass me. And he didn't."

Everything went well with the melodrama, except for the one detail.

Bennett Clontz finished second.

Wanda Tallent won the race.

Tallent probably had enough talent to eventually get to NASCAR's elite stock car racing division. She con-quered the Power Puff derbies and felt the Sportsman class was the next step up. "A man offered to set me up with a car and pay for my expenses," said Tallent. "I'm not scared to drive against the men, but those boys down at Hickory Speedway just drive like they don't have any sense."

Tallent was near-sighted -- and poor vision was probably the main reason she never attempted to hit the big leagues. "I can't drive without my glasses," she once said. "That was no big deal against other women. I think most of them drove with their eyes closed."

Grand National Race No. 1
200 Laps at Concord Speedway
Concord, NC
100 Miles on Half-mile Dirt Track
November 5, 1961

Fin	St	No.	Driver	Team / Car	Laps	Money	Status
1	2	46	Jack Smith	Smith '61 Pontiac	200	$800	Running
2	1	8	Joe Weatherly	Bud Moore '61 Pontiac	200	525	Running
3	7	6	Cotton Owens	Owens '61 Pontiac	198	375	Running
4	4	4	Rex White	White-Clements '61 Chevrolet	198	275	Running
5	8	11	Ned Jarrett	B G Holloway '61 Chevrolet	196	350	Running
6	13	23	Doug Yates	Yates '61 Plymouth	183	215	Running
7	18	62	Curtis Crider	Crider '61 Mercury	183	175	Running
8	14	93	Lee Reitzel	Reitzel '60 Ford	183	150	Running
9	21	36	Larry Thomas	Wade Younts '60 Ford	178	140	Running
10	22	19	Herman Beam	Beam '60 Ford	169	130	Running
11	25	68	Ed Livingston	Curtis Crider '60 Ford	157	125	Running
12	11	48	G C Spencer	'60 Chevrolet	156	110	Running
13	6	42	Richard Petty	Petty Eng '61 Plymouth	152	100	Rear End
14	23	34	Wendell Scott	Scott '60 Chevrolet	145	85	A Frame
15	5	86	Buck Baker	Baker '61 Chrysler	139	70	Axle
16	12	85	Tommy Irwin	Monroe Shook '60 Chevrolet	137	60	Running
17	20	1	George Green	Jess Potter '60 Chevrolet	136	50	Running
18	15	89	Mark Hurley	'59 Pontiac	129	50	Rear End
19	16	97	Harry Leake	'60 Chevrolet	98	50	Running
20	10	59	Ralph Earnhardt	Lynn Holloway '61 Pontiac	94	50	Oil Leak
21	24	77	Joe Jones	'60 Ford	82	50	Axle
22	26	54	Jimmy Pardue	Pardue '60 Chevrolet	59	50	A Frame
23	19	74	L D Austin	Austin '61 Chevrolet	53	---	A Frame
24	3	27	Junior Johnson	Holly Farms '61 Pontiac	42	---	Engine
25	9	17	Fred Harb	Harb '61 Ford	38	---	Engine
26	17	43	Maurice Petty	Petty Eng '61 Plymouth	16	---	Fuel Tank

Time of Race: 1 hour, 41 minutes
Average Speed: 59.405 mph
Pole Winner: Joe Weatherly - 68.543 mph
Lap Leaders: ....Joe Weatherly -199, Jack Smith 200
Cautions:
Margin of Victory:
Attendance: 3,000

Race No. 1

Smith Bumps Weatherly; Wins Battle of Concord

CONCORD, NC (Nov 5, 1961) -- Jack Smith bumped Joe Weatherly into the infield in the final lap and scampered home first in the 100-mile Grand National race at Concord Speedway.

The 200 lapper was the opener for the 1962 NASCAR season and was Smith's 17th career Grand National triumph.

Weatherly paced the 26 car field most of the way, but was the victim of the Smith nudge in the first turn of the final lap around the half-mile dirt track. Smith went on to win by more than a half lap as Weatherly recovered to finish second. Third place fell to Cotton Owens as Rex White finished fourth and Ned Jarrett fifth. As the cars came to a halt in the pits, both princi-

ple drivers approached each other. A few choice words were exchanged and fans rushed onto the track to support their personal favorite.

Quivering with emotion, Smith told the 3,000 spectators via the Public Address, "Joe crossed up in front of me so I bumped him. I don't like to rough anyone up, but I couldn't help what happened."

Later, afraid his emotional voice might be mistaken for fear, Smith quickly squared the record by saying, "If Joe isn't satisfied with my explanation, I'm always ready to settle it with fists."

Weatherly had his own version. "He came in at the bottom of the turn and his right front bumper hit my left rear wheel, causing me to spin out. If a guy rides me clean, that's all right. But not this. I promise you this isn't the last time Smith and I will run together."

High ranking NASCAR official John Bruner, Sr. said he saw no basis for a protest. "The way I saw it, both men were driving hard."

Smith covered the 100 miles at an average speed of 59.405 mph.

Grand National Race No. 2
200 Laps at Asheville-Weaverville Speedway
Weaverville, NC
100 Miles on Half-mile Paved Track
November 12, 1961

Fin	St	No.	Driver	Team / Car	Laps	Money	Status
1	5	4	Rex White	White-Clements '61 Chevrolet	200	$800	Running
2	12	86	Buck Baker	Baker '61 Chrysler	200	525	Running
3	1	8	Joe Weatherly	Bud Moore '61 Pontiac	200	375	Running
4	6	46	Jack Smith	Smith '61 Pontiac	200	275	Running
5	4	11	Ned Jarrett	B G Holloway '61 Chevrolet	200	350	Running
6	3	85	Tommy Irwin	Monroe Shook '61 Chevrolet	200	215	Running
7	8	43	Richard Patty	Petty Eng '61 Plymouth	199	175	Running
8	9	44	Jim Paschal	J H Petty '61 Pontiac	198	150	Running
9	15	64	Bill Morton	'60 Chevrolet	192	140	Running
10	20	36	Larry Thomas	Wade Younts '60 Chevrolet	187	130	Running
11	19	55	Tom Cox	Ray Herlocker '60 Plymouth	187	125	Running
12	16	19	Herman Beam	Beam '60 Ford	183	110	Running
13	13	54	Jimmy Pardue	Pardue '59 Chevrolet	183	100	Running
14	25	62	Curtis Crider	Crider '61 Mercury	179	85	Running
15	27	58	Bob Cooper	'60 Ford	178	70	Running
16	22	1	George Green	Jess Potter '60 Chevrolet	169	60	Rear End
17	21	77	Joe Jones	'60 Ford	168	50	Running
18	23	68	Ed Livingston	Curtis Crider '60 Ford	163	50	Running
19	14	71	Bob Waddell	'60 Dodge	161	50	Running
20	26	25	Lester Hicks	'60 Dodge	158	50	Engine
21	18	23	Doug Yates	Yates '61 Plymouth	152	50	Spindle
22	11	48	G C Spencer	'60 Chevrolet	149	50	Running
23	17	89	Mark Hurley	'59 Pontiac	145	---	Bearing
24	24	93	Lee Reitzel	Reitzel '60 Ford	137	---	Axle
25	10	59	Fred Harb	Lynn Holloway '61 Pontiac	60	---	Brakes
26	2	27	Junior Johnson	Holly Farms '61 Pontiac	35	---	Pan
27	7	14	Joe Lee Johnson	Johnson '61 Chevrolet	8	---	T Bar

Time of Race: 1 hour, 27 minutes, 38 seconds
Average Speed: 68.467 mph
Pole Winner: Joe Weatherly - 81.743 mph
Lap Leaders: Joe Weatherly 1-16, Rex White 17-32, Jim Paschal 33-63, Buck Baker 64-69
   Paschal 70-93, White 94-200
Cautions: 3 for 14 laps
Margin of victory: 60 yards
Attendance: 6,500

Race No. 2

Weaverville 100 to White; 3-way Tie for Point Lead

WEAVERVILLE, NC (Nov 12, 1961) -- Rex White hammered down his 21st career win in the 100-mile Grand National race at Asheville-Weaverville Speedway, an event tagged the "Rain Check 200". Most of the 6,500 spectators were admitted free, having held ticket stubs from the August 13th Western North Carolina 500, which was curtailed at 258 laps when the track tore up.

White grabbed the lead for good in the 94th lap and crossed the finish line a scant 60 yards in front of runner-up Buck Baker. Joe Weatherly was a close third, Jack Smith was fourth with Ned Jarrett fifth and Tommy Irwin sixth. The first six finishers were all running in the lead lap, the first time that has been done in a 100-mile Grand National race on a short track.

Weatherly led the first 16 laps before White jumped into the lead. Veteran Jim Paschal led for 31 laps after getting around White in the 33rd lap. Baker took the lead on lap 64, but Paschal came right back on lap 70. Once White made his move, he held command the rest of the way.

Paschal fell off the pace with tire problems in the closing stages and wound up eighth. Three caution flags consumed 14 laps, lowering White's average speed to 68.467 mph.

White, Smith and Weatherly were all deadlocked for the Grand National point lead with 752 points.

Grand National Race No. 3
40 Laps at Daytona International Speedway
Daytona Beach, FL
100 Miles on 2.5-mile Paved Track
February 16, 1962

Fin	St	No.	Driver	Team / Car	Laps	Money	Status
1	1	22	Fireball Roberts	Jim Stephens '62 Pontiac	40	$1,000	Running
2	2	47	Jack Smith	Smith '62 Pontiac	40	600	Running
3	4	6	Cotton Owens	Owens '62 Pontiac	40	400	Running
4	6	0	Dan Gurney	LaFayette '62 Ford	40	300	Running
5	3	27	Junior Johnson	Holly Farms '62 Pontiac	40	300	Running
6	7	66	Larry Frank	Ratus Walters '62 Ford	40	250	Running
7	11	53	Bob Burdick	Roy Burdick '61 Pontiac	40	225	Running
8	9	86	Buddy Baker	Buck Baker '62 Chrysler	39	175	Running
9	10	84	Ernie Gahan	Ed Hinton '61 Ford	39	150	Running
10	22	25	Jim Bennett	Thurman Wilkes '61 Ford	39	140	Running
11	21	75	Ralph Earnhardt	Robert Smith '61 Pntiac	39	135	Running
12	17	14	Charley Griffith	Adcox-Kirby '62 Chevrolet	39	125	Running
13	15	42	Bunkie Blackburn	Petty Eng '62 Plymouth	39	115	Running
14	13	31	Jim McGuirk	'61 Ford	39	100	Running
15	14	2	Jim Paschal	Cliff Stewart '62 Pontiac	38	85	Running
16	20	36	Larry Thomas	Wade Younts '62 Dodge	38	75	Running
17	8	32	Bill Wimble	Dave McCredy '62 Pontiac	38	75	Running
18	24	95	Jim Cushman	Jack Russell '61 Plymouth	37	75	Running
19	18	88	Sal Tovella	Tom Hawkins '61 Ford	36	50	Running
20	16	58	John Roger	'61 Pontiac	35	50	Fan Belt
21	23	38	G C Spencer	Mat DeMatthews '61 Ford	35	50	Fuel
22	25	60	Thomas Cox	Ray Herlocker '60 Plymouth	22	50	Running
23	19	01	Harlan Richardson	Luther Costales '62 Ford	17	50	Oil Pres
24	5	28	Fred Lorenzen	LaFayette '62 Ford	8	50	Engine
25	12	92	Gerald Duke	Donald Harrison '62 Ford	5	---	Running

Time of Race: 38 minutes, 13 seconds
Average Speed: 156.999 mph
Pole Winner: Fireball Roberts - 158.744 mph
Lap Leaders: - - - - - - - - - - - - - - - Fireball Roberts   -40
Cautions: None
Margin of Victory:
Attendance:

Race No. 3

Roberts Shakes Johnson; Grabs Daytona 100 Qualifying Race

DAYTONA BEACH, FL (Feb 16) -- Fireball Roberts put his Pontiac on the point early in the race and won the scorching 100-mile qualifying race in preparation for the Daytona 500 at Daytona International Speedway.

Roberts and Junior Johnson had broken away from the pack in the 40 lap sprint around the 2.5-mile track, and Fireball's Stephens-Yunick Pontiac breezed home first when his rival's fuel tank ran low. The 38 minute race was run without a caution flag.

Jack Smith finished in second place, with Cotton Owens third. Dan Gurney, driving his first Grand National, finished fourth with Junior Johnson fifth.

Both Roberts and Johnson took turns drafting each other, which somewhat miffed Roberts. "I pulled him more than he pulled me," he remarked. "We evened it out though. I let him lead for a while and refused to go any faster. I just followed him like he did me."

With the drafting art still in its developmental stage, the lead driver usually would claim the car in his wake would slow him down.

There were no accidents, which helped Roberts establish an all time Grand National race record of 156.999 mph.

It was the 26th career win for the hometown throttle-stomper.

Grand National Race No. 4
40 Laps at Daytona International Speedway
Daytona Beach, FL
100 Miles on 2.5-mile Paved Track
February 16, 1962

Fin	St	No.	Driver	Team / Car	Laps	Money	Status
1	3	8	Joe Weatherly	Bud Moore '62 Pontiac	40	$1,000	Running
2	5	29	Nelson Stacy	Holman-Moody '62 Ford	40	600	Running
3	7	4	Rex White	Louis Clements '62 Chevrolet	40	400	Running
4	12	43	Richard Petty	Petty Eng '62 Plymouth	39	300	Running
5	11	7	Johnny Allen	B G Holloway '62 Chevrolet	39	300	Running
6	16	37	Wally Dallenbach	Don House '61 Ford	39	250	Running
7	15	5	Woodie Wilson	Leroy Faucett '61 Pontiac	39	225	Running
8	13	44	Bob Welborn	J H Petty '62 Pontiac	38	175	Tire
9	20	63	George Alsobrook	Ratus Walters '61 Ford	38	150	Running
10	18	52	Cale Yarborough	Julian Buesink '61 Ford	38	140	Running
11	24	23	Red Farmer	Frank Rhoads '61 Ford	38	135	Running
12	21	68	Ed Linvingtston	Livingston '61 Ford	38	125	Running
13	23	62	Curtis Crider	Crider '61 Mercury	37	115	Running
14	22	19	Herman Beam	Beam '62 Ford	35	100	Running
15	2	94	Banjo Matthews	Matthews '62 Pontiac	30	85	Fuel Pmp
16	9	11	Ned Jarrett	B G Holloway '62 Chevrolet	22	75	Rock Arm
17	14	87	Buck Baker	Baker '62 Chrysler	12	75	Timing
18	25	98	Paul Burrow	'62 Ford	8	75	U Joint
19	17	77	Elmo Langley	Ratus Walters '61 Ford	5	50	Engine
20	10	90	Marvin Panch	Bob Osiecki '62 Dodge	4	50	Crash
21	4	72	Bobby Johns	Shorty Johns '62 Pontiac	4	50	Crash
22	1	39	Darel Dieringer	Ray Fox '61 Pontiac	3	50	Crash
23	6	15	Speedy Thompson	Holman-Moody '62 Ford	3	50	Crash
24	19	9	Art Brady	Ewell Williams '62 Ford	3	50	Crash
25	8	85	Tommy Irwin	Monroe Shook '62 Chevrolet	1	---	Crash

Time of Race: 41 minutes, 16 seconds
Average Speed: 145.395 mph
Pole Winner: Darel Dieringer - 155.086 mph
Fastest Qualifier: Joe Weatherly - 156.862 mph
Lap Leaders: Banjo Matthews 1-11, Joe Weatherly 12-40
Cautions:
Margin of victory:
Attendance:

Pole sitter Darel Dieringer's Pontiac is crunched early in Daytona Qualifier

crash in the opening laps. Marvin Panch, Speedy Thompson and Bobby Johns were also knocked out.

After the race, Dieringer was replaced as the driver of the primary Fox entry by David Pearson. Pearson, who did not compete in either of the 100-milers, had not logged an official qualifying lap for the second Fox entry. Dieringer was therefore not eligible for the main event in the other Fox car.

Matthews, who has come close to winning his first Grand National race many times, was running second when his Pontiac lost fuel pressure. He wound up 15th.

Weatherly averaged 145.395 mph in his Bud Moore Pontiac.

Race No. 4

Joe Outlasts Banjo to Win 2nd Qualifier

DAYTONA BEACH, FL (Feb 16) -- Joe Weatherly zipped past Banjo Matthews in the 12th lap and led the rest of the way to take top honors in the second 100-mile Grand National sprint race at Daytona International Speedway. It was the 14th career win for the stubby 39 year-old Norfolk, VA Pontiac driver.

Nelson Stacy finished second in a Holman-Moody Ford and Rex White third. Fourth place went to Richard Petty and fifth to Johnny Allen.

Darel Dieringer won the pole for the 100-miler by winning a special 25-mile pole position race 5 days earlier. The Indianapolis, IN speedster, wheeling a Ray Fox Pontiac, was eliminated in a spectacular six car

Tommy Irwin #85 skids out of control in Daytona's 100-mile Qualifier. Wally Dallenbach #37 breezes past on the outside

Race No. 5

Roberts Survives Petty Protest; Wins Daytona 500

DAYTONA BEACH, FL (Feb 18) -- Glenn "Fireball" Roberts, the hometown favorite, gunned his Stephens/Yunick Pontiac into the lead for good with 50 laps remaining and sprinted to a 27 second victory over young Richard Petty in the fourth annual Daytona 500.

It was the first 500 that Roberts had finished. He was the dominant factor during SpeedWeeks -- earning the pole position, winning a 100-mile qualifier and taking the 500. Roberts led for 144 of the 200 laps around the 2.5-mile tri-oval superspeedway.

For the third time in the four runnings, the celebrated event was run without a caution flag. Roberts averaged 152.529 mph for his 27th career win.

Fireball, the clear cut favorite, fought off the pesky Petty in the late stages. Petty, only 24 years old, tucked the nose of his underpowered Plymouth behind Roberts' tailpipes and got a free ride into second place. From the 67th lap until the finish, Petty was the only driver other than Roberts to lead the race.

Smokey Yunick, chief mechanic on Fireball Roberts' winning Pontiac

After the race, the Petty Engineering crew filed a protest against Roberts' victory. They claimed the Smokey Yunick led crew had used more than the six crewmen during pit stops. Three days later, Roberts' victory was upheld with this formal announcement from NASCAR: "Investigation revealed the protest was made on hearsay and was groundless and is hereby denied."

Joe Weatherly boosted his point lead to 136 by taking third place. Jack Smith, second in the point race, was fourth. Fred Lorenzen came in fifth and David Pearson sixth.

Roberts and Yunick mapped "flat out" strategy for the race and the swift pace caused Roberts to run out of

Grand National Race No. 5
200 Laps at Daytona International Speedway
Daytona Beach, FL
"Daytona 500"
500 Miles on 2.5-mile Paved Track
February 18, 1962

Fin	St	No.	Driver	Team / Car	Laps	Money	Status
1	1	22	Fireball Roberts	Jim Stephens '62 Pontiac	200	$24,190	Running
2	10	43	Richard Petty	Petty Eng '62 Plymouth	200	10,250	Running
3	4	8	Joe Weatherly	Bud Moore '62 Pontiac	199	7,100	Running
4	3	47	Jack Smith	Smith '62 Pontiac	199	4,025	Running
5	34	28	Fred Lorenzen	LaFayette '62 Ford	199	2,975	Running
6	2	39	David Pearson	Ray Fox '62 Pontiac	198	2,075	Running
7	8	4	Rex White	Louis Clements '62 Chevrolet	197	1,550	Running
8	35	94	* Banjo Matthews	Matthews '62 Pontiac	197	1,050	Running
9	38	11	Ned Jarrett	B G Holloway '62 Chevrolet	196	850	Running
10	17	44	Bob Welborn	J H Petty '62 Pontiac	194	750	Running
11	36	32	Bill Wimble	Dave McCredy '61 Pontiac	193	600	Running
12	16	84	Ernie Gahan	Ed Hinton '61 Ford	192	500	Running
13	24	42	Bunkie Blackburn	Petty Eng '62 Plymouth	192	500	Running
14	28	2	Jim Paschal	Cliff Stewart '61 Pontiac	186	475	Running
15	42	95	Jim Cushman	Jack Russell '61 Plymouth	186	475	Running
16	12	7	Johnny Allen	B G Holloway '62 Chevrolet	183	450	Running
17	33	15	Speedy Thompson	Holman-Moody '62 Ford	182	450	Engine
18	45	01	Billy Wade	Luther Costales '62 Ford	182	425	Running
19	46	98	Paul Burrow	'62 Ford	181	425	Running
20	47	60	Thomas Cox	Ray Herlocker '60 Plymouth	180	425	Running
21	43	9	Art Brady	Ewell Williams '62 Ford	176	400	Running
22	29	19	Herman Beam	Beam '62 Ford	175	400	Running
23	27	62	Curtis Crider	Crider '61 Mercury	173	400	Running
24	26	31	Jim McGuirk	'61 Ford	157	400	Engine
25	44	92	Gerald Duke	Don Harrison '62 Ford	150	400	Engine
26	19	63	George Alsobrook	Ratus Walters '61 Ford	144	400	Running
27	7	0	Dan Gurney	Holman-Moody '62 Ford	134	400	Engine
28	31	87	Buck Baker	Baker '62 Chrysler	89	400	Crash
29	15	86	Buddy Baker	Buck Baker '62 Chrysler	83	400	Heating
30	30	72	Bobby Johns	Shorty Johns '62 Pontiac	81	400	Trans
31	40	36	Larry Thomas	Wade Younts '62 Dodge	76	400	Distrib
32	25	68	Ed Livingston	Livingston '61 Ford	75	400	Oil Pres
33	5	6	Cotton Owens	Owens '62 Pontiac	73	400	Clutch
34	9	27	Junior Johnson	Holly Farms '62 Pontiac	72	400	Engine
35	13	53	Bob Burdick	Roy Burdick '62 Pontiac	55	400	Crankshft
36	20	75	Ralph Earnhardt	Robert Smith '61 POntiac	54	400	Engine
37	14	37	Wally Dallenbach	Don House '61 Ford	53	400	Engine
38	22	14	Charley Griffith	Adcox-Kirby '62 Chevrolet	53	400	Rock Arm
39	41	88	Sal Tovella	Tom Hawkins '61 Ford	41	400	H Gasket
40	23	23	Red Farmer	Frank Rhoads '61 Ford	34	400	Spindle
41	18	85	Jim Bennett	Thurman Wilkes '61 Ford	31	400	H Gasket
42	32	85	Tommy Irwin	Monroe Shook '62 Chevrolet	26	400	Piston
43	6	29	Nelson Stacy	Holman-Moody '62 Ford	25	400	Engine
44	37	90	Marvin Panch	Bob Osiecki '62 Dodge	19	400	Rear End
45	48	38	G C Spencer	Matthew DeMathews '61 Ford	15	400	Clutch
46	11	66	Larry Frank	Ratus Walters '61 Ford	14	400	Engine
47	39	77	Elmo Langley	Ratus Walters '61 Ford	4	400	Engine
48	21	52	Cale Yarbrough	Julian Buesink '61 Ford	4	400	Electric

* Relieved by Darel Dieringer
Time of Race: 3 hours, 10 minutes, 41 seconds
Average Speed: 152.529 mph
Pole Winner: Fireball Roberts - 156.999 mph
Lap Leaders: Joe Weatherly 1, Fireball Roberts 2-3, Junior Johnson 4, Roberts 5-15, Cotton Owens 16, Johnson 17, Roberts 18-19, Johnson 20-25, Roberts 26-34, Johnson 35-41, Richard Petty 42-46, Roberts 47-48, Johnson 49-52, Roberts 53-63, Johnson 64-66, Roberts 67-80, Petty 81-88, Roberts 89-112, Petty 113-130, Roberts 131-149, Petty 150, Roberts 151-200
Cautions: None
Margin of Victory: 27 seconds
Attendance: 58,070

gas twice in the early going. Weatherly, Cotton Owens and Junior Johnson all led for brief stages before Roberts worked his way into command with Petty in his

Bill Amick's practice crash kept the Wood Brothers Ford out of the Daytona 500

slip-stream.

Buck Baker crashed his Chrysler into the wall in the 83rd lap. He was taken to the hospital with minor rib injuries.

Darel Dieringer, who was left without a ride when only one of the Ray Fox Pontiacs was allowed to start, relieved Banjo Matthews and brought his Pontiac home eighth.

Cale Yarborough, a spunky kid out of Timmonsville, SC, made his first Daytona 500 in a Julian Buesink Ford. Buesink owned the Oldsmobile that Bill Rexford drove to the 1950 Grand National championship. Yarborough made only four laps before the wires shorted out, leaving him with a last place effort.

Race No. 6

Little Joe Pockets 39-miler After 2 Rain-outs

CONCORD, NC (Feb 25) -- A heavy thundershower washed out the 100-mile Grand National race at Concord Speedway with Joe Weatherly in front after 78 of the scheduled 200 laps had been completed. Since less than half the laps had been completed, the race was not originally declared official. However, the scheduled completion was again rained out and sanctioning NASCAR paid the drivers half the prize money based on the running order at 78 laps.

Weatherly started on the pole and led the entire 78 laps before 8,000 spectators. A three-car wreck took

out contenders Fred Lorenzen and Rex White along with Stick Elliott, who was three laps behind. Weatherly averaged 53.161 mph for his 15th career win.

Richard Petty was credited with second place with Ralph Earnhardt third, Jack Smith fourth and Buddy Baker fifth.

Ned Jarrett's car was the first out of the race, departing after 17 laps with a blown engine.

Grand National Race No. 6
200 Laps at Concord Speedway
Concord, NC
100 Miles on Half-mile Dirt Track
February 25, 1962

Fin	St	No.	Driver	Team / Car	Laps	Money	Status
1	1	8	Joe Weatherly	Bud Moore '61 Pontiac	78	$500	Running
2		43	Richard Petty	Petty Eng '62 Plymouth	78	300	Running
3		75	Ralph Earnhardt	Robert Smith '61 Pontiac	77	200	Running
4		47	Jack Smith	Smith '61 Pontiac	77	150	Running
5		87	Buddy Baker	Buck Baker '61 Chrysler	77	138	Running
6		2	Jim Paschal	Cliff Stewart '62 Pontiac	76	120	Running
7		48	G C Spencer	'61 Chevrolet	76	100	Running
8		34	Wendell Scott	Scott '61 Chevrolet	75	88	Running
9		85	Tommy Irwin	Monroe Shook '61 Chevrolet	72	75	Running
10		60	Tom Cox	Ray Herlocker '60 Plymouth	72	70	Running
11		62	Curtis Crider	Crider '61 Mercury	71	65	Running
12		19	Herman Beam	Beam '60 Ford	71	60	Running
13		6	Cotton Owens	Owens '62 Pontiac	69	55	Engine
14		148	Bill McDonald	'61 Chevrolet	69	50	Running
15		4	Rex White	Louis Clements '61 Chevrolet	51	43	Crash
16		28	Fred Lorenzen	LaFayette '62 Ford	51	38	Crash
17		18	Stick Elliott	Toy Bolton '60 Ford	48	33	Crash
18		93	Lee Reitzel	Reitzel '60 Ford	38	30	Radiator
19		51	Bob Cooper	'60 Ford	31	25	Engine
20		1	Ned Jarrett	B G Holloway '60 Chevrolet	17	25	Engine

* Race shortened to 78 laps due to rain
Time of Race: 44 minutes, 01 second
Average Speed: 53.161 mph
Pole Winner: Joe Weatherly
Lap Leaders: Joe Weatherly 1-78
Cautions:
Margin of Victory:
Attendance: 8,000

Race No. 7

White Wrecks; Weatherly Wins Weaverville

WEAVERVILLE, NC (March 4) -- Joe Weatherly took the lead in the 144th lap when leader Rex White crashed and went on to win the 100-mile Grand National race at the Asheville-Weaverville Speedway.

Weatherly had his hands full for the first 140 laps, then swept to a three lap victory over Jim Paschal at the finish. Buddy Baker wound up third, Maurice Petty was fourth, and Jack Smith came in fifth.

White grabbed the lead at the outset and held on for the first 119 laps in a bumper-to-bumper, crowd pleasing duel with upstart driver Tommy Irwin. Irwin started second and zoomed into the lead on lap 120. Ten laps later White was back in front, but he hit the wall while holding a narrow lead.

Irwin, making one of his finest efforts, had problems in the pits and lost a lap under caution when his Monroe Shook pit crew had trouble changing a tire. Weatherly took the lead during the yellow and led the rest of the way.

Irwin had scrambled back up to second place when a right rear wheel broke in the final 10 laps. He wound up getting seventh place money.

A crowd of 5,000 braved bleak and overcast conditions to see Weatherly average 75.471 mph. The Norfolk, VA speedster had now won three of the first seven races in the 1962 season.

Grand National Race No. 8
200 Laps at Savannah Speedway
Savannah, GA
"St. Patrick's Day 200"
100 Miles on Half-mile Dirt Track
March 17, 1962

Fin	St	No.	Driver	Team / Car	Laps	Money	Status
1	4	47	Jack Smith	Smith '61 Pontiac	200	$1,000	Running
2	9	6	Cotton Owens	Owens '60 Pontiac	200	600	Running
3	3	8	Joe Weatherly	Bud Moore '61 Pontiac	198	400	Running
4	13	62	Curtis Cruder	Crider '61 Mercury	190	300	Running
5	1	4	Rex White	Louis Clements '61 Chevrolet	183	275	Axle
6	10	60	Tom Cox	Ray Herlocker '60 Plymouth	182	240	Running
7	11	34	Wendell Scott	Scott '61 Chevrolet	177	200	Running
8	15	19	Herman Beam	Beam '60 Ford	173	175	Running
9	5	87	Buddy Baker	Buck Baker '61 Chrysler	161	150	Running
10	14	1	George Green	Jess Potter '60 Chevrolet	156	140	Tie Rod
11	7	2	Jim Paschal	Cliff Stewart '62 Pontiac	155	130	Oil Pan
12	12	48	G C Spencer	Floyd Powell '60 Chevrolet	150	120	Drive Sh
13	6	11	Ned Jarrett	B G Holloway '62 Chevroelt	134	310	Oil Pan
14	8	43	Richard Petty	Petty Eng '62 Plymouth	52	100	Ball Joint
15	2	86	Darel Dieringer	Buck Baker '61 Chrysler	36	85	Crash
16	16	68	Ed Livingston	Livingston '61 Ford	6	75	H Gasket

Time of Race: 1 hour, 41 minutes, 45 seconds
Average Speed: 58.775 mph
Pole Winner: Rex White - 70.588 mph
Lap Leaders: Joe Weatherly 1-36, Ned Jarrett 37-117, Cotton Owens 118-152,
    Jack Smith 153-200
Cautions: 3
Margin of Victory: 3/4 lap
Attendance: 7,000

Grand National Race No. 7
200 Laps at Asheville-Weaverville
Speedway
Weaverville, NC
100 Miles on Half-mile Paved Track
March 4, 1962

Fin	St	No.	Driver	Team / Car	Laps	Money	Status
1	3	8	Joe Weatherly	Bud Moore '61 Pontiac	200	$1,000	Running
2	5	2	Jim Paschal	Cliff Stewart '62 Pontiac	197	600	Running
3	12	87	Buddy Baker	Buck Baker '61 Chrysler	197	400	Running
4	15	41	Maurice Petty	Petty Eng '62 Plymouth	192	300	Running
5	4	47	Jack Smith	Smith '61 Pontiac	191	275	Running
6	14	75	Ralph Earnhardt	Robert Smith '61 Pontiac	191	240	Running
7	2	85	Tommy Irwin	Monroe Shook '61 Chevrolet	190	200	Wheel
8	7	43	Richard Petty	Petty Eng '62 Plymouth	190	175	Running
9	17	95	Jim Cushman	Jack Russell '61 Plymouth	189	150	Running
10	20	1	George Green	Jess Potter '60 Chevrolet	187	140	Running
11	13	19	Herman Beam	Beam '60 Ford	185	130	Running
12	11	34	Wendell Scott	Scott '61 Chevrolet	185	120	Running
13	19	60	Tom Cox	Ray Herlocker '60 Plymouth	184	110	Running
14	18	62	Curtis Crider	Crider '61 Mercury	182	100	Running
15	21	51	Bob Cooper	'60 Ford	176	85	Running
16	10	11	Ned Jarrett	B G Holloway '62 Chevrolet	169	75	Running
17	6	14	Joe Lee Johnson	Adcox-Kirby '62 Chevrolet	148	65	Engine
18	1	4	Rex White	Louis Clements '61 Chevrolet	143	60	Crash
19	16	148	Bill McDonald	'61 Chevrolet	52	50	Rear End
20	8	48	G C Spencer	Floyd Powell '61 Chevrolet	36	50	Axle
21	9	86	Junior Johnson	Buck Baker '61 Chrysler	8	50	Crash

Time of Race: 1 hour, 19 minutes, 30 seconds
Average Speed: 75.471 mph
Pole Winner: Rex White - 80.46 mph
Lap Leaders: Rex White 1-119, Tommy Irwin 120-129, White 130-143, Weatherly 144-200
Cautions: 1
Margin of Victory: 3 laps plus
Attendance: 5,000

Race No. 8

Jack Smith Limps to Victory In St. Patrick's Day 200

SAVANNAH, GA (Mar. 17) -- Gushing oil like a Texas well, Jack Smith's Pontiac limped across the finish line nearly a lap ahead of Cotton Owens to win the St. Patrick's Day 200 at the new Savannah Speedway. It was the second win of the year for the Sandy Springs, GA driver.

Smith took the lead from Owens in the 153rd lap and led the rest of the way despite a severe oil leak that surfaced in the final laps. Third place went to point leader Joe Weatherly who endured three pit stops in the 100-miler. Curtis Crider came in fourth and pole sitter Rex White, who was on the sidelines when the checkered flag fell, got credit for fifth.

Three caution flags flew as the new track peeled badly. The third caution was thrown to allow officials to water down the track. Dust conditions held drivers' visibility to near zero.

Weatherly led the opening 36 laps before Ned Jarrett

flashed past in his Chevrolet. The Newton, NC defending Grand National champion was holding down first place when he began to show smoke which eventually put him out of the race. Owens led for 35 laps before Smith assumed command.

Smith averaged 58.775 mph before a crowd of 7,000. Darel Dieringer, filling in for the injured Buck Baker, qualified a Chrysler on the front row but crashed after 36 laps.

Rex White celebrates victory at Hillsboro

Grand National Race No. 9
110 Laps at Orange Speedway
Hillsboro, NC
99 Miles on .9-mile Dirt Track
March 18, 1962

Fin	St	No.	Driver	Team / Car	Laps	Money	Status
1	3	4	Rex White	Louis Clements '61 Chevrolet	110	$1,000	Running
2	2	43	Richard Petty	Petty Eng '62 Plymouth	110	600	Running
3	7	2	Jim Paschal	Cliff Stewart '62 Pontiac	110	400	Running
4	21	47	Jack Smith	Smith '61 Pontiac	110	300	Running
5	6	87	Buddy Baker	Buck Baker '61 Chrysler	109	275	Running
6	8	41	Maurice Petty	Petty Eng '62 Plymouth	107	240	Running
7	13	75	Ralph Earnhardt	Robert Smith '61 Pontiac	105	200	Running
8	14	60	Tom Cox	Ray Herlocker '60 Plymouth	105	175	Running
9	11	86	Buck Baker	Baker '61 Chrysler	105	150	Running
10	9	11	Ned Jarrett	B G Holloway '62 Chevrolet	105	340	Running
11	1	8	Joe Weatherly	Bud Moore '61 Pontiac	102	130	Trans
12	12	34	Wendell Scott	Scott '61 Chevrolet	102	120	Running
13	15	68	Ed Livingston	Livingston '61 Ford	99	110	Running
14	18	1	George Green	Jess Potter '60 Chevrolet	97	100	Running
15	16	19	Herman Beam	Beam '60 Ford	94	85	Running
16	17	62	Curtis Crider	Crider '61 Mercury	84	75	Oil Leak
17	20	51	Bob Cooper	'60 Ford	72	65	Rear End
18	19	18	Stick Elliott	Toy Bolton '60 Ford	68	60	Distributor
19	10	48	G C Spencer	Floyd Powell '60 Chevrolet	36	50	Radiator
20	4	6	Cotton Owens	Owens '60 Pontiac	28	50	Heating
21	5	85	Tommy Irwin	Monroe Shook '61 Chevrolet	0	50	Crash

Time of Race: 1 hour, 08 minutes, 19 seconds
Average Speed: 86.948 mph
Pole Winner: Joe Weatherly - 96.285 mph
Lap Leaders: Joe Weatherly 1-24, Richard Petty 25-47, Weatherly 48-102, Petty 103-105, White 106-110
Cautions:
Margin of Victory: 2 car lengths
Attendance: 9,000

Jim Paschal finished third, Jack Smith was fourth and Buddy Baker fifth.

Point leader Joe Weatherly was leading by almost a full lap when the transmission of his Bud Moore Pontiac gave out with only eight laps to go. Petty took the lead when Weatherly departed but could hold off White for only three laps.

White beat Petty by a mere two car lengths at the stripe.

Tommy Irwin and Buck Baker crashed in the opening lap as a cloud of dust shrouded the first turn. Baker blamed the accident on the dust, and officials red flagged the race for an hour to water the track.

Weatherly, whose point lead was cut to 80 points over Smith, wound up 11th in the 21 car field. White averaged 86.948 mph for his 22nd career win.

Race No. 10

Muddy Richmond 200 to Rex White

RICHMOND, VA (Apr 1) -- Rex White outlasted two dozen rivals, layers of thick mud and impending darkness to win the Richmond 250 at the Atlantic Rural Fairgrounds Raceway. It was the second win in a row for the Silver Spring, Md veteran.

White pushed his Chevrolet across the finish line a full lap ahead of runner-up Ned Jarrett as darkness curtailed the event at 180 laps. An all night rain left the track surface in less than ideal condition. But with

Race No. 9

White Nabs Petty in Late Race Pass. Takes 99-miler

Hillsboro, NC (Mar 18) -- Rex White galloped into the lead with five laps left and scored a narrow victory over Richard Petty in the 99-mile Grand National race at the refurbished Orange Speedway. It was his second win in the 1962 campaign.

intermittent sunshine, a road grader and several fans using their family cars to iron out the track, the event got underway at 5:03 pm, more than two hours after the scheduled kick-off.

The 25 competitors had to deal with a literal sea of mud. The lead changed hands seven times among six drivers before White took the lead for good with what amounted to eight laps to go.

Junior Johnson wound up third and Joe Weatherly was fourth. Fireball Roberts made a rare short track appearance and took fifth place. After the race, Roberts turned down an offer to drive a Mickey Thompson rear-engine car in the Indianapolis 500.

Five caution flags for 32 laps held White's winning speed to 51.363 mph.

Drivers were forced to draw for their starting positions and Herman "The Turtle" Beam drew the pole. On the pace lap, the Johnson City Ford driver came into the pits, allowing the entire field to pass him. He rejoined the race in last position. Later he remarked that he didn't like the idea of starting in front of all the "hot dogs". Beam eventually wound up in 12th place, 44 laps behind the winner.

Ralph Moody ended a lengthy retirement but parked his Ford after one lap with overheating problems. Clumps of mud had covered his radiator. Larry Frank, Moody's teammate on the Ratus Walters squad, crashed 17 laps later.

Grand National Race No. 10
250 Laps at Atlantic Rural Fairgrounds
Richmond, VA
"Richmond 250"
125 Miles on Half-mile Dirt Track
April 1, 1962

Fin	St	No.	Driver	Team / Car	Laps	Money	Status
1	20	4	Rex White	Louis Clements '61 Chevrolet	180	$1,850	Running
2	2	11	Ned Jarrett	B G Holloway '62 Chevrolet	179	1,300	Running
3	12	27	Junior Johnson	Holly Farms '61 Pontiac	178	800	Running
4	19	8	Joe Weatherly	Bud Moore '61 Pontiac	168	600	Running
5	7	22	Fireball Roberts	Holly Farms '61 Pontiac	163	450	Running
6	21	0	Harold Carmac	Ray Herlocker '60 Plymouth	160	375	Running
7	8	6	Cotton Owens	Owens '60 Pontiac	157	300	Engine
8	9	48	G C Spencer	Floyd Powell '60 Chevrolet	154	250	Engine
9	16	1	George Green	Jess Potter '61 Chevrolet	152	200	Running
10	23	62	Curtis Crider	Crider '61 Mercury	141	200	Drive Sh
11	5	60	Tom Cox	Ray Herlocker '60 Plymouth	140	100	Trans
12	1	19	Herman Beam	Beam '60 Ford	136	100	Running
13	25	76	Jim Bray	'61 Ford	124	100	Runing
14	6	47	Jack Smith	Smith '61 Pontiac	105	100	Running
15	13	17	Fred Harb	Harb '61 Ford	84	100	Heating
16	22	2	Jim Paschal	Cliff Stewart '62 Pontiac	83	75	Heating
17	10	20	Marvin Panch	'61 Ford	67	75	Heating
18	18	34	Wendell Scott	Scott '61 Chevrolet	62	75	Engine
19	15	84	Ernie Gahan	Ed Hinton '61 Ford	53	75	Rear End
20	3	43	Richard Petty	Petty Eng '61 Plymouth	34	75	Radiator
21	11	18	Stick Elliott	Toy Bolton '60 Ford	28	75	Running
22	17	81	Dick Dixon	'61 Ford	23	75	Engine
23	14	77	Larry Frank	Ratus Walters '61 Ford	18	75	Crash
24	4	87	Buck Baker	Baker '61 Chrysler	2	75	Brakes
25	24	66	Ralph Moody	Ratus Walters '62 Ford	1	75	Heating

* Race shortened to 180 laps due to darkness
Time of Race: 1 hour, 45 minutes, 08 seconds
Average Speed: 51.363 mph
Pole Winner: Drew for position
Lap Leaders: Richard Petty 1-34, Ned Jarrett 35-41, Junior Johnson 42-51,
    Marvin Panch 52-67, Jim Paschal 68-83, Jarrett 84-172, White 173-180
Cautions: 5 for 32 laps
Margin of Victory:
Attendance:

Race No. 11

Jarrett Gets First '62 Win in Arclite 200 at Columbia

COLUMBIA, SC (Apr 13) -- Ned Jarrett drove the Bee Gee Holloway Chevrolet to his first win of the year in the Arclite 200 at Columbia Speedway.

Pole winner and point leader Joe Weatherly, driving in the lead lap, finished second to Jarrett. Jack Smith was third, Jim Paschal fourth and G.C. Spencer fifth.

Weatherly continued to lead the standings as Jarrett moved into fifth place, 1,520 points behind the leader.

Fifteen of the 19 cars that started the race were running at the finish. Wendell Scott, the only black driver on the major league stock car racing circuit, crashed his Chevrolet after 166 laps. Rookie Jim Bennett qualified a surprising third, but his Thurman Wilkes Ford was the first car out of the race.

Jarrett averaged 56.710 mph for his ninth career Grand National win.

Race No. 12

Petty Wilkesboro Champ; Herb Thomas Makes Return

NORTH WILKESBORO, NC (Apr 15) -- Richard Petty pushed his Plymouth into the lead on lap 319 and led the rest of the way to win the Gwyn Staley Memorial 400 at North Wilkesboro Speedway. It was Petty's first win of the year and the sixth of his career.

Fred Lorenzen finished second, just four car lengths behind Petty's blue Plymouth. Junior Johnson started on the pole and finished third. Fireball Roberts was fourth and Darel Dieringer fifth in a lightly regarded Dodge.

Grand National Race No. 11
200 Laps at Columbia Speedway
Columbia, SC
"Arclite 200"
100 Miles on Half-mile Dirt Track
April 13, 1962

Fin	St	No.	Driver	Team / Car	Laps	Money	Status
1	7	11	Ned Jarrett	B G Holloway '62 Chevrolet	200	$1,200	Running
2	1	8	Joe Weatherly	Bud Moore '61 Pontiac	200	600	Running
3	2	47	Jack Smith	Smith '61 Pontiac	198	400	Running
4	8	2	Jim Paschal	Cliff Stewart '62 Pontiac	198	300	Running
5	10	48	G C Spencer	Floyd Powell '60 Chevrolet	197	275	Running
6	5	4	Rex White	Louis Clements '61 Chevrolet	197	240	Running
7	6	43	Richard Petty	Petty Eng '61 Plymouth	197	200	Running
8	18	87	Buck Baker	Baker '62 Chrysler	195	175	Running
9	4	75	Ralph Earnhardt	Robert Smith '61 Pontiac	194	150	Running
10	15	60	Tom Cox	Ray Herlocker '60 Plymouth	186	140	Running
11	17	62	Curtis Crider	Crider '61 Mercury	185	130	Running
12	19	18	Stick Elliott	Toy Bolton '61 Ford	185	120	Running
13	13	86	Buddy Baker	Buck Baker '61 Chrysler	184	110	Running
14	9	19	Herman Beam	Beam '60 Ford	183	100	Running
15	14	1	George Green	Jess Potter '61 Chevrolet	183	85	Running
16	11	34	Wendell Scott	Scott '61 Chevrolet	166	75	Crash
17	16	31	Frank Sessons	Gene Stokes '61 Studebaker	160	65	Running
18	12	6	Cotton Owens	Owens '60 Pontiac	33	60	Heating
19	3	25	Jim Bennett	Thurman Wilkes '61 Ford	27	50	Oil Pres

Time of Race: 1 hour, 45 minutes, 48 seconds
Average Speed: 56.710 mph
Pole Winner: Joe Weatherly 64.423 mph
Lap Leaders: - - - - - - - - - - - - - - - Ned Jarrett   -200
Cautions:
Margin of Victory:
Attendance:

and held onto a 322 point lead over Jack Smith, who finished ninth.

Roberts lost three laps on a green flag pit stop but made one of them up as he appeared to have the fastest car in the second half of the race.

An unusual emergency spiced the action. The fuel trucks ran dry of racing gasoline just after the half-way point of the race. Some members of pit crews were seen scurrying around the infield with buckets and hoses in hand, siphoning gas from passenger cars. A caution flag was thrown on lap 250 so that a fuel truck could go get more gas. However it never made it back to the track. Track officials said the large number of cars running at the finish (23 of 35 starters) was

Grand National Race No. 12
400 Laps at North Wilkesboro
Speedway
North Wilkesboro, NC
"Gwyn Staley 400"
250 Miles on .625-mile Paved Track
April 15, 1962

Fin	St	No.	Driver	Team / Car	Laps	Money	Status
1	15	43	Richard Petty	Petty Eng '62 Plymouth	400	$2,725	Running
2	6	28	Fred Lorenzen	LaFayette '62 Ford	400	1,450	Running
3	1	27	Junior Johnson	Holly Farms '61 Pontiac	399	1,110	Running
4	4	22	Fireball Roberts	Banjo Matthews '62 Pontiac	398	850	Running
5	17	90	Darel Dieringer	Bob Osiecki '62 Dodge	396	675	Running
6	21	87	Buck Baker	Baker '62 Chrysler	395	500	Running
7	20	66	Larry Frank	Ratus Walters '62 Ford	391	475	Running
8	2	8	Joe Weatherly	Bud Moore '62 Pontiac	389	590	Running
9	13	47	Jack Smith	Smith '62 Pontiac	387	375	Running
10	3	24	Billy Wade	James Turner '61 Pontiac	382	375	Crash
11	18	48	G C Spencer	Floyd Powell '60 Chevrolet	382	300	Running
12	28	60	Tom Cox	Ray Herlocker '60 Plymouth	381	250	Running
13	19	30	J C Hendricks	Fred Clark '62 Chevrolet	379	250	Running
14	23	91	Herb Thomas	'62 chevrolet	377	200	Running
15	16	36	Larry Thomas	Wade Younts '62 Dodge	373	175	Running
16	11	72	Bobby Johns	Shorty Johns '62 Pontiac	370	175	Running
17	30	95	Jim Cushman	Jack Russell '61 Plymouth	370	150	Running
18	7	85	Tommy Irwin	Monroe Shook '62 Chevrolet	365	175	Running
19	33	62	Curtis Crider	Crider '61 Mercury	362	150	Running
20	27	19	Herman Beam	Beam '62 Ford	360	150	Running
21	26	92	Gerald Duke	Don Harrison '62 Ford	356	100	Running
22	35	1	George Green	Jess Potter '61 Chevrolet	353	100	Runing
23	32	51	Bob Cooper	'60 Plymouth	349	100	Running
24	14	11	Ned Jarrett	B G Holloway '62 Chevrolet	318	375	Engine
25	8	29	Nelson Stacy	Holman-Moody '62 Ford	289	125	Trans
26	24	2	Jim Pascal	Cliff Stewart '62 Pontiac	281	100	Trans
27	25	34	Wendell Scott	Scott '61 Chevrolet	240	100	Running
28	5	54	Jimmy Pardue	Pardue '62 Pontiac	198	150	Crash
29	31	79	Johnny Nave	'60 Ford	169	100	Withdrew
30	9	6	Cotton Owens	Owens '62 Pontiac	163	125	Trans
31	12	4	Rex White	Louis Clements '62 Chevrolet	162	25	Oil Pres
32	10	21	Marvin Panch	Wood Bros '62 Ford	140	25	Rear End
33	22	44	David Pearson	J H Petty '62 Pontiac	90	---	Oil Pres
34	29	23	Doug Yates	Yates '60 Plymouth	23	---	Oil Leak
35	34	50	Bobby Waddell	'60 Dodge	6	---	Distrib

Time of Race: 2 hours, 57 minutes, 01 second
Average Speed: 84.737 mph
Pole Winner: Junior Johnson - 94.142 mph
Lap Leaders: Junior Johnson 1-19, Fireball Roberts 20-114, Joe Weatherly 115-204, Richard Petty 205-264, Ned Jarrett 265-318, Petty 319-400
Cautions: 5
Margin of Victory: 4 car lengths
Attendance: 9,228

Herb Thomas, two time Grand National champion, ended a five year retirement and finished 14th in a Chevrolet, 23 laps off the pace.

Joe Weatherly and Fireball Roberts had engaged in a tight struggle in the middle stages of the 400 lap event on the .625-mile oval. After leading for 90 laps, Roberts tapped the rear of Weatherly's Pontiac. Weatherly scooted up the track and nudged the wall as Petty took the lead for the first time.

Ned Jarrett passed Petty in the 265th lap and led for 54 laps before Petty regained the lead for good. Weatherly lost several laps in the pits getting repairs and was penalized one lap for jumping the green flag on a restart after a caution. The Norfolk, VA driver eventually finished eighth

Richard Petty - winner at North Wilkesboro

responsible for the dwindling supply of gas.

Young Texas hot-shot Billy Wade qualified a stunning third and ran with the leaders in the early going. A tire blew on Wade's Pontiac and he slapped the wall, knocking him down to a 10th place finish. A crowd of 9,228 braved the numbing cold to watch Petty win at an average speed of 84.737 mph.

across the finish line in second place with Joe Weatherly third. Wendell Scott broke into the top five, finishing fourth, with Jim Bennett fifth.

Richard Petty pressed Jarrett in the early going, but the Randleman, NC Plymouth driver fell out on lap 139 with a broken ball joint. Jack Smith, Buck Baker and Rex White were other contenders on the sidelines when the checkered flag fell.

Jarrett averaged 57.480 mph for his 10th career win.

Grand National Race No. 13
200 Laps at Greenville-Pickens Speedway
Greenville, SC
100 Miles on Half-mile Dirt Track
April 19, 1962

Fin	St	No.	Driver	Team / Car	Laps	Money	Status
1	1	11	Ned Jarrett	B G Holloway '62 Chevrolet	200	$1,200	Running
2	8	2	Jim Paschal	Cliff Stewart '62 Pontiac	200	600	Running
3	7	8	Joe Weatherly	Bud Moore '61 Pontiac	200	400	Running
4	6	34	Wendell Scott	Scott '61 Chevrolet	194	300	Running
5	10	25	Jim Bennett	Thurman Wilkes '61 Ford	191	275	Running
6	15	19	Herman Beam	Beam '60 Ford	186	240	Running
7	11	62	Curtis Crider	Crider '61 Mercury	182	200	Running
8	12	18	Stick Elliott	Toy Bolton '60 Ford	172	175	Running
9	17	60	Tom Cox	Ray Herlocker '60 Plymouth	170	150	Running
10	5	48	G C Spencer	Floyd Powell '60 Chevrolet	148	140	Ball Joint
11	2	43	Richard Petty	Petty Eng '62 Plymouth	139	230	Ball Joint
12	9	17	Fred Harb	Harb '61 Ford	104	120	Heating
13	3	47	Jack Smith	Smith '61 Pontiac	89	110	Lug Bolts
14	19	51	Bob Cooper	'60 Ford	81	100	Trans
15	18	55	Neil Castles	'60 Ford	61	85	Running
16	14	86	Buck Baker	Baker '61 Chrysler	44	75	Rear End
17	4	4	Rex White	Louis Clements '61 Chevrolet	41	65	Engine
18	16	1	George Green	Jess Potter '61 Chevrolet	39	60	Engine
19	13	63	George Alsobrook	Ratus Walters '61 Ford	36	50	Heating

Time of Race: 1 hour, 44 minutes, 23 seconds
Average Speed: 57.480 mph
Pole Winner: Ned Jarrett - 66.568 mph
Lap Leaders: - - - - - - - - - - - - - - - Ned Jarrett   -200
Cautions:
Margin of Victory:
Attendance:

Grand National Race No. 14
200 Laps at Rambi Raceway
Myrtle Beach, SC
100 Miles on Half-mile Dirt Track
April 21, 1962

Fin	St	No.	Driver	Team / Car	Laps	Money	Status
1	3	47	Jack Smith	Smith '61 Pontiac	200	$1,000	Running
2	7	43	Richard Petty	Petty Eng '60 Plymouth	198	600	Running
3	1	11	Ned Jarrett	B G Holloway '62 Chevrolet	195	600	Running
4	14	60	Tom Cox	Ray Herlocker '60 Plymouth	188	300	Running
5	12	62	Curtis Crider	Crider '61 Mercury	183	275	Running
6	10	17	Fred Harb	Harb '61 Ford	183	240	Running
7	13	1	George Green	Jess Potter '61 Chevrolet	179	200	Running
8	15	6	Frank Graham	'60 Ford	178	175	Running
9	6	34	Wendell Scott	Scott '61 Chevrolet	176	150	A Frame
10	11	76	Neil Castles	'60 Ford	173	140	Running
11	18	19	Herman Beam	Beam '60 Ford	163	130	Running
12	19	31	Frank Sessons	Gene Stokes '61 Studebaker	159	120	Running
13	2	8	Joe Weatherly	Bud Moore '61 Pontiac	132	110	Rear Axle
14	16	51	Bob Cooper	'60 Ford	129	100	Running
15	4	25	Jim Bennett	Thurman Wilkes '61 Ford	114	85	Flagged
16	5	86	Buck Baker	Baker '61 Chrysler	112	75	Crash
17	9	48	G C Spencer	Floyd Powell '60 Chevrolet	96	65	Cont Arm
18	8	2	Jim Paschal	Cliff Stewart '62 Pontiac	73	60	Piston
19	17	68	Ed Livingston	Livingston '61 Ford	1	50	Trans

Time of Race: 1 hour, 35 minutes, 11 seconds
Average Speed: 63.036 mph
Pole Winner: Ned Jarrett - 68.939 mph
Lap Leaders: - - - - - - - - - - - - - - - Jack Smith   -200
Cautions:
Margin of Victory:
Attendance:

Race No. 13

Ned 'Loves the Lights' -- Wins 2nd Night Race

GREENVILLE, SC (Apr 19) -- Ned Jarrett of Newton, NC tooled his Chevrolet to a narrow win over a pair of Pontiacs in the 200-lap event at Greenville-Pickens Speedway. It was Jarrett's second win of the season, both of them coming under the lights in night races.

Jim Paschal, driving a Cliff Stewart Pontiac, came

Race No. 14

Smith Wins Myrtle Beach As Rookies Shine

MYRTLE BEACH, SC (Apr 21) -- Jack Smith drove his Pontiac to victory in the 100-mile Grand National race at Rambi Raceway for his third win of the year.

Richard Petty was two laps back in second place and Ned Jarrett was third. Rookie Tom Cox wound up fourth and Curtis Crider fifth.

Rookie Jim Bennett, who has been turning in some fine qualifying efforts, started fourth but was out of the race by the 114th lap. Sophomore driver Wendell Scott qualified sixth and was running in the top five when an A-frame snapped on his Chevrolet, knocking him down to a ninth place finish.

Buck Baker crashed his Chrysler in the 112th lap, but the Charlotte, NC veteran was not hurt.

Smith averaged 63.036 mph for his 19th career win.

Race No. 15

Richard Petty Outlasts Rivals in Virginia 500

MARTINSVILLE, VA (Apr 22) -- Richard Petty, 24 year-old driver out of Randleman, NC, outlasted the faster Pontiacs and cruised home first in the Virginia 500 at Martinsville Speedway.

Petty's Plymouth beat Joe Weatherly's Pontiac by a half-lap to take the $3,400 first prize. Rex White finished third, Fred Lorenzen was fourth and Lee Petty, with relief help from Jim Paschal, wound up fifth.

It was the elder Petty's first start since February 24, 1961, when he was gravely injured in a flip over the guard rail at Daytona International Speedway.

Junior Johnson and Fireball Roberts combined to lead 300 of the first 379 laps in their powerful Pontiacs. Neither one, however, was around at the finish. Johnson started 26th in the field of 32 and used an unaccustomed outside groove to rim-ride past his rivals. He took the lead on lap 56 and led for 56 laps before being passed by Petty during one of the two caution periods. Johnson eventually fell out with rear gearing failure on lap 204.

Roberts started back in the 18th spot and worked his way up to the lead by lap 136. From that point on the Daytona fleet-foot proceeded to make a runaway of the race, building up a four lap lead. He was heading for the checkered flag when the rear end of his Pontiac burned out with 85 laps to go.

Petty's second win of the year moved him to third place in the point standings, only 32 points out of second place. Weatherly leads Jack Smith by 430 points.

Petty averaged 66.425 mph before a capacity crowd of 14,500.

Grand National Race No. 15
500 Laps at Martinsville Speedway
Martinsville, VA
"Virginia 500"
250 Miles on Half-mile Paved Track
April 22, 1962

Fin	St	No.	Driver	Team / Car	Laps	Money	Status
1	7	43	Richard Petty	Petty Eng '62 Plymouth	500	$3,400	Running
2	27	8	Joe Weatherly	Bud Moore '62 Pontiac	500	1,625	Running
3	8	4	Rex White	Louis Clements '62 Chevrolet	499	1,210	Running
4	1	28	Fred Lorenzen	LaFayette '61 Ford	499	860	Running
5	5	41	* Lee Petty	Petty Eng '62 Plymouth	499	750	Running
6	3	21	Marvin Panch	Wood Bros '62 Ford	492	650	Running
7	6	47	Jack Smith	Smith '62 Pontiac	492	550	Running
8	10	24	Billy Wade	James Turner '61 Pontiac	487	500	Running
9	13	66	Larry Frank	Ratus Walters '62 Ford	487	400	Running
10	19	90	Darel Dieringer	Bob Osiecki '62 Dodge	469	365	Running
11	20	19	Herman Beam	Beam '62 Ford	461	325	Running
12	29	48	G C Spencer	Floyd Powell '60 Chevrolet	456	275	Coil
13	16	11	Ned Jarrett	B G Holloway '62 Chevrolet	456	450	Running
14	25	34	Wendell Scott	Scott '61 Chevrolet	456	225	Running
15	22	36	Larry Thomas	Wade Younts '62 Dodge	451	150	Running
16	9	54	Jimmy Pardue	Pardue '62 Pontiac	438	150	Rear End
17	12	60	Tom Cox	Ray Herlocker '60 Plymouth	430	150	Ball Joint
18	18	22	Fireball Roberts	Banjo Matthews '62 Pontiac	415	390	Rear End
19	24	62	Curtis Crider	Crider '61 Mercury	410	150	Brakes
20	11	85	Johnny Allen	Monroe Shook '62 Chevrolet	282	150	Rear End
21	2	29	Nelson Stacy	Holman-Moody '62 Ford	248	180	Rear End
22	26	27	Junior Johnson	Holly Farms '61 Pontiac	204	210	Rear End
23	15	87	Buck Baker	Baker '62 Chrysler	202	150	Trans
24	21	1	George Green	Jess Potter '61 Chevrolet	194	150	Engine
25	4	72	Bobby Johns	Shorty Johns '62 Pontiac	111	150	Brakes
26	30	65	Lester Hicks	'60 Dodge	106	100	Engine
27	23	18	Stick Elliott	Toy Bolton '60 Ford	98	100	Rock Arm
28	14	17	Fred Harb	Harb '61 Ford	20	100	Clutch
29	28	51	Bob Cooper	'60 Ford	18	100	Rear End
30	17	75	Ralph Earnhardt	Robert Smith '61 Pontiac	18	100	Fan Belt
31	31	76	Neil Castles	'60 Ford	1	100	Brakes
32	32	79	Johnny Nave	'60 Ford	1	100	Trans

* Relieved by Jim Paschal
Time of Race: 3 hours, 45 minutes, 49 seconds
Average Speed: 66.425 mph
Pole Winner: Fred Lorenzen - 71.287 mph
Lap Leaders: Fred Lorenzen 1-18, Nelson Stacy 19-48, Rex White 49-55, Junior Johnson 56-111, Richard Petty 112-135, Fireball Roberts 136-379, R Petty 380-500
Cautions: 2
Margin of Victory: 1/2 lap   Attendance: 14,500

The beautiful Martinsville Speedway situated in the rolling hills of Southern Virginia

Race No. 16

White in Front When Rains Interrupt Easter Parade

WINSTON-SALEM, NC (Apr 23) -- Rex White of Silver Spring, MD drove his Louis Clements Chevrolet to his fourth win of the year in the rain-abbreviated Easter Monday Grand National race at Bowman-Gray Stadium.

Rain forced officials to stop the race after 108 of the scheduled 200 laps had been completed. Jack Smtih was flagged in second place with Joe Weatherly third, George Dunn fourth and Richard Petty fifth.

Junior Johnson, a crowd favorite, qualified second but was in the pits with two flat tires when the rains came. He got credit for 15th place in the field of 19.

Weatherly held a 414 point lead over Smith in the Grand National point standings.

White averaged 43.392 mph for his 37 minute ride.

Grand National Race No. 16
200 Laps at Bowman-Gray Stadium
Winston-Salem, NC
50 Miles on Quarter-mile Paved Track
April 23, 1962

Fin	St	No.	Driver	Team / Car	Laps	Money	Status
1	1	4	Rex White	Louis Clements '62 Chevrolet	108	$565	Running
2	5	47	Jack Smith	Smith '61 Pontiac	108	475	Running
3	3	8	Joe Weatherly	Bud Moore '62 Poontiac	108	370	Running
4	7	97	George Dunn	Lewis Osborne '62 Chevrolet	108	305	Running
5	6	43	Richard Petty	Petty Eng '61 Plymouth	107	225	Running
6	11	54	Jimmy Pardue	Pardue '62 Pontiac	107	250	Running
7	4	11	Ned Jarrett	B G Holloway '62 Chevrolet	107	410	Running
8	10	2	Jim Paschal	Cliff Stewart '62 Pontiac	106	210	Running
9	8	48	G C Spencer	Floyd Powell '60 Chevrolet	106	170	Running
10	9	17	Fred Harb	Harb '61Ford	105	155	Running
11	12	36	Larry Thomas	Wade Younts '62 Dodge	104	145	Running
12	13	19	Herman Beam	Beam '60 Ford	102	120	Running
13	16	62	Curtis Crider	Crider '60 Ford	102	125	Running
14	17	60	Tom Cox	Ray Herlocker '60 Plymouth	102	100	Running
15	2	27	Junior Johnson	Holly Farms '61 Pontiac	100	100	Tires
16	15	34	Wendell Scott	Scott '61 Chevrolet	96	75	Running
17	18	76	Neil Castles	'60 Ford	31	75	Heating
18	19	7	Bill Delaney	'62 Pontiac	3	60	Handling
19	14	24	Billy Wade	James Turner '61 Pontiac	3	50	Handling

* Race shortened to 108 laps due to rain
Time of Race: 37 minutes, 20 seconds
Average Speed: 43.392 mph
Pole Winner: Rex White - 48417 mph
Lap Leaders:- - - - - - - - - - - - - - Rex White   -108
Cautions:
Margin of Victory:
Attendance:

Grand National Race No. 17
500 Laps at Bristol International Speedway
Bristol, TN
"Volunteer 500"
250 Miles on Half-mile Paved Track
April 29, 1962

Fin	St	No.	Driver	Team / Car	Laps	Money	Status
1	6	72	Bobby Johns	Shorty Johns '62 Pontiac	500	$4,405	Running
2	1	22	Fireball Roberts	Banjo Matthews '62 Pontiac	494	2,500	Running
3	10	47	Jack Smith	Smith '62 Pontiac	492	1,635	Running
4	12	11	Ned Jarrett	B G Holloway '62 Chevrolet	475	1,400	Running
5	25	60	Tom Cox	Ray Herlocker '60 Plymouth	470	850	Running
6	22	19	Herman Beam	Beam '62 Ford	469	850	Running
7	14	6	David Pearson	Cotton Owens '62 Pontiac	461	650	Lug bolts
8	31	34	Wendell Scott	Scott '61 Chevrolet	460	550	Running
9	28	61	Bill Morton	'62 Ford	459	475	Running
10	33	62	Curtis Crider	Crider '61 Mercury	447	400	Running
11	8	8	Joe Weatherly	Bud Moore '62 Pontiac	444	400	Rear End
12	20	86	Buddy Baker	Buck Baker '62 Chrysler	430	275	Engine
13	7	54	Jimmy Pardue	Pardue '62 Pontiac	419	325	Running
14	36	1	George Green	Jess Potter '61 Che;vrolet	417	225	Running
15	27	17	Fred Harb	Harb '61 Ford	370	200	H Gasket
16	11	43	Richard Petty	Petty Eng '62 Plymouth	368	300	Engine
17	13	26	Bunkie Blackburn	'61 Pontiac	359	175	Rear End
18	4	29	Nelson Stacy	Holman-Moody '62 Ford	302	200	Crash
19	18	41	Maurice Petty	Petty Eng '62 Plymouth	297	150	Crash
20	30	64	Gene Blackburn	'60 Chevrolet	274	150	Axle
21	17	85	Johnny Allen	Monroe Shook '62 Chevrolet	225	125	Engine
22	23	14	Joe Lee Johnson	Adcox-Kirby '62 Chevrolet	223	125	Engine
23	19	90	Darel Dieringer	Bob Osiecki '62 Dodge	191	225	Oil Line
24	24	30	Tiny Lund	Fred Clark '62 Chevrolet	187	125	Hub
25	26	48	G C Spencer	Floyd Powell '60 Chevrolet	161	125	Engine
26	3	21	Marvin Panch	Wood Bros '62 Ford	154	200	Rear End
27	21	87	Buck Baker	Baker '62 Chrysler	139	125	Distributo
28	35	49	Charley Griffith	J C Parkett '61 Pontiac	137	100	Rear End
29	9	4	Rex White	Louis Clements '62 Chevrolet	109	125	Rock Arm
30	5	27	Junior Johnson	Holly Farms '62 Pontiac	96	175	Trans
31	34	18	Stick Elliott	Toy Bolton '60 Ford	81	100	Oil Pres
32	16	2	Jim Paschal	Cliff Stewart '62 Pontiac	77	100	Crank Sh
33	29	75	Ralph Earnhardt	Robert Smith '62 Pontiac	68	---	Heating
34	2	28	Fred Lorenzen	LaFayette '62 Ford	61	100	Engine
35	15	36	Larry Thomas	Wade Younts '62 Dodge	60	---	Engine
36	32	66	Larry Frank	Ratus Walters '62 Ford	29	---	Heating

Time of Race: 3 hours, 24 minutes, 22 seconds
Average Speed: 73.397 mph
Pole Winner: Fireball Roberts - 81.374 mph
Lap Leaders: Fireball Roberts 1-61, Bobby Johns 62-159, Richard Petty 160-162, Johns 163-320, Petty 321-326, Johns 327-500
Cautions: 4 for 37 laps
Margin of Victory: 6 laps plus
Attendance: 17,000

Race No. 17

Johns' Pontiac Victorious in Volunteer 500

BRISTOL, TN (Apr 29) -- Bobby Johns of Miami led an amazing 430 laps en route to a six lap victory in the Bristol International Speedway's second annual

Volunteer 500. It was Johns' second career Grand National win and his first since the 1960 Atlanta 500.

Fireball Roberts led the opening 61 laps, then faltered as the coil in his Pontiac malfunctioned. He lost 12 laps in the pits getting repairs but stormed back to finish second. He made up six laps on the field under green flag conditions.

Third place went to Jack Smith as Ned Jarrett finished fourth and rookie Thomas Cox fifth.

Richard Petty, who led on two occasions when Johns pitted, fell out with a blown engine while running second on lap 368.

Bobby Johns

He was credited with 16th place in the final order.

Only 11 cars in the field of 36 managed to go the distance. Other top contenders Fred Lorenzen, Junior Johnson, Nelson Stacy, Rex White, David Pearson and Joe Weatherly were on the sidelines when the checkered flag ended the 250 mile contest.

Four caution flags broke the action for 37 laps. The most serious altercation came on lap 302 when Stacy's Ford was T-boned by Maurice Petty's Plymouth. Stacy was examined at the infield hospital and released.

A crowd of 17,000 watched the 30 year-old Johns average 73.397 mph. He started sixth on the grid and led from the 62nd lap except for nine laps when he made routine pit stops.

Weatherly wound up 11th when the rear end of his Pontiac burned out with 56 laps to go. He still held a 142 point lead over Jack Smith after the 17th event of the 1962 schedule.

G.C. Spencer spins off banking as Bill Morton slips by

Grand National Race No. 18
200 Laps at Southside Speedway
Richmond, VA
66.7 Miles on .333-Mile Paved Track
May 4, 1962

Fin	St	No.	Driver	Team / Car	Laps	Money	Status
1	12	54	Jimmy Pardue	Pardue '62 Pontiac	200	$550	Running
2	4	47	Jack Smith	Smith '61 Pontiac	200	480	Running
3	7	43	Richard Petty	Petty Eng '60 Plymouth	199	375	Running
4	9	17	Joe Weatherly	Fred Harb '61 Ford	197	290	Running
5	3	2	Jim Paschal	Cliff Stewart '62 Pontiac	196	275	Running
6	5	20	Emanuel Zervakis	'62 Mercury	195	220	Running
7	8	85	Johnny Allen	Monroe Shook '61 Chevrolet	192	200	Running
8	11	34	Wendell Scott	Scott '61 Chevrolet	190	175	Running
9	16	62	Curtis Crider	Crider '60 Ford	180	150	Running
10	14	19	Herman Beam	Beam '61 Ford	180	155	Running
11	13	224	Bob Devine	'61 Chevrolet	177	130	Running
12	10	112	Ronny Fones	'60 Chevrolet	170	135	Running
13	1	4	Rex White	Louis Clements '62 Chevrolet	142	140	Engine
14	6	11	Ned Jarrett	B G Holloway '62 Chevrolet	79	350	Engine
15	2	36	Larry Thomas	Wade Younts '62 Dodge	66	100	Engine
16	15	76	Jim Bray	'61 Ford	34	75	Brakes

Time of Race: 58 minutes, 59 seconds
Average Speed: 67.747 mph
Pole Winner: Rex White - 71.145 mph
Lap Leaders: Rex White 1-134, Jimmy Pardue 135-200
Cautions:
Margin of Victory:
Attendance: 4,500

Race No. 18

Pardue Pockets $550 for First Grand National Triumph

RICHMOND, VA (May 4) -- Good Samaritan Jimmy Pardue of North Wilkesboro, NC powered his Pontiac into the lead on lap 135 and went on to win the 66.7-mile Grand National race at Southside Speedway. It was the first big league triumph for the 31 year-old independent.

Pardue edged out Jack Smith to take the $550 winner's prize. Richard Petty finished third, Joe Weatherly was fourth and Jim Paschal fifth.

Pardue very nearly did not compete in the race. He offered Weatherly his seat since the Bud Moore Pontiac which Weatherly normally drives was not ready from

Jimmy Pardue won at Richmond with a disabled car

the mechanical beating it took at Bristol. However, during a shake-down session, Pardue's Pontiac broke a transmission. Weatherly then struck a deal with Fred Harb to drive his Ford in the race.

Pardue went to work on his transmission, but had recurring problems in another practice session. In order to simply start the race, the 5'11" veteran wired the transmission in third gear with a sturdy wire. He started 12th in the 16 car field in a car that had only a third gear. Chances for a strong run were remote at best.

Rex White led the first 134 laps after starting on the pole. Pardue's unspectacular but steady pace gradually brought him up to second place. He forged to the front on the .333-mile paved oval when engine problems put White in the pits for a lengthy stay. Pardue led the rest of the way, earning a big cheer from the 4,500 in attendance. He averaged 67.747 mph while winning his first Grand National in his 92nd start.

White retired eight laps later with engine problems and wound up 13th.

Grand National Race No. 19
250 Laps at Hickory Speedway
Hickory, NC
"Hickory 250"
100 Miles on .4-mile Dirt Track
May 5, 1962

Fin	St	No.	Driver	Team / Car	Laps	Money	Status
1	1	47	Jack Smith	Smith '61 Pontiac	250	$1,000	Running
2	3	4	Rex White	Louis Clements '62 Chevrolet	248	600	Running
3	7	8	Joe Weatherly	Bud Moore '61 Pontiac	246	400	Running
4	13	2	Jim Paschal	Cliff Stewart '62 Pontiac	240	300	Running
5	6	75	Ralph Earnhardt	Robert Smith '61 Pontiac	237	275	Running
6	4	43	Richard Petty	Petty Eng '62 Plymouth	234	240	Running
7	16	60	Tom Cox	Ray Herlocker '60 Plymouth	231	200	Running
8	18	1	George Green	Jess Potter '60 Chevrolet	229	175	Running
9	19	19	Herman Beam	Beam '60 Ford	223	150	Running
10	5	85	Johnny Allen	Monroe Shook '61 Chevrolet	221	140	Running
11	17	X	John V Hamby	'60 Ford	197	130	Running
12	11	17	Fred Harb	Harb '61 Ford	172	120	Heating
13	9	11	Ned Jarrett	B G Holloway '62 Chevrolet	167	110	Rear End
14	2	27	Junior Johnson	Holly Farms '61 Pontiac	145	100	Cont Arm
15	10	48	G C Spencer	'60 Chevrolet	145	85	Spindle
16	12	34	Wendell Scott	Scott '61 Chevrolet	141	75	Running
17	8	6	Cotton Owens	Owens '61 Pontiac	126	65	Heating
18	14	18	Stick Elliott	Toy Bolton '60 Ford	96	60	Oil Leak
19	15	62	Curtis Crider	Crider '61 Mercury	31	50	H Gasket
20	20	50	Bobby Waddell	'60 Dodge	1	50	Engine

Time of Race: 1 hour, 24 minutes, 15 seconds
Average Speed: 71.216 mph
Pole Winner: Jack Smith - 74.074 mph
Lap Leaders: Jack Smith 1-250
Cautions: 1 for 5 laps
Margin of Victory: 2 laps plus
Attendance: 10,000

Race No. 19
Jack Smith Tightens Point Race with Hickory 250 Win

HICKORY, NC (May 5) -- Jack Smith of Sandy Springs, GA closed the gap on Joe Weatherly's point lead with a flag-to-flag triumph in the Hickory 250 at Hickory Speedway.

Smith's Pontiac outraced the 20 car field by two full laps to stake claim to his fourth win of the season. It was also the 20th of his 14 year career.

Rex White came in second with Weatherly third, Jim Paschal fourth and Ralph Earnhardt fifth. Smith sliced Weatherly's point lead to just 78 points after 19 races.

Smith, giving Pontiac its 11th win in 19 races thus far in the 1962 season, averaged 71.216 mph for the 100 miles on the .4-mile dirt track.

Richard Petty lost a wheel on his Plymouth and spun out midway through the race. His mishap brought out the lone caution flag which lasted only five laps. Petty returned to action and wound up sixth, 16 laps off the pace.

Second fastest qualifier Junior Johnson went 145 laps before his Pontiac was sidelined by a broken control arm. Defending Grand National champion Ned Jarrett went 167 laps before his Chevrolet fell out with differential problems.

Race No. 20
Weatherly Survives in Concord Car-killer

CONCORD, NC (May 6) -- Joe Weatherly emerged victorious after a car beating, 100-mile spectacle at Concord Speedway. It was Little Joe's fourth win of the year as he padded his point lead to 126 points over Jack Smith, who finished fourth.

Deplorable dust conditions and a severely rutted surface left only seven cars running at the finish. Twenty cars were on the starting grid.

Cotton Owens wound up second, a half lap behind. Sophomore Wendell Scott came in third, Smith was fourth and Maurice Petty fifth.

The track was torn with what some newspaper reporters described as "fox holes". Defending series champion Ned Jarrett drove his Chevy around the track once, collecting $150, and withdrew in disgust.

The 8,000 fans who attended the 200 lapper were

Grand National Race No. 20
200 Laps at Concord Speedway
Concord, NC
100 Miles on Half-mile Dirt Track
May 6, 1962

Fin	St	No.	Driver	Team / Car	Laps	Money	Status
1	7	8	Joe Weatherly	Bud Moore '61 Pontiac	200	$1,000	Running
2	8	6	Cotton Owens	Owens '60 Pontiac	200	600	Running
3	3	34	Wendell Scott	Scott '61 Chevrolet	192	400	Running
4	12	47	Jack Smith	Smith '61 Pontiac	191	300	Running
5	9	41	Maurice Petty	Petty Eng '62 Plymouth	188	275	Running
6	18	19	Herman Beam	Beam '60 Ford	171	240	Running
7	14	44	Bob Welborn	J H Petty '62 Pontiac	154	200	Housing
8	16	1	George Green	Jess Potter '60 Chevrolet	140	175	Rod
9	1	43	Richard Petty	Petty Eng '62 Plymouth	134	150	Axle
10	5	60	Tom Cox	Ray Herlocker '60 Plymouth	131	140	A Frame
11	19	18	Stick Elliott	Toy Bolton '60 Ford	118	130	Running
12	17	75	Ralph Earnhardt	Robert Smith '61 Pontiac	70	120	Brakes
13	11	21	Marvin Panch	Wood Bros '62 Ford	66	110	Heating
14	20	85	Johnny Allen	Monroe Shook '61 Chevrolet	43	100	Withdrew
15	6	48	G C Spencer	'60 Chevrolet	39	85	Axle
16	15	2	Jim Paschal	Cliff Stewart '62 Pontiac	33	75	Withdrew
17	2	62	Curtis Crider	Crider '61 Mercury	20	65	
18	13	X	John V Hamby	'60 Ford	6	60	Trans
19	10	11	Ned Jarrett	B G Holloway '62 Chevrolet	1	150	Withdrew
20	4	4	Rex White	Louis Clements '62 Chevrolet	1	50	Fire

Time of Race: 1 hour, 45 minutes, 10 seconds
Average Speed: 57.052 mph
Pole Winner: Drew for positions
Lap Leaders: Richard Petty 1-134, Joe Weatherly 135-200
Cautions:
Margin of Victory: 1/2 lap
Attendance: 8,000

covered head to toe with dust when the checkered flag fell.

Time trials were not held due to the poor track conditions. Richard Petty drew the pole position out of a hat. The Randleman Plymouth jockey led the first 134 laps before a broken axle, which he blamed on the track, dropped him from contention.

Weatherly ran the last 50 laps with a jammed accelerator. In order to negotiate the turns, he would turn the ignition key off to slow the car, then turn it back on to accelerate through the straightaways.

Weatherly led the rest of the way, averaging 57.052 mph for his 17th career victory.

Race No. 21

Stacy Nabs Panch Near Finish In Darlington's Rebel 300

DARLINGTON, SC (May 12) -- Nelson Stacy, finding a new frontier of racing in the South, made

Nelson Stacy - won Rebel 300

Darlington Raceway history repeat itself in a breathtaking victory over Marvin Panch in the sixth annual Rebel 300.

Stacy, a 40 year-old grandfather out of Cincinnati, wheeled his Holman-Moody Ford around Panch's Wood Brothers Ford with two laps left and sped to a two car length victory before 35,000 screaming spectators. Fred Lorenzen was credited with third place despite flipping his Ford in the final lap. Jack Smith got credit for fourth and fifth place went to Cotton Owens who tangled with Lorenzen in the final lap.

Smith, driving only two laps before turning the wheel of his Pontiac over to relief driver Johnny Allen, took the point lead by 882 points over Joe Weatherly, who struggled to an 18th place finish.

It was Stacy's second career victory. He won the 1961 Southern 500 with a dramatic pass around Panch at this same storied 1.375-mile oval.

Weatherly was involved in a fourth lap collision with Fireball Roberts. Roberts was sidelined and Weatherly spent many laps in the pits while his Bud Moore pit crew did major surgical work. Weatherly returned to the fray but finished some 29 laps off the pace.

Darel Dieringer pulled the day's biggest surprise by putting his lightly regarded Bob Owiecki Dodge into the lead for 17 laps. Rear end problems sidelined the Indianapolis, IN driver with 14 laps to go. He wound up 12th.

Pole sitter Lorenzen led 51 of the first 52 laps, but was penalized a lap when he passed the pace car during one of the early caution periods. He worked his way back into the lead lap but crashed in the final lap when his Ford broke loose, struck the wall and flipped over. Crashes also took out Jim Paschal, G C Spencer, Jim Reed and Rex White.

Stacy averaged 117.429 mph in what was slated to be the final Convertible race. The old rag-top division ran its final championship season in 1959, but Darlington officials wanted to keep the open-topped cars for the annual 300 mile spring race. Since 1960, points awarded in the Rebel have counted toward the Grand National championship. From 1957-1959, points were awarded strictly to the Convertible Division championship.

Grand National Race No. 21
219 Laps at Darlington Raceway
Darlington, SC
"Rebel 300"
300 Miles on 1.375 Mile Paved Track
May 12, 1962

Fin	St	No.	Driver	Team / Car	Laps	Money	Status
1	3	29	Nelson Stacy	Holman-Moody '62 Ford	219	$7,900	Running
2	5	21	Marvin Panch	Wood Bros '62 Ford	219	4,890	Running
3	1	28	Fred Lorenzen	LaFayette '62 Ford	218	3,400	Crash
4	11	47	* Jack Smith	Smith '62 Pontiac	217	2,270	Running
5	14	6	Cotton Owens	Owens '62 Pontiac	216	1,765	Crash
6	32	66	Larry Frank	Ratus Walters '62 ford	215	1,300	Running
7	6	3	David Pearson	Ray Fox '62 Pontiac	215	1,025	Running
8	9	72	Bobby Johns	Shorty Johns '62 Pontiac	214	925	Tire
9	29	11	Ned Jarrett	B G Holloway '62 Chevrolet	214	1,000	Running
10	16	54	Jimmy Pardue	Pardue '62 Pontiac	213	750	Running
11	15	86	Buddy Baker	Buck Baker '62 Chrysler	208	700	Running
12	10	90	Darel Dieringer	Bob Osiecki '62 Dodge	205	650	Rear End
13	17	52	Cale Yarborough	Julian Buesink '62 Ford	205	600	Running
14	12	87	Buck Baker	Baker '62 Chrysler	203	615	Running
15	7	43	Richard Petty	Petty Eng '62 Plymouth	201	500	Running
16	22	68	Ed Livingston	Livingston '61 Ford	195	450	Running
17	26	1	George Green	Jess Potter '61 Chevrolet	193	400	Running
18	4	8	Joe Weatherly	Bud Moore '62 Pontiac	190	370	Running
19	25	80	Tubby Gonzales	Gonzales '61 Ford	190	300	Running
20	27	60	Tom Cox	Ray Herlocker '60 Plymouth	186	300	Running
21	31	62	Curtis Crider	Crider '62 Mercury	178	200	Running
22	19	2	Jim Paschal	Cliff Stewart '62 Pontiac	154	200	Crash
23	28	93	Lee Reitzel	Reitzel '62 Ford	143	200	Crash
24	20	64	Elmo Langley	Woodfield '62 Ford	137	200	Rear End
25	21	75	Ralph Earnhardt	Robert Smith '61 Pontiac	130	200	Push Rod
26	18	77	Jim Reed	Ratus Walters '62 Ford	129	200	Crash
27	13	4	Rex White	Louis Clements '62 Chevrolet	48	200	Crash
28	24	38	G C Spencer	Mat DeMatthews '61 Ford	45	200	Crash
29	23	20	Emanuel Zervakis	'62 Mercury	28	200	Handling
30	30	97	Lee Roy Yarbrough	Lewis Osborne '62 Chevrolet	23	200	Engine
31	8	39	Junior Johnson	Ray Nichels '61 Pontiac	7	200	Oil Leak
32	2	22	Fireball Roberts	Banjo Matthews '62 Pontiac	4	265	Crash

* Relieved by Johnny Allen
Time of Race: 2 hours, 33 minutes, 17 seconds
Aveage Speed: 117.429 mph
Pole Winner: Fred Lorenzen - 129.810 mph
Lap Leaders: Fireball Roberts 1, Fred Lorenzen 2-52, Bobby Johns 53-54,
    David Pearson 55-110, Darel Dieringer 111-127, Lorenzen 128-147,
    Nelson Stacy 148-161, Marvin Panch 162-218, Stacy 219
Cautions: 6 for 22 minutes, 44 seconds
Margin of Victory: 2 car lengths
Attendance: 35,000

Grand National Race No. 22
200 Laps at Piedmont Interstate Fairgrounds
Spartanburg, SC
100 Miles on Half-mile Dirt Track
May 19, 1962

Fin	St	No.	Driver	Team / Car	Laps	Money	Status
1	2	11	Ned Jarrett	B G Holloway '62 Chevrolet	200	$1,200	Running
2	6	2	Jim Paschal	Cliff Stewart '62 Pontiac	200	600	Running
3	7	43	Richard Petty	Petty Eng '60 Plymouth	200	400	Running
4	9	48	G C Spencer	Floyd Powell '60 Chevrolet	198	300	Running
5	5	8	Joe Weatherly	Bud Moore '61 Pontiac	197	275	Running
6	10	60	Tom Cox	Ray Herlocker '60 Plymouth	193	240	Running
7	4	47	Jack Smith	Smith '61 Pontiac	189	200	Running
8	14	19	Herman Beam	Beam '60 Ford	183	175	Running
9	11	1	George Green	Jess Potter '61 Chevrolet	182	150	Running
10	8	62	Curtis Crider	Crider '62 Mercury	167	140	Running
11	13	68	Ed Livingston	Livingston '61 Ford	152	130	Heating
12	12	58	Paul Lewis	'62 Chevrolet	147	120	Running
13	15	17	Fred Harb	Harb '61 Ford	60	110	Heating
14	3	3	David Pearson	Ray Fox '61 Pontiac	30	100	Engine
15	1	6	Cotton Owens	Owens '61 Pontiac	20	85	Engine

Time of Race: 1 hour, 39 minutes, 52 seconds
Average Speed: 60.080 mph
Pole Winner: Cotton Owens - 64.423 mph
Lap Leaders: - - - - - - - - - - - - - - Ned Jarrett   -200
Cautions:
Margin of Victory:
Attendance:

Race No. 22
Jarrett Takes Spartanburg 100 For 3rd Win of Year

SPARTANBURG, SC (May 19) -- Ned Jarrett of Newton, NC drove his Chevrolet to victory in the 100-mile Grand National race at the Piedmont Interstate Fairgrounds in Spartanburg, SC. It was the third win of the season for the defending Grand National champion.

Jim Paschal finished second in a Pontiac and Richard Petty brought his Plymouth home third. The first three finishers were all in the lead lap at the finish of the 200-lapper on the half-mile dirt track. G.C. Spencer came in fourth with Joe Weatherly fifth.

Point leader Jack Smith wound up seventh and held a 850 point lead over Weatherly.

Cotton Owens set a new qualifying record of 64.423 mph, but the veteran hometowner was the first car out of the race. His Pontiac popped an engine after just 20 laps.

David Pearson, star of the 1961 campaign, fell victim to a blown engine after 30 laps and was forced to park his potent Ray Fox Pontiac.

Jarrett averaged 60.080 mph for his 11th career Grand National win.

Race No. 23

Stacy Bags Second Straight Superspeedway Race in World 600

CHARLOTTE, NC (May 27) -- Nelson Stacy, driving his yellow Holman-Moody Ford into the lead with eight laps to go, scooted home first in the third annual World 600 at Charlotte Motor Speedway. Stacy, of Cincinnati, breezed into the lead when front-running David Pearson blew an engine in his Pontiac with about 10 miles left in the 600-mile marathon. The 27 year-old Spartanburg speedster had led on six occasions for 217 laps around the 1.5-mile high-banked oval.

Joe Weatherly wound up second, 32.35 seconds behind the winner. Third place was claimed by Fred Lorenzen with Richard Petty fourth and Larry Franks fifth.

Weatherly, driving the Bud Moore Pontiac, reclaimed command in the point race by 896 points over Richard Petty, who moved into second spot in the point standings.

Stacy and Lorenzen, stable-mates on the Holman-Moody team, were forced to drive Fords set up for dirt tracks when NASCAR outlawed the new 'fastback' sloped roofs which Ford had unveiled for the 600. Sanctioning NASCAR said the roof lines were not in mass production and did not conform to "stock" car racing.

A crowd of 45,875 was on hand to watch Stacy win at a record speed of 125.552 mph leading only 13 laps, including the last eight. Pontiac automobiles led 382 of the 400 laps while Plymouth's Richard Petty led twice for five trips around the tri-oval.

Pearson and Fireball Roberts swapped the lead three times in the first 28 laps. Then popular independent Jimmy Pardue stormed to the front for 36 laps. Johnny Allen and Bobby Johns were stout contenders until their mounts failed under the strain or faded. Pardue blew a tire and crashed on lap 190; Johns encountered engine problems on lap 284; Allen fell off the pace and finished 20 laps down in 15th place; Roberts encountered tire problems and wound up ninth, seven laps off the pace.

Allen was driving the Holly Farms Pontiac owned by the Lovette Brothers. The seat had been vacated by Junior Johnson who opted to move over to Cotton Owens' Pontiac team. Johnson went only 72 laps before clutch failure put him out of the race.

Jack Smith fell to fourth place in the point standings when he was forced to park his Pontiac after 355 laps with brake failure.

Roberts and Pearson won special 50-mile, no-point

Grand National Race No. 23
400 Laps at Charlotte Motor Speedway
Charlotte, NC
"World 600"
600 Miles on 1.5-mile Paved Track
May 27, 1962

Fin	St	No.	Driver	Team / Car	Laps	Money	Status
1	18	29	Nelson Stacy	Holman-Moody '62 Ford	400	$25,505	Running
2	4	8	Joe Weatherly	Bud Moore '62 Pontiac	400	11,105	Running
3	15	0	Fred Lorenzen	LaFayette '62 Ford	399	6,870	Running
4	21	43	Richard Petty	Petty Eng '62 Plymouth	397	5,400	Running
5	12	66	Larry Frank	Ratus Walters '62 Ford	395	3,475	Running
6	14	11	Ned Jarrett	B G Holloway '62 Chevrolet	394	3,600	Running
7	2	3	David Pearson	Ray Fox '62 Pontiac	393	4,695	Engine
8	11	21	Marvin Panch	Wood Bros '62 Ford	393	1,600	Running
9	1	22	Fireball Roberts	Banjo Matthews '62 Pontiac	393	2,095	Running
10	24	41	Bunkie Blackburn	Petty Eng '62 Plymouth	393	1,100	Running
11	10	4	Rex White	Louis Clements '62 Chevrolet	392	1,075	Running
12	31	39	LeeRoy Yarbrough	Ray Nichels '61 Pontiac	386	1,300	Running
13	19	44	Bob Welborn	J H Petty '62 Pontiac	385	850	Running
14	8	20	Emanuel Zervakis	'62 Mercury	383	1,150	Running
15	6	46	Johnny Allen	Holly Farms '62 Pontiac	380	590	Running
16	22	36	Larry Thomas	Wade Younts '62 Dodge	378	1,000	Running
17	26	84	Red Foote	Ed Hinton '61 Ford	369	575	Running
18	46	61	Bill Morton	'62 Ford	368	485	Running
19	37	30	Tiny Lund	Fred Clark '62 Chevrolet	365	500	Running
20	28	9	Jimmy Thompson	Ewell Williams '62 Ford	364	475	Running
21	27	79	G C Spencer	'62 Chevrolet	363	500	Running
22	38	1	George Green	Jess Potter '61 Chevrolet	360	425	Running
23	34	90	Darel Dieringer	Bob Osiecki '62 Dodge	358	500	Coil Wire
24	25	47	Jack Smith	Smith '62 Pontiac	355	475	Brakes
25	39	19	Herman Beam	Beam '62 Ford	348	375	Running
26	47	5	Stick Elliott	'61 Pontiac	341	350	Running
27	42	62	Curtis Crider	Crider '62 Mercury	284	375	Wheel
28	5	72	Bobby Johns	Shorty Johns '62 Pontiac	284	615	Push Rod
29	17	77	Jim Reed	Ratus Walters '62 Ford	284	475	Engine
30	41	34	Wendell Scott	Scott '61 Chevrolet	277	325	Engine
31	20	87	Buck Baker	Baker '62 Chrysler	259	825	Oil Press
32	32	2	Jim Paschal	Cliff Stewart '62 Pontiac	227	600	Fuel Pmp
33	33	91	Herb Tillman	Bob Osiecki '62 Dodge	194	500	Clutch
34	7	54	Jimmy Pardue	Pardue '62 Pontiac	190	1,400	Crash
35	16	86	Buddy Baker	Buck Baker '62 Chrysler	176	300	Oil Pres
36	29	68	Ed Livingston	Livingston '61 Ford	118	325	Engine
37	23	92	Gerald Duke	Don Harrison '62 Ford	96	300	Engine
38	9	6	Junior Johnson	Cotton Owens '62 Pontiac	72	500	Clutch
39	40	93	Lee Reitzel	Reitzel '62 Ford	69	325	Trans
40	35	38	John Dodd, Jr	Mat DeMatthews '61 Ford	68	375	Engine
41	36	58	Paul Lewis	'61 Chevrolet	57	350	Engine
42	44	60	Tom Cox	Ray Herlocker '60 Plymouth	45	320	Crank Sh
43	3	94	Banjo Matthews	Matthews '62 Pontiac	13	350	Crash
44	13	81	Roscoe Thompson	'62 Mercury	12	325	Engine
45	30	16	Ralph Earnhardt	Happy Steigel '61 Pontiac	11	300	Crash
46	40	80	Tubby Gonzales	Gonzales '61 Ford	6	300	Vibration
47	43	96	Johnny Sudderth	'61 Chevrolet	5	320	Engine
48	45	50	Bobby Waddell	'60 Dodge	2	320	Freeze Pl

Time of Race: 4 hours, 46 minutes, 44 seconds
Average Speed: 125.552 mph
Pole Winner: Fireball Roberts - 140.150 mph
Lap Leaders: David Pearson 1-21, Fireball Roberts 22-26, Pearson 27-28, Jimmy Pardue 29-64, Johnny Allen 65-68, Pardue 69-77, Bobby Johns 78-81, Richard Petty 82-85, Pardue 86-134, Pearson 135-139, Johns 140-159, Petty 160, Pardue 161-185, Roberts 186-207, Pearson 208-273, Nelson Stacy 274-278, Pearson 279-392, Stacy 393-400
Cautions: 2 for 14 laps
Margin of Victory: 32.35 seconds
Attendance: 45,875

qualifying races staged one week before the 600.

Pearson was in the process of lapping Stacy when his engine bit the dust in the closing laps. "I heard his engine burp when he was going around me," said Stacy. "I couldn't believe it. He had us all beat."

Race No. 24

Lorenzen Declared Victor in Disputed, Rain-shortened Atlanta 500

HAMPTON, GA (June 10) -- A hard hitting rain squall ended the Atlanta 500 after 328.5 miles, but NASCAR officials could not determine a clearcut winner for almost five hours. Fred Lorenzen was given the nod after sanctioning officials carefully studied the score cards.

Ray Fox and his driver David Pearson were convinced they had won the race. "Freddy never passed me the entire race," said Pearson, who started third to Lorenzen's seventh. "I remember who passes me, especially if they are among the faster cars."

In the final decision, Pearson was dropped to seventh, two laps behind. "Can't be," muttered Pearson.

It was the third straight big track win for the Holman-Moody team and the first for the 27 year-old Elmhurst, IL Ford driver.

The race was an electrifying contest from start to the abbreviated finish. The lead changed hands 23 times among seven drivers with Banjo Matthews having the upper hand for 73 laps.

Long pit stop foiled Banjo Matthews bid for Atlanta 500 victory

Lorenzen and Matthews, the principles in the late-race showdown, were both forced to make green flag pit stops with blackened skies coming in rapidly from the west. Matthews lost several precious seconds in the pits which proved the difference for the hard-luck Asheville, NC veteran. He was awarded second place in the final rundown.

Third place went to Bobby Johns, Fireball Roberts was fourth and USAC driver Troy Ruttman was fifth.

When the skies opened up, the score board operators ran for shelter, and at the time they scampered to safety, Pearson's number "3" was listed in first place. Officials dropped the red flag on lap 218 as Pearson pulled off the track, blinded by the storm. NASCAR said later he failed to come around to finish the 219th lap and thus fell a lap off the pace. After combing the score cards, it was found he was another lap off the pace.

"I was never worried," said Lorenzen. "I know I passed Pearson once on the track and I got a better pit stop than Matthews. I knew I won."

Lorenzen averaged 101.983 mph after three caution flags were dropped for 61 laps, most of them rain related. A record Georgia crowd of 55,000 was on hand for the race, which had been rained out twice.

Grand National Race No. 24
334 Laps at Atlanta International Raceway
Hampton, GA
"Atlanta 500"
500 Miles on 1.5-mile Paved Track
June 10, 1962

Fin	St	No.	Driver	Team / Car	Laps	Money	Status
1	7	28	Fred Lorenzen	Lafayette '62 Ford	219	$15,555	Running
2	1	02	Banjo Matthews	Matthews '62 Pontiac	219	9,490	Running
3	4	72	Bobby Johns	Shorty Johns '62 Pontiac	218	5,220	Running
4	14	22	Fireball Roberts	Banjo Matthews '62 Pontiac	218	2,525	Running
5	22	98	Troy Ruttman	Bill Stroppe '62 Mercury	218	1,750	Running
6	19	01	Paul Goldsmith	Ray Nichels '62 pontiac	218	1,375	Running
7	3	3	David Pearson	Ray Fox '62 Pontiac	217	1,420	Running
8	10	21	Marvin Panch	Wood Bros '62 Ford	217	1,250	Running
9	11	6	Junior Johnson	Cotton Owens '62 Pontiac	216	1,025	Running
10	30	2	Jim Paschal	Cliff Stewart '62 Pontiac	214	900	Running
11	25	86	Buddy Baker	Buck Baker '62 Chrysler	213	800	Running
12	12	12	Bob Welborn	B G Holloway '62 Pontiac	213	750	Running
13	16	47	Jack Smith	Smith '62 Pontiac	213	625	Running
14	18	81	Roscoe Thompson	'62 Mercury	212	500	Running
15	21	30	Tiny Lund	Fred Clark '62 Chevrolet	212	400	Running
16	15	20	Emanuel Zervakis	'62 Mercury	212	350	Running
17	35	97	LeeRoy Yarbrough	Lewis Osborne '62 Chevrolet	211	300	Running
18	9	8	Joe Weatherly	Bud Moore '62 Pontiac	210	375	Running
19	39	36	Larry Thomas	Wade Younts '62 Dodge	210	300	Running
20	24	87	Buck Baker	Baker '62 Chrysler	209	300	Running
21	2	4	Rex White	Louis Clements '62 Chevrolet	207	325	Running
22	34	61	Bill Morton	'62 Ford	207	250	Running
23	27	43	Richard Petty	Petty Eng '62 Plymouth	207	250	Running
24	31	80	Tubby Gonzales	Gonzales '61 Ford	206	250	Running
25	20	54	Jimmy Pardue	Pardue '62 Pontiac	205	250	Running
26	32	79	G C Spencer	'62 Chevrolet	204	250	Running
27	38	49	Friday Hassler	J C Parker '62 Pontiac	202	250	Running
28	40	62	Curtis Crider	Crider '62 Mercury	202	250	Running
29	26	19	Herman Beam	Beam '62 Ford	199	250	Running
30	6	66	Larry Frank	Ratus Walters '62 Ford	199	525	Running
31	43	1	George Green	Jess Potter '61 Chevrolet	199	225	Running
32	33	90	Darel Dieringer	Bob Osiecki '62 Dodge	183	225	Rear End
33	41	68	Ed Livingston	Livingston '61 Ford	181	225	Engine
34	42	63	George Alsobrook	Ratus Walters '61 Ford	156	225	H Gasket
35	45	32	Jim Locke	'61 Ford	140	225	Running
36	28	16	Ralph Earnhardt	Happy Steigel '62 Pontiac	132	225	Trans
37	17	46	Johnny Allen	Holly Farms '62 Pontiac	130	250	Trans
38	44	60	Tom Cox	Ray Herlocker '60 Plymouth	130	200	Axle
39	13	11	Ned Jarrett	B G Holloway '62 Chevrolet	114	475	Engine
40	23	92	Cale Yarborough	Julian Buesink '62 Ford	89	200	Engine
41	5	7	Cotton Owens	Owens '62 Pontiac	81	425	Trans
42	36	18	Stick Elliott	Toy Bolton '61 Pontiac	66	200	Engine
43	29	9	Bunkie Blackburn	Ewell Williams '62 Ford	23	200	Crash
44	37	10	T C Hunt	Fred Wheat '61 Dodge	6	200	Engine
45•	8	29	Nelson Stacy	Holman-Moody '62 Ford	2	250	Steering
46	46	50	A F Nichols	'60 Plymouth	1	200	Oil Pres

* Race shortened to 219 laps due to rain
Time of Race: 3 hours, 13 minutes, 16 seconds
Average Speed: 101.983 mph
Pole Winner: Banjo Matthews - 137.640 mph
Fastest Qualifier: Cotton Owens - 138.063 mph
Total Laps Led: Banjo Matthews 73 laps, Fred Lorenzen 48 laps, Joe Weatherly 36 laps, Bobby Johns 32 laps, David Pearson 14 laps, Tiny Lund 8 laps, Emanuel Zervakis 5 laps -- 23 Total lead changes
Cautions: 3 for 61 laps
Margin of Victory:
Attendance: 55,000

Grand National Race No. 25
200 Laps at Bowman-Gray Stadium
Winston-Salem, NC
"Myers Brothers Memorial"
50 Miles on Quarter-mile Paved Track
June 16, 1962

Fin	St	No.	Driver	Team / Car	Laps	Money	Status
1	2	58	Johnny Allen	Fred Lovette '61 Pontiac	200	$580	Running
2	1	4	Rex White	Louis Clements '62 Chevrolet	200	500	Running
3	4	43	Richard Petty	Pety Eng '62 Plymouth	196	375	Running
4	9	36	Larry Thomas	Wade Younts '62 Dodge	195	305	Running
5	12	8	Joe Weatherly	Bud Moore "61 Pontiac	194	275	Running
6	10	34	Wendell Scott	Scott '61 Chevrolet	193	215	Running
7	17	17	Fred Harb	Harb '61 Ford	192	195	Running
8	3	54	Jimmy Pardue	Pardue '62 Pontiac	190	160	Running
9	13	97	Harry Leake	Lewis Osborne '60 Chevrolet	189	150	Running
10	5	47	Jack Smith	Smith '61 Pontiac	189	155	Running
11	6	11	Ned Jarrett	B G Holloway '62 Chevrolet	188	350	Running
12	19	62	Curtis Crider	Crider '60 Ford	182	120	Running
13	15	19	Herman Beam	Beam '60 Ford	179	110	Running
14	11	48	G C Spencer	Floyd Powell '60 Chevrolet	172	125	Trans
15	8	2	Jim Paschal	Cliff Stewart '62 Pontiac	153	90	Rear End
16	14	1	George Green	Jess Potter '60 Chevrolet	145	75	A Frame
17	18	18	Stick Elliott	Toy Bolton '60 Ford	122	75	W Bearing
18	7	87	Buck Baker	Baker '61 Chrysler	112	80	Tires
19	16	60	Tom Cox	Ray Herlocker '60 Plymouth	51	50	Brakes

Time of Race: 1 hour, 05 minutes, 59 seconds
Average Speed: 45.466 mph
Pole Winner: 48.179 mph
Lap Leaders: Rex White 1-22, Johnny Allen 23-200
Cautions:
Margin of Victory: 6 inches
Attendance: 14,000

Race No. 25

Johnny Allen Crashes;
Still Wins on Final Lap

WINSTON-SALEM, NC (June 16) -- Johnny Allen of Fayetteville, NC scored his first Grand National win on a bizarre note as he nipped Rex White in a stirring duel in the Myers Brothers Memorial 50-mile event at Bowman-Gray Stadium.

Allen, wheeling a Pontiac owned by Fred Lovette, nosed out White by six inches on the small quarter-mile flat oval. He gunned his car so hard to win the race that he couldn't make the sharp first turn and over the wall he went.

The finish was so close that no immediate

Johnny Allen won and crashed

announcement was made. Don Matlock, assistant to Chief Scorer Morris Metcalfe, had seen the electrifying finish and carved his way through the masses of fans and onto the scoring podium. Matlock advised Metcalfe that Allen had won by the narrowest of margins.

Richard Petty wound up third, four laps back. Larry Thomas was fourth and Joe Weatherly fifth.

White started on the pole and led the first 22 laps. Allen whipped his mount under White on lap 23 and led the remaining distance. White mustered a stout challenge in the final lap as the two principles crossed the finish line in a near dead heat.

Allen collected only $580 for his win, which left him with a crunched race car. "I've had worse wrecks and gotten less out of them," remarked Allen.

A crowd of 14,000 jammed the stadium to watch Allen win at an average speed of 45.466 mph.

Grand National Race No. 26
200 Laps at Augusta Speedway
Augusta, GA
100 Miles on Half-mile Dirt Track
June 19, 1962

Fin	St	No.	Driver	Team / Car	Laps	Money	Status
1	1	8	Joe Weatherly	Bud Moore '61 Pontiac	200	$1,000	Running
2	8	11	Ned Jarrett	B G Holloway '62 Chevrolet	199	800	Running
3	5	43	Richard Petty	Petty Eng '62 Plymouth	198	400	Running
4	6	2	Jim Paschal	Cliff Stewart '62 Pontiac	193	300	Running
5	11	48	G C Spencer	Floyd Powell '60 Chevrolet	193	275	Running
6	15	86	Buddy Baker	Buck Baker '61 Chrysler	193	240	Running
7	13	62	Curtis Crider	Crider '62 Mercury	180	200	Running
8	9	60	Tom Cox	Ray Herlocker '60 Plymouth	177	175	Running
9	7	34	Wendell Scott	Scott '61 Chevrolet	177	150	Running
10	16	19	Herman Beam	Beam '60 Ford	175	140	Running
11	10	1	George Green	Jess Potter '61 Chevrolet	166	130	Running
12	2	47	Jack Smith	Smith '62 Pontiac	143	120	A Frame
13	3	97	LeeRoy Yarbrough	Lewis Osborne '62 Chevrolet	136	110	Electric
14	4	87	Buck Baker	Baker '62 Chrysler	100	100	Brakes
15	14	6	Weldon Adams	'60 Ford	90	85	Axle
16	12	18	Stick Elliott	Toy Bolton '60 Ford	79	75	H Gasket

Time of Race: 1 hour, 40 minutes, 15 seconds
Average Speed: 59.850 mph
Pole Winner: Joe Weatherly 63.069 mph
Lap Leaders: - - - - - - - - - - - - - - - Joe Weatherly   -200
Cautions:
Margin of Victory: 1 lap plus
Attendance:

Race No. 26

Weatherly Waxes
Field in Augusta 100

AUGUSTA, GA (June 19) -- Joe Weatherly of Norfolk, VA started on the pole and had little trouble disposing of the field in the 100-mile Grand National event at Augusta Speedway. It was the fifth win of the season for the 40 year-old veteran.

Finishing second, a lap behind, was Ned Jarrett. Richard Petty wound up third with Jim Paschal fourth and G C Spencer fifth.

Weatherly's triumph enabled him to open a 1,346 point lead over Petty. Jack Smith still held third in the point talley despite falling out with a broken A Frame.

LeeRoy Yarbrough qualified third in a lightly re-garded Chevrolet owned by Lewis Osborne and ran with the leaders until electrical problems forced him to the sidelines on lap 136.

Weldon Adams of Augusta made a return to Grand National racing in the 200 lapper on the half-mile dirt track. Adams had not made a Grand National appear-ance since 1953. He wound up 15th in the 16 car field when an axle knocked his Ford out of the race.

Weatherly averaged 59.850 mph for his 18th career victory.

Race No. 27

Paschal Takes Southside Victory after Pardue Blows Tire

RICHMOND, VA (June 22) -- Jim Paschal became the 12th different winner of the 1962 season with a late race surge in the 100-miler at Southside Speedway. It was the 10th career win for the High Point, NC speed-ster.

Paschal motored his Cliff Stewart owned Pontiac into the lead nine laps from the finish and beat runner-up Rex White by one lap and 10 seconds. Jimmy Par-due came in third, Johnny Allen was fourth and Jim Reed fifth.

White started on the pole--the 30th time he has earned the inside front row starting position--and led the first 276 laps. But his Louis Clements Chevrolet ran out of fuel 24 laps from the finish and he had to

Grand National Race No. 27
300 Laps at Southside Speedway
Richmond, VA
100 Miles on .333-mile Paved Track
June 22, 1962

Fin	St	No.	Driver	Team / Car	Laps	Money	Status
1	3	2	Jim Paschal	Cliff Stewart '62 Pontiac	300	$1,010	Running
2	1	4	Rex Whtie	Louis Clements '62 Chevrolet	299	650	Running
3	6	54	Jimmy Pardue	Pardue '62 Pontiac	298	400	Running
4	9	58	Johnny Allen	Fred Lovette '61 Pontiac	297	300	Running
5	4	77	Jim Reed	Ratus Walters '62 Pontiac	296	290	Running
6	7	11	Ned Jarrett	B G Holloway '62 Chevrolet	294	440	Running
7	11	8	Joe Weatherly	Bud Moore '61 Pontiac	294	200	Running
8	5	47	Jack Smith	Smith '61 Pontiac	290	175	Running
9	8	27	Tommy Irwin	'62 Chevrolet	288	150	Running
10	23	87	Buck Baker	Baker '62 Chrysler	284	140	Running
11	24	48	G C Spencer	Floyd Powell '60 Chevrolet	278	130	Running
12	16	60	Tom Cox	Ray Herlocker '60 Plymouth	278	120	Running
13	17	224	Bob Devine	'61 Chevrolet	276	110	Running
14	20	34	Wendell Scott	Scott '61 Chevrolet	275	100	Running
15	25	1	George Green	Jess Potter '61 Chevrolet	272	85	Running
16	19	19	Herman Beam	Beam '60 Ford	267	75	Running
17	21	112	Ronnie Fones	'60 Chevrolet	264	65	Running
18	18	62	Curtis Crider	Crider '60 Ford	262	60	Running
19	2	43	Richard Petty	Petty Eng '62 Plymouth	111	75	Rear End
20	12	17	Fred Harb	Harb '61 Ford	89	50	Heating
21	15	57	Jack Deniston	'62 Chevrolet	81	50	Frame
22	22	76	Neil Castles	'60 Ford	76	50	Running
23	10	20	Emanuel Zervakis	'62 Mercury	74	---	Rear End
24	13	36	Larry Thomas	Wade Younts '62 Dodge	41	---	Crash
25	14	86	Buddy Baker	Buck Baker '61 Chrysler	41	---	Crash

Time of Race: 1 hour, 30 minutes, 25 seconds
Average Speed: 66.293 mph
Pole Winner: Rex White - 70.435 mph
Lap Leaders: Rex Whie 1-276, Jimmy Pardue 277-291, Jim Paschal 292-300
Cautions: 1
Margin of Victory: 1 lap plus 10 seconds
Attendance: 5,000

Grand National Race No. 28
267 Laps at South Boston Speedway
South Boston, VA
100 Miles on .375-mile Paved Track
June 23, 1962

Fin	St	No.	Driver	Team / Car	Laps	Money	Status
1	2	4	Rex White	Louis Clements '62 Chevrolet	267	$1,000	Running
2	1	47	Jack Smith	Smith '61 Pontiac	267	600	Running
3	5	43	Richard Petty	Petty Eng '62 Plymouth	267	400	Running
4	9	58	Johnny Allen	Fred Lovette '61 Pontiac	265	300	Running
5	12	36	Larry Thomas	Wade Younts '62 Dodge	262	275	Running
6	4	11	Ned Jarrett	B G Holloway '62 Chevrolet	262	440	Running
7	10	8	Joe Weatherly	Bud Moore '61 Pontiac	260	200	Running
8	7	27	Tommy Irwin	Holly Farms '62 Chevrolet	256	175	Running
9	6	87	Buck Baker	Baker '62 Chrysler	253	150	Running
10	16	34	Wendell Scott	Scott '62 Chevrolet	249	140	Running
11	17	19	Herman Beam	Beam '60 Ford	241	130	Running
12	18	62	Curtis Crider	Crider '60 Ford	241	120	Running
13	13	60	Tom Cox	Ray Herlocker '60 Plymouth	240	110	Running
14	23	83	Worth McMillion	McMillion '62 Pontiac	236	100	Running
15	22	86	Buddy Baker	Buck Baker '61 Chrysler	223	85	Running
16	3	54	Jimmy Pardue	Pardue '62 Pontiac	222	75	Running
17	8	77	Jim Reed	Ratus Walters '62 Ford	210	65	Crash
18	19	1	George Green	Jess Potter '61 Chevrolet	201	60	Running
19	15	48	G C Spencer	Floyd Powell '60 Chevrolet	146	50	Rear End
20	21	2	Jim Paschal	Cliff Stewart '62 Pontiac	77	50	Engine
21	11	20	Emanuel Zervakis	'62 Mercury	53	50	Trans
22	20	76	Neil Castles	'60 Ford	14	50	Oil Pres
23	14	17	Fred Harb	Harb '61 Ford	8	---	Clutch
24	24	3	Earl Brooks	'60 Chevrolet	3	---	Flagged

Time of Race: 1 hour, 22 minutes, 49 seconds
Average Speed: 72.540 mph
Pole Winner: Jack Smith - 79.458 mph
Lap Leaders: Jack Smith 1-152, Rex White 153-267
Cautions:
Margin of Victory: 1/2 lap
Attendance:

make an emergency pit stop. Pardue, who started sixth, assumed command as White chugged into the pits. He appeared to be on his way to victory when his Pontiac blew a tire on lap 291. The North Wilkesboro hot-shot limped to the pits and lost two laps getting a replacement. Paschal took the lead at that point and led the rest of the way.

Larry Thomas and Buck Baker, who started side-by-side, crashed together in the 41st lap. Neither driver was injured.

A crowd of 5,000 watched Paschal average 66.293 mph as one caution flag interrupted the pace.

Race No. 28

White Beats Smith in South Boston Two Car Show

S. BOSTON, VA (June 23) -- Rex White out-dueled Jack Smith in what turned out to be a two car show in the 100-mile Grand National race at South Boston Speedway.

It was White's fifth win of the year and the 25th in the last six seasons on NASCAR's major league stock car racing tour.

Smith finished a half lap back in second place after starting on the pole. The Sandy Springs, GA Pontiac driver led the first 152 laps before White set sail in his Chevrolet. Richard Petty came in third, Johnny Allen was fourth and Larry Thomas fifth.

Point leader Joe Weatherly wound up seventh and held a 1,474 point advantage over Petty.

Smith's bid to lead the 300 lapper from flag-to-flag came to a halt when he spun from the lead on lap 152. He was never able to make up the deficit.

Jim Reed was taken out of the race in a 210th lap accident, but he was not hurt in the mishap.

White averaged 72.540 mph in the 267 lap event on the .375-mile paved oval.

Race No. 29

Crafty Fireball Annexes Firecracker 250

DAYTONA BEACH, FL (July 4) -- Fireball Roberts uncharacteristically played the waiting game, then roared into the lead late in the race and sped to victory in the fourth annual Firecracker 250 at Daytona Interna-

Grand National Race No. 29
100 Laps at Daytona International Speedway
Daytona Beach, FL
"Firecracker 250"
250 Miles on 2.5-mile Paved Track
July 4, 1962

Fin	St	No.	Driver	Team / Car	Laps	Money	Status
1	4	22	Fireball Roberts	Banjo Matthews '62 Pontiac	100	$9,850	Running
2	7	6	Junior Johnson	Cotton Owens '62 Pontiac	100	5,450	Running
3	10	21	Marvin Panch	Wood Bros '62 Ford	98	3,400	Running
4	8	47	Jack Smith	Smith '62 Pontiac	98	1,675	Running
5	12	54	Jimmy Pardue	Pardue '62 Pontiac	97	1,225	Running
6	16	66	Larry Frank	Ratus Walters '62 Ford	96	900	Running
7	23	11	Ned Jarrett	B G Holloway '62 Chevrolet	96	775	Running
8	5	3	David Pearson	Ray Fox '62 Pontiac	96	1,075	Running
9	19	36	Larry Thomas	Wade Younts '62 Dodge	95	650	Running
10	13	41	Art Malone	'62 Pontiac	95	600	Running
11	21	4	Rex White	Louis Clements '62 Chevrolet	93	450	Running
12	26	87	Buck Baker	Baker '62 Chrysler	92	350	Running
13	27	19	Herman Beam	Beam '62 Ford	89	320	Running
14	29	60	Thomas Cox	Ray Herlocker '60 Plymouth	89	300	Running
15	33	1	George Green	Jess Potter '61 Chevrolet	89	220	Running
16	32	62	Curtis Crider	Crider '62 Mercury	88	220	Running
17	18	16	Ralph Earnhardt	Happy Steigel '62 Chevrolet	85	275	Running
18	25	86	Buddy Baker	Buck Baker '62 Chrysler	84	250	Running
19	2	72	Bobby Johns	Shorty Johns '62 Pontiac	82	275	Trans
20	28	90	Darel Dieringer	Bob Osiecki '62 Dodge	76	250	Engine
21	1	02	Banjo Matthews	Matthews '62 Pontiac	73	400	Engine
22	22	81	Roscoe Thompson	'62 Mercury	42	250	Engine
23	6	8	Joe Weatherly	Bud Moore '62 Pontiac	34	600	Crash
24	9	28	Fred Lorenzen	LaFayette '62 Ford	34	400	Crash
25	14	39	LeeRoy Yarbrough	Ray Nichels '61 Pontiac	34	300	Crash
26	15	29	Nelson Stacy	Holman-Moody '62 Ford	32	250	Crash
27	3	46	Johnny Allen	Holly Farms '62 Pontiac	24	600	Trans
28	31	80	Tubby Gonzales	Gonzales '62 Ford	20	200	Oil Pres
29	24	38	Johnny Dodd, Jr	Mat DeMatthews '60 Ford	10	250	Engine
30	11	43	Richard Petty	Petty Eng '62 Plymouth	6	275	Crash
31	20	97	Tom Pistone	Lewis Osborne '62 Chevrolet	2	250	Crash
32	30	27	Tommy Irwin	'62 Chevrolet	1	200	Oil Pres
33	17	12	Bob Welborn	Cliff Stewart '62 Pontiac	1	275	Lug Bolts

Time of Race: 1 hour, 37 minutes, 36 seconds
Average Speed: 153.688 mph
Pole Winner: Banjo Matthews 160.499 mph
Lap Leaders: Fireball Roberts 1, Banjo Matthews 2-18, Bobby Johns 19-21, Matthews 22-31, Johns 32, Matthews 33, Johns 34, Matthews 35, Johns 36-40, Matthews 41-72, Johns 73, Roberts 74, Johns 75-80, Roberts 81-100
Cautions: 2 for 7 laps
Margin of Victory: 12 seconds
Attendance: 22,591

tional Raceway.

It was Roberts' third win of the season and his first since he romped to victory in the Daytona 500. Oddly, all three of his 1962 Grand National wins have come at the 2.5-mile ultra fast oval at Daytona.

Junior Johnson finished second, 12 seconds behind Roberts' Banjo Matthews Pontiac. Johnson was wheeling a Cotton Owens Pontiac. Third place went to Marvin Panch with Jack Smith fourth and Jimmy Pardue fifth.

Point leader Joe Weatherly was involved in a four car crack-up in the 34th lap and saw his lead in the standings slice to 1,272 points over Smith, who moved into second place. Also involved in the mishap were-

Banjo Matthews and Bobby Johns on front row for the Firecracker 250

Fred Lorenzen, LeeRoy Yarbrough and Nelson Stacy.

Richard Petty, who fell to third place in the point standings, fell victim to a sixth lap crash.

Banjo Matthews and Bobby Johns dueled for top

Richard Petty's crumpled Plymouth after Firecracker 250 wreck. "I just got a little behind in my steering," said Petty

honors most of the way in the 100-lap sprint contest. Matthews, who led on five occasions for a total of 61 laps, was bidding for his first Grand National win. But the engine in his Pontiac blew on lap 73, putting him out.

Johns took over the lead at Matthews' departure, but he pitted on lap 80 with transmission problems. He had to park his Pontiac two laps later and Roberts was home free.

A holiday crowd of 22,591 watched Roberts average 153.688 mph in winning his 11th superspeedway race. Matthews had earned the pole at 160.499 mph. Two caution flags for seven laps were waved for accidents.

Art Malone of Tampa, FL, who gained notoriety by driving Bob Osiecki's winged Mad Dog IV over Daytona's high banks at 181.561 mph in August of 1961, finished 10th in a Pontiac.

Grand National Race No. 30
200 Laps at Columbia Speedway
Columbia, SC
100 Miles on Half-mile Dirt Track
July 7, 1962

Fin	St	No.	Driver	Team / Car	Laps	Money	Status
1	4	4	Rex White	Louis Clements '62 Chevrolet	200	$1,000	Running
2	3	8	Joe Weatherly	Bud Moore '61 Pontiac	200	600	Running
3	1	47	Jack Smith	Smith '61 Pntiac	199	400	Running
4	9	6	Cotton Owens	Owens '62 Pontiac	199	300	Running
5	5	11	Ned Jarrett	B G Holloway '62 Chevrolet	199	475	Running
6	11	27	Tommy Irwin	Holly Farms '62 Chevrolet	198	240	Running
7	6	60	Tom Cox	Ray Herlocker '60 Plymouth	197	200	Running
8	12	61	Sherman Utsman	'62 Ford	189	175	Running
9	10	34	Wendell Scott	Scott '61 Chevrolet	186	150	Tire
10	19	1	George Green	Jess Potter '61 Chevrolet	185	140	Running
11	13	19	Herman Beam	Beam '60 Ford	183	130	Running
12	15	18	Stick Elliott	Toy Bolton '61 Pontiac	183	120	Running
13	17	62	Curtis Crider	Crider '62 Mercury	182	110	Running
14	18	87	Buddy Baker	Buck Baker '61 Chrysler	177	100	Rear End
15	20	48	Joe Penland	Floyd Powell '60 Chevrolet	160	85	Running
16	7	2	Jim Paschal	Cliff Stewart '62 Pontiac	104	75	Rad Fan
17	8	17	Fred Harb	Harb '61 Ford	95	65	H Gasket
18	16	76	Neil Castles	'60 Ford	73	60	Rear End
19	14	36	Larry Thomas	Wade Younts '62 Dodge	60	50	Crash
20	2	43	Richard Petty	Petty Eng '62 Plymouth	20	50	Engine

Time of Race: 1 hour, 36 minutes, 12 seconds
Average Speed: 62.370 mph
Pole Winner: Jack Smith - 66.667 mph
Lap Leaders: - - - - - - - - - - - - - - - Rex White   -200
Cautions:
Margin of Victory:
Attendance:

Race No. 30
White Wins 6th of Year
In Columbia 100

COLUMBIA, SC (July 7) -- Rex White bagged his sixth win of the year by taking first place in the 100-

miler at Columbia Speedway. The Silver Spring, MD Chevrolet driver became the winningest driver of the 1962 Grand National campaign with his triumph.

White started fourth on the grid and beat Joe Weatherly's Pontiac by less than a lap on the half-mile dirt track. Pole winner Jack Smith took third. Cotton Owens was fourth and Ned Jarrett came in fifth.

Weatherly maintained a comfortable 1,288 point lead over Smith in the race for the national driving championship.

Richard Petty, who started next to Smith on the front row, ran only 20 laps before the engine in his Plymouth expired. He finished last in the 20 car field.

Larry Thomas crashed his Dodge into the retaining barrier on lap 60. It was the only accident of the race.

White averaged 62.370 mph for his 26th career victory.

Speedway and Jack Smith of Sandy Springs, GA came out on top of the 250 lap scramble. It was Smith's fifth win of the season.

Point leader Joe Weatherly finished second, a lap behind. Richard Petty took third place, Buck Baker was fourth and Ned Jarrett fifth.

White earned the pole position and led the first 118 laps in his Chevrolet. While leading, the shock mounts broke, sidelining the 1960 Grand National champ. Smith breezed into the lead and went virtually unchallenged the rest of the way.

A crowd of 5,000 watched Smith win the caution-free event at an average speed of 78.294 mph.

Grand National Race No. 31
250 Laps at New Asheville Speedway
Asheville, NC
100 Miles on .4-mile Paved Track
July 13, 1962

Fin	St	No.	Driver	Team / Car	Laps	Money	Status
1	3	47	Jack Smith	Smith '61 Pontiac	250	$1,000	Running
2	5	8	Joe Weatherly	Bud Moore '61 Pontiac	249	600	Running
3	2	43	Richard Petty	Petty Eng '62 Plymouth	248	400	Running
4	9	87	Buck Baker	Baker '62 Chrysler	244	300	Running
5	4	11	Ned Jarrett	B G Holloway '62 Chevrolet	241	475	Running
6	10	61	Sherman Utsman	'62 Ford	239	240	Running
7	13	60	Tom Cox	Ray Herlocker '60 Plymouth	238	200	Running
8	14	1	George Green	Jess Potter '60 Chevrolet	231	175	Running
9	17	34	Wendell Scott	Scott '61 Chevrolet	221	150	Running
10	12	26	Earl Brooks	'60 Chevrolet	220	140	Running
11	6	54	Jimmy Pardue	Pardue '62 Pontiac	219	130	Running
12	16	62	Curtis Crider	Crider '60 Ford	218	120	Running
13	19	18	Stick Elliott	Toy Bolton '60 Ford	203	110	Running
14	18	19	Herman Beam	Beam '60 Ford	201	100	Running
15	7	49	Bob Welborn	J C Parker '62 Pontiac	163	85	Oil Pres
16	8	41	Bunkie Blackburn	Petty Eng '62 Plymouth	128	75	Steering
17	1	4	Rex White	Louis Clements '62 Chevrolet	118	65	Shocks
18	11	86	Buddy Baker	Buck Baker '61 Chrysler	21	60	Fuel Pmp
19	15	36	Larry Thomas	Wade Younts '62 Dodge	4	50	H Gasket

Time of Race: 1 hour, 16 minutes, 38 seconds
Average Speed: 78.294 mph
Pole Winner: Jack Smith - 82.285 mph
Lap Leaders: Rex White 1-118, Jack Smith 119-250
Cautions: None
Margin of Victory:
Attendance: 5,000

Grand National Race No. 32
200 Laps at Greenville-Pickens
Speedway
Greenville, SC
100 Miles on Half-mile Dirt Track
July 14, 1962

Fin	St	No.	Driver	Team / Car	Laps	Money	Status
1	4	43	Richard Petty	Petty Eng '62 Plymouth	200	$1,000	Running
2	2	47	Jack Smith	Smith '61 Pontiac	197	600	Running
3	11	34	Wendell Scott	Scott '61 Chevrolet	194	400	Running
4	3	27	Tommy Irwin	'62 Chevrolet	194	300	Running
5	1	4	Rex White	Louis Clements '62 Chevrolet	192	275	Running
6	14	62	Curtis Crider	Crider '62 Mercury	190	240	Running
7	10	61	Sherman Utsman	'62 Ford	186	200	Running
8	20	19	Herman Beam	Beam '60 Ford	185	175	Running
9	15	86	Buddy Baker	Buck Baker '61 Chrysler	176	150	Running
10	12	60	Tom Cox	Ray Herlocker '60 Plymouth	172	140	Running
11	16	118	Bob Cooper	Toy Bolton '60 Ford	167	130	Running
12	17	18	Stick Elliott	Toy Bolton '61 Pontiac	147	120	Distributo
13	13	48	Floyd Powell	Powell '60 Chevrolet	142	110	Brakes
14	9	49	Bob Welborn	J C Parker '62 Pontiac	124	100	Running
15	7	11	Ned Jarrett	B G Holloway '62 Chevrolet	118	285	Engine
16	8	1	George Green	Jess Potter '61 Chevrolet	104	75	Running
17	18	26	Earl Brooks	'60 Chevrolet	91	65	A Frame
18	6	87	Buck Baker	Baker '62 Chrysler	57	60	Oil Line
19	5	8	Joe Weatherly	Bud Moore '62 Pontiac	45	50	Fuel Pmp
20	21	6	Mark Hurley	'60 Ford	15	50	Flagged
21	19	36	Larry Thomas	Wade Younts '62 Dodge	15	50	Eng Mnt

Time of Race: 1 hour, 36 minutes, 26 seconds
Average Speed: 62.219 mph
Pole Winner: Rex White - 66.055 mph
Lap Leaders: - - - - - - - - - - - - - - Richard Petty   -200
Cautions:
Margin of Victory: 3 laps plus
Attendance:

Race No. 31
White Breaks, Smith Wins Asheville 100

ASHEVILLE, NC (July 13) -- The Grand National touring pros made their first stop at the New Asheville

Race No. 32
Richard Petty Runs Away With Greenville 100

GREENVILLE, SC (July 14) -- Richard Petty hustled to his third win of the season in the 100-mile Grand National event at Greenville-Pickens Speedway.

It was a virtual runaway for the 25 year-old Randleman, NC speedster with the toothy grin. Finishing second was Jack Smith, who was three full laps behind. Wendell Scott made a strong run from 11th starting position to finish third. Tommy Irwin came in fourth and Rex White was fifth.

Joe Weatherly got credit for 19th in the final order when fuel pump failure put his Bud Moore Pontiac out of action. His point lead was shaved to an even 1,000 points over Smith after 32 races on the 1962 slate.

Buck Baker, who qualified a Chrysler sixth fastest, fell victim to a broken oil line. He wound up 18th in the field of 21. Ned Jarrett fell out after 118 laps with a blown engine.

Petty averaged 62.219 mph for his eighth career victory.

Race No. 33

Weatherly Again In Augusta 100

AUGUSTA, GA (July 17) -- Joe Weatherly outsped Richard Petty in a stretch duel and won the 100 mile event at Augusta International Speedway. It was the sixth win of the season for the 5'7" Pontiac driver.

Petty finished second, a quarter lap behind the winner. Buck Baker got the most out of his Chrysler and finished third. Buddy Baker came in fourth in another Chrysler and Bob Welborn was fifth.

Jack Smith won the pole and led in the early going, but engine problems developed in his Pontiac after 160 laps. Second fastest qualifier Larry Frank lost a wheel on lap 108 and went to the showers. Rookie Rock Harn crashed his Ford in the second lap for the evening's only accident.

Weatherly upped his point advantage to 1,208 over Smith.

Weatherly covered the 200 laps on the half-mile dirt track at an average speed of 55.104 mph

Grand National Race No. 33
200 Laps at Augusta International Speedway
Augusta, GA
100 Miles on Half-mile Dirt Track
July 17, 1962

Fin	St	No.	Driver	Team / Car	Laps	Money	Status
1	4	8	Joe Weatherly	Bud Moore '61 Pontiac	200	$1,000	Running
2	3	43	Richard Petty	Petty Eng '62 Plymouth	200	600	Running
3	7	87	Buck Baker	Baker '62 Chrysler	198	400	Running
4	13	86	Buddy Baker	Buck Baker '61 Chrysler	196	300	Running
5	9	49	Bob Welborn	J C Parker '62 Pontiac	195	275	Running
6	14	60	Tom Cox	Ray Herlocker '60 Plymouth	194	240	Running
7	6	54	Jimmy Pardue	Pardue '62 Pontiac	192	200	Running
8	18	26	Earl Brooks	'60 Chevrolet	187	175	Running
9	11	27	Tommy Irwin	'62 Chevrolet	182	150	Axle
10	17	62	Curtis Crider	Crider '62 Mercury	180	140	Running
11	10	1	George Green	Jess Potter '61 Chevrolet	180	130	Running
12	16	36	Larry Thomas	Wade Younts '62 Dodge	177	120	Running
13	20	19	Herman Beam	Beam '60 Ford	176	110	Running
14	1	47	Jack Smith	Smith '61 Pontiac	160	100	Piston
15	5	11	Ned Jarrett	B G Holloway '62 Chevrolet	152	285	Lug Bolts
16	8	96	Tiny Lund	'61 Chevrolet	124	75	Engine
17	15	61	H G Rosier	Curtis Crider '61 Mercurey	119	65	Rear End
18	2	77	Larry Frank	Ratus Walters '62 Ford	108	60	Wheel
19	21	97	LeeRoy Yarbrough	Lewis Osborne '62 Chevrolet	69	50	Oil Leak
20	12	48	Joe Penland	Floyd Powell '60 Chevrolet	64	50	Ball Joint
21	19	18	Bob Cooper	Toy Bolton '60 Ford	38	50	Cylinder
22	22	6	Rock Harn	'60 Ford	2	50	Crash

Time of Race: 1 hour, 48 minutes, 53 seconds
Average Speed: 55.104 mph
Pole Winner: Jack Smith - 65.885 mph
Lap Leaders: Jack Smith 1 --------, Joe Weatherly ---- 200
Cautions:
Margin of Victory: 1/4 lap
Attendance:

Grand National Race No. 34
200 Laps at Savannah Speedway
Savannah, GA
100 Miles on Half-mile Dirt Track
July 20, 1962

Fin	St	No.	Driver	Team / Car	Laps	Money	Status
1	6	8	Joe Weatherly	Bud Moore '61 Pontiac	200	$1,000	Running
2	7	27	Tommy Irwin	'62 Chevrolet	200	600	Runing
3	9	43	Richard Petty	Petty Eng '62 Plymouth	200	400	Running
4	2	49	Bob Welborn	J C Parker '62 Pontiac	199	300	Running
5	14	2	Jim Paschal	Cliff Stewart '62 Pontiac	198	275	Running
6	3	11	Ned Jarrett	B G Holloway '62 Chevrolet	193	340	Running
7	15	60	Tom Cox	Ray Herlocker '60 Plymouth	193	200	Running
8	1	34	Wendell Scott	Scott '61 Chevrolet	188	175	Running
9	11	62	Curtis Crider	Crider '62 Mercury	187	150	Running
10	19	19	Herman Beam	Beam '60 Ford	183	140	Running
11	12	1	George Green	Jess Potter '61 Chevrolet	177	130	Running
12	21	79	Harry Leake	'60 Chevrolet	176	120	Running
13	16	96	Tiny Lund	'60 Chevrolet	170	110	Rear End
14	18	36	Larry Thomas	Wade Younts '62 Dodge	169	100	Running
15	17	61	Frank Brantley	Curtis Crider '61 Mercury	164	85	Running
16	10	86	Buddy Baker	Buck Baker '61 Chrysler	162	75	Electric
17	20	26	Earl Brooks	'60 Chevrolet	160	65	Running
18	5	47	Jack Smith	Smith '61 Pontiac	115	50	Housing
19	13	87	Buck Baker	Baker '62 Chrysler	107	50	Engine
20	8	97	LeeRoy Yarbrough	Lewis Osborne '62 Chevrolet	21	50	Heating
21	4	77	Larry Frank	Ratus Walters '62 Ford	17	50	Heating

Time of Race: 1 hour, 29 minutes, 14 seconds
Average Speed: 67.239 mph
Pole Winner: Wendell Scott - 71.627 mph
Lap Leaders: - - - - - - - - - - - - - - Joe Weatherly   -200
Cautions:
Margin of Victory:
Attendance:

Race No. 34

Weatherly Wins Again; Wendell Scott Fades From Pole

SAVANNAH, GA (July 20) -- Title-bound Joe Weatherly, hitting stride in the crucial mid-summer events, stormed to victory in the 100-mile Grand National race at Savannah Speedway. It was the second win in a row and the seventh of the season for the Norfolk, VA driver.

Finishing second was Keysville, VA driver Tommy Irwin, who has been close to his first Grand National win on many occasions but has yet to crack victory circle. Richard Petty grabbed third place money, Bob Welborn was fourth and Jim Paschal fifth.

The biggest surprise of the warm, humid evening was Wendell Scott's capture of the pole position at 71.627 mph. Scott faded and finished eighth, 12 laps off the pace.

Hard-luck Larry Frank qualified fourth, but fell out with overheating problems after just 17 laps. Jack Smith and LeeRoy Yarbrough encountered mechanical problems and failed to finish.

Weatherly averaged 67.239 mph for his 20th career win.

Race No. 35

Rambi Hundred to Ned Jarrett

MYRTLE BEACH, SC (July 21) -- Ned Jarrett whisked past Jim Paschal in the 161st lap and led the rest of the way to win the 200 lap race at Rambi Raceway. It was win number four for the Newton, NC Chevrolet driver in the 1962 Grand National season.

Joe Weatherly was a full lap behind in second place. Jack Smith came in third and Buddy Baker was fourth. Fifth place went to

Ned Jarrett - tops at Myrtle Beach

Grand National Race No. 35
200 Laps at Rambi Raceway
Myrtle Beach, SC
100 Miles on Half-mile Dirt Track
July 21, 1962

Fin	St	No.	Driver	Team / Car	Laps	Money	Status
1	1	11	Ned Jarrett	B G Holloway '62 Chevrolet	200	$1,200	Running
2	4	8	Joe Weatherly	Bud Moore '60 Pontiac	199	600	Running
3	11	47	Jack Smith	Smith '62 Pontiac	196	400	Running
4	19	86	Buddy Baker	Buck Baker '61 Chrysler	195	300	Running
5	7	49	Bob Welborn	J C Parker '62 Pontiac	190	275	Running
6	3	54	Jimmy Pardue	Pardue '62 Pontiac	188	240	Running
7	15	34	Wendell Scott	Scott '61 Chevrolet	177	200	Running
8	17	19	Herman Beam	Beam '60 Ford	175	175	Running
9	18	26	Earl Brooks	'60 Chevrolet	173	150	Running
10	13	60	Tom Cox	Ray Herlocker '60 Plymouth	170	140	Running
11	16	79	Harry Leake	'60 Chevrolet	170	130	Running
12	9	62	Curtis Crider	Crider '62 Mercury	169	120	Vapor Lk
13	6	2	Jim Paschal	Cliff Stewart '62 Pontiac	163	110	Engine
14	12	48	Joe Penland	Floyd Powell '60 Chevrolet	155	100	Running
15	14	36	Larry Thomas	Wade Younts '62 Dodge	148	85	Battery
16	5	43	Richard Petty	Petty Eng '62 Plymouth	130	75	Idler Arm
17	8	1	George Green	Jess Potter '61 Chevrolet	89	65	Frame
18	2	27	Tommy Irwin	'62 Chevrolet	27	60	Engine
19	10	17	Fred Harb	Harb '61 Ford	13	50	Heating

Time of Race: 1 hour, 33 minutes, 30 seconds
Average Speed: 64.171 mph
Pole Winner: Ned Jarrett - 68.467 mph
Lap Leaders: Ned Jarrett 1-151, Jim Paschal 152-160, Jarrett 161-200
Cautions:
Margin of Victory:
Attendance:

Bob Welborn.

Jarrett started on the pole and led the first 151 laps. When he made his pit stop for tires and fuel, Paschal grabbed the lead for nine laps. Jarrett took command on lap 161 when Paschal ducked into the pits; he was never headed.

Paschal's engine blew three laps after his pit stop and he wound up 13th in the 19 car field.

Second fastest qualifier Tommy Irwin's engine let go in his Chevrolet just 27 laps into the 200 lapper. A broken idler arm sent Richard Petty to the showers after 130 laps.

Jarrett averaged 64.171 mph for his 12th Grand National victory.

Race No. 36

Paschal Lands Petty Ride; Wins Southeastern 500

BRISTOL, TN (July 29) -- Jim Paschal applied a healthy dose of finesse and outran his rough riding rivals in the second annual Southeastern 500 at Bristol International Speedway.

Grand National Race No. 36
500 Laps at Bristol International Speedway
Bristol, TN
"Southeastern 500"
250 Miles on Half-Mile Paved Track
July 29, 1962

Fin	St	No.	Driver	Team / Car	Laps	Money	Status
1	12	42	Jim Paschal	Petty Eng '62 Plymouth	500	$3,930	Running
2	4	20	Fred Lorenzen	Holman-Moody '62 Ford	500	2,370	Running
3	16	43	Richard Petty	Petty Eng '62 Plymouth	500	1,540	Running
4	14	46	Johnny Allen	Holly Farms '62 Pontiac	498	1,270	Running
5	8	29	Nelson Stacy	Holman-Moody '62 Ford	498	875	Running
6	12a	8	Joe Weatherly	Bud Moore '62 Pontiac	498	900	Running
7	11	4	Rex White	Louis Clements '62 Chevrolet	494	650	Running
8	21	41	Bunkie Blackburn	Petty Eng '62 Plymouth	491	550	Running
9	19	11	Ned Jarrett	B G Holloway '62 Chevrolet	491	675	Running
10	6	54	Jimmy Pardue	Pardue '62 Pontiac	491	450	Running
11	7	21	Marvin Panch	Wood Bros '62 Ford	489	375	Running
12	17	49	Bob Welborn	J C Parker '62 Pontiac	486	275	Running
13	18	87	Buck Baker	Baker '62 Chrysler	486	350	Running
14	5	61	Sherman Utsman	'62 Ford	483	275	Running
15	27	86	Buddy Baker	Buck Baker '62 Chrysler	483	200	Running
16	34	36	Larry Thomas	Wade Younts '62 Dodge	468	290	Running
17	26	1	George Green	Jess Potter '61 Chevrolet	467	175	Running
18	31	2	Ken Rush	Cliff Stewart '62 Pontiac	463	150	Running
19	33	34	Wendell Scott	Scott '61 Chevrolet	454	150	Running
20	25	19	Herman Beam	Beam '62 Ford	453	150	Running
21	9	47	Jack Smith	Smith '62 Pontiac	444	175	Running
22	32	35	Ray Hendrick	Rebel Racing '61 Pontiac	438	125	Running
23	40	63	John Hardy	Curtis Crider '61 Mercury	435	125	Running
24	35	83	Worth McMillion	McMillion '62 Pontiac	432	125	Running
25	29	60	Tom Cox	Ray Herlocker '60 Plymouth	430	125	Hub
26	44	79	Ralph Smith	'62 Chevrolet	392	125	Rear End
27	37	17	Fred Harb	Harb '61 Ford	385	125	Axle
28	3	72	Bobby Johns	Shorty Johns '62 Pontiac	324	375	Engine
29	2	6	Junior Johnson	Cotton Owens '62 Pontiac	283	370	Crash
30	10	20	Emanuel Zervakis	'62 Mercury	258	225	Engine
31	20	27	Tommy Irwin	'62 Chevrolet	247	100	Rear End
32	24	48	G C Spencer	Floyd Powell '62 Chevrolet	241	100	Rear End
33	39	93	Doc Reitzel	'62 Ford	228	---	Rear End
34	36	18	Stick Elliott	Toy Bolton '61 Pontiac	225	---	Engine
35	38	62	Curtis Crider	Crider '62 Mercury	213	---	Rear End
36	1	22	Fireball Roberts	Jim Stephens '62 Pontiac	185	270	Ignition
37	22	3	David Pearson	Ray Fox '62 Pontiac	135	---	Wat Pmp
38	28	64	Bill Morton	'60 Chevrolet	133	---	W Bearing
39	41	67	Reb Wickersham	Wickersham '60 Olds	133	---	Engine
40	42	89	Earl Brooks	'60 Chevrolet	110	---	Rear End
41	15	66	Larry Frank	Ratus Walters '62 Ford	78	---	Brakes
42	23	97	LeeRoy Yarbrough	Lewis Osborne '62 Chevrolet	69	---	Rear End
43	30	9	T C Hunt	Ewell Williams '62 Ford	63	---	Bearing
44	43	65	Allan Harley	'60 Dodge	5	---	Handling

Time of Race: 3 hours, 19 minutes 16 seconds
Average Speed: 75.276 mph
Pole Winner: Fireball Roberts 80.321 mph
Lap Leaders: Fireball Roberts 1-29, Junior Johnson 30-155, Fred Lorenzen 156-168,
    Richard Petty 169-171, Lorenzen 172-176, Johnny Allen 177-236, Petty 237-243,
    Johnson 244-283, Petty 284-320, Lorenzen 321-411, Paschal 412-462,
    Lorenzen 463-474, Paschal 475-500
Cautions: 4 for 21 laps
Margin of Victory: 1/2 Lap
Attendance: 15,000

In his first driving assignment for the Petty Engineering stable of the '62 campaign, the High Point, NC veteran motored past Fred Lorenzen with 26 laps to go and pulled away to a half-lap advantage at the end of the 500 lap contest around the half-mile paved track.

Lorenzen's Holman-Moody Ford tossed a wheel in the final lap, but still finished second in a shower of sparks. Third place went to Richard Petty. Johnny Allen finished fourth with Nelson Stacy fifth.

Junior Johnson slugged his way to the front and led on two occasions for a total of 246 laps. However, his Pontiac popped a tire and he crammed head first into the retaining wall on lap 283, putting him out of action.

Petty and Lorenzen fought for the lead after Johnson's departure and trackside witnesses said Lorenzen leaned heavily on Petty's rear bumper. On lap 321, the Elmhurst, IL Ford driver eased into the side of the Petty Plymouth and cut the left rear tire. The 'rub down' sent Richard to the pits and he was unable to make a run for the lead for the remainder of the race.

Lorenzen led for a 91 lap stretch, but Paschal ran him down in the final 100 laps. After an exchange of pit stops, Lorenzen held a three second advantage, which Paschal erased in a matter of eight laps.

On lap 475, Paschal whipped his car in a four wheel drift coming off the fourth turn and spurted ahead of Lorenzen for the final pass of the race.

Three Plymouths were entered by the Petty clan, with Bunkie Blackburn finishing eighth in the third entry.

Fireball Roberts led the first 29 laps from the pole, but he fell out with ignition problems after 185 laps.

A crowd of 15,000 watched Paschal win at an average speed of 75.276 mph. Four caution flags consumed 21 laps. Forty-four cars started the race and 11 went home without earning a dime.

Joe Weatherly's sixth place finish left him 1,786 points ahead of Petty in the point standings. Little Joe almost did not start the race. Qualifying 13th, he refused to line his Pontiac up on the starting grid because of an ingrained superstition about the number 13. The promoter graciously allowed him to use the starting postions designated "12a" instead of 13.

Race No. 37

Petty Falters; Weatherly Wins Confederate 200

CHATTANOOGA, TN (Aug 3) -- Joe Weatherly slipped past the faltering Plymouth of Richard Petty in the 182nd lap and went on to win the Confederate 200 at Boyd Speedway. It was the eighth win of the year for Weatherly.

Joe Weatherly - Choo Choo Champ

Fireball Roberts, the only other driver to complete the 200 laps around the .333-mile paved track, wound up second. Jim Paschal was third, Petty sputtered to a fourth place finish and Sherman Utsman was fifth.

Ned Jarrett led the first nine laps but fell steadily back and wound up ninth. Junior Johnson, taking a ride in the Ray Fox Pontiac, was sidelined by overheating problems after 123 laps. Johnson was in line to take the Fox ride when the veteran mechanic and car owner dismissed David Pearson.

Weatherly, wheeling Bud Moore's Pontiac, averaged 71.145 mph in the 66.7-mile event.

Grand National Race No. 37
200 Laps at Boyd Speedway
Chattanooga, TN
"Confederate 200"
66.7 Miles on .333-mile Paved Track
August 3, 1962

Fin	St	No.	Driver	Team / Car	Laps	Money	Status
1	5	8	Joe Weatherly	Bud Moore '61 Pontiac	200	$1,000	Running
2	3	22	Fireball Roberts	Jim Stephens '62 Pntiac	200	600	Running
3	9	2	Jim Paschal	Cliff Stewart '62 Pontiac	197	400	Running
4	1	42	Richard Petty	Petty Eng '62 Plymouth	197	300	Running
5	10	61	Sherman Utsman	'62 Ford	196	275	Running
6	6	48	G C Spencer	Floyd Powell '62 Chevrolet	195	240	Running
7	21	149	Bob Welborn	J C Parker '62 Pontiac	192	200	Running
8	2	11	Ned Jarrett	B G Holloway '62 Chevrolet	192	375	Running
9	13	87	Buck Baker	Baker '62 Chrysler	192	150	Running
10	4	47	Jack Smith	Smith '62 Pontiac	191	140	Running
11	17	86	Buddy Baker	Buck Baker '61 Chrysler	189	130	Running
12	15	34	Wendell Scott	Scott '61 Chevrolet	188	120	Running
13	12	79	Harold Fryar	'62 Chevrolet	187	110	Running
14	14	62	Curtis Crider	Crider '62 Mercury	186	100	Running
15	16	1	George Green	Jess Potter '61 Chevrolet	184	85	Running
16	18	19	Herman Beam	Beam '62 Ford	172	75	Running
17	7	3	Junior Johnson	Ray Fox '62 Pontiac	123	65	Heating
18	19	63	Jerry Smith	Curtis Crider '61 Mercury	109	60	Lug Bolts
19	11	9	T C Hunt	Ewell Williams '62 Ford	94	50	Rear End
20	8	49	Friday Hassler	J C Parker '61 Pontiac	55	50	Rear End
21	20	39	Nero Steptoe	'60 Chevrolet	36	50	W Bearing

Time of Race: 56 min, 10 seconds
Average Speed: 71.145 mph
Pole Winner: Richard Petty - 73.365 mph
Lap Leaders: Ned Jarrett 1-9, Richard Petty 10-181, Joe Weatherly 182-200
Cautions:
Margin of Victory:
Attendance:

Race No. 38

Paschal Perfect in Petty Plymouth

NASHVILLE, TN (Aug 5) -- Jim Paschal's smooth and steady pace netted a four lap victory in the sweltering Nashville 500 Grand National race at the Nashville Fairgrounds Speedway.

Grand National Race No. 38
500 Laps at Fairgrounds Speedway
Nashville, TN
"Nashville 500"
250 Miles on Half-mile Paved Track
August 5, 1962

Fin	St	No.	Driver	Team / Car	Laps	Money	Status
1	3	42	Jim Paschal	Petty Eng '62 Plymouth	500	$3,250	Running
2	2	43	Richard Petty	Petty Eng '62 Pontiac	489	1,875	Running
3	9	87	Buck Baker	Baker '62 Chrysler	493	1,350	Running
4	10	8	Joe Weatherly	Bud Moore '62 Pontiac	489	800	Running
5	11	2	Tom Cox	Cliff Stewart '62 Pontiac	471	700	Running
6	13	1	George Green	Jess Potter '61 Chevrolet	463	600	Running
7	16	19	Herman Beam	Beam '62 Ford	452	500	Running
8	12	36	Larry Thomas	Wade Younts '62 Dodge	422	500	Running
9	8	11	Ned Jarrett	B G Holloway '62 Chevrolet	387	550	Engine
10	17	62	Curtis Crider	Crider '62 Mercury	384	365	Rock Arm
11	5	48	G C Spencer	Floyd Powell '62 Chevrolet	357	350	Running
12	15	149	Bob Welborn	J C Parker '62 Pontiac	333	225	Running
13	6	61	Sherman Utsman	'62 Ford	330	240	Hub
14	24	79	Ralph Smith	'62 Chevrolet	292	175	Drive Sh
15	19	34	Wendell Scott	Scott '61 Chevrolet	244	150	Crash
16	4	54	Jimmy Pardue	Pardue '62 Pontiac	204	150	Engine
17	1	46	Johnny Allen	Holly Farm '62 Pontiac	179	175	Crash
18	7	47	Jack Smith	Smith '62 Pontiac	119	150	Heating
19	20	22	Fireball Roberts	Jim Stephens '62 Pontiac	78	150	Steering
20	18	49	Nero Steptoe	J C Parker '61 Pontiac	78	150	Crash
21	14	86	Buddy Baker	Buck Baker '61 Chrysler	60	150	H Gasket
22	22	60	Harold Carmac	Ray Herlocker '60 Plymouth	12	150	Oil Pres
23	23	63	Earl Brooks	Curtis Crider '61 Mercury	2	150	Handling
24	25	41	Joe Lee Johnson	'61 Pontiac	2	150	Clutch
25	21	74	Hank Grilliot	'62 Studebaker	1	150	Handling

Time of Race: 3 hours, 52 minutes, 41 seconds
Average Speed: 64.469 mph
Pole Winner: Johnny Allen - 77.854 mph
Lap Leaders: Johnny Allen 1-46, Richard Petty 47-180, Jim Paschal 181-189, Petty 190,
   Buck Baker 191-202, Paschal 203-500
Cautions: 3 for 108 laps
Margin of Victory: 4 laps plus
Attendance: 12,596

The 35 year-old High Point, NC veteran poked the nose of his Petty Engineering Plymouth into the lead in the 203rd lap and was never headed in the wreck-marred 500 lapper. Three caution flags for a whopping 108 laps kept the winning average speed down to 64.469 mph.

It was Paschal's second start in a Plymouth out of the Lee Petty stable of Randleman, NC -- and it was his second straight triumph.

Richard Petty finished second with Buck Baker third. Joe Weatherly took another step closer to the national driving title by coming home fourth. Fifth place went to rookie Thomas Cox.

Johnny Allen started on the pole for the third time in his career and led the first 46 laps. Petty and Paschal traded the lead for the rest of the race except for a 12 lap stint led by Buck Baker's Chrysler. Tire problems foiled Allen. A blown tire sent him to the pits while leading, which gave the lead to Petty. Allen got back out on the track and was hustling to make up lost time when another tire blew, sending his Holly Farms Pontiac into the wall.

Wendell Scott broke a spindle on lap 256 on his Chevrolet and ripped out 20 wooden fence posts. The caution flag was out for almost a half hour while track maintenance workers repaired the retaining barrier. Nero Steptoe slugged the wall early in the race after a tire blew on his Pontiac. No drivers were injured.

A crowd of 12,596 showed up on the humid afternoon as temperatures reached into the upper 90's. Paschal's victory was the 12th of his career.

tional race at Huntsville Speedway.

Petty started on the pole and led the entire 200 laps on the compact quarter-mile paved track. Bob Welborn wound up in second place, a full lap behind Petty when the checkered flag fell. Jim Paschal, back in Cliff Stewart's Pontiac, came in third with Buck Baker and Ned Jarrett rounding out the top five.

Joe Weatherly wound up in seventh place and held a 1,690 point lead over Petty in the NASCAR point standings.

G.C. Spencer surprised everyone with a solid third fastest qualifying time. However, the 37 year-old Jonesboro TN Chevrolet driver fell out after only two laps and finished dead last.

Petty averaged 54.644 mph in the caution-free event.

Grand National Race No. 39
200 Laps at Huntsville Speedway
Huntsville, AL
50 Miles on Quarter-mile Paved Track
August 8, 1962

Fin	St	No.	Driver	Team / Car	Laps	Money	Status
1	1	43	Richard Petty	Petty Eng '62 Plymouth	200	$580	Running
2	5	49	Bob Welborn	J C Parker '62 Pontiac	199	475	Running
3	7	2	Jim Paschal	Cliff Stewart '62 Pontiac	198	400	Running
4	8	87	Buck Baker	Baker '62 Chrysler	198	325	Running
5	2	11	Ned Jarrett	B G Holloway '62 Chevrolet	198	450	Running
6	4	47	Jack Smith	Smith '62 Pontiac	195	230	Running
7	6	8	Joe Weatherly	Bud Moore '61 Pontiac	193	195	Running
8	9	86	Buddy Baker	Buck Baker '61 Chrysler	193	180	Running
9	12	36	Larry Thomas	Wade Younts '62 Dodge	186	165	Running
10	13	79	T C Hunt	'62 Chevrolet	182	140	Running
11	11	62	Curtis Crider	Crider '62 Mercury	179	145	Running
12	10	19	Herman Beam	Beam '61 Ford	179	120	Running
13	15	1	George Green	Jess Potter '61 Chevrolet	179	110	Running
14	16	89	Wendell Scott	Scott '60 Chevrolet	56	115	Brake Cyl
15	14	39	Nero Steptoe	'60 Chevrolet	54	75	Rear End
16	3	48	G C Spencer	Floyd Powell '62 Chevrolet	2	75	Timing

Time of Race: 54 minutes, 54 seconds
Average Speed: 54.644 mph
Pole Winner: Richard Petty - 54.086 mph
Lap Leaders: Richard Petty 1-200
Cautions:
Margin of Victory: 1 lap plus
Attendance:

Race No. 40

3 P's Again -- Paschal in a Petty Plymouth Takes Weaverville 500

WEAVERVILLE, NC (Aug 12) -- Jim Paschal made it 3-for-3 in the saddle of the potent Petty Engineering Plymouth by capturing first place in the fifth annual Western North Carolina 500 at Asheville-Weaverville Speedway.

Paschal led the final 337 laps en route to his fourth win of the year -- and his third straight since joining the Petty team in selected major events on NASCAR's premier stock car racing circuit. Joe Weatherly finished in second place, three laps behind. Rex White took third, Ned Jarrett was fourth and Jack Smith fifth.

Two caution flags did not keep Paschal from setting a new record for the 250-mile distance. The High Point, NC furniture salesman hung a new standard of 77.492 mph for the 500-lapper on the half mile track located in the rural Carolina mountains.

Smith started on the pole and led the first 163 laps. The Sandy Springs, GA veteran made several pit stops for tires and wound up 12 laps of the pace.

A crowd of 6,000 -- far below Weaverville standards -- watched Paschal win his fourth race of the year. His previous best was three wins in 1955.

Race No. 39

Petty Crushes 'Em in Huntsville 50-miler

HUNTSVILLE, AL (Aug 8) -- Richard Petty scored his fourth win of the year in convincing fashion as he blitzed the 16 car field in the 50-mile Grand Na-

Grand National Race No. 40
500 Laps at Asheville-Weaverville Speedway
Weaverville, NC
"Western North Carolina 500"
250 Miles on Half-mile Paved Track
August 12, 1962

Fin	St	No.	Driver	Team / Car	Laps	Money	Status
1	2	42	Jim Paschal	Petty Eng '62 Plymouth	500	$2,350	Running
2	7	8	Joe Weatherly	Bud Moore '62 Pontiac	497	1,625	Running
3	5	4	Rex White	Louis Clements '62 Chevrolet	495	1,150	Running
4	11	11	Ned Jarrett	B G Holloway '62 Chevrolet	494	1,150	Running
5	1	47	Jack Smith	Smith '62 Pontiac	488	800	Running
6	3	54	Jimmy Pardue	Pardue '62 Pontiac	487	650	Running
7	6	43	Richard Petty	Petty Eng '62 Plymouth	485	600	Running
8	14	1	George Green	Jess Potter '61 Chevrolet	456	550	Running
9	15	2	Tom Cox	Cliff Stewart '62 Pontiac	454	450	Running
10	17	36	Larry Thomas	Wade Younts '62 Dodge	451	400	Running
11	21	63	Curtis Crider	Crider '61 Mercury	438	375	Running
12	18	83	Worth McMillion	McMillion '62 Pontiac	413	375	Running
13	16	19	Herman Beam	Beam '62 Ford	377	325	Running
14	25	89	Wendell Scott	Scott '60 Chevrolet	371	275	Running
15	24	00	Eddie Pagan	'62 Chevrolet	354	250	Running
16	9	61	Sherman Utsman	'62 Ford	273	250	Rear End
17	19	60	Ray Hughes	Ray Herlocker '60 Plymouth	235	250	Clutch
18	4	27	Tommy Irwin	'62 Chevrolet	151	225	Rear End
19	10	49	Bob Welborn	J C Parker '62 Pontiac	116	225	Fuel Line
20	22	51	Bob Cooper	'60 Ford	106	225	Trans
21	20	79	Bill Smith	'62 Chevrolet	60	200	Crash
22	12	48	G C Spencer	Floyd Powell '62 Chevrolet	46	200	Valve
23	8	87	Buck Baker	Baker '62 Chrysler	26	175	Oil Leak
24	13	86	Buddy Baker	Buck Baker '61 Chrysler	18	150	Oil Press
25	23	65	Allan Harley	'60 Dodge	10	150	Oil Line

Time of Race: 3 hours, 13 minutes, 34 seconds
Average Speed: 77.492 mph
Pole Winner: Jack Smith - 82.720 mph
Lap Leaders: Jack Smith 1-163, Jim Paschal 164-500
Cautions: 2
Margin of Victory: 3 laps plus
Attendance: 6,000

The victory was Petty's fifth of the year and 10th of his career. He covered the 50 miles at a 51.165 mph clip after Smith had won the pole at 54.086 mph.

Weatherly still held a comfortable 1,814 point lead over Petty in the Grand National point standings.

Grand National Race No. 41
200 Laps at Roanoke Raceway
Roanoke, VA
50 Miles on Quarter-mile Paved Track
August 15, 1962

Fin	St	No.	Driver	Team / Car	Laps	Money	Status
1	2	42	Richard Petty	Petty Eng '62 Plymouth	200	$550	Running
2	7	8	Joe Weatherly	Bud Moore '62 Pontiac	200	480	Running
3	3	11	Ned Jarrett	B G Holloway '62 Chevrolet	200	575	Running
4	4	49	Bob Welborn	J C Parker '62 Pontiac	200	325	Running
5	1	47	Jack Smith	Smith '62 Pontiac	200	245	Running
6	6	2	Tom Cox	Cliff Stewart '62 Pontiac	197	225	Running
7	8	54	Jimmy Pardue	Pardue '62 Pontiac	196	210	Running
8	12	36	Larry Thomas	Wade Younts '62 Dodge	190	180	Running
9	9	60	Ray Hughes	Ray Herlocker '60 Plymouth	189	165	Running
10	5	48	G C Spencer	Floyd Powell '62 Chevrolet	186	190	Trans
11	10	63	Curtis Crider	Crider '61 Mercury	186	145	Rear End
12	14	89	Wendell Scott	Scott '60 Chevrolet	180	120	Running
13	11	19	Herman Beam	Beam '60 Ford	176	125	Running
14	16	17	Fred Harb	Harb '60 Ford	154	115	Tires
15	13	97	Harry Leake	Lewis Osborne '60 Chevrolet	36	75	Engine
16	17	83	Worth McMillion	McMillion '62 Pontiac	24	75	Handling
17	15	1	George Green	Jess Potter '60 Chevrolet	17	75	Drive Sh
18	18	00	Dick Getty	'62 Chevrolet	8	60	Handling

Time of Race: 58 minutes, 38 seconds
Average Speed: 51.165 mph
Pole Winner: Jack Smith - 54.086 mph
Lap Leaders: - - - - - - - - - - - - - - Richard Petty   -200
Cautions:
Margin of Victory: 4 seconds
Attendance:

Race No. 41

Richard Runs Rapid At Roanoke

ROANOKE, VA (Aug 15) -- Richard Petty made it five out of six for the powerful Petty Plymouth team by stomping the competition in the 50-mile event at Roanoke Raceway.

The 200 lapper on the tiny quarter-mile paved oval was a hard fought contest as the top five finishers all completed the prescribed distance. Joe Weatherly wound up second, 4.0 seconds behind the winner. Ned Jarrett took third spot, Bob Welborn was fourth and Jack Smith fifth.

Thomas Cox, leading candidate for Rookie of the Year honors, finished sixth in the Cliff Stewart Pontiac recently vacated by Jim Paschal.

Race No. 42

Petty Survives Protest; Wins International 200

WINSTON-SALEM, NC (Aug 18) -- Richard Petty and Jack Smith waged a furious duel for most of the way; then Petty ran off and hid in the late stages and won the International 200 at Bowman-Gray Stadium. It was the sixth win of the year for the 25 year-old sensation, but this one was shrouded by controversy.

Smith finished second after losing a full lap to Petty in the final 44 laps. Joe Weatherly wound up third, Jimmy Pardue was fourth and G.C. Spencer fifth.

Smith and Weatherly protested the Petty Plymouth

in unison immediately after the race, and both put up the protest fee to take a look at the engine in the winning car. Dick Beaty presided over the inspection since NASCAR Chief Inspector Norris Friel was not on hand. A big question mark was raised over the possible illegality of Petty's manifold. Beaty took the manifold to Charlotte where it was ruled 'legal' a day later. Smith and Weatherly objected to the manner in which NASCAR handled the situation.

A crowd of 13,000 was on hand to watch 10 compact sports cars tackle the big bore Grand Nationals. Bill Whitley drove a Corvette to a 12th place finish 29 laps behind Petty. It was the best effort of the small cars.

Smith started on the pole and swapped the lead three times with Petty, who averaged a record 48.875 mph for the 200 laps on the flat quarter-mile oval.

Grand National Race No. 43
200 Laps at Hub City Speedway
Spartanburg, SC
100 Miles on Half-mile Dirt Track
August 21, 1962

Fin	St	No.	Driver	Team / Car	Laps	Money	Status
1	1	43	Richard Petty	Petty Eng '62 Plymouth	200	$1,000	Running
2	6	8	Joe Weatherly	Bud Moore '61 Pontiac	200	600	Running
3	5	47	Jack Smith	Smith '61 Pontiac	197	400	Running
4	2	6	Cotton Owens	Owens '60 Pontiac	197	300	Running
5	4	48	G C Spencer	Floyd Powell '62 Chevrolet	195	275	Running
6	13	36	Larry Thomas	Wade Younts '62 Dodge	192	240	Running
7	15	51	Bob Copper	'60 Ford	184	200	Running
8	10	19	Herman Beam	Beam '60 Ford	181	175	Running
9	11	1	George Green	Jess Potter '60 Chevrolet	171	150	Running
10	3	11	Ned Jarrett	B G Holloway '62 Chevrolet	158	230	Crash
11	12	89	Wendell Scott	Scott '60 Chevrolet	155	130	Clutch
12	14	60	Ray Hughes	Ray Herlocker '60 Plymouth	143	120	Trans
13	7	27	Tommy Irwin	'62 Chevrolet	123	100	Crash
14	9	63	Curtis Crider	Crider '61 Mercury	118	100	Rear End
15	8	2	Tom Cox	Cliff Stewart '62 Pontiac	107	85	Steering
18	16	00	Dick Getty	'62 Ford	18	75	A Frame

Time of Race: 1 hour, 40 minutes, 13 seconds
Average Speed: 59.870 mph
Pole Winner: Richard Petty - 61.59 mph
Lap Leaders: - - - - - - - - - - - - - - Richard Petty   -200
Cautions:
Margin of Victory:
Attendance:

Grand National Race No. 42
200 Laps at Bowman-Gray Stadium
Winston-Salem, NC
"International 200"
50 Miles on Quarter-mile Paved Trck
August 18, 1962

Fin	St	No.	Driver	Team / Car	Laps	Money	Status
1	3	43	Richard Petty	Petty Eng '62 Plymouth	200	$600	Running
2	1	47	Jack Smith	Smith '61 Pontiac	199	450	Running
3	2	8	Joe Weatherly	Bud Moore '61 Pontiac	199	400	Running
4	4	54	Jimmy Pardue	Pardue '62 Pontiac	199	290	Running
5	6	48	G C Spencer	Floyd Powell '62 Chevrolet	196	250	Running
6	7	49	Ned Jarrett	J C Parker '62 Pontiac	196	430	Running
7	5	00	Dick Getty	'62 Chevrolet	192	205	Running
8	11	63	Curtis Crider	Crider '61 Mercury	188	175	Running
9	15	89	Wendell Scott	Scott '60 Chevrolet	186	165	Running
10	12	60	Ray Hughes	Ray Herlocker '60 Plymouth	182	170	Running
11	14	19	Herman Beam	Beam '60 Ford	177	130	Running
12	13	17X	Bill Whitely	Corvette	171	370	Running
13	8	2	Tom Cox	Cliff Stewart '62 Pontiac	137	110	Timing
14	9	17	Fred Harb	Harb '61 Ford	102	120	Heating
15	24	32	Robert Berrier	MG	100	250	Running
16	10	36	Larry Thomas	Wade Younts '62 Dodge	84	95	Engine
17	18	71	Warren Scott	Austin Healey	79	175	
18	21	21	Doug Duval	Sprite	59	160	
19	20	9	Bill Faulkner	MGA	43	125	
20	22	114	Steve Garrett	MGA	40	75	
21	23	53	Kelly Ryan	Sprite	34	75	
22	16	7	Bill Block	Alfa Romeo	32	75	
23	19	27	Paul Lyons	Sprite	9	25	
24	17	4	Jim Street	MGA	8	50	

Time of Race: 1 hour, 4 minutes
Average Speed: 46.875 mph
Pole Winner: Jack Smith - 48.102 mph
Lap Leaders: Jack Smith 1-138, Richard Petty 139-147, Smith 148-155, Petty 156-200
Cautions: None
Margin of Victory: 1 lap plus
Attendance: 13,000

Race No. 43

Petty Nips Weatherly at Spartanburg

SPARTANBURG, SC (Aug 21) -- Richard Petty continued his hot streak by driving his blue Plymouth to victory in the 100-miler at Hub City Speedway. It was his seventh win of the season and the third in seven days.

Joe Weatherly trailed Petty at the finish line by nearly a half lap. Jack Smith came in third, Cotton Owens was fourth and G.C. Spencer fifth.

Ned Jarrett qualified third and ran with the leaders for three-quarters of the race. But the Newton, NC former champion popped a tire and his Chevrolet splintered the guard rail. He was not hurt.

Hard-luck Tommy Irwin also had a bout with the retaining wall.

Petty averaged 59.870 mph for his 13th career victory.

Grand National Race No. 44
200 Laps at Valdosta 75 Speedway
Valdosta, GA
100 Miles on Half-mile Dirt Track
August 25, 1962

Fin	St	No.	Driver	Team / Car	Laps	Money	Status
1	5	11	Ned Jarrett	B G Holloway '62 Chevrolet	200	$1,200	Running
2	1	43	Richard Petty	Petty Eng '62 Plymouth	199	600	Running
3	2	8	Joe Weatherly	Bud Moore '61 Pontiac	197	400	Running
4	11	48	G C Spencer	Floyd Powell '62 Chevrolet	191	300	Running
5	4	179	LeeRoy Yarbrough	'62 Chevrolet	191	275	Running
6	6	36	Larry Thomas	Wade Younts '62 Dodge	189	240	Running
7	8	89	Wendell Scott	Scott '60 Chevrolet	183	200	Steering
8	10	63	Curtis Crider	Crider '62 Mercury	182	175	Running
9	7	1	George Green	Jess Potter '60 Chevrolet	182	150	Running
10	12	19	Herman Beam	Beam '60 Ford	161	140	Running
11	3	47	Jack Smith	Smith '61 Pontiac	130	130	Oil Leak
12	9	62	Sam McQuagg	'60 Ford	51	120	Engine
13	13	38	Sam Packard	Matt DeMatthews '61 Ford	45	110	Piston

Time of Race: 1 hour, 37 minutes, 38 seconds
Average Speed: 61.454 mph
Pole Winner: Richard Petty - 59.386 mph
Lap Leaders: - - - - - - - - - - - - - - Ned Jarrett   -200
Cautions:
Margin of Victory: 1 lap plus
Attendance:

Race No. 44

Jarrett Snaps Petty Streak At Valdosta

VALDOSTA, GA (Aug 25) -- Ned Jarrett broke Richard Petty's three race winning streak by taking a one lap win in the 100-miler at Valdosta 75 Speedway. It was the fifth win of the year for the 29 year-old Newton, NC Chevrolet driver.

Petty drove his Plymouth into second place and Joe Weatherly finished third. Petty dipped slightly into Weatherly's point lead, now trailing by 1,750 points. G.C. Spencer came in fourth and LeeRoy Yarbrough was fifth.

Only 13 cars showed up for the 200 lapper on the half-mile dirt track. Local star Sam McQuagg drove a Ford 51 laps before blowing his engine. He had qualified ninth fastest.

Petty won the pole at 59.386 mph and Jarrett average 61.454 mph for the entire 100 miles. The track was watered heavily just before time trials, holding down qualifying speeds.

Race No. 45

Larry Frank Declared Southern 500 Winner After Scoring Re-check

Larry Frank

DARLINGTON, SC (Sept 3) -- Larry Frank of Indianapolis was declared the winner of the controversial 12th renewal running of the Southern 500 at Darlington Raceway after Junior Johnson had been flagged the winner. In an official statement made at midnight on Labor Day, the first six positions were shuffled in perhaps the most embarrassing scoring foul-up NASCAR has ever encountered.

Originally Frank, a 32 year-old ex-Marine, had not been credited with leading a single lap in the 364 lap event on the 1.375-mile egg-shaped oval. Johnson had been flagged in first place with Marvin Panch, David Pearson, Frank Jim Paschal and Richard Petty in that order.

Johnny Allen skids along guard rail in Southern 500

Grand National Race No. 45
364 Laps at Darlington Raceway
Darlington, SC
"Southern 500"
500 Miles on 1.375 Mile Paved Track
September 3, 1962

Fin	St	No.	Driver	Team / Car	Laps	Money	Status
1	10	66	Larry Frank	Ratus Walters '62 Ford	364	$21,730	Running
2	2	3	Junior Johnson	Ray Fox '62 Pontiac	364	10,155	Running
3	8	21	Marvin Panch	Wood Bros '62 Ford	364	5,150	Running
4	7	6	David Pearson	Cotton Owens '62 Pontiac	364	3,325	Running
5	6	43	Richard Petty	Petty Eng '62 Plymouth	363	5,450	Running
6	14	42	Jim Paschal	Petty Eng '62 Plymouth	363	2,025	Running
7	12a	29	Nelson Stacy	Holman-Moody '62 Ford	363	1,525	Running
8	30	11	Ned Jarrett	B G Holloway '62 Chevrolet	360	1,575	Running
9	18	4	Rex White	Louis Clement '62 Chevrolet	359	1,355	Running
10	5	8	Joe Weatherly	Bud Moore '62 Pontiac	357	1,025	Running
11	23	87	Buck Baker	Baker '62 Chrysler	357	950	Running
12	12	54	Jimmy Pardue	Pardue '62 Pontiac	357	900	Running
13	16	20	Emanuel Zervakis	'62 Mercury	355	800	Running
14	28	49	Bob Welborn	J C Parker '62 Pontiac	354	700	Running
15	31	61	Sherman Utsman	'62 Ford	346	650	Running
16	27	82	Elmo Langley	'61 Ford	344	620	Running
17	24	5	H G Rosier	'61 Pontiac	343	550	Wheel
18	42	97	Paul Lewis	Louis Osborne '62 Chevrolet	340	500	Running
19	11	30	Tiny Lund	Fred Clark '62 Chevrolet	335	470	Running
20	34	84	Red Foote	G Hinton '61 Ford	334	450	Running
21	33	1	George Green	Jess Potter '61 Chevrolet	332	400	Running
22	32	68	Ed Livingston	Livingston '61 Ford	330	400	Running
23	38	62	Curtis Crider	Crider '62 Mercury	304	400	Running
24	3	28	Fred Lorenzen	LaFayette '62 Ford	291	730	Engine
25	39	19	Herman Beam	Beam '61 Ford	286	400	Running
26	9	46	Johnny Allen	Holly Farms '62 Pontiac	275	550	Crash
27	29	83	LeeRoy Yarbrough	Worth McMillion '62 Pontiac	259	400	Engine
28	22	48	G C Spencer	Floyd Powell '62 Chevrolet	200	400	W Bearing
29	37	96	T C Hunt	'61 Chevrolet	196	400	Engine
30	15	26	Darel Dieringer	Mamie Reynolds '62 Ford	184	450	Crash
31	4	72	Bobby Johns	Shorty Johns '62 Pontiac	184	1,070	Crash
32	21	41	Bunkie Blackburn	Petty Eng '62 Plymouth	181	400	Crash
33	36	93	Doc Reitzel	Reitzel, '62 Ford	161	400	Trans
34	17	47	Jack Smith	Smith '62 Pontiac	111	550	Crash
35	30	36	Larry Thomas	Wade Younts '62 Dodge	95	400	Trans
36	1	22	Fireball Roberts	Jim Stephens '62 Pontiac	74	1,030	Crash
37	20	86	Buddy Baker	Buck Baker '62 Chrysler	58	400	Distributor
38	25	92	Cale Yarborough	Donald Harrison '62 Ford	39	650	Heating
39	26	81	Roscoe Thompson	'62 Mercury	39	530	Crash
40	41	79	Bill Champion	'62 Chevrolet	15	400	Trans
41	35	18	Stick Elliott	Toy Bolton '61 Pontiac	14	400	Engine
42	40	91	Gary Sain	Bob Osiecki '62 Dodge	11	400	Fuel Pmp
43	43	2	Thomas Cox	Cliff Stewart '62 Pontiac	4	400	Oil Pres
44	44	38	Mat DeMatthews	DeMatthews '61 Ford	2	400	Oil Pres

Time of Race: 4 hours, 14 minutes, 34 seconds
Average Speed: 117.965 mph
Pole Winner: Fireball Roberts - 130.246 mph
Lap Leaders: Fireball Roberts 1-58, Bobby Johns 59-75, Richard Petty 76,
    Jim Paschal 77-85, Johns 86-125, Fred Lorenzen 126-156, Petty 157-160,
    Junior Johnson 161-189, Petty 190-279, Larry Frank 280-364
Cautions: 4 for 27 laps
Margin of Victory: 5 seconds
Attendance: 60,000

Morris Metcalfe was independently scoring the South-ern 500. While most of the scorers had Junior Johnson leading and eventually winning the Labor Day Classic, Metcalfe's sheets indicated Larry Frank was in front. A few weeks later Metcalfe was promoted by NASCAR.

The media and most of the 60,000 fans in attendance felt that Frank had been the leader for at least the final 80 laps. Lee Petty was the first to actually file an official protest on the finishing order NASCAR had posted. Frank, suffering from dehydration and blisters on his eyes, immediately left the track and went to Horne's Motor Lodge in Florence.

After cross-checking the score cards, NASCAR chief scorer, Joe Epton, made a prepared statement that one of Frank's scorers had shortened him a lap. He was credited with winning his first Grand National race. It came in his 64th big league start.

Despite Frank's claim that Johnson wasn't even in the lead lap, Johnson got credit for second place, 5.0 seconds behind the winner. Panch was lowered to third, Pearson dropped to fourth, Petty elevated to fifth and Paschal dropped to sixth. Officially, Frank led the final 66 trips around the "Lady in Black" and won $21,730.

Petty had been in a position to grab his first super-speedway win. He had led for 90 laps and was hounding Frank in the late stages. A blown tire four laps from the finish removed him from the hunt and he wound up a lap off the pace.

After the check of the score cards, Johnson led only 29 laps. Midway in the race his Pontiac whacked the guard rail and he spent at least two laps getting the fender pried off the tires.

Accidents were the by-word on the terribly hot day in which track temperatures soared to 140 degrees. Johnny Allen's Pontiac bounced off the guard rail and rode the narrow steel plate for a few hundred feet, dragging the undercarriage of his car along the rail. The car burst into flames as the fuel tank was punctured.

Frank's Ratus Walters-owned Ford had broken a wheel on what turned out to be his safety lap and limped across the finish line nearly a lap behind the leaders. "I got past the checkered flag, pulled my car down into the grass and parked it," Frank said later. "I never went to victory lane. I walked past it when Junior was there and I was pretty bitter about it. Junior wasn't even on the same lap."

After several agonizing moments, the Fayetteville, NC driver scrambled out unhurt.

Darel Dieringer's Ford went up in flames after a collision with Bunkie Blackburn and Bobby Johns on lap 186. Jack Smith and Fireball Roberts were also taken out by accidents.

Frank set a new record for the 500 miler at 117.965 mph. Roberts had won the pole at a speed of 130.246 mph.

Joe Weatherly finished 10th and held on to a 1,190 point lead over Petty.

The race was the 13th Southern 500 to be run, but promoter Bob Colvin officially tabbed it the "12th 'Renewal' Southern 500". Joe Weatherly, a supersticious driver, had threatened not to enter a race that had anything to do with the number "13".

Race No. 46

White Wins Shuman Memorial 250 by 9 Laps

HICKORY, NC (Sept 7) -- Rex White steered his Chevrolet past Junior Johnson in the 73rd lap and went on to score a lopsided victory in the Buddy Shuman Memorial race at Hickory Speedway.

White finished nine laps in front of runner-up Jimmy Pardue to stake claim to his seventh win of the season. Buck Baker was third, Larry Thomas fourth and Joe Weatherly fifth. There were seven different makes of cars filling the top 10 positions.

Overheating problems played havoc with a number of the 24 starters. Pit crews were kept busy battling geysers of steam and smoke. Johnson started on the pole and led the first 72 laps, but his Pontiac was kayoed by overheating problems while leading.

Fred Lorenzen, making a rare short track appearance in a Ford owned by Mamie Reynolds, fell victim to overheating gremlins after 106 laps. Jack Smith was another favorite to fall out due to a boiling radiator.

An overflow crowd of 12,000 jammed their way into the 7,000 seats and the infield at the .4-mile dirt track to watch White cover the 100 miles at a speed of 70.574 mph.

Grand National Race No. 46
250 Laps at Hickory Speedway
Hickory, NC
"Buddy Shuman Memorial"
100 Miles on .4-mile Dirt Track
September 7, 1962

Fin	St	No.	Driver	Team / Car	Laps	Money	Status
1	3	4	Rex White	Louis Clements '62 Chevrolet	250	$1,000	Running
2	4	54	Jimmy Pardue	Pardue '62 Pontiac	241	600	Running
3	9	87	Buck Baker	Baker '62 Chrysler	240	400	Running
4	13	36	Larry Thomas	Wade Younts '62 Dodge	240	300	Running
5	7	8	Joe Weatherly	Bud Moore '61 Pontiac	239	275	Running
6	14	62	Curtis Crider	Crider '62 Mercury	236	240	Running
7	2	48	G C Spencer	Floyd Powell '62 Chevrolet	233	200	Running
8	18	2	Bill Foster	Cliff Stewart '62 Pontiac	228	175	Running
9	21	19	Herman Beam	Beam '60 Ford	224	150	Running
10	5	42	Richard Petty	Petty Eng '62 Plymouth	220	140	Running
11	20	17	Fred Harb	Harb '61 Ford	206	130	Running
12	6	49	Bob Welborn	J C Parker '61 Pontiac	172	120	Running
13	17	60	Ray Hughes	Ray Herlocker '60 Plymouth	159	110	Running
14	24	1	George Green	Jess Potter '60 Chevrolet	152	100	Running
15	13	34	Wendell Scott	Scott '61 Chevrolet	150	85	H Gasket
16	12	67	Jerry Burnett	Reb's Sport Shop '60 Chevy	143	75	Oil Pres
17	11	11	Ned Jarrett	B G Holloway '62 Chevrolet	130	265	Piston
18	22	76	Neil Castles	'61 Ford	118	60	Running
19	23	51	Bob Cooper	'60 Ford	115	50	Heating
20	10	26	Fred Lorenzen	Mamie Reynolds '62 Ford	106	50	Radiator
21	1	3	Junior Johnson	Ray Fox '62 Pontiac	72	50	Radiator
22	8	91	Gary Sain	Bob Osiecki '62 Dodge	66	50	Rear End
23	16	47	Jack Smith	Smith '61 Pontiac	62	50	Radiator
24	19	63	Glenn Killian	Curtis Crider '61 Mercury	3	50	Drive Sh

Time of Race: 1 hour, 26 minutes, 01 second
Average Speed: 70.574 mph
Pole Winner: Junior Johnson - 71.357 mph
Lap Leaders: Junior Johnson 1-72, Rex White 73-250
Cautions:
Margin of Victory: 9 laps plus
Attendance: 12,000

Race No. 47

Scoring Snafu Mars Weatherly Win at Richmond

RICHMOND, VA (Sept 9) -- Joe Weatherly powered his way past Fred Lorenzen in the 227th lap and ran away from the pack to win the inaugural Capital City 300 at the Atlantic Rural Fairgrounds Speedway. It was the ninth win of the year for the title bound Weatherly.

Jim Paschal finished second, Lorenzen was third and Richard Petty fourth. Rex White nabbed fifth spot.

Once again, scoring foul-ups marred Weatherly's victory. The official rundown with Weatherly atop the 33 car field, was not announced until most of the 13,000 spectators had left the track. In the original rundown, Weatherly was left entirely out of the top 10. The stubby Norfolk, VA Pontiac driver immediately

Grand National Race No. 47
300 Laps at Atlantic Rural Fairgrounds Speedway
Richmond, VA
"Capital City 300"
150 Miles on Half-mile Dirt Track
September 9, 1962

Fin	St	No.	Driver	Team / Car	Laps	Money	Status
1	2	8	Joe Weatherly	Bud Moore '62 Pontiac	300	$2,000	Running
2	4	41	Jim Paschal	Petty Eng '62 Plymouth	299	1,350	Running
3	14	26	Fred Lorenzen	LaFayette '62 Ford	296	950	Running
4	9	42	Richard Petty	Petty Eng '62 Plymouth	296	675	Running
5	1	4	Rex White	Louis Clements '62 Chevrolet	294	510	Running
6	6	11	Ned Jarrett	B G Holloway '62 Chevrolet	292	625	Running
7	19	27	Mel Bradley	'62 Chevrolet	287	350	Running
8	16	49	Bob Welborn	J C Parker '62 Pontiac	282	300	Running
9	24	00	Dick Getty	'62 Chevrolet	281	250	Running
10	12	54	Jimmy Pardue	Pardue '62 Pontiac	277	250	Running
11	8	35	Ray Hendrick	Rebel Racing '61 Pontiac	276	150	Running
12	15	62	Curtis Crider	Crider '62 Mercury	270	150	Running
13	18	36	Larry Thomas	Wade Younts '62 Dodge	269	150	Running
14	3	48	G C Spencer	Floyd Powell '62 Chevrolet	269	150	Running
15	21	98	Bill Dennis	'61 Chevrolet	268	150	Running
16	17	2	Bill Foster	Cliff Stewart '62 Pontiac	257	125	Running
17	10	22	Fireball Roberts	Jim Stephens '62 Pontiac	256	125	Running
18	25	19	Herman Beam	Beam '60 Ford	254	125	Running
19	20	17	Fred Harb	Harb '61 Ford	246	125	Running
20	28	31	Al White	'62 Ford	233	125	Distributor
21	32	34	Wendell Scott	Scott '61 Chevrolet	220	125	Ball Joint
22	33	1	George Green	Jess Potter '60 Chevrolet	220	125	Running
23	29	5	Jim Bray	'60 Ford	204	125	Radiator
24	5	20	Emanuel Zervakis	'62 Mercury	190	125	Steering
25	11	91	Gary Sain	Bob Osiecki '62 Dodge	173	---	Lug Bolts
26	27	79	T C Hunt	'62 Chevrolet	138	---	Shocks
27	31	50	Bobby Waddell	'60 Dodge	80	---	Radiator
28	26	63	Runt Harris	Curtis Crider '61 Mercury	73	---	Pistons
29	13	47	Jack Smith	Smith '62 Pontiac	50	---	Crash
30	22	87	Buck Baker	Baker '62 Chrysler	47	---	Radiator
31	23	7	Bill Champion	'60 Ford	40	---	H Gasket
32	7	64	Elmo Langley	'62 Ford	24	---	Trans
33	30	66	Larry Frank	Ratus Walters '62 Ford	2	---	Rear End

Time of Race: 2 hours, 18 minutes, 30 seconds
Average Speed: 64.981 mph
Pole Winner: Rex White-66.127 mph
Lap Leaders: - - - - - - - - - - - - - - Joe Weatherly   -300
Cautions: 1 for 9 laps
Margin of Victory: 1 lap plus
Attendance: 13,000

behind Weatherly at the finish. Modified star Ray Hendrick wound up 11th after starting eighth.

One caution flag was out for a total of nine laps. Jack Smith's Pontiac, with the accelerator stuck open down the backstretch, plunged wildly through the guard rail and down a 15 foot embankment. Smith walked away unhurt.

Grand National Race No. 48
250 Laps at Dog Track Speedway
Moyock, NC
62.5 Miles on Quarter-mile Dirt Track
September 11, 1962

Fin	St	No.	Driver	Team / Car	Laps	Money	Status
1	1	11	Ned Jarrett	B G Holloway '62 Chevrolet	250	$775	Running
2	6	8	Joe Weatherly	Bud Moore '61 Pontiac	249	500	Running
3	14	62	Curtis Crider	Crider '62 Mercury	240	380	Running
4	8	27	Mel Bradley	'62 Chevrolet	235	290	Running
5	2	1	George Green	Jess Potter '60 Chevrolet	228	245	Trans
6	12	19	Herman Beam	Beam '60 Ford	221	215	Running
7	13	34	Wendell Scott	Scott '61 Chevrolet	209	180	Running
8	7	40	Roy Hallquist	'62 Chevrolet	183	175	Rear End
9	11	23	Doug Yates	Yates '61 Plymouth	163	150	Axle
10	5	87	Buck Baker	Baker '62 Chrysler	159	190	H Gasket
11	4	42	Richard Petty	Petty Eng '62 Plymouth	151	155	Axle
12	10	49	Bob Welborn	J C Parker '62 Pntiac	143	150	Oil Pres
13	3	66	Larry Frank	Ratus Walters '62 Ford	119	130	Axle
14	15	63	Runt Harris	Curtis Crider '61 Mercury	57	100	H Gasket
15	9	36	Larry Thomas	Wade Younts '62 Dodge	53	90	Torsion B

Time of Race: 1 hour, 27 minutes, 03 seconds
Average Speed: 43.078 mph
Pole Winner: Ned Jarrett - 45.569 mph
Lap Leaders: Ned Jarrett 1-250
Cautions:
Margin of Victory: 1 lap plus
Attendance:

Race No. 48

Jarrett Flag-to-Flag at Dog Track Speedway

MOYOCK, NC (Sept 11) -- Ned Jarrett wheeled his Bee Gee Holloway Chevrolet to a decisive triumph in the 62.5-mile Grand National race at Dog Track Speedway. It was the sixth win of the year for the Newton, NC veteran, each one coming on a dirt track.

Joe Weatherly finished second and extended his point lead to 1,474 points over Richard Petty, who wound up 11th after an axle broke on his Plymouth. Third place went to Curtis "Crawfish" Crider, who turned in one of his finer efforts in his independent Mercury. Mel Bradley came in fourth and George

filed a protest, claiming scorer error. The NASCAR recheck discovered that individual scorers had "forgotten" to count almost two dozen of Weatherly's laps. He had been scored 11th, finishing after Jimmy Pardue who was 23 laps off the pace.

The lead changed hands nine time among five drivers as Weatherly collected $2,000 for his 64.981 mph ride.

A number of celebrated drivers made rare appearances on dirt, including Southern 500 winner Larry Frank. The Indianapolis driver fell out with rear gearing failure after two laps and finished dead last. Fireball Roberts finished 17th, laboring some 44 laps

Green was fifth as lightly regarded privateers gained a measurable degree of the spotlight.

Only six cars in the starting field of 15 were able to finish the race. Suspension parts and axles broke on the rough quarter-mile clay oval.

Top contenders Larry Frank, Bob Welborn and Buck Baker failed to finish.

Jarrett averaged only 43.078 mph for his 14th career Grand National win.

Grand National Race No. 49
200 Laps at Augusta Speedway
Augusta, GA
100 Miles on Half-mile Dirt Track
September 13, 1962

Fin	St	No.	Driver	Team / Car	Laps	Money	Status
1	4	26	Fred Lorenzen	Mamie Reynolds '62 Ford	200	$1,000	Running
2	5	41	Richard Petty	Petty Eng '62 Plymouth	200	600	Running
3	1	8	Joe Weatherly	Bud Moore '62 Pontiac	197	400	Running
4	2	11	Ned Jarrett	B G Holloway '62 Chevrolet	190	500	Running
5	7	34	Wendell Scott	Scott '61 Chevrolet	190	275	Running
6	15	5	H G Rosier	'61 Pontiac	189	240	Running
7	12	1	George Green	Jess Potter '60 Chevrolet	181	200	Running
8	14	19	Herman Beam	Beam '60 Ford	174	175	Running
9	10	79	T C Hunt	'62 Chevrolet	158	150	Running
10	11	62	Curtis Crider	Crider '62 Mercury	131	140	Running
11	9	87	Buck Baker	Baker '62 Chrysler	114	130	H Gasket
12	6	47	Jack Smith	Smith '61 Pontiac	94	120	Housing
13	3	92	Cale Yarborough	Donald Harrison '62 Ford	56	110	Fuel Pmp
14	13	63	George Alsobrook	'61 Ford	32	100	Spring
15	16	00	Dick Getty	'62 Chevrolet	26	85	Oil Pres
16	8	97	Bubba Farr	Lewis Osborne '62 Chevrolet	22	75	Manifold

Time of Race: 1 hour, 38 minutes, 45 seconds
Average Speed: 60.759 mph
Pole Winner: Joe Weatherly - 65.241 mph
Lap Leaders: Ned Jarrett 1-181, Fred Lorenzen 182-200
Cautions:
Margin of Victory: 1/3 lap
Attendance:

Race No. 49

Lorenzen Gives Lady Car Owner Her First GN Victory

AUGUSTA, GA (Sept 13) -- Fred Lorenzen gunned his Ford past Ned Jarrett 19 laps from the finish and sped to victory in the 100-mile event at Augusta Speedway. The Elmhurst, IL hot-shot, driving a Ford owned by wealthy heiress Mamie Reynolds, presented the lady with her first Grand National victory. It was Lorenzen's fifth Grand National win, but his first on a dirt track.

Richard Petty wound up second, one-third of a lap behind Lorenzen. Joe Weatherly was third, Ned Jarrett fourth and Wendell Scott fifth.

Jarrett started second on the grid and jumped out to an early lead. He led the first 181 laps, but went wide in a turn in the final 10 miles and slapped the wall. After a lengthy pit stop, he returned to the track, salvaging fourth place 10 laps off the pace.

Cale Yarborough, a blond-haired 22 year-old newcomer out of Timmonsville, SC, qualified a Ford owned by Donald Harrison in the third spot. His time trial was faster than heavy hitters Lorenzen, Petty, Jack Smith and Buck Baker. His bid for victory ended on lap 56 when his fuel pump died. Cale got credit for 13th place and earned $110.

Lorenzen, starting fourth, covered the 100 miles at an average speed of 60.759 mph

Race No. 50

Stacy Wins Old Dominion 500; Roberts 'Parks' Lorenzen

MARTINSVILLE, VA (Sept 23) -- A ferocious bumping duel between Fireball Roberts and Fred Lorenzen overshadowed a superlative drive by Nelson Stacy in the Old Dominion 500 at Martinsville Speedway. It was the third win of the year for the Cincinnati veteran -- all in "major" events of 250 miles or more.

Old Pro Roberts, starting on the pole, took the lead at the green flag. Lorenzen, in his third year on the Grand National tour, moved into third place early behind Roberts and his teammate Stacy. Lorenzen was eager to get to the front. He tapped the rear of Stacy's Ford a few laps before making a pass shortly before the 100 lap mark.

The day's first caution flag came out for a minor spin out. As the green fell, Lorenzen started "knocking" on Fireball's bumper. Roberts shook his finger at the "Golden Boy", but the bumping became more pronounced. After a few laps of playing bumper tag, Roberts used the oldest trick in the book for tailgaters -- a quick application of the brakes. Coming off the second turn of lap 105, Roberts jammed his brakes and Lorenzen plowed into him full bore. Both cars momentarily veered out of control. Lorenzen had to park his Ford a lap later with a busted radiator. Roberts limped home seventh in his ill-handling Pontiac. Stacy led the final 411 laps and beat runner-up Richard Petty by three laps. He won $3,655 for his Holman-Moody team. Ned Jarrett came in third, Jack Smith was fourth and Joe Weatherly fifth.

Grand National Race No. 50
500 Laps at Martinsville Speedway
Martinsville, VA
"Old Dominion 500"
250 Miles on Half-mile Paved Track
September 23, 1962

Fin	St	No.	Driver	Team / Car	Laps	Money	Status
1	3	29	Nelson Stacy	Holman-Moody '62 Ford	500	$3,655	Running
2	13	43	Richard Petty	Petty Eng '672 Plymouth	497	1,650	Running
3	21	11	Ned Jarrett	B G Holloway '62 Chevrolet	496	1,500	Running
4	34	47	Jack Smith	Smith '62 Pontiac	495	850	Running
5	2	8	Joe Weatherly	Bud Moore '62 Pontiac	495	920	Running
6	17	26	Darel Dieringer	Mamie Reynolds '62 Pontiac	495	675	Running
7	1	22	Fireball Roberts	Jim Stephens '62 Pontiac	492	800	Running
8	22	54	Jimmy Pardue	Pardue '62 Pontiac	492	550	Running
9	8	41	Jim Paschal	Petty Eng '62 Plymouth	489	425	Running
10	12	49	Bob Welborn	J C Parker '62 Pontiac	489	390	Running
11	15	27	Mel Bradley	'62 Chevrolet	485	350	Running
12	36	58	Tiny Lund	'62 Chevrolet	482	275	Running
13	23	86	Buddy Baker	Baker '62 Chrysler	479	285	Running
14	6	61	Sherman Utsman	'62 Chevrolet	476	250	Running
15	18	36	Larry Thomas	Wade Younts '62 Dodge	474	175	Running
16	16	19	Herman Beam	Beam '62 Ford	465	175	Running
17	5	3	Junior Johnson	Ray Fox '62 Pontiac	455	200	Axle
18	25	2	Bill Foster	Cliff Stewart '62 Pontiac	452	175	Running
19	27	34	Wendell Scott	Scott '61 Chevrolet	452	175	Running
20	31	91	Gary Sain	Bob Osiecki '62 Dodge	437	150	Running
21	32	37	Tom Cox	'60 Chevrolet	437	150	Running
22	14	66	Larry Frank	Ratus Walters '62 Ford	416	175	Running
23	37	60	Ray Hughes	Ray Herlocker '60 Plymouth	381	150	Running
24	29	18	Stick Elliott	Toy Bolton '61 Pontiac	337	150	Fuel Pmp
25	28	23	Doug Yates	'60 Plymouth	256	150	Engine
26	19	97	Paul Lewis	Lewis Osborne '62 Chevrolet	239	125	Rear End
27	10	4	Rex White	Louis Clements '62 Chevrolet	203	125	Engine
28	4	28	Fred Lorenzen	LaFayette '62 Ford	106	150	Crash
29	24	1	George Green	Jess Potter '61 Chevrolet	102	125	Engine
30	9	48	G C Spencer	Floyd Powell '62 Chevrolet	98	125	Crash
31	30	93	Doc Reitzel	'62 Ford	97	100	Rear End
32	11	46	Johnny Allen	Holly Farms '62 Pontiac	84	125	Crash
33	7	21	Marvin Panch	Wood Bros '62 Ford	83	125	Brakes
34	33	17	Fred Harb	Harb '61 Ford	77	100	Engine
35	26	79	T C Hunt	'62 Chevrolet	45	125	Rear End
36	20	62	Curtis Crider	Crider '62 Mercury	43	125	Oil Pres
37	35	0	E J Trivette	'61 Chevrolet	29	100	Brakes

Time of Race: 3 hours, 44 minutes, 18 seconds
Average Speed: 66.874 mph
Pole Winner: Fireball Roberts - 71.513 mph
Lap Leaders: Fireball Roberts 1-102, Fred Lorenzen 103-106, Stacy 107- 108,
   Joe Weatherly 109-189, Stacy 190-500
Cautions: 2
Margin of Victory: 3 laps plus
Attendance:11,500

Grand National Race No. 51
320 Laps at North Wilkesboro
Speedway
North Wilkesboro, NC
"Wilkes 320"
200 Miles on .625-mile Paved Track
September 30, 1962

Fin	St	No.	Driver	Team / Car	Laps	Money	Status
1	5	43	Richard Petty	Petty Eng '62 Plymouth	320	$2,560	Running
2	3	21	Marvin Panch	Wood Bros '62 Ford	320	1,400	Running
3	9	8	Joe Weatherly	Bud Moore '62 Pntiac	320	875	Running
4	7	27	Junior Johnson	Holly Farms '62 Pontiac	319	765	Running
5	4	41	Jim Paschal	Petty Eng '62 Plymouth	319	650	Running
6	1	28	Fred Lorenzen	LaFayette '62 Ford	318	770	Running
7	2	29	Nelson Stacy	Holman-Moody '62 Ford	318	500	Running
8	11	4	Rex White	Louis Clements '62 Chevrolet	318	375	Running
9	6	46	Johnny Allen	Holly Farms '62 Pontiac	318	325	Running
10	15	54	Jimmy Pardue	Pardue '62 Pontiac	316	250	Running
11	12	11	Ned Jarrett	B G Holloway '62 Chevrolet	315	425	Running
12	13	26	Darel Dieringer	Mamie Reynolds '62 Ford	315	200	Running
13	30	47	Jack Smith	Smith '62 Pontiac	314	150	Running
14	20	66	Larry Frank	Ratus Walters '62 Ford	314	165	Running
15	14	49	Bob Welborn	J C Parker '62 Pontiac	313	150	Running
16	19	36	Larry Thomas	Wade Younts '62 Dodge	309	135	Running
17	21	91	Gary Sain	Bob Osiecki '62 Dodge	299	100	Running
18	22	1	George Green	Jess Potter '61 Chevrolet	296	100	Running
19	17	48	G C Spencer	Floyd Powell '62 Chevrolet	294	125	Running
20	23	19	Herman Beam	Beam '62 Ford	288	100	Running
21	25	62	Curtis Crider	Crider '62 Mercury	258	100	Running
22	28	37	Tom Cox	'60 Chevrolet	208	100	Crash
23	18	86	Buddy Baker	Buck Baker '62 Chrysler	203	125	H Gasket
24	16	61	Sherman Utsman	'62 Ford	176	125	Crash
25	26	58	Tiny Lund	'62 Chevrolet	167	100	Manifold
26	24	2	Bill Foster	Cliff Stewart '62 Pontiac	166	50	Radiator
27	10	87	Buck Baker	Baker '62 Chrysler	137	75	W Pump
28	31	34	Wendell Scott	Scott '61 Chevrolet	110	50	Engine
29	8	22	Fireball Roberts	Jim Stephens '62 Pontiac	75	75	H Gasket
30	27	50	Bobby Waddell	'60 Dodge	53	50	Gas Tank
31	29	5	George Fox	'60 Dodge	3	50	Trans

Time of Race: 2 hours, 19 minutes, 14 seconds
Average Speed: 86.186 mph
Pole Winner: Fred Lorenzen - 94.657 mph
Lap Leaders: Fred Lorenzen 1-124, Junior Johnson 125-160, Richard Petty 161-320
Cautions: 3
Margin of Victory: 14 seconds
Attendance: 11,000

Banjo Matthews, who owns the Roberts Pontiac, was hot under the collar with what he described as "unnecessary antics" by Lorenzen. Roberts explained the incident after the race. "I warned Freddy by shaking my finger at him," he said. "That must have made him mad because he shook his finger back at me and began bumping again. I waved my hand at him and told him to lay off. But he kept it up. I didn't tell him again because I knew how to get him off me."

Lorenzen left the track and was unavailable for comment.

A crowd of 11,500 watched Stacy average 66.874 mph.

Race No. 51

Richard Petty Wins Wilkesboro on 'Fireball Roberts Day'

NORTH WILKESBORO, NC (Sept 30) -- Richard Petty shook off an early spin and drove his electric blue Plymouth to a 14 second victory in the Wilkes 320 at North Wilkesboro Speedway.

Fireball Roberts was honored in prerace ceremonies that commemorated the 15th anniversary of the track and Roberts' career - both of which began in 1947. The 33 year-old Daytona Beach Pontiac driver was one of the first men out of the race -- falling victim to a blown head gasket after just 75 laps.

Petty finished about a half-lap in front of runner-up Marvin Panch, who was driving the Wood Brothers Ford. Joe Weatherly came in third, Junior Johnson was fourth and Jim Paschal fifth.

The eventual winner spun out in the 18th lap but came back strong in the second half of the 200 miler on the .625 mile oval. He took the lead for keeps in the 161st lap and led the rest of the way. It was the eighth win of the season for the second generation driver.

Fred Lorenzen started on the pole and led the first 124 laps. His Holman-Moody Ford fell two laps off the pace in the late stages and wound up sixth in the final order.

Thomas Cox was shaken up and suffered minor leg injuries when his Chevrolet whacked the retaining wall on lap 224. Sherman Utsman was uninjured when his Ford struck the wall on lap 184.

Three caution flags slowed Petty's average speed to 86.186 mph. Weatherly's point lead was cut to 1,334 points over Petty with two races left on the 1962 slate.

Race No. 52

Johnson Wins National 400; Weatherly Cops Championship

CHARLOTTE, NC (Oct 14) -- Junior Johnson, the robust chicken farmer out of Ronda, NC, ended a 12 month famine with an impressive victory in Charlotte Motor Speedway's National 400. Consistent Joe Weatherly clinched the 1962 NASCAR Grand National championship.

Junior Johnson - winner of National 400

Grand National Race No. 52
267 Laps at Charlotte Motor Speedway
Charlotte, NC
"National 400"
400 Miles on 1.5-mile Paved Track
October 14, 1962

Fin	St	No.	Driver	Team / Car	Laps	Money	Status
1	3	3	Junior Johnson	Ray Fox '62 Pntiac	267	$11,355	Running
2	1	22	Fireball Roberts	Jim Stephens '62 Pontiac	265	5,420	Running
3	8	28	Fred Lorenzen	LaFayette '62 Ford	264	3,230	Running
4	27	83	Bunkie Blackburn	Worth McMillion '262	262	2,425	Running
5	7	8	Joe Weatherly	Bud Moore '62 Pontiac	261	1,725	Running
6	15	42	Jim Paschal	Petty Eng '62 Plymouth	259	1,250	Running
7	20	20	Emanuel Zervakis	'62 Mercury	258	1,125	Running
8	33	91	Ralph Earnhardt	Bob Osiecki '62 Dodge	258	1,225	Running
9	23	41	Speedy Thompson	Petty Eng '62 Plymouth	258	900	Running
10	19	49	Bob Welborn	J C Parker '62 Pontiac	258	825	Running
11	31	11	Ned Jarrett	B G Holloway '61 Chevrolet	255	1,300	Running
12	28	36	Larry Thomas	Wade Younts '62 Dodge	255	625	Running
13	32	90	Jimmy Thompson	Bob Osiecki '62 Dodge	254	850	Running
14	36	61	Sherman Utsman	'62 Ford	251	600	Running
15	5	21	Marvin Panch	Wood Bros '62 Ford	250	760	Block
16	12	43	Richard Petty	Petty Eng '62 Plymouth	250	475	Running
17	40	68	Ed Livingston	Livingston '61 Ford	243	475	Running
18	11	87	Buck Baker	Baker '62 Chrysler	243	450	Running
19	43	1	George Green	Jess Potter '61 Chevrolet	242	425	Running
20	18	54	Jimmy Pardue	Pardue '62 Pontiac	238	425	Running
21	30	62	Curtis Crider	Crider '62 Mercury	237	350	Running
22	44	19	Herman Beam	Beam '62 Ford	233	375	Running
23	2	6	David Pearson	Cotton Owens '62 Pontiac	230	460	Ball Joint
24	9	47	Jack Smith	Smith '62 Pontiac	223	450	Fan Belt
25	39	9	Cale Yarborough	Ewell Williams '62 Ford	212	375	W Bearing
26	34	48	G C Spencer	Floyd Powell '62 Chevrolet	204	400	Engine
27	16	12	Tiny Lund	Cliff Stewart '62 Pontiac	194	400	Timing
28	6	72	Bobby Johns	Shorty Johns '62 Pontiac	185	360	Distributo
29	29	84	Red Foote	E Hinton '61 Ford	181	300	H Gasket
30	26	4	Rex White	Louis Clements '62 Chevrolet	178	350	Engine
31	17	29	Nelson Stacy	Holman-Moody '62 Ford	177	300	Crash
32	35	30	John Sudderth	Fred Clark '62 Chevrolet	171	325	Engine
33	24	86	Buddy Baker	Buck Baker '62 Chrysler	168	250	Oil Pres
34	14	18	Stick Elliott	Toy Bolton '62 Pontiac	154	250	Engine
35	25	97	Paul Lewis	Lewis Osborne '62 Chevrolet	142	350	Crash
36	42	96	Bruce Brantley	'62 Chevrolet	139	275	Rear End
37	38	2	Bill Foster	Cliff Stewart '61 Pontiac	127	275	Brakes
38	10	26	Darel Dieringer	Mamie Reynolds '62 Ford	72	325	Engine
39	41	79	T C Hunt	'62 Ford	38	275	Engine
40	22	27	Doug Yates	'62 Chevrolet	31	250	Engine
41	13	5	H G Rosier	'61 Pontiac	22	400	Trans
44	37	38	Woody Wilson	Mat DeMatthews '61 Ford	19	275	Axle
43	21	81	LeeRoy Yarbrough	'62 Mercury	17	250	Oil Leak
44	4	46	Johnny Allen	Holly Farms '62 Pontiac	8	350	H Gasket

Time of Race: 3 hours, 01 minute, 42 seconds
Average Speed: 132.085 mph
Pole Winner: Fireball Roberts - 140.287 mph
Lap Leaders: David Pearson 1-2, Junior Johnson 3-70, Bobby Johns 71-74, Marvin Panch 75-98, Johnson 99-125, Panch 126-136, Johns 137-146, Johnson 147-183, Panch 184-195, Johnson 196-267
Cautions: 1 for 6 laps
Margin of Victory: 2 laps plus
Attendance: 40,211

Johnson drove his Ray Fox Pontiac into the lead for the final time in the 196th lap and beat Fireball Roberts by two laps to pocket the $11,355 first prize. Fred Lorenzen came in third and Bunkie Blackburn was a surprising fourth in a Pontiac owned by Worth McMillion. Champ Weatherly scampered home fifth.

Blackburn, who recently lost his assignment as third driver on the Petty Engineering team, started back in 27th place but drove his heart out. Speedy Thompson

Paul Lewis spins in 3rd turn at Charlotte

Grand National Race No. 53
267 Laps at Atlanta International Raceway
Hampton, GA
"Dixie 400"
400 Miles on 1.5-mile Paved Track
October 28, 1962

Fin	St	No.	Driver	Team / Car	Laps	Money	Status
1	5	4	Rex White	Louis Clements '62 Chevrolet	267	$10,315	Running
2	7	8	Joe Weatherly	Bud Moore '62 Pntiac	267	5,270	Running
3	3	21	Marvin Panch	Wood Bros '62 Ford	267	3,535	Running
4	15	43	Richard Petty	Petty Eng '62 Plymouth	266	2,415	Running
5	2	28	Fred Lorenzen	LaFayette '62 Ford	266	2,000	Running
6	28	77	Larry Frank	Ratus Walters '62 Ford	264	1,300	Running
7	39	18	Stick Elliott	Toy Bolton '62 Pontiac	263	1,175	Running
8	27	47	Buck Baker	Jack Smith '62 Pontiac	263	1,125	Running
9	12	17	Jack Smith	Smith '62 Pontiac	262	900	Running
10	1	22	Fireball Roberts	Jim Stephens '62 Pontiac	262	2,425	Running
11	10	08	David Pearson	Bud Moore '62 Pontiac	261	750	Running
12	23	49	Bob Welborn	J C Parker '62 Pontiac	261	600	Running
13	30	66	Elmo Langley	Ratus Walters '62 Ford	260	525	Running
14	34	91	Ralph Earnhardt	Bob Osiecki '62 Dodge	259	450	Running
15	40	87	Buddy Baker	Buck Baker '62 Chrysler	258	425	Running
16	18	48	G C Spencer	Floyd Powell '62 Chevrolet	257	350	Running
17	20	42	Jim Paschal	Petty Eng '62 Plymouth	257	350	Running
18	16	83	Bunkie Blackburn	Worth McMillion '62 Pontiac	257	350	Running
19	38	12	Tiny Lund	Cliff Stewart '62 Pontiac	251	425	Running
20	8	46	Johnny Allen	Holly Farms '62 Pontiac	251	350	Running
21	32	19	Herman Beam	Beam '62 Ford	241	325	Running
22	26	90	Jimmy Thompson	Bob Osiecki '62 Dodge	229	325	Oil Pres
23	19	26	Darel Dieringer	Mamie Reynolds '62 Ford	196	325	Engine
24	6	72	Bobby Johns	Shorty Johns '62 Pontiac	188	515	Crash
25	22	54	Jimmy Pardue	Pardue '62 Pontiac	158	325	H Gasket
26	36	61	Sherman Utsman	'62 Ford	148	300	Engine
27	21	20	Emanuel Zervakis	'62 Mercury	145	300	Trans
28	13	40	Tommy Irwin	'62 Chevrolet	124	300	Crash
29	35	36	Larry Thomas	Wade Younts '621 Dodge	104	300	A Frame
30	37	24	H B Bailey	'61 Pontiac	101	300	Crash
31	33	5	H G Rosier	'61 Pontiac	99	250	Rear End
32	17	30	John Sudderth	Fred Clark '62 Chevrolet	85	250	Sway Bar
33	31	92	Cale Yarborough	Donald Harrison '62 Ford	84	250	Engine
34	29	27	Doug Yates	'62 Chevrolet	75	275	Engine
35	9	29	Nelson Stacy	Holman-Moody '62 Ford	71	250	Crash
36	4	3	Junior Johnson	Ray Fox '62 Pontiac	66	560	Crash
37	14	81	LeeRoy Yarbrough	'62 Mercury	62	250	Crash
38	41	84	Red Foote	E Hinton '61 Ford	55	275	Engine
39	42	97	Paul Lewis	Lewis Osborne '62 Chevrolet	20	250	Engine
40	11	11	Ned Jarrett	B G Holloway '62 Chevrolet	12	550	Engine
41	44	38	Woody Wilson	Mat DeMatthews '61 Ford	12	250	Axle
42	24	86	Tom Cox	Buck Baker '62 Chrysler	11	250	Oil Pres
43	25	62	Curtis Crider	Crider '62 Mercury	6	250	Fr Plug
44	43	1	George Green	Jess Potter '61 Chevrolet	3	250	Engine

Time of Race: 3 hours, 12 minutes, 24 seconds
Average Speed: 124.740 mph
Pole Winner: Fireball Roberts - 138.978 mph
Lap Leaders: Fireball Roberts 1-3, Junior Johnson 4-5, Roberts 6-34, Johnson 35-46,
   Bobby Johns 47-52, Johnson 53-65, Johns 66-67, Richard Petty 68-70, Marvin Panch
   71-95, Roberts 96-102, Johns 103-132, Panch 133-134, Johnson 135-192, Panch 193,
   Roberts 194-240, Panch 241-264, White 265-267.
Cautions: 3
Margin of Victory: 12 seconds
Attendance: 25,000

replaced Blackburn in Lee Petty's Plymouth stable and wound up ninth.

A crowd of 40,211 watched the lead change hands 10 times in the 267 lap contest on the mile-and-a-half at Charlotte. Johnson, starting third, was clearly the class of the field as he led on four occasions for a total of 204 laps. Marvin Panch loomed as Johnson's only threat, but his bid was ruined 17 laps from the finish when he parked his Wood Brothers Ford with a blown head gasket.

Ralph Earnhardt and Jimmy Thompson, a pair of old warriors from the Modified and Sportsman ranks, were picked to drive the Bob Osiecki-owned Dodges in the 400 miler. Earnhardt wound up an inpressive eighth after starting 33rd, and Thompson was 13th after lining up 32nd.

Johnson averaged a record 132.085 mph as only six laps were run under caution. Nelson Stacy and Paul Lewis tangled in the second half of the race, bringing out the lone yellow flag.

Race No. 53

Hitch-hiking White Surprise Winner in Dixie 400

HAMPTON, GA (Oct 28) -- Little Rex White, admittedly having a "slim to none" chance of winning, hitch-hiked 400 miles on a non-stop highway and scored an upset victory in the season-ending Dixie 400 at Atlanta International Raceway. It was the 28th victory for the 33 year-old Chevrolet driver, but his first on a superspeedway.

White, starting fifth on the grid, spent the entire day riding the draft of his speedier rivals. He gained the

Johnny Sudderth loses the grip on Atlanta

acs after tires blew out, forcing them into the wall. The same fate struck Nelson Stacy, Tommy Irwin, and LeeRoy Yarbrough, who was making his first Grand National superspeedway start. Rookie H B Bailey flipped his Pontiac near the midway point, but escaped unharmed.

Weatherly was officially crowned Grand National champion by a 2,396 point margin of Richard Petty.

White averaged 124.740 mph for his eighth win of the season.

Junior Johnson #3 darts toward the wall after a blowout in Dixie 400

lead with only three laps to go as leader Marvin Panch had to pit for fuel. White then outran Joe Weatherly by 12 seconds to bag the $10,315 top prize. Panch gunned his Ford back onto the track and salvaged third place. Richard Petty was fourth and Fred Lorenzen fifth.

White's trusty Chevy was clearly outmuscled by three factory backed Pontiacs and an industry supported Ford. Fireball Roberts, Junior Johnson and Bobby Johns -- in a trio of fleet Pontiacs -- battled with Panch's Ford most of the way. White watched the epic battle as he ran as hard as he could to stay in the slipstream.

White had mapped out his strategy with his car owner and chief mechanic, Louis Clements. "I knew I couldn't run with those guys," explained White, "so I drafted all I could."

As the laps wound down, White's strategy made the difference. By running in Panch's draft for 28 laps, he was able to conserve fuel and make one less pit stop. "I really didn't outrun anybody," the 5'4" Silver Spring, Md driver confessed. "I just ran with them."

Several of the top contenders were washed out in accidents. Johnson and Johns lost control of their Ponti-

Nelson Stacy backwards at 140 mph in Dixie 400

Marvin Panch #21 and Rex White #4 battle close in late laps of Dixie 400

1962 NASCAR Season
Final Point Standings - Grand National Division

Rank	Driver	Points	Starts	Wins	Top 5	Top 10	Winnings
1	Joe Weatherly	30,836	52	9	39	45	$70,742.10
2	Richard Petty	28,440	52	8	31	38	60,763.30
3	Ned Jarrett	25,336	52	6	19	35	43,443.12
4	Jack Smith	22,870	51	5	28	36	34,747.74
5	Rex White	19,424	37	8	18	23	36,245.36
6	Jim Paschal	18,128	38	4	17	24	27,347.88
7	Fred Lorenzen	17,554	19	2	11	12	46,100.00
8	Fireball Roberts	16,380	19	3	9	12	66,151.22
9	Marvin Panch	15,138	17	0	5	8	26,745.84
10	David Pearson	14,404	12	0	1	7	19,031.44
11	Herman Beam	13,650	51	0	0	18	12,570.94
12	Curtis Crider	13,050	52	0	3	18	12,015.94
13	Buck Baker	12,838	37	0	6	14	12,786.44
14	Larry Frank	12,814	19	1	2	8	32,986.44
15	Bob Welborn	12,368	25	0	5	12	10,346.44
16	George Green	12,132	46	0	1	15	9,220.96
17	Larry Thomas	11,946	37	0	3	12	9,485.96
18	Thomas Cox	11,688	42	0	3	20	10,180.96
19	Jimmy Pardue	11,414	28	1	5	15	12,065.96
20	Junior Johnson	11,140	23	1	7	8	34,840.96
21	Nelson Stacy	10,934	15	3	5	7	43,080.00
22	Wendell Scott	9,906	41	0	4	19	7,133.00
23	Buddy Baker	9,828	31	0	5	10	7,578.00
24	G C Spencer	9,788	42	0	6	13	7,995.00
25	Bunkie Blackburn	8,016	10	0	1	3	5,890.00
26	Johnny Allen	7,602	20	1	5	8	7,230.00
27	Emanuel Zervakis	6,406	11	0	0	2	4,545.00
28	Bobby Johns	5,670	13	1	2	3	15,863.00
29	Ralph Earnhardt	5,472	17	0	2	6	4,545.00
30	Cotton Owens	4,984	16	1	7	8	5,905.00
31	Banjo Matthews	4,956	5	0	1	2	11,375.00
32	Sherman Utsman	4,896	12	0	1	4	3,580.00
33	Darel Dieringer	4,548	14	0	1	3	4,880.00
34	Tiny Lund	4,384	10	0	0	0	2,880.00
35	Stick Elliott	4,254	22	0	0	2	3,928.00
36	LeeRoy Yarbrough	4,240	12	0	1	1	3,285.00
37	Tommy Irwin	3,980	19	0	2	9	3,305.00
38	Ed Livingston	3,604	13	0	0	0	2,940.00
39	Fred Harb	3,430	21	0	0	3	2,220.00
40	Elmo Langley	2,556	6	0	0	0	1,795.00
41	Bill Morton	2,522	5	0	0	2	1,350.00
42	Speedy Thompson	2,522	3	0	0	1	1,400.00
43	Jimmy Thompson	2,346	3	0	0	0	1,650.00
44	Red Foote	2,274	4	0	0	0	1,600.00
45	Ernie Gahan	2,092	3	0	0	1	725.00
46	Billy Wade	2,008	4	0	0	2	1,350.00
47	Jim Cushman	1,954	4	0	0	1	850.00
48	Bill Wimble	1,944	2	0	0	0	675.00
49	Troy Ruttman	1,890	1	0	1	1	1,750.00
50	Cale Yarborough	1,884	8	0	0	1	2,725.00

The 1963 Season
The 'Golden Boy' and the 'Hitchhiking Champion'

Volume two of a four volume series . . . . . The Superspeedway Boom 1959 - 1964

1963

When Fred Lorenzen was 15 years old, he had his first experience in a beefed up stock car. He and a bunch of his buddies from the Elmhurst, IL area took an old 1937 Plymouth out to an abandoned field and cranked it around in circles. The idea of this teenage game was to see who could flip the automobile first. Lorenzen claimed he did the "honors" first.

A few months later, a much more "refined" Lorenzen got out of the fields and into a more established environment -- a narrow strip of asphalt that had sign posts that read "County Line Road".

By that time, Lorenzen had a 1952 Oldsmobile that he had "hopped" up at a service station where he worked part time. He would often brag about how his "four wheel bomb" could outrun anything the neighborhood "wild dawgs" could find to run against him. Once he had a baited taker, Lorenzen would slip down to the gas station, chop off a couple hundred pounds of what he determined was "unnecessary weight", hustle back to the County Line Road and commence to whip 'em in an ear-piercing display of juvenile delinquency and burned rubber. "I didn't lose too many races," Lorenzen once boasted.

It was six years later that Lorenzen, then 21, would drive a car in NASCAR Grand National competition. Having purchased a '56 Chevrolet from Tom Pistone, one of the best known and successful drivers in the Chicago area, Lorenzen left for Langhorne, PA "with no change of clothing and less money."

Lorenzen qualified his Chevy in the 39th starting spot in the 41 car field. If he were entertaining thoughts of getting back home after the race, he would have to

run like hell. Only the top 30 finishers earned any prize money.

On the day Lorenzen arrived at Langhorne, he saw John McVitty, another driver trying to make the grade in NASCAR's major league stock car racing circuit, kill himself in a crash while qualifying. "I really shuddered," said Lorenzen. "My assigned pit was next to the empty one that other guy (McVitty) was supposed to have. I thought about not racing. But I had already qualified and I had to somehow get back home."

Lorenzen struggled for 76 laps before the fuel pump broke on his car. He finished in 26th place and earned a "whopping" $25. Evidently, he made it back home to Elmhurst.

Fred Lorenzen won $122,587.28 in 1963

The sandy-haired youngster entered six more Grand National races in 1956 -- and won less than $250 all year long. His average take per start was $33.57. Dreams of fame and fortune seldom develop on such meager winnings.

Lorenzen packed up and trudged back to the midwest -- to lick his wounds.

Lorenzen kicked around the USAC stock car circuit for a few seasons, winning the late model championship in 1958 and 1959. "The best year I had," recalled Lorenzen, "I won $14,000, a trophy and a gold watch." It was not taking him where he wanted to go.

In 1960, he moved South and took up residence in a tiny trailer in a friend's back yard. He also took on a job at the Holman-Moody plant in Charlotte. Moody had seen the rustic 5'11", 185 pounder in action and he befriended the determined youngster.

But Lorenzen was stubborn. Instead of working on all the cars Holman-Moody was producing for a variety of teams in NASCAR, Lorenzen wanted the whole pie. "I was bull-headed," Lorenzen confessed. "That was one of my problems. I thought I could make all the money for myself." So, he quit Holman-Moody, built his own Ford and hit the Grand National trail.

His first start in 1960 was at Speed-Weeks at Daytona. Having be-

Lorenzen won 1958 and 1959 USAC stock car titles in this Ford

come accustomed to the short tracks, a facility like Daytona with its enormous dimensions and ultra high speeds "scared me to death," Lorenzen admitted. NASCAR vets Fireball Roberts and Joe Weatherly tutored the green rookie; they told him and showed him what to do and not to do on the steep banks and the speedy straightaways.

Lorenzen, a quick learner, went out and ran third in the 100-mile qualifier. He backed that up with an eighth in the Daytona 500. But it went downhill after that. His funds lasted long enough to run in eight more races. In 10 races, he earned a total of $9,135.94, including point money. He spent twice that much in doing so.

Toward the tail end of the 1960 season, Fred Lorenzen was out of racing, hungry, disgusted and discouraged.

Before the year was out, he sold his car for $7,500, paid off some of his debts and went begging for a ride. Bud Moore turned him down. So did Smokey Yunick. Still owing $5,500, Lorenzen packed up and went home -- a broken man. He went back to hammering nails in the carpenter "industry".

On Christmas Eve, 1960, Ralph Moody called Loren-

zen and asked him to drive the Holman-Moody car in the 1961 season. "I was really surprised. I couldn't imagine what I had done to impress them. I'm sure a lot of people thought they were crazy to hire me," said Lorenzen.

The Holman-Moody Ford wasn't ready for Speed-Weeks in Daytona, so Lorenzen bummed a ride from Tubby Gonzales. The deal was struck just a day before the Daytona 500. He ran fourth in the 500 in a car that probably shouldn't have finished in the top 15. Maybe John Holman and Ralph Moody weren't so crazy after all.

Lorenzen's first ride in the Holman-Moody car was in the March 26, 1961 Atlanta 500. He qualified third and took the lead from Marvin Panch in the 34th lap. He had led straight through the 106th lap when a tire blew sending the car into the wall. He was out for the day, but had left his mark on the superspeedways.

In his next start, on April 9, he won what was scheduled to be the Virginia 500. Rain washed the race out after 149 laps. Instead of picking the race up at that point the following week, NASCAR officials paid the field according to a 100-mile race. Lorenzen got his first win. The Virginia 500 was rescheduled later that

Fred Lorenzen battled Junior Johnson all year long

month.

It was on May 6, 1961 that Lorenzen's star began to shine. In a stirring and memorable duel with Curtis Turner in Darlington Raceway's Rebel 300, Lorenzen outfoxed the 'Grand Ole Master' to take the win. Turner had taken the lead from Fireball Roberts in the 199th lap of the 219 lap contest and appeared to be headed for victory. The only other driver left in the lead lap late in the race was fair-haired Freddy Lorenzen. The 32,000 spectators were certain Turner would notch his third win at the 1.375-mile oval. Lorenzen didn't have a chance against a man like Turner. They thought!

But things got a little more interesting in the late stages. Lorenzen sliced the deficit each and every lap and moved in on the rear of Turner's red Wood Brothers Ford. Despite Lorenzen's late race strength, Turner was in the cat-bird seat. Darlington was strictly a one groove race track in those days, and no one was better at keeping a foe at bay than Turner.

Lorenzen made several attempts to pass Turner on the outside. Turner blocked them all. Turner hogged the groove -- which was not an unusual practice at Darlington. The leader of the race had the right to use defensive tactics -- the reasoning went -- and Turner was surely stretching the rules of the race track to the limits.

As the pair roared down the front chute with two laps to go, Lorenzen once again poked his nose to the high side of Turner. Turner drifted up to block the move as the two cars neared the first turn.

Fireball Roberts beat new teammate Lorenzen to the line in Firecracker 400

At the last moment, Lorenzen darted to the inside of Turner and the two cars fused together. Side-by-side they went -- each trying to grasp the single groove. Sparks flew. Tire smoke shot skyward. The grinding of metal could be heard over the roar of the engines. Turner's car clanged against the steel guard rail. Lorenzen skated sideways, but got straightened out. Turner gave chase to Lorenzen the

Fred Lorenzen and Joe Weatherly, the two headliners of the 1963 NASCAR season

final lap and a half, but fell six car lengths short at the finish line. Lorenzen became an instant hero.

Turner finally caught up to Lorenzen -- on the back-stretch of the cool-off lap. And he laid a heavy front bumper on the rear of Lorenzen's Ford.

"That was my biggest win," Lorenzen said years lat-er. "I caught Turner with two laps to go and made the pass. I was determined to pass him. He had blocked me for 15 laps. Ralph Moody had told me all week how to do it. He told me I'd have to make the pass on Turner low going into the turn. How did he know it would be between me and Turner? Ralph was a genius. He knew things would happen long before they did happen. I learned so much from him."

Lorenzen won three times in 1961 and twice in 1962. He won over $76,000 in his first two seasons with Holman-Moody. It turned out to be only a drop in the bucket compared to what lay ahead in 1963.

Lorenzen started the season off with Holman-Moody by running third in the qualifier and second in the Daytona 500 during the Speed-Weeks festival. He won the Atlanta 500 for the second year in a row and things looked rosy.

But in the spring Holman-Moody lured Fireball Roberts away from the Pontiac camp and he joined the famed car builders for the Southeastern 500 at Bristol. Lorenzen was leading Roberts in the late stages when he had to make an extra pit stop for fuel. Lorenzen raised cain at his pit crew for not giving him a full tank on his last scheduled pit stop. Rumors were that the respective pit crews were informed before hand that Roberts was supposed to win his first race in a Ford.

An intense rivalry between teammates was forecast by many. Roberts and Lorenzen both had a burning desire to win -- particularly since they were driving for the same team. Each wanted to win the most races for Holman-Moody. Despite the personal rivalry, both Roberts and Lorenzen held each other in very high esteem.

"He's the best there is," said Lorenzen. "That's why I like to beat him more than anyone else. He's got so many records you can't call him anything but the best. I'd rather beat Fireball than eat. I envy him more than anyone else," Freddy added. "I want to hold all the records he holds. Each time I beat him, it makes me the best, doesn't it?"

Lorenzen became the best in 1963. And he set records that were judged to be unattainable. He started 29 races in the 1963 Grand National season and won six times. His victories included the Atlanta 500 and the World 600 -- and a clean sweep at Martinsville. He finished in the top five on 21 occasions -- and he finished third in the point standings despite missing 26 races. His total winnings for the year came to $122,587.28 including $9,017.28 in point fund earnings. The previous high was Joe Weatherly's total of just a shade over $70,000 in 1962. The $100,000 mark was considered a plateau that wasn't reachable for the better part of a decade. Lorenzen did it in a flash while running only half the races.

Herb Nab, Lorenzen's crew chief in 1963, shared his driver's love for beating Roberts. But he didn't share Lorenzen's view of who was the best driver.

"That's the best driver there is," said Nab, pointing to Lorenzen during a lull one afternoon. "He can drive a race car better than any of the others, including Fireball. Don't let anyone tell you different."

Sharing the spotlight in the 1963 NASCAR season was a stubby 5'7", 140 pound bundle of energy who went by the name of Joe Weatherly. The Norfolk, VA native won the Grand National championship for the second straight season -- the third driver to take the title two years in a row. But Weatherly did it in a most unconventional way. He did not have a regular ride the full year -- and he had to 'hitchhike' his way into the starting line-up in 18 races. He drove equipment far below the potential of a champion. He spent hours on the phone trying to line up a ride -- talking back-markers out of their car so he could drive for the points.

"Sometimes I would get in a car that I knew couldn't win," said Weatherly. "But I did the best I could and tried to take it easy on the fellow's equipment."

Weatherly drove for nine different teams in 1963.

Due to the General Motors factory retreat in the early part of the season, car owner Bud Moore, who had run the full campaign in 1962, said it was not financially feasible to make a run for the championship again. Moore told Weatherly he would provide a Pontiac in the 'major' races, but that was all he could do.

On ten occasions, Weatherly hitched a ride in a Pontiac owned by furniture magnate Cliff Stewart. He registered five top 10 finishes, including a second and a third. When Stewart's year-old Pontiac was not available, he drove for a variety of car owners -- names like Fred Harb, Pete Stewart, Major Melton, Worth McMillion and Wade Younts -- names not associated with championship drivers. Weatherly also drove once for Petty Engineering and in one race he drove a #05 Pontiac, whose owner could not be traced.

Joe Weatherly did not have a full-time ride in 1963, but he repeated as the Grand National champion by "bumming" rides in lightly regarded cars

Weatherly had the tenacity of a pit bull. He was one of the most dedicated and determined champions ever to wear the NASCAR crown. Quitting was not a term he could understand -- nor did he care to. If his car was maimed, Joe Weatherly persevered. And often, he won anyway.

In the 1961 Firecracker 250, the transmission of his Pontiac kept hopping out of gear. Running the high speeds that Daytona International Speedway can generate, a balking transmission can be terminal. But not when Joe Weatherly was at the wheel.

In order to cope with the crisis, Weatherly wrapped his right leg around the gear shift lever -- to hold it securely in place -- and he proceeded to drive with his left foot on the throttle. He finished sixth that afternoon.

On May 6, 1962, Weatherly started seventh on the grid in a 100-miler at Concord, NC. For 134 laps he worked his way into contention and spent several laps chasing leader Richard Petty. When Petty was sidelined by a broken axle, Weatherly took over the lead. With about 50 laps to go, the little man who was once described by a relative as being "so ugly he's cute", was exposed to an element of danger all race drivers fear. The throttle hung wide open when he went into the turn.

With instant reflexes, Weatherly cut the ignition switch. Once that task was out of the way, he spent the majority of the turn wrestling the car back under control Miraculously, he didn't sail into the guard rail or over the bank.

He saved his car, and perhaps his life in one fell swoop.

It worked once, so he tried it again. And again. Twice each lap -- going into the first and third turns.

The man drove for 50 laps with a throttle that was lying on the floor. He would turn the ignition key going into each turn and guide the car through the corners with one hand. He beat runner-up Cotton Owens by a half lap.

It was the same determination that carried 41 year-old Joe Weatherly to the 1963 title. In the first part of the year, he drove a Pontiac wrenched by Moore. Without new state of the art engine development, the car was short of power. Yet, Weatherly still won the Rebel 300 at Darlington. It was Pontiac's only superspeedway win of the year. Late in the season, Moore struck a deal with Mercury and the new car made its debut in the Southern 500. Weatherly finished seventh in the caution free event.

But it didn't thrill Moore in the least. He claimed his driver was 'stroking' the car -- not running flat out and employing a more conservative nature than Moore liked. Weatherly admitted he was deeply hurt.

"When we set the car up in practice it was running and handling fine," Weatherly said. "But we put a new motor in the car that was stronger. That changed the way the car handled. The front end was pushing. I could smell the rubber burning on the right front tire. So I had to back off where I couldn't smell the rubber.

"I could have gone for a while, but that right front tire wouldn't have stood up and I knew it. I had to accept that and do the best I could. Bud didn't understand it, but I told him that it is one thing to direct strategy from the pits and another to carry it out on the track."

In spite of the disagreement with Moore, Weatherly held his car owner in very high esteem. "I'll say one thing for Moore. He won't put a race car on the track until he is sure it is solid in every respect," said Weatherly. That's why he parked the Pontiac for the small races. We couldn't get proper parts and Bud wouldn't do a half-way job. He is a great mechanic and he must

have quality products to work with. He doesn't complain when you wreck his car. The only time he complains is when you don't win. I can understand that.

"There are so many good cars now that you have to play some percentages. Some of the hot cars are going to blow, but not all of them. If you can't go to the lead and stay there, you've got to try to run hard enough to be in a position to go for the bundle at the end.

"Listen," Weatherly continued, "I'd rather play the rabbit than the dog any day. But if I can't be the rabbit, it doesn't mean I'm going to give up the chase. Any time my car has speed and handling, you can look for me at the front."

Weatherly diced it out with Richard Petty for the 1963 title. The little dynamo didn't clinch the championship until the final race of the year at Riverside.

Weatherly took the role of a modest champ. "My luck was better than Richard's," he said. "I had greater luck, rather than greater skill. In the first place, I was lucky to get rides. Lots of guys in racing helped me. I don't know how to thank each and every one for their help. I tried to split up the money so they would be satisfied."

In the season finale -- the Golden State 400 at Riverside International Raceway, Weatherly and Petty were lined up nose-to-tail on the starting grid -- Weatherly in ninth and Petty in eleventh. Just before saddling up for the 400-miler on Riverside's twisting road course -- with all the championship marbles on the line, Petty walked up to his friendly rival and said, "I don't know whether to wish you luck, play it cool or what. Just don't get hurt, Joe."

"That made me feel a hell of a lot better," said Weatherly. "I had more pressure on me going into that race than ever before. Richard is a fine sport and a clean driver. He has all it takes to make a great champion."

Weatherly finished seventh in the race. It was a first round knockout as Petty suffered transmission failure after just five laps. Weatherly earned 1,216 points for seventh, while Petty got only 64. Weatherly bagged the title by 2,228 points.

The following year a tragic paradox occurred. Weatherly was killed on his next visit to Riverside and Petty wound up winning the first of seven NASCAR championships.

Race No. 1

Paschal and Petty Sweep '63 Opener at Birmingham

BIRMINGHAM, AL (Nov 4, 1962) -- Jim Paschal led a one-two sweep for Petty Engineering Plymouths with a victory in the season opening 100-miler at Birmingham Speedway. It was the 14th career Grand National win for the 36 year-old High Point, NC driver.

Paschal led all but eight of the 200 laps around the half-mile paved track and finished over a lap ahead of Petty to win the $1,000 top prize. Buck Baker wound up third in a Chrysler as Jimmy Pardue's Pontiac finished fourth. Darel Dieringer was fifth in a Ford.

The Holman-Moody factory Ford team entered two potent cars, but neither took the green flag. Marvin Panch blew an engine in a practice session and did not start the feature. Fred Lorenzen, driver of the other car, failed to appear for the race. Rather than finding a last-minute substitute for the Elmhurst, IL star, John Holman and Ralph Moody withdrew the car.

One caution for four laps held Paschal's winning

speed to 68.350 mph. Maurice Petty spun his Plymouth in the 189th lap and was T-boned by Ned Jarrett's Chevrolet. Jarrett wound up 11th in the final rundown; Maurice was 14th.

Grand National Race No. 1
200 Laps at Birmingham Speedway
Birmingham, AL
100 Miles on Half-mile Dirt Track
November 4, 1962

Fin	St	No.	Driver	Team / Car	Laps	Money	Status
1	1	41	Jim Paschal	Petty Eng '62 Plymouth	200	$1,000	Running
2	6	43	Richard Petty	Petty Eng '62 Plymouth	199	600	Running
3	12	87	Buck Baker	Baker 62 Chrysler	196	400	Running
4	5	54	Jimmy Pardue	Pardue '62 Pontiac	196	300	Running
5	3	26	Darel Dieringer	Mamie Reynolds '62 Ford	197	275	Running
6	2	47	Jack Smith	Smith '62 Pontiac	197	240	Running
7	4	4	Rex White	Louis Clements '62 Chevrolet	197	200	Running
8	11	8	Joe Weatherly	Bud Moore '62 Pontiac	197	375	Running
9	8	61	Sherman Utsman	'62 Ford	196	150	Running
10	10	36	Larry Thomas	Wade Younts '62 Dodge	194	140	Running
11	7	11	Ned Jarrett	B G Holloway '62 Chevrolet	188	130	Crash
12	17	2	Bill Foster	Cliff Stewart '62 POntiac	187	120	Running
13	18	18	Stick Elliott	Toy Bolton '62 Pontiac	186	110	Running
14	9	42	Maurice Petty	Petty Eng '62 Plymouth	186	100	Crash
15	15	19	Herman Beam	Beam '62 Ford	186	85	Running
16	13	1	George Green	Jess Potter '62 Chevrolet	185	75	Running
17	20	79	T C Hunt	'62 Chevrolet	184	65	Running
18	19	30	Charley Griffith	'62 Pontiac	182	60	Running
19	14	62	Curtis Crider	Crider '62 Mercury	148	50	Rear End
20	16	81	LeeRoy Yarbrough	'62 Mercury	114	50	Brakes
21	21	9	Cotton Hodges	Ewell Williams '62 Ford	9	50	Oil Leak

Time of Race: 1 hour, 27 minutes, 47 seconds
Average Speed: 68.350 mph
Pole Winner: Jim Paschal - 73.952 mph
Lap Leaders: Jim Paschal 1-146, Richard Petty 147-154, Paschal 155-200
Cautions: 1 for 4 laps
Margin of Victory: 1 lap plus
Attendance: 5,000

Grand National Race No. 2
200 Laps at Golden Gate Speedway
Tampa, FL
66.7 Miles on .3-mile Dirt Track
November 11, 1962

Fin	St	No.	Driver	Team / Car	Laps	Money	Status
1	5	43	Richard Petty	Petty Eng '62 Plymouth	200	$780	Running
2	2	41	Jim Paschal	Petty Eng '62 Plymouth	200	490	Running
3	7	8	Joe Weatherly	Bud Moore '62 Pontiac	200	580	Running
4	8	54	Jimmy Pardue	Pardue '62 Pontiac	199	275	Running
5	9	21	Tommy Irwin	Wood Bros '62 Ford	198	240	Running
6	11	42	Maurice Petty	Petty Eng '62 Plymouth	198	200	Running
7	15	6	Possum Jones	'60 Pontiac	196	180	Running
8	12	61	Sherman Utsman	'62 Ford	193	175	Running
9	17	1	George Green	Jess Potter '61 Chevrolet	192	150	Running
10	18	22A	Buzzy Reutimann	'60 Chevrolet	192	140	Running
11	10	62	Curtis Crider	Crider '62 Mercury	191	145	Running
12	3	87	Buck Baker	Baker '62 Chrysler	189	150	Running
13	1	4	Rex White	Louis Clements '62 Chevrolet	186	125	Running
14	16	2	Bill Foster	Cliff Stewart '62 Pontiac	183	100	Running
15	24	58	Lyle Stelter	'62 Chevrolet	182	75	Running
16	20	19	Herman Beam	Beam '61 Ford	181	75	Running
17	23	12	Henry Montgomery	'60 Chevrolet	166	75	Running
18	22	67	Reb Wickersham	Reb's Sport Shop '60 Olds	137	60	Running
19	14	11	Ned Jarrett	B G Holloway '62 Chevrolet	92	70	Rear End
20	4	22	Fireball Roberts	Banjo Matthews '62 Pontiac	88	75	Crash
21	6	48	G C Spencer	Floyd Powell '62 Chevrolet	83	75	Rear End
22	19	82	Darel Dieringer	'61 Ford	68	50	Heating
23	21	23	Stan Parker	'60 Dodge	59	---	Handling
24	13	36	Larry Thomas	Wade Younts '62 Dodge	56	---	Ignition

Time of Race: 1 hour, 9 minutes, 54 seconds
Average Speed: 57.167 mph
Pole Winner: Rex White - 60.090 mph
Lap Leaders: Rex White 1-41, Richard Petty 42-111, Jim Paschal 112, Petty 113-200
Cautions: 2
Margin of Victory: 1 car length
Attendance: 6,000

Race No. 2

Richard Petty Sparkles at Golden Gate

TAMPA, FL (Nov 11, 1962) -- Richard Petty turned the tables on teammate Jim Paschal by winning the 66.7-mile Grand National race at Golden Gate Speedway. The two Plymouth drivers found themselves deadlocked for the 1963 point lead -- each having one win and one runner-up finish.

Joe Weatherly finished in third place with Jimmy Pardue fourth and Tommy Irwin fifth. Maurice Petty was sixth, giving the Petty Engineering team a 1-2-6 finish.

Fireball Roberts was a surprise entry in the Banjo Matthews Pontiac. The Daytona Beach charger qualified fourth and was holding that position when he hit the wall on lap 88 after a tap from Buck Baker.

Richard Petty

Baker and Paschal sideswiped each other several laps later and Paschal's car lifted momentarily on two wheels. Baker went on to finish 12th after starting third.

Rex White led the opening 41 laps. Richard Petty moved into the lead on lap 42 and was in front the rest of the way except for one lap.

A crowd of 6,000 watched Petty nose out Paschal by a single car length. It was his 14th career win, coming at an average speed of 57.167 mph. Two cautions broke the action.

Race No. 3

Thanksgiving Day Feast to Jim Paschal

RANDLEMAN, NC (Nov. 22, 1962) -- Jim Paschal scooted past a faltering Glen Wood 27 laps from the finish and captured the Thanksgiving Turkey Day 200 at Tar Heel Speedway. It was the third straight Grand National win for the Petty Engineering Plymouth team.

Joe Weatherly was a distant second followed by Tommy Irwin across the finish line. David Pearson wound up fourth with Maurice Petty fifth.

Wood, the crafty Ford driver out of Stuart, VA, started on the pole and threatened to lead the 50-mile race from start to finish. But a blown tire sent the popular driver to the sidelines. Wood did not re-enter the race. Lap times on the quarter-mile paved track, located in the Petty hometown of Randleman, were in the neighborhood of 17 seconds and he figured it was not worth the effort. Wood got credit for 15th place finish, earning $125.

A crowd of 3,500 braved wintry weather to watch Paschal win at an average speed of 47.544 mph.

Grand National Race No. 3
200 Laps at Tar Heel Speedway
Randleman, NC
"Turkey Day 200"
50 Miles on Quarter-mile Dirt Track
November 22, 1962

Fin	St	No.	Driver	Team / Car	Laps	Money	Status
1	2	41	Jim Paschal	Petty Eng '62 Plymouth	200	$575	Running
2	7	8	Joe Weatherly	Bud Moore '62 Pontiac	198	650	Running
3	8	44	Tommy Irwin	S McKinney '62 Ford	197	350	Running
4	15	6	David Pearson	Cotton Owens '62 Dodge	197	290	Running
5	6	42	Maurice Petty	Petty Eng '62 Plymouth	196	225	Running
6	10	62	Curtis Crider	Crider '62 Mercury	196	220	Running
7	14	61	Sherman Utsman	'62 Ford	193	230	Running
8	3	49	Jimmy Pardue	J C Parker '672 Pntiac	193	160	Running
9	9	1	George Green	Jess Potter '62 Chevrolet	192	200	Running
10	16	34	Wendell Scott	Scott '61 Chevrolet	191	140	Running
11	5	43	Richard Petty	Petty Eng '62 Plymouth	188	145	Trans
12	18	33	Jack Deniston	C L Kilpatrick '62 Chevrolet	187	135	Running
13	21	60	Ray Hughes	Ray Herlocker '60 Plymouth	183	110	Running
14	17	2	Bill Foster	Cliff Stewart '62 Pontiac	180	100	Running
15	1	21	Glen Wood	Wood Bros '62 Ford	173	125	Engine
16	24	5	Jim Bray	'60 Ford	171	100	Running
17	22	31	Sonny Fogle	'61 Mercury	162	100	Running
18	12	48	G C Spencer	Floyd Powell 62 Chevrolet	156	100	Oil Pres
19	19	58	Lyle Stelter	'62 Chevrolet	122	100	Tire
20	11	17	Fred Harb	Harb '61 Ford	117	100	Drive Sh
21	20	19	Herman Beam	Beam '60 Ford	111	100	Running
22	23	32	John Hoffman	'60 Ford	51	100	Handling
23	13	36	Larry Thomas	Wade Younts '62 Dodge	27	100	Trans
24	4	11	Ned Jarrett	Burton-Robinson '62 Ford	6	100	Handling

Time of Race: 1 hour, 03 minutes, 06 seconds
Average Speed: 47.544 mph
Pole Winner: Glen Wood - 51.933 mph
Lap Leaders: Glen Wood 1-173, Jim Paschal 174-200
Cautions: None (1 restart)
Margin of Victory:
Attendance: 3,500

Race No. 4

Gurney Grabs 6-hour Marathon at Riverside

RIVERSIDE, CA (Jan 20) -- Dan Gurney, skillful 31 year-old driver out of Costa Mesa, CA, blazed a path of glory around the twisting 2.7-mile road course and won the Riverside 500 in a 1963 Ford Sport Coupe. Gurney bagged $14,400 for his first Grand National win. The triumph came in only his third NASCAR start.

Dan Gurney - Riverside winner

Another stranger to NASCAR circles, A. J. Foyt, finished in second place. Foyt's Pontiac was 36 seconds behind Gurney when the day's sixth and final caution forced a 40 mph finish. Third place went to Troy Ruttman with Fireball Roberts fourth and Bobby Johns fifth. Joe Ruttman, 18 year-old younger brother of the third place finisher, drove in his first Grand National race, finishing 10th in a superlative effort.

A.J. Foyt finishes second at Riverside

Gurney's Holman-Moody Ford was in front for 110 of the 185 laps. He took the lead for the final time when he passed Roberts in the 101st lap. Gurney stretched his advantage from that point on and averaged 84.965 mph before 52,500 spectators. The race lasted nearly six hours.

Richard Petty tried an experimental automatic transmission in his Plymouth. However, he retired from the race after 27 laps with transmission failure.

Danny Weinberg crashed heavily in turn six at the same moment Petty limped to the pits. Weinberg flipped three times but escaped injury. Point leader Jim Paschal flipped his Plymouth a dozen times after his brakes failed and wound up 36th in the 44 car field. He was not hurt but fell to 14th place in the point standings.

Jimmy Pardue finished eighth in his Pontiac and took the lead in the NASCAR point race, 432 points ahead of Ned Jarrett, who wound up sixth in the 500-miler.

Billy Wade, rookie driver who has hooked up with car owner Cotton Owens for the 1963 campaign, finished seventh in a new Dodge.

Paul Goldsmith started on the pole and led for three laps, but the St. Clair Shores, MI driver departed after 59 laps with engine problems.

Grand National Race No. 4
185 Laps at Riverside International Raceway
Riverside, CA
"Riverside 500"
500 Miles on 2.7-mile Paved Road Course
January 20, 1963

Fin	St	No.	Driver	Team / Car	Laps	Money	Status
1	11	28	Dan Gurney	Holman-Moody '63 Ford	185	$14,400	Running
2	2	02	A J Foyt	Ray Nichels '63 Pontiac	185	6,570	Running
3	17	14	Troy Ruttman	Bill Stroppe '63 Mercury	184	3,980	Running
4	3	22	Fireball Roberts	Banjo Matthews '63 Pontiac	184	2,630	Running
5	25	7	Bobby Johns	Shorty Johns '63 Pontiac	182	1,750	Running
6	8	11	Ned Jarrett	Burton-Robinson '63 Ford	181	1,225	Running
7	21	5	Billy Wade	Cotton Owens '63 Dodge	180	1,850	Running
8	6	54	Jimmy Pardue	Pete Stewart '62 Pontiac	179	1,050	Running
9	28	1	Danny Letner	'63 Dodge	179	950	Running
10	30	98	Joe Ruttman	Bill Stroppe '62 Mercury	176	850	Running
11	26	97	Ron Hornaday	'62 Ford	176	750	Running
12	13	0	Dave MacDonald	Holman-Moody '62 Chevrolet	176	675	Running
13	39	38	Bob Perry	'62 Mercury	175	575	Running
14	32	70	Bob Ross	'60 Pontiac	175	575	Running
15	18	4	Rex White	Louis Clements '62 Chevrolet	173	575	Engine
16	27	19	John Rostek	'62 Ford	172	500	Crash
17	10	12	Art Watts	'62 Ford	171	475	Running
18	33	34	Wendell Scott	Scott 62 Chevrolet	169	425	Running
19	43	61	Richard Bown	'62 Chevrolet	166	425	Running
20	41	50	Hal Beal	'62 Dodge	164	425	Running
21	31	51	Scotty Cain	'61 Ford	162	375	Running
22	16	21	Fred Lorenzen	Wood Bros '63 Ford	158	530	Engine
23	34	27	Marshall Sargent	60 Pontiac	157	375	Crash
24	5	8	Joe Weatherly	Bud Moore '63 Pontiac	148	925	Oil Pan
25	40	26	Carl Joiner	'62 Chevrolet	143	375	Crash
26	38	10	Jim Cook	'62 Dodge	143	325	Crash
27	9	75	Jim Hurtubise	'61 Pontiac	142	325	Engine
28	42	20	Jack Norton	'62 Chevrolet	140	325	Carb
29	35	15	Eddie Pagan	'63 Chevrolet	137	325	Running
30	24	88	Don Noel	'63 Mercury	126	450	Engine
31	7	33	Clem Proctor	'62 Pontiac	122	275	Crash
32	23	80	Sal Tovella	Tubby Gonzales '63 Ford	116	500	Engine
33	20	6	David Pearson	Cotton Owens '63 Dodge	113	275	Oil Pres
34	44	25	Bill Clifton	'61 Ford	111	275	Running
35	37	2	Bill Foster	Cliff Stewart '62 Pontiac	91	275	Trans
36	19	41	Jim Paschal	Petty Eng '63 Plymouth	81	300	Crash
37	12	15	Parnelli Jones	Bill Stroppe '63 Mercury	78	525	Trans
38	22	77	Marvin Porter	'63 Ford	67	650	Rear End
39	1	01	Paul Goldsmith	Ray Nichels '63 Pontiac	59	680	Con Rod
40	4	07	Len Sutton	Ray Nichels '63 Pntiac	49	350	Con Rod
41	15	43	Richard Petty	Petty Eng '63 Plymouth	27	300	Trans
42	14	23	Danny Weinberg	'62 Pontiac	27	300	Crash
43	36	62	Curtis Crider	Crider '62 Mercury	26	275	Clutch
44	29	44	Lloyd Dane	'62 Chevrolet	8	300	Trans

Time of Race: 5 hours, 53 minutes, 20 seconds
Average Speed: 84.965 mph
Pole Winner: Dan Gurney - 99.590 mph
Lap Leaders: A J Foyt 1-2, Paul Goldsmith 3-5, Parnelli Jones 6-34, Fred Lorenzen 35-42, Dan Gurney 43-60, Jones 61-70, Gurney 71-87, Fireball Roberts 88-100, Gurney 101-185.
Cautions: 6
Margin of Victory: 36 seconds (prior to caution)
Attendance: 52,500

Race No. 5
Junior Johnson Grabs
Daytona 100-mile Qualifier

DAYTONA BEACH, FL (Feb 22) -- Junior Johnson took the lead in the 24th lap and held off a pack of

In the driver's seat with Larry Frank at Daytona International Speedway

challengers to capture the first 100-mile qualifying race for Daytona International Speedway's Daytona 500. The Ronda, NC veteran was behind the wheel of a Chevrolet tuned to perfection by Ray Fox.

G.C. Spencer, Johnson's running mate, crossed the finish line a close second, but was penalized two laps for failure to heed a black flag thrown for a misplaced gas cap. Spencer officially got paid for 11th place. USAC star Paul Goldsmith was elevated to second place, 70 yards behind Johnson. A.J.Foyt came in third, Larry Frank survived a spin to finish fourth and Dan Gurney was fifth.

Fireball Roberts won the pole in a special 25-mile event five days earlier, but his Banjo Matthews Pontiac was short on horsepower. Roberts wound up sixth in the 40 lap sprint, one lap off the pace.

Johnson averaged a stunning 164.083 mph for the race which was one mile per hour faster than he qualified. The lead pack hooked up in a speedy, dizzy draft that set records from the first lap.

Paul Clark was involved in a solo accident in the 11th lap. He was not hurt. Jack Smith spun his Chrysler on lap 18 and flat-spotted the tires. He pulled into the pits and parked his car for the afternoon.

Grand National Race No. 5
40 Laps at Daytona International Speedway
100 Miles on 2.5-mile Paved Track
February 22, 1963

Fin	St	No.	Driver	Team / Car	Laps	Money	Status
1	2	3	Junior Johnson	Ray Fox '63 Chevrolet	40	$1,100	Running
2	11	01	Paul Goldsmith	Ray Nichels '63 Pontiac	40	600	Running
3	10	02	A J Foyt	Ray Nichels '63 Pontiac	40	400	Running
4	4	06	Larry Frank	Holman-Moody '63 Ford	40	300	Running
8	8	0	Dan Gurney	Holman Moody '63 Ford	40	300	Running
6	1	22	Fireball Roberts	Banjo Matthews '63 Pontiac	39	230	Running
7	18	44	Tommy Irwin	S McKinney '63 Ford	39	225	Running
8	14	14	Troy Ruttman	Bill Stroppe '63 Ford	39	200	Running
9	19	60	Johnny Allen	Lou Sidoit '63 Mercury	39	150	Running
10	17	31	Dick Goode	Romy '63 Ford	39	150	Running
11	3	03	G C Spencer	Ray Fox '63 Chevrolet	38	150	Running
12	22	43	Richard Petty	Petty '63 Plymouth	38	125	Running
13	16	80	Sal Tovella	Tubby Gonzales '63 Frod	38	125	Running
14	6	32	Bob James	Roscoe Sanders '63 Plym	38	100	Running
15	20	70	Floyd Powell	Powell '62 Pontiac	38	100	Running
16	21	34	Red Foote	E Hinton '63 Ford	38	100	Running
17	23	42	Jim Hurtubise	Petty Eng '63 Plymouth	38	100	Running
18	24	57	Pete Stewart	Stewart '62 Pontiac	37	100	Running
19	27	36	Larry Thomas	Wade Younts '62 Dodge	37	75	Running
20	15	25	Chuck Daigh	Bill Stroppe '63 Mercury	37	75	Running
21	9	67	Reb Wickersham	Reb's Sport Shop '62 Pontiac	36	75	Running
22	25	19	Herman Beam	Beam '63 Ford	36	75	Running
23	31	95	Jim Cushman	Jack Russell '63 Plymouth	35	75	Running
24	13	24	Whitey Gerken	Bill Stroppe '63 Mercury	23	75	
25	29	47	Jack Smith	Smith '63 Chrysler	17	---	Flat Tires
26	12	71	Bubba Farr	W M Harrison '63 Chevrolet	12	---	
27	7	62	Curtis Crider	Crider '62 Mercury	12	---	Heating
28	5	74	Paul Clark	Clark '62 Pntiac	11	---	Crash
29	30	5	Billy Wade	Cotton Owens '63 Dodge	7	---	Piston
30	28	68	Frank Graham	Ed Livingston '61 Ford	4	---	Spin out
31	26	9	Al Terrell	Wildcat Williams '62 Ford	4	---	Spin out

Time of Race: 36 minutes, 34 seconds
Average Speed: 164.083
Pole Winner: Fireball Roberts
Fastest Qualifier: Junior Johnson 163.681 mph
Lap Leaders: ---- Junior Johnson 24-40
Cautions:
Margin of Victory: 70 yards
Attendance: 27,000

Race No. 6

Johnny Rutherford Stuns Favorites in Second Daytona Qualifier

DAYTONA BEACH, FL (Feb 22) -- Johnny Rutherford, young USAC driver who had been assigned to drive the potent Smokey Yunick Chevrolet, zipped past Rex White with five laps remaining and drove to a three car length victory in the second 100-miler at Daytona International Speedway. The 24 year-old Fort Worth, Texas sprint car specialist became the sixth driver to win his first Grand National start.

White finished second and pole sitter Fred Lorenzen was third. Ned Jarrett was fourth with Nelson Stacy fifth. Tiny Lund finished sixth, driving the Wood Brothers Ford in place of the injured Marvin Panch.

Johnny Rutherford wins 100 mile qualifier in his first NASCAR start

Rutherford qualified at a record 165.183 mph but started back in ninth position. He led briefly in the 33rd lap before running down White in the stretch duel. White led for 26 laps in his surprisingly powerful Chevrolet.

Point leader Jimmy Pardue lasted only three laps before the engine blew in his Pontiac.

Rutherford covered the 40 laps at an average speed of 162.969 mph as a crowd of 27,000 watched the unknown newcomer stick it to the NASCAR regulars.

Race No. 7

Tiny Lund Wins Big in Daytona 500

DAYTONA BEACH, FL (Feb 24) -- DeWayne "Tiny" Lund of Cross, SC took the lead with eight laps

Grand National Race No. 6
40 Laps at Daytona International Speedway
Daytona Beach, FL
100 Miles on 2.5-mile Paved Track
February 22, 1963

Fin	St	No	Driver	Team / Car	Laps	Money	Status
1	9	13	Johnny Rutherford	Smokey Yunick '63 Chevrolet	40	$1,100	Running
2	8	4	Rex White	Louis Clements '63 Chevrolet	40	600	Running
3	1	28	Fred Lorenzen	Holman-Moody '63 Ford	40	400	Running
4	3	11	Ned Jarrett	Burton-Robinson '63 Ford	40	300	Running
5	6	29	Nelson Stacy	Holman-Moody '63 Ford	40	300	Running
6	2	21	Tiny Lund	Wood Bros '63 Ford	40	250	Running
7	11	7	Bobby Johns	Shorty Johns '63 Pontiac	39	225	Running
8	15	15	Parnelli Jones	Bill Stroppe '63 Mercury	39	200	Running
9	14	26	Darel Dieringer	Bill Stroppe '63 Mercury	39	150	Running
10	16	10	Bunkie Blackburn	Jim Stephens '62 Pontiac	39	150	Running
11	7	30	LeeRoy Yarbrough	E A McQuaig '62 Pontiac	39	150	Running
12	18	72	Ted Hairfield	Parker Snead '63 Ford	39	125	Running
13	10	8	Joe Weatherly	Bud Moore '63 Pontiac	38	125	Running
14	22	51	Bob Cooper	Cooper 62 Pontiac	38	100	Running
15	20	18	Stick Elliott	Toy Bolton '62 pontiac	38	100	Running
16	24	33	Roy Mayne	C L Kilpatrick '62 Chevrolet	38	100	Running
17	25	04	H B Bailey	Bailey '61 Pontiac	38	100	Running
18	29	6	David Pearson	Cotton Owens '63 Dodge	37	100	Running
19	26	58	John Rogers	Rogers '61 Pontiac	37	75	Running
20	21	52	Cale Yarborough	Julian Buesink '63 Ford	37	75	Heating
21	28	2	Bill Foster	Cliff Stewart '62 Ford	36	75	Running
22	27	90	Bobby Isaac	Bondy Long '62 Plymouth	31	75	Too Slow
23	23	41	Jim Paschal	Petty Eng '63 Plymouth	28	75	Engine
24	19	73	Ralph Earnhardt	Acey Taylor '62 Pontiac	26	75	H Gasket
25	31	34	Wendell Scott	Scott '62 Chevrolet	25	---	Too Slow
26	14	56	Ed Livingston	Marnie Reynolds '62 Ford	21	---	Heating
27	17	36	Rodger Ward	Bill Stroppe '63 Mercury	9	---	Engine
28	4	54	Jimmy Pardue	Pete Stewart '62 Pontiac	3	---	Engine
29	30	05	Jim McGuirk	Ray Nichels '62 Pontiac	3	---	
30	13	97	Len Sutton	Ray Nichels '63 Pontiac	3	---	Distributo
31	12	87	Buck Baker	Baker '63 Pontiac	1	---	Distributo

Time of Race: 36 minutes, 49 seconds
Average Speed: 162.969 mph
Fastest Qualifier: John Rutherford 165.183 mph
Pole Winner: Fred Lorenzen - 160.943 mph
Lap Leaders: Fred Lorenzen 1-8, Rex White 9-32, John Rutherford 33, White 34-35, Rutherford 36-40
Cautions:
Margin of Victory: 3 car lengths
Attendance: 27,000

Chris Economaki interviews Tiny Lund after Daytona 500

remaining and edged Fred Lorenzen for a storybook victory in the fifth annual Daytona 500 at Daytona International Speedway.

Lund, scoring his first Grand National triumph in his 134th big league start, was filling in for the injured Marvin Panch and gave the Wood Brothers their first superspeedway win since Speedy Thompson won the 1960 National 400 at Charlotte.

Panch was seriously injured in a flaming crash 10 days before the 500. Panch was testing a Maserati sports car when he veered out of control, flipped and caught fire. Lund was one of the five bystanders who ran to the aid of Panch. From his hospital bed, the 36 year-old Oakland, CA native asked Glen and Leonard Wood to let Lund drive

Grand National Race No. 7
200 Laps at Daytona International Speedway
Daytona Beach, FL
"Daytona 500"
500 Miles on 2.5-mile Paved Track
February 24, 1963

Fin	St	No.	Driver	Team / Car	Laps	Money	Status
1	12	21	Tiny Lund	Wood Bros '63 Ford	200	$24,550	Running
2	2	28	Fred Lorenzen	Holman-Moody '63 Ford	200	15,450	Running
3	8	11	Ned Jarrett	Burton-Robinson '63 Ford	200	8,700	Running
4	10	29	Nelson Stacy	Holman-Moody '63 Ford	199	8,275	Running
5	11	0	Dan Gurney	Holman-Moody '63 Ford	199	3,550	Running
6	23	43	Richard Petty	Petty Eng '63 Plymouth	198	2,500	Running
7	14	7	Bobby Johns	Shorty Johns 63 Pontiac	198	2,600	Running
8	26	8	Joe Weatherly	Bud Moore '63 Pontiac	197	1,500	Running
9	4	13	Johnny Rutherford	Smokey Yunick '63 Chevrolet	196	1,250	Running
10	13	44	Tommy Irwin	S McKinney '63 Ford	195	1,000	Running
11	9	06	Larry Frank	Holman-Moody '63 Ford	195	1,500	Running
12	15	14	Troy Ruttman	Bill Stroppe '63 Mercury	195	1,000	Running
13	22	39	LeeRoy Yarbrough	E A McQuaig '62 Pontiac	194	1,000	Running
14	6	4	Rex White	Louis Clements '63 Chevrolet	194	1,100	Running
15	16	19	Parnelli Jones	Bill Stroppe '63 Mercury	194	1,000	Running
16	18	26	Darel Dieringer	Bill Stroppe '63 Mercury	192	675	Running
17	25	80	Sal Tovella	Tubby Gonzales '63 Ford	192	675	Running
18	27	32	Bob James	Roscoe Sanders '63 Plym	191	675	Running
19	49	04	H B Bailey	Bailey '61 Pontiac	188	675	Running
20	30	18	Stick Elliott	Toy Bolton '62 Pontiac	188	675	Running
21	1	22	Fireball Roberts	Banjo Matthews '63 Pontiac	182	650	Engine
22	42	56	Ed Livingston	Mamie Reynolds '62 Ford	180	550	Running
23	47	95	Jim Cushman	Jack Russell '63 Plymouth	176	550	Running
24	45	19	Herman Beam	Beam '63 Ford	175	550	Running
25	39	54	Jimmy Pardue	Pete Stewart '62 Pontiac	169	550	Trans
26	41	34	Wendell Scott	Scott '62 Chevrolet	168	550	Engine
27	7	02	A J Foyt	Ray Nichels '62 Pontiac	143	550	Spin Out
28	37	41	Jim Hurtubise	Petty Eng '63 Plymouth	113	550	Engine
29	35	84	Red Foote	E Hinton '63 Ford	113	550	Con Rod
30	17	69	Johnny Allen	Lou Sidoit '63 Mercury	111	550	Engine
31	33	07	Len Sutton	Ray Nichels '63 Pontiac	97	550	Engine
32	21	03	G C Spencer	Ray Fox '63 Chevrolet	95	1,550	Engine
33	29	70	Floyd Powell	Powell '62 Pontiac	94	550	W Studs
34	44	68	Frank Graham	Ed Livingston '61 Ford	93	550	Engine
35	36	51	John Rogers	Rogers '61 Pontiac	72	550	Handling
36	34	42	Jim Paschal	Petty Eng '63 Plymouth	72	550	Ignition
37	19	81	Dick Goode	Romy '63 Ford	68	550	Spin Out
38	43	05	Jim McGuirk	Ray Nichels '62 Pontiac	67	550	Fumes
39	28	51	Bob Cooper	Cooper '62 Pontiac	53	550	Engine
40	5	01	Paul Goldsmith	Ray Nichels '63 Pontiac	39	1,250	Piston
41	46	5	Billy Wade	Cotton Owens '63 Dodge	32	550	Valves
42	3	3	Junior Johnson	Ray Fox '63 Chevrolet	26	1,750	Distributor
43	31	71	Bubba Farr	W M Harrison '63 Chevrolet	22	550	Fuel Pmp
44	38	47	Jack Smith	Smith '63 Chrysler	19	550	Flywheel
45	20	10	Bunkie Blackburn	Jim Stephens '62 Pntiac	18	550	W Pump
46	40	67	Reb Wickersham	Reb's Sport Shop '62 Pontiac	18	550	Engine
47	32	73	Ralph Earnhardt	Acey Taylor '62 Pontiac	15	550	Fuel Pmp
48	50	6	David Pearson	Cotton Owens '63 Dodge	12	550	Handling
49	24	72	Ted Hairfield	Parker Snead '63 Ford	11	550	Clutch
50	48	62	Curtis Crider	Crider '62 Mercury	4	550	Heating

Time of Race: 3 hours, 17 minutes, 56 seconds
Average Speed: 151.566 mph
Pole Winner: Fireball Roberts - 160.943
Fastest Qualifier: Junior Johnson - 165.183
Lap Leaders: Fireball Roberts 1-10, Bobby Johns 11-22, Paul Goldsmith 23-33,
   A J Foyt 34-38, G C Spencer 39-40, Rex White 41-42, Spencer 43-45, White 46-47,
   Spencer 48-50, Larry Frank 51-55, Spencer 56-63, Foyt 64, Spencer 65-69,
   Fred Lorenzen 70-105, Johns 106, Lorenzen 107-108, Johns 109-114, Roberts 115,
   Johns 116-118, Ned Jarrett 119-141, Lorenzen 142-155, Jarrett 156-157,
   Tiny Lund 158-162, Lorenzen 163-184, Lund 185, Lorenzen 186, Lund 187-189,
   Lorenzen 190-191, Jarrett 192, Lund 193-200
Cautions: 2 for 10 laps
Margin of Victory: 24 seconds
Attendance: 70,780

his car in the 500.

Lund and the Wood Brothers outfoxed their rivals and outlasted the field as the Fords made a 1-2-3-4-5 sweep of the nation's premier stock car racing event. Lund, 33, crossed under the checkered flag with his fuel tank dry, 24 seconds in front of Lorenzen. Ned Jarrett, who pitted with nine laps remaining while holding down the lead, wound up third. Nelson Stacy was fourth and Dan Gurney fifth. Richard Petty was sixth in his Plymouth.

Lund made one fewer pit stop, and it proved the difference. He won $24,550, finishing on the same set of tires he started on. It was the first time the Daytona 500 winner did not change rubber en route to victory.

Eleven different drivers led the race and swapped first place 30 times in front of a record audience of 70,780. Chevrolets driven by Junior Johnson and G.C. Spencer exercised amazing speed but lacked durability. Johnson, lead driver for the Ray Fox team, departed after 26 laps with distributor problems. He wound up 42nd in the field of 50. Spencer, starting 21st, scampered to first place by the 43rd lap, but pulled behind the wall on lap 95 with a blown engine. He got paired for 32nd place.

Johnny Rutherford, wheeling Smokey Yunick's Chevrolet, was biding his time -- running effortlessly in the lead lap. Late in the race a wind gust caught his car and he grazed the wall in turn two. A long pit stop, consuming four laps, dropped him to ninth in the final rundown.

Jarrett took the lead in the point standings with an 854 point lead over Bobby Johns who wound up seventh. Previous point leader Jimmy Pardue wound up 25th when transmission failure sidelined his Pontiac.

The Fords didn't enter the picture until the 125-mile mark when Larry Frank took the lead. Frank, winner of the Southern 500 in 1962, struggled to finish 11th.

Lund led on four occasions for a total of 17 laps, averaging 151.566 mph. Two caution flags for ten laps broke the action. It was only the second Daytona 500 to be interrupted by a yellow flag.

Fred Lorenzen #28 and Tiny Lund side-by-side in Daytona 500

Grand National Race No. 8
200 Laps at Piedmont Interstate Fairgrounds
Spartanburg, SC
100 Miles on Half-mile Dirt Track
March 2, 1963

Fin	St	No.	Driver	Team / Car	Laps	Money	Status
1	2	43	Richard Petty	Petty Eng '63 Plymouth	200	$1,000	Running
2	3	11	Ned Jarrett	Burton-Robinson '63 Ford	199	600	Running
3	7	42	Jim Paschal	Petty Eng '63 Plymouth	199	400	Running
4	14	17	Joe Weatherly	Fred Harb '62 Pontiac	194	500	Running
5	9	34	Wendell Scott	Scott '61 Chevrolet	190	275	Running
6	13	104	Bruce Brantley	'61 Pontiac	188	240	Running
7	11	2	Bill Foster	Cliff Stewart '62 Pntiac	188	200	Running
8	21	54	Jimmy Pardue	Pete Stewart '62 Pontiac	185	175	Running
9	12	19	Herman Beam	Beam '61 Ford	184	150	Running
10	19	62	Curtis Crider	Crider '62 Mercury	174	140	Running
11	4	99	Bobby Isaac	Bondy Long '62 Plymouth	167	130	Running
12	15	65	Frank Waite	'61 Dodg	167	120	Running
13	18	18	Stick Elliott	Toy Bolton '62 Pontiac	135	110	Running
14	10	98	Johnny Clements	'61 Ford	132	100	Crash
15	17	31	Sammy Fogle	'61 Mercury	96	85	Fuel Pmp
16	5	5	Billy Wade	Cotton Owens '62 Dodge	48	75	Clutch
17	1	3	Junior Johnson	Ray Fox '63 Chevrolet	42	65	Rear End
18	20	6	David Pearson	Cotton Owens '63 Dodge	34	60	Handling
19	16	88	Major Melton	Melton '61 Chrysler	27	50	Fuel Pmp
20	8	90	Gary Sain	'62 Dodge	26	50	Axle
21	6	33	Roy Mayne	C L Kilpatrick '62 Chevrolet	---	50	Crash

Time of Race: 1 hour, 47 minutes, 55 seconds
Average Speed: 55.598 mph
Pole Winner: Junior Johnson - 64.47 mph
Lap Leaders: Junior Johnson 1-42, Ned Jarrett 43-198, Richard Petty 199-200
Cautions: 2
Margin of Victory: 1 lap plus
Attendance:

Race No. 8

Jarrett Runs Dry; Petty Wins at Spartanburg

SPARTANBURG, SC (Mar 2) -- Richard Petty rolled his Plymouth into the lead two laps from the finish and went on to post a one lap victory in the 100-mile Grand National race at the Piedmont Interstate Fairgrounds.

Ned Jarrett, who had led from the 43rd lap when he passed Junior Johnson's disabled Chevrolet, ran out of gas with the checkered flag in sight. He still managed to finish second in his Burton & Robinson Ford. Jim Paschal finished third, Joe Weatherly was fourth and Wendell Scott fifth.

Weatherly was driving a Pontiac belonging to Floyd Powell. His regular car owner, Bud Moore, had decided not to seek the championship again but would furnish a Pontiac for Weatherly to drive in selected 'major' events. Weatherly, guaranteed $200 apearance fee at each race as defending champion, said he would seek

the title by borrowing rides whenever he could secure a car for the short track races.

Two caution flags held Petty's average speed to 55.598 mph. It was his second win of the year and the 15th of his career.

Tommy Irwin, who signed on with a factory backed Ford team for the 1963 season suffered serious injuries to his left eye and shoulder when he flipped three times in a warm-up session.

Race No. 9

Petty Unstoppable On Weaverville Short Track

WEAVERVILLE, NC (Mar 3) -- Richard Petty racked up his fifth straight win on short tracks for the Petty Engineering team by beating out Buck Baker in a close finish in the 100-miler at the Asheville-Weaverville Speedway. It was Petty's third win of the

Grand National Race No. 9
200 Laps at Asheville Weaverville Speedway
Weaverville, NC
100 Miles on Half-mile Paved Track
March 3, 1963

Fin	St	No.	Driver	Team / Car	Laps	Money	Status
1	3	43	Richard Petty	Petty Eng '63 Plymouth	200	$1,000	Running
2	2	87	Buck Baker	Baker '62 Chrysler	200	600	Running
3	1	3	Junior Johnson	Holly Farms '63 Chevrolet	200	400	Running
4	5	17	Joe Weatherly	Fred Harb '62 Pontiac	200	500	Running
5	9	19	Ned Jarrett	Herman Beam '62 Ford	195	275	Running
6	4	99	Bobby Isaac	Bondy Long '62 Plymouth	195	240	Running
7	7	5	Billy Wade	Cotton Owens '62 Dodge	194	200	Running
8	15	2	Bill Foster	Cliff Stewart '62 Pontiac	191	175	Running
9	10	18	Stick Elliott	Toy Bolton '62 Pontiac	191	150	Running
10	8	70	Floyd Powell	Powell '62 Pontiac	187	140	Engine
11	14	62	Curtis Crider	Crider '62 Mercury	182	130	Running
12	13	34	Wendell Scott	Scott '62 Chevrolet	174	120	Running
13	18	33	Roy Mayne	C L Kilpatrick '62 Cdhevrolet	172	110	Fuel
14	19	65	Frank Waite	'61 Dodge	167	100	Running
15	17	90	Gary Sain	'62 Dodge	144	85	A Frame
16	12	36	Larry Thomas	Wade Younts '62 Dodge	143	75	Lug Bolts
17	21	51	Bob Cooper	Cooper '62 Pontiac	140	65	Crash
18	6	6	David Pearson	Cotton Owens '63 Dodge	57	60	Wheel
19	11	42	Jim Paschal	Petty Eng '63 Plymouth	45	50	Engine
20	16	104	Bruce Brantley	'61 Pontiac	13	50	A Frame
21	20	93	Jerome Warren	'62 Ford	3	50	Handling
22	22	88	Major Melton	'61 Chrysler	3	50	Handling

Time of Race: 1 hour, 15 minutes, 19 seconds
Average Speed: 76.664 mph
Pole Winner: Junior Johnson - 82.75 mph
Lap Leaders: - - - - - - - - - - - - - - Richard Petty   - 200
Cautions:
Margin of Victory:
Attendance: 10,000

year. Teammate Jim Paschal won the other two short track events in the 1963 season, giving Petty Engineering a full sweep.

Baker was driving his own Chrysler, the company which ditched its factory-backed efforts after a dismal 1962 season. Baker was financing his own operation. Junior Johnson was third, Joe Weatherly fourth and Ned Jarrett fifth. Rookie driver Bobby Isaac, who has won many Modified-Sportsman races on this half-mile paved oval, wound up sixth.

Weatherly was driving a Pontiac owned by independent Fred Harb in his quest to garner as many points as possible.

An unexpectedly large crowd of 10,000 attended the early spring event, and a massive traffic jam forced officials to delay the start of the race for 30 minutes to let the throng fill the confines of the infield. All the grandstand seats were filled beyond capacity.

Johnson set a new qualifying record of 82.75 mph. He led the early going, but was no match for Petty's electric blue Plymouth in the stretch duel.

Race No. 10

Johnson Gets $1,550 and Jayne Mansfield for Hillsboro Win

HILLSBORO, NC (Mar 10) -- Junior Johnson fought back a late challenge from Jim Paschal and won the 148.5-mile race at Orange Speedway in his speedy Chevrolet. The triumph on the dusty .9-mile oval netted

Joe Weatherly #8 and Jim Paschal #91 on front row for start of Hillsboro race

the well fed mountain kid $1,550 in prize money and a kiss from actress Jayne Mansfield. The buxom blond watched the race from the press box and diverted the attention of most of the media in attendance away from the race.

Paschal's Plymouth wound up 2.0 seconds behind the fleet Johnson at the finish of the 165 lap event. Race officials called the event a 150-miler, although only 148.5 miles were scheduled. Richard Petty finished third with Ned Jarrett fourth and Jimmy Pardue fifth.

Joe Weatherly started on the pole in his Bud Moore Pontiac. The defending Grand National champ finished 15th in the field of 23 after being sidelined with a faulty fuel pump. Bobby Isaac's Plymouth climbed over the bank and landed in a clump of pine trees after a spectacular crash on lap 40.

Herman Beam of

Grand National Race No. 10
165 Laps at Orange Speedway
Hillsboro, NC
148.5 Miles on .9-mile Dirt Track
March 10, 1963

Fin	St	No.	Driver	Team / Car	Laps	Money	Status
1	4	3	Junior Johnson	Ray Fox '63 Chevrolet	165	$1,550	Running
2	2	41	Jim Paschal	Petty Eng '62 Plymouth	165	1,100	Running
3	3	43	Richard Petty	Petty Eng '63 Plymouth	165	750	Running
4	6	11	Ned Jarrett	Burton-Robinson '63 Ford	161	575	Running
5	8	54	Jimmy Pardue	Pete Stewart '62 Pontiac	157	425	Running
6	12	33	Roy Mayne	C L Kilpatrick '62 Chevrolet	155	325	Running
7	14	17	Floyd Powell	Fred Harb '62 Pontiac	154	275	Running
8	17	X	Larry Manning	'62 Chevrolet	151	225	Running
9	16	19	Herman Beam	Beam '62 Ford	149	200	Running
10	23	0	E J Trivette	'62 Chevrolet	138	175	Running
11	9	2	Bill Foster	Cliff Stewart '62 Pontiac	119	100	Engine
12	10	87	Buck Baker	Baker '62 Chrysler	115	100	Running
13	20	90	Gary Sain	'62 Dodge	112	100	Running
14	11	62	Curtis Crider	Crider '62 Mercury	110	100	Running
15	1	8	Joe Weatherly	Bud Moore '63 Pontiac	90	300	Fuel Pres
16	21	31	Sonny Fogle	'61 Mercury	83	75	Heating
17	7	29	Nelson Stacy	Holman-Moody '63 Ford	70	75	Engine
18	15	64	Elmo Langley	Woodfield '62 Ford	61	75	Engine
19	18	5	David Pearson	Cotton Owens '62 Dodge	50	75	Front End
20	5	99	Bobby Isaac	Bondy Long '62 Plymouth	40	75	Crash
21	22	88	Major Melton	Melton '61 Chrysler	22	75	Rear End
22	19	18	Stick Elliott	Toy Bolton '62 Pontiac	15	75	Engine
23	13	34	Wendell Scott	Scott '61 Chevrolet	10	75	Axle

Time of Race: 1 hour, 47 minutes, 11 seconds
Average Speed: 83.129 mph
Pole Winner: Joe Weatherly - 95.716 mph
Lap Leaders: Joe Weatherly 1, Junior Johnson 2-42, Weatherly 43, Johnson 44-71, Petty 72-86, Johnson 87-165
Cautions: 3
Margin of Victory: 2 seconds
Attendance: 15,000

Jayne Mansfield plants kiss on cheek of Hillsboro winner, Junior Johnson

Johnson City, TN finished ninth. It was the 84th consecutive Grand National race in which Beam was running at the finish -- a record of extraordinary magnitude.

The lead changed hands six times among three drivers. Johnson led on three occasions and took the lead for the final time on lap 87 when he sped past Petty. He averaged 83.129 mph before 15,000 spectators.

Jarrett continued to lead the point standings with a 1,528 point margin over Petty. Weatherly stood third, 1,796 points out of first place.

Race No. 11

Fearless Freddy Fantastic in Fast Atlanta 500

HAMPTON, GA (Mar 17) -- Fred Lorenzen bided his time in the early going and then poured on the coals to win the fourth annual Atlanta 500 at Atlanta International Speedway. It was Lorenzen's sixth career win and his fourth on a superspeedway.

Fearless Freddy ducked under Bobby Johns and took the lead for keeps in the 268th lap. He wound up a lap and six seconds in front of runner-up Fireball Roberts. Lorenzen gave Ford its fourth straight 500-mile win.

Third place went to Johns with Joe Weatherly fourth. Tiny Lund was fifth.

Roberts removed himself from contention with an unusual mistake. After making a pit stop in the 268th lap, he gunned his car out of the pits, spinning out in the second turn. He lost a lap righting his path and Lorenzen coasted home after that. Roberts nosed out Johns by two feet to gain runner-up honors.

Fred Lorenzen in Atlanta 500 victory lane with Linda Vaughn

The General Motors products dominated the first part of the race, leading all but one of the first 131 laps. A. J. Foyt took the wheel of Smokey Yunick's Chev-

Grand National Race No. 11
334 Laps at Atlanta International Raceway
Hampton, GA
"Atlanta 500"
500 Miles on 1.5-mile Paved Track
March 17, 1963

Fin	St	No.	Driver	Team / Car	Laps	Money	Status
1	2	28	Fred Lorenzen	Holman-Moody '63 Ford	334	$16,855	Running
2	17	22	Fireball Roberts	Banjo Matthews '63 Pontiac	333	8,655	Running
3	3	7	Bobby Johns	Shorty Johns '63 Pontiac	333	5,700	Running
4	16	8	Joe Weatherly	Bud Moore '63 Pontiac	333	3,790	Running
5	15	21	Tiny Lund	Wood Bros '63 Ford	331	1,875	Running
6	14	4	Rex White	Louis Clements '63 Chevrolet	329	1,305	Running
7	12	39	LeeRoy Yarbrough	E A McQuaig '62 Pontiac	329	1,100	Running
8	8	43	Richard Petty	Petty Eng "62 Plymouth	328	1,000	Running
9	7	14	Troy Ruttman	Bill Stroppe '63 Mercury	328	900	Running
10	20	11	Ned Jarrett	Burton-Robinson '63 Ford	328	800	Running
11	6	01	Paul Goldsmith	Ray Nichels '63 Pontiac	325	740	Running
12	36	44	Larry Frank	S McKinney '63 Ford	323	625	Running
13	40	6	Billy Wade	Cotton Owens '63 Dodge	317	500	Running
14	11	41	Jim Paschal	Petty Eng '63 Plymouth	315	450	Engine
15	30	55	Elmo Langley	'62 Mercury	314	400	Running
16	31	50	T C Hunt	'62 Pontiac	306	350	Running
17	32	67	Reb Wickersham	Reb's Sport Shop '62 Pontiac	303	350	Running
18	27	73	Ralph Earnhardt	Acey Taylor '62 Pontiac	303	350	Running
19	28	18	Stick Elliott	Toy Bolton '62 Pontiac	297	350	Running
20	21	99	Bobby Isaac	Bondy Long '63 Ford	295	350	Engine
21	46	56	Ed Livingston	Marnie Reynolds '62 Ford	294	325	Running
22	10	42	Jim Hurtubise	Petty Eng '63 Plymouth	290	325	Engine
23	38	51	Bob Cooper	Cooper '62 Pontiac	285	325	Con Rod
24	41	62	Curtis Crider	Crider '62 Mercury	265	325	Running
25	9	26	Darel Dieringer	Bill Stroppe '63 Mercury	261	325	Lug Bolt
26	34	02	David Pearson	Ray Nichels '63 Pontiac	255	550	Engine
27	24	16	Rodger Ward	Bill Stroppe '63 Mercury	242	325	Engine
28	37	54	Jimmy Pardue	Pete Stewart '63 Ford	189	350	Cam Sh
29	22	47	Jack Smith	Smith '63 Plymouth	182	325	Clutch
30	29	19	Herman Beam	Beam '63 Ford	181	325	Clutch
31	23	84	Red Foote	E Hinton '62 Ford	165	300	RF Whee
32	44	2	Larry Thomas	Cliff Stewart '62 Pontiac	157	300	Timing
33	5	87	Buck Baker	Baker '63 Pontiac	157	325	Engine
34	13	32	Bob James	Roscoe Sanders '63 Plym	150	300	Engine
35	35	72	Johnny Allen	Parker Snead '63 ford	134	350	Engine
36	19	15	Parnelli Jones	Bill Stroppe '63 Mercury	133	275	Tire
37	4	13	A J Foyt	Smokey Yunick '63 Chevrolet	126	580	Trans
38	18	07	Len Sutton	Ray Nichels '63 Pontiac	125	275	Engine
39	43	49	Buddy Baker	J C Parker '63 Dodge	85	275	Fuel Pmp
40	33	65	James Norton	'61 Dodge	84	275	Engine
41	25	70	Floyd Powell	Powell '62 Pontiac	70	250	Engine
42	1	3	Junior Johnson	Ray Fox '63 Chevrolet	65	1,370	Pistons
43	42	89	Bruce Brantley	'61 Pontiac	27	250	Fuel Pmp
44	39	74	Paul Clark	Clark '62 Pontiac	17	250	Bearings
45	26	30	Johnny Sudderth	Fred Clark '62 Chevrolet	16	250	Spin
46	45	68	Thomas Cox	Ed Livingston '61 Ford	2	250	Handling

Time of Race: 3 hours, 50 minutes, 12 seconds
Average Speed: 130.582 mph
Pole Winner: Junior Johnson - 141.038 mph
Lap Leaders: Junior Johnson 1-59, Fireball Roberts 60-61, Paul Goldsmith 62-69, Fred Lorenzen 70, A J Foyt 71-126, Roberts 127-130, Rex White 131, Lorenzen 132-135 Bobby Johns 136-143, Joe Weatherly 144-211, Lorenzen 212-215, Johns 216-267, Lorenzen 268-334
Cautions:
Margin of Victory: 1 lap plus 6 seconds
Attendance: 55,000

rolet and led for 55 laps before being sidelined with a balky transmission. Junior Johnson set a record qualifying lap of 141.038 mph and led the first 59 laps. But six laps after making his first pit stop, the white Ray Fox prepared Chevy lost an engine. Herman

Grand National Race No. 12
250 Laps at Hickory Speedway
Hickory, NC
"Hickory 250"
100 Miles on .4-mile Dirt Track
March 24, 1963

Fin	St	No.	Driver	Team / Car	Laps	Money	Status
1	1	3	Junior Johnson	Ray Fox '63 Chevrolet	250	$1,150	Running
2	3	43	Richard Petty	Petty Eng '63 Plymouth	249	700	Running
3	2	11	Ned Jarrett	Burton-Robinson '63 Ford	248	450	Running
4	8	41	Jim Paschal	Petty Eng '62 Plymouth	246	300	Running
5	18	33	Roy Mayne	C L Kilpatrick '62 Chevrolet	237	275	Running
6	7	62	Curtis Crider	Crider '62 Mercury	236	240	Running
7	11	87	Buck Baker	Baker '62 Chrysler	230	200	Dif
8	12	34	Wendell Scott	Scott '61 Chevrolet	228	175	Runing
9	10	19	Herman Beam	Beam '62 Ford	221	150	Running
10	15	68	Ed Livingston	Livingston '61 Ford	209	140	Crash
11	19	88	Major Melton	Melton '61 Chrysler	209	130	Crash
12	16	49	Buddy Baker	J C Parker '63 Dodge	204	120	Engine
13	20	0	E J Trivette	'63 Chevrolet	173	110	Valve
14	9	54	Jimmy Pardue	Pete Stewart '63 Ford	140	100	Trans
15	17	18	Stick Elliott	Toy Bolton '61 Pontiac	57	85	Engine
16	4	90	Gary Sain	'62 Dodge	52	75	Engine
17	14	2	Bill Foster	Cliff Stewart '62 Pontiac	33	65	Engine
18	21	31	Sammy Fogle	'61 Ford	30	60	Crash
19	5	57	Joe Weatherly	Pete Stewart '62 Pontiac	23	250	Oil Cooler
20	13	89	Joel Davis	'61 Pontiac	2	50	Crash
21	6	47	Jack Smith	Smith '63 Plymouth	1	50	Crash

Time of Race: 1 hour, 26 minutes, 38 seconds
Average Speed: 67.950 mph
Pole Winner: Junior Johnson - 75.235 mph
Lap Leaders: Junior Johnson 1-40, Richard Petty 41-124, Johnson 125-250
Cautions: 2
Red Flags: 1
Margin of Victory: 1 lap plus
Attendance: 13,500

Beam's Ford was knocked out with a clutch failure after 181 laps. It was the first time the Johnson City, TN veteran has failed to finish a Grand National race since April 23, 1961 at Richmond, VA

A crowd of 55,000 watched the lead change hands 13 times among eight drivers. Lorenzen established a new 500 mile record at the 1.5-mile oval with a speed of 130.582 mph.

A heavy downpour delayed the start of the race for an hour and a half. The first 10 laps were run under the caution flag. Lorenzen, playing the role of a thinking man, kicked his car out of gear and coasted through the turns to conserve fuel.

Race No. 12

Johnson Takes Hickory; Announces Indy 500 Plans

HICKORY, NC (Mar 24) -- Junior Johnson mastered his old home track for the fifth time and took first place in the Hickory 250 at Hickory Speedway. It was Johnson's third win of the year and only the fourth time he has finished in 1963.

In a post race interview, Johnson declared he had signed a contract to drive in the May 30 Indianapolis 500 for car owner John Chalik.

The powerful Ray Fox Chevrolet manned by Johnson led the first 40 laps from the pole. He gave up first place to Richard Petty, who led for 84 laps, then got back in front on lap 125 and led to the checkered flag.

Petty finished a lap behind in second place as Ned Jarrett protected his point lead with a third place effort. Jim Paschal finished fourth and rookie Roy Mayne grabbed fifth place in a fine performance.

The race was red-flagged in the second lap when Jack Smith spun his Plymouth into the wall. Paschal and Jimmy Pardue spun to avoid contact and mayhem developed behind them. Rookie Joel Davis fish-tailed his Pontiac, hooked the retaining wall and flipped four times down the front chute. The top was ripped off in the second roll-over and all the glass was knocked out of the car. Davis escaped injury, but officials flagged the field to a halt to clean up the glass.

Johnson averaged 67.950 mph before an overflow crowd of 13,500.

Race No. 13

Fireball Joins Holman-Moody; Wins Bristol in Ford

BRISTOL, TN (Mar 31) -- Fireball Roberts made his return to Ford a victorious one as he took the lead in the closing laps from enraged teammate Fred Lorenzen

Fireball Roberts grazes Bristol wall as Junior Johnson rides past

Billy Wade #5, Fireball Roberts #22, Fred Lorenzen #28 and LeeRoy Yarbrough #69 duel at Bristol

Grand National Race No. 13
500 Laps at Bristol Internatiuonal Speedway
Bristol, TN
"Southeastern 500"
250 Miles on Half-mile Paved Track
March 31, 1963

Fin	St	No.	Driver	Team / Car	Laps	Money	Status
1	3	22	Fireball Roberts	Holman-Moody '63 Ford	500	$4,060	Running
2	1	28	Fred Lorenzen	Holman-Moody '63 Ford	500	2,395	Running
3	4	3	Junior Johnson	Ray Fox '63 Chevrolet	497	1,725	Running
4	16	43	Richard Petty	Petty Eng '63 Plymouth	495	1,225	Running
5	10	69	LeeRoy Yarbrough	Lou Sodoit '62 Mercury	490	975	Running
6	20	54	Jimmy Pardue	Pete Stewart '63 Ford	488	775	Running
7	5	26	Darel Dieringer	Bill Stroppe '63 Mercury	486	675	Running
8	11	5	Billy Wade	Cotton Owens '63 Dodge	465	650	Engine
9	19	60	Bud Harless	'62 Pontiac	464	500	Running
10	13	8	Joe Weatherly	Bud Moore '63 Pontiac	456	915	Diff
11	22	67	Reb Wickersham	Reb's Sport Shop '62 Pontiac	444	375	Running
12	18	19	Herman Beam	Beam '63 Ford	444	300	Running
13	24	36	Larry Thomas	Wade Younts '62 Dodge	443	250	Dist Cap
14	2	21	Tiny Lund	Wood Bros '63 Ford	434	305	Engine
15	15	11	Ned Jarrett	Burton-Robinson '63 Ford	430	225	Engine
16	28	09	Larry Manning	'62 Chevrolet	429	215	Wheel
17	29	2	Bill Foster	Cliff Stewart '62 Pontiac	420	200	Running
18	26	56	Ed Livingston	Mamie Reynolds '62 Ford	389	200	Diff
19	27	34	Wendell Scott	Scott '62 Chevrolet	371	185	Running
20	9	74	Paul Clark	Clark '62 Pontiac	346	175	Wheel
21	14	41	Jim Paschal	Petty Eng '63 Plymouth	342	200	Engine
22	30	90	Gary Sain	'62 Dodge	328	175	Diff
23	17	87	Buck Baker	Baker '63 Pontiac	299	175	Engine
24	7	4	Rex White	Louis Clements '63 Chevrolet	291	175	Piston
25	33	18	Stick Elliott	Toy Bolton '62 Pontiac	262	175	Engine
26	25	12	Fred Harb	Harb '62 Pontiac	242	250	Con Rod
27	6	99	Bobby Isaac	Bondy Long '63 Ford	176	175	Diff
28	32	62	Curtis Crider	Crider '62 Mercury	176	150	Engine
29	21	47	Jack Smith	Smith '63 Plymouth	147	150	Oil Pres
30	34	33	Roy Mayne	C L Kilpatrick '62 Chevrolet	133	125	Oil Leak
31	8	6	David Pearson	Cotton Owens '63 Dodge	123	150	Engine
32	32	1	Bill Morton	'62 Chevrolet	115	125	Piston
33	12	32	Bob James	Roscoe Sanders '63 Plym	95	125	Con Rod
34	31	88	Major Melton	Melton '61 Chrysler	2	150	Handling
35	35	93	Jerome Warren	'62 Ford	1	125	Handling

Time of Race: 3 hours, 15 minutes, 2 seconds
Average Speed: 76.910 mph
Pole Winner: Fred Lorenzen - 80.681 mph
Lap Leaders: Tiny Lund 1-3, Jimmy Pardue 4, Lund 5-75, Joe Weatherly 76-163,
Lund 164-171, Fireball Roberts 172-328, Fred Lorenzen 329-492, Roberts 493-500
Cautions: 1 for 9 laps
Margin of Victory: 5.0 seconds
Attendance: 28,000

and sputtered across the finish line with an empty gas tank to win the Southeastern 500 at Bristol International Speedway.

Roberts motored past Lorenzen as the Elmhurst, IL driver had to dip into the pits for a few gulps of fuel. Lorenzen, pounding his fist on the steering wheel, peeled out of the pits and wound up 5.0 seconds behind Roberts' lavender Ford in the final rundown.

Lorenzen was irked at his pit crew for the turn of events. "I got 110 miles out of that first tank of gas (after the first pit stop) and only 85 miles out of the second. How can you figure that?" he raged. Roberts added he was surprised to see Lorenzen pit. "I figured he had enough gas to finish."

Third place went to Junior Johnson, three laps behind. Richard Petty was fourth and LeeRoy Yarbrough fifth.

Lorenzen and Roberts, principles in a fender banging incident six months earlier at Martinsville, VA, rekindled their feud in the middle portions of the race. Lorenzen tapped his new running mate several times while battling for the lead. On one occasion, the jolt was so hard that it knocked the gas cap off Roberts' Ford. He had to observe the black flag to get it replaced. Roberts spent the next 164 lap working his way back up to the lead.

A record crowd of 28,000 sat in perfect racing weather to watch Roberts average a record 76.910 mph.

Grand National Race No. 14
200 Laps at New Augusta Speedway
Augusta, GA
100 Miles on Half-mile Dirt Track
April 4, 1963

Fin	St	No.	Driver	Team / Car	Laps	Money	Status
1	3	11	Ned Jarrett	Burton-Robinson '63 Ford	112	$1,000	Running
2	2	43	Richard Petty	Petty Eng '62 Plymouth	112	600	Running
3	15	62	Curtis Crider	Crider '62 Mercury	110	400	Running
4	6	5	H G Rosier	'61 Pontiac	108	300	Running
5	4	87	Buck Baker	Baker '62 Chrysler	106	275	Running
6	9	54	Jimmy Pardue	Pete Stewart '63 Ford	106	240	Running
7	7	99	Bobby Isaac	Bondy Long '62 Plymouth	106	200	Running
8	8	03	G C Spencer	Holly Farms '62 Chevrolet	105	175	Running
9	1	55	LeeRoy Yarbrough	'62 Mercury	101	150	Running
10	5	34	Wendell Scott	Scott '61 Chevrolet	100	140	Running
11	14	88	Joe Weatherly	Major Melton '61 Chrysler	98	330	Running
12	13	65	Frank Waite	'61 Dodge	98	120	Running
13	11	19	Herman Beam	Beam '62 Ford	96	110	Running
14	12	31	Sammy Fogle	'61 Mercury	86	100	Running
15	10	68	Tiny Lund	Ed Livingston '61 Ford	71	85	Crash

* Race scheduled for 200 laps; halted because of dust after 112 laps
Time of Race: 55 minutes, 55 seconds
Average Speed: 60.089 mph
Pole Winner: LeeRoy Yarbrough - 64.61 mph
Lap Leaders: LeeRoy Yarbrough 1-8, Ned Jarrett 9-112
Cautions:
Margin of Victory
Attendance: 4,000

Race No. 14

Jarrett Dusts Field in Dusty Augusta Race

AUGUSTA, GA (Apr 4) -- Ned Jarrett took the lead from upstart LeeRoy Yarbrough in the ninth lap and went on to win the dusted out 56 mile Grand National race at the New Augusta Speedway. The Newton, NC Ford driver became the ninth different winner in the 14 Grand National events in the 1963 season.

The race was scheduled for 200 laps on the half-mile dirt track. Officials opted to flag the race to a halt after 112 laps because of heavy dust conditions. Some 4,000 spectators voiced loud complaints about having to pay $4 to watch an abbreviated event.

Richard Petty was flagged in second place and Curtis Crider third. Newcomer H.G. Rosier took fourth, just ahead of fifth place finisher Buck Baker.

One caution flag came out early when Sammy Fogle spun and Bobby Isaac, Baker and G.C.Spencer made contact. All were able to continue. Tiny Lund wrecked in the 71st lap -- an incident which did not bring out a yellow flag.

Yarbrough of Jacksonville, FL, surprised everyone

by earning his first Grand National pole. He led the first eight laps before giving way to Jarrett. Yarbrough eventually finished ninth.

Jarrett's 15th career win came at an average speed of 60.089 mph

Grand National Race No. 15
250 Laps at Atlantic Rural Fairgrounds
Richmond, VA
"Richmond 250"
125 Miles on Half-mile Dirt Track
April 7, 1963

Fin	St	No.	Driver	Team / Car	Laps	Money	Status
1	3	8	Joe Weatherly	Bud Moore '63 Pontiac	250	$2,400	Running
2	14	11	Ned Jarrett	Burton-Robinson '63 Ford	249	1,300	Running
3	1	4	Rex White	Louis Clements '62 Chevrolet	247	900	Running
4	7	5	Billy Wade	Cotton Owens '63 Dodge	245	625	Running
5	6	3	Junior Johnson	Ray Fox '63 Chevrolet	242	450	Engine
6	11	41	Richard Petty	Petty Eng '63 Plymouth	240	375	Running
7	18	62	Curtis Crider	Crider '62 Mercury	234	300	Running
8	20	96	Jim Massey	'62 Chevrolet	230	250	Running
9	13	34	Wendell Scott	Scott '62 Chevrolet	228	200	Running
10	25	83	Worth McMillion	McMillion '62 Chevrolet	227	200	Running
11	21	33	Roy Mayne	C L Kilpatrick '62 Chevrolet	223	175	Running
12	22	47	Jack Smith	Smith '63 Plymouth	220	175	Radiator
13	23	19	Herman Beam	Beam '62 Ford	213	175	Running
14	2	6	David Pearson	Cotton Owens '63 Dodge	196	150	Spindle
15	10	66	Johnny Allen	Ratus Walters '62 Ford	196	150	Engine
16	4	87	Buck Baker	Baker '63 Pontiac	173	125	Engine
17	17	03	G C Spencer	Holly Farms '62 Chevrolet	166	125	Engine
18	24	27	Bob James	'63 Dodge	155	125	Crash
19	8	43	Jim Paschal	Petty Eng '63 Plymouth	129	125	Diff
20	19	2	Fred Harb	Pete Stewart '62 Pontiac	95	125	Crash
21	5	54	Jimmy Pardue	Pete Stewart '63 Ford	81	100	Engine
22	15	44	Fred Lorenzen	S McKinney '63 Ford	80	100	Engine
23	9	22	Fireball Roberts	Holman-Moody '63 Ford	70	100	Engine
24	12	20	Emanuel Zervakis	'62 Mercury	68	100	Diff
25	16	09	Larry Manning	'62 Chevrolet	35	75	Engine

Time of Race: 2 hours, 6 minutes, 16 seconds
Average Speed: 58.624 mph
Pole Winner: Rex White - 69.151 mph
Lap Leaders: David Pearson 1-4, Joe Weatherly 5-9, Junior Johnson 10-70, Weatherly 71-81, Jim Paschal 82-129, Johnson 130-163, Pearson 164-169, Johnson 170-186, Weatherly 187-190, Johnson 191-207, Weatherly 208-250
Cautions: 6 for 37 laps
Margin of Victory: 1 lap plus
Attendance: 15,000

Race No. 15

Weatherly Breaks Ice with Comeback at Richmond

RICHMOND, VA (Apr 7) -- Joe Weatherly battled back from a lap behind and disposed of his challengers one-by-one to win the Richmond 250 at the Atlantic Rural Fairgrounds. It was the first win of the year for the defending Grand National champ.

Grand National Race No. 16
200 Laps at Greenville-Pickens Speedway
Greenville, SC
100 Miles on Half-mile Dirt Track
April 13, 1963

Fin	St	No.	Driver	Team / Car	Laps	Money	Status
1	9	87	Buck Baker	Baker '63 Pontiac	200	$1,000	Running
2	4	11	Ned Jarrett	Burton-Robinson '63 Ford	200	600	Running
3	5	03	G C Spencer	'62 Chevrolet	200	400	Running
4	3	41	Richard Petty	Petty Eng '62 Plymouth	199	300	Running
5	7	6	David Pearson	Cotton Owens '63 Dodge	199	275	Running
6	17	86	Neil Castles	Buck Baker '62 Chrysler	197	240	Running
7	1	54	Jimmy Pardue	Pete Stewart '63 Ford	196	200	Running
8	16	43	Jim Paschal	Petty Eng '63 Plymouth	194	175	Running
9	10	9	Gary Sain	'62 Dodge	191	150	Running
10	11	5	Billy Wade	Cotton Owens '62 Dodge	190	140	Running
11	18	0	E J Trivette	'62 Chevrolet	189	130	Running
12	20	19	Herman Beam	Beam '62 Ford	188	120	Running
13	8	12	Fred Harb	Harb '62 Pontiac	187	110	Running
14	21	68	Ed Livingston	Livingston '62 Ford	187	100	Running
15	23	65	Frank Waite	'62 Dodge	185	85	Running
16	6	99	Bobby Isaac	Bondy Long '62 Plymouth	181	75	Crash
17	24	31	Sonny Fogle	'62 Chevrolet	175	65	Running
18	14	88	Major Melton	Melton '61 Chrysler	169	60	Running
19	2	44	Fred Lorenzen	S McKinney '63 Ford	158	50	Crash
20	13	62	Curtis Crider	Crider '62 Mercury	154	50	Running
21	22	18	Stick Elliott	Toy Bolton '62 Pontiac	106	50	Rear End
22	15	09	Larry Manning	'62 Chevrolet	94	50	Rear End
23	12	34	Wendell Scott	Scott '61 Chevrolet	52	50	Crash
24	19	2	Joe Weatherly	Cliff Stewart '62 Pontiac	28	250	Heating

Time of Race: 1 hour, 49 minutes, 23 seconds
Average Speed: 54.853 mph
Pole Winner: Jimmy Pardue - 66.27 mph
Lap Leaders: Jimmy Pardue 1, Richard Petty 2-45, Ned Jarrett 46-70, David Pearson 71-90, Buck Baker 91-150, Jarrett 151-198, Baker 199-200
Cautions: 7
Margin of Victory:
Attendance: 9,000

Race No. 16

Bad Luck Foils Jarrett; Baker Ends 2-year Drought

GREENVILLE, SC (Apr 13) -- Old pro Buck Baker needed a stroke of luck to end a two year winless streak in the 100-mile Grand National event at Greenville-Pickens Speedway. It was the 44th career win for the Charlotte, NC Pontiac driver.

Ned Jarrett was holding down first place when his Ford blew a tire with two laps to go. Baker zoomed into the lead as Jarrett got a quick replacement. Jarrett returned to the track and finished second. G.C. Spencer was third with Richard Petty fourth. David Pearson grabbed fifth place.

Pearson was flagged in fourth place in Cotton Owens' Dodge. Owens protested, claiming his driver had finished third. NASCAR officials checked the score cards and discovered he had actually finished fifth. Owens said he was not convinced.

Jimmy Pardue earned his first career Grand National pole position and led the first lap. The North Wilkesboro, NC speedster drifted to seventh at the finish of the 100-miler.

A crowd of 9,000 watched an unusually hard fought short track race as the lead changed hands six times among five drivers. Seven cautions held Baker's winning speed to 54.853 mph.

Fred Lorenzen wrecked his Ford on lap 158 and wound up 19th. Lorenzen was driving the factory supported McKinney Racing Ford which was assigned to Tommy Irwin. Irwin was still recovering from injuries he suffered at Spartanburg.

Ned Jarrett finished second and Rex White was third. Rookie Billy Wade nabbed fourth spot with Junior Johnson fifth. Johnson was not running at the finish.

Weatherly started third and diced for the lead early with David Pearson and Johnson. In the 84th lap, Weatherly pitted during the first of six caution flags. Car owner Bud Moore cross-threaded a lug nut while changing a tire, costing Weatherly a lap. But within 103 laps on the half-mile dirt track he was back in the lead. Johnson, who led on four occasions for 129 laps, was running just two seconds behind Weatherly when his engine let go with only eight laps left.

Jimmy Massey, a strong soldier of the 1950's, made a return to racing and finished eighth in a Chevrolet. Fred Harb plunged his Pontiac through the retaining barrier and flipped in a nasty series of roll overs. Harb escaped injury.

Weatherly averaged 58.624 mph for his 23rd career victory. Jarrett held a 1,118 point lead over Petty in the point standings. Weatherly stood third, 1,543 behind.

Race No. 17

Petty's Fourth of Year Comes in South Boston 400

SOUTH BOSTON, VA (Apr 14) -- Richard Petty, 25 year-old Randleman, NC Ply-

Richard Petty

mouth driver, grabbed the lead from Ned Jarrett in the 76th lap and went on to take a decisive triumph in the South Boston 400 at South Boston Speedway. It was Petty's fourth win of the year.

Jim Paschal wound up second, giving the Petty Engineering team its third 1-2 finish of the 1963 NASCAR Grand National season. Jarrett came in third, Larry Manning was fourth and Earl Brooks fifth.

Jarrett led the first 75 laps after winning the pole for the 14th time in his career. During an exchange of pit stops, Jarrett lost the lead to Petty and never was able to catch back up. He eventually wound up six laps off the pace in the 400 lapper staged at the .375-mile paved oval.

A crowd of 5,000 watched the caution-free event. Petty had lapped the field by the 100th lap in the uneventful race. The average speed for the 150-miler was 75.229 mph.

Joe Weatherly borrowed a Pontiac from privateer Worth McMillion and finished last in the 16 car field.

Grand National Race No. 17
400 Laps at South Boston Speedway
South Boston, VA
"South Boston 400"
150 Miles on .375-mile Paved Track
April 14, 1963

Fin	St	No.	Driver	Team / Car	Laps	Money	Status
1	2	43	Richard Petty	Petty Eng '63 Plymouth	400	$1,500	Running
2	3	41	Jim Paschal	Petty Eng '62 Plymouth	398	900	Running
3	1	11	Ned Jarrett	Burton-Robinson '63 Ford	394	700	Running
4	9	09	Larry Manning	'62 Chevrolet	374	550	Running
5	16	134	Earl Brooks	'61 Chevrolet	369	450	Running
6	7	19	Herman Beam	Beam '62 Ford	368	350	Running
7	12	34	Wendell Scott	Scott '62 Chevrolet	365	250	Running
8	5	6	David Pearson	Cotton Owens '63 Dodge	358	175	Running
9	6	87	Buck Baker	Baker '62 Chrysler	347	150	Running
10	14	0	E J Trivette	'62 Chevrolet	346	140	Running
11	13	62	Curtis Crider	Crider '62 Mercury	325	130	Running
12	15	49	Larry Thomas	J C Parker '63 Dodge	254	120	Rear End
13	4	5	Billy Wade	Cotton Owens '62 Dodge	210	110	Engine
14	10	86	Neil Castles	Buck Baker '62 Chrysler	145	100	Engine
15	8	54	Jimmy Pardue	Pete Stewart '63 Ford	64	90	Rear End
16	11	83	Joe Weatherly	Worth McMillion '62 Pontiac	48	380	Rear End

Time of Race: 1 hour, 59 minutes, 38 seconds
Average Speed: 75.229 mph
Pole Winner: Ned Jarrett - 78.72 mph
Lap Leaders: Ned Jarrett 1-75, Richard Petty 76-400
Cautions: 0
Margin of Victory: 2 laps plus
Attendance: 5,000

Race No. 18

Jim Paschal Beats Fred Harb at Bowman-Gray

WINSTON-SALEM, NC (April 15) -- Jim Paschal, muscular High Point, NC pioneer, battled back the challenge of Fred Harb and won the 50 mile Grand National race at Bowman-Gray Stadium. It was Paschal's third win of the year.

Harb, a 31 year-old driver who is a neighbor of Paschal, drove his best race and took runner-up position. Harb was the winner of a 1959 Sportsmanship award for saving the life of fellow driver Bill Morton.

Third place went to Larry Thomas with Buck Baker fourth and Ned Jarrett fifth.

Paschal won only $575 for his 16th career NASCAR big league win. Harb pocketed $465 for his best career finish.

G.C. Spencer, driving a Chevrolet, qualified fourth but wrecked in the first lap as the 16 car field became congested on the start.

Joe Weatherly drove a Cliff Stewart Pontiac to 10th place to protect his third ranking spot in the point standings.

Paschal average 46.814 mph in giving Petty Engineering its seventh win of the season.

Grand National Race No. 18
200 Laps at Bowman-Gray Stadium
Winston Salem, NC
50 Miles on Quarter-mile Paved Track
April 15, 1963

Fin	St	No.	Driver	Team / Car	Laps	Money	Status
1	3	43	Jim Paschal	Petty Eng '62 Plymouth	200	$575	Running
2	8	12	Fred Harb	Harb '62 Pontiac	198	465	Running
3	10	36	Larry Thomas	Wade Younts '62 Dodge	195	370	Running
4	7	87	Buck Baker	Baker '62 Chrysler	195	290	Running
5	2	11	Ned Jarrett	Burton-Robinson '63 Ford	194	275	Running
6	5	44	Fred Lorenzen	S McKinney '63 Ford	193	230	Running
7	11	34	Wendell Scott	Scott '61 Chevrolet	190	195	Running
8	13	18	Stick Elliott	Toy Bolton '62 Pontiac	190	185	Running
9	6	54	Jimmy Pardue	Pete Stewart '63 Ford	185	180	Running
10	12	2	Joe Weatherly	Cliff Stewart '62 Pontiac	181	340	Running
11	1	41	Richard Petty	Petty Eng '63 Plymouth	146	130	Fuel Pmp
12	9	62	Curtis Crider	Crider '62 Mercury	62	170	Fuel Pmp
13	14	49	Hank Thomas	J C Parker '63 Dodge	44	125	Fuel Pmp
14	16	88	Neil Castles	Buck Baker '61 Chrysler	11	100	Clutch
15	15	0	Billy Wade	'62 Chevrolet	10	95	Trans
16	4	03	G C Spencer	Holly Farms '62 Chevrolet	1	75	Crash

Time of Race: 1 hour, 04 minutes, 05 seconds
Average Speed: 46.814 mph
Pole Winner: Richard Petty - 48.28 mph
Lap Leaders: - - - - - - - - - - - - - Jim Paschal   -200
Cautions:
Margin of Victory:
Attendance:

Grand National Race No. 19
500 Laps at Martinsville Speedway
Martinsville, VA
"Virginia 500"
250 Miles on Half-mile Paved Track
April 21, 1963

Fin	St	No.	Driver	Team / Car	Laps	Money	Status
1	8	43	Richard Petty	Petty Eng '63 Plymouth	500	$3,375	Running
2	4	21	Tiny Lund	Wood Bros '63 Ford	499	1,675	Running
3	7	26	Darel Dieringer	Bill Stroppe '63 Mercury	496	1,225	Running
4	16	11	Ned Jarrett	Burton-Robinson '63 Ford	495	875	Running
5	5	28	Fred Lorenzen	Holman-Moody '63 Ford	494	1,150	Running
6	21	8	Joe Weatherly	Bud Moore '63 Pontiac	494	1,000	Running
7	17	5	Billy Wade	Cotton Owens '63 Dodge	493	575	Running
8	12	41	* Jim Paschal	Petty Eng '63 Plymouth	493	525	Running
9	11	6	David Pearson	Cotton Owens '63 Dodge	489	425	Running
10	14	47	Jack Smith	Smith '63 Plymouth	489	390	Running
11	1	4	Rex White	Louis Clements '63 Chevrolet	484	475	Crash
12	15	54	Jimmy Pardue	Pete Stewart '63 Ford	300	484	Running
13	24	96	Jimmy Massey	'62 Chevrolet	477	275	Running
14	29	86	Neil Castles	Buck Baker '62 Chrysler	454	225	Running
15	33	33	Roy Mayne	C L Kilpatrick '62 Chevrolet	450	175	Running
16	27	83	Worth McMillion	McMillion '62 Pontiac	442	175	Running
17	9	69	LeeRoy Yarbrough	Lou Sidoit '63 Mercury	414	175	Handling
18	33	93	Curtis Crider	'62 Ford	397	150	Running
19	32	09	Larry Manning	'62 Chevrolet	369	150	Running
20	26	1	E J Trivette	'61 Chevrolet	360	175	Running
21	10	99	Bobby Isaac	Bondy long '63 Ford	358	175	Engine
22	28	134	Earl Brooks	'61 Chevrolet	346	175	Rear End
23	20	19	Herman Beam	Beam '63 Ford	340	175	Rear End
24	6	87	Buck Baker	Baker '63 Pontiac	331	175	Engine
25	18	34	Wendell Scott	Scott '62 Chevrolet	277	175	Rear End
26	13	44	Larry Frank	S McKinney '63 Ford	250	125	Handling
27	23	18	Slick Elliott	Toy Bolton '62 Pontiac	234	135	Engine
28	2	22	Fireball Roberts	Holman-Moody '63 Ford	223	350	Crash
29	22	49	Larry Thomas	J C Parker '63 Dodge	131	150	Heating
30	31	68	Ed Livingston	Livingston '62 Ford	58	100	Rear End
31	19	60	Bud Harless	'62 Pontiac	26	125	Heating
32	30	62	Jerome Warren	Curtis Crider '62 Mercury	25	100	H Gasket
33	3	3	Junior Johnson	Ray Fox '63 Chevrolet	23	175	Crash

* Relieved by Lee Petty
Time of Race: 3 hours, 51 minutes, 24 seconds
Average Speed: 64.823 mph
Pole Winner: Rex White 72.000 mph
Lap Leaders: Fireball Roberts 1-177, Fred Lorenzen 178-459, Richard Petty 460-500
Cautions: 5
Margin of Victory: 1 lap plus
Attendance: 18,500

*Larry Frank backs into the wall at Martinsville as field
scrambles for an opening*

six laps, but it put the Elmhurst Express hopelessly out
of contention.

Tiny Lund finished second with Darel Dieringer
third. Ned Jarrett took fourth and Lorenzen came back
to finish fifth.

Fireball Roberts started on the pole and led the first
177 laps. However, the fiery Daytonan departed in the
253rd lap after hitting the second turn wall.

Junior Johnson brought out the first of five caution
flags when he lost control of his Chevrolet in the 23rd
lap and smacked the wall in the second turn. He was
taken to the hospital for observation, but was not believed to be seriously hurt.

LeeRoy Yarbrough and Larry Frank also made contact with the wall in solo accidents.

Jim Paschal pulled his Plymouth into the pits on lap
218 and collapsed on the ground with heat exhaustion .

Race No. 19

Petty Tops Lorenzen, Lund In Virginia 500

MARTINSVILLE, VA (Apr 21) -- Short track
King, Richard Petty, tooled his Plymouth into the
lead late in the race and outdistanced Tiny Lund to
win the eighth annual Virginia 500 at Martinsville
Speedway.

Petty took command in the 460th lap when Fred
Lorenzen, seemingly on his way to victory, broke
an axle in his Ford. Lorenzen's Holman-Moody pit
crew did a magnificent job of repairing the car in

Rex White #4 and Fireball Roberts on Virginia 500 pace lap

A roar went up from the 18,500 spectators when his relief driver -- Lee Petty -- hopped over the pit wall with helmet in hand. The Old Master finished the race and brought Paschal's car home eighth.

Petty, who led only the final 41 laps, averaged 64.823 mph for his 18th career victory.

Grand National Race No. 20
400 Laps at North Wilkesboro Speedway
North Wilkesboro, NC
"Gwyn Staley Memorial 400"
250 Miles on .625-mile Paved Track
April 28, 1963

Fin	St	No.	Driver	Team / Car	Laps	Money	Status
1	7	43	Richard Petty	Petty Eng '63 Plymouth	257	$3,575	Running
2	1	28	Fred Lorenzen	Holman-Moody '63 Ford	256	2,575	Running
3	2	21	Tiny Lund	Wood Bros '63 Ford	256	1,300	Running
4	9	41	Jim Paschal	Petty Eng '63 Plymouth	254	825	Running
5	5	87	Buck Baker	Baker '63 Pontiac	254	700	Running
6	11	6	David Pearson	Cotton Owens '63 Dodge	253	525	Running
7	6	4	Rex White	Louis Clements '63 Chevrolet	252	475	Running
8	10	99	Bobby Isaac	Bondy Long '63 Ford	250	425	Running
9	13	5	Billy Wade	Cotton Owens '63 Dodge	249	375	Running
10	12	47	Jack Smith	Smith '63 Plymouth	248	325	Running
11	17	49	Larry Thomas	J C Parker '63 Dodge	247	300	Running
12	23	62	Curtis Crider	Crider '62 Mercury	244	250	Running
13	30	7	Buddy Baker	Buck Baker '62 Chrysler	241	225	Running
14	18	96	Jimmy Massey	'62 Chevrolet	241	225	Running
15	19	09	Larry Manning	'62 Chevrolet	240	175	Running
16	22	1	E J Trivette	'62 Chevrolet	237	150	Running
17	20	19	Herman Beam	Beam '63 Ford	234	175	Running
18	21	51	Bob Cooper	Cooper '62 Pontiac	234	150	Running
19	16	18	Stick Elliott	Toy Bolton '62 Pontiac	231	175	Running
20	14	57	Jimmy Pardue	Pete Stewart '62 Pontiac	229	175	Running
21	27	34	Wendell Scott	Scott '62 Chevrolet	225	100	Running
22	26	33	Roy Mayne	C L Kilpatrick '62 Chevrolet	222	100	Running
23	3	8	Joe Weatherly	Bud Moore '63 Pontiac	213	425	Rear End
24	15	58	G C Spencer	'62 Chevrolet	183	125	Rear End
25	8	11	Ned Jarrett	Burton-Robinson '63 Ford	156	125	Engine
26	24	55	LeeRoy Yarbrough	'62 Mercury	138	100	Rear End
27	4	3	Junior Johnson	Ray Fox '63 Chevrolet	98	250	Crash
28	25	86	Neil Castles	Buck Baker '62 Chrysler	71	100	Piston
29	28	134	Earl Brooks	'61 Chevrolet	68	100	A Frame
30	29	93	Jerome Warren	'62 Ford	29	100	Handling
31	31	31	Sammy Fogle	'61 Mercury	20	50	Handling

* Race shortened to 257 laps due to rain
Time of Race: 1 hour, 57 minutes, 06 seconds
Average Speed: 83.301 mph
Pole Winner: Fred Lorenzen - 96.15 mph
Lap Leaders: Fred Lorenzen 1-19, Junior Johnson 20-98, Lorenzen 99-102, Tiny Lund 103-127, Richard Petty 128-257
Cautions:
Margin of Victory: 1 lap plus
Attendance: 13,500

Race No. 20
Rapid Richard Runs Right
In Rainy North Wilkesboro

NORTH WILKESBORO, NC (Apr 28) -- Rapid Richard Petty motored past Tiny Lund in the 128th lap

and held first place until rain curtailed the Gwyn Staley 400 after 257 laps. It was the sixth win of the year for the 25 year-old Plymouth driver and his third straight at this .625-mile paved track.

Left in Petty's wake was runner-up Fred Lorenzen, a lap behind. Tiny Lund was flagged in third place with Jim Paschal fourth and Buck Baker fifth.

Promoter Enoch Staley waited an hour standing in the hard rain before calling the race off. Only a few of the 13,500 spectators had left the speedway. They all hoped to see the rest of the event.

Lorenzen started on the pole and led the first 19 laps. Junior Johnson, driving a fleet but seldom reliable Chevrolet, stormed into the lead on lap 20 and was stretching his advantage when he sailed into the wall after his engine blew. Johnson took out a 15-foot section of wooden guard rail, reducing it to splinters. He was not hurt.

Joe Weatherly started third on the grid but encountered rear end problems on his Bud Moore Pontiac. He left the race after 213 laps, good only for a 23rd place finish in the field of 31.

Petty averaged 83.301 mph for his 19th career victory.

Grand National Race No. 21
200 Laps at Columbia Speedway
Columbia, SC
100 Miles on Half-mile Dirt Track
May 2, 1963

Fin	St	No.	Driver	Team / Car	Laps	Money	Status
1	1	41	Richard Petty	Petty Eng '63 Plymouth	200	$1,000	Running
2	2	87	Buck Baker	Baker '63 Pontiac	200	600	Running
3	3	11	Ned Jarrett	Burton-Robinson '63 Ford	200	400	Running
4	8	7	Buddy Baker	Buck Baker '62 Chrysler	200	300	Running
5	23	47	Jack Smith	Smith '63 Plymouth	200	275	Running
6	14	86	Neil Castles	Buck Baker '62 Chrysler	198	240	Running
7	22	34	Wendell Scott	Scott '61 Chevrolet	194	200	Running
8	17	51	Bob Cooper	Cooper '62 Pontiac	191	175	Running
9	5	18	Stick Elliott	Toy Bolton '62 Pontiac	191	150	Running
10	15	55	LeeRoy Yarbrough	'62 Mercury	191	140	Running
11	12	19	Herman Beam	Beam '62 Ford	191	130	Running
12	16	68	Ed Livingston	Livingston '62 Ford	190	120	Running
13	7	57	Jimmy Pardue	Pete Stewart '62 Pontiac	187	110	Running
14	6	12	Fred Harb	Harb '62 Pontiac	156	100	Axle
15	11	62	Curtis Crider	Crider '62 Mercury	147	85	Running
16	24	96	Jimmy Massey	'62 Chevrolet	137	75	Crash
17	19	31	Sammy Fogle	'62 Mercury	127	65	Engine
18	20	93	Jerome Warren	'62 Ford	113	60	Running
19	10	2	Joe Weatherly	Cliff Stewart '62 Pontiac	87	250	Crash
20	9	43	Maurice Petty	Petty Eng '62 Plymouth	74	50	Crash
21	13	99	Bobby Isaac	Bondy Long '62 Plymouth	56	50	Crash
22	4	03	G C Spencer	'62 Chevrolet	54	50	Piston
23	18	5	H G Rosier Jr	'61 Pontiac	54	50	Engine
24	21	1	E J Trivette	'62 Chevrolet	25	50	Piston

Time of Race: 1 hour, 56 minutes, 10 seconds
Average Speed: 51.650 mph
Pole Winner: Richard Petty - 68.08 mph
Lap Leaders: - - - - - - - - - - - - - - Richard Petty   -200
Cautions: 13
Margin of Victory: 3 car lengths
Attendance: 5,000

Race No. 21

Thirteen Cautions Fail to Slow Petty at Columbia

COLUMBIA, SC (May 2) -- Richard Petty ran his winning streak to three as he prevailed in a close decision over Buck Baker in the 100-mile Grand National race at Columbia Speedway.

The 200 lapper over the half-mile dirt track was a caution-marred contest with the yellow flag unfurled 13 times. Petty and Baker swapped the lead on numerous occasions and the front runners drove in a tight cluster all night.

Petty edged Baker by three car lengths at the wire. Baker squeezed past Ned Jarrett in the final lap to gain second place with Jarrett finishing third. Buddy Baker turned in a fine effort and took fourth. Jack Smith was fifth as each of the top five finishers completed all 200 laps.

Accidents took out three drivers. Jimmy Massey wrecked his Chevy after 98 laps, Bobby Isaac crashed on lap 57 and Maurice Petty went out in the 76th lap. No injuries were reported.

Petty averaged 51.650 mph before a crowd of 5,000. Jarrett led Petty by 522 points in the Grand National point standings.

Grand National Race No. 22
200 Laps at Tar Heel Speedway
Randleman, NC
50 Miles on Quarter-mile Dirt Track
May 5, 1963

Fin	St	No.	Driver	Team / Car	Laps	Money	Status
1	3	43	Jim Paschal	Petty Eng '62 Plymouth	200	$570	Running
2	9	2	Joe Weatherly	Cliff Stewart '62 Pontiac	196	675	Running
3	1	11	Ned Jarrett	Burton-Robinson '63 Ford	196	400	Running
4	8	57	Jimmy Pardue	Pete Stewart '62 Pontiac	195	290	Running
5	4	36	Larry Thomas	Wade Younts '62 Dodge	195	240	Running
6	7	12	Fred Harb	Harb '62 Pontiac	195	225	Running
7	15	58	G C Spencer	'62 Chevrolet	195	200	Running
8	11	34	Wendell Scott	Scott '61 Chevrolet	194	175	Running
9	10	96	Jimmy Massey	'61 Chevrolet	190	165	Running
10	13	62	Curtis Crider	Crider '62 Mercury	188	170	Running
11	5	49	Joe Jones	J C Parker '63 Dodge	186	130	Running
12	12	19	Herman Beam	Beam '62 ford	184	120	Running
13	2	41	Richard Petty	Petty Eng '63 Plymouth	171	160	Running
14	6	87	Buck Baker	Baker '62 Chrysler	80	105	Gas Tank
15	14	86	Neil Castles	Buck Baker '62 Chrysler	3	75	Clutch

Time of Race: 1 hour, 02 minutes, 16 seconds
Average Speed: 48.605 mph
Pole Winner: Ned Jarrett - 50.856 mph
Lap Leaders: Ned Jarrett 1-130, Jim Paschal 131-200
Cautions: None
Margin of Victory: 4 laps plus
Attendance: 4,000

Race No. 22

Paschal Gives Petty Engineering 6th Straight Win

RANDLEMAN, NC (May 5) -- Jim Paschal took the lead in the 131st lap and cruised to a four lap victory in the 50-mile race at Tar Heel Speedway. The steady High Point driver gave the Petty Engineering team its sixth straight Grand National win.

Joe Weatherly finished second in a Pontiac owned by Cliff Stewart, who just happened to be the promoter of the little quarter-mile paved track, located just a stone's throw from the Petty shops. Third place went to Ned Jarrett, fourth to Jimmy Pardue and fifth to Larry Thomas.

Jarrett started on the pole and led the first 130 laps. He had his Ford comfortably in front when a tire blew, forcing him to the pits. He wound up four laps behind Paschal.

It was Paschal's second straight win at Tar Heel. His strategy, he said, was "to follow a faster Ford and just wait until something happens to the front runner." He had won the Thanksgiving Day race last November by following Glen Wood until a tire blew. "The same thing happened to Jarrett in this race," said Paschal.

Richard Petty had qualified second, but he pulled into the pits after one lap. His family-oriented pit crew went to work on a faulty fuel pump and he got back in the race 30 laps later. He wound up 13th in the 15 car field. Only two cars fell out of the race.

Race No. 23

Weatherly Prevails in Two-Part Rebel 300

DARLINGTON, SC (May 11) -- Joe Weatherly parlayed consistent driving in two 151-mile races and emerged victorious in the seventh annual Rebel 300 at Darlington Raceway. It was his second win of the year and the first for Pontiac on superspeedways in the 1963 campaign.

Weatherly said car owner Bud Moore installed a "Ford eater engine to calm down those Brand X (Ford) drivers."

Raceway President Bob Colvin devised a complicated and confusing system of determining the Rebel 300 winner. The event was broken into a pair of 110 lap races. This was the first time the spring race was not

Grand National Race No. 23
220 Laps at Darlington Raceway
Darlington, SC
"Rebel 300"
302.5 Miles on 1.375-mile Paced Track
May 11, 1963

Fin	St	No.	Driver	Team / Car	Laps	Money	Status
1	6	8	Joe Weatherly	Bud Moore '63 Pontiac	220	$11,100	Running
2	5	22	Fireball Roberts	Holman-Moody '63 Ford	219	6,200	Running
3	9	42	Richard Petty	Petty Eng '63 Plymouth	219	4,980	Running
4	2	21	Tiny Lund	Wood Bros '63 Ford	219	2,665	Running
5	10	7	Bobby Johns	Shorty Johns	218	1,965	Running
6	11	41	Jim Paschal	Petty Eng '63 Plymouth	216	1,470	Running
7	7	26	Darel Dieringer	Bill Stroppe '63 Mercury	217	1,250	Running
8	14	87	Buck Baker	Baker '63 Pontiac	216	1,000	Running
9	16	54	Jimmy Pardue	Pete Stewart '63 Ford	215	850	Running
10	18	5	Billy Wade	Cotton Owens '63 Dodge	213	650	Running
11	22	52	Cale Yarborough	Julian Buesink '62 Ford	211	600	Running
12	13	6	David Pearson	Cotton Owens '63 Dodge	180	600	Crash
13	21	16	G C Spencer	Cotton Owens '63 Dodge	210	500	Running
14	24	73	Curtis Crider	Acey Taylor '62 Pontiac	205	450	Running
15	19	47	Stick Elliott	Jack Smith '63 Plymouth	155	400	Engine
16	20	71	LeeRoy Yarbrough	W M Harrison '63 Chevrolet	130	420	Push Rod
17	8	24	Larry Frank	Bill Stroppe '63 Mercury	155	350	Running
18	29	09	Larry Manning	'62 Chevrolet	198	300	Running
19	27	66	Ed Livingston	Mamie Reynolds '62 Ford	193	300	Running
20	15	11	Ned Jarrett	Burton-Robinson '63 Ford	197	300	Running
21	17	99	Bobby Isaac	Bondy Long '63 ford	112	390	Handling
22	23	27	Bob James	Roscoe Sanders '63 Plym	196	300	Running
23	25	67	Reb Wickersham	Reb's Sport Shop '62 Pontiac	132	300	Crash
24	26	19	Herman Beam	Beam '62 Ford	57	300	Handling
25	4	3	Junior Johnson	Ray Fox '63 Chevrolet	110	1,300	Rear End
26	28	86	Neil Castles	Buck Baker '63 Chrysler	8	300	Engine
27	12	66	Johnny Allen	Ratus Walters '63 Ford	69	300	Con Rod
28	30	51	Bob Cooper	Cooper '62 Pontiac	41	300	Crash
29	31	97	Possum Jones	Lewis Osborne '62 Chevrolet	3	300	Sway Bar
30	1	28	Fred Lorenzen	Holman-Moody '63 Ford	6	415	Crash
31	3	4	Rex White	Louis Clements '63 Chevrolet	2	320	Crash

Time of Race: 2 hours, 27 minutes, 36 seconds
Average Speed: 122.745 mph
Pole Winner: Fred Lorenzen - 131.718 mph
First Race:
  Lap Leaders: Junior Johnson 1-47, Joe Weatherly 48-50, Jim Paschal 51-76
    Junior Johnson 77-109, Weatherly 110
  Cautions: 2 for 8 laps
  Margin of Victory: 6 seconds
Second Race:
  Lap Leaders: Richard Petty 1-67, Bobby Johns 68-69, Fireball Roberts 70-76,
    Petty 77-110
  Cautions: 1 for 6 laps
  Margin of Victory: 8 seconds
Attendance: 25,000

points. Tiny Lund got fourth place overall with 185.6 points earned in fifth and fourth place finishes. Bobby Johns, who finished seventh and fifth, accumulated 177.5 points and was fifth overall.

It was possible for a driver to pocket first place money wtihout ever leading a lap. Fortunately, Grand National racing and sanctioning NASCAR saved face since Weatherly fully earned his 24th career win.

Bob Cooper's Pontiac jumps on guard rail in Rebel 300

A crowd of 25,000 watched Weatherly prevail by six seconds over the coasting Johnson in the first race. The lead changed hands five times. Petty's margin over Weatherly in the second event was eight seconds. Weatherly's average speed for the 302.5 miles was a record 122.745 mph

Pole sitter Fred Lorenzen was kayoed in a second lap crash with Rex White. No driver injuries were reported, and Lorenzen accepted blame for the accident. "I got a little over anxious," he admitted.

The official rundown released by NASCAR was even more confusing than the races themselves. Johnson completed 110 laps and finished in 25th place, yet Herman Beam was listed one spot ahead of Johnson while running only 57 laps. Ned Jarrett completed 197 laps and got paid for 20th place while David Pearson's 180 laps were good enough for 12th place.

Only days after the race, NASCAR "suggested" to Colvin and Raceway officials that such a system had to go.

Petty overtook Jarrett in the point race and now leads by 652 points.

Race No. 24

Point Leader Petty Back on Winning Track at Manassas

MANASSAS, VA (May 18) -- Richard Petty drove a flawless race and won the non-stop 112.5-mile Grand National race at the new Old Dominion Speedway. It

staged for Convertible stock cars, and Colvin felt it was necessary to conceive a new twist to attract a good crowd.

Weatherly took the lead in the final lap of the first 151-miler when the Chevrolet of Junior Johnson stripped its rear gearing. The 5'7" Norfolk, VA veteran wound up second to Richard Petty in the second half of the race. Weatherly's consistency enabled him to rack up 197.8 points in the 'involved' point system used solely to determine the winner of the race.

Fireball Roberts, who finished third in both events, wound up with 191.7 points and finished second ovrall. Richard Petty, sixth in the opener and winner of the second 151-miler, was third overall with 187.9

was his eighth win of the year and the seventh in the last eight races for Petty Engineering Plymouths.

The toothy Petty throttled his Plymouth into the lead in the opening lap and outdistanced Ned Jarrett by a full lap to win the $1,000 first place check. Petty was driving the #41 Plymouth, which had appeared more potent in practice times. Jim Paschal took Petty's #43 and wound up third. Paschal seemed a bit irked that he had to give up the #41 for this reason. Fourth place went to Larry Thomas with Elmo Langley fifth.

The caution-free contest was completed at an average speed of 70.275 mph. A crowd of 4,000 turned out to watch the 300 lapper on the .375-mile paved track.

Grand National Race No. 24
300 Laps at Old Dominion Speedway
Manassas, VA
112.5 Miles on .375-mile Dirt Track
May 18, 1963

Fin	St	No.	Driver	Team / Car	Laps	Money	Status
1	1	41	Richard Petty	Petty Eng '63 Pontiac	300	$1,000	Running
2	3	11	Ned Jarrett	Burton-Robinson '63 Ford	299	600	Running
3	2	43	Jim Paschal	Petty Eng '63 Plymouth	298	400	Running
4	5	36	Larry Thomas	Wade Younts '62 Dodge	292	300	Running
5	8	64	Elmo Langley	Woodfield '62 Ford	289	275	Running
6	6	88	Nace Mattingly	Major Melton '62 Chrysler	288	240	Running
7	10	12	Fred Harb	Harb '63 Ford	288	200	Running
8	11	96	Curtis Crider	'62 Chevrolet	285	175	Running
9	7	2	Joe Weatherly	Cliff Stewart '62 Pontiac	284	350	Running
10	15	09	Larry Manning	'62 Chevrolet	282	140	Running
11	16	33	Roy Mayne	C L Kilpatrick '62 Chevrolet	279	130	Running
12	12	83	Worth McMillion	McMillion '62 Chevrolet	279	120	Running
13	13	34	Wendell Scott	Scott '62 Chevrolet	279	120	Running
14	14	19	Herman Beam	Beam '63 Ford	270	100	Running
15	4	57	Jimmy Pardue	Pete Stewart '62 Pontiac	136	85	Diff
16	9	66	Johnny Allen	Ratus Walters '63 Ford	97	75	Trans

Time of Race: 1 hour, 36 minutes, 03 seconds
Average Speed: 70.275 mph
Pole winner: Richard Petty - 71.580 mph
Lap Leaders: -------------- Richard Petty -300
Cautions: None
Margin of Victory: 1 lap plus
Attendance: 4,000

Race No. 25

Jarrett Outlasts Petty at Richmond's Southside Speedway

RICHMOND, VA (May 19) -- Ned Jarrett prevailed in a see-saw struggle with Richard Petty and won the 100-mile event at Southside Speedway before a disappointing crowd of 2,000.

It was Jarrett's second win of the year and the 16th of his career -- but his first Grand National win on a

Grand National Race No. 25
300 Laps at Southside Speedway
Richmond, VA
100 Miles on .333-mile Paved Track
May 19, 1963

Fin	St	No.	Driver	Team / Car	Laps	Money	Status
1	1	11	Ned Jarrett	Burton-Robinson '63 Ford	300	$1,000	Running
2	2	41	Richard Petty	Petty Eng '63 Plymouth	298	600	Running
3	6	36	Larry Thomas	Wade Younts '62 Dodge	294	400	Running
4	3	57	Jimmy Pardue	Pete Stewart '62 Pontiac	291	300	Running
5	5	35	Ray Hendrick	Rebel Racing '61 Pontiac	288	275	Running
6	8	09	Larry Manning	'62 Chevrolet	286	240	Running
7	10	96	Jimmy Massey	'62 Chevrolet	286	200	Running
8	7	12	Fred Harb	Harb '62 Pontiac	283	175	Trans
9	14	34	Wendell Scott	Scott '61 Chevrolet	282	150	Running
10	13	83	Worth McMillion	McMillion '62 Pontiac	274	140	Running
11	12	33	Roy Mayne	C L Kilpatrick '62 Chevrolet	272	130	Running
12	15	19	Herman Beam	Beam '62 Ford	271	120	Running
13	16	88	Major Melton	Melton '61 Chrysler	263	110	Running
14	4	43	Jim Paschal	Petty Eng '62 Plymouth	258	100	Running
15	11	64	Elmo Langley	Woodfield '62 Ford	223	85	Diff
16	17	38	Bob Hurt	Mat DeMatthews '62 Chevy	144	75	Brakes
17	9	2	Curtis Crider	Cliff Stewart '62 Pontiac	93	65	Clutch

Time of Race: 1 hour, 32 minutes, 14 seconds
Average Speed: 65.052 mph
Pole Winner: Ned Jarrett - 70.642 mph
Lap Leaders: Ned Jarrett 1-108, Richard Petty 109-199, Jarrett 200-240, Petty 241-256, Jarrett 257-300
Cautions: 1 for 6 laps
Margin of Victory: 2 laps, 8 seconds
Attendance: 2,000

paved track. The Newton, NC former Sportsman champion drove past Petty for the final time in the 257th lap of the 300 lap affair. He wound up two laps and eight seconds in front of his friendly rival as Petty was forced to slacken his pace with worn tires. Larry Thomas came in third, Jimmy Pardue was fourth and Ray Hendrick fifth.

Joe Weatherly was unable to secure a ride for the 300 lapper on the .333-mile paved oval. He fell 2,274 points behind leader Petty in the Grand National standings.

One caution flag, lasting only six laps, interrupted the hot Jarrett-Petty contest. Jarrett averaged 65.052 mph

In other news, Junior Johnson decided to turn down the offer to drive owner John Chalik's car in the forthcoming Indianapolis 500.

Race No. 26
Lorenzen Snares World 600; Blown Tire Foils Johnson

CHARLOTTE, NC (June 2) -- Fred Lorenzen of Elmhurst, IL took the lead four laps from the finish and grabbed a $27,780 check in the fourth annual World

Grand National Race No. 26
400 Laps at Charlotte Motor Speedway
Charlotte, NC
"World 600"
600 Miles on 1.5-mile Paved Track
June 2, 1963

Fin	St	No.	Driver	Team / Car	Laps	Money	Status
1	2	28	Fred Lorenzen	Holman-Moody '63 Ford	400	$27,780	Running
2	1	3	Junior Johnson	Ray Fox '63 Chevrolet	400	17,460	Running
3	6	4	Rex White	Louis Clements '63 Chevrolet	398	8,310	Running
4	7	8	Joe Weatherly	Bud Moore '63 Pontiac	397	6,275	Running
5	23	6	David Pearson	Cotton Owens '63 Dodge	396	4,425	Running
6	5	29	Nelson Stacy	Holman-Moody '63 Ford	395	3,000	Running
7	3	21	Marvin Panch	Wood Bros '63 Ford	395	2,620	Running
8	12	26	Darel Dieringer	Bill Stroppe '63 Mercury	394	1,750	Running
9	15	25	G C Spencer	Bill Stroppe '63 Mercury	392	1,450	Running
10	4	22	Fireball Roberts	Holman-Moody '63 Ford	391	1,580	Running
11	14	99	Bobby Isaac	Bondy Long '63 Ford	385	1,200	Running
12	19	44	Tiny Lund	S McKinney '62 Ford	384	1,150	Running
13	10	0	Jimmy Pardue	Holman-Moody '63 Ford	384	1,050	Running
14	28	19	Larry Thomas	Herman Beam '63 Ford	373	1,000	Running
15	27	60	Bob Cooper	'62 Pontiac	373	900	Running
16	34	20	Emanuel Zervakis	'63 Ford	367	800	Engine
17	9	13	Banjo Matthews	Smokey Yunick '63 Chevrolet	358	700	Diff
18	25	48	Stick Elliott	Jack Smith '63 Plymouth	355	650	Crash
19	36	09	Larry Manning	'62 Chevrolet	354	600	Running
20	43	34	Wendell Scott	Scott '62 Chevrolet	350	550	Running
21	39	83	Worth McMillion	McMillion '62 Pontiac	350	500	Running
22	30	97	Possum Jones	Lewis Osborne '62 Chevrolet	338	500	Running
23	41	18	Cale Yarborough	Toy Bolton '62 Pontiac	336	500	Running
24	20	5	Billy Wade	Cotton Owens '63 Dodge	335	500	Diff
25	13	24	Larry Frank	Bill Stroppe '63 Mercury	321	500	Bearing
26	37	1	E J Trivette	'62 Chevrolet	288	450	Engine
27	32	50	T C Hunt	'62 Pontiac	264	450	Engine
28	16	7	Bobby Johns	Shorty Johns '63 Pontiac	259	450	Piston
29	8	06	Bob Welborn	'63 Pontiac	253	450	Engine
30	22	11	Ned Jarrett	Burton-Robinson '63 Ford	228	450	Engine
31	40	86	Neil Castles	Buck Baker '62 Chrysler	200	450	Engine
32	35	30	Bunkie Blackburn	Fred Clark '62 Chevrolet	194	450	Engine
33	31	39	LeeRoy Yarbrough	E A McQuaig '61 Pontiac	188	450	Engine
34	24	41	Bob James	Petty Eng '63 Plymouth	111	450	Fuel Pmp
35	29	74	Paul Clark	Clark '62 Pontiac	96	450	Engine
36	18	43	Richard Petty	Petty '63 Plymouth	90	450	Camshaft
37	38	56	Ed Livingston	Mamie Reynolds '62 Ford	81	450	Engine
38	44	2	Buddy Baker	Cliff Stewart '62 Pontiac	61	450	Engine
39	26	54	Ralph Earnhardt	Pete Stewart '63 Ford	59	450	Crash
40	17	66	Johnny Allen	Ratus Walters '63 Ford	53	450	Crash
41	33	47	Jack Smith	Smith '63 Plymouth	27	450	Wheel
42	20	42	Jim Paschal	Petty Eng '63 Plymouth	24	450	Crash
43	11	87	Buck Baker	Baker '63 Pontiac	23	450	Crash
44	42	62	Curtis Crider	Crider '63 Mercury	2	450	Withdrew

Time of Race: 4 hours, 31 minutes, 52 seconds
Average Speed: 132.417 mph
Pole Winner: Junior Johnson -- 141.148 mph
Lap Leaders: Junior Johnson 1-56, Fireball Roberts 57-71, Johnson 72-100,
   Rex White 101, Johnson 102-122, Fred Lorenzen 123-129, G C Spencer 130,
   Marvin Panch 131, Johnson 132-192, Panch 193-194, Lorenzen 195-201,
   Panch 202-216, Johnson 217-261, Lorenzen 262-319, Johnson 320-396,
   Lorenzen 397-400
Relief Drivers: Yarbrough for Matthews, James for Wade, Elmo Langley for Zervakis,
   Petty for James, Baker for Welborn, Allen for Stacy
Cautions: 2 for 14 laps
Margin of Victory: 35 seconds
Attendance: 58,722

He was forced to pit for fresh rubber in the 397th lap of the 400 lap race. Lorenzen drove uncontested into the lead and kept it to the finish.

Johnson wound up second, 35 seconds behind Lorenzen's Ford. Rex White finished third, two laps back. Joe Weatherly came in fourth and leaped into the Grand National point standings lead. Fifth place went to David Pearson.

Lorenzen received a chill himself when his engine sputtered as he took the white flag. "I was out of gas," said the 28-year old driver. "I was praying harder than I ever have before, and I couldn't have been going more than 20 mph when I got the checkered flag."

Out of gas, Lorenzen cuts across infield to get to victory lane after World 600

Johnson, who led for a total of 289 laps, held a 16 second advantage over Lorenzen with 20 laps to go. However, he saw his lead sliced each lap in the closing stages. The deficit was being cut by about a second per lap. Lorenzen was about four seconds behind when Johnson's white Chevrolet popped the tire.

"He couldn't have caught me," muttered a disappointed Johnson after the race. "He hadn't caught me all day. How was he gonna make that big hunk of track in just three laps?"

Lorenzen disagreed. "I feel like I would have caught him," he offered. "We probably would have run the last two laps neck-and-neck. It would have been a heck of a finish."

The potent Petty Engineering team suffered through a miserable day. Jim Paschal's car was wiped out in a three-car wreck, which also involved Buck Baker and Larry Frank. Richard Petty went only 90 laps before a broken cam shaft put him out of action. He also lost his lead in the standings, falling 1,338 points behind Weatherly.

Marvin Panch, about 90 percent recovered from

600 at Charlotte Motor Speedway. It was the second big track win of the year for the former carpenter and it pushed his season's earnings to $69,480.

Junior Johnson, the crowd favorite, had led for 77 laps and was running a couple car lengths in front of Lorenzen when a right rear tire blew on his Chevrolet.

Larry Frank #24, Buck Baker #87 and Jim Paschal #42 tango in World 600

burns suffered at Daytona, made his return to racing. The 37 year-old Oakland, CA Ford driver started third and finished seventh. Tiny Lund joined the McKinney Ford factory team, and wound up 12th.

Lorenzen established a new standard for a 600-mile race by averaging 132.417 mph before a record crowd of 58,722.

Grand National Race No. 27
200 Laps at Birmingham International Raceway
Birmingham, AL
100 Miles on Half-mile Dirt Track
June 9, 1963

Fin	St	No.	Driver	Team / Car	Laps	Money	Status
1	2	41	Richard Petty	Petty Eng '63 Plymouth	200	$1,000	Running
2	3	3	Junior Johnson	Ray Fox '63 Chevrolet	200	600	Running
3	6	87	Buck Baker	Baker '63 Pontiac	198	400	Running
4	5	11	Ned Jarrett	Burton-Robinson '63 Ford	196	300	Running
5	1	47	Jack Smith	Smith '63 Plymouth	195	275	Running
6	8	62	Curtis Crider	Crider '63 Mercury	193	240	Running
7	15	34	Wendell Scott	Scott '62 Chevrolet	186	200	Running
8	14	39	Fred Thompson	E A McQuaig '61 Pontiac	186	175	Running
9	13	19	Herman Beam	Beam '62 Ford	185	150	Running
10	12	67	Reb Wickersham	Reb's Sport Shop '62 Pontiac	180	140	Running
11	11	86	Neil Castles	Buck Baker '62 Chrysler	169	130	Running
12	16	88	Major Melton	Melton '61 Chrysler	168	120	Running
13	10	6	David Pearson	Cotton Owens '62 Dodge	162	110	Vapor Lk
14	9	21W	Bob Perry	'63 Mercury	79	100	Vapor Lk
15	7	2	Joe Weatherly	Cliff Stewart '62 Pontiac	71	300	Wheel
16	4	57	Jimmy Pardue	Pete Stewart '62 Pontiac	36	100	Drive Sh

Time of Race: 1 hour, 27 minutes, 59 seconds
Average speed: 68.195 mph
Pole Winner: Jack Smith 71.146 mph
Lap Leaders: Jack Smith 1-22, Richard Petty 23-200
Cautions: 1 for 3 laps
Margin of Victory: 2.0 seconds
Attendance: 7,000

Race No. 27

Petty Cars 13 for 27 After Richard's Win at Birmingham

BIRMINGHAM, AL (June 9) -- Richard Petty returned to victory lane in the more comfortable confines of a short track by taking first place honors in the 100-miler at Birmingham International Raceway. It was his ninth win of the year and the 13th in 27 Grand National races for the Petty Engineering Plymouths.

Junior Johnson made it close at the finish as his Chevrolet was 2.0 seconds behind when the checkered flag waved on the half-mile dirt track. Buck Baker came in third, Ned Jarrett was fourth and Jack Smith fifth.

Smith won the pole position and led the first 22 laps. Petty slipped into the lead in the 23rd lap and led the rest of the way.

A hefty crowd of 7,000 was on hand to watch Petty average 68.195 mph. Only one caution flag for three laps interrupted his brisk pace.

Joe Weatherly was back in the saddle of the Cliff Stewart Pontiac for the short tracks. However, he wound up 15th in the field of 16 when a right rear wheel broke in the 71st lap. Weatherly's point lead dropped to 938 points over Petty.

Race No. 28

Johnson Beats Lorenzen at Atlanta; Allen in Nasty Crash

HAMPTON, GA (June 30) -- Junior Johnson, a man accustomed to riding the bumpy road of misfortune, finally made it to victory lane on a superspeedway by taking a narrow decision over Fred Lorenzen in the fourth annual Dixie 400.

Johnson whipped his Chevrolet around Lorenzen in the 235th lap and led the final 33 laps at Atlanta International Raceway. It was his fourth win of the year and his first super track victory in eight months. Lorenzen's Ford was trailing Johnson by 3.0 seconds at the end of the 267-lap race.

Marvin Panch finished third in another inspiring drive since his serious Daytona accident. Darel Dieringer came in fourth with point leader Joe Weatherly fifth.

The lead changed hands 18 times among six drivers. The most eye-popping drive was turned in by rookie

Johnny Allen's Ford explodes on top of Atlanta's guard rail

Grand National Race No. 28
267 Laps at Atlanta International Raceway
Hampton, GA
"Dixie 400"
400 Miles on 1.5-mile Paved Track
June 30, 1963

Fin	St	No.	Driver	Team / Car	Laps	Money	Status
1	2	3	Junior Johnson	Ray Fox '63 Chevrolet	267	$12,445	Running
2	4	28	Fred Lorenzen	Holman-Moody '63 Ford	267	6,190	Running
3	1	21	Marvin Panch	Wood Bros '63 Ford	267	3,370	Running
4	11	26	Darel Dieringer	Bill Stroppe '63 Mercury	266	2,245	Running
5	8	8	Joe Weatherly	Bud Moore '63 Pontiac	266	2,050	Running
6	17	4	Rex White	Louis Clements '63 Chevrolet	266	1,200	Running
7	5	29	Nelson Stacy	Holman-Moody '63 Ford	264	1,200	Running
8	18	5	Billy Wade	Cotton Ownes '63 Dodge	264	1,085	Running
9	10	87	Buck Baker	Baker '63 Pontiac	263	900	Running
10	13	11	Ned Jarrett	Burton-Robinson '63 Ford	263	800	Running
11	21	99	Bobby Isaac	Bondy Long '63 Ford	262	700	Running
12	14	43	Richard Petty	Petty Eng '63 Plymouth	262	600	Running
13	19	25	G C Spencer	Bill Stroppe '63 Mercury	262	500	Running
14	20	54	Jimmy Pardue	Pete Stewart '63 Ford	261	450	Running
15	12	41	Bob James	Petty Eng '63 Plymouth	260	400	Running
16	22	39	Bob Welborn	E A McQuaig '62 Pontiac	259	350	Running
17	24	48	Stick Elliott	Jack Smith '63 Plymouth	258	350	Running
18	25	67	Reb Wickersham	Reb's Sport Shop '63 Pontiac	252	350	Running
19	27	62	Curtis Crider	Crider '63 Mercury	246	350	Running
20	32	34	Wendell Scott	Scott '62 Chevrolet	244	350	Running
21	26	1	Bob Perry	'63 Mercury	244	325	Running
22	31	56	Ed Livingston	Mamie Reynolds '63 Ford	236	325	Running
23	29	19	Herman Beam	Beam '62 Ford	232	325	Running
24	15	47	Jack Smith	Smith '62 Plymouth	163	325	Oil Pres
25	37	12	Bunkie Blackburn	Fred Harb '63 Pontiac	161	325	Crash
26	33	36	Larry Thomas	Wade Younts '62 dodge	140	325	Engine
27	9	0	Tiny Lund	Holman-Moody '63 Ford	127	325	Tie Rod
28	28	86	Neil Castles	Buck Baker '63 Chrysler	101	325	Clutch
29	23	2	Buddy Baker	Cliff Stewart '63 Pontiac	87	325	Engine
30	16	42	Jim Paschal	Petty Eng '63 Plymouth	83	325	Diff
31	3	22	Fireball Roberts	Holman-Moody '62 Ford	47	300	Engine
32	30	66	Johnny Allen	Ratus Walters '62 Ford	44	300	Crash
33	6	7	Bobby Johns	Shorty Johns '63 Ford	25	300	Heating
34	7	6	David Pearson	Cotton Owens '63 Plymouth	24	300	Engine
35	34	63	Bruce Brantley	'63 Pontiac	3	300	Handling
36	35	33	Roy Mayne	'63 Dodge	3	275	Engine

Time of Race: 3 hours, 18 minutes, 42 seconds
Average speed: 121.139 mph
Pole Winner: Marvin Panch 140.753 mph
Lap Leaders: Junior Johnson 1-33, Billy Wade 34-35, Johnson 36-41, Wade 42-56,
    Marvin Panch 57 -............................. Johnson 235-267
Total Laps led: Junior Johnson 169 laps, Fred Lorenzen 35 laps, Nelson Stacy 20 laps,
    Billy Wade 17 laps, Darel Dieringer 14 laps, Marvin Panch 12 laps. Total 18 lead
    changes
Cautions: 2 for 32 laps
Margin of Victory: 3.0 seconds
Attendance: 20,000

Billy Wade of Houston, Texas, who shoved his lightly regarded Cotton Owens Dodge around Johnson twice in the early going. Wade was victimized by a faulty front end alignment which forced him to make six pit stops for tires. Wade finished eighth, three laps behind.

Johnny Allen, driving the same Ratus Walters-owned Ford that took Larry Frank to victory in the 1962 Southern 500, blew a right front tire in the 46th lap. His car gyrated on top of and over the guard rail -- tearing the metal rail to shavings as he cartwheeled outside the track. The engine landed some 100 feet from the mutilated remains of his car. Allen was treated for a small cut on the bridge of his nose but otherwise was unhurt.

Fireball Roberts ran over a bumper from Allen's car and snapped the driveshaft of his Ford.

Smokey Yunick entered his fast and mysterious Chevrolet prepared for LeeRoy Yarbrough. After several practice sessions of less than anticipated results, Yunick withdrew the car. The famed mechanic and car builder said the car was too difficult for anyone to drive. "It'll just clog up the track," he grumbled.

Two caution flags for 32 laps held Johnson's winning speed to 121.139 mph.

Weatherly increased his point lead to 1,688 points over Richard Petty, who finished 12th.

Race No. 29

Three-car Blanket Finish at Daytona; Roberts Wins

DAYTONA BEACH, FL (July 4) -- Cagey Fireball Roberts swooped under Fred Lorenzen in the final turn and roared home first in the fifth annual Firecracker 400 at Daytona International Speedway. It was the 12th superspeedway win for Roberts since he bagged

Grand National Race No. 29
160 Laps at Daytona International Speedway
Daytona Beach, FL
"Firecracker 400"
500 Miles on 2.5-mile Paved Track
July 4, 1963

Fin	St	No.	Driver	Team / Car	Laps	Money	Status
1	3	22	Fireball Roberts	Holman-Moody '63 Ford	160	$12,100	Running
2	4	28	Fred Lorenzen	Holman-Moody '63 Ford	160	8,015	Running
3	8	21	Marvin Panch	Wood Bros '63 Ford	160	5,310	Running
4	5	16	Darel Dieringer	Bill Stroppe '63 Mercury	158	3,175	Running
5	26	11	Ned Jarrett	Burton-Robinson '63 Ford	156	1,900	Running
6	13	6	David Pearson	Cotton Owens '63 Dodge	156	1,550	Running
7	17	54	Jimmy Pardue	Pete Stewart '63 Ford	154	1,350	Running
8	18	43	Richard Petty	Petty Eng '63 Plymouth	154	1,250	Running
9	16	25	G C Spencer	Bill Stroppe '63 Mercury	149	1,150	Engine
10	10	0	Tiny Lund	Holman-Moody '63 Ford	145	1,100	Crash
11	31	13	A J Foyt	Smokey Yunick '63 Chevrolet	145	750	Engine
12	24	05	Jim McGuirk	'62 Pontiac	142	650	Running
13	21	1	Herman Beam	Beam '63 ford	142	650	Running
14	27	34	Wendell Scott	Scott '62 Chevrolet	135	550	Running
15	15	87	Buck Baker	Baker '63 Pontiac	124	550	Engine
16	30	99	Bobby Isaac	Bondy Long '63 Ford	112	450	Engine
17	1	3	Junior Johnson	Ray Fox '63 Chevrolet	111	1,500	Piston
18	12	8	Joe Weatherly	Bud Moore '63 Pontiac	102	850	Engine
19	23	5	Billy Wade	Cotton Owens '63 Dodge	95	450	Clutch
20	20	36	Larry Thomas	Wade Younts '63 Dodge	84	450	Fuel Pmp
21	7	4	Rex White	Louis Clements '63 Mercury	79	500	Engine
22	25	56	Ed Livingston	Mamie Reynolds '62 Ford	79	350	Timing
23	2	03	Jim Paschal	Ray Fox '63 Chevrolet	61	900	Piston
24	29	1	Bob Perry	'63 Mercury	58	350	Engine
25	9	02	Pedro Rodriguez	Ray Nichels '63 Pontiac	54	400	Engine
26	11	14	Troy Ruttman	Bill Stroppe '63 Mercury	50	350	Crash
27	6	01	Paul Goldsmith	Ray Nichels '63 Pontiac	40	600	Windshld
28	14	7	Bobby Johns	Shorty Johns '63 Pontiac	25	350	Radiator
29	32	39	Bob Welborn	E A McQuaig '62 Pontiac	23	325	Clutch
30	19	86	Neil Castles	Buck Baker '61 Chrysler	21	350	Vibration
31	33	48	Stick Elliott	Jack Smith '63 Plymouth	16	300	Heating
32	34	47	Jack Smith	Smith '63 Plymouth	14	275	Heating
33	28	29	Nelson Stacy	Holman-Moody '63 Ford	11	300	Engine
34	35	97	Cale Yarborough	Lewis Osborne '62 Chevrolet	9	250	Engine
35	22	62	Curtis Crider	Crider '62 Mercury	4	300	Engine

Time of Race: 2 hours, 39 minutes, 01 second
Average Speed: 150.927 mph
Pole Winner: Junior Johnson - 166.005 mph
Lap Leaders: Jim Paschal 1, Junior Johnson 2-3, Fred Lorenzen 4, Johnson 5-8,
   Lorenzen 9, Fireball Roberts 10-13, Johnson 14, Lorenzen 15, Johnson 16-17,
   Paschal 18, Lorenzen 19, Roberts 20-21, Paschal 22-23, Johnson 24-26, Paschal 27
   Roberts 28, Johnson 29-33, Roberts 34-35, Paschal 36-37, Lorenzen 38, Johnson 39,
   Lorenzen 40-44, Paschal 45, Marvin Panch 46-50, Johnson 51-63, Roberts 64-65,
   Johnson 66-77, Roberts 78-80, Johnson 81-87, Lorenzen 88-90, Tiny Lund 91-92,
   Johnson 93-106, Roberts 107-108, Johnson 109-110, Roberts 111-155,
   Lorenzen 156 Roberts 157, Lorenzen 158-159, Roberts 160
Cautions: 3 for 19 laps
Margin of Victory: 3/4 car length
Attendance: 26,640

Fireball Roberts #22, Fred Lorenzen #28 and Marvin Panch #21 in fantastic last lap duel in Firecracker 400

"Fireball knew what I was planning to do," said Lorenzen. "He just didn't let me do it."

Roberts lifted the throttle and kept his purple Ford poised on Lorenzen's rear bumper as they toured the track. Coming off the fourth turn of the 160th and final lap, Roberts exercised the famed "slingshot" move and drove past Lorenzen on the short chute. "Instead of passing him, I just slowed down and waited until we got to the third turn to make my move."

Panch was trapped behind the two leaders and couldn't make a move himself. "I was going with Fireball," said Panch. "I didn't care where he went. But I was going with him."

Darel Dieringer finished fourth with Ned Jarrett fifth.

Junior Johnson started on the pole for the sixth time in the 1963 season. But his fleet Chevrolet was once again on the sidelines after 111 laps. Engine problems put him behind the wall while leading. He had led on 12 occasions before the mechanical gremlins struck.

Jim Paschal accepted car owner Ray Fox's invitation to drive a Chevrolet identical to that of running mate Johnson. Paschal led on six occasions but lost an engine after 61 laps.

his first on July 4, 1956 at Raleigh, NC.

Roberts, Lorenzen and third place finisher Marvin Panch crossed the finish line so close that a blanket could have covered them all. All three of the Ford drivers were playing a 160 mph game of poker, each trying to out-think the other two. Roberts held the trump card, however, and won by a car length with a nifty move on the final lap.

Lorenzen, who led with two laps to go, purposely slowed -- wanting Roberts to move into first place.

Junior Johnson pits his Chevrolet at Daytona

Troy Ruttman, driving a Bill Stroppe Mercury, tagged the front stretch retaining wall and flipped on his side. He was not hurt. Tiny Lund was uninjured when his Ford crashed with 12 laps left.

The lead changed hands a record 39 times among six drivers. Only a dozen cars were running at the finish. A foot-stomping, arm-waving crowd of 26,640 cheered Roberts' 150.927 mph victory. Nineteen laps were run under the yellow flag.

Grand National Race No. 30
200 Laps at Rambi Raceway
Myrtle Beach, SC
"Speedorama 200"
100 Miles on Half-mile Dirt Track
July 7, 1963

Fin	St	No.	Driver	Team / Car	Laps	Money	Status
1	3	11	Ned Jarrett	Burton-Robinson '63 Ford	200	$1,000	Running
2	8	87	Buck Baker	Baker '63 Pontiac	193	600	Running
3	7	2	Joe Weatherly	Cliff Stewart '62 Pontiac	191	600	Running
4	10	86	Neil Castles	Buck Baker '62 Chrysler	190	300	Running
5	6	19	Cale Yarborough	Herman Beam '62 Ford	185	275	Running
6	11	09	Larry Manning	'62 Chevrolet	179	240	Running
7	15	96	Jimmy Massey	'62 Chevrolet	178	200	Running
8	16	88	Curtis Crider	Buck Baker '61 Chrysler	171	175	Running
9	18	62	Chuck Huckabee	Curtis Crider '62 Mercury	165	150	Running
10	13	18	Stick Elliott	Toy Bolton '62 Pontiac	155	140	Running
11	4	54	Jimmy Pardue	Pete Stewart '63 Ford	119	130	Engine
12	14	X	J D McDuffie	'61 Ford	113	120	Running
13	17	68	Ed Livingston	Livingston '61 Ford	102	110	Running
14	5	93	Lee Reitzel	'63 Ford	94	100	Engine
15	1	41	Richard Petty	Petty Eng '63 Plymouth	60	100	Crash
16	9	34	Wendell Scott	Scott '62 Chevrolet	46	100	Engine
17	12	61	Mark Hurley	'63 Ford	31	100	Engine
18	2	99	Bobby Isaac	Bondy Long '63 Ford	30	100	Engine

Time of Race: 1 hour, 38 minutes, 22 seconds
Average Speed: 60.996 mph
Pole Winner: Richard Petty - 68.70 mph
Lap Leaders: Bobby Isaac 1-30, Richard Petty 31-60, Ned Jarrett 61-200
Cautions:
Margin of Victory: 7 laps plus
Attendance: 4,000

Race No. 30

Jarrett Outlasts Upstart Isaac at Myrtle Beach

MYRTLE BEACH, SC (July 7) -- Ned Jarrett ran a steady pace and waited for two chargers to run themselves into trouble, then motored to an overwhelming victory in the 100-mile race at Rambi Raceway.

Jarrett breezed into the lead in the 61st lap and led the rest of the way to capture the Speedorama 200 on the half-mile dirt track. Buck Baker wound up second, seven laps behind Jarrett's Ford. Joe Weatherly came in third, Neil Castles was fourth and Cale Yarborough fifth.

Bobby Isaac, a professed short track wizard, buzzed into the lead at the outset in Bondy Long's Plymouth. He led for 30 laps and was pulling away when the engine went sour. He had to accept last place money.

Petty took up the lead when Isaac limped to the pits and stayed in front until he crashed in the 60th lap. Jarrett was home free after that.

J.D. McDuffie, driving a two year-old Ford with a big 'X' on the doors, drove in his first Grand National event and finished 12th.

A crowd of 4,000 watched Jarrett average 60.996 mph. It was his 17th career victory.

Race No. 31

Jarrett Wins Savannah; Petty Tangles With Alligator

SAVANNAH, GA (July 10) -- Ned Jarrett grabbed his second straight win in the 100-mile Grand National Race at Savannah Speedway. The Newton, NC Ford driver led all but six laps on the half-mile dirt track and

Grand National Race No. 31
200 Laps at Savannah Speedway
Savannah, GA
100 Miles on Half-mile Dirt Track
July 10, 1963

Fin	St	No.	Driver	Team / Car	Laps	Money	Status
1	2	11	Ned Jarrett	Burton-Robinson '63 Ford	200	$1,000	Running
2	5	6	David Pearson	Cotton Owens '63 Dodge	200	600	Running
3	3	57	Jimmy Pardue	Pete Stewart '62 Pontiac	199	400	Running
4	4	48	Jack Smith	Smith '63 Plymouth	199	300	Running
5	7	19	Cale Yarborough	Herman Beam '62 Ford	198	275	Running
6	6	39	LeeRoy Yarbrough	E A McQuaig '62 Ponitac	197	240	Running
7	10	09	Larry Manning	'62 Chevrolet	194	200	Running
8	12	62	Curtis Crider	Crider '62 Mercury	193	175	Running
9	11	87	Buck Baker	Baker '63 Pontiac	190	150	Running
10	13	86	Neil Castles	Buck Baker '63 Chrysler	187	140	Running
11	15	68	Ed Livingston	Livingston '61 Ford	182	130	Running
12	14	89	Joel Davis	'62 Pontiac	174	120	Running
13	8	34	Wendell Scott	Scott '61 Chevrolet	155	110	Running
14	9	2	Joe Weatherly	Cliff Stewart '62 Pontiac	57	300	Crash
15	1	42	Richard Petty	Petty Eng '63 Plymouth	38	85	Crash

Time of Race: 1 hour, 40 minutes, 38 seconds
Average Speed: 59.622 mph
Pole Winner: Richard Petty - 71.34 mph
Lap Leaders: Richard Petty 1-6, Ned Jarrett 7-200
Cautions:
Margin of Victory: 3/4 lap
Attendance:

wound up almost a lap in front of runner-up David Pearson.

Third place went to Jimmy Pardue with Jack Smith fourth and Cale Yarborough fifth. Yarborough, a stubby blond-thatched kid out of Timmonsville, SC, has been driving a Ford owned by Herman "The Turtle" Beam with enlightening results.

Pole sitter Richard Petty led the first six laps and was running second when his Plymouth broke through the retaining wall. The car wound up in an adjoining swamp, which he termed "a pretty scary looking place. I don't mind a little wreck, but alligators I don't like!" A rather large reptile has been rumored to spend considerable time in and around the marsh.

Point leader Joe Weatherly was the only other driver in the 15 car field not to finish. His Pontiac crashed in the 57th lap.

Jarrett's fourth win of the year came at a speed of 59.622 mph.

62.5-mile race at Dog Track Speedway after Ned Jarrett had been flagged in first place.

Pardue's Ford had fallen two full laps behind Jarrett in the middle stages of the 250 lapper on the quarter-mile dirt track. When Jarrett was forced to make a green flag pit stop to replace a flat tire, Pardue zoomed into the lead. The 32 year-old journeyman driver led the final 72 laps, but scorers were uncertain whether he was ahead of or behind Jarrett in the final laps.

Jarrett was flagged in first place with Pardue second. Third place went to Buck Baker with Mark Hurley fourth and Neil Castles fifth.

Score cards were re-examined by NASCAR officials and Pardue was given the nod an hour after the race.

Pardue became the 12th different winner of the 1963 season.

Junior Johnson started on the pole, but never led. His Chevrolet wound up 10th in the field of 14, falling victim to overheating after 179 laps.

One caution flag held Pardue's winning speed to 45.464 mph.

Grand National Race No. 32
250 Laps at Dog Track Speedway
Moyock, NC
62.5 Miles on Quarter-mile Dirt Track
July 11, 1963

Fin	St	No.	Driver	Team / Car	Laps	Money	Status
1	6	54	Jimmy Pardue	Pete Stewart '63 Ford	250	$550	Running
2	2	11	Ned Jarrett	Burton Robinson '63 Ford	250	500	Running
3	3	87	Buck Baker	Baker '63 Pontiac	246	365	Running
4	9	61	Mark Hurley	'63 Ford	241	300	Running
5	10	86	Neil Castles	Buck Baker '62 Chrysler	236	255	Running
6	11	64	Elmo Langley	Woodfield '62 Ford	232	250	Running
7	5	19	Herman Beam	Beam '62 Ford	222	195	Running
8	12	09	Larry Manning	'62 Chevrolet	214	175	Crash
9	8	62	Curtis Crider	Crider '62 Mercury	182	170	Rear End
10	1	3	Junior Johnson	Ray Fox '63 Chevrolet	179	170	Heating
11	4	43	Richard Petty	Petty Eng '63 Plymouth	145	145	Diff
12	7	X	J D McDuffie	'61 Ford	117	140	Diff
13	14	2	Joe Weatherly	Cliff Stewart '62 Pontiac	19	335	Engine
14	13	34	Wendell Scott	Scott '61 Chevrolet	---	100	Piston

Time of Race: 1 hour, 22 minutes, 29 seconds
Average Speed: 45.464 mph
Pole Winner: Junior Johnson - 47.12 mph
Lap Leaders: Ned Jarrett 1-178, Jimmy Pardue 179-250
Cautions: 1
Margin of Victory:
Attendance:

Race No. 32
Pardue Pockets Disputed 250-lapper at Dog Track

MOYOCK, NC (July 11) -- Jimmy Pardue of North Wilkesboro, NC was declared the winner of the

Grand National Race No. 33
200 Laps at Bowman-Gray Stadium
Winston-Salem, NC
50 Miles on Quarter-mile Paved Track
July 13, 1963

Fin	St	No.	Driver	Team / Car	Laps	Money	Status
1	1	21	Glenn Wood	Wood Bros '63 Ford	200	$575	Running
2	4	11	Ned Jarrett	Burton-Robinson '63 Ford	200	480	Running
3	5	87	Buck Baker	Baker '63 Pontiac	198	350	Running
4	6	41	Lee Petty	Petty Eng '63 Plymouth	197	300	Running
5	13	48	Jack Smith	Smith '63 Plymouth	195	240	Running
6	14	36	Larry Thomas	Wade Younts '62 Dodge	194	215	Running
7	12	2	Joe Weatherly	Cliff Stewart '62 Pontiac	194	400	Running
8	3	42	Richard Petty	Petty Eng '63 Plymouth	193	180	Running
9	8	57	Perk Brown	Pete Stewart '62 Poontiac	192	165	Running
10	21	12	Fred Harb	Harb '62 Pontiac	191	140	Running
11	10	6	David Pearson	Cotton Owens '63 Dodge	191	180	Running
12	16	54	Jimmy Pardue	Pete Stewart '63 Ford	190	120	Running
13	18	34	Wendell Scott	Scott '61 Chevrolet	184	110	Running
14	17	18	Stick Elliott	Toy Bolton '62 Ford	173	150	Running
15	23	96	Jimmy Massey	'62 Chevrolet	165	75	Engine
16	9	44	Tommy Irwin	S McKinney '63 Ford	151	90	Tire
17	2	3	Junior Johnson	Ray Fox '63 Chevrolet	117	75	Tire
18	7	03	G C Spencer	'62 Chevrolet	69	60	Crash
19	20	88	Major Melton	Melton '61 Chrysler	62	50	Tire
20	15	64	Elmo Langley	Woodfield '62 Ford	53	50	Fuel Pmp
21	22	86	Neil Castles	Buck Baker '62 Chrysler	9	25	Trans
22	11	62	Curtis Crider	Crider '62 Mercury	3	25	Engine
23	19	61	Billy Wade	'63 Ford	1	55	Oil Pres

Time of Race: 1 hour, 7 minutes, 35 seconds
Average Speed: 44.390 mph
Pole Winner: Glen Wood - 48.387 mph
Lap Leaders: Glen Wood 1, Junior Johnson 2-80, Ned Jarrett 81-106, Wood 107-200
Cautions: 3
Margin of Victory: 5 seconds
Attendance: 15,000

Race No. 33

Lee Petty Makes Racing Return; Glen Wood Wins

WINSTON-SALEM, NC (July 13) -- Glen Wood took the lead from Ned Jarrett in the 107th lap and sped to victory in the 50-mile Grand National race at Bowman-Gray Stadium. It was Wood's first win of the year and the fourth of his career.

Biggest news of the overcast evening was the return of Lee Petty, three-time Grand National champ who was seriously injured at Daytona Beach two-and-a-half years earlier. The 49 year-old Randleman, NC veteran wound up fourth behind runner-up Jarrett and Buck Baker. Jack Smith finished fifth.

"Old Man" Petty started sixth and was in contention for most of the way. Eventually he fell three laps off the pace but gave a fine account of himself considering the long lay-off.

Perk Brown of Spray, NC, who campaigned regularly on the Grand National tour in 1952, made a come-back of his own. Driving a Pete Stewart-owned Pontiac, Brown finished ninth.

Wood spun his Ford in a congested fifth lap melee and dropped to 14th place. He made a miraculous comeback considering the tight turns and narrow grooves for passing. The likeable "Woodchopper" squeezed past Jarrett in the 107th lap and led the rest of the way.

Junior Johnson rooted Wood out of the lead in the first turn of the second lap. The Ronda, NC throttle-stomper led for 80 laps before Jarrett made his pass. Johnson left the race after 117 laps with a tire problem.

Wood averaged 44.390 mph as three caution flags broke the action.

Race No. 34

Jarrett, Petty Tangle at Asheville; Ned Wins

ASHEVILLE, NC (July 14) -- Ned Jarrett continued his hot summer pace and closed to within 580 points of standings leader Joe Weatherly with a victory in the 100-miler at the New Asheville Speedway. It was the fifth win of the year for the Newton, NC Ford driver.

The lead changed hands six times in the hard fought 300 lapper on the .333-mile paved track. Jarrett took the lead for good on lap 281 after a motorized rubdown with Richard Petty as they were overtaking the lapped car of Major Melton. Petty's right front tire spit smoke during the final 20 laps and he settled for second place. David Pearson wound up third after starting on the pole. Joe Weatherly was fourth in a Petty Engineering Plymouth. Fifth place went to Darel Dieringer.

After the race, Jarrett and Petty squared off. Petty shook his fist at Jarrett as the victory lane proceedings were about to get underway. Bud Allman, Jarrett's crew chief stepped in -- just as Petty's brother Maurice arrived at the scene. Maurice restrained Allman while NASCAR officials separated Jarrett and Richard.

Jarrett averaged 63.384 mph before a crowd of 4,500.

Race No. 35

Roberts Aces Old Bridge; Heartbreaker for Weatherly

OLD BRIDGE, NJ (July 19) -- Fireball Roberts, who usually confines his activity below the Mason-Dixon line, gave the Northern fans a glimpse of his

---

Grand National Race No. 34
300 Laps at New Asheville Speedway
Asheville, NC
100 Miles on .333-mile Paved Track
July 14, 1963

Fin	St	No.	Driver	Team / Car	Laps	Money	Status
1	5	11	Ned Jarrett	Burton-Robinson '63 Ford	300	$1,000	Running
2	3	43	Richard Petty	Petty Eng '63 Plymouth	300	600	Running
3	1	6	David Pearson	Cotton Owens '63 Dodge	297	400	Running
4	9	41	Joe Weatherly	Petty Eng '63 Plymouth	296	500	Running
5	7	87	Buck Baker	Baker '63 Pontiac	291	275	Running
6	6	61	Darel Dieringer	'63 Ford	291	240	Running
7	8	18	Stick Elliott	Toy Bolton '62 Pontiac	290	200	Running
8	16	76	J D McDuffie	'61 Ford	271	175	Running
9	15	34	Wendell Scott	Scott '61 Chevrolet	270	150	Running
10	4	54	Jimmy Pardue	Pete Stewart '63 Ford	269	140	Diff
11	13	88	Major Melton	Melton '61 Chrysler	262	130	Running
12	19	64	Elmo Langley	'62 Ford	260	120	Running
13	11	36	Larry Thomas	Wade Younts '62 Dodge	235	110	Heating
14	10	48	Jack Smith	Smith '63 Plymouth	96	100	Handling
15	2	3	Junior Johnson	Ray Fox '63 Chevrolet	90	85	Handling
16	14	99	Bobby Isaac	Bondy Long '62 Plymouth	86	75	Handling
17	20	86	Neil Castles	Buck Baker '62 Chrysler	34	65	Trans
18	12	03	G C Spencer	'61 Chevrolet	23	60	Fuel Pmp
19	17	57	Bobby Keck	Pete Stewart '63 Ford	16	50	Crash
20	18	1	E J Trivette	'62 Chevrolet	1	50	Crash

Time of Race: 1 hour, 34 minutes, 34 seconds
Average Speed: 63.384 mph
Pole Winner: David Pearson - 67.235 mph
Lap Leaders: David Pearson 1, Junior Johnson 2-31, Pearson 32-33, Ned Jarrett 34-160, Richard Petty 161-280, Jarrett 281-300
Cautions:
Margin of Victory:
Attendance: 4,500

Grand National Race No. 35
200 Laps at Old Bridge Stadium
Old Bridge, NJ
100 Miles on Half-mile Paved Track
July 19, 1963

Fin	St	No.	Driver	Team / Car	Laps	Money	Status
1	5	22	Fireball Roberts	Holman-Moody '63 Ford	200	$1,000	Running
2	6	4	Rex White	Louis Clements '63 Mercury	200	600	Running
3	2	28	Fred Lorenzen	Holman-Moody '63 Ford	199	400	Running
4	7	11	Ned Jarrett	Burton-Robinson '63 Ford	199	300	Running
5	9	99	Bobby Isaac	Bondy Long '63 Ford	196	275	Running
6	3	21	Marvin Panch	Wood Bros '63 Ford	196	240	Running
7	1	8	Joe Weatherly	Bud Moore '63 Pontiac	194	400	Running
8	12	12	Fred Harb	Harb '63 Ford	194	175	Running
9	17	34	Wendell Scott	Scott '62 Chevrolet	188	150	Running
10	15	86	Neil Castles	Buck Baker '62 Chrysler	188	140	Running
11	18	83	Worth McMillion	McMillion '62 Pontiac	186	130	Running
12	20	2	Mal Delometer	'63 Ford	183	120	Running
13	13	54	Jimmy Pardue	Pete Stewart '62 Pontiac	182	110	Running
14	10	87	Buck Baker	Baker '63 Pontiac	180	100	Running
15	11	63	Joe Kelly	'63 Ford	120	85	Brakes
16	4	43	Richard Petty	Petty Eng '63 Plymouth	83	75	Brakes
17	16	64	Elmo Langley	Woodfield '63 Ford	75	65	Rear End
18	14	41	Lee Petty	Petty Eng '63 Plymouth	59	60	Oil Line
19	8	66	Jim Reed	Ratus Walters '63 Ford	29	50	Rear End
20	19	27	Dom Persicketti	'61 Ford	16	50	Crash

Time of Race: 1 hour, 22 minutes, 10 seconds
Average Speed: 73.022 mph
Pole Winner: Joe Weatherly - 75.85 mph
Lap Leaders: Joe Weatherly 1-179, Fireball Roberts 180-200
Cautions: 4
Margin of Victory: 6 car lengths
Attendance: 5,400

Grand National Race No. 36
35 Laps at Bridgehampton Race Circuit
Bridgehampton, NY
100 Miles on 2.85-mile Paved Road Course
July 21, 1963

Fin	St	No.	Driver	Team / Car	Laps	Money	Status
1	1	43	Richard Petty	Petty Eng '63 Plymouth	35	$1,000	Running
2	2	28	Fred Lorenzen	Holman-Moody '63 Ford	35	600	Running
3	7	21	Marvin Panch	Wood Bros '63 Ford	35	400	Running
4	3	6	David Pearson	Cotton Owens '63 Dodge	35	300	Running
5	5	22	Fireball Roberts	Holman-Moody '63 Ford	35	275	Running
6	12	41	Lee Petty	Petty Eng '63 Plymouth	35	240	Running
7	17	4	Rex White	Louis Clements '63 Mercury	35	200	Running
8	8	11	Ned Jarrett	Burton-Robinson '63 Ford	34	175	Running
9	9	99	Bobby Isaac	Bondy Long '63 Ford	34	150	Running
10	11	87	Buck Baker	Baker '63 Pontiac	34	140	Running
11	10	45	Roy Hallquist	'63 Ford	34	130	Running
12	6	5	Billy Wade	Cotton Owens '63 Dodge	33	120	Tire
13	4	8	Joe Weatherly	Bud Moore '63 Pontiac	32	310	Spin Out
14	14	83	Worth McMillion	McMillion '62 Pontiac	29	100	Running
15	13	86	Neil Castles	Buck Baker '62 Chrysler	28	85	Running
16	15	34	Wendell Scott	Scott '62 Chevrolet	28	75	Running
17	16	54	Jimmy Pardue	Pete Stewart '62 Pontiac	24	65	Spin Out

Time of Race: 1 hour, 9 minutes, 4 seconds
Average Speed: 86.047 mph
Pole Winner: Richard Petty - 86.301 mph
Lap Leaders: Fred Lorenzen 1-2, Richard Petty 3-35
Cautions:
Margin of Victory: 25 seconds
Attendance: 11,200

Race No. 36

Petty Wins Bridgehampton; First Road Course Victory

BRIDGEHAMPTON, NY (July 21) -- Richard Petty ended a six week slump and captured the 100-mile race staged over the twisting 2.85-mile Bridgehampton Race Circuit. It was his 10th win of the 1963 season.

Fred Lorenzen led the first two laps, but settled for second place, 25 seconds behind the fleet, lightweight blue Plymouth. Marvin Panch was third, David Pearson fourth and Fireball Roberts fifth.

Petty led 33 of the 35 laps around the scenic course, His Plymouth, which was light and nimble, was never seriously threatened in the second half of the race. Fifth place finisher Roberts said it best: "It was no contest. Richard just ran off and hid. That light Plymouth shot out of the corners like a bullet. We didn't have enough straightaways to use our advantage in power."

Petty averaged 86.047 mph for his first win on a road course. A crowd of 11,200 was on hand to watch the NASCAR stocks tackle the seven year-old facility, which was built and designed for sports cars.

driving prowess as he scored a close victory in the 100-miler at Old Bridge Stadium. It was the third win of the year for the 34 year-old Daytona Beach Ford driver.

Rex White, who shifted to the Mercury camp, finished second, six car lengths behind the winner. Fred Lorenzen was third, Ned Jarrett fourth and Bobby Isaac fifth.

Joe Weatherly earned the pole position and led the first 179 laps in his Pontiac. When the Norfolk, VA driver made his one scheduled pit stop for fuel, the motor stalled. The Bud Moore pit crew had trouble getting it re-fired and Weatherly lost six laps. He got back on the track and wound up seventh.

A crowd of 5,400 was on hand to watch the NASCAR stars make the first of two stops in the Northeast. Four caution flags held Roberts' average speed to 73.022 mph.

Lee Petty, continuing his comeback, went 59 laps in his Plymouth before a broken oil line sidelined him. He wound up 18th in the field of 20.

David Pearson leads Fred Lorenzen at Bridgehampton's road course

climbed out of his car, walked to the infield, then fell to his knees. He was taken to a nearby hospital and released several hours later.

Junior Johnson led all but one of the first 161 laps, but his Chevrolet eventually went behind the wall with engine problems. It was the 12th time in 20 starts that Johnson has failed to finish -- and the ninth time in his last 12 starts that engine problems have knocked him out of action.

Thirty-six laps were run under the caution flag, keeping Lorenzen's average speed to 74.844 mph. He had won the pole at 82.229 mph.

Point leader Joe Weatherly finished sixth and held a 724 point lead over Petty in the championship standings.

David Pearson #6 misses spinning car at Bristol

Race No. 37

Lorenzen Rim-rides Way to Victory in Volunteer 500

BRISTOL, TN (July 28) -- Record-wrecking Fred Lorenzen held off Richard Petty in a tenacious late race battle and scored a popular victory in the third annual Volunteer 500 at Bristol International Speedway. It was Lorenzen's third win of the year and moved him over the $90,000 mark in winnings.

Lorenzen stuck his Ford in the upper groove, passed Petty in the 320th lap and led the rest of the way. Petty finished second, 3.0 seconds behind. Jim Paschal came in third with Marvin Panch fourth and David Pearson fifth.

"I ran real high all day while just about everybody else ran in the low groove," said the Elmhurst Express. "By going high, I could really get going while coming down the inclines (banking). I really got up a head of steam down the straightaways."

Fireball Roberts suffered a wrenched back in the most spectacular crack-up in the three year history of this half-mile paved track. His Holman-Moody Ford hit the wall in the 312th lap and flipped end over end four times. Roberts

Fireball Roberts flips at Bristol as Joe Weatherly dives low to avoid contact

Grand National Race No. 37
500 Laps at Bristol International Speedway
Bristol, TN
"Volunteer 500"
250 Miles on Half-mile Paved Track
July 28, 1963

Fin	St	No.	Driver	Team / Car	Laps	Money	Status
1	1	28	Fred Lorenzen	Holman-Moody '63 Ford	500	$4,540	Running
2	15	43	Richard Petty	Petty Eng '63 Plymouth	500	2,365	Running
3	13	42	Jim Paschal	Petty Eng '63 Plymouth	499	1,825	Running
4	4	21	Marvin Panch	Wood Bros '63 ford	492	1,225	Running
5	9	6	David Pearson	Cotton Owens '63 Dodge	491	1,075	Running
6	8	8	Joe Weatherly	Bud Moore '62 Pontiac	488	1,175	Running
7	6	0	Tiny Lund	Holman-Moody '63 Ford	488	775	Running
8	20	26	Darel Dieringer	Bill Stroppe '63 Mercury	488	775	Running
9	14	4	Rex White	Louis Clements '63 Mercury	486	700	Running
10	7	44	Tommy Irwin	S McKinney '63 Ford	484	525	Running
11	16	99	Bobby Isaac	Bondy Long '63 Ford	482	475	Running
12	23	36	Larry Thomas	Wade Younts '62 Dodge	475	400	Running
13	12	5	Billy Wade	Cotton Owens '63 Dodge	473	350	Clutch
14	22	19	Cale Yarborough	Herman Beam '63 Ford	471	300	Running
15	11	7	Bobby Johns	Shorty Johns '63 Pontiac	469	350	Running
16	28	86	Neil Castles	Buck Baker '62 Chrysler	467	275	Running
17	30	56	Ed Livingston	Mamie Reynolds '62 Ford	436	275	Running
18	32	67	Reb Wickersham	Reb's Sport Shop '62 Pontiac	430	275	Engine
19	33	76	J D McDuffie	'61 Ford	425	250	Running
20	35	83	Worth McMillion	McMillion '62 Pontiac	423	200	Running
21	34	88	Major Melton	Melton '61 Chrysler	418	225	Running
22	3	3	Junior Johnson	Ray Fox '63 Chevrolet	407	485	Engine
23	31	57	Bobby Keck	Pete Stewart '63 Ford	406	225	Running
24	21	47	Jack Smith	Smith '63 Plymouth	401	225	Engine
25	10	11	Ned Jarrett	Burton-Robinson '63 Ford	399	225	Running
26	27	32	Mark Hurley	'63 Ford	396	235	Wheel
27	24	05	Possum Jones	'62 Pontiac	364	200	Brakes
28	19	48	Stick Elliott	Jack Smith '63 Plymouth	349	225	Diff
29	2	22	Fireball Roberts	Holman-Moody '63 Ford	312	250	Crash
30	18	54	Jimmy Pardue	Pete Stewart '63 Ford	187	225	Crash
31	26	75	Bunkie Blackburn	'62 Pontiac	135	200	Tire
32	17	87	Buck Baker	Baker '63 Pontiac	62	225	Ignition
33	29	62	Curtis Crider	Crider '63 Mercury	51	200	Engine
34	5	29	Nelson Stacy	Holman-Moody '63 Ford	47	225	Crash
35	25	03	G C Spencer	'62 Chevrolet	11	300	Fuel Pmp
36	36	63	Huck Huckabee	Curtis Crider '62 Mercury	4	200	Diff

Time of Race: 3 hours, 20 minutes, 25 seconds
Average Speed: 74.844 mph
Pole Winner: Fred Lorenzen - 82.229 mph
Lap Leaders: Fred Lorenzen 1, Junior Johnson 2-161, Lorenzen 162-240, Jim Paschal 241, Lorenzen 242-316, Richard Petty 317-319, Lorenzen 320-500
Cautions: 7 for 36 laps
Margin of Victory: 3 seconds
Attendance: 23,000

Grand National Race No. 38
200 Laps at Greenville-Pickens Speedway
Greenville, SC
100 Miles on Half-mile Dirt Track
July 30, 1963

Fin	St	No.	Driver	Team / Car	Laps	Money	Status
1	7	41	Richard Petty	Petty Eng '63 Plymouth	200	$1,000	Running
2	1	11	Ned Jarrett	Burton-Robinson '63 Ford	200	600	Running
3	5	87	Buck Baker	Baker '63 Pontiac	199	400	Running
4	11	2	Fred Harb	Cliff Stewart '62 Pontiac	195	300	Running
5	6	99	Bobby Isaac	Bondy Long '63 Ford	195	275	Running
6	4	6	David Pearson	Cotton Owens '63 Dodge	195	240	Running
7	3	32	Tiny Lund	'63 Ford	192	200	Running
8	12	05	Joe Weatherly	'62 Pontiac	191	175	Running
9	22	X	Frank Warren	'61 Pontiac	190	150	Running
10	16	34	Wendell Scott	Scott '62 Chevrolet	190	140	Running
11	19	56	Ed Livingston	Mamie Reynolds '62 Ford	190	130	Running
12	15	54	Jimmy Pardue	Pete Stewart '63 Ford	190	120	Running
13	14	1	E J Trivette	'62 Chevrolet	181	110	Running
14	17	86	Neil Castles	Buck Baker '62 Chrysler	172	100	Spindle
15	13	19	Cale Yarborough	Herman Beam '62 Ford	123	85	Running
16	18	89	Curtis Crider	'62 Pontiac	90	75	Fuel Pmp
17	8	18	Stick Elliott	Toy Bolton '62 Pontiac	71	55	V Gasket
18	2	5	Billy Wade	Cotton Owens '63 Dodge	23	60	Diff
19	10	75	Bunkie Blackburn	'62 Pontiac	23	50	Engine
20	9	48	Jack Smith	Smith '63 Dodge	10	50	Heating
21	21	76	J D McDuffie	'61 Ford	1	50	Crash

Time of Race: 1 hour, 36 minutes, 4 seconds
Average Speed: 62.456 mph
Pole Winner: Ned Jarrett 65.526 mph
Lap Leaders: Ned Jarrett 1-69, David Pearson 70-105, Jarrett 106-148, Richard Petty 149-200
Cautions: 2
Margin of Victory:
Attendance:

Jarrett, who started on the pole and led twice for a total of 112 laps, was a close second. Buck Baker came in third, Richard Harb fourth and Bobby Isaac fifth.

Outstanding rookie driver Billy Wade qualified the Cotton Owens Dodge in second place and challenged for the lead early. But the Houston, Texas hot-shot fell out with differential problems after 23 laps and wound up 18th in the field of 21.

J. D. McDuffie, freshman driver out of Sanford, NC, crashed his Ford in the first lap. He escaped unharmed.

Petty's 24th career Grand National win came at an average speed of 62.456 mph.

Race No. 38

Petty's 11th of Year Comes In Greenville 100

GREENVILLE, SC (July 30) -- Richard Petty wheeled his Plymouth around Ned Jarrett in the 149th lap and led the rest of the way to win the 100-miler at Greenville-Pickens Speedway. It was the 11th win of the year for the popular Randleman, NC pilot and gave him an outside chance at challenging Tim Flock's all-time win total of 18 in one season set in 1955.

Race No. 39

Paschal First in Fiery Nashville 400

NASHVILLE, TN (Aug 4) -- Jim Paschal found the Nashville Fairgrounds to his liking as he scored his third Grand National win in the 175-mile August 4

Grand National Race No. 39
400 Laps at Nashville Raceway
Nashville, TN
"Nashville 400"
200 Miles on Half-mile Paved Track
August 4, 1963

Fin	St	No.	Driver	Team / Car	Laps	Money	Status
1	3	42	Jim Paschal	Petty Eng '63 Plymouth	350	$2,500	Running
2	7	5	Billy Wade	Cotton Owens '63 Dodge	349	1,350	Running
3	5	8	Joe Weatherly	Bud Moore '63 Pontiac	349	1,025	Running
4	1	43	Richard Petty	Petty Eng '63 Plymouth	348	675	Running
5	9	87	Buck Baker	Baker '63 Pontiac	348	475	Running
6	11	18	Stick Elliott	Toy Bolton '63 Pontiac	346	450	Running
7	8	11	Ned Jarrett	Burton-Robinson '63 Ford	344	425	Running
8	13	19	Cale Yarborough	Herman Beam '62 Ford	335	375	Running
9	10	54	Jimmy Pardue	Pete Stewart '63 Ford	334	325	Running
10	12	36	Larry Thomas	Wade Younts '62 Dodge	309	300	Running
11	20	34	Wendell Scott	Scott '62 Chevrolet	309	270	Running
12	14	45	Jimmy Griggs	'63 Mercury	304	240	Running
13	15	86	Neil Castles	Buck Baker '62 Chrysler	286	245	Engine
14	16	99	Bobby Isaac	Bondy Long '63 Ford	257	200	Crash
15	6	32	Tiny Lund	'63 Ford	194	170	Crash
16	19	6	David Pearson	Cotton Owens '63 Dodge	194	150	Crash
17	2	4	Rex White	Louis Clements '63 Mercury	194	230	Crash
18	4	28	Fred Lorenzen	LaFayette '63 Ford	158	170	Engine
19	21	68	Ed Livingston	Livingston '62 Ford	27	100	Handling
20	17	63	Chuck Huckabee	Curtis Crider '62 Mercury	2	100	Engine
21	18	03	G C Spencer	'62 Chevrolet	1	100	Piston

* Race was flagged to a halt after 350 laps due to impending darkness
Time of Race: 2 hours, 54 minutes, 38 seconds
Average Speed: 60.126 mph
Pole Winner: Richard Petty - 78.878 mph
Lap Leaders: Richard Petty 1-96, Tiny Lund 97- .... Jim Paschal -350
Cautions: 98 Laps
Margin of Victory:
Attendance: 12,875

race. It was High Point Jim's fifth win of the year. Rain, impending darkness and a fiery accident played havoc with the scheduled 400 lap distance -- and the event was flagged to a halt after 350 laps.

Billy Wade, freshman Texas driver with lightning reflexes, finished second to post his best career finish. Joe Weatherly garnered third spot with Richard Petty fourth and Buck Baker fifth.

Daytona 500 winner Tiny Lund survived a savage crash in the 194th lap. Lund's Ford blew an engine in the fourth turn and David Pearson, directly behind, skidded in the oil deposited on the track. Lund's car clipped the guard rail and busted through two huge wooden billboards. The errant Ford then bounded back onto the track and landed on top of Rex White's Mercury -- slicing the top in half. The roll bars in White's car were crushed, but fortunately the 5'4" Silver Spring, MD driver ducked and avoided catastrophic injuries.

NASCAR officials said it was the first time they could recall a roll bar crushed like that. To which Weatherly responded, "And I bet that's the first time you've seen a two-ton car land on one."

Lund's car caught fire, and it was several moments before the 6'5", 270-pound driver scrambled out.

Cale Yarborough, driving Herman Beam's Ford, charged as hard as he could and wound up eighth. Beam, noted for his conservatism, repeatedly gave Yarborough the "E-Z" sign on the pit board. Cale failed to heed the instructions and kept charging.

When Lund had his accident, Yarborough backed off and was driving slow on the apron to miss the river of flaming fuel. Lund, who had gotten tangled up in his seat belt, stormed out of his car when he finally freed himself, and ran smack into the side of Yarborough's passenger side door. The impact dented the door. Later, Beam stressed his point to Yarborough: "You see there? If you would've slowed down he'd missed you!" Yarborough was puzzled by Beam's remark.

A total of 98 laps were run under the caution flag as Paschal averaged 60.126 mph. The race was also red-flagged for an hour and 24 minutes because of a thunderstorm.

Wreckers extract Tiny Lund's Ford from billboards and fence at Nashville

Race No. 40
Columbia's Sandlapper 200 Won By Richard Petty

COLUMBIA, SC (Aug 8) -- Richard Petty sped to his 12th win of the season as Junior Johnson swallowed another

Grand National Race No. 40
200 Laps at Columbia Speedway
Columbia, SC
"Sandlapper 200"
100 Miles on Half-mile Dirt Track
August 8, 1963

Fin	St	No.	Driver	Team / Car	Laps	Money	Status
1	1	43	Richard Petty	Petty Eng '63 Plymouth	200	$1,140	Running
2	12	6	David Pearson	Cotton Owens '63 Dodge	200	600	Running
3	3	99	Bobby Isaac	Bondy Long '63 Ford	200	400	Running
4	5	11	Ned Jarrett	Burton-Robinson '63 Ford	200	350	Running
5	8	03	G C Spencer	'62 Chevrolet	198	275	Running
6	9	5	Billy Wade	Cotton Owens '63 Dodge	198	240	Running
7	13	48	Jack Smith	Smith '63 Plymouth	197	200	Running
8	10	19	Cale Yarborough	Herman Beam '62 Ford	196	175	Running
9	16	34	Wendell Scott	Scott '62 Chevrolet	191	150	Running
10	21	57	Bobby Keck	Pete Stewart '63 Ford	186	140	Running
11	2	8	Joe Weatherly	Bud Moore '63 Pontiac	185	340	Sway Bar
12	14	62	Curtis Crider	Crider '63 Mercury	185	120	Running
13	18	X	Frank Warren	'61 Pontiac	183	110	Running
14	6	76	J D McDuffie	'61 Ford	127	100	Axle
15	7	87	Buck Baker	Baker '63 Pontiac	108	85	Tie Rod
16	20	89	Joel Davis	'62 Pontiac	104	75	Crash
17	4	3	Junior Johnson	Ray Fox '63 Chevrolet	102	65	Crash
18	22	31	Billy Oswald	'61 Mercury	61	60	Engine
19	17	2	Fred Harb	Cliff Stewart '62 Pontiac	46	50	Ignition
20	11	54	Jimmy Pardue	Pete Stewart '62 Pontiac	41	50	Engine
21	19	68	Ed Livingston	Livingston '61 Ford	10	50	Crash
22	15	05	Possum Jones	'61 Pontiac	5	50	Tires

Time of Race: 1 hour, 47 minutes, 55 seconds
Average Speed: 55.598 mph
Pole Winner: Richard Petty - 69.014 mph
Lap Leaders: Richard Petty 1-103, David Pearson 104-165, Petty 166-200
Cautions:
Margin of Victory: 9 seconds
Attendance: 8,500

Grand National Race No. 41
500 Laps at Asheville-Weaverville Speedway
Weaverville, NC
"Western North Carolina 500"
250 Miles on Half-mile Paved Track
August 11, 1963

Fin	St	No.	Driver	Team / Driver	Laps	Money	Status
1	2	28	Fred Lorenzen	Holman-Moody '63 Ford	500	$2,550	Running
2	10	43	Richard Petty	Petty Eng '63 Plymouth	499	1,425	Running
3	9	42	Jim Paschal	Petty Eng '63 Plymouth	498	1,150	Running
4	23	6	David Pearson	Cotton Owens '63 Dodge	494	950	Running
5	22	5	Billy Wade	Cotton Owens '63 Dodge	493	800	Running
6	15	47	Jack Smith	Smith '63 Plymouth	493	650	Running
7	17	87	Buck Baker	Baker '63 Pontiac	478	600	Running
8	8	36	Joe Weatherly	Wade Younts '62 Dodge	473	800	Running
9	1	11	Ned Jarrett	Burton-Robinson '63 Ford	467	450	Running
10	18	2	Buddy Baker	Cliff Stewart '62 Pontiac	467	400	Running
11	27	34	Wendell Scott	Scott '62 Chevrolet	452	375	Running
12	24	67	Reb Wickersham	Reb's Sport Shop '62 Pontiac	448	375	Running
13	6	83	Worth McMillion	McMillion '62 Pontiac	437	325	Running
14	16	19	Cale Yarborough	Herman Beam '63 Ford	434	275	Running
15	5	09	Elmo Langley	'62 Chevrolet	379	250	Ening
16	26	33	Roy Mayne	C L Kilpatrick '62 Chevrolet	369	250	Running
17	19	88	Major Melton	Melton '61 Chrysler	324	250	Seal
18	7	99	Bobby Isaac	Bondy Long '63 Ford	303	225	Clutch
19	3	44	Tommy Irwin	S McKinney '63 Ford	264	225	Vibration
20	25	62	Curtis Crider	Crider '63 Mercury	258	225	Heating
21	4	48	G C Spencer	Jack Smith '63 Plymouth	216	200	Crash
22	14	93	Lee Reitzel	'62 Ford	199	175	Crash
23	21	3	Junior Johnson	Ray Fox '63 Chevrolet	161	150	Batt Cable
24	12	57	Bobby Keck	Pete Stewart '63 Pontiac	52	150	Brakes
25	11	54	Jimmy Pardue	Pete Stewart '62 Ford	38	150	Oil Leak
26	20	18	Stick Elliott	Toy Bolton '62 Pontiac	30	150	Crash
27	13	05	Possum Jones	'61 Pontiac	8	150	Fuel Leak

Time of Race: 3 hours, 13 minutes, 7 seconds
Average Speed: 77.673 mph
Pole Winner: None. Starting positions by sign-in
Lap Leaders: Ned Jarrett 1-13, Fred Lorenzen 14-188, Richard Petty 189-223, Lorenzen 224-500
Cautions: 2
Margin of Victory: 1 lap plus
Attendance: 14,500

bitter-tasting pill in the Sandlapper 200 at Columbia Speedway.

Petty hustled past David Pearson in the 166th lap and led the rest of the way before a wall-to-wall crowd of 8,500. Pearson's effort to give Dodge its first win of the year was short by 9.0 seconds. Bobby Isaac made a strong showing by taking third place. Ned Jarrett finished fourth with G. C. Spencer fifth.

Junior Johnson started fourth and spent the early laps chasing Petty, Isaac and Joe Weatherly. He was running in the top five in the 102nd lap when his Chevrolet skidded sideways and sailed upside down over an embankment. The car disappeared into the dark Carolina night bottom up. Johnson was shaken but uninjured in the nasty wreck. He won $65 to ease the hurt -- the payoff for 17th place.

Ed Livingston and Joel Davis were knocked out in separate crashes.

Petty, who led twice for 138 laps, averaged 55.598 mph.

Fred Lorenzen #28 leads an unpainted Plymouth driven by Richard Petty in Western North Carolina 500

Race No. 41

Lorenzen Wins at Weaverville; Moore and Weatherly In Rift

WEAVERVILLE, NC (Aug 11) -- With Fred Lorenzen entered, a standing-room-only crowd of 14,500 fans crammed into the Asheville-Weaverville Speedway for the Western North Carolina 500. The fair-haired Ford driver did not disappoint them as he trounced the field to pick up his fourth win of the year. Lorenzen's earnings stood at $92,220 for the 1963 season -- an all time NASCAR record.

In second place, a full lap behind, was Richard Petty, who moved to within 304 points of leader Joe Weatherly. Little Joe finished eighth in a Dodge borrowed from owner Wade Younts and driver Larry Thomas. Third place went to Jim Paschal with David Pearson fourth and Billy Wade fifth.

Weatherly and car owner Bud Moore were rumored to be near a split after an unusual turn of events at Weaverville. The time trials were rained out and starting positions were assigned by order of sign-in at the track. Moore said he was the first at the gate at 10:00 am, but no NASCAR official was there to sign him in. When he returned, he was told his car would start 18th in the field of 27. "It's not right for my car to have a starting position back in the pack because officials were tardy," huffed Moore.

Weatherly was late in showing up for the race. In disgust, Moore loaded up his Pontiac and returned to Spartanburg. When Weatherly finally showed up, he had to make a last minute deal for the Younts-Thomas ride.

Lorenzen was on top of the leader board for 452 of the 500 laps around the half-mile paved oval. He had clear sailing most of the way except for one scare in the 188th lap. Lorenzen's Holman-Moody Ford glanced off the concrete retaining wall, and he was forced to come into the pits to have a fender pried off the right front tire. He returned to the track a half lap behind Petty, but he ran him down by the 224th lap.

It was the 41st Grand National race run in the 1963 season. Lorenzen stood fourth in the point standings although he had started only 19 races. His deficit was 2,528 points -- a small number considering the upcoming Southern 500 with its 3,050 points to the winner.

Freddy the Magnificent averaged 77.673 mph. After the race the 28 year-old driver signed autographs for nearly four hours.

Grand National Race No. 42
200 Laps at Piedmont Interstate Fairgrounds
Spartanburg, SC
100 Miles on Half-mile Dirt Track
August 14, 1963

Fin	St	No.	Driver	Team / Car	Laps	Money	Status
1	2	11	Ned Jarrett	Burton-Robinson '63 Ford	200	$1,000	Running
2	3	43	Richard Petty	Petty Eng '63 Plymouth	200	600	Running
3	12	87	Buck Baker	Baker '63 Pontiac	200	400	Running
4	7	5	Billy Wade	Cotton Owens '63 Dodge	199	300	Running
5	8	19	Cale Yarborough	Herman Beam '62 Ford	195	275	Running
6	16	86	Neil Castles	Buck Baker '62 Chrysler	191	240	Running
7	9	75	G C Spencer	'62 Pontiac	177	200	Running
8	10	16	Cotton Owens	Owens '63 Dodge	170	175	Crash
9	17	57	Bobby Keck	Pete Stewart '63 Ford	152	150	Crash
10	13	18	Stick Elliott	Toy Bolton '62 Pontiac	117	140	Housing
11	5	54	Jimmy Pardue	Pete Stewart '63 Ford	100	130	H Gasket
12	11	62	Curtis Crider	Crider '63 Mercury	100	120	Diff
13	15	33	Roy Mayne	C L Kilpatrick '62 Chevrolet	85	110	H Gasket
14	6	99	Bobby Isaac	Bondy Long '63 Ford	70	100	Spindle
15	14	34	Wendell Scott	Scott '62 Chevrolet	65	85	Crash
16	4	6	David Pearson	Cotton Owens '63 Dodge	43	75	Oil Line
17	1	8	Joe Weatherly	Bud Moore '63 Pontiac	33	265	Engine

Time of Race: 1 hour, 54 minutes, 27 seconds
Average Speed: 52.424 mph
Pole Winner: Joe Weatherly - 64.958 mph
Lap Leaders: Joe Weatherly 1-33, Ned Jarrett 34- , Richard Petty - , Buck Baker - , Ned Jarrett -200
Cautions:
Margin of Victory:
Attendance:

Race No. 42

Owens Ends Retirement; Jarrett Wins at Spartanburg

SPARTANBURG, SC (Aug 14) -- Ned Jarrett racked up his sixth win of the year with a close victory in the 100-mile Grand National race at the Piedmont Interstate Fairgrounds.

Jarrett gunned his Burton-Robinson Ford past Buck Baker in the late stages and went on to edge Richard Petty at the finish of the 200 lapper. Baker took third place, Billy Wade fourth and Cale Yarborough fifth.

Cotton Owens, who has spent most of his time tuning Dodges for David Pearson and Wade Younts this year, ended his retirement at his hometown track. The 39 year-old Owens crashed in the final laps, but still wound up eighth in the final rundown.

Joe Weatherly started on the pole but engine failure sent him to the showers after just 33 laps. Pearson's Dodge broke an oil line early, and Bobby Isaac's Ford broke a spindle.

Jarrett averaged 52.424 mph for his 20th career win.

Grand National Race No. 43
200 Laps at Bowman-Gray Stadium
Winston-Salem, NC
"International 200"
50 Miles on Quarter-mile Paved Track
August 16, 1963

Fin	St	No.	Driver	Team / Car	Laps	Money	Status
1	1	3	Junior Johnson	Ray Fox '63 Plymouth	200	$580	Running
2	3	43	Richard Petty	Petty Eng '63 Plymouth	199	500	Running
3	2	21	Glen Wood	Wood Bros '63 Ford	198	370	Running
4	6	6	David Pearson	Cotton Owens '63 Dodge	196	275	Running
5	4	11	Ned Jarrett	Burton-Robinson '63 Ford	196	225	Running
6	10	03	G C Spencer	'62 Chevrolet	194	250	Running
7	11	62	Curtis Crider	Crider '63 Mercury	193	205	Running
8	9	36	Larry Thomas	Wade Younts '62 Dodge	193	175	Running
9	5	361	Joe Weatherly	Wade Younts '62 Dodge	191	350	Running
10	7	87	Buck Baker	Baker '63 Pontiac	188	160	Running
11	17	34	Wendell Scott	Scott '62 Chevrolet	188	145	Running
12	13	76	J D McDuffie	'61 Ford	181	135	Running
13	16	86	Neil Castles	Buck Baker '62 Chrysler	79	110	Spindle
14	14	57	Bob Keck	Pete Stewart '63 Ford	64	115	Engine
15	8	18	Stick Elliott	Toy Bolton '62 Pontiac	46	100	Engine
16	12	2	Fred Harb	Cliff Stewart '62 Pntiac	29	105	Brakes
17	18	32	Smokey Cook	MG	12	75	Heating
18	15	9	Roy Tyner	Tyner '62 Chevrolet	7	60	Axle
19	19	17X	Bill Whitley	Corvette	1	50	Crash

Time of Race: 1 hour, 4 minutes, 46 seconds
Average Speed: 46.320 mph
Pole Winner: Junior Johnson - 49.806 mph
Lap Leaders: Junior Johnson 1-200
Cautions: 1 for 4 laps
Margin of Victory:
Attendance: 11,500

Race No. 43

International 200 Won By Junior Johnson's Chevrolet

WINSTON-SALEM, NC (Aug 16) -- Junior Johnson kept the 'innards' of his Chevrolet intact for the entire race and won the International 200 at Bowman-Gray Stadium. It was the 32nd career win for the 32 year-old chicken rancher.

It was only the ninth time in 23 starts that the Ray Fox Chevrolet has finished in the 1963 campaign, and the fifth time it has ended up in victory circle. Richard Petty finished second and took a 48 point lead in the standings. Glen Wood came in third with David Pearson fourth and Ned Jarrett fifth.

Joe Weatherly hitched a ride in the Dodge owned by Wade Younts and wound up ninth.

Johnson started on the pole and quickly stormed to first place. He lapped the second place Petty by the 62nd lap and breezed to an uncontested triumph.

Only two cars fitting 'international' status started -- and both of them were out of the race after 12 laps. Bill Whitley wrecked his Corvette in the opening lap and

Smokey Cook's MG overheated after 12 laps.

One caution flag for four laps held Johnson's average speed to 46.320 mph. A crowd of 11,500 was on hand.

Grand National Race No. 44
300 Laps at West Virginia International Speedway
Huntington, WV
"Mountaineer 300"
112.5 Miles on .375-mile Paved Track
August 18, 1963

Fin	St	No.	Driver	Team / Car	Laps	Money	Status
1	1	28	Fred Lorenzen	Holman-Moody '63 Ford	300	$1,600	Running
2	6	8	Joe Weatherly	Bud Moore '63 Pontiac	299	1,225	Running
3	7	42	Jim Paschal	Petty Eng '63 Plymouth	299	750	Running
4	8	11	Ned Jarrett	Burton-Robinson '63 Ford	297	600	Running
5	13	87	Buck Baker	Baker '63 Pontiac	296	450	Running
6	11	03	G C Spencer	'62 Chevrolet	291	375	Running
7	9	2	Nelson Stacy	'63 Ford	288	300	Running
8	16	62	Curtis Crider	Crider '63 Mercury	288	250	Running
9	5	21	Marvin Panch	Wood Bros '63 Ford	288	225	Running
10	3	43	Richard Petty	Petty Eng '63 Plymouth	286	250	Running
11	18	60	Bud Harless	'62 Pontiac	283	175	Running
12	15	20	Jack Anderson	'63 Ford	277	175	Running
13	19	36	Larry Thomas	Wade Younts '62 Dodge	275	175	Running
14	10	54	Jimmy Pardue	Pete Stewart '63 Ford	272	150	Wheel
15	12	67	Reb Wickersham	Reb's Sport Shop '62 Pontiac	269	150	Running
16	14	34	Wendell Scott	Scott '62 Chevrolet	268	125	Running
17	2	47	Jack Smith	Smith '63 Plymouth	206	200	Crash
18	20	14	Jim Bray	'62 Chevrolet	206	125	Running
19	17	36	Neil Castles	Buck Baker '62 Chrysler	128	125	Brakes
20	4	3	Junior Johnson	Ray Fox '63 Chevrolet	90	150	Brakes

Time of Race: 1 hour, 53 minutes, 45 seconds
Average Speed: 59.340 mph
Pole Winner: Fred Lorenzen - 66.568 mph
Lap Leaders: Fred Lorenzen 1-62, Richard Petty 63-115, Jim Paschal 116-132, Joe Weatherly 133-197, Lorrenzen 198-300
Cautions: 7 for 30 laps
Margin of Victory: 1 lap plus
Attendance: 16,000

Race No. 44

Lorenzen Snatches Loot in Mountaineer 300

HUNTINGTON, WV (Aug 18) -- Fred Lorenzen skillfully steered his Holman-Moody Ford around a rash of spin-outs and minor crack-ups and won the first annual Mountaineer 300 at the brand new West Virginia International Speedway. It was the fifth win of the year for Lorenzen, and the first place pot of $1,600 hiked his seasonal earnings to $93,820.

Lorenzen passed Joe Weatherly for the lead in the 198th lap and steered clear of large chunks of pavement en route to the one-lap win. Weatherly was declared runner-up after NASCAR studied the score cards for two hours. Jim Paschal accepted third place money, Ned Jarrett was fourth and Buck Baker fifth.

Weatherly moved back on top of the point standings by a 112 point margin over Richard Petty who struggled to finish 10th.

A crowd of 16,000 was present for the first race at the new .375-mile paved oval. The track came apart badly in the first and second turns. Most of the spins and seven caution flags were attributed to the poor track conditions.

"My tires were getting bald and the chunks of pavement didn't make that problem any better," explained Lorenzen. "I knew I had a big lead, so I slowed up the last 50 laps. I concentrated on missing the holes and the loose chunks of pavement."

The lead changed hands five times among four drivers with Lorenzen on top for 169 laps. He averaged 59.340 mph.

Race No. 45

Fireball Roberts Wins Non-stop Southern 500 at 129 mph

DARLINGTON, SC (Sept 2) -- Fireball Roberts established a record judged to be unbeatable as he captured the non-stop 14th annual Southern 500 at Darlington Raceway. The average speed for the 500 miles was an eye-popping 129.784 mph. Roberts' record erased the old standard of 117.960 mph set a year ago by Larry Frank.

Roberts nosed his lavender Ford past Fred Lorenzen in the 332nd lap and led the remaining 33 circuits to snare his 13th career victory on the South's high banked superspeedways. It was his fourth win of the

Nelson Stacy leads the field off the 2nd turn at Darlington

year and the 32nd of his career.

Marvin Panch wound up second, 17 seconds behind Roberts. Lorenzen took third place with Nelson Stacy fourth and Darel Dieringer fifth.

Junior Johnson led for 163 of the first 234 laps, but once again barbecued the engine in his Chevrolet. He wound up 20th in the final order, but lap money boosted his day's earnings to $4,705, fourth best of the hot and humid afternoon.

Panch took the lead when Johnson departed, and the Oakland, CA native waged a nip-and-tuck battle with Roberts and Lorenzen. Lorenzen scooted into first place on lap 314 and was pulling away when fuel pump problems forced a long pit stop. He got back into the race a lap down, but rapidly made up lost ground. He was back on the lead lap at the end of the race.

Lorenzen won $6,550 to push his 1963 earnings over the $100,000 figure -- a plateau previously thought to be unreachable.

Roberts sailed into the lead 33 laps from the finish and coasted to the $22,150 pay-off. "I really wanted to win this race," said an exhausted Roberts afterwards. "I wanted to show these younger guys that I can still do it. After my wreck at Bristol, I heard the talk that I was washed up. I really wanted to show them they were wrong."

Joe Weatherly finished seventh in a new Bud Moore Mercury and boosted his point lead to 712 points over Richard Petty, who finished 12th.

After the race there was unrest in both the Petty and Moore camps. Petty and Jim Paschal, driving the #41 Plymouth, swapped cars on the first pit stop because head honcho Lee Petty felt Paschal's car was faster. When the #41 fell out after 166 laps, Petty was placed back in the car he started.

Paschal quit the Petty team two days later. "I don't feel there is any use in continuing under the present set-up," said Paschal. "I'll be shopping around for something to drive next year."

Moore was upset that Weatherly was only able to run seventh. "There's nothing wrong with the car," Moore grunted. "I've got to feel Joe is stroking. At times he could turn laps of 134 mph, then in a few laps I'd look up and see cars going by him in bunches."

Weatherly said the car wasn't handling on the crusty old Darlington surface. "This is a brand new car and it wasn't handling right. I was running the car as hard as I safely could. We won over $2,000 and kept the lead in the championship. Maybe Bud would have been happier if I had piled the car up and finished last."

Billy Wade suffered facial cuts when his Dodge slammed into the wall and was hit by Ned Jarrett and Bob James on lap 59. A lack of communication between observers in the crash area and the flagstand prevented a caution being thrown.

A crowd of 62,000 watched the contest, in which only 16 of the original starting field of 41 cars finished. Nine cars dropped out in the first seven laps.

Grand National Race No. 45
364 Laps at Darlington Raceway
Darlington, SC
"Southern 500"
500 Miles on 1.375-mile Paved Track
September 2, 1963

Fin	St	No.	Driver	Team / Car	Laps	Money	Status
1	10	22	Fireball Roberts	Holman-Moody '63 Ford	364	$22,150	Running
2	6	21	Marvin Panch	Wood Bros '63 Ford	364	12,650	Running
3	1	28	Fred Lorenzen	Holman-Moody Ford '73 Ford	364	6,550	Running
4	7	29	Nelson Stacy	Holman -Moody '63 Ford	363	3,500	Running
5	4	26	Darel Dieringer	Bill Stroppe '63 Mercury	360	2,625	Running
6	10	4	Rex White	Louis Clements '63 Mercury	358	2,155	Running
7	3	8	Joe Weatherly	Bud Moore '63 Mercury	358	2,345	Running
8	24	0	Tiny Lund	Pulliam Motor Co '63 Ford	356	1,775	Running
9	5	7	Bobby Johns	Shorty Johns '63 Pontiac	356	1,275	Running
10	8	13	Buck Baker	Smokey Yunick '63 Chevrolet	356	1,025	Running
11	16	99	Bobby Isaac	Bondy Long '63 Ford	353	950	Running
12	18	43	* Richard Petty	Petty Eng '63 Plymouth	341	1,030	Running
13	22	70	Bunkie Blackburn	'62 Pontiac	339	800	Running
14	17	6	David Pearson	Cotton Owens '63 Dodge	339	950	Running
15	20	54	Jimmy Pardue	Pete Stewart '63 Ford	332	650	Diff
16	27	62	Curtis Crider	Crider '63 Mercury	332	600	Running
17	21	19	Cale Yarborough	Herman Beam '63 Ford	306	500	Running
18	35	09	Elmo Langley	'62 Chevrolet	302	500	Trans
19	28	60	Bud Harless	'62 Pontiac	274	500	A Frame
20	2	3	Junior Johnson	Ray Fox '63 Chevrolet	257	4,705	Heating
21	11	11	Ned Jarrett	Burton-Robinson '63 Ford	208	570	Engine
22	14	41	* Jim Paschal	Petty Eng '63 Plymouth	166	500	Carb
23	19	87	Buddy Baker	Baker & Son '63 Pontiac	133	570	Clutch
24	12	47	G C Spencer	Jack Smith '63 Plymouth	123	500	Engine
25	26	17	Ralph Earnhardt	Fred Harb '62 Pontiac	88	570	Engine
26	29	H G Rosier		'62 Plymouth	66	500	Handling
27	15	42	Bob James	Petty Eng '63 Plymouth	59	500	Spindle
28	13	5	Billy Wade	Cotton Owens '63 Dodge	59	500	Crash
29	25	92	LeeRoy Yarbrough	'63 Ford	19	630	Diff
30	23	36	Larry Thomas	Wade Younts '62 Dodge	16	500	Fuel Pmp
31	34	9	Roy Tyner	Tyner '62 Chevrolet	15	500	Trans
32	30	76	Larry Manning	'61 Ford	11	500	Handling
33	32	57	Bobby Keck	Pete Stewart '63 Ford	7	500	Clutch
34	31	86	Neil Castles	Buck Baker '62 Chrysler	6	500	Oil Pres
35	36	2	Bob Welborn	Cliff Stewart '62 Pontiac	4	500	H Gasket
36	39	05	Possum Jones	'61 Pontiac	3	500	Oil Pres
37	37	53	Paul Lewis	'63 Ford	2	500	Handling
38	40	68	Frank Graham	Ed Livingston '61 Ford	2	500	Clutch
39	41	56	Ed Livingston	Mamie Reynolds '62 Ford	2	500	Oil Pres
40	38	93	Lee Reitzel	'62 Ford	2	500	Brakes
41	33	20	Emanuel Zervakis	'63 Ford	1	500	Handling

* Jim Paschal relieved Richard Petty; Richard Petty relieved Jim Paschal
Time of Race: 3 hours, 51 minutes, 23 seconds
Average Speed: 129.784 mph
Pole Winner: Fred Lorenzen - 133.648 mph
Fastest Qualifier: Fireball Roberts - 133.819 mph
Lap Leaders: Fred Lorenzen 1, Junior Johnson 2-73, Marvin Panch 74, Lorenzen 75,
    Panch 76-143, Johnson 144-234, Panch 235-288, Fireball Roberts 289-313,
    Lorenzen 314-331, Roberts 332-364
Cautions: None
Margin of Victory: 17 seconds
Attendance: 62,000

Grand National Race No. 46
250 Laps at Hickory Speedway
Hickory, NC
"Buddy Shuman Memorial"
100 Miles on .4-mile Dirt Track
September 6, 1963

Fin	St	No.	Driver	Team / Car	Laps	Money	Status
1	7	3	Junior Johnson	Ray Fox '63 Chevrolet	250	$1,775	Running
2	14	03	G C Spencer	'62 Chevrolet	246	700	Running
3	8	17	Bob Welborn	Fred Harb '62 Pontiac	237	450	Running
4	9	96	Jimmy Massey	'61 Chevrolet	232	300	Running
5	20	36	Larry Thomas	Wade Younts '62 Dodge	232	275	Running
6	18	87	Buck Baker	Baker '63 Pontiac	225	240	Running
7	17	86	Neil Castles	Buck Baker '62 Chrysler	224	200	Running
8	24	76	J D McDuffie	'61 Ford	224	175	Running
9	2	28	Fred Lorenzen	Holman-Moody '63 Ford	218	150	Running
10	15	19	Cale Yarborough	Herman Beam '62 Ford	210	140	Running
11	12	32	Tiny Lund	'63 Ford	210	130	Running
12	16	54	Jimmy Pardue	Pete Stewart '63 Ford	202	120	Running
13	23	62	Curtis Crider	Crider '63 Mercury	201	110	Running
14	13	11	Ned Jarrett	Burton-Robinson '63 Ford	197	395	Running
15	5	43	Richard Petty	Petty Eng '63 Plymouth	196	85	Oil Line
16	22	88	Major Melton	Melton '61 Chrysler	141	75	Diff
17	11	90	Gary Sain	'62 Dodge	141	65	Brakes
18	1	6	David Pearson	Cotton Owens '63 Dodge	123	295	Engine
19	4	47	Jack Smith	Smith '63 Plymouth	74	65	Engine
20	25	23	Bill Widenhouse	'62 Plymouth	68	50	Engine
21	3	8	Joe Weatherly	Bud Moore '63 Mercury	58	330	Crash
22	6	4	Rex White	Louis Clements '63 Mercury	56	50	Crash
23	21	9	Roy Tyner	Tyner '62 Chevrolet	53	50	Crash
24	10	5	Pete Stewart	'62 Pontiac	41	50	Brakes
25	19	34	Wendell Scott	Scott '62 Chevrolet	14	50	Crash
26	26	97	Bill Whitley	'62 Chevrolet	4	50	Brakes

Time of Race: 1 hour, 35 minutes, 21 seconds
Average Speed: 62.926 mph
Pole Winner: David Pearson - 72.471 mph
Lap Leaders: David Pearson 1-3, Joe Weatherly 4-19, Pearson 20-55, Jack Smith 56-58,
    Pearson 59-65, Ned Jarrett 66-122, Pearson 123, Jarrett 124-125, Johnson 126-250
Cautions: 3 for 16 laps
Margin of Victory: 4 laps plus
Attendance: 12,000

Race No. 46

Johnson Flips in Practice; Then Wins Shuman Memorial

HICKORY, NC (Sept 6) -- Junior Johnson survived a roll-over in practice, then drove his Chevrolet to a popular victory in the Buddy Shuman Memorial 250 at Hickory Speedway.

In a surprising departure from his customary charging, Johnson used his head and drove past Ned Jarrett

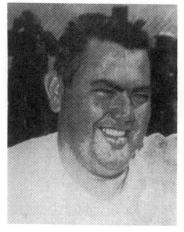

Junior Johnson

in the 126th lap and scampered to a four lap victory. He won $1,775 for his sixth win of the year. It was only the 10th race all year he has finished.

G.C. Spencer wound up in second place as Bob Welborn was third. Jimmy Massey came in fourth and Larry Thomas fifth.

Fred Lorenzen spun his Ford in the 18th lap and was hit broadside by Wendell Scott. There were no injuries and Lorenzen got back in the race after a 35 lap pit stop to repair sheet metal damage. He eventually finished ninth, 32 laps behind winner Johnson.

Point leaders Joe Weatherly and Richard Petty fell victims to separate problems. Weatherly crashed after 58 laps and Petty's car fell out on lap 196 with a broken oil line.

A crowd of 12,000 braved soggy weather to watch Johnson complete the 250 laps on the .4-mile dirt track at a speed of 62.926 mph.

Race No. 47

Jarrett Blisters Field in Capital City 300

RICHMOND, VA (Sept 8) -- Ned Jarrett rallied from a two-lap deficit and won the Capital City 300 at the Atlantic Rural Fairgrounds going away. It was the seventh win of the year for the cagey Newton, NC Ford driver.

Rex White finished second, two laps down. Larry Frank, who replaced Bobby Isaac in the Bondy Long Ford, wound up third. G.C. Spencer took fourth place with Fred Lorenzen fifth.

Jarrett started seventh on the grid, but hustled through the field and was in front by the 99th lap. While leading on lap 118, he ran over a piece of metal and had to make an unscheduled pit stop. Jarrett lost two laps while his Burton-Robinson pit crew scrambled to repair the car.

Jarrett returned to the race two laps in arrears as Joe Weatherly took over the lead. Weatherly was sidelined by engine failure while leading in the 165th lap and White took over for a 98 lap stint. Jarrett worked his way past White's Mercury on lap 264 and led the rest of the way.

Weatherly's misfortune, which left him with a 21st place finish, reduced his point lead to 326 over Richard Petty, who finished sixth.

A crowd of 15,000 watched Jarrett average 66.339 mph for his 21st career Grand National victory.

Grand National Race No. 47
300 Laps at Atlantic Rural Fairgrounds
Richmond, VA
"Capital City 300"
150 Miles on Half-mile Dirt Track
September 8, 1963

Fin	St	No.	Driver	Team / Car	Laps	Money	Status
1	7	11	Ned Jarrett	Burton-Robinson '63 Ford	300	$2,200	Running
2	5	4	Rex White	Louis Clements '63 Mercury	298	1,475	Running
3	12	99	Larry Frank	Bondy Long '63 Ford	293	1,050	Running
4	9	03	G C Spencer	'62 Chevrolet	291	775	Running
5	8	28	Fred Lorenzen	Holman-Moody '63 Ford	289	560	Running
6	3	41	Richard Petty	Petty Eng '63 Plymouth	286	425	Distrib
7	18	35	Ray Hendrick	Rebel Racing '61 Pontiac	285	350	Running
8	15	83	Worth McMillion	McMillion '62 Pontiac	275	300	Running
9	16	32	Tiny Lund	'63 Ford	275	250	Running
10	19	16	Larry Thomas	Wade Younts '62 Dodge	273	250	Running
11	14	19	Cale Yarborough	Herman Beam '62 Ford	260	225	Running
12	2	47	Jack Smith	Smith '63 Plymouth	266	225	Diff
13	23	96	Jimmy Massey	'62 Chevrolet	266	225	Wheel
14	11	34	Wendell Scott	Scott '62 Chevrolet	262	200	Running
15	4	6	David Pearson	Cotton Owens '63 Dodge	254	200	Running
16	21	20	Jack Anderson	'63 Ford	242	175	Diff
17	24	33	Roy Mayne	C L Kilpatrick '62 Chevrolet	240	175	Running
18	17	62	Curtis Crider	Crider '63 Mercury	237	175	Clutch
19	22	17	Bob Welborn	Fred Harb '62 Pontiac	233	175	Running
20	20	54	Jimmy Pardue	Pete Stewart '63 Ford	175	175	Heating
21	1	8	Joe Weatherly	Bud Moore '63 Mercury	165	350	Engine
22	6	87	Buck Baker	Baker '63 Pontiac	124	150	Heating
23	10	09	Larry Manning	'62 Chevrolet	98	150	Heating
24	25	86	Neil Castles	Buck Baker '62 Chrysler	90	150	Crash
25	13	3	Junior Johnson	Ray Fox '63 Chevrolet	62	100	Wheel Cy
26	26	66	Elmo Langley	Ratus Walters '63 Ford	8	100	H Gasket

Time of Race: 2 hours, 15 minutes, 4 seconds
Average Speed: 66.339 mph
Pole Winner: Joe Weatherly - 68.104 mph
Lap Leaders: Joe Weatherly 1-98, Ned Jarrett 99-118, Weatherly 119-165, White 166-263, Jarrett 264-300
Cautions:
Margin of Victory: 2 laps, 2 seconds
Attendance: 15,000

Race No. 48

Junior, Stacy Irked with Freddy's Drive at Martinsville

MARTINSVILLE, VA (Sept 22) -- Fred Lorenzen breezed into the lead in the 81st lap and was never headed as he romped to victory in the Old Dominion 500 at Martinsville Speedway. The 28 year-old Ford driver accepted a $3,800 first place check, which boosted his record earnings to $104,380. It was Lorenzen's sixth win of the year.

Marvin Panch finished second a lap behind. Joe Weatherly was third, David Pearson fourth and Richard

Grand National Race No. 48
500 Laps at Martinsville Speedway
Martinsville, VA
"Old Dominion 500"
250 Miles on Half-mile Paved Track
September 22, 1963

Fin	St	No.	Driver	Team / Car	Laps	Money	Status
1	2	28	Fred Lorenzen	Holman-Moody '63 Ford	500	$3,800	Running
2	5	21	Marvin Panch	Wood Bros '63 Ford	499	1,675	Running
3	7	8	Joe Weatherly	Buck Moore '63 Mercury	497	1,475	Running
4	8	6	David Pearson	Cotton Owens '63 Dodge	496	875	Running
5	9	41	Richard Petty	Petty Eng '63 Plymouth	496	775	Running
6	10	5	Billy Wade	Cotton Owens '63 Dodge	495	675	Running
7	3	22	Fireball Roberts	Holman-Moody '63 Ford	489	625	Running
8	21	29	Nelson Stacy	Holman-Moody '63 Ford	488	600	Running
9	14	47	Jack Smith	Smith '63 Plymouth	488	425	Running
10	17	87	Buck Baker	Baker '63 Pontiac	477	390	Running
11	18	36	Larry Thomas	Wade Younts '62 Dodge	477	350	Running
12	19	19	Cale Yarborough	Herman Beam '63 Ford	474	300	Running
13	25	62	Curtis Crider	Crider '63 Mercury	461	275	Running
14	27	60	Bud Harless	'62 Pontiac	461	250	Running
15	24	09	Larry Manning	'62 Chevrolet	459	175	Running
16	23	83	Worth McMillion	McMillion '62 Pontiac	447	150	Running
17	11	67	Reb Wickersham	Reb's Sport Shop '62 Pontiac	430	175	Crash
18	29	34	Wendell Scott	Scott '62 Chevrolet	403	150	Running
19	6	11	Ned Jarrett	Burton-Robinson '63 Ford	362	200	Engine
20	16	99	Larry Frank	Bondy Long '63 Ford	300	175	Heating
21	1	3	Junior Johnson	Ray Fox '63 Chevrolet	296	350	Crash
22	15	26	Darel Dieringer	Bill Stroppe '63 Mercury	250	175	Push Rod
23	12	48	G C Spencer	Jack Smith '63 Plymouth	250	175	Pin Seal
24	36	31	Al White	'63 Ford	211	150	Heating
25	4	4	Rex White	Louis Clements '63 Mercury	183	200	Crash
26	34	9	Roy Tyner	Tyner '62 Chevrolet	130	100	Valve
27	30	23	Bill Widenhouse	'63 Plymouth	101	100	Ball Joint
28	31	33	Roy Mayne	C L Kilpatrick '62 Chevrolet	93	100	Rock Arm
29	26	76	J D McDuffie	'61 Ford	82	125	Hub
30	35	92	Fred Harb	Harb '63 Ford	53	100	Brakes
31	33	88	Major Melton	Melton '61 Chrysler	53	100	Brakes
32	23	14	Perk Brown	'63 Ford	41	135	Bearing
33	32	93	Bobby Keck	'62 Ford	26	100	Oil Leak
34	20	20	Jack Anderson	'63 Ford	13	125	H Gasket
35	22	54	Jimmy Pardue	Pete Stewart '62 Pontiac	0	150	Crash
36	13	43	Jimmy Massey	Petty Eng '63 Plymouth	0	125	Crash

Time of Race: 3 hours, 42 minutes, 16 seconds
Average speed: 67.486 mph
Pole Winner: Junior Johnson 73.379 mph
Lap Leaders: Junior Johnson 1-51, Fred Lorenzen 52, Johnson 53-80, Lorenzen 81-500
Cautions: 5 for 18 laps
Margin of Victory: 1 lap, 2 seconds
Attendance: 20,000

'tailgater' trick which Roberts used on Lorenzen in last year's 500 lappper at this half-mile paved track. This time, however, Lorenzen darted to the inside and swept to first place.

Lorenzen led the 52nd lap, then backed off and let Johnson back in front. Lorenzen made the decisive pass in the 81st lap and was never headed.

"I played a little bumper tag with Junior," smiled Lorenzen after the race. "Junior has been known to do that, you know. He must have resented it though because he hit the brakes. I let him back in front, then passed him clean like a racer should."

The 250-miler was an unusual event -- normally Lorenzen follows Johnson until the Chevrolet breaks. This time, he flat-footed it all the way. "Fans have been writing me asking why I let Junior outrun me all the time," Freddy said. "So I wanted to prove I could outrun Junior."

Lorenzen survived a couple of other close calls. He glanced off the stalled car of Reb Wickersham and hooked bumpers with stablemate Stacy. Stacy later delivered a message to crew chief Herb Nab: "I'm sick and tired of being roughed up by Lorenzen. This is my last warning."

Johnson chased Lorenzen futilely and eventually crashed while trying to run him down. In all, five cautions slowed the field for 18 laps. Lorenzen averaged 67.486 mph for his 11th career NASCAR win.

Petty fifth.

Lorenzen had to survive a furious bumping duel with pole sitter Junior Johnson; then endured a tongue-lashing from teammate Nelson Stacy. The Elmhurst, IL chauffeur has risen from virtually nowhere to the pinnacle of stock car racing in just over two years, and he found that everyone takes pot shots at someone who wins too much.

Johnson sprang from the starting blocks and led the early going. Lorenzen fell in behind Johnson and hugged his rear bumper. By the 40th lap, Lorenzen began tapping on Johnson's rear bumper. The "knocking on the door" persisted for 11 laps.

On lap 51, Johnson jammed his brakes -- the old

Grand National Race No. 49
300 Laps at Dog Track Speedway
Moyock, NC
75 Miles on Quarter-mile Dirt Track
September 24, 1963

Fin	St	No.	Driver	Team / Car	Laps	Money	Status
1	2	11	Ned Jarrett	Burton-Robinson '63 Ford	300	$645	Running
2	1	8	Joe Weatherly	Bud Moore '63 Mercury	300	680	Running
3	4	5	David Pearson	Cotton Owens '63 Dodge	291	375	Running
4	5	42	Richard Petty	Petty Eng '63 Plymouth	290	300	Running
5	10	28	Fred Lorenzen	Holman-Moody '63 Ford	289	250	Running
6	6	19	Cale Yarborough	Herman Beam '62 Ford	288	225	Running
7	8	87	Buck Baker	Baker '63 Pontiac	284	200	Running
8	14	67	Jimmy Pardue	'62 Pontiac	283	175	Running
9	13	83	Worth McMillion	McMillion '62 Pontiac	279	150	Running
10	15	09	Larry Manning	'62 Chevrolet	257	140	Diff
11	12	34	Wendell Scott	Scott '62 Chevrolet	229	130	Running
12	9	76	J D McDuffie	'61 Ford	127	120	Crash
13	7	62	Curtis Crider	Crider '63 Mercury	102	110	Spindle
14	3	32	Tiny Lund	'63 Ford	82	100	Heating
15	11	23	Bill Widenhouse	'62 Plymouth	67	75	Carb

Time of Race: 1 hour, 44 minutes, 39 seconds
Average Speed: 43.000 mph
Pole Winner: Joe Weatherly - 45.988 mph
Lap Leaders: - - - - - - - - - - - - - - - Ned Jarrett   -300
Cautions:
Margin of Victory:
Attendance:

Race No. 49

Jarrett Wins Moyock; Joe Yells Foul

MOYOCK, NC (Sept 24) -- Ned Jarrett outdueled Joe Weatherly and won a disputed 75-mile Grand National stock car race at Dog Track Speedway.

Jarrett was flagged in first place, but Weatherly yelled foul, claiming he had finished the 300 laps first. Score cards were sent to Daytona Beach, and NASCAR said no error was found. Jarrett kept the $645 first place pay check.

Weatherly got second place and David Pearson third. Richard Petty came in fourth with Fred Lorenzen fifth.

Weatherly won the pole for the 18th time in his career as Jarrett joined him in the front row. It was strictly a two-car show as the pair lapped third place Pearson nine times. Jarrett and Weatherly "leaned" on each other heavily at times, but no one spun out.

"Our cars were about equal," said Jarrett. "There's bound to be a little rubbing with cars that close in speed on a little quarter-mile track like this."

Jarrett averaged 43.000 mph.

Race No. 50

Panch Comeback Complete With N. Wilkesboro Win

NORTH WILKESBORO, NC (Sept 29) -- Marvin Panch made his auto racing comeback complete with a victory in the Wilkes 250 at North Wilkesboro Speedway. It was his first win since February 26, 1961 when he won a 100-mile qualifying race at Daytona. It was also Panch's first trip to victory lane since being injured in a sports car practice session seven months earlier.

Fred Lorenzen gave Panch a run for his money, finishing just six seconds behind. Nelson Stacy came in third with Fireball Roberts and Ned Jarrett filling out the top five.

Panch gave a brilliant exhibition of steady driving

Marvin Panch

Grand National Race No. 50
400 Laps at North Wilkesboro Speedway
North Wilkesboro, NC
"Wilkes 250"
250 Miles on .625-mile Paved Track
September 29, 1963

Fin	St	No.	Driver	Team / Car	Laps	Money	Status
1	3	21	Marvin Panch	Wood Bros '63 Ford	400	$3,225	Running
2	1	28	Fred Lorenzen	Holman-Moody '62 Ford	400	2,050	Running
3	4	29	Nelson Stacy	Holman-Moody '63 Ford	398	1,450	Running
4	2	22	Fireball Roberts	Holman-Moody '63 Ford	397	1,225	Running
5	7	11	Ned Jarrett	Burton-Robinson '63 Ford	397	625	Running
6	5	8	Joe Weatherly	Bud Moore '63 Mercury	397	800	Running
7	13	4	Rex White	Louis Clements '63 Mercury	390	475	Running
8	10	6	David Pearson	Cotton Owens '63 Dodge	389	425	Running
9	15	32	Tiny Lund	'63 Ford	384	375	Running
10	16	36	Larry Thomas	Wade Younts '62 Dodge	383	325	Running
11	18	14	Darel Dieringer	'63 Ford	378	300	Running
12	27	17	Bob Welborn	Fred Harb '62 Pontiac	375	250	Running
13	23	62	Curtis Crider	Crider '63 Mercury	368	225	Running
14	28	67	Reb Wickersham	Reb's Sport Shop '62 Pontiac	358	200	Running
15	24	34	Wendell Scott	Scott '62 Chevrolet	354	150	Running
16	26	88	Major Melton	Melton '61 Chrysler	351	150	Running
17	20	09	Larry Manning	'62 Chevrolet	344	175	Running
18	21	33	Roy Mayne	C L Kilpatrick '62 Chevrolet	326	150	Running
19	17	87	Buck Baker	Baker '63 Pontiac	276	175	Crash
20	14	99	Larry Frank	Bondy Long '63 Ford	243	175	Brakes
21	11	7	Bobby Johns	Shorty Johns '63 Pntiac	236	125	Piston
22	19	54	Jimmy Pardue	Pete Stewart '63 Ford	236	125	Diff
23	22	93	Lee Reitzel	'62 Ford	201	100	Crash
24	6	47	Jack Smith	Smith '63 Plymouth	151	125	Diff
25	12	43	Jimmy Massey	Petty Eng '63 Plymouth	78	125	Engine
26	3	41	Richard Petty	Petty Eng '63 Plymouth	45	125	Engine
27	25	96	Bobby Keck	'61 Chevrolet	26	100	Heating
28	9	3	Junior Johnson	Ray Fox '63 Chevrolet	4	125	Brake Cyl

Time of Race: 2 hours, 47 minutes, 44 seconds
Average Speed: 89.428 mph
Pole Winner: Fred Lorenzen - 96.566 mph
Lap Leaders: Fireball Roberts 1-153, Fred Lorenzen 154-158, Nelson Stacy 159-214,
     Lorenzen 215-226, Roberts 227-228, Lorenzen 229-230, Panch 231-312,
     Lorenzen 313-351, Panch 352-400
Cautions: 2 for 17 laps
Margin of Victory: 6 seconds
Attendance: 14,000

---

under heavy pressure from Lorenzen, the "Golden Boy" who has had a year for the dreamers in 1963. Panch made the final pass of the afternoon in the 352nd lap and held on for the $3,225 first prize.

"All this time without a win and this is one we were least prepared to win," sighed Panch as he wiped his brow in victory circle. "I had a terrible head cold and I took some tablets that upset my stomach. But the Wood Brothers got the car working better on each pit stop. They are the ones who won this race."

Lorenzen, who had a tire go bad in the last 100 laps, offered no alibis. "I have no excuses," he said. "You can't win 'em all. I try to, but Marvin was best today."

Junior Johnson, who has given the Fords fits in 1963, only lasted four laps on this pleasant autumn afternoon. His Chevy broke a brake cylinder, and he wound up last in the 28 car field.

Panch's ninth career win came at an average speed of 89.428 mph.

Grand National Race No. 51
200 Laps at Tar Heel Speedway
Randleman, NC
50 Miles on Quarter-mile Paved Track
October 5, 1963

Fin	St	No.	Driver	Team / Car	Laps	Money	Status
1	2	43	Richard Petty	Petty Eng '63 Plymouth	200	$580	Running
2	3	8	Joe Weatherly	Bud Moore '63 Mercury	200	670	Running
3	6	42	Bob Welborn	Petty Eng '63 Plymouth	199	380	Running
4	9	14	Darel Dieringer	'63 Ford	196	290	Running
5	1	28	Fred Lorenzen	LaFayette '63 Ford	194	275	Diff
6	14	67	Buck Baker	Baker '63 Pontiac	192	200	Running
7	13	96	Jimmy Massey	'62 Chevrolet	189	180	Running
8	19	33	Roy Mayne	C L Kilpatrick '62 Chevrolet	188	160	Running
9	4	11	Ned Jarrett	Burton-Robinson '63 Ford	187	200	Running
10	17	76	J D McDuffie	'62 Ford	184	155	Running
11	15	09	Larry Manning	'62 Chevrolet	180	130	Running
12	11	54	Jimmy Pardue	Pete Stewart '62 Pntiac	150	120	Radiator
13	12	34	Wendell Scott	Scott '62 Chevrolet	134	125	Engine
14	5	5	David Pearson	Cotton Owens '63 Dodge	107	125	Crash
15	10	62	Curtis Crider	Crider '63 Mercury	95	55	Diff
16	7	2	Jim Paschal	Cliff Stewart '62 Pontiac	32	100	Trans
17	18	53	Tiny Lund	'63 Ford	18	75	Handling
18	8	36	Larry Thomas	Wade Younts '62 Dodge	17	80	Engine
19	16	9	Roy Tyner	Tyner '62 Chevrolet	8	65	No report

Time of Race: 1 hour, 5 minutes, 13 seconds
Average Speed: 46.001 mph
Pole Winner: Fred Lorenzen - 51.724 mph
Lap Leaders: Fred Lorenzen 1-159, Richard Petty 160-200
Cautions:
Margin of Victory:
Attendance: 3,000

Race No. 51

Jarrett-Pearson Brawl Overshadows Petty Win At Randleman

RANDLEMAN, NC (Oct 5) -- A thundering bumping duel between Ned Jarrett and David Pearson stole the spotlight as Richard Petty won the 50-mile Grand National race at his homeown Tar Heel Speedway. It was Petty's 13th win of the year.

The incident between Jarrett and Pearson began in the first lap. The front of Pearson's Dodge hooked Jarrett's rear bumper, knocking him into the wall. Jarrett's Ford received repairs within 10 laps and he was back on the track. Just past the halfway point in the 200 lapper on the tight quarter-mile paved track, Jarrett drove his car into the side of Pearson, taking him out of the race.

Verbal sparring occurred after the race. "I think this 'nice guy' label has been carried too far," Jarrett growled. "It seems some of the drivers are getting the idea they can drive over me. That's not the case. I can be just as mean as anybody, and I will if I have to be."

Pearson claimed, "I bumped Ned on the first lap, but I didn't mean to. Then he came back later and forced me into the wall."

Joe Weatherly finished second, four car lengths behind Petty. Bob Welborn, recent addition to the Petty Engineering team, came in third. Darel Dieringer was fourth and Fred Lorenzen fifth.

Lorenzen led the first 159 laps before Petty sailed into the lead. Petty averaged 46.001 mph for his 26th career win.

Grand National Race No. 52
267 Laps at Charlotte Motor Speedway
Charlotte, NC
"National 400"
400 Miles on 1.5-mile Paved Track
October 13, 1963

Fin	St	No.	Driver	Team / Car	Laps	Money	Status
1	2	3	Junior Johnson	Ray Fox '63 Chevrolet	267	$11,720	Running
2	9	28	Fred Lorenzen	Holman-Moody '63 Ford	267	6,215	Running
3	1	21	Marvin Panch	Wood Bros '63 Ford	267	3,596	Running
4	3	22	Fireball Roberts	Holman-Moody '63 Ford	263	2,225	Running
5	11	8	Joe Weatherly	Bud Moore '63 Mercury	261	2,075	Running
6	15	43	Richard Petty	Petty Eng '63 Plymouth	257	1,200	Running
7	28	48	G C Spencer	Jack Smith '63 Plymouth	257	1,400	Running
8	6	26	Bill Stroppe	Darel Dieringer '63 Mercury	256	1,175	Running
9	12	4	Rex White	Louis Clements '63 Mercury	256	925	Running
10	7	29	Nelson Stacy	Holman-Moody '63 Ford	253	800	Wheel
11	14	6	David Pearson	Cotton Owens '63 Dodge	252	775	Running
12	25	19	Cale Yarborough	Herman Beam '63 Ford	251	675	Running
13	19	99	Larry Frank	Bondy Long '63 Ford	250	575	Running
14	17	2	Jimmy Pardue	Pete Stewart '63 Pontiac	249	625	Running
15	27	47	Jack Smith	Smith '63 Plymouth	237	900	Engine
16	37	34	Wendell Scott	Scott '62 Chevrolet	231	525	Running
17	31	56	Ed Livingston	Marnie Reynolds '62 Ford	228	575	Running
18	24	23	Bill Widenhouse	'62 Plymouth	225	450	Running
19	20	62	Curtis Crider	Crider '63 Ford	223	475	Engine
20	34	02	Bob Cooper	Cooper '62 Pontiac	204	550	Running
21	8	0	Tiny Lund	Holman-Moody '63 Ford	183	400	Heating
22	13	03	Jim Paschal	Ray Fox '63 Chevrolet	170	400	Heating
23	16	42	Bob James	Petty Eng '63 Plymouth	159	400	Engine
24	23	36	Larry Thomas	Wade Younts '62 Dodge	138	400	Ignition
25	40	7	Bobby Johns	Shorty Johns '63 Pontiac	93	425	Crank Sh
26	21	41	Bob Welborn	Petty Eng '63 Plymouth	78	400	Engine
27	10	33	Buck Baker	Holly Farms '63 Chevrolet	67	450	H Gasket
28	33	87	Reb Wickersham	Reb's Sport Shop '63 Pontiac	64	425	Engine
29	35	83	Worth McMillion	McMillion '62 Pontiac	59	425	Handling
30	34	1	E J Trivette	'62 Chevrolet	58	425	Ex Pipe
31	5	13	Bobby Isaac	Smokey Yunick '63 Chevrolet	57	425	Crash
32	4	11	Ned Jarrett	Burton-Robinson '63 Ford	46	425	Crash
33	18	5	Billy Wade	Cotton Owens '63 Dodge	32	450	Oil Pres
34	29	92	LeeRoy Yarbrough	'63 Ford	20	600	Clutch
35	38	9	Roy Tyner	Tyner '62 Chevrolet	15	425	Heating
36	22	18	Stick Elliott	Toy Bolton '62 Pontiac	11	400	Engine
37	26	09	Larry Manning	'62 Chevrolet	8	450	Heating
38	32	75	Thomas Cox	'62 Pontiac	6	450	Handling
39	36	86	Ronnie Bristow	Buck Baker '62 Chrysler	5	425	Clutch
40	39	61	Roy Mayne	'63 Mercury	3	425	Engine

Time of Race: 3 hours, 1 minute, 54 seconds
Average Speed: 132.105 mph
Pole Winner: Fred Lorenzen - 143.017 mph
Lap Leaders: Marvin Panch 1, Junior Johnson 2-49, Panch 50, Darel Dieringer 51-85,
  Lorenzen 86-93, Fireball Roberts 94, Lorenzen 95, Johnson 96-153, Lorenzen 154-157,
  Johnson 158-163, Lorenzen 164, Johnson 165-218, Lorenzen 219-224,
  Johnson 225-267
Cautions: 3 for 17 miles
Margin of Victory: 12 seconds
lAttendance: 46,531

Race No. 52

Chevy Fans Cheer Johnson Romp in National 400

CHARLOTTE, NC (Oct 13) -- Junior Johnson gained a large measure of revenge for a season laced with frustration by driving his Chevrolet to a big win in Charlotte Motor Speedway's National 400. It was the 34th career win for the Ronda Road Runner.

The victory was an emotional farewell for Johnson and car owner Ray Fox, who learned earlier in the week that Chevrolet was going to disband their factory efforts in stock car racing. Fox and Johnson announced they would probably move over to the Mercury camp for the 1964 campaign.

Fred Lorenzen finished second, 12.0 seconds behind the winner when the checkered flag was waved. Third place went to Marvin Panch. Fireball Roberts was fourth and Joe Weatherly fifth.

Johnson was a proud man in victory lane. "I knew I had to run wide open all the way to stay ahead of the Fords," he said. "They have been improving until they're awfully close to a Chevrolet in speed. At the first of the season, I could shake them, but I've got to run wide open to beat them now."

Johnson added that the victory may ease some of the

A crowd of 46,531 fans turned out for Charlotte's National 400

Farms team, led 209 of the 267 laps. Jim Paschal and Buck Baker, other drivers on the Fox team, both failed to finish.

Bobby Isaac, promising freshman driver out of Catawba, NC, hooked up with Smokey Yunick for the 400-miler. He qualified fifth, but stuffed the car into the wall after 57 laps. He was not hurt.

Three caution flags for 17 laps held Johnson's winning speed to 132.105 mph.

A record crowd of 46,531 turned out on a crisp day to watch the final superspeedway race of the year.

Junior Johnson's Chevy held together at Charlotte

talk about the Ford superiority on the NASCAR superspeedways. "I don't guess Freddy will be doing any more of his bragging about him outrunning me. He had his chance today, but he didn't do it," Johnson added.

Johnson, one of three entrants on Fox's Holly

Race No. 53

Richard Petty Beats Weary Junior Johnson at S. Boston

SOUTH BOSTON, VA (Oct 20) -- Richard Petty drove his Plymouth past a fatigued Junior Johnson in the 114th lap and breezed to an easy win in the South Boston 400 at South Boston Speedway. It was the 14th win of the year for the popular Plymouth pilot.

David Pearson finished second three laps behind. Joe Weatherly inched toward his second straight Grand National championship by taking third place. Bob Welborn was fourth and Larry Thomas fifth.

G.C. Spencer started second in a Jack Smith Plymouth and led the first eight laps. Billy Wade passed Spencer and led for four laps before Johnson, who started third, stormed into first place. Johnson led for

Grand National Race No. 53
400 Laps at South Boston Speedway
South Boston, VA
"South Boston 400"
150 Miles on .375-mile Paved Track
October 20, 1963

Fin	St	No.	Driver	Team / Car	Laps	Money	Status
1	4	41	Richard Petty	Petty Eng '63 Plymouth	400	$1,550	Running
2	7	6	David Pearson	Cotton Owens '63 Dodge	397	900	Running
3	5	8	Joe Weatherly	Bud Moore '63 Pntiac	396	925	Running
4	8	42	Bob Welborn	Petty Eng '63 Plymouth	394	550	Running
5	10	36	Larry Thomas	Wade Younts '62 Dodge	388	450	Running
6	9	2	Jimmy Pardue	Cliff Stewart '62 Pontiac	388	350	Running
7	12	14	Darel Dieringer	'63 Ford	372	250	Running
8	13	96	Jimmy Massey	'61 Chevrolet	369	175	Running
9	14	33	Roy Mayne	C L Kilpatrick '62 Chevrolet	369	150	Running
10	20	62	Curtis Crider	Crider '63 Mercury	368	140	Running
11	19	83	Worth McMillion	McMillion 62 Pontiac	364	130	Running
12	18	34	Wendell Scott	Scott '62 Chevrolet	361	120	Running
13	17	88	Major Melton	Melton '61 Chrysler	267	110	Running
14	11	09	Larry Manning	'62 Chevrolet	262	100	Diff
15	3	3	Junior Johnson	Ray Fox '63 Chevrolet	204	165	Fatigue
16	2	48	G C Spencer	Jack Smith '63 Plymouth	181	180	H Gasket
17	21	9	Roy Tyner	Tyner '63 Chevrolet	149	70	H Gasket
18	16	86	Ronnie Bristow	Buck Baker '63 Chrysler	107	60	Clutch
19	6	5	Billy Wade	Cotton Owens 63 Dodge	55	50	H Gasket
20	15	87	Buck Baker	Baker '63 Pontiac	44	50	Engine
21	1	47	Jack Smith	Smith '63 Plymouth	24	200	Oil Line
22	22	02	Doug Cooper	Bob Cooper '62 Pontiac	0	50	H Gasket

Time of Race: 1 hour, 57 minutes, 55 seconds
Average speed: 76.325 mph
Pole Winner: Jack Smith 81.081 mph
Lap Leaders: G C Spencer 1-8, Billy Wade 9-12, Junior Johnson 13-113, Petty 114-300
Cautions: None
Margin of Victory: 3 laps plus
Attendance: 5,500

Grand National Race No. 54
167 Laps at Orange Speedway
Hillsboro, NC
150 Miles on .9-mile Dirt Track
October 27, 1963

Fin	St	No.	Driver	Team / Car	Laps	Money	Status
1	1	8	Joe Weatherly	Bud Moore '63 Pontiac	167	$1,600	Running
2	9	41	Bob Welborn	Petty Eng '63 Plymouth	166	1,000	Running
3	18	02	Doug Cooper	Bob Cooper '62 POntiac	154	700	Running
4	21	87	Buck Baker	Baker '63 Pontiac	152	550	Running
5	16	62	Curtis Crider	Crider '63 Mercury	149	425	Running
6	5	42	Richard Petty	Petty Eng '63 Plymouth	146	325	Running
7	14	96	Jimmy Massey	'61 Chevrolet	141	275	Running
8	12	36	Larry Thomas	Wade Younts '63 Dodge	124	225	Crash
9	19	09	Larry Manning	'62 Chevrolet	120	200	Running
10	17	23	Bill Widenhouse	'62 Plymouth	114	175	Running
11	15	34	Wendell Scott	Scott '62 Chevrolet	110	100	Spindle
12	23	83	Worth McMillion	McMillion '62 Pontiac	106	100	A Frame
13	2	3	Junior Johnson	Ray Fox '63 Chevrolet	104	100	Engine
14	22	86	Fred Harb	Buck Baker '62 Chrysler	94	100	Engine
15	4	6	David Pearson	Cotton Owens '63 Dodge	86	100	Crash
16	11	2	Jimmy Pardue	Cliff Stewart '62 Pntiac	74	75	Egnine
17	7	48	G C Spencer	Jack Smith '63 Plymouth	71	75	Engine
18	13	76	J D McDuffie	'61 Ford	66	75	Axle
19	20	88	Major Melton	Melton '61 Chrysler	39	75	Brakes
20	3	11	Ned Jarrett	Burton-Robinson '63 Ford	38	75	Engine
21	6	5	Billy Wade	Cotton Owens '62 Dodge	28	75	Heating
22	8	99	Larry Frank	Bondy Long '63 Ford	22	75	Heating
23	10	32	Tiny Lund	'63 Ford	5	75	H Gasket
24	24	9	Roy Tyner	Tyner '62 Chevrolet	4	75	Heating

Time of Race: 1 hour, 45 minutes, 24 seconds
Average Speed: 85.559 mph
Pole Winner: Joe Weatherly - 93.156 mph
Lap Leaders: Joe Weatherly 1-84, Junior Johnson 85-90, Richard Petty 91-124,
    Joe Weatherly 125-167
Cautions: 2 for 14 laps
Margin of Victory: 1 lap plus
Attendance: 6,800

101 laps but began tiring well before the half-way point.

Johnson pulled his Chevrolet into the pits on lap 204 and told car owner Ray Fox he was too tired to continue. No relief driver was sought.

Petty averaged 76.325 mph in the 400 lap race on the .375-mile paved oval. A crowd of 5,500 watched the caution-free event.

Race No. 54

Weatherly Silences Critics With Hillsboro Victory

HILLSBORO, NC (Oct 27) -- Joe Weatherly gunned his Pontiac around Richard Petty in the 125th lap and sped to victory in the 150-mile Grand National race at Orange Speedway. It was the third win of the year

Joe Weatherly dismounts his Pontiac after Hillsboro 150 victory. It was to be Little Joe's final Grand National triumph

for the stubby Norfolk, VA veteran and he all but clinched the 1963 NASCAR driving title.

Weatherly's triumph, worth $1,600, also silenced many of his critics, who felt the 41 year-old former motorcycle champ had been "stroking" his way to the title.

Bob Welborn, who replaced Jim Paschal on the Petty Engineering team, finished second a lap behind. Doug Cooper was third, Buck Baker fourth and Curtis Crider fifth. Petty wound up sixth.

Weatherly had heard the whispers from fellow drivers, media members and most of all his car owner, Bud Moore, that he wasn't putting out 100 percent. Weatherly scoffed at the rumors. "There's more to racing than floorboarding the accelerator and holding it there until you win or blow up," stressed Weatherly. "What do you prove by blowing it up? I won nine races last year. Does that sound like stroking? When the car had it, I did my best to put it in the winner's circle. But there were times I had to settle for less. And in the long run, it paid off. The championship is worth better than $30,000. Racing is my business and that kind of money is good business."

Weatherly charged all the way at the historic .9-mile dirt track. He started on the pole and led the first 84 laps. Junior Johnson and Petty enjoyed brief stints in the lead, but it was Weatherly in the final analysis.

Two caution flags held Weatherly's average speed down to 85.559 mph. A crowd of 6,800 watched the final East Coast Grand National race of the year.

Grand National Race No. 55
148 Laps at Riverside Raceway
Riverside, CA
"Golden State 400"
400 Miles on 2.7-mile Paved Road Course
November 3, 1963

Fin	St	No.	Driver	Team / Car	Laps	Money	Status
1	3	16	Darel Dieringer	Bill Stroppe '63 Mercury	148	$7,875	Running
2	6	21	Dave MacDonald	Wood Bros '63 Ford	147	4,655	Running
3	1	121	Marvin Panch	Wood Bros '63 Ford	147	2,860	Running
4	2	22	Fireball Roberts	Holman-Moody '63 Ford	147	1,775	Running
5	19	26	Junior Johnson	Bill Stroppe '63 Mercury	145	1,300	Running
6	15	47	Jack Smith	Smith '63 Plymouth	144	1,175	Running
7	9	8	Joe Weatherly	Bud Moore '63 Mercury	143	1,475	Running
8	22	62	Bill Amick	'63 Mercury	142	1,000	Running
9	40	18	Bob Ross	'63 Mercury	140	950	Running
10	33	97	Ron Hornaday	'63 Ford	140	850	Running
11	10	281	Ken Miles	'63 Ford	139	710	Running
12	8	33	Clem Proctor	'63 Pontiac	138	575	Running
13	12	6	David Pearson	Cotton Owens '63 Dodge	136	580	Running
14	27	15	Bill Clifton	'63 Ford	136	450	Running
15	14	77	Marvin Porter	'63 Ford	135	450	Running
16	26	211	Pete Brock	'63 Mercury	134	350	Fuel
17	21	88	Don Noel	'63 Ford	133	350	Crash
18	24	72	Jim Cook	'63 Ford	131	300	Running
19	38	44	Lloyd Dane	'63 Ford	131	250	Running
20	20	98	Eddie Gray	'63 Mercury	131	225	Running
21	31	7	Dick Mitchell	'63 Mercury	126	200	Running
22	23	2	Jimmy Pardue	Cliff Stewart '63 Pntiac	117	400	Trans
23	29	61	Bob Perry	'61 Olds	112	200	Running
24	36	13	Gene Davis	'62 Ford	95	200	Running
25	25	58	Oren Prosser	'62 Pontiac	95	200	Running
26	17	02	Skip Hudson	'63 Dodge	75	275	Trans
27	41	40	Chuck Shore	'63 Chevrolet	74	200	Engine
28	30	162	Scotty Cain	'63 Ford	67	200	Engine
29	35	0	Bob Bondurant	'62 Chevrolet	44	200	Crash
30	39	12	Frank Denny	'62 Ford	44	200	Drive Sh
31	16	1	Paul Goldsmith	Ray Nichels '63 Plymouth	42	300	Crash
32	4	28	Fred Lorenzen	Holman-Moody '63 Ford	25	400	Trans
33	13	5	Billy Wade	Cotton Owens '63 Dodge	23	400	Trans
34	7	11	Ned Jarrett	Burton-Robinson '63 ford	21	400	Trans
35	18	29	Augie Pabst	'63 Ford	18	250	Clutch
36	11	43	Richard Petty	Petty Eng '63 Plymouth	5	400	Trans
37	5	4	Rex White	Louis Clements '63 Mercury	1	400	Crash
38	29	771	Jack McCoy	'63 Plymouth	1	200	Diff
39	37	64	Al Self	'62 ford	1	200	Engine
40	32	20	Al Brand	'62 Chevrolet	1	200	Engine
41	34	48	Bruce Worrell	'62 Chevrolet	1	200	Engine

Time of Race: 4 hours, 21 minutes, 37 seconds
Average Speed: 91.465 mph
Pole Winner: Dan Gurney - 101.050 (Car driven in race by Marvin Panch)
Fastest Qualifier: Paul Goldsmith - 101.620 mph
Lap Leaders: Fred Lorenzen 1-21, Dave MacDonald 22-76, Darel Dieringer 77-79,
    MacDonald 80-115, Dieringer 116-117, MacDonald 118, Dieringer 119-148
Cautions: 1
Margin of Victory: I lap plus
Attendance: 32,500

Race No. 55

Dieringer Drives Stroppe Mercury to Golden State 400 Win

RIVERSIDE, CA (Nov 3) -- The twisting Riverside road course was the scene of the 1963 NASCAR

Paul Goldsmith confers with car owner Ray Nichels at Riverside. Goldsmith raced in Golden State 400 and was kicked out of USAC for a year

season finale and upset-minded Darel Dieringer drove a Bill Stroppe-owned Mercury to victory. It was the first career Grand National win for the Indianapolis driver.

The 37 year-old Dieringer took the lead from Dave MacDonald in the 119th lap and led the rest of the way. He won $7,875 and gave the Mercury nameplate its only '63 win. MacDonald, a newcomer with unlimited promise, drove the Wood Brothers Ford to second place. Marvin Panch, in a car teamed with MacDonald, wound up third. Fireball Roberts was fourth and Junior Johnson, taking his first ride in a Mercury, was fifth.

Johnson got out of the car early and Richard Petty finished the race. Petty had fallen out after only five laps with transmission failure.

Joe Weatherly finished seventh and locked up the NASCAR Grand National championship. He finished 2,228 points in front of Petty in the final point tally.

Biggest news of the week was USAC headquarters' announcement refusing to allow their drivers to compete despite international approval by the FIA. Track General Manager Les Richter applied for and received the FIA license, which permitted drivers from other sanctioning bodies to compete in the race. Despite the FIA approval, USAC officials clamped the lid on the race -- even after the USACers had qualified.

Dan Gurney had won the pole, but was forced to comply with the 11th hour USAC ruling. He withdrew and Marvin Panch took over the car. A.J.Foyt, Parnelli Jones and Rodger Ward were other USAC drivers who had qualified and then left -- under USAC pressure.

"USAC's attitude was shortsighted for racing as a whole," declared Richter. "USAC let down the fans, the drivers and the Raceway with which it had an agreement."

Paul Goldsmith refused to go along with the USAC ban and competed. "I have an obligation to the fans and my car owner Ray Nichels to drive in this race," said Goldsmith. "Besides, I have a right to drive at Riverside because of the FIA."

Immediately after the race, USAC suspended Goldsmith indefinitely. Along with the suspension, Goldsmith lost hopes of competing in the 1964 Indianapolis 500, which USAC sanctions. Goldsmith logged the fastest time trial but crashed his Plymouth in the 42nd lap. He won $300 -- and paid dearly for it.

MacDonald and Dieringer swapped the lead six times before the Mercury driver took first place for good. Dieringer, who was released from a factory Ford ride, averaged 91.465 mph.

1963 NASCAR Season
Final Point Standings - Grand National Division

Rank	Driver	Points	Starts	Wins	Top 5	Top 10	Winnings
1	Joe Weatherly	33,398	53	3	20	35	$74,623.76
2	Richard Petty	31,170	54	14	30	34	55,964.00
3	Fred Lorenzen	29,684	29	6	21	23	122,587.28
4	Ned Jarrett	27,214	53	8	32	39	45,843.29
5	Fireball Roberts	22,642	20	4	11	14	73,059.30
6	Jimmy Pardue	22,228	52	1	7	20	20,358.34
7	Darel Dieringer	21,418	20	1	7	15	29,724.50
8	David Pearson	21,156	41	0	13	19	24,985.66
9	Rex White	20,976	25	0	5	14	27,240.76
10	Tiny Lund	19,624	22	1	5	12	49,396.36
11	Buck Baker	18,114	46	1	16	29	18,615.61
12	Junior Johnson	17,720	33	7	13	14	67,350.61
13	Marvin Panch	17,156	12	1	9	12	39,101.61
14	Nelson Stacy	14,974	12	0	4	9	18,265.61
15	Wendell Scott	14,814	47	0	1	15	10,965.61
16	Billy Wade	14,646	31	0	5	15	15,203.74
17	Curtis Crider	13,996	49	0	2	15	11,643.74
18	G C Spencer	13,744	31	0	4	12	13,513.74
19	Jim Paschal	13,456	32	5	15	18	20,978.74
20	Bobby Isaac	12,858	27	0	3	7	9,528.74
21	Bobby Johns	12,652	12	0	3	6	15,915.00
22	Larry Thomas	11,010	32	0	6	12	8,945.00
23	Stick Elliott	9,582	28	0	0	7	6,235.00
24	Jack Smith	8,218	28	0	3	10	8,645.00
25	Cale Yarborough	8,062	18	0	2	7	5,550.00
26	LeeRoy Yarbrough	7,872	14	0	1	5	6,680.00
27	Herman Beam	7,742	25	0	0	6	5,255.00
28	Larry Frank	7,582	11	0	2	2	5,450.00
29	Larry Manning	6,952	23	0	1	9	5,405.00
30	Ed Livingston	6,818	20	0	0	1	4,930.00
31	Neil Castles	5,928	28	0	2	8	5,165.00
32	Tommy Irwin	5,176	7	0	2	5	2,655.00
33	Reb Wickersham	4,812	14	0	0	1	3,800.00
34	Worth McMillion	4,614	15	0	0	4	3,145.00
35	Bob James	4,316	10	0	0	0	3,375.00
36	Roy Mayne	4,188	20	0	1	4	3,490.00
37	Bob Cooper	4,164	9	0	0	0	3,115.00
38	Jimmy Masset	4,016	15	0	1	8	2,870.00
39	Elmo Langley	3,982	11	0	1	2	2,170.00
40	Bob Welborn	3,484	11	0	4	4	4,830.00
41	Fred Harb	3,286	16	0	2	7	2,720.00
42	Dave MacDonald	2,944	2	0	1	1	5,330.00
43	Major Melton	2,806	17	0	0	0	1,910.00
44	Sal Tovella	2,570	3	0	0	0	1,300.00
45	Ron Hornaday	2,520	2	0	0	1	1,600.00
46	J D McDuffie	2,498	12	0	0	3	1,620.00
47	Bob Perry	2,478	5	0	0	0	1,550.00
48	Bunkie Blackburn	2,454	7	0	0	1	2,525.00
49	Bill Foster	2,168	10	0	0	2	1,410.00
50	Bud Harless	2,156	5	0	0	1	1,550.00

The 1964 Season
Speed, Danger on the Rise - Three Heroes Die

Volume two of a four volume series . . . . . The Superspeedway Boom 1959 - 1964

1964

In 1961 and 1962, Pontiac Division of General Motors was tossing fresh batches of racing options into the bins of such builders as Smokey Yunick, Cotton Owens, Bud Moore, Ray Fox, Ray Nichels and Banjo Matthews. The big, swaggering machines were virtually unbeatable in major races on the NASCAR Grand National Circuit.

All of this was going on during the supposed ban on auto racing imposed by the Automobile Manufacturers Association in June of 1957.

When Ford announced that it was going to "go racing" in the summer of 1962, despite the outlines of the AMA resolution, General Motors said they would "continue to abide by the spirit of the AMA ban." This meant they would not participate directly in any stock car racing events.

What happened was all the development at GM halted. It stopped in the General Motors corner of Detroit when they said it wasn't going on in the first place.

With the umbilical cord cut, by the middle of the 1963 season Nichels had switched to Plymouth, Owens went to Dodge, Moore and Matthews to Ford. Yunick raced a Chevrolet briefly before he dropped out of racing to devote full time to his GMC truck agency.

In 1963, General Motors took one parting shot before disappearing from the racing scene. They built a few potent 427 cubic inch "high lift" engines and delivered them to Ray Fox in Daytona Beach, who got throttle-stomper Junior Johnson to do just that -- stomp the throttle. They ran like a scalded dog in most of the superspeedway races, but seldom finished. For 1964, Fox faced the reality that without factory help, racing a car in NASCAR was a hopeless cause. He switched to Dodge.

Prior to General Motors' throwing in the towel came

the famous cannonball plunge of Ford into the racing puddle. The enormous injection of resources produced a record-wrecking year in 1963 -- with Fred Lorenzen going over the $100,000 mark in winnings, a 1-2-3-4-5 sweep of the prestigious Daytona 500, and a thorough shellacking of the competition all year long.

In the major league of stock car racing, Chrysler had traditionally been content to dabble along in a somewhat intoxicated manner, occasionally delivering small packages to the ever-loyal Petty Engineering plant in Randleman, NC. In 1963, they upgraded a 426 cubic inch motor that generated some 400 brute horsepower. However, on the big superspeedways, the boxy Plymouth bodies couldn't run their way out of a thick fog. On the short tracks, they were quite potent. All they needed in 1964 was a little refining in the right places.

Their first step was to streamline the Plymouth and Dodge bodies. And then they dusted off some blueprints from 1951 and came up with a "new" engine to

Fireball Roberts won on Augusta road course in the 1964 season

go racing with. It was called the "Super-Commando" by Plymouth and the "Hemi-Charger" by Dodge. Actually it was the hemispherical combustion engine that had been in Chrysler's bag of tricks since 1951, but hadn't been utilized on the race track since before the AMA ban in 1956.

Also out of the closet came a double-rocker arm system used in conjunction with the hemi-heads. Chrysler engineers came up with the layout that placed the huge valves on opposite sides of the combustion chamber, rather than side by side. In essence, it was a free-breathing combustion chamber which produced lots of power at the top end -- about 500 or so brute horsepower on a facility which breeds high speeds.

A series of "top secret" tests were made at Goodyear's test oval in San Angelo, TX during the winter of 1963-64 -- on a gigantic five-mile track. Word leaked out that certain Plymouths and Dodges were recording speeds of around 180 mph -- a figure unheard of in that day.

In the first major event of the 1964 season at Riverside, CA, Ford Motor Company products dusted the field and enjoyed another 1-2-3-4-5 sweep. The Plymouths were quite silent.

However, when the teams unloaded their new cars at Daytona International Speedway for the annual SpeedWeeks events, Paul Goldsmith, in the Nichels mount and Petty were whipping their Plymouths around the Big D at an alarming rate. Petty qualified at 174.418 mph -- which was earth shattering compared to his 1963 clocking of 154.785 mph. Goldsmith was tops at 174.910 mph.

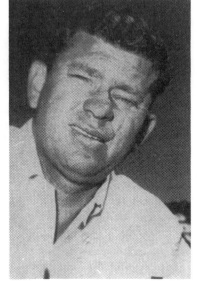

Joe Weatherly

The Fords, which had only peripheral refinements made for the 1964 season, were lumbering around in the high 160's. They found it was nearly impossible to even draft their swift counterparts. The high-ranking Ford executives were awe-struck. It was now apparent that the deeds on the Texas plains had been the gospel truth.

In the Daytona 500, Richard Petty won his first superspeedway race in impressive fashion. He led for a total of 184 of the 200 laps and Plymouths finished 1-2-3. A Ford product

led only two laps of the Daytona 500 -- when Petty was making a scheduled pit stop. Ford had its fanny flayed.

Before the Daytona 500, the touring pros were in Riverside for the second annual Motor Trend 500. Driving Bud Moore's red and black Mercury, Joe Weatherly had qualified for the 16th starting position. Weatherly, two-time defending Grand National champion, was leading the point standings entering the 500-miler on the 2.7-mile road course.

A lengthy pit stop had put the 41 year-old Norfolk, VA veteran miles behind the leaders. He had no chance of winning -- or even placing high. But he was back out on the track speeding around the tight corners chasing after the valuable championship points. In his 86th lap, Joe Weatherly failed to come out of turn six.

Witnesses said a puff of smoke was visible as Weatherly cranked the steering wheel through the "esses". Whether it was a mechanical problem or tire smoke from heavy braking, no one will ever know. Weatherly lost control and struck the concrete retaining barrier. The car slid across the track and wound up in a grassy area off the track surface.

The impact was not a direct, head-on shot at high speed. It was more of a glancing blow at no more than 85 mph. Such accidents are considered "routine" -- and the driver is expected to climb from his car and signal he is okay.

Something was wrong at Riverside on that cloudy afternoon. There was no movement from the cockpit of the Mercury. Little Joe was slumped over the wheel.

Rescue workers reached the scene and found the driver lifeless -- his helmet badly cracked down the side. The injuries in the "ordinary looking" wreck were fatal. Speculation was that Weatherly's head flopped out the window and hit the cement wall on impact.

Weatherly had not driven that day with a shoulder harness in place. In fact, he never even had one installed in his car. "The thing I fear the most is fire," Weatherly once said. "If my car catches on fire, I can get out a lot quicker if I only have my lap belt to unfasten."

The racing fraternity mourned the loss of its champion. Weatherly became the first driver to get cut down in race day traffic in nearly seven years.

Following the Daytona 500, Ford won 11 out of 15 races. Plymouth and Dodge won twice apiece. Of the 15 races, 13 were on short tracks. It became evident that the high-powered

Joe Weatherly's Mercury being towed off at Riverside. The 2-time Grand National champ was killed in the crash

Fireball Roberts

Jimmy Pardue

Chrysler cars were "too strong" for their own good on the short tracks. The Fords handled better and had a better balance of power all the way around the track.

In the Atlanta 500, only 10 cars finished as tires blew like firecrackers on the Fourth of July. Seven cars were badly crashed -- and all of them were being driven by top drivers in speedy, factory-backed entries. The victims were such headliners as Fireball Roberts, David Pearson, Paul Goldsmith, Darel Dieringer, Jimmy Pardue, Dan Gurney and Parnelli Jones. Most wrecks are caused by blowouts. The tremendous jump in speeds had overtaxed the available tire technology.

Goldsmith's crash was scary. While leading, a right front tire blew on his Plymouth, sending it into the guard rail -- hard. So hard that the car became airborne. Goldsmith slid through the third and fourth turns on his roof -- a shower of sparks shoot-

Fireball Roberts' Ford was burnt to a crisp in fiery World 600 wreck

ing out like a sparkler. Goldsmith was uninjured, but the top and half of the roll bars were reduced to 'too hot to handle', smouldering iron.

Richard Petty became concerned after the brutal Atlanta 500. He expressed particular anxiety if a similar incident occurred to a Ford driver. "The Fords should be at least 400 pounds heavier than the Plymouths and Dodges," said Petty. "But they are a couple of hundred pounds lighter. Some of us think they have lightened up their cars to a dangerous point from a safety standpoint.

"I'm afraid that someone may die before any safety measures are taken," warned Petty.

The second jewel of the so-called "Triple Crown" of the superspeedways was the World 600 at Charlotte Motor Speedway. Speeds were up about four mph over the 1963 qualifications.

Jimmy Pardue grabbed his first career superspeedway pole with a speed of 144.346 mph in the Burton-Robinson Plymouth. The North Wilkesboro, NC driver considered it his biggest thrill in racing -- better than his two short track Grand National triumphs and better than finishing second in the Daytona 500 three months earlier.

On the second day of time trials, Junior Johnson, wheeling Banjo Matthews' Ford, topped Pardue's mark. Johnson blitzed the timing lights at 145.102 mph, which earned him the ninth starting spot. Fireball Roberts was bumped on pole day and settled for 11th starting spot -- third fastest on the second day.

Pardue jumped out of the starting blocks and led the early laps. The green flag was out for only a few laps. By the seventh time around, starter Roby Combs was frantically waving the yellow flag. A terrible accident had occurred on the backstretch.

Fastest qualifier Junior Johnson, hustling toward the front, had hooked the rear of Ned Jarrett's Ford spinning both sideways. Roberts, running directly behind, looped his car to avoid hitting Jarrett and Johnson directly.

The lavender Holman-Moody Ford slid down the backstretch and struck an opening in the concrete wall, designed to accommodate over-the-track infield traffic. Jarrett's car spun into the inside wall and caught on fire. Roberts' Ford, having a full load of fuel on board, exploded and flipped as it hit the edge of the concrete wall.

"I knew I was on fire and I leaped out as soon as I stopped," explained Jarrett. "I had an advantage in that my car was rightside up and it wasn't burning inside.

"But Fireball's car was upside down and the gas from his punctured tank was dripping inside setting the whole inside on fire. I ran to the wall about six to eight feet away and turned around. He had started out of his car. Flames were four to five feet all around and I went back to help him.

"He said, 'My God, Ned, help me, I'm on fire'. I pulled him free of the flames and tore off everything I could get a hand on. He was conscious and helped me," said Jarrett.

Roberts was burned badly. "The flames first got to the bottom of his legs," Jarrett added. "He was burned around his hands, neck... any loose part of the uniform. His legs were burned worse than any other part. It was a miracle he could get out at all."

The rescue squad was quickly on the scene and administered to Roberts. "Once they got there I just wanted to get away," said Jarrrett. "They were trained in what to do. There was nothing more I could do. I just couldn't stand it any longer. It was a terrible experience."

Roberts arrived at Charlotte Memorial Hospital by

Fred Lorenzen suffered injuries in Firecracker 400 Qualifying Race

helicopter at about 1:15 pm, Sunday, May 24. He was listed in "extremely critical condition" with burns over nearly 80% of his body. The surgeon's report was issued later that night:

"At first we felt that about 80% of his body had been burned -- 40% second degree burns and about 40% third degree. A rule of thumb is that it is usually fatal if a person has third degree burns over 50% of his body.

"All of his legs except where his shoes were, were burned -- both front and back. His face was burned slightly except where the helmet was. His hands were burned badly. His back was also burned, as well as his arms up to the shoulders and on one side. The deepest burns were on the legs and hands -- about 30% of his body is third degree burns, the kind that burns through the skin into the tissue. It is difficult to say what percentage of burns are second or third degree. This changes each day."

Johnson, who was near tears, said: "I guess it was all my fault. I lost control coming off the second turn and spun. Then I saw Jarrett hit the wall and catch on fire. By the time I got out of my car, Roberts' car was on fire. I've known Fireball since my first race." Johnson was checked and released from the infield hospital.

"Junior was coming up on me, trying to pass me," reflected Jarrett. "He got a nose on me. He hit a bump, hit me and got crossways. There's a lot of turbulence at that speed (145 mph) and it's very easy to lose control."

Roberts' Ford was destroyed in the crash. The entire rear section was gone. All the paint was burned off and the remains had to be studied very hard to be able to tell it was at one time an American made automobile.

The car was dragged back to the garage area and a brown tarpolin placed over it. It was placed in the corner of the garage area and the entire area was sealed off by the NASCAR technical inspector. Many people -- including newsmen with garage area credentials -- were refused admission.

Lee Petty, one of the few allowed to go into the garage area, reportedly snipped a piece of metal from one of the Fords in the wreck. He was said to have sent the metal to Chrysler engineers who reported the metal was approximately half the thickness

Jimmy Pardue's Plymouth that carried him to the pole in the World 600 -- and to death in a tire test

that it should have been.

"The quarter-paneling and fenders on the Fords are like tissue paper," said Richard Petty.

Petty was on the track directly in front of the crash, but he saw it all unfold in his rear view mirror. "I saw Johnson and Jarrett spinning and then I saw a third car get airborne and catch on fire," said Petty, who finished second to teammate Jim Paschal in the World 600. "The next time I came around, I recognized Fireball's car. He was on the ground and Ned was trying to tear off his burning clothes. The next time around, I couldn't look."

Roberts fought for his life -- and the Charlotte Hospital released daily statements that the 35 year-old Daytonan was "improving". After a week or so, he was taken off the critrical list. "He is a remarkable patient," said a hospital spokesman. "Barring tragic infection, this man will come through."

Roberts, who had rallied tremendously from his May 24 accident, succumbed to the injuries on July 2, 1964. His condition had suddenly worsened on Tuesday, June 30 after an operation to remove the burned tissue from his body. He lapsed into a coma and never regained consciousness. He died of the burns, pneumonia and blood poisoning.

The Grand National tour was arriving in Daytona for the Firecracker 400 -- in which Roberts was to be the defending champion -- when the news hit.

"It's hard to believe Fireball is gone," said Richard Petty. "He was a man first, a competitor second and a teacher third. I saw him take young guys aside many times and tell them something that would help. I guess he helped the sport more than anybody."

"Fireball was the most respected driver there ever was -- or maybe ever will be," said Jarrett. "He was ideal. A lot of drivers copied him, but few had his ability. I believe that he had as much to do with making stock car racing what it is today as anyone else in the world."

The day after Roberts died, Daytona International Speedway hosted a pair of 50-mile qualifying races to determine starting positions for the 400. In the first 20-lap sprint, a five-car crash sent Ford star Fred Lorenzen to the hospital with injuries. Paul Goldsmith spun off the fourth turn and was nipped by Darel Dieringer. A.J. Foyt and Johnny Rutherford were also involved. Lorenzen tried to duck under the mishap, but plowed into Goldsmith's Plymouth, demolishing both cars.

Lorenzen climbed dazedly out of his car and got on the hood of his Ford. Then, he jumped to the ground and collapsed. "I climbed out of the car," Lorenzen later said. "There was blood all over the place. I took one look and passed out."

An artery had been cut and Lorenzen was bleeding profusely. Surgery was performed on his hand and he was out of the hospital in a few days.

Half-way through the 1964 season, outcries could

be heard from the contestants.

"It's reached the point at the superspeedways where it's a big relief when a race ends and you're okay, no matter where you finished," said Buck Baker. "It's become a pretty jumpy game."

"The cars are going too fast for the tracks," said Junior Johnson. "We haven't learned enough to keep the cars handling safely at the speeds we can now travel. And the tire companies are having trouble developing compounds that will give adequate tire wear."

Lorenzen claimed the 1964 speeds "are just too fast. I'll never run another race unless they slow the speeds down."

Having several days to think things over, Lorenzen changed his tune -- just a little.

"When I return and just how long I continue in racing will be affected a great deal by what NASCAR decides to do about speeds. That incident at Daytona (in the 50-mile qualifier) has taken a lot out of me."

Pat Purcell, NASCAR's Executive Manager, said in the summer that the sanctioning body would take steps to make Grand National stock car racing safer -- and slower. "I don't know what the answer will be," Purcell said. "But in my opinion, we have simply got to find out something to do. We will see what we can come up with."

Talk centered around a reduction of engine size for the 1965 season. A 396 cubic inch limit on engines was discussed openly, along with expanding the minimum wheel base to 116 inches. However, these talks came up with a number of stumbling blocks, including the fact that the change would be a severe financial burden on indpendent teams, who rely heavily on hand-me-down parts from the factory teams -- and most of them could not afford to engage in the costly process of building and maintaining new power plants. Besides, the United States Auto Club had intentions of sticking with the 427 cubic inch engine limit and NASCAR feared there would be mass defection.

In order to cope with the problem, the tire companies began to conduct an extensive series of tire tests. Nearly every factory backed driver -- and there were up to 17 of them who had industry support -- participated in the tire tests at all of the superspeedways.

Jimmy Pardue was scheduled to make a series of short test runs at Charlotte Motor Speedway on Tuesday, September 22, 1964. He took his bright red Plymouth to the mile-and-a-half at Charlotte and was testing a new tire compound.

He was scheduled for a 10-lap test. Only the 10th lap never came. On the seventh time around -- the same lap in which Fireball Roberts wrecked at the same track four months earlier -- there was a sickening sound of a tire exploding. Pardue, who had been clocked at 149 mph -- four mph faster than the track record the lap before -- shot up the banking in the third turn and broke through the guard rail. Wooden posts which anchored the rail were splintered. Forty-eight feet of railing were torn away.

Pardue's car sailed off the 75-foot embankment and apparently dived nose first into a chain-link fence 150 yards away. Reports said the car turned over once and landed in a dried up creek near a tunnel entrance to the infield.

Parts of the car were scattered all over the Speedway's acreage. The engine was torn from the chassis and the front bumper was wadded up 75 yards across the infield entrance road.

Drivers Darel Dieringer, Larry Thomas and Billy Wade, along with track official Roby Combs, helped remove Pardue from the wreckage. He was taken semi-conscious to Cabarrus Memorial Hospital in Concord at 2:10 pm.

Jimmy Pardue, 33, died at 4:38 pm, moments after his wife Betty arrived at his bedside. Dr R.C. Bailey, the attending surgeon, said Pardue died of "massive brain damage and a crushed chest". It was speculated that a steel post supporting the fence had come through the windshield and struck Pardue in the head.

Within two weeks, sanctioning NASCAR issued a new set of rules for the 1965 season. The engine displacement was kept at 427 cubic inches -- guarding against losing their drivers to the USAC ranks -- but the engines must be of production design only. Thus, no overhead cams, high risers and hemispherical heads. For the superspeedways, NASCAR said, the minimum wheelbase would be upped to 119 inches. The standard 116 inch wheelbase would remain in effect for short tracks.

The new rules would effectively put Chrysler cars "out to lunch". Dodge's Cotton Owens said, "This puts us out of racing."

Richard Petty wound up winning the 1964 Grand National championship by an enormous margin. He won nine races and $114,771.45 in prize and point money. Ned Jarrett won 15 races and was second in the point standings.

Three heroes lost their lives on the NASCAR tracks in 1964. And five days into the 1965 calendar year, Billy Wade was killed in tire tests at Daytona.

NASCAR addressed the situation and adjusted the 1965 rules accordingly. But the new rules triggered a series of boycotts, led by Chrysler Corporation, which pulled out of NASCAR for most of the 1965 season.,

Richard Petty
1964 Grand National Champion

Race No. 1

Jarrett Takes '64 Opener; Weatherly, Lund Feud

CONCORD, NC (Nov 10, 1963) -- Ned Jarrett won NASCAR's 1964 Grand National season opener at Concord Speedway -- but Joe Weatherly and Tiny Lund stole the show with an on-track feud.

Jarrett raced past Weatherly in the 231st lap of the Textile 250 and led the rest of the way. Weatherly recovered from a spin and finished second, 12 seconds behind the winning Ford. Richard Petty came in third with David Pearson fourth and Maurice Petty fifth.

The fender crunching session between Weatherly and Lund provided most of the thrills for the 3,000 spectators in attendance. The feud began with Weather-ly leading in the closing stages. Lund, running almost 30 laps behind, refused to allow the leader to pass. Lund's Ford and Weatherly's Pontiac brushed together on lap 230 as Jarrett swept into first place.

Lund spun around in the turn. He then motored to the pits and returned to the track directly in front of Weatherly, who was trying to chase down Jarrett.

With less than 10 laps to go, Lund veered into Weatherly's car in the first turn, nearly pushing it over the bank. Weatherly righted his path and crashed into Lund in the fourth turn. As the two cars raced down the home chute, Bud Moore, owner of Weatherly's Pontiac threw a rock which struck the side of Lund's car.

Tension was thick as a London fog after the race. "Joe had run over me once before in the race," huffed Lund. "And he's knocked me around at other tracks."

"Sure, I tapped Tiny," Weatherly explained. "He had been holding me up for 10 laps and Jarrett had cut my lead to nothing. The last thing I wanted to do was tangle with him because I was trying to outrun Jarrett to the flag. Tiny was out of contention. He's supposed to move over and let the contenders race. I don't know why the flagman didn't black flag him off the track."

When the two principles drove to the pit area, Bud Moore casually dropped a large wrench in his hip pocket -- just in case he needed it. However, spectators seeking autographs closed in and around their favorite drivers keeping Lund and Weatherly apart.

Jarrett averaged 56.897 mph -- a remarkable time considering the foot-deep furrows which developed in the half-mile dirt track as the race progressed.

Grand National Race No. 1
250 Laps at Concord International Speedway
Concord, NC
"Textile 250"
125 Miles on Half-mile Dirt Track
November 10, 1963

Fin	St	No.	Driver	Team / Car	Laps	Money	Status
1	3	11	Ned Jarrett	Burton-Robinson '63 Ford	250	$1,350	Running
2	6	8	Joe Weatherly	Bud Moore '63 Pontiac	250	1,000	Running
3	4	42	Richard Petty	Petty Eng '63 Plymouth	248	650	Running
4	1	5	David Pearson	Cottton Owens '63 Dodge	241	500	Running
5	12	41	Maurice Petty	Petty Eng '63 Plymouth	241	400	Running
6	16	20	Jack Anderson	'63 Ford	233	300	Running
7	18	16	Larry Thomas	Wade Younts '62 Dodge	230	250	Running
8	14	09	Larry Manning	'62 Chevrolet	229	200	Running
9	22	62	Curtis Crider	Crider '63 Mercury	221	165	Running
10	7	32	Tiny Lund	'63 Ford	215	150	Running
11	20	02	Doug Cooper	Bob Cooper '62 Pontiac	213	140	Running
12	21	87	Buck Baker	Baker '63 Pontiac	205	130	Fuel Tank
13	23	9	Roy Tyner	Tyner '62 Chevrolet	201	120	Running
14	17	83	Worth McMillion	McMillion '62 Pontiac	194	110	Running
15	8	6	Billy Wade	Cotton Owens '63 Dodge	185	100	Oil Pres
16	15	23	Bill Widenhouse	'62 Plymouth	153	90	Engine
17	19	34	Wendell Scott	Scott '62 Chevrolet	134	80	Crash
18	13	67	Jimmy Pardue	'62 Pontiac	111	70	Rear End
19	2	3	Junior Johnson	Holly Farms '63 Chevrolet	109	55	Heating
20	9	75	G C Spencer	'62 Pontiac	95	50	Rear End
21	5	48	Jack Smith	Smith '63 Plymouth	57	50	A Frame
22	10	14	Darel Dieringer	'63 Ford	57	50	Trans
23	24	18	Lee Roy Bolton	Toy Bolton '61 Pontiac	48	---	Rear End
24	25	86	Neil Castles	Buck Baker '62 Chrysler	27	---	Engine
25	26	68	Ed Livingston	Livingston '61 Ford	13	---	Heating
26	11	96	Jimmy Massey	'62 Chevrolet	---	---	Crash

Time of Race: 2 hours, 11 minutes, 49 seconds
Average Speed: 56.897 mph
Pole Winner: David Pearson - 69.257 mph
Lap Leaders: David Pearson 1-39, Ned Jarrett 40-133, Joe Weatherly 134-135,
  Richard Petty 136-148, Weatherly 149-230, Jarrett 231-250
Cautions:
Margin of Victory: 12 seconds
Attendance: 3,000

Race No. 2

Roberts Paces Augusta Field; First to Win 2 Road Races

AUGUSTA, GA (Nov 17,1963) -- Fireball Roberts steered clear of trouble and maintained a steady pace as he netted victory in the 417-mile Grand National event at Augusta

Dave MacDonald -- 2nd at Augusta, later to lose life at Indy

Grand National Race No. 2
139 Laps at Augusta International Speedway
Augusta, GA
417 Miles on 3-mile Paved Road Course
November 17, 1963

Fin	St	No.	Driver	Team / Car	Laps	Money	Status
1	2	22	Fireball Roberts	Holman-Moody '63 Ford	139	$13,190	Running
2	11	29	Dave MacDonald	Holman-Moody '63 Ford	138	6,745	Running
3	6	5	Billy Wade	Cotton Owens '63 Dodge	137	3,730	Running
4	8	26	Joe Weatherly	Bill Stroppe '63 Mercury	137	2,650	Running
5	7	11	Ned Jarrett	Burton-Robinson '63 Ford	132	1,675	Running
6	22	2	Jimmy Pardue	Cliff Stewart '63 Pontiac	132	1,800	Running
7	16	36	Larry Thomas	Wade Younts '62 Dodge	130	1,250	Running
8	19	62	Curtis Crider	Crider '63 Ford	129	1,100	Running
9	3	21	Marvin Panch	Wood Bros '63 Ford	128	1,220	Trans
10	26	87	Buddy Baker	Buck Baker '63 Pontiac	127	1,050	Running
11	14	12	Graham Shaw	Shaw '61 Ford	126	900	Running
12	36	32	Tiny Lund	'63 Ford	125	800	Running
13	17	80	Frank Warren	'61 Pontiac	125	625	Running
14	18	20	Jack Anderson	'63 Ford	120	775	Running
15	24	19	Cale Yarborough	Herman Beam '63 Ford	119	650	Running
16	28	02	Doug Cooper	Bob Cooper '62 Pontiac	117	575	Running
17	4	6	David Pearson	Cotton Owens '63 Dodge	115	670	Engine
18	30	34	Wendell Scott	Scott '62 Chevrolet	115	525	Running
19	15	43	Richard Petty	Petty Eng '63 Plymouth	94	820	Pinion G
20	23	92	Johnny Allen	'63 Ford	66	700	Engine
21	10	3	Junior Johnson	Holly Farms '63 Chevrolet	52	620	Trans
22	31	86	Neil Castles	Buck Baker '62 Chrysler	47	525	Clutch
23	25	30	Larry Frank	'62 Chevrolet	37	575	Engine
24	27	70	G C Spencer	'62 Pontiac	33	525	Engine
25	9	9	Roy Tyner	Tyner '62 Chevrolet	25	525	Rear End
26	13	4	Rex White	Louis Clements '63 Mercury	17	575	Engine
27	5	16	Darel Dieringer	Bill Stroppe '63 Mercury	14	525	Engine
28	1	28	Fred Lorenzen	LaFayette '63 Ford	12	625	Piston
29	9	42	Buck Baker	Petty Eng '63 Plymouth	12	575	Engine
30	33	156	Jim Bray	'62 Chevrolet	7	525	Trans
31	35	03	Elmo Henderson	'62 Chevrolet	6	525	Oil Pres
32	12	47	Jack Smith	Smith '63 Plymouth	4	525	Engine
33	32	05	Joe Penland	'61 Pontiac	4	525	Oil Pres
34	20	56	Ed Livingston	Livingston '62 Ford	3	575	Engine
35	21	7	Bobby Johns	Shorty Johns '63 Pontiac	2	900	Crash
36	34	23	Weldon Adams	'62 Plymouth	2	525	Distributo

Time of Race: 4 hours, 49 minutes, 51 seconds
Average Speed: 86.320 mph
Pole Winner: Buck Baker - 89.545 mph
Lap Leaders: Fireball Roberts 1-3, David Pearson 4-22, Junior Johnson 23-27,
   Richard Petty 28, Johnson 29-35, Petty 36-48, Johnson 49-51, Petty 52-93,
   Marvin Panch 94-128, Roberts 129-139
Cautions:
Margin of Victory: 1 lap plus 28 seconds
Attendance: 15,000

for 510 miles. However, it was changed to a five-hour event when qualifying times made it obvious that speeds would not be fast enough to complete 510 miles before the 5:00 pm Sunday curfew.

Roberts started second and led the opening three laps. He dropped off the pace and watched David Pearson, Richard Petty and Junior Johnson dice it out. Pearson blew an engine on lap 115, and Johnson lost a transmission after 52 laps. Petty had led for 42 straight laps when a pinion gear broke on his Plymouth as he was pulling away from the field.

Marvin Panch took up first place when Petty departed and was nursing a comfortable lead when his Ford snapped a transmission. Roberts drove into the lead in the 129th lap and led the final 11 laps. He won $13,190 for his 86.320 mph victory. It was the 33rd time he had earned a trip to victory lane.

David Pearson ran well at Augusta until engine problem put him out of the race

Thirty-six cars started but only 16 were running at the finish. Among those contenders watching from the sidelines when the checkered flag fell included Bobby Johns, Buck Baker, Fred Lorenzen, Rex White, Jack Smith and Darel Dieringer.

Weatherly took the lead in the point race with an 84 point cushion over Jarrett.

International Speedway's new road course. The 34 year-old Ford driver became NASCAR's first two-time winner on a road course. He had won a 100-miler on December 30, 1956 at Titusville, FL.

Dave MacDonald wound up second, a lap behind Roberts. Billy Wade was third with Joe Weatherly fourth and Ned Jarrett fifth.

The race, run over a difficult 21-turn course, was originally scheduled

The giant 3-mile road course at Augusta, GA. It was used only once by the NASCAR Grand Nationals

Race No. 3

Wendell Scott Surprise Winner in Jacksonville 100

JACKSONVILLE, FL (Dec 1, 1963) -- Wendell Scott of Danville, VA was declared the winner of the 100-mile Grand National Race at Jacksonville Speedway Park. It was the first Grand National win for the 42 year-old black driver.

Buck Baker was flagged the winner and Jack Smith was originally hailed as runner-up. Scott jumped out of his 1962 Chevrolet and insisted he had won. "I knew I had won that race," claimed Scott. "I had lapped Buck three times."

Protests and counter protests were filed as NASCAR officials deliberated for four hours. Finally the announcement came. Scott had won the race -- actually completing 202 laps in a scheduled 200 lap event. "The lengthy delay in posting the official results was caused by a scorer missing two of Scott's laps," said NASCAR's Johnny Bruner, Sr.

Wendell Scott

When the score cards were straightened out, Scott was given credit for taking the lead in the 176th lap from Richard Petty. Baker got paid for second and Smith third. Ed Livingston came in fourth while Petty fell to fifth as engine problems slowed him in the late stages.

Nearly all of the 5,000 spectators had left the track when Scott was officially given the nod. "Someone took off with my trophy," said Scott. "I wish I had gotten the trophy for winning the race."

Five cautions for 24 laps slowed Scott's average speed to 58.252 mph. Larry Thomas was the author of the day's most spectacular wreck -- a solo job which saw him tumble his Dodge into a protective screen above the guard rail.

Ned Jarrett finished seventh and took the lead in the standings.

Maurice Petty crashed in qualifying and did not compete in the 200 lapper.

Grand National Race No. 3
200 Miles at Jacksonville Speedway Park
Jacksonville, FL
100 Laps on Half-mile Dirt Track
December 1, 1963

Fin	St	No.	Driver	Team / Car	Laps	Money	Status
1	15	34	Wendell Scott	Scott '62 Chevrolet	202	$1,000	Running
2	14	87	Buck Baker	Baker '63 Pontiac	200	600	Running
3	1	47	Jack Smith	Smith '63 Plymouth	199	400	Running
4	18	68	Ed Livingston	Livingston '62 Ford	195	300	Running
5	2	42	Richard Petty	Petty Eng '63 Plymouth	193	275	Running
6	17	86	Neil Castles	Buck Baker '62 Chrysler	190	240	Running
7	5	11	Ned Jarrett	Burton-Robinson '63 Ford	183	200	W Bolts
8	20	78	Buddy Arrington	Arrington '63 Dodge	182	175	Running
9	19	92	Johnny Allen	'63 Ford	179	150	Running
10	4	5	Billy Wade	Cotton Owens '63 Dodge	163	140	Diff
11	21	05	Possum Jones	'61 Pontiac	156	130	Running
12	10	32	Tiny Lund	'63 Ford	124	120	Diff
13	7	20	Jack Anderson	'63 Ford	121	110	Radiator
14	22	61	Joe Weatherly	'62 Ford	120	300	Running
15	16	9	Roy Tyner	Tyner '62 Chevrolet	99	85	Axle
16	9	6	David Pearson	Cotton Owens '63 Dodge	70	75	Oil Pan
17	6	03	G C Spencer	'62 Chevrolet	60	65	Diff
18	13	36	Larry Thomas	Wade Younts '62 Dodge	60	60	Crash
19	3	90	Jimmy Lee Capps	'63 Plymouth	50	50	Crash
20	11	39	LeeRoy Yarbrough	E A McQuaig '62 Pontiac	23	50	Axle
21	12	62	Curtis Crider	Crider '63 Ford	8	50	Engine
22	8	2	Jimmy Pardue	Cliff Stewart '63 Pontiac	6	50	Axle

* Race scheduled for 200 laps. Due to scoring error, 202 laps were actually run. Buck Baker flagged winner, but scoring re-check revealed Wendell Scott was not scored for 4 laps in race.
Time of Race: 1 hour, 43 minutes, 0 seconds
Average Speed: 58.252 mph
Pole Winner: Jack Smith - 70.921 mph
Lap Leaders: Jack Smith 1-20, Ned Jarrett 21-........... Richard Petty ....-175, Wendell Scott 176-202
Cautions: 5 for 24 laps
Margin of Victory: 2 laps plus
Attendance: 5,000

Race No. 4

Petty's Powerful Plymouth Stout at Savannah

SAVANNAH, GA (Dec 29, 1963) -- Richard Petty coaxed his Plymouth across the finish line first and won the Sunshine 200 at Savannah Speedway. The 200 lap event had been rained out three times, yet 3,500 fans showed up for the 'between the holidays' event.

Jack Smith was flagged in second place with Tiny Lund third, Maurice Petty fourth and Curtis Crider fifth.

Ned Jarrett started on the pole for the 18th time in his career and the Newton, NC veteran led the first 67

Grand National Race No. 4
200 Laps at Savannah Speedway
Savannah, GA
"Sunshine 200"
100 Miles on Half-mile Dirt Track
December 29, 1963

Fin	St	No.	Driver	Team / Car	Laps	Money	Status
1	5	43	Richard Petty	Petty Eng '63 Plymouth	200	$1,000	Running
2	2	47	Jack Smith	Smith '63 Plymouth	199	600	Running
3	6	32	Tiny Lund	'63 Ford	196	400	Running
4	3	42	Maurice Petty	Petty Eng '63 Plymouth	195	300	Running
5	15	62	Curtis Crider	Crider '63 Ford	194	275	Running
6	17	36	Larry Thomas	Wade Younts '62 Dodge	189	240	Running
7	18	86	Neil Castles	Buck Baker '62 Chrysler	188	200	Running
8	13	81	John Sears	John Black '63 Dodge	188	175	Running
9	22	9	Roy Tyner	Tyner '62 Chevrolet	182	150	Running
10	16	92	Joe Weatherly	'63 Ford	175	340	Running
11	21	68	Mitch Walker	Ed Livingston '61 Ford	174	130	Running
12	10	5	David Pearson	Cotton Owens '63 Dodge	156	120	Con Rod
13	12	80	Frank Warren	'61 Pontiac	141	110	Diff
14	20	23	Leland Colvin Jr	'62 Plymouth	118	100	Spindle
15	11	34	Wendell Scott	Scott '62 Chevrolet	112	85	Axle
16	7	87	Buck Baker	Baker '63 Pontiac	104	75	H Gasket
17	4	90	LeeRoy Yarbrough	'63 Plymouth	96	65	Crash
18	8	20	Jack Anderson	'63 Ford	72	60	Crash
19	9	30	Buddy Baker	'62 Chevrolet	69	50	Ignition
20	1	11	Ned Jarrett	Burton-Robinson '63 Ford	67	50	Engine
21	14	2	Doug Cooper	Cliff Stewart '62 Pontiac	57	50	Piston
22	19	91	Rod Eulenfeld	'62 Chevrolet	1	50	Carb

Time of Race: 1 hour, 28 minutes, 3 seconds
Average Speed: 68.143 mph
Pole Winner: Ned Jarrett - 73.529 mph
Lap Leaders: Ned Jarrett 1-67, Richard Petty 68-200
Cautions: 3
Margin of Victory: 1 lap plus
Attendance: 3,500

Grand National Race No. 5
185 Laps at Riverside International Raceway
Riverside, CA
"Motor Trend 500"
500 Miles on 2.7-mile Paved Road Course
January 19, 1964

Fin	St	No.	Driver	Team / Car	Laps	Money	Status
1	4	121	Dan Gurney	Wood Bros '64 Ford	185	$12,870	Running
2	6	21	Marvin Panch	Wood Bros '64 Ford	184	6,650	Running
3	14	22	Fireball Roberts	Holman-Moody '64 Ford	183	3,900	Running
4	10	9W	Bill Amick	Bill Stroppe '63 Mercury	181	2,470	Running
5	21	11	Ned Jarrett	Bondy Long '64 Ford	180	1,750	Running
6	3	6	David Pearson	Cotton Owens '63 Dodge	179	1,500	Running
7	31	77W	Marvin Porter	'63 Ford	179	1,150	Running
8	9	06	Skip Hudson	Holman-Moody '64 Ford	178	1,075	Running
9	8	16	Darel Dieringer	Bill Stroppe '64 Mercury	177	975	Running
10	17	02	Troy Ruttman	Ray Nichels '63 Plymouth	177	850	Running
11	13	0	Don White	Holman-Moody '64 Ford	176	825	Running
12	39	98W	Eddie Gray	'63 Mercury	174	650	Running
13	15	4	Billy Wade	Bud Moore '63 Mercury	174	625	Running
14	40	2W	Jim Cook	'63 Ford	170	575	Running
15	18	32	Tiny Lund	'63 Ford	164	575	Running
16	38	60W	Bruce Worrell	'63 Olds	161	575	Running
17	1	28	Fred Lorenzen	Holman-Moody '64 Ford	159	1,005	Running
18	37	56	Jim Bray	Nick Rampling '62 Chevrolet	156	525	Running
19	20	44W	Lloyd Dane	'63 Ford	154	525	Engine
20	22	7W	Dick Mitchell	'63 Ford	152	525	Running
21	12	00	A J Foyt	Banjo Matthews '64 Ford	151	650	Crash
22	35	151	Bill Clifton	'63 Ford	150	525	Running
23	36	92	Jack Anderson	'63 Ford	145	525	Running
24	5	14	Dave MacDonald	Bill Stroppe '64 Mercury	137	600	Crash
25	33	10	Don Walker	'63 Ford	106	525	A Frame
26	2	43	Richard Petty	Petty Eng '63 Plymouth	101	940	Trans
27	24	33W	Jim Blomgren	'62 Pontiac	94	500	Engine
28	29	58W	Oren Prosser	'62 Pontiac	87	500	Engine
29	16	8	Joe Weatherly	Bud Moore '64 Mercury	86	1,000	Crash
30	44	25	Paul Goldsmith	Ray Nichels '63 Dodge	83	500	Engine
31	23	05W	Dave James	'63 Dodge	79	500	Engine
32	11	15	Parnelli Jones	Bill Stroppe '64 Mercury	68	685	Trans
33	27	18W	Chuck Daigh	'63 Mercury	62	500	Clutch
34	32	1W	Joe Ruttman	'63 Mercury	46	500	Engine
35	41	63W	Walt Price	'62 Ford	43	500	Engine
36	19	27	Curtis Crider	63 Plymouth	32	500	Trans
37	30	162	Joe Clark	'63 Ford	26	500	Oil Pres
38	7	26	Rodger Ward	Bill Stroppe '64 Mercury	24	525	Trans
39	25	51W	Clem Proctor	'64 Ford	15	500	Crash
40	34	61W	Don Noel	'61 Olds	10	500	Engine
41	28	3W	Danny Weinberg	'63 Plymouth	9	500	Oil Pres
42	42	12W	Frank Deiny	'61 Ford	9	500	Oil Pres
43	43	64W	Al Self	'62 Ford	9	500	Engine
44	26	20W	Al Brand	'62 Chevrolet	7	500	Wheel

Time of Race: 5 hours, 28 minutes, 47 seconds
Average Speed: 91.245 mph
Pole Winner: Fred Lorenzen - 102.433 mph
Lap Leaders: Fred Lorenzen 1-7, Richard Petty 8-18, Dan Gurney 19-28, Parnelli Jones 29-37, Petty 38-53, Dan Gurney 54-185
Cautions: 2
Margin of Victory: 1 lap plus
Attendance: 58,265

laps. Engine problems sent his car to the pits and Petty took over for good. He wound up over a lap ahead of Smith at the finish.

At one time, Richard and Maurice Petty were running first and second -- bidding to become the first 1-2 brother finish in almost a decade. But Maurice slid high in the turn and was passed by three cars. Eventually he fell five laps off the pace.

LeeRoy Yarbrough was challenging Richard for the lead in the 96th lap when his Plymouth sailed nose first over the first turn. His car got stuck in a pile of mud, and he was through for the day.

For the fourth time in as many races, there was a new point leader. Joe Weatherly finished 10th in a borrowed Ford and took a 132 point lead over Jarrett in the national standings.

Petty averaged 68.143 mph as he streaked to his 28th career triumph.

Race No. 5
Weatherly Dies as Gurney Wins Motor Trend 500

RIVERSIDE, CA (Jan 19) -- Dan Gurney took the lead in the 54th lap and led the rest of the way to win the tragic Motor Trend 500 -- an event which took the life of two-time Grand National champion Joe Weatherly.

Weatherly met instant death when his Bud Moore Mercury wobbled through the "esses" and struck the

Rescue workers tend to Joe Weatherly after late race wreck in Motor Trend 500

retaining wall with a solid blow. The 41 year-old Norfolk, VA driver, who did not wear a shoulder harness, hit his head on the retaining wall at the moment of impack. Witnesses said they saw a puff of smoke seep from under the black and red Mercury just before the car broke loose in the turn. It took rescue workers over five minutes to get the former motorcycle champ out of the mangled remains of his car.

Gurney's victory drive, his second in two starts on the 2.7-mile road course, held little suspense. The Costa Mesa, CA Ford driver led all but 43 of the 185 laps as he finished over a lap ahead of runner-up Mar-

Parnelli Jones' Mercury was out early at Riverside with transmission problems

vin Panch. Fireball Roberts came in third with Bill Amick fourth and Ned Jarrett fifth. Jarrett took the point lead, 200 points ahead of Roberts, who had missed three of the first five 1964 season events.

Fred Lorenzen started on the pole and led the first seven laps. But the Elmhurst, IL Ford chauffeur dropped back and eventually wound up 17th. "There's no sense in chasing Gurney unless something is wrong with his car," declared Lorenzen. "There's no catching him when everything is right."

Clem Proctor, established West Coast star, flipped his Ford in a series of end-over-end cartwheels in the

Skip Hudson #06 gets out of shape at Riverside

15th lap. He emerged dazed, but unhurt. A.J. Foyt was holding down third place with 34 laps to go when his Ford went into a dirt bank.

A crowd of 58,265 watched Gurney win at an average speed of 91.245 mph. It took nearly five and a half hours to complete the 500 miles.

Grand National Race No. 6
40 Laps at Daytona International Speedway
Daytona Beach, FL
100 Miles on 2.5-mile Paved Track
February 21, 1964

Fin	St	No.	Driver	Team / Car	Laps	Money	Status
1	2	3	Junior Johnson	Ray Fox '64 Dodge	40	$1,100	Running
2	9	41	Buck Baker	Petty Eng '64 Plymouth	40	600	Running
3	3	6	David Pearson	Cotton Owens '64 Dodge	40	400	Running
4	5	21	Marvin Panch	Wood Bros '64 Ford	40	300	Running
5	4	16	Darel Dieringer	Bill Stroppe '64 Mercury	40	300	Running
6	7	32	Tiny Lund	Graham Shaw '64 Ford	40	250	Running
7	8	22	Fireball Roberts	Holman-Moody '64 Ford	40	225	Running
8	6	11	Ned Jarrett	Bondy Long '64 Ford	40	200	Running
9	12	17	Dave MacDonald	Bill Stroppe '64 Mercury	40	150	Running
10	10	1	Billy Wade	Bud Moore '64 Mercury	39	150	Running
11	13	7	Bobby Johns	Shorty Johns '64 Pontiac	39	150	Running
12	21	27	Larry Thomas	'63 Plymouth	38	125	Running
13	15	04	R B Chumley	'63 Pontiac	38	125	Running
14	14	84	Nathan Boutwell	Edgar Hinton '63 Ford	37	100	Running
15	16	60	Doug Cooper	Bob Cooper '63 Ford	37	100	Running
16	17	71	Ray Gemberling	Roscoe Sanders '63 Plym	34	100	Heating
17	1	25	Paul Goldsmith	Ray Nichels '64 Plymouth	28	100	Engine
18	11	01	Johnny Rutherford	Bud Moore '64 Mercury	17	100	Engine
19	22	70	Elmo Henderson	'63 Pontiac	4	100	Oil Pres
20	23	95	Reb Wickersham	Ken Spikes '64 Dodge	3	100	Valves
21	18	61	Bob Cooper	Cooper '62 Pontiac	2	100	Gasket
22	19	97	Joe Clark	'64 Ford	2	100	Handling
23	20	56	Jim Bray	Nick Rampling '62 Chevrolet	2	100	Handling

Time of Race: 35 minutes, 08 seconds
Average Speed: 170.777 mph
Pole Winner: Paul Goldsmith - 174.910 mph
Lap Leaders: Paul Goldsmith 1-17, Buck Baker 18-21, Goldsmith 22, Baker 23-39, Junior Johnson 40
Cautions:
Margin of Victory: 1 car length
Attendance: 17,500

Race No. 6

Johnson Gets a 'Goat' Into the 'Pen'

DAYTONA BEACH, FL (Feb 21) -- Junior Johnson, who was set to drive a Mercury in the 1964 NASCAR season, switched to a Dodge and won the first 100-mile Grand National qualifier at Daytona International Speedway. The pudgy Ronda, NC veteran established an all-time race record by averaging 170.777 mph for the 40 trips around the 2.5-mile Big D.

"It's been a long time since a 'Goat' has been in this pen," declared Johnson in victory lane ceremonies. He used to rib the Dodges by calling them 'Goats', and the

Race No. 7

Bobby Isaac Wins First Start For Factory Dodge Team

DAYTONA BEACH, FL (Feb 21) -- Bobby Isaac of Catawba, NC made his first start with the factory Dodge team a victorious one by streaking to a one-foot win in the second 100-mile qualifying race at Daytona International Speedway.

Isaac, Jimmy Pardue and Richard Petty crossed the finish line three-abreast in perhaps the closest finish in the six year history of Bill France's ultra fast speed

Bobby Isaac #26, a sideways Jimmy Pardue and an out-of-gas Richard Petty #43 in close Daytona 100 finish

Ray Fox and Junior Johnson collect trophies after 170.777 mph victory in 100-mile qualifier

pen is the winner's circle.

Buck Baker, taking a ride in a Petty Engineering Plymouth, came in second, one car length behind the fleet Johnson. David Pearson was third, Marvin Panch fourth and Darel Dieringer fifth.

Chrysler Corporation unveiled a new Hemi engine, and its brute speed left the Ford teams scratching their heads. Panch, the highest finisher in a Ford product, remarked that the Dodge and Plymouth cars "ran disgustingly good."

Johnson started second but led only one lap -- the final one. Baker led on two occasions for 21 laps, but Johnson pulled the "slingshot" off the final corner.

Paul Goldsmith started on the pole with a record 174.910 mph lap. The St. Clair Shores, MI Plymouth driver led the first 17 laps, but left the race in the 28th lap with a blown engine.

For awhile, three drivers huddled the winning trophy: Bobby Isaac, Richard Petty and Jimmy Pardue

cathedral.

NASCAR officials waited until the photo-finish camera pictures were printed before making a decision on who won. The camera produced blank paper so France solicited still photos from trackside shutterbugs. Three hours later, Isaac was named the winner.

Pardue got second place with Petty third. A.J. Foyt was fourth and Jim Paschal fifth.

Petty jumped out of the starting blocks like a bullet and proceeded to make a mockery of the 40-lap sprint race. His Plymouth was nearly a half lap ahead when it ran out of gas in the final lap. Petty hugged the inside groove, hoping his car would coast over the finish line first. It was not to be as Isaac and Pardue came roaring toward the checkered flag side by side. They overtook number 43 at the finish line. Petty crossed the line at 40 mph. "I knew I was running low on fuel four laps earlier," said Petty. "I was just hoping for the best."

Isaac averaged 169.811 mph in the Ray Nichels-owned Dodge.

Grand National Race No. 7
40 Laps at Daytona International Speedway
Daytona Beach, FL
40 Miles on 2.5-mile Paved Track
February 21, 1964

Fin	St	No.	Driver	Team / Car	Laps	Money	Status
1	4	26	Bobby Isaac	Ray Nichels '64 Dodge	40	$1,100	Running
2	2	54	Jimmy Pardue	Burton-Robinson '64 Plym	40	600	Running
3	1	43	Richard Petty	Petty Eng '64 Plymouth	40	400	Running
4	11	00	A J Foyt	Banjo Matthews '64 Ford	40	300	Running
5	9	5	Jim Paschal	Cotton Owens '64 Dodge	40	300	Running
6	3	15	Parnelli Jones	Bill Stroppe '64 Mercury	40	250	Running
7	12	29	Larry Frank	Holman-Moody '64 Ford	40	225	Running
8	7	06	Bobby Marshman	Holman-Moody '64 Ford	39	200	Running
9	8	77	Joe Schlesser	Bondy Long '64 Ford	39	150	Running
10	10	12	Dan Gurney	Wood Bros '64 Ford	39	150	Running
11	13	19	Cale Yarborough	Herman Beam '64 Ford	38	150	Running
12	14	09	Sal Tovella	Herb Onash '64 Ford	38	125	Running
13	6	14	Jim McElreath	Bill Stroppe '64 Mercury	37	125	Running
14	16	31	Ralph Earnhardt	Tom Spell '63 Ford	36	100	Running
15	17	62	Curtis Crider	Crider '63 Mercury	36	100	Running
16	15	2	G C Spencer	Cliff Stewart '63 Pontiac	32	100	Fuel
17	5	28	Fred Lorenzen	Holman-Moody '64 Ford	31	100	Tire
18	18	92	Jack Anderson	Ray Osborne '63 Ford	10	100	Heating
19	22	86	Neil Castles	Buck Baker '62 Chrysler	4	100	Plugs
20	21	34	Wendell Scott	Scott '62 Chevrolet	4	100	Handling
21	23	89	LeeRoy Yarbrough	David Walker '64 Plymouth	3	100	Oil Leak
22	19	82	Bill McMahan	Casper Hensley '63 Pontiac	3	100	Bearing
23	20	20	Jim Cook	'63 Ford	3	100	Vibration

Time of Race: 35 minutes, 20 seconds
Average Speed: 169.811 mph
Pole Winner: Richard Petty - 174.418 mph
Lap Leaders: Richard Petty 1-39, Bobby Isaac 40
Cautions:
Margin of Victory: 1 foot
Attendance: 17,500

Grand National Race No. 8
200 Laps at Daytona International Speedway
Daytona Beach, FL
"Daytona 500"
500 Miles on 2.5-mile Paved Track
February 23, 1964

Fin	St	No.	Driver	Team / Car	Laps	Money	Status
1	2	43	Richard Petty	Petty Eng '64 Plymouth	200	$33,300	Running
2	6	54	Jimmy Pardue	Burton-Robinson '64 Plym	199	11,600	Running
3	1	25	Paul Goldsmith	Ray Nichels '64 Plymouth	198	8,600	Running
4	9	21	Marvin Panch	Wood Bros '64 Ford	198	4,350	Running
5	10	5	Jim Paschal	Cotton Owens '64 Dodge	197	3,700	Running
6	21	1	Billy Wade	Bud Moore '64 Mercury	197	2,500	Running
7	11	16	Darel Dieringer	Bill Stroppe '64 Mercury	197	2,000	Running
8	14	29	Larry Frank	Holman-Moody '64 Ford	197	1,750	Running
9	3	3	Junior Johnson	Ray Fox '64 Dodge	197	1,500	Running
10	19	17	Dave MacDonald	Bill Stroppe '64 Mercury	196	1,200	Running
11	13	32	Tiny Lund	Graham Shaw '64 Ford	195	1,200	Running
12	5	41	Buck Baker	Petty Eng '64 Plymouth	194	1,200	Running
13	18	77	Joe Schlesser	Bondy Long '64 Ford	192	1,200	Running
14	20	12	Dan Gurney	Wood Bros '64 Ford	192	1,200	Running
15	4	26	Bobby Isaac	Ray Nichels '64 Dodge	189	1,500	Fuel
16	25	27	Larry Thomas	'63 Plymouth	188	1,000	Running
17	22	19	Cale Yarborough	Herman Beam '64 Ford	187	1,000	Running
18	31	60	Doug Cooper	Bob Cooper '63 Ford	186	1,000	Running
19	28	31	Ralph Earnhardt	Tom Spell '63 Ford	180	1,000	Running
20	29	84	Nathan Boutwell	Edgar Hinton '63 Ford	180	1,000	Running
21	30	62	Curtis Crider	Crider '63 Ford	177	725	Running
22	39	95	Reb Wickersham	Ken Spikes '64 Dodge	131	725	Sway bar
23	24	09	Sal Tovella	Herb Onash '64 Ford	129	725	Engine
24	8	00	A J Foyt	Banjo Matthews '64 Ford	127	825	Engine
25	26	14	Jim McElreath	Bill Stroppe '64 Mercury	126	725	Crash
26	35	01	Johnny Rutherford	Bud Moore '64 Mercury	107	725	Crash
27	17	11	Ned Jarrett	Bondy Long '64 Ford	106	725	Crash
28	12	15	Parnelli Jones	Bill Stroppe '64 Mecury	77	725	Engine
29	42	89	Buddy Baker	David Walker '64 Plymouth	64	725	Engine
30	7	6	David Pearson	Cotton Owens '64 Dodge	52	725	Crash
31	34	28	Fred Lorenzen	Holman-Moody '64 Ford	49	725	Engine
32	36	92	Jack Anderson	Ray Osborne '63 Ford	41	725	Rear End
33	32	2	G C Spencer	Cliff Stewart '63 Pontiac	31	725	Engine
34	27	04	R B Chumley	'63 Pontiac	21	725	Engine
35	16	06	Bobby Marshman	Holman-Moody '64 Ford	17	725	Heating
36	23	7	Bobby Johns	Shorty Johns '64 Pontiac	15	725	Engine
37	15	22	Fireball Roberts	Holman-Moody '64 Ford	13	725	Trans
38	40	34	Wendell Scott	Scott '62 Chevrolet	7	725	Heating
39	37	70	Elmo Henderson	'63 Pontiac	4	725	Engine
40	43	97	Joe Clark	'64 Ford	4	725	H Gasket
41	44	82	Bill McMahan	Casper Hensley '63 Pontiac	3	725	Handling
42	45	56	Jim Bray	Nick Rampling '62 Chevrolet	2	725	Handling
43	33	71	Bunkie Blackburn	Roscoe Sanders '63 Plym	1	725	Crank Sh
44	41	61	Bob Cooper	Cooper '62 Pontiac	1	725	Oil Pres
45	46	20	Jim Cook	'63 Ford	1	725	Handling
46	38	86	Neil Castles	Buck Baker '62 Chrysler	1	725	Trans

Time of Race: 3 hours, 14 minutes, 23 seconds
Average Speed: 154.334 mph
Pole Winner: Paul Goldsmith - 174.910 mph
Lap Leaders: Paul Goldsmith 1, Richard Petty 2-6, Bobby Isaac 7-9, Petty 10-39,
     A J Foyt 40-41, Goldsmith 42-51, Petty 52-200
Cautions: 3 for 19 laps
Margin of Victory: 1 lap plus 9 seconds
Attendance: 69,738

Race No. 8

Plymouths 1-2-3 in Daytona 500; Petty on Top

DAYTONA BEACH, FL (Feb 23) -- A record audience of 69,738 filled every seat at the Daytona International Speedway and sat through a lopsided 500-mile affair as Richard Petty stomped tail in the sixth annual Daytona 500. The 26 year-old Plymouth driver led all but 16 laps and finished three miles in front of runner-up Jimmy Pardue. Paul Goldsmith was third to complete the 1-2-3 sweep for the Plymouth nameplate.

Marvin Panch salvaged fourth place for Ford and Jim Paschal finished fifth in a Dodge.

Petty, of Randleman, NC, took the lead for keeps in the 52nd lap. He was never threatened after that. "I wasn't exactly enjoying myself out there," Petty confessed. "You've got to stay right with the car every second at the speeds we're going now."

Petty averaged a record 154.334 mph and pocketed

Paul Goldsmith leads opening lap of Daytona 500 with Richard Petty in hot pursuit

$33,300 for his first superspeedway victory. "I was sweating it out at the finish. I've been awfully close to winning a big one several times only to have something happen," he said.

The lead changed hands only six times and Chrysler products led 198 of the 200 laps. A.J. Foyt, one of Ford's top hopes, led two laps, but a blown engine

Richard Petty laps Jack Anderson #92 en route to Daytona 500 win

ended his bid after 127 laps.

The caution came out three times, two for crashes. David Pearson blew a tire and slammed into the wall in the 52nd lap. Johnny Rutherford survived a wild ride on lap 107. His car broke loose and was tapped by Ned Jarrett exiting turn two. Air currents got underneath Rutherford's Mercury and lifted it up in the air. It landed on its roof and slid some 800 feet. "Boy, when I started sliding upside down," said Rutherford, "I covered my eyes with my arm. That grinding was terrible. I thought it never would stop."

Panch took the lead in the point standings by 352 points over sophomore Billy Wade. Wade shifted over to the Bud Moore team and wound up sixth after starting 21st.

Richard Petty beams from Daytona 500 victory lane

Race No. 9

Pearson Wins Two-day Richmond 250

RICHMOND, VA (Mar 10) -- David Pearson won his first race in two and a half years in the two-day Richmond 250 at the Atlantic Rural Fairgrounds Speedway. One hundred laps were run on Sunday before the half-mile dirt track was hit by a soft but steady rain. The event was completed on Tuesday night with 10,000 of the original 15,000 spectators returning for the balance of the event.

Pearson's Cotton Owens Dodge finished a half lap in front of Richard Petty to win the $1,500 top prize. Third place went to Billy Wade with Junior Johnson fourth and Doug Yates fifth. Point leader Marvin Panch took sixth place.

The lead changed hands six times among four drivers. Pearson passed Petty for the final time in the 215th lap and led the rest of the way. It was his first win since September 17, 1961 when he won the Atlanta Dixie 400.

Two caution periods slowed Pearson's winning speed to 60.233 mph. Cale Yarborough brought out one of the cautions when he spun his Ford into the path of Panch, who was running second at the time. Panch retreated to the pits where his Wood Brothers pit crew made repairs. He lost only one lap and finished one lap down.

Grand National Race No. 9
250 Laps at Atlantic Rural Fairgrounds
Richmond, VA
"Richmond 250"
125 Miles on Half-mile Dirt Track
March 10, 1964

Fin	St	No.	Driver	Team / Car	Laps	Money	Status
1	10	6	David Pearson	Cotton Owens '64 Dodge	250	$1,500	Running
2	6	43	Richard Petty	Petty Eng '64 Plymouth	250	1,000	Running
3	2	1	Billy Wade	Bud Moore '64 Mercury	250	750	Running
4	13	3	Junior Johnson	Ray Fox '64 Dodge	249	600	Running
5	7	45	Doug Yates	Louie Weathersby '63 Plym	249	450	Running
6	3	21	Marvin Panch	Wood Bros '64 Ford	249	375	Running
7	4	41	Maurice Petty	Petty Eng '63 Plymouth	248	300	Running
8	17	09	Larry Manning	'62 Chevrolet	241	250	Running
9	20	60	Doug Cooper	Bob Cooper '63 Ford	239	200	Running
10	11	62	Curtis Crider	Crider '63 Mercury	232	200	Running
11	16	78	Buddy Arrington	Arrington '63 Plymouth	232	175	Running
12	22	97	Joe Clark	'64 Ford	232	175	Running
13	1	11	Ned Jarrett	Bondy Long '64 Ford	224	175	Engine
14	14	5	Jim Paschal	Cotton Owens '64 Dodge	223	150	Cylinder
15	24	92	Jim Cook	Ray Osborne '63 Ford	222	150	Running
16	18	19	Cale Yarborough	Heman Beam '64 Ford	218	125	Crash
17	23	7	E J Trivette	'62 Chevrolet	216	125	Engine
18	25	83	Worth McMillion	McMillion '62 Pontiac	176	125	A Frame
19	19	32	Tiny Lund	Graham Shaw '63 Ford	170	125	Rear End
20	12	54	Jimmy Pardue	Burton-Robinson '64 Plym	140	125	Crash
21	9	36	Larry Thomas	Wade Younts '63 Dodge	116	125	A Frame
22	5	31	Ralph Earnhardt	Tom Spell '63 Ford	73	125	Rear End
23	21	20	Jack Anderson	'63 Ford	22	125	Engine
24	15	34	Wendell Scott	Scott '62 Chevrolet	9	125	Cam Sh
25	26	86	Neil Castles	Buck Baker '62 Chrysler	1	125	Con Rod
26	18	71	Bunkie Blackburn	Roscoe Sanders '63 Plym	0	125	Crash
DNS		61	Bob Cooper	Cooper '62 Pontiac	---	125	---

Time of Race: 2 hours, 07 minutes, 51 seconds
Average Speed: 60.233 mph
Pole Winner: Ned Jarrett - 69.07 mph
Lap Leaders: Ned Jarrett 1-104, Billy Wade 105-137, Richard Petty 138-162,
  Billy Wade 163-210, Petty 211-214, David Pearson 215-250
Cautions: 2
Margin of Victory: 1/2 lap
Attendance: 15,000 on Sunday - 10,000 on Tuesday

Grand National Race No. 10
500 Laps at Bristol International
Speedway
Bristol, TN
"Southeastern 500"
250 Miles on Half-mile Paved Track
March 22, 1964

Fin	St	No.	Driver	Team / Car	Laps	Money	Status
1	2	28	Fred Lorenzen	Holman-Moody '64 Ford	500	$4,300	Running
2	3	22	Fireball Roberts	Holman-Moody '64 Ford	500	2,150	Running
3	13	25	Paul Goldsmith	Ray Nichels '64 Plymouth	497	1,685	Running
4	11	41	Buck Baker	Petty Eng '64 Plymouth	496	1,075	Running
5	1	21	Marvin Panch	Wood Bros '64 Ford	494	1,075	Running
6	9	11	Ned Jarrett	Bondy Long '64 Ford	493	800	Running
7	14	5	Jim Paschal	Cotton Owens '64 Dodge	491	890	Running
8	4	43	Richard Petty	Petty Eng '64 Plymouth	489	675	Running
9	6	4	Rex White	Bud Moore '64 Mercury	488	650	Running
10	10	1	Billy Wade	Bud Moore '64 Mercury	485	500	Running
11	20	71	LeeRoy Yarbrough	Roscoe Sanders '63 Plym	482	450	Running
12	19	19	Cale Yarborough	Herman Beam '63 Ford	477	400	Running
13	23	64	Curtis Crider	Crider '63 Mercury	465	350	Running
14	28	40	Bud Harless	'62 Pontiac	461	275	Running
15	8	3	Junior Johnson	Ray Fox '64 Dodge	461	250	Trans
16	26	81	John Sears	John Black '63 Dodge	459	300	Running
17	30	92	Jack Anderson	Ray Osborne '63 Ford	440	275	Running
18	21	32	Tiny Lund	Graham Shaw '63 Ford	423	250	Rear End
19	31	34	Wendell Scott	Scott '62 Chevrolet	422	275	Running
20	12	54	Jimmy Pardue	Burton-Robinson '64 Plym	418	250	Rear End
21	24	60	Doug Cooper	Bob Cooper '63 Ford	365	250	Running
22	7	16	Darel Dieringer	Bill Stroppe '64 Mercury	336	250	Clutch
23	33	31	Ralph Earnhardt	Tom Spell '63 Ford	242	275	Engine
24	22	82	Bill McMahan	Casper Hensley '63 Pontiac	203	250	Oil Pres
25	35	78	Buddy Arrington	Arrington '63 Dodge	170	250	Gas Leak
26	16	27	Larry Thomas	'63 Dodge	161	275	Crash
27	17	26	Bobby Isaac	Ray Nichels '64 Dodge	110	275	Rear End
28	15	6	David Pearson	Cotton Owens '64 Dodge	102	275	Trans
29	25	25	Buddy Baker	'63 Ford	69	250	Engine
30	18	49	G C Spencer	'64 Chevrolet	52	350	Engine
31	29	7	E J Trivette	'62 Chevrolet	43	275	Oil Pres
32	5	17	Johnny Allen	Bill Stroppe '64 Mercury	34	275	Engine
33	27	9	Roy Tyner	Tyner '62 Chevrolet	31	285	Engine
34	32	62	John V Hamdy	'63 Mercury	5	275	Rear End
35	34	97	Joe Clark	'64 Ford	5	275	Freeze Pl
36	36	99	Gene Hobby	'62 Dodge	2	250	Flagged

Time of Race: 3 hours, 27 minutes, 46 seconds
Average Speed: 72.196 mph
Pole Winner: Marvin Panch - 80.64 mph
Lap Leaders: Marvin Panch 1-6, Fred Lorenzen 7-500
Cautions: 4 for 54 laps
Margin of Victory: 1/2 lap
Attendance: 26,500

Race No. 10

Lorenzen Blasts Bristol Rivals in Smoky Ford

BRISTOL, TN (Mar 22) -- Fred Lorenzen led 494 of the 500 laps in Bristol International Speedway's Southeastern 500, but had to nurse his smoky Ford across the finish line at 60 mph to beat teammate Fireball Roberts by a half-lap. It was the first win of the season for the flashy Elmhurst, IL speedster.

Paul Goldsmith took third place with Buck Baker and Marvin Panch rounding out the top five.

Clumps of sod fly as Larry Thomas clips outside track in Southeastern 500

Lorenzen passed Panch in the seventh lap and was never headed. There was little suspense for the sell-out crowd of 26,500 until the final 24 laps when smoke began seeping from the undercarriage of the white Ford. "I didn't know if I could make it or not," Lorenzen said afterwards. "It was something in the engine. I had to lower my speed to about 60 mph. When I gave it the gas, it would slow down. I held it at about 4,000 rpm and held it there."

Four cautions for a total of 54 laps held Lorenzen's winning speed to 72.196 mph. Forty-one laps were run under the yellow when Larry Thomas' Dodge broke through the guard rail and slid down a steep embankment. The Thomasville, NC driver escaped unharmed.

Panch, who won the pole at 80.64 mph, extended his point lead to 502 points over Billy Wade in the Grand National point standings.

Lorenzen survived another engine related malfunction earlier in the week when his Beech Bonanza private aircraft blew an engine at 11,000 feet. "I heard the engine go 'ka-pow-wee'," said Lorenzen. When I heard the engine go, I backed off -- just like in a stock car. I made it to Chicago, though. It was a close call."

Race No. 11

Pearson Wins Greenville; Hutcherson Arrives

GREENVILLE, SC (Mar 28) -- David Pearson throttled his Dodge past Ned Jarrett 23 laps from the finish and won the 100-miler at Greenville-Pickens Speedway. It was the second win of the year for the 29 year-old driver.

Jarrett, who led twice for 89 laps, came in second a quarter lap behind. Marvin Panch finished third, LeeRoy Yarbrough fourth and Tiny Lund fifth.

Dick Hutcherson of Keokuk, IA, a former IMCA champion, was a surprise entry and he put his Ford on the pole. However, failure of lug bolts on his right front wheel forced him to the pits after his 109th lap. He led the first 60 laps before Richard Petty moved into

Grand National Race No. 11
200 Laps at Greenville-Pickens Speedway
Greenville, SC
100 Miles on Half-mile Dirt Track
March 28, 1964

Fin	St	No.	Driver	Team / Car	Laps	Money	Status
1	9	6	David Pearson	Cotton Owens '64 Dodge	200	$1,100	Running
2	3	11	Ned Jarrett	Bondy Long '64 Ford	200	700	Running
3	10	21	Marvin Panch	Wood Bros '64 Ford	200	450	Running
4	2	45	LeeRoy Yarbrough	Louie Weathersby '63 Plym	197	300	Running
5	20	19	Tiny Lund	Herman Beam '63 Ford	196	275	Running
6	17	81	John Sears	John Black '63 Dodge	196	240	Running
7	16	41	Maurice Petty	Petty Eng '63 Plymouth	195	200	Running
8	19	62	Curtis Crider	Crider '63 Mercury	190	175	Running
9	11	75	Elmo Henderson	'62 Pontiac	190	150	Running
10	8	5	Jim Paschal	Cotton Owens '64 Dodge	189	150	Air Clean
11	14	82	Bill McMahan	Casper Hensley '63 Pontiac	184	130	Running
12	18	86	Neil Castles	Buck Baker '62 Chrysler	183	120	Running
13	12	34	Wendell Scott	Scott '62 Chevrolet	151	110	Spindle
14	13	78	Buddy Arrington	Arrington '63 Dodge	136	100	Tie Rod
15	1	1	Dick Hutcherson	'64 Ford	109	100	Lug bolts
16	7	43	Richard Petty	Petty Eng '64 Plymouth	87	100	Rear End
17	4	54	Jimmy Pardue	Burton-Robinson '64 Plym	80	100	Rear End
18	5	31	Ralph Earnhardt	Tom Spell '63 Ford	69	100	Rear End
19	21	9	Roy Tyner	Tyner '62 Chevrolet	34	100	Battery
20	15	18	Stick Elliott	Toy Bolton '62 Pontiac	19	100	Coil
21	22	60	Doug Cooper	Bob Cooper '63 Ford	4	100	Rear End
22	6	98	Graham Shaw	Shaw '63 Ford	1	100	Bearing

Time of Race: 1 hour, 44 minutes, 15 seconds
Average Speed: 57.554 mph
Pole Winner: Dick Hutcherson - 66.74 mph
Lap Leaders: Dick Hutcherson 1-60, Richard Petty 61-87, Ned Jarrett 88-115, David Pearson 116, Jarrett 117-177, David Pearson 178-200
Cautions: 4
Margin of Victory 1/4 lap
Attendance: 6,000

the lead. Petty led until the 87th lap when his Plymouth suffered rear end failure. Jarrett picked up first place and led virtually all the way until the final 23 laps.

Time trials on the half-mile dirt track provided more surprises than Hutcherson's pole. Yarbrough put a lightly regarded Louie Weathersby Plymouth on the outside of the front row. Ralph Earnhardt was fifth fastest, and Graham Shaw, wealthy sports car enthusiast, qualified sixth. Shaw, who had said he would "purchase" Ford factory backing if necessary, fell out after one lap with engine problems.

native.

Ned Jarrett chased Panch all afternoon, but had to settle for second. Richard Petty came in third, Jim Paschal was fourth and David Pearson fifth.

Only 3,323 spectators braved the icy winds on a day when the temperatures only got up to 40 degrees.

It was the first time Panch had driven on a quarter-mile oval since 1956. "I tried to get Glen (Wood, car owner) to drive the car, but he wouldn't do it," said Panch. "He would have done better than I did. He would have lapped the field at least once.."

Panch averaged 47.796 mph in an event uninterrupted by the caution flag. His point lead grew to 1,270 over Billy Wade who was not entered.

Junior Johnson started fifth in a Dodge but broke an axle after 121 laps and retired. The rumor mill was saying that Johnson is disgusted with the Dodge cars and is itching for a change.

Grand National Race No. 12
200 Laps at Bowman-Gray Stadium
Winston-Salem, NC
50 Miles on Quarter-mile Paved Track
March 30, 1964

Fin	St	No.	Driver	Team / Car	Laps	Money	Status
1	1	21	Marvin Panch	Wood Bros '64 Ford	200	$820	Running
2	2	11	Ned Jarrett	Bondy Long '64 Ford	200	530	Running
3	3	43	Richard Petty	Petty Eng '64 Plymouth	199	425	Running
4	8	5	Jim Paschal	Cotton Owens '64 Dodge	198	325	Running
5	6	6	David Pearson	Cotton Owens '64 Dodge	197	290	Running
6	10	54	Jimmy Pardue	Burton-Robinson '64 Plym	192	290	Running
7	12	81	John Sears	John Black '63 Dodge	190	215	Running
8	9	12	Fred Harb	Harb '61 Pontiac	188	180	Running
9	7	36	Larry Thomas	Wade Younts '62 Dodge	183	200	Running
10	16	86	Neil Castles	Buck Baker '62 Chrysler	182	140	Running
11	14	99	Gene Hobby	'62 Dodge	172	130	Running
12	13	34	Wendell Scott	Scott '62 Chevrolet	137	120	Trans
13	5	3	Junior Johnson	Ray Fox '64 Dodge	121	140	Axle
14	11	62	Curtis Crider	Crider '63 Mercury	106	115	Rear End
15	4	2	Ken Rush	Cliff Stewart '63 Pontiac	76	120	Engine
16	15	9	Roy Tyner	Tyner '62 Chevrolet	32	100	H Gasket

Time of Race: 1 hour, 02 minutes, 46 seconds
Average Speed: 47.796 mph
Pole Winner: Marvin Panch - 49.83 mph
Lap Leaders: Marvin Panch 1-200
Cautions: None
Margin of Victory: 3/4 lap
Attendance: 3,323

Race No. 12

Panch Start-to-Finish in Easter Monday 50-miler

WINSTON-SALEM, NC (Mar 30) -- Point leader Marvin Panch became the season's 10th different winner by leading all the way in the chilly Easter Monday 50-mile Grand National race at Bowman-Gray Stadium. It was the 10th career victory for the California

Race No. 13

Magician Lorenzen Wins Tire-popping Atlanta 500

HAMPTON, GA (Apr 5) -- Fred Lorenzen pulled a disappearing act and ran away from the field to win the fifth annual Atlanta 500 before 50,000 shivering fans at Atlanta International Raceway. It was the 13th career win for 'Fearless Freddy' and his sixth on a superspeedway.

Fred Lorenzen leads Fireball Roberts down the front chute at Atlanta

*Richard Petty and Paul Goldsmith duel in
Atlanta 500*

Lorenzen drove his Holman-Moody Ford around
Bobby Isaac's Dodge in the 167th lap and sped to a
two-lap victory on the 1.5-mile oval. Isaac came in second with Ned Jarrett third. Junior Johnson was fourth
despite rumors that he would be fired from Dodge after
the race. Fifth place went to Buck Baker.

Johnson had claimed his Ray Fox-led Dodge team
"can't get the good engines and parts that the other
Chrysler teams are getting", and it was reported that the
MoPar executives didn't much care for Johnson's re-
marks. Johnson drove the car less than 100 laps, and
USAC driver Jim Hurtubise carried it to the finish.

Four caution flags for 19 laps failed to keep Lorenzen from setting a record 134.137 mph for the 500
miles. Paul Goldsmith jumped past Lorenzen at the
start and led the first 55 laps. While leading, a tire exploded on Goldsmith's Plymouth. He climbed the wall
and flipped -- sliding through the third turn upside
down. Lorenzen scooted into the lead, narrowly missing the errant car of Goldsmith. "He nearly came down
right on top of me," Lorenzen said later. "I thought I
was a goner."

*Paul Goldsmith's Plymouth skids on its roof as
Fred Lorenzen #28 scoots by at Atlanta*

It was a tough day for car owners. Bill Stroppe, for
example, entered 4 factory-backed Mercurys -- all driv-
en by nationally known drivers. Two were casualties of
blown engines while the other two were destroyed in
crashes.

David Pearson and Fireball Roberts were eliminated in another crash. A tire blew on Pearson's Dodge
and he shot into Roberts and the wall. Blown tires also
caused Jimmy Pardue and Darel Dieringer to crash.

Grand National Race No. 13
334 Laps at Atlanta International Raceway
Hampton, GA
"Atlanta 500"
500 Miles on 1.5-mile Paved Track
April 5, 1964

Fin	St	No.	Driver	Team / Car	Laps	Money	Status
1	1	28	Fred Lorenzen	Holman-Moody '64 Ford	334	$18,000	Running
2	6	26	Bobby Isaac	Ray Nichels '64 Dodge	332	8,065	Running
3	18	11	Ned Jarrett	Bondy Long '64 Ford	331	4,500	Running
4	9	3	* Junior Johnson	Ray Fox '64 Dodge	330	2,925	Running
5	14	41	Buck Baker	Petty Eng '64 Plymouth	327	1,850	Running
6	22	35	Tiny Lund	'64 Plymouth	326	1,275	Running
7	8	43	Richard Petty	Petty Eng '64 Plymouth	325	1,100	Running
8	24	5	Jim Paschal	Cotton Owens '64 Dodge	315	1,050	Running
9	28	82	Bill McMahan	Casper Hensley '63 Pontiac	279	925	Running
10	30	95	Ken Spikes	Spikes '64 Dodge	269	925	Running
11	2	00	A J Foyt	Banjo Matthews '64 Ford	246	775	Engine
12	5	1	Billy Wade	Bud Moore '64 Mercury	225	750	Engine
13	26	66	Bay Darnell	Holman-Moody '64 Ford	205	625	Push Rod
14	12	21	Marvin Panch	Wood Bros '64 Ford	190	755	Engine
15	16	14	Jim McElrath	Bill Stroppe '64 Mercury	173	500	Engine
16	19	17	Dave MacDonald	Bill Stroppe '64 Mercury	150	500	Engine
17	23	7	Bobby Johns	Shorty Johns '64 Pontiac	149	600	H Gasket
18	15	01	Rex White	Bud Moore '64 Mercury	119	550	Engine
19	10	06	Larry Frank	Holman-Moody '64 Ford	110	500	A Frame
20	4	22	Fireball Roberts	Holman-Moody '64 Ford	107	640	Crash
21	20	6	David Pearson	Cotton Owens '64 Dodge	106	550	Crash
22	29	89	LeeRoy Yarbrough	David Walker '64 Plymouth	78	650	Engine
23	21	2	Jim Hurtubise	Norm Nelson '64 Plymouth	77	585	Rear End
24	37	92	Cale Yarborough	Ray Osborne '64 Ford	74	540	Gas leak
25	25	49	G C Spencer	Spencer '64 Chevrolet	73	525	Rock arm
26	33	62	Curtis Crider	Crider '63 Mercury	60	580	Heating
27	31	52	E J Trivette	Jess Potter '62 Chevrolet	58	600	Rear End
28	34	9	Roy Tyner	Tyner '62 Chevrolet	58	570	Rear End
29	3	25	Paul Goldsmith	Ray Nichels '64 Plymouth	55	1,075	Crash
30	38	02	Roy Mayne	Curtis Crider '63 Mercury	42	530	Handling
31	17	16	Darel Dieringer	Bill Stroppe '64 Mercury	41	500	Crash
32	27	36	Larry Thomas	Wade Younts '63 Plymouth	31	525	Ignition
33	36	20	Jack Anderson	'63 Ford	26	550	Ignition
34	32	88	Jimmie Helms	Buck Baker '62 Chrysler	22	590	Rear End
35	13	54	Jimmy Pardue	Burton-Robinson '64 Plym	19	525	Crash
36	11	12	Dan Gurney	Wood Bros '64 Ford	17	550	Crash
37	7	15	Parnelli Jones	Bill Stroppe '64 Mercury	17	450	Crash
38	40	97	Joe Clark	'64 Ford	3	475	A Frame
39	39	86	Neil Castles	Buck Baker '62 Chrysler	2	475	Handling

* Relieved by Jim Hurtubise

Time of Race: 3 hours, 46 minutes, 05 seconds

Average Speed: 134.137 mph

Pole Winner: Fred Lorenzen - 146.470 mph

Lap Leaders: Paul Goldsmith 1-55, Fireball Roberts 56-58, Jim Hurtubise 59-60,
    Marvin Panch 61-91, Lorenzen 92-112, Bobby Isaac 113, Lorenzen 114-129,
    Isaac 130-149, Lorenzen 150, Isaac 151-166, Lorenzen 167-334

Cautions: 4 for 19 laps

Margin of Victory: 2 laps plus

Attendance: 50,000

Only 10 cars in the starting field of 39 finished. Tenth place in the final order went to rookie Ken Spikes, trailing the winner by 65 laps.

The lead changed hands 11 times with Lorenzen on top for a total of 216 laps.

A.J. Foyt established a NASCAR precedent by turning three of his four qualifying laps at an identical 145.945 mph.

Grand National Race No. 14
200 Laps at Asheville-Weaverville Speedway
Weaverville, NC
100 Miles on Half-mile Paved Track
April 11, 1964

Fin	St	No.	Driver	Team / Car	Laps	Money	Status
1	2	21	Marvin Panch	Wood Bros '64 Ford	200	$1,150	Running
2	6	3	Junior Johnson	Ray Fox '64 Dodge	199	700	Running
3	2	1	Billy Wade	Bud Moore '64 Mercury	199	450	Running
4	5	6	David Pearson	Cotton Owens '64 Dodge	198	300	Running
5	7	54	Jimmy Pardue	Burton-Robinson '64 Plym	198	275	Running
6	9	41	Maurice Petty	Petty Eng '63 Plymouth	196	240	Running
7	8	2	Ken Rush	Cliff Stewart '63 Pontiac	192	200	Running
8	12	45	LeeRoy Yarbrough	Louie Weathersby '63 Plymo	188	175	Running
9	11	36	Larry Thomas	Wade Younts '62 Dodge	187	150	Running
10	15	02	Curtis Crider	Crider '63 Mercury	187	140	Running
11	14	82	Bill McMahan	Casper Hensley '63 Pontiac	187	130	Running
12	16	01	Bob Cooper	Curtis Crider '63 Mercury	185	120	Running
13	19	34	Wendell Scott	Scott '62 Chevrolet	178	110	Running
14	20	56	Ken Anderson	'62 Chevrolet	176	100	Running
15	17	91	E J Trivette	'62 Chevrolet	170	100	Running
16	3	11	Ned Jarrett	Bondy Long '64 Ford	159	100	Engine
17	4	43	Richard Petty	Petty Eng '64 Plymouth	146	100	Rear End
18	10	19	Cale Yarborough	Herman Beam '64 Ford	79	100	Engine
19	21	9	Roy Tyner	Tyner '62 Chevrolet	79	100	Piston
20	24	86	Jimmy Helms	Buck Baker '62 Chrysler	69	100	Heating
21	18	75	Elmo Henderson	'62 Pontiac	61	100	Lug bolts
22	23	88	Neil Castles	Buck Baker '62 Chrysler	49	100	Ignition
23	22	18	Stick Elliott	Toy Bolton '62 Pontiac	28	---	Heating
24	13	20	Jack Anderson	'63 Ford	24	---	Engine

Time of Race: 1 hour, 13 minutes, 28 seconds
Average Speed: 81.669 mph
Pole Winner: Marvin Panch - 84.905 mph
Lap Leaders: Marvin Panch 1-200
Cautions: None
Margin of Victory: 1 lap plus
Attendance: 7,000

Race No. 14

Panch Sets Record with Weaverville 100 Win

WEAVERVILLE, NC (Apr 11) -- Marvin Panch set a world's record for a 100 mile race on a half-mile track with a flag-to-flag triumph in the 200 lapper at Asheville-Weaverville Speedway. Panch's Wood Brothers Ford was flagged at a speed of 81.669 mph in the caution free event. It was the second time in the 1964 season that Panch has led a race from start to finish.

Marvin Panch - winner at Weaverville

Junior Johnson enjoyed his best outing since Daytona by taking second place, a lap behind. Billy Wade was third, David Pearson fourth and Jimmy Pardue fifth.

A crowd of 7,000 filled the grandstands of the little mountain village's main claim to fame and watched Panch pocket $1,150 for his effortless ride. He increased his point lead to 1,204 over Mercury driver Wade.

Fifteen cars in the starting field of 24 were running at the finish. Ned Jarrett and Richard Petty, who started in the second row, went out with mechanical problems and did not finish.

Race No. 15

Pearson Beats Independents In Joe Weatherly Memorial

HILLSBORO, NC (Apr 12) -- David Pearson rolled his Cotton Owens Dodge past Richard Petty in the 53rd lap and went on to win the Joe Weatherly Memorial 150 at Orange Speedway.

It was the third win of the season for the Spartanburg, SC driver.

Dick Hutcherson, IMCA stock car champ, wound up second, three laps behind the fleet Pearson. Larry Thomas enjoyed his best career finish by taking third. Ralph Earnhardt was fourth and Bobby Keck fifth as independents had a good pay day.

The 167 lap contest on the .9-mile dirt oval was named in honor of the two-time Grand National champion, who won his final race here on October 27, 1963 in a Bud Moore Pontiac. Oddly, Moore did not enter a car in this event, despite the fact that his driver, Billy Wade, was holding down second place in the point standings.

Twenty-seven cars started the race but only nine finished. Petty was running second when clutch failure sidelined his Plymouth on lap 117. Ignition problems put Junior Johnson out, and Ned Jarrett was sidelined with rear gearing failure.

Pearson averaged 83.319 mph for his sixth career Grand National win.

Grand National Race No. 15
167 Laps at Orange Speedway
Hillsboro, NC
"Joe Weatherly Memorial 150"
150 Miles on .9-mile Dirt Track
April 12, 1964

Fin	St	No.	Driver	Team / Car	Laps	Money	Status
1	1	6	David Pearson	Cotton Owens '64 Dodge	167	$1,400	Running
2	7	1	Dick Hutcherson	'64 Ford	164	1,100	Running
3	11	36	Larry Thomas	Wade Younts '62 Dodge	160	700	Running
4	26	31	Ralph Earnhardt	Tom Spell '63 Ford	160	575	Running
5	19	23	Bobby Keck	Leland Colvin '63 Ford	155	425	Running
6	12	02	Curtis Crider	Crider '63 Mercury	155	325	Running
7	14	34	Wendell Scott	Scott '62 Chevrolet	152	275	Running
8	23	83	Worth McMillion	McMillion '62 Pontiac	143	225	Running
9	3	3	Junior Johnson	Ray Fox '64 Dodge	131	200	Ignition
10	22	86	Neil Castles	Buck Baker '62 Chrysler	127	175	Con Rod
11	13	66	Elmo Langley	Ratus Walters '63 Ford	119	100	Engine
12	2	43	Richard Petty	Petty '64 Plymouth	117	100	Clutch
13	15	78	Buddy Arrington	Arrington '63 Dodge	106	100	Running
14	18	45	LeeRoy Yarbrough	Louie Weathersby '63 Plym	102	100	Heating
15	17	99	Gene Hobby	'62 Dodge	101	100	Trans
16	16	01	Bob Cooper	Curtis Crider '63 Mercury	78	100	Heating
17	4	21	Marvin Panch	Wood Bros '64 Ford	75	100	Heating
18	10	98	Tiny Lund	Graham Shaw '64 Ford	72	100	Gas Leak
19	24	81	John Sears	John Black '62 Dodge	72	100	Axle
20	5	11	Ned Jarrett	Bondy Long '64 Ford	64	100	Rear End
21	9	2	Doug Yates	'63 Plymouth	62	100	Heating
22	8	41	Maurice Petty	Petty Eng '63 Plymouth	55	100	Trans
23	25	92	Buddy Baker	Ray Osborne '64 Ford	43	100	Engine
24	6	54	Jimmy Pardue	Burton-Robinson '64 Plym	27	100	Drive Sh
25	21	9	Roy Tyner	Tyner '62 Chevrolet	20	---	R Housing
26	20	33	Roy Mayne	C L Kilpatrick '72 Chevrolet	13	---	Heating
27	27	19	Larry Frank	Herman Beam '62 Ford	12	---	Heating

Time of Race: 1 hour, 48 minutes, 14 seconds
Average Speed: 83.319 mph
Pole Winner: David Pearson - 99.784 mph
Lap Leaders: David Pearson 1, Richard Petty 2-52, Pearson 53-167
Cautions:
Margin of Victory: 3 laps plus
Attendance:

Race No. 16

Jarrett Noses Out Panch In Spartanburg 100

SPARTANBURG, SC (Apr 14) -- Ned Jarrett and his Bondy Long Ford whistled past Billy Wade in the 162nd lap and held off Marvin Panch in a late race battle to win the 100-mile Grand National race at the Piedmont Interstate Fairgrounds. It was his second win of the year.

Panch finished a close second -- 1.35 seconds behind Jarrett's dark blue Ford. David Pearson was a distant third with Ken Rush fourth and Elmo Henderson fifth.

Wade got sixth place money when his Mercury developed rear end problems in the closing laps.

Dick Hutcherson started on the pole and led the first 15 laps. Wade took over on lap 16 and held first place until Jarrett made the decisive pass.

Hutcherson's Ford went out on lap 121 with a broken wheel bearing. Richard Petty qualified third but encountered rear end problems on lap 83. Ralph Earnhardt's Ford was an early retiree with overheating troubles.

Three caution flags held Jarrett's average speed to 58.852 mph. Panch continued to hold the point lead with a cushion of 1,448 points over Wade.

Grand National Race No. 16
200 Laps at Piedmont Interstate
Fairgrounds
Spartanburg, SC
100 Miles on Half-mile Dirt Track
April 14, 1964

Fin	St	No.	Driver	Team / Car	Laps	Money	Status
1	4	11	Ned Jarrett	Bondy Long '64 Ford	200	$1,150	Running
2	5	21	Marvin Panch	Wood Bros '64 Ford	200	700	Running
3	6	6	David Pearson	Cotton Owens '64 Dodge	197	400	Running
4	9	2	Ken Rush	Cliff Stewart '63 Pontiac	195	300	Running
5	10	75	Elmo Henderson	'62 Pontiac	191	275	Running
6	2	1	Billy Wade	Bud Moore '64 Mercury	185	240	R Housing
7	16	86	Neil Castles	Buck Baker '62 Chrysler	184	200	Running
8	17	87	Buddy Baker	J C Parker '63 Dodge	183	175	Running
9	12	34	Wendell Scott	Scott '62 Chevrolet	173	150	Running
10	19	91	E J Trivette	'62 Chevrolet	168	140	Running
11	15	23	Bobby Keck	'63 Ford	163	130	Running
12	7	54	Jimmy Pardue	Burton-Robinson '64 Plym	146	120	Axle
13	1	7	Dick Hutcherson	'64 Ford	121	110	W Bearing
14	8	45	LeeRoy Yarbrough	Louie Weathersby '63 Plym	95	100	Ignition
15	3	43	Richard Petty	Petty Eng '64 Plymouth	83	100	Rear End
16	11	31	Ralph Earnhardt	Tom Spell '63 Ford	24	100	Heating
17	14	01	Bob Cooper	Curtis Crider '63 Mercury	23	100	Heating
18	12	02	Curtis Crider	Crider '63 Mercury	10	100	Crash
19	18	18	Stick Elliott	Toy Bolton '62 Pontiac	9	100	H Gasket

Time of Race: 1 hour, 41 minutes, 57 seconds
Average Speed: 58.852 mph
Pole Winner: Dick Hutcherson - 69.044 mph
Lap Leaders: Dick Hutcherson 1-15, Billy Wade 16-161, Ned Jarrett 162-200
Cautions: 3
Margin of Victory: 1.35 seconds
Attendance: 6,500

Race No. 17

Jarrett's Comeback Nets Victory in Columbia 200

COLUMBIA, SC (Apr 16) -- Ned Jarrett recovered from an early mishap, fell a lap behind then ran down the field to win the Columbia 200 at Columbia Speedway. It was Jarrett's 25th career win in Grand National competition.

David Pearson led the first 18 laps from the pole position. Jarrett brought out the first of six caution flags when his Ford broke loose and rapped the inside pit wall. Repairs were made and he went back out on the track running 19th. However, the Newton, NC driver masterfully picked off every car in the field and moved past Billy Wade in the 137th lap. He then proceeded to lap the field.

Marvin Panch finished second with LeeRoy Yarbrough third. Wade came in fourth and Dick Hutcherson fifth.

Tiny Lund took the lead from Pearson when Jarrett spun early. The Cross, SC driver put his Graham Shaw Ford on the point until lap 32 when overheating problems ended his bid for an upset win. Yarbrough, Pearson and Wade battled for first place until Jarrett zipped by for good.

For the fifth straight short track race, Richard Petty failed to finish. A faulty rear end forced his Plymouth out after 129 laps, but he still held on to third place in the Grand National point standings.

Grand National Race No. 17
200 Laps at Columbia Speedway
Columbia, SC
"Columbia 200"
100 Miles on Half-mile Dirt Track
April 16, 1964

Fin	St	No.	Driver	Team / Car	Laps	Money	Status
1	2	11	Ned Jarrett	Bondy Long '64 Ford	200	$1,150	Running
2	6	21	Marvin Panch	Wood Bros '64 Ford	199	700	Running
3	5	45	LeeRoy Yarbrough	Louie Weathersby '63 Plym	198	400	Running
4	4	1	Billy Wade	Bud Moore '64 Mercury	198	300	Running
5	8	7	Dick Hutcherson	'64 Ford	198	275	Running
6	1	6	David Pearson	Cotton Owens '64 Dodge	198	240	Running
7	14	75	Elmo Henderson	'62 Pontiac	193	200	Running
8	16	54	Jimmy Pardue	Burton-Robinson '64 Plym	190	175	Rear End
9	17	01	Curtis Crider	Crider '63 Mercury	190	150	Running
10	12	23	Bobby Keck	'63 Ford	188	140	Running
11	11	31	Ralph Earnhardt	Tom Spell '63 Ford	188	130	Running
12	18	2	Ken Rush	Cliff Stewart '63 Pontiac	187	120	Running
13	13	91	E J Trivette	'62 Chevrolet	186	110	Running
14	15	34	Wendell Scott	Scott '62 Chevrolet	180	100	Running
15	3	43	Richard Petty	Petty Eng '64 Plymouth	129	100	Rear End
16	10	81	John Sears	John Black '62 Dodge	95	100	Trans
17	20	86	Neil Castles	Buck Baker '62 Chrysler	48	100	Brakes
18	9	79	Larry Frank	Speedy Spiers '62 Ford	35	100	Heating
19	7	98	Tiny Lund	Graham Shaw '64 Ford	32	100	Heating
20	19	18	Stick Elliott	Toy Bolton '62 Ford	13	100	Radiator
21	21	87	Buddy Baker	J C Parker '63 Dodge	1	100	Shift
22	22	88	Jimmy Helms	Buck Baker '62 Chrysler	0	100	Carb

Time of Race: 1 hour, 33 minutes, 09 seconds
Average Speed: 64.412 mph
Pole Winner: David Pearson - 71.485 mph
Lap Leaders: David Pearson 1-18, Tiny Lund 19-32, LeeRoy Yarbrough 33-57, Pearson 58-74, Billy Wade 75-136, Ned Jarrett 137-200
Cautions: 6 for 14 laps
Margin of Victory: 1 lap plus
Attendance:

Race No. 18

Engine Blows; Freddy Still Wins Wilkesboro 400

NORTH WILKESBORO, NC (Apr 19) -- Fred Lorenzen stumbled across the finish line with a blown engine just ahead of on-rushing Ned Jarrett to win the Gwyn Staley Memorial 400 at North Wilkesboro Speedway. It was his third win of the season and his second with a sputtering engine.

Holman-Moody team quickly services Fred Lorenzen's Ford at North Wilkesboro. Lorenzen won the race

Lorenzen had taken the lead for keeps in the 170th lap of the 400 lap affair and built a solid lead. With five laps to go the engine in his white Ford wheezed and smoke poured from the exhaust pipes. He managed to nurse the car across the finish line 200 yards ahead of the speeding Jarrett just as the engine let go with a big bang. "I couldn't have gone another lap," said Lorenzen. "We had a 250-mile engine in the car -- and no more."

Third place went to point leader Marvin Panch. Junior Johnson came in fourth with Darel Dieringer fifth. Petty teammates Buck Baker and Richard Petty took sixth and seventh.

The lead changed hands only six times and Lorenzen was on top for 368 of the 400 laps on the .625-mile oval. Dieringer, Jarrett and Petty enjoyed brief and small leads, but Lorenzen had the quickest car in the race. Jarrett started last in the 30 car field when he was unable to post a qualifying speed due to engine problems.

The caution flag came out seven times and trackside reporters said there were 13 spin-outs along the first turn which did not bring out the yellow. Lorenzen averaged 81.930 mph before a crowd of 17,000.

Fireball Roberts was unable to start the race. He crashed through the wooden guard rail in time trials and wrecked his Ford beyond repair.

Panch extended his point lead to 1,630 points over Billy Wade who finished eighth.

Grand National Race No. 18
400 Laps at North Wilkesboro Speedway
North Wilkesboro, NC
"Gwyn Staley Memorial"
250 Miles on .625-mile Paved Track
April 19, 1964

Fin	St	No.	Driver	Team / Car	Laps	Money	Status
1	1	28	Fred Lorenzen	Holman-Moody '64 Ford	400	$3,950	Running
2	30	11	Ned Jarrett	Bondy Long '64 Ford	400	1,900	Running
3	3	21	Marvin Panch	Wood Bros '64 Ford	399	1,250	Running
4	6	3	Junior Johnson	Ray Fox '64 Dodge	395	850	Running
5	4	16	Darel Dieringer	Bill Stroppe '64 Mercury	395	625	Running
6	7	41	Buck Baker	Petty Eng '64 Plymouth	393	525	Running
7	2	43	Richard Petty	Petty Eng '64 Plymouth	392	550	Running
8	5	1	Billy Wade	Bud Moore '64 Mercury	390	450	Running
9	13	7	Bobby Johns	Shorty Johns '64 Pontiac	389	375	Running
10	12	5	Jim Paschal	Cotton Owens '64 Dodge	389	325	Running
11	9	6	David Pearson	Cotton Owens '64 Dodge	386	300	Running
12	14	49	G C Spencer	Spencer '64 Chevrolet	382	275	Running
13	8	54	Jimmy Pardue	Burton-Robinson '64 Plym	382	250	Running
14	22	01	Curtis Crider	Crider '63 Mercury	371	200	Running
15	18	82	Bill McMahan	Casper Hensley '62 Pontiac	366	200	Running
16	20	34	Wendell Scott	Scott '62 Chevrolet	365	175	Running
17	17	87	Buddy Baker	J C Parker '63 Dodge	355	200	Running
18	16	78	Buddy Arrington	Arrington '63 Dodge	352	200	Running
19	15	40	Bud Harless	'62 Pontiac	345	200	Running
20	23	88	Neil Castles	Buck Baker '62 Chrysler	342	175	Running
21	21	56	Ken Anderson	'62 Chevrolet	312	150	Brakes
22	26	53	Don Tilley	'63 Ford	240	150	Oil Pres
23	11	19	Cale Yarborough	Herman Beam '64 Ford	220	175	Engine
24	10	36	Larry Thomas	Wade Younts '62 Dodge	158	175	Drive Sh
25	24	23	Bobby Keck	'63 Ford	138	150	Rear End
26	29	77	LeeRoy Yarbrough	'62 Pontiac	69	150	Brakes
27	28	60	Bob Cooper	Cooper '63 Ford	28	150	Crash
28	27	18	Stick Elliott	Toy Bolton '62 Pontiac	4	150	Push Rod
29	25	86	Jimmy Helms	Buck Baker '62 Chrysler	2	150	Heating
30	19	91	E J Trivette	'62 Chevrolet	0	175	Engine
DNS		22	Fireball Roberts	Holman-Moody '64 Ford		75	Crash

Time of Race: 3 hours, 03 minutes, 05 seconds
Average Speed: 81.930 mph
Pole Winner: Fred Lorenzen - 94.024 mph
Lap Leaders: Fred Lorenzen 1-61, Darel Dieringer 62-86, Lorenzen 87-162,
    Ned Jarrett 163-165, Richard Petty 166-169, Lorenzen 170-400
Cautions: 7 for 35 laps
Margin of Victory: 200 yards
Attendance: 17,000

Race No. 19

Lorenzen Mows 'em Down At Martinsville

MARTINSVILLE, VA (Apr 26) -- Fred Lorenzen continued his mastery of the major short track events by leading all but 13 laps of the Virginia 500 at Martinsville Speedway. It was the fourth win in a row for the Elmhurst Express.

In the three 250-mile short track races, Lorenzen has led 1,349 of a possible 1,400 laps. He started on the pole and lost the lead only when he made scheduled pit stops. Marvin Panch was second, a lap behind. Junior Johnson drove a Banjo Matthews Ford into third place -- his first start since quitting the Ray Fox Dodge team. Ned Jarrett finished fourth with Fireball

Clay Earles
Martinsville Speedway Promoter

Roberts fifth.

A crowd of 23,500 watched Lorenzen average a record 70.098 mph for his 15th career victory.

Billy Wade, who entered the race second in the point standings, did not compete. Technical inspectors said car owner Bud Moore would have to make some corrective work on the air scoops. Moore refused to comply and loaded his car up. He left for Spartanburg before the race started. That dropped Wade to fourth in the Grand National standings. Richard Petty moved into second place, 2,040 points behind Panch.

Buck Baker quit as driver of the second Petty Engineering Plymouth a few days before the Virginia 500. Paul Goldsmith was a temporary replacement, but he wrecked the car in practice and did not start.

his Louie Weathersby Plymouth to victory in the Savannah 200 for his first Grand National win. It was the first big league win for both driver and car owner.

Point leader Marvin Panch came in second with Richard Petty third, Buddy Baker fourth and Cale Yarborough fifth.

LeeRoy Yarbrough

Jimmy Pardue of North Wilkesboro, NC, started his Burton-Robinson Plymouth on the pole and took off like a shot at the green flag. The 33 year-old likeable veteran was running away from the field when rear end failure forced him out in the 137th lap.

Yarbrough, of Jacksonville, FL, took over at that point and led the rest of the way. The 25 year-old driver became the 11th different winner in the 1964 Grand National season.

Only 12 cars showed up for the 100-miler on the half-mile dirt track. Eight were running at the finish. Two cars not running at the end were fifth place finisher Yarborough, who stripped the lug nuts of his Herman Beam Ford in the last few laps and Ned Jarrett, who blew his engine after 127 laps and finished last in the rundown.

Grand National Race No. 19
500 Laps at Martinsville Speedway
Martinsville, VA
"Virginia 500"
250 Miles on Half-mile Paved Track
April 26, 1964

Fin	St	No.	Driver	Team / Car	Laps	Money	Status
1	1	28	Fred Lorenzen	Holman-Moody '64 Ford	500	$4,175	Running
2	2	21	Marvin Panch	Wood Bros '64 Ford	499	1,925	Running
3	3	00	Junior Johnson	Banjo Matthews '64 Ford	497	1,250	Running
4	4	11	Ned Jarrett	Bondy Long '64 Ford	495	850	Running
5	20	22	Fireball Roberts	Holman-Moody '64 Ford	494	800	Running
6	6	43	Richard Petty	Petty Eng '64 Plymouth	490	675	Running
7	9	19	Cale Yarborough	Herman Beam '64 Ford	474	575	Running
8	12	36	Larry Thomas	Wade Younts '62 Dodge	470	525	Running
9	17	23	Bobby Keck	'63 Ford	450	425	Running
10	19	34	Wendell Scott	Scott '62 Chevrolety	437	390	Engine
11	31	83	Worth McMillion	McMilion '62 Pontiac	426	325	Running
12	16	20	Jack Anderson	'63 Ford	394	300	Running
13	21	49	G C Spencer	Spencer '64 Chevrolet	389	300	Engine
14	28	09	Roy Mayne	'62 Chevrolet	387	225	Running
15	22	01	Curtis Crider	Crider '63 Mercury	382	235	Running
16	32	56	Ken Anderson	'62 Chevrolet	360	200	Rear End
17	14	72	Doug Yates	Yates '63 Plymouth	355	225	Rear End
18	7	6	David Pearson	Cotton Owens '64 Dodge	317	225	Rear End
19	29	99	Gene Hobby	'62 Dodge	305	200	Running
20	5	16	Darel Dieringer	Bill Stroppe '64 Mercury	275	250	Crash
21	13	5	Jim Paschal	Cotton Owens '64 'Dodge	263	225	Rear End
22	24	87	Buddy Baker	J C Parker '63 Dodge	213	225	Heating
23	18	82	Bill McMahan	Casper Hensley '63 Pontiac	153	225	Oil Pan
24	26	9	Roy Tyner	Tyner '62 Chevrolet	138	225	Trans
25	10	54	Jimmy Pardue	Burton-Robinson '64 Plym	133	225	Rear End
26	30	88	Jimmy Helms	Buck Baker '62 Chrysler	117	175	Heating
27	15	78	Buddy Arrington	Arrington '63 Dodge	74	200	Oil Cooler
28	11	2	Ken Rush	Cliff Stewart '63 Pontiac	50	175	Brakes
29	27	91	E J Trivette	'62 Chevrolet	49	150	Brakes
30	8	7	Bobby Johns	Shorty Johns '64 Pontiac	35	200	Rear End
31	25	86	Neil Castles	Buck Baker '62 Chrysler	2	150	Handling
32	23	40	Bud Harless	'62 Pontiac	2	175	Oil Pres
DNS		1	Billy Wade	Bud Moore '64 Mercury	---	25	Technical

Time of Race: 3 hours, 33 minutes, 59 minutes
Average Speed: 70.098 mph
Pole Winner: Fred Lorenzen - 74.472 mph
Lap Leaders: Fred Lorenzen 1-153, Junior Johnson 154-155, Marvin Panch 156-161,
    Lorenzen 162-431, Panch 432-436, Lorenzen 437-500
Cautions: 2 for 14 laps
Margin of Victory: 1 lap plus
Attendance: 23,500

Race No. 20
Pardue Breaks; LeeRoy Wins First GN Race

SAVANNAH, GA (May 1) -- Daring LeeRoy Yarbrough, a product of the rugged Modified ranks, drove

---

Grand National Race No. 20
200 Laps at Savannah Speedway
Savannah, GA
"Savannah 200"
100 Miles on Half-mile Dirt Track
May 1, 1964

Fin	St	No.	Driver	Team / Car	Laps	Money	Status
1	4	45	LeeRoy Yarbrough	Louie Weathersby '63 Plym	200	$1,000	Running
2	6	21	Marvin Panch	Wood Bros '64 Ford	199	600	Running
3	2	43	Richard Petty	Petty Eng '64 Plymouth	197	400	Running
4	8	87	Buddy Baker	J C Parker '63 Dodge	197	300	Running
5	7	19	Cale Yarborough	Herman Beam '64 Ford	185	275	Lug bolts
6	9	01	Curtis Crider	Crider '63 Mercury	182	240	Running
7	5	6	David Pearson	Cotton Owens '64 Dodge	176	200	Rear End
8	10	71	Andy Buffington	'62 Ford	173	175	Runing
9	11	9	Roy Tyner	Tyner '62 Chevrolet	172	150	Running
10	12	88	Jimmy Helms	Buck Baker '62 Chrysler	152	150	Running
11	1	54	Jimmy Pardue	Burton-Robinson '64 Plym	137	150	Rear End
12	3	11	Ned Jarrett	Bondy Long '64 Ford	127	150	Engine

Time of Race: 1 hour, 25 minutes, 19 seconds
Average Speed: 70.326 mph
Pole Winner: Jimmy Pardue - 73.111 mph
Lap Leaders: Jimmy Pardue 1-137, LeeRoy Yarbrough 138-200
Cautions:
Margin of Victory: 1 lap plus
Attendance:

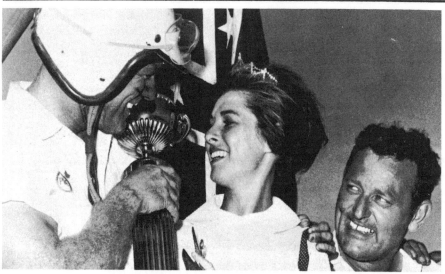

Fred Lorenzen in Rebel 300 victory lane with Nancy Sanders and Herb Nab - chief mechanic.
Nab was fired by John Holman after the race -- then rehired two days later

Race No. 21

Lorenzen's Rebel 300 Win His 5th Straight; Crew Chief Herb Nab Fired

DARLINGTON, SC (May 9) -- Fred Lorenzen passed Richard Petty in the 134th lap and breezed to his fifth straight Grand National win in Darlington Raceway's eighth annual Rebel 300. Lorenzen led a 1-2 sweep for Holman-Moody vehicles as Fireball Roberts came in second. Third place went to Junior Johnson and Ned Jarrett finished fourth -- giving Ford a 1-2-3-4 day. Fifth place went to Plymouth driver Jimmy Pardue.

Herb Nab, crew chief for Lorenzen, was fired by Ford boss John Holman for refusing to obey an order to bring Lorenzen into the pits for a tire change late in the going. "It's my job to see that the Fords win," said Holman. "No matter who is driving them. We were in such good command of the situation that I didn't want to take any chances."

Nab said he didn't feel Lorenzen needed a tire change -- and a late pit stop would mean no better than a second place finish. "I came here to win the race," Nab responded. "None of us on this team came here to run second."

Two days after the firing, Nab was re-hired.

The 300 triumph was Lorenzen's fifth straight finish -- and his fifth straight win. "This streak is fantastic," he beamed in victory lane. "Every time I see the checkered flag I sort of shake my head and marvel. I think to myself, 'now, really, how long can this go on'? Then I answer, 'I hope forever'."

Only one caution flag broke the action. Jim Pas-

Grand National Race No. 21
219 Laps at Darlington Raceway
Darlington, SC
"Rebel 300"
300 Miles on 1.375-mile Paved Track
May 9, 1964

Fin	St	No.	Driver	Team / Car	Laps	Money	Status
1	1	28	Fred Lorenzen	Holman-Moody '64 Ford	219	$10,265	Running
2	5	22	Fireball Roberts	Holman-Moody '64 Ford	219	5,990	Running
3	4	27	Junior Johnson	Banjo Matthews '64 Ford	218	4,510	Running
4	10	11	Ned Jarrett	Bondy Long '64 Ford	216	2,995	Running
5	3	54	Jimmy Pardue	Burton-Robinson '64 Plym	215	2,170	Running
6	6	6	David Pearson	Cotton Owens '64 Dodge	215	1,500	Running
7	18	1	Billy Wade	Bud Moore '64 Mercury	214	1,270	Running
8	14	03	LeeRoy Yarbrough	Ray Fox '64 Dodge	213	1,000	Running
9	20	25	Paul Goldsmith	Ray Nichels '64 Plymouth	212	900	Running
10	2	43	Richard Petty	Petty Eng '64 Plymouth	211	840	Running
11	8	21	Marvin Panch	Wood Bros '64 Ford	211	750	Running
12	7	41	Jim Paschal	Petty Eng '64 Plymouth	209	700	Crash
13	12	16	Johnny Allen	Bill Stroppe '64 Mercury	205	650	Running
14	13	5	Larry Thomas	Cotton Owens '64 Dodge	204	600	Crash
15	22	82	Bunkie Blackburn	Casper Hensley '63 Pontiac	202	550	Running
16	16	49	G C Spencer	Spencer '64 Chevrolet	189	500	Running
17	24	56	J T Putney	'62 Chevrolet	187	450	Running
18	25	95	Ken Spikes	Spikes '64 Plymouth	177	400	Running
19	15	19	Cale Yarborough	Herman Beam '64 Ford	172	350	Running
20	21	89	Tiny Lund	David Walker '64 Plymouth	167	300	Engine
21	9	4	Rex White	Bud Moore '64 Mercury	161	415	H Gasket
22	27	52	E J Trivette	Jess Potter '62 Chevrolet	140	300	Engine
23	23	60	Bob Cooper	Cooper '63 Ford	109	300	Rear End
24	24	09	Roy Mayne	'62 Chevrolet	86	300	Rear End
25	17	14	Darel Dieringer	Bill Stroppe '64 Mercury	81	415	Bearing
26	11	3	Buck Baker	Ray Fox '64 Dodge	59	340	Battery
27	19	26	Bobby Isaac	Ray Nichels '64 Dodge	35	340	Crash
28	26	01	Curtis Crider	Crider '63 Mercury	18	300	Handling
29	25	87	Buddy Baker	J C Parker '63 Dodge	7	300	Trans
30	28	88	Neil Castles	Buck Baker '62 Chrysler	5	300	Oil Pres
31	31	78	Buddy Arrington	Arrington '62 Dodge	4	300	Handling
32	32	86	Jimmy Helms	Buck Baker '62 Chrysler	2	300	Bearing

Time of Race: 2 hours, 18 minutes, 51 seconds
Average Speed: 130.013 mph
Pole Winner: Fred Lorenzen - 135.727 mph
Lap Leaders: Richard Petty 1-57, Fred Lorenzen 58-74, Petty 75-98, Lorenzen 99-101,
    Petty 102-103, Lorenzen 104-106, Petty 107-108, Lorenzen 109-123, Petty 124-133,
    Lorenzen 134-219
Cautions: 1 for 5 laps
Margin of Victory: 1/4 mile
Attendance: 30,000

Bobby Allison got out of a Ray Fox Dodge at Darlington due to lack of experience

chal, back in the Petty Engineering stable, lost an engine and crashed on lap 214. He was running in sixth place.

Bobby Allison, Modified champion out of Miami, FL, was slated to drive one of the two Ray Fox Dodges in the race. But after one practice session, the 26 year-old driver admitted he did not have the experience to attempt to tackle Darlington. LeeRoy Yarbrough, fresh off a win at Savannah, took over for Allison. Buck Baker drove the other car. Yarbrough finished eighth and Baker went out early with ignition problems.

Lorenzen averaged 135.013 mph for his 16th career Grand National win. A crowd of 30,000 was on hand.

Race No. 22

Jarrett Wins Easily In Tidewater 250

HAMPTON, VA (May 15) -- Ned Jarrett drove past David Pearson in the 24th lap and scored a three lap victory in the Tidewater 250 at Langley Field Speedway. It was the fourth win of the season for the 31 year-old Ford driver.

Marvin Panch came in second and Buddy Baker was third. Wendell Scott finished fourth with Curtis Crider fifth. All of the cars in the race were running in separate laps. "It's nice to win by a comfortable margin" said Jarrett. "But it must have been dull for the fans. You race for more than money. It's a real thrill when you've got a battle going for the lead."

Pearson started on the pole and led the first 23 laps. His Dodge was running in second place when the oil pressure dropped, putting him out after 87 laps. Richard Petty blew an engine as the green flag came out and wound up dead last in the 17 car field.

Jarrett averageed 65.300 mph in the caution free event.

Race No. 23

Jarrett Triumphs at Hickory Before 10,000

HICKORY, NC (May 16) -- Ned Jarrett broke a six-year jinx at his former home town track and emerged victorious in the Hickory 250 at Hickory Speedway. It was his fifth win of the 1964 season.

Jarrett pushed his Ford into the lead in the 236th lap

Grand National Race No. 22
250 Laps at Langley Field Speedway
Hampton, VA
"Tidewater 250"
100 Miles on .4-mile Dirt Track
May 15, 1964

Fin	St	No.	Driver	Team / Car	Laps	Money	Status
1	4	11	Ned Jarrett	Bondy Long '64 Ford	250	$1,000	Running
2	7	21	Marvin Panch	Wood Bros '64 Ford	247	600	Running
3	9	87	Buddy Baker	J C Parker '63 Dodge	242	400	Running
4	11	34	Wendell Scott	Scott '63 Ford	240	300	Running
5	12	02	Curtis Crider	Crider '63 Mercury	234	275	Running
6	8	08	Elmo Langley	'63 Ford	228	240	Running
7	10	4	Earl Brooks	'62 Chevrolet	221	200	Running
8	16	83	Worth McMillion	McMillion '62 Pontiac	220	275	Running
9	5	45	LeeRoy Yarbrough	Louie Weathersby '63 Plym	216	150	Running
10	13	88	Neil Castles	Buck Baker '62 Chrysler	204	140	Running
11	6	01	Gene Lovelace	Curtis Crider '63 Mercury	125	130	Ball Jnt
12	1	6	David Pearson	Cotton Owens '64 Dodge	87	120	Oil Pres
13	14	72	Doug Yates	Yates '63 Plymouth	60	110	Brakes
14	3	54	Jimmy Pardue	Burton-Robinson '64 Plym	43	100	Spring
15	17	09	Roy Mayne	'62 Chevrolet	22	100	Rear End
16	2	60	Doug Cooper	Bob Cooper '63 Ford	5	100	Rear End
17	15	43	Richard Petty	Petty Eng '64 Plymouth	1	100	Engine

Time of Race:1 hour, 31 minutes, 53 seconds
Average Speed: 65.300 mph
Pole Winner: David Pearson - 67.542 mph
Lap Leaders: David Pearson 1-23, Ned Jarrett 24-250
Cautions: None
Margin of Victory: 3 laps plus
Attendance:

Grand National Race No. 23
250 Laps at Hickory Speedway
Hickory, NC
"Hickory 250"
100 Miles on .4-mile Dirt Track
May 16, 1964

Fin	St	No.	Driver	Team / Car	Laps	Money	Status
1	2	11	Ned Jarrett	Bondy Long '64 Ford	250	$1,150	Running
2	5	6	David Pearson	Cotton Owens '64 Dodge	249	600	Running
3	9	43	Richard Petty	Petty Eng '64 Plymouth	249	400	Running
4	4	45	LeeRoy Yarbrough	Louie Weathersby '63 Plym	248	300	Running
5	7	87	Buddy Baker	J C Parker '63 Dodge	244	275	Running
6	13	4	Earl Brooks	'62 Chevrolet	230	240	Running
7	18	88	Neil Castles	Buck Baker '62 Chrysler	229	200	Running
8	12	08	Elmo Langley	'63 Ford	227	175	Running
9	14	34	Wendell Scott	Scott '63 Ford	223	150	Running
10	8	60	Doug Cooper	Bob Cooper '63 Frod	217	140	Rear End
11	10	03	Buck Baker	Ray Fox '64 Dodge	190	130	Rear End
12	3	54	Jimmy Pardue	Burton-Robinson '64 Plym	140	120	Rear End
13	6	21	Marvin Panch	Wood Bros '64 Ford	108	110	Piston
14	16	52	E J Trivette	Jess Potter '62 Chevrolet	65	100	Oil Pres
15	11	53	Don Tilley	'63 Ford	35	100	Lug Bolts
16	13	20	Jack Anderson	'63 Ford	18	100	Crash
17	1	28	Junior Johnson	LaFayette '64 Ford	8	100	Gas tank
18	17	86	Jimmy Helms	Buck Baker '62 Chrysler	2	100	Axle

Time of Race: 1 hour, 26 minutes, 30 seconds
Average Speed: 69.364 mph
Pole Winner: Junior Johnson - 76.882 mph
Lap Leaders: Junior Johnson 1-2, Ned Jarrett 3-45, David Pearson 46-136, Jarrett 137-147, Pearson 148-235, Jarrett 236-250
Cautions: 3 for 19 laps
Margin of Victory: 1 lap plus
Attendance: 10,000

when leader David Pearson went to the pits with a flat tire. Pearson got back on the track and finished second, a lap behind. Richard Petty came in third, LeeRoy Yarbrough fourth and Buddy Baker fifth.

Junior Johnson drove the #28 Holman-Moody Ford usually driven by Fred Lorenzen. Johnson started on the pole but pulled into the pits after eight laps with a badly sputtering engine. The pit crew discovered water was in the fuel.

In other news, racing pioneer Bob Flock died in his Atlanta home on May 16 of a heart seizure following a digestive disorder. He was 47 and had won four Grand National races in his career.

Grand National Race No. 24
267 Laps at South Boston Speedway
South Boston, VA
100 Miles on .375-mile Paved Track
May 17, 1964

Fin	St	No.	Driver	Team / Car	Laps	Money	Status
1	7	43	Richard Petty	Petty Eng '63 Plymouth	267	$1,000	Running
2	1	21	Marvin Panch	Wood Bros '64 Ford	267	600	Running
3	4	11	Ned Jarrett	Bondy Long '64 Ford	265	400	Running
4	3	6	David Pearson	Cotton Owens '64 Dodge	260	300	Running
5	10	09	Roy Mayne	'62 Chevrolet	256	275	Running
6	16	02	Curtis Crider	Crider '63 Mercury	251	240	Running
7	8	34	Wendell Scott	Scott '63 Ford	246	200	Running
8	14	83	Worth McMillion	McMillion '62 Pontiac	241	175	Running
9	18	4	Earl Brooks	'62 Chevrolet	240	150	Running
10	11	01	John V Hamby	Curtis Crider '63 Mercury	235	140	Running
11	17	99	Gene Hobby	'62 Plymouth	234	130	Running
12	5	78	Buddy Arrington	Arrington '63 Dodge	214	120	Running
13	2	54	Jimmy Pardue	Burton-Robinson '64 Plym	207	110	Running
14	12	72	Doug Yates	Yates '63 Plymouth	134	100	Axle
15	6	36	Larry Thomas	Wade Younts '63 Dodge	116	100	Filter
16	9	08	Elmo Langley	'63 Ford	42	100	Heating
17	15	88	Neil Castles	Buck Baker '62 Chrysler	23	100	Crash
18	13	87	Buddy Baker	J C Parker '63 dodge	9	100	Clutch

Time of Race: 1 hour, 23 minutes, 23 seconds
Average Spee: 71.957 mph
Pole Winner: Marvin Panch - 80.023 mph
Lap Leaders: Marvin Panch 1-2, Jimmy Pardue 3-17, Ned Jarrett 18-54,
  Richard Petty 55-116, Panch 117-148, Petty 149-267
Cautions: 3 for 14 laps
Margin of Victory: 8 seconds
Attendance: 3,000

Race No. 24

Petty Ends Skid; Outruns Panch for S. Boston Victory

SOUTH BOSTON, VA (May 17) -- The friendly confines of the South Boston Speedway welcomed Richard Petty as he drove his Plymouth to victory in the 100-mile Grand National event. The Randleman, NC driver ended a 15 race losing streak with a narrow win over Ford's Marvin Panch.

Ned Jarrett finished third, David Pearson fourth and Roy Mayne fifth.

Petty credited tires with the difference in winning and losing. Lee Petty had brought a number of tires designed for the Atlanta International Raceway and decided to give them a tryout on the .375-mile paved track in South Boston. "I just figured they would be about right for this track," said Papa Lee. "Nobody else here had any like them -- not even the tire company people."

"We did not have quite as much speed with the tires," said Richard. "But we figured they would make up the differnce by lasting, and they did."

Petty took the lead for the final time in the 149th lap of the 267 lap event. Panch got back on the track a lap behind and gained steadily on Petty, but the laps ran out.

Petty averaged 71.957 mph and beat Panch by 8.0 seconds. It was the 30th career win for the lanky speed artist.

Race No. 25

Jim Paschal Wins World 600; Fireball Badly Burned

CHARLOTTE, NC (May 24) -- Jim Paschal made his return to the Petty Engineering team a successful one by taking the rich World 600 at Charlotte Motor Speedway, an event marred by the fiery crash which left racing great Fireball Roberts near death.

Roberts was severely burned in a seventh lap incident when he spun backwards into the edge of a concrete wall on the backstretch. The 35 year-old Daytona Beach, FL Ford star was trying to miss the spinning cars of Junior Johnson and Ned Jarrett. Roberts' car exploded on impact, flipped and burned. Jarrett jumped out of his flaming car and ran to the aid of Roberts, who had managed to half-free himself on his own. When he recognized Jarrett, Roberts cried out, "My God, Ned, help me! I'm on fire!" The winner of 33 NASCAR Grand National races was airlifted to Charlotte Memorial Hospital where his condition was "extremely critical".

It was Paschal's second start since accepting an

*Ned Jarrett leaps from his burning car after 7th lap World 600 crash. Fireball Roberts'
car is engulfed in flames at right. Roberts died of complications on July 2*

Race No. 26

Yarbrough's Independent Plymouth Outruns Petty's Factory Mount

GREENVILLE, SC (May 30) --
LeeRoy Yarbrough hopped in his Louie
Weathersby independent Plymouth and
outran Richard Petty's factory mount in
a thrilling 100-miler at Greenville-
Pickens Speedway.

Yarbrough of Jacksonville, FL
nosed out Petty by two car lengths.
The finish was so thrilling that the flagman accidentally threw the checkered
flag one lap too early. "It wouldn't have mattered if we
ran that other lap," boasted Yarbrough. "I would have
beat him."

J.T. Putney came in third, two laps behind. Bobby
Keck finished fourth and G.C. Spencer was fifth.

Marvin Panch started on the pole and led early, but
his day ended against the wall in the 179th lap. His
Ford was given credit for 11th place in the field of 22.

Crashes also took out Ned Jarrett, Buddy Baker,
Doug Cooper and Earl Brooks. No injuries were reported.

On another subject, Fireball Roberts, critically
burned six days earlier, was reported to be improving
slightly.

invitation to drive one of Lee Petty's potent Plymouths.
He had quit the team eight months earlier when he was
continually lifted from the saddle for relief drivers. This
time, insiders said, Paschal made an arrangement to
keep the wheel as long as he wanted in each race.

Finishing second was Richard Petty, four laps behind. The Petty Engineering cash awards amounted to
$35,240 for the 1-2 sweep. Rex White came in third
with Fred Lorenzen fourth and Billy Wade fifth. White
and Wade were driving Bud Moore-prepared
Mercurys.

Jimmy Pardue won the pole at 144.346 mph and led
the first 33 laps. A blown engine put the North Wilkesboro, NC native out just before the half-way point.

Attrition took many contenders out of contention.
Lorenzen had worked his way to the front after 189
laps and paced the field for 44 laps around the 1.5-mile
tri-oval. But a series of pit stops dropped him nine laps
off the pace. He made four pit stops within a nine lap
stretch to correct an assortment of maladies from paper
in the carburetor, a flat tire and a misplaced gas cap.

Paschal first appeared in the lead on lap 275 -- and
he never gave it up. Darel Dieringer loomed as Paschal's final threat, but his Bill Stroppe Mercury popped
its engine after 344 laps.

Marvin Panch blew a tire and crashed in the 52nd
lap and lost his point lead. Petty picked up 4,224 points
while Panch only got 176 -- and Petty emerged the
leader by 1,008 points.

Seven cautions for 48 laps held Paschal's winning
speed to 125.772 mph. It was his 19th career win, but
his first on a superspeedway. A crowd of 66,311 was
on hand to view the action.

*LeeRoy Yarbrough won his 2nd race at Greenville.
David Pearson was 10th*

Grand National Race No. 25
400 Laps at Charlotte Motor Speedway
Charlotte, NC
"World 600"
600 miles on 1.5-mile Paved Track
May 24, 1964

Fin	St	No.	Driver	Team / Car	Laps	Money	Status
1	12	41	Jim Paschal	Petty Eng '64 Plymouth	400	$24,785	Running
2	5	43	Richard Petty	Petty Eng '64 Plymouth	396	10,455	Running
3	13	4	Rex White	Bud Moore '64 Mercury	393	8,095	Running
4	2	28	Fred Lorenzen	Holman-Moody '64 Ford	393	6,425	Running
5	14	1	Billy Wade	Bud Moore '64 Mercury	390	4,050	Running
6	33	49	G C Spencer	Spencer '64 Chevrolet	376	2,950	Running
7	31	76	Larry Frank	Frank '63 Ford	364	2,650	Running
8	10	6	David Pearson	Cotton Owens '64 Dodge	363	2,085	Running
9	40	34	Wendell Scott	Scott '63 Ford	359	1,775	Running
10	24	20	Jack Anderson	Anderson '63 Ford	358	1,500	Running
11	26	02	Curtis Crider	Crider '63 Mercury	358	1,450	Running
12	21	46	J T Putney	Walt Hunter '62 Chevrolet	358	1,325	Running
13	7	16	Darel Dieringer	Bill Stroppe '64 Mercury	344	1,250	Engine
14	37	83	Worth McMillion	McMillion '62 Pontiac	340	1,200	Running
15	32	60	Doug Cooper	Bob Cooper '63 Ford	338	1,350	Running
16	41	9	Roy Tyner	R Southerlund '64 Chevrolet	329	925	Running
17	42	68	Bob Derrington	'63 Ford	305	825	Running
18	25	42	Bunkie Blackburn	Casper Hensley '62 Pontiac	255	850	Rear end
19	4	25	Paul Goldsmith	Ray Nichels '64 Plymouth	253	1,915	Engine
20	17	3	Buck Baker	Ray Fox '64 Dodge	238	990	Engine
21	30	82	Bill McMahan	Casper Hensley '64 Pontiac	231	625	Clutch
22	20	95	Ken Spikes	Spikes '64 Plymouth	217	625	Flagged
23	16	5	Larry Thomas	Cotton Owens '64 Dodge	199	600	Axle
24	1	54	Jimmy Pardue	Burton-Robinson '64 Plym	195	1,280	Engine
25	3	26	Bobby Isaac	Ray Nichels '64 Dodge	169	775	Eng Mnt
26	15	03	LeeRoy Yarbrough	Ray Fox '64 Dodge	151	620	Pinion B
27	23	18	Stick Elliott	Toy Bolton '63 Pontiac	137	600	Engine
28	18	19	Cale Yarborough	Herman Beam '64 Ford	117	650	Crash
29	6	21	Marvin Panch	Wood Bros '64 Ford	52	625	Crash
30	28	09	Roy Mayne	'62 Chevrolet	50	625	Oil Leak
31	19	2	Ken Rush	Cliff Stewart '63 Pontiac	28	625	Itnition
32	27	39	Mark Hurley	'63 Ford	11	625	Trans
33	8	11	Ned Jarrett	Bondy Long '64 Ford	7	700	Crash
34	9	27	Junior Johnson	Banjo Matthews '64 Ford	7	700	Crash
35	11	22	Fireball Roberts	Holman-Moody '64 Ford	7	650	Crash
36	22	87	Buddy Bker	J C Parker '63 Dodge	6	625	Heating
37	35	70	Ralph Earnhardt	'62 Pontiac	5	675	Engine
38	36	88	Neil Castles	Buck Baker '62 Chrysler	4	650	Radiator
39	43	86	Jimmy Helms	Buck Baker '62 Chrysler	4	625	Oil Line
40	34	01	Bob Cooper	Curtis Crider '63 Mercury	4	700	Radiator
41	39	40	Bud Harless	'62 Pontiac	3	650	Engine
42	29	64	Elmo Langley	Woodfield '63 Ford	1	625	Engine
43	38	52	E J Trivette	Jess Potter '62 Chevrolet	1	650	Engine
44	44	84	Pete Stewart	'63 Pontiac	1	600	Con Rod

Time of Race: 4 hours, 46 minutes, 14 seconds
Average Speed: 125.772 mph
Fastest Qualifier: Junior Johnson - 145.102 mph
Pole Winner: Jimmy Pardue - 144.346 mph
Lap Leaders: Jimmy Pardue 1-33, Bobby Isaac 34-43, Paul Goldsmith 44-59, LeeRoy Yarbrough 60-66, Goldsmith 67-69, Pardue 70-79, Goldsmith 80-121, Yarbrough 122, David Pearson 123, Buck Baker 124-147, Goldsmith 148-188, Fred Lorenzen 189-232, Goldsmith 233-253, Lorenzen 254-274, Paschal 275-400
Cautions: 7 for 48 laps
Margin of Victory: 4 laps plus
Attendance: 66,311

Race No. 27
Jarrett Takes 6th of Year At Asheville

ASHEVILLE, NC (May 31) -- Ned Jarrett wheeled his dark blue Bondy Long-owned Ford to a two lap

Grand National Race No. 26
200 Laps at Greenville-Pickens Speedway
Greenville, SC
100 Miles on Half-mile Dirt Track
May 30, 1964

Fin	St	No.	Driver	Team / Car	Laps	Money	Status
1	8	45	LeeRoy Yarbrough	Louie Weathersby '63 Plym	199	$1,000	Running
2	4	43	Richard Petty	Petty Eng '63 Plymouth	199	600	Running
3	11	46	J T Putney	Walt Hunter '62 Chevrolet	197	400	Running
4	17	23	Bobby Keck	'63 Ford	197	300	Running
5	16	75	G C Spencer	'62 Pontiac	193	275	Running
6	18	88	Neil Castles	Buck Baker '62 Chrysler	192	240	Running
7	7	78	Buddy Arrington	Arrington '63 Dodge	190	200	Running
8	14	9	Roy Tyner	R Southerlund '64 Chevrolet	190	175	Running
9	3	19	Cale Yarborough	Herman Beam '64 Ford	189	150	Running
10	2	6	David Pearson	Cotton Owens '64 Dodge	187	140	Engine
11	1	21	Marvin Panch	Wood Bros '64 Ford	179	130	Crash
12	21	34	Wendell Scott	Scott '63 Ford	174	120	Running
13	20	4	Earl Brooks	'62 Chevrolet	173	110	Crash
14	6	11	Ned Jarrett	Bondy Long '64 Ford	106	100	Crash
15	13	87	Buddy Baker	J C Parker '63 Dodge	91	100	Crash
16	10	54	Jimmy Pardue	Burton-Robinson '64 Plym	81	100	Rear End
17	5	3	Buck Baker	Ray Fox '64 Dodge	79	100	Tie Rod
18	9	31	Ralph Earnhardt	Tom Spell '63 Ford	75	100	Heating
19	15	01	Curtis Crider	Crider '63 Mercury	37	100	Heating
20	12	60	Doug Cooper	Bob Cooper '64 Ford	5	100	Crash
21	19	02	John V Hamby	Curtis Crider '63 Mercury	3	100	Heating
22	22	86	Jimmy Helms	Buck Baker '62 Chrysler	2	100	Handling

Time of Race: 1 hour, 46 minutes, 05 seconds
Average Speed: 56.559 mph
Pole Winner: Marvin Panch - 68.050 mph
Lap Leaders: - - - - - - - - - - - - - - LeeRoy Yarbrough - 199
Cautions:
Margin of Victory: 2 car lengths
Attendance:

victory in the 100-miler at the New Asheville Speedway. it was the sixth win of the year for the Newton, NC driver.

Richard Petty started on the pole and wound up second. Marvin Panch was third and David Pearson fourth. Fifth place went to spunky Cale Yarborough.

Jimmy Helms was the only victim of a crash. The Salisbury, NC newcomer, who drove a Buck Baker owned Chrysler, wound up in the guard rail after just two laps.

Petty still held the lead in the point standings with a commanding 2,168 point lead over Panch. Billy Wade still ranked third despite missing 12 races and Jarrett was fourth.

Fireball Roberts, in a hospital bed in Charlotte, was 12th in the standings. Dave MacDonald, who died the day before the Indianapolis 500, still ranked 19th although he started only five of the 27 races in the 1964 season.

Grand National Race No. 27
300 Laps at New Asheville Speedway
Asheville, NC
100 Miles on .333-mile Paved Track
May 31, 1964

Fin	St	No.	Driver	Team / Car	Laps	Money	Status
1	2	11	Ned Jarrett	Bondy Long '64 Ford	300	$1,000	Running
2	1	43	Richar Petty	Petty Eng '674 Plymouth	298	600	Running
3	3	21	Marvin Panch	Wood Bros '64 Ford	297	400	Running
4	4	6	David Pearson	Cotton Owens '64 Dodge	293	300	Running
5	5	19	Cale Yarborough	Herman Beam '64 Ford	293	275	Running
6	18	34	Wendell Scott	Scott '63 Ford	286	240	Running
7	9	3	Buck Baker	Ray Fox '64 Dodge	284	200	Running
8	7	75	G C Spencer	'62 Pontiac	283	175	Running
9	8	36	Larry Thomas	Wade Younts '62 Dodge	280	150	Running
10	11	78	Buddy Arrington	Arrington '63 Dodge	277	140	Running
11	14	23	Bobby Keck	'63 Ford	250	130	Running
12	13	01	John V Hamby	Curtis Crider '63 Mercury	238	120	Running
13	15	88	Neil Castles	Buck Baker '62 Chrysler	131	110	Clutch
14	10	02	Curtis Crider	Crider '63 Mercury	123	100	Running
15	6	54	Jimmy Pardue	Burton-Robinson '64 Plym	63	100	Heating
16	19	4	Earl Brooks	'62 Chevrolet	4	100	Handling
17	17	87	Buddy Baker	J C Parker '62 Dodge	4	100	Exhaust
18	16	86	Jimmy Helms	Buck Baker '62 Chrysler	2	100	Crash
19	12	9	Roy Tyner	R Southerlund '64 Chevrolet	1	100	Trans

Time of Race: 1 hour, 30 minutes, 05 seconds
Average Speed: 66.538 mph
Pole Winenr: Richard Petty - 69.889 mph
Lap Leaders:- - - - - - - - - - - - - - Ned Jarrett   -300
Cautions:
Margin of Victory:
Attendance:

Ned Jarrett and wife, Martha, celebrate first superspeedway win in Dixie 400

Three caution flags for a total of 63 laps held Jarrett's speed to 112.535 mph. Forty-seven of those laps were used to clean up the debris from Doug Cooper's frightful crash in the 44th lap. Cooper's Ford blew a tire and sailed into the guard rail, ripping 30 fence posts out of the ground. He sent splinters of wood spiraling off into the heavens. He escaped uninjured.

Bobby Johns, driving a Bud Moore Mercury, blew a tire in the 27th lap and slugged the retaining barrier. He, too, was not hurt in the mishap.

Race No. 28

Southern Gentleman Jarrett First in Dixie 400

HAMPTON, GA (June 7) -- Gentleman Ned Jarrett overcame a poor week of practice and collared his first superspeedway victory in the fifth annual Dixie 400 at Atlanta International Raceway.

The Ford driver took the lead from Rex White in the 241st lap and was in front the final 27 circuits to nail down the $11,500 winner's share of the $56,000 purse. Richard Petty, beset with tire problems, settled for second place over a half lap behind. Paul Goldsmith came in third with Darel Dieringer fourth and White fifth.

White, driving in what would be his final Grand National race, had passed Jarrett in the 232nd lap and was pulling away. However, the engine stalled during his final pit stop and he fell a lap off the pace.

After the race, Bill Stroppe, Dieringer's car owner, withdrew from the NASCAR circuit citing financial reasons. Dieringer moved over to the Bud Moore team, replacing White.

Doug Cooper blew a tire and destroyed the fence at Atlanta

LeeRoy Yarbrough, promising driver out of Jacksonville, FL, had moved up to second place late in the race. However, his Ray Fox Dodge blew two tires at once. The young lad made a miraculous save and went to the pits. He eventually wound up 11th.

Jarrett was anything but optimistic after initial practice sessions. His qualifying speed was good enough for 17th place in the starting grid. "I was pretty appre-

Grand National Race No. 28
267 Laps at Atlanta International Raceway
Hampton, GA
"Dixie 400"
400 Miles on 1.5-mile Paved Track
June 7, 1964

Fin	St	No.	Driver	Team / Car	Laps	Money	Status
1	17	11	Ned Jarrett	Bondy Long '64 Ford	267	$11,500	Running
2	13	43	Richard Petty	Petty Eng '64 Plymouth	267	5,790	Running
3	4	25	Paul Goldsmith	Ray Nichels '64 Plymouth	266	3,530	Running
4	8	16	Darel Dieringer	Bill Stroppe '64 Mercury	266	2,425	Running
5	11	4	Rex White	Bud Moore '64 Mercury	266	2,025	Running
6	5	41	Jim Paschal	Petty Eng '64 Plymouth	266	1,300	Running
7	10	26	Bobby Isaac	Ray Nichels '64 Dodge	266	1,250	Running
8	12	1	Billy Wade	Bud Moore '64 Mercury	264	1,050	Running
9	9	54	Jimmy Pardue	Burton-Robinson '64 Plym	257	1,175	Engine
10	25	10	Larry Thomas	Bernard Alvarez '64 Ford	254	825	Running
11	7	03	LeeRoy Yarbrough	Ray Fox '64 Dodge	254	750	Running
12	24	34	Wendell Scott	Scott '63 Ford	252	675	Running
13	27	32	E J Trivette	'62 Chevrolet	247	600	Running
14	23	95	Ken Spikes	Spikes '64 Dodge	244	600	Running
15	26	02	Curtis Crider	Crider '63 Mercury	244	500	Running
16	20	46	J T Putney	Walt Hunter '62 Chevrolet	242	450	Running
17	30	68	Bob Derrington	'64 Ford	241	425	Running
18	21	42	Bill McMahan	Casper Hensley '63 Pontiac	239	450	Running
19	34	9	Roy Tyner	R Southerlund '64 Chevrolet	234	425	Running
20	6	3	Buck Baker	Ray Fox '64 Dodge	224	500	Rear End
21	28	92	Reb Wickersham	Ray Osborne '64 Ford	186	400	Engine
22	18	82	Bunkie Blackburn	Casper Hensley '64 Pontiac	177	475	Engine
23	2	6	David Pearson	Cotton Owens '64 Dodge	139	675	Trans
24	31	76	Larry Frank	Frank '64 Ford	126	400	Valve
25	22	89	Tiny Lund	David Walker '64 Plymouth	80	475	Rear End
26	19	60	Doug Cooper	Bob Cooper '63 Ford	42	450	Crash
27	1	27	Junior Johnson	Banjo Matthews '64 Ford	37	925	Valve
28	16	7	Bobby Johns	Bud Moore '64 Mercury	27	500	Crash
29	15	21	Marvin Panch	Wood Bros '64 Ford	14	400	Engine
30	14	5	Earl Balmer	Cotton Owens '64 Dodge	12	425	Engine
31	3	28	Fred Lorenzen	Holman-Moody '64 Ford	8	450	Valve
32	29	88	Neil Castles	Buck Baker '62 Chrysler	5	400	Oil Pres
33	32	86	Bob Gray	Buck Baker '62 Chrusler	2	400	Oil Pres
34	33	01	Bob Cooper	Curtis Crider'63 Mercury	2	400	Oil Pres
35	35	49	G C Spencer	Spencer '64 Chevrolet	1	400	Piston

Time of Race: 3 hours, 33 minutes, 32 seconds
Average Speed: 112.535 mph
Fastest Qualifier: Rex White - 146.024 mph
Pole Winner: Junior Johnson 145.906 mph
Lap Leaders: Junior Johnson 1, David Pearson 2-27, Jimmy Pardue 28-44, Buck Baker 45,
  Billy Wade 46, Pearson 47-48, Bobby Isaac 49-88, Marvin Panch 89-90,
  Richard Petty 91-104, Darel Dieringer 105, Petty 106-108, Paul Goldsmith 109-111,
  Petty 112-115, Goldsmith 116,Petty 117-119,Dieringer 120, Petty 121-130,
  Jim Paschal 131-132, Godsmith 133-147, Petty 148-149, Goldsmith 150, Petty 151-152,
  Pardue 153-156, Goldsmith 157, Pardue 158-160, Petty 161, Pardue 162,
  Petty 163-164, Goldsmith 165-168, Petty 169, Pardue 170-173, Baker 174,
  Rex White 175-192, Ned Jarrett 193-231, White 232-240, Jarrett 241-267
Cautions: 3 for 63 laps
Margin of Victory: Half-lap plus
Attendance: 40,000

---

drivers swap the lead 35 times. Petty's lead in the point standings grew to 3,382 points over Billy Wade, who moved past Marvin Panch into second place. Wade finished eighth; Panch 29th.

Race No. 29

Petty Outduels Pearson at Concord; Cale Runs Strong

CONCORD, NC (June 11) -- Richard Petty ran down David Pearson in the 116th lap and went on to win the 100-mile Grand National race at Concord International Speedway. It was the fourth win of the season for the Grand National point leader.

Pearson, who led on two occasions for a total of 100 laps, finished second. Ned Jarrett crossed the finish line in third place with Wendell Scott fourth and Curtis Crider fifth.

Grand National Race No. 29
200 Laps at Concord International Speedway
Concord, NC
100 Miles on Half-mile Dirt Track
June 11, 1964

Fin	St	No.	Driver	Team / Car	Laps	Money	Status
1	1	43	Richard Petty	Petty Eng '64 Plymouth	200	$1,000	Running
2	2	6	David Pearson	Cotton Owens '64 Dodge	200	600	Running
3	4	11	Ned Jarrett	Bondy Long '64 Frod	198	400	Running
4	7	34	Wendell Scott	Scott '63 Ford	191	300	Running
5	14	02	Curtis Crider	Crider '63 Mercury	185	275	Running
6	18	88	Neil Castles	Buck Baker '62 Chrysler	181	240	Running
7	11	23	Bobby Keck	'63 Ford	176	200	Running
8	17	9	Roy Tyner	R Southerlund '64 Chevrolet	175	175	Running
9	15	87	Buddy Baker	J C Parker '63 Dodge	161	150	Steering
10	10	44	Earl Brooks	'62 Chevrolet	158	140	Wheel
11	9	54	Jimmy Pardue	Burton-Robinson '64 Plym	138	130	Rear End
12	8	45	LeeRoy Yarbrough	Louie Weathersby '63 Plym	84	120	Engine
13	5	31	Ralph Earnhardt	Tom Spell '63 Ford	55	110	Engine
14	3	19	Cale Yarborough	Herman Beam '64 Ford	41	100	Heating
15	13	78	Buddy Arrington	Arrington '63 Dodge	29	100	Heating
16	6	2	Ken Rush	Cliff Stewart '63 Pontiac	28	100	Engine
17	12	40	Bud Harless	'62 Pontiac	26	100	Exhaust
18	16	01	John V Hamby	Curtis Crider '63 Mercury	3	100	Trans
19	19	86	Jimmy Helms	Buck Baker '62 Chrysler	1	100	Handling
DNS		3	Buck Baker	Ray Fox '64 Dodge	---	100	Tie Rod

Time of Race: 1 hour, 32 minutes, 14 seconds
Average Speed: 66.352 mph
Pole Winner: Richard Petty - 68.233 mph
Lap Leaders: Richard Petty 1-5, David Pearson 6-31, Cale Yarborough 32-41,
  Pearson 42-115, Petty 116-200
Cautions: 1
Margin of Victory: 1/4 lap
Attendance:

---

hensive about things until the green flag," Jarrett admitted. "I was in a new Ford and it wasn't handling right." But help came from unexpected sources. Fred Lorenzen fell out after only five laps and the Holman-Moody team moved over to Jarrett's pits for the remainder of the day. "When I came in and saw Herb (Nab), Freddy (Lorenzen) and their tires, I knew things were going to be all right," said Jarrett. "I finished the race on Lorenzen's tires."

A crowd, announced at 40,000, watched a dozen

Petty Engineering crew services Richard Petty at Nashville

Cale Yarborough, aspiring youngster out of Timmonsville, SC, qualified the Herman Beam Ford in third spot and dogged Petty and Pearson in the early going. The crowd came to its feet when he muscled his way into the lead in the 32nd lap. Cale was fending off his more famous rivals when overheating problems put him out after 41 laps.

Car owner Beam spoke about his 24 year-old driver after the race. "That boy sure does run a car hard. He might have run it too hard tonight."

One caution flag held Petty's speed to 66.352 mph. Buck Baker crashed his Ray Fox Dodge in practice and was unable to start due to a broken tie-rod.

Petty's lead in the point standings rose to 3,782 over the idle Billy Wade.

Race No. 30

Quick Pit Stop Nets Victory For Petty at Nashville

NASHVILLE, TN (June 14) -- Richard Petty made a quick pit stop for fuel with 58 laps to go and edged David Pearson in the 100-miler at Nashville Fairgrounds Speedway. It was the fifth win of the year for Petty.

Petty and Pearson started on the front row and had

Grand National Race No. 30
200 Laps at Fairgrounds Speedway
Nashville, TN
100 Miles on Half-mile Paved Track
June 14, 1964

Fin	St	No.	Driver	Team / Car	Laps	Money	Status
1	2	43	Richard Petty	Petty Eng '64 Plymouth	200	$1,000	Running
2	1	6	David Pearson	Cotton Owens '64 Dodge	199	600	Running
3	4	3	Buck Baker	Ray Fox '64 Dodge	199	400	Running
4	3	54	Jimmy Pardue	Burton-Robinson '64 Plym	195	300	Running
5	6	49	G C Spencer	Spencer '64 Chevrolet	191	275	Running
6	5	36	Larry Thomas	Wade Younts '63 Dodge	191	240	Running
7	7	34	Wendell Scott	Scott '63 Ford	188	200	Running
8	11	02	Curtis Crider	Crider '63 Mercury	185	175	Running
9	10	42	Bill McMahan	Casper Hensley '63 Pontiac	184	150	Running
10	15	44	Earl Brooks	'62 Chevrolet	178	140	Running
11	8	40	Bud Harless	'62 Pontiac	169	130	Running
12	14	99	Gene Hobby	Hobby '62 Dodge	168	120	Running
13	13	88	Neil Castles	Buck Baker '62 Chrysler	80	110	Axle
14	12	9	Roy Tyner	R Southerlund '64 Chevrolet	79	100	Trans
15	9	87	Buddy Baker	J C Parker '63 Dodge	30	100	Heating
16	16	01	Frank Tanner	Curtis Crider '63 Mercury	2	100	Handling
DNS		11	Ned Jarrett	Bondy Long '64 Ford	---	100	Engine

Time of Race: 1 hour, 18 minutes, 26 seconds
Average Speed: 76.498 mph
Pole Winner: David Pearson - 80.142 mph
Lap Leaders: Richard Petty 1-65, David Pearson 66-138, Petty 139-200
Cautions:
Margin of Victory:
Attendance: 9,000

the race virtually to themselves throughout the 200 lapper on the half-mile paved track. The event came down to a battle of pit crews. Pearson was leading when he whipped down pit road on lap 138. His Cotton Owens pit crew put in eight gallons of fuel and the Spartanburg

Dodge driver was back on the track after 26 seconds. Petty pitted on lap 142 and his Petty Engineering crew added 10 gallons in just 19 seconds.

Car owner Owens admitted the race between pit crews was the difference. "We added eight gallons of gas, but we spilled 10 more gallons on the ground," said Owens.

Buck Baker wound up third with Jimmy Pardue fourth and G.C. Spencer fifth.

Ned Jarrett blew an engine in his Ford in practice and was unable to start the race.

Petty's point lead was upped to 4,182 points over Billy Wade, who did not enter.

Race No. 31

Pearson Turns Tables on Petty in Confederate 300

CHATTANOOGA, TN (June 19) -- David Pearson passed Richard Petty with 140 laps to go and sped to victory in the 100-mile Grand National at Chattanooga

Grand National Race No. 31
300 Laps at Chattanooga International Raceway
Chattanooga, TN
"Confederate 300"
100 Miles on .333-mile Paved Track
June 19, 1964

Fin	St	No.	Driver	Team / Car	Laps	Money	Status
1	2	6	David Pearson	Cotton Owens '64 Dodge	300	$1,000	Running
2	1	43	Richard Petty	Petty Eng '64 Plymouth	298	600	Running
3	4	3	Buck Baker	Ray Fox '64 Dodge	293	400	Running
4	3	11	Ned Jarrett	Bondy Long '64 Ford	290	300	Crash
5	11	49	G C Spencer	Spencer '64 Chevrolet	289	275	Running
6	5	54	Jimmy Pardue	Burton-Robinson '64 Plym	286	240	Running
7	8	02	Curtis Crider	Crider '63 Mercury	281	200	Running
8	18	44	Earl Brooks	'62 Chevrolet	274	175	Running
9	14	9	Toy Tyner	R Southerlund '64 Chevrolet	270	150	Running
10	16	99	Gene Hobby	'62 Dodge	254	140	Running
11	13	68	Bob Derrington	'64 Ford	196	130	Brakes
12	6	34	Wendell Scott	Scott '63 Ford	151	120	Crash
13	15	01	Chuck Huckabee	Curtis Crider '63 Mercury	131	110	Handling
14	7	36	Larry Thomas	Wade Younts '63 Plymouth	112	100	Crash
15	12	87	Buddy Baker	J C Parker '63 Dodge	99	100	Crash
16	17	52	E J Trivette	Jess Potter '62 Chevrolet	99	100	Rear End
17	0	46	J T Putney	Walt Hunter '62 Chevrolet	68	100	Handling
18	10	88	Neil Castles	Buck Baker '62 Chrysler	33	100	Coil

Time of Race: 1 hour, 25 minutes, 34 seconds
Average Speed: 70.051 mph
Pole Winner: Richard Petty - 75.235 mph
Lap Leaders: David Pearson 1-100, Richard Petty 101-160, Pearson 161-300
Cautions:
Margin of Victory:
Attendance:

Grand National Race No. 32
200 Laps at Birmingham International Raceway
Birmingham, AL
100 Miles on Half-mile Paved Track
June 21, 1964

Fin	St	No.	Driver	Team / Car	Laps	Money	Status
1	2	11	Ned Jarrett	Bondy Long '64 Ford	200	$1,150	Running
2	4	43	Richard Petty	Petty Eng '64 Plymouth	199	600	Running
3	3	1	Billy Wade	Bud Moore '64 Mercury	198	450	Running
4	1	6	David Pearson	Cotton Owens '64 Dodge	198	300	Running
5	5	3	Buck Baker	Ray Fox '64 Dodge	194	275	Running
6	6	19	Cale Yarborough	Herman Beam '64 Ford	193	240	Running
7	9	36	Larry Thomas	Wade Younts '63 Plymouth	191	200	Running
8	7	54	Jimmy Pardue	Burton-Robinson '64 Plym	188	175	Vapor Lk
9	20	34	Wendell Scott	Scott '63 Ford	187	150	Running
10	10	46	J T Putney	Walt Hunter '62 Chevrolet	187	140	Runnng
11	19	60	Doug Cooper	Bob Cooper '63 Ford	185	130	Running
12	16	44	Earl Brooks	'62 Chevrolet	184	120	Running
13	18	9	Roy Tyner	R Southerlund '64 Chevrolet	184	110	Running
14	15	99	Gene Hobby	'62 Dodge	174	100	Running
15	17	01	Chuck Huckabee	Curtis Crider '63 Mercury	134	100	Running
16	14	52	E J Trivette	'62 Chevrolet	110	100	Lug Bolts
17	12	68	Bob Derrington	'64 Ford	89	100	Brakes
18	13	88	Neil Castles	Buck Baker '62 Chrysler	67	100	Heating
19	11	87	Buddy Baker	J C Parker '63 Dodge	50	100	Heating
20	8	02	Curtis Crider	Crider '63 Mercury	18	100	Axle

Time of Race: 1 hour, 28 minutes, 42 seconds
Average Speed: 67.643 mph
Pole Winner: David Pearson - 72.115 mph
Lap Leaders: Ned Jarrett 1-200
Cautions:
Margin of Victory: 1 1/2 laps
Attendance: 8,000

International Raceway. It was the fourth win of the year for the Spartanburg, SC Dodge driver.

Petty finished second, two laps behind. Buck Baker was third and Ned Jarrett fourth despite wrecking his Ford in the final laps. Fifth place went to G.C. Spencer.

The .333-mile paved oval was rough on tires. Larry Thomas blew a tire and slammed into the wall on lap 116. Thomas was not hurt. Wendell Scott suffered a similar fate on lap 164, and Buddy Baker went into the wall after a tire failure.

Cale Yarborough lost his transmission in practice and was unable to start.

Pearson moved into fifth place in the point standings with his seventh career victory.

Race No. 32

Jarrett Wins Sleeper at Birmingham

BIRMINGHAM, AL (June 21) -- Ned Jarrett led from start to finish and won the 100-mile Grand National race at Birmingham International Raceway for his eighth win of the year.

A crowd of 8,000 showed up and watched Jarrett bolt to a five car length lead by the first turn of the first lap. From that point on, he stretched his advantage each and every lap. Jarrett's margin of victory was nearly two laps at the end of the 100-miler.

Richard Petty finished second and Billy Wade was third. David Pearson wound up fourth with Buck Baker fifth.

Jarrett held second in the point standings, but he was 4,284 points out of first place.

Jimmy Pardue, running in the top five, encountered mechanical problems which sidelined his Plymouth in the final 10 laps.

Jarrett averaged 67.643 mph for his 30th career

Billy Wade #1 and Ned Jarrett #11 feud at Spartanburg

Race No. 33

Baker Takes Valdosta 100 As Yarbrough Runs Out of Gas

VALDOSTA, GA (June 23) -- Buck Baker of Charlotte, NC took his first win of the year at Valdosta

"75" Speedway, giving car owner Ray Fox his first Grand National win since Daytona's SpeedWeeks.

Baker grabbed the lead with five laps to go when leader LeeRoy Yarbrough's Plymouth ran out of gas. The independent driver was going for his third win of the year after starting 20th. He sliced through thick clumps of traffic with bold, daring moves and had taken the lead just past the half-way point.

Baker, who is Yarbrough's teammate in superspeedway races, started second and was never out of contention. He had led 44 laps in the early going before making the final pass less than three miles from the finish.

Yarbrough made a quick pit stop and salvaged second place. Tiny Lund was third, Wendell Scott fourth and Curtis Crider fifth.

Ned Jarrett started on the pole and led the first 62 laps. He was out in front when the rear end went out on his Ford. Point leader Richard Petty never got untracked and finished 13th.

Grand National Race No. 33
200 Laps at Valdosta "75" Speedway
Valdosta, GA
100 Miles on Half-mile Dirt Track
June 23, 1964

Fin	St	No.	Driver	Team / Car	Laps	Money	Status
1	2	3	Buck Baker	Ray Fox '64 Dodge	200	$1,000	Running
2	20	45	LeeRoy Yarbrough	Louie Weathersby '63 Plym	200	600	Running
3	8	89	Tiny Lund	David Walker '64 Plymouth	196	400	Running
4	5	34	Wendell Scott	Scott '63 Ford	195	300	Running
5	6	02	Curtis Crider	Crider '63 Mercury	193	275	Running
6	21	88	Neil Castles	Buck Baker '62 Chrysler	190	240	Running
7	10	60	Doug Cooper	Bob Cooper '63 Ford	189	200	Running
8	3	6	David Pearson	Cotton Owens '64 Dodge	185	175	Running
9	15	9	Roy Tyner	R Southerlund '64 Chevrolet	184	150	Running
10	17	44	Earl Brooks	'62 Chevrolet	184	140	Running
11	9	87	Buddy Baker	J C Parker '63 Dodge	183	130	A Frame
12	14	52	E J Trivette	'62 Chevrolet	180	120	Running
13	11	43	Richard Petty	Petty Eng '64 Plymouth	179	110	Running
14	7	36	Larry Thomas	Wade Younts '63 Plymouth	176	100	Rear End
15	18	99	Gene Hobby	'62 Dodge	163	100	Running
16	12	72	Sam McQuasg	J C Thomas '63 Ford	111	100	Rear end
17	22	68	Bob Derrington	'63 Ford	83	100	Handling
18	13	49	Doug Moore	G C Spencer '64 Chevrolet	70	100	Crash
19	1	11	Ned Jarrett	Bondy Long '64 Ford	62	100	Rear End
20	16	54	Jimmy Pardue	Burton-Robinson '64 Plym	51	100	A Frame
21	19	95	Ken Spikes	Spikes '64 Dodge	23	100	Clutch
22	4	19	Cale Yarborough	Herman Beam '64 Ford	13	100	Rear End
23	23	01	Rodney Bottinger	Curtis Crider '63 Mercury	8	100	Handling

Time of Race: 1 hour, 37 minutes, 50 seconds
Average Speed: 61.328 mph
Pole Winner: Ned Jarrett - 65.146 mph
Lap Leaders: Ned Jarrett 1-62, Buck Baker 63-106, LeeRoy Yarbrough 107-195, Baker 196-200
Cautions:
Margin of Victory: 15 seconds
Attendance:

Race No. 34

Four Cars Flip; Petty Wins Spartanburg 100

SPARTANBURG, SC (June 26) -- Richard Petty steered clear of trouble in the car-bashing 100-mile Grand National race at Piedmont Interstate Fairgrounds for his sixth win of the year.

LeeRoy Yarbrough was flagged in second place with Doug Cooper third. Wendell Scott pushed his Ford into fourth place. Ned Jarrett, Billy Wade and Cale Yarborough, finishing fifth, sixth and seventh respectively, were all victims of wrecks on a spill-filled evening of stock car racing.

A crowd of 6,000 turned out to watch the spine-tingling episode on the half-mile dirt track. The lead changed hands seven times among four drivers -- and four cars flipped during the course of the race.

Pole sitter David Pearson led the first 72 laps in what appeared to be a fairly routine event. Petty took the lead when Pearson fell out with a broken axle.

The fun started on lap 126. J.T. Putney and Buddy Baker got together in a turn and both cars performed a series of barrel rolls.

Jarrett and Wade, who started side-by-side in the second row, moved to the front and engaged in a spirited duel for top honors. Wade slid into the wall while trying to pass Jarrett with about 50 laps to go. He finally got past on lap 164 and led for 10 laps before the two tangled. Jarrett, with years of track know-how, blocked Wade's pass on the outside. Wade lost it and spun out. Jarrett took over the lead, but Wade was not ready to give up. He caught back up, riding Jarrett's bumper. Then with 15 laps to go he banged into the rear of Jarrett's Ford sending both cars tumbling end over end. Neither driver was injured, but both cars were demolished.

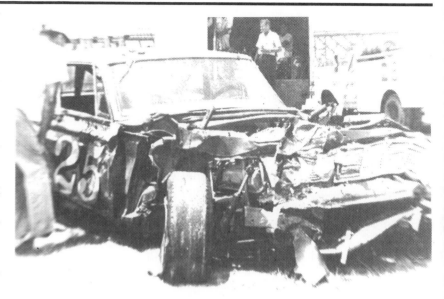

Paul Goldsmith's Plymouth was badly damaged after qualifying race crash prior to the Firecracker 400

Petty moved past the scramble and took the lead on lap 186, leading the rest of the way.

"Jarrett deliberately spun me out on the backstretch after I had passed him clean," said Wade. "I made up my mind to get even with him."

Jarrett said, "There was nothing intentional on my part. It was just hard racing."

Petty averaged 58.233 mph for his 33rd career win.

Grand National Race No. 34
200 Laps at Piedmont Interstate Fairgrounds
Spartanburg, SC
100 Miles on Half-mile Dirt Track
June 26, 1964

Fin	St	No.	Driver	Team / Car	Laps	Money	Status
1	2	43	Richard Petty	Petty Eng '64 Plymouth	200	$1,000	Running
2	6	45	LeeRoy Yarbrough	Louie Weathersby '63 Plym	199	600	Running
3	7	60	Doug Cooper	Bob Cooper '63 Ford	193	400	Running
4	13	34	Wendell Scott	Scott '63 Ford	190	300	Running
5	4	11	Ned Jarrett	Bondy Long '64 Ford	185	275	Crash
6	3	1	Billy Wade	Bud Moore '64 Mercury	183	240	Crash
7	8	19	Cale Yarborough	Herman Beam '64 Ford	179	200	Crash
8	16	99	Gene Hobby	'62 Dodge	175	175	Running
9	18	02	Curtis Crider	Crider '63 Mercury	161	150	Rear end
10	21	52	E J Trivette	'62 Chevrolet	156	140	Running
11	20	88	Neil Castles	Buck Baker '62 Chrysler	142	130	Axle
12	12	87	Buddy Baker	J C Parker '63 Dodge	122	120	Crash
13	15	46	J T Putney	Walt Hunter '62 Chevrolet	118	110	Crash
14	11	78	Buddy Arrington	Arrington '63 Dodge	106	100	Rear End
15	9	36	Larry Thomas	Wade Younts '63 Dodge	87	100	Oil Pres
16	1	6	David Pearson	Cotton Owens '64 Dodge	72	100	Axle
17	5	3	Buck Baker	Ray Fox '64 Dodge	67	100	Brakes
18	14	83	Worth McMillion	McMillion '62 Pontiac	27	100	RF Hub
19	10	75	Elmo Henderson	'62 Pontiac	12	100	Engine
20	19	86	Jimmy Helms	Buck Baker '62 Chrysler	1	100	Coil
21	17	01	Rodney Bottinger	Curtis Crider '63 Mercury	1	100	Trans

Time of Race: 1 hour, 43 minutes, 02 seconds
Average Speed: 58.233 mph
Pole Winner: David Pearson - 66.939 mph
Lap Leaders: David Pearson 1-72, Richard Petty 73-115, Ned Jarrett 116-127,
  Billy Wade 128, Jarrett 129-163, Wade 164-173, Jarrett 174-185, Petty 186-200
Cautions: 3
Margin of Victory: 1 lap plus
Attendance: 6,000

Bobby Isaac leads Buck Baker in Firecracker 400

Grand National Race No. 35
160 Laps at Daytona International Speedway
Daytona Beach, FL
"Firecracker 400"
400 Miles on 2.5-mile Paved Track
July 4, 1964

Fin	St	No.	Driver	Team / Car	Laps	Money	Status
1	19	47	A J Foyt	Ray Nichels '64 Dodge	160	$13,000	Running
2	4	26	Bobby Isaac	Ray Nichels '64 Dodge	160	8,895	Running
3	9	54	Jimmy Pardue	Burton-Robinson '64 Plym	160	5,430	Running
4	5	3	Buck Baker	Ray Fox '64 Dodge	158	3,475	Running
5	2	41	* Jim Paschal	Petty Eng '64 Plymouth	158	2,200	Running
6	7	6	David Pearson	Cotton Owens '64 Dodge	158	1,900	Running
7	21	0	Johnny Rutherford	Holman-Moody '64 Ford	156	1,350	Running
8	8	5	Earl Balmer	Cotton Owens '64 Dodge	156	1,450	Running
9	1	16	Darel Dieringer	Bud Moore '64 Mercury	153	1,250	Running
10	13	82	Bunkie Blackburn	Casper Hensley '64 Pontiac	152	1,050	Running
11	15	03	LeeRoy Yarbrough	Ray Fox '64 Dodge	144	750	Fuel Pmp
12	26	71	Sam McQuagg	J L Thomas '63 Ford	144	650	Running
13	30	02	Curtis Crider	Crider '63 Mercury	141	650	Running
14	10	7	Bobby Johns	Holman-Moody '64 Ford	114	600	Engine
15	22	10	Larry Thomas	'64 Ford	111	550	Crash
16	3	43	Richard Petty	Petty Eng '64 Plymouth	103	1,400	Engine
17	32	34	Wendell Scott	Scott '63 Ford	103	400	Engine
18	12	76	Larry Frank	Frank '63 Ford	103	450	Running
19	20	95	Kenneth Spikes	Spikes '64 Dodge	88	450	Crash
20	6	1	Billy Wade	Bud Moore '64 Mercury	69	900	Engine
21	24	89	Tiny Lund	David Walker '64 Plymouth	62	450	Ignition
22	27	46	J T Putney	Walt Hunter '62 Chevrolet	44	450	Valve
23	14	11	Ned Jarrett	Bondy Long '64 Ford	35	450	Engine
24	16	27	Junior Johnson	Banjo Matthews '64 Ford	17	450	Engine
25	18	42	Bill McMahan	Casper Hensley '63 Pontiac	13	450	Oil Temp
26	17	2	Reb Wickersham	Cliff Stewart '64 Pontiac	10	450	Vibration
27	11	21	Marvin Panch	Wood Bros '64 Ford	9	500	Distributo
28	25	92	Rodney Williams	Ray Osborne '64 Ford	5	450	Oil Pres
29	30	86	Neil Castles	Buck Baker '62 Chrysler	3	450	Fuel Pmp
30	23	9	Roy Tyner	R Southerlund '64 Chevrolet	1	400	Distributo
31	29	01	Roy Mayne	Curtis Crider '63 Mercury	1	400	Oil Pres
32	31	49	Doug Moore	G C Spencer '64 Chevrolet	1	400	Distributo
DNS		25	Paul Goldsmith	Ray Nichels 64 Plymouth	---	50	Crash
DNS		28	Fred Lorenzen	LaFayette '64 Ford	---	50	Crash

* Relieved by Paul Goldsmith
Time of Race: 2 hours, 38 minutes, 28 seconds
Average Speed: 151.451 mph
Pole Winner: Darel Dieringer - 172.678 mph
Lap Leaders: Richard Petty 1-39, Earl Balmer 40, Petty 41-103, Bobby Isaac 104,
   A J Foyt 105, Isaac 106, Foyt 107-110, Isaac 111-119, Foyt 120, Isaac 121-135,
   Foyt 136-138, Isaac 139-145, Foyt 146, Isaac 147, Foyt 148, Isaac 149-155,
   Foyt 156-157, Isaac 158-159, Foyt 160
Cautions: 5 for 25 laps
Margin of Victory: 1 car length
Attendance: 34,681

Race No. 35
Foyt Beats Isaac in Thriller; Roberts Succumbs to Injuries

DAYTONA BEACH, FL (July 4) -- A.J. Foyt of Houston nabbed Bobby Isaac in the final lap and stormed home first in the sixth annual Firecracker 400 at Daytona International Speedway. It was Foyt's 10th career Grand National start and his first victory.

A somber crowd of 34,681 was on hand to watch Foyt and Isaac battle down to the wire in their team Ray Nichels' Dodges. Racing great Fireball Roberts died two days earlier as the result of critical burns suffered May 24 during the World 600. Funeral services were held July 5 with more than 1,000 persons attending the ceremony. He was laid to rest at Bellevue Memorial Park.

Foyt and Isaac swapped the lead 16 times during the final 56 laps. Foyt tagged along in Isaac's draft and made the final pass down the backstretch of the last lap. Jimmy Pardue came in third with Buck Baker fourth. Jim Paschal took fifth place with Paul Goldsmith driving in relief. David Pearson was sixth giving Chrysler products a sweep for the first six places.

Richard Petty dominated the race until he left with a blown engine after 103 laps. He had led all but one lap until that point.

Petty's departure set up the thrilling Foyt-Isaac duel. "I didn't want to be ahead of Isaac going into the last lap," said Foyt, 29. "I went way down low on the backstretch and managed to get by before we hit the corner."

"I was going to try to slingshot off the fourth turn in the inside groove," said Isaac. "That's the fastest one. A.J. took it and I had to go high. All I needed was about 30 more feet."

Car owner Nichels said he was somewhat uneasy watching his two cars run so close. "It's a heck of a feeling when you worry about two of your own drivers getting each other into trouble. But it sure makes you feel good to know they're running up front. That's the best racing duel I've ever seen," he said.

Ken Spikes of Cordele, GA crashed his Dodge hard in the 117th lap. He was taken to Halifax Hospital with a broken leg and internal injuries.

Fred Lorenzen and Goldsmith did not start the race. Their cars were taken out of the 400 miler in a preliminary qualifying race. Lorenzen suffered a cut tendon in his wrist and was admitted to the hospital.

Darel Dieringer earned the pole position at 172.678 mph. Only two cars made time trials the first day of qualifying. Rain wiped out the afternoon session and starting positions were determined in the qualifying races.

Race No. 36
Ned Jarrett Nabs 9th of Year at Manassas

MANASSAS, VA (July 8) -- Ned Jarrett got past David Pearson in the 223rd lap and led the rest of the way to win the Old Dominion 400 at Old Dominion Speedway. It was his ninth win of the year and the 31st of his career.

Pearson finished second a lap behind. Jimmy

Pardue was third with Curtis Crider fourth and Buddy Arrington fifth.

A crowd of 5,560 turned out for the 400 lapper on the .375-mile paved track. Jarrett won at an average speed of 67.652 mph

Jarrett started on the pole and led until he made his first pit stop on lap 181. Pearson took over and led for 41 laps before Jarrett sailed past for good.

Point leader Richard Petty started second and was running third when the differential broke on his Plymouth on lap 366. He still held a 5,046 point lead over Jarrett.

Billy Wade - won Fireball Roberts 200

first Grand National win for the sophomore driver.

Wade started on the pole and led the first 16 laps. After that, he backed off, paced himself and let Richard Petty, David Pearson and Ned Jarrett fight for the lead. Wade went the distance without a pit stop and that was the difference.

"I planned to go all the way," said Wade. "That's why I let Petty, Pearson and Jarrett go at the start of the race. I knew they couldn't go the distance on one tank going that hard.

"Fireball Roberts won here last year by going all the way on one tank," added Wade. The 200 lapper on the half-mile paved track was named in honor of the late

Grand National Race No. 36
400 Laps at Old Dominion Speedway
Manassas, VA
"Old Dominion 400"
150 Miles on .375-mile Paved Track
July 8, 1964

Fin	St	No.	Driver	Team / Car	Laps	Money	Status
1	1	11	Ned Jarrett	Bondy Long '64 Ford	400	$1,100	Running
2	3	6	David Pearson	Cotton Owens '64 Dodge	399	625	Running
3	4	54	Jimmy Pardue	Burton-Robinson '64 Plym	388	450	Running
4	7	02	Curtis Crider	Crider '63 Mercury	371	350	Running
5	6	78	Buddy Arrington	Arrington '63 Dodge	370	325	Running
6	5	64	Elmo Langley	Woodfield '63 Ford	370	290	Running
7	19	9	Roy Tyner	R Southerlund '63 Mercury	368	250	Running
8	2	43	Richard Petty	Petty Eng '64 Plymouth	366	225	Diff
9	16	55	Earl Brooks	'63 Chevrolet	353	200	Running
10	8	49	Doug Moore	G C Spencer '64 Chevrolet	346	190	Running
11	13	99	Gene Hobby	'62 Dodge	337	180	Running
12	20	45	LeeRoy Yarbrough	Louie Weathersby '63 Plym	190	170	Trans
13	14	83	Worth McMillion	McMillion '62 Pontiac	180	160	Engine
14	9	88	Neil Castles	Buck Baker '62 Chrysler	70	150	Spindle
15	12	01	Buddy Baker	Curtis Crider '63 Mercury	51	135	Piston
16	17	09	Roy Mayne	'63 Chevrolet	30	125	Heating
17	18	60	Doug Cooper	Bob Cooper '64 Ford	30	115	Engine
18	15	34	Wendell Scott	Scott '63 Ford	4	110	Ignition
19	11	71	James Hylton	Bondy Long '64 Ford	4	100	Handling
20	10	68	Bob Derrington	'63 Ford	2	100	Diff

Time of Race: 2 hours, 13 minutes, 02 seconds
Average Speed: 67.652 mph
Pole Winner: Ned Jarrett - 73.609 mph
Lap Leaders: Ned Jarrett 1-181, David Pearson 182-222, Jarrett 223-400
Cautions:
Margin of Victory:
Attendance: 5,560

Race No. 37

Billy Wade Captures Fireball Roberts 200 at Old Bridge

OLD BRIDGE, NJ (July 10) -- Billy Wade, Houston native, throttled his Bud Moore Mercury past Richard Petty in the 157th lap and went on to win the Fireball Roberts 200 at Old Bridge Speedway. It was the

Grand National Race No. 37
200 Laps at Old Bridge Speedway
Old Bridge, NJ
"Fireball Roberts 200"
100 Miles on Half-mile Paved Track
July 10, 1964

Fin	St	No.	Driver	Team / Car	Laps	Money	Status
1	1	1	Billy Wade	Bud Moore '63 Mercury	200	$1,000	Running
2	4	11	Ned Jarrett	Bondy Long '64 Ford	199	600	Running
3	3	43	Richard Petty	Petty Eng '64 Plymouth	198	400	Running
4	5	54	Jimmy Pardue	Burton-Robinson '64 Plym	195	300	Running
5	2	6	David Pearson	Cotton Owens '64 Dodge	193	275	Running
6	6	45	LeeRoy Yarbrough	Louie Weathersby '63 Plym	192	240	Running
7	19	64	Elmo Langley	Woodfield '63 Ford	190	200	Running
8	12	9	Roy Tyner	R Southerlund '64 Chevrolet	184	175	Running
9	8	34	Wendell Scott	Scott '63 Ford	182	150	Running
10	21	31	Al White	'63 Ford	177	140	Running
11	10	88	Neil Castles	Buck Baker '62 Chrysler	177	130	Running
12	13	49	Doug Moore	G C Spencer '64 Chevrolet	157	120	Running
13	14	01	Wally Dallenbach	Currtis Crider '63 Mercury	142	110	Engine
14	16	55	Earl Brooks	'63 Chevrolet	90	100	Bearing
15	15	02	Curtis Crider	Crider '63 Mercury	42	100	Axle
16	7	71	James Hylton	Bondy Long '64 Ford	22	100	A Frame
17	17	41	Lee Petty	Petty Eng '64 Plymouth	19	100	Itnition
18	11	68	Bob Derrington	'63 Ford	18	100	Handling
19	9	60	Doug Cooper	Bob Cooper '64 Ford	15	100	Valve
20	18	16	Darel Dieringer	Bud Moore '64 Mercury	11	100	Fuel Pmp
21	20	03	Buddy Baker	Ray Fox '64 Dodge	7	100	Engine
22	22	10	Bernard Alvarez	Alvarez '64 Ford	1	100	Rear end

Time of Race: 1 hour, 21 minutes, 12 seconds
Average Speed: 73.891 mph
Pole Winner: Billy Wade - 76.660 mph
Lap Leaders: Billy Wade 1-16, Richard Petty 17-43, David Pearson 44-128, Petty 129-156, Wade 157-200
Cautions: None
Margin of Victory: 1 lap plus 12 seconds
Attendance: 5,000

Roberts, who had died eight days earlier from burns suffered in the World 600.

Lee Petty drove in his first race of the year. The 50 year-old three-time champ started 17th and finished 17th -- going only 19 laps before ignition problems hit his Plymouth.

Wade became the 15th different winner on the

Race No. 38

Pearson Blows -- Wade Wins Again at Bridgehampton

BRIDGEHAMPTON, NY (July 12) -- Billy Wade scooted into first place 12 laps from the finish when engine failure sidelined leader David Pearson and won his

second straight Grand National at Bridgehampton Raceway.

Wade finished 20 seconds in front of Buck Baker in the 142.5-mile event on the 2.85-mile road course. Road racing specialist Walt Hansgen took third spot with Marvin Panch fourth and Curtis Crider fifth.

It was the 17th Grand National race held on a road course and Wade became the 15th different winner. By road racing standards, the race was exciting as the lead changed hands nine times among four drivers in the 50-lapper. Wade started third and led on four occasions for 31 laps. He averaged a record 87.707 mph.

Point leader Richard Petty won the pole in a special 10-lap pole position race at 90.60 mph and led only the final lap in so doing. He wound up 13th in the feature, blowing an engine after 21 laps.

Bobby Isaac started 12th and was competing in his second road race. The Catawba, NC Dodge driver had difficulty getting the hang of the twisting course. "I was off the course and in the woods so much that the animals were beginning to recognize me," he said. Transmission failure ended his futile drive after 15 laps.

Petty's point lead was cut to 4,890 over Ned Jarrett who wound up sixth in the field of 24.

Grand National Race No. 38
50 Laps at Bridgehampton Raceway
Bridgehampton, NY
142.5 Miles on 2.85-mile Road Course
July 12, 1964

Fin	St	No.	Driver	Team / Car	Laps	Money	Status
1	3	1	Billy Wade	Bud Moore '64 Mercury	50	$1,225	Running
2	7	3	Buck Baker	Ray Fox '64 Dodge	50	675	Running
3	9	46	Walt Hansgen	'64 Ford	48	500	Running
4	22	06	Marvin Panch	Holman-Moody '64 Ford	44	350	Running
5	10	02	Curtis Crider	Crider '63 Mercury	42	350	Running
6	6	11	Ned Jarrett	Bondy Long '64 Ford	41	340	Engine
7	21	88	Neil Castles	Buck Baker '62 Chrysler	41	250	Running
8	2	6	David Pearson	Cotton Owens '64 Dodge	38	400	Engine
9	17	9	Roy Tyner	R Southerlund '64 Chevrolet	38	200	Running
10	23	68	Bob Derrington	'63 Ford	31	190	Running
11	14	45	Louie Weathersby	Weathersby '63 Plymouth	31	180	Running
12	4	16	Darel Dieringer	Bud Moore '64 Mercury	25	270	Oil Pmp
13	1	43	Richard Petty	Petty Eng '64 Plymouth	21	385	Engine
14	19	71	James Hylton	Bondy Long '64 Ford	21	150	Oil Pres
15	24	55	Earl Brooks	'62 Chevrolet	21	135	Spindle
16	8	54	Jimmy Pardue	Burton-Robinson '64 Plym	17	175	Trans
17	12	26	Bobby Isaac	Ray Nichels '64 Dodge	15	115	Trans
18	11	03	LeeRoy Yarbrough	Ray Fox '64 Dodge	14	110	Diff
19	5	25	Paul Goldsmith	Ray Nichels '64 Plymouth	13	175	Trans
20	16	01	Buddy Baker	Curtis Crider '62 Mercury	5	100	Con Rod
21	13	10	Bernard Alvarez	Alvarez '64 Ford	5	100	Brakes
22	15	31	Al White	'62 Ford	3	100	Oil Pres
23	20	34	Wendell Scott	Scott '63 Ford	2	---	Clutch
24	18	49	Doug Moore	G C Spencer '64 Chevrolet	1	---	Spin

Time of Race: 1 hour, 37 minutes, 29 seconds
Average Speed: 87.707 mph
Pole Winner: Richard Petty 90.60 (Average in 10-mile Qualifier race)
Lap Leaders: Richard Petty 1, Billy Wade 2-7, David Pearson 8-11, Wade 12-14, Pearson 15-24, Derrington 25, Wade 26-35, Pearson 36-38, Wade 39-50
Cautions:
Margin of Victory: 20 seconds
Attendance: 6,500

Grand National Race No. 39
300 Laps at Islip Speedway
Islip, NY
60 Miles on .20-mile Paved Track
July 15, 1964

Fin	St	No.	Driver	Team / Car	Laps	Money	Status
1	1	1	Billy Wade	Bud Moore '64 Mercury	300	$1,000	Running
2	2	11	Ned Jarrett	Bondy Long '64 Ford	299	600	Running
3	3	41	Richard Petty	Petty Eng '64 Plymouth	295	400	Running
4	5	54	Jimmy Pardue	Burton-Robinson '64 Plym	283	300	Running
5	7	06	Bob Welborn	Holman-Moody '64 Ford	273	275	Running
6	11	88	Neil Castles	Buck Baker '62 Chrysler	270	240	Running
7	13	60	Doug Cooper	Bob Cooper '64 Ford	266	200	Running
8	16	9	Roy Tyner	R Southerlund '64 Chevrolet	265	175	Running
9	12	49	Doug Moore	G C Spencer '64 Chevrolet	262	150	Running
10	15	31	Al White	'62 Ford	257	140	Running
11	8	34	Wendell Scott	Scott '63 Ford	229	130	Running
12	10	55	Earl Brooks	'63 Chevrolet	167	120	Steering
13	9	02	Curtis Crider	Crider '63 Mercury	139	110	Steering
14	4	6	David Pearson	Cotton Owens '64 Dodge	135	100	Crash
15	6	45	LeeRoy Yarbrough	Louie Weathersby '63 Plym	112	100	Diff
16	19	10	Rene Charland	Bernard Alvarez '64 Ford	9	100	Brakes
17	18	16	Darel Dieringer	Bud Moore '64 Mercury	8	100	Handling
18	14	68	Bob Derrington	'63 Ford	5	100	Engine
19	22	03	Bobby Schuyler	Ray Fox '64 Dodge	3	100	Spindle
20	21	3	Buddy Baker	Ray Fox '64 Dodge	3	100	Radiator
21	20	66	Frank Tanner	'63 Ford	3	100	tie Rod
22	17	01	Pete Boland	Curtis Crider '63 Mercury	3	100	Heating

Time of Race: 1 hour, 17 minutes, 50 seconds
Average Speed: 46.252 mph
Pole Winner: Billy Wade - 51.100 mph
Lap Leaders: Billy Wade 1-97, Ned Jarrett 98-192, Billy Wade 193-300
Cautions: 1
Margin of Vicotry: 1 lap plus
Attendance:

Race No. 39

Wade-Jarrett Re-light Feud; Wade Wins Third Straight

ISLIP, NY (July 15) -- Billy Wade and Ned Jarrett renewed their feud on the tight .2-mile Islip Speedway, and Wade came home with his third straight Grand National win.

With the two sharing the front row, Wade got the jump and took the lead at the green flag with Jarrett close behind. Jarrett made his pass in lap 98 and led until lap 193 when Wade grabbed the lead for good. He beat his rival to the finish line by just over a lap. The two drivers engaged in a fender tapping battle that had the packed crowd on its feet. "We were both driving to win," said Wade. "That happens on a short track. Sometimes you have to lean

Grand Nationals climb hill at Watkins Glen

on each other a bit." Wade averaged 46.252 mph.

Richard Petty finished third with Jimmy Pardue fourth. Bob Welborn, one of the top pilots in the '50's, accepted a Holman-Moody Ford ride and finished fifth.

Buddy Baker got a ride on the powerful Ray Fox Dodge, but his day was over as soon as it began. He pulled the car behind the wall in the third lap with a radiator leak.

Grand National Race No. 40
66 Laps at Watkins Glen International
Watkins Glen, NY
150 Miles on 2.3-mile Paved Road Course
July 19, 1964

Fin	St	No.	Driver	Team / CAr	Laps	Money	Status
1	1	1	Billy Wade	Bud Moore '64 Mercury	66	$1,400	Running
2	8	03	LeeRoy Yarbrough	Ray Fox '64 Dodge	66	800	Running
3	10	46	Walt Hansgen	'64 Chevrolet	65	600	Running
4	9	3	Buck Baker	Ray Fox '64 Dodge	65	500	Running
5	11	06	Bob Welborn	Holman-Moody '64 Ford	64	400	Running
6	5	6	David Pearson	Cotton Owens '64 Dodge	63	350	Running
7	7	54	Jimmy Pardue	Burton-Robinson 64 Plymouth	59	300	Engine
8	2	11	Ned Jarrett	Bondy Long '64 Ford	58	240	Engine
9	23	02	Curtis Crider	Crider '63 Mercury	57	220	Running
10	15	60	Doug Cooper	Bob Cooper '64 Ford	56	200	Running
11	12	45	Louie Weathersby	Weathersby '63 Plymouth	54	200	Running
12	14	34	Wendell Scott	Scott '63 Ford	53	195	Running
13	16	49	Doug Moore	G C Spencer '64 Chevrolet	51	180	Running
14	6	16	Darel Dieringer	Bud Moore '64 Mercury	49	150	Engine
15	21	9	Roy Tyner	R Southerlund '64 Chevrolet	39	150	Running
16	25	55	Earl Brooks	'63 Chevrolet	35	150	Steering
17	18	88	Neil Castles	Buck Baker '62 Chrysler	33	150	Rear Wind
18	17	68	Bob Derrington	'63 Ford	26	150	Heating
19	13	10	Bernie Alvarez	Alvarez '64 Ford	25	150	Shift Lev
20	3	25	Paul Goldsmith	Ray Nichels '64 Plymouth	13	150	Oil Pres
21	4	43	Richard Petty	Petty Eng '64 Plymouth	10	150	Crash
22	20	41	Lee Petty	Petty Eng '64 Plymouth	9	150	Handling
23	24	31	Al White	'63 Ford	5	---	Rear End
24	19	71	Marvin Panch	Bondy Long '64 Ford	3	---	Handling
25	26	66	Frank Tanner	'63 Ford	2	---	Handling
26	22	01	Pete Boland	Curtis Crider '63 Mercury	2	---	Brakes

Time of Race: 1 hour, 32 minutes, 57 seconds
Average speed: 97.988 mph
Pole Winner: Billy Wade - 102.222 mph
Lap Leaders: Ned Jarrett 1-6, Darel Dieringer 7-14, Billy Wade 15-24, Jarrett 25-35, Wade 36-66
Cautions:
Margin of Victory: 6 seconds
Attendance: 10,000

Race No. 40

Confident Billy Wade Snares 4th Straight at Watkins Glen

WATKINS GLEN, NY (July 19) -- Billy Wade charged past Ned Jarrett in the 36th lap and went on to grab his fourth straight win in the 150-miler at Watkins Glen International. Wade became the first man in NAS-CAR history to win four straight Grand National races.

LeeRoy Yarbrough quickly adapted to a road course and finished second, 6.0 seconds behind Wade's black and red Mercury. Walt Hansgen came in third, Buck Baker was fourth and Bob Welborn fifth.

The lead changed hands five times with Wade holding the front spot for 41 of

Lee Petty drove his last Grand National at Watkins Glen

Billy Wade en route to Watkins Glen victory

			Grand National Race No. 41 200 Laps at Lincoln Speedway New Oxford, PA "Pennsylvania 200" 100 Miles on Half-mile Dirt Track July 21, 1964				
Fin	St	No.	Driver	Team / Car	Lasp	Money	Status
1	1	6	David Pearson	Cotton Owens '64 Dodge	200	$1,000	Running
2	3	41	Richard Petty	Petty Eng '64 Plymouth	200	600	Running
3	6	54	Jimmy Pardue	Burton-Robinson '64 Plym	194	400	Running
4	21	34	Wendell Scott	Scott '63 Ford	193	300	Running
5	7	72	Doug Yates	Yates '64 Plymouth	192	275	Running
6	9	02	Curtis Crider	Crider '63 Mercury	190	240	Running
7	14	31	Al White	'63 Ford	183	200	Running
8	5	60	Doug Cooper	Bob Cooper '63 Ford	181	175	Running
9	18	9	Roy Tyner	R Southerlund '64 Chevrolet	177	150	Running
10	12	68	Bob Derrington	'63 Ford	173	140	Running
11	2	06	Bob Welborn	Holman-Moody '64 Ford	169	130	Engine
12	10	55	Earl Brooks	'63 Chevrolet	109	120	Trans
13	8	88	Neil Castles	Buck Baker '62 Chrysler	107	110	Rear End
14	17	64	Elmo Langley	Woodfield '63 Ford	50	100	Brakes
15	4	11	Ned Jarrett	Bondy Long '64 Ford	32	100	Engine
16	15	45	Louie Weathersby	Weathersby '63 Plymouth	10	100	Crash
17	11	49	Doug Moore	G C Spencer '64 Chevrolet	4	100	Itnition
18	13	03	LeeRoy Yarbrough	Ray Fox '64 Dodge	3	100	H Gasket
19	16	10	Bernie Alvarez	Alvarez '64 Ford	3	100	Heating
20	20	01	Pete Boland	Curtis Crider '63 Mercury	2	100	Steering
21	19	66	Frank Tanner	'63 Ford	2	100	Oil Pres

Time of Race: 1 hour, 12 minutes, 40 seconds
Average Speed: 82.568 mph
Pole Winner: David Pearson - 86.289 mph
Lap Leaders: Bob Welborn 1-125, David Pearson 126-200
Cautions:
Margin of Victory: 11 seconds
Attendance:

the 66 laps on the 2.3-mile road course.

The streaking Wade said winning has changed his attitude. "Winning races changes your outlook," he remarked. "Back in Texas, I won regularly in Modified races. I expected to win and was disappointed when I didn't. We've been trying to catch up in these Grand Nationals. My spirits are up right now. I'm looking for ways to win now, rather than expecting something to happen that will make you lose. I've got a new attitude."

Point leader Richard Petty crashed in the 10th lap and wound up 21st. His point lead was reduced to 4,614 points over Ned Jarrett, who wound up seventh after blowing an engine late in the race.

In a less distinct honor, Pete Boland finished last in the 26 car field. His car, the #01 Mercury owned by Curtis Crider, has now finished last in 5 of the last 11 Grand National races.

Race No. 41

Welborn's Bid Foiled by Blown Engine; Pearson Wins New Oxford

NEW OXFORD, PA (July 21) -- David Pearson guided his Dodge under a bobbling Bob Welborn in the 126th lap and went on to win the Pennsylvania 200 at Lincoln Speedway. It was the fifth win of the season for the 29 year-old Pearson.

Richard Petty finished second, 11 seconds behind. Third place went to Jimmy Pardue as Wendell Scott came in fourth and Doug Yates fifth.

Welborn, who recently re-joined the Grand National circuit, started second and got the jump on pole sitter Pearson at the drop of the green flag. Bidding for his first Grand National win in five years, Welborn kept his burgandy Ford on the rails the first part of the race. The Summerfield, NC driver was holding down second place when his engine blew on lap 169, relegating him to an 11th place finish.

Louie Weathersby, forced to drive his own Plymouth for the second race in a row when he couldn't find a driver, wrecked in the 10th lap after a tire blew. He was not hurt. LeeRoy Yarbrough had driven the Weathersby Plymouth earlier in the year on short track races but elected to drive Ray Fox's Dodge. LeeRoy went only three laps before dropping out with a blown head gasket.

Race No. 42

Lorenzen Leads Only Final Lap in Volunteer 500

BRISTOL, TN (July 26) -- Heartbreaking engine failure put Richard Petty out of the race a half-mile from the finish, and Fred Lorenzen rode his Ford home first in the Volunteer 500 at Bristol International Speedway. It was the sixth win of the year for the blonde bachelor.

Grand National Race No. 42
500 Laps at Bristol International Speedway
Bristol, TN
"Volunteer 500"
250 Miles on Half-mile Paved Track
July 26, 1964

Fin	St	No.	Driver	Team / Car	Laps	Money	Status
1	8	28	* Fred Lorenzen	Holman-Moody '64 Ford	500	$4,185	Running
2	1	43	Richard Petty	Petty Eng '64 Plymouth	499	2,730	Rear End
3	11	41	** Jim Paschal	Petty Eng '64 Plymouth	499	1,500	Running
4	13	03	LeeRoy Yarbrough	Ray Fox '64 Dodge	489	1,260	Running
5	15	19	Larry Thomas	Herman Beam '64 Ford	482	975	Running
6	17	54	Jimmy Pardue	Burton-Robinson '64 Plym	479	825	Running
7	4	21	Marvin Panch	Wood Bros '64 Ford	463	775	Rear End
8	20	09	Roy Mayne	'62 Chevrolet	461	650	Running
9	18	78	Buddy Arrington	Arrington '63 Dodge	455	550	Rear End
10	22	46	J T Putney	'62 Chevrolet	449	500	Running
11	28	88	Neil Castles	Buck Baker '62 Chrysler	446	475	Running
12	24	42	Bill McMahan	Casper Hensley '63 Pontiac	440	400	Running
13	33	53	Pete Stewart	'63 Ford	426	375	Running
14	14	5	Earl Balmer	Cotton Owens '64 Dodge	420	315	Rear End
15	36	83	Worth McMillion	McMillion '62 Pontiac	420	250	Running
16	29	49	Doug Moore	G C Spencer '64 Chevrolet	418	375	Running
17	6	6	David Pearson	Cotton Owens '64 Dodge	363	250	Rear End
18	7	27	Junior Johnson	Banjo Matthews '64 Ford	352	300	Engine
19	12	3	Buck Baker	Ray Fox '64 Dodge	309	250	Heating
20	35	48	Doug Wilson	'63 Ford	284	250	Rear End
21	2	25	Paul Goldsmith	Ray Nichels '64 Plymouth	148	310	Trans
22	3	1	Billy Wade	Bud Moore '64 Mercury	77	375	Engine
23	9	26	Bobby Isaac	Ray Nichels '64 Dodge	74	250	Trans
24	16	82	Bunkie Blackburn	Casper Hensley '64 Pontiac	70	375	Engine
25	5	11	Ned Jarrett	Bondy Long '64 Ford	62	275	Heating
26	10	16	Darel Dieringer	Bud Moore '64 Mercury	42	250	Engine
27	19	34	Wendell Scott	Scott '63 Ford	41	250	Oil Pres
28	26	20	Jack Anderson	'64 Ford	15	300	Oil Pres
29	24	55	Earl Brooks	'62 Chevrolet	10	275	Trans
30	23	52	E J Trivette	Jess Potter '62 Chevrolet	9	250	Trans
31	27	60	Doug Cooper	Bob Cooper '63 Ford	9	285	Handling
32	30	02	Curtis Crider	Crider '63 Mercury	4	275	Clutch
33	32	9	Roy Tyner	R Southerlund '64 Chevrolet	4	275	Valve
34	25	86	Jimmy Helms	Buck Baker '62 Chrysler	2	350	Fuel Pres
35	21	39	Johnny Nave	'64 Ford	2	250	Heating
36	31	36	Darrell Bryant	Wade Younts "62 Dodge	1	275	Fuel Pres

* Relieved by Ned Jarrett (laps 276-443)
** Relieved by Billy Wade
Time of Race: 3 hours, 12 minutes, 12 seconds
Average Speed: 78.044 mph
Pole Winner: Richard Petty - 82.91 mph
Lap Leaders: Paul Goldsmith 1-12, Richard Petty 13-305, Junior Johnson 306-350, Petty 351-499, Fred Lorenzen 500
Cautions: 1 for 14 laps
Margin of Victory:
Attendance: 25,500

Petty had driven his Plymouth around Junior Johnson in the 351st lap and was holding down a full three lap advantage over Lorenzen when smoke belched from beneath his car on lap 496. He coaxed the dying machine three more laps before it finally expired on pit road after completing his 499th lap. Lorenzen circled the track two more times and received the checkered flag. He led only one lap in the race -- the one that counted most.

Fred Lorenzen led only the final lap to win at Bristol

"I felt real sorry for Petty," said Lorenzen. "But the same thing happened to me at Martinsville once. I blew an engine and Richard was in second place and went on to win the race."

Petty was philosophical about the defeat. "That's just the way racing goes," he said, managing a smile. "You never have it won until you see that checkered flag. I won a race at Martinsville when Fred had trouble. I guess this just makes us even."

Petty got credit for second and Jim Paschal, with relief help from Billy Wade, took third place. LeeRoy Yarbrough came in fourth with Larry Thomas fifth.

Lorenzen was competing in his first race since being injured in a July 3 crash at Daytona. Ned Jarrett, who departed after 62 laps, relieved Lorenzen from lap 276 to 443. A refreshed Lorenzen got back in the saddle for the closing stages.

Lorenzen averaged 78.044 mph despite one caution flag for 14 laps.

Bobby Johns, who replaced Freball Roberts on the Holman-Moody Ford team, suffered facial lacerations from a crash during a practice lap. He spent one night in the hospital.

Race No. 43

Petty Leads All 400 Laps In Nashville Win

NASHVILLE, TN (Aug 2) -- Richard Petty leaped into the lead in the opening lap and was on the point for all 400 laps as he won the scorching 200-mile event at Nashville Fairgrounds Speedway.

Petty left little excitement for the crowd of 13,128 as he led all the way on the hot afternoon as temperatures

Front row starters Richard Petty and Billy Wade lead charge in Nashville 400

rose into the upper 90's. David Pearson was flagged in second place, but after a scoring check, Jim Paschal was moved up a notch into the runner-up slot. Pearson got paid for third place. Earl Balmer ran fourth with Ned Jarrett fifth.

The Petty team finished first and second and won $3,150. Paschal was driving one of the newfangled "cool suits". "It was fine in the early going," said Paschal, 37. "But it quit working after about 175 laps. After that it was hotter than blazes."

Richard didn't wear one in the race. "What's he need one for," queried Papa Lee. "Hell, he's still young."

Billy Wade started second but fell out after 171 laps with a bad alternator. "Those cool suits cost $1,500, I hear. But I've got to get me one. This heat is murder," he said.

Petty averaged 73.208 mph despite three caution flags for 26 laps.

Richard Petty celebrates 200 -mile victory at Nashville

Grand National Race No. 43
400 Laps at Fairgrounds Speedway
Nashville, TN
200 Miles on Half-mile Paved Track
August 2, 1964

Fin	St	No.	DRiver	Team / Car	Laps	Money	Status
1	1	43	Richard Petty	Petty Eng '64 Plymouth	400	$2,150	Running
2	3	41	Jim Paschal	Petty Eng '64 Plymouth	400	1,000	Running
3	5	6	David Pearson	Cotton Owens '64 Dodge	399	800	Running
4	6	5	Earl Balmer	Cotton Owens '64 Dodge	392	500	Running
5	4	11	Ned Jarrett	Bondy Long '64 Ford	392	575	Running
6	7	16	Darel Dieringer	Bud Moore '64 Mercury	390	450	Running
7	9	19	Larry Thomas	Herman Beam '64 Ford	385	425	Running
8	8	54	Jimmy Pardue	Burton-Robinson '64 Plym	375	375	Running
9	14	49	Doug Moore	G C Spencer '64 Chevrolet	358	350	Running
10	15	88	Neil Castles	Buck Baker '62 Chrysler	355	350	Running
11	11	42	Bill McMahan	Buck Baker '64 Pntiac	348	270	Running
12	20	02	Curtis Crider	Crider '63 Mercury	339	265	Running
13	17	20	Jack Anderson	'64 Ford	337	220	Running
14	19	52	E J Trivette	Jess Potter '62 Chevrolet	320	200	Running
15	23	17	Junior Spencer	'64 Ford	288	170	Rear End
16	12	34	Wendell Scott	Scott '63 Ford	251	150	Engine
17	16	9	Roy Tyner	R Southerlund '64 Chevrolet	233	130	Itnition
18	10	82	Bunkie Blackburn	Casper Hensley '63 pontiac	171	100	Clutch
19	2	1	Billy Wade	Bud Moore '64 Mercury	171	100	Alternator
20	27	81	Henley Gray	John Black '64 Ford	126	100	Flagged
21	18	60	Doug Cooper	Bob Cooper '63 Ford	48	100	Heating
22	21	32	Mark Hurley	'63 Ford	34	100	Heating
23	13	78	Buddy Arrington	Arrington '63 Dodge	17	100	Hub
24	24	92	Rodney Bottinger	Ray Osborne '64 Ford	8	100	Trans
25	22	01	Chuck Huckabee	Curtis Crider '63 Mercury	7	100	Fuel Pmp
26	25	86	Steve Young	Buck Baker '62 Chrysler	3	100	Clutch
27	26	66	Bud Moore	'63 Ford	3	100	Heating

Time of Race: 2 hours, 43 minutes, 55 seconds
Average Speed: 73.208 mph
Pole Winner: Richard Petty - 80.826
Lap Leaders: Richard Petty 1-400
Cautions: 3 for 26 laps
Margin of Victory:
Attendance: 13,128

Grand National Race No. 44
200 Laps at Rambi Raceway
Myrtle Beach, SC
100 Miles on Half-mile Dirt Track
August 7, 1964

Fin	St	No.	Driver	Team / Car	Laps	Money	Status
1	1	6	David Pearson	Cotton Owens '64 Dodge	200	$1,000	Running
2	2	43	Richard Petty	Petty Eng '64 Plymouth	199	600	Running
3	3	45	LeeRoy Yarbrough	Louie Weathersby '63 Plym	195	400	Running
4	5	11	Ned Jarrett	Bondy Long '64 Ford	192	300	Running
5	8	88	Neil Castles	Buck Baker '62 Chrysler	187	275	Running
6	12	34	Wendell Scott	Scott '63 Ford	186	240	Running
7	6	72	Doug Yates	Yates '63 Plymouth	182	200	Running
8	9	49	Doug Moore	G C Spencer '64 Chevrolet	173	175	Running
9	4	54	Jimmy Pardue	Burton-Ronbins '64 Plymouth	150	150	Rear End
10	10	9	Roy Tyner	R Southerlund '64 Chevrolet	117	140	A Frame
11	7	60	Doug Cooper	Bob Cooper '63 Ford	30	130	Engine
12	11	20	Jack Anderson	'64 Ford	1	120	Radiator

Time of Race: 1 hour, 37 minutes, 10 seconds
Average Speed: 61.750 mph
Pole Winner: David Pearson - 69.659 mph
Lap Leaders: David Pearson 1-78, Ned Jarrett 79-162, Pearson 163-200
Cautions:
Margin of Victory: 1 lap plus
Attendance:

Race No. 44

Pearson Beats Slim Field At Myrtle Beach

MYRTLE BEACH, SC (Aug 7) -- David Pearson of Spartanburg, SC out-sped a slim field and won the 100-mile Grand National race at Rambi Raceway. It was his sixth win of the season.

Pearson pedaled his Cotton Owens Dodge around Ned Jarrett in the 163rd lap and led the rest of the way. He wound up better than a lap ahead of Richard Petty in second place. Third place went to LeeRoy Yarbrough with Jarrett fourth and Neil Castles fifth.

Only a dozen cars went to the starting post. Pearson led the first 78 laps from the pole, then lost the lead to Jarrett for 84 laps. Once Pearson gained the lead for the second time, he set sail. It was the ninth win of his career.

Pearson averaged 61.750 mph over the half-mile dirt track.

Petty's point lead over Jarrett was extended to 5,900 points.

Race No. 45

Jarrett Beats Pearson In Western North Carolina 500

WEAVERVILLE, NC (Aug 9) -- Ned Jarrett, saying he "needed to win one badly", outran David Pearson in a late race showdown and came home first in the Western North Carolina 500 at Asheville-Weaverville Speedway. It was his 10th win of the year and his first in nearly five weeks.

Benny Parsons got a chance at a factory Ford at Weaverville but showed inexperience

Jarrett passed Pearson in the 429th lap and led the remaining distance on the half-mile paved oval. He crossed under the checkered flag 9.0 seconds in front of his Dodge rival. Jarrett picked up $2,550 for his Bondy Long Ford

team.

"We've got a good solid team," said Jarrett. "My chassis man, James Hylton, has done an outstanding job this year. It takes time for a racing team to be successful. We've come together in a relatively short period of time."

The lead changed hands five times among three driver. Junior Johnson started on the pole and led the first 105 laps. He wound up third, four laps off the pace. Darel Dieringer came in fourth with Buck Baker fifth.

Ford Motor Company assigned two young drivers to wheel factory-backed cars in the race for future refer-

Grand National Race No. 45
500 Laps at Asheville-Weaverville Speedway
Weaverville, NC
"Western North Carolina 500"
250 Miles on Half-mile Paved Track
August 9, 1964

Fin	St	No.	Drvier	Team / Car	Laps	Money	Status
1	4	11	Ned Jarrett	Bondy Long '64 Ford	500	$2,550	Running
2	10	6	David Pearson	Cotton Owens '64 Dodge	500	1,400	Running
3	1	27	Junior Johnson	Banjo Matthews '64 Ford	496	1,100	Running
4	3	16	Darel Dieringer	Bud Moore '64 Mercury	494	875	Running
5	8	3	Buck Baker	Ray Fox '64 Dodge	485	750	Running
6	14	19	Larry Thomas	Herman Beam '64 Ford	470	650	Running
7	16	42	Bill McMahan	Casper Hensley '64 Pontiac	450	600	Running
8	29	49	Doug Moore	G C Spencer '64 Chevrolet	450	550	Running
9	20	34	Wendell Scott	Scott '63 Frod	449	450	Running
10	18	46	J T Putney	Walt Hunter '62 Chevrolet	455	400	Running
11	22	88	Neil Castles	Buck Baker '62 Chrysler	444	375	Running
12	33	02	Curtis Crider	Crider '63 Mercury	440	375	Running
13	23	32	Mark Hurley	'63 Ford	424	325	Running
14	31	99	Gene Hobby	'62 Dodge	406	275	Running
15	11	54	Jimmy Pardue	Burton-Robinson '64 Plym	388	250	Brakes
16	24	48	Doug Wilson	'64 Ford	342	250	Gen Brkt
17	19	20	Jack Anderson	'64 Ford	327	250	Brakes
18	25	86	Steve Young	Buck Baker '62 Chrysler	300	250	Shocks
19	15	78	Buddy Arrington	Arrington '63 Dodge	289	250	Shocks
20	5	00	Cale Yarborough	Holman-Moody '64 Ford	267	250	Radiator
21	9	06	Benny Parsons	Holman -Moody '64 Ford	258	250	Heating
22	12	5	Earl Balmer	Cotton Owens '64 Dodge	253	250	Shocks
23	30	9	Roy Tyner	R Southerlund '64 Chevrolet	201	250	Rear End
24	27	55	Earl Brooks	'62 Chevrolet	165	250	Clutch
25	6	43	Richard Petty	Petty Eng '64 Plymouth	140	250	Crash
26	7	1	Billy Wade	Bud Moore '64 Mercury	138	100	Engine
27	35	60	Doug Cooper	Bob Cooper '63 Frod	135	100	Heating
28	32	01	Chuck Huckabee	Curtis Crider '63 Mercury	123	100	Rear End
29	28	92	Rod Wiliams	Ray Osborne '64 Ford	110	100	Engine
30	2	41	Jim Paschal	Petty Eng '64 Plymouth	85	100	Brakes
31	21	52	E J Trivette	Jess Potter '62 Che;vrolet	66	100	H Gasket
32	26	53	Pete Stewart	'64 Ford	51	100	Brakes
33	17	10	Bernard Alvarez	Alvarez '64 Ford	19	100	Heating
34	34	04	Don Branson	'63 Ford	16	100	Engine
35	13	82	Bunkie Blackburn	Casper Hensley '63 Pontiac	12	100	Engine
36	36	61	Jim Dineo	'62 Pontiac	4	100	Handling

Time of Race: 3 hours, 13 minutes, 18 seconds
Average Speed: 77.600 mph
Pole Winner: Junior Johnson - 84.626 mph
Lap Leaders: Junior Johnson 1-105, Ned Jarrett 106-145, David Pearson 146-180,
    Jarrett 181-418, Pearson 419-428, Jarrett 429-500
Cautions: 2
Margin of Victory: 9 seconds
Attendance: 10,000

Cale Yarborough impressed the FoMoCo brass at Weaverville

ence. Benny Parsons, an ARCA driver out of Detroit, MI, and Cale Yarborough drew the assignments. Cale started fifth and Parsons lined up ninth.

Parsons had difficulty in getting oriented with the powerful car on the speedy track and was generally unimpressive in his big chance. Yarborough ran with the leaders at times and drew raves until a broken radiator sent him to the sidelines. "I thought Cale was excellent," said John Holman, entrepreneur of the Ford racing efforts.

A crowd of 10,000 was on hand to watch Jarrett average 77.600 mph for his 32nd career win.

Race No. 46

Jarrett Ignores Peeling Tire; Wins Moyock 300

MOYOCK, NC (Aug 13) -- Ned Jarrett ignored orders from his pit crew and rode the wing of a prayer to victory in the Moyock 300 at Dog Track Speedway.

The Newton, NC driver drove his Bondy Long Ford around David Pearson six laps from the finish with white threads showing through his right front tire and a fuel tank registering empty.

The two veteran drivers had run close all night with Pearson leading all but the first 37 laps and the last six. As the final laps approached, Pearson pulled into the pits for fuel and tires. Jarrett stayed out. "When Pearson pitted, I figured I'd try to make it," said Jarrett. "I really slowed up and was lucky I made it."

Pearson fell a lap back but still managed to finish second. Richard Petty was third with Bunkie Blackburn fourth and Bill McMahan fifth.

Jarrett led the opening 37 laps from the pole position. Pearson slid past in the 38th lap and was in front when rain forced a red flag. The race had to be resumed the following night.

Jarrett averaged 63.965 mph.

Grand National Race No. 46
300 Laps at Dog Track Speedway
Moyock, NC
"Moyock 300"
100 Miles on .333-mile Paved Track
August 13, 1964

Fin	St	No.	Driver	Team / Car	Laps	Money	Status
1	1	11	Ned Jarrett	Bondy Long '64 Ford	300	$1,000	Running
2	3	6	David Pearson	Cotton Owens '64 Dodge	299	600	Running
3	2	43	Richard Petty	Petty Eng '64 Plymouth	296	400	Running
4	5	82	Bunkie Blackburn	Casper Hensley '64 Pontiac	294	300	Running
5	8	42	Bill McMahan	Casper Hensley '63 Pontiac	286	275	Running
6	4	72	Doug Yates	Yates '63 Plymouth	283	240	Running
7	9	88	Neil Castles	Buck Baker '62 Chrysler	277	200	Running
8	17	55	Wendell Scott	'62 Chevrolet	273	175	Running
9	10	83	Worth McMillion	McMillion '62 Pontiac	272	150	Running
10	7	02	Curtis Crider'	Crider '63 Mercury	257	140	Rear End
11	13	9	Roy Tyner	R Southerlund '64 Chevrolet	111	130	Rear End
12	15	01	Chuck Huckabee	Curtis Crider '63 Mercury	67	120	Brakes
13	16	04	Don Branson	'63 Ford	44	110	Oil Pres
14	11	78	Ray Carter	'63 Dodge	37	100	Handling
15	6	10	Bernard Alvarez	Alvarez '64 Ford	36	100	Sway Bar
16	14	86	Steve Young	Buck Baker '62 Chrysler	12	100	Axle
17	12	49	Doug Moore	G C Spencer '64 Chevrolet	11	100	Engine
DNS		34	Earl Brooks	'63 Ford	---	100	Clutch

Time of Race: 1 hour, 33 minutes, 48 seconds
Average Speed: 63.965 mph
Pole Winner: Ned Jarrett - 67.643 mph
Lap Leaders: Ned Jarrett 1-37, David Pearson 38-294, Jarrett 295-300
Cautions:
Margin of Victory: 1 lap plus 12 seconds
Attendance:

Race No. 47

Petty Nears Title With Mountaineer 500 Victory

HUNTINGTON, WV (Aug 16) -- Richard Petty scampered past David Pearson in the 221st lap and breezed to victory in the Mountaineer 500 at the West Virginia International Speedway. It was the eighth win of the year for the Randleman, NC Plymouth driver and it virtually assured him of the 1964 NASCAR championship.

Petty increased his point lead over Ned Jarrett to 5,300 points after 47 races.

Junior Johnson wound up second in his Ford, three laps off the pace. Jarrett got third place money despite blowing his engine with two laps to go. Fourth place went to Jim Paschal, also in a Petty Plymouth, with Earl Balmer fifth.

The lead changed hands four times among four drivers with Petty on top twice for a total of 396 laps. "I figured there were about six drivers capable of winning

*Richard Petty seems very happy after winning
Mountaineer 500*

Grand National Race No. 47
500 Laps at West Virginia International Speedway
Huntington, WV
"Mountaineer 500"
218.75 miles on .4375-mile Paved Track
August 16, 1964

Fin	St	No.	Driver	Team / Car	Laps	Money	Status
1	3	43	Richard Petty	Petty Eng '64 Plymouth	500	$2,550	Running
2	5	27	Junior Johnson	Banjo Matthews '64 Ford	497	1,600	Running
3	2	11	Ned Jarrett	Bondy Long '64 Ford	494	1,225	Engine
4	9	41	Jim Paschal	Petty Eng '64 Plymouth	494	1,000	Running
5	7	5	Earl Balmer	Cotton Owens '64 Dodge	489	800	Running
6	1	1	Billy Wade	Bud Moore '64 Mercury	488	800	Running
7	6	16	Darel Dieringer	Bud Moore '64 Mercury	485	550	Running
8	8	39	Larry Thomas	Thomas '64 Ford	478	450	Running
9	11	82	Bunkie Blackburn	Capser Hensley '64 Pontiac	477	375	Running
10	13	78	Buddy Arrington	Arrington '63 Dodge	458	350	Running
11	19	17	Junior Spencer	'64 Ford	448	300	Running
12	21	83	Worth McMillion	McMillion '62 Pontiac	432	275	Running
13	27	31	Al White	'63 Ford	418	250	Running
14	16	46	J T Putney	Walt Hunter '62 Chevrolet	414	250	Engine
15	18	60	Doug Cooper	Bob Cooper '63 Ford	393	250	Running
16	10	54	Jimmy Pardue	Burton-Robinson '64 Plym	380	200	Axle
17	4	6	David Pearson	Cotton Owens '64 Dodge	367	225	Crash
18	14	40	Bud Harless	'62 Pontiac	365	300	Engine
19	26	86	Steve Young	Buck Baker '62 Chrysler	337	200	Running
20	29	02	Curtis Crider	Crider '63 Mercury	336	200	Oil Press
21	17	20	Jack Anderson	'64 Ford	290	200	Rear End
22	24	34	Wendell Scott	Scott '63 Ford	248	200	Rear End
23	25	61	Pop McGinnis	'62 Pontiac	238	200	Brakes
24	12	42	Bill McMahan	Casper Hensley '63 Pontiac	235	200	Clutch
25	30	01	Chuck Huckabee	Curtis Crider '63 Mercury	131	---	Rear End
26	28	10	Bernard Alvarez	'64 Ford	73	---	Engine
27	22	52	E J Trivette	Jess Potter '62 Chevrolet	71	---	Engine
28	23	55	Earl Brooks	'62 Chevrolet	71	---	Engine
29	31	04	Don Branson	'62 Ford	46	---	Engine
30	15	88	Neil Castles	Buck Baker '62 Chrysler	38	---	Trans
31	20	32	Mark Hurley	'63 Ford	30	---	Trans

Time of Race: 3 hours, 06 minutes, 12 seconds
Average Speed: 70.488 mph
Pole Winner: Billy Wade - 79.505 mph
Lap Leaders: Billy Wade 1-58, Ned Jarrett 59-100, Richard Petty 101-216,
    David Pearson 217-220, Petty 221-500
Cautions: 6 for 36 laps
Margin of Victory: 3 laps plus
Attendance: 12,000

this race," said the 27 year-old Petty. "I was the one who got through without any trouble."

Petty averaged 70.488 mph for the 218.75-mile race on the .4375-mile oval. "I like the long races because they pay more money," Petty said as he flashed his famous grin. He won $2,550 for his 35th career Grand National win.

Thirty-one cars started the race but only 13 were running at the finish. David Pearson led four laps but was taken out in a solo crash wnen a tire blew.

Race No. 48

Pearson Takes Columbia 200 For 7th Win of Season

COLUMBIA, SC (Aug 21) -- David Pearson overcame a punctured tire and took the lead late in the race to win the Sandlapper 200 at Columbia Speedway. It was the seventh win of the season for the dark-haired Dodge driver.

Pearson, 29, started ninth and spent most of the race working his way into contention. After he suffered a flat tire early, Pearson had to work to stay within sight of leaders Junior Johnson, Billy Wade and Ned Jarrett.

Jarrett seemingly was on his way to his 12th win of the season, but a blown engine put the Newton, NC Ford driver out in the final laps. Pearson took the lead for the first time with 10 laps remaining and outran Doug Yates by two laps to snare the $1,000 top prize.

Jimmy Pardue came in third and Jarrett got credit for fourth based on laps completed. Doug Cooper wrecked late in the race, but still got fifth place money.

Five caution flags broke the action. In one incident, Buddy Arrington, rookie out of Martinsville, VA, spun his Dodge into the infield dirt embankment. Arrington then backed out into traffic where Bobby Isaac and E.J. Trivette slammed into him. There were no injuries.

All top threats except Pearson fell out. Richard Petty led the first seven laps, but retired early with oil pressure problems. Junior Johnson went behind the wall with engine problems at the half-way point. Billy Wade, who led for 45 laps, called it a day after his Mercury suffered rear end problems.

Pearson averaged 61.697 mph before a crowd of 9,000.

Grand National Race No. 48
200 Laps at Columbia Speedway
Columbia, SC
"Sandlapper 200"
100 Miles on Half-mile Dirt Track
August 21, 1964

Fin	St	No.	Driver	Team / Car	Laps	Money	Status
1	9	6	David Pearson	Cotton Owens '64 Dodge	200	$1,000	Running
2	3	72	Doug Yates	Yates '63 Plymouth	198	600	Running
3	5	54	Jimmy Pardue	Burton-Robinson '64 Plym	196	400	Running
4	1	11	Ned Jarrett	Bondy Long '64 Ford	193	300	Engine
5	11	60	Doug Cooper	Bob Cooper '63 Ford	186	275	Crash
6	16	49	Doug Moore	G C Spencer '64 Chevrolet	182	240	Running
7	10	34	Wendell Scott	Scott '64 Ford	177	200	Running
8	21	61	Jim Dimeo	'62 Pontiac	171	175	Running
9	13	20	Jack Anderson	'64 Ford	159	150	Running
10	6	1	Billy Wade	Bud Moore '64 Mercury	149	140	R Housing
11	8	45	Bobby Isaac	Louie Weathersby '63 Plym	120	130	Crash
12	7	78	Buddy Arrington	Arrington '63 Dodge	117	120	Crash
13	12	52	E J Trivette	Jess Potter '62 Chevrolet	114	110	Crash
14	4	27	Junior Johnson	Banjo Matthews '64 Ford	100	100	Engine
15	18	88	Neil Castles	Buck Baker '62 Chrysler	57	100	Rear End
16	14	02	Curtis Crider	Crider '63 Mercury	53	100	Balve
17	2	43	Richard Petty	Petty Eng '64 Plymouth	17	100	Oil Pres
18	15	9	Roy Tyner	R Southerlund '64 Chevrolet	11	100	Heating
19	19	01	Chuck Huckabee	Curtis Crider '63 Mercury	8	100	Oil Pres
20	20	04	Don Branson	'62 Ford	2	100	Engine
21	17	86	Steve Young	Buck Baker '62 Chrysler	1	100	Coil

Time of Race: 1 hour, 37 minutes, 15 seconds
Average Speed: 61.697 mph
Pole Winner: Ned Jarrett - 69.150 mph
Lap Leaders: Richard Petty 1-17, Junior Johnson 18-100, Billy Wade 101-145,
    Ned Jarrett 146-190, David Pearson 191-200
Cautions: 5
Margin of Victory: 2 laps plus
Attendance: 9,000

Race No. 49

Johnson Ends Famine with Flag-to-Flag Victory

WINSTON-SALEM, NC (Aug 22) -- Junior Johnson of Ronda, NC ended a season-long slump by taking the Myers Brothers Memorial Race at Bowman-Gray Stadium in impressive fashion. It was Johnson's first win since February and his first since returning to Ford.

Johnson put his Banjo Matthews Ford on the pole and led the entire distance. He finished a lap ahead of runner-up Richard Petty. Ned Jarrett came in third with David Pearson fourth and Fred Harb fifth.

A crowd of 15,000 watched Johnson notch his 36th career Grand National triumph at a speed of 46.192 mph. One caution flag for four laps interrupted the hot

pace.

Glen Wood made his annual return to racing on the quarter-mile track and started fourth. But the 'Old Woodchopper' went only 106 laps before he pulled his Ford in with handling problems.

Grand National Race No. 49
250 Laps at Bowman-Gray Stadium
Winston-Salem, NC
"Myers Brothers Memorial"
62.5 Miles on Quarter-Mile Paved Track
August 22, 1964

Fin	St	No.	Driver	Team / Car	Laps	Money	Status
1	1	27	Junior Johnson	Banjo Matthews '64 Ford	250	$1,000	Running
2	2	43	Richard Petty	Petty Eng '64 Plymouth	249	600	Running
3	3	11	Ned Jarrett	Bondy Long '64 Ford	249	400	Running
4	6	6	David Pearson	Cotton Owens '64 Dodge	245	300	Running
5	7	2	Fred Harb	Cliff Stewart '63 Pontiac	240	275	Running
6	9	36	Larry Thomas	Wade Younts '62 Dodge	239	240	Running
7	10	72	Doug Yates	Yates '63 Plymouth	239	200	Running
8	8	60	Doug Cooper	Bob Cooper '64 Ford	233	175	Running
9	11	02	Curtis Crider	Crider '64 Mercury	231	150	Running
10	13	88	Neil Castles	Buck Baker '62 Chrysler	228	140	Running
11	17	9	Roy Tyner	R Southerlund '64 Chevrolet	218	130	Running
12	12	32	Jack Anderson	'63 Ford	216	120	Running
13	21	61	Jim Dimeo	'62 Pontiac	193	110	Running
14	16	99	Gene Hobby	'62 Dodge	191	100	Running
15	22	01	Chuck Huckabee	Curtis Crider '63 Mercury	179	100	Oil Pres
16	5	54	Jimmy Pardue	Burton-Robinson '64 Plym	171	100	Linkage
17	14	49	Doug Moore	G C Spencer '64 Chevrolet	149	100	Handling
18	23	34	Wendell Scott	Scott '63 Ford	119	100	Diff
19	4	21	Glen Wood	Wood Bros '64 Ford	106	100	Handling
20	19	20	Mark Hurley	'64 Ford	99	100	Diff
21	15	97	Bill Whitley	'62 Chevrolet	98	100	Brakes
22	20	52	E J Trivette	Jess Potter '62 Chevrolet	82	100	Heating
23	18	78	Buddy Arrington	Arrington '63 Dodge	52	---	Diff
24	24	55	Earl Brooks	'62 Chevrolet	49	---	Oil Pres

Time of Race: 1 hour, 11 minutes, 11 seconds
Average Speed: 46.192 mph
Pole Winner: Junior Johnson 49.846 mph
Lap Leaders: Junior Johnson 1-250
Cautions: 1 for 4 laps
Margin of Victory: 1 lap plus
Attendance: 15,000

Race No. 50

Johnson Outruns Wood For 2nd Straight Win

ROANOKE VA (Aug 23) -- Junior Johnson whipped his Ford past Glen Wood in the sixth lap and led the rest of the way to win the 50-mile Grand National event at Roanoke Raceway. It was the second straight win for the portly Ronda, NC Ford driver.

Wood started on the pole but fell to third place at the finish. Ned Jarrett wound up second, a lap behind

Grand National Race No. 50
200 Laps at Roanoke Raceway
Roanoke, VA
50 Miles on Quarter-mile Paved Track
August 23, 1964

Fin	St	No.	Driver	Team / Car	Laps	Money	Status
1	3	27	Junior Johnson	Banjo Matthews '64 Ford	200	$850	Running
2	13	11	Ned Jarrett	Bondy Long '64 Ford	199	530	Running
3	1	21	Glen Wood	Wood Bros '64 Ford	199	430	Running
4	2	6	David Pearson	Cotton Owens '64 dodge	199	350	Running
5	5	54	Jimmy Pardue	Burton-Robinson '64 Plym	199	300	Running
6	9	72	Doug Yates	Yates '63 Plymouth	195	240	Running
7	4	36	Larry Thomas	Wade Younts '62 Dodge	192	215	Running
8	16	9	Roy Tyner	R Southerlund '64 Chevrolet	186	180	Running
9	10	80	Neil Castles	Buck Baker '62 Chrysler	185	150	Running
10	20	83	Worth McMillion	McMillion '62 Pontiac	178	140	Running
11	15	49	Doug Moore	G C Spencer '64 Chevrolet	176	145	Running
12	12	99	Gene Hobby	'62 Dodge	174	120	Running
13	11	32	Jack Anderson	'63 Ford	167	130	Running
14	19	02	Curtis Crider	Crider '63 Mercury	164	120	Trans
15	6	41	Richard Petty	Petty Eng '64 Plymouth	148	125	Engine
16	8	2	Fred Harb	Cliff Stewart '63 Pntiac	122	100	Housing
17	21	34	Wendell Scott	Scott '63 Ford	43	100	Heating
18	7	60	Doug Cooper	Bob Cooper '64 Ford	21	100	Trans
19	18	01	Chuck Huckabee	Curtis Crider '63 Mercury	8	100	Brakes
20	14	61	Bob Cooper	Cooper '62 Pontiac	2	115	Elngine
21	17	20	Mark Hurley	'64 Ford	2	100	Handling
22	22	55	Earl Brooks	'62 Chevrolet	2	100	Trans

Time of Race: 1 hour, 11 seconds
Average Speed: 49.847 mph
Pole Winner: Glen Wood - 55.970 mph
Lap Leaders: Glen Wood 1-5, Junior Johnson 6-200
Cautions:
Margin of Victory: 1 lap plus
Attendance: 4,500

Johnson. David Pearson was fourth with Jimmy Pardue fifth.

A crowd of 4,500 was on hand for the 200 lapper on the quarter-mile oval. Johnson averaged 49.847 mph.

Richard Petty started sixth on the grid but went only 148 laps before the engine blew in his Plymouth. His point lead over Jarrett was 'sliced' to 4,900

Race No. 51

Baker's Steady Drive Nets 3rd Southern 500 Victory

DARLINGTON, SC (Sept 7) -- Old Pro Buck Baker ignored the roars of the young lions and won his third Southern 500 before a Labor Day crowd of 65,000 at Darlington Raceway. The 45 year-old Charlotte driver carefully steered his Ray Fox Dodge through the wreck-plagued 15th staging of the event to pocket $21,230. It was his 46th career Grand National win.

Baker started sixth on the grid and patiently bided his time. Young hot-shots Richard Petty, David Pear-

Old Pro Buck Baker drove Ray Fox's Dodge #3 to his 3rd Southern 500 win

Grand National Race No. 51
364 Laps at Darlington Raceway
Darlington, SC
"Southern 500"
500 Miles on 1.375-mile Paved Track
September 7, 1964

Fin	St	No.	Driver	Team / Car	Laps	Money	Status
1	6	3	Buck Baker	Ray Fox '64 Dodge	364	$21,230	Running
2	4	41	Jim Paschal	Petty Eng '64 Plymouth	362	8,960	Running
3	1	43	Richard Petty	Petty Eng '64 Plymouth	360	8,170	Running
4	16	11	Ned Jarrett	Bondy Long '64 Ford	359	3,575	Running
5	5	54	Jimmy Pardue	Burton-Robinson '64 Plym	358	2,955	Running
6	17	1	Billy Wade	Bud Moore '64 Mercury	351	2,375	Running
7	22	19	Larry Thomas	Herman Beam '64 Ford	351	1,775	Running
8	14	06	Cale Yarborough	Holman-Moody '64 Ford	344	1,525	Running
9	27	46	J T Putney	Walt Hunter '63 Chevrolet	337	1,345	Running
10	38	53	Bob Cooper	Cooper '63 Ford	305	1,025	Running
11	36	02	Curtis Crider	Crider '63 Mercury	301	950	Running
12	2	6	David Pearson	Cotton Owens '64 Dodge	298	1,130	Crash
13	27	48	Bobby Keck	W S Jenkins '63 Ford	280	850	Running
14	41	9	Roy Tyner	R Southerlund '64 Chevrolet	264	800	Rear End
15	32	36	Major Melton	Wade Younts '63 Dodge	253	750	Crash
16	30	09	Roy Mayne	'62 Chevrolet	247	700	Engine
17	11	03	LeeRoy Yarbrough	Ray Fox '64 Dodge	233	720	Vibration
18	15	49	G C Spencer	Spencer '64 Ford	186	600	Engine
19	33	71	Sam McQuagg	J L Thomas '63 Ford	179	550	Rear End
20	10	26	Bobby Isaac	Ray Nichels '64 dodge	176	530	Axle
21	23	64	Elmo Langley	Woodfield Ford '64 Ford	167	500	Hub Bolts
22	3	28	Fred Lorenzen	Holman-Moody '64 Ford	154	620	Crash
23	12	27	Junior Johnson	Banjo Matthews '64 Ford	149	610	Crash
24	7	16	Darel Dieringer	Bud Moore '64 Mercury	149	600	Crash
25	24	45	Bud Moore	Louie Weathersby '63 Plym	142	500	Crash
26	29	04	H B Bailey	Alemeda Auto '64 Pontiac	135	500	Crash
27	18	7	Bobby Johns	Holman-Moody '64 Ford	131	500	Engine
28	9	25	Paul Goldsmith	Ray Nichels '64 Plymouth	129	790	Vibration
29	19	76	Larry Frank	Frank '64 Ford	119	620	Running
30	21	82	Bunkie Blackburn	Casper Hensley '64 Pontiac	114	600	Clutch
31	20	10	Buddy Baker	Bernard Alvarez '64 Ford	112	500	Engine
32	18	5	Earl Balmer	Cotton Owens '64 Dodge	109	580	Engine
33	25	55	Tiny Lund	'64 Ford	71	750	Crash
34	39	58	Doug Moore	Moore '64 Chevrolet	66	500	Oil Pres
35	35	86	Neil Castles	Buck Baker '62 Chrysler	17	500	Trans
36	31	42	Bill McMahan	Casper Hensley '63 Pontiac	17	500	Brakes
37	26	60	Doug Cooper	Bob Cooper '64 Ford	16	630	Valve
38	28	63	Don Hume	Don House '63 Ford	9	500	Crash
39	13	21	Nelson Stacy	Wood Bros '64 Ford	5	500	Drive Sh
40	34	52	E J Trivette	Jess Potter '62 Chevrolet	4	500	Handling
41	44	13	Bud Harless	'64 Ford	2	500	Engine
42	40	88	Jimmy Helms	Buck Baker '62 Chrysler	2	500	Fuel Pmp
43	43	01	Ed Livingston	Curtis Crider '63 Mercury	2	500	Oil Pres
44	42	0	Frank Graham	Curtis Crider '62 Ford	1	500	Heting

Time of Race: 4 hours, 15 minutes, 01 second
Average Speed: 117.757 mph
Pole Winner: Richard Petty - 136.815 mph
Lap Leaders: Richard Petty 1-32, David Pearson 33-37, Petty 38-56, Jimmy Pardue 57,
Petty 58-84, Junior Johnson 85, Jim Paschal 86-111, Paul Goldsmith 112-114,
Petty 115-151, Goldsmith 152, Petty 153-289, Pardue 290-301, Buck Baker 302-364
Cautions: 7 for 50 laps
Margin of Victory: 2 laps plus
Attendance: 65,000

Jim Paschal finished second to Baker, two laps down. Petty was third, Ned Jarrett fourth and Pardue fifth.

"This is a tricky track," said Baker. "I could run at

Buck Baker chats with Jim Hunter and Joe Whitlock prior to Southern 500

135 (mph) without straining, and I felt confident at that speed. I'm not a flashy guy. I don't feel I have to blow everbody off the track to prove I can drive."

Petty won the pole at 136.815 mph and led almost at will. "We had 'em covered," he said. "But the big thing was that $20,000 ignition wire that burned in two."

Junior Johnson triggered the day's biggest crash, spinning his Ford on lap 149. Bud Moore's Plymouth smashed into Johnson, driving the rear bumper of the yellow Ford into the back seat compartment. Miraculously there was no fire.

Darel Dieringer had a rough afternoon, spinning or wrecking his Mercury no less than four times. After the fourth incident, car owner Bud Moore told Dieringer to

Darel Dieringer's #16 Mercury tangles with Bobby Isaac's #26 Dodge. Paul Goldsmith, fighting a vibration, slides underneath

Pearson, Jimmy Pardue and Junior Johnson battled tooth-and-nail for top honors. Petty had led for 252 laps and was the dominating factor in the race. On lap 289, he came into the pits where his Petty Engineering pit crew went to work under the hood to repair a faulty ignition wire. He lost two laps and dropped out of contention. He was making a desperate bid to regain his lost time, but collided with Pearson and lost two more laps.

park the car. Dieringer, however, wanted to continue in the race. Moore prevailed in the argument. "Only a fool would drive that car out there again," muttered the car owner.

Baker averaged 117.757 mph as 50 laps were run under the caution flag.

Race No. 52

Pearson Wins Hickory; Thomas Comes From Last to 2nd

HICKORY, NC (Sept 11) -- David Pearson inched past Junior Johnson in the 65th lap and won the Buddy Shuman Memorial 250 at Hickory Speedway. It was the eighth win of the year for the Spartanburg, SC veteran.

Larry Thomas, driving Herman Beam's Ford, pulled the day's biggest surprise. He started last in the 27 car field, but came charging up through the pack. He wound up second, three laps behind Pearson. Buck Baker was third, Jimmy Pardue fourth and Richard Petty fifth.

Johnson led for 43 laps in his Ford, but overheating problems put him out after 89 laps. Bobby Isaac retired early when his Plymouth sheared off the lug nuts.

A crowd of 11,000 watched Pearson average 67.797 mph for the 250 trips around the .4-mile dirt oval.

Grand National Race No. 52
250 Laps at Hickory Speedway
Hickory, NC
"Buddy Shuman Memorial"
100 Miles on .4-mile Dirt Track
September 11, 1964

Fin	St	No.	Driver	Team / Car	Laps	Money	Status
1	1	6	David Pearson	Cotton Owens '64 Dodge	250	$2,035	Running
2	27	19	Larry Thomas	Herman Beam '64 Ford	247	600	Running
3	6	3	Buck Baker	Ray Fox '64 Dodge	246	400	Running
4	3	54	Jimmy Pardue	Burton-Robinson '64 Plym	246	300	Running
5	2	43	Richard Petty	Petty Eng '64 Plymouth	238	275	Running
6	16	02	Curtis Crider	Crider '63 Mecury	237	240	Running
7	21	5	Tiny Lund	'64 Ford	235	200	Running
8	14	88	Neil Castles	Buck Baker '62 Chrysler	229	175	Running
9	10	34	Wendell Scott	Scott '63 Ford	220	150	Running
10	26	61	Jimmy Helms	'62 Pontiac	218	140	Running
11	8	78	Buddy Arrington	Arrington '63 Dodge	217	130	Running
12	12	32	Mark Hurley	'63 Ford	217	120	Running
13	15	9	Roy Tyner	R Southerlund '64 Chevrolet	211	110	Running
14	17	58	Doug Moore	'64 Chevrolet	205	100	Running
15	20	48	Doug Wilson	'63 Ford	200	100	Running
16	18	68	Bob Derrington	'63 Ford	177	100	Rear End
17	19	86	Steve Young	Buck Baker '62 Chrysler	177	100	Running
18	7	60	Doug Cooper	Bob Cooper '64 Ford	170	100	Engine
19	24	97	Bill Whitley	'62 Chevrolet	142	100	Running
20	25	55	Earl Brooks	'62 Chevrolet	113	100	Heating
21	22	0	Don Branson	'62 Ford	96	100	Engine
22	4	27	Junior Johnson	Banjo Matthews '64 Ford	89	315	Heating
23	13	52	E J Trivette	Jess Potter '62 Chevrolet	59	100	Heating
24	11	81	Frank Weathers	'63 Dodge	52	100	Lug Bolts
25	9	53	Pete Stewart	'63 Ford	48	100	Piston
26	5	45	Bobby Isaac	Louie Weathersby '63 Plym	7	100	Lug Bolts
27	23	01	Joe Cotes	Curtis Crider '63 Mercury	5	100	Radiator

Time of Race: 1 hour, 28 minutes, 30 seconds
Average Speed: 67.797 mph
Pole Winner: David Pearson - 74.418 mph
Lap Leaders: David Pearson 1-21, Junior Johnson 22-64, Pearson 65-250
Cautions: 5
Margin of Victory: 3 laps plus
Attendance: 11,000

Grand National Race No. 53
300 Laps at Virginia State Fairgrounds
Richmond, VA
"Capital City 300"
150 Miles on Half-mile Dirt Track
September 14, 1964

Fin	St	No.	Driver	Team / Car	Laps	Money	Status
1	3	5	Cotton Owens	Owens '64 Dodge	300	$2,400	Running
2	9	6	David Pearson	Cotton Owens '64 Dodge	299	1,600	Running
3	10	41	Richard Petty	Petty Eng '64 Plymouth	292	1,200	Running
4	12	19	Larry Thomas	Herman Beam '64 Ford	289	900	Running
5	1	11	Ned Jarrett	Bondy Long '64 Ford	280	710	Engine
6	27	88	Neil Castles	Buck Baker '62 Chrysler	271	525	Running
7	15	9	Roy Tyner	R Southerlund '64 Chevrolet	270	400	Running
8	4	27	Junior Johnson	Banjo Matthews '64 Ford	264	300	Engine
9	7	32	Mark Hurley	'63 Ford	262	250	Running
10	21	52	E J Trivette	Jess Potter '62 Chevrolet	254	250	Running
11	17	54	Jimmy Pardue	Burton-Robinson '64 Plym	223	225	Rear End
12	14	78	Buddy Arrington	Arrington '63 Dodge	219	225	Running
13	32	83	Worth McMillion	McMillion '62 Pontiac	206	225	Rear End
14	2	1	Billy Wade	Bud Moore '64 Mercury	203	225	Engine
15	23	60	Doug Cooper	Bob Cooper '64 Ford	203	200	Running
16	31	64	Elmo Langley	Woodfield '64 Ford	186	200	Oil Cooler
17	5	45	Bobby Isaac	Louie Weathersby '63 Plym	184	200	Con Rod
18	6	16	Darel Dieringer	Bud Moore '64 Mercury	182	175	Engine
19	33	99	Gene Hobby	'62 Plymouth	177	175	A Frame
20	16	09	Roy Mayne	'62 Chevrolet	175	175	Engine
21	20	34	Wendell Scott	Scott '63 Ford	159	175	Radiator
22	8	43	Jim Paschal	Petty Eng '64 Plymouth	116	150	Rear end
23	26	02	Curtis Crider	Crider '63 Mercury	103	150	Shocks
24	13	3	Buck Baker	Ray Fox '64 Dodge	101	150	Rear End
25	28	20	Jack Anderson	'64 Ford	99	150	Oil Pres
26	19	58	Doug Moore	'64 Chevrolet	67	150	Crash
27	24	0	Don Branson	'62 Ford	65	150	Crash
28	29	61	Bob Cooper	Cooper '62 Pontiac	41	150	Rear End
29	25	01	Joe Cotes	Curtis Crider '63 Mercury	15	150	Handling
30	22	86	Steve Young	Buck Baker '62 Chevrolet	11	150	Oil Line
31	11	55	Tiny Lund	'64 Ford	10	150	Rock Arm
32	30	68	Bob Derrington	'63 Ford	1	150	Oil Pres
33	18	72	Doug Yates	Yates '63 Plymouth	1	150	Oil Pres

Time of Race: 2 hours, 25 minutes, 16 seconds
Average Speed: 61.955 mph
Pole Winner: Ned Jarrett - 66.89 mph
Lap Leaders: Billy Wade 1-9, Junior Johnson 10-65, Wade 66-131, Johnson 132-169, Cotton Owens 170-187, Johnson 188-264, Owens 265-300
Cautions: 5 for 23 laps
Margin of Victory: 1 lap plus
Attendance: 8,500

Race No. 53

Cotton Owens Wins Capital City 300 in Return to Action

RICHMOND, VA   (Sept 14) -- Cotton Owens returned to the driver's seat and emerged with a popular victory in the attrition-sapped Capital City 300 at the

Virginia State Fairgrounds. It was the ninth career win for the sandy-haired 40 year-old veteran.

David Pearson, Owens' regular driver, finished second to his talented tutor. Richard Petty came in third with Larry Thomas and Ned Jarrett rounding out the top five.

Owens came out of retirement for mere exercise. "I love the dirt tracks," he said. "We're running fewer and fewer dirt tracks on the Grand National circuit these days. That's a shame. I don't care anything about driving on asphalt. I just did this for fun."

Owens took the lead for the final time in the 265th lap when leader Junior Johnson blew an engine. Only 10 cars finished the race, which had 33 starters. One car, Doug Cooper's Ford, was 97 laps behind at the finish.

Owens, the diminutive 5'6" pioneer of the sport of speed, became the 16th different winner in the 1946 NASCAR season. He averaged 61.955 mph as the caution flag was waved five times for 23 laps.

Doug Moore crashed his Chevrolet through the board fence on lap 69, but he was not hurt.

Race No. 54

Jarrett Beats Pearson, Rain In Manassas 500

MANASSAS, VA (Sept 18) -- A steady light rain failed to stop Ned Jarrett from racking up his 12th win of the season in the 500-lapper at Old Dominion Speedway.

Jarrett drove his Bondy Long Ford past David Pearson in the 299th lap and led the rest of the way. Nearly 230 laps were run on the .375-mile paved oval while it was raining, but officials said the misty rain was insufficient to halt the race.

Pearson finished a lap-and-a-second behind Jarrett to take second place. Richard Petty was third, Larry Thomas fourth and Bert Robbins fifth in his first Grand National start. Robbins had started dead last in the 20 car field.

After Pearson led the first six laps from the pole, Petty took the lead on lap 7, holding it for 20 laps. Then Jarrett and Pearson took the spotlight. Jarrett led all but 50 laps after he took the lead from Petty.

Jarrett averaged 68.842 mph for his 34th career win.

Grand National Race No. 54
500 Laps at Old Dominion Speedway
Manassas, VA
187.5-Miles on .375-mile Paved Track
September 18, 1964

Fin	St	No.	Driver	Team / Car	Laps	Money	Status
1	3	11	Ned Jarrett	Bondy Long '64 Ford	500	$1,500	Running
2	1	6	David Pearson	Cotton Owens '64 Dodge	499	1,000	Running
3	2	41	Richard Petty	Petty Eng '64 Plymouth	496	725	Running
4	6	19	Larry Thomas	Herman Beam '64 Ford	480	600	Running
5	20	84	Bert Robbins	'63 Ford	467	400	Running
6	7	34	Wendell Scott	Scott '63 Ford	457	325	Running
7	17	83	Worth McMillion	McMillion '62 Pontiac	443	250	Running
8	4	64	Elmo Langley	Woodfield '64 Ford	433	200	Diff
9	12	9	Roy Tyner	R Southerlund '64 Chevrolet	420	150	Running
10	8	02	Curtis Crider	Crider '63 Mercury	414	125	Running
11	11	99	Gene Hobby	'62 Ford	414	125	Runing
12	13	88	Neil Castles	Buck Baker '62 Chrysler	354	100	Engine
13	19	55	Earl Brooks	'62 Chevrolet	309	100	Engine
14	5	54	Jimmy Pardue	Burton-Robinson '64 Plym	210	100	Engine
15	10	09	Dennis Zimmerman	'62 Ford	209	100	Oil Pres
16	9	68	Bob Derrington	'63 Ford	80	100	Diff
17	18	20	Jack Anderson	'64 Ford	9	100	Oil Pres
18	14	86	Steve Young	Buck Baker '62 Chrysler	3	100	Trans
19	16	0	Don Branson	'62 Ford	1	100	Steering
20	15	01	Joe Cotes	Curtis Crider '63 Mercury	1	100	Steering

Time of Race: 2 hours, 43 minutes, 25 seconds
Average Speed: 68.842 mph
Pole Winner: David Pearson - 74.626 mph
Lap Leaders: David Pearson 1-6, Richard Petty 7-26, Ned Jarrett 27-248,
    Pearson 249-298, Jarrett 299-500
Cautions:
Margin of Victory: 1 lap plus 1 second
Attendance:

Race No. 55

Jarrett Edges Owens in Hillsboro 150

HILLSBORO, NC (Sept 20) -- Ned Jarrett took the lead from David Pearson with 39 laps to go and held off Cotton Owens to win the 150-miler at Orange Speedway. It was the 13th win of the season for Jarrett.

Owens, competing in his second race since ending a lengthy retirement, insisted he isn't back in the driver's seat for good. "This was another race on the dirt tracks, so I decided I'd go out and have some more fun." he said. Owens started fifth and wound up second. He won his other race at Richmond.

Larry Thomas grabbed third spot -- his fourth straight top five finish in Herman Beam's Ford. Wendell Scott was fourth and Buddy Arrington fifth.

Jarrett covered the 150 miles at a 86.725 clip. Pearson had led for 118 laps when a broken fan belt sent his Dodge to the pits for good. He got 14th in the final order.

Jimmy Pardue, who ranks fourth in the point

standings, qualified second and wound up 13th after making several unscheduled pit stops. The North Wilkesboro, NC Plymouth driver was competing in his final Grand National race. Two days later, he was killed while testing tires at Charlotte Motor Speedway. He became the third NASCAR driver to lose his life in the 1964 season.

Grand National Race No. 55
167 Laps at Orange Speedway
Hillsboro, NC
150 Miles on .9-mile Dirt Track
September 20, 1964

Fin	St	No.	Driver	Team / Car	Laps	Money	Status
1	6	11	Ned Jarrett	Bondy Long '64 Ford	167	$1,550	Running
2	5	5	Cotton Owens	Owens '64 Dodge	166	1,000	Running
3	8	19	Larry Thomas	Herman Beam '64 Ford	162	750	Running
4	10	34	Wendell Scott	Scott '63 Ford	156	575	Running
5	11	78	Buddy Arrington	Arrington '63 Dodge	153	425	Running
6	15	02	Curtis Crider	Crider '63 Mercury	148	325	Vapor Lk
7	16	86	Steve Young	Buck Baker '62 Chrysler	147	275	Running
8	24	9	Roy Tyner	R Southerlund '64 Chevrolet	146	225	Running
9	27	36	Major Melton	Wade Younts '62 Dodge	145	200	Running
10	17	99	Gene Hobby	'62 Dodge	142	175	Running
11	9	48	Bobby Keck	'63 Ford	140	100	Running
12	23	83	Worth McMillion	McMillion '62 Pontiac	136	100	Running
13	2	54	Jimmy Pardue	Burton-Robinson '64 Plym	132	100	Running
14	1	6	David Pearson	Cotton Owens '64 Dodge	130	100	Fan Belt
15	22	68	Bob Derrington	'63 Ford	112	100	Running
16	4	43	Richard Petty	Petty Eng '64 Plymouth	111	100	Heating
17	12	52	E J Trivette	Jess Potter '62 Chevrolet	102	100	Engine
18	13	61	Doug Cooper	Bob Cooper '62 Pontiac	89	100	Engine
19	18	97	Bill Whitley	'62 Chevrolet	62	100	Heating
20	26	89	Buck Baker	David Walker '64 Plymouth	54	100	Brakes
21	19	20	Jack Anderson	'64 Ford	51	100	Engine
22	20	31	Cale Yarborough	'63 Ford	41	100	Crash
23	28	55	Earl Brooks	'62 Chevrolet	17	100	Heating
24	3	72	Doug Yates	Yates '63 Plymouth	14	100	Heating
25	7	2	Ken Rush	Cliff Stewart '63 Pontiac	12	000	Heating
26	14	88	Neil Castles	Buck Baker '62 Chrysler	8	---	Crank Sh
27	21	01	Joe Cotes	Curtis Crider '63 Mercury	2	---	Brakes
28	25	0	Don Branson	'62 Ford	1	---	Heating

Time of Race: 1 hour, 43 minutes, 59 seconds
Average Speed: 86.725 mph
Pole Winner: David Pearson - 89.28 mph
Lap Leaders: David Pearson 1-46, Richard Petty 47-53, Ned Jarrett 54-56, Pearson 57-128, Jarrett 129-167
Cautions:
Margin of Victory: 1 lap plus
Attendance:

Grand National Race No. 56
500 Laps at Martinsville Speedway
Martinsville, VA
"Old Dominion 500"
250 Miles on Half-mile Paved Track
September 27, 1964

Fin	St	No.	Driver	Team / Car	Laps	Money	Start
1	1	28	Fred Lorenzen	Holman-Moody '64 Ford	500	$4,175	Running
2	21	43	Richard Petty	Petty Eng '64 Plymouth	500	1,725	Running
3	2	27	Junior Johnson	Banjo Matthews '64 Ford	500	1,250	Running
4	5	21	Marvin Panch	Wood Bros '64 Ford	499	850	Running
5	3	11	Ned Jarrett	Bondy Long '64 Ford	497	775	Running
6	12	16	Darel Dieringer	Bud Moore '64 Mercury	491	675	Running
7	18	26	Bobby Isaac	Ray Nichels '64 Dodge	491	600	Running
8	13	6	David Pearson	Cotton Owens '64 dodge	491	525	Running
9	8	1	Billy Wade	Bud Moore '64 Mercury	490	425	Running
10	9	00	Cale Yarborough	Holman-Moody '64 Ford	489	415	Running
11	15	5	Earl Balmer	Cotton Owens '64 Dodge	487	375	Running
12	10	49	G C Spencer	Spencer '64 Ford	486	325	Running
13	19	3	Buck Baker	Ray Fox '64 Dodge	484	275	Running
14	14	19	Larry Thomas	Herman Beam '64 Ford	480	250	Running
15	24	46	J T Putney	Walt Hunter '62 Chevrolet	452	200	Running
16	30	84	Bert Robbins	'63 Ford	451	200	Running
17	37	31	Al White	'63 Ford	441	200	Running
18	27	09	Roy Mayne	'62 Chevrolet	436	200	Running
19	31	17	Junior Spencer	'64 Ford	436	200	Running
20	26	83	Worth McMillion	McMillion '62 Pontiac	436	200	Running
21	36	99	Gene Hobby	'62 Dodge	424	200	Running
22	23	02	Curtis Crider	Crider '63 Mercury	414	235	Rear End
23	32	55	Earl Brooks	'62 Chevrolet	402	200	Running
24	17	64	Elmo Langley	Woodfield '64 Ford	397	225	Rear end
25	7	41	Jim Paschal	Petty Eng '64 Plymouth	383	250	Rear End
26	29	34	Wendell Scott	Scott '63 Ford	380	150	Rear End
27	16	03	LeeRoy Yarbrough	Ray Fox '64 Dodge	344	175	Handling
28	39	36	Major Melton	Wade Younts '63 Dodge	339	150	Engine
29	22	60	Doug Cooper	Bob Cooper '64 Ford	338	175	Brakes
30	4	7	Bobby Johns	Holman-Moody '64 Ford	325	225	Crash
31	25	42	Bill McMahan	Casper Hensley '63 Pontiac	268	200	W Bearing
32	28	48	Doug Wilson	'63 Ford	260	150	Heating
33	6	25	Paul Goldsmith	Ray Nichels '64 Plymouth	184	200	Vibration
34	38	88	Neil Castles	Buck Baker '62 Chrysler	165	150	Trans
35	35	68	Bob Derrington	'63 Ford	128	150	Rear End
36	20	82	Bunkie Blackburn	Casper Hensley '64 Pontiac	124	205	Clutch
37	11	10	Buddy Baker	Bernard Alvarez '64 Ford	44	175	Heating
38	34	13	Jack Anderson	'64 Ford	18	150	Brakes
39	33	20	Ronnie Croy	'64 Ford	11	150	Oil Pres
40	40	97	Bill Whitley	'62 Chevrolet	6	150	Trans
DNS		72	Doug Yates	Yates '63 Plymouth	---	50	Engine
DNS		78	Buddy Arrington	Arrington '63 Dodge	---	25	

Time of Race: 3 hours, 42 minutes, 49 seconds
Average Speed: 67.320 mph
Pole Winner: Fred Lorenzen - 74.196 mph
Lap Leaders: Fred Lorenzen 1-163, Ricahrd Petty 164-168, Lorenzen 169-170, Ned Jarrett 171, Lorenzen 172-339, Junior Johnson 340, Lorenzen 341-500
Cautions: 6 for 28 laps
Margin of Victory: 1/3 lap
Attendance: 18,214

Race No. 56

Petty Clinches Title; Lorenzen Wins Martinsville

MARTINSVILLE, VA (Sept 27) -- Fred Lorenzen bagged his seventh victory in 14 starts, but 27 year-old Richard Petty grabbed the big prize by clinching the 1964 Grand National driving championship in the Old Dominion 500 at Martinsville Speedway.

Lorenzen started on the pole and led 493 of the 500 laps on the half-mile paved oval. Petty charged from 21st starting spot to finish second, one-third of a lap behind. Junior Johnson came in third, Marvin Panch fourth and Ned Jarrett fifth.

Petty held a 5,170 point lead over Jarrett when the points were tallied. Six races were remaining on the 1964 slate with total winner's points of 4,650.

Lorenzen said the 500 lapper was a seemingly

Bobby Johns, the replacement for the late Fireball Roberts in the Holman-Moody Ford, pits at Martinsville

endless event. "I don't know how much money I won," he said afterwards, "but I earned every dime of it. It was hotter than blue blazes out there. The heat was coming through the firewall and it was cooking me. I thought this race would never end."

A crowd of 18,214 watched the former carpenter from Elmhurst, IL average 67.320 mph for his 18th career Grand National win.

The night before the race, former driver Jimmy Thompson suffered a fatal heart attack at his home in Monroe, NC. He was 47.

Race No. 57

Jarrett Fends Off Petty for 14th Win of Year

SAVANNAH, GA (Oct 9) -- Ned Jarrett survived a scrape with Richard Petty and went on to win the 100-miler at Savannah Speedway. It was his 14th win of the season.

Jarrett started on the pole and led all the way. Midway through the race, Petty offered a stout challenge and the two raced side-by-side for just over a lap. Petty's rear tires almost came around and his car bounced off Jarrett's Ford. Jarrett wobbled while righting his path as Petty dropped several car lengths back. Richard had to settle for second place, a lap behind Jarrett when the checkered flag fell.

David Pearson came in third, Jack Anderson was fourth and Wendell Scott fifth.

Curtis Crider, journeyman driver out of Charleston, SC, qualified his tired Mercury fourth and chased the factory drivers with all his heart. He retired just after 18 laps and wound up 10th in the field of 12.

A crowd of 4,500 watched Jarrett average 68.663 mph on the half-mile dirt track.

Grand National Race No. 57
200 Laps at Savannah Speedway
Savannah, GA
100 Miles on Half-mile Dirt Track
October 9, 1964

Fin	St	No.	Driver	Team / Car	Laps	Money	Status
1	1	11	Ned Jarrett	Bondy Long '64 Ford	200	$1,000	Running
2	3	43	Richard Petty	Petty Eng '64 Plymouth	199	600	Running
3	2	6	David Pearson	Cotton Owens '64 Dodge	198	400	Running
4	8	32	Jack Anderson	'64 Ford	193	300	Running
5	5	34	Wendell Scott	Scott '63 Ford	192	275	Running
6	9	0	Larry Thomas	'62 Ford	190	240	Running
7	11	01	Darrell Bryant	Curtis Crider '63 Mercury	178	200	Running
8	10	88	Neil Castles	Buck Baker '62 Chrysler	177	175	Running
9	7	89	Marshall Sargent	David Walker '64 Plymouth	77	150	Engine
10	4	02	Curtis Crider	Cruder '63 Mercury	18	140	Rear end
11	6	18	Frank Brantley	'62 Plymouth	10	130	Oil Pres
12	12	68	Bob Derrington	Derrington '63 Ford	8	120	Fuel Pmp

Time of Race: 1 hour, 27 minutes, 23 seconds
Aveaage Speed: 68.663 mph
Pole Winner: Ned Jarrett - 68.886 mph
Lap Leaders: Ned Jarrett 1-200
Cautions:
Margin of Victory: 1 lap plus
Attendance: 4,500

Race No. 58

Panch Sneaks in Back Door To Win Wilkes 400

NORTH WILKESBORO, NC (Oct 11) -- Fred Lorenzen, Junior Johnson, Richard Petty and David Pearson engaged in a dramatic duel at North Wilkesboro Speedway, but steady Marvin Panch sneaked home the winner in the Wilkes 400.

"How about that?" Panch said, shaking his head. "I get outrun all day on the track and I come up the winner."

Johnson and Lorenzen led most of the way with Petty and Pearson running in their wake until their Chrysler products fell by the wayside. Johnson led on four occasions for 201 laps; Lorenzen led twice for 123 laps.

The brisk pace caused Petty to fall out after 153 laps with rear gearing failure. Pearson followed on lap 205 with a blown head gasket. That left Johnson and Lorenzen, with Panch tagging along well behind, to battle

Grand National Race No. 58
400 Laps at North Wilkesboro Speedway
North Wilkesboro, NC
"Wilkes 400"
250 Miles on .625-mile Paved Track
October 11, 1964

Fin	St	No.	Driver	Team / Car	Laps	Money	Status
1	5	21	Marvin Panch	Wood Bros '64 Ford	400	$3,225	Running
2	4	28	Fred Lorenzen	Hooman-Moody '64 Ford	400	2,150	Running
3	8	16	Darel Dieringer	Bud Moore '64 Mercury	397	1,225	Running
4	14	1	Billy Wade	Bud Moore '64 Mercury	394	850	Running
5	10	3	Buck Baker	Ray Fox '64 Dodge	390	625	Running
6	9	00	Cale Yarborough	Holman-Moody '64 Ford	389	525	Running
7	18	02	Curtis Crider	Crider '63 Mercury	370	475	Running
8	15	19	Larry Thomas	Herman Beam '64 Ford	366	425	Running
9	20	88	Neil Castles	Buck Baker '62 Chrysler	356	350	Running
10	11	7	Bobby Johns	Holman-Moody '64 Ford	348	325	Rear End
11	30	32	Jack Anderson	'63 Ford	344	275	Running
12	31	9	Roy Tyner	R Southerlund '64 Chevrolet	311	250	Running
13	1	27	Junior Johnson	Banjo Matthews '64 Ford	297	775	Engine
14	27	34	Wendell Scott	Scott '63 Ford	294	200	Engine
15	16	72	Doug Yates	Yates '63 Plymouth	265	200	Running
16	24	53	Pete Stewart	Stewart '63 Ford	208	175	Rear End
17	2	6	David Pearson	Cotton Owens '64 Dodge	205	275	H Gasket
18	12	5	Earl Balmer	Cotton Owens '64 Dodge	200	200	W Bearing
19	3	43	Richard Petty	Petty Eng '64 Plymouth	153	250	Rear End
20	17	46	J T Putney	Walt Hunter '62 Chevrolet	125	200	Drive Sh
21	6	41	Jim Paschal	Petty Eng '64 Plymouth	87	175	Engine
22	13	10	Buddy Baker	Bernard Alvarez '64 Ford	51	175	Engine
23	26	01	Darrell Bryant	Curtis Crider '63 Mercury	48	150	Trans
24	25	0	Larry Manning	'62 Ford	38	150	Brakes
25	32	58	Doug Moore	'64 Chevrolet	36	150	Fuel Line
26	23	52	Paul Lewis	Jess Potter '62 Chevrolet	27	150	Heating
27	28	55	Earl Brooks	'62 Chevrolet	26	150	Rear End
28	29	97	Bill Whitley	'62 Chevrolet	22	150	Tire rub
29	7	11	Ned Jarrett	Bondy Long '64 Ford	5	175	Fuel
30	22	20	Mark Hurley	'63 Ford	3	150	Engine
31	19	78	Buddy Arrington	Arrington '63 Dodge	2	---	Crash
32	21	60	Doug Cooper	Bob Cooper '64 Ford	2	---	Crash

Time of Race: 2 hours, 44 minutes, 07 seconds
Average Speed: 91.398 mph
Pole Winner: Junior Johnson - 100.761 mph
Lap Leaders: Junior Johnson 1-91, Darel Dieringer 92-93, Johnson 94-194,
   Fred Lorenzen 195- 245, Johnson 246-251, Marvin Panch 252-294, Johnson 295-297,
   Panch 298-303, Lorenzen 304-375, Panch 376-400
Cautions: 2 for 28 laps
Margin of Victory: 5.8 seconds
Attendance: 12,000

Jim Paschal's Plymouth in the marbles at N. Wilkesboro

it out. Johnson was leading in the 297th lap when the engine blew in his Banjo Matthews Ford. That put Lorenzen into the lead. The 29 year-old Ford driver had things well in hand until he had to make a quick stop for fuel with 25 laps to go.

Panch drove his Wood Brothers Ford into the lead and was 11 seconds ahead of Lorenzen once his pit stop was completed. In the final 25 laps on the .625-mile paved oval, Lorenzen cut the deficit to 5.8 seconds.

"We weren't gambling," said Panch. "We knew we could run 150 laps on a tank of gas. Actually I was surprised when Lorenzen stopped."

Darel Dieringer came in third, three laps behind the Panch-Lorenzen shoot-out. Billy Wade finished fourth with Buck Baker fifth. Cale Yarborough drove a factory backed Ford into sixth place.

Panch averaged 91.398 mph before a crowd of 12,000. Two caution flags consumed 28 laps; 21 of which were required to clean up oil from Jim Paschal's blown engine.

Race No. 59

Petty Crash Opens Door for Lorenzen in National 400

CHARLOTTE, NC (Oct 18) -- Fred Lorenzen squeaked into the lead two miles from the finish when leader Richard Petty blew a tire and clobbered the wall. He went on to win the National 400 at Charlotte Motor Speedway.

Petty had led for 188 of the 267 laps in his blue Petty Engineering Plymouth. He had fended off Lorenzen in a stirring 65 lap duel in the late stages. Then disaster struck. Petty's right front tire blew in the third turn as the white flag was about to fall. The car shot up the banking and hit the guard rail with a thundering blow. It lifted high in the air and came down on all four wheels. Petty had been jerked out of the shoulder harness and was lying down in the front seat when the car stopped.

Lorenzen coasted around and finished a full lap ahead of runner-up Jim Paschal. Petty got credit for third with Ned Jarrett fourth and LeeRoy Yarbrough fifth.

"The tire just went," said Petty. "When it blew, it seemed like it took two hours to get to that fence. I went the same route Pardue did. I was just lucky enough to stay inside the race track."

Jimmy Pardue was killed a month earlier in tire tests

in the same location. Pardue's Plymouth shot through the guard rail and tumbled down a 40 foot embankment.

"I may be sore all over for the next few days," added Petty. "But all that is hurting right now is my pocketbook."

Lorenzen had tried to get around his friendly rival for nearly 100 miles. "I saw Richard keep looking at the floorboard (presumably at the trap door which opens to check tire wear)." said Lorenzen. "It was a shame that the race ended the way it did. I feel sorry for him, but I'm glad he wasn't hurt.

"I was lucky I won this one," he continued. "But have you ever seen a winner of a race who wasn't lucky?"

Lorenzen averaged 134.475 mph as the throng of 63,399 was on its collective feet for the last 40 laps.

Heavy rains on Thursday and Friday washed the rubber off the track and made the newly repaved third turn exceptionally hard on tires. Cale Yarborough and Wendell Scott were wiped out in collisions with the wall after tires had blown.

Richard Petty slumped in his car after National 400 crash

Only 16 cars in the starting field of 44 finished the race. Four caution flags for 21 laps slowed the pace.

Race No. 60

New Champ Petty Harnesses Harris Hundred

HARRIS, NC (Oct 25) -- Richard Petty outlasted a pair of early chargers and rode home first in the 100-miler at Harris Speedway. It was the ninth win of the year for the new 1964 Grand National champion.

Grand National Race No. 59
267 Laps at Charlotte Motor Speedway
Charlotte, NC
"National 400"
400 Miles on 1.5-mile Paved Track
October 18, 1964

Fin	St	No.	Drvier	Team / Car	Laps	Money	Status
1	3	28	Fred Lorenzen	Holman-Moody '64 Ford	267	$11,185	Running
2	5	41	Jim Paschal	Petty Eng '64 Plymouth	266	5,725	Running
3	1	43	Richard Petty	Petty Eng '64 Plymouth	265	4,245	Crash
4	11	11	Ned Jarrett	Bondy Long '64 Ford	265	2,375	Running
5	16	03	LeeRoy Yarbrough	Ray Fox '64 Dodge	264	1,650	Running
6	10	16	Darel Dieringer	Bud Moore '64 Mercury	263	1,225	Running
7	25	6	David Pearson	Cotton Owens '64 Dodge	263	1,100	Running
8	6	3	Buck Baker	Ray Fox '64 Dodge	261	1,025	Running
9	24	5	Earl Balmer	Cotton Owens '64 Dodge	253	900	Running
10	32	82	Bunkie Blackburn	Casper Hensley '64 Pontiac	246	800	Running
11	15	64	Elmo Langley	Woodfield '64 Ford	245	850	Running
12	37	53	Pete Stewart	Stewart '63 Ford	235	650	Running
13	23	7	Bobby Johns	Holman-Moody '64 Ford	232	600	Itnition
14	22	02	Curtis Crider	Crider '63 Mercury	223	550	Running
15	26	68	Bob Derrington	'63 Ford	222	500	Running
16	30	9	Roy Tyner	R Southerlund '64 Chevrolet	217	425	Running
17	34	83	Worth McMillion	McMillion '62 Pontiac	211	425	Running
18	2	25	Paul Goldsmith	Ray Nichels '64 Plymouth	202	855	Engine
19	13	00	Cale Yarborough	Holman-Moody '64 Ford	192	425	Crash
20	7	36	Larry Thomas	Burton-Robinson '64 Plym	183	450	Heating
21	38	46	J T Putney	Walt Hunter '62 Chevrolet	158	400	Rear end
22	42	34	Wendell Scott	Scott '63 Ford	145	475	Crash
23	14	76	Larry Frank	Frank '64 Ford	143	400	Running
24	18	47	A J Foyt	Ray Nichels '64 Dodge	127	400	W Bearing
25	39	52	Jack Anderson	Jess Potter '62 Chevrolet	118	400	Engine
26	27	71	Sam McQuagg	J L Thomas '63 Ford	71	400	Fuel Pmp
27	4	26	Bobby Isaac	Ray Nichels '64 Dodge	68	425	W Bearing
28	25	10	Buddy Baker	Bernard Alvarez '64 Ford	65	400	Piston
29	33	49	G C Spencer	Spencer '64 Ford	64	400	Engine
30	40	60	Doug Cooper	Bob Cooper '64 Ford	63	400	Flagged
31	12	21	Marvin Panch	Wood Bros '64 Ford	52	400	Oil Temp
32	31	42	Bill McMahan	Casper Hensley '63 Pontiac	45	400	Handling
33	29	58	Doug Moore	'64 Chevrolet	37	400	Fuel Pmp
34	9	27	Junior Johnson	Banjo Matthews '64 Ford	36	425	Handling
35	36	63	Don Hume	Don House '63 Ford	9	400	Heating
36	19	88	Neil Castles	Buck Baker '62 Chrysler	8	400	Engine
37	8	1	Billy Wade	Bud Moore '64 Mercury	6	400	Windsh
38	43	19	H B Bailey	Herman Beam '64 Ford	6	400	Handling
39	44	31	Possum Jones	'63 Ford	5	400	Oil Cooler
40	28	86	Jimmy Helms	Buck Baker '62 Chrysler	4	400	Brakes
41	41	61	Bob Cooper	Cooper '62 Pontiac	3	400	Handling
42	17	81	Frank Weathers	'63 Plymouth	1	400	Engine
43	21	01	Stick Elliott	Curtis Crider '63 Mercury	1	400	Handling
44	20	0	Roy Mayne	'62 Ford	1	400	Oil Pres

Time of Race: 2 hours, 58 minutes, 35 seconds
Average Speed: 134.475 mph
Pole Winner: Richard Petty - 150.711 mph
Lap Leaders: Paul Goldsmith 1, Richard Petty 2-28, Goldsmith 29-68, Fred Lorenzen 69-73, Petty 74-105, Goldsmith 106-135, Petty 136-198, Jim Paschal 199, Petty 200-265, Lorenzen 266-267
Cautions: 4 for 21 laps
Margin of Victory: 1 lap plus

Ned Jarrett finished a lap behind in second place. Curtis Crider was third, nine laps off the pace. Bobby Isaac was fourth and Larry Thomas fifth.

Billy Wade started on the pole and led the first 100 laps. He began to drop off the pace and was out of the race six laps later with rear gearing failure. David Pearson took the lead when Wade faltered and led until the 159th lap when his Dodge blew an engine. Petty took over at that point and led the rest of the way.

"I didn't feel so good when Billy and David were

outrunning me," confessed Petty. "I felt better when I saw Billy go out and still better when David fell out."

A crowd of 5,000 watched Petty average 59.009 mph on the .333-mile paved oval. It was his 36th career Grand National win.

The Mercury Division had announced they were pulling out of stock car racing. Dieringer took the lead in the 228th lap and led the rest of the way. "Hell yes I was driving like it was my last race," Dieringer responded to questioning. "It might have been. I know it was the last for Mercury."

Isaac, driving Cotton Owens' Dodge, started seventh and wound up second. It was his third runner-up effort of the year. Larry Thomas, new driver for the Burton-Robinson team in the wake of Jimmy Pardue's death, was third despite crashing in the final lap. Billy Wade took fourth and Doug Cooper fifth.

David Pearson set a brisk pace early, but he lost control of his Dodge and banged the wall after just nine laps. Wade, Dieringer and Ned Jarrett traded the lead

Grand National Race No. 60
334 Laps at Harris Speedway
Harris, NC
100 Miles on .333-mile Paved Track
October 25, 1964

Fin	St	No.	Driver	Team / Car	Laps	Money	Status
1	4	41	Richard Petty	Petty Eng '64 Plymouth	334	$1,000	Running
2	3	11	Ned Jarrett	Bondy Long '64 Ford	333	600	Running
3	6	02	Curtis Crider	Crider '63 Mercury	325	400	Running
4	5	5	Bobby Isaac	Cotton Owens '64 Dodge	324	300	Running
5	8	36	Larry Thomas	Wade Younts '63 Dodge	321	275	Running
6	11	34	Wendell Scott	Scott '63 Ford	317	240	Running
7	15	09	Larry Manning	'62 Chevrolet	313	200	Running
8	19	88	Neil Castles	Buck Baker '62 Chrysler	304	175	Running
9	9	78	Buddy Arrington	Arrington '63 Dodge	304	150	Running
10	21	9	Roy Tyner	R Southerlund '63 Chevrolet	290	140	Running
11	12	45	Louie Weathersby	Weathersby '63 Plymouth	290	130	Running
12	18	58	Doug Moore	'64 Chevrolet	280	120	Running
13	10	31	Possum Jones	'63 Ford	259	110	RR Hub
14	13	60	Doug Cooper	Bob Cooper '64 Ford	195	100	Trans
15	2	6	David Pearson	Cotton Owens '64 Dodge	159	100	Engine
16	7	46	J T Putney	Walt Hunter '62 Chevrolet	154	100	Rear End
17	20	97	Bill Whitley	'62 Chevrolet	125	100	Trans
18	1	1	Billy Wade	Bud Moore '64 Mercury	106	100	Rear End
19	14	01	Darrell Bryant	Curtis Crider '63 Mercury	69	100	Heating
20	16	70	Al Farmer	'62 Pontiac	49	100	Steering
21	17	0	Jack Anderson	'62 Ford	33	100	Trans

Time of Race: 1 hour, 41 minutes, 53 seconds
Average Speed: 59.009 mph
Pole Winner: Billy Wade - 64.787 mph
Lap Leaders: Billy Wade 1-100, David Pearson 101-159, Richard Petty 160-334
Cautions: 3 for 16 laps
Margin of Victory; 1 lap plus
Attendance: 5,000

Race No. 61

Dieringer Dashes to Victory At Augusta in Mercury's Final Fling

AUGUSTA, GA (Nov 1) -- Darel Dieringer of Indianapolis averted several spine-tingling crashes and beat Bobby Isaac by a half lap in the Jaycee 300 at Augusta Speedway. It was Dieringer's first win of the year and the final race for the Mercury factory-backed team.

Grand National Race No. 61
300 Laps at Augusta Speedway
Augusta, GA
"Jaycee 300"
150 Miles on Half-mile Paved Track
November 1, 1964

Fin	St	No.	Driver	Team / Car	Laps	Money	Status
1	5	16	Darel Dieringer	Bud Moore '64 Mercury	300	$1,750	Running
2	7	5	Bobby Isaac	Cotton Owens '64 Dodge	300	800	Running
3	6	36	Larry Thomas	Burton-Robinson '64 Plym	298	600	Crash
4	4	1	Billy Wade	Bud Moore '64 Mercury	293	525	Running
5	16	60	Doug Cooper	Bob Cooper '64 Ford	283	500	Running
6	17	46	J T Putney	Walt Hunter '62 Chevrolet	281	475	Fuel
7	12	02	Curtis Crider	Crider '63 Mercury	281	450	Running
8	11	55	Tiny Lund	'64 Ford	278	435	Running
9	8	10	Buddy Baker	Bernard Alvarez '64 Ford	278	400	Running
10	14	88	Neil Castles	Buck Baker '62 Chrysler	276	390	Running
11	20	58	Doug Moore	'64 Chrysler	275	380	Running
12	18	53	Pete Stewart	Stewart '63 Ford	274	365	Running
13	19	9	Roy Tyner	R Southerlund '64 Chevrolet	269	350	Running
14	25	78	Buddy Arrington	Arrington '63 Dodge	263	330	Running
15	23	89	Buck Baker	David Walker '64 Plymouth	260	310	Rear end
16	26	0	Frank Graham	'62 Ford	252	200	Running
17	13	18	Frank Brantley	'62 Plymouth	252	160	Running
18	28	70	Al Farmer	'62 Pontiac	240	160	Running
19	1	11	Ned Jarrett	Bondy Long '64 Ford	227	260	Engine
20	9	76	Larry Frank	Frank '64 Ford	197	160	Axle
21	22	155	Earl Brooks	'62 Chevrolet	182	160	Push Rod
22	29	91	Bubba Into	'62 Plymouth	170	160	Engine
23	24	45	LeeRoy Yarbrough	Louie Weathersby '63 Plym	155	---	Rear End
24	10	71	Sam McQuagg	J L Thomas '63 Ford	148	---	Rear End
25	2	41	Richard Petty	Petty Eng '64 Plymouth	109	50	Crash
26	21	01	Darrell Bryant	Curtis Crider '63 Mercury	70	---	Oil Pres
27	30	34	Wendell Scott	Scott '63 Ford	57	---	Rear End
28	15	31	Possum Jones	'63 Ford	31	---	Engine
29	3	6	David Pearson	Cotton Owens '64 Dodge	9	30	Crash
30	27	20	Jack Anderson	'64 Ford	1	---	Engine

Time of Race: 2 hours, 11 minutes, 07 seconds
Average Speed: 68.641 mph
Pole Winner: Ned Jarrett - 82.455 mph
Lap Leaders: Ned Jarrett 1, David Pearson 2-9, Billy Wade 10-47, Darel Dieringer 48-111, Jarrett 112-128, Dieringer 129-192, Jarrett 193-227, Dieringer 228-300
Cautions: 6 for 45 laps
Margin of Victory: Half lap
Attendance: 13,000

six times before Dieringer took command. He steered clear of the spins and wrecks to post a 68.641 mph triumph.

The caution flag was out six times for a total of 45 laps. A crowd of 13,000 was on hand at the neatly contoured half-mile paved track.

Race No. 62

Jarrett Cops Finale at Jacksonville

JACKSONVILLE, NC (Nov 8) -- The 62-race season came to a close under heavily overcast skies at the Jacksonville Speedway, and Ned Jarrett drove his brakeless Ford to his 15th win of the season.

Jarrett slipped past David Pearson in the 104th lap and led the rest of the way. He wound up a lap ahead of runner-up Richard Petty, who won the championship by an official margin of 5,302 points over Jarrett. G.C. Spencer finished third in the 100-miler on the half-mile dirt track with Doug Cooper fourth and Larry Thomas fifth.

Doug Yates, veteran Modified driver, won the pole in his independent Plymouth and led the first nine laps. Jarrett, Petty and Pearson swapped the lead four times the rest of the way. Yates fell off the pace and eventually finished 15th.

Jarrett averaged 57.535 mph for his 37th career Grand National win.

Storm clouds were brewing on the horizon. NASCAR issued a statement that new rules would be adopted for the 1965 season, in which no super engines or intermediate bodies would be allowed to compete on the big tracks. This in effect would wipe out the Chrysler cars, rendering them uncompetitive, said Chrysler racing boss Ronney Householder. Chrysler threatened a boycott of all 1965 races as the 1964 season came to a close.

Grand National Race No. 62
200 Laps at Jacksonville Speedway
Jacksonville, NC
100 Miles on Half-mile Dirt Track
November 8, 1964

Fin	St	No.	Driver	Team / Car	Laps	Money	Status
1	2	11	Ned Jarrett	Bondy Long '64 Ford	200	$1,000	Running
2	4	43	Richard Petty	Petty Eng '64 Plymouth	199	600	Running
3	5	49	G C Spencer	Spencer '64 Ford	196	400	Running
4	11	60	Doug Cooper	Bob Cooper '64 Ford	195	300	Running
5	18	36	Larry Thomas	Burton-Robinson '64 Plym	190	275	Running
6	20	88	Neil Castles	Buck Baker '62 Chrysler	190	240	Running
7	15	02	Curtis Crider	Crider '63 Mercury	188	200	Running
8	24	78	Buddy Arrington	Arrington '63 Dodge	184	175	Running
9	3	55	Tiny Lund	'64 Ford	174	150	Running
10	10	6	David Pearson	Cotton Owens '64 Dodge	172	140	Rear End
11	9	34	Wendell Scott	Scott '63 Ford	162	130	Running
12	16	0	Frank Graham	'62 Ford	157	120	Rear end
13	25	09	Larry Manning	'62 Chevrolet	150	110	Crash
14	22	86	Jim Helms	Buck Baker '62 Chrysler	148	100	Running
15	1	72	Doug Yates	Yates '63 Plymouth	144	100	Running
16	19	58	Doug Moore	'64 Chevrolet	119	100	R Housing
17	7	5	Bobby Isaac	Cotton Owens '64 Dodge	103	100	R Housing
18	17	64	Elmo Langley	Woodfield '64 Ford	84	100	R Housing
19	13	31	Possum Jones	'63 Ford	80	100	Oil Leak
20	6	45	Bud Moore	Louie Weathersby '63 Plym	64	100	Fuel Tank
21	23	9	Roy Tyner	R Southerlund '64 Chevrolet	59	100	Engine
22	14	10	Buddy Baker	Bernard Alvarez '64 Ford	54	100	R Housing
23	8	89	Buck Baker	David Walker '64 Plymouth	38	50	R Housing
24	21	155	Earl Brooks	'62 Chevrolet	21	50	Heating
25	12	91	Bubba Into	'62 Dodge	15	50	Engine

Time of Race: 1 hour, 44 minutes, 17 seconds
Average Speed: 57.535 mph
Pole Winner: Doug Yates - 64.285 mph
Lap Leaders: Doug Yates 1-9, Ned Jarrett 10-38, Richard Petty 39-64,
    David Pearson 65-103, Jarrett 104-200
Cautions: 4 for 22 laps
Margin of Victory: 1 lap plus
Attendance: 3,500

1964 NASCAR Season
Final Point Standings - Grand National Division

Rank	Driver	Points	Starts	Wins	Top 5	Top 10	Winnings
1	Richard Petty	40,252	61	9	37	43	$114,771.45
2	Ned Jarrett	34,950	59	15	40	45	71,924.05
3	David Pearson	32,146	61	8	29	42	45,541.65
4	Billy Wade	28,474	35	4	12	25	36,094.58
5	Jimmy Pardue	26,570	50	0	14	24	41,597.18
6	Curtis Crider	25,606	59	0	7	30	22,170.46
7	Jim Paschal	25,450	22	1	10	15	60,115.68
8	Larry Thomas	22,950	43	0	9	27	21,225.64
9	Buck Baker	22,366	34	2	15	18	43,780.88
10	Marvin Panch	21,480	31	3	18	21	34,835.88
11	Darel Dieringer	19,972	27	1	6	13	20,684.23
12	Wendell Scott	19,574	56	1	8	25	16,494.23
13	Fred Lorenzen	18,098	16	8	10	10	73,859.23
14	Junior Johnson	17,066	29	3	12	15	26,974.23
15	LeeRoy Yarbrough	16,172	34	2	11	15	16,629.23
16	Roy Tyner	13,922	46	0	0	17	11,487.82
17	Neil Castles	13,372	58	0	1	24	14,317.82
18	Bobby Isaac	13,252	19	1	5	7	26,732.82
19	Cale Yarborough	12,618	24	0	2	9	10,377.82
20	Tiny Lund	12,598	22	0	3	9	9,912.82
21	Doug Cooper	11,942	39	0	4	11	10,445.00
22	Paul Goldsmith	11,700	14	0	3	4	20,835.00
23	J T Putney	10,744	17	0	1	6	7,295.00
24	Larry Frank	10,314	12	0	0	3	7,830.00
25	Jack Anderson	10,040	31	0	1	4	8,510.00
26	G C Spencer	10,012	21	0	4	6	9,490.00
27	Fireball Roberts	9,900	9	1	5	6	28,345.00
28	Rex White	8,222	6	0	2	3	12,310.00
29	Dave MacDonald	7,650	5	0	1	3	9,195.00
30	Worth McMillion	7,586	18	0	0	6	4,700.00
31	Buddy Baker	7,314	35	0	3	7	8,460.00
32	Bunkie Blackburn	7,264	14	0	1	4	6,630.00
33	Bill McMahan	7,240	20	0	1	4	7,205.00
34	Buddy Arrington	6,364	24	0	2	9	4,715.00
35	Earl Balmer	6,170	10	0	2	4	5,795.00
36	Bob Derrington	5,896	17	0	0	2	2,755.00
37	Bobby Johns	5,436	12	0	0	2	5,700.00
38	E J Trivette	5,118	26	0	0	3	5,495.00
39	Doug Moore	4,970	24	0	0	6	5,175.00
40	Kenny Spikes	4,934	6	0	0	1	3,100.00
41	Earl Brooks	4,820	28	0	0	8	3,925.00
42	Elmo Langley	4,400	14	0	0	5	3,905.00
43	Roy Mayne	4,278	13	0	1	2	4,705.00
44	Gene Hobby	4,054	18	0	0	3	2,795.00
45	Doug Yates	3,778	15	0	3	7	3,290.00
46	Ralph Earnhardt	3,720	11	0	1	1	3,290.00
47	Bob Cooper	3,602	12	0	0	0	3,360.00
48	Joe Weatherly	3,132	5	0	2	3	5,290.00
49	Sam McQuagg	2,928	5	0	0	0	1,700.00
50	Bobby Keck	2,754	10	0	2	5	2,850.00

Special Events
The 1961, 1962 and 1963 NASCAR All-Star Races

Volume two of a four volume series . . . . . The Superspeedway Boom 1959 - 1964

In its first half dozen years of operation, the Daytona International Speedway conducted a wide variety of automobile races. Indy Cars, compact cars, big bore NASCAR stocks, Europeon sporty cars -- they all had their day in the sun at the Big D.

Big Bill France, President of the elaborate racing palace, jammed his SpeedWeeks full of stock car racing events every February. In addition to the Daytona 500, the Modified-Sportsman race and the 100-mile qualifiers, there were a pair of 25-mile pole position races, a consolation race and even a contest titled the "Air Lift Challenge" -- in which selected Grand National pilots wheeled a passenger car around the 2.5-mile track trying to drive as close as they could to a predetermined speed.

In 1961, a new idea cut across the brainwaves of Big Bill, who was perhaps the most promotionally inclined individual of his era.

Joe Weatherly
1961 Winner
Pontiac - 154.905

Fireball Roberts
1962 Winner
Pontiac - 157.081

Fred Lorenzen
1963 Winner
Ford - 163.297

France figured a special race -- open by invitation only -- would spice up the activities of the classic SpeedWeeks. The drivers who won "major" Grand National races in the 1960 NASCAR season would be invited to compete in a 10-lap, 25-mile "American Challenge Cup" race. A purse of $2,500 would be up for grabs with the winner taking home $1,000.

It was NASCAR's first staging of an All-Star race -- ala The Winston, which would arrive on the scene two-and-a-half decades later.

The 1960 Grand National season produced 18 different winners, 17 of whom were extended an invitation to compete in the inaugural American Challenge Cup. Glen Wood, winner of three Grand Nationals in 1960, was not eligible since sanctioning NASCAR said the Bowman-Gray Stadium did not host "major" races. Wood won all three of his races on the flat quarter-mile oval in Winston-Salem, NC.

Eleven of the eligible drivers accepted the invitation to compete in the 10-lapper held on February 19, 1961. West Coast drivers Jim Cook, John Rostek and Marvin Porter, each of whom won in 1960, were not in Daytona for SpeedWeeks. Neither was Speedy Thompson, who did not have a ride lined up for the 1961 season. Lee Petty and Johnny Beauchamp were racing in Daytona, but neither one wanted to drive in the 25-miler. They decided against participating in a slice of little-known history on the NASCAR front.

Ironically, Petty and Beauchamp, principles in the famed '59 Daytona 500 finish, crashed together in an alarming incident five days later during the 100-mile qualifying race. Both Petty's Plymouth and Beauchamp's Chevrolet hurtled over the wall in one of the most spectacular crashes in the annals of stock car racing. Petty, the most seriously injured of the two, eventually was able to race again. Beauchamp, however, would never race again in NASCAR. It was the last time he ever strapped on a helmet in a NASCAR sanctioned event.

A crowd of 4,500 turned out in overcast conditions

to watch the first NASCAR All-Star race. Eleven cars took the flag at 2:30 pm and the lead changed hands four times among three drivers.

Joe Weatherly, who drew the coveted pole position from a hat, dropped back in the first couple of laps then made a bold charge to the front in the last lap. "Only one lap paid the money -- the last one," said Little Joe.

Weatherly nipped Fireball Roberts in a stirring duel of powerful Pontiacs. Johnson and Cotton Owens were third and fourth in Pontiacs. Richard Petty was fifth in a Plymouth with his dad Lee cheering him on from the pits.

Buck Baker surprised everyone by finishing 4th in the 1962 All-Star race in a big Chrysler

The race was exciting enough for Bill France to schedule another American Challenge Cup race in 1962.

There were a record tying 19 different winners in the 1961 Grand National season -- and 19 invitations went out. West Coasters Lloyd Dane and Eddie Gray were not about to haul a race car 3,000 miles to run for a top prize of $1,000, so they declined.

Lee Petty was still recuperating from his 1961 injuries and did not compete. Emanuel Zervakis had lost his ride to Tommy Irwin and did not drive in the 1962 Daytona races.

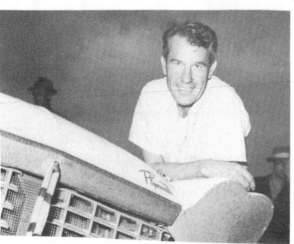

Lee Petty was eligible for the first two NASCAR All-Star Races but did not compete in either

Chevy driver Rex White, who ran eighth in the field of 11 in 1961, figured his car had no chance of keeping up with the Pontiacs. Instead of risking his machinery for a fourth or

fifth place pay-off of $100, he kept it in the garage on race day.

Also having the opportunity to compete, but declining, were Cotton Owens, Bob Burdick, Junior Johnson and Jack Smith.

A crowd of 5,500, up a 'grand' from the year before, came out for the second annual American Challenge Cup event. They were treated to another wingding of a race.

Roberts, starting last for the second year in a row, boldly charged around the field in the first lap and had the lead by the backstretch. He led for nine of the 10 laps. Weatherly, bidding for his second consecutive win, tried the slingshot but came up a fender short. Roberts claimed he "got even" for 1961. David Pearson was third in a Pontiac and Buck Baker gunned a bulky Chrysler home fourth. Fred Lorenzen was fifth in a Ford.

Larry Frank's fine showing in the 1963 All-Star race earned himself a ride in the Daytona 500

The final All-Star event, renamed the "Race of Champions", was staged in 1963. Only 14 drivers had won races in 1962 and one of those -- Johnny Allen -- had won at Bowman Gray Stadium in Winston-Salem , which still was not considered a "major" race.

The 13 invited drivers were all in Daytona, but only seven of them accepted the challenge. Among those sitting out in 1963 were Weatherly, who rarely passed up a chance to race anywhere. "Gotta consider the risks," he said. "I'd be goin' for a thousand bucks, but I might wreck my Daytona 500 car, which could win me $25,000."

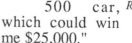

Richard Petty drove in the first two NASCAR All-Star races, finishing 5th and 7th

Rex White did not go to the post for much the same

Fred Lorenzen leaps pit wall to saddle up for 3rd annual Race of Champions in 1963.
Lorenzen won the race

Johnson sat it out, too.

Five Fords and a pair of Pontiacs took the green flag before a crowd of 3,500, which merely dotted the massive Daytona grandstands. Fred Lorenzen held off Nelson Stacy's last lap charge to win the third and final "Race of Champions". Larry Frank wound up third -- and his sparkling effort earned him a ride in the Daytona 500. Roberts wound up fourth in his trusty Pontiac.

While the early editions of the NASCAR All-Star race have been, for the most part completely forgotten, they underscored the importance of having an event for 'winners only'. R.J. Reynolds would pick up on the idea more than 20 years later and promote it in the right way.

The American Challenge Cup and Race of Champions did not draw a tremendous amount of interest and attention, but their electrifying finishes will be hard to top -- for as many years as an All-Star type race is run under NASCAR sanction.

reasons he didn't in 1962 -- his Chevy couldn't keep up. Jack Smith turned down the offer for the second year in a row, and Richard Petty declined the offer after competing in the first two. Jim Paschal and Junior

1961 All-Star Race

Weatherly Snookers Roberts in First Challenge Cup

DAYTONA BEACH, FL (Feb. 19, 1961) -- Joe Weatherly gunned his Bud Moore Pontiac around Fireball Roberts a quarter-mile from the finish and won the inaugural American Challenge Cup -- an All-Star race for NASCAR Grand National race winners.

Weatherly, who started on the pole but led only one lap before the final trip around Daytona International Speedway's 2.5-mile tri-oval, shot his car to the high side of Roberts as the pair came off the fourth turn for the last time. "I was just watching and waiting to see how much I could pull ahead," said Weatherly, who averaged 154.905 mph in the nine minute sprint. "Everybody thinks the groove is at the bottom coming down hill (off the banking). I think it's faster on the outside. That's where I made my move. I don't reckon anybody will argue that I had the fastest groove."

Joe Weatherly won the first All-star race in 1961

Junior Johnson, who led the first two laps, came in third in the Holly Farms Pontiac. Cotton Owens was fourth in another Pontiac, giving the 'Big Indians' a

First NASCAR All-Star Race American Challenge Cup
Daytona International Speedway
February 19, 1961

Fin	St	No.	Driver	Team / Car	Laps	Money	Status
1	1	8	Joe Weatherly	Bud Moore '61 Pontiac	10	$1,000	Running
2	11	22	Fireball Roberts	Smokey Yunick '61 Pontiac	10	500	Running
3	5	27	Junior Johnson	Holly Farms '61 Pontiac	10	250	Running
4	4	6	Cotton Owens	Owens '61 Pontiac	10	150	Running
5	2	43	Richard Petty	Petty Eng '61 Plymouth	10	100	Running
6	10	72	Bobby Johns	Shorty Johns '61 Ford	10	100	Running
7	7	49	Jack Smith	Bob Welborn '61 Pontiac	10	100	Running
8	8	4	Rex White	White '61 Chevrolet	10	100	Running
9	9	87	Buck Baker	Baker '61 Chrysler	10	50	Running
10	6	11	Ned Jarrett	B G Holloway '61 Chevrolet	10	50	Running
11	3	89	Joe Lee Johnson	Johnson '61 Chevrolet	10	50	Running

Time of Race: 9 minutes, 41 Seconds
Average Speed: 154.905 mph
Lap Leaders: Junior Johnson 1-2, Joe Weatherly 3, Fireball Roberts 4-9, Weatherly 10
Cautions: None
Margin of Victory: 36 inches
Attendance: 4,500

1-2-3-4 sweep. Richard Petty's Plymouth took fifth place.

Roberts started last by virtue of a blind draw, but charged through the pack. He had the lead by the fourth lap. Weatherly, regarded as an expert of the newfangled 'draft', hugged Roberts' rear bumper until the final lap.

"I didn't open it up until the last lap," Weatherly said. "That was the only lap that pays. There wasn't any lap money today."

Car owner Moore, who was standing on pit wall when the two cars crossed the finish line door-to-door, remarked, "He (Weatherly) ran the race just like we planned it."

Bobby Johns finished sixth in the lone Ford entry. Jack Smith, Rex White, Buck Baker and Ned Jarrett rounded out the top 10. Joe Lee Johnson was last in the 11 car field.

Weatherly won $1,000 from the $2,500 purse. A crowd of 4,500 watched the fast-paced 25-miler.

1962 All-Star Race

Fireball Turns Tables on Little Joe; Wins 2nd Challenge Cup

DAYTONA BEACH, FL (Feb. 10, 1962) -- Fireball Roberts hustled from last to first in less than two miles, then held off Joe Weatherly's last lap surge to win the second annual American Challenge Cup at Daytona International Speedway.

Roberts' half-car length victory was sweet revenge for the hometown Pontiac driver, who ran second to Weatherly in the 1961 All-Star event staged for winning NASCAR drivers.

Third place went to David Pearson's Ray Fox Pontiac. Buck Baker took his huge Chrysler into fourth place and Fred Lorenzen finished fifth in a Ford.

Roberts said Weatherly made one small mistake which was a major factor in the outcome. "I'm not going to say what he did wrong," he remarked. "Let's just say that he did. Anyway, that makes us even for last year."

Roberts took off like a shot when Johnny Bruner, Sr. waved the green flag. "I cheated a little," admitted the 33 year-old veteran. "When I went by the (start-finish) line, I was in high gear and already hitting 4,000 rpm while the rest of the field was in third gear.

Fireball Roberts -- last to first in one lap!

I really accelerated."

Roberts whipped past his rivals on the high side in the first turn. "I'll tell you," he said. "I was so close to that rail I was putting body english on the door to keep 'er off."

Nelson Stacy, Richard Petty and Marvin Panch finished in positions six through eight. Ned Jarrett's Chevrolet and Jim Paschal's Pontiac fell out and were not running at the finish.

Roberts' black and gold Pontiac completed the 25 miles at an average speed of 157.081 mph. The crowd was estimated at 5,500.

Second NASCAR All-Star Race
American Challenge Cup
Daytona International Speedway
February 10, 1962

Fin	St	No.	Driver	Team / Car	Laps	Money	Status
1	10	22	Fireball Roberts	Jim Stephens '62 Pontiac	10	$1,000	Running
2	1	8	Joe Weatherly	Bud Moore '62 Pontiac	10	500	Running
3		39	David Pearson	Ray Fox '62 Pontiac	10	250	Running
4		87	Buck Baker	Baker '62 Chrysler	10	150	Running
5		0	Fred Lorenzen	Holman-Moody '62 Ford	10	100	Running
6		29	Nelson Stacy	Holman-Moody '62 Ford	10	100	Running
7		43	Richard Petty	Petty Eng '62 Plymouth	10	100	Running
8		70	Marvin Panch	'62 Chevrolet	10	100	Running
9		11	Ned Jarrett	B G Holloway '62 Chevrolet		50	DNF
10		2	Jim Paschal	Cliff Stewart '62 Pontiac		50	DNF

Time of Race: 9 minutes, 32.95 seconds
Average Speed: 157.081 mph
Lap Leaders: Fireball Roberts 1-6, Joe Weatherly 7, Roberts 8-10
Cautions: None
Margin of Victory: Half-car length
Attendance: 5,500

1963 All-Star Race

Lorenzen Beats Stacy by an Eyelash in Race of Champions

DAYTONA BEACH, FL (Feb. 10, 1963) -- Fred Lorenzen of Elmhurst, IL nosed out Nelson Stacy and Larry Frank to win the third annual Race of Champions at Daytona International Speedway. It gave the powerful Holman-Moody Ford team out of Charlotte, NC a 1-2-3 sweep in NASCAR's All-Star event.

Fred Lorenzen drives toward victory lane

Fireball Roberts lagged a short chute behind in fourth place with his lumbering Pontiac. Ned Jarrett was fifth in a Ford.

Lorenzen averaged a record 163.297 mph as he and Stacy dueled for the entire 10 laps. "I couldn't shake him," said the blond bachelor. "I knew he would be there at the finish, so I concentrated on keeping him behind me. He almost got by me on the last lap but I held on."

Stacy led the first lap, then followed Lorenzen the final nine laps. The Cincinnati veteran was driving a Ford reserved for Dan Gurney in the Daytona 500.

The 1963 All-Star event for NASCAR Grand Na-

Third NASCAR All-Star Race
Race of Champions
Daytona International Speedway
February 10, 1963

Fin	St	No.	Driver	Team / Car	Laps	Money	Status
1	28	Fred Lorenzen	Holman-Moody '63 Ford	10	$1,000	Running
2	0	Nelson Stacy	Holman-Moody '63 Ford	10	500	Running
3	06	Larry Frank	Holman-Moody '63 Ford	10	250	Running
4	22	Fireball Roberts	Banjo Matthews '63 Pontiac	10	150	Running
5	11	Ned Jarrett	Burton-Robinson '63 Ford	10	100	Running
6	54	Jimmy Pardue	Pete Stewart '63 Ford	10	100	Running
7	7	Bobby Johns	Shorty Johns '63 Pontiac	10	100	Running

Time of Race: 9 minutes, 11.14 seconds
Average Speed: 163.297 mph
Lap Leaders: Nelson Stacy 1, Fred Lorenzen 2-10
Cautions: None
Margin of Victory: Half-car length
Attendance: 3,500

Nelson Stacy drove Dan Gurney's Ford in 1963 Race of Champions

tional drivers was the final such contest staged during Speedweeks. Bill France had noticed that the starting fields had gotten smaller, and fewer drivers were willing to risk their primary Daytona 500 car for comparatively "pocket change".

Race Winners and Pole Winners
NASCAR Winston Cup Grand National Series
1949 - 1987

Race #	Year #	Date	Site	Track	Surface	Miles	Race Winner	Car	Speed	Pole Winner	Car	Speed
1949												
1	1	6/19/49	Charlotte NC	0.750	D	150.00	Jim Roper	Lincoln	---	Bob Flock	Hudson	67.958
2	2	7/10/49	Daytona Beach FL	4.150	B-R	166.00	Red Byron	Olds	80-.883	Gober Sosebee	Olds	---
3	3	8/7/49	Hillsboro NC	1.000	D	200.00	Bob Flock	Olds	76.800	---	---	---
4	4	9/11/49	Langhorne PA	1.000	D	200.00	Curtis Turner	Olds	69.403	Red Byron	Olds	77.482
5	5	9/18/49	Hamburg NY	0.500	D	100.00	Jack White	Lincoln	---	---	---	---
6	6	9/25/49	Martinsville VA	0.500	D	100.00	Red Byron (2)	Olds	---	Curtis Turner	Olds	---
7	7	10/2/49	Heidelberg PA	0.500	D	100.00	Lee Petty	Plymouth	57.458	Al Bonnell	Olds	61.475
8	8	10/16/49	N Wilkesboro NC	0.500	D	100.00	Bob Flock (2)	Olds	53.364	Ken Wagner	Lincoln	57.563
1950												
9	1	2/5/50	Daytona Beach FL	4.167	B-R	200.00	Harold Kite	Lincoln	89.894	Joe Littlejohn	Olds	98.840
10	2	4/3/50	Charlotte NC	0.750	D	150.00	Tim Flock	Lincoln	---	Red Byron (2)	Olds	67.839
11	3	4/16/50	Langhorne PA	1.000	D	150.00	Curtis Turner (2)	Olds	69.399	Tim Flock	Lincoln	---
12	4	5/21/50	Martinsville VA	0.500	D	75.00	Curtis Turner (3)	Olds	---	Buck Baker	Ford	54.216
13	5	5/30/50	Canfield OH	0.500	D	100.00	Bill Rexford	Olds	---	Jimmy Florian	Ford	---
14	6	6/18/50	Vernon NY	0.500	D	100.00	Bill Blair	Mercury	---	Chuck Mahoney	Mercury	---
15	7	6/25/50	Dayton OH	0.500	D	100.00	Jimmy Florian	Ford	63.354	Dick Linder	Olds	66.543
16	8	7/2/50	Rochester NY	0.500	D	100.00	Curtis Turner (4)	Olds	50.614	Curtis Turner (2)	Olds	54.974
17	9	7/23/50	Charlotte NC	0.750	D	150.00	Curtis Turner (5)	Olds	---	Curtis Turner (3)	Olds	---
18	10	8/13/50	Hillsboro NC	1.000	D	100.00	Fireball Roberts	Olds	---	Dick Linder (2)	Olds	---
19	11	8/20/50	Dayton OH	0.500	D	97.50	Dick Linder	Olds	None	Curtis Turner (4)	Olds	---
20	12	8/27/50	Hamburg NY	0.500	D	100.00	Dick Linder (2)	Olds	50.747	Dick Linder (3)	Olds	53.113
21	13	9/4/50	Darlington SC	1.250	P	500.00	Johnny Mantz	Plymouth	75.250	Curtis Turner (5)	Olds	82.034
22	14	9/17/50	Langhorne PA	1.000	D	200.00	Fonty Flock	Olds	72.801	Wally Campbell	Olds	---
23	15	9/24/50	N Wilkesboro NC	0.625	D	125.00	Leon Sales	Plymouth	---	Fireball Roberts	Olds	73.266
24	16	10/1/50	Vernon NY	0.500	D	100.00	Dick Linder (3)	Olds	---	Dick Linder (4)	Olds	---
25	17	10/15/50	Martinsville VA	0.500	D	100.00	Herb Thomas	Plymouth	---	Fonty Flock	Olds	54.761
26	18	10/15/50	Winchester IN	0.500	D	100.00	Lloyd Moore	Mercury	---	---	---	---
27	19	10/29/50	Hillsboro NC	1.000	D	200.00	Lee Petty (2)	Plymouth	---	Fonty Flock (2)	Olds	85.898
1951												
28	1	2/11/51	Daytona Beach FL	4.100	B-R	160.00	Marshall Teague	Hudson	82.328	Tim Flock (2)	Lincoln	102.200
29	2	4/1/51	Charlotte NC	0.750	D	112.50	Curtis Turner (6)	Nash	70.545	Fonty Flock (3)	Olds	68.337
30	3	4/8/51	Mobile AL	0.750	D	112.50	Tim Flock (2)	Olds	50.260	No Time Trials	NTT	NTT
31	4	4/8/51	Gardena CA	0.500	D	100.00	Marshall Teague (2)	Hudson	61.047	Andy Pierce	Buick	62.959
32	5	4/15/51	Hillsboro NC	1.000	D	95.00	Fonty Flock (2)	Olds	80.889	Fonty Flock (4)	Olds	88.278
33	6	4/29/51	Phoenix AZ	1.000	D	150.00	Marshall Teague (3)	Hudson	60.153	Fonty Flock (5)	Olds	---
34	7	4/29/51	N Wilkesboro NC	0.625	D	93.75	Fonty Flock (3)	Olds	None	Fonty Flock (6)	Olds	72.184
35	8	5/6/51	Martinsville VA	0.500	D	100.00	Curtis Turner (7)	Olds	---	Tim Flock (3)	Olds	55.062
36	9	5/30/51	Canfield OH	0.500	D	100.00	Marshall Teague (4)	Hudson	49.308	Bill Rexford	Olds	54.233
37	10	6/10/51	Columbus OH	0.500	D	100.00	Tim Flock (3)	Olds	---	Gober Sosebee (2)	Cadillac	57.766
38	11	6/16/51	Columbia SC	0.500	D	100.00	Frank Mundy	Studebaker	50.683	Frank Mundy	Studebaker	57.563
39	12	6/24/51	Dayton OH	0.500	P	100.00	Curtis Turner (8)	Olds	---	Tim Flock (4)	Olds	70.838
40	13	6/30/51	Gardena CA	0.500	D	100.00	Lou Figaro	Hudson	---	Lou Figaro	Hudson	76.988
41	14	7/1/51	Grand Rapids MI	0.500	D	100.00	Marshall Teague (5)	Hudson	---	---	---	---
42	15	7/8/51	Bainbridge OH	0.500	D	100.00	Fonty Flock (4)	Olds	65.753	Fonty Flock (7)	Olds	---
43	16	7/15/51	Heidelberg PA	0.500	D	100.00	Herb Thomas (2)	Olds	None	Fonty Flock (8)	Olds	61.983
44	17	7/29/51	Weaverville NC	0.500	D	100.00	Fonty Flock (5)	Olds	---	Billy Carden	Olds	64.608
45	18	7/31/51	Rochester NY	0.500	D	100.00	Lee Petty (3)	Plymouth	---	Fonty Flock (9)	Olds	---
46	19	8/1/51	Altamont NY	0.500	D	100.00	Fonty Flock (6)	Olds	---	---	---	---
47	20	8/12/51	Detroit MI	1.000	D	250.00	Tommy Thompson	Chrysler	57.588	Marshall Teague	Hudson	69.131
48	21	8/19/51	Toledo OH	0.500	D	100.00	Tim Flock (4)	Olds	50.847	Fonty Flock (10)	Olds	55.521
49	22	8/24/51	Morristown NJ	0.500	D	100.00	Tim Flock (5)	Olds	---	Tim Flock (5)	Olds	58.670
50	23	8/25/51	Greenville SC	0.500	D	100.00	Bob Flock (3)	Olds	---	---	---	---
51	24	9/3/51	Darlington SC	1.250	P	500.00	Herb Thomas (3)	Hudson	76.906	Frank Mundy (2)	Studebaker	84.173
52	25	9/7/51	Columbia SC	0.500	D	100.00	Tim Flock (6)	Olds	---	Tim Flock (6)	Olds	58.843
53	26	9/8/51	Macon GA	0.500	D	100.00	Herb Thomas (4)	Oldsmobile	53.222	Bob Flock (2)	Olds	---

Race #	Year #	Date	Site	Track	Surface	Miles	Race Winner	Car	Speed	Pole Winner	Car	Speed
54	27	9/15/51	Langhorne PA	1.000	D	150.00	Herb Thomas (5)	Hudson	71.043	Fonty Flock (11)	Olds	81.773
55	28	9/23/51	Charlotte NC	0.750	D	150.00	Herb Thomas (6)	Hudson	---	Billy Carden (2)	Olds	66.914
56	29	9/23/51	Dayton OH	0.500	P	100.00	Fonty Flock (7)	Olds	---	Fonty Flock (12)	Olds	---
57	30	9/30/51	Wilson NC	0.500	D	100.00	Fonty Flock (8)	Olds	---	Fonty Flock (13)	Olds	---
58	31	10/7/51	Hillsboro NC	1.000	D	150.00	Herb Thomas (7)	Hudson	72.454	Herb Thomas	Hudson	79.628
59	32	10/21/51	Thompson CT	0.500	P	100.00	Neil Cole	Olds	---	Neil Cole	Olds	59.269
60	33	10/14/51	Shippenville PA	0.500	D	100.00	Tim Flock (7)	Olds	---	---	---	---
61	34	10/14/51	Martinsville VA	0.500	D	100.00	Frank Mundy (2)	Olds	---	Herb Thomas (2)	Hudson	56.109
62	35	10/14/51	Oakland CA	0.625	D	250.00	Marvin Burke	Mercury	---	---	---	---
63	36	10/21/51	N Wilkesboro NC	0.625	D	125.00	Fonty Flock (9)	Olds	67.791	Herb Thomas (3)	Hudson	68.828
64	37	10/28/51	Hanford CA	0.500	D	100.00	Danny Weinberg	Studebaker	---	---	---	---
65	38	11/4/51	Jacksonville FL	0.500	D	100.00	Herb Thomas (8)	Hudson	53.412	Herb Thomas (4)	Hudson	64.818
66	39	11/11/51	Atlanta GA	1.000	D	100.00	Tim Flock (8)	Hudson	59.960	Frank Mundy (3)	Studebaker	74.013
67	40	11/11/51	Gardena CA	0.500	D	100.00	Bill Norton	Mercury	---	Fonty Flock (14)	Olds	---
68	41	11/25/51	Mobile AL	0.750	D	112.50	Frank Mundy (3)	Studebaker	---	Frank Mundy (4)	Studebaker	61.113

1952

Race #	Year #	Date	Site	Track	Surface	Miles	Race Winner	Car	Speed	Pole Winner	Car	Speed
69	1	1/20/52	W Palm Beach FL	0.500	D	100.00	Fim Flock (9)	Hudson	None	Tim Flock (7)	Hudson	67.794
70	2	2/10/52	Daytona Beach FL	4.100	B-R	200.90	Marshall Teague (6)	Hudson	85.612	Pat Kirkwood	Chrysler	110.970
71	3	3/6/52	Jacksonville FL	0.500	D	100.00	Marshall Teague (7)	Hudson	55.197	Marshall Teague (2)	Hudson	60.100
72	4	3/30/52	N Wilkesboro NC	0.625	D	125.00	Herb Thomas (9)	Hudson	58.593	Herb Thomas (5)	Hudson	75.075
73	5	4/6/52	Martinsville VA	0.500	D	100.00	Dick Rathmann	Hudson	42.862	Buck Baker (2)	Hudson	54.945
74	6	4/12/52	Columbia SC	0.500	D	100.00	Buck Baker	Hudson	53.460	Buck Baker (3)	Hudson	---
75	7	4/20/52	Atlanta GA	1.000	D	100.00	Bill Blair (2)	Olds	66.877	Tim Flock (8)	Hudson	71.613
76	8	4/27/52	Macon GA	0.500	D	99.00	Herb Thomas (10)	Hudson	53.853	Jack Smith	Studebaker	54.429
77	9	5/4/52	Langhorne PA	1.000	D	150.00	Dick Rathmann (2)	Hudson	67.669	Herb Thomas (6)	Hudson	76.045
78	10	5/10/52	Darlington SC	1.375	P	100.00	Dick Rathmann (3)	Hudson	83.818	No Time Trials	NTT	NTT
79	11	5/18/52	Dayton OH	0.500	P	100.00	Dick Rathmann (4)	Hudson	65.526	Fonty Flock (15)	Olds	71.884
80	12	5/30/52	Canfield OH	0.500	D	100.00	Herb Thomas (11)	Hudson	48.057	Dick Rathmann	Hudson	58.102
81	13	6/1/52	Augusta GA	0.500	D	100.00	Gober Sosebee	Chrysler	None	Tommy Moon	Hudson	51.561
82	14	6/1/52	Toledo OH	0.500	D	100.00	Tim Flock (10)	Hudson	47.175	Fonty Flock (16)	Olds	57.034
83	15	6/8/52	Hillsboro NC	1.000	D	100.00	Tim Flock (11)	Hudson	81.008	Fonty Flock (17)	Olds	91.977
84	16	6/15/42	Charlotte NC	0.750	D	112.50	Herb Thomas (12)	Hudson	64.820	Fonty Flock (18)	Olds	70.038
85	17	6/29/52	Detroit MI	1.000	D	250.00	Tim Flock (12)	Hudson	59.908	Dick Rathmann (2)	Hudson	70.230
86	18	7/1/52	Niagara Falls ONT	0.500	D	100.00	Buddy Shuman	Hudson	45.620	Herb Thomas (7)	Hudson	52.401
87	19	7/4/52	Owego NY	0.500	D	100.00	Tim Flock (13)	Hudson	56.603	Tim Flock (9)	Hudson	67.669
88	20	7/6/52	Monroe MI	0.500	D	100.00	Tim Flock (14)	Hudson	44.499	Tim Flock (10)	Hudson	57.600
89	21	7/11/52	Morristown NJ	0.500	D	100.00	Lee Petty (4)	Plymouth	59.661	Herb Thomas (8)	Hudson	60.996
90	22	7/20/52	South Bend IN	0.500	D	100.00	Tim Flock (15)	Hudson	41.889	Herb Thomas (9)	Hudson	58.120
91	23	8/15/52	Rochester NY	0.500	D	88.00	Tim Flock (16)	Hudson	None	No Time Trials	NTT	NTT
92	24	8/17/52	Weaverville NC	0.500	D	100.00	Bob Flock (3)	Hudson	57.288	Herb Thomas (10)	Hudson	64.888
93	25	9/1/52	Darlington SC	1.375	P	500.00	Fonty Flock (10)	Olds	74.512	Fonty Flock (19)	Olds	88.550
94	26	9/7/52	Macon GA	0.500	D	150.00	Lee Petty (5)	Plymouth	48.404	Fonty Flock (20)	Olds	50.113
95	27	9/14/52	Langhorne PA	1.000	D	250.00	Lee Petty (6)	Plymouth	72.463	Herb Thomas (11)	Hudson	85.287
96	28	9/21/52	Dayton OH	0.500	P	150.00	Dick Rathmann (5)	Hudson	61.643	Fonty Flock (21)	Olds	72.741
97	29	9/28/52	Wilson NC	0.500	D	100.00	Herb Thomas (13)	Hudson	35.398	Herb Thomas (12)	Hudson	55.883
98	30	10/12/52	Hillsboro NC	1.000	D	150.00	Fonty Flock (11)	Olds	73.489	Bill Blair	Olds	75.901
99	31	10/29/52	Martinsville VA	0.500	D	100.00	Herb Thomas (14)	Hudson	47.556	Perk Brown	Hudson	55.333
100	32	10/26/52	N Wilkesboro NC	0.625	D	125.00	Herb Thomas (15)	Hudson	67.044	Herb Thomas (13)	Hudson	76.013
101	33	11/16/52	Atlanta GA	1.000	D	100.00	Donald Thomas	Hudson	64.853	Donald Thomas	Hudson	72.874
102	34	11/30/52	W Palm Beach FL	0.500	D	100.00	Herb Thomas (16)	Hudson	58.008	Herb Thomas (14)	Hudson	63.716

1953

Race #	Year #	Date	Site	Track	Surface	Miles	Race Winner	Car	Speed	Pole Winner	Car	Speed
103	1	2/1/53	W Palm Beach FL	0.500	D	100.00	Lee Petty (7)	Dodge	60.220	Dick Rathmann (3)	Hudson	65.028
104	2	2/15/53	Daytona Beach FL	4.100	B-R	160.00	Bill Blair (3)	Olds	89.789	Bob Pronger	Olds	115.770
105	3	3/8/53	Spring Lake NC	0.500	D	100.00	Herb Thomas (17)	Hudson	48.826	Herb Thomas (15)	Hudson	51.918
106	4	3/29/53	N Wilkesboro NC	0.625	D	125.00	Herb Thomas (18)	Hudson	71.907	Herb Thomas (16)	Hudson	78.108
107	5	4/5/53	Charlotte NC	0.750	D	112.50	Dick Passwater	Olds	---	Tim Flock (11)	Hudson	71.108
108	6	4/19/53	Richmond VA	0.500	D	100.00	Lee Petty (8)	Dodge	45.535	Buck Baker (4)	Olds	48.465
109	7	4/26/53	Macon GA	0.500	D	100.00	Dick Rathmann (6)	Hudson	56.417	---	---	---
110	8	5/3/53	Langhorne PA	1.000	D	150.00	Buck Baker (2)	Olds	72.743	No Time Trials	---	---
111	9	5/9/53	Columbia SC	0.500	D	100.00	Buck Baker (3)	Olds	53.707	Herb Thomas (17)	Hudson	58.670
112	10	5/9/53	Hickory NC	0.500	D	100.00	Tim Flock (17)	Hudson	---	---	---	---
113	11	5/17/53	Martinsville VA	0.500	D	100.00	Lee Petty (9)	Dodge	---	---	---	---
114	12	5/24/53	Columbus OH	0.500	D	100.00	Herb Thomas (19)	Hudson	56.127	Fonty Flock (22)	Olds	59.288
115	13	5/30/53	Raleigh NC	1.000	P	300.00	Fonty Flock (12)	Hudson	70.629	Slick Smith	Olds	76.230
116	14	6/7/53	Shreveport LA	0.500	D	100.00	Lee Petty (10)	Dodge	53.199	Herb Thomas (18)	Hudson	58.727
117	15	6/14/53	Pensacola FL	0.500	D	70.00	Herb Thomas (20)	Hudson	63.316	Dick Rathmann (4)	Hudson	67.039
118	16	6/21/53	Langhorne PA	1.000	D	200.00	Dick Rathmann (7)	Hudson	64.434	Lloyd Shaw	Jaguar	82.200

Race #	Year #	Date	Site	Track	Surface	Miles	Race Winner	Car	Speed	Pole Winner	Car	Speed
119	17	6/23/53	High Point NC	0.500	D	100.00	Herb Thomas (21)	Hudson	58.186	Herb Thomas (19)	Hudson	66.152
120	18	6/28/53	Wilson NC	0.500	D	100.00	Fonty Flock (13)	Hudson	53.803	---	---	---
121	19	7/3/53	Rochester NY	0.500	D	100.00	Herb Thomas (22)	Hudson	56.939	No Time Trials	NTT	NTT
122	20	7/4/53	Spartanburg SC	0.500	D	100.00	Lee Petty (11)	Dodge	56.934	Buck Baker (5)	Olds	58.027
123	21	7/10/53	Morristown NJ	0.500	D	100.00	Dick Rathmann (8)	Hudson	69.417	Herb Thomas (20)	Hudson	61.016
124	22	7/12/53	Atlanta GA	1.000	D	100.00	Herb Thomas (23)	Hudson	70.685	Herb Thomas (21)	Hudson	72.756
125	23	7/22/53	Rapid City SD	0.500	D	100.00	Herb Thomas (24)	Hudson	57.720	Herb Thomas (22)	Hudson	55.727
126	24	7/26/53	N Platte NE	0.500	D	100.00	Dick Rathmann (9)	Hudson	54.380	Herb Thomas (23)	Hudson	54.397
127	25	8/2/53	Davenport IA	0.500	D	100.00	Herb Thomas (25)	Hudson	62.500	Buck Baker (6)	Olds	54.397
128	26	8/9/53	Hillsboro NC	1.000	D	100.00	Curtis Turner (9)	Olds	75.125	Curtis Turner (6)	Olds	89.078
129	27	8/16/53	Weaverville NC	0.500	D	100.00	Fonty Flock (14)	Hudson	62.434	Curtis Turner (7)	Olds	---
130	28	8/23/53	Norfolk VA	0.500	D	100.00	Herb Thomas (26)	Hudson	51.040	Curtis Turner (8)	Olds	54.200
131	29	8/29/53	Hickory NC	0.500	D	100.00	Fonty Flock (15)	Hudson	---	Tim Flock (12)	Hudson	79.362
132	30	9/7/53	Darlington SC	1.375	P	500.00	Buck Baker (4)	Olds	92.881	Fonty Flock (23)	Hudson	107.893
133	31	9/13/53	Macon GA	0.500	D	100.00	Speedy Thompson	Olds	55.172	Joe Eubanks	Hudson	60.810
134	32	9/20/53	Langhorne PA	1.000	D	250.00	Dick Rathmann (10)	Hudson	67.046	Herb Thomas (24)	Hudson	---
135	33	10/3/53	Bloomsburg PA	0.500	D	100.00	Herb Thomas (27)	Hudson	---	Jim Paschal	Dodge	55.953
136	34	10/4/53	Wilson NC	0.500	D	100.00	Herb Thomas (28)	Hudson	56.022	Herb Thomas (25)	Hudson	56.962
137	35	10/11/53	N Wilkesboro NC	0.625	D	100.00	Speedy Thompson (2)	Olds	71.202	Buck Baker (7)	Olds	78.288
138	36	10/18/53	Martinsville VA	0.500	D	100.00	Jim Paschal	Dodge	56.013	Fonty Flock (24)	Hudson	58.958
139	37	11/1/53	Atlanta GA	1.000	D	100.00	Buck Baker (5)	Olds	63.180	Tim Flock (13)	Hudson	73.580

1954

Race #	Year #	Date	Site	Track	Surface	Miles	Race Winner	Car	Speed	Pole Winner	Car	Speed
140	1	2/7/54	W Palm Beach FL	0.500	D	100.00	Herb Thomas (29)	Hudson	58.958	Dick Rathmann (5)	Hudson	66.371
141	2	2/21/54	Daytona Beach FL	4.100	B-R	160.00	Lee Petty (12)	Chrysler	89.108	Lee Petty	Chrysler	123.410
142	3	3/7/54	Jacksonville FL	0.500	D	100.00	Herb Thomas (30)	Hudson	56.561	Curtis Turner (9)	Olds	63.581
143	4	3/21/54	Atlanta GA	1.000	D	100.00	Herb Thomas (32)	Hudson	60.494	Herb Thomas (26)	Hudson	73.514
144	5	3/28/54	Savannah GA	0.500	D	100.00	Al Keller	Hudson	59.820	Herb Thomas (27)	Hudson	63.202
145	6	3/28/54	Oakland CA	0.500	D	125.00	Dick Rathmann (11)	Hudson	50.692	Hershel McGriff	Olds	55.624
146	7	4/4/54	N Wilkesboro NC	0.625	D	100.00	Dick Rathmann (12)	Hudson	68.545	Gober Sosebee (3)	Olds	78.698
147	8	4/18/54	Hillsboro NC	1.000	D	100.00	Herb Thomas (32)	Hudson	77.386	Buck Baker (8)	Olds	86.767
148	9	4/25/54	Macon GA	0.500	D	100.00	Gober Sosebee (2)	Olds	55.410	Dick Rathmann (6)	Hudson	57.859
149	10	5/2/54	Langhorne PA	1.000	D	150.00	Herb Thomas (33)	Hudson	74.883	Lee Petty (2)	Chrysler	87.217
150	11	5/9/54	Wilson NC	0.500	D	100.00	Buck Baker (6)	Olds	52.279	Jim Paschal (2)	Olds	55.469
151	12	5/16/54	Martinsville VA	0.500	D	100.00	Jim Paschal (2)	Olds	46.153	No Time Trials	NTT	NTT
152	13	5/23/54	Sharon PA	0.500	D	100.00	Lee Petty (13)	Chrysler	None	Dick Rathmann (7)	Hudson	62.090
153	14	5/29/54	Raleigh NC	1.000	P	250.00	Herb Thomas (34)	Hudson	73.909	Herb Thomas (28)	Hudson	76.660
154	15	5/30/54	Charlotte NC	0.750	D	100.00	Buck Baker (7)	Olds	49.805	Al Keller	Hudson	68.947
155	16	5/30/54	Gardena CA	0.500	D	248.00	John Soares	Dodge	53.438	Danny Letner	Hudson	62.849
156	17	6/6/54	Columbia SC	0.500	D	100.00	Curtis Turner (10)	Olds	56.719	Buck Baker (9)	Olds	62.240
157	18	6/13/54	Linden NJ	2.000	P	100.00	Al Keller (2)	Jaguar	77.469	Buck Baker (10)	Olds	80.536
158	19	6/19/54	Hickory NC	0.500	D	100.00	Herb Thomas (35)	Hudson	82.872	Herb Thomas (29)	Hudson	81.669
159	20	6/25/54	Rochester NY	0.500	D	100.00	Lee Petty (14)	Chrysler	52.455	Herb Thomas (30)	Hudson	60.422
160	21	6/27/54	Mechanicsburg PA	0.500	D	100.00	Herb Thomas (36)	Hudson	51.085	Dick Rathmann (8)	Hudson	54.945
161	22	7/3/54	Spartanburg SC	0.500	D	100.00	Herb Thomas (37)	Hudson	59.181	Hershel McGriff (2)	Olds	58.120
162	23	7/4/54	Weaverville NC	0.500	D	100.00	Herb Thomas (38)	Hudson	61.318	Herb Thomas (31)	Hudson	67.771
163	24	7/10/54	Willow Springs IL	0.500	D	100.00	Dick Rathmann (13)	Hudson	72.216	Buck Baker (11)	Olds	75.662
164	25	7/11/54	Grand Rapids MI	0.500	D	100.00	Lee Petty (15)	Chrysler	52.090	Herb Thomas (32)	Hudson	59.055
165	26	7/30/54	Morristown NJ	0.500	D	100.00	Buck Baker (8)	Olds	58.968	Buck Baker (12)	Olds	66.667
166	27	8/1/54	Oakland CA	0.500	D	150.00	Danny Letner	Hudson	53.045	Marvin Panch	Dodge	55.248
167	28	8/13/54	Charlotte NC	0.500	D	100.00	Lee Petty (16)	Chrysler	51.362	Buck Baker (13)	Olds	57.270
168	29	8/22/54	San Mateo CA	1.000	D	250.00	Hershel McGriff	Olds	64.710	Hershel McGriff (3)	Olds	75.566
169	30	8/29/54	Corbin KY	0.500	D	100.00	Lee Petty (17)	Chrysler	63.080	Jim Paschal (3)	Olds	65.789
170	31	9/6/54	Darlington SC	1.375	P	500.00	Herb Thomas (39)	Hudson	95.026	Buck Baker (14)	Olds	108.261
171	32	9/12/54	Macon GA	0.500	D	100.00	Hershel McGriff (2)	Olds	50.526	Tim Flock (14)	Olds	56.907
172	33	9/24/54	Charlotte NC	0.500	D	100.00	Hershel McGriff (3)	Olds	53.167	Hershel McGriff (4)	Olds	54.054
173	34	9/26/54	Langhorne PA	1.000	D	250.00	Herb Thomas (40)	Hudson	71.186	Herb Thomas (33)	Hudson	89.418
174	35	10/10/54	LeHi AR	1.500	D	250.00	Buck Baker (9)	Olds	89.013	Junior Johnson	Cadillac	---
175	36	10/17/54	Martinsville VA	0.500	D	82.50	Lee Petty (18)	Chrysler	44.547	Lee Petty (3)	Chrysler	53.191
176	37	10/24/54	N Wilkesboro NC	0.625	D	98.10	Hershel McGriff (4)	Olds	65.175	Hershel McGriff (5)	Olds	77.612

1955

Race #	Year #	Date	Site	Track	Surface	Miles	Race Winner	Car	Speed	Pole Winner	Car	Speed
177	1	11/7/54	High Point NC	0.500	D	100.00	Lee Petty (19)	Chrysler	62.882	Herb Thomas (34)	Hudson	71.942
178	2	2/6/55	W Palm Beach FL	0.500	D	100.00	Herb Thomas (41)	Hudson	56.013	Dick Rathmann (9)	Hudson	65.454
179	3	2/13/55	Jacksonville FL	0.500	D	100.00	Lee Petty (20)	Chrysler	69.031	Dick Rathmann (10)	Hudson	63.514
180	4	2/27/55	Daytona Beach FL	4.100	B-R	160.00	Tim Flock (18)	Chrysler	91.999	Tim Flock (15)	Chrysler	130.293
181	5	3/6/55	Savannah GA	0.500	D	100.00	Lee Petty (21)	Chrysler	60.150	Dick Rathmann (11)	Hudson	62.805
182	6	3/26/55	Columbia SC	0.500	D	100.00	Fonty Flock (16)	Chevy	None	Tim Flock (16)	Chrysler	---
183	7	3/27/55	Hillsboro NC	1.000	D	100.00	Jim Paschal (3)	Olds	82.304	Tim Flock (17)	Chrysler	91.696

Race #	Year #	Date	Site	Track	Surface	Miles	Race Winner	Car	Speed	Pole Winner	Car	Speed
184	8	4/3/55	N Wilkesboro NC	0.625	D	100.00	Buck Baker (10)	Olds	73.126	Dink Widenhouse	Olds	77.720
185	9	4/17/55	Montgomery AL	0.500	D	100.00	Tim Flock (19)	Chrysler	60.872	Jim Paschal (4)	Olds	64.290
186	10	4/24/55	Langhorne PA	1.000	D	150.00	Tim Flock (20)	Chrysler	72.893	Tim Flock (18)	Chrysler	86.699
187	11	5/1/55	Charlotte NC	0.750	D	100.00	Buck Baker (11)	Buick	52.630	Herb Thomas (35)	Buick	70.184
188	12	5/7/55	Hickory NC	0.500	D	100.00	Junior Johnson	Olds	65.502	Tim Flock (19)	Chrysler	67.748
189	13	5/8/55	Phoenix AZ	1.000	D	100.00	Tim Flock (21)	Chrysler	71.485	Bill Amick	Dodge	75.519
190	14	5/15/55	Tucson AZ	0.500	D	100.00	Danny Letner (2)	Olds	51.428	Bill Amick (2)	Dodge	56.179
191	15	5/15/55	Martinsville VA	0.500	D	100.00	Tim Flock (22)	Chrysler	52.554	Jim Paschal (5)	Olds	58.823
192	16	5/22/55	Richmond VA	0.500	D	100.00	Tim Flock (23)	Chrysler	54.298	No Time Trials	NTT	NTT
193	17	5/28/55	Raleigh NC	0.500	D	100.00	Junior Johnson (2)	Olds	50.522	Tim Flock (20)	Chrysler	58.612
194	18	5/29/55	Winston Salem NC	0.500	D	100.00	Lee Petty (22)	Chrysler	50.583	Fonty Flock (25)	Chrysler	56.710
195	19	6/10/55	New Oxford PA	0.500	D	100.00	Junior Johnson (3)	Olds	65.371	Junior Johnson (2)	Olds	75.853
196	20	6/17/55	Rochester NY	0.500	D	100.00	Tim Flock (24)	Chrysler	57.710	Buck Baker (15)	Chrysler	61.141
197	21	6/18/55	Fonda NY	0.500	D	100.00	Junior Johnson (4)	Olds	58.413	Fonty Flock (26)	Chrysler	61.770
198	22	6/19/55	Plattsburg NY	0.500	D	100.00	Lee Petty (23)	Chrysler	59.074	Lee Petty (4)	Chrysler	55.744
199	23	6/24/55	Charlotte NC	0.500	D	100.00	Tim Flock (25)	Chrysler	51.289	Tim Flock (21)	Chrysler	57.915
200	24	7/6/55	Spartanburg SC	0.500	D	100.00	Tim Flock (26)	Chrysler	49.106	Tim Flock (22)	Chrysler	58.517
201	25	7/9/55	Columbia SC	0.500	D	100.00	Jim Paschal (4)	Olds	55.469	Jimmie Lewallen	Olds	59.741
202	26	7/10/55	Weaverville NC	0.500	D	100.00	Tim Flock (27)	Chrysler	62.739	Tim Flock (23)	Chrysler	69.310
203	27	7/15/55	Morristown NJ	0.500	D	100.00	Tim Flock (28)	Chrysler	58.092	Tim Flock (24)	Chrysler	63.649
204	28	7/29/55	Altamont NY	0.500	D	88.50	Junior Johnson (5)	Olds	None	Tim Flock (25)	Chrysler	56.603
205	29	7/30/55	Syracuse NY	0.500	D	100.00	Tim Flock (29)	Chrysler	76.522	Tim Flock (26)	Chrysler	78.311
206	30	7/31/55	San Mateo CA	1.000	D	252.00	Tim Flock (30)	Chrysler	68.571	Fonty Flock (27)	Chrysler	79.330
207	31	8/5/55	Charlotte NC	0.500	D	100.00	Jim Paschal (5)	Olds	48.806	Tim Flock (27)	Chrysler	57.859
208	32	8/7/55	Winston-Salem NC	0.500	D	100.00	Lee Petty (24)	Dodge	50.111	Tim Flock (28)	Chrysler	59.016
209	33	8/14/55	LeHi AR	1.500	D	250.00	Fonty Flock (17)	Chrysler	89.892	Fonty Flock (28)	Chrysler	99.944
210	34	8/20/55	Raleigh NC	1.000	P	100.00	Herb Thomas (42)	Buick	76.400	Tim Flock (29)	Chrysler	78.752
211	35	9/5/55	Darlington SC	1.375	P	500.00	Herb Thomas (43)	Chevy	92.281	Fireball Roberts (2)	Buick	110.682
212	36	9/11/55	Montgomery AL	0.500	D	100.00	Tim Flock (31)	Chrysler	62.773	Tim Flock (30)	Chrysler	68.728
213	37	9/18/55	Langhorne PA	1.000	D	250.00	Tim Flock (32)	Chrysler	77.888	Tim Flock (31)	Chrysler	92.095
214	38	9/30/55	Raleigh NC	1.000	P	100.00	Fonty Flock (18)	Chrysler	73.289	Fonty Flock (29)	Chrysler	82.098
215	39	10/6/55	Greenville SC	0.500	D	100.00	Tim Flock (33)	Chrysler	57.942	Bob Welborn	Chevy	58.027
216	40	10/9/55	LeHi AR	1.500	D	300.00	Speedy Thompson (3)	Ford	83.898	Fonty Flock (30)	Chrysler	100.390
217	41	10/15/55	Columbia SC	0.500	D	100.00	Tim Flock (34)	Chrysler	55.393	Junior Johnson (3)	Olds	61.728
218	42	10/16/55	Martinsville VA	0.500	P	100.00	Speedy Thompson (4)	Chrysler	59.210	No Time Trials	NTT	NTT
219	43	10/16/55	Las Vegas NV	1.000	D	111.00	Norm Nelson	Chrysler	44.449	Norm Nelson	Chrysler	74.518
220	44	10/23/55	N Wilkesboro NC	0.625	D	100.00	Buck Baker (12)	Ford	72.347	Buck Baker (16)	Ford	79.815
221	45	10/30/55	Hillsboro NC	1.000	D	100.00	Tim Flock (35)	Chrysler	70.465	Tim Flock (32)	Chrysler	81.673

1956

Race #	Year #	Date	Site	Track	Surface	Miles	Race Winner	Car	Speed	Pole Winner	Car	Speed
222	1	10/30/55	Hickory NC	0.500	D	80.00	Tim Flock (36)	Chrysler	56.962	Tim Flock (33)	Chrysler	---
223	2	11/20/55	Charlotte NC	0.750	D	100.00	Fonty Flock (19)	Chrysler	61.825	Fonty Flock (31)	Chrysler	70.496
224	3	11/20/55	Lancaster CA	0.500	D	200.00	Chuck Stevenson	Ford	66.512	Jim Reed	Chevy	76.556
225	4	12/11/55	W Palm Beach FL	0.500	D	100.00	Herb Thomas (44)	Chevy	65.009	Fonty Flock (32)	Chrysler	78.912
226	5	1/22/56	Phoenix AZ	1.000	D	150.00	Buck Baker (13)	Chrysler	64.408	Joe Weatherly	Ford	71.315
227	6	2/26/56	Daytona Beach FL	4.100	B-R	151.70	Tim Flock (37)	Chrysler	90.657	Tim Flock (34)	Chrysler	135.747
228	7	3/4/56	W Palm Beach FL	0.500	D	100.00	Billy Myers	Mercury	68.990	Buck Baker (17)	Dodge	81.081
229	8	3/18/56	Wilson NC	0.500	D	53.00	Herb Thomas (45)	Chevy	46.287	Herb Thomas (36)	Chevy	57.157
230	9	3/25/56	Atlanta GA	1.000	D	100.00	Buck Baker (14)	Chrysler	70.643	Tim Flock (35)	Chrysler	82.154
231	10	4/8/56	N Wilkesboro NC	0.625	D	100.00	Tim Flock (38)	Chrysler	71.034	Junior Johnson (4)	Pontiac	78.370
232	11	4/22/56	Langhorne PA	1.000	D	150.00	Buck Baker (15)	Chrysler	75.928	Buck Baker (18)	Chrysler	104.590
233	12	4/29/56	Richmond VA	0.500	D	100.00	Buck Baker (16)	Dodge	56.232	Buck Baker (19)	Dodge	67.091
234	13	5/5/56	Columbia SC	0.500	D	100.00	Speedy Thompson (5)	Dodge	54.545	Buck Baker (20)	Dodge	63.224
235	14	5/6/56	Concord NC	0.500	D	100.00	Speedy Thompson (6)	Chrysler	61.633	Speedy Thompson	Chrysler	65.241
236	15	5/10/56	Greenville SC	0.500	D	100.00	Buck Baker (17)	Dodge	60.362	Rex White	Chevy	61.100
237	16	5/12/56	Hickory NC	0.400	D	80.00	Speedy Thompson (7)	Chrysler	59.442	Speedy Thompson (2)	Chrysler	67.447
238	17	5/13/56	Hillsboro NC	0.900	D	90.00	Buck Baker (18)	Chrysler	83.720	Buck Baker (21)	Chrysler	89.305
239	18	5/20/56	Martinsville VA	0.500	P	250.00	Buck Baker (19)	Dodge	60.824	Buck Baker (22)	Dodge	66.103
240	19	5/25/56	Abbottstown PA	0.500	D	100.00	Buck Baker (20)	Dodge	69.619	Speedy Thompson (3)	Dodge	76.628
241	20	5/27/56	Charlotte NC	0.750	D	100.00	Speedy Thompson (8)	Chrysler	64.866	Speedy Thompson (4)	Chrysler	76.966
242	21	5/27/56	Portland OR	0.500	P	75.00	Herb Thomas (46)	Chrysler	63.815	John Kieper	Olds	67.239
243	22	5/30/56	Eureka CA	0.625	D	78.10	Herb Thomas (47)	Chrysler	38.814	John Kieper (2)	Olds	66.040
244	23	5/30/56	Syracuse NY	1.000	D	150.00	Buck Baker (21)	Chrysler	86.179	Buck Baker (23)	Chrysler	83.975
245	24	6/3/56	Merced CA	0.500	D	100.00	Herb Thomas (48)	Chrysler	47.325	Herb Thomas (37)	Chrysler	58.234
246	25	6/10/56	LeHi AR	1.500	D	250.00	Ralph Moody	Ford	74.313	Buck Baker (24)	Chrysler	98.512
247	26	6/15/56	Charlotte NC	0.500	D	100.00	Speedy Thompson (9)	Chrysler	56.022	Fireball Roberts (3)	Ford	59.661
248	27	6/22/56	Rochester NY	0.500	D	100.00	Speedy Thompson (10)	Chrysler	57.288	Jim Paschal (6)	Mercury	57.434
249	28	6/24/56	Portland OR	0.500	P	100.00	John Kieper	Olds	62.586	Herb Thomas (38)	Chrysler	65.934
250	29	7/1/56	Weaverville NC	0.500	D	100.00	Lee Petty (25)	Dodge	56.435	Fireball Roberts (4)	Ford	72.260
251	30	7/4/56	Raleigh NC	1.000	P	250.00	Fireball Roberts (2)	Ford	79.822	Lee Petty (5)	Dodge	82.587
252	31	7/7/56	Spartanburg SC	0.500	D	100.00	Lee Petty (26)	Dodge	50.483	Fireball Roberts (5)	Ford	58.900
253	32	7/8/56	Sacramento CA	1.000	D	100.00	Lloyd Dane	Mercury	74.074	Eddie Pagan	Ford	76.612

Race #	Year #	Date	Site	Track	Surface	Miles	Race Winner	Car	Speed	Pole Winner	Car	Speed
254	33	7/21/56	Chicago IL	0.500	P	100.00	Fireball Roberts (3)	Ford	61.037	Billy Myers	Mercury	---
255	34	7/17/56	Shelby NC	0.500	D	100.50	Speedy Thompson (11)	Dodge	53.699	Ralph Moody	Ford	55.658
256	35	7/29/56	Montgomery AL	0.500	D	100.00	Marvin Panch	Ford	67.252	Marvin Panch (2)	Ford	69.444
257	36	8/3/56	Oklahoma City OK	0.500	D	100.00	Jim Paschal (6)	Mercury	60.100	Speedy Thompson (5)	Dodge	64.655
258	37	8/12/56	Elkhart Lake WI	4.100	P	258.30	Tim Flock (39)	Mercury	73.858	Buck Baker (25)	Dodge	---
259	38	8/17/56	Old Bridge NJ	0.500	P	100.00	Ralph Moody (2)	Ford	65.170	Jim Reed (2)	Chevy	72.028
260	39	8/19/56	San Mateo CA	1.000	D	241.00	Eddie Pagan	Ford	68.161	Eddie Pagan (2)	Ford	81.614
261	40	8/22/56	Norfolk VA	0.500	D	100.00	Billy Myers (2)	Mercury	56.408	Ralph Moody (2)	Ford	58.631
262	41	8/23/56	Spartanburg SC	0.500	D	100.00	Ralph Moody (3)	Ford	54.372	Ralph Moody (3)	Ford	61.433
263	42	8/25/56	Myrtle Beach SC	0.500	D	100.00	Fireball Roberts (4)	Ford	50.576	Ralph Moody (4)	Ford	58.346
264	43	8/26/56	Portland OR	0.500	P	123.00	Royce Haggerty	Dodge	None	John Kieper (3)	Olds	65.861
265	44	9/3/56	Darlington SC	1.375	P	500.00	Curtis Turner (11)	Ford	95.167	Speedy Thompson (6)	Chrysler	118.683
266	45	9/9/56	Montgomery AL	0.500	D	100.00	Buck Baker (22)	Chrysler	60.893	Tim Flock (36)	Ford	64.864
267	46	9/12/56	Charlotte NC	0.500	D	100.00	Ralph Moody (4)	Ford	52.847	Joe Eubanks (2)	Ford	59.464
268	47	9/23/56	Langhorne PA	1.000	D	300.00	Paul Goldsmith	Chevy	70.615	Buck Baker (26)	Chrysler	93.628
269	48	9/23/56	Portland OR	0.500	P	125.00	Lloyd Dane (2)	Ford	None	Royce Haggerty	Dodge	---
270	49	9/29/56	Columbia SC	0.500	D	100.00	Buck Baker (23)	Dodge	61.193	Tim Flock (37)	Ford	61.940
271	50	9/30/56	Hillsboro NC	0.900	D	99.00	Fireball Roberts (5)	Ford	72.734	Speedy Thompson (7)	Chrysler	88.067
272	51	10/7/56	Newport TN	0.500	D	100.00	Fireball Roberts (6)	Ford	61.475	Joe Eubanks (3)	Ford	65.597
273	52	10/14/56	Charlotte NC	0.750	D	100.00	Buck Baker (24)	Chrysler	72.268	Ralph Moody (5)	Ford	75.041
274	53	10/23/56	Shelby NC	0.500	D	100.00	Buck Baker (25)	Chrysler	54.054	Doug Cox	Ford	58.479
275	54	10/28/56	Martinsville VA	0.500	P	200.00	Jack Smith	Dodge	61.136	Buck Baker (27)	Chrysler	67.643
276	55	11/11/56	Hickory NC	0.400	D	100.00	Speedy Thompson (12)	Chrysler	66.420	Ralph Earnhardt	Ford	68.278
277	56	11/18/56	Wilson NC	0.500	D	100.00	Buck Baker (26)	Chrysler	50.579	Buck Baker (28)	Chrysler	60.160

1957

Race #	Year #	Date	Site	Track	Surface	Miles	Race Winner	Car	Speed	Pole Winner	Car	Speed
278	1	11/11/56	Lancaster CA	2.500	P	150.00	Marvin Panch (2)	Ford	78.648	Marvin Panch (3)	Ford	78.596
279	2	12/2/56	Concord NC	0.500	D	100.00	Marvin Panch (3)	Ford	55.883	Curtis Turner (10)	Ford	62.586
280	3	12/30/56	Titusville FL	1.700	P	89.60	Fireball Roberts (7)	Ford	None	Paul Goldsmith	Chevy	69.106
281	4	2/17/57	Daytona Beach FL	4.100	B-R	160.00	Cotton Owens	Pontiac	101.541	Banjo Matthews	Pontiac	134.382
282	5	3/3/57	Concord NC	0.500	D	100.00	Jack Smith (2)	Chevy	59.860	Mel Larson	Ford	62.225
283	6	3/17/57	Wilson NC	0.500	D	100.00	Ralph Moody (5)	Ford	55.079	Fireball Roberts (6)	Ford	59.269
284	7	3/24/57	Hillsboro NC	0.900	D	99.00	Buck Baker (27)	Chevy	82.233	Fireball Roberts (7)	Ford	87.828
285	8	3/31/57	Weaverville NC	0.500	D	100.00	Buck Baker (28)	Chevy	65.693	Marvin Panch (4)	Ford	73.649
286	9	4/7/57	N Wilkesboro NC	0.625	D	100.00	Fireball Roberts (8)	Ford	75.015	Fireball Roberts (8)	Ford	81.521
287	10	4/14/57	Langhorne PA	1.000	D	150.00	Fireball Roberts (9)	Ford	85.850	Paul Goldsmith (2)	Ford	93.701
288	11	4/19/57	Charlotte NC	0.500	D	100.00	Fireball Roberts (10)	Ford	52.083	Marvin Panch (5)	Ford	60.060
289	12	4/27/57	Spartanburg SC	0.500	D	100.00	Marvin Panch (4)	Ford	55.130	Speedy Thompson (8)	Chevy	61.538
290	13	4/28/57	Greensboro NC	0.333	D	83.25	Paul Goldsmith (2)	Ford	49.905	Buck Baker (29)	Chevy	50.120
291	14	4/28/57	Portland OR	0.500	P	50.00	Art Watts	Ford	64.754	Art Watts	Ford	65.813
292	15	5/4/57	Shelby NC	0.500	D	100.00	Fireball Roberts (11)	Ford	54.861	Tiny Lund	Pontiac	57.544
293	16	5/5/57	Richmond VA	0.500	D	100.00	Paul Goldsmith (3)	Ford	62.445	Russ Hepler	Pontiac	64.239
294	17	5/19/57	Martinsville VA	0.500	P	220.50	Buck Baker (29)	Chevy	57.318	Paul Goldsmith (3)	Ford	65.693
295	18	5/26/57	Portland OR	0.500	P	75.00	Eddie Pagan (2)	Ford	64.732	Art Watts (2)	Ford	66.347
296	19	5/30/57	Eureka CA	0.625	D	96.63	Lloyd Dane (3)	Ford	55.957	Parnelli Jones	Ford	63.920
297	20	5/30/57	New Oxford PA	0.500	D	100.00	Buck Baker (30)	Chevy	76.126	Marvin Panch (6)	Ford	78.238
298	21	6/1/57	Lancaster SC	0.500	D	100.00	Paul Goldsmith (4)	Ford	61.622	Buck Baker (30)	Chevy	67.365
299	22	6/8/57	Los Angeles CA	0.500	D	75.00	Eddie Pagan (3)	Ford	None	Eddie Pagan (3)	Ford	67.290
300	23	6/15/57	Newport TN	0.500	D	100.00	Fireball Roberts (12)	Ford	60.687	Speedy Thompson (9)	Chevy	61.813
301	24	6/20/57	Columbia SC	0.500	D	100.00	Jack Smith (3)	Chevy	58.045	Buck Baker (31)	Chevy	64.585
302	25	6/22/57	Sacramento CA	0.500	D	99.50	Bill Amick	Ford	59.580	Art Watts (3)	Ford	69.337
303	26	6/29/57	Spartanburg SC	0.500	D	100.00	Lee Petty (27)	Olds	46.287	Lee Petty (6)	Olds	59.642
304	27	6/30/57	Jacksonville NC	0.500	D	100.00	Buck Baker (31)	Chevy	55.342	Lee Petty (7)	Olds	61.328
305	28	7/4/57	Raleigh NC	1.000	P	250.00	Paul Goldsmith (5)	Ford	75.693	Frankie Schneider	Chevy	83.371
306	29	7/12/57	Charlotte NC	0.500	D	100.00	Marvin Panch (5)	Ford	56.302	Tiny Lund (2)	Pontiac	60.913
307	30	7/14/57	LeHi AR	1.500	D	200.00	Marvin Panch (6)	Pontiac	67.167	Speedy Thompson (10)	Chevy	98.991
308	31	7/14/57	Portland OR	0.500	P	100.00	Eddie Pagan (4)	Ford	64.539	Art Watts (4)	Ford	66.396
309	32	7/20/57	Hickory NC	0.500	D	100.00	Jack Smith (4)	Chevy	58.737	Gwyn Staley	Chevy	66.085
310	33	7/24/57	Norfolk VA	0.500	D	100.00	Buck Baker (32)	Chevy	47.987	Bill Amick (3)	Ford	56.338
311	34	7/30/57	Lancaster SC	0.500	D	100.00	Speedy Thompson (13)	Chevy	66.543	Speedy Thompson (11)	Chevy	67.694
312	35	8/4/57	Watkins Glen NY	2.300	P	101.20	Buck Baker (33)	Chevy	83.064	Buck Baker (32)	Chevy	87.071
313	36	8/4/47	Bremerton WA	0.900	P	72.00	Parnelli Jones	Ford	38.959	Art Watts (5)	Ford	62.657
314	37	8/10/57	New Oxford PA	0.500	P	100.00	Marvin Panch (7)	Ford	77.569	Tiny Lund (3)	Pontiac	80.971
315	38	8/16/57	Old Bridge NJ	0.500	P	100.00	Lee Petty (28)	Olds	65.813	Rex White (2)	Chevy	71.599
316	39	8/26/57	Myrtle Beach SC	0.500	D	100.00	Gwyn Staley	Chevy	50.782	Johnny Allen	Plymouth	58.139
317	40	9/2/57	Darlington SC	1.375	P	500.00	Speedy Thompson (14)	Chevy	100.094	Cotton Owens	Pontiac	117.416
318	41	9/5/57	Syracuse NY	1.000	D	100.00	Gwyn Staley (2)	Chevy	80.591	Gwyn Staley (2)	Chevy	83.045
319	42	9/8/57	Weaverville NC	0.500	D	100.00	Lee Petty (29)	Olds	67.950	Bill Amick (4)	Ford	77.687
320	43	9/8/57	Sacramento CA	1.000	D	100.00	Danny Graves	Chevy	68.663	Danny Graves	Chevy	78.007
321	44	9/15/57	San Jose CA	0.500	D	100.00	Marvin Porter	Ford	None	No Time Trials	NTT	NTT
322	45	9/15/57	Langhorne PA	1.000	D	300.00	Gwyn Staley (3)	Chevy	72.759	Paul Goldsmith (4)	Ford	92.072

Race #	Year #	Date	Site	Track	Surface	Miles	Race Winner	Car	Speed	Pole Winner	Car	Speed
323	46	9/19/57	Columbia SC	0.500	D	100.00	Buck Baker (34)	Chevy	60.514	Buck Baker (33)	Chevy	63.649
324	47	9/21/57	Shelby NC	0.500	D	100.00	Buck Baker (35)	Chevy	53.699	Buck Baker (34)	Chevy	58.177
325	48	10/5/57	Charlotte NC	0.500	D	100.00	Lee Petty (30)	Olds	51.583	Lee Petty (8)	Olds	60.585
326	49	10/6/57	Martinsville VA	0.500	P	250.00	Bob Welborn	Chevy	63.025	Eddie Pagan (4)	Ford	65.837
327	50	10/12/57	Newberry SC	0.500	D	100.00	Fireball Roberts (13)	Ford	50.398	Jack Smith (2)	Chevy	56.514
328	51	10/13/57	Concord NC	0.500	D	100.00	Fireball Roberts (14)	Ford	59.553	Jack Smith (3)	Chevy	65.052
329	52	10/20/57	N Wilkesboro NC	0.625	P	100.00	Jack Smith (5)	Chevy	69.902	Fireball Roberts (9)	Ford	81.640
330	53	10/27/57	Greensboro NC	0.333	D	83.25	Buck Baker (36)	Chevy	38.927	Ken Rush	Ford	48.358

1958

Race #	Year #	Date	Site	Track	Surface	Miles	Race Winner	Car	Speed	Pole Winner	Car	Speed
331	1	11/3/57	Fayetteville NC	0.333	P	50.00	Rex White	Chevy	59.170	Jack Smith (4)	Chevy	62.665
332	2	2/23/58	Daytona Beach FL	4.100	B-R	160.00	Paul Goldsmith (6)	Pontiac	101.113	Paul Goldsmith (5)	Pontiac	140.570
333	3	3/2/58	Concord NC	0.500	D	100.00	Lee Petty (31)	Olds	58.555	Speedy Thompson (12)	Chevy	---
334	4	3/15/58	Fayetteville NC	0.333	P	50.00	Curtis Turner (12)	Ford	56.141	Lee Petty (9)	Olds	62.600
335	5	3/16/58	Wilson NC	0.500	D	100.00	Lee Petty (32)	Olds	48.459	Marvin Panch (7)	Ford	58.901
336	6	3/23/58	Hillsboro NC	0.900	D	99.00	Buck Baker (37)	Chevy	78.502	Buck Baker (35)	Chevy	83.076
337	7	4/5/58	Fayetteville NC	0.333	P	50.00	Bob Welborn (2)	Chevy	50.229	Lee Petty (10)	Olds	60.576
338	8	4/10/58	Columbia SC	0.500	D	100.00	Speedy Thompson (15)	Chevy	None	Possum Jones	Chevy	66.201
339	9	4/12/58	Spartanburg SC	0.500	D	100.00	Speedy Thompson (16)	Chevy	56.613	Speedy Thompson (13)	Chevy	61.412
340	10	4/13/58	Atlanta GA	1.000	D	100.00	Curtis Turner (13)	Ford	79.016	Joe Weatherly (2)	Ford	81.577
341	11	4/18/58	Charlotte NC	0.500	D	100.00	Curtis Turner (14)	Ford	53.254	Curtis Turner (11)	Ford	54.471
342	12	4/20/58	Martinsville VA	0.500	P	250.00	Bob Welborn (3)	Chevy	61.166	Buck Baker (36)	Chevy	66.007
343	13	4/25/58	Manassas VA	0.375	P	56.25	Frankie Schneider	Chevy	67.590	Eddie Pagan (5)	Ford	69.018
344	14	4/27/58	Old Bridge NJ	0.500	P	93.50	Jim Reed	Ford	68.438	Jim Reed (3)	Ford	71.371
345	15	5/3/58	Greenville SC	0.500	D	100.00	Jack Smith (6)	Chevy	62.295	Jack Smith (5)	Chevy	60.484
346	16	5/11/58	Greensboro NC	0.333	D	50.00	Bob Welborn (4)	Chevy	45.628	Bob Welborn (2)	Chevy	46.250
347	17	5/15/58	Roanoke VA	0.250	P	37.50	Jim Reed (2)	Ford	49.504	Jim Reed (4)	Ford	51.963
348	18	5/18/58	N Wilkesboro NC	0.625	P	100.00	Junior Johnson (6)	Ford	78.636	Jack Smith (6)	Chevy	82.056
349	19	5/24/58	Winston-Salem NC	0.250	P	37.50	Bob Welborn (5)	Chevy	40.407	Rex White (3)	Chevy	46.851
350	20	5/30/58	Trenton NJ	1.000	P	500.00	Fireball Roberts (15)	Chevy	84.522	Marvin Panch (8)	Ford	89.020
351	21	6/1/58	Riverside CA	2.631	D	500.00	Eddie Gray	Ford	79.481	Danny Graves (2)	Chevy	---
352	22	6/5/58	Columbia SC	0.500	D	100.00	Junior Johnson (7)	Ford	54.752	Buck Baker (37)	Chevy	64.308
353	23	6/12/58	Bradford PA	0.333	D	50.00	Junior Johnson (8)	Ford	59.840	Bob Duell	Ford	65.831
354	24	6/15/58	Reading PA	0.500	D	100.00	Junior Johnson (9)	Ford	53.763	Speedy Thompson (14)	Chevy	60.687
355	25	6/25/58	New Oxford PA	0.500	D	100.00	Lee Petty (33)	Olds	69.726	Ken Rush (2)	Chevy	82.796
356	26	6/28/58	Hickory NC	0.400	D	100.00	Lee Petty (34)	Olds	62.413	Speedy Thompson (15)	Chevy	68.768
357	27	6/29/58	Weaverville NC	0.500	P	100.00	Rex White (2)	Chevy	73.892	Rex White (4)	Chevy	76.857
358	28	7/4/58	Raleigh NC	1.000	P	250.00	Fireball Roberts (16)	Chevy	73.691	Cotton Owens (2)	Pontiac	83.896
359	29	7/12/58	Asheville NC	0.250	P	37.50	Jim Paschal (7)	Chevy	46.440	Jim Paschal (7)	Chevy	50.336
360	30	7/16/58	Busti, NY	0.333	D	50.00	Shorty Rollins	Ford	47.110	Lee Petty (11)	Olds	---
361	31	7/18/58	Toronto CAN	0.333	P	33.30	Lee Petty (35)	Olds	43.184	Rex White (5)	Chevy	51.406
362	32	7/19/58`	Buffalo NY	0.250	P	25.00	Jim Reed (3)	Ford	46.972	Rex White (6)	Chevy	38.593
363	33	7/25/58	Rochester NY	0.500	D	100.00	Cotton Owens (2)	Pontiac	59.990	Rex White (7)	Chevy	62.871
364	34	7/26/58	Belmar NJ	0.333	P	100.00	Jim Reed (4)	Ford	65.395	Rex White (8)	Chevy	68.936
365	35	8/3/58	Bridgehampton NY	2.850	P	100.00	Jack Smith (7)	Chevy	80.696	Jack Smith (7)	Chevy	82.001
366	36	8/7/58	Columbia SC	0.500	D	100.00	Speedy Thompson (17)	Chevy	54.820	Speedy Thompson (16)	Chevy	64.240
367	37	8/10/58	Nashville TN	0.500	P	100.00	Joe Weatherly	Ford	59/269	Rex White (9)	Chevy	71.315
368	38	8/17/58	Weaverville NC	0.500	P	250.00	Fireball Roberts (17)	Chevy	66.780	Jimmy Massey	Pontiac	76.596
369	39	8/22/58	Winston-Salem NC	0.250	P	50.00	Lee Petty (36)	Olds	39.158	George Dunn	Mercury	46.680
370	40	8/23/58	Myrtle Beach SC	0.500	D	100.00	Bob Welborn (6)	Chevy	60.443	Speedy Thompson (17)	Chevy	66.667
371	41	9/1/58	Darlington SC	1.375	P	500.00	Fireball Roberts (18)	Chevy	102.585	Eddie Pagen (6)	Ford	116.952
372	42	9/5/58	Charlotte NC	0.500	D	100.00	Buck Baker (38)	Chevy	52.280	Lee Petty (12)	Olds	57.879
373	43	9/7/58	Birmingham AL	0.500	D	100.00	Fireball Roberts (19)	Chevy	60.678	Cotton Owens (3)	Pontiac	64.034
374	44	9/7/58	Sacramento CA	1.000	D	100.00	Parnelli Jones (2)	Ford	65.550	Parnelli Jones (2)	Ford	77.922
375	45	9/12/58	Gastonia NC	0.333	D	66.70	Buck Baker (39)	Chevy	47.856	Tiny Lund (4)	Chevy	52.650
376	46	9/14/58	Richmond VA	0.500	D	100.00	Speedy Thompson (18)	Chevy	57.878	Speedy Thompson (18)	Chevy	62.915
377	47	9/29/58	Hillsboro NC	0.900	D	99.00	Joe Eubanks	Pontiac	72.439	Tiny Lund (5)	Chevy	87.308
378	48	10/5/58	Salisbury NC	0.625	D	100.00	Lee Petty (37)	Olds	58.271	Gober Sosebee (4)	Chevy	72.162
379	49	10/12/58	Martinsville VA	0.500	P	175.00	Fireball Roberts (20)	Chevy	64.344	Glen Wood	Ford	67.950
380	50	10/19/58	N Wilkesboro NC	0.625	P	100.00	Junior Johnson (10)	Ford	84.906	Glen Wood (2)	Ford	86.805
381	51	10/26/58	Atlanta GA	1.000	D	150.00	Junior Johnson (11)	Ford	69.570	Glen Wood (3)	Ford	81.522

1959

Race #	Year #	Date	Site	Track	Surface	Miles	Race Winner	Car	Speed	Pole Winner	Car	Speed
382	1	11/9/58	Fayetteville NC	0.333	D	50.00	Bob Welborn (7)	Chevy	56.001	Bob Welborn (3)	Chevy	61.985
383	2	2/20/59	Daytona Beach FL	2.500	P	100.00	Bopb Welborn (8)	Chevy	143.198	Fireball Roberts (10)	Pontiac	140.581
384	3	2/22/59	Daytona Beach FL	2.500	P	500.00	Lee Petty (38)	Olds	135.521	Bob Welborn (4)	Chevy	140.120
385	4	3/1`/59	Hillsboro NC	0.900	D	99.00	Curtis Turner (15)	T-Bird	81.612	Curtis Turner (12)	T-Bird	87.544
386	5	3/8/59	Concord NC	0.500	D	100.00	Curtis Turner (16)	T-Bird	59.239	Buck Baker (38)	Chevy	66.420
387	6	3/22/59	Atlanta GA	1.000	D	100.00	Johnny Beauchamp	T-Bird	75.172	Buck Baker (39)	Chevy	77.888
388	7	3/29/59	Wilson NC	0.500	D	100.00	Junior Johnson (12)	Ford	50.300	No Time Trials	NTT	NTT
389	8	3/30/59	Winston-Salem NC	0.250	P	50.00	Jim Reed (5)	Ford	43.562	Rex White (10)	Chevy	46.296
390	9	4/4/59	Columbia SC	0.500	D	100.00	Jack Smith (8)	Chevy	87.343	Jack Smith (8)	Chevy	60.730

302

Race	Year #	Date	Site	Track	Surface	Miles	Race Winner	Car	Speed	Pole Winner	Car	Speed
391	10	4/5/59	N Wilkesboro NC	0.625	P	100.00	Lee Petty (39)	Olds	71.985	Speedy Thompson (19)	Chevy	85.746
392	11	4/26/59	Reading PA	0.500	D	100.00	Junior Johnson (13)	Ford	53.011	---	---	---
393	12	5/2/59	Hickory, NC	0.400	D	100.00	Junior Johnson (14)	Ford	62.165	Junior Johnson (5)	Ford	68.900
394	13	5/3/59	Martinsville, VA	0.500	P	250.00	Lee Petty (40)	Olds	59.512	Bobby Johns	Chevry	66.030
395	14	5/17/59	Trenton, NJ	1.000	P	150.00	Tom Pistone	T-Bird	87.350	Bob Burdick	T-Bird	88.950
396	15	5/22/59	Charlotte NC	0.500	D	100.00	Lee Petty (41)	Olds	55.300	Bob Welborn (5)	Chevy	57.950
397	16	5/24/59	Nashville TN	0.500	P	100.00	Rex White (3)	Chevy	71.006	Rex White (11)	Chevy	70.890
398	17	5/30/59	Los Angeles CA	0.400	D	200.00	Parnelli Jones (3)	Ford	50.982	Jim Reed (5)	Chevy	53.590
399	18	6/5/59	Spartanburg SC	0.500	D	100.00	Jack Smith (9)	Chevy	55.547	Cotton Owens (4)	Pontiac	63.180
400	19	6/13/59	Greenville, SC	0.500	D	100.00	Junior Johnson (15)	Ford	51.480	Jack Smith (9)	Chevy	65.838
401	20	6/14/59	Atlanta GA	1.000	D	150.00	Lee Petty (42)	Olds	58.499	No Time Trials	NTT	NTT
402	21	6/18/59	Columbia SC	0.500	D	100.00	Lee Petty (43)	Plymouth	58.726	Bob Burdick (2)	T-Bird	64.865
403	22	6/20/59	Wilson NC	0.500	D	100.00	Junior Johnson (16)	Ford	58.065	No Time Trials	NTT	NTT
404	23	6/21/59	Richmond VA	0.500	D	100.00	Tom Pistone (2)	T-Bird	56.881	Buck Baker (40)	Chevy	66.420
405	24	6/27/59	Winston-Salem NC	0.250	P	50.00	Rex White (4)	Chevy	41.228	Lee Petty (13)	Plymouth	47.071
406	25	6/28/59	Weaverville NC	0.500	P	100.00	Rex White (5)	Chevy	72.934	Glen Wood (4)	Ford	76.820
407	26	7/4/59	Daytona Beach FL	2.500	P	250.00	Fireball Roberts (21)	Pontiac	140.581	Fireball Roberts (11)	Pontiac	144.900
408	27	7/21/59	Heidelberg PA	0.250	D	50.00	Jim Reed (6)	Chevy	45.000	Dick Bailey	Plymouth	47.970
409	28	7/26/59	Charlotte NC	0.500	D	100.00	Jack Smith (10)	Chevy	49.553	Buck Baker (41)	Chevy	63.070
410	29	8/1/59	Myrtle Beach SC	0.500	D	100.00	Ned Jarrett	Ford	52.941	Bob Welborn (6)	Chevy	66.470
411	30	8/2/59	Charlotte NC	0.500	D	100.00	Ned Jarrett (2)	Ford	52.794	Bob Welborn (7)	Chevy	62.540
412	31	8/2/59	Nashville TN	0.500	P	150.00	Joe Lee Johnson	Chevy	63.343	Rex White (12)	Chevy	74.044
413	32	8/16/59	Weaverville NC	0.500	P	250.00	Bob Welborn (9)	Chevy	71.833	Rex White (13)	Chevy	77.687
414	33	8/21/59	Winston-Salem NC	0.250	P	50.00	Rex White (6)	Chevy	44.085	Rex White (14)	Chevy	47.443
415	34	8/22/59	Greenville SC	0.500	D	100.00	Buck Baker (40)	Chevy	58.055	Lee Petty (14)	Plymouth	63.313
416	35	8/29/59	Columbia SC	0.500	D	100.00	Lee Petty (44)	Plymouth	48.264	No Time Trials	NTT	NTT
417	36	9/7/59	Darlington SC	1.375	P	500.00	Jim Reed (7)	Chevy	111.836	Fireball Roberts (12)	Pontiac	123.734
418	37	9/11/59	Hicory NC	0.400	D	100.00	Lee Petty (45)	Plymouth	63.380	No Time Trials	NTT	NTT
419	38	9/13/59	Richmond VA	0.500	D	100.00	Cotton Owens (3)	T-Bird	60.382	Cotton Owens (5)	%-Bird	62.674
420	39	9/13/59	Sacramento CA	1.000	D	100.00	Eddie Gray (2)	Ford	54.753	No Time Trials	NTT	NTT
421	40	9/20/59	Hillsboro NC	0.900	D	99.00	Lee Petty (46)	Plymouth	77.868	Jack Smith (10)	Chevy	85.533
422	41	9/27/59	Martinsville VA	0.500	P	250.00	Rex White (7)	Chevy	60.500	Glen Wood (5)	Ford	69.471
423	42	10/11/59	Weaverville NC	0.500	P	100.00	Lee Petty (47)	Plymouth	76.433	Tommy Irwin	T-Bird	78.568
424	43	10/18/59	N Wilkesboro NC	0.625	P	100.00	Lee Petty (48)	Plymouth	74.829	Glen Wood (6)	Ford	86.806
425	44	10/25/59	Concord NC	0.500	D	150.00	Jack Smith (11)	Chevy	54.005	No Time Trials	NTT	NTT

1960

Race	Year #	Date	Site	Track	Surface	Miles	Race Winner	Car	Speed	Pole Winner	Car	Speed
426	1	11/8/59	Charlotte NC	0.500	D	100.00	Jack Smith (12)	Chevy	52.409	Buck Baker (42)	Chevy	64.103
427	2	11/26/59	Columbia SC	0.500	D	100.00	Ned Jarrett (3)	Ford	55.071	Junior Johnson (6)	Dodge	65.217
428	3	2/12/60	Daytona Beach FL	2.500	P	100.00	Fireball Roberts (22)	Pontiac	137.614	Cotton Owens (6)	Pontiac	149.892
429	4	2/12/60	Daytona Beach FL	2.500	P	100.00	Jack Smith (13)	Pontiac	146.520	Jack Smith (11)	Pontiac	148.157
430	5	2/14/60	Daytona Beach FL	2.500	P	500.00	Junior Johnson (17)	Chevy	124.740	Cotton Owens (7)	Pontiac	149.892
431	6	2/28/60	Charlotte NC	0.500	P	100.00	Richard Petty	Plymouth	53.404	Lee Petty (15)	Plymouth	62.110
432	7	3/27/60	N Wilkesboro NC	0.625	P	100.00	Lee Petty (49)	Plymouth	66.347	Junior Johnson (7)	Chevy	83.860
433	8	4/3/60	Phoenix AZ	1.000	D	100.00	John Rostek	Ford	71.889	Mel Larson (2)	Pontiac	78.930
434	9	4/5/60	Columbia SC	0.500	D	100.00	Rex White (8)	Chevy	50.697	Doug Yates	Plymouth	66.030
435	10	4/10/60	Martinsville VA	0.500	P	250.00	Richard Petty (2)	Plymouth	63.943	Glen Wood (7)	Ford	60.150
436	11	4/16/60	Hickory NC	0.500	D	100.00	Joe Weatherly (2)	Ford	66.347	Rex White (15)	Chevy	71.080
437	12	4/17/60	Wilson NC	0.500	D	100.00	Joe Weatherly (3)	Ford	55.113	Emanuel Zervakis	Chevy	60.500
438	13	4/18/60	Winston Salem NC	0.250	P	50.00	Glen Wood	Ford	43.082	Glen Wood (8)	Ford	47.240
439	14	4/23/60	Greenville SC	0.500	D	100.00	Ned Jarrett (4)	Ford	62.337	Curtis Turner (13)	Ford	64.720
440	15	4/24/60	Weavervile NC	0.500	D	83.50	Lee Petty (50)	Plymouth	63.368	Junior Johnson (8)	Ford	78.090
441	16	5/14/60	Darlington SC	1.375	P	300.00	Joe Weatherly (4)	Ford	102.640	Fireball Roberts (13)	Pontiac	127.750
442	17	5/28/60	Spartanburg SC	0.500	D	100.00	Ned Jarrett (5)	Ford	51.843	Jack Smith (12)	Pontiac	64.220
443	18	5/29/60	Hillsboro NC	0.900	D	99.00	Lee Petty (51)	Plymouth	83.583	Richard Petty	Plymouth	88.190
444	19	6/5/60	Richmond VA	0.500	D	100.00	Lee Petty (52)	Plymouth	62.251	Ned Jarrett	Ford	64.560
445	20	6/12/60	Hanford CA	1.500	P	250.00	Marvin Porter (2)	Ford	88.032	Frank Secrist	Ford	93.040
446	21	6/19/60	Charlotte NC	1.500	P	600.00	Joe Lee Johnson (2)	Chevy	107.735	Fireball Roberts (14)	Pontiac	133.904
447	22	6/26/60	Winston-Salem NC	0.250	P	50.00	Glen Wood (2)	Ford	45.872	Lee Petty (16)	Plymouth	47.850
448	23	7/4/60	Daytona Beach FL	2.500	P	250.00	Jack Smith (14)	Pontiac	146.842	Jack Smith (13)	Pontiac	152.129
449	24	7/10/60	Heidelberg PA	0.500	D	94.00	Lee Petty (53)	Plymouth	67.450	Lee Petty (17)	Plymouth	91.650
450	25	7/17/60	Montgomery NY	2.000	P	200.00	Rex White (9)	Chevy	88.626	John Rostek	Ford	96.650
451	26	7/23/60	Myrtle Beach SC	0.500	D	100.00	Buck Baker (41)	Chevy	60.985	Ned Jarrett (2)	Ford	64.610
452	27	7/31/60	Atlanta GA	1.500	P	300.00	Fireball Roberts (23)	Pontiac	112.652	Fireball Roberts (15)	Pontiac	133.129
453	28	8/3/60	Birmingham AL	0.250	P	50.00	Ned Jarrett (3)	Ford	54.463	Ned Jarrett (3)	Ford	55.866
454	29	8/7/60	Nashville TN	0.500	P	166.50	Johnny Beauchamp (2)	Chevy	56.966	Rex White (16)	Chevy	74.810
455	30	8/14/60	Weaverville NC	0.500	P	250.00	Rex White (10)	Chevy	65.024	Jack Smith (14)	Pontiac	77.850
456	31	8/16/60	Spartanburg SC	0.500	D	100.00	Cotton Owens (4)	Pontiac	59.681	Cotton Owens (8)	Pontiac	63.250
457	32	8/18/60	Columbia SC	0.500	D	150.00	Rex White (11)	Chevy	54.265	Tommy Irwin (2)	T-Bird	60.360
458	33	8/20/60	South Boston VA	0.250	D	37.50	Junior Johnson (18)	Chevy	50.732	Ned Jarrett (4)	Ford	51.903
459	34	8/23/60	Winston-Salem NC	0.250	P	50.00	Glen Wood (3)	Ford	44.389	Glen Wood (9)	Ford	46.970
460	35	9/5/60	Darlington SC	1.375	P	500.00	Buck Baker (42)	Pontiac	105.901	Fireball Roberts (16)	Pontiac	125.549

Race	Year #	Date	Site	Track	Surface	Miles	Race Winner	Car	Speed	Pole Winner	Car	Speed
461	36	9/9/60	Hickory NC	0.400	D	100.00	Junior Johnson (19)	Chevy	69.998	Buck Baker (43)	Chevy	71.180
462	37	9/11/60	Sacramento CA	1.000	D	100.00	Jim Cook	Dodge	70.629	Jim Cook	Dodge	78.450
463	38	9/15/60	Sumter SC	0.250	D	50.00	Ned Jarrett (7)	Ford	41.208	David Pearson	Chevy	45.070
464	39	9/18/60	Hillsboro NC	0.900	D	0.00	Richard Petty (3)	Plymouth	80.161	Richard Petty (2)	Plymouth	75.285
465	40	9/25/60	Martinsville VA	0.500	P	250.00	Rex White (12)	Chevy	60.439	Glen Wood (10)	Ford	68.440
466	41	10/2/60	N Wilkesboro NC	0.625	P	200.00	Rex White (13)	Chevy	77.444	Rex White (17)	Chevy	93.399
467	42	10/16/60	Charlotte NC	1.500	P	400.00	Speedy Thompson (19)	Ford	112.905	Fireball Roberts (17)	Pontiac	133.465
468	43	10/23/60	Richmond VA	0.500	D	100.00	Speedy Thompson (20)	Ford	63.739	Ned Jarrett (5)	Ford	64.410
469	44	10/30/60	Atlanta GA	1.500	P	500.00	Bobby Johns	Pontiac	108.408	Fireball Roberts (18)	Pontiac	134.596

1961

Race	Year #	Date	Site	Track	Surface	Miles	Race Winner	Car	Speed	Pole Winner	Car	Speed
470	1	11/6/60	Charlotte NC	0.500	D	100.00	Joe Weatherly (5)	Ford	59.435	Lee Petty (18)	Plymouth	63.581
471	2	11/20/60	Jacksonville FL	0.500	D	100.00	Lee Petty (54)	Plymouth	64.400	Junior Johnson (9)	Pontiac	68.623
472	3	2/24/61	Daytona Beach FL	2.500	P	100.00	Fireball Roberts (24)	Pontiac	133.037	Fireball Roberts (19)	Pontiac	155.709
473	4	2/24/61	Daytona Beach FL	2.500	P	100.00	Joe Weatherly (6)	Pontiac	152.671	Joe Weatherly (3)	Pontiac	154.122
474	5	2/26/61	Daytona Beach FL	2.500	P	500.00	Marvin Panch (8)	Pontiac	149.601	Fireball Roberts (20)	Pontiac	155.709
475	6	3/4/61	Spartanburg SC	0.500	D	100.00	Cotton Owens (5)	Pontiac	59.152	Ned Jarrett (6)	Ford	63.920
476	7	3/5/61	Weaverville NC	0.500	P	100.00	Rex White (14)	Chevy	72.492	Rex White (18)	Chevy	79.295
477	8	3/12/61	Hanford CA	1.400	P	250.00	Fireball Roberts (25)	Pontiac	95.621	Bob Ross	Ford	98.370
478	9	3/26/61	Atlanta GA	1.500	P	500.00	Bob Burdick	Pontiac	124.172	Marvin Panch (9)	Pontiac	135.755
479	10	4/1/61	Greenville SC	0.500	D	100.00	Emanuel Zervakis	Chevy	52.189	Junior Johnson (10)	Pontiac	62.090
480	11	4/2/61	Hillsboro NC	0.900	D	99.00	Cotton Owens (6)	Pontiac	84.695	Ned Jarrett (7)	Chevy	91.836
481	12	4/3/61	Winston-Salem NC	0.250	P	37.50	Rex White (15)	Chevy	45.500	Glen Wood (11)	Ford	48.700
482	13	4/9/61	Martinsville VA	0.500	P	74.50	Fred Lorenzen	Ford	68.366	Rex White (19)	Chevy	70.280
483	14	4/16/61	N Wilkesboro NC	0.625	P	250.00	Rex White (16)	Chevy	83.248	Junior Johnson (11)	Pontiac	95.660
484	15	4/20/61	Columbia SC	0.500	D	100.00	Cotton Owens (7)	Pontiac	51.940	Ned Jarrett (8)	Chevy	64.380
485	16	4/22/61	Hickory NC	0.400	D	100.00	Junior Johnson (20)	Pontiac	66.654	Junior Johnson (12)	Pontiac	74.074
486	17	4/23/61	Richmond VA	0.500	D	100.00	Richard Petty (4)	Plymouth	62.456	Richard Petty (3)	Plymouth	66.667
487	18	4/30/61	Martinsville VA	0.500	P	250.00	Junior Johnson (21)	Pontiac	66.287	Rex White (20)	Chevy	71.320
488	19	5/6/61	Darlington SC	1.375	P	300.00	Fred Lorenzen (2)	Ford	119.520	Fred Lorenzen	Ford	128.965
489	20	5/21/61	Charlotte NC	1.500	P	100.00	Richard Petty (5)	Plymouth	133.554	Fred Lorenzen (2)	Ford	137.509
490	21	5/21/61	Charlotte NC	1.500	P	100.00	Joe Weatherly (7)	Pontiac	115.591	Junior Johnson (13)	Pontiac	136.951
491	22	5/21/61	Riverside CA	2.580	P	100.00	Lloyd Dane (4)	Chevy	82.512	Eddie Gray	Ford	85.210
492	23	5/27/61	Los Angeles CA	0.500	D	100.00	Eddie Gray (3)	Ford	68.833	Danny Weinberg	Ford	71.940
493	24	5/28/61	Charlotte NC	1.500	P	600.00	David Pearson	Pontiac	111.633	Richard Petty (4)	Plymouth	131.611
494	25	6/2/61	Spartanburg SC	0.500	D	100.00	Jim Paschal (8)	Pontiac	55.495	Joe Weatherly (4)	Pontiac	61.250
495	26	6/4/61	Birmingham AL	0.500	D	100.00	Ned Jarrett (8)	Chevy	61.068	Johnny Allen (2)	Chevy	65.910
496	27	6/8/61	Greenville SC	0.500	D	100.00	Jack Smith (15)	Pontiac	58.441	Ned Jarrett (9)	Chevy	65.480
497	28	6/10/61	Winston-Salem NC	0.250	P	50.00	Rex White (17)	Chevy	42.714	Junior Johnson (14)	Pontiac	47.720
498	29	6/17/61	Norwood MA	0.250	P	125.00	Emanuel Zervakis (2)	Chevy	53.827	Rex White (21)	Chevy	55.870
499	30	6/23/61	Hartsville SC	0.333	P	50.00	Buck Baker (43)	Chrysler	46.234	Emanuel Zervakis (2)	Chevy	54.970
500	31	6/24/61	Roanoke VA	0.250	P	37.50	Junior Johnson (22)	Pontiac	49.907	Rex White (22)	Chevy	53.700
501	32	7/4/61	Daytona Beach FL	2.500	P	250.00	David Pearson (2)	Pontiac	154.294	Fireball Roberts (21)	Pontiac	157.150
502	33	7/9/61	Atlanta GA	1.500	P	250.00	Fred Lorenzen (3)	Ford	118.067	Fireball Roberts (22)	Pontiac	136.088
503	34	7/20/61	Columbia SC	0.500	D	100.00	Cotton Owens (8)	Pontiac	62.198	Cotton Owens (9)	Pontiac	67.650
504	35	7/22/61	Myrtle Beach SC	0.500	D	100.00	Joe Weatherly (8)	Pontiac	57.655	Joe Weatherly (5)	Pontiac	66.690
505	36	7/29/61	Bristol TN	0.500	P	250.00	Jack Smith (16)	Pontiac	68.373	Fred Lorenzen (3)	Ford	70.225
506	37	8/6/61	Nashville TN	0.500	P	201.50	Jim Paschal (9)	Pontiac	56.455	Rex White (23)	Chevy	76.600
507	38	8/9/61	Winston-Salem NC	0.250	P	37.50	Rex White (18)	Chevy	42.452	Junior Johnson (15)	Pntiac	48.050
508	39	8/13/61	Weaverville NC	0.500	P	129.00	Junior Johnson (23)	Pntiac	64.704	Jim Paschal (8)	Pontiac	80.430
509	40	8/18/61	Richmond VA	0.500	P	37.50	Junior Johnson (24)	Pontiac	51.605	Junior Johnson (16)	Pontiac	52.630
510	41	8/27/61	South Boston VA	0.250	P	50.00	Junior Johnson (25)	Pontiac	48.348	Cotton Owens (10)	Pntiac	52.630
511	42	9/4/61	Darlington SC	1.375	P	500.00	Nelson Stacy	Ford	117.787	Fireball Roberts (23)	Pontiac	128.680
512	43	9/8/61	Hickory NC	0.400	D	100.00	Rex White (10)	Chevy	67.529	Rex White (24)	Chevy	72.290
513	44	9/10/61	Richmond VA	0.500	P	125.00	Joe Weatherly (9)	Pontiac	61.677	Junior Johnson (17)	Pontiac	65.010
514	45	9/10/61	Sacramento CA	1.000	D	100.00	Eddie Gray (4)	Ford	None	Bill Amick (5)	Ford	79.260
515	46	9/17/61	Atlanta GA	1.500	P	400.00	David Pearson (3)	Pontiac	125.384	Fireball Roberts (24)	Pontiac	136.294
516	47	9/24/61	Martinsville VA	0.500	P	250.00	Joe Weatherly (10)	Pontiac	62.586	Fred Lorenzen (4)	Ford	70.730
517	48	10/1/61	N Wilkesboro NC	0.625	P	200.00	Rex White (20)	Chevy	84.675	Junior Johnson (18)	Pontiac	94.540
518	49	10/15/61	Charlotte NC	1.500	P	400.00	Joe Weatherly (11)	Pontiac	119.950	David Pearson (2)	Pontiac	138.577
519	50	10/22/61	Bristol TN	0.500	P	250.00	Joe Weatherly (12)	Pontiac	72.452	Bobby Johns (2)	Pontiac	80.645
520	51	10/28/61	Greenville SC	0.500	D	100.00	Junior Johnson (26)	Pontiac	63.346	Buck Baker (44)	Chrysler	66.667
521	52	10/29/61	Hillsboro NC	0.900	D	148.50	Joe Weatherly (13)	Pontiac	85.249	Joe Weatherly (6)	Pontiac	95.154

1962

Race	Year #	Date	Site	Track	Surface	Miles	Race Winner	Car	Speed	Pole Winner	Car	Speed
522	1	11/5/61	Concord NC	0.500	D	100.00	Jack Smith (17)	Pontiac	59.405	Joe Weatherly (7)	Pontiac	68.543
523	2	11/12/61	Weaverville NC	0.500	P	100.00	Rex White (21)	Chevy	68.467	Joe Weatherly (8)	Pontiac	81.743
524	3	2/16/61	Daytona Beach FL	2.500	P	100.00	Fireball Roberts (26)	Pontiac	156.999	Fireball Roberts 25	Pontiac	155.774
525	4	2/16/62	Daytona Beach FL	2.500	P	100.00	Joe Weatherly (14)	Pontiac	145.395	Darel Dieringer	Pontiac	155.086
526	5	2/18/62	Daytona Beach FL	2.500	P	500.00	Fireball Roberts (27)	Pontiac	152.529	Fireball Roberts (26)	Pontiac	158.774

Race Winners Pole Winners

Race	Year #	Date	Site	Track	Surface	Miles	Race Winner	Car	Speed	Pole Winner	Car	Speed
527	6	2/25/62	Concord NC	0.500	D	39.00	Joe Weatherly (15)	Pontiac	53.161	Joe Weatherly (9)	Pontiac	---
528	7	3/4/62	Weaverville NC	0.500	P	100.00	Joe Weatherly (16)	Pontiac	75.471	Rex White (25)	Chevy	80.460
529	8	3/17/62	Savannah GA	0.500	D	100.00	Jack Smith (18)	Pontiac	58.775	Rex White (26)	Chevy	70.588
530	9	3/18/62	Hillsboro NC	0.900	D	99.00	Rex White (22)	Chevy	86.948	Joe Weatherly (10)	Pontiac	96.588
531	10	4/1/62	Richmond VA	0.500	D	90.00	Rex White (23)	Chevy	51.363	No Time Trials	NTT	NTT
532	11	4/13/62	Columbia SC	0.500	D	100.00	Ned Jarrett (9)	Chevy	56.710	Joe Weatherly (11)	Pontiac	64.423
533	12	4/15/62	N Wilkesboro NC	0.625	P	250.00	Richard Petty (6)	Plymouth	84.737	Junior Johnson (19)	Pontiac	94.142
534	13	4/19/62	Greenville SC	0.500	D	100.00	Ned Jarrett (10)	Chevy	57.480	Ned Jarrett (10)	Chevy	66.568
535	14	4/21/62	Myrtle Beach SC	0.500	D	100.00	Jack Smith (19)	Pontiac	63.036	Ned Jarrett (11)	Chevy	68.939
536	15	4/22/62	Martinsville VA	0.500	P	250.00	Richard Petty (7)	Plymouth	66.425	Fred Lorenzen (5)	Ford	71.287
537	16	4/23/62	Winston-Salem NC	0.250	P	27.00	Rex White (24)	Chevy	43.392	Rex White (27)	Chevy	48.417
538	17	4/29/62	Bristol TN	0.500	P	250.00	Bobby Johns (2)	Pontiac	73.397	Fireball Roberts (27)	Pontiac	81.374
539	18	5/4/62	Richmond VA	0.500	P	66.70	Jimmy Pardue	Pontiac	67.747	Rex White '(28)	Chevy	71.145
540	19	5/5/62	Hickory NC	0.400	D	100.00	Jack Smith (20)	Pontiac	71.216	Jack Smith (15)	Pontiac	74.074
541	20	5/6/62	Concord NC	0.500	D	100.00	Joe Weatherly (17)	Pontiac	57.052	Not Time Trials	NTT	NTT
542	21	5/12/62	Darlington SC	1.375	P	300.00	Nelson Stacy (2)	Ford	117.429	Fred Lorenzen (6)	Ford	129.810
543	22	5/19/62	Spartanburg SC	0.500	D	100.00	Ned Jarrett (11)	Chevy	60.080	Cotton Owens (11)	Pontiac	64.423
544	23	5/27/62	Charlotte NC	1.500	P	600.00	Nelson Stacy (3)	Ford	125.552	Fireball Roberts (28)	Pontiac	140.150
545	24	6/10/62	Atlanta GA	1.500	P	328.50	Fred Lorenzen (4)	Ford	101.983	Banjo Matthews (2)	Pontiac	137.640
546	25	6/16/62	Winston-Salem NC	0.250	P	50.00	Johnny Allen	Pontiac	45.466	Rex White (29)	Chevy	48.179
547	26	6/19/62	Augusta GA	0.500	D	100.00	Joe Weatherly (18)	Pontiac	59.850	Joe Weatherly (12)	Pontiac	63.069
548	27	6/22/62	Richmond VA	0.333	P	100.00	Jim Paschal (10)	Pontiac	66.293	Rex White (30)	Chevy	70.435
549	28	6/23/62	South Boston VA	0.375	P	100.00	Rex White (25)	Chevy	72.540	Jack Smith (16)	Pontiac	79.458
550	29	7/4/62	Daytona Beach FL	2.500	P	250.00	Fireball Roberts (28)	Pontiac	153.688	Banjo Matthews (3)	Pontiac	160.499
551	30	7/7/62	Columbia SC	0.500	D	100.00	Rex White (26)	Chevy	62.370	Jack Smith (17)	Pontiac	66.667
552	31	7/13/62	Asheville NC	0.400	P	100.00	Jack Smith (21)	Pontiac	78.294	Rex White (31)	Chevy	82.885
553	32	7/14/62	Greensville SC	0.500	D	100.00	Richard Petty (8)	Plymouth	62.219	Rex White (32)	Chevy	66.055
554	33	7/17/62	Augusta GA	0.500	D	100.00	Joe Weatherly (19)	Pontiac	55.104	Jack Smith (18)	Pontiac	65.885
555	34	7/20/62	Savannah GA	0.500	D	100.00	Joe Weatherly (20)	Pontiac	67.239	Wendell Scott	Chevy	71.627
556	35	7/21/62	Myrtle Beach SC	0.500	D	100.00	Ned Jarrett (12)	Chevy	64.171	Ned Jarrett (12)	Chevy	68.467
557	37	7/29/62	Bristol TN	0.500	P	250.00	Jim Paschal (11)	Plymouth	75.276	Fireball Roberts (29)	Pontiac	80.321
558	37	8/3/62	Chattanooga TN	0.333	P	66.70	Joe Weatherly (21)	Pontiac	71.145	Richard Petty (5)	Plymouth	73.365
559	38	8/5/62	Nashville TN	0.500	P	250.00	Jim Paschal (12)	Plymouth	64.469	Johnny Allen (3)	Pontiac	77.854
560	39	8/8/62	Huntsville AL	0.250	P	50.00	Richard Petty (9)	Plymouth	54.644	Richard Petty (6)	Plymouth	54.086
561	40	8/12/62	Weaverville NC	0.500	P	250.00	Jim Paschal (13)	Plymouth	77.492	Jack Smith (19)	Pontiac	82.720
562	41	8/15/62	Roanoke VA	0.250	P	50.00	Richard Petty (10)	Plymouth	51.165	Jack Smith (20)	Pontiac	54.086
563	42	8/18/62	Winston-Salem NC	0.250	P	50	Richard Petty (11)	Plymouth	46.88	Jack Smith (21)	Pontiac	48.102
564	43	8/21/62	Spartanburg SC	0.500	D	100.00	Richard Petty (12)	Plymouth	59.870	Richard Petty (7)	Plymouth	61.590
565	44	8/25/62	Valdosta GA	0.500	D	100.00	Ned Jarrett (13)	Chevy	61.454	Richard Petty (8)	Plymouth	59.386
566	45	9/3/62	Darlington SC	1.375	P	500.00	Larry Frank	Ford	117.965	Fireball Roberts (30)	Pontiac	130.246
567	46	9/7/62	Hickory NC	0.400	D	100.00	Rex White (27)	Chevrolet	70.574	Junior Johnson (20)	Pontiac	71.357
568	47	9/9/62	Richmond VA	0.500	D	100.00	Joe Weatherly (22)	Pontiac	64.981	Rex White (33)	Chevy	66.127
569	48	9/11/62	Moyock, NC	0.250	D	62.50	Ned Jarrett (14)	Chevy	43.078	Ned Jarrett (13)	Chevy	45.569
570	49	9/13/62	Augusta GA	0.500	D	100.00	Fred Lorenzen (5)	Ford	60.759	Joe Weatherly (13)	Pontiac	65.421
571	50	9/23/62	Martinsville VA	0.500	P	250.00	Nelson Stacy (4)	Ford	66.874	Fireball Roberts (31)	Pontiac	71.513
572	51	9/30/62	N Wilkesboro NC	0.625	P	200.00	Richard Petty (13)	Plymouth	86.186	Fred Lorenzen (7)	Ford	94.657
573	52	10/14/62	Charlotte NC	1.500	P	400.00	Junior Johnson (27)	Pontiac	132.085	Fireball Roberts (32)	Pontiac	140.287
574	53	10/28/62	Atlanta GA	1.500	P	400.00	Rex White (28)	Chevy	124.740	Fireball Roberts (33)	Pontiac	138.978

1963

Race	Year #	Date	Site	Track	Surface	Miles	Race Winner	Car	Speed	Pole Winner	Car	Speed
575	1	11/4/62	Birmingham AL	0.500	D	100.00	Jim Paschal (14)	Plymouth	68.350	Jim Paschal (9)	Plymouth	73.592
576	2	11/11/62	Tampa FL	0.333	P	66.70	Richard Petty (14)	Plymouth	57.167	Rex White (34)	Chevy	60.090
577	3	11/22/62	Randleman NC	0.250	P	50.00	Jim Paschal (15)	Plymouth	47.544	Glen Wood (12)	Ford	51.933
578	4	1/20/63	Riverside CA	2.700	P	500.00	Dan Gurney	Ford	84.965	Paul Goldsmith (6)	Pontiac	98.809
579	5	2/22/63	Daytona Beach FL	2.500	P	100.00	Junior Johnson (28)	Chevy	164.083	Fireball Roberts (34)	Pontiac	160.943
580	6	2/22/63	Daytona Beach FL	2.500	P	100.00	Johnny Rutherford	Chevy	162.969	Fred Lorenzen (8)	Ford	161.870
581	7	2/24/63	Daytona Beach FL	2.500	P	500.00	Tiny Lund	Ford	151.566	Fireball Roberts (35)	Pontiac	160.943
582	8	3/2/63	Spartanburg SC	0.500	D	100.00	Richard Petty (15)	Plymouth	55.598	Junior Johnson (21)	Chevy	64.670
583	9	3/3/63	Weaverville NC	0.500	P	100.00	Richard Petty (16)	Plymouth	79.664	Junior Johnson (22)	Chevy	82.750
584	10	3/10/63	Hillsboro NC	0.900	D	148.50	Junior Johnson (29)	Chevy	83.129	Joe Weatherly (14)	Pontiac	95.716
585	11	3/17/63	Atlanta GA	1.500	P	500.00	Fred Lorenzen (6)	Ford	130.582	Junior Johnson (23)	Chevy	141.038
586	12	3/24/63	Hickory NC	0.500	D	100.00	Junior Johnson (30)	Chevy	67.950	Junior Johnson (24)	Chevy	75.235
587	13	3/31/63	Bristol TN	0.500	P	250.00	Fireball Roberts (29)	Ford	76.910	Fred Lorenzen (9)	Ford	80.681
588	14	4/4/63	Augusta GA	0.500	D	56.00	Ned Jarrett (15)	Ford	60.089	LeeRoy Yarbrough	Mercury	64.610
589	15	4/7/63	Richmond VA	0.500	D	125.00	Joe Weatherly (23)	Pontiac	58.624	Rex White (35)	Chevy	69.151
590	16	4/13/63	Greenville SC	0.500	D	100.00	Buck Baker (44)	Pontiac	54.853	Jimmy Pardue	Ford	66.250
591	17	4/14/63	South Boston VA	0.333	P	150.00	Richard Petty (17)	Plymouth	75.229	Ned Jarrett (14)	Ford	78.720
592	18	4/15/63	Winston-Salem NC	0.250	P	50.00	Jimmy Pardue (16)	Plymouth	46.814	Richard Petty (9)	Plymouth	48.280
593	19	4/21/63	Martinsville VA	0.500	P	250.00	Richard Petty (18)	Plymouth	64.823	Rex White (36)	Chevy	72.000
594	20	4/28/63	N Wilkesboro NC	0.625	P	160.60	Richard Petty (19)	Plymouth	83.302	Fred Lorenzen (10)	Ford	96.150
595	21	5/2/63	Columbia SC	0.500	D	100.00	Richard Petty (20)	Plymouth	51.650	Richard Petty (10)	Plymouth	68.080
596	22	5/5/63	Randleman NC	0.250	P	50.00	Jim Paschal (17)	Plymouth	48.605	Ned Jarrett (15)	Ford	50.856

305

Race	Year #	Date	Site	Track	Surface	Miles	Race Winner	Car	Speed	Pole Winner	Car	Speed
597	23	5/11/63	Darlington SC	1.375	P	302.50	Joe Weatherly (24)	Pontiac	122.745	Fred Lorenzen (11)	Ford	131.718
598	24	5/18/63	Manassas VA	0.333	P	112.50	Richard Petty (21)	Plymouth	70.275	Richard Petty (11)	Plymouth	71.580
599	25	5/19/63	Richmond VA	0.333	P	100.00	Ned Jarrett (16)	Ford	65.052	Ned Jarrett (16)	Ford	70.642
600	26	6/2/63	Charlotte NC	1.500	P	600.00	Fred Lorenzen (7)	Ford	132.417	Junior Johnson (25)	Chevy	141.148
601	27	6/9/63	Birmingham AL	0.500	D	100.00	Richard Petty (22)	Plymouth	68.195	Jack Smith (22)	Plymouth	71.146
602	28	6/30/63	Atlanta GA	1.500	P	400.00	Junior Johnson (31)	Chevy	121.139	Marvin Panch (10)	Ford	140.753
603	29	7/4/63	Daytona Beach FL	2.500	P	400.00	Fireball Roberts (30)	Ford	150.927	Junior Johnson (26)	Chevy	166.005
604	30	7/7/63	Myrtle Beach SC	0.500	D	100.00	Ned Jarrett (17)	Ford	60.996	Richard Petty (12)	Plymouth	68.700
605	31	7/10/63	Savannah GA	0.500	D	100.00	Ned Jarrett (18)	Ford	59.622	Richard Petty (13)	Plymouth	71.340
606	32	7/11/63	Moyock NC	0.250	D	62.50	Jimmy Pardue (2)	Ford	45.464	Junior Johnson (27)	Chevy	47.120
607	33	7/13/63	Winston-Salem NC	0.250	P	50.00	Glen Wood (4)	Ford	44.390	Glen Wood (13)	Ford	48.387
608	34	7/14/63	Asheville NC	0.333	P	100.00	Ned Jarrett (19)	Ford	63.384	David Pearson (3)	Dodge	67.235
609	35	7/19/63	Old Bridge NJ	0.500	P	100.00	Fireball Roberts (31)	Ford	73.022	Joe Weatherly (15)	Pontiac	75.850
610	36	7/21/63	Bridgehampton NY	2.850	P	99.00	Richard Petty (23)	Plymouth	86.047	Richard Petty (14)	Plymouth	86.301
611	37	7/28/63	Bristol TN	0.500	P	250.00	Fred Lorenzen (8)	Ford	74.844	Fred Lorenzen (12)	Ford	82.229
612	38	7/30/63	Greenville SC	0.500	D	100.00	Richard Petty (24)	Plymouth	62.456	Ned Jarrett (17)	Ford	65.526
613	39	8/4/63	Nashville TN	0.500	P	175.00	Jim Paschal (18)	Plymouth	60.126	Richard Petty (15)	Plymouth	78.878
614	40	8/8/63	Columbia SC	0.500	D	100.00	Richard Petty (25)	Plymouth	55.l598	Richard Petty (15)	Plymouth	60.014
615	41	8/11/63	Weaverville NC	0.500	P	250.00	Fred Lorenzen (9)	Ford	77.673	No Time Trials	NTT	NTT
616	42	8/14/63	Spartanburg SC	0.500	D	100.00	Ned Jarrett (20)	Ford	52.424`	Joe Weatherly (16)	Pontiac	64.958
617	43	8/16/63	Winston-Salem NC	0.250	P	50.00	Junior Johnson (32)	Chevy	46.320	Junior Johnson (28)	Chevy	66.568
618	44	8/18/63	Huntington WV	0.375	P	112.50	Fred Lorenzen (10)	Ford	59.340	Fred Lorenzen (13)	Ford	66.569
619	45	9/2/63	Darlington SC	1.375	P	500.00	Fireball Roberts (32)	Ford	129.784	Fred Lorenzen (14)	Ford	133.648
620	46	9/6/63	Hickory NC	0.400	D	100.00	Junior Johnson (33)	Chevy	62.926	David Pearson (4)	Dodge	72.471
621	47	9/8/63	Richmond VA	0.500	P	150.00	Ned Jarrett (21)	Ford	66.339	Joe Weatherly (17)	Mercury	68.104
622	48	9/22/63	Martinsville VA	0.500	P	250.00	Fred Lorenzen (11)	Ford	67.486	Junior Johnson (29)	Chevy	73.379
623	49	9/24/63	Moyock NC	0.250	D	75.00	Ned Jarrett (22)	Ford	43.000	Joe Weatherly (18)	Mercury	45.988
624	50	9/29/63	N Wilkesboro NC	0.625	P	250.00	Marvin Panch (9)	Ford	89.428	Fred Lorenzen (15)	Ford	96.566
625	52	10/5/63	Randleman NC	0.250	P	50.00	Richard Petty (26)	Plymouth	46.001	Fred Lorenzen (16)	Ford	51.724
626	52	10/13/63	Charlotte NC	1.500	P	400.00	Junior Johnson (34)	Chevy	132.105	Marvin Panch (11)	Ford	142.461
627	53	10/20/63	South Boston VA	0.333	P	150.00	Richard Petty (27)	Plymouth	76.325	Jack Smith (23)	Plymouth	81.081
628	54	10/27/63	Hillsboro NC	0.900	D	150.00	Joe Weatherly (25)	Pontiac	85.559	Joe Weatherly (19)	Pontiac	93.156
629	55	11/3/63	Riverside CA	2.700	P	400.00	Darel Dieringer	Mercury	91.465	Dan Gurney	Ford	101.050

1964

Race	Year #	Date	Site	Track	Surface	Miles	Race Winner	Car	Speed	Pole Winner	Car	Speed
630	1	11/10/63	Concord NC	0.500	D	125.00	Ned Jarrett (23)	Ford	56.897	David Pearson (5)	Dodge	69.257
631	2	11/10/63	Augusta GA	3.000	P	417.00	Fireball Roberts (33)	Ford	86.320	Fred Lorenzen (17)	Ford	88.590
632	3	12/1/63	Jacksonville FL	0.500	D	101.00	Wendell Scott	Chevy	58.252	Jack Smith (24)	Plymouth	70.921
633	4	12/29/63	Savannah GA	0.500	D	100.00	Richard Petty (28)	Plymouth	68.143	Ned Jarrett (18)	Ford	73.529
634	5	1/19/64	Riverside CA	2.700	P	500.00	Dan Gurney (2)	Ford	91.245	Fred Lorenzen (18)	Ford	102.433
635	6	2/21/64	Daytona Beach FL	2.500	P	100.00	Junior Johnson (35)	Dodge	170.777	Paul Goldsmith (7)	Plymouth	173.910
636	7	2/21/64	Daytona Beach FL	2.500	P	100.00	Bobby Isaac	Dodge	169.811	Richard Petty (17)	Plymouth	174.l81
637	8	2/23/64	Daytona Beach FL	2.500	P	500.00	Richard Petty (29)	Plymouth	154.334	Paul Goldsmith (8)	Plymouth	174.910
638	9	3/10/64	Richmond VA	0.500	D	125.00	David Pearson (4)	Dodge	60.233	Ned Jarrett (19)	Ford	69.070
639	10	3/22/64	Bristol TN	0.500	P	250.00	Fred Lorenzen (12)	Ford	72.196	Marvin Panch (12)	Ford	80.640
640	11	3/28/64	Greenville SC	0.500	D	100.00	David Pearson (5)	Dodge	57.554	Dick Hutcherson	Ford	66.740
641	12	3/30/64	Winston-Salem NC	0.250	P	50.00	Marvin Panch (10)	Ford	47.796	Marvin Panch (13)	Ford	49.830
642	13	4/5/64	Atlanta GA	1.500	P	500.00	Fred Lorenzen (13)	Ford	134.137	Fred Lorenzen (19)	Ford	146.470
643	14	4/11/64	Weaverville NC	0.500	P	100.00	Marvin Panch (11)	Ford	81.669	Marvin Panch (14)	Ford	84.905
644	15	4/12/64	Hillsboro NC	0.900	D	150.00	David Pearson (6)	Dodge	83.319	David Pearson (6)	Dodge	99.784
645	16	4/14/64	Spartanburg SC	0.500	D	100.00	Ned Jarrett (24)	Ford	58.852	Dick Hutcherson (2)	Ford	69.044
646	17	4/16/64	Columbia SC	0.500	D	100.00	Ned Jarrett (25)	Ford	64.412	David Pearson (7)	Dodge	71.485
647	18	4/19/64	N Wilkesboro NC	0.625	P	250.00	Fred Lorenzen (14)	Ford	81.930	Fred Lorenzen (20)	Ford	94.024
648	19	4/26/64	Martinsville VA	0.500	P	250.00	Fred Lorenzen (15)	Ford	70.098	Fred Lorenzen (21)	Ford	74.472
649	20	5/1/64	Savannah GA	0.500	D	100.00	LeeRoy Yarbrough	Plymouth	70.326	Jimmy Pardue (2)	Plymouth	73.111
650	21	5/9/64	Darlington SC	1.375	P	300.00	Fred Lorenzen (16)	Ford	130.013	Fred Lorenzen (22)	Ford	135.727
651	22	5/15/64	Hampton VA	0.400	D	100.00	Ned Jarrett (26)	Ford	65.300	David Pearson (8)	Dodge	67.542
652	23	5/16/64	Hickory NC	0.400	D	100.00	Ned Jarrett (27)	Ford	69.364	Junior Johnson (30)	Ford	76.882
653	24	5/17/64	South Boston VA	0.333	P	100.00	Richard Petty (30)	Plymouth	72.957	Marvin Panch (15)	Ford	80.023
654	25	5/24/64	Charlotte NC	1.500	P	600.00	Jim Paschal (19)	Plymouth	125.772	Jimmy Pardue (3)	Plymouth	144.346
655	26	5/30/64	Greenville SC	0.500	D	99.50	LeeRoy Yarbrough (2)	Plymouth	56.559	Marvin Panch (16)	Ford	68.050
656	27	5/31/64	Asheville NC	0.333	P	100.00	Ned Jarrett (28)	Ford	66.538	Richard Petty (18)	Plymouth	69.889
657	28	6/7/64	Atlanta GA	1.500	P	400.00	Ned Jarrett (29)	Ford	112.535	Junior Johnson (31)	Ford	145.906
658	29	6/11/64	Concord NC	0.500	D	100.00	Richard Petty (31)	Plymouth	66.352	Richard Petty (19)	Plymouth	68.233
659	30	6/14/64	Nashville TN	0.500	P	100.00	Richard Petty (32)	Plymouth	76.498	David Pearson (9)	Dodge	80.142
660	31	6/19/64	Chattanooga TN	0.333	P	100.00	David Pearson (7)	Dodge	70.051	Richard Petty (20)	Plymouth	75.235
661	32	6/21/64	Birmingham AL	0.500	P	100.00	Ned Jarrett (30)	Ford	67.643	David Pearson (10)	Dodge	72.115
662	33	6/23/64	Valdosta GA	0.500	D	100.00	Buck Baker (45)	Dodge	61.328	Ned Jarrett (20)	Ford	65.146
663	34	6/26/64	Spartanburg SC	0.500	D	100.00	Richard Petty (33)	Plymouth	58.233	David Pearson (11)	Dodge	66.939
664	35	7/4/64	Daytona Beach FL	2.500	P	400.00	A.J. Foyt	Dodge	151.451	Darel Dieringer (2)	Mercury	172.678
665	36	7/8/64	Manassas VA	0.375	P	150.00	Ned Jarrett (31)	Ford	67.652	Ned Jarrett (21)	Ford	73.609
666	37	7/10/64	Old Bridge NJ	0.500	P	100.00	Billy Wade	Mercury	73.891	Billy Wade	Mercury	76.660

Race Winners Pole Winners

Race	Year #	Date	Site	Track	Surface	Miles	Race Winner	Car	Speed	Pole Winner	Car	Speed
667	38	7/12/64	Bridgehampton NY	2.850	P	142.50	Billy Wade (2)	Mercury	87.707	Richard Petty (21)	Plymouth	90.600
668	39	7/15/64	Islip NY	0.200	P	60.00	Billy Wade (3)	Mercury	46.252	Billy Wade (2)	Mercury	51.100
669	40	7/19/64	Watkins Glen NY	2.300	P	151.80	Billy Wade (4)	Mercury	97.988	Billy Wade (3)	Mercury	102.222
670	41	7/21/64	New Oxford PA	0.500	D	100.00	David Pearson (8)	Dodge	82.568	David Pearson (12)	Dodge	86.289
671	42	7/26/64	Bristol TN	0.500	P	250.00	Fred Lorenzen (17)	Ford	78.044	Richard Petty (22)	Plymouth	82.910
672	43	8/2/64	Nashville TN	0.500	P	200.00	Richard Petty (34)	Plymouth	73.208	Richard Petty (23)	Plymouth	80.826
673	44	8/7/64	Myrtle Beach SC	0.500	D	100.00	David Pearson (9)	Dodge	61.750	David Pearson (13)	Dodge	69.659
674	45	8/9/64	Weaverville NC	0.500	P	250.00	Ned Jarrett (32)	Ford	77.600	Junior Johnson (32)	Ford	84.626
675	46	8/13/64	Moyock NC	0.333	P	100.00	Ned Jarrett (33)	Ford	63.965	Ned Jarrett (22)	Ford	67.643
676	47	8/16/64	Huntington WV	0.375	P	218.75	Richard Petty (35)	Plymouth	70.488	Billy Wade (4)	Mercury	79.505
677	48	8/21/64	Columbia SC	0.500	D	100.00	David Pearson (10)	Dodge	61.697	Ned Jarrett (23)	Ford	69.150
678	49	8/22/64	Winston-Salem NC	0.250	P	62.50	Junior Johnson (36)	Ford	46.192	Junior Johnson (33)	Ford	49.846
679	50	8/23/64	Roanoke VA	0.250	P	50.00	Junior Johnson (37)	Ford	49.847	Glen Wood (14)	Ford	55.970
680	51	9/7/64	Darlington SC	1.375	P	500.00	Buck Baker (46)	Dodge	117.757	Richard Petty (24)	Plymouth	136.815
681	52	9/11/64	Hickory NC	0.400	D	100.00	David Pearson (11)	Dodge	67.797	David Pearson (14)	Dodge	74.418
682	53	9/14/64	Richmond VA	0.500	D	150.00	Cotton Owens (9)	Dodge	61.955	Ned Jarrett (24)	Ford	66.890
683	54	9/18/64	Manassas VA	0.375	P	187.50	Ned Jarrett (34)	Ford	68.842	David Pearson (15)	Dodge	74.626
684	55	9/20/64	Hillsboro NC	0.900	D	150.00	Ned Jarrett (35)	Ford	86.725	David Pearson (16)	Dodge	89.280
685	56	9/27/64	Martinsville VA	0.500	P	250.00	Fred Lorenzen (18)	Ford	67.320	Fred Lorenzen (23)	Ford	74.196
686	57	10/9/64	Savannah GA	0.500	D	100.00	Ned Jarrett (36)	Ford	68.663	Ned Jarrett (25)	Ford	68.886
687	58	10/11/64	N Wilkesboro NC	0.625	P	250.00	Marvin Panch (12)	Ford	91.398	Junior Johnson (34)	Ford	100.761
688	59	10/18/64	Charlotte NC	1.500	P	400.00	Fred Lorenzen (19)	Ford	134.475	Richard Petty (25)	Plymouth	150.711
689	60	10/25/64	Harris NC	0.300	P	100.00	Richard Petty (36)	Plymouth	59.009	Billy Wade (5)	Mercury	64.787
690	61	11/1/64	Augusta GA	0.500	P	150.00	Darel Dieringer (2)	Mercury	68.641	Ned Jarrett (26)	Ford	82.455
691	62	11/8/64	Jacksonville NC	0.500	D	100.00	Ned Jarrett (37)	Ford	57.535	Doug Yates (2)	Plymouth	64.285

1965

Race	Year #	Date	Site	Track	Surface	Miles	Race Winner	Car	Speed	Pole Winner	Car	Speed
692	1	1/17/65	Riverside CA	2.700	P	500.00	Dan Gurney (3)	Ford	87.708	Junior Johnson (35	Ford	102.846
693	2	2/12/65	Daytona Beach FL	2.500	P	100.00	Darel Dieringer (3)	Mercury	165.669	Darel Dieringer (3)	Mercury	171.151
694	3	2/12/65	Daytona Beach FL	2.500	P	100.00	Junior Johnson (38)	Ford	111.706	Fred Lorenzen (24)	Ford	170.551
695	4	2/14/65	Daytona Beach FL	2.500	P	332.50	Fred Lorenzen (20)	Ford	141.539	Darel Dieringer (4)	Mercury	171.151
696	5	2/27/65	Spartanburg SC	0.500	D	100.00	Ned Jarrett (38)	Ford	66.367	Dick Hutcherson (3)	Ford	70.644
697	6	2/28/65	Weaverville NC	0.500	P	100.00	Ned Jarrett (39)	Ford	75.678	Ned Jarrett (27)	Ford	84.230
698	7	3/7/65	Richmond VA	0.500	D	125.00	Junior Johnson (39)	Ford	61.416	Junior Johnson (36)	Ford	67.847
699	8	3/14/65	Hillsboro NC	0.900	D	150.00	Ned Jarrett (40)	Ford	90.663	Junior Johnson (37)	Ford	98.570
700	9	4/11/65	Atlanta GA	1.500	P	500.00	Marvin Panch (13)	Ford	129.410	Marvin Panch (17)	Ford	145.581
701	10	4/17/65	Greenville SC	0.500	D	100.00	Dick Hutcherson	Ford	56.899	Bud Moore	Plymouth	67.695
702	11	4/18/65	N Wilkesboro NC	0.625	P	250.00	Junior Johnson (40)	Ford	95.047	Junior Johnson (38)	Ford	101.033
703	12	4/25/65	Martinsville VA	0.500	P	250.00	Fred Lorenzen (21)	Ford	66.765	Junior Johnson (39)	Ford	74.503
704	13	4/28/65	Columbia SC	0.500	D	62.00	Tiny Lund (2)	Ford	55.591	Ned Jarrett (28)	Ford	71.061
705	14	5/2/65	Bristol TN	0.500	P	250.00	Junior Johnson (41)	Ford	74.937	Marvin Panch (18)	Ford	84.626
706	15	5/8/65	Darlington SC	1.375	P	300.00	Junior Johnson (42)	Ford	111.849	Fred Lorenzen (25)	Ford	138.133
707	16	5/14/65	Hampton VA	0.400	D	100.00	Ned Jarrett (41)	Ford	57.815	Dick Hutcherson (4)	Ford	66.790
708	17	5/15/65	Winston-Salem NC	0.250	P	50.00	Junior Johnson (43)	Ford	47.911	Junior Johnson (40)	Ford	49.261
709	18	5/16/65	Hickory NC	0.400	D	100.00	Junior Johnson (44)	Ford	72.130	G.C. Spencer	Ford	76.312
710	19	5/23/65	Charlotte NC	1.500	P	600.00	Fred Lorenzen (22)	Ford	121.722	Fred Lorenzen (26)	Ford	145.268
711	20	5/27/65	Shelby NC	0.500	D	100.00	Ned Jarrett (42)	Ford	63.909	Dick Hutcherson (5)	Ford	65.862
712	21	5/29/65	Asheville NC	0.333	P	100.00	Junior Johnson (45)	Ford	66.293	Junior Johnson (41)	Ford	70.601
713	22	5/30/65	Harris NC	0.300	P	100.00	Ned Jarrett (43)	Ford	56.851	Paul Lewis	Ford	61.644
714	23	6/3/65	Nashville TN	0.500	P	100.00	Dick Hutcherson (2)	Ford	71.386	Tom Pistone	Ford	79.155
715	24	6/6/65	Birmingham AL	0.500	P	54.00	Ned Jarrett (44)	Ford	56.364	Ned Jarrett (29)	Ford	71.575
716	25	6/13/65	Atlanta GA	1.500	P	400.00	Marvin Panch (14)	Ford	110.120	Fred Lorenzen (27)	Ford	143.407
717	26	6/19/65	Greenville SC	0.500	D	100.00	Dick Hutcherson (3)	Ford	55.274	Ned Jarrett (30)	Ford	65.574
718	27	6/24/65	Myrtle Beach SC	0.500	D	100.00	Dick Hutcherson (4)	Ford	59.701	Dick Hutcherson (6)	Ford	66.421
719	28	6/27/65	Valdosta GA	0.500	D	100.00	Cale Yarborough	Ford	58.862	Dick Hutcherson (7)	Ford	64.540
720	29	7/4/65	Daytona Beach FL	2.500	P	400.00	A.J. Foyt (2)	Ford	150.046	Marvin Panch (19)	Ford	171.510
721	30	7/8/65	Manassas VA	0.375	P	150.00	Junior Johnson (46)	Ford	68.165	Ned Jarrett (31)	Ford	73.569
722	31	7/9/65	Old Bridge NJ	0.500	P	100.00	Junior Johnson (47)	Ford	72.087	Marvin Panch (20)	Ford	77.286
723	32	7/14/65	Islip NY	0.200	P	50.00	Marvin Panch (15)	Ford	43.838	Marvin Panch (21)	Ford	51.246
724	33	7/18/65	Watkins Glen NY	2.300	P	151.80	Marvin Panch (16)	Ford	98.182	No Time Trials	NTT	NTT
725	34	7/25/65	Bristol TN	0.500	P	250.00	Ned Jarrett (45)	Ford	61.826	Fred Lorenzen (28)	Ford	84.348
726	35	7/31/65	Nashville TN	0.500	P	200.00	Richard Petty (37)	Plymouth	72.383	Richard Petty (26)	Plymouth	82.117
727	36	8/5/65	Shelby NC	0.500	D	100.00	Ned Jarrett (46)	Ford	64.748	David Pearson (17)	Dodge	67.797
728	37	8/6/65	Weaverville NC	0.500	P	250.00	Richard Petty (38)	Plymouth	74.343	Richard Petty (27)	Plymouth	86.455
729	38	8/13/65	Maryville TN	0.500	D	100.00	Dick Hutcherson (5)	Ford	65.455	Ned Jarrett (32)	Ford	77.620
730	39	8/14/65	Spartanburg SC	0.500	D	100.00	Ned Jarrett (47)	Ford	56.926	Dick Hutcherson (8)	Ford	66.890
731	40	8/15/65	Augusta GA	0.500	P	100.00	Dick Hutcherson (6)	Ford	71.499	Ned Jarrett (33)	Ford	81.118
732	41	8/19/65	Columbia SC	0.500	D	100.00	David Pearson (12)	Dodge	57.361	Dick Hutcherson (9)	Ford	71.343
733	42	8/24/65	Moyock NC	0.333	P	100.00	Dick Hutcherson (7)	Ford	63.047	Richard Petty (28)	Plymouth	68.493
734	43	8/25/65	Beltsville MD	0.500	P	100.00	Ned Jarrett (48)	Ford	74.165	Ned Jarrett (34)	Ford	79.260
735	44	8/28/65	Winston-Salem NC	0.250	P	62.50	Junior Johnson (48)	Ford	46.632	Richard Petty (29)	Plymouth	50.195
736	45	9/6/65	Darlington SC	1.375	P	500.00	Ned Jarrett (49)	Ford	115.878	Junior Johnson (42)	Ford	137.571

Race Winners Pole Winners

Race #	Year #	Date	Site	Track	Surface	Miles	Race Winner	Car	Speed	Pole Winner	Car	Speed
737	46	9/10/65	Hickory NC	0.400	D	100.00	Richard Petty (39)	Plymouth	74.365	Junior Johnson (43)	Ford	74.766
738	47	9/14/65	New Oxford PA	0.500	D	100.00	Dick Hutcherson (8)	Ford	82.607	Richard Petty (30)	Plymouth	86.705
739	48	9/17/65	Manassas VA	0.375	P	150.00	Richard Petty (40)	Plymouth	67.890	Ned Jarrett (35)	Ford	73.851
740	49	9/18/65	Richmond VA	0.500	D	150.00	David Pearson (13)	Dodge	60.983	Dick Hutcherson (10)	Ford	67.340
741	50	9/26/65	Martinsville VA	0.500	P	250.00	Junior Johnson (49)	Ford	67.056	Richard Petty (31)	Plymouth	74.503
742	51	10/3/65	N Wilkesboro NC	0.625	P	250.00	Junior Johnson (50)	Ford	88.801	Fred Lorenzen (29)	Ford	101.580
743	52	10/17/65	Charlotte NC	1.500	P	400.00	Fred Lorenzen (23)	Ford	119.117	Fred Lorenzen (30)	Ford	147.773
744	53	10/24/65	Hillsboro NC	0.900	D	100.80	Dick Hutcherson (9)	Ford	87.462	Dick Hutcherson (11)	Ford	98.810
745	54	10/31/65	Rockingham NC	1.000	P	500.00	Curtis Turner (17)	Ford	101.942	Richard Petty (32)	Plymouth	116.260
746	55	11/7/65	Moyock NC	0.333	P	100.00	Ned Jarrett (50)	Ford	63.773	Bobby Isaac	Ford	68.143

1966

Race #	Year #	Date	Site	Track	Surface	Miles	Race Winner	Car	Speed	Pole Winner	Car	Speed
747	1	11/14/65	Augusta GA	0.500	P	150.00	Richard Petty (41)	Plymouth	73.569	Richard Petty (33)	Plymouth	82.987
748	2	1/23/66	Riverside CA	2.700	P	500.00	Dan Gurney (4)	Ford	97.952	David Pearson (18)	Dodge	106.078
749	3	2/25/66	Daytona Beach FL	2.500	P	100.00	Paul Goldsmith (7)	Plymouth	160.427	Richard Petty (34)	Plymouth	175.165
750	4	2/25/66	Daytona Beach FL	2.500	P	100.00	Earl Balmer	Dodge	153.191	Dick Hutcherson (12)	Ford	174.317
751	5	2/27/66	Daytona Beach FL	2.500	P	495.00	Richard Petty (42)	Plymouth	160.627	Richard Petty (35)	Plymouth	175.165
752	6	3/13/66	Rockingham NC	1.000	P	500.00	Paul Goldsmith (8)	Plymouth	100.027	Paul Goldsmith (9)	Plymouth	116.684
753	7	3/20/66	Bristol TN	0.500	P	250.00	Dick Hutcherson (10)	Ford	69.952	David Pearson (19)	Dodge	86.248
754	8	3/27/66	Atlanta GA	1.500	P	500.00	Jim Hurtubise	Plymouth	131.247	Richard Petty (36)	Plymouth	147.742
755	9	4/3/66	Hickory NC	0.400	D	100.00	David Pearson (14)	Dodge	68.428	Elmo Langley	Ford	75.117
756	10	4/7/66	Columbia SC	0.500	D	100.00	David Pearson (15)	Dodge	65.574	Tom Pistone (2)	Ford	72.202
757	11	4/9/66	Greenville SC	0.500	D	100.00	David Pearson (16)	Dodge	65.850	Tiny Lund (6)	Ford	68.208
758	12	4/11/66	Winston-Salem NC	0.250	P	50.00	David Pearson (17)	Dodge	51.341	David Pearson (20)	Dodge	54.479
759	13	4/17/66	N Wilkesboro NC	0.625	P	250.00	Jim Paschal (20)	Plymouth	89.045	Jim Paschal (10)	Plymouth	102.693
760	14	4/24/66	Martinsville VA	0.500	P	250.00	Jim Paschal (21)	Plymouth	69.156	Jim Paschal (11)	Plymouth	76.345
761	15	4/30/66	Darlington SC	1.375	P	400.00	Richard Petty (43)	Plymouth	131.993	Richard Petty (37)	Plymouth	140.815
762	16	5/7/66	Hampton VA	0.400	D	100.00	Richard Petty (44)	Plymouth	60.616	Richard Petty (38)	Plymouth	66.812
763	17	5/10/66	Macon GA	0.500	P	100.00	Richard Petty (45)	Plymouth	82.023	Richard Petty (39)	Plymouth	85.026
764	18	5/13/66	Monroe NC	0.500	D	100.00	Darel Dieringer (4)	Ford	60.140	James Hylton	Dodge	65.099
765	19	5/15/66	Richmond VA	0.500	D	125.00	David Pearson (18)	Dodge	66.539	Tom Pistone (3)	Ford	70.978
766	20	5/22/66	Charlotte NC	1.500	P	600.00	Marvin Panch (17)	Plymouth	135.042	Richard Petty (40)	Plymouth	148.637
767	21	5/29/66	Moyock NC	0.333	P	100.00	David Pearson (19)	Dodge	61.913	Richard Petty (41)	Plymouth	69.164
768	22	6/2/66	Asheville NC	0.333	P	100.00	David Pearson (20)	Dodge	64.917	Richard Petty (42)	Plymouth	72.964
769	23	6/4/66	Spartanburg SC	0.500	D	100.00	Elmo Langley	Ford	60.050	David Pearson (21)	Dodge	68.027
770	24	6/9/66	Maryville TN	0.500	D	100.00	David Pearson (21)	Dodge	71.986	Tom Pistone (4)	Ford	78.947
771	25	6/12/66	Weaverville NC	0.500	P	150.00	Richard Petty (46)	Plymouth	81.423	Richard Petty (43)	Plymouth	86.455
772	26	6/15/66	Beltsville MD	0.500	P	100.00	Tiny Lund (3)	Ford	73.409	Richard Petty (44)	Plymouth	80.250
773	27	6/25/66	Greensville SC	0.500	D	100.00	David Pearson (22)	Dodge	66.286	David Pearson (22)	Dodge	69.364
774	28	7/4/66	Daytona Beach FL	2.500	P	400.00	Sam McQuagg	Dodge	153.813	Lee Roy Yarbrough (2)	Dodge	176.660
775	29	7/7/66	Manassas VA	0.375	P	150.00	Elmo Langley (2)	Ford	68.079	Bobby Allison	Chevy	73.973
776	30	8/10/66	Bridgehampton NY	2.850	P	148.20	David Pearson (23)	Dodge	86.949	David Pearson (23)	Dodge	---
777	31	7/12/66	Oxford ME	0.333	P	100.00	Bobby Allison	Chevy	56.782	Bobby Allison (2)	Chevy	65.681
778	32	7/14/66	Fonda NY	0.500	D	100.00	David Pearson (24)	Dodge	61.010	Richard Petty (45)	Plymouth	71.514
779	33	7/16/66	Islip NY	0.200	P	60.00	Bobby Allison (2)	Chevy	47.285	Tom Pistone (5)	Ford	55.919
780	34	7/24/66	Bristol TN	0.500	P	250.00	Paul Goldsmith (9)	Plymouth	77.693	Curtis Turner (14)	Chevy	84.309
781	35	7/28/66	Maryville TN	0.500	D	100.00	Paul Lewis	Plymouth	69.822	Buddy Baker	Dodge	77.821
782	36	7/30/66	Nashville TN	0.500	P	200.00	Richard Petty (47)	Plymouth	71.770	Richard Petty (46)	Plymouth	82.493
783	37	8/7/66	Atlanta GA	1.500	P	400.00	Richard Petty (48)	Plymouth	130.244	Curtis Turner (15)	Chevy	148.331
784	38	8/18/66	Columbia SC	0.500	D	100.00	David Pearson (25)	Dodge	66.128	Bobby Allison (3)	Chevy	73.469
785	39	8/21/66	Weaverville NC	0.500	P	250.00	Darel Dieringer (5)	Mercury	76.700	Junior Johnson (44)	Ford	86.831
786	40	8/24/66	Beltsville MD	0.500	P	100.00	Bobby Allison (3)	Chevy	68.899	Bobby Allison (4)	Chevy	79.330
787	41	8/27/66	Winston-Salem NC	0.250	P	62.50	David Pearson (26)	Dodge	45.928	Richard Petty (47)	Plymouth	54.348
788	42	9/5/66	Darlington SC	1.375	P	500.00	Darel Dieringer (6)	Mercury	114.830	LeeRoy Yarbrough (3)	Dodge	140.058
789	43	9/9/66	Hickory NC	0.400	D	100.00	David Pearson (27)	Dodge	70.533	Richard Petty (48)	Plymouth	76.923
790	44	9/11/66	Richmond VA	0.500	D	150.00	David Pearson (28)	Dodge	62.886	David Pearson (24)	Dodge	70.644
791	45	9/18/66	Hillsboro NC	0.900	D	150.00	Dick Hutcherson (11)	Ford	90.603	Dick Hutcherson (13)	Ford	95.716
792	46	9/25/66	Martinsville VA	0.500	P	250.00	Fred Lorenzen (24)	Ford	69.177	Junior Johnson (45)	Ford	75.598
793	47	10/2/66	N Wilkesboro NC	0.625	P	250.00	Dick Hutcherson (12)	Ford	89.012	Junior Johnson (46)	Ford	103.069
794	48	10/16/66	Charlotte NC	1.500	P	500.00	LeeRoy Yarbrough (3)	Dodge	130.576	Fred Lorenzen (31)	Ford	150.533
795	49	10/30/66	Rockingham NC	1.000	P	500.00	Fred Lorenzen (25)	Ford	104.348	Fred Lorenzen (32)	Ford	115.988

1967

Race #	Year #	Date	Site	Track	Surface	Miles	Race Winner	Car	Speed	Pole Winner	Car	Speed
796	1	11/13/66	Augusta GA	0.500	P	150.00	Richard Petty (49)	Plymouth	71.809	Dick Hutcherson (14)	Ford	84.112
797	2	1/22/67	Riverside CA	2.700	P	500.00	Parnelli Jones (4)	Ford	91.080	Dick Hutcherson (15)	Ford	106.951
798	3	2/24/67	Daytona Beach FL	2.500	P	100.00	LeeRoy Yarbrough (4)	Ford	163.934	Curtis Turner (16)	Chevy	180.831
799	4	2/24/67	Daytona Beach FL	2.500	P	100.00	Fred Lorenzen (26)	Ford	174.587	Richard Petty (49)	Plymouth	179.068
800	5	2/26/67	Daytona Beach FL	2.500	P	500.00	Mario Andretti	Ford	146.926	Curtis Turner (17)	Chevy	180.831
801	6	3/5/67	Weaverville NC	0.500	P	150.00	Richard Petty (50)	Plymouth	83.360	Darel Dieringer (5)	Ford	88.626
802	7	3/19/67	Bristol TN	0.500	P	250.00	David Pearson (29)	Dodge	77.937	Darel Dieringer (6)	Ford	87.124

308

Race #	Year #	Date	Site	Track	Surface	Miles	Race Winner	Car	Speed	Pole Winner	Car	Speed
803	8	3/25/67	Greenville SC	0.500	D	100.00	David Pearson (30)	Dodge	61.824	Dick Hutcherson (16)	Ford	70.313
804	9	3/27/67	Winston-Salem NC	0.250	P	50.00	Bobby Allison (4)	Chevy	49.248	Bobby Allison (5)	Chevy	53.476
805	10	4/2/67	Atlanta GA	1.500	P	500.00	Cale Yarborough (2)	Ford	131.238	Cale Yarborough	Ford	148.996
806	11	4/6/67	Columbia SC	0.500	D	100.00	Richard Petty (51)	Plymouth	65.455	Dick Hutcherson (17)	Ford	74.166
807	12	4/9/67	Hickory NC	0.400	D	100.00	Richard Petty (52)	Plymouth	69.699	Richard Petty (50)	Plymouth	79.120
808	13	4/16/67	N Wilkesboro NC	0.625	P	250.00	Darel Dieringer (7)	Ford	93.594	Darel Dieringer (7)	Ford	104.603
809	14	4/23/67	Martinsville VA	0.500	P	250.00	Richard Petty (53)	Plymouth	67.446	Darel Dieringer (8)	Ford	77.319
810	15	4/28/67	Savannah GA	0.500	D	100.00	Bobby Allison (5)	Chevy	66.802	John Sears	Ford	72.173
811	16	4/30/67	Richmond VA	0.500	D	125.00	Richard Petty (54)	Plymouth	65.982	Richard Petty (51)	Plymouth	70.038
812	17	5/13/67	Darlington SC	1.375	P	400.00	Richard Petty (55)	Plymouth	125.738	David Pearson (25)	Ford	144.536
813	18	5/19/67	Beltsville MD	0.500	P	100.00	Jim Paschal (22)	Plymouth	71.036	Richard Petty (52)	Plymouth	80.286
814	19	5/20/67	Hampton VA	0.400	D	100.00	Richard Petty (56)	Plymouth	66.704	Richard Petty (53)	Plymouth	68.214
815	20	5/28/67	Charlotte NC	1.500	P	600.00	Jim Paschal (23)	Plymouth	135.832	Cale Yarborough (2)	Ford	154.385
816	21	6/2/67	Asheville NC	0.333	P	100.00	Jim Paschal (24)	Plymouth	63.080	Richard Petty (54)	Plymouth	73.710
817	22	6/6/67	Macon GA	0.500	P	150.00	Richard Petty (57)	Plymouth	80.321	Richard Petty (55)	Plymouth	86.538
818	23	6/8/67	Maryville TN	0.500	D	100.00	Richard Petty (58)	Plymouth	72.919	Jim Hunter	Chevy	79.051
819	24	6/10/67	Birmingham AL	0.500	P	100.00	Bobby Allison (6)	Dodge	88.999	Jim Paschal (12)	Plymouth	94.142
820	25	6/18/67	Rockingham NC	1.000	P	500.00	Richard Petty (59)	Plymouth	104.682	Dick Hutcherson (18)	Ford	116.486
821	26	6/24/67	Greenville SC	0.500	D	100.00	Richard Petty (60)	Plymouth	61.781	Richard Petty (56)	Plymouth	69.498
822	27	6/27/67	Montgomery AL	0.500	P	100.00	Jim Paschal (25)	Plymouth	72.435	Richard Petty (57)	Plymouth	77.088
823	28	7/4/67	Daytona Beach FL	2.500	P	400.00	Cale Yarborough (3)	Ford	143.583	Darel Dieringer (9)	Ford	179.802
824	29	7/9/67	Trenton NJ	1.500	P	300.00	Richard Petty (61)	Plymouth	95.322	Richard Petty (58)	Plymouth	101.208
825	30	7/11/67	Oxford ME	0.330	P	100.00	Bobby Allison (7)	Chevy	61.697	James Hylton (2)	Dodge	66.043
826	31	7/13/67	Fonda NY	0.500	D	100.00	Richard Petty (62)	Plymouth	65.826	Richard Petty (59)	Plymouth	72.173
827	32	7/15/67	Islip NY	0.200	P	60.00	Richard Petty (63)	Plymouth	42.428	Richard Petty (60)	Plymouth	51.136
828	33	7/23/67	Bristol TN	0.500	P	250.00	Richard Petty (64)	Plymouth	78.705	Richard Petty (61)	Plymouth	86.621
829	34	7/27/67	Maryville TN	0.500	D	100.00	Dick Hutcherson (13)	Ford	65.765	Dick Hutcherson (19)	Ford	79.540
830	35	7/29/67	Nashville TN	0.500	P	200.00	Richard Petty (65)	Plymouth	70.866	Dick Hutcherson (20)	Ford	84.260
831	36	8/6/67	Atlanta GA	1.500	P	500.00	Dick Hutcherson (14)	Ford	132.286	Darel Dieringer (10)	Ford	150.417
832	37	8/12/67	Winston-Salem NC	0.250	P	62.50	Richard Petty (66)	Plymouth	50.893	Richard Petty (62)	Plymouth	53.160
833	38	8/17/67	Columbia SC	0.500	D	100.00	Richard Petty (67)	Plymouth	64.274	Richard Petty (63)	Plymouth	74.968
834	39	8/25/67	Savannah GA	0.500	D	100.00	Richard Petty (68)	Plymouth	65.041	Richard Petty (64)	Plymouth	71.942
835	40	9/4/67	Darlington SC	1.375	P	500.00	Richard Petty (69)	Plymouth	130.423	Richard Petty (65)	Plymouth	143.436
836	41	9/8/67	Hickory NC	0.400	P	100.00	Richard Petty (70)	Plymouth	71.414	Dick Hutcherson (21)	Ford	86.538
837	42	9/10/67	Richmond VVA	0.500	D	150.00	Richard Petty (71)	Plymouth	57.631	No Time Trials	NTT	NTT
838	43	9/15/67	Beltsville MD	0.500	P	150.00	Richard Petty (72)	Plymouth	76.563	Richard Petty (66)	Plymouth	81.044
839	44	9/17/67	Hillsboro NC	0.900	D	150.00	Richard Petty (73)	Plymouth	81.574	Richard Petty (67)	Plymouth	94.159
840	45	9/24/67	Martinsville VA	0.500	P	250.00	Richard Petty (74)	Plymouth	69.605	Cale Yarborough (3)	Ford	77.386
841	46	10/1/67	N Wilkesboro NC	0.625	P	250.00	Richard Petty (75)	Plymouth	94.837	Dick Hutcherson (22)	Ford	104.312
842	47	10/15/67	Charlotte NC	1.500	P	500.00	Buddy Baker	Dodge	130.317	Cale Yarborough (4)	Ford	154.872
843	48	10/29/67	Rockingham NC	1.000	P	500.00	Bobby Allison (8)	Ford	98.420	David Pearson (26)	Ford	117.120
844	49	11/5/67	Weaverville NC	0.500	P	250.00	Bobby Allison (9)	Ford	76.291	Bobby Allison (6)	Ford	90.407

1968

Race #	Year #	Date	Site	Track	Surface	Miles	Race Winner	Car	Speed	Pole Winner	Car	Speed
845	1	11/12/67	Macon GA	0.500	P	267.00	Bobby Allison (10)	Ford	81.001	LeeRoy Yarbrough (4)	Ford	94.323
846	2	11/26/67	Montgomery AL	0.500	P	100.00	Richard Petty (76)	Plymouth	70.644	Richard Petty (68)	Plymouth	79.694
847	3	1/21/68	Riverside CA	2.700	P	500.00	Dan Gurney (5)	Ford	100.598	Dan Gurney (2)	Ford	110.971
848	4	2/25/68	Daytona Beach FL	2.500	P	500.00	Cale Yarborough (4)	Mercury	143.251	Cale Yarborough (5)	Mercury	189.222
849	5	3/17/68	Bristol TN	0.500	P	250.00	David Pearson (31)	Ford	77.247	Richard Petty (69)	Plymouth	88.582
850	6	3/24/68	Richmond VA	0.500	D	125.00	David Pearson (32)	Ford	65.217	Bobby Isaac (2)	Dodge	67.822
851	7	3/31/68	Atlanta GA	1.500	P	500.00	Cale Yarborough (5)	Mercury	125.564	LeeRoy Yarbrough (5)	Mercury	155.646
852	8	4/7/68	Hickory NC	0.400	P	100.00	Richard Petty (77)	Plymouth	79.435	David Pearson (27)	Ford	86.957
853	9	4/13/68	Greenville SC	0.500	P	100.00	Richard Petty (78)	Plymouth	63.347	David Pearson (28)	Ford	67.848
854	10	4/18/68	Columbia SC	0.500	D	100.00	Bobby Isaac (2)	Dodge	71.358	Richard Petty (70)	Plymouth	75.282
855	11	4/21/68	N Wilkesboro NC	0.625	P	250.00	David Pearson (33)	Ford	90.425	David Pearson (29)	Ford	104.993
856	12	4/28/68	Martinsville VA	0.500	P	250.00	Cale Yarborough (6)	Mercury	66.686	David Pearson (30)	Ford	78.230
857	13	5/3/68	Augusta, GA	0.500	P	125.00	Bobby Isaac (3)	Dodge	73.099	Bobby Isaac (3)	Dodge	83.877
858	14	5/5/68	Weaverville NC	0.500	P	150.00	David Pearson (34)	Ford	75.167	David Pearson (31)	Ford	89.708
859	15	5/11/68	Darlington SC	1.375	P	400.00	David Pearson (35)	Ford	132.699	LeeRoy Yarbrough (6)	Ford	148.850
860	16	5/17/68	Beltsville MD	0.500	P	150.00	David Pearson (36)	Ford	74.844	Richard Petty (71)	Plymouth	83.604
861	17	5/18/68	Hampton VA	0.400	P	100.00	David Pearson (37)	Ford	71.457	Richard Petty (72)	Plymouth	80.801
862	18	5/26/68	Charlotte NC	1.500	P	382.50	Buddy Baker (2)	Dodge	104.207	Donnie Allison	Ford	159.223
863	19	5/31/68	Asheville NC	0.333	P	100.00	Richard Petty (79)	Plymouth	64.741	Richard Petty (73)	Plymouth	74.349
864	20	6/2/68	Macon GA	0.500	P	150.00	David Pearson (38)	Ford	79.342	David Pearson (32)	Ford	86.873
865	21	6/6/68	Maryville TN	0.500	P	100.00	Richard Petty (80)	Plymouth	76.743	David Pearson (33)	Ford	88.583
866	22	6/8/68	Birmingham AL	0.500	P	100.00	Richard Petty (81)	Plymouth	89.153	David Pearson (34)	Ford	97.784
867	23	6/16/68	Rockingham NC	1.000	P	500.00	Donnie Allison	Ford	99.338	LeeRoy Yarbrough (7)	Ford	118.644
868	24	6/22/68	Greenville SC	0.500	D	100.00	Richard Petty (82)	Plymouth	64.609	David Pearson (35)	Ford	68.834
869	25	7/4/68	Daytona Beach FL	2.500	P	400.00	Cale Yarborough (7)	Mercury	167.247	Charlie Glotzbach	Dodge	185.156
870	26	7/7/68	Islip NY	0.200	P	60.00	Bobby Allison (11)	Chevy	48.561	Buddy Baker (2)	Dodge	51.873
871	27	7/9/68	Oxford ME	0.333	P	100.00	Richard Petty (83)	Plymouth	63.717	Buddy Baker (3)	Dodge	67.835
872	28	7/11/68	Fonda NY	0.500	P	100.00	Richard Petty (84)	Plymouth	64.935	David Pearson (36)	Ford	73.800

Race #	Year #	Date	Site	Track	Surface	Miles	Race Winner	Car	Speed	Pole Winner	Car	Speed
873	29	7/14/68	Trenton NJ	1.500	P	300.00	LeeRoy Yarbrough (5)	Ford	89.079	LeeRoy Yarbrough (8)	Ford	103.717
874	30	7/21/68	Bristol TN	0.500	P	250.00	David Pearson (39)	Ford	76.310	LeeRoy Yarbrough (9)	Ford	87.421
875	31	7/25/68	Maryville TN	0.500	P	100.00	Richard Petty (85)	Plymouth	72.513	Bobby Isaac (4)	Dodge	86.538
876	32	7/27/68	Nashville TN	0.500	P	151.50	David Pearson (40)	Ford	72.980	Richard Petty (74)	Plymouth	85.066
877	33	8/4/68	Atlanta GA	1.500	P	500.00	LeeRoy Yarbrough (6)	Mercury	127.068	Buddy Baker (4)	Dodge	153.361
878	34	8/8/68	Columbia SC	0.500	D	100.00	David Pearson (41)	Ford	67.039	Buddy Baker (5)	Dodge	74.196
879	35	8/10/68	Winston-Salem NC	0.250	P	62.50	David Pearson (42)	Ford	42.940	Richard Petty (75)	Plymouth	53.828
880	36	8/17/68	Weaverville NC	0.500	P	250.00	David Pearson (43)	Ford	73.686	Darel Dieringer (11)	Plymouth	88.409
881	37	8/23/68	South Boston VA	0.375	P	100.00	Richard Petty (86)	Plymouth	75.916	Richard Petty (76)	Plymouth	84.428
882	38	8/24/68	Hampton VA	0.400	P	100.00	David Pearson (44)	Ford	75.582	David Pearson (37)	Ford	78.007
883	39	9/2/68	Darlington, SC	1.375	P	500.00	Cale Yarborough (8)	Mercury	126.132	Charlie Glotzbach (2)	Dodge	144.830
884	40	9/6/68	Hickory NC	0.400	P	100.00	David Pearson (45)	Ford	80.357	Richard Petty (77)	Plymouth	85.868
885	41	9/8/68	Richmond VA	0.500	P	187.50	Richard Petty (87)	Plymouth	85.659	Richard Petty (78)	Plymouth	103.178
886	42	9/13/68	Beltsville MD	0.500	P	150.00	Bobby Isaac (4)	Dodge	71.033	Cale Yarborough (6)	Mercury	81.311
887	43	9/15/68	Hillsboro NC	0.900	P	150.00	Richard Petty (88)	Plymouth	87.681	Richard Petty (79)	Plymouth	93.245
888	44	9/22/68	Martinsville VA	0.500	P	250.00	Richard Petty (89)	Plymouth	64.808	Cale Yarborough (7)	Mercury	77.279
889	45	9/29/68	N Wilkesboro NC	0.625	P	250.00	Richard Petty (90)	Plymouth	94.103	Bobby Allison (7)	Plymouth	104.525
890	46	10/5/68	Augusta GA	0.500	P	100.00	David Pearson (46)	Ford	75.821	Bobby Allison (8)	Plymouth	84.822
891	47	10/20/68	Charlotte NC	1.500	P	500.00	Charlie Glotzbach	Dodge	135.324	Charlie Glotzbach (3)	Dodge	156.060
892	48	10/27/68	Rockingham NC	1.000	P	500.00	Richard Petty (91)	Plymouth	105.060	Cale Yarborough (8)	Mercury	118.717
893	49	11/3/68	Jefferson GA	0.500	P	100.00	Cale Yarborough (9)	Mercury	77.737	David Pearson (38)	Ford	90.694

1969

Race #	Year #	Date	Site	Track	Surface	Miles	Race Winner	Car	Speed	Pole Winner	Car	Speed
894	1	11/17/68	Macon GA	0.500	P	250.00	Richard Petty (92)	Plymouth	85.121	David Pearson (39)	Ford	95.472
895	2	12/8/68	Montgomery AL	0.500	P	100.00	Bobby Allison (12)	Plymouth	73.200	Richard Petty (80)	Plymouth	80.899
896	3	2/1/69	Riverside CA	2.700	P	500.00	Richard Petty (93)	Ford	105.498	A.J.Foyt	Ford	110.323
897	4	2/20/69	Daytona Beach FL	2.500	P	125.00	David Pearson (47)	Ford	152.181	Buddy Baker (6)	Dodge	188.901
898	5	2/20/69	Daytona Beach FL	2.500	P	125.00	Bobby Isaac (5)	Dodge	151.668	Bobby Isaac (5)	Dodge	188.726
899	6	2/23/69	Daytona Beach FL	2.500	P	500.00	LeeRoy Yarbrough (7)	Ford	157.950	Buddy Baker (7)	Dodge	188.901
900	7	3/9/69	Rockingham NC	1.000	P	500.00	David Pearson (48)	Ford	102.569	David Pearson (40)	Ford	119.619
901	8	3/16/69	Augusta GA	0.500	P	100.00	David Pearson (49)	Ford	77.586	Bobby Isac (6)	Dodge	86.901
902	9	3/23/69	Bristol TN	0.500	P	250.00	Bobby Allison (13)	Dodge	81.455	Bobby Isaac (7)	Dodge	88.669
903	10	3/30/69	Atlanta GA	1.500	P	500.00	Cale Yarborough (10)	Mercury	132.191	David Pearson (41)	Ford	156.794
904	11	4/3/69	Columbia SC	0.500	D	100.00	Bobby Isaac (6)	Dodge	68.558	Bobby Isaac (8)	Dodge	73.806
905	12	4/6/69	Hickory NC	0.400	P	100.00	Bobby Isaac (7)	Dodge	79.086	Bobby Isaac (9)	Dodge	85.612
906	13	4/8/69	Greenville SC	0.500	D	100.00	Bobby Isaac (8)	Dodge	64.389	David Pearson (42)	Ford	70.359
907	14	4/13/69	Richamond VA	0.500	P	250.00	David Pearson (50)	Ford	73.752	David Pearson (43)	Ford	82.538
908	15	4/20/69	N Wilkesboro NC	0.625	P	250.00	Bobby Allison (14)	Dodge	95.268	Bobby Isaac (10)	Dodge	106.731
909	16	4/27/69	Martinsville VA	0.500	P	250.00	Richard Petty (94)	Ford	64.405	Bobby Allison (9)	Dodge	78.260
910	17	5/4/69	Weaverville NC	0.500	P	150.00	Bobby Isaac (9)	Dodge	72.581	Bobby Isaac (11)	Dodge	90.361
911	18	5/10/69	Darlington SC	1.375	P	400.00	LeeRoy Yarbrough (8)	Mercury	131.572	Cale Yarborough (9)	Mercury	152.293
912	19	5/16/69	Beltsville MD	0.500	P	150.00	Bobby Isaac (10)	Dodge	73.059	Bobby Isaac (12)	Dodge	83.329
913	20	5/17/69	Hampton VA	0.400	P	150.00	David Pearson (51)	Ford	75.789	David Pearson (44)	Ford	80.236
914	21	5/25/69	Charlotte NC	1.500	P	600.00	LeeRoy Yarbrough (9)	Mercury	134.361	Donnie Allison (2)	Ford	159.296
915	22	6/1/69	Macon GA	0.500	P	150.00	Bobby Isaac (11)	Dodge	73.717	David Pearson (45)	Ford	87.946
916	23	6/5/69	Maryville TN	0.500	P	150.00	Bobby Isaac (12)	Dodge	81.706	David Pearson (46)	Ford	87.976
917	24	6/15/69	Brooklyn MI	2.000	P	500.00	Cale Yarborough (11)	Mercury	139.254	Donnie Allison (3)	Ford	160.135
918	25	6/19/69	Kingsport TN	0.400	P	100.00	Richard Petty (95)	Ford	73.619	Bobby Isaac (13)	Dodge	90.112
919	26	6/21/69	Greenville SC	0.500	D	100.00	Bobby Isaac (13)	Dodge	61.813	Bobby Isaac (14)	Dodge	66.030
920	27	6/26/69	Raleigh NC	0.500	D	100.00	David Pearson (52)	Ford	65.418	Bobby Isaac (15)	Dodge	72.942
921	28	7/4/69	Daytona Beach FL	2.500	P	400.00	LeeRoy Yarbrough (10)	Ford	160.875	Cale Yarborough (10)	Mercury	190.706
922	29	7/6/69	Dover DE	1.000	P	300.00	Richard Petty (96)	Ford	115.772	David Pearson (47)	Ford	130.430
923	30	7/10/69	Thompson CT	0.625	P	125.00	David Pearson (53)	Ford	89.498	David Pearson (48)	Ford	99.800
924	31	7/13/69	Trenton NJ	1.500	P	300.00	David Pearson (54)	Ford	121.000	Bobby Isaac (16)	Dodge	132.668
925	32	7/15/69	Beltsville MD	0.500	P	150.00	Richard Petty (97)	Ford	77.253	Richard Petty (81)	Ford	82.094
926	33	7/20/69	Bristol TN	0.500	P	250.00	David Pearson (55)	Ford	79.737	Cale Yarborough (11)	Mercury	103.432
927	34	7/26/69	Nashville TN	0.500	P	200.00	Richard Petty (98)	Ford	78.740	Richard Petty (82)	Ford	84.918
928	35	7/27/69	Maryville TN	0.500	P	200.00	Richard Petty (99)	Ford	82.417	David Pearson (49)	Ford	87.434
929	36	8/10/69	Atlanta GA	1.500	P	500.00	LeeRoy Yarbrough (11)	Ford	133.001	Cale Yarborough (12)	Mercury	155.413
930	37	8/17/69	Brooklyn MI	2.000	P	330.00	David Pearson (56)	Ford	115.508	David Pearson (50)	Ford	161.714
931	38	8/21/69	South Boston VA	0.500	P	100.00	Bobby Isaac (14)	Dodge	76.906	Bobby Isaac (17)	Dodge	84.959
932	39	8/22/69	Winston-Salem NC	0.250	P	62.50	Richard Petty (100)	Ford	47.458	Richard Petty (83)	Ford	54.253
933	40	8/24/69	Weaverville NC	0.500	P	250.00	Bobby Isaac (15)	Dodge	80.450	Bobby Isaac (18)	Dodge	89.000
934	41	9/1/69	Darlington SC	1.375	P	316.25	LeeRoy Yarbrough (12)	Ford	105.612	Cale Yarborough (13)	Mercury	151.985
935	42	9/5/69	Hickory NC	0.400	P	100.00	Bobby Isaac (16)	Dodge	80.519	Bobby Isaac (19)	Dodge	86.212
936	43	9/7/69	Richmond VA	0.563	P	250.00	Bobby Allison (15)	Dodge	76.388	Richard Petty (84)	Ford	91.257
937	44	9/14/69	Talladega AL	2.660	P	500.00	Richard Brickhouse	Dodge	153.778	Bobby Isaac (20)	Dodge	196.386
938	45	9/18/69	Columbia SC	0.500	D	100.00	Bobby Isaac (17)	Dodge	70.230	Richard Petty (85)	Ford	73.108
939	46	9/28/69	Martinsville VA	0.500	P	250.00	Richard Petty (101)	Ford	63.127	David Pearson (51)	Ford	83.197
940	47	10/5/69	N Wilkesboro NC	0.625	P	250.00	David Pearson (57)	Ford	93.429	Bobby Isaac (21)	Dodge	106.032
941	48	10/12/69	Charlotte NC	1.500	P	500.00	Donnie Allison (2)	Ford	131.271	Cale Yarborough (14)	Mercury	162.162
942	49	10/17/69	Savannah GA	0.500	P	100.00	Bobby Isaac (18)	Dodge	78.432	Bobby Isaac (22)	Dodge	86.095

Race #	Year #	Date	Site	Track	Surface	Miles	Race Winner	Car	Speed	Pole Winner	Car	Speed
943	50	10/19/69	Augusta GA	0.500	P	100.00	Bobby Isaac (19)	Dodge	78.740	Bobby Isaac (23)	Dodge	85.689
944	51	10/26/69	Rockingham NC	1.017	P	500.00	LeeRoy Yarbrough (13)	Ford	111.938	Charlie Glotzbach (4)	Dodge	136.972
945	52	11/2/69	Jefferson GA	0.500	P	100.00	Bobby Isaac (20)	Dodge	85.106	David Pearson (52)	Ford	89.565
946	53	11/9/69	Macon GA	0.548	P	274.00	Bobby Allison (16)	Dodge	81.079	Bobby Isaac (24)	Dodge	98.148
947	54	12/7/69	College Station TX	2.000	P	500.00	Bobby Isaac (21)	Dodge	144.277	Buddy Baker (8)	Dodge	176.284

1970

Race #	Year #	Date	Site	Track	Surface	Miles	Race Winner	Car	Speed	Pole Winner	Car	Speed
948	1	1/18/70	Riverside CA	2.700	P	500.00	A.J. Foyt (3)	Ford	97.450	Dan Gurney (3)	Plymouth	112.060
949	2	2/19/70	Daytona Beach FL	2.500	P	125.00	Cale Yarborough (12)	Mercury	183.295	Cale Yarborough (15)	Mercury	194.015
950	**3**	**2/19/70**	**Daytona Beach FL**	**2.500**	**P**	**125.00**	**Charlie Glotzbach (2)**	**Dodge**	**147.734**	**Buddy Baker (9)**	**Dodge**	**192.624**
951	4	2/22/70	Daytona Beach FL	2.500	P	500.00	Pete Hamilton	Plymouth	149.601	Cale Yarborough (16)	Mercury	194.015
952	5	3/1/70	Richmond VA	0.542	P	250.00	James Hylton	Ford	82.044	Richard Petty (86)	Plymouth	89.137
953	6	3/8/70	Rockingham NC	1.017	P	500.00	Richard Petty (102)	Plymouth	116.117	Bobby Allison (10)	Dodge	139.048
954	7	3/15/70	Savannah GA	0.500	P	100.00	Richard Petty (103)	Plymouth	82.418	Richard Petty (87)	Plymouth	85.874
955	8	3/29/70	Atlanta GA	1.522	P	500.00	Bobby Allison (17)	Dodge	139.554	Cale Yarborough (17)	Mercury	159.929
956	9	4/5/70	Bristol TN	0.533	P	266.50	Donnie Allison (3)	Ford	87.543	David Pearson (53)	Ford	107.079
957	10	4/12/70	Talladega AL	2.660	P	500.00	Pete Hamilton (2)	Plymouth	152.321	Bobby Isaac (25)	Dodge	199.658
958	11	4/18/70	N Wilkesboro NC	0.625	P	250.00	Richard Petty (104)	Plymouth	94.246	Bobby Isaac (26)	Dodge	107.041
959	12	4/30/70	Columbia SC	0.500	D	100.00	Richard Petty (105)	Plymouth	62.685	Larry Baumel	Ford	72.329
960	13	5/9/70	Darlington SC	1.366	P	400.00	David Pearson (58)	Ford	129.668	Charlie Glotzbach (5)	Dodge	153.822
961	14	5/15/70	Beltsville MD	0.500	P	150.00	Bobby Isaac (22)	Dodge	76.370	James Hylton (3)	Ford	83.128
962	15	5/18/70	Hampton VA	0.400	P	120.00	Bobby Isaac (23)	Dodge	73.245	Bobby Isaac (27)	Dodge	79.659
963	16	5/24/70	Charlotte NC	1.500	P	600.00	Donnie Allison (4)	Ford	129.680	Bobby Isaac (28)	Dodge	159.277
964	17	5/28/70	Maryville TN	0.520	P	104.00	Bobby Isaac (24)	Dodge	82.558	Bobby Allison (11)	Dodge	92.094
965	18	5/31/70	Martinsville VA	0.525	P	197.90	Bobby Isaac (25)	Dodge	68.584	Donnie Allison (4)	Ford	82.609
966	19	6/7/70	Brooklyn MI	2.040	P	400.00	Cale Yarborough (13)	Mercury	138.302	Pete Hamilton	Plymouth	162.737
967	20	6/14/70	Riverside CA	2.620	P	400.00	Richard Petty (106)	Plymouth	101.120	Bobby Allison (12)	Dodge	111.621
968	21	6/20/70	Hickory NC	0.363	P	100.00	Bobby Isaac (26)	Dodge	68.011	Bobby Isaac (29)	Dodge	79.596
969	22	6/26/70	Kingsport TN	0.337	P	100.00	Richard Petty (107)	Plymouth	65.583	Richard Petty (88)	Plymouth	75.056
970	23	6/27/70	Greenville SC	0.500	P	100.00	Bobby Isaac (27)	Dodge	75.345	Bobby Isaac (30)	Dodge	82.327
971	24	7/4/70	Daytona Beach FL	2.500	P	400.00	Donnie Allison (5)	Ford	162.235	Cale Yarborough (18)	Mercury	191.640
972	25	7/7/70	Malta NY	0.362	P	90.50	Richard Petty (108)	Plymouth	68.589	Bobby Isaac (31)	Dodge	73.213
973	26	7/9/70	Thompson CT	0.542	P	108.40	Bobby Isaac (28)	Dodge	80.296	Bobby Isaac (32)	Dodge	87.029
974	27	7/12/70	Trenton NJ	1.500	P	300.00	Richard Petty (109)	Plymouth	120.724	Bobby Isaac (33)	Dodge	131.749
975	28	7/19/70	Bristol TN	0.533	P	266.50	Bobby Allison (18)	Dodge	84.880	Cale Yarborough (19)	Mercury	107.375
976	29	7/24/70	Maryville TN	0.520	P	104.00	Richard Petty (110)	Plymouth	84.956	Richard Petty (89)	Plymouth	91.264
977	30	7/25/70	Nashville TN	0.596	P	250.00	Bobby Isaac (29)	Dodge	87.943	LeeRoy Yarbrough (10)	Ford	114.115
978	31	8/2/70	Atlanta GA	1.522	P	500.00	Richard Petty (111)	Plymouth	142.712	Fred Lorenzen (33)	Dodge	157.625
979	32	8/6/70	Columbia SC	0.500	D	100.00	Bobby Isaac (30)	Dodge	67.101	Richard Petty (90)	Plymouth	72.695
980	33	8/11/70	Ona WV	0.455	P	131.25	Richard Petty (112)	Plymouth	78.358	Bobby Allison (13)	Ford	150.555
981	34	8/16/70	Brooklyn MI	2.040	P	400.00	Charlie Glotzbach (3)	Dodge	147.571	Charlie Glotzbach (6)	Dodge	157.363
982	35	8/23/70	Talladega AL	2.660	P	500.00	Pete Hamilton (3)	Plymouth	158.517	Bobby Isaac (34)	Dodge	186.834
983	36	8/28/70	Winston-Salem NC	0.250	P	62.50	Richard Petty (113)	Plymouth	51.527	Richard Petty (91)	Plymouth	54.553
984	37	8/29/70	South Boston VA	0.357	P	100.00	Richard Petty (114)	Plymouth	73.060	Richard Petty (92)	Plymouth	81.187
985	38	9/7/70	Darlington SC	1.366	P	500.00	Buddy Baker (3)	Dodge	128.817	David Pearson (54)	Ford	150.555
986	39	9/11/70	Hickory NC	0.363	P	100.00	Bobby Isaac (31)	Dodge	73.365	Bobby Isaac (35)	Dodge	78.411
987	40	9/13/70	Richmond VA	0.542	P	271.00	Richard Petty (115)	Plymouth	81.476	Richard Petty (93)	Plymouth	87.014
988	41	9/20/70	Dover DE	0.500	P	300.00	Richard Petty (116)	Plymouth	112.103	Bobby Isaac (36)	Dodge	129.538
989	42	9/30/70	Raleigh NC	1.000	D	100.00	Richard Petty (117)	Plymouth	68.376	John Sears (2)	Ford	71.380
990	43	10/4/70	N Wilkesboro NC	0.625	P	250.00	Bobby Isaac (32)	Dodge	90.162	Bobby Isaac (37)	Dodge	105.406
991	44	10/11/70	Charlotte NC	1.500	P	500.00	LeeRoy Yarbrough (14)	Mercury	123.246	Charlie Glotzbach (7)	Dodge	147.273
992	45	10/18/70	Martinsville VA	0.525	P	262.50	Richard Petty (118)	Plymouth	72.235	Bobby Allison (14)	Dodge	82.167
993	46	11/8/70	Macon GA	0.548	P	274.00	Richard Petty (119)	Plymouth	83.284	Richard Petty (94)	Plymouth	94.064
994	47	11/15/70	Rockingham NC	1.017	P	500.00	Cale Yarborough (14)	Mercury	117.811	Charlie Glotzbach (8)	Dodge	136.498
995	48	11/22/70	Hampton VA	0.395	P	118.50	Bobby Allison (19)	Dodge	69.585	Benny Parsons	Ford	78.239

1971

Race #	Year #	Date	Site	Track	Surface	Miles	Race Winner	Car	Speed	Pole Winner	Car	Speed
996	1	1/10/71	Riverside CA	2.620	P	500.00	Ray Elder	Dodge	100.783	Richard Petty (95)	Plymouth	107.084
997	2	2/11/71	Dayton Beach FL	2.500	P	125.00	Pete Hamilton (4)	Plymouth	175.029	A.J. Foyt (2)	Mercury	182.744
998	2	2/11/71	Daytona Beach FL	2.500	P	125.00	David Pearson (59)	Mercury	168.278	Bobby Isaac (38)	Dodge	180.050
999	4	2/14/71	Daytona Beach FL	2.500	P	500.00	Richard Petty (120)	Plymouth	144.744	A.J. Foyt (3)	Mercury	182.744
1000	5	2/28/71	Ontario CA	2.500	P	500.00	A.J. Foyt (4)	Mercury	134.168	A.J. Foyt (4)	Mercury	151.711
1001	6	3/7/71	Richmond VA	0.542	P	271.00	Richard Petty (121)	Plymouth	79.838	Dave Marcis	Dodge	87.178
1002	7	3/14/71	Rockingham NC	1.017	P	500.00	Richard Petty (122)	Plymouth	118.696	Fred Lorenzen (34)	Plymouth	133.892
1003	8	3/21/71	Hickory NC	0.363	P	100.00	Richard Petty (123)	Plymouth	67.700	Bobby Allison (15)	Dodge	79.001
1004	9	3/28/71	Bristol TN	0.533	P	276.00	David Pearson (60)	Ford	91.704	David Pearson (55)	Ford	105.525
1005	10	4/4/71	Atlanta GA	1.522	P	500.00	A.J. Foyt (5)	Mercury	131.375	A.J. Foyt (5)	Mercury	155.152
1006	11	4/8/71	Columbia SC	0.500	P	100.00	Richard Petty (124)	Plymouth	76.513	James Hylton (4)	Ford	84.229
1007	12	4/10/71	Greenville SC	0.500	P	100.00	Bobby Isaac (33)	Dodge	78.159	David Pearson (56)	Ford	82.257
1008	13	4/15/71	Maryville TN	0.520	P	104.00	Richard Petty (125)	Plymouth	88.697	Friday Hassler	Chevy	91.464

Race #	Year #	Date	Site	Track Surface		Miles	Race Winner	Car	Speed	Pole Winner	Car	Speed
1009	14	4/18/71	N Wilkesboro NC	0.625	P	250.00	Richard Petty (126)	Plymouth	98.479	Bobby Isaac (39)	Dodge	106.217
1010	15	4/25/71	Martinsville VA	0.525	P	262.50	Richard Petty (127)	Plymouth	77.707	Donnie Allison (5)	Mercury	82.529
1011	16	5/2/71	Darlington SC	1.366	P	400.00	Buddy Baker (4)	Dodge	130.678	Donnie Allison (6)	Mercury	149.826
1012	17	5/9/71	South Boston VA	0.357	P	100.00	Benny Parsons	Ford	72.271	Bobby Isaac (40)	Dodge	81.548
1013	18	5/16/71	Talladega AL	2.660	P	500.00	Donnie Allison (6)	Mercury	147.419	Donnie Allison (7)	Mercury	185.869
1014	19	5/21/71	Asheville NC	0.333	P	100.00	Richard Petty (128)	Plymouth	71.231	Richard Petty (96)	Plymouth	79.598
1015	20	5/23/71	Kingsport TN	0.337	P	101.00	Bobby Isaac (34)	Dodge	63.242	Bobby Isaac (41)	Dodge	75.167
1016	21	5/30/71	Charlotte NC	1.500	P	600.00	Bobby Allison (20)	Mercury	140.422	Charlie Glotzbach (9)	Chevy	157.788
1017	22	6/6/71	Dover DE	1.000	P	500.00	Bobby Allison (21)	Mercury	123.119	Richard Petty (97)	Plymouth	129.486
1018	23	6/13/71	Brooklyn MI	2.000	P	400.00	Bobby Allison (22)	Mercury	149.567	Bobby Allison (16)	Mercury	161.190
1019	24	6/20/71	Riverside CA	2.620	P	400.00	Bobby Allison (23)	Dodge	93.427	Bobby Allison (17)	Dodge	107.315
1020	25	6/23/71	Houston TX	0.500	P	150.00	Bobby Allison (24)	Dodge	73.489	Bobby Allison (18)	Dodge	78.226
1021	26	6/26/71	Greenville SC	0.500	P	150.00	Richard Petty (129)	Plymouth	74.297	Bobby Allison (19)	Ford	81.555
1022	27	7/4/71	Daytona Beach FL	2.500	P	400.00	Bobby Isaac (35)	Dodge	161.947	Donnie Allison (8)	Mercury	183.228
1023	28	7/11/71	Bristol TN	0.533	P	266.50	Charlie Glotzbach (4)	Chevy	101.074	Richard Petty (98)	Plymouth	104.589
1024	29	7/14/71	Malta NY	0.362	P	90.50	Richard Petty (130)	Plymouth	66.748	Richard Petty (99)	Plymouth	74.896
1025	30	7/15/71	Islip NY	0.200	P	46.00	Richard Petty (131)	Plymouth	49.925	Richard Petty (100)	Plymouth	46.133
1026	31	7/18/71	Trenton NJ	1.500	P	300.00	Richard Petty (132)	Plymouth	120.347	Friday Hassler (2)	Chevy	129.134
1027	32	7/24/71	Nashville TN	0.596	P	250.00	Richard Petty (133)	Plymouth	89.667	Richard Petty (101)	Plymouth	114.628
1028	33	8/1/71	Atlanta GA	1.522	P	500.00	Richard Petty (134)	Plymouth	129.061	Buddy Baker (10)	Dodge	155.796
1029	34	8/6/71	Winston-Salem NC	0.250	P	62.50	Bobby Allison (25)	Mustang	44.792	Richard Petty (102)	Plymouth	55.283
1030	35	8/8/71	Ona WV	0.455	P	219.00	Richard Petty (135)	Plymouth	83.805	Bobby Allison (20)	Mustang	84.053
1031	36	8/15/71	Brooklyn MI	2.000	P	400.00	Bobby Allison (26)	Mercury	149.862	Pete Hamilton (2)	Plymouth	161.901
1032	37	8/22/71	Talladega AL	2.660	P	500.00	Bobby Allison (27)	Mercury	145.945	Donnie Allison (9)	Mercury	187.323
1033	38	8/27/71	Columbia SC	0.500	P	102.00	Richard Petty (136)	Plymouth	64.831	Richard Petty (103)	Plymouth	85.137
1034	39	8/28/71	Hickory NC	0.363	P	100.00	Tiny Lund (4)	Camaro	72.937	Dave Marcis (2)	Dodge	80.147
1035	40	9/6/71	Darlington SC	1.366	P	500.00	Bobby Allison (28)	Mercury	131.398	Bobby Allison (21)	Mercury	147.915
1036	41	9/26/71	Martinsville VA	0.525	P	262.50	Bobby Isaac (36)	Dodge	73.681	Bobby Isaac (42)	Dodge	83.635
1037	42	10/10/71	Charlotte NC	1.500	P	347.00	Bobby Allison (29)	Mercury	126.140	Charlie Glotzbach (10)	Chevy	157.085
1038	43	10/17/71	Dover DE	1.000	P	500.00	Richard Petty (137)	Plymouth	123.254	Bobby Allison (22)	Mercury	132.811
1039	44	10/24/71	Rockingham NC	1.017	P	500.00	Richard Petty (138)	Plymouth	113.405	Charlie Glotzbach (11)	Chevy	135.167
1040	45	11/7/71	Macon GA	0.548	P	274.00	Bobby Allison (30)	Ford	80.859	Bobby Allison (23)	Ford	95.334
1041	46	11/14/71	Richmond VA	0.542	P	271.00	Richard Petty (139)	Plymouth	80.025	Bill Dennis	Mercury	---
1042	47	11/21/71	N Wilkesboro NC	0.625	P	250.00	Tiny Lund (5)	Camaro	96.174	Charlie Glotzbach (12)	Chevy	107.558
1043	48	12/12/71	College Station TX	2.000	P	500.00	Richard Petty (140)	Plymouth	144.000	Pete Hamilton (3)	Plymouth	170.830

1972

Race #	Year #	Date	Site	Track Surface		Miles	Race Winner	Car	Speed	Pole Winner	Car	Speed
1044	1	1/23/72	Riverside CA	2.620	P	387.76	Richard Petty (141)	Plymouth	104.016	A.J. Foyt (6)	Mercury	110.033
1045	2	2/20/72	Daytona Beach FL	2.500	P	500.00	A.J. Foyt (6)	Mercury	161.550	Bobby Isaac (43)	Dodge	186.632
1046	3	2/27/72	Richmond VA	0.542	P	271.00	Richard Petty (142)	Plymouth	76.258	Bobby Allison (24)	Chevy	90.573
1047	4	3/5/72	Ontario CA	2.500	P	500.00	A.J. Foyt (7)	Mercury	127.082	A.J. Foyt (7)	Mercury	153.217
1048	5	3/12/72	Rockingham NC	1.017	P	500.00	Bobby Isaac (37)	Dodge	113.895	Bobby Allison (25)	Chevy	137.539
1049	6	3/26/72	Atlanta GA	1.522	P	500.00	Bobby Allison (31)	Chevy	128.214	Bobby Allison (26)	Chevy	156.245
1050	7	4/9/72	Bristol TN	0.533	P	266.50	Bobby Allison (32)	Chevy	92.826	Bobby Allison (27)	Chevy	106.875
1051	8	4/16/72	Darlington SC	1.366	P	400.00	David Pearson (61)	Mercury	124.406	David Pearson (57)	Mercury	148.209
1052	9	4/23/72	N Wilkesboro NC	0.625	P	250.00	Richard Petty (143)	Plymouth	86.381	Bobby Isaac (44)	Dodge	107.506
1053	10	4/30/72	Martinsville VA	0.525	P	262.50	Richard Petty (144)	Plymouth	72.657	Bobby Allison (28)	Chevy	84.163
1054	11	5/7/72	Talladega AL	2.660	P	500.00	David Pearson (62)	Mercury	134.400	Bobby Isaac (45)	Dodge	192.428
1055	12	5/28/72	Charlotte NC	1.500	P	600.00	Buddy Baker (5)	Dodge	142.255	Bobby Allison (29)	Chevy	158.162
1056	13	6/4/72	Dover DE	1.000	P	500.00	Bobby Allison (33)	Chevy	118.019	Bobby Isaac (46)	Dodge	130.809
1057	14	6/11/72	Brooklyn MI	2.000	P	400.00	David Pearson (63)	Mercury	146.639	Bobby Isaac (47)	Dodge	160.764
1058	15	6/18/72	Riverside CA	2.620	P	400.00	Ray Elder (2)	Dodge	98.761	Richard Petty (104)	Plymouth	108.688
1059	16	6/25/72	College Station TX	2.000	P	500.00	Richard Petty (145)	Plymouth	144.185	Richard Petty (105)	Plymouth	169.412
1060	17	7/4/72	Daytona Beach FL	2.500	P	400.00	David Pearson (64)	Mercury	160.821	Bobby Isaac (48)	Dodge	186.277
1061	18	7/9/72	Bristol TN	0.533	P	266.50	Bobby Allison (34)	Chevy	92.735	Bobby Allison (30)	Chevy	107.279
1062	19	7/16/72	Trenton NJ	1.500	P	300.00	Bobby Allison (35)	Chevy	114.030	Bobby Isaac (49)	Dodge	133.126
1063	20	7/23/72	Atlanta GA	1.522	P	500.00	Bobby Allison (36)	Chevy	131.295	David Pearson (58)	Mercury	158.353
1064	21	8/6/72	Talladega AL	2.660	P	500.00	James Hylton (2)	Mercury	148.728	Bobby Isaac (50)	Dodge	190.677
1065	22	8/20/72	Brooklyn MI	2.000	P	400.00	David Pearson (65)	Mercury	134.416	Richard Petty (106)	Dodge	157.607
1066	23	8/27/72	Nashville TN	0.596	P	250.00	Bobby Allison (37)	Chevy	92.578	Bobby Allison (31)	Chevy	116.932
1067	24	9/4/72	Darlington SC	1.366	P	500.00	Bobby Allison (38)	Chevy	128.124	Bobby Allison (32)	Chevy	152.228
1068	25	9/10/72	Richmond VA	0.542	P	271.00	Richard Petty (146)	Plymouth	75.899	Bobby Allison (33)	Chevy	89.669
1069	26	9/17/72	Dover DE	1.000	P	500.00	David Pearson (66)	Mercury	120.506	Bobby Allison (34)	Chevy	133.323
1070	27	9/24/72	Martinsville VA	0.525	P	262.50	Richard Petty (147)	Plymouth	69.989	Bobby Allison (35)	Chevy	85.890
1071	28	10/1/72	N Wilkesboro NC	0.625	P	250.00	Richard Petty (148)	Plymouth	95.816	Buddy Baker (11)	Dodge	105.922
1072	29	10/8/72	Charlotte NC	1.500	P	500.00	Bobby Allison (39)	Chevy	133.234	David Pearson (59)	Mercury	158.539
1073	30	10/22/72	Rockingham NC	1.017	P	500.00	Bobby Allison (40)	Chevy	118.275	David Pearson (60)	Mercury	127.528
1074	31	11/12/72	College Station TX	2.000	P	500.00	Buddy Baker (6)	Dodge	147.059	A.J. Foyt (8)	Mercury	170.273

1973

Race #	Year #	Date	Site	Track Surface		Miles	Race Winner	Car	Speed	Pole Winner	Car	Speed
1075	1	1/21/73	Riverside CA	2.620	P	500.00	Mark Donohue	Matador	104.055	David Pearson (61)	Mercury	110.856

312

Race #	Year #	Date	Site	Track	Surface	Miles	Race Winner	Car	Speed	Pole Winner	Car	Speed
1076	2	2/18/73	Daytona Beach FL	2.500	P	500.00	Richard Petty (149)	Dodge	157.205	Buddy Baker (12)	Dodge	185.662
1077	3	2/25/73	Richmond VA	0.542	P	271.00	Richard Petty (150)	Dodge	74.764	Bobby Allison (36)	Chevy	90.952
1078	4	3/18/73	Rockingham NC	1.017	P	500.00	David Pearson (67)	Mercury	118.649	David Pearson (62)	Mercury	134.021
1079	5	3/25/73	Bristol TN	0.533	P	266.50	Cale Yarborough (15)	Chevy	88.952	Cale Yarborough (20)	Chevy	107.608
1080	6	4/1/73	Atlanta GA	1.522	P	500.00	David Pearson (68)	Mercury	139.351	No Time Trials	NTT	NTT
1081	7	4/8/73	N Wilkesboro NC	0.625	P	250.00	Richard Petty (151)	Dodge	97.224	Bobby Allison (37)	Chevy	106.750
1082	8	4/15/73	Darlington SC	1.366	P	500.00	David Pearson (69)	Mercury	122.655	David Pearson (63)	Mercury	153.463
1083	9	4/29/73	Martinsville VA	0.525	P	262.50	David Pearson (70)	Mercury	70.251	David Pearson (64)	Mercury	86.369
1084	10	5/6/73	Talladega AL	2.660	P	500.00	David Pearson (71)	Mercury	131.956	Buddy Baker (13)	Dodge	193.435
1085	11	5/12/73	Nashville TN	0.596	P	250.00	Cale Yarborough (16)	Chevy	98.419	Cale Yarborough (21)	Chevy	105.741
1086	12	5/27/73	Charlotte NC	1.500	P	600.00	Buddy Baker (7)	Dodge	124.890	Buddy Baker (14)	Dodge	158.051
1087	13	6/3/73	Dover DE	1.000	P	500.00	David Pearson (72)	Mercury	119.745	David Pearson (65)	Mercury	133.111
1088	14	6/10/73	College Station TX	2.000	P	500.00	Richard Petty (152)	Dodge	142.114	Buddy Baker (15)	Dodge	169.248
1089	15	6/17/73	Riverside CA	2.620	P	400.00	Bobby Allison (41)	Chevy	100.215	Richard Petty (107)	Dodge	110.027
1090	16	6/24/73	Brooklyn Mi	2.000	P	400.00	David Pearson (73)	Mercury	153.485	Buddy Baker (16)	Dodge	158.273
1091	17	7/4/73	Daytona Beach FL	2.500	P	400.00	David Pearson (74)	Mercury	158.468	Bobby Allison (38)	Chevy	179.619
1092	18	7/8/73	Bristol TN	0.533	P	266.50	Benny Parsons (2)	Chevy	91.342	Cale Yarborough (22)	Chevy	106.472
1093	19	7/22/73	Atlanta GA	1.522	P	500.00	David Pearson (75)	Mercury	130.211	Richard Petty (108)	Dodge	157.163
1094	20	8/12/73	Talladega AL	2.660	P	500.00	Dick Brooks	Plymouth	145.454	Bobby Allison (39)	Chevy	187.064
1095	21	8/25/73	Nashville TN	0.596	P	250.00	Buddy Baker (8)	Dodge	89.310	Cale Yarborough (23)	Chevy	103.024
1096	22	9/3/73	Darlington SC	1.366	P	500.00	Cale Yarborough (17)	Chevy	134.033	David Pearson (66)	Mercury	150.366
1097	23	9/9/73	Richmond VA	0.542	P	271.00	Richard Petty (153)	Dodge	63.215	Bobby Allison (40)	Chevy	90.245
1098	24	9/16/73	Dover DE	1.000	P	500.00	David Pearson (76)	Mercury	112.852	David Pearson (67)	Mercury	124.649
1099	25	9/23/73	N Wilkesboro NC	0.625	P	250.00	Bobby Allison (42)	Chevy	95.198	Bobby Allison (41)	Chevy	105.619
1100	26	9/30/73	Martinsville VA	0.525	P	252.00	Richard Petty (154)	Dodge	68.831	Cale Yarborough (24)	Chevy	85.922
1101	27	10/7/73	Charlotte NC	1.500	P	500.00	Cale Yarborough (18)	Chevy	145.240	David Pearson (68)	Mercury	158.315
1102	28	10/21/73	Rockingham NC	1.017	P	500.00	David Pearson (77)	Mercury	117.749	Richard Petty (109)	Dodge	135.748

1974

Race #	Year #	Date	Site	Track	Surface	Miles	Race Winner	Car	Speed	Pole Winner	Car	Speed
1103	1	1/26/74	Riverside CA	2.620	P	500.00	Cale Yarborough (19)	Chevy	101.140	David Pearson (69)	Mercury	110.098
1104	2	2/17/74	Daytona Beach FL	2.500	P	450.00	Richard Petty (155)	Dodge	140.894	David Pearson (70)	Mercury	185.817
1105	3	2/24/74	Richmond VA	0.542	P	243.90	Bobby Allison (43)	Chevy	80.095	Bobby Allison (42)	Chevy	90.353
1106	4	3/3/74	Rockingham NC	1.017	P	450.50	Richard Petty (156)	Dodge	121.622	Cale Yarborough (25)	Chevy	134.868
1107	5	3/17/74	Bristol TN	0.533	P	239.90	Cale Yarborough (20)	Chevy	64.533	Donnie Allison (10)	Chevy	107.785
1108	6	3/24/74	Atlanta GA	1.522	P	450.50	Cale Yarborough (21)	Chevy	136.910	David Pearson (71)	Mercury	159.242
1109	7	4/7/74	Darlington SC	1.366	P	450.00	David Pearson (78)	Mercury	117.543	Donnie Allison (11)	Chevy	150.689
1110	8	4/21/74	N Wilkesboro NC	0.625	P	225.00	Richard Petty (157)	Dodge	96.200	Bobby Allison (43)	Chevy	105.669
1111	9	4/28/74	Martinsville VA	0.525	P	236.70	Cale Yarborough (22)	Chevy	70.427	Cale Yarborough (26)	Chevy	84.362
1112	10	5/5/74	Talladega AL	2.660	P	450.00	David Pearson (79)	Mercury	130.220	David Pearson (72)	Mercury	186.086
1113	11	5/11/74	Nashville TN	0.596	P	238.00	Richard Petty (158)	Dodge	84.240	Bobby Allison (44)	Chevy	100.088
1114	12	5/19/74	Dover DE	1.000	P	450.00	Cale Yarborough (23)	Chevy	119.990	David Pearson (73)	Mercury	134.403
1115	13	5/26/74	Charlotte NC	1.500	P	540.00	David Pearson (80)	Mercury	135.720	David Pearson (74)	Mercury	157.498
1116	14	6/9/74	Riverside CA	2.620	P	361.60	Cale Yarborough (24)	Chevy	102.489	George Follmer	Matador	109.093
1117	15	6/16/74	Brooklyn Mi	2.000	P	360.00	Richard Petty (159)	Dodge	127.098	David Pearson (75)	Mercury	156.426
1118	16	7/4/74	Daytona Beach FL	2.500	P	400.00	David Pearson (81)	Mercury	138.310	David Pearson (76)	Mercury	180.759
1119	17	7/14/74	Bristol TN	0.533	P	266.50	Cale Yarborough (25)	Chevy	75.430	Richard Petty (110)	Dodge	107.351
1120	18	7/20/74	Nashville TN	0.596	P	250.00	Cale Yarborough (26)	Chevy	76.368	Darrell Waltrip	Chevy	101.274
1121	19	7/28/74	Atlanta GA	1.522	P	500.00	Richard Petty (160)	Dodge	131.651	Cale Yarborough (27)	Chevy	156.750
1122	20	8/4/74	Pocono PA	2.500	P	480.00	Richard Petty (161)	Dodge	115.593	Buddy Baker (17)	Ford	144.122
1123	21	8/11/74	Talladega AL	2.660	P	500.00	Richard Petty (162)	Dodge	148.637	David Pearson (77)	Mercury	184.926
1124	22	8/25/74	Brooklyn Mi	2.000	P	400.00	David Pearson (82)	Mercury	133.045	David Pearson (78)	Mercury	157.946
1125	23	9/2/74	Darlington SC	1.366	P	500.00	Cale Yarborough (27)	Chevy	111.075	Richard Petty (111)	Dodge	150.132
1126	24	9/8/74	Richmond VA	0.542	P	271.00	Richard Petty (163)	Dodge	64.430	Richard Petty (112)	Dodge	88.852
1127	25	9/15/74	Dover DE	1.000	P	500.00	Richard Petty (164)	Dodge	113.640	Buddy Baker (18)	Ford	133.640
1128	26	9/22/74	N Wilkesboro NC	0.625	P	250.00	Cale Yarborough (28)	Chevy	80.782	Richard Petty (113)	Dodge	105.087
1129	27	9/29/74	Martinsville VA	0.525	P	262.50	Earl Ross	Chevy	66.232	Richard Petty (114)	Dodge	84.119
1130	28	10/6/74	Charlotte NC	1.500	P	500.00	David Pearson (83)	Mercury	119.912	David Pearson (79)	Mercury	158.749
1131	29	10/20/74	Rockingham NC	1.017	P	500.00	David Pearson (84)	Mercury	118.493	Richard Petty (115)	Dodge	135.297
1132	30	11/24/74	Ontario CA	2.500	P	500.00	Bobby Allison (44)	Matador	134.963	Richard Petty (116)	Dodge	149.940

1975

Race #	Year #	Date	Site	Track	Surface	Miles	Race Winner	Car	Speed	Pole Winner	Car	Speed
1133	1	1/19/75	Riverside CA	2.620	P	500.00	Bobby Allison (45)	Matador	98.627	Bobby Allison (45)	Matador	110.382
1134	2	2/16/75	Daytona Beach FL	2.500	P	500.00	Benny Parsons (3)	Chevy	153.649	Donnie Allison (12)	Chevy	185.827
1135	3	2/23/75	Richmond VA	0.542	P	271.00	Richard Petty (165)	Dodge	74.913	Richard Petty (117)	Dodge	93.340
1136	4	3/2/75	Rockingham NC	1.017	P	500.00	Cale Yarborough (29)	Chevy	117.588	Buddy Baker (19)	Ford	137.611
1137	5	3/16/75	Bristol TN	0.533	P	266.50	Richard Petty (166)	Dodge	97.053	Buiddy Baker (20)	Ford	110.951
1138	6	3/25/75	Atlanta GA	1.522	P	500.00	Richard Petty (167)	Dodge	133.496	Richard Petty (118)	Dodge	159.029
1139	7	4/6/75	N Wilkesboro NC	0.625	P	250.00	Richard Petty (168)	Dodge	90.009	Darrell Waltrip (2)	Chevy	105.520
1140	8	4/13/75	Darlington SC	1.366	P	500.00	Bobby Allison (46)	Matador	117.597	David Pearson (80)	Mercury	155.433
1141	9	4/27/75	Martinsville VA	0.525	P	262.50	Richard Petty (169)	Dodge	69.282	Benny Parsons (2)	Chevy	85.789
1142	10	5/4/75	Talladega AL	2.660	P	500.00	Buddy Baker (9)	Ford	144.948	Buddy Baker (21)	Ford	189.947
1143	11	5/10/75	Nashville TN	0.596	P	250.00	Darrell Waltrip	Chevy	94.107	Darrell Waltrip (3)	Chevy	103.793

Race #	Year #	Date	Site	Track	Surface	Miles	Race Winner	Car	Speed	Pole Winner	Car	Speed
1144	12	5/19/75	Dover DE	1.000	P	500.00	David Pearson (85)	Mercury	100.820	David Pearson (81)	Mercury	136.612
1145	13	5/25/74	Charlotte NC	1.500	P	600.00	Richard Petty (170)	Dodge	145.327	David Pearson (82)	Mercury	159.353
1146	14	6/8/75	Riverside CA	2.620	P	400.00	Richard Petty (171)	Dodge	101.028	Bobby Allison (46)	Matador	110.353
1147	15	6/15/75	Brooklyn MI	2.000	P	400.00	David Pearson (86)	Mercury	131.398	Cale Yarborough (28)	Chevy	158.541
1148	16	7/4/75	Daytona Beach FL	2.500	P	400.00	Richard Petty (172)	Dodge	158.381	Donnie Allison (13)	Chevy	186.737
1149	17	7/20/75	Nashville TN	0.596	P	250.00	Cale Yarborough (30)	Chevy	89.792	Benny Parsons (3)	Chevy	103.247
1150	18	8/3/75	Pocono PA	2.500	P	500.00	David Pearson (87)	Mercury	111.179	Bobby Allison (47)	Matador	146.491
1151	19	8/17/75	Talladega AL	2.660	P	500.00	Buddy Baker (10)	Ford	130.892	Dave Marcis (3)	Dodge	191.340
1152	20	8/24/75	Brooklyn MI	2.000	P	400.00	Richard Petty (173)	Dodge	107.583	David Pearson (83)	Mercury	159.798
1153	21	9/1/75	Darlington SC	1.366	P	500.00	Bobby Allison (47)	Matador	116.825	David Pearson (84)	Mercury	153.401
1154	22	9/14/75	Dover DE	1.000	P	500.00	Richard Petty (174)	Dodge	111.372	Dave Marcis (4)	Dodge	133.953
1155	23	9/21/75	N Wilkesboro NC	0.625	P	250.00	Richard Petty (175)	Dodge	88.986	Richard Petty (119)	Dodge	105.500
1156	24	9/28/75	Martinsville VA	0.525	P	262.50	Dave Marcis	Dodge	75.819	Cale Yarborough (29)	Chevy	86.199
1157	25	10/5/75	Charlotte NC	1.500	P	500.00	Richard Petty (176)	Dodge	132.209	David Pearson (85)	Mercury	161.071
1158	26	10/12/75	Richmond VA	0.542	P	271.00	Darrell Waltrip (2)	Chevy	81.886	Benny Parsons (4)	Chevy	91.071
1159	27	10/19/75	Rockingham NC	1.017	P	500.00	Cale Yarborough (31)	Chevy	120.129	Dave Marcis (5)	Dodge	132.021
1160	28	11/2/75	Bristol TN	0.533	P	266.50	Richard Petty (177)	Dodge	97.016	Cale Yarborough (30)	Chevy	110.162
1161	29	11/9/75	Atlanta GA	1.522	P	500.00	Buddy Baker (11)	Ford	130.990	Dave Marcis (6)	Dodge	160.662
1162	30	11/23/75	Ontario CA	2.500	P	500.00	Buddy Baker (12)	Ford	140.712	David Pearson (86)	Mercury	153.525

1976

Race #	Year #	Date	Site	Track	Surface	Miles	Race Winner	Car	Speed	Pole Winner	Car	Speed
1163	1	1/18/76	Riverside CA	2.620	P	500.00	David Pearson (88)	Mercury	99.180	Bobby Allison (48)	Matador	112.416
1164	2	2/15/76	Daytona Beach FL	2.500	P	500.00	David Pearson (89)	Mercury	152.181	Ramo Stott	Chevy	183.456
1165	3	2/29/76	Rockingham NC	1.017	P	500.00	Richard Petty (178)	Dodge	113.665	Dave Marcis (7)	Dodge	138.287
1166	4	3/7/76	Richmond VA	0.542	P	216.80	Dave Marcis (2)	Dodge	72.792	Bobby Allison (49)	Mercury	92.715
1167	5	3/14/76	Bristol TN	0.533	P	213.20	Cale Yarborough (32)	Chevy	87.377	Buddy Baker (22)	Ford	110.720
1168	6	3/21/76	Atlanta GA	1.522	P	500.00	David Pearson (90)	Mercury	128.904	Dave Marcis (8)	Dodge	160.709
1169	7	4/4/76	N Wilkesboro NC	0.625	P	250.00	Cale Yarborough (33)	Chevy	96.858	Dave Marcis (9)	Dodge	108.585
1170	8	4/11/76	Darlington SC	1.366	P	500.00	David Pearson (91)	Mercury	122.973	David Pearson (87)	Mercury	154.171
1171	9	4/25/76	Martinsville VA	0.525	P	262.50	Darrell Waltrip (3)	Chevy	71.759	Dave Marcis (10)	Dodge	86.286
1172	10	5/2/76	Talladega AL	2.660	P	500.00	Buddy Baker (13)	Ford	169.887	Dave Marcis (11)	Dodge	189.197
1173	11	5/8/76	Nashville TN	0.596	P	250.00	Cale Yarborough (34)	Chevy	84.512	Benny Parsons (5)	Chevy	104.328
1175	12	5/16/76	Dover DE	1.000	P	500.00	Benny Parsons (4)	Chevy	115.436	Dave Marcis (12)	Dodge	136.013
1176	13	5/30/76	Charlotte NC	1.500	P	600.00	David Pearson (92)	Mercury	137.352	David Pearson (88)	Mercury	159.132
1176	14	6/6/76	Riverside CA	2.620	P	248.90	David Pearson (93)	Mercury	106.279	David Pearson (89)	Mercury	111.437
1177	15	6/13/76	Brooklyn MI	2.000	P	400.00	David Pearson (94)	Mercury	141.148	Richard Petty (120)	Dodge	158.569
1178	16	7/4/76	Daytona Beach FL	2.500	P	400.00	Cale Yarborough (35)	Chevy	160.966	A.J. Foyt (9)	Chevy	183.090
1179	17	7/16/76	Nashville TN	0.596	P	250.00	Benny Parsons (5)	Chevy	86.908	Neil Bonnett	Mercury	103.049
1180	18	8/1/76	Pocono PA	2.500	P	500.00	Richard Petty (179)	Dodge	115.875	Cale Yarborough (31)	Chevy	147.865
1181	19	8/8/76	Talladega AL	2.660	P	500.00	Dave Marcis (3)	Dodge	157.547	Dave Marcis (13)	Dodge	190.651
1182	20	8/22/76	Brooklyn MI	2.000	P	400.00	David Pearson (95)	Mercury	140.078	David Pearson (90)	Mercury	160.875
1183	21	8/29/76	Bristol TN	0.533	P	213.20	Cale Yarborough (36)	Chevy	99.175	Darrell Waltrip (4)	Chevy	110.300
1184	22	9/6/76	Darlington SC	1.366	P	500.00	David Pearson (96)	Mercury	120.534	David Pearson (91)	Mercury	154.699
1185	23	9/12/76	Richmond VA	0.542	P	216.80	Cale Yarborough (37)	Chevy	77.993	Benny Parsons (6)	Chevy	92.460
1186	24	9/19/76	Dover DE	1.000	P	500.00	Cale Yarborough (38)	Chevy	115.740	Cale Yarborough (32)	Chevy	133.377
1187	25	9/26/76	Martinsville VA	0.525	P	178.50	Cale Yarborough (39)	Chevy	75.370	Darrell Waltrip (5)	Chevy	88.484
1188	26	10/3/76	N Wilkesboro NC	0.625	P	250.00	Cale Yarborough (40)	Chevy	96.380	Darrell Waltrip (6)	Chevy	107.449
1189	27	10/10/76	Charlotte NC	1.500	P	500.00	Donnie Allison (7)	Chevy	141.266	David Pearson (92)	Mercury	161.223
1190	28	10/24/76	Rockingham NC	1.017	P	500.00	Richard Petty (180)	Dodge	117.718	David Pearson (93)	Mercury	139.117
1191	29	11/7/76	Atlanta GA	1.522	P	500.00	Dave Marcis (4)	Dodge	127.396	Buddy Baker (23)	Ford	161.652
1192	30	11/21/76	Ontario CA	2.500	P	500.00	David Pearson (97)	Mercury	137.101	David Pearson (94)	Mercury	153.964

1977

Race #	Year #	Date	Site	Track	Surface	Miles	Race Winner	Car	Speed	Pole Winner	Car	Speed
1193	1	1/16/77	Riverside CA	2.620	P	311.78	David Pearson (98)	Mercury	107.038	Cale Yarborough (33)	Chevy	112.686
1194	2	2/20/77	Daytona Beach FL	2.500	P	500.00	Cale Yarborough (41)	Chevy	153.218	Donnie Allison (14)	Chevy	188.048
1195	3	2/27/77	Richmond VA	0.542	P	133.00	Cale Yarborough (42)	Chevy	73.084	Neil Bonnett (2)	Dodge	93.632
1196	4	3/13/77	Rockingham NC	1.017	P	500.00	Richard Petty (181)	Dodge	97.860	Donnie Allison (15)	Chevy	135.387
1197	5	3/20/77	Atlanta GA	1.522	P	500.00	Richard Petty (182)	Dodge	144.093	Richard Petty (121)	Dodge	162.501
1198	6	3/27/77	N Wilkesboro NC	0.625	P	250.00	Cale Yarborough (43)	Chevy	88.950	Neil Bonnett (3)	Dodge	107.537
1199	7	4/3/77	Darlington SC	1.366	P	500.00	Darrell Waltrip (4)	Chevy	128.817	David Pearson (95)	Mercury	151.269
1200	8	4/17/77	Bristol TN	0.533	P	266.50	Cale Yarborough (44)	Chevy	100.989	Cale Yarborough (34)	Chevy	110.168
1201	9	4/24/77	Martinsville VA	0.525	P	201.60	Cale Yarborough (45)	Chevy	77.405	Neil Bonnett (4)	Dodge	88.923
1202	10	5/1/77	Talladega AL	2.660	P	500.00	Darrell Waltrip (5)	Chevy	164.877	A.J. Foyt (10)	Chevy	192.424
1203	11	5/7/77	Nashville TN	0.596	P	250.00	Benny Parsons (6)	Chevy	87.490	Darrell Waltrip (7)	Chevy	103.643
1294	12	5/15/77	Dover DE	1.000	P	500.00	Cale Yarborough (46)	Chevy	123.327	Richard Petty (122)	Dodge	136.033
1205	13	5/29/77	Charlotte NC	1.500	P	600.00	Richard Petty (183)	Dodge	137.676	David Pearson (96)	Mercury	161.435
1206	14	6/12/77	Riverside CA	2.620	P	248.90	Richard Petty (184)	Dodge	105.021	Richard Petty (123)	Dodge	112.432
1207	15	6/19/77	Brooklyn MI	2.000	P	400.00	Cale Yarborough (47)	Chevy	135.033	David Pearson (97)	Mercury	159.175
1208	16	7/4/77	Daytona Beach FL	2.500	P	400.00	Richard Petty (185)	Dodge	142.716	Neil Bonnett (5)	Dodge	187.191
1209	17	7/16/77	Nashville TN	0.596	P	250.00	Darrell Waltrip (6)	Chevy	78.999	Benny Parsons (7)	Chevy	104.210

314

Race #	Year #	Date	Site	Track	Surface	Miles	Race Winner	Car	Speed	Pole Winner	Car	Speed
1210	18	7/31/77	Pocono PA	2.500	P	500.00	Benny Parsons (7)	Chevy	128.379	Darrell Waltrip (8)	Chevy	147.591
1211	19	8/7/77	Talladega AL	2.660	P	500.00	Donnie Allison (8)	Chevy	162.524	Benny Parsons (8)	Chevy	192.684
1212	20	8/22/77	Brooklyn MI	2.000	P	400.00	Darrell Waltrip (7)	Chevy	137.944	David Pearson (98)	Mercury	160.346
1213	21	8/28/77	Bristol TN	0.533	P	213.00	Cale Yarborough (48)	Chevy	79.726	Cale Yarborough (35)	Chevy	109.746
1214	22	9/5/77	Darlington SC	1.366	P	500.00	David Pearson (99)	Mercury	106.797	Darrell Waltrip (9)	Chevy	153.493
1215	23	9/11/77	Richmond VA	0.542	P	216.80	Neil Bonnett	Dodge	80.644	Benny Parsons (9)	Chevy	92.281
1216	24	9/18/77	Dover DE	1.000	P	500.00	Benny Parsons (8)	Chevy	114.708	Neil Bonnett (7)	Dodge	134.233
1217	25	9/25/77	Martinsville VA	0.525	P	262.50	Cale Yarborough (49)	Chevy	73.447	Neil Bonnett (8)	Dodge	87.637
1218	26	10/2/77	N Wilkesboro NC	0.625	P	250.00	Darrell Waltrip (8)	Chevy	86.713	Richard Petty (124)	Dodge	108.350
1219	27	10/9/77	Charlotte NC	1.500	P	500.00	Benny Parsons (9)	Chevy	142.780	David Pearson (99)	Mercury	160.892
1220	28	10/23/77	Rockingham NC	1.017	P	500.00	Donnie Allison (9)	Chevy	113.584	Donnie Allison (16)	Chevy	138.685
1221	29	11/6/77	Atlanta GA	1.522	P	408.00	Darrell Waltrip (9)	Chevy	110.052	Sam Sommers	Chevy	160.229
1222	30	11/20/77	Ontario CA	2.500	P	500.00	Neil Bonnett (2)	Dodge	128.296	Richard Petty (125)	Dodge	154.905

1978

Race #	Year #	Date	Site	Track	Surface	Miles	Race Winner	Car	Speed	Pole Winner	Car	Speed
1223	1	1/22/78	Riverside CA	2.620	P	311.78	Cale Yarborough (50)	Olds	102.269	David Pearson (100)	Mercury	113.204
1224	2	2/19/78	Daytona Beach FL	2.500	P	500.00	Bobby Allison (48)	Ford	159.730	Cale Yarborough (36)	Olds	187.536
1225	3	2/26/78	Richmond VA	0.542	P	216.80	Benny Parsons (10)	Chevy	80.304	Neil Bonnett (8)	Dodge	93.382
1226	4	3/5/78	Rockingham NC	1.017	P	500.00	David Pearson (100)	Mercury	116.681	Neil Bonnett (9)	Dodge	141.940
1227	5	3/19/78	Atlanta GA	1.522	P	500.00	Bobby Allison (49)	Ford	142.520	Cale Yarborough (37)	Olds	162.006
1228	6	4/2/78	Bristol TN	0.533	P	266.50	Darrell Waltrip (10)	Chevy	92.401	Neil Bonnett (10)	Dodge	110.409
1229	7	4/9/78	Darlington SC	1.366	P	500.00	Benny Parsons (11)	Chevy	127.544	Bobby Allison (50)	Ford	151.862
1230	8	4/16/78	N. Wilkesboro NC	0.625	P	250.00	Darrell Waltrip (11)	Chevy	92.345	Benny Parsons (10)	Chevy	108.510
1231	9	4/23/78	Martinsville VA	0.525	P	262.50	Darrell Waltrip (12)	Chevy	77.971	Lennie Pond	Chevy	88.637
1232	10	5/14/78	Talladega AL	2.660	P	500.00	Cale Yarborough (51)	Olds	159.699	Cale Yarborough (38)	Olds	191.904
1233	11	5/21/78	Dover DE	1.000	P	500.00	David Pearson (101)	Mercury	114.664	Buddy Baker (24)	Chevy	135.452
1234	12	5/28/78	Charlotte NC	1.500	P	600.00	Darrell Waltrip (13)	Chevy	138.355	David Pearson (101)	Mercury	160.551
1235	13	6/3/78	Nashville TN	0.596	P	250.00	Cale Yarborough (52)	Olds	87.541	Lennie Pond (2)	Chevy	105.094
1236	14	6/11/78	Riverside CA	2.620	P	248.90	Benny Parsons (12)	Chevy	104.311	David Pearson (102)	Mercury	112.882
1237	15	6/18/78	Brooklyn MI	2.000	P	400.00	Cale Yarborough (53)	Olds	149.563	David Pearson (103)	Mercury	163.036
1238	16	7/4/78	Daytona Beach FL	2.500	P	400.00	David Pearson (102)	Mercury	154.340	Cale Yarborough (39)	Olds	186.803
1239	17	7/15/78	Nashville TN	0.596	P	250.00	Cale Yarborough (54)	Olds	88.924	Lennie Pond (3)	Chevy	104.257
1240	18	7/30/78	Pocono PA	2.500	P	500.00	Darrell Waltrip (14)	Chevy	142.540	Benny Parsons (11)	Chevy	149.917
1241	19	8/6/78	Talladega AL	2.660	P	500.00	Lennie Pond	Olds	174.700	Cale Yarborough (40)	Olds	192.917
1242	20	8/20/78	Brooklyn MI	2.000	P	400.00	David Pearson (109)	Mercury	129.566	David Pearson (104)	Mercury	164.073
1243	21	8/26/78	Bristol TN	0.533	P	266.50	Cale Yarborough (55)	Olds	88.628	Lennie Pond (4)	Olds	110.958
1244	22	9/4/78	Darlington SC	1.266	P	500.00	Cale Yarborough (56)	Olds	116.828	David Pearson (105)	Mercury	153.685
1245	23	9/10/78	Richmond VA	0.542	P	216.80	Darrell Waltrip (15)	Chevy	79.568	Darrell Waltrip (10)	Chevy	92.964
1246	24	9/17/78	Dover DE	1.000	P	500.00	Bobby Allison (50)	Ford	119.323	J.D. McDufffie	Chevy	135.480
1247	25	9/24/78	Martinsville VA	0.525	P	262.50	Cale Yarborough (57)	Olds	79.185	Lennie Pond (5)	Chevy	86.558
1248	26	10/1/78	N Wilkesboro NC	0.625	P	150.00	Cale Yarborough (58)	Olds	97.847	Darrell Waltrip (11)	Chevy	109.397
1249	27	10/8/78	Charlotte NC	1.500	P	500.00	Bobby Allison (51)	Ford	141.826	David Pearson (106)	Mercury	161.355
1250	28	10/22/78	Rockingham NC	1.017	P	500.00	Cale Yarborough (59)	Olds	117.288	Cale Yarborough (41)	Olds	142.067
1251	29	11/5/78	Atlanta GA	1.522	P	500.00	Donnie Allison (10)	Chevy	124.312	Cale Yarborough (42)	Olds	168.425
1252	30	11/19/78	Ontario CA	2.500	P	500.00	Bobby Allison (52)	Ford	137.783	Cale Yarborough (43)	Olds	156.190

1979

Race #	Year #	Date	Site	Track	Surface	Miles	Race Winner	Car	Speed	Pole Winner	Car	Speed
1253	1	1/14/79	Riverside CA	2.620	P	311.78	Darrell Waltrip (16)	Chevy	107.820	David Pearson (107)	Mercury	113.659
1254	2	2/18/79	Daytona Beach FL	2.500	P	500.00	Richard Petty (186)	Olds	143.977	Buddy Baker (25)	Olds	196.049
1255	3	3/4/79	Rockingham NC	1.017	P	500.00	Bobby Allison (53)	Ford	121.727	Bobby Allison (51)	Ford	136.790
1256	4	3/11/79	Richmond VA	0.542	P	216.80	Cale Yarborough (60)	Olds	83.608	Bobby Allison (52)	Ford	92.957
1257	5	3/18/79	Atlanta GA	1.522	P	500.00	Buddy Baker (14)	Olds	135.136	Buddy Baker (26)	Olds	165.951
1258	6	3/25/79	N Wilkesboro NC	0.625	P	0.63	Bobby Allison (54)	Ford	88.400	Benny Parsons (12)	Chevy	108.136
1259	7	4/1/79	Bristol TN	0.533	P	266.50	Dale Earnhardt	Chevy	91.033	Buddy Baker (27)	Chevy	111.610
1260	8	4/8/79	Darlington SC	1.366	P	500.00	Darrell Waltrip (17)	Chevy	121.721	Donnie Allison (17)	Chevy	154.797
1261	9	4/22/79	Martinsville VA	0.525	P	262.50	Richard Petty (187)	Chevy	76.562	Darrell Waltrip (12)	Chevy	87.383
1262	10	5/6/79	Talladega AL	2.660	P	500.00	Bobby Allison (55)	Ford	154.770	Darrell Waltrip (13)	Olds	195.644
1263	11	5/12/79	Nashvile TN	0.596	P	150.00	Cale Yarborough (61)	Olds	88.652	Joe Millikan	Chevy	104.155
1264	12	5/20/79	Dover DE	1.000	P	500.00	Neil Bonnett (3)	Mercury	111.269	Darrell Waltrip (14)	Chevy	136.103
1265	13	5/27/79	Charlotte NC	1.500	P	600.00	Darrell Waltrip (18)	Chevy	136.674	Neil Bonnett (11)	Mercury	160.125
1266	14	6/3/79	College Station TX	2.000	P	400.00	Darrell Waltrip (19)	Chevy	156.216	Buddy Baker (28)	Chevy	167.903
1267	15	6/10/79	Riverside CA	2.620	P	248.90	Bobby Allison (56)	Ford	103.732	Dale Earnhardt	Chevy	113.039
1268	16	6/17/79	Brooklyn MI	2.000	P	400.00	Buddy Baker (15)	Chevy	135.798	Neil Bonnett (12)	Mercury	162.371
1269	17	7/4/79	Daytona Beach FL	2.500	P	400.00	Neil Bonnett (4)	Mercury	172.890	Buddy Baker (20)	Olds	193.196
1270	18	7/14/79	Nashville TN	0.596	P	250.00	Darrell Waltrip (20)	Chevy	92.227	Darrell Waltrip (15)	Chevy	105.430
1271	19	7/30/79	Pocono PA	2.500	P	500.00	Cale Yarborough (62)	Chevy	115.207	Harry Gant	Chevy	148.711
1272	20	8/5/79	Talladega AL	2.660	P	500.00	Darrell Waltrip (21)	Olds	161.229	Neil Bonnett (13)	Mercury	193.600
1273	21	8/19/79	Brooklyn MI	2.000	P	400.00	Richard Petty (188)	Chevy	130.376	David Pearson (108)	Chevy	162.992
1274	22	8/25/79	Bristol TN	0.533	P	266.50	Darrell Waltrip (22)	Chevy	91.493	Richard Petty (126)	Chevy	110.524
1275	23	9/3/79	Darlington SC	1.366	P	500.00	David Pearson (104)	Chevy	126.259	Bobby Allison (52)	Ford	154.880

315

Race #	Year #	Date	Site	Track	Surface	Miles	Race Winner	Car	Speed	Pole Winner	Car	Speed
1276	24	9/9/79	Richmond VA	0.542	P	216.80	Bobby Allison (57)	Ford	80.604	Dale Earnhardt (2)	Chevy	92.605
1277	25	9/16/79	Dover DE	1.000	P	500.00	Richard Petty (189)	Chevy	114.366	Dale Earnhardt (3)	Chevy	135.726
1278	26	9/23/79	Martinsville VA	0.525	P	262.50	Buddy Baker (16)	Chevy	75.119	Darrell Waltrip (16)	Chevy	88.265
1279	27	10/7/79	Charlotte NC	1.500	P	500.00	Cale Yarborough (63)	Chevy	134.266	Neil Bonnett (14)	Mercury	164.304
1280	28	10/14/79	N Wilkesboro NC	0.625	P	250.00	Benny Parsons (13)	Chevy	91.454	Dale Earnhardt (4)	Chevy	112.783
1281	29	10/21/79	Rockingham NC	1.017	P	500.00	Richard Petty (190)	Chevy	108.356	Buddy Baker (30)	Chevy	141.315
1282	30	11/4/79	Atlanta GA	1.522	P	500.00	Neil Bonnett (5)	Mercury	140.120	Buddy Baker (31)	Chevy	164.813
1283	31	11/18/79	Ontario CA	2.500	P	500.00	Benny Parsons (14)	Chevy	132.822	Cale Yarborough (44)	Olds	154.902

1980

Race #	Year #	Date	Site	Track	Surface	Miles	Race Winner	Car	Speed	Pole Winner	Car	Speed
1284	1	1/19/80	Riverside CA	2.620	P	311.78	Darrell Waltrip (23)	Chevy	94.974	Darrell Waltrip (17)	Chevy	113.404
1285	2	2/17/80	Daytona Beach, FL	2.500	P	500.00	Buddy Baker (17)	Olds	177.602	Buddy Baker (32)	Olds	194.009
1286	3	2/24/80	Richmond VA	0.542	P	216.80	Darrell Waltrip (24)	Chevy	67.703	Darrell Waltrip (18)	Chevy	93.695
1287	4	3/9/80	Rockingham NC	1.017	P	500.00	Cale Yarborough (64)	Olds	108.735	Darrell Waltrip (19)	Chevy	136.765
1288	5	3/16/80	Atlanta GA	1.522	P	500.00	Dale Earnhardt (2)	Chevy	134.808	Buddy Baker (33)	Olds	166.212
1289	6	3/30/80	Bristol TN	0.533	P	266.50	Dale Earnhardt (3)	Chevy	96.977	Cale Yarborough (45)	Chevy	111.688
1290	7	4/13/80	Darlington SC	1.366	P	258.17	David Pearson (105)	Chevy	112.397	Benny Parsons (13)	Chevy	155.866
1291	8	4/20/80	N Wilkesboro NC	0.625	P	250.00	Richard Petty (191)	Chevy	95.501	Bobby Allison (54)	Ford	113.797
1292	9	4/27/80	Martinsville VA	0.525	P	262.50	Darrell Waltrip (25)	Chevy	69.049	Darrell Waltrip (20)	Chevy	88.566
1293	10	5/4/80	Talladega AL	2.660	P	500.00	Buddy Baker (18)	Olds	170.481	David Pearson (109)	Olds	197.704
1294	11	5/10/80	Nashville TN	0.596	P	150.00	Richard Petty (192)	Chevy	89.471	Cale Yarborough (46)	Chevy	106.581
1295	12	5/18/80	Dover DE	1.000	P	500.00	Bobby Allison (58)	Ford	113.866	Cale Yarborough (47)	Chevy	138.814
1296	13	5/15/80	Charlotte NC	1.500	P	600.00	Benny Parsons (15)	Chevy	119.265	Cale Yarborough (48)	Chevy	165.194
1297	14	6/1/80	College Station TX	2.000	P	400.00	Cale Yarborough (65)	Chevy	159.046	Cale Yarborough (49)	Chevy	170.709
1298	15	6/8/80	Riverside CA	2.620	P	248.90	Darrell Waltrip (26)	Chevy	101.846	Cale Yarborough (50)	Chevy	113.792
1299	16	6/15/80	Brooklyn MI	2.000	P	400.00	Benny Parsons (16)	Chevy	131.808	Benny Parsons (14)	Chevy	163.662
1300	17	7/4/80	Daytona Beach FL	2.500	P	400.00	Bobby Allison (59)	Ford	173.473	Cale Yarborough (51)	Olds	194.670
1301	18	7/12/80	Nashville TN	0.596	P	250.00	Dale Earnhardt (4)	Chevy	93.821	Cale Yarborough (52)	Chevy	104.817
1302	19	7/17/80	Pocono PA	2.500	P	500.00	Neil Bonnett (6)	Mercury	124.395	Cale Yarborough (53)	Chevy	151.469
1303	20	8/3/80	Talladega AL	2.660	P	500.00	Neil Bonnett (7)	Mercury	166.894	Buddy Baker (33)	Olds	198.545
1304	21	8/17/80	Brooklyn MI	2.000	P	400.00	Cale Yarborough (66)	Chevy	145.352	Buddy Baker (34)	Chevy	162.693
1305	22	8/23/80	Bristol TN	0.533	P	266.50	Cale Yarborough (67)	Chevy	86.973	Cale Yarborough (54)	Chevy	110.990
1306	23	9/1/80	Darlington SC	1.366	P	500.00	Terry Labonte	Chevy	115.210	Darrell Waltrip (21)	Chevy	153.838
1307	24	9/7/80	Richmond VA	0.542	P	216.80	Bobby Allison (60)	Ford	79.722	Cale Yarborough (55)	Chevy	93.466
1308	25	9/14/80	Dover DE	1.000	P	500.00	Darrell Waltrip (27)	Chevy	116.024	Cale Yarborough (56)	Chevy	137.583
1309	26	9/21/80	N Wilkesboro NC	0.625	P	250.00	Bobby Allison (61)	Ford	75.510	Cale Yarborough (57)	Chevy	111.996
1310	27	9/28/80	Martinsville VA	0.525	P	262.50	Dale Earnhardt (5)	Chevy	69.654	Buddy Baker (35)	Chevy	88.500
1311	28	10/5/80	Charlotte NC	1.500	P	500.00	Dale Earnhardt (6)	Chevy	135.243	Buddy Baker (36)	Buick	165.634
1312	29	10/19/80	Rockingham NC	1.017	P	500.00	Cale Yarborough (68)	Chevy	114.159	Donnie Allison (18)	Chevy	142.648
1313	30	11/2/80	Atlanta GA	1.522	P	500.00	Cale Yarborough (69)	Chevy	131.190	Bobby Allison (55)	Mercury	165.620
1314	31	11/15/80	Ontario CA	2.500	P	500.00	Benny Parsons (17)	Chevy	129.441	Cale Yarborough (58)	Chevy	155.499

1981

Race #	Year #	Date	Site	Track	Surface	Miles	Race Winner	Car	Speed	Pole Winner	Car	Speed
1315	1	1/11/81	Riverside CA	2.620	P	311.78	Bobby Allison (62)	Chevy	95.263	Darrell Waltrip (22)	Chevy	114.711
1316	2	2/15/81	Daytona Beach FL	2.500	P	500.00	Richard Petty (193)	Buick	169.651	Bobby Allison (56)	Pontiac	194.624
1317	3	2/22/81	Richmond VA	0.542	P	216.80	Darrell Waltrip (28)	Buick	76.570	Morgan Shepherd	Pontiac	92.821
1318	4	3/1/81	Rockingham NC	1.017	P	500.00	Darrell Waltrip (29)	Buick	114.594	Cale Yarborough (59)	Buick	140.448
1319	5	3/15/81	Atlanta GA	1.522	P	500.00	Cale Yarborough (70)	Buick	133.619	Terry Labonte	Buick	162.940
1320	6	3/29/81	Bristol TN	0.533	P	266.50	Darrell Waltrip (30)	Buick	85.530	Darrell Waltrip (23)	Buick	112.125
1321	7	4/5/81	N Wilkesboro NC	0.625	P	250.00	Richard Petty (194)	Buick	85.381	Dave Marcis (14)	Chevy	114.647
1322	8	4/12/81	Darlington SC	1.366	P	500.00	Darrell Waltrip (31)	Buick	126.703	Bill Elliott	Ford	153.896
1323	9	4/26/81	Martinsville VA	0.525	P	262.50	Morgan Shepherd	Pontiac	75.019	Ricky Rudd	Buick	89.056
1324	10	5/3/81	Talladega AL	2.660	P	500.00	Bobby Allison (63)	Buick	149.376	Bobby Allison (56)	Buick	195.864
1325	11	5/9/81	Nashville TN	0.596	P	250.00	Benny Parsons (18)	Ford	89.756	Ricky Rudd (2)	Buick	104.409
1326	12	5/17/81	Dover DE	1.000	P	500.00	Jody Ridley	Ford	116.595	David Pearson (110)	Olds	138.475
1327	13	5/24/81	Charlotte NC	1.500	P	600.00	Bobby Allison (64)	Buick	129.326	Neil Bonnett (15)	Ford	158.115
1328	14	6/7/81	College Station TX	2.000	P	400.00	Benny Parsons (19)	Ford	132.475	Terry Labonte (2)	Buick	167.543
1329	15	6/17/81	Riverside CA	2.660	P	248.90	Darrell Waltrip (32)	Buick	93.957	Darrell Waltrip (23)	Buick	114.378
1330	16	6/21/81	Brooklyn MI	2.000	P	400.00	Bobby Allison (65)	Buick	130.589	Darrell Waltrip (24)	Buick	160.471
1331	17	7/4/81	Daytona Beach FL	2.500	P	400.00	Cale Yarborough (71)	Buick	142.588	Cale Yarborough (60)	Buick	192.852
1332	18	7/11/81	Nashville TN	0.596	P	250.00	Darrell Waltrip (33)	Buick	90.052	Mark Martin	Pontiac	104.353
1333	19	7/26/81	Pocono PA	2.500	P	500.00	Darrell Waltrip (34)	Buick	119.111	Darrell Waltrip (25)	Buick	150.148
1334	20	8/2/81	Talladega AL	2.660	P	500.00	Ron Bouchard	Buick	156.737	Harry Gant (2)	Buick	195.897
1335	21	8/16/81	Brooklyn MI	2.000	P	400.00	Richard Petty (195)	Buick	123.457	Ron Bouchard	Buick	161.501
1336	22	8/22/81	Bristol TN	0.533	P	266.50	Darrell Waltrip (35)	Buick	84.723	Darrell Waltrip (26)	Buick	110.818
1337	23	9/7/81	Darlington SC	1.366	P	500.00	Neil Bonnett (8)	Ford	126.446	Harry Gant (3)	Pontiac	152.693
1338	24	9/13/81	Richmond VA	0.542	P	216.80	Benny Parsons (20)	Ford	69.998	Mark Martin (2)	Pontiac	93.435
1339	25	9/20/81	Dover DE	1.000	P	500.00	Neil Bonnett (9)	Ford	119.561	Ricky Rudd (3)	Chevy	136.757
1340	26	9/27/81	Martinsville VA	0.525	P	262.50	Darrell Waltrip (36)	Buick	70.089	Darrell Waltrip (27)	Buick	89.014
1341	27	10/4/81	N Wilkesboro NC	0.625	P	250.00	Darrell Waltrip (37)	Buick	93.091	Darrell Waltrip (28)	Buick	113.065

Race #	Year #	Date	Site	Track	Surface	Miles	Race Winner	Car	Speed	Pole Winner	Car	Speed
1342	28	10/11/81	Charlotte NC	1.500	P	500.00	Darrell Waltrip (38)	Buick	117.483	Darrell Waltrip (29)	Buick	162.744
1343	29	1/1/81	Rockingham NC	1.017	P	500.00	Darrell Waltrip (39)	Buick	107.399	Darrell Waltrip (30)	Buick	136.164
1344	30	11/8/81	Atlanta GA	1.522	P	500.00	Neil Bonnett (10)	Ford	130.391	Harry Gant (4)	Pontiac	163.266
1345	31	11/22/81	Riverside CA	2.620	P	311.78	Bobby Allison (66)	Buick	95.288	Darrell Waltrip (31)	Buick	114.981

1982

Race #	Year #	Date	Site	Track	Surface	Miles	Race Winner	Car	Speed	Pole Winner	Car	Speed
1346	1	2/14/82	Daytona Beach FL	2.500	P	500.00	Bobby Allison (67)	Buick	153.991	Benny Parsons (15)	Pontiac	196.317
1347	2	2/21/82	Richmond VA	0.533	P	135.50	Dave Marcis (5)	Chevy	72.914	Darrell Waltrip (32)	Buick	93.256
1348	3	3/14/82	Bristol TN	0.533	P	266.50	Darrell Waltrip (40)	Buick	94.025	Darrell Waltrip (33)	Buick	111.068
1349	4	3/21/82	Atlanta GA	1.522	P	436.80	Darrell Waltrip (41)	Buick	124.824	Dale Earnhardt (3)	Ford	163.774
1350	5	3/28/82	Rockingham NC	1.017	P	500.00	Cale Yarborough (72)	Buick	108.992	Benny Parsons (16)	Pontiac	141.577
1351	6	4/4/82	Darlington SC	1.366	P	500.00	Dale Earnhardt (7)	Ford	123.554	Buddy Baker (37)	Buick	153.979
1352	7	4/18/82	N Wilkesboro NC	0.625	P	250.00	Darrell Waltrip (42)	Buick	97.646	Darrell Waltrip (34)	Buick	114.801
1353	8	4/25/82	Martinsville VA	0.525	P	262.50	Harry Gant	Buick	75.073	Terry Labonte (3)	Chevy	89.988
1354	9	5/2/82	Talladega AL	2.660	P	500.00	Darrell Waltrip (43)	Buick	156.697	Benny Parsons (17)	Pontiac	200.176
1355	10	5/8/82	Nashville TN	0.596	P	250.00	Darrell Waltrip (44)	Buick	83.502	Darrell Waltrip (35)	Buick	102.773
1356	11	5/16/82	Dover DE	1.000	P	500.00	Bobby Allison (68)	Chevy	120.136	Darrell Waltrip (36)	Buick	139.308
1357	12	5/30/82	Charlotte NC	1.500	P	600.00	Neil Bonnett (11)	Ford	130.058	David Pearson (111)	Buick	162.511
1358	13	6/6/82	Pocono PA	2.500	P	500.00	Bobby Allison (69)	Buick	113.579	No Time Trials	NTT	NTT
1359	14	6/13/82	Riverside CA	2.620	P	248.90	Tim Richmond	Buick	103.816	Terry Labonte (4)	Buick	114.352
1360	15	6/20/82	Brooklyn MI	2.000	P	400.00	Cale Yarborough (73)	Buick	118.101	Ron Bouchard (2)	Buick	162.404
1361	16	7/4/82	Daytona Beach, FL	2.500	P	400.00	Bobby Allison (70)	Buick	163.099	Geoff Bodine	Pontiac	194.721
1362	17	7/10/82	Nashville TN	0.596	P	250.00	Darrell Waltrip (45)	Buick	86.524	Morgan Shepherd (2)	Pontiac	103.959
1363	18	7/25/82	Pocono PA	2.500	P	500.00	Bobby Allison (71)	Buick	115.496	Cale Yarborough (61)	Buick	150.764
1364	19	8/1/82	Talladega AL	2.660	P	500.00	Darrell Waltrip (46)	Buick	168.157	Geoff Bodine (2)	Pontiac	199.400
1365	20	8/22/82	Brooklyn MI	2.000	P	400.00	Bobby Allison (72)	Buick	136.454	Bill Elliott (2)	Ford	162.173
1366	21	8/28/82	Bristol TN	0.533	P	266.50	Darrell Waltrip (47)	Buick	94.318	Tim Richmond	Buick	112.507
1367	22	9/6/82	Darlington SC	1.366	P	500.00	Cale Yarborough (74)	Buick	115.224	David Pearson (112)	Buick	155.739
1368	23	9/12/82	Richmond VA	0.542	P	216.80	Bobby Allison (73)	Chevy	82.800	Bobby Allison (57)	Chevy	93.435
1369	24	9/19/82	Dover DE	1.000	P	500.00	Darrell Waltrip (48)	Buick	107.642	Ricky Rudd (4)	Pontiac	139.384
1370	25	10/3/82	N Wilkesboro NC	0.625	P	250.00	Darrell Waltrip (49)	Buick	98.071	Darrell Waltrip (37)	Buick	113.860
1371	26	10/10/82	Charlotte NC	1.500	P	500.00	Harry Gant (2)	Buick	137.208	Harry Gant (5)	Buick	164.694
1372	27	10/17/82	Martinsville VA	0.525	P	262.50	Darrell Waltrip (50)	Buick	71.315	Ricky Rudd (5)	Pontiac	89.132
1373	28	10/31/82	Rockingham NC	1.017	P	500.00	Darrell Waltrip (51)	Buick	115.122	Cale Yarborough (62)	Buick	143.220
1374	29	11/7/82	Atlanta GA	1.522	P	500.00	Bobby Allison (74)	Buick	130.884	Morgan Shepherd (3)	Buick	166.779
1375	30	11/21/82	Riverside CA	2.620	P	311.78	Tim Richmond (2)	Buick	99.823	Darrell Waltrip (38)	Buick	122.021

1983

Race #	Year #	Date	Site	Track	Surface	Miles	Race Winner	Car	Speed	Pole Winner	Car	Speed
1376	1	2/20/83	Daytona Beach FL	2.500	P	500.00	Cale Yarborough (75)	Pontiac	155.979	Ricky Rudd (6)	Chevy	198.864
1377	2	2/27/83	Richmond VA	0.542	P	216.80	Bobby Allison (75)	Chevy	79.584	Ricky Rudd (7)	Chevy	93.439
1378	3	3/13/83	Rockingham NC	1.017	P	500.00	Richard Petty (196)	Pontiac	113.055	Ricky Rudd (8)	Chevy	143.413
1379	4	3/27/83	Atlanta GA	1.522	P	500.00	Cale Yarborough (76)	Chevy	124.055	Geoff Bodine (3)	Pontiac	167.703
1380	5	4/10/83	Darlington SC	1.366	P	500.00	Harry Gant (3)	Buick	130.406	Tim Richmond (2)	Pontiac	157.818
1381	6	4/17/83	N Wilkesboro NC	0.625	P	250.00	Darrell Waltrip (52)	Chevy	91.436	Neil Bonnett (16)	Chevy	112.332
1382	7	4/24/83	Martinsville VA	0.525	P	262.50	Darrell Waltrip (53)	Chevy	66.460	Ricky Rudd (9)	Chevy	89.910
1383	8	5/1/83	Talladega AL	2.660	P	500.00	Richard Petty (197)	Pontiac	153.936	Cale Yarborough (63	Chevy	202.650
1384	9	5/7/83	Nashville TN	0.596	P	250.00	Darrell Waltrip (54)	Chevy	70.717	Darrell Waltrip (39)	Chevy	103.119
1385	10	5/15/83	Dover DE	1.000	P	500.00	Bobby Allison (76)	Buick	114.847	Joe Ruttman	Buick	139.616
1386	11	5/21/83	Bristol TN	0.533	P	266.50	Darrell Waltrip (55)	Chevy	93.445	Neil Bonnett (17)	Chevy	110.409
1387	12	5/29/83	Charlotte NC	1.500	P	600.00	Neil Bonnett (12)	Chevy	140.707	Buddy Baker (38)	Ford	162.841
1388	13	6/5/83	Riverside CA	2.620	P	248.90	Ricky Rudd	Chevy	88.063	Darrell Waltrip (40)	Chevy	116.421
1389	14	6/12/83	Pocono PA	2.500	P	500.00	Bobby Allison (77)	Buick	128.636	Darrell Waltrip (41)	Chevy	152.315
1390	15	6/19/83	Brooklyn MI	2.000	P	400.00	Cale Yarborough (77)	Chevy	138.728	Terry Labonte (5)	Chevy	161.965
1391	16	7/4/83	Daytona Beach FL	2.500	P	400.00	Buddy Baker (19)	Ford	167.442	Cale Yarborough (64)	Chevy	196.635
1392	17	7/16/83	Nashville TN	0.596	P	250.00	Dale Earnhardt (8)	Ford	85.726	Ron Bouchard (3)	Buick	103.020
1393	18	7/24/83	Pocono PA	2.500	P	500.00	Tim Richmond (3)	Pontiac	114.818	Tim Richmond (3)	Pontiac	151.981
1394	19	7/31/83	Talladega AL	2.660	P	500.00	Dale Earnhardt (9)	Ford	170.611	Cale Yarborough (65)	Chevy	201.981
1395	20	8/21/83	Brooklyn MI	2.000	P	400.00	Cale Yarborough (78)	Chevy	147.511	Terry Labonte (6)	Chevy	162.437
1396	21	8/27/83	Bristol TN	0.533	P	266.50	Darrell Waltrip (56)	Chevy	89.430	Joe Ruttman (2)	Pontiac	111.437
1397	22	9/5/83	Darlington SC	1.366	P	500.00	Bobby Allison (78)	Buick	123.343	Neil Bonnett (18)	Chevy	157.187
1398	23	9/11/83	Richmond VA	0.542	P	216.80	Bobby Allison (79)	Buick	79.381	Darrell Waltrip (42)	Buick	96.069
1399	24	9/18/83	Dover DE	1.000	P	500.00	Bobby Allison (80)	Buick	116.077	Terry Labonte (7)	Chevy	139.573
1400	25	9/25/83	Martinsville VA	0.525	P	262.50	Ricky Rudd (2)	Chevy	76.134	Darrell Waltrip (43)	Chevy	89.342
1401	26	10/2/83	N Wilkesboro NC	0.625	P	250.00	Darrell Waltrip (57)	Chevy	100.716	Darrell Waltrip (44)	Chevy	114.539
1402	27	10/9/83	Charlotte NC	1.500	P	500.00	Richard Petty (198)	Pontiac	139.998	Tim Richmond (4)	Pontiac	163.073
1403	28	10/30/83	Rockingham NC	1.017	P	500.00	Terry Labonte (2)	Chevy	119.324	Neil Bonnett (19)	Chevy	143.876
1404	29	11/6/83	Atlanta GA	1.522	P	500.00	Neil Bonnett (13)	Chevy	137.643	Tim Richmond (5)	Pontiac	168.151
1405	30	11/20/83	Riverside CA	2.620	P	311.78	Bill Elliott	Ford	95.859	Darrell Waltrip (45)	Chevy	116.782

Race Winners Pole Winners

Race #	Year #	Date	Site	Track	Surface	Miles	Race Winner	Car	Speed	Pole Winner	Car	Speed
1984												
1406	1	2/19/84	Daytona Beach FL	2.500	P	500.00	Cale Yarborough (79)	Chevy	150.994	Cale Yarborough (66)	Chevy	102.848
1407	2	2/26/84	Richmond VA	0.542	P	216.80	Ricky Rudd (3)	Ford	76.736	Darrell Waltrip (46)	Chevy	95.817
1408	3	3/4/84	Rockingham NC	0.542	P	500.00	Bobby Allison (81)	Buick	122.931	Harry Gant (6)	Chevy	145.084
1409	4	3/18/84	Atlanta GA	1.522	P	500.00	Benny Parsons (21)	Chevy	144.945	Buddy Baker (39)	Ford	166.642
1410	5	4/1/84	Bristol TN	0.533	P	26.50	Darrell Waltrip (58)	Chevy	93.967	Ricky Rudd (10)	Ford	111.390
1411	6	4/8/84	N Wilkesboro NC	0.625	P	250.00	Tim Richmond (4)	Pontiac	97.830	Ricky Rudd (11)	Ford	113.487
1412	7	4/15/84	Darlington SC	1.366	P	500.00	Darrell Waltrip (59)	Chevy	119.925	Benny Parsons (18)	Chevy	156.328
1413	8	4/29/84	Martinsville VA	0.525	P	262.50	Geoff Bodine	Chevy	73.264	Joe Ruttman (3)	Chevy	89.426
1414	9	5/6/84	Talladega AL	2.660	P	500.00	Cale Yarborough (80)	Chevy	172.988	Cale Yarborough (67)	Chevy	202.692
1415	10	5/12/84	Nashville TN	0.596	P	250.00	Darrell Waltrip (60)	Chevy	85.702	Darrell Waltrip (47)	Chevy	104.439
1416	11	5/20/84	Dover DE	1.000	P	500.00	Richard Petty (199)	Pontiac	118.717	Ricky Rudd (12)	Ford	140.807
1417	12	5/27/84	Charlotte NC	1.500	P	600.00	Bobby Allison (82)	Buick	129.233	Harry Gant (7)	Chevy	162.496
1418	13	6/3/84	Riverside CA	2.620	P	248.90	Terry Labonte (3)	Chevy	102.910	Terry Labonte (8)	Chevy	115.921
1419	14	6/10/84	Pocono PA	2.500	P	500.00	Cale Yarborough (81)	Chevy	138.164	David Pearson (113)	Chevy	150.921
1420	15	6/17/84	Brooklyn MI	2.000	P	400.00	Bill Elliott (2)	Ford	134.705	Bill Elliott (3)	Ford	164.339
1421	16	7/4/84	Daytona Beach FL	2.500	P	400.00	Richard Petty (200)	Pontiac	171.204	Cale Yarborough (68)	Chevy	199.743
1422	17	7/14/84	Nashville TN	0.596	P	250.00	Geoff Bodine (2)	Chevy	80.908	Ricky Rudd (13)	Ford	104.120
1423	18	7/22/84	Pocono PA	2.500	P	500.00	Harry Gant (4)	Chevy	121.351	Bill Elliott (4)	Ford	152.184
1424	19	7/29/84	Talladega AL	2.660	P	500.00	Dale Earnhardt (10)	Chevy	155.485	Cale Yarborough (69)	Chevy	202.474
1425	20	8/12/84	Brooklyn MI	2.000	P	400.00	Darrell Waltrip (61)	Chevy	153.863	Bill Elliott (5)	Ford	165.217
1426	21	8/25/84	Bristol TN	0.533	P	266.50	Terry Labonte (4)	Chevy	85.365	Geoff Bodine (4)	Chevy	111.734
1427	22	9/2/84	Darlington SC	1.366	P	500.00	Harry Gant (5)	Chevy	128.270	Harry Gant (8)	Chevy	155.502
1428	23	9/9/84	Richmond VA	0.542	P	216.80	Darrell Waltrip (62)	Chevy	74.780	Darrell Waltrip (48)	Chevy	92.518
1429	24	9/16/84	Dover DE	1.000	P	500.00	Harry Gant (6)	Chevy	111.856	No Time Trials	NTT	NTT
1430	25	9/23/84	Martinsville VA	0.525	P	262.50	Darrell Waltrip (63)	Chevy	75.532	Geoff Bodine (5)	Chevy	89.523
1431	26	10/7/84	Charlotte NC	1.500	P	500.00	Bill Elliott (3)	Ford	146.861	Benny Parsons (19)	Chevy	165.579
1432	27	10/14/84	N Wilkesboro NC	0.625	P	250.00	Darrell Waltrip (64)	Chevy	90.525	Darrell Waltrip (49)	Chevy	113.304
1433	28	10/21/84	Rockingham NC	1.017	P	500.00	Bill Elliott (4)	Ford	112.617	Geoff Bodine (6)	Chevy	144.415
1434	29	11/11/84	Atlanta GA	1.522	P	500.00	Dale Earnhardt (11)	Chevy	134.610	Bill Elliott (6)	Ford	170.198
1435	30	11/18/84	Riverside CA	2.620	P	311.78	Geoff Bodine (3)	Chevy	98.448	Terry Labonte	Chevy	116.714
1985												
1436	1	2/17/85	Daytona Beach FL	2.500	P	500.00	Bill Elliott (5)	Ford	172.265	Bill Elliott (7)	Ford	205.114
1437	2	2/24/85	Richmond VA	0.542	P	216.80	Dale Earnhardt (12)	Chevy	67.945	Darrell Waltrip (50)	Chevy	95.218
1438	3	3/3/85	Rockingham NC	1.017	P	500.00	Neil Bonnett (14)	Chevy	114.953	Terry Labonte (10)	Chevy	145.067
1439	4	3/17/85	Atlanta GA	1.522	P	500.00	Bill Elliott (6)	Ford	140.273	Neil Bonnett (20)	Chevy	170.278
1440	5	4/6/85	Bristol TN	0.533	P	266.50	Dale Earnhardt (13)	Chevy	81.790	Harry Gant (9)	Chevy	112.778
1441	6	4/14/85	Darlington SC	1.366	P	500.00	Bill Elliott (7)	Ford	126.295	Bill Elliott (8)	Ford	157.454
1442	7	4/21/85	N Wilkesboro NC	0.625	P	250.00	Neil Bonnett (15)	Chevy	93.818	Darrell Waltrip (51)	Chevy	111.899
1443	8	4/28/85	Martinsville VA	0.525	P	262.50	Harry Gant (7)	Chevy	73.022	Darrell Waltrip (52)	Chevy	90.279
1444	9	5/5/85	Talladega AL	2.660	P	500.00	Bill Elliott (8)	Ford	186.288	Bill Elliott (9)	Ford	209.398
1445	10	5/19/85	Dover DE	1.000	P	500.00	Bill Elliott (9)	Ford	123.094	Terry Labonte (11)	Chevy	138.106
1446	11	5/26/85	Charlotte NC	1.500	P	600.00	Darrell Waltrip (65)	Chevy	141.807	Bill Elliott (10)	Ford	164.703
1447	12	6/2/85	Riverside CA	2.620	P	248.90	Terry Labonte (5)	Chevy	104.276	Darrell Waltrip (53)	Chevy	115.533
1448	13	6/9/85	Pocono PA	2.500	P	500.00	Bill Elliott (10)	Ford	138.974	Bill Elliott (11)	Ford	152.563
1449	14	6/15/85	Brooklyn MI	2.000	P	400.00	Bill Elliott (11)	Ford	144.724	No Time Trials	NTT	NTT
1450	15	7/4/85	Daytona Beach FL	2.500	P	400.00	Greg Sacks	Chevy	158.730	Bill Elliott (12)	Ford	201.523
1451	16	7/21/85	Pocono PA	2.500	P	500.00	Bill Elliott (12)	Ford	134.008	Darrell Waltrip (54)	Chevy	152.523
1452	17	7/28/85	Talladega AL	2.660	P	500.00	Cale Yarborough (82)	Ford	148.772	Bill Elliott (13)	Ford	107.578
1453	18	8/11/85	Brooklyn MI	2.000	P	400.00	Bill Elliott (13)	Ford	137.430	Bill Elliott (14)	Ford	165.479
1454	19	8/24/85	Bristol TN	0.533	P	266.50	Dale Earnhardt (14)	Chevy	82.388	Dale Earnhardt (6)	Chevy	113.586
1455	20	9/1/85	Darlington SC	1.366	P	500.00	Bill Elliott (14)	Ford	121.254	Bill Elliott (15)	Ford	156.641
1456	21	9/8/85	Richmond VA	0.542	P	216.80	Darrell Waltrip (66)	Chevy	72.508	Geoff Bodine (7)	Chevy	94.535
1457	22	9/15/85	Dover DE	1.000	P	500.00	Harry Gant (8)	Chevy	120.538	Bill Elliott (16)	Ford	141.543
1458	23	9/22/85	Martinsville VA	0.525	P	262.50	Dale Earnhardt (15)	Chevy	70.694	Geoff Bodine (8)	Chevy	90.521
1459	24	9/29/85	N Wilkesboro NC	0.625	P	250.00	Harry Gant (9)	Chevy	95.077	Geoff Bodine (9)	Chevy	113.967
1460	25	10/6/85	Charlotte NC	1.500	P	500.00	Cale Yarborough (83)	Ford	136.761	Harry Gant (10)	Chevy	166.139
1461	26	10/25/85	Rockingham NC	1.017	P	500.00	Darrell Waltrip (67)	Chevy	118.344	Terry Labonte (12)	Chevy	141.841
1462	27	11/3/85	Atlanta GA	1.522	P	500.00	Bill Elliott (15)	Ford	139.597	Harry Gant (11)	Chevy	167.940
1463	28	11/17/85	Riverside CA	2.620	P	311.78	Ricky Rudd (4)	Ford	105.065	Terry Labonte (13)	Chevy	116.938
1986												
1464	1	2/16/86	Daytona Beach FL	2.500	P	500.00	Geoff Bodine (4)	Chevy	148.124	Bill Elliott (17)	Ford	205.039
1465	2	2/23/86	Richmond VA	0.542	P	216.80	Kyle Petty	Ford	71.078	No Time Trials	NTT	NTT
1466	3	3/2/86	Rockingham NC	1.017	P	500.00	Terry Labonte (6)	Olds	120.468	Terry Labonte (14)	Olds	146.348
1467	4	3/16/86	Atlanta GA	1.522	P	500.00	Morgan Shepherd (2)	Buick	132.126	Dale Earnhardt (7)	Chevy	170.713
1468	5	4/6/86	Bristol TN	0.533	P	266.50	Rusty Wallace	Pontiac	89.747	Geoff Bodine ((10)	Chevy	114.850

Race Winners Pole Winners

Race #	Year #	Date	Site	Track	Surface	Miles	Race Winner	Car	Speed	Pole Winner	Car	Speed
1469	6	4/13/86	Darlington SC	1.366	P	500.00	Dale Earnhardt (16)	Chevy	128.994	Geoff Bodine (11)	Chevy	159.197
1470	7	4/20/86	N Wilkesboro NC	0.625	P	250.00	Dale Earnhardt (17)	Chevy	86.408	Geoff Bodine (12)	Chevy	112.419
1471	8	4/27/86	Martinsville VA	0.525	P	262.50	Ricky Rudd (5)	Ford	76.882	Tim Richmond (6)	Chevy	90.716
1472	9	5/4/86	Talladega AL	2.660	P	500.00	Bobby Allison (83)	Buick	157.698	Bill Elliott (18)	Ford	212.229
1473	10	5/18/86	Dover DE	1.000	P	500.00	Geoff Bodine (5)	Chevy	115.009	Ricky Rudd (14)	Ford	138.217
1474	11	5/15/86	Charlotte NC	1.500	P	600.00	Dale Earnhardt (18)	Chevy	140.406	Geoff Bodine (13)	Chevy	164.511
1475	12	6/1/86	Riverside CA	2.620	P	248.90	Darrell Waltrip (68)	Chevy	105.083	Darrell Waltrip (55)	Chevy	117.006
1476	13	6/8/86	Pocono PA	2.500	P	500.00	Tim Richmond (5)	Chevy	113.279	Geoff Bodine (14)	Chevy	153.625
1477	14	6/15/86	Brooklyn MI	2.000	P	400.00	Bill Elliott (16)	Ford	138.581	Tim Richmond (7)	Chevy	172.031
1478	15	7/4/86	Daytona Beach FL	2.500	P	400.00	Tim Richmond (6)	Chevy	131.916	Cale Yarborough (70)	Ford	203.519
1479	16	7/20/86	Pocono PA	2.500	P	375.00	Tim Richmond (7)	Chevy	124.218	Harry Gant (12)	Chevy	154.392
1480	17	7/27/86	Talladega AL	2.660	P	500.00	Bobby Hillin Jr	Buick	151.552	Bill Elliott (19)	Ford	209.005
1481	18	8/10/86	Watkins Glen NY	2.438	P	218.50	Tim Richmond (8)	Chevy	90.463	Tim Richmond (8)	Chevy	117.563
1482	19	8/17/86	Brooklyn MI	2.000	P	400.00	Bill Elliott (17)	Ford	135.376	Benny Parsons (20)	Olds	171.924
1483	20	8/23/86	Bristol TN	0.533	P	266.50	Darrell Waltrip (69)	Chevy	86.934	Geoff Bodine (15)	Chevy	114.665
1484	21	8/31/86	Darlington SC	1.366	P	500.00	Tim Richmond (9)	Chevy	121.068	Tim Richmond (9)	Chevy	158.489
1485	22	9/7/86	Richmond VA	0.542	P	216.80	Tim Richmond (10)	Chevy	70.161	Harry Gant (13)	Chevy	93.966
1486	23	9/14/86	Dover DE	1.000	P	500.00	Ricky Rudd (6)	Ford	114.329	Geoff Bodine (16)	Chevy	146.205
1487	24	9/21/86	Martinsville VA	0.525	P	262.50	Rusty Wallace (2)	Pontiac	73.191	Geoff Bodine (17)	Chevy	90.599
1488	25	9/28/86	N Wilkesboro NC	0.625	P	250.00	Darrell Waltrip (70)	Chevy	95.612	Tim Richmond (10)	Chevy	113.447
1489	26	10/3/86	Charlotte NC	1.500	P	500.00	Dale Earnhardt (19)	Chevy	132.403	Tim Richmond (11)	Chevy	167.078
1490	27	10/10/86	Rockingham NC	1.017	P	500.00	Neil Bonnett (16)	Chevy	126.381	Tim Richmond (12)	Chevy	146.948
1491	28	11/2/86	Atlanta GA	1.522	P	500.00	Dale Earnhardt (20)	Chevy	152.523	Bill Elliott (20)	Ford	172.905
1492	29	11/16/86	Riverside CA	2.620	P	311.78	Tim Richmond (11)	Chevy	101.246	Tim Richmond (13)	Chevy	118.247

1987

Race #	Year #	Date	Site	Track	Surface	Miles	Race Winner	Car	Speed	Pole Winner	Car	Speed
1492	1	2/15/87	Daytona Beach FL	2.500	P	500.00	Bill Elliott (18)	Ford	176.263	Bill Elliott (21)	Ford	210.364
1494	2	3/1/87	Rockingham NC	1.017	P	500.00	Dale Earnhardt (21)	Chevy	117.556	Davey Allison	Ford	146.989
1495	3	3/8/87	Richmond VA	0.542	P	216.80	Dale Earnhardt (22)	Chevy	81.420	Alan Kulwicki	Ford	95.153
1496	4	3/15/87	Atlanta GA	1.522	P	500.00	Ricky Rudd (7)	Ford	133.689	Dale Earnhardt (8)	Chevy	175.497
1497	5	3/29/87	Darlington SC	1.366	P	500.00	Dale Earnhardt (23)	Chevy	122.540	Ken Shrader	Ford	158.387
1498	6	4/5/87	N Wilkesboro NC	0.625	P	250.00	Dale Earnhardt (24)	Chevy	94.103	Bill Elliott (22)	Ford	116.003
1499	7	4/12/87	Bristol TN	0.533	P	266.50	Dale Earnhardt (25)	Chevy	75.621	Harry Gant (14)	Chevy	115.674
1500	8	4/26/87	Martinsville VA	0.525	P	262.50	Dale Earnhardt (26)	Chevy	72.808	Morgan Shepherd (4)	Buick	92.355
1501	9	5/3/87	Talladega AL	2.660	P	473.48	Davey Allison	Ford	154.228	Bill Elliott (23)	Ford	212.809
1502	10	5/24/87	Charlotte NC	1.500	P	600.00	Kyle Petty (2)	Ford	131.483	Bill Elliott (24)	Ford	170.901
1503	11	5/31/87	Dover DE	1.000	P	500.00	Davey Allison (2)	Ford	112.958	Bill Elliott (25)	Ford	145.056
1504	12	6/14/87	Pocono PA	2.500	P	500.00	Tim Richmond (12)	Chevy	122.166	Terry Labonte (15)	Chevy	155.502
1505	13	6/21/87	Riverside CA	2.620	P	248.90	Tim Richmond (13)	Chevy	102.183	Terry Labonte (16)	Chevy	117.541
1506	14	6/28/87	Brooklyn MI	2.000	P	400.00	Dale Earnhardt (27)	Chevy	148.454	Rusty Wallace	Pontiac	170.746
1507	15	7/4/87	Daytona Beach FL	2.500	P	400.00	Bobby Allison (84)	Buick	161.074	Davey Allison (2)	Ford	198.085
1508	16	7/9/87	Pocono PA	3.500	P	500.00	Dale Earnhardt (28)	Chevy	121.745	Tim Richmond (14)	Chevy	155.979
1509	17	7/16/87	Talladega AL	2.660	P	500.00	Bill Elliott (19)	Ford	171.293	Bill Elliott (26)	Ford	203.827
1510	18	8/10/87	Watkins Glen NY	2.438	P	218.50	Rusty Wallace (3)	Pontiac	90.682	Terry Labonte (17)	Chevy	117.956
1511	19	8/16/87	Brooklyn MI	2.000	P	400.00	Bill Elliott (20)	Ford	138.648	Davey Allison (3)	Ford	170.705
1512	20	8/22/87	Bristol TN	0.533	P	266.50	Dale Earnhardt (29)	Chevy	90.373	Terry Labonte (18)	Chevy	115.758
1513	21	9/6/87	Darlington SC	1.366	P	275.90	Dale Earnhardt (30)	Chevy	115.520	Davey Allison (4)	Ford	157.232
1514	22	9/13/87	Richmond VA	0.542	P	216.80	Dale Earnhardt (31)	Chevy	67.074	Alan Kulwicki (2)	Ford	94.052
1515	23	9/20/87	Dover DE	1.000	P	500.00	Ricky Rudd (8)	Ford	124.706	Alan Kulwicki (3)	Ford	145.826
1516	24	9/27/87	Martinsville VA	0.525	P	262.50	Darrell Waltrip (71)	Chevy	76.410	Geoff Bodine (18)	Chevy	91.218
1517	25	10/4/87	N Wilkesboro NC	0.625	P	250.00	Terry Labonte (7)	Chevy	96.051	Bill Elliott (27)	Ford	115.196
1518	26	10/11/87	Charlotte NC	1.500	P	500.00	Bill Elliott (20)	Ford	128.443	Bobby Allison (58)	Buick	145.609
1519	27	10/25/87	Rockingham NC	1.017	P	500.00	Bill Elliott (21)	Ford	118.258	Davey Allison (5)	Ford	145.609
1520	28	11/8/87	Riverside CA	2.620	P	311.78	Rusty Wallace (4)	Pontiac	98.035	Geoff Bodine (19)	Chevy	117.934
1521	29	11/22/87	Atlanta GA	1.522	P	500.00	Bill Elliott (22)	Ford	139.047	Bill Elliott (28)	Ford	174.341